ALSO BY EDWARD DE GRAZIA

Censorship Landmarks
Banned Films: Movies, Censors and the First Amendment
(with Roger K. Newman)

GIRLS LEAN BACK EVERYWHERE

GIRLS
LEAN BACK
EVERYWHERE

The Law
of Obscenity
and the Assault
on Genius

Edward de Grazia

RANDOM HOUSE   NEW YORK

Owing to limitations of space, all acknowledgments of
permission to use previously published material will
be found following the index.

All rights reserved under International and Pan-American Copyright Conventions.
Published in the United States by Random House, Inc., New York, and
simultaneously in Canada by Random House of Canada Limited, Toronto.

Library of Congress Cataloging-in-Publication Data

de Grazia, Edward.
Girls lean back everywhere: the law of obscenity and the assault
on genius/Edward de Grazia.
p.   cm.
Includes index.
ISBN 0-394-57611-X
1. Censorship—United States. 2. Obscenity (Law)—United States.
3. Law and literature. I. Title.
KF4775.D44 1991
344.73'0547—dc20   90-53153
[347.304547]

Manufactured in the United States of America

24689753

FIRST EDITION

This book was set in 10/12 Galliard.

For
Justice William J. Brennan, Jr.

Girls lean back everywhere, showing lace and silk stockings; wear low-cut sleeveless blouses, breathless bathing suits; men think thoughts and have emotions about these things everywhere—seldom as delicately and imaginatively as Mr. Bloom—and no one is corrupted.

—JANE HEAP
The Little Review

Introduction

THIS book is about the long struggle to "solve" the intractable problem of obscenity in this country, and to some extent in Britain. There, in the closing years of the last century, the distinguished publisher Henry Vizetelly was twice prosecuted, and in his seventieth year was sent to prison, for publishing English translations of the novels of Emile Zola. Vizetelly's trials are of great significance because they are the first examples in an English-speaking country of the use by government of the law of obscenity to suppress plainly meritorious literary works. Vizetelly was convicted under a legal rule known as the *Hicklin* doctrine, fashioned in 1868 by Queen's Bench; this based the test for obscenity on whether the material in question had a "tendency" to "deprave and corrupt those whose minds are open to such immoral influences"—a test that subordinated the freedom of writers, publishers, and readers to the imagined effects books might have upon impressionable young girls. *Hicklin* thereafter became the legal standard by which the freedom of authors and publishers in the United States was measured—until 1933, when an enlightened federal judge sitting in New York ruled that James Joyce's *Ulysses* might enter the country and be published here without legal risk. Twelve years earlier, two brave American women had been convicted (and could have gone to jail) for publishing the Gertie McDowell ("Nausicaa") episode from *Ulysses* in their magazine, *The Little Review*. My book takes its title from their spirited defense of the right to publish Joyce's description of Gertie's posture, and the "erotic musings" it inspired in Leopold Bloom.

In the *Ulysses* case the judge, John M. Woolsey, fashioned a new legal rule to replace *Hicklin*. Woolsey took the position that the freedom to publish *Ulysses* should be judged not by any tendency the novel might have to corrupt the morals of young girls, but rather by its effect on the judge himself—and two friends, whom he privately consulted. When all three gentlemen—in Woolsey's estimation *hommes moyens sensuels*—found that reading *Ulysses* failed to arouse them sexually, Joyce's masterpiece was set free. The capacity to arouse lust in the "average person" now became the prevailing American legal test of whether literature ought to be suppressed for being "obscene." This was a marked improvement, but the law was still subject to the personal reactions of this or that judge.

In 1957, for the first time, the Supreme Court spoke to the question of whether literature dealing with sex was meant to be protected by the First Amendment; the Court said that literature was protected, but that "obscenity" was *not*. The justices defined "obscenity" much as Judge Woolsey had, subjectively, in terms of its ability to arouse the "average person's" prurient interest in sex. Then, in a 1964 case involving Henry Miller's erotic novel *Tropic of Cancer,* the wise and courageous Justice William J. Brennan, Jr., produced a more objective and much more liberal rule by which the freedom of literature and other arts might be measured.

In fact, the rule that Brennan announced (referred to in this book as "the Brennan doctrine") was so generously fashioned to protect literature and art that it led to the freeing of hard-core pornography. In order to ensure freedom for valued cultural expression the Supreme Court had found it necessary to free what was "obscene" as well. It did this by effectively (although not formally) abandoning the effort to define what in a literary or artistic context was undefinable—"the obscene"—and providing an efficient, because nearly absolute, defense for expression "not utterly without" literary, artistic, scientific, or other social value. Thus the Court made it close to impossible for prosecutors to prove that targeted literary or artistic works were obscene but easy for defense lawyers to demonstrate that the works of literature or art created or disseminated by their clients were entitled to First Amendment protection.

Soon the Court's critics found in the Brennan doctrine grounds to blame the Court for the "tides of pornography" that were now "seeping into the sanctity of the home." The spread of pornography was cited as evidence not that entrepreneurial capitalism had made sex a multibillion-dollar industry, but that the Supreme Court had mocked the founding fathers' intentions with regard to freedom of the press.

In 1973, the Court's new chief justice, Warren E. Burger, redefined obscenity in a way he hoped would be more palatable to conservative opinion, and this led Brennan and three others who had served on the Warren Court (Stewart, Marshall, and Douglas) to disassociate themselves from Burger's position and move into deep dissent. At that point Brennan, disdaining Burger's effort to fashion an improved definition of "the obscene," called for the abandonment of attempts to define and suppress obscenity through law. It was plain to Brennan that people who express themselves through literature and art could not be fully safe from government control unless the Court constrained government to forgo any attempt to punish purveyors of pornography and obscenity to adults.

The wisdom of Brennan's 1973 position (which he reiterated frequently in dissent) recently was confirmed when the director of a Cincinnati art gallery, the leader of a Miami rap music group, and the owner of a Fort Lauderdale record store all found themselves arrested under the Burger Court's revised definition for showing, singing, and selling what police officials and prosecutors claimed was obscene because in their judgment it did not qualify as "serious" art, or even art. Splendid as Brennan's achievements of the sixties were, they have not dispelled fears that literature and art can subvert and even destroy deeply entrenched political and religious values. And they have by no means discouraged ambitious public officials and zealous religious leaders from invoking the law to suppress artistic expression they find repellent.

We have no doubt come a long way from the time, a century ago, when Vizetelly was imprisoned and Zola's novels were burned—as were, later, those of Lawrence, Joyce, Radclyffe Hall, Edmund Wilson, and many lesser authors. Yet freedom of literature and art in this country cannot be taken for granted. Last year, Dennis Barrie, the director of the Contemporary Arts Center in Cincinnati, was acquitted by a jury in a criminal proceeding that could have sent him to prison—it would have been the first such incident in our history—for exhibiting "obscene" and "pornographic" works by the artist Robert Mapplethorpe. Barrie may be pardoned if he felt in his bones, while those proceedings against him were unraveling, what Vizetelly must have felt in his one hundred years earlier—fear of the sting of the criminal law. In Vizetelly's case, members of the National Vigilance Association goaded police and prosecutors to take action; in Barrie's case it was the Cincinnati Citizens for Community Values.

In Miami, in June 1990, Luther Campbell, the leader of 2 Live Crew, was arrested for singing and playing "obscene" songs; thereafter he was acquitted by jurors who, aided by experts, felt they knew artistic expression when they heard it. But in Fort Lauderdale, record-store owner Charles Freeman, who was arrested around the same time for selling a recording of the same music—the 2 Live Crew album *As Nasty As They Wanna Be*—to an undercover sheriff, was convicted by a jury that failed to see the serious artistic and political value that many other people saw in the songs. Yet the First Amendment has for the past twenty-five years been put forward by the Supreme Court as a barrier to this sort of censorship. One had hoped the issue was settled.

In historical perspective, it can be remarked that under Justice Brennan's leadership the Supreme Court interpreted the First Amendment's guarantees of speech and press in ways that permitted authors and artists, their publishers and promoters, to communicate on the subjects of sex, religion, politics, and anything else in almost limitless ways—much as the Court (equally controversially, and again following Brennan's lead) privileged this country's newspaper press. Here admittedly is a degree of freedom or license that many people prefer to deny themselves and others. The liberty asserted by American artists and writers is nothing less than the right to upset the basic assumptions upon which our family, social, political, religious, and cultural life is based.

The First Amendment's framers must have anticipated a situation such as this—one that right-wing conservatives especially decry. This is, in fact, the best explanation of why the speech and press guarantees were couched by the founders in unprecedentedly sweeping terms. Of course, they would have had little notion of what ingenious forms speech and press would take in this country two hundred years later, nor of the remarkable inventions that would come to amplify and disperse words and images among a great, diverse, and polyglot people.

It occurred to me some eight years ago to write this book. I wanted to find out, and describe, how the persons who were most immediately affected by literary censorship—authors and publishers—responded to and felt about it, and to present their reactions as much as possible in words of their own. I also wanted to say what I could about the nature of the legal and constitutional process that has framed the struggle against censorship in our country, and about the one person above all others who is responsible for the only real gains that have been made, over the past one hundred years, in the freedom with which authors and artists are able to express themselves. I mean, of course, Supreme Court Justice William J. Brennan, Jr.

Contents

Introduction   *xi*

1. Girls Lean Back Everywhere   *3*
2. Fuck Up, Love!   *20*
3. A Judicial Murder   *40*
4. A Sermon-on-the-Mount—of Venus   *54*
5. It's Such an Ugly Cemetery   *72*
6. L'Affaire Doubleday   *98*
7. Mencken's Lead Zeppelins   *109*
8. I Took a Girl Away from You Once   *128*
9. Dear Comrade Dreiser   *150*
10. The Knopfs "Ratted" on John   *165*
11. Ungrateful England   *186*
12. Like a Phallus Made of Dough   *209*
13. She Always Called It "It"   *230*
14. With Your Little Claws, Lolita   *243*
15. I'm Just Going to Feed Adolphe   *273*
16. Clear and Present Danger of *What*?   *295*
17. I Was Getting Hard-ons   *327*
18. El Hombre Invisible   *343*
19. Like a Piece of Lead with Wings on It   *366*
20. This Was "Star Wars"   *384*
21. Who Is His Parish Priest?   *398*
22. Because We Never Could Agree on a Definition   *417*
23. If All Mankind Minus One   *434*
24. The Ideas I Have Are Now Imprisoned Within Me   *444*

xvi • Contents

25. Any Writer Who Hasn't Jacked Off   480
26. Sex Life of a Cop   496
27. Playing the Role of Revolutionaries   525
28. A Magna Charta for Pornographers   551
29. Like the Towel-Boy in a Whorehouse   577
30. Just a Pro-Choice Kind of Gal   622

    Acknowledgments   689
    Endnotes   691
    Select Bibliography   773
    Index   783

GIRLS LEAN BACK EVERYWHERE

1

Girls
Lean Back
Everywhere

I DA CRADDOCK was forty-five years old when in 1902 she took her own life. She had come to New York a few years earlier, leaving Philadelphia and shorthand teaching behind. On the door of her flat on West Twenty-third Street a sign read: INSTRUCTOR IN DIVINE SCIENCE.

Her friends said she experienced erotic hallucinations that led her to imagine she was the earthly sweetheart of an angel. On the basis of those conjugal relations she wrote, in 1900 or 1901, a booklet called *The Wedding Night,* containing suggestions for affianced women, and another called *Advice to a Bridegroom,* intended for affianced men. She also published a pamphlet of essays that included a defense of the *danse du ventre.*

There were doctors who thought Ida Craddock insane, but she wrote intelligently, and with feeling. When Anthony Comstock read what Craddock wrote he said it was "the science of seduction" and arranged for her to be arrested and prosecuted in state and federal courts. A remnant of Craddock's "science of seduction" exists in the New York Public Library.

IDA CRADDOCK *(Advice to a Bridegroom): I am so glad that you are about to marry. It is not good for man to be alone. And there is a sweet and wholesome satisfaction attending intercourse with a woman whom a man rejoices to openly acknowledge as his wife. . . .*

In the marital relation the sexual nature manifests through two distinct functions—the love function and the parental function. These two functions are not always exercised conjointly. There are also different sets of organs for these two different functions.

For the parental function the organs are, in women, the ovaries and uterus. In men they are the testicles and the vesiculae seminales.

For the love function the organs are those which contact, the organ in man, the vulva and vagina in women . . .

Upon no account use the hand to arouse excitement at the woman's genitals. There is but one lawful finger of love with which to approach her sexual organs for purposes of excitation—the erectile organ of the male. Many men, in order to arouse passion quickly in the woman, are accustomed to titillate the clitoris with the finger—a proceeding which is distinctly masturbative. . . . The orgasm aroused by excitation within the vagina appears to be the one which satisfies the woman most completely, because it awakens her sweetest and most womanly, most maternal instincts. . . .

———

Anthony Comstock was secretary of the New York Society for the Suppression of Vice for forty-three years. He was only twenty-eight years old when the society was chartered, in 1873, a fatal year for literary freedom. That same year the U.S. Post Office made Comstock a "special agent" (unpaid), which permitted him to go to any post office and inspect mail he suspected was obscene; and the Congress, after vigorous lobbying by Comstock,* amended an 1865 law† that made it a crime knowingly to send obscene publications through the mails. As amended, the law also made it a crime knowingly to send information and advertisements about obscene publications, contraception, or abortion through the mails. Thereafter the law was known as the Comstock law. In its first six months of operation, Comstock said, the law made it possible for him to seize 194,000 obscene pictures and photographs, 134,000 pounds of books, 14,200 stereopticon plates, 60,300 "rubber articles," 5,500 sets of playing cards, and 31,150 boxes of pills and powders, mostly "aphrodisiacs."

By the time of Ida Craddock's prosecutions, the Supreme Court had said that the obscenity provisions of the federal postal law were adopted to punish any use of the mails "to corrupt the morals of the people," particularly "that form of immorality which has relation to sexual impurity." This was the meaning given by English courts to obscenity at common law, in prosecutions for obscene libel. A publication was obscene if there was "in it anything of a lewd, lascivious and obscene tendency, calculated to cor-

———

*In his congressional lobbying efforts Comstock took "a great cloth bag" full of "lowbrow publications and their advertisements, gadgets purportedly designed to stimulate sexual potency, and 'fancy books,' the bogus sex literature, contraceptive and abortifacient matter, and other 'abominations' which were sold via the ads"—to Washington to show to congressmen. While there he also set up the first of what became known as "chambers of horrors," in Vice President Schuyler Colfax's office. Colfax may have agreed to this as a distraction from his involvement in the Crédit-Mobilier affair.

†The 1865 legislation was evidently enacted in response to a report by the postmaster general that "great numbers" of "obscene books and pictures" were being sent via the mails to the army. The daguerreotype and the photograph had only recently been developed, and one of the first uses to which they were put was the visual communication of the visible charms of ladies of questionable virtue.

rupt and debauch the mind and morals of those into whose hands it might fall."*

Comstock claimed to have destroyed, over the course of his long career, more than "sixteen tons of vampire literature" and convicted of obscenity "enough persons to fill a passenger train of sixty-one coaches—sixty coaches containing sixty passengers each and the sixty-first coach not quite full." Some of those persons were female: his biographers have counted fifteen women whom Comstock drove to "self-destruction," among them Ida Craddock.

According to Comstock, Ida Craddock had escaped to New York from the Asylum for the Insane in Frankford, Pennsylvania. In New York she sold her "vile literature" at fifty cents a copy, advertising by means of circulars that she handed out. This "instructor in divine science" thought it was *good* for young men and women to read her books and attend the public lectures she gave. Comstock thought otherwise:

ANTHONY COMSTOCK: Any refined person reading her books would find all the finer and sweeter sensibilities violently shocked; while to the ordinary mind, it would be regarded as the science of seduction and a most dangerous weapon in the hands of young men, as educating them in a manner that would enable them to practice the wiles of the seducer to perfection upon innocent girls.

———

Ida Craddock's first case pitting her against Anthony Comstock, complainant, was a prosecution in 1902 in New York for putting a copy of *The Wedding Night* into the mails; it landed her in state prison for three months because she could not pay a $500 fine. The lawyer who appeared at the sentencing on her behalf pleaded in extenuation that it was apparent "that no woman in her right mind would write such a book." Almost immediately after she had served her time, a federal judge convicted Craddock for putting *Advice to a Bridegroom* into the mails. The judge would not let the jurors see the booklet because, he said, it was "indescribably obscene." The jury found Ida Craddock guilty "without leaving their seats."

Judicial legerdemain of this sort was characteristic of the way the obscenity laws were applied by the courts in those days to purveyors of allegedly obscene literature. The judges professed such horror of the stuff the police brought before them that they usually did not allow it into the record, let the jurors take it into the jury room, or let lawyers read it aloud in the courtroom. This made especially problematic the defense in an obscenity case, and next to useless any appeal from a guilty verdict: the reviewing judges had no way of testing the trial judge's or jury's conclusions that the material in question was obscene.

When the day arrived for Ida Craddock to appear in federal court for

———

*The quoted language is from an 1896 Supreme Court opinion, *Swearingen* v. *United States,* reprinted in de Grazia, *Censorship Landmarks* (1969), 46.

sentencing, she stayed home instead; she cut her wrists and gassed herself, in this way asserting a right to die as she pleased. Craddock left a note behind:

IDA CRADDOCK: I am taking my life because a judge, at the instigation of Anthony Comstock, has declared me guilty of a crime I did not commit—the circulation of obscene literature.*

———

The work of Comstock and his New York anti-vice society received generous support from such tycoons as J. Pierpont Morgan, William E. Dodge, Jr., and Samuel Colgate,† and from the press during his lifetime and after his death.

THE NEW YORK TIMES: All through his long career, Anthony Comstock suffered because the popular impression of him was based not on the large amount of his work, about the merits of which there never has been or could be any question by decent people, but on the small part of it that was, with more or less reason, considered by such people at best unnecessary or unwise and at worst the manifestation of ignorant fanaticism. . . . That Mr. Comstock never made mistakes, that he did not sometimes allow himself to be carried away by excessive zeal, that he was not an occasional persecutor as well as a frequent prosecutor, not even his best friends and most sincere appreciators could truthfully deny, and they do not. They can and do claim for him, however, the credit due to a thoroughly honest man who through a long life, for the scantiest of material rewards, devoted his courage and energy, both remarkable, to the protecting of society from a detestable and dangerous group of enemies.

———

The earliest English prosecutions of the publishers of serious fiction were directed at the works of French authors: Zola, Flaubert, Bourget, and de Maupassant. Similarly, Comstock's earliest literary targets were the works of foreigners: Balzac's *Droll Stories,* Tolstoy's *The Kreutzer Sonata,* and

———

*Craddock had already been in trouble because of her writings. Five years earlier in Chicago she was sentenced to three months, but the sentence was suspended. The judge at her New York trial, a man named McKean, seemed to think what Craddock wrote in *The Wedding Night* was "extremely blasphemous" rather than "obscene," but this did not deter him from convicting her for "obscenity" and sending her to prison "on The Island" for three months.

Her book had been "partially indorsed" by Rev. W. S. Rainsford, who thought "she had been too broad in some of her phrases, but that she had meant to do a great ethical work." After Craddock's suicide, Rainsford severely criticized Comstock in a letter to "The Roundsman of the Lord," saying: "I would not like to be in your shoes. You hounded an honest, not a bad woman to her death. I would not like to have to answer to God for what you have done." Stung by the "unpleasant newspaper attacks" that followed, Comstock wrote to Rainsford, challenging him to a duel of words before his anti-vice society's executive committee, but reported to the society that the minister "treated this letter with silent contempt." The 1902 Report of the New York Society for the Suppression of Vice (9–20) contains an extended account of this affair.

†John Tebbel points out that it was not the Roman Catholic Church that was behind Comstock's "rise to the throne of censorship power" but the WASP establishment. *A History of Book Publishing in the United States* 2 (1975), 611.

D'Annunzio's *The Triumph of Death*. Selling Balzac cost a mail-order publisher named John A. Wilson two years in jail, but the prosecutions directed at the other two works were unsuccessful. *The New York Times* characteristically aligned itself with Comstock when dirty books were in question, but it took the anti-vice crusader to task for stimulating demand for the D'Annunzio and Tolstoy works: "Both Signor D'Annunzio and the American publisher owe a lasting debt of gratitude to Mr. Anthony Comstock. Until that illustrious maker of reputations took the matter in hand the Italian's books were a drug on the market." Comstock's handling of Tolstoy was even more frustrating for the *Times:* "If not for the censorship of the United States mails relating to *The Kreutzer Sonata,* this last insanity of Tolstoi's would have had but a few thousand readers. As it is . . . it looks as if New York would supply 300,000 copies of the book. At the beginning of the run . . . the book publishers in New York streets alone bought $800 worth a day."

In 1915, after Comstock died, John Sumner took his place. Sumner had gone to New York University Law School at night and considered himself a literary man. He claimed to regard Comstock's activities as excessive and tried to carry out the society's work in a more subdued way. Like his predecessor, however, Sumner enjoyed reporting to the society's members and the press the annual tonnage of "obscene" and "immoral" material that he had suppressed, and he did not hesitate to attack women when he found them disseminating literature likely to corrupt young boys or girls. One of his earliest successful cases was the prosecution of the two feminists who ran the Washington Square Bookstore in Greenwich Village, from which they published *The Little Review.* * Their names: Margaret Anderson and Jane Heap.

Margaret Anderson started *The Little Review* in Chicago in the winter of 1914. She published the magazine on a shoestring, without any financial plan or backing, on sheer willpower; it was one of the best of our avant-garde literary journals and reflected its publisher's sudden shifts of interest: first, feminism; next, Emma Goldman and anarchism; then imagism, symbolism, dadaism, the machine. Anderson was drawn to "experimentalism," the more advanced the better, and so to Joyce and his revolutionary novel.

The expatriate American poet Ezra Pound, who energetically promoted Joyce from London during and after the war years, and from 1921 to 1924, when both men lived in Paris, advised Anderson and Heap that they should publish Joyce's *Ulysses.* He told them Joyce was better than Flaubert, and it was certainly worth running a magazine like *The Little Review* if they could

---

*They were lovers as well. Shari Benstock, *Women of the Left Bank: Paris 1900–1940* (1986), 22, 239, 379, 443. According to Benstock, Heap and Anderson became lovers in 1916, when Heap joined *The Little Review.* In the early Greenwich Village period, Djuna Barnes hated Anderson "for having taken Jane Heap away from her." When the journal moved to Paris, Anderson found a new lover, Georgette Leblanc, and turned *The Little Review* over to Heap for the duration.

publish material of this quality. Reading the first three installments caused Anderson to cry out to Heap:

MARGARET ANDERSON: This is the most beautiful thing we'll ever have to publish. Let us print it if it's the last effort of our lives!

—

It was not easy for *The Little Review* to find a printer in New York willing to print the episodes of *Ulysses* that came from Joyce's pen in Paris. Anderson wrote: "We found a Serbian who with his two daughters were the shop." The man's mother had been the poet laureate of Serbia and so "he knew the beautiful words." Once, in his troubled English, he asked Anderson about certain words in Joyce's manuscript. When she explained their meaning, he responded: "Ah, yes, I know! In Serbia those words are good for people but in America it is not good. Here the people are not brave about words, they are not healthy about words. . . . You can go to prison."

Ezra Pound became their foreign editor. Later, when they went to Paris, they found him living in a garden studio in the rue Notre Dame des Champs. Jane Heap said he "went around dressed in the large beret and flowering tie of The Latin Quarter artist of the 1830's." Pound sent them other writers, whose prose and poetry they published in *The Little Review*.

Pound also introduced the women who ran *The Little Review* to one of Joyce's financial supporters and the man "who became their lawyer and benefactor," John Quinn. Born in 1870 in Ohio into an impoverished Irish-Catholic immigrant family, Quinn rose through Harvard Law School to become a distinguished member of the New York bar and a wealthy Tammany lawyer. He did it "through hard work and the fighting spirit of the Irish."

MARGARET ANDERSON: He fought everybody, from his office boys—who trembled visibly and were in consequence the most inefficient office boys in the world—to his friend and protege, James Joyce, who sat calmly in Paris and ignored Quinn's cutting suggestions about how *Ulysses* ought to be written.

—

Quinn used the fortune he made at law to satisfy his love for literature and art (for a while he considered purchasing the right to publish *Ulysses*),* and this led him to defend censorship cases and so to represent Anderson and Heap when, in 1920, they were brought to trial for publishing episodes from *Ulysses* in *The Little Review*. Opposed was John Sumner, representing the people of the State of New York.

Margaret Anderson had first noticed Sumner in 1915, five years before

---

*Quinn provided financial support for two years to *The Little Review*, giving Ezra Pound a salary of $750 per year—$300 for editorial duties and $450 for his own contributions; he also often gave Anderson and Heap donations from his own pocket. Noel Stock, *The Life of Ezra Pound* (1970), 203.

her arrest and trial, when the young anti-vice–society agent obliged a young publisher named Alfred A. Knopf to withdraw the novel *Homo Sapiens* from sale—because Sumner pronounced it obscene. To ensure that he would not repeat the crime, Knopf was also made to melt down the book's plates. In the pages of *The Little Review* Anderson exclaimed: "This is the most inexcusably ridiculous thing that has happened for months. It is incredible!"

Young Knopf's humiliation at the hands of Sumner did not stop Anderson and Heap from publishing James Joyce's *Ulysses,* episode by episode. The first installment appeared in the Spring 1918 number of *The Little Review.*

Said Anderson about the event: "We were the first to publish this masterpiece and the first to be arrested for it."

On October 4, 1920, Sumner had them arrested and charged with publishing obscenity. The offense consisted of printing and distributing the July/August 1920 number of *The Little Review* containing the "Nausicaa" episode from *Ulysses,* in which Leopold Bloom was inspired to indulge in "some erotic musings," as Anderson delicately phrased it, when a young girl named Gertie McDowell let Bloom see her uncovered legs. Gertie's friends had just trotted off to get a better view of some fireworks:

JAMES JOYCE *(Ulysses): At last they were left alone without the others to pry and pass remarks and she knew he could be trusted to the death, steadfast, a man of honour to his fingertips. She leaned back far to look up where the fireworks were and she caught her knee in her hands so as not to fall back looking up and there was no one to see only him and her when she revealed all her graceful beautifully shaped legs like that, supply soft and delicately rounded, and she seemed to hear the panting of his heart his hoarse breathing, because she knew about the passion of men like that, hotblooded, because Bertha Supple told her once in secret about the gentleman lodger that was staying with them out of the record office that had pictures cut out of papers of those skirtdancers and she said he used to do something not very nice that you could imagine sometimes in the bed. But this was different from a thing like that because there was all the difference because she could almost feel him draw her face to his and the first quick hot touch of his handsome lips. Besides there was absolution so long as you didn't do the other thing before being married and there ought to be women priests that would understand without telling out and Cissy Caffrey too sometimes had that dreamy kind of dreamy look in her eyes so that she too, my dear, and besides it was on account of that other thing coming on the way it did.*

And Jacky Caffrey shouted to look, there was another and she leaned back and the garters were blue to match on account of the transparent and they all saw it and shouted to look, look there it was and she leaned back ever so far to see the fireworks and something queer was flying about through the air, a soft thing to and fro, dark. And she saw a long Roman candle going up over the trees up, up, and they were all breathless with excitement as it went higher and higher and she had to lean back more and more to look up after it, high, high, almost out of *sight, and her face was suffused with a divine, an entrancing blush from straining back and he could see her other things too, nainsook knickers, four and eleven, on account of being white and she let him and she saw that he saw and then it went so high it went out of sight a moment and she was trembling in every limb from being bent so far back that he could see high up above her knee where no-one ever and she wasn't ashamed and he wasn't either to look in that immodest way like that because he couldn't resist the sight like those skirtdancers behaving so immodest before gentlemen looking and he kept on looking, looking. She would fain have cried to him chokingly, held out her snowy slender arms to him to come, to feel his lips laid on her white brow. . . . **

———

The episode culminated in Bloom's orgasm, but probably only the careful reader noticed that. Jane Heap defended what Joyce had done, in *The Little Review*.

JANE HEAP: Mr. Joyce was not teaching early Egyptian perversions nor inventing new ones. Girls lean back everywhere, showing lace and silk stockings; wear low-cut sleeveless blouses, breathless bathing suits; men think thoughts and have emotions about these things everywhere—seldom as delicately and imaginatively as Mr. Bloom—and no one is corrupted.†

MARGARET ANDERSON: John Quinn's strategy in defending us was to argue that *Ulysses* was not indecent, merely disgusting, and that the mannequins in Fifth Avenue shop windows exhibited more than Gertie McDowell did, in the way of underdrawers.

———

Although they were not required by law to do so, the judges allowed Quinn to put on the stand three literary experts, to defend what Joyce had written.‡ Anderson commented upon the futility of their contributions. When Phillip Moeller (of the Theatre Guild) was called, he tried to explain the Freudian method of unveiling the unconscious mind, which James Joyce used.

MARGARET ANDERSON: The court gasps and one of the judges calls out— "Here, here, you might as well talk Russian. Speak plain English if you want us to understand what you're saying!"

———

*This is the text as published in the July/August 1920 issue of *The Little Review*, which provided the basis for the prosecution of Anderson and Heap by Sumner, and their conviction.

†The male-oriented perspective suggested by Heap in this passage (from which my book takes its title) may be understood as an aspect of what Harriet Monroe of *Poetry* magazine called *The Little Review*'s "male-identified character." When Heap and Anderson arrived in Paris in 1923, men among the literary community there—including Pound—found Heap "a frightening specimen of the lesbian cross-dresser." Shari Benstock, *Women of the Left Bank* (1986), 379.

‡Anderson was "informed" that "the judges are being especially tolerant to admit witnesses at all—that such is not the custom in the Special Sessions Court." *The Little Review Anthology* (1953), 306.

The next witness was Scofield Thayer, editor of the magazine *The Dial.*

MARGARET ANDERSON: Scofield Thayer was forced to admit that if he had had the desire to publish *Ulysses* he should have consulted a lawyer first— and not published it.

———

The final witness was John Cowper Powys, the famous English poet, novelist, and critic; he made a better impression, declaring *Ulysses* to be "a beautiful piece of work in no way capable of corrupting a young girl."

Afterward, Jane Heap tossed barbs at the court and its process from the pages of *The Little Review:*

JANE HEAP: The heavy farce and sad futility of trying a creative work in a court of law appalled me. Was there ever a judge qualified to judge even the simplest psychic outburst? How then a work of Art? What man not a nincompoop has ever been heard by a jury of his peers? . . . The society for which Mr. Sumner is agent, I am told, was founded to protect the public from corruption. When asked *what public?* its defenders spring to the rock on which America was founded: the cream-puff of sentimentality, and answer chivalrously: "Our young girls!" So the mind of the young girl rules this country? . . . If there is anything really to be feared it is the mind of a young girl.*

MARGARET ANDERSON: Mr. Sumner is . . . a serious, sincere man, very much interested in proving his conviction that James Joyce is filthy to read and contaminating to those who read him. . . . [But the man] is operating in realms in which it can be proved that he cannot function intelligently, legitimately, or with any relation to the question which *should* be up for discussion in the court. That question is the relation of the artist—the great writer—to the public. . . . *I state clearly that the (quite unnecessary!) defense of beauty is the only issue involved.*

James Joyce has never written anything, and will never be able to write anything, that is not beautiful.

———

The law, however, did not concede that beauty could be a defense against an imputation of obscenity;† most English and American judges refused

———

*Heap had fine insight into the workings of obscenity law. Elsewhere she remarked that in seeking to protect the public against obscenity the law actually creates "an artificial market for pornography." Hugh Ford, *Published in Paris* (1975), 287. I find it plausible that in declining to entirely free literary and artistic expression from obscenity laws in 1973, the Supreme Court stimulated the production of inartistic (not to say ugly) illicit pornography, which still looms large in the field of sexual expression. See Chapters 28 and 29.

†Beauty would not become a "defense" to an imputation of obscenity until Justice William J. Brennan, Jr., led the Supreme Court to adopt what became known as the Brennan doctrine in a series of rulings from 1957 to 1966. This doctrine stated that any work with literary or social value could not be branded obscene.

The opposition of the beautiful and the obscene and paradoxically, their *apposition,* was even to let in evidence of literary or artistic merit. The test for obscenity was whether a writing tended to deprave and corrupt the morals of young or immature persons—"those whose minds are open to such immoral influences, and into whose hands a publication of this sort may fall." The language is from the leading English case, followed by most American courts well into the twentieth century, *Regina* v. *Hicklin,* decided in 1868. This being the tenor of the law, some judges maintained that literary merit merely compounded the crime of obscenity by enhancing a book's capacity to deprave and corrupt.

During the trial, Margaret Anderson's "worst moments" came when John Quinn saw fit to apologize to the judges for what *Ulysses'* author and publishers had done. He addressed the "merits" of *Ulysses* "in terms he thought our judges could understand." And so Quinn pontificated that Joyce's *Ulysses* might be called "futuristic literature." It was "neither written for, nor read by, school girls." It was "disgusting in portions, perhaps, but not more so than Swift, Rabelais, Shakespeare, the Bible." It was doubtless "inciting to anger or repulsion but not to lascivious acts." And, Anderson charged, "as his ultimate bit of nauseating and diabolical forensic psychology, aiming at that dim stirring of human intelligence which for one moment lit up the faces of our three judges," Quinn confessed: "I myself do not understand *Ulysses;* I think Joyce has carried his method too far."

At this nadir in Quinn's defense of *Ulysses,* the "most bewildered of the three judges" chimed in: "Yes, it sounds to me like the ravings of a disordered mind. I can't see why anyone would want to publish it!" Feeling wounded and betrayed, having been dissuaded by her lawyer from taking the witness stand, Anderson "almost leapt" from her chair beside him, shouting at the judges: "Let me tell you *why*!" Later she described in *The Little Review* what she fervently wished she had said:

MARGARET ANDERSON: Since I *am* the publisher it may be apropos for me to tell you why I have wanted to publish it more than anything else that has ever been offered to me. Let me tell you *why* I regard it as the masterpiece of my generation. Let me tell you *what* it's about and *why* it was written and *for whom* and *why* you don't understand it and why it is just as well that you don't and *why* you have no right to pit the dullness of your brain against the fineness of mine.

—

suggested by Freud: "There is to my mind no doubt that the concept of 'beautiful' has its roots in sexual excitation and that its original meaning was 'sexually stimulating.' This is related to the fact that we never regard the genitals themselves, which produce the strongest sexual excitation, as really 'beautiful.' " *Three Essays on the Theory of Sexuality* (1962), 22. The legally obscene is that which excites lust or sexual feeling but is patently offensive. Exposed genitalia no doubt epitomize what is obscene. Art, however, effectively renders what is otherwise "obscene" beautiful, and this suggests the insight that possessed Justice Brennan when he fashioned the constitutional doctrine that artistic value will cancel out (or "purify") an imputation that expression is obscene. See Chapters 16 and 22.

She felt, she said, "as though I had been run over by a subway train." And then, Jane Heap, her "distinguished co-publisher," was "pounding me violently in the ribs."

JANE HEAP: Don't try to talk! Don't put yourself in their hands!

And so the publisher of *The Little Review* shut up.

MARGARET ANDERSON: With that look of being untouched by the surrounding stupidities which sends me into paroxysms, I sat back and smiled vacuously at my judges.

Of course the verdict went against the obstreperous women; attitudes of esthetic superiority and intellectual disdain, voiced by or for litigants, make a bad impression on many of those who have charge of the law. Anderson and Heap were fined a hundred dollars—paid, they said, "by a lady from Chicago who detested 'Ulysses' "—and, despite John Quinn's "furious remonstrances," were "led off to have our fingerprints taken."

MARGARET ANDERSON: If they had imagined that registering my digits was going to be a simple matter they were quickly disillusioned. I examined the thick fluid into which I was supposed to dip my well-kept fingers and insisted upon elaborate advance preparations to guarantee its removal. They hadn't enough towels to reassure me. They rushed out to find more. I didn't like their soap. They produced another kind. I insisted on a nail brush. This gave them more difficulty but they found one. Then I managed to make them suffer for my indignity until they were all in a state bordering on personal guilt. I finally offered my fingers with the distaste of a cat and it became their responsibility to convince me that there would be no permanent disfigurement.

Their friend Mary Garden reproached them for paying the fine: "I'm disappointed in you. I thought you'd go to jail."

JOHN QUINN: And now for God's sake, don't publish any more obscene literature!
MARGARET ANDERSON: How am I to know when it's obscene?
JOHN QUINN: I'm sure I don't know. But don't do it!

They did not do it. The magazine stopped carrying episodes from *Ulysses*—"Nausicaa" was the last *The Little Review*'s readers would see.

MARGARET ANDERSON: The trial of *The Little Review* for printing a masterpiece is now over—lost, of course, but if anyone thought there was a chance of winning . . . in the United States of America . . .

The Little Review had serialized about half of Joyce's novel by the time that Sumner struck, but even before that happened, the United States Post

Office had seized from the mails and burned three issues of the magazine because of Joyce's "obscene" prose.* The first seizure was in January 1919 (the "Lestrygonians" episode), the second in May ("Scylla and Charybdis"), the third in January 1920 ("Cyclops").

MARGARET ANDERSON: It was like a burning at the stake as far as I was concerned. The care we had taken to preserve Joyce's text intact; the worry over the bills that accumulated when we had no advance funds; the tears, prayers, hysterics and rages we used on printer, binder, paper houses; the addressing, wrapping, stamping, mailing; the excitement of anticipating the world's response to the literary masterpiece of our generation . . .

And then a notice from the Post Office: BURNED.

———

They received almost no support from intellectuals on behalf of the masterpiece, for months or years.

MARGARET ANDERSON: A desultory appreciation arrived from time to time—usually from the West. New York was especially cold. *The New York Times* was the worst. It took pleasure in insulting us as purveyors of lascivious literature. That must have brought a great deal of satisfaction to Mr. Sumner.

———

Jane Heap expressed this thought in the trial's wake:

JANE HEAP: It was the poet, the artist, who discovered love, created the lover, made sex everything that it is beyond a function. It was the Mr. Sumners who have made it an obscenity.

———

The New York Times was not unhappy with the New York criminal court's decision and was relieved to see that Anderson and Heap were not martyred:

THE NEW YORK TIMES: There will be, doubtless, the usual outcry from circles self-styled artistic and literary over the fining of the two women who edit and publish *The Little Review* for printing in it a presentation of life in Dublin as seen by a writer by the name of Joyce. . . . It is a curious production, not wholly uninteresting, especially to psychopathologists. Its offending lies in its occasional violations of what by common consent is decency in the use of words. Mr. Joyce and the editors of *The Little Review* probably would defend them as "realistic," but that does not make them the more tolerable in print, and certainly does not make them either artistic or literary. . . . That most people would find the story incomprehensible and therefore dull is, perhaps, a reason for letting anybody who wants to print such stuff do it. To make martyrs, even pseudo-martyrs, unnecessarily, is not wise.

———

*Another issue, the October 1917 number, was seized and destroyed for being "obscene" because of an antiwar story in it, "Cattleman's Spring Mate," by Wyndham Lewis. Judge Augustus Hand upheld the Post Office's action. See endnotes to this chapter.

For years Anderson brooded over her decision not to go to jail:

MARGARET ANDERSON: If I had refused to permit the payment of the fine I might have circulated some intelligent propaganda about *Ulysses*, from my jail cell. Still I suppose that *The New York Times* and the others would have refused to give it space. It was not until much later when Sylvia Beach published *Ulysses* in book form in Paris that our three-year propaganda began to have its effect. *The New York Times* must have astonished its readers when finally it began to devote columns to James Joyce's masterpiece.

From then on books of criticism appeared every week lauding *Ulysses*, interpreting it for the general public, often misunderstanding it, and always omitting to mention in spite of our copyright and our trial that it had first been published in *The Little Review*. . . .

It is impossible to go anywhere or read anything without getting into some gibberish about *Ulysses*. *Ulysses* ran serially in *The Little Review* for three years . . . scarcely a peep from the now swooning critics except to mock it. . . . Burton Rascoe, who runs the Bookman's Day Book in the *New York Tribune*, perhaps speaks for them all: When challenged for a past valuation of the book he explained that he didn't know it was a masterpiece when it was running in *The Little Review* because some of the words were misspelled, etc.*

In the summer of 1924, Anderson published in *The Chicago Tribune* a stinging rebuke of the critics and papers that had scorned *The Little Review*'s services to arts and letters with its bold publication of *Ulysses*. She was, she said, "a bit fed-up" with the literary critics who were now themselves taking credit for having discovered *Ulysses*.

MARGARET ANDERSON: Especially as I happen to possess all the inside information as to their refusal for three years to recognize Joyce as anything but an excrescence upon the judicial horizon. As editor, publisher, and founder of *The Little Review* I may be said to be more or less *au courant* with the fact that it was I who published Joyce's *Ulysses* serially in *The Little Review* some five years ago. This was in the days before the professional critics knew that Joyce existed—in spite of the opportunities he had given them with his "Exiles," "Portrait of the Artist as a Young Man," etc. No, I am unjust: several of them have already denounced him thoroughly on

---

*Even the Shakespeare and Company edition of *Ulysses*, personally supervised by Joyce, contained hundreds of errata. Eventually, over 5,000 "imperfections" in that edition—most involving errors of punctuation and spelling—were uncovered by Professor Hans Walter Gabler. His changes were incorporated into *Ulysses (The Corrected Text)*, published by Random House in 1986. However, many "errors" were not errors at all but represented Joyce's intentions. More recently, John Kidd condemned *Ulysses (The Corrected Text)* as being "not a purified text" but "a different version from what Joyce conceived, authorized, and saw into print." "The Scandal of 'Ulysses,'" *The New York Review of Books*, June 30, 1988.

the grounds that in the "Portrait" he wrote of natural functions . . . naturally. When we urged *The New York Times* to help us in spreading a little publicity about this great book our requests were ignored completely, except for sneers at "a decadent art magazine that delights in publishing the filth of diseased contemporary writers," etc. We ran *Ulysses* serially for almost three years, and from the first were attacked by the combined forces of literary, social, and civic America. The Post Office Department suppressed five different issues of *The Little Review*—not only suppressed them but burned them up—each issue of some 4,000 copies, so that we were almost unable to carry on our business.

—

Finding herself "penniless again," Anderson went to see the financier Otto Kahn, hoping that he would help.

OTTO KAHN: Yes, some intelligent help ought to be arranged for *The Little Review*. I'll come up and talk with you both about it.

MARGARET ANDERSON: He came to see us in Eighth Street, admired the magenta floor and the black walls (against which his yellow tea rose boutonnière was effective) and talked with genius about *The Little Review*'s financial problems. He made a summary of ten points which covered the ground.

OTTO KAHN: I'm interested in your personalities. Do you exploit them sufficiently? Do you go about a lot?

MARGARET ANDERSON: I answered that one cannot go about comfortably without being well dressed.

OTTO KAHN: Yes, of course. I should say *The Little Review* needs about four thousand dollars to start with. That will remove your worries about the publication end of it and provide a few pretty dresses.

MARGARET ANDERSON: Wonderful! Then we can go everywhere. And we can talk everywhere. We really can make most interesting talk.

OTTO KAHN: Oh, no one wants to hear any talk. Just go about. Let people see the color of your eyes and your hair and the way you wear your clothes. No one cares about anything else nowadays. Of course your *Ulysses* affair was badly managed. John Quinn is rather old-fashioned, I'm afraid. I should have given you Morris Guest as a publicity agent and had the case on all the front pages. That would have helped you. . . .*

---

*Why did not Quinn appeal the case, if need be, up to the Supreme Court? I suppose because he did not consider the suppression of *The Little Review*, nor the branding of the "Gertie McDowell" issue as "obscene," to raise any judicially cognizable constitutional issue of freedom of speech or press. The struggle for literary freedom was led throughout the first half of the century by lawyers like Quinn who did not press First Amendment arguments upon the courts. By this time (1920) the Supreme Court had recognized in cases like *Schenck* v. *United States* that the free speech and press guarantees could be raised in defense of *political* speech in federal criminal prosecutions for speaking or writing "subversive" words. In 1925, the Court went on to hold the guarantees were also enforceable against prosecutions under state laws, in *Gitlow* v. *New York*.

That the argument for applying the First Amendment to works of literature was available is shown by a letter that *Poetry* publisher Harriet Monroe sent to Margaret Anderson, who published it in *The Little Review* shortly after the trial had been lost: "I want to send a word

MARGARET ANDERSON: Yes, that would have helped. So would have the promised four thousand dollars which for a reason we have never been able to explain did not materialize. I had tea with Otto Kahn once or twice after his visit, and found him charming and interesting. We talked of the four thousand dollars as a foregone conclusion . . . but finally received a letter saying that it would not be forthcoming. Otto Kahn being a man of his word, this was an enigma as well as a shock. We discussed all the possible reasons for the disaster, and could find none.

Margaret Anderson and Jane Heap's *Little Review* survived for another eight years, but the spirit drained out of their magazine after they had to stop publishing *Ulysses.* When they could publish no more of Joyce's masterpiece, they packed up and moved to Paris. It was there, in 1929, the year of the Crash, that the last issue of *The Little Review* came out. Looking back, Anderson realized that "it was because of *Ulysses*," and Pound, that her magazine had been such a success.

After *The Little Review* case was lost, Joyce would not find a man in England or the United States who was brave enough to publish his masterpiece for over ten years. It was another woman who gave the novel new life, in France. From there it made its way to fame and fortune by being smuggled into England and the States.

BENNETT CERF:* For several years after Miss Margaret Anderson and Miss Jane Heap ran afoul of the law for publishing parts of *Ulysses* in their magazine, *The Little Review,* even the most liberal and daring publishers in America recognized the futility of making a fight to legalize James Joyce's greatest book in America. . . . Mr. Joyce did not receive a single overture from a reputable American publisher for *Ulysses* from 1920 until 1931. Copies of the Paris edition, in the familiar Columbia blue paper, continued to be smuggled into the country in ever increasing numbers, and the literary reputation of the book grew apace, but from a strictly legal standpoint, the taboo remained absolute and unchallenged.

None of the "new breed" of American book publishers who emerged in the aftermath of World War I—many of them young Jews and all of them men—dared publish *Ulysses* unexpurgated. Even the scrappy young publishers Albert Boni and Horace Liveright dropped the idea when they learned

---

of cheer," Monroe wrote, "for your courage in the fight against the Society for the Prevention of Vice. My father was a lawyer, and his blood in me longs to carry the battle to the Supreme Court of the United States, in order to find out whether the Constitution permits the assumption of a self-appointed group of citizens, of a restriction of the freedom of the press which only the state, through proper channels, should have any right even to attempt. I wish you a triumphant escape out of their clutches." Monroe evidently felt that it was particularly outrageous that John Sumner was empowered (by his power of "private" prosecution) to deprive Anderson and *The Little Review* of their constitutional right to freedom of the press.

*Founder of Random House, with Donald Klopfer.

that the distinguished B. W. ("Ben") Huebsch—who had proved venture-some enough in 1916 to publish Joyce's *Portrait of the Artist as a Young Man* unexpurgated—had declined to publish *Ulysses* unchanged.

In England, twelve printers had refused to set up Joyce's *Portrait of the Artist as a Young Man* the way Joyce wrote it,* and Harriet Weaver, who had published parts of the work serially in her avant-garde magazine *The Egoist,* would not go along with Ezra Pound's proposal that blank spaces be left and, after printing, the offending passages be filled in with a type-writer. The difficulty was exacerbated because, as everyone knew, only a year earlier, in England, the entire edition of D. H. Lawrence's novel *The Rainbow* had been destroyed by the police.† Publishers and printers on both sides of the Atlantic were intimidated. It was after Ben Huebsch went ahead and published *Portrait* in the States that Weaver brought out her edition in England.

Huebsch was the first Jew in the twentieth century to enter general publishing in the United States. (The first book he published was safe enough—E. H. Grigg's *A Book of Meditations,* published in 1902.) His entry cracked the solidly Gentile façade of the book publishing business and rebuked the unacknowledged anti-Semitism prevalent in the trade. Estab-lished American book publishers of the time would not employ Jews, who thus were able to engage in publishing only by starting their own firms. Between the two world wars a significant number of publishing houses headed by Jews were founded. Not all, however, managed to weather the legal and financial storms that wracked the industry during those years.

Women were discriminated against even more than Jews in book publish-ing, notwithstanding that they had been prominently involved, as both writers and readers, "in the manic surge toward fiction" that took place in the last quarter of the nineteenth century. In 1872, according to John Tebbel's definitive *History of Book Publishing in the United States,* nearly three fourths of American novels published were written by women. By 1880 the flood of fiction was so strong that a backlash set in from people who feared that novels "were the opiate of the masses and productive of social degener-acy." A magazine called *The Hour* warned in 1880: "Millions of young girls and hundreds of thousands of young men are *novelized* into absolute idiocy. Novel-readers are like opium-smokers: the more they have of it the more they want of it, and the publishers, delighted at this state of affairs, go on corrupting public taste and understanding and making fortunes out of this corruption."‡

---

*Typically, printers were liable along with publishers under criminal anti-obscenity laws in France, England, and the United States.

†The censorship is described below in Chapter 4.

‡John Tebbel, *A History of Book Publishing* 2 (1975), 170ff. According to Tebbel, the fiction that was most read and discussed in the nineties came from British authors; much of it was sensational novels that were not even reviewed. Foreign literature could be published without the payment of royalties until the enactment of the Copyright Law of 1891. Tebbel says that

From the beginning, American publishers refused to admit women—other than their wives—as owners, managers, or editors. Notable among the wives in publishing were Blanche Knopf and Frances Brentano. A few other women were able to work their way up from secretarial jobs to positions of assistants, but there was no significant entry of women into the upper echelons of book publishing before the political and cultural upheavals of the 1960s. The family that controlled the distinguished old Boston publishing house Little, Brown did not let women own stock or hire them as editors until after World War II, in the 1950s.* Excluded from roles of influence in established houses and denied the capital needed to start firms of their own, women interested in writing and in bringing other new writers to the public—and interested also in radical social and political change—resorted to the "little magazine," or moved to Paris, where they set up small "alternative" presses† and published some of the best, most innovative and radical literature of the time.

When Ben Huebsch informed Joyce that he wanted to publish *Ulysses*, but only if "some changes are made in the manuscript," Joyce refused to let Huebsch go ahead, and turned his book over to a woman.

---

the absence of international copyright protection helped the growth of the American publishing industry, for "piracy, whatever its ethics, unquestionably gave many American publishers their start and so created the economic conditions in which the industry could grow" (641).

*According to Angus Cameron, editor in chief of Little, Brown at that time. For more about Cameron and Little, Brown, see Chapter 26.

†Shari Benstock documents their fruitful innovative activity as expatriate authors, booksellers, and alternative publishers in Paris in *Women of the Left Bank: Paris 1900–1940* (1986).

2

Fuck Up,
Love!

I N PARIS, Sylvia Beach was relieved to hear that John Quinn's "brilliant defense" had kept Margaret Anderson and Jane Heap from going to jail but was saddened at the news that their publication of *Ulysses* had been stopped. When James Joyce dropped by Shakespeare and Company, her Left Bank bookshop, to tell Beach the news, she saw immediately that "it was a heavy blow for him, and I felt, too, that his pride was hurt." In a tone of complete discouragement, Joyce sat down and said: "My book will never come out now." He had been working at *Ulysses* for seven years.

Joyce had run into trouble publishing almost everything he wrote, including his first volume of prose, *Dubliners.*

JAMES JOYCE: Publishers and printers alike seemed to agree among themselves, no matter how divergent their point of view in other matters, not to publish anything of mine as I wrote it.

Twenty-two publishers and printers had read the manuscript of *Dubliners.*

JAMES JOYCE: When at last it was printed some very kind person bought out the entire edition and had it burnt in Dublin—a new and private auto-da-fé.

In her bookshop that day in early 1921, hoping to buck the author up, Beach asked Joyce if he would let Shakespeare and Company "have the honor of bringing out your *Ulysses.*"* He accepted her offer on the spot,

---

*This is according to Beach, *Shakespeare and Company* (1959), 47. Brenda Maddox considers this scene "a bit like Mickey Rooney and Judy Garland deciding to do their own show, and Beach—"undeterred by her lack of capital, experience, and all the other requisites"—plunged straight into its publication.

She had first arrived in Paris when she was fifteen years old, leaving Bridgeton, New Jersey, behind; her father had been named associate pastor of the American Church in Paris, with a special concern for American students living in the Latin Quarter. This brought Sylvia and her two sisters into contact with famous artists.

SYLVIA BEACH: We were exceedingly fond of Paris, my sisters and I, and this was the fault of my parents, who took us there and gave us a taste of it when we were very young.

———

In November 1919, Beach opened Shakespeare and Company, using $3,000 that her mother gave her; she was thirty-two years old.

SYLVIA BEACH: [M]y mother in Princeton got a cable from me, saying simply: "Opening bookshop in Paris. Please send money," and she sent me all her savings.

———

It was chiefly a lending library, like the one run by her friend and lover Adrienne Monnier,* La Maison des Amis des Livres, around the corner. Monnier's shop was already four years old and she was by then a skillful businesswoman; she advised Beach on the affairs of Shakespeare and Company and introduced her to the Left Bank literary world. Joyce once referred to Monnier as "Beach's more intelligent partner." When the expatriate American resolved to publish *Ulysses*, Monnier encouraged the venture and introduced her to her printer, Maurice Darantière, who removed the last obstacle to the Shakespeare and Company publication of Joyce's masterwork by setting the manuscript in type.

SYLVIA BEACH: Darantière was much interested in what I told him about the banning of *Ulysses* in the English-speaking countries. . . . I laid bare my financial situation and warned him that there could be no question of paying for the printing till the money from the subscriptions came in—if it did come in. . . . M. Darantière agreed to take on the printing of *Ulysses* on those terms.

JAMES JOYCE: My friend Ezra Pound and good luck brought me into contact with a very clever and energetic person Miss Sylvia Beach who had

---

'right here, in the barn!' " and contends: "In reality, it was Joyce who took the initiative and suggested the idea. He knew that Adrienne Monnier had done some publishing under the imprint of her shop and suggested that Sylvia Beach could be persuaded to follow suit." *Nora* (1988), 183-84. Noel Riley Fitch quotes a passage from an early draft of Beach's memoirs: "I accepted with enthusiasm Joyce's suggestion that I publish his book." *Sylvia Beach and the Lost Generation* (1983), 78.

*Shari Benstock, *Women of the Left Bank* (1986), 206ff. Benstock speculates that Monnier seduced Beach "to sexual love" not long after Monnier's lover, Suzanne Bonnierre, suddenly died. Noel Riley Fitch describes Beach's first meetings with Monnier and Joyce in *Sylvia Beach and the Lost Generation* (1983), 11.

been running for some years previously a small English book shop and lending library in Paris under the name of Shakespeare and Co. This brave woman risked what professional publishers did not wish to, she took the manuscript and handed it to the printers. These were very scrupulous and understanding French printers in Dijon, the capital of the French printing press. In fact I attached no small importance to the work being done well and quickly. My eyesight still permitted me at the time to read the proofs myself and thus it came about that thanks to extra work and the kindness of Mr. Darantière the well known Dijon printer *Ulysses* came out a very short time after the manuscript had been delivered and the first printed copy was sent to me for my fortieth birthday on the second of February 1922.

———

Joyce's portrayals of Gertie McDowell's girlish seductiveness and Leopold Bloom's lusting voyeurism—images that had brought *The Little Review* down in New York—were tame compared with later passages in the book, notably the "Penelope" episode; these forty-odd pages, in the form of a soliloquy by Molly Bloom, concluded Joyce's masterpiece. Ezra Pound called it Joyce's "Mollylogue" and claimed it was one of the best things Joyce had ever done. In London, T. S. Eliot concurred, wondering how *anyone* could even write again "after the immense prodigy of that last chapter."*

T. S. ELIOT: I wish, for my sake, that I had not read it.

———

George Moore, the English novelist and essayist, publicly deprecated Joyce's "immense prodigy" but privately exerted himself to obtain for Joyce a coveted English literary award, the King's Purse, worth £100. In England Moore had his own censors to deal with—not the police but the heads of the giant private circulating libraries, who took it upon themselves to protect England's young girls from corruption. The librarians, who had practically a monopoly on the public distribution of popular literature, regularly refused to stock novels that they considered immoral or obscene; most of Moore's novels were of this type. Once it was known that a librarian would not handle an author's work, the author was bereft of a publisher.

"*Ulysses* is hopeless," Moore said, full of envy.

---

*Later, in discussions that took place between the lawyers for Random House, the American publisher of *Ulysses,* and the U.S. attorney preparing for a legal battle to persuade a federal court to find *Ulysses* obscene, the government—faced with the difficult prospect of having to discount a wealth of critical acclaim for Joyce's masterpiece—almost threw in the towel. According to Random House's Bennett Cerf, the authorities decided finally to proceed against them "because there were too many dirty words in the last section of the book." Letter from Bennett Cerf to Paul Léon, dated August 30, 1933, published in *The United States of America v. One Book Entitled Ulysses by James Joyce,* edited by Michael Moscato and Leslie LeBlanc, with an introduction by Richard Ellmann (1984), 221.

GEORGE MOORE: It is absurd to imagine that any good can be served by trying to record every single thought and sensation of any human being. That's not art, it's like trying to copy the *London Directory*.

———

Moore was sure that Joyce had got his idea for the "interior monologue" from Moore's friend the French author Edouard Dujardin. Another theory holds that Joyce copied the style of his wife, Nora, in the letters she wrote to him—"very long, rambling, unpunctuated sentences."* The entire "Penelope" episode consists of eight such sentences. Richard Ellmann thought that the idea came to Joyce via a chance reading of a Dujardin novel, *Les Lauriers Sont Coupés,* which Joyce picked up at a railroad station kiosk in Tours. He was in Tours to hear a tenor he respected sing at the cathedral because, at the time, he was thinking about taking singing lessons himself, again. An Italian musician in Dublin once told him his voice was like that of Jean de Reszke, whom Joyce had heard in *I Pagliacci* at the Paris opera.

Nora loved music and loved the way her husband sang more than the way he wrote. She never would read *Ulysses* and showed little interest or pride in her husband's writings until after he was dead.

NORA JOYCE: Jim should have stuck to music instead of bothering with writing.

———

Nora's indifference, even aversion, to her husband's writing did not bother Joyce except when—in retaliation for Joyce's drunken roistering with his friends Frank Budgen and Paul Suter—she notified him: "I've torn up your book." Joyce reportedly turned stone-cold sober and did not take another drop until he found his manuscript intact. Later, during the writing of *Ulysses,* Budgen and Suter came to call and Nora said: "My husband is writing a book. I tell you *das Buch ist ein Schwein.*" Joyce responded by showing his friends what Nora liked to read: a trashy magazine called *Perl-Romane.*

Nora Joyce also claimed that her husband knew "nothing at all about women." That was her comment after Joyce showed her a flattering letter he received from the psychoanalyst Dr. Carl Jung, who called the "Penelope" episode a "a string of veritable peaches."

DR. CARL JUNG: I suppose the devil's grandmother knows so much about the real psychology of women, I didn't.

———

Although Joyce never said so, some people, including Sylvia Beach, believed that his main model for the character of Molly Bloom was Nora. After Joyce died and his widow went to live in Zurich, someone asked her if she was Molly Bloom. Said Nora: "I'm not. *She* was much fatter." Joyce

———

*Brenda Maddox, *Nora* (1988), 199.

weighed Molly in at "eleven stone nine," or 163 pounds. Brenda Maddox's biography of Nora has as its thesis that Nora *was* Molly Bloom.

Nora liked to say that her husband's writing "baffled" her. She could not see that it made any sense to rewrite sentences again and again. Joyce is known to have read aloud to her at least once from a chapter of *Ulysses,* although she told him straight out that she cared nothing about his "so-called art." She accepted his writing because she expected that eventually it would allow them to live a rich life in Paris. When he copied his changes from a notebook into his manuscript, she was pained.

NORA JOYCE: Will all that paper be wasted?

———

She felt the same way about George Moore's writing. Once Joyce set her to reading Moore's story "Mildred Lawson," which ended with a woman musing in her bed—an ending about as inconclusive as that of *Ulysses,* or the stories in *Dubliners.* Said Nora about Moore: "That man doesn't know how to finish a story."

Here is the way Joyce finished *Ulysses;* Molly is ruminating in bed:

JAMES JOYCE *(Ulysses): the sun shines for you he said the day we were lying among the rhododendrons on Howth head in the grey tweed suit and his straw hat the day I got him to propose to me yes first I gave him the bit of seedcake out of my mouth and it was leapyear like now yes 16 years ago my God after that long kiss I near lost my breath yes he said I was a flower of the mountain yes so we are flowers all a woman's body yes that was one true thing he said in his life and the sun shines for you today yes that was why I liked him because I saw he understood or felt what a woman is and I knew I could always get round him and I gave him all the pleasure I could leading him on till he asked me to say yes and I wouldnt answer first only looked out over the sea and the sky I was thinking of so many things he didnt know of Mulvey and Mr Stanhope and Hester and father and old captain Groves and the sailors playing all birds fly and I say stoop and washing up dishes they called it on the pier and the sentry in front of the governors house with the thing round his white helmet poor devil half roasted and the Spanish girls laughing in their shawls and their tall combs and the auctions in the morning the Greeks and the jews and the Arabs and the devil knows who else from all the ends of Europe and Duke street and the fowl market all clucking outside Larby Sharons and the poor donkeys slipping half asleep and the vague fellows in the cloaks asleep in the shade on the steps and the big wheels of the carts of the bulls and the old castle thousands of years old yes and those handsome Moors all in white and turbans like kings asking you to sit down in their little bit of a shop and Ronda with the old windows of the posadas 2 glancing eyes a lattice hid for her lover to kiss the iron and the wineshops half open at night and the castanets and the night we missed the boat at Algeciras the watchman going about serene with his lamp and O that awful deepdown torrent O and the sea the sea crimson sometimes like fire and the glorious sunsets and the figtrees in the Alameda gardens yes and all the queer little streets and the pink and blue and yellow houses and the rosegardens and the jessamine and geraniums and cactuses and Gibraltar as a girl where I was a*

Flower of the mountain yes when I put the rose in my hair like the Andalusian girls used or shall I wear a red yes and how he kissed me under the Moorish wall and I thought well as well him as another and then I asked him with my eyes to ask again yes and then he asked me would I yes to say yes my mountain flower and first I put my arms around him yes and drew him down to me so he could feel my breasts all perfume yes and his heart was going like mad and yes I said yes I will Yes.

———

Sylvia Beach had a prospectus printed up, announcing that *Ulysses* by James Joyce would be published by Shakespeare and Company "complete as written," in a limited edition of one thousand copies; on the back of the prospectus was a subscription form. The book was produced rapidly so that it could be in the author's hands on Joyce's fortieth birthday, February 2, 1921. The night before, while Joyce waited at home "in a state of energetic prostration," the printer, Darantière, entrusted two copies of the book to the conductor of the Dijon–Paris express; Beach met the train at seven the next morning and in ten minutes by taxi was at Joyce's door. She gave the author one copy and kept the other for herself, to exhibit at Shakespeare and Company. Richard Ellmann says: "Everyone crowded in from nine o'clock until closing to see it."

SYLVIA BEACH: André Gide [was] the first of our French friends to rush to my bookshop and fill in one of the subscription blanks.

———

Then Ernest Hemingway—one of her bookstore's "best customers"— put himself down for several copies; and Ezra Pound personally handed over a subscription blank filled in by W. B. Yeats. The literati were testifying to their interest in Joyce's underground novel.

GERTRUDE STEIN: Joyce is good. He is a good writer. People like him because he is incomprehensible and anybody can understand him. But who came first, Gertrude Stein or James Joyce?

ERNEST HEMINGWAY: Joyce has a most goddamn wonderful book. Meantime the report is that he and all his family are starving but you can find the whole celtic crew of them every night in Michaud's where Binney [his wife, Hadley] and I can only afford to go about once a week. . . . The damned Irish, they have to moan about something or other, but you never heard of an Irishman starving.

J. MIDDLETON MURRY: The driving impulse of this remarkable book is an immense, an unprecedented, liberation of the suppressions of an adult man who has lived under the shadow of the Roman-Catholic Church in a country where that Church is at its least European, and is merely an immense reinforcement of Puritanism.

———

Gilbert Seldes said, "Whole chapters in *Ulysses* are monuments to the power and the glory of the written word. It is a victory of the creative intelligence over the chaos of uncreated things and a triumph of devotion, to my mind one of the most significant and beautiful of our time." Edmund Wilson commented that "*Ulysses'* importance is in once more setting the standard of the novel so high that it needn't be ashamed to take its place beside poetry and drama."

The verdict was not unanimous.

EDMUND GOSSE: He is a sort of Marquis de Sade, but does not write so well.

GEORGE MOORE: A sort of Zola gone to seed.

VIRGINIA WOOLF: A queasy undergraduate scratching his pimples.

———

And, in the *Sunday Express,* James Douglas castigated what Joyce had done: "I have read it, and I say that it is the most infamously obscene book in ancient or modern literature. The obscenity of Rabelais is innocent compared with its leprous and scabrous horrors. All the secret sewers of vice are canalized in its flood of unimaginable thoughts, images and pornographic words. And its unclean lunacies are larded with appalling and revolting blasphemies directed against the Christian religion and against the holy name of Christ—blasphemies hitherto associated with the most degraded orgies of Satanism and the Black Mass."

Douglas's review ensured that *Ulysses* would not be published in England for a long time, for the literary reviewers systematically inspired action by the government and the vigilantes—groups of private citizens who raised money to finance the prosecution of publications they considered obscene. The sort of thing that made the obscenity of Rabelais seem to Douglas "innocent" by comparison can be found a short way into the "Penelope" episode. Molly Bloom is musing in bed:

JAMES JOYCE (*Ulysses*): *Ines told me that one drop even if it got into you at all after I tried with the Banana but I was afraid it might break and get lost up in me somewhere because they once took something down out of a woman that was up there for years covered with limesalts theyre all mad to get in there where they come out of youd think they could never go far enough up and then theyre done with you in a way till the next time yes because theres a wonderful feeling there so tender all the time how did we finish it off yes O yes I pulled him off into my handkerchief pretending not to be excited but I opened my legs I wouldn't let him touch me inside my petticoat because I had a skirt opening up the side I tormented the life out of him first tickling him I loved rousing that dog in the hotel rrrsssstt awokwokawok his eyes shut and a bird flying below us he was shy all the same I liked him like that moaning I made him blush a little when I got over him that way when I unbuttoned him and took his out and drew back the skin it had a kind of eye in it theyre all Buttons men down the middle on the wrong side of them Molly darling he called me what was his name Jack Joe Harry Mulvey was it yes. . . .*

Within a month of the Shakespeare and Company publication, the first printing of *Ulysses* was practically sold out, and within a year James Joyce had become a well-known figure. *Ulysses* was explosive in its impact on the literary world of 1922. Probably no significant novelist, poet, or dramatist from that time on has been untouched by Joyce's *Ulysses*.

Then began the great game of smuggling the Shakespeare and Company edition into countries where it was forbidden, especially England and the United States. The contraband article was transported across the seas and national borders in all sorts of cunning ways: in the bottom of hatboxes, hidden in underwear, stuck under the traveler's waistcoat, even with the covers of the Bible pasted over it. So many copies left Sylvia Beach's bookshop for dissemination abroad in surreptitious ways that eight months after the initial printing of one thousand copies a second printing appeared. By December 1925 Shakespeare and Company had issued five more printings. The eleventh and last edition was brought out by Beach in May 1929.

Joyce lived to see *Ulysses* published freely in the United States and England. Ten years after the first Shakespeare and Company edition, the novel was published in New York by Random House, a five-year-old firm founded by two of the "new breed," Bennett Cerf and Donald Klopfer. Random House beat out half a dozen competitors to get the right to publish *Ulysses;* the prospect of persuading an American court that the masterpiece was not "obscene" was much better in 1932 than it had been a decade earlier. For one thing, a short time before, another young firm, Covici-Friede, had won a well-publicized legal battle with John Sumner in New York—over Radclyffe Hall's "lesbian novel," *The Well of Loneliness*. For another, Joyce's underground book by now had acquired the status of a classic.

The idea that the time had come to fight for *Ulysses'* freedom was suggested to Cerf by a New York financier, Robert Kastor, whose sister Helen was married to Joyce's son, George ("Giorgio"). The publisher told this story, which is elsewhere unrecorded, in the February 15, 1934, issue of a "review of books and personalities" called *Contempo*.

BENNETT CERF: High up in one of lower Broadway's mightiest sky-scrapers there is hidden a brokerage office that is unlike any other I have seen, and is presided over by two of the most remarkable figures in this town. One of them is named Irving Sartorius, famous in Yale crew annals, and today noted for his uncanny skill at bridge and sailing. The other is Robert Kastor, who, tho he is so shy that few outsiders have heard his name, and tho he speaks in such a low, gentle voice that companions must strain continually to hear what he is saying, is said to possess one of the great fortunes of this new era, and who has made the literary reputation of more than one name that the reader would recognize very readily today. Together, these two men preside over a brokerage office that might be mistaken, were it not for the hum of the tickers, for an old Southern club, with a liveried old negro flunkey at the door, and a handful of distinguished looking gentlemen watching the stock quotations with what might be described at best as indifferent attention.

Into this rather precious atmosphere I was summoned one day in December 1931, by Mr. Kastor himself. He had watched the progress of Random House since its first book had appeared in 1927. (I recognized some of our books, in fact, on the shelves behind him while he spoke to me. Two volumes of the Nonesuch Shakespeare, I remember, were on Mr. Sartorius' desk.) He believed that the time had come to make the fight for *Ulysses* in America. He was leaving for Europe in a few weeks to visit his sister Helen, who is married to James Joyce's son. Would we like him to tell Mr. Joyce that Random House was ready to take up the battle?

Would we!

I tore uptown, talked the matter over with Donald Klopfer, my partner, and before five that evening we were closeted with Morris Ernst, the lawyer, outlining a contract to offer to Mr. Joyce, and laying the plans for the legal battle that lay before us.

———

Those plans had at their core the idea of obtaining a judicial determination regarding *Ulysses'* obscenity from a New York federal court in advance of any American publication of the book. This promised to eliminate the large legal costs and financial risks that would be entailed if the court test was secured instead through a post-publication criminal prosecution. With some help from friends of Joyce's in Paris, Cerf and New York lawyer Morris Ernst would eventually arrange to get a copy of the Shakespeare and Company edition seized by U.S. Customs officials in New York, setting the stage for the test case.

BENNETT CERF: I had heard Morris Ernst, the great lawyer, say one night that the banning of *Ulysses* was a disgrace, and that he'd like to wage a fight to legalize it. So in March, 1932, I had lunch with Ernst and said, "If I can get Joyce signed up to do an American edition of *Ulysses,* will you fight the case for us in Court?" I added, "We haven't got the money to pay your fancy prices"—he was a very high-powered lawyer—"but I'd like to make you a proposition. We'll pay all the court expenses, and if you win the case, you'll get a royalty on *Ulysses* for the rest of your life." Ernst said "Great, great."

———

So Cerf wrote Joyce in Paris, in care of Shakespeare and Company, "where I knew he made his headquarters," to say he was coming over and would love to meet him in Paris "to see if we could work out a way of publishing *Ulysses* officially in America." But before that, Kastor opened the way through a personal visit with Joyce.

BENNETT CERF: Mr. Kastor sailed for Europe early in February, and pleaded our case with such eloquence before Joyce that he signed a contract with us early in March. The advance that we paid him on the signing of the contract was the first money he had ever received from America for the book that is universally recognized as one of the most important of all time!

—

In Paris, Cerf went straight to Joyce's headquarters at Shakespeare and Company.

BENNETT CERF: On the morning agreed upon I walked into Sylvia Beach's and there was James Joyce sitting with a bandage around his head, a patch over his eye, his arm in his sling and his foot all bound up and stretched out on a chair. He looked like one of those characters in "The Spirit of '76." I retreated a pace.

SYLVIA BEACH: "Oh, Mr. Cerf, don't think he always looks that way. He was so excited about meeting you, on the way here he was run over by a taxicab. But he insisted on seeing you today, because he needs money and he thinks maybe you're going to get some for him."

BENNETT CERF: I said, "Well, I'm certainly ready to give him some. . . . I don't really know whether we can win this case or not, but I do think the climate is changing in America, and I'm willing to gamble on it. I'll give you fifteen hundred dollars,* with the understanding that if we legalize the book, this is an advance against regular royalties of fifteen percent. If we lose the case, you keep the fifteen hundred." He was delighted with that; it was a lot more money than it would be today.

JAMES JOYCE: "I don't think you'll manage it. And you're not going to get the fifteen hundred back."

—

The contract that they signed on March 31, 1932, actually provided for an advance of $1,000.00 with an additional $1,500.00 promised "on the day of publication." *Ulysses* would become Random House's "first really important trade publication." Cerf said, "It did a lot for Random House."

After the customs seizure of the Shakespeare and Company edition in New York, Random House went into federal court to try to free the book for American publication by getting the seized copy declared not obscene.† To get the case removed from a "straight-laced Catholic judge" to a "liberal" one, Ernst was able to "time" the proceedings to come up when Judge John M. Woolsey was sitting.‡ The stratagem worked, and in the first of

---

*Brenda Maddox has a somewhat different version: Cerf at first "offered only a miserly two-hundred-dollar advance on *Ulysses*," but Robert Kastor, "who outperformed Joyce's literary agent [Pinker] shamed him into quintupling it and into paying top royalties—15 percent— as well. Joyce could not resist going round to boast to Sylvia and Adrienne. From then on, he admitted Kastor to that tight circle of people he considered as family." *Nora* (1988), 277.

†The method Cerf and Ernst used to get testimony of *Ulysses'* literary value before the court is described below in Chapter 2.

‡The lawyer would have had no way to have the trial assigned to Woolsey except by requesting adjournments or postponements of proceedings called before other judges of the district court, until the case reached the judge whom Cerf understood was "the most liberal-minded judge on the circuit." In a letter to Paul Léon dated August 30, 1933, Cerf reported: "The *Ulysses* case is finally underway, after almost innumerable postponements. The last few postponements, as a matter of fact, however, were engineered by our own attorneys for the

two *Ulysses* decisions destined to become landmarks in the struggle for literary freedom, Woolsey, sitting in federal district court in New York, held that the work as a whole had literary merit but no aphrodisiacal impact on the average person and was therefore not obscene. This was a new and, for its time, liberal approach to the definition of the obscene. It followed a suggestion federal district judge Learned Hand had made twenty years before to modernize the rule laid down in 1868 in *Regina* v. *Hicklin*, which made the test of obscenity whether a publication had any tendency to morally corrupt the young or otherwise "susceptible."

Later, Ernst would write a foreword to the Random House edition of *Ulysses* in which he characterized Judge Woolsey's decision as "a body-blow for the censors" and predicted that "the necessity for hypocrisy and circumlocution in literature was eliminated." Writers, Ernst buoyantly mused, would no longer need "to seek refuge in euphemisms" and might "describe basic human functions without fear of the law." In fact, the *Ulysses* decision did not open the doors of American publishers to already contraband meritorious literary works, such as D. H. Lawrence's unexpurgated *Lady Chatterley's Lover* or Henry Miller's *Tropic of Cancer* and *Tropic of Capricorn*,* and it would not forestall the banning as obscene of new meritorious literary works, including Theodore Dreiser's *An American Tragedy,* Erskine Caldwell's *God's Little Acre,* Lillian Smith's *Strange Fruit,* and Edmund Wilson's *Memoirs of Hecate County.* In part this was because a federal rule, even one such as Woolsey's that was upheld on appeal, could not control the behavior of state legislatures in defining the obscene, nor the decisions of state courts in identifying the obscene.†

In the foreword he wrote for the first American edition of *Ulysses,* Morris

---

purpose of getting the case before the most liberal-minded judge on the circuit. This is Judge Woolsey and the case is now in his hands." *United States of America v. One Book Entitled Ulysses by James Joyce* (1984), 221. Ernst knew Woolsey was "liberal-minded" because two years earlier, in two separate cases, the judge had been persuaded by Ernst to free from customs seizure books by Dr. Marie C. Stopes: one was called *Married Love,* on its way to the publishers G. P. Putnam's Sons from their London branch; the other was titled *Contraception.* The cases, *United States* v. *One Book Entitled "Married Love"* and *United States* v. *One Book Entitled "Contraception,"* are reprinted in de Grazia, *Censorship Landmarks* (1969), 88, 90.

*Events of censorship regarding *Lady Chatterley's Lover* and *Tropic of Cancer* are described in Chapters 5 and 19. In his foreword to *Ulysses* Ernst cited Judge Woolsey's decision freeing *Ulysses* as the latest in a series of decisions "which have served to liberalize the law of obscenity." The other cases he mentioned were "the victory over the New York Vice Society" in the *Mademoiselle de Maupin* case in 1922, the *Well of Loneliness* case, the *Dennett* case, the cases involving Dr. Stopes's books, the *Frankie and Johnnie* case, and the *God's Little Acre* case. The texts of these cases may be found in de Grazia, *Censorship Landmarks* (1969), 71, 78, 83, 88, 90, 91, and 93. It should be noted, however, that this "salutary forward march of our court," as Ernst called it, failed to produce an authoritative constitutional doctrine like that later adumbrated by Supreme Court Justice William J. Brennan, Jr., which would result in a national freeing of all literature having even the slightest merit. It was only a "salutary forward march" by the Warren Court that brought this achievement about. See especially Chapter 22.

†Even trial and appellate courts in other federal districts were not "bound" to follow Woolsey's rule, as adapted on appeal. Nor are federal courts sitting in different districts today bound to follow one another. Today, such courts (as well as state courts) are bound to follow a federal rule only to the extent that the rule has been approved of, affirmed, or announced by the Supreme Court as an aspect of federal constitutional law.

Ernst flattered the judge who had tried and freed Joyce's book, proclaiming that Woolsey's opinion "raises him to the level of former Supreme Court Justice Oliver Wendell Holmes as a master of judicial prose." The opinion was printed immediately after Ernst's foreword.* According to Woolsey, the "correct" federal test for obscenity was whether literature "tended to stir the sex impulse or to lead to impure and lustful thoughts." While this was certainly a narrower definition of obscenity than traditional formulations that were based on *Hicklin,* it still left judges and jurors room to find obscene whatever struck *them* as obscene. The new test was almost as subjective as the old; it essentially required the obscenity detector to inquire of himself whether *he* was aroused by reading the stuff. In those days this must have seemed a brave undertaking, and one that only the spread of Freud's new ideas on human sexuality and the unconscious could have induced grown men, at least if they were judges,† to engage in. More "objectively," Woolsey said, the question should be: Was the *average* reader, or "the man on the street," or the person "with average sex instincts"—what the French call *"l'homme moyen sensuel"*—likely to be aroused by reading the work in question. Such a person, Woolsey speculated, would be "objective" and "fair" and not "too much subservient" to the inquirer's "own idiosyncrasies."

Faced now with the need to apply to *Ulysses* the legal rule he had decided ought to control his decision, Judge Woolsey proceeded by "checking my impressions with two friends of mine who in my opinion answered to the requirements of *l'homme moyen sensuel.*" From these two unknown and invisible men (certainly they would not have been women) Woolsey learned that "they found as I did that reading *Ulysses* in its entirety did not tend to excite sexual impulses or lustful thoughts." "Indeed," Woolsey concluded, "the net effect" on those consulted was "only that of a somewhat tragic and very powerful commentary on the inner lives of men and women." We can take it that reading *Ulysses* did not stir either man to tumescence.‡

Writing in *Scribner's Magazine* for May 1934, Ben Ray Redman took incisive issue with the accolades that greeted Woolsey's decision, with Ernst's "victory dance over the graves of Bowdler, Anthony Comstock and Mrs. Grundy," and with the "critics everywhere" who, "with pagan piety,

---

*It may also be found in de Grazia, *Censorship Landmarks* (1969), 94.

†I am not sure Woolsey and other enlightened judges such as Learned and Augustus Hand would have trusted the average juror to apply such a test. There was no jury in the *Ulysses* case, although either side might have had one for the asking. I suspect a jury would have proved fatal to *Ulysses* if the government had been allowed to read particularly daring passages.

‡In 1962, the United States Supreme Court would add to the definition of the "obscene" a necessity that it be "patently offensive." The case is *Manual Enterprises* v. *Day* (1962), reprinted in de Grazia, *Censorship Landmarks* (1969), 360. The opinion was written by Justice John Marshall Harlan, who sometimes competed with Justice Brennan in trying to define the indefinable "obscene" for the Court. The current definition was set forth in the 1973 case of *Miller* v. *California.* In *Miller,* Justice Brennan and three other dissenting members of the Warren Court bench advocated abandonment of the fruitless job of trying to define (in a constitutionally acceptable way) the "obscene." See Chapter 22.

have conscientiously hymned the dawn of a new freedom." Redman's thesis is remarkable for its modernity; it holds good even as a criticism of the contemporary Supreme Court's continuing attempt to define the obscene.

BEN RAY REDMAN: We have here, certainly, an admirable example of judicial reasoning in a worthy cause, but I fail utterly to find the useful formula to which Mr. Ernst refers; and I do not believe that such a formula can be forged until the legal definition of obscenity, under which Judge Woolsey worked, is abolished as hypocritical and ridiculous. So long as that definition remains in force, the best we can do is to evade its teeth by ingenious special pleading. . . .

Let me repeat that the legal definition of obscenity enunciated by Judge Woolsey in the course of duty bears no relation to the facts of life and the realities of literature, and that we cannot even begin to talk of satisfactory formulas for censorial judgement until this definition is abolished or altered beyond recognition. To deny literature the right of stirring the sex impulses of man is to deny it one of its prime and proper functions; for these impulses are fundamental, necessary and energizing, and there are no strings within us more vital and more vitalizing upon which art can play. . . .

So long as a large portion of mankind clings to the idea that there is something inherently sinful or dirty about sex, so long as numberless persons insist upon believing that they have been conceived in iniquity, there is no hope of framing a censorial formula that will be proof against the onslaught of such believers. They may agree, in general, that the function of literature is to enrich, enlarge and intensify our experience of life; but the instant literature presumes to deal (in a manner they consider over-frank) with the experience from which life itself stems, they will be ready with their whip and scorpions. In other words, between you and me, I think there is almost no hope of the desired formula being found. Judge Woolsey's average man stands squarely across the path that leads to legalized freedom, and the best that literature can expect is that its romps in the open fields will be paid for, periodically, in hair shirt and in chains.

———

Woolsey's decision that *Ulysses* was not obscene was appealed by the United States attorney Martin Conboy, who had approved the customs bureau's seizure of *Ulysses*. Conboy, a prominent lay Catholic, had used his office two years earlier to bar from importation into the United States the Czechoslovakian film *Ecstasy,* directed by the experimental Czech filmmaker Gustav Machaty and starring the immortal Hedy Lamarr.* While the distributor's appeal from the trial court's decision in that case was pending before the higher court, the copy of the film seized by customs was burned by impatient federal officials.

In due course Joyce's book was vindicated on appeal, as at trial. The

---

*The movie and its censorship in the United States are described in de Grazia and Newman, *Banned Films: Movies, Censors and the First Amendment* (1982).

three-man panel of judges who heard the case included two of the most enlightened judges in the country: Learned Hand and Augustus Hand.* In upholding the claim by Random House that *Ulysses* should be set free, the Hands made use of the same "test" for obscenity that Woolsey had applied: Did reading *Ulysses* in its entirety have "the effect of promoting lust"? In an opinion written by Augustus Hand, the court announced that it had read the book and concluded that it was "a work of originality and sincerity of treatment" which "had not the effect of promoting lust." There-fore—and "even though it justly might offend many"—*Ulysses* was not "obscene" and could lawfully be brought into the United States.

The court's decision did not turn on any argument of counsel that the importation of a meritorious literary work was protected by the constitu-tional guarantees of freedom of speech or press, although Ernst diligently advanced that argument. Presented in an obscenity case, this contention would not seriously be listened to by American judges until after World War II. But the Hand opinion recognized that "progress" in literature and art was threatened by governmental decisions to suppress "the obscene," and so the definition of what was "obscene" was narrowed by a declaration that literature might lawfully be found obscene only if, *taken as a whole*, it tended to arouse lust; and then only if such a tendency was the book's *dominant effect*. That *some passages*† were thought "filthy," or sexually "im-moral" or likely to "corrupt" or to have an aphrodisiacal quality would not be a sufficient ground to condemn literature—at least not in a federal court in the Hands' federal circuit.‡ In applying their rules, Augustus Hand said, they had considered "the relevancy of the objectionable parts to the theme"

---

*The third judge on the panel, Martin Manton, dissented. Ellmann reports he was later imprisoned for "corruption in office." Richard Ellmann, *James Joyce* (1982), 679. The *Ulysses* decision on appeal is reprinted in de Grazia, *Censorship Landmarks* (1969), 96.

†Ben Ray Redman intelligently scorned the value of this "liberal" rule: "[W]hy niggle over arguments as to whether a certain work of art is sexually stirring only in parts or in its entirety? The part serves its purpose for good or evil as potently as the whole. Four lines of *Venus and Adonis* can do as much damage, if there is damage to be done, as all the lines of Carew's *A Rapture*. And are we to condemn a first-rate work of literature because it stirs the sex impulses in its entirety, while we condone a tenth-rate piece of writing because only a quarter of it happens to tickle our erogenous zones? The rule proves asinine the moment we attempt to apply it. Indeed, it is no rule at all, but only a casuist's trick for outwitting hypocrisy. So far as it accomplished its end, it is not to be despised, but it can never be looked upon as anything better than evasion." "Obscenity and Censorship," *Scribner's Magazine*, May 1934, 344.

‡Obscenity law was not "constitutionalized"—which is to say, the administrative or judicial determination that a publication was obscene was not made a constitutional question ulti-mately for the Supreme Court to decide—until 1957, when Justice Brennan began the process in *Roth* v. *United States*. Obscenity law was not "nationalized" until 1964, when the Supreme Court, again speaking through Justice Brennan, did that in cases involving the Henry Miller novel *Tropic of Cancer* and a Louis Malle movie, *The Lovers*, in which the Court held that state and local communities could not constitutionally disagree with the Court's own determina-tion (or approval of a lower court's determination) that a particular work was entitled to be free and could not be branded "obscene." Brennan's move to nationalize the constitutional law of obscenity was to a degree (but only to a degree) frustrated by subsequent decisions of the Burger Court emphasizing the importance of "local community standards." Local commu-nity standards do *not* control the decision whether a work has literary or artistic value serious enough to preclude its being banned as obscene. See Chapter 28 below.

and "the established reputation of the work in the estimation of approved critics"—thereby validating the use and enhancing the weight of literary experts like those who had futilely come to the defense of *Ulysses,* and Margaret Anderson and Jane Heap, fifteen years earlier.*

If the tests articulated by Judges John Woolsey and Augustus and Learned Hand had been applied to a series of early letters exchanged between Joyce and his sweetheart, Nora, those letters would have been found obscene, because their dominant purpose *was* to arouse lust, and the absence of literary, artistic, or historical value would not become an element in the definition of the obscene for another thirty years.

According to Julian Symons, in *Makers of the New* (1987), these letters written by Joyce to Nora in 1909 exposed his "sexual desires and torments," including his "delight in seeing her stained bloomers, his longing for her to write him wicked words like *arse* and *fuck,* and his desire to be flogged by her and see her eyes blazing with anger." Brenda Maddox's biography *Nora* depicts these letters—they passed between Joyce and Nora during several months of separation—as "masturbatory," beginning with the frank declaration by Nora that she was "longing to be fucked" by him. When Joyce "replied in a frenzy of obscenity," the lovers were off on a pornographic spree, each striving to outdo the other in writing "the dirtiest things" they could think of, and with Joyce demanding of them both what Freud seemed to be "asking of his patients in the new art of psychoanalysis: to put every thought, however shameful, into words without flinching." For Maddox, the wonder was not that Joyce could do it, but that Nora Barnacle, "schooled only at the Convent of Mercy, confidently matched him and, by his own judgement, sometimes bettered him."

That Nora in the beginning *did* better Joyce becomes clear from a long, beautiful letter of December 3, 1909, in which Joyce sought to excite his "darling convent girl" by recalling moments in which she had taken the lead. One evening in Ringsend, he reminded her, it was she who slid her hand down inside Joyce's trousers.

JAMES JOYCE: You . . . gradually took it all, fat and stiff as it was, into your hand and frigged me slowly until I came off through your fingers, all the time bending over me and gazing at me out of your quiet saintlike eyes.

—

Another time, in bed in Pola, Nora, tired of lying under Joyce, ripped her nightgown off "violently" and climbed atop him naked, to ride him "up and down."

JAMES JOYCE: Perhaps the horn I had was not big enough for you. I remember that you bent down to my face and murmured tenderly "Fuck up, love! Fuck up, love!"

*Eventually, a literary work's defender would have a "due process" right to introduce such testimony of literary value, and such testimony would become practically a ticket to freedom under the "Brennan doctrine." See Chapter 22.

Joyce told Nora to keep his letters secret and let no one see her excitement. He was afraid that she would get so aroused reading them that she would give herself to somebody else.

BRENDA MADDOX: The letters were designed as aids to self-stimulation. . . .* They give no sign of having been written during the act of masturbation; indeed the clarity of the filthiest pages, compared with the more mundane, suggests that Joyce may even have copied them from rough drafts he wrote during the day.

———

The favorable federal decisions, coming so long after *Ulysses* had exploded on the literary scene, had little effect on James Joyce's already enormous literary standing, thanks to the Shakespeare and Company publication of *Ulysses* in Paris and the remarkably widespread and effective smuggling of the book into England and America. And although the much larger American sales that followed the Random House publication, together with the royalties on the first French, Swedish, Polish, and Japanese editions, vastly improved Joyce's financial situation, most of what came in to Joyce was spent on experiences connected with the mental illness of his daughter, Lucia, and his own increasingly debilitating eye problems. Despite the news that the government had lost its appeal from Woolsey's decision freeing *Ulysses,* Joyce fell into melancholy and depression. The years between the first Shakespeare and Company edition of *Ulysses* and the free publication of the book in America were ravaged by the author's worsening sight and insoluble family and financial problems. More than anything else, Lucia's illness tortured him: none of the psychiatric nostrums he tried could help her, nor could Carl Jung, the psychoanalyst. Said Lucia about the celebrated Jung's efforts at therapy: "To think that such a big fat materialistic Swiss man should try to get hold of my soul."†

---

*Maddox speaks of them as the "dirty letters," saying they "are still dirty today, a sexual revolution later" (*Nora,* 107). The impression this gives, however, is that some elements of the sexual revolution passed Maddox by. She suggests that Nora participated in the exchange mainly in order to keep Joyce from visiting prostitutes in her absence and as a method of controlling Joyce's allegiance to her. It was, supposes Maddox, another "tactic" that Nora used to keep Joyce in love with her, dependent upon her sexual favors. Says Maddox, in explaining Nora's indulgence of the "dirty letter" exchange: "[S]he wanted to hold her man, she wanted to extract money, and she loved sexual games" (105).

Murray S. Davis has investigated some interesting anatomical and sociological relationships between "sex" and "dirt," and how people think and feel about them, in *Smut: Erotic Reality/ Obscene Ideology* (1983), 87–96, and his notes to those pages.

†Lucia's letters were destroyed by Stephen Joyce, James Joyce's grandson, because he "didn't want to have greedy little eyes and greedy little fingers going over them," as, presumably, they went over Joyce's "lust" letters to Nora. Said Stephen Joyce in justification: "My aunt may have been many things, but to my knowledge she was not a writer." See "The Fate of Joyce Family Letter Causes Angry Literary Debate" in *The New York Times,* August 15, 1988. Brenda Maddox points to evidence that Gertie McDowell (see Chapter 1) and the Blooms' fifteen-year-old daughter, Millie (with whom Bloom thrice committed sexual improprieties), were modeled by Joyce after his daughter, Lucia, somewhat in the way that Molly Bloom was modeled after Joyce's wife, Nora. *Nora* (1988), 205.

When Jung told Joyce that the poems Lucia wrote contained schizoid elements, Joyce replied that they were anticipations of a new literature, and that Lucia was an innovator not yet understood. After that, Joyce removed Lucia to a different sanatorium. Later Jung commented: "They were like two people going to the bottom of a river, one falling, the other diving."

Lucia's episodes of madness finally led to her permanent hospitalization.* In Paris, on November 19, 1934, not long after the Random House victory in New York, the author noted that during the previous three years Lucia had had twenty-four doctors, twelve nurses, and eight companions, and had been in three different mental institutions. He spent £4,000, during that time, on her care. A friend estimated that three fourths of Joyce's income went for Lucia. Joyce wrote his friend Budgen: "If anything lies ahead of us except ruin, I wish someone would point it out."

On January 7, 1941, while Europe was aflame with war, Joyce, in Zurich, wrote his last postcard to his brother Stanislaus, in Florence; he listed the names of some people who might be helpful to his brother in case of need. That evening he and Nora had dinner at the Kronenhalle restaurant, where, apropos of nothing, Joyce remarked to his hostess, Frau Zumsteg: "Perhaps I won't be here much longer." A week later he was dead: the cause was a perforated ulcer and generalized peritonitis.

He had emerged momentarily from a coma to ask that Nora's bed be placed close to his, but the doctors urged her and Giorgio, their son, to go home.

RICHARD ELLMANN: At one o'clock in the morning Joyce awoke and asked the nurse to call his wife and son, then relapsed into coma. Nora and George were summoned at two o'clock to the hospital. But at 2:15 on January 13, 1941, before they arrived, Joyce died.

——

When Nora and Giorgio made preparations for the funeral, a Catholic priest asked them if they wanted a religious service. Nora said: "I wouldn't do that to him." Joyce's wooden coffin and his grave were simple. Because Joyce did not like flowers, a green wreath with a lyre woven in it, standing for Ireland, was laid on the grave. Otherwise Ireland, like the Catholic Church, had no place in Joyce's funeral.

An interesting essay by Richard Ellmann into the question of whether the publication of Joyce's "lust" letters to Nora amounted to a "gross invasion of privacy" may be found in "Diary" by Ruth Dudley Edwards, in *London Review of Books,* September 1, 1988, 25.

*Lucia was born in the pauper ward of a hospital in Trieste at a time when Joyce was desperately looking for work elsewhere, including Dublin and South Africa. When Nora left the hospital she was given twenty crowns in charity. The child was born on St. Anne's day "and so, since Anne was also the name of Nora's mother, they added Anne to the first name of Lucia, the patron saint of eyesight, which Joyce had decided on earlier." Ellmann, *James Joyce* (1982), 262. Joyce later wondered whether his forced nomadic existence had not generated Lucia's madness. According to Shari Benstock, on September 1, 1939—with all Paris fearful of bombing by the Germans—Margaret Anderson fled Paris with Georgette Leblanc, while Joyce tried to transport Lucia to a *maison de santé* in Switzerland. *Women of the Left Bank* (1986), 443.

When Lucia, by now quite mad, was told of her father's death, she demanded: "What is he doing under the ground, that idiot?"

Nora took visitors to see where Joyce was buried; it was next to the zoological garden.

NORA JOYCE: My husband is buried there. He was awfully fond of the lions. I imagine him lying there, listening to them roar.

———

Until Joyce's estate was settled and royalties on the Random House edition of *Ulysses* began coming in to Nora, she was hard up. She had a longing to return to Ireland but would not leave Jim behind, and in Ireland, Church and State proved as unwilling to have Joyce's remains brought back as they had been to let his books enter the country. At one point, Nora asked Robert Kastor in New York to sell her own manuscript copy of Joyce's *Chamber Music* (he had copied the poems onto parchment for her in 1909, when she was in Trieste and he in Dublin). But she changed her mind, and later, when things were better for her, she said:

NORA JOYCE: I had others but I have given them away or people have borrowed them and kept them. But I will not part with *Chamber Music* because Joyce made this copy in his own writing for me. Once, when I needed money badly, I sent it off to America to be sold, but I missed it so much that I wrote and said to send it back, that I would not part with it for any money.

———

After Joyce's death, Nora expressed greater appreciation for her husband's art.

BRENDA MADDOX: As she came to play the part of the widow Joyce, Nora began at last to believe in her husband's genius. She was interested in literary news and pleased to see the number of books appearing about Joyce's work. She asked for three copies of the *Portable James Joyce* to give as gifts, and for herself, she asked for a copy of Lucia's *Chaucer ABC.* *

———

Maddox has provided another example of Nora's posthumous pride in her husband's work. During Joyce's lifetime André Gide had been uncomplimentary to Joyce's talent. After his death, the wife of Ignazio Silone asked Nora for her opinion of André Gide, and got it:

NORA JOYCE: Sure, when you've been married to the greatest writer in the world, you don't remember all the little fellows.

———

---

*Evidently a book consisting of a Chaucer poem called "An ABC," in which each stanza begins with a successive letter of the alphabet. Lucia drew twenty-six decorative letters to go with the poem, and Joyce had it published at his expense, with a preface by Louis Gillet, in July 1936. Ellmann, *James Joyce* (1982), 658, 690. Maddox, in *Nora* (1988), 288, says that Joyce "pressed his friends to praise, then to buy [Lucia's] *Chaucer ABC* with her illustrations. When they declined or hesitated, he broke with them."

Joyce's estate had amounted to less than one thousand pounds. A court case was necessary because of doubts concerning the author's legal domicile. This gave a Dublin judge and the Dublin press a chance to laugh at Joyce. The *Dublin Evening Herald* reported this exchange:

MR. JUSTICE BENNETT: What sort of books did he write?

MR. VANNECK (for the administrators of the will): I think his best-known book was called *Ulysses.*

MR. JUSTICE BENNETT: It sounds Greek to me (*laughter*).

———

Ten years later, Nora died. When close to death, she asked that a priest be brought to the convent hospital; he gave her the last rites. At her burial, the priest gave a speech in front of Nora's grave. He said: "She was a great sinner."*

Before Joyce died, and after signing over to him her interest in the American rights to publish *Ulysses,* Sylvia Beach was forced to sell precious items, including Joyce manuscripts, in order to keep Shakespeare and Company afloat and a roof over her head. To maintain La Maison des Amis des Livres, Adrienne Monnier had to do much the same thing. Then, in the winter of 1936, the two women took into Monnier's apartment a young German photographer named Gisele Freund, who was without a passport and had just been ordered to leave France. The next year, Beach went to the States for the first time in twenty-two years, to visit her eighty-four-year-old father in California. A hysterectomy detained her for several weeks, and upon her return to Paris she found that Gisele Freund had replaced her as Monnier's lover. So she moved into the rooms above Shakespeare and Company until the Germans came. In 1940, with the advance of the Germans, Gisele Freund fled Paris. In December 1941, Sylvia Beach closed her bookshop after an altercation with a German officer who wanted to buy her last copy of Joyce's *Finnegans Wake.* Then, in July 1942, she was taken to an internment camp south of Paris.

When the war was over, Beach returned to Paris but did not reopen Shakespeare and Company. In 1955, after a long and painful illness, Adrienne Monnier took her own life, much as Beach's mother had in 1927. Eleanor Beach overdosed on her medication; Adrienne Monnier took too many sleeping pills.

On June 16, 1962 (Bloomsday, a name she coined), Sylvia Beach went to Ireland to dedicate the Martello Tower at Sandycove, near Dublin, the setting of the opening passage of *Ulysses.* The tower would now be a center for Joyce studies, the James Joyce Tower. That fall she returned to Paris and on October 6 died in her apartment, alone, of a

———

*Brenda Maddox questions whether the priest really said this, or meant it the way it sounds. *Nora* (1988), 371–73.

heart attack. A simple funeral was held at the Père-Lachaise cemetery. After her body was cremated, her ashes were sent to her sister Holly in Greenwich, Connecticut. Her closest friends silently protested, feeling Sylvia Beach should have stayed in Paris; she had lived there forty-five years.

3

A
Judicial
Murder

LONDON. 1888. The accused was an English publisher of the highest distinction who specialized in French literature. His family had immigrated from Italy at the close of the seventeenth century. Henry Vizetelly pioneered the illustrated press and was the son of printers and the grandson of members of the Stationers' Company. By breaking with the tradition of publishing novels in expensive three-volume editions only, he assisted authors like George Moore to escape the "private" censorship of the giant circulating libraries. The best works of Gogol, Dostoevsky, and Tolstoy, of Balzac, Flaubert, and Zola, were brought out by Vizetelly in inexpensive English-language editions, as were Harriet Beecher Stowe's *Uncle Tom's Cabin* and Edgar Allan Poe's *Tales*. It was when he brought out an English translation of Emile Zola's novel about the French peasantry, *The Earth* (*La Terre*), that the vigilantes, the government, and the press went after him and brought him down. He was sixty-nine years old at the time. The accusation against Vizetelly and Company: publishing obscene literature.

La Terre was conceived by Zola as "a kind of poem on the soil," specifically the rich land of the Beauce, along the river Loire, the region from which his mother and her forebears had come. It is a portrait of the French peasant, based on visits to the countryside, on Joseph Bonnemère's *Histoire des paysans,* and on the socialist ideas of Jules Guesde, the controversial Marxist editor of *Le Cri du peuple.* Written in one year, from 1886 to 1887, and published by Charpentier, *La Terre* provoked a great outcry and the usual protests from critics, who charged that Zola's documentary novel was false.

EMILE ZOLA: Will you allow me to be stubborn about my work? Everyone throws out *his* concept of what the peasant is really like. Then why should mine, alone, be false?

———

Edmond de Goncourt said *La Terre* was "painted by the hand of a master" and Huysmans wrote that it possessed "an incontestable grandeur." But in *Le Temps* there was this from Anatole France:

ANATOLE FRANCE: His work is bad and of these unfortunate tomes one might best say that it would have been better if they had never been written. I cannot deny his detestable glory. No one before him has ever created such a heap of filth. That is his monument, the size of which no one can contest. Never has a man made such an effort to vilify humanity, to insult every aspect of beauty and love, to deny all that is good and decent.

———

When Zola fled to England in 1898, after the publication of "J'accuse!," Vizetelly's son Ernest helped to hide and safeguard him from his French and English enemies. Zola lived in an old cottage called "Penn" in Oatlands Chase, and Ernest's daughter, Violette, stayed there with him; she was only fifteen years old but had charge of the household, including two servants.

The Vizetelly family's friendship with Zola had developed during the years when Ernest, the son, translated Zola's novels into English and Henry, the father, published them at his London firm, Vizetelly and Company, and sold them throughout Britain. According to Ernest, his father came to publish Zola because, having lived in Paris for many years, he was aware of Zola's immense popularity in France and most other European countries. In England, he had noticed that "a tolerably large market existed even for the few wretchedly translated and mutilated American editions" of Zola's works that had appeared; and so Vizetelly decided to issue an unabridged one-volume English edition of *Nana,* which Ernest helped translate—"Suppressing nothing, and merely throwing a slight veil" over passages likely to excite difficulties. The success of Vizetelly's English publication of *Nana* induced the firm to translate into English and publish all of Zola's previously published novels and purchase the English copyrights to his new ones.

George Moore, then living in Paris, had spoken to Zola about *La Terre* on behalf of Vizetelly and Company, Moore's own English publisher. At that time, Vizetelly "knew nothing of *La Terre* other than the fact that it would deal with the French peasantry." When Ernest read the manuscript he "was struck by the boldness of Zola's story, which seemed to surpass in outspokenness any of the novelist's previous works," including *Nana.* He recommended that certain "excisions and alterations" be made in the text because, although his father had no personal prejudice against Zola's writing—life in Paris "having inclined him to the outspokenness of the French"—he knew, as did his son, "that English literature, like English journalism, was under the thumb of Mrs. Grundy."

In England, well into the twentieth century, novels were ordinarily published in three volumes at the high price of one and a half guineas, and distributed through a few giant private circulating libraries, which frequently bought up 75 percent of an issue. As long as the novel was published in this expensive "three-decker" form, the heads of the circulating libraries exercised a widespread private censorship over literature by the simple expedient of declining to stock a book of which they disapproved. Publishers apprehensive about outspoken manuscripts sent them to the librarians in advance of issuing them. After the largest libraries—Mudie's and W. A. Smith's—consistently declined to stock and sell George Moore's novels, the author threatened to "wreck their big houses" by getting Henry Vizetelly to publish his works in inexpensive one-volume editions. Moore hoped, for the most part in vain, that other writers and publishers would soon follow suit, and thus abolish the censorship of literature by the heads of the circulating libraries.

In 1888, a campaign against obscene literature and pornography raged in the English press. In a letter to *The Guardian,* then a Church of England newspaper, Lord Mount-Temple launched an attack on pornography that even included a condemnation of Sir Richard Burton's translation of the *Arabian Nights.* A Roman Catholic newspaper, *The Tablet,* and the *Whitehall Review* both attacked Zola personally, saying that he not only "wallowed in immorality" but "sapped the foundations of manhood and womanhood."* The publisher of the *Whitehall Review* demanded that Zola's London publisher be immediately prosecuted.

The trouble with Zola's *La Terre,* as published by Vizetelly and Company, is suggested by the following passage describing how a young girl brought her cow to a bull on a neighboring farm—one of the excerpts the prosecutor was allowed to read to the jury in Vizetelly's first case:

EMILE ZOLA *(La Terre): Carefully, as though undertaking something of great importance, Françoise stepped quickly forward with pursed lips and set face; her concentration made her eyes seem even darker. She had to reach right across with her arm as she grasped the bull's penis firmly in her hand and lifted it up. And when the bull felt that he was near the edge, he gathered his strength and, with one simple thrust of his loins, pushed his penis right in. Then it came out again. It was all over; the dibble had planted the seed. . . . And now Caesar slipped down from her back, making the ground shake again.*

Françoise had released her grip but was still holding her arm in the air. Finally, she let it drop, saying "That's that."

---

*This last, perhaps, by inciting young men and women to masturbation, a practice notoriously feared during the nineteenth century for its supposed baleful effects on mental and physical health.

The press was furious:

THE METHODIST TIMES: Zolaism is a disease. It is a study of the putrid. No one can read Zola without moral contamination.

THE LIVERPOOL MERCURY: There is nothing likely to do more injury to the morals of the people than the free publication of cheap works which pander to prurient tastes: and there cannot be the slightest doubt that the novels of M. Zola as published by Vizetelly & Co. are among the worst of their kind.

THE LONDON STAR: It is true that Rabelais is obscene, that Chaucer is coarse, and that Boccaccio's ladies and gentlemen are all too frank. But M. Zola's *La Terre* has none of the charm, the humour, the style which redeem the works of the authors named. It is simply unrelieved and morbid filth.

In Parliament, the lawmakers fulminated. One of the loudest was Samuel Smith of Flintshire, who gave a long speech about the corrupting use to which indecent literature was being put, and the role in this played by certain English booksellers and publishers, notably Henry Vizetelly.

SAMUEL SMITH: A lady of my acquaintance has brought to my attention facts of so shocking a nature that I scarcely feel fit to place them before the House but which I believe to be thoroughly authenticated; this lady has investigated them with care. . . . It has become a rule with a class of low booksellers in London to provide indecent literature for young girls, to offer them every inducement to come into the shops and read the books, to provide them with private rooms stocked with the vilest class of literature where, on making the small deposit of 6d., they are supplied with this literature. And in many cases these shops are in league with houses of the worst class, to which the girls, when their minds are sufficiently polluted and depraved, are consigned. . . .

Are we to sit still while the country is wholly corrupted by literature of this kind? Are we to wait until the moral fibre of the English race is eaten out, as that of the French is almost? Look what such literature has done for France! It overspread that country like a torrent, and its poison is destroying the whole national life. . . .

There can be no doubt that there has been of late years in London and throughout the country an immense increase of vile literature, and that this literature is working terrible effects upon the morals of the young. I need only refer to the public confession of one whom I believe to be the chief culprit in the spread of this pernicious literature—I have reference, of course, to Mr. Henry Vizetelly. In the *Pall Mall Gazette* of a short time ago, this fellow boasted that his house had been the means of translating and selling in the English market more than one million copies of French novels, some of them of the worst class. . . . Vizetelly has also confessed that he has been selling 1,000 copies weekly of the books of Zola, in England alone! . . .

Regrettably, the police are very inactive and they allow things to go on which ought not to be permitted. We ought to have an active Public Prosecutor. I do not know where the official who is called the Public Prosecutor is to be found. I believe there is some one known by this title; but he seems to be asleep, he seems to have had his wings clipped. . . .

—

In England the common-law courts had always permitted private citizens who had the necessary means to retain counsel to commence criminal proceedings. This mode of "private" prosecution was in fact the ordinary method for prosecuting criminals. Although in practice the local police instituted most criminal proceedings, they acted nominally as private citizens interested in the preservation of public order and the peace. It was not until the Public Prosecution Act of 1879 was enacted that centralized government officials, public prosecutors, were enabled by law to prosecute persons suspected of having committed "public wrongs," which is to say, crimes. This authority was less than ten years old when Henry Vizetelly published *La Terre*.

As the prosecution of criminals is expensive and offenses against manners, morals, and religion have no victims motivated to prosecute, associations were formed to raise funds to pay for lawyers necessary to prosecute the perpetrators of crimes such as blasphemy and obscenity.

The private prosecution of Vizetelly was begun by the National Vigilance Association, which retained a firm of private solicitors, Collette and Collette, to obtain from the Bow Street police court a summons directed against Henry Vizetelly for having published three obscene novels by Zola: *The Soil (La Terre), Nana,* and *Piping Hot (Pot-bouille)*. The summons was issued on August 10, 1888. When the Crown later intervened in the case, Herbert Asquith—soon to become prime minister—referred to these works as "the three most immoral books ever published." The London *Times* for October 31, 1888, however, mentioned only *La Terre:*

THE TIMES: Mr. Henry Vizetelly, the publisher, surrendered to his recognisances today to answer an indictment charging him with publishing an obscene libel. The book which forms the subject-matter of the indictment is an English translation of a French novel, and entitled *The Soil.*

—

In his book *Emile Zola,* published in 1904, Ernest Vizetelly wrote about his father's terrifying trials:

ERNEST VIZETELLY: He first had felt fairly confident respecting the issue of the case, and, as an old journalist, had entertained nothing but contempt for the terriers of the profession who barked at his heels.

—

That was before the government stepped in. Vizetelly had anticipated making his trial "a demonstration in favor of free speech," but when the Crown intervened in his case, taking over the prosecution started by the vigilantes, his "confidence was roughly shaken."

ERNEST VIZETELLY: There was an incessant *chassé-croisé* of advice; and Vizetelly, now resolving on one course, and now on another, was at a loss what to do. . . . [H]e was now sixty-eight years old, and though he was still of most industrious habit, the strenuous life he had led had left its mark upon him. Moreover, a complaint from which he suffered had taken a very serious turn, and frequent physical suffering was not conducive to perspicuity and energy of mind. Again, there was the position of his business to be considered.

—

In consequence of the prosecution, and the calumny heaped upon Zola and Vizetelly by the newspapers and the vigilantes, the trade stopped handling books published by Vizetelly and Company. At the same time, the publisher found it "virtually impossible to obtain adequate counsel" for his trial. One barrister would not represent him because he frankly did not like the case and would, he said, "therefore prove a poor advocate in my cause." Eventually, Mr. Francis B. Williams, a Queen's Counsel and the recorder of Cardiff, was retained, with Mr. A. R. Cluer as his junior.

The trial occurred at the Old Bailey before the recorder, Sir Thomas Chambers. The man who took charge of the Crown's case against Vizetelly was the solicitor-general himself, Sir Edward Clarke. He had a considerable reputation "because of certain cross-examinations." Sir Edward opened the proceedings by urging upon the recorder two propositions: One, at law it was no excuse for the publication of obscenity that it might be published for good motive (this had been a main point of the *Hicklin* case), or that other literature—especially that of two or three centuries previous—might contain passages conflicting with contemporary judgment as to what was fit for circulation. Second, Zola's *The Earth* "was a novel full of bestial obscenity, without a spark of literary genius or the expression of an elevated thought."

When he had concluded his opening speech the solicitor-general announced that he would read some passages from *La Terre* for the benefit of the jurymen. This Sir Thomas was disposed to allow. The solicitor-general also cautioned the gentlemen of the press in the courtroom—both English and French—that if any of them published in England a report of this proceeding containing the passages he was going to read, they too would be liable to be prosecuted. The fact that it was merely the report of the case would, he assured them, be no justification.* The recorder took no exception to the solicitor-general's presentation.

---

*The English press regularly reported legal proceedings in some detail and profited from particularly salacious or scandalous trials; these reports were not, however, exempted from obscenity law.

When Sir Edward Clarke was halfway through the reading of the passage about the mating of the bull, quoted earlier, a juryman interrupted the reading: "Is it necessary to read all of the objectionable passages?"

SIR THOMAS CHAMBERS: They are charged in the indictment as being the substance and essence of the case. They are revolting to a degree, but they are charged in the indictment and must be proved.

———

Sir Edward Clarke had informed the jurors that it was not the Crown's position that a single, isolated passage of an immoral tendency would be a sufficient justification for finding the publisher of the book guilty.

SIR EDWARD CLARKE: The book in my hand does not contain one, two or three filthy passages such as this one, but 21 of them, located in different parts—some of them very long passages extending over several pages. There can be no question here of a novel written with a wholesome purpose of teaching about the conditions of the French peasantry; this book is filthy from beginning to end. I do not believe there was ever collected between the covers of a book so much bestial obscenity.

EMILE ZOLA *(La Terre): And so, as soon as they were alone anywhere for a minute, in the cowshed or the kitchen, Buteau would spring to the attack and Françoise would defend herself tooth and nail. And there was always the same scenario; he pushed his arm up her skirt and caught hold of a handful of naked flesh and hair, as when mounting an animal.*

———

The solicitor-general's reading was interrupted again by another upset juryman. "Is it necessary to read all of them?" Sir Edward responded sympathetically:

SIR EDWARD CLARKE: I hope you will understand that it is at least as unpleasant for me to read them as it is for you to listen to them. If you think, subject to what may be said by my learned friend on the part of the defense, that these passages are obscene, I will stop reading them at once.

———

At this juncture Vizetelly's lawyer, Francis B. Williams, "showed a strong desire" to interrupt the trial in order to confer with his client. After a moment, he notified the solicitor-general and the recorder that it was the defendant Vizetelly's wish to withdraw his plea of "not guilty" and enter one of "guilty." It was a complete rout.

FRANCIS WILLIAMS, Q.C.: Acting upon my advice, the defendant Vizetelly will plead "Guilty" to having published these books. It would seem there is no doubt that the work which forms the subject matter of the indictment contains passages which the jury had intimated are very disgusting and unpleasant even in the discharge of their public duty to have to listen to. Therefore, it is not for the defendant to contend that these works are not obscene. That being so, Mr. Vizetelly will undertake at once to withdraw all those translations of M. Zola's works from circulation. I understand that the Solicitor-General does not ask that any imprisonment should be inflicted.

———

Although the solicitor-general did not ask for any imprisonment of Vizetelly on this occasion, he set a trap for the distraught publisher:

SIR EDWARD CLARKE: Of course I am very glad that a course has been taken which will not only stop from circulation the three books contained in these indictments, but which carries with it an undertaking by Mr. Vizetelly that he will be no party to the circulation of any other of the works which M. Zola has produced, any others—I should like to say—which are at least as objectionable as those which are indicted before Your Lordship today.

———

The solicitor-general also "pointed out" that after such warning, proceedings under Lord Campbell's Act would be taken "in the event of any other person attempting to circulate" these books. This meant that any copies of the Zola novels found by police at Vizetelly and Company or with booksellers would be seized and destroyed by order of the magistrate.

It was in view of the defendant's "good character"—a matter conceded by the solicitor-general—that Vizetelly was not on this trial sent to jail. However, the undertaking to discontinue circulation of the Zola books, craftily phrased by the solicitor-general to embrace any Zola novel that was "at least as objectionable" as the three that were indicted, effectively enjoined Vizetelly altogether from publishing or republishing Zola's work.

During the trial, the publisher's lawyer, Francis Williams, seems not to have attempted to introduce any evidence of literary merit.* However, this arch dialogue took place when he asked the court to take note that the indicated works were "works of a *great* French author."

SIR EDWARD CLARKE: A *voluminous* French author . . .

SIR THOMAS CHAMBERS: A *popular* French author . . .

FRANCIS WILLIAMS, Q.C.: Of an author who ranks high among the literary men of France.

———

The day after Vizetelly's conviction, the London *Times* commented pontifically:

---

*The English scholar Norman St. John-Stevas numbered among the "anomalies of English" obscenity law three that, by and large, also characterized American obscenity law, as applied by many courts, during this period and up to 1957: (1) It was doubtful whether there was any "defense" in a work's having literary merit, or whether this was a relevant consideration to be taken into account by a judge or jury in deciding whether to declare a book "obscene" under the law. (2) Expert evidence on literary or artistic merit was not admissible in court, and it was doubtful whether evidence of scientific value was admissible. (3) No certainty in theory or practice existed as to the meaning of the words "deprave or corrupt," nor to which class of persons these words applied. *Obscenity and the Law* (1956), Appendix I.

THE TIMES: Henceforth, anyone who publishes translations of Zola's novels and works of similar character will do so at his peril, and must not expect to escape so easily as Mr. Vizetelly.

———

The vigilantes now printed up and distributed a pamphlet urging the public to boycott Vizetelly and Company books, in order to put the publisher into bankruptcy. Extracts from all the attacks on Zola and Vizetelly that the newspapers had published were reproduced in this document, along with an account of the criminal proceedings against the publisher. From the standpoint of the firm's fortunes, the timing could not have been worse. The company had several thousand pounds locked up in illustrated books which were not ready for publication. Further, because of the prosecution and the boycott, sales of existing books had sharply declined. There were "also the normal liabilities weighing down the company." Under these straitened circumstances, according to Ernest Vizetelly, with the company "threatened with collapse," it was decided that the Zola publications "could not be sacrificed." Thus did Henry Vizetelly step into the government's trap. The undertaking given by Vizetelly in court "was interpreted to mean" that the firm was free to sell Zola's books if they were made unobjectionable by further expurgation. It was decided to put a large group of Zola novels back on the market as soon as they could be revised.

Much of the work was entrusted to Ernest, who spent two months deleting and modifying 325 pages of the fifteen volumes that were given him to "tone down." Although Henry Vizetelly was in poor health at the time, he also revised a few volumes, and read all of his son's work before forwarding it to the printers. No sooner did Vizetelly move forward again with the publication of Zola than the vigilantes sprang the legal trap. This time Vizetelly and Company editions of eight Zola novels and four other French works were branded as "obscene."*

ERNEST VIZETELLY: [O]n the day of his new committal Father took the only course consistent with integrity. He assigned everything he possessed for the benefit of his creditors, in order that his business might be liquidated. It was impossible to carry it on any longer. The wreckers had resolved to ruin him, and had succeeded to their hearts' desire. . . . Not a newspaper dared to print a word on behalf of this old servant of the press whom the "Vigilantes" had chosen for their victim.

———

An attempt by George Moore to publish in the *Fortnightly Review* a defense of Henry Vizetelly—excoriating the prosecution as a violent cen-

---

*The newly indicted Zola novels included *Germinal, The Fortune of the Rougons,* and *L' Assommoir.* The other works were: *Madame Bovary,* by Flaubert; *A Love Crime,* by Paul Bourget; and two novels by de Maupassant, *A Woman's Life* and *A Ladies' Man (Bel-Ami).* After a few objections had been raised in the press apropos the prosecution of *Madame Bovary,* the summons with respect to it (and with respect to *L'Assommoir, Germinal,* and *The Fortune of the Rougons*) was eventually adjourned. E. A. Vizetelly, *Emile Zola* (1904), 286.

sorship of the press—was completely frustrated; the journal would not print it. For all the country at large knew, Vizetelly was just another Hollywell Street smut peddler.

The trustees of Henry Vizetelly's estate now took over Vizetelly and Company. They resolved to fight the censorship and provided funds to defend Vizetelly in the Old Bailey. They thought it critical that a Queen's Counsel again be engaged, for "it would be ridiculous to pit a stuff-gowns-man such as Mr. Cluer against the Solicitor General!" And so, after many delays—it was even more difficult on this occasion than on the former to secure counsel for Vizetelly's defense—one Mr. Cock, Q.C., was retained, Mr. Cluer again being relegated to the position of junior counsel.

Ernest Vizetelly in particular was disturbed by this decision because, although he feared a fresh conviction was inevitable, he also felt that Cluer, "who had a perfect knowledge of the French language and an appreciation of Zola's works," would "do his best," and that "if the Vizetelly ship went down it would at least do so with colours flying."* Against Ernest's better judgement, no sooner was Mr. Cock's fee established than it was voluntarily increased by the trustees, in order to induce Queen's Counsel "to do his utmost." Mr. Cock, however, was nowhere to be found until half an hour before the new prosecution commenced at the Central Criminal Court. It was May 30, 1889.

On that occasion the Vizetellys, father and son, were introduced for the first time to the barrister by Mr. Cluer, in a room adjoining the robing room at the Old Bailey.

ERNEST VIZETELLY: Mr. Cock, Q.C., was a fat unwieldy man with a startling red face.

———

He opened the discussion by announcing that there "could be no defense." Henry Vizetelly, who had come to the Old Bailey expecting something very different, almost fell down. Cock, Q.C., did not pause to explain or argue; he sought "to dispose of the distasteful matter as quickly as possible." To Vizetelly he said: "You must throw yourself on the mercy of the court. That is the only thing to do."

ERNEST VIZETELLY: The blow was a *coup de massue* for him, and at first he could say nothing. His son, likewise very much amazed, and, in particular, disgusted with this blustering barrister who threw up the sponge at the moment of going into court, tried to interject a few words, but was curtly silenced.

———

*Frank Harris, then editor of the *Fortnightly Review* and the author of the notorious *My Life and Loves* (published by Grove Press in the States in 1963), appreciated the threat to literary freedom that was presented by the Vizetelly prosecutions and offered to bear all Vizetelly's expenses; however, he had wanted Mr. Cluer to take over the defense. E. A. Vizetelly, *Emile Zola* (1904), 288. Concerning *My Life and Loves,* see endnotes to Chapter 4.

Said Cock, Q.C.: "There is nothing, nothing to be done."

Ernest thought "Queen's Counsel" at least might have returned to the trustees the extra fee which had been given him to make a good fight. This, however, was never done. Instead, Cock proposed to ascertain what would be the results of a plea of guilty on his client's behalf. And, before anyone could question him, he vanished.

ERNEST VIZETELLY: He rolled out of the room.

———

Ernest was not certain whom Cock, Q.C., actually saw, and wrote that "in case of uncertainty it is best to stay one's pen." I suppose Cock went to speak to the solicitor-general and the recorder, for when he returned he said—in the presence of the Vizetellys and Cluer—that the recorder felt "there must be some imprisonment."

ERNEST VIZETELLY: Did Henry Vizetelly hear those last words? According to his own account, afterwards, he never did; for had he done so, in spite of all Mr. Cock's bluster, he would never, he said, have pleaded guilty. But the poor man may well have misunderstood his counsel.

———

But Vizetelly was in a condition "little short of actual physical collapse" and "in a dreamy sort of way gave, or appeared to give, a feeble assent to everything." At that very moment his son's brain was racing, for it occurred to him that, even then, one might dispense with Mr. Cock's services and induce Mr. Cluer to undertake the defense unaided. But there was no opportunity for further deliberation; "the court was almost waiting and one went downstairs to meet the inevitable."

ERNEST VIZETELLY: The proceedings were brief. Vizetelly took his stand at the foot of the solicitor's table, his son, who sat there, and who at every moment feared to see him fall, holding his hand the while. For an instant, when challenged, he hesitated, then ejaculated the word "Guilty," much as if he were expectorating—while Ernest prayed to hear him utter instead the two words which might help resuce the family from ruin—"Not Guilty."

———

The solicitor-general maintained that the previous undertaking on Vizetelly's part not to publish any more Zola works that were "at least as objectionable" as those indicted had been violated and, therefore, his recognizances of 200 pounds ought to be escheated. On the defendant's behalf, Mr. Cock, Q.C., solicited a mitigation of punishment by referring to the expurgation of the Zola books that had been accomplished, although he allowed that they "had not gone sufficiently far." Still, Mr. Cock, Q.C., added unctuously: "The defendant *is* in his seventieth year and in delicate health."

Ernest was asked to testify concerning the very serious character of the defendant's illness, which, he said, could not be adequately treated in prison. Before being permitted to leave the witness box, however, he was cross-examined by the solicitor-general concerning his relationship to the firm of Vizetelly and Company. The government wished to extract undertakings from him that, with Henry Vizetelly gone, the company would engage in no further sale of Zola's novels and would destroy existing stock. But these were matters out of Ernest's control. Wishing to say nothing that might lead to assurances of such a sort being given by any others, Ernest exclaimed from the witness box: "You have made the defendant a pauper! What more do you want?"

SIR EDWARD CLARKE: Now, now, we want none of that!
ERNEST VIZETELLY: Well, I have nothing else to say. I do not belong to the firm of Vizetelly and Company, and I know nothing about it.
SIR THOMAS CHAMBERS: It is useless to fine the defendant as he has no means to pay a fine. But his recognizances must be escheated and he must go to prison, as a first class misdemeanant, for three months.

———

While Mr. Cock busied himself with his papers, Henry Vizetelly was taken below. The defendant's solicitor, Mr. Lickfold, asked the recorder whether the son might talk to his father before he was put in jail. The recorder agreed to this and told them to apply at the barred gate of Newgate, immediately adjoining the Old Bailey. A guard, admitting them, went and asked but returning in a moment, said: "The Governor's answer is that you cannot see the prisoner. The judge has no power to give leave to see any prisoner once he has left the court."

GEORGE MOORE: This poor old gentleman, in the seventieth year of his life, could not find a lawyer to defend him. If he had poisoned half a dozen nieces and nephews, brothers and sisters, he could have had the best advice of the bar to prove him an innocent man. Because his crime was that he published Zola's novels, he could find nobody. The counsel he employed took the fees, but the counsel was a very pious man, who said that he could not go on with the case because to do so he would have to read the books with their immoral passages, and he persuaded Mr. Vizetelly to plead guilty. . . . The case made an ineffaceable impression on me. Henry Vizetelly was not merely a book publisher. He was a man of letters, the author of several historical works. And two years after Vizetelly's death, brought on prematurely from the effects of his prison, Zola was received in London as a hero, entertained by public bodies and invited everywhere.*

———

Moore visited Vizetelly in Holloway Gaol where the publisher (according to Moore) said this to his author:

---

*Henry Vizetelly died on January 1, 1894. Zola made his hero's visit to London in April 1899, five years later.

HENRY VIZETELLY: There was a good jury,* and I should have been acquitted if the counsel had gone on with the case. But he advised me to plead
guilty and I was in great bodily pain and mental pain as well, and thought
that all the world was against me and that I had better give way.

GEORGE MOORE: Since then I have oft times wished I were a lawyer so that
I might have defended Henry Vizetelly before a jury who abhorred to hear
Emile Zola's words. Were I not the only Irishman living or dead who
cannot make a speech, I should have had no difficulty in getting a verdict
of acquittal from Vizetelly's jury. . . . I looked upon Henry Vizetelly's death
as a judicial murder. And I sometimes wondered if the members of the
Vigilance Society ever turned over in their graves, asking themselves were
they murderers?

If you ask what significance that prosecution of so many years ago has
today I will answer: Some things are for all time and never lose their
significance, being part and parcel of humanity. I believe Vizetelly's case to
be one of those, so packed was it with subterfuge, evasion, lies, hypocrisy,
cunning, and ill-smelling midden, humanity at its very worst.

———

The last decades of the nineteenth century were a difficult time in England for authors and publishers. In 1886, George Moore went into exile
in Paris. In 1889, Henry Vizetelly was imprisoned in London for publishing the novels of Emile Zola.† Six years later Oscar Wilde was imprisoned
in connection with a homosexual love affair, after a series of sensational
trials that aroused intense popular hostility against homosexuals. When the
psychologist Havelock Ellis attempted, in 1897, to enlighten the English
public about the sorts of persons who committed the "nameless crime,"‡
the publisher of his book *Sexual Inversion* was tried and convicted for
publishing "obscenity," and all copies of the book were destroyed;§ later
editions were published only in the United States.

E. M. Forster did not dare publish his homosexually oriented novel
Maurice, or his short stories having the same theme, in England or the
United States during his lifetime. The taboo in England against any literary
discussion of sex, including homosexuality, was an inflamed aspect of English Francophobia. Louis Crompton has shown that the great English
philosopher and reformer Jeremy Bentham was afraid to publish the argu-

---

*Vizetelly (or Moore) erred here since, according to Ernest Vizetelly's detailed account,
there was no jury impaneled at Vizetelly's brief second trial.

†According to Donald Thomas (*A Long Time Burning* [1969], 244), the first English
translation of Sade's *Justine* appeared in England the year that Vizetelly went to prison.

‡Byron's phrase. See Louis Crompton's *Byron and Greek Love: Homophobia in Nineteenth-
Century England* (1985), 65. Ellis's wife was an "invert," and a disguised "case study" of her
condition was included in *Sexual Inversion. The Well of Loneliness* cases were benchmarks in the
struggle for the freedom to portray gay lives and behavior in fiction, in England and the
United States, as described in Chapters 10 and 11. The freedom to publish this literature is
directly related to the freedom of homosexually oriented persons to live free of fears of
punishment for their sexual orientation.

§ See Chapter 10.

ment that "utilitarianism" and the "greatest happiness principle" required the abolition of the laws making sodomy a crime because such publication would have given his opponents an invincible weapon for discrediting his whole program of reform.*

Zola's *La Terre* was not republished in England until 1954. Cyril Connolly commented in *The Sunday Times* of August 8, 1954: "It is excellent that such a book should have at last been translated for the English public." The English public, however, had been deprived of it for over sixty years by the Vizetelly prosecutions, unreformed English obscenity law, and the fears that the law put into the breasts of English publishers.†

---

*Louis Crompton, *Byron and Greek Love: Homophobia in Nineteenth-Century England* (1985), Chapter 1 and Appendix.

†In the United States, according to Tebbel, a copy of *La Terre* in French was seized at customs in November 1888 and burned by the Treasury Department, which had commissioned and read an "official" literal translation.

The National Union Catalogue shows that an edition of *La Terre (The Soil)* was published in Philadelphia in 1888 by T. B. Peterson and Brothers, and that in the same year it was published under the same title in Chicago by Laird and Lee.

In 1894, customs authorities in New York are said to have admitted *La Terre,* but every copy "in the vernacular or in translation" was reported "confiscated" by New York police. John Tebbel, *A History of Publishing in the United States* 2 (1975), 620, 622.

In 1924, Boni and Liveright published *La Terre* (translated from the French by Ernest Dowson), with an essay by Harry Thurston Peck. In 1955, Grove Press published it under the title *The Earth,* in a translation by Ann Lindsay.

4

A Sermon-
on-the-
Mount—of Venus

D URING THE FIRST QUARTER of the twentieth century it was
possible in France to publish "obscene" books in the English language, but no reputable publishing house did that. In Paris, Sylvia Beach
brought out *Ulysses* in English, using a Shakespeare and Company imprint,
but she ran a bookstore, not a publishing house, and Joyce was the only
author whose work she published. In 1922, the year of *Ulysses'* first publication, four hundred copies shipped to the United States were burned at
customs; the next year, five hundred copies entering England at Folkestone
"went up the King's Chimney."

As the fame of Joyce and *Ulysses* spread, so did the reputation of Sylvia
Beach, her bookshop, and her press. Writers flocked to Shakespeare and
Company on the assumption that Beach specialized in erotica.

SYLVIA BEACH: They brought me their most erotic efforts. And not only
that; they insisted on reading me passages that couldn't, they thought, fail
to tempt a person with my supposed tastes.

———

One day "a small man with whiskers" drove up to the bookshop in a
carriage—a barouche and pair hired for the occasion to impress the bold
new female publisher.

SYLVIA BEACH: His long arms swinging apelike in front of him, he walked
into the shop, deposited on my table a parcel that had the look of a
manuscript, and introduced himself as Frank Harris. I had liked his book
The Man Shakespeare. I had also liked the volume on Wilde, and especially
Shaw's preface about Wilde's gigantism. So had Joyce. I asked Harris what
his manuscript was about.

The author undid the parcel and showed Beach what it was that she ought to publish. It was called *My Life and Loves*.* In it, Harris said, he went "much further than Joyce." He told her that he was really the only English writer who has got "under a woman's skin." And then he read aloud from it to Beach:

FRANK HARRIS *(My Life and Loves): I kept a buggy and horse at a livery stable and used to drive Lily or Rose out nearly every day. . . . In the evening Rose came straight to my office, told me it was the very thing she had most wanted, and let me study her beauties one by one; but when I turned her around and kissed her bottom, she wanted me to stop. "You can't possibly like or admire that," was her verdict. "Indeed I do," I cried. But I confessed to myself that she was right, her bottom was adorably dimpled but it was a little too fat, and the line underneath was not perfect. One of her breasts, too, was prettier than the other, though both were small and stuck out boldly: my critical sense would find no fault with her triangle or her sex; the lips of it were perfect, very small and rose-red and her clitoris was like a tiny, tiny button. I often wished it were half an inch long like Mrs. Mayhew's.*

SYLVIA BEACH: [W]hen he gave up trying to make me listen to *My Life and Loves* . . . I suggested that he try Jack Kahane,† who was always looking for "hot books."

The next "hot book" offered to Sylvia Beach was D. H. Lawrence's *Lady Chatterley's Lover*.

SYLVIA BEACH: I was obliged to turn [it] down. . . . I didn't admire this work, which I found the least interesting of its author's productions.

Privately Beach called Lawrence's *Lady C.* a "kind of Sermon-on-the-Mount—of Venus." But it was hard for her to refuse Lawrence's appeal.

---

*Published unexpurgated in the United States by Grove Press in 1963, edited and with an introduction by John F. Gallagher. An American edition of the second volume of Frank Harris's *My Life and Loves*, published in English in Germany in 1924, is known to have been seized by New York police at the Up-To-Date Printing Company in June 1925. The next year John Sumner led a raid on a bindery, where 680 additional copies were seized. No effective defense of the book seems to have been mounted, and Harris's American agent, Esar Levine, was sent to prison ("the workhouse"). The censorship did not upset the publishing industry; *Publishers Weekly* observed that Harris's work was "unfit for publication under the standards of any country." Paul Boyer, *Purity in Print* (1968), 136–37; John Tebbel, *A History of Book Publishing in the United States* 3 (1978), 415.

†Kahane was the founder of the Obelisk Press in Paris and became the first publisher of Henry Miller's *Tropic of Cancer* in English, in 1934. His son Maurice Girodias adopted his mother's name when the Germans went to war against France. He established the Olympia Press, also in Paris, and was the first publisher of later "obscene" novels by Miller, as well as Vladimir Nabokov's *Lolita*, William Burroughs's *Naked Lunch*, Samuel Beckett's *Watt*, and a long series of "dirty books" ("d.b.'s") in English. In 1957, during de Gaulle's reign, Girodias was prosecuted for publishing *Lolita* and the d.b.'s, his little firm was destroyed, and he barely escaped imprisonment, as described in Chapter 14.

She was told by two friends of Lawrence's, Richard Aldington and Aldous Huxley—who came to Paris expressly to ask Beach to take over *Lady C.*'s publication—that the situation was "desperate." The problem was that Lawrence's last novel was not protected by copyright, in England or the United States, and publishing pirates easily undersold the edition that Lawrence had privately printed in Italy with the help of the Florentine printer Pino Orioli. When his friends' mission failed, Lawrence and his wife, Frieda, went to Paris to see Sylvia Beach themselves.

SYLVIA BEACH: It was sad refusing Lawrence's *Lady,* particularly because he was so ill . . . he had got out of bed to come to the bookshop and had a flushed, feverish look. It was distressing trying to explain to him my reasons for not undertaking other publications than *Ulysses*—lack of capital . . . and that we lacked space, personnel, and time. It was difficult to tell him that I didn't want to get a name as a publisher of erotica, and impossible to say that I wanted to be a one-book publisher—what could anybody offer after *Ulysses*?

———

The first of Lawrence's novels to be suppressed in England was *The Rainbow,* published in 1915 by Methuen and Company. It was the successor to *Sons and Lovers,* the novel that had gained Lawrence an international reputation. *The Rainbow* was written in England, during the war, as "a kind of working up to the dark sensual or Dionysic or Aphrodisic ecstasy which actually bursts the world-consciousness in every individual." And *Women in Love,* its sequel, was "very wonderful and terrifying, even to me who had written it, and I knew it could be a long time before it would be printed—if ever."

A first reading of *The Rainbow* manuscript caused Methuen to send it back "for alteration" to the author's agent, J. B. Pinker.* Lawrence's second version was scarcely better, so the publisher returned it also, marking portions he thought should be cut. Finally, on July 26, 1915, Lawrence wrote to Pinker:

D. H. LAWRENCE: I send you back the slips and pages. I have cut out as I said I would, all the *phrases* objected to. The passages and paragraphs marked I cannot alter. . . . Tell Methuen, he need not be afraid.

———

Pinker told Methuen that Lawrence now refused to "mutilate" his work any further, and so Methuen decided to go ahead. *The Rainbow* appeared on September 30, 1915.

There is no doubt that Lawrence self-censored the manuscript that Methuen finally published. It is also clear that the author refused to cut as many as thirteen passages that Methuen considered likely to cause trouble.† In

---

*Pinker had been agent as well for Joseph Conrad, Henry James, Arnold Bennett, and Ford Madox Ford.

†Pinker, however, told the Society of Authors that Lawrence "only left unchanged, I think, one passage of which [Methuen] complained." Pinker's remark, made in a letter in November 1915, was published for the first time in the *Times Literary Supplement* for February 27, 1969,

any event, no sooner was the Methuen edition out than the reviewers alerted the circulating libraries and the prosecutive authorities to *The Rainbow*'s foul character, and Methuen was filled with forebodings.*

In the *Daily News,* Robert Lynd called Lawrence's novel "windy, tedious, boring and nauseating" and to boot "a monstrous wilderness of phallicism." In the *Sphere,* Clement Shorter invoked the imprisonment of Vizetelly and said that Zola's novels were as "child's food compared with the strong meat" of *The Rainbow;* it was "an orgy of sexiness" that omitted "no form of viciousness, of suggestiveness." The most dangerous notice came from the book critic of the *Star,* James Douglas: "These people are not human beings," he wrote of *The Rainbow*'s characters. "They are creatures who are immeasurably lower than the lowest animal in the Zoo." Douglas recommended prosecution, for when literature refuses to "conform to the ordered laws that govern human society . . . it must pay the penalty. The sanitary inspector of literature must notify it and call for its isolation."†

And so, on November 3, 1915, Albert Draper, detective-inspector of the criminal investigation department of New Scotland Yard, went knocking on Methuen's door. He had in hand a warrant from the chief magistrate at Bow Street police court to seize all copies of *The Rainbow*. The policeman passed along to Methuen information that Messrs. Wontner and Sons of Bow Street, the Yard's solicitors, had given him:

ALGERNON METHUEN: The solicitors, in consideration of the reputation of our firm, kindly suggested that we might prefer to hand over the books rather than submit to actual search, and this we did.

—

After Draper left, Methuen called Pinker, but he reported nothing to Lawrence, who learned what happened a few days later from a friend. By then the police had removed from Methuen and their printers, Hazell, Watson, and Viney, 1,011 copies of *The Rainbow*. Then, on Thursday, November 11, Draper called again on Methuen, this time with a summons to show cause why "the said books should not be destroyed."

ALGERNON METHUEN: We understood from Inspector Draper that this was merely a formal matter to obtain our formal consent on the destruction of

---

in a piece by John Carter, "The 'Rainbow' Prosecution." In court Methuen had sought to placate the magistrate by saying, "Lawrence was unyielding on the question of alterations." Commented Pinker in his letter to the Society of Authors: "This is not the case."

The passages that Lawrence refused to cut from *The Rainbow* are thought to be among thirteen that publisher B. W. Huebsch cut—without Lawrence's permission—from the American edition of *The Rainbow*, published in New York in December 1915. The endnotes to this chapter take these up.

*A letter of October 18 from Methuen to Pinker said: "The result is that . . . the book has earned in royalties roughly £60, against an advance of £300. . . . We shall decline to accept his next book if it at all approaches the present book in outspokenness." Another letter from Methuen to Pinker reported that none of the big libraries or booksellers "would touch it," and called their publication of *The Rainbow* "a disastrous fiasco." *The Rainbow,* edited by Mark Kinkead-Weekes (1989), xiv.

†Douglas later became book critic and editor of the London *Daily Express*.

the book; the impression we received was that it would not be heard in a public court, and we did not therefore obtain legal assistance or arrange to be legally represented.

We asked Inspector Draper if the author could have a voice in the destruction of the books, and understood him to say that the action of the Police Court was taken against us and the author had no right to appear in the matter.*

———

Algernon Methuen played the game of the police in the hope of emerging from the censorship with his gentlemanly reputation intact, possibly even enhanced. However, as Emile Delavenay said: "The net effect of [Meuthen's] malleability was that neither they nor Pinker nor Lawrence were represented by counsel in Bow Street court, on November 13, the field thus being clear for the prosecution."

EMILE DELAVENAY:† The proceedings read, in retrospect . . . like a ritual execution, performed in accordance with an arranged scenario.

———

The police action against *The Rainbow* was not a criminal proceeding, which could have resulted in a jail term; it was taken under Lord Campbell's Act of 1857, which authorized the seizure and destruction of all copies of an "obscene" publication. That act was concerned not with providing judges with a definition of the "obscene"—that had been accomplished satisfactorily to those who supported literary censorship by the *Hicklin* case—but with giving them an efficient means for the destruction of books and prints suspected to be obscene—without the need to get the assent of a jury. Although the act was supposed to be used to stamp out pornography, given the utter vagueness of the *Hicklin* definition of what was "obscene," its procedures could easily be used against literature too. A magistrate, under the act, might issue a search warrant merely on being shown or told about a suspicious book. Armed with the warrant, the police could raid the premises of printer, publisher, or bookseller, seize any "obscene" or "immoral" books, and take them to the magistrate, who would then set a hearing for their destruction. For the government and the anti-vice societies, the great virtue of a Lord Campbell Act proceeding, compared with common-law criminal prosecution, was not only that no jury needed to be convened but that the former could, whereas the latter could not, bring about the destruction of a publisher's entire stock of a

———

*Although Methuen claimed they let Pinker know of the proceedings by the police, Lawrence's agent said he knew nothing "until I read of them in the newspapers." Pinker said he spoke by telephone with a Mr. Mueller of the publishing firm, who expressed Methuen's wish to hush up the affair. "Mueller told me that he had discussed the question with one of the Directors, and they felt very strongly that the matter should be hushed up. I pointed out to him that they do not seem to have considered Mr. Lawrence's point of view, and we were going to try and get the order reversed. Mr. Mueller said that they hoped I should do nothing in the matter." *The Rainbow,* edited by Mark Kinkead-Weekes (1989), xlix.

†Author of *D. H. Lawrence: The Man and His Work* (1972).

particular book or books. As the British scholar and barrister Geoffrey Robertson has observed: "The new system was a boon to prosecuting authorities and the vice-suppression societies, who could thereafter proudly boast of the tonnage of literature which had been consigned to the flames by their efforts."* It was a most efficient and terrifying way to suppress books.

The advantage to a reputable publisher faced with a Lord Campbell Act proceeding was that it carried for him no risk of being stigmatized by the government as a criminal. Nor need the publisher suffer fine or the great distress of imprisonment, as Vizetelly did, whether he protested the proceedings or not. The books seized and destroyed were Methuen's property but also Lawrence's art and work; yet the author was given no notice of the proceedings, nor any opportunity to contest them. The law made no provision for such things.† When Lawrence learned about the action from a friend—who had been alerted to the seizure by the disappearance of Methuen's ad for *The Rainbow*—he did not seek legal advice or assistance. Instead he sought to mobilize in defense of his novel a member of Parliament, Philip Morrell, and Prime Minister Herbert Asquith; Morrell's wife and Asquith's daughter-in-law were Lawrence's friends.

D. H. LAWRENCE: My dear Lady Cynthia [Asquith]. . . . [A] magistrate has suppressed the sale of *The Rainbow,* and Methuen's are under orders to deliver up all existing copies. This is most irritating. Some interfering person goes to a police magistrate and says, "This book is indecent, listen here." Then the police magistrate says, "By Jove, we'll stop that." Then the thing is suppressed. But I think it is possible to have the decision reversed.‡ If it is possible, and you and Herbert Asquith can help, would you do so? You know quite well that the book is not indecent, though I heard of you saying to a man that it was like the second story in *The Prussian Officer,* only *much worse.* Still, one easily says those things.

———

Asquith, at the time, was preoccupied with matters of state, notably with "perilous political negotiations over the impending withdrawal from Gallipoli." Later, when Philip Morrell raised a question in Parliament with regard to the proceedings, Home Secretary Sir John Simon laid the matter to rest by mentioning that the police had acted "in the pursuance of their ordinary duty," and the publishers in accordance with their right.

SIR JOHN SIMON: [T]he publishers and not the author were the defendants, and they had the customary opportunity to produce such evidence as they

*Obscenity (1979), 28ff.

†According to Geoffrey Robertson, amendments to Lord Campbell's Act, adopted some fifty years later in 1977, "accord to the authors, publishers and distributors a right to intervene in forfeiture proceedings to argue that publications in which they have an interest should not be destroyed." However, even these amendments provided "no machinery for notifying authors or publishers of the [destruction] hearing." *Obscenity* (1979), 97–98.

‡An appeal from the magistrate's destruction order was permitted under the statute; however, only Methuen might have appealed—an entitlement useless to the author.

considered necessary in defence. . . . [S]o far from resisting the proceedings they said they thought it right that the order [of destruction] should be issued.

———

A solicitor named Herbert G. Muskett, senior partner in Wontner and Sons, the firm that regularly represented Scotland Yard, had appeared at Bow Street Court for the commissioner of police. He read aloud denunciations by newspaper reviewers of Lawrence's novel, adding one or two of his own. Muskett saw fit to praise Methuen as "a publishing house of old standing and the highest repute" which had finally behaved "with the strictest propriety." He found it difficult, nonetheless, to see why they had lent their "great name" to such a work in the first place. Sir John Dickinson, the recorder, feigned surprise to see publishers "of such old standing" brought before him, and agreed with Solicitor Muskett that the novel was "just a mass of obscenity of thought, idea, and action throughout." Conceding it to be "nicely wrapped up in a language which would be regarded in some quarters as an artistic and intellectual effort," he nonetheless believed Methuen "ought to have known better than lend their name to such a publication." Others of the magistrate's views were reported in the *Telegraph*.

THE DAILY TELEGRAPH: [Sir John] had never read anything more disgusting than this book, and how it could ever have passed through Messrs Methuen's hands he failed to understand. . . . It was appalling to think of the harm that such a book might have done. It was utter filth, nothing else would describe it. He was very glad to hear that the libraries refused to circulate it.

———

Methuen stated that at their request the author had twice made deletions, but then refused to cooperate further. Sir John, seeing the firm apologize so abjectly for having published the book, "mingled his regrets with theirs" and added that they should have listened to what the reviewers said and withdrawn the book straightaway. Under the circumstances, Methuen could find no reason to object to the judicial destruction of the entire edition of *The Rainbow,* and of the plates—notwithstanding that an advance *had* been paid to Lawrence* and a considerable sum spent to have the work printed up and shipped to the usual outlets. More gratifying to Methuen, the recorder elected merely to "scold" them, and order a payment by them of "costs" amounting to ten guineas.† Methuen's total out-of-pocket expense for the proceeding came to £40. As Jeffrey Meyers

———

*The publishers asked Lawrence to return his advance. The contract that Pinker had arranged with Methuen called for an advance of £300: £150 on receipt of manuscript and £150 on publication. All was paid. With the advance, Lawrence opened a bank account. *The Rainbow,* edited by Mark Kinkead-Weekes (1989), xxix. Kinkead-Weekes says Methuen initially had been "eager for the book." There is no evidence that Lawrence repaid the advance.

†This has sometimes incorrectly been referred to as a fine.

observed, "Algernon Methuen's gentlemanly contribution paid off, for he avoided a fine and placed all the blame on Lawrence. The following year he was made a baronet."*

Lawrence believed that the passages mainly responsible for *The Rainbow*'s destruction were those memorable ones in which a pregnant Anna danced naked.†

D. H. LAWRENCE *(The Rainbow): As she sat by her bedroom window, watching the steady rain, her spirit was somewhere far off.*

She sat in pride and curious pleasure. When there was no one to exult with, and the unsatisfied soul must dance and play, then one danced before the Unknown.

Suddenly she realized that this was what she wanted to do. Big with child as she was, she danced there in the bedroom by herself, lifting her hands and her body to the Unseen, to the unseen Creator who had chosen her, to Whom she belonged.

She would not have had any one know. She danced in secret, and her soul rose in bliss. She danced in secret before the Creator, she took off her clothes and danced in the pride of her bigness.

It surprised her, when it was over. She was shrinking and afraid. To what was she now exposed? She half wanted to tell her husband. Yet she shrank from him. . . .

On a Saturday afternoon, when she had a fire in the bedroom, again she took off her things and danced, lifting her knees and her hands in a slow, rhythmic exulting. He was in the house, so her pride was fiercer. She would dance his nullification, she would dance to her unseen Lord. She was exalted over him, before the Lord.

She heard him coming up the stairs, and she flinched. She stood with the firelight on her ankles and feet, naked in the shadowy, late afternoon, fastening up her hair. He was startled. He stood in the doorway, his brows black and lowering. "What are you doing?" he said, gratingly. "You'll catch a cold."

And she lifted her hands and danced again, to annul him, the light glanced on her knees as she made her slow, fine movements down the far side of the room, across the firelight. He stood away near the door in blackness of shadow, watching, transfixed. And with slow, heavy movements she swayed backwards and forwards, like a full ear of corn, pale in the dusky afternoon, threading before the firelight, dancing his non-existence, dancing herself to the Lord, to exultation.

He watched, and his soul burned in him. He turned aside, he could not look, it hurt his eyes. Her fine limbs lifted and lifted, her hair was sticking out all fierce,

---

**D. H. Lawrence: A Biography (1990), 190.

†In a letter written in 1920 to publisher Martin Secker, then proposing to reissue an expurgated *The Rainbow* and its sequel, *Women in Love*, Lawrence advised that *The Rainbow* be republished "as a new book, with a new title, anyhow," and referred to the prior censorship: "The magistrates proceeded on the reviews by James Douglas, in the *Star*, and one by Clement Shorter, I think in *Pall Mall*. The scene to which exception was *particularly* taken was the one where Anna dances naked, when she is with child. I don't think it's very important, anyhow sufficiently past."

and her belly, big, strange, terrifying, uplifted to the Lord. Her face was rapt and beautiful, she danced exulting before her Lord, and knew no man.

It hurt him as he watched as if he were at the stake. He felt he was being burned alive. The strangeness, the power of her in her dancing consumed him, he was burned, he could not grasp, he could not understand. He waited obliterated. Then his eyes became blind to her, he saw her no more. And through the unseeing veil between them he called to her, in his jarring voice: "What are you doing that for?"

"Go away," she said. "Let me dance by myself."

"That isn't dancing," he said harshly. "What do you want to do that for?"

"I don't do it for you," she said. "You go away."

Her strange, lifted belly, big with his child! Had he no right to be there? He felt his presence a violation. Yet he had his right to be there. He went and sat on the bed.

She stopped dancing, and confronted him, again lifting her slim arms and twisting at her hair. Her nakedness hurt her, opposed to him.

"I can do as I like in my bedroom," she cried.

———

There was reason to suspect, however, that the suppression was related to the wartime atmosphere in England. The book was published in autumn 1915, when the war was not going well: there was the Gallipoli failure, the first big Zeppelin raids, and the coming fall of the Asquith cabinet. On the day that *The Rainbow* was ordered burned, Winston Churchill's resignation from the cabinet was announced; and a noted literary figure, Augustine Birrell, who was chief secretary of Ireland, said in a speech at Bristol that he "for one would forbid the use, during the war, of poetry." The day's news included a report that not enough unmarried Englishmen had volunteered, and now Lord Derby threatened conscription. Richard Aldington wrote in 1931 that he believed "the real reason for the attack" on Lawrence's book "was that he denounced war. . . . They can say what they like about obscenity."

A government propaganda campaign had been launched to improve recruiting with posters screeching at British women: "Is your 'best boy' wearing Khaki? . . . If your young man neglects his duty to his King and Country, the time may come when he will NEGLECT YOU!" This could only have made Lawrence's Ursula laugh. In the novel, Ursula makes fun of her "best boy" for taking the war seriously: "I hate soldiers," she cries, "they are stiff and wooden."

The book's reviewers had argued that *The Rainbow* was tainted by Lawrence's "pro-Germanism."* In the *New Statesman,* Lawrence was said by

———

*At the same time, in the United States, Theodore Dreiser was receiving similar treatment from American reviewers of his new novel, *The "Genius."* This was two years before America would enter the war against Germany, on England's side. See Chapter 7.

That Lawrence was not pro-German but was angry at, and terrified by, the warmongers may be surmised from the letters Lawrence wrote to friends during the war. Writing to Lady Ottoline Morrell, he said: "I cannot bear it much longer, to let the madness get stronger and stronger possession. Soon we in England shall go fully mad, with hate. I too hate the Germans

J. C. Squire to be "under the spell of German psychologists," and in the *Athenaeum,* George William de Tungelmann suggested he had accepted German "materialistic pseudophilosophy," an attitude that the critic allowed was responsible for "many of the humiliating weaknesses which have so hampered [England's] action against Germany." It was widely known that Lawrence's wife, Frieda, was German and it was widely but mistakenly said that she was the daughter of a general in the kaiser's army. In fact, Frieda's father, Friedrich von Richthofen, was an officer who had served in the Franco-Prussian War and been seriously wounded and captured. His disability "kept him from ever again being a soldier."

Lawrence would do nothing, however, to disabuse his countrymen of the notion that he was pro-German (and anti-British). To top the matter off, *The Rainbow* appeared with a dedication to a German, Frieda's sister, Else.

HARRY T. MOORE: Many of the other sensitive literary men of Europe refused, like Lawrence, to support the war effort of their own countries; men such as Romain Rolland in France and Heinrich Mann in Germany. In England, most of the imaginative writers had at once rushed into uniform, or government bureaux, or espionage; among them Lawrence's antiwar stand was almost unique. . . . To officials and to officious patriots, Lawrence soon became a man who, physically unfit for military service, was dangerous to have behind one's lines.

—

After Methuen's submission, Lawrence's spirit lay wounded; the man tried to beg and borrow money to leave England. "I am so sick, in body and soul, that if I don't go away I shall die," he said in a letter to his friend Edward Marsh, adding:

D. H. LAWRENCE: A man said we could live on his little estate in Florida. I want you, if you can, to give me a little money to go with: if you can, easily, that is. God knows I don't want to mulct you. I'll give it you back if ever I have any money: I owe you £10 already. And I will give you full and final possession of some poems, when I have any you like. . . . But I feel so sick I shall never be able to get through a winter here.

---

so much, I could kill every one of them. Why should they goad us to this frenzy of hatred, why should we be tortured to (*bloody*) madness, when we are only grieved in our souls, and heavy? They will drive our heaviness and our grief away in a fury of rage. And we don't want to be worked up to this fury, this destructive madness of rage. Yet we must, we are goaded on and on. I am mad with rage myself. I would like to kill a million Germans—two millions." *Selected Letters of D. H. Lawrence,* edited by Diana Trilling (1958), 108–10. See also the letter dated November 2, 1915, to Lady Cynthia Asquith published in *The Collected Letters of D. H. Lawrence,* edited by Harry T. Moore, vol. 1 (1962), 374–76.

Lady Ottoline Morrell, who served Lawrence as one of his many typists, was described by Diana Trilling as "a noted hostess and friend of writers and painters." She was one of Lawrence's aristocratic friends with whose help Lawrence hoped to establish "a vitalistic religious revolution" and a new kind of community (201 n.). It was Lady Ottoline's husband, Philip Morrell, who raised questions in Parliament concerning the government's suppression of *The Rainbow.*

He wrote Pinker on the same day, November 6, 1915:

D. H. LAWRENCE: I hope to be going away in about a fortnight's time: to America: there is a man who more or less offers us a cottage in Florida: but nothing is settled yet. We have got passports. It is the end of my writing for England. I will try to change my public.

No English publisher would now touch his work. (The Oxford University Press, having commissioned Lawrence to do a book on European history, did publish it, but under a pseudonym.) To Lawrence, English publishers seemed a spineless lot. The possibility of being accused of publishing immoral literature frightened them to death. Of course, they remembered "how Vizetelly was imprisoned and his house brought down in ruins, for the crime of publishing Zola. But not even a fight?" Lawrence was certain now that his next book, *Women in Love,* would never find an English publisher.

D. H. LAWRENCE: I believe that England is . . . capable of not seeing anything but badness in me, for ever and ever. I believe America is my virgin soil: truly.

Unlike George Moore and so many other authors and artists who went into voluntary exile in France, Lawrence decided it was to America that he "must go as a seed that falls into the new ground."

D. H. LAWRENCE: I don't think America is a paradise. But I know I can sell my stories there, and get a connection with publishers. And what I want is for us to have sufficient to go far West, to California or the South Seas, and live apart, away from the world. . . . I hope in the end other people will come, and we can be a little community, a monastery, a school—a little Hesperides of the soul and body.

At the time, Lawrence was still hoping that America would stay out of the war, and this was another reason why he thought to go there. On September 18, 1915, Lawrence wrote to Harriet Monroe (who published *Poetry* magazine): "Pray to heaven to keep America always out of this war. God knows what will be the end of Europe."*

The idea of going to America hung fire for six years. With the intervention of Lady Cynthia at the Foreign Office, Lawrence and Frieda received passports to go to the United States in November 1915, but the crisis over *The Rainbow* led them to postpone the trip, and by the time of their next effort, it proved necessary to obtain an exit visa, which required a certificate of Lawrence's exemption from military service. This the author was incapa-

---

*When, two years later, America entered the war on the side of England, Lawrence lost a reason for going there. *The Collected Letters of D. H. Lawrence,* edited by Harry T. Moore, vol. 1 (1962), 369.

ble of securing; after standing in line for two hours at the Battersea recruiting office, he suddenly "broke out of the queue, in face of the table where one's name was to be written, and went across the hall away from all the underworld of spectral submission."

And so Lawrence and Frieda went as "far away as possible" to live in remote Cornwall,* where, in a mood of hatred for "putrescent mankind" and without thought of publication at first, Lawrence would resume the story of Ursula Brangwen in the novel to be published as *Women in Love.* But for years the effects of England's destruction of *The Rainbow* disturbed, almost devastated, the man.

In the United States the first of Lawrence's works to appear was not *The Rainbow* but the author's earlier novel, *Sons and Lovers,* the book many consider Lawrence's finest novel. Published by William Heinemann in England, it was brought out successfully in the States by a now almost forgotten Scotsman, Mitchell Kennerley.† Heinemann had unsuccessfully sought to persuade Lawrence to alter some of the "erotic" matter in *Sons and Lovers;* Kennerley, an expatriate Britisher, was cut from a different cloth. By 1913, when he published *Sons and Lovers* in New York, he already had a reputation for welcoming the "better uninhibited" authors, whose works the established houses were reluctant to take on. The next year he was toasted for winning a full-fledged court battle against Anthony Comstock, involving a book he published called *Hagar Revelly.* It was Comstock's last important legal battle; the next year "Old Antonio" died.

In the initial stage of that case, *United States* v. *Kennerley,* Kennerley went into federal court to stop Comstock's prosecution. There, Learned Hand, sitting as a federal district judge, declined to interfere with the state case but expressed some intelligent ideas, thereafter often quoted, on the subject of obscenity.‡ This was some twenty years before Hand took part in the revolutionary judicial act of freeing James Joyce's *Ulysses,* and only a few years before he tried, valiantly but unsuccessfully, on free press grounds, to save the socialist antiwar magazine *The Masses* from suppression for obstructing the war effort and the draft. There was, however, little in Hand's opinion in Kennerley's case to indicate that freedom of speech or press was at stake, and the New York State court judge who tried the criminal case seems to have disregarded some of Hand's enlightened dicta. Nevertheless, *Little Review* lawyer John Quinn was permitted at the criminal trial to give each member of Kennerley's jury a copy of *Hagar Revelly* to read, and to put on the stand expert witnesses to talk about the book's "reformist" design and social value. Although the judge charged the jury concerning the meaning of "obscenity" in *Regina* v. *Hicklin*'s hoary terms—this was the

---

*Eventually, he and Frieda were expelled from Cornwall, as suspected German spies.

†Matthew Bruccoli has remembered the publisher in his book *The Fortunes of Mitchell Kennerley, Bookman* (1986).

‡Some of Hand's dicta are quoted in the endnotes for this chapter.

main respect in which he ignored Learned Hand's admonitions—the verdict returned by the jury on the criminal charge was "not guilty." Publisher B. W. Huebsch hailed Kennerley's achievement in the pages of the trade journal *Publishers Weekly:*

B. W. HUEBSCH: Mr. Kennerley was prosecuted for publishing and mailing a book in which freedom of expression went no further than in a hundred novels of the past decade. Nobody seriously denied that it possessed both literary merit and social significance. It would have been a simple matter for Mr. Kennerley to plead guilty (following precedent in the cases of booksellers) and pay a fine, but to his credit he chose the difficult, hazardous, and expensive alternative of standing trial. His acquittal by a jury is a vindication of a free press and a triumph for democracy. Specifically the case concerned Mr. Kennerley alone, but actually he fought for a principle and thus made every American publisher his debtor.

———

Kennerley had come to New York from England at the age of eighteen to help open a branch of the John Lane Company. This was the firm that in 1894 brought out in England Oscar Wilde's *Salomé,* with illustrations by Aubrey Beardsley, and in the same year founded *The Yellow Book* magazine, with Beardsley as its art editor.* Lane also brought out early works by Lionel Johnson, Ernest Dowson, Lord Alfred Douglas, Max Beerbohm, and George Moore. In New York he would publish Theodore Dreiser's novels.†

In 1902, in New York, Kennerley launched his own literary magazine, a twenty-five-cent monthly called *The Reader.* He was now twenty-four years old. Eight years later he took over "a respected but unprosperous" journal of political and social opinion called *The Forum,* also selling for twenty-five cents, and enlarged the space devoted to literature and art. He published Vachel Lindsay, Maurice Maeterlinck, Leo Tolstoy, Ezra Pound, Jack London, John Reed, W. B. Yeats, Robert Frost, D. H. Lawrence, H. L. Mencken, Sherwood Anderson, and Edna St. Vincent Millay, among others, in its pages; a number of these later became Kennerley authors.

In 1907 he opened his own publishing house; at the same time he started a bookstore, the Little Bookshop Around the Corner, which took its name from a church across the street called the Little Church Around the Corner. In those days a good bookstore became a gathering place for poets and writers, artists and typographers, and this is what Kennerley had in mind.

The young Alfred A. Knopf worked for a year, at twenty-five dollars a

———

*Lane is said to have had "a rather nerve-racking time" with Beardsley who, "for the fun of it, was always trying to slip some indecency into his covers, not apparent without close scrutiny, so that Lane used to go over them with a microscope and submit them to a jury of his friends before he ventured to publish them." Frank Arthur Mumby, *Publishing and Bookselling* (1931), 359. For more about Beardsley, see Chapter 15.

†It was John Lane's New York branch manager, J. Jefferson Jones, who gave up the entire first printing of Dreiser's novel *The "Genius"* to John Sumner, as described in Chapter 7.

week, as Kennerley's general factotum, before going off on his own in 1915—"with $3000 and a desk in his father's office." He was not overly grateful to the Scotsman for his apprenticeship. Said Knopf: "I learned how not to publish by working for Kennerley. . . . I think that if Mitchell had been honest, I never would have become a publisher." Within three years, Knopf said, he "was beating Kennerley at his own publishing game."

Kennerley hoped to be remembered for being the first to publish in America nonconformist new writers like D. H. Lawrence and Edna St. Vincent Millay, as well as Frank Harris, whose *The Man Shakespeare* and *Oscar Wilde: His Life and Confessions* he published.* He was also the first to publish Walter Lippmann, bringing out his *Preface to Politics*. When he published what many consider Lawrence's best book, *Sons and Lovers,* he promoted it vigorously, using "a personal touch" that worked so well that Knopf was said to have copied it. An ad that Kennerley ran in *Publishers Weekly* had this pitch: "I do not ask you to buy it but I do tell you that *Sons and Lovers* by D. H. Lawrence is one of the great novels of the age."

Kennerley had trouble, however, keeping Lawrence on his list. After publishing *Sons and Lovers,* he had an option to publish Lawrence's next books as well, but now the author spoke of him to others as "a swine, a young Britisher of advanced publishing ideas but shady business ethics."† Lawrence complained that the man had not paid him any royalties for *Sons and Lovers,* and that when B. W. Huebsch was willing to bring it out in a new edition, Kennerley would not stop selling his own. After the Methuen debacle concerning *The Rainbow,* Lawrence and Frieda were definitely hard up. Frieda's divorce had been costly, and nothing was coming in from England or America from sales of *The Rainbow* or its sequel, *Women in Love.* Lawrence had been thinking about going to Florida to start a new life, but he did not have funds for passage. When he pressed Kennerley for an accounting, the publisher responded by sending the author a check for £20 or £25 (the reports disagree) and the next month another for £10. According to Lawrence, neither check could be cashed.

D. H. LAWRENCE: [Mitchell Kennerley] published *Sons and Lovers* in America, and one day, joyful, arrived a check for twenty pounds. Twenty pounds in those days was a little fortune: and as it was a windfall, it was handed over to Madame; the first pin-money she had seen. Alas and alack, there was an alteration in the date of the cheque, and the bank would not cash it. It was returned to Mitchell Kennerley, but that was the end of it. He never made good, and never to this day made any further payment for *Sons*

---

*Sylvia Beach seems to have read both of these books, as mentioned above in Chapter 2.
†This was Lawrence's public view of Kennerley, which he probably hoped might assist him to collect what was owed him by his first American publisher. Privately, as in a letter to Amy Lowell written in 1915, he seemed to hold Kennerley in some affection: "I don't want him ever to publish me anything ever any more as long as either of us lives. So you can say what you like to him. But I think that really he is rather nice." Harry T. Moore, *The Intelligent Heart: The Story of D. H. Lawrence* (1962), 221–22.

and Lovers. Till this year of grace 1924, America has had that, my most popular book, for nothing—as far as I am concerned.*

FRIEDA LAWRENCE: [Kennerley] is a jug—He gave Lawrence £25 for 'Sons and Lovers,' promised him another £25, then. arrived the bad check. . . . L. hates the whole business so much that he shouts at me every time he thinks of it! I feel a grudge against Kennerley, not only has he done me out of £25, but every time L thinks of *Kennerley* he gets in a rage with *me,* the logic of men and husbands.

———

Later, Van Wyck Brooks, who published three books with Kennerley,† expressed great appreciation for the publisher—although he himself had come close to suing Kennerley in 1916:

VAN WYCK BROOKS: What did it matter in the end that he sometimes played a double game. He made nothing out of his exasperated authors, and who else would have printed them, who else would have looked at their first little books, which Kennerley delightedly acclaimed and so charmingly published? . . . [H]e backed books often at a loss, with a feeling for talents that no one but he distinguished; and he should be remembered as the friend of a whole generation of writers whom, in surprising numbers, he first brought out.

HARRY T. MOORE: These are kind thoughts but the lovers at Fiascherino would doubtless have preferred some hard cash.

———

Lawrence had sent Kennerley the manuscript of *The Rainbow,* but after their falling out over the royalties for *Sons and Lovers,* the author's agent, Pinker, contracted with George H. Doran for American rights to Lawrence's next three books, including *The Rainbow* and *Women in Love,* and tried to get *The Rainbow* manuscript out of Kennerley's hands. But Doran turned out to be "a prude" and would not publish *The Rainbow.* (Later he would also refuse to publish Theodore Dreiser.‡)

GEORGE H. DORAN: I barely escaped becoming publisher for D. H. Lawrence. After reading his *Sons and Lovers,* I was all eagerness to have the distinction of his name on my list. The opportunity came, and I had arranged a three-book contract with his literary agent. The first book offered under that contract was *The Rainbow,* a grand book and after the

———

*Later Lawrence did obtain ownership of Mabel Luhan's Taos, New Mexico, ranch in exchange for the ms. of *Sons and Lovers.* Said Lawrence: "Everyone is very mad with me for giving that MS. The ranch was only worth about $1000, and the MS. of *Sons and Lovers* worth three or four thousand—so everybody says. But I don't care." *The Collected Letters of D. H. Lawrence,* edited by Harry T. Moore, vol. 2 (1962), 805.

† *The Wine of the Puritans* (1909), *John Addington Symonds: A Biographical Study* (1914), and *The World of H. G. Wells* (1915).

‡See Chapter 7 below.

manner of *Sons and Lovers*, but Lawrence could not resist the temptation to drag in some Lesbianism not in the slightest degree essential to the novel itself. It was issued in London first, and there it was so quickly suppressed as immoral that there was not the slightest chance of its publication being permitted in America. The London publisher was fined a modest sum upon his agreeing completely to withdraw the book from sale. I do not know of its ever being reissued in England in its original form. Upon my contention that no contract could oblige me to violate the laws of my country, the book and the contract were taken from me. B. W. Huebsch, then a publisher in his own name, issued it privately in an edition limited to 1,000 copies. As I have closely followed the work of Lawrence since that time, I have congratulated myself that I have not been his publisher. Artist he may have been, possibly always was to the end of his days, but his art took the form of the vulgar nudity of intellectualism. Very few of us would want to become members of a nudist colony. Even fewer of us would choose the language of the besmirched walls of the privy for our dinner-table conversation.

———

When Doran declined to go ahead with *The Rainbow*, Lawrence at first despaired of publishing any further in the States. He wrote Pinker:

D. H. LAWRENCE: It doesn't seem to me that it is any use altering *The Rainbow* for the Americans. Curse them, what good is it to them, altered or not. Don't you think it is best . . . not to publish in America at all?

———

But Doran showed the manuscript to Ben Huebsch and proposed to Lawrence that he proceed under the same terms with Huebsch, understanding, however, that what Doran referred to as "precarious conditions" precluded any advance being paid to Lawrence on account of royalties. Having never heard of Huebsch, Lawrence wrote Pinker:

D. H. LAWRENCE: Is he disreputable, or what? And why will he publish the novel if Doran won't?

———

Satisfied by what Pinker told him, Lawrence agreed to let Huebsch go ahead.

On December 15, 1915, the American poet Amy Lowell wrote Lawrence to say that she had heard that *The Rainbow* "is to be issued over here, and now that Anthony Comstock is dead, I do not suppose you have anything to fear." But American publishers knew that the New York Society for the Suppression of Vice was not dead, and that a lawyer named John Sumner had been appointed secretary in Comstock's place.

When Huebsch set the book up from corrected proofs of the Methuen edition, he deleted thirteen passages from the novel's text without consulting Lawrence. At first Lawrence noticed only five, and he wondered whether Pinker had authorized Huebsch to make the expurgations. There is a letter from Lawrence to Pinker that asks: "Did Huebsch have your permission to cut out certain parts of *The Rainbow*? He never had mine."*

Among the passages Huebsch deleted were three short paragraphs from a "lesbian" bathing scene that Harry T. Moore and others believed had caused Methuen the most trouble—the text between a paragraph in which Winifred Inger says to Ursula, "I shall carry you into the water," and one that begins, "After a while the rain came down on their flushed, hot limbs, startling, delicious." Huebsch also excluded the following lines, which were said to have "generated the most complaints" about the Methuen edition, and which foreshadowed and far exceeded in explicitness a line that, some twenty years later, would trigger proceedings in England and the United States against Radclyffe Hall's "lesbian novel," *The Well of Loneliness*. †

D. H. LAWRENCE *(The Rainbow): Ursula lay still in her mistress's arms, her forehead against the beloved, maddening breast.*
"I shall put you in," said Winifred.
—But Ursula twined her body about her mistress.

———

John Sumner's activities had made Huebsch very cautious. The publisher was getting ready to take a trip with the Ford Peace Expedition only days before *The Rainbow* was to be published. Learning of the Bow Street proceedings against the British edition of the book, and the court order to Methuen to destroy the stock, Huebsch feared similar action from John Sumner and instructed his small staff (he later said they "included none who could face the expected proceedings"‡) to "do no more than make such sale as to give validity to the copyright and to lock up the stock until my return."

B. W. HUEBSCH: Surmising that the then current Comstock§ was lying in wait I told my travellers‖ . . . to let the book dribble out to the trade with a caution against talking too much about it, and thus the edition . . . was eventually sold out without, I think, any advertising or copies for review. Perhaps there were some reviews at that stage but if so the editors must have asked for copies; I know that I did not offer any because that would have balked my plan. The book having gone out of stock there were demands for more, of course, but I was still timid and decided to take refuge in the old trick of a limited edition, a little larger in dimensions and a little more expensively produced than the first. . . .

In justice to myself let me add that I did not try to deceive anybody by the term "limited" edition, but made it clear through the travellers that I

———

*The Letters of D. H. Lawrence 3 (1979), 652. The editor of the Cambridge edition of *The Rainbow* examines in detail the passages that Huebsch cut out and the extent to which Lawrence was pressed by Methuen and Pinker to expurgate the novel. D. H. Lawrence, *The Rainbow,* edited by Mark Kinkead-Weekes (1989), xxxviii-xxxix.

†Described in Chapters 10 and 11. The line in Hall's novel reads simply: "and that night they were not divided." It appears at the end of Chapter 38 of *The Well of Loneliness*.

‡I.e., defend themselves and the book against criminal prosecution.

§John Sumner, who replaced Comstock the year Huebsch brought out *The Rainbow,* 1915.

‖Of "travellers" (traveling salesmen), Huebsch confessed, there were no more than two.

was feeling my way, printing a lot at a time during a ticklish period. I wanted to fulfill my obligation to Lawrence by keeping the book available but I was in no position then, working almost single handed, to defend a suit which following on the London suppression, might have had serious consequences for me.

———

The "serious consequences" in Huebsch's mind no doubt were those that Vizetelly had suffered: criminal prosecution, prison, and the destruction of his firm and, virtually, his life. For, unlike Methuen—and even if he had been prepared to appear before his judges in an equally craven way— Huebsch would have been deemed put on notice, by the Bow Street proceedings and the English reviews, that the Lawrence novel was "disgusting," "utter filth," and legally "obscene."

Seven years later, "a little man" named Thomas Seltzer—who was to publish *Women in Love* and nineteen other books by Lawrence, more than anyone else in the States—reissued *The Rainbow*. This time, although the novel seems to have been brought out once more in a "limited" edition, it quickly sold 15,000 copies. But it would be only a matter of time before Seltzer, "poor devil, went broke"—in large measure because of the heavy expense of defending himself against repeated criminal prosecutions—and Lawrence abandoned him. The author's last American publisher would be the man who learned the book trade at Mitchell Kennerley's knee, Alfred A. Knopf.

In 1950 Kennerley hanged himself in the Manhattan hotel room where he had been living. Amos Basel, his lawyer, said "there were suicide notes all over the place," including "a note to call me, clippings and quotations about the quiet and peace of death." Kennerley's estate was valued at fifty dollars. After his death *Publishers Weekly* gave him credit for having brought "a fresh spirit of venture" to New York publishing, and said he had "helped pave the way" for the literary renaissance of the twenties.

5

It's Such an
Ugly Cemetery

THOMAS SELTZER was the first American publisher of Proust's *Remembrance of Things Past*. He was the translator of the Polish novel *Homo Sapiens*, published in 1915 by young Alfred A. Knopf, a novel that young John Sumner persuaded Knopf to withdraw from circulation because it was "obscene." Seltzer's nephews, Albert and Charles Boni, opened a bookshop in Greenwich Village, started the literary magazine *The Globe*, and joined with Horace Liveright to launch the most exciting publishing venture of the twenties, Boni and Liveright. For a few years Seltzer held a third interest in that firm; then, in 1922, he established his own house and subsequently issued three books that John Sumner pronounced "obscene" because they were "saturated" with sex—"sex during childhood, sex in mature women and sex in old age!"—all calculated "to drum up the country's post-war obsession with sex." In Sumner's estimation the worst of the three Seltzer books was D. H. Lawrence's sequel to *The Rainbow, Women in Love*.

A warrant the New York Society for the Suppression of Vice obtained to search Seltzer's premises was used to seize 722 copies of *Women in Love* ("sex in mature women"), Arthur Schnitzler's *Casanova's Homecoming* ("sex in old age"), and a "charming book written by a little Austrian girl" that Seltzer published anonymously, *A Young Girl's Diary* ("sex during childhood"); this last had a preface by Sigmund Freud. Seltzer himself trucked the books to police headquarters, possibly in an effort to prevent Sumner from purloining copies.

The publisher engaged a lawyer, Jonah Goldstein, who mounted a first-rate defense at the trial, which took place in 1923 in the Jefferson Market courthouse in New York before Magistrate George Simpson. An enlightened judge, Simpson permitted Goldstein to bring on a line of expert witnesses, including a psychiatrist, Adolph Stern; Columbia University professor Carl Van Doren, who was literary editor of *The Nation;* Gilbert Seldes, from *The Dial;* and Dorothea Brand, who wrote for *The New Republic.* Not surprisingly, the trial received plenty of publicity. When the case was over and the magistrate freed all three books, *The New York Times* and the trade press hailed the decision as a great victory for freedom of the press. Seltzer celebrated by reissuing *Women in Love* in a popular $1.50 edition and filing a $30,000 malicious-prosecution suit against John Sumner—acts that hardly endeared him to Sumner and may have provoked the fatal legal attack against him that was later mounted by a New York prosecutor. But for the moment, Seltzer rode high and so did Lawrence. Adele Seltzer, Thomas's wife, who served him as a sort of assistant publisher, was thrilled by her husband's defeat of the people whom Lawrence referred to as "censor-morons"; she mistakenly supposed there would be no recrudescence.

ADELE SELTZER: So Thomas has come out with colors flying, you may say tri-colors flying: a color for vindication, a color for courage, and a color for the excellence of the books he has made it a practice to publish. It was a regular cause célèbre. . . .

The Vice Society has become very much hated of late because it has diverged from its original object, which was merely to suppress pornographic postal cards, and began to mess in the fine field of literature. . . . We are getting congratulations on all sides and the weak-kneed publishers are all delighted that Thomas has fought their battle for them. . . .

The favorable verdict meant a tremendous inrush of business. Everybody wanted the three "obscene" books and all of them are now quite sold out, and going into new editions.

———

Lawrence was pleased with what Seltzer had done for *Women in Love,* but before another year was up, he learned that Seltzer had been criminally indicted for publishing the two other judicially "cleared" books. This time—it was January 1924—a reactionary New York judge, Robert F. Wagner, sat in judgment on Seltzer and convicted him. Lawrence's novel was not directly involved, but the proceedings seem to have been instigated because the sixteen-year-old daughter of another New York judge had brought home a copy of *Women in Love,* bearing the Seltzer imprint; she had borrowed it from Womrath's lending library. Her father, Judge John Ford, was appalled.

JUDGE JOHN FORD: What can ail our magistrates? This book is a terrible thing. It is loathsome. The fact that a Magistrate [i.e., Simpson] may have approved of it doesn't alter the fact. A Grand Jury can still act. . . . I'll find some way of acting, or I'll go to the Legislature with a law that will stop this sort of thing.

D. H. LAWRENCE *(Women in Love): They threw off their clothes, and he gathered her to him, and found her, found the pure lambent reality of her forever invisible flesh. . . . She had her desire of him, she touched, she received the maximum of unspeakable communication in touch, dark, subtle, positively silent, a magnificent gift and give again, a perfect acceptance and yielding, a mystery, the reality of that which can never be known, mystic, sensual reality that can never be transmuted into mind content, but remains outside, living body of darkness and silence and subtlety, the mystic body of reality. She had her desire fulfilled. He had his desire fulfilled. . . .*

———

The problem, of course, was not simply an "ailing" magistrate; the larger trouble was that the bite of New York's obscenity law had been softened by recent liberal decisions reached not only by trial court magistrates but by New York appellate judges; taken together, these decisions allowed judicial notice to be taken of a book's literary standing and its author's reputation, suggested that a book ought to be judged as a whole, and— perhaps most significant—indicated that a work of fiction could not properly be found obscene merely because it "passed" the *Hicklin* test of tending to "corrupt the morals" of young and susceptible persons; it must also pass the *Ulysses* test of tending to "excite lustful or lecherous desire in the average person."*

To repair the situation Ford moved on two fronts: he exhorted the district attorney to obtain a grand jury indictment of Seltzer for publishing *A Young Girl's Diary* and *Casanova's Homecoming,* † and he joined with John Sumner to organize a "Clean Books League" to persuade the New York legislature to pass a new law that would eliminate the restrictions on obscenity law prosecutions established by New York's appellate courts. Initial members of the league included high-ranking officials of Catholic, Jewish, and Protestant organizations, representatives of the YMCA and the Boy Scouts, and Martin Conboy, a Catholic U.S. attorney. Judge Ford was the group's chairman. He announced the league's aims: to make the New York obscenity law "horse-high, pig-tight, and bull-strong."

The most drastic of the proposed changes were: first, that "opinion or expert testimony shall not be received for any purpose whatever upon any hearing, examination or trial"; and second, that a judicial finding that a

———

*The cases were *Halsey* v. *New York Society for the Suppression of Vice,* decided in 1922, reprinted in de Grazia, *Censorship Landmarks* (1969), 71–74; and *People* v. *Brainard,* decided in 1924, reprinted in de Grazia, *Censorship Landmarks* (1969), 68–70. In 1957, the Supreme Court ruled unconstitutional a Michigan law making criminal the sale (to adults) of books that might have a deleterious effect on youth. Michigan argued that its restraint on the reading matter of the general public in order to protect juveniles was a proper exercise of the power to promote the general welfare. Said Justice Frankfurter, for the Court, in one of his rare pro-free-speech opinions: "Surely, this is to burn the house to roast the pig." The constitutional guarantees do not permit a state to reduce its adult population "to reading only what is fit for children." *Butler* v. *Michigan* (1957), reprinted in de Grazia, *Censorship Landmarks* (1969), 301–2.

†It is unclear why the New York prosecutor did not secure an indictment of *Women in Love* as well; perhaps the grand jury was not persuaded that there was cause to believe it obscene.

book was obscene might be based "exclusively upon a part or parts, of any publication," and that in any prosecution based only on a part of a book, "only such part . . . shall be admissible in evidence." Thus, even a single phrase or sentence might be enough to condemn a book and fine or imprison its printer, publisher, or distributor; and no critic, writer, or other expert could speak in defense of a work; it would have been rendered doubtful even whether judicial notice might be taken of the reputation of a challenged book's author or of the literary merit of a work. In Massachusetts, where such rules represented the law as late as 1930, Theodore Dreiser's two-volume novel *An American Tragedy* was held obscene by the state's highest court on the basis of allegedly indecent passages and phrases contained in one of the large volumes.*

The New York Times recoiled from the Clean Books League's proposals:

THE NEW YORK TIMES: But profane writers . . . would be wholly at Mr. Sumner's mercy. He could suppress such classics as he dislikes; he could and certainly would suppress such modern works as he dislikes. For under this law almost every book is guilty, and all evidence for the defense is excluded. If this bill is passed, Mr. Sumner will be an absolute and irresponsible censor of all modern literature. We hardly want that.

———

Lawrence was by now living in the little ranch house in Taos, New Mexico, that he and Frieda had bought. Hearing of the uproar concerning his book in New York, the author shot a barbed telegram off to the newspapers seeking to put the irate father and judge in his place:

D. H. LAWRENCE: Let Judge Ford confine his judgment to court of law, and not try to perch in seats that are too high for him. And let him take away the circulating library tickets from Miss Ford, lest worse befall her. She evidently needs an account at a candy shop.

———

The Clean Books League bill sailed through the New York assembly and passed its first and second readings in the state senate without a hitch. At senate judiciary committee hearings testimony in favor of the bill was heard from the Salvation Army, the New York Federation of Churches, the Society for the Suppression of Vice, the YMCA, the Holy Name Society, the Minerva Club, the League of Catholic Women, and leaders of the Roman Catholic archdiocese and the Protestant Episcopal Church, among others. The *Times* disgustedly reported that not a single person or group appeared at the initial hearings to oppose the league's legislation.† The bill

———

*See Chapter 8.
†The American Civil Liberties Union, for one, did not get involved, presumably because prosecutions for the publication or sale of allegedly obscene books did not "officially" raise a civil liberty question. The ACLU first began directly—as a policy matter—to involve itself in the defense of such books and their distributors in the late forties, when the ACLU officer (and playwright) Elmer Rice offered legal assistance to Doubleday and Company on the occasion of its prosecution for publishing Edmund Wilson's *Memoirs of Hecate County*, de-

was stopped only after "a small, determined band of insurgents" requested and obtained—with the help of New York State Senator Jimmy Walker—a last-minute hearing to oppose the insidious measure. The insurgents, led by Horace Liveright, included novelist Gertrude Atherton, Max Fleischer of the *New York American,* Thomas E. McEntegart of the Hearst Corporation, a psychology instructor from Union Theological Seminary, and a lawyer and former New York City parks commissioner, Francis D. Gallatin. Upon being introduced to the motley crew, Senator Walker exclaimed (aside) to Horace Liveright:

SENATOR JAMES J. WALKER: For God's sake, Horace, what's this? What did you bring these nuts for?

___

Each member of Liveright's entourage had a set point to make. Max Fleischer read aloud the *New York Times* editorial quoted above, which had been timed to appear on the day of the hearings, warning that the Clean Books League bill would make John Sumner's vice society "an absolute and irresponsible censor of all modern literature." Horace Liveright deplored the proponents of the legislation as anti-American and anti-religious, because under its terms even the Bible could be banned as "obscene." Francis D. Gallatin warned the legislators that if the bill was enacted, (anti-religious) "Reds and Communists" might use it to bring Liveright's prediction to pass. And closer to home, Thomas E. McEntegart warned that the bill might destroy New York's preeminence as a magazine-publishing center, because publishers like William Randolph Hearst* would move their mass-circulation periodicals out of the state rather than risk capricious prosecutions. Finally, novelist Gertrude Atherton informed the judiciary committee members that when she read the *Decameron* at age sixteen she did not understand it, and that even if she had understood it, "what harm does the book do that hasn't already been done?" Judge John Ford berated the witness, and John Sumner handed around to interested legislators sealed envelopes containing "hot" tidbits from contemporary novels.

Although some New York newspaper and magazine publishers had spo-

___

scribed in Chapter 12. The offer was turned down. In 1952, the ACLU provided volunteer lawyers in an unsuccessful attempt to prevent the customs bureau from barring entry into the country of Henry Miller's novels *Tropic of Cancer* and *Tropic of Capricorn* (*Besig* v. *United States,* reprinted in de Grazia, *Censorship Landmarks,* 233). During the early sixties, when the Grove Press edition of *Tropic of Cancer* was attacked by police, prosecutors, and judges all over the country, I counseled the ACLU for the adoption of a policy that enabled its staff, state affiliates, and volunteer lawyers to take part in many such actions. I also acted as an ACLU volunteer lawyer. See Chapters 19 and 22, and Samuel Walker's *In Defense of American Liberties: A History of the ACLU* (1990).

*In addition to his magazine empire, Hearst had a large interest in the book-publishing business: first, because of his ownership of the International Library Company, established in 1914, which published Dickens, Emerson, Shakespeare, Plutarch, Plato, Poe, the *Arabian Nights,* and other works; and second, because of "the adroit use of his magazines to secure the rights to books, both fiction and non-fiction, that would reach the mass market." John Tebbel, *A History of Book Publishing in the United States* 3 (1978), 19.

ken out against the dangers to freedom of expression presented by the proposed legislation, the New York book-publishing industry, whose membership was predominantly conservative, for the most part kept still. It was rumored that some mainline publishers were privately aiding and abetting passage of the Clean Books League law; two under suspicion were George Doran and Frank Doubleday. *Publishers Weekly* neatly registered the industry's ambivalence with an editorial that criticized Womrath's for letting Judge Ford's daughter take home *Women in Love* but also criticized Judge Ford for his moral crusade. It went on to appeal to each publisher and bookdealer to "reexamine his attitude," and asked all concerned to "accept a personal responsibility for cleaning his own business."

When a coalition of magazine and newspaper publishers and printers' associations was provoked by the Liveright group to issue a strong public statement denouncing the proposed legislation as striking "at the fundamental constitutional amendments prohibiting the abridgement of the freedom of the press," captains of the book-publishing industry retorted by deploring "the growing tendency on the part of some publishers unduly to exploit books of a salacious character for purely pecuniary gain." And when the liberal George Palmer Putnam and Alfred Harcourt resigned in disgust from the National Association of Book Publishers' executive committee, the conservative George Doran and Frank Doubleday acted quickly to take their places.

The most decisive blow against the censorship bill was struck not by a witness but by Jimmy Walker, the senate minority whip, during the floor debate that followed the committee hearings. When his speech was over, a vote was called and the bill was defeated by a two-to-one majority that crossed party lines. Here are excerpts from the speech; the italicized line made Jimmy Walker legendary:

SENATOR JAMES J. WALKER: There is not one among us who cannot tell the story of my dad's sweetheart who afterward became Dad's wife, and who lived in days when there were as many salacious books as there are today and who for all that grew into a life of saintliness and went down to her last resting place just as clean and pure in mind and heart as the day she was born. That is all there is to this talk about books of the kind against which this bill is directed ruining our young girls. They haven't got to read them and they won't read them if proper influences dominate their home.

No woman was ever ruined by a book. It is one of those strong men who are worrying about salacious books in the hands of little girls who are ruining them. This debate makes me think of the Volstead Act* and in connection with that of how many vote one way and drink another. Some of the best tellers of shabby stories in this Senate have been worrying their

---

*The law (named after Representative Andrew Volstead of Minnesota) passed by Congress in 1919 to enforce the Eighteenth Amendment, which prohibited the manufacture, sale, or transportation of all alcoholic beverages. The act became void only after the Eighteenth Amendment was repealed in 1933.

hearts out during the debate today about somebody reading something which may not have been good for him or her.

———

The New York Times praised the speech as the best Walker had ever made, one that promised "a return of common sense to our legislative bodies, from which pessimists thought it had been exiled forever." Later, at a testimonial dinner given in Horace Liveright's honor at the Hotel Brevoort, Walker graciously allowed that Liveright was "solely responsible for defending the freedom of the press." The publisher was honored officially "in recognition of his unselfish and untiring efforts in fighting and eventually defeating the recent Book and Press Censorship Bill before the New York Senate." In his own speech, Liveright thanked those present and announced that he had formally resigned from the National Association of Book Publishers because of its failure to take part in the struggle against the censorship bill.

HORACE LIVERIGHT: [T]he only publishers who helped at all were Seltzer (who had three books on the list which Justice Ford issued); Huebsch (who had one) and Macrae of Dutton who had been attacked by Sumner in the public prints. Fortunately, none of my books was mentioned in any of the recent rumpus so I could lead the opposition with fairly clean hands.

———

The New York Times scolded both the book publishers' association and the Authors' League of America for standing back and letting "three or four authors and a single publisher . . . do all the work" of dragging the Ford bill into the light of publicity, "which it could hardly survive."

THE NEW YORK TIMES: If A and B stand calmly by and allow themselves to be made criminals under the impression that the law will be enforced only against X and Y, they are making [a big] mistake.*

———

The Clean Books League's pressures on the New York legislature did not end with this defeat; they continued for another two years: During this period, the criminal proceedings that had been launched against Seltzer went ahead. At his new trial for publishing *Casanova's Homecoming* and *A Young Girl's Diary,* Judge Wagner deemed immaterial that in the prior case involving the same books, presided over by Magistrate Simpson, experts had been permitted to testify to the books' merits, and the books themselves had been found not obscene. Seltzer's new judge could not be moved from the position that literary and social values were not relevant, and this spelled the difference between conviction and acquittal. Refusing to listen to the testimony of any expert, Judge Wagner found Thomas Seltzer's books "obscene."

———

*While the *Times*'s opposition to the Ford legislation appears not to have been expressly rooted in free press concerns, that of the periodical publishers and printers who spoke out against the bill was.

Only a year earlier, Seltzer had so roundly defeated John Sumner that the *Times* editorially applauded him, and *Publishers Weekly* said the decision was "the worst set-back" the Society for the Suppression of Vice had ever suffered. Now, however, the publisher's situation became desperate. His damage action against John Sumner was stalled and the financial condition of his publishing firm was so precarious that he found it impossible to bear the expense of further litigation. For these reasons he agreed to withdraw his suit against Sumner, to remove the condemned books from circulation, and to destroy the plates. In return, the criminal case against him was withdrawn. But the decision was a blow from which Seltzer's firm never recovered.

And soon another blow was struck, this time by Lawrence himself, whom Thomas and Adele Seltzer had come to think of as "their friend and benefactor." It was Seltzer's publishing house that had "put across" Lawrence in America by publishing *Women in Love* and fighting successfully to free the novel. Seltzer also by then had published more than a dozen of Lawrence's other works.

In the beginning Lawrence trusted Seltzer more than he trusted his previous publishers, Mitchell Kennerley (who he believed had cheated him out of money) and B. W. Huebsch (who he knew had secretly "mutilated" his work). On December 30, 1922, with the Seltzers as his Christmas guests in Taos, Lawrence wrote to a friend:

D. H. LAWRENCE: Thomas Seltzer and his wife are here. He's a tiny man,* I think I trust him really.

———

For his part, Seltzer saw Lawrence as "as great a man as he was a writer . . . natural, without pose and, at bottom sane . . . yet how distinguished." Adele Seltzer was bowled over; to her, Frieda Lawrence was "a Norse goddess," and . . .

ADELE SELTZER: Lawrence is a Titan, and I go about with an ever-present sense of wonder that we, Thomas and I, little, little Jews, should be the publishers of the great English giant of this age, publishers of him, not because with Jewish shrewdness we outwitted some other publishers & got Lawrence first, but because Lawrence's *Women in Love* went begging for a publisher, and we were the only people who understood its greatness & had faith in him as a writer.†

---

*Seltzer was barely five feet tall.

†These remarks were made in a letter from Adele Seltzer to Dorothy Hoskins, a literary agent and friend. Hoskins must have questioned the "anti-Semitic" connotations of the words that Adele used, because Adele returned to the point in a later letter to her friend: "[Y]ou didn't get the fun with which I said that about us little Jews publishing the English Titan. If you'd ever talked with me face to face you'd have seen me wink when I said it. I'm not humble about being a Jew. Heavens no! I haven't got an inferiority complex, racial, national or individual. The Jews, I feel, are the aristocrats of the intellect, as the English are the aristocrats of breeding and character. It tickled my sense of the drama of things to think of us publishing the works of the great English genius, just as it tickled my sense of drama to

Their relationship with D. H. Lawrence was a source of pride and joy to Adele and Thomas Seltzer for years.

ADELE SELTZER: You should see Thomas when he comes home with a letter or Mss. from Lawrence, or even a letter from a sort of agent-friend of his, or a letter from a brilliant young South African artist who has illustrated one of Lawrence's books. I can tell the moment Thomas walks in the door by the schmunzeln on his face. . . . "Quick," I say, "what is it now? Show it to me!" Then, "Isn't he a wonder? Isn't he this, and isn't he that?"

We say these things to each other again and again, and for once Fate seems kind, that she has granted to the little Russian Jew, Thomas Seltzer, to be the publisher of the works of a century-marvel. And Lawrence appreciates Thomas and feels very friendly to him and writes him glorious letters. For Lawrence, before Thomas got him, suffered at the hands of publishers. He had two in America, Huebsch and Mitchell Kennerley, both of whom *cheated* him, and at the same time did nothing to promote him.

Best of all, Adele Seltzer thought, was that Lawrence had such great confidence in Seltzer, who had held his little company together while many of the old ones crashed.

ADELE SELTZER: I think Lawrence means to be absolutely loyal to Thomas. I simply cannot get over the wonder that we are the publisher of this greatest genius of our age and that we are his publishers not by having snatched him away from somebody else but because he really needed us, because we came at a time when he could not get any other publisher.

The falling out came when Seltzer caved in after his second obscenity prosecution. Lawrence "could see things were not going well at all for Seltzer." The author didn't hear from his publisher for six weeks, during the Christmas period, and "wondered if something were wrong with his business." By spring Lawrence was sure his publisher was failing. He decided to go to New York to see about it. Seltzer met Lawrence at the wharf.

D. H. LAWRENCE: Landed at last, and got all the things through Customs— such a fuss! . . . We struggled up to 100th St. buried in luggage, in a taxi, in half a blizzard, snow and rain on a gale of N.E. wind. New York looking vile. Seltzer was at the wharf, though I hadn't told him I was coming. He'd got it from Curtis Brown.* He looked very diminished, and him so small already. Apparently his business has gone very badly this winter, and he has

---

see Trotsky, the little Jewish Soviet war lord, dictating terms to the German junkers. I was looking at the situation from the outside, as an anti-Semite world might see it. You know, there really is a terribly strong feeling among the older publishers against the three rising Jewish firms—Knopf, Seltzer, Boni & Liveright." *D. H. Lawrence, Letters to Thomas and Adele Seltzer,* edited by Gerald M. Lacy (1976), 258.

*Lawrence's new agent, replacing Pinker.

sleepless nights. So, it seems, might I. My money is at present in thin air.
. . . Damn it all and damn everything.

———

Despite Lawrence's coldness, Seltzer invited him, Frieda, and their friend
Dorothy Brett to stay at his New York flat. This was too small for all of
them so Frieda and Brett stayed there for a week, while Lawrence put up
in a nearby hotel and the Seltzers camped at their office. But Lawrence had
soured on his publisher and his wife.

D. H. LAWRENCE: Seltzer and Mrs. Seltzer are not so nice. She is the bad
influence. He says he lost $7000 last year. And simply no money in the
bank for me. I don't like the look of their business at all.

———

By the middle of September 1924, Lawrence was acknowledging that
Seltzer was slowly paying up what he owed him in royalties, and that he
(Lawrence) now had "plenty." Evidently, the author had collected about
$3,000 from his American publisher that year. But he still feared that
Seltzer would go bankrupt. And by the end of the month Frieda wrote her
mother that "Seltzer still owes Lawr so much money, it's really irritating.
Says he hasn't got it and still brings so many books out." A few days later,
Lawrence reported that his agent, Curtis Brown, "with a great struggle, has
just got another $1000 from Seltzer." After Brown met with Seltzer,
Lawrence wrote his agent:

D. H. LAWRENCE: I'm glad you saw Seltzer. I'm sure he's in a bad way, poor
devil: though he did help to bring it on himself, trying to be a big publisher
when God cut him out a little one, if not tiny.

———

In November, Lawrence wrote his agent again to say he was "a bit out
of patience with Seltzer" because "he's been so furtive with me."

D. H. LAWRENCE: And I'm sure he'll never do much good with me any more.
But I leave it to you and Barmby* to decide whether to go to Knopf with
a book of mine, or not.

———

And then, on November 15, in a letter to his sister:

D. H. LAWRENCE: My agent has started to leave Seltzer—he is not giving him
the *Memoirs of the Foreign Legion*. Poor Thomas will squeal, but then he's
deserved it.

———

On January 10, 1925, Lawrence lowered the boom.

D. H. LAWRENCE: I wired Barmby to proceed with Knopf for the next book.
As for Seltzer, if only he'd been open and simple with me, I'd have borne
with him through anything. But a furtive little flea who hides his hand from

———

*Curtis Brown's New York manager.

me as if I was going to fleece him—whether fleas have hands and fleece or not—why—Basta!

———

When Seltzer heard that his prize author was thinking of moving over to Knopf, he asked Lawrence if it was true. Lawrence would only say that another book might be offered to him. The author had decided that it wasn't good for him to be "monopolized by one publisher in each country." Two publishers would stimulate sales better than one. When Adele Seltzer wrote Lawrence begging him to come back with a "best-seller" under his arm, Lawrence responded: "Don't look to me for your best-seller. I'm not that sort of bird."

To his friend Catherine Carswell, Lawrence wrote:

D. H. LAWRENCE: I have left Seltzer, who hangs, like a creaking gate, long; and gone to Knopf, who is a better business man. But, of course, I still have to live on what is squeezed out of poor Seltzer.

———

A little later Adele sent this word to the Norse goddess:

ADELE SELTZER: All I want is to pay our debts and DIE.

———

In May 1925, Lawrence notified Seltzer that he had definitely promised his next book to Knopf and could promise Seltzer nothing for the future. In reply, Seltzer wrote that he would pay Lawrence the arrears in royalties if the author came back, but not if he didn't. Lawrence took this as a threat.

D. H. LAWRENCE: You say you will pay me the arrears [about $5,000] if I come back, but not if I don't: which is a sort of threat. And you know why I left you: because you left *me* quite in the dark. And Adele says I am to come back with a best seller under my arm. When I have written "Sheik II" or "Blondes Prefer Gentlemen," I'll come. Why does anybody look to me for a best seller? I'm the wrong bird. I'm awfully sorry things went to pieces. Blame me, if you like, for leaving you. But blame yourself, now as ever, for not knowing how to be simple and open with me.

———

On April 21, Lawrence wrote a friend that he had signed up "a new publisher over here." He went on: "Knopf—a Jew again*—but *rich* and enterprising—seems very nice. Seltzer is staggering, staggering."

For his part, Knopf lost no time in advertising his new author in *Publishers Weekly:* "D. H. Lawrence permanently joins the Borzoi list with the publication of his latest novel ST. MAWR. . . . Mr. Lawrence's work will henceforth appear exclusively under the Borzoi imprint."

This was somewhat misleading: Lawrence's contract with Knopf was not an exclusive one. The Knopfs, according to an admiring Lawrence, were

———

*Lawrence's relations with and attitude toward his Jewish friends and publishers are explored in Jeffrey Meyers, *D. H. Lawrence: A Biography* (1990), 128ff. and 405–6.

"set up in great style, in their offices on Fifth Avenue—deep carpets, and sylphs in a shred of black satin and a shred of brilliant undergarment darting by." What Lawrence put out of mind was that, unlike Kennerley and Seltzer, Alfred A. Knopf would not fight for the freedom of his books, having no taste for "this business" of mixing it up with the likes of John Sumner, Judge Wagner, or Judge Ford.

Seltzer felt sorry for himself when Lawrence "dished him" at a time when his fortunes were at their lowest, but he did not express anger toward the unfaithful author. Instead he told Lawrence that he considered himself "a sacrifice to the arts." Lawrence replied cruelly that if so, he was "an unwilling sacrifice," and was "not born for success in the Knopf sense, any more than the arts." From France, on December 3, 1928, Lawrence wrote one of his last personal letters to Seltzer, an almost apologetic one, asking for a release of the copyright on a volume of poems, and commenting upon the defeated publisher's unbusinesslike character, and his own.

D. H. LAWRENCE: I think of you and Adele often, and always with affection. People are so fond of blaming one another—and they blame you for this that and the other. But I know it was neither your fault nor mine. It is just that we are neither of us in line with modern business. I don't intend to be—and you can't be. I hate modern business, and always did. You wanted to make a success in it—and it's not really in your nature. You aren't tough enough. I can afford *not* to succeed—but you, being in business, needed to. Which makes me very sorry things went as they did. I myself know I shall never be a real business success. But I can always make as much money as I need: so why should I bother. I care about my books—I want them to stand four-square *there,* even if they don't sell many. That's why I want to rescue my poems.

How are you both? I hope, well. How is Adele? is she good and cheerful?—I was ill last year with bad bronchial hemorrhages, and am still slowly getting better. But I *am* getting better, nearly my old self. We have given up the Italian villa, which was not good for my health—and now I don't quite know what next.

You have heard of *Lady Chatterley*—wonder if you read it. I lost most of the copies sent to America—and now there are *two* pirated editions, I hear—so there we are, same old story. But I sold the bulk to England—and lost nothing—& put the book into the world.

Do you still have the 96 St. flat? and Carrie? and those good baked hams so shiny?—Why didn't things turn out nicer?

Remembrances from us both to you both . . .

———

Lawrence left America in September 1925 and never returned. He became afraid that his tuberculosis and the notoriety of his next and final book, *Lady Chatterley's Lover,* would lead the immigration authorities to bar his readmission to the States. The author had five more years to live, although a doctor in Mexico City, diagnosing TB, would give him one or two years at most. After the Seltzer debacle he and Frieda went for a while to Mexico, where "Lawr" worked on the book that was later published as *The Plumed Serpent;* but there, according to Frieda, "he became so ill with tuberculosis and malaria that he feared he might die and have to be buried in the local cemetery."

FRIEDA LAWRENCE: No, No, it's such an ugly cemetery, don't you think of it!

———

They had decided to seek out the cool air and quiet foothills of the Sangre de Christo mountains in Italy. By the time they arrived Lawr was weak and wasted and assured Frieda he would never write another novel. But eleven days later he was forty-one manuscript pages into *Lady Chatterley's Lover.* This would become his last book, one he arranged with Pino Orioli to publish privately in Florence.

Frieda described the way Lawr worked at Villa Mirenda, near Florence, in the "beautiful, warm, vineyard-covered Tuscany hills":

FRIEDA LAWRENCE: After breakfast—we had it at seven or so—he would take his book and pen and a cushion, followed by John the dog, and go into the woods behind the Mirenda and come back to lunch with what he had written. I read it day by day and wondered . . . how it all came to him. I wondered at his courage and daring to face and write those hidden things that people dare not write or say.

———

Seated against a tree in the shade of the umbrella pines, "with his knees drawn up, a child's thick exercise notebook resting on them and almost touching his beard," Lawrence wrote what some people said was "the foulest book in the English language." It was there also, at Villa Mirenda, that Lawrence did the series of watercolor paintings that would be raided by the police when they were exhibited in London*—one of the episodes that inspired the essay "Pornography and Obscenity," published in 1929, in which Lawrence excoriated the nineteenth century as "the eunuch century, the century of the mealy-mouthed lie, the century that has tried to destroy humanity."

In November of 1928, Lawrence was working on a series of poems, which would be published by Martin Secker as *Pansies*—he described them as "a sort of loose little poem form: Frieda says with joy: real doggerel—But meant for *Pensées,* not poetry, especially not lyrical poetry."†

———

*Among them: *Fire Dance*—"two naked men—rather nice I think—not particularly 'natural' "; *Dandelions*—"a charming picture of a man pissing"; *The Rape of the Sabine Women* or *A Study in Arses; Yawning; The Lizard;* and *Under the Haystacks. Dandelions* was not shown at the London exhibition. Harry T. Moore, *The Intelligent Heart* (1962), 462; Jeffrey Meyers, *D. H. Lawrence: A Biography* (1990), 366ff.

†Compare James Joyce's little book of poetry *Pomes Penyeach,* published in 1927. Ezra Pound did not think them worth printing but Archibald MacLeish raved about them. Richard Ellmann, *James Joyce* (1982), 591.

HARRY T. MOORE: He wrote these *Pansies* sitting up in bed in the mornings, wearing a small African straw cap ("to keep my brain warm"), and he would between chuckles read them to visitors.

———

Meanwhile, in London, his paintings were assembled for exhibition. On January 7, 1929, Lawrence sent two copies of the *Pansies* manuscript by registered mail to Curtis Brown in London, and a week later sent him by registered mail an essay meant to serve as an introduction to a projected volume of reproductions of his paintings.* Three weeks later, neither shipment had arrived, and Lawrence began to worry about them, with good cause.

Both manuscripts had been seized from the mails on the instructions of the home secretary, Sir William Joynson-Hicks, whom everyone called Jix. At the time Jix's police were also busily searching the mails, and the homes of Lawrence's friends, for copies of the Orioli edition of *Lady Chatterley's Lover.* Any found were peremptorily seized.

The Labour Party (soon to win the national elections) raised a question in Parliament concerning the government's seizure of the *Pansies* manuscript and the essay. The home secretary was asked (by F. W. Pethick-Lawrence, representing West Leicester) who had acted "before any question of publication arose" to seize Lawrence's manuscripts in the post, and "if he will give the names and official positions of the persons on whose advice he causes books and manuscripts to be seized and banned; what are the qualifications of such persons for literary censorship; and whether, to assist authors and publishers, he will state what are the rules and regulations, the contravention of which causes a book to be seized and banned by his Department?"

Jix proved nearly as deft at circumventing accountability for the censorship as Home Secretary Simon had, almost fifteen years before, on the occasion of *The Rainbow*'s seizure; he pointed to the censorship powers implied by Lord Campbell's Act, under which, he noted, a metropolitan police magistrate or any two justices of the peace, "on sworn information," might issue a search warrant to seize a book or picture. But, he was asked, what did that have to do with the government's confiscating things put in the mails?

JAMES RAMSEY MacDONALD: Will the right hon. Gentleman make it quite clear whose responsibility it is to put the law into operation?

———

Jix said it was the police's responsibility, of course, but would not deny his own involvement. Somewhat as in the case of U.S. postal laws, British

———

*The essay, "Introduction to These Paintings" contained what Sir Kenneth Clark said was "the best criticism ever written on Cézanne." The essay and the reproductions were privately published "for subscribers only" by P. R. Stephenson's Mandrake Press (which also published "the mildly pornographic *London Aphrodite*") to coincide with the exhibition. Jeffrey Meyers, *D. H. Lawrence: A Biography* (1990), 368.

law stated that the postmaster general should "refuse to take part in the conveyance of any indecent matter." Jix claimed that Lawrence's objectionable manuscripts were discovered during a routine inspection of packages for concealed letters sent through the mails at lower than lawful postal rates, and that they "were sent to the Home Office and by my directions were then forwarded to the Director of Public Prosecutions."

SIR WILLIAM JOYNSON-HICKS: I am advised that there is no possible doubt whatever that these [Lawrence manuscripts] contain indecent matter and, as such, are liable to seizure. I have, however, given two months to enable the author to establish the contrary if he desires to do so.*

Pethick-Lawrence now expressed a wish to be informed who had determined the matter to be "obscene."

SIR WILLIAM JOYNSON-HICKS: In the first place, in this case the Postmaster-General makes the first determination that this is prima facie a case of indecency. He then sends it to me, and, if I agree, I send it on to the Director of Public Prosecutions. It is not a question of literary merit at all, and, if the hon. Member has any doubt, I will show him the book in question. It contains grossly indecent matter.

HARRY T. MOORE: Like Simon nearly fifteen years before, Jix insisted that there was no literary censorship, and like the parliamentary debates over *The Rainbow* at that time, this one faded away, ending on a note of inquiry as to the right of the Postmaster-General to open packets.†

Of course the publicity given the poems as a result of the government's censorship made them alluring; so when Secker went ahead and issued *Pansies* in book form—apparently minus fourteen poems that had been identified as too "indecent" by Jix—the collection sold very well indeed, for poetry. From this expurgated edition, and from an unexpurgated one that Lawrence's friend P. R. Stephenson brought out in collaboration with bookseller Charles Lahr, Lawrence cleared more than £500.

The scheduled exhibition of Lawrence's paintings went forward at the

---

*This suggests that Lawrence was being offered the opportunity to protest the seizure and destruction of his writings as a matter of grace, not legal right. As noted above, the procedures authorized under Lord Campbell's Act appear to have allowed only the possessor of books seized—not the author, or anyone else—to be heard on the question of why they should not be destroyed. Jix may have been advised that in the case of a seizure of writings in transit through the mails, the mailer—here Lawrence—should be given the same opportunity to be heard as a possessor. It seems possible that Jix fabricated his authority over the mails to harass Lawrence and censor his expression.

†A similar question long existed in the States. In general the Post Office police exercised the "right" to open and inspect other than first-class mail to see if it met the conditions for lower rates; upon opening they used this right also to look for and seize any written, published, or printed "obscene" material found within. It was learned that during the sixties and the anti–Vietnam War struggle, the Post Office also collaborated with the CIA in searching the contents even of first-class mail for messages subversive of the government's war policies.

Warren Gallery in London and proved a great success. (The gallery was owned by Dorothy Warren, a niece of Philip Morrell's; the young Henry Moore had his first one-man show there.) More than twelve thousand persons paid to see Lawrence's pictures between June 14 and July 5. Finally Jix could restrain himself no longer. A squad of police was dispatched to the galleries with a warrant to remove thirteen of the Lawrence watercolors, along with four copies of Stephenson's published reproductions and a volume of drawings by Blake.*

RICHARD ALDINGTON: Hearing that William Blake had been dead for a century, the prosecution withdrew the charge† against him.

———

As possessors of the Lawrence paintings, the exhibition's curator, Philip Trotter, and the gallery's owner, Dorothy Warren, were duly notified to come to court if they wished to show cause why the confiscated paintings should not be destroyed. A hearing took place on August 9, 1929, and Lawrence's old nemesis, the solicitor Muskett, who had prosecuted *The Rainbow* fourteen years before, reappeared to engineer the destruction of Lawrence's watercolors. Muskett informed the magistrate that Lawrence's pictures were "gross, coarse, hideous, unlovely and obscene." In answer, the gallery's curator sought to put forward the opinions of people more knowledgeable about art than Muskett—particularly the impressions of Augustus John‡—but the eighty-two-year-old presiding magistrate, Frederick Meade, would not listen to him or any other "defense" witness, remarking: "It is utterly immaterial whether they are works of art. That is a collateral question which I have not to decide. The most splendidly painted picture in the universe might be obscene." With these words he found Lawrence's paintings obscene: "I would destroy these pictures, as I would destroy wild beasts."

That sort of legal reasoning, on the part of other English judges, had aborted the attempt a year earlier, by the lawyers for publisher Jonathan

---

*In the United States today local policemen and prosecutors are constrained by the First Amendment (as interpreted by the Supreme Court) not to pull down or close any exhibition of paintings without *first* obtaining a decision by a judge, made after an adversary hearing, that the paintings suspected to be obscene are obscene as a matter of constitutional law, which means (among other things) that they have no "serious artistic value." It is thus not for any policeman, bureaucrat, or prosecutor, nor any ministerial or executive officer—whatever the rank—to decide, as Jix did, that "there is no possible doubt" that such and such a book or painting is obscene; the judges must decide, and not (as of old) on the basis of their own impressions of what is and is not obscene, but upon expert testimony concerning artistic and other merit. Thus, the Cincinnati, Ohio, police recently were constrained not to close down or interfere with an exhibition of the artist Robert Mapplethorpe's pictures thought by them and a local prosecutor and grand jury to contain obscene items until after the conclusion of a criminal trial of the director of the gallery. See the stories on this almost unprecedented incident in *The New York Times,* March 29 and April 7, 8, and 9, 1990; and see Chapter 30.

†This would not have been a criminal "charge" since the seizure was not in anticipation or pursuit of a prosecution.

‡The English painter and etcher, whose works included portraits of Elizabeth II, Lloyd George, and George Bernard Shaw.

Cape and author Radclyffe Hall, to produce literary experts and knowledge-able persons from all walks of life to testify to the literary and social importance of Hall's *Well of Loneliness.* In fact, not until 1959 would British judges let in any testimony of this kind as defense to, or in mitigation of, a charge of obscenity; and then only because Parliament finally acted to overrule the judges' age-old practice in this regard.

Lawrence obtained a poet's revenge when he published the following lines:

D. H. LAWRENCE:

> Lately I saw a sight most quaint:
> London's lily-white policemen faint
> in virgin outrage as they viewed
> the nudity of a Lawrence nude.
>
> Oh what a pity, Oh! don't you agree
> that fig-trees aren't found in the land of the free!
> Fig-trees don't grow in my native land;
> there's never a fig-leaf near at hand
> when you want one; so I did without;
> and that is what the row's about.
> Virginal, pure policemen came
> and hid their faces for very shame,
> while they carried the shameless things away
> to gaol, to be hid from the light of day.
> And Mr. Mead, that old, old lily
> said: "Gross! Coarse! hideous!"—and I, like a silly,
> thought he meant the faces of the police-court officials,
> and how right he was. . . .

—

Dorothy Warren wanted to appeal the magistrate's decision but Lawrence "was weary of the martyr's role," and a dying man. He persuaded Warren to accept an offer by the government to give back the pictures on condition that they never again be shown in England.

D. H. LAWRENCE: [T]hat they may never pollute that island of lily-livered angels again. What hypocrisy and poltroonery, and how I detest and despise my England. I had rather be a German or anything than belong to such a nation of craven, cowardly hypocrites. My curse on them!

—

Recently uncovered documents show that the police raid against the Warren Gallery and Lawrence's paintings was instigated by the publisher Grant Richards, and condemnatory reviews in the *Evening Standard* newspaper and *The Observer.* *

In Florence, working on *Lady C.,* Lawrence had trouble with his typist,

---

*See Jeffrey Meyers, *D. H. Lawrence: A Biography* (1990), 369–70.

Nelly Morrison. She typed as far as Chapter 6, then refused to type on. "It's too indecent," she said. So Lawrence had to use two friends to complete the typing job: Catherine Carswell, who worked on it in England, and Aldous Huxley's wife, Maria, in Italy. Lawrence told Catherine that the book "was very verbally improper but very truly moral as well." Catherine sat up nights, despite influenza, and typed half the book. Maria typed the other half over the violent objections of her sister-in-law Juliette, who suggested in disgust that Lawrence should rename the book "John Thomas and Lady Jane"—the terms he sometimes used in the novel to refer to the male and female genitals. Actually, Lawrence almost had called it that.

It took Lawrence only three months to write *Lady C.,* in its first complete version, at a time when he was slowly dying of tuberculosis. He rewrote it twice, completing the third version—the one Pino Orioli published—within another three months; the writing took six months in all. By January 1928 he was finished. Still, he was under no illusions that any reputable English or American publisher would dare to publish the book. It was "much too shocking—verbally—for any publisher."

D. H. LAWRENCE: Says shit! and fuck! in so many syllables.* So if it's going to be published I'll have to do it myself—therefore think of bringing it out this spring privately in Florence—1,000 copies, half for England, half for America—at two guineas. So perhaps earn some money, very welcome.

———

But for a time he was in a quandary. He "always labored at the same thing, to make sex relation valid and precious, instead of shameful." And this novel was the furthest he had gone. To Lawrence, it was "beautiful and tender and frail as the naked self." He knew, however, that the world would call it very improper.

One morning Lawrence spoke to Frieda about it:

D. H. LAWRENCE: Shall I publish it, or will it only bring me abuse and hatred again?
FRIEDA LAWRENCE: You have written it. You believe in it, all right, then publish it!

———

And he did. With the help of Pino Orioli, an old friend who ran a Florence bookstore, Lawrence personally "took care of all aspects of the printing, distributing and financing of a pure and undiluted edition meant for the non-vulgar public"; he even helped with shipping the books, until he became too ill.

A first edition of one thousand copies, which Lawrence signed, was to be sold, by subscription only, at a price of $10.00 in America and $2.00

---

*Felice Flannery Lewis has pointed out that it was not the mere use of such four-letter words that helped make *Lady C.* an "unpublishable" novel; it was rather Lawrence's use of the word "fuck" "in its biological sense of copulation," in scenes depicting a couple engaged in intercourse. *Literature, Obscenity and Law* (1976), 199.

elsewhere. They sent copies to critics in England and America and mailed order forms to all their European and American friends, asking them to hand them around "to all others who might be interested." The printed forms said this: "Mr. Orioli begs to thank you for your order for *Lady Chatterley's Lover,* with enclosed check for _____, and will forward the book by registered post immediately it is ready." Subscribers took the risk of the book's being confiscated in transit by police. Lawrence's plan—and it worked—was to make £1,000 from the first printing of *Lady C.*

According to Lawrence's letters, his English agent at the time, Curtis Brown, was "scared stiff of *Lady C.*" The publisher William Heinemann, who in 1910 had bravely brought out the author's first novel, *The White Peacock,* without wanting Lawrence "to alter anything," would not bring out an unaltered edition of Lawrence's *Lady C.* until 1956, almost two decades after Lawrence's death; even then, Heinemann took the precaution of issuing the book in the Netherlands, for distribution wherever it would go—except to the British Empire or the U.S.A. The law in the United Kingdom regarding the publication of "obscene" books would not be reformed to provide a defense of literary merit until 1959.

Lawrence's "ancient enemy," the paper *John Bull,* called *Lady Chatterley's Lover* "A Landmark in Evil," and ran a photograph of "the bearded satyr" who wrote the book, accompanied by an article saying that it was "the most evil outpouring that has ever besmirched the literature of our country. The sewers of French pornography would be dragged in vain to find a parallel in beastliness."

RICHARD ALDINGTON: Why the book was ever sent out for review or why Lawrence's agent in England ever sent him [Lawrence] the vile journalistic trash I have never been able to understand. I have never read such disgusting abuse and vulgarity, such hypocrisy. Here are some of the phrases: "Most evil outpouring—sewers of French pornography—beastliness—muddy-minded pervert—diseased mind—literary cesspool—shameful inspiration—this bearded satyr—book snapped up by degenerate booksellers and British decadents—the foulest book in English literature—poisoned genius." And so forth . . .

What astonished me at the time was that Lawrence was seriously disturbed by utterances which the rest of us received with complete contempt. Perhaps he disliked the thought that his sisters might read them.

———

Lady Chatterley's Lover was published in Florence in the summer of 1928. The following year, word of the book's publication having got around, the Dunster House Bookshop in Cambridge, catering especially to Harvard faculty and students, received a number of requests for the book. The proprietor, James A. DeLacey, ordered five copies, at five dollars apiece, even though he personally "didn't care" for Lawrence's writing. The copies he received carried Lawrence's Phoenix colophon and signature and had a mulberry-colored binding, with black lettering and a white paper label printed in black on the spine—the "Orioli" edition. DeLacey knew there were four or five different pirated editions floating around, from which Lawrence received not a penny; those he would not sell.

In New York, learning that the Dunster House Bookshop had received copies of the Orioli edition, John Sumner alerted the New England Watch and Ward Society.* An agent of the Watch and Ward, John Tate Slaymaker, was sent off to buy a copy, but since DeLacey did not recognize him as a regular customer, neither he nor his clerk, Joe Sullivan, would sell a copy of the book to him. Returning to the store twice more, Slaymaker finally managed to buy a copy, for fifteen dollars. Within a matter of days DeLacey and Sullivan were arrested, and soon thereafter tried, for selling *Lady C.*

Although the Harvard community expressed support for the defendants, the judge convicted both men. DeLacey's lawyer seems to have conceded his clients' guilt by stating that the book they had sold was "not fit for publication or circulation." The lawyer also allowed DeLacey to admit that although he "had never read it through, [he] was fully familiar with the reviews of it; he knew the substance of it and did not consider the book fit to sell." DeLacey was sentenced to serve four months in jail and pay an $800 fine; Sullivan received a sentence of two weeks' imprisonment plus a $200 fine.

DeLacey fruitlessly appealed his conviction and sentence. The supreme judicial court of Massachusetts (which a few years later would also hold Dreiser's *An American Tragedy* obscene) said of the bookseller: "[H]e knew what he was putting out and could not defend the book." At sentencing, the prosecutor—who had referred to Lawrence as "a filthy degenerate with a sewer brain"—recommended mercy. The judge suspended the defendants' jail sentences, and the Harvard community paid the two men's fines.

DeLacey is said to have emerged from the criminal proceedings with his morale shattered and his reputation in shreds. Soon his Dunster House Bookshop closed its doors. Then his wife left him. After that, the bookseller became an alcoholic and within a few years died.

Here is some of the obscenity that brought about DeLacey's ruin:

D. H. LAWRENCE *(Lady Chatterley's Lover): "But what do you believe in?" she insisted.*

"I believe in being warm hearted. I especially believe in being warm hearted in love, in fucking with a warm heart. . . ."

She softly rubbed her cheek on his belly, and gathered his balls in her hand. The penis stirred softly, with strange life, but did not rise up. . . .

"Thou's got a real soft sloping bottom on thee, as a man loves in 'is guts. It's a bottom as could hold the world up, it is."

---

*A "vice society" that had been founded by a group of ministers in 1873, only months after Anthony Comstock founded the New York Society for the Suppression of Vice. The men who financed the Boston organization were "almost a roll call of the Brahmin aristocracy." Paul Boyer's *Purity in Print* (1968) is the best guide to the vice societies of old.

All the while he spoke he exquisitely stroked the rounded tail, till it seemed as if a slippery sort of fire came from it into his hands. And his finger-tips touched the two secret openings of her body, time after time, with a soft little brush of fire.

"An' if tha shits an' if tha pisses, I'm glad. I don't want a woman as couldna shit nor piss. . . ."

With quiet fingers he threaded a few forget-me-not flowers in the fine brown fleece of the mount of Venus.

———

Once, Lawrence explained to his friend Lady Ottoline Morrell why he wrote *Lady C.*:

D. H. LAWRENCE: I was not advocating perpetual sex. Far from it. Nothing nauseated me more than promiscuous sex in and out of season. But I wanted, with *Lady C.,* to make an *adjustment in consciousness* to the basic physical realities. I realized that one of the reasons why the common people often kept the good *natural glow* of life, just warm life, longer than educated people, was because it was still possible for them to say fuck or shit without either a shudder or a sensation. If a man had been able to say to you when you were young and in love: "An' if tha shits an' if tha pisses, I'm glad, I shouldna want a woman who couldna shit nor piss. . . ." surely it would have helped to keep your heart warm.

———

Lawrence thought of *Lady C.*—"in the latter half at least"—as "a phallic novel, but tender and delicate." He "believed in the phallic reality, and the phallic consciousness: as distinct from our irritable cerebral consciousness of today. But it wasn't just sex. Sex, alas, was one of the worst phenomena of the day: all cerebral reaction, and itch and not a bit of the real phallic insouciance and spontaneity. But in my novel there was."

D. H. LAWRENCE *(Lady Chatterley's Lover): "Let me see you!"*

He dropped the shirt and stood still, looking towards her. The sun through the low window sent a beam that lit up his thighs and slim belly, and the erect phallus rising darkish and hot-looking from the little cloud of vivid gold-red hair. She was startled and afraid.

"How strange!" she said slowly. "How strange he stands there! So big! and so dark and cocksure! Is he like that?"

The man looked down the front of his slender white body, and laughed. Between the slim breasts the hair was dark, almost black. But at the root of the belly, where the phallus rose thick and arching, it was gold-red, vivid in a little cloud.

"So proud!" she murmured, uneasy. "And so lordly! Now I know why men are so overbearing. But he's lovely, really, like another being! A bit terrifying! But lovely really! And he comes to me!—" She caught her lower lip between her teeth, in fear and excitement.

The man looked down in silence at his tense phallus, that did not change. . . . "Cunt, that's what tha'rt after. Tell lady Jane tha' wants cunt. John Thomas, an' th' cunt o' lady Jane!—"

"Oh, don't tease him," said Connie, crawling on her knees on the bed towards
him and putting her arms round his white slender loins, and drawing him to her
so that her hanging swinging breasts touched the top of the stirring, erect phallus,
and caught the drop of moisture. She held the man fast.
"Lie down!" he said. "Lie down! Let me come!"
He was in a hurry now.

———

Like the 1922 "subscription-only" edition of Joyce's *Ulysses* published by
Sylvia Beach in Paris, the 1928 Orioli edition of Lawrence's *Lady Chatterley's Lover* was long contraband in England and the United States: police
and customs officials routinely searched for and destroyed any copies of the
books they could find; bookdealers caught selling the book from under
the counter were prosecuted and punished. Nevertheless, Lawrence and the
printer Orioli quickly succeeded in getting more than a thousand copies of
Lady C. into the hands of friends in both countries willing to help distribute the book privately, and into those of many others wishing to read it.
Although Jix furiously beat the bushes in England for hidden copies of *Lady
C.,* the underground distribution was quite successful; by the end of 1928,
Lawrence notified Orioli that *Lady C.*'s gross profits so far came to £1,024.

Lawrence had been deeply distressed by the pirated editions of *Lady C.*
that were being sold everywhere by unscrupulous booksellers.* In New
York alone five different pirated editions and thousands of copies were
reportedly being sold, from which Lawrence received nothing. More than
one of the publishers of those editions wrote to Lawrence offering to pay
royalties if he would "authorize" their edition. Although the prospect gave
him pause—"for in a world of: Do him or you will be done by him—why
not?"—Lawrence could not stand the idea of ratifying their editions and
elected to lose thousands of dollars instead. And during his lifetime nothing came of his discussions with Martin Secker in London and Alfred A.
Knopf in New York regarding the publication of expurgated editions.†

Lawrence was tempted to try expurgating *Lady C.* himself:

D. H. LAWRENCE: I did a fair amount of blanking out and changing, then
I got sort of colour-blind, and didn't know any more what was supposed
to be proper and what not. I felt blind to the purple of propriety. I
expurgated what I could—all the man's touching address to his penis, and

---

*He describes these at length in "A Propos of 'Lady Chatterley's Lover,'" in D. H.
Lawrence, *Sex, Literature and Censorship,* edited by Harry T. Moore (1953), 89ff.

†Fourteen years after his death, in 1944, Dial published an expurgated American edition,
entitled *The First Lady Chatterley,* with a foreword by Frieda Lawrence. John Sumner commenced a prosecution against the publisher that same year, and a magistrate, pretending to
apply to the book the test for obscenity laid down by the federal court of appeals in the *Ulysses*
case, refused to consider the novel's "literary merit or demerit," found it obscene, and held
the defendant for trial in the court of special sessions. There, in an unreported decision, the
book was found not obscene. The magistrate's decision is fully reported in *Censorship Landmarks* (1969), 121–23; the incident is also recounted in Felice Flannery Lewis, *Literature,
Obscenity and Law* (1976), 155–59.

things like that—and sent on the MSS, one to Alfred Knopf and one to Martin Secker. But it never worked. It was impossible. I might as well try to clip my own nose into shape with scizzors. The book bleeds.

———

Lawrence did arrange to publish an unexpurgated inexpensive edition of *Lady C.,* pocket-size, in Paris—an effort to undersell the pirates. After Sylvia Beach declined to do the job, he turned to two other Paris-based firms having reputations for publishing erotica: Pegasus Press and Fanfrolico Press; they never responded. Finally Edward Titus—who may have been recommended to Lawrence by Sylvia Beach—printed it up in his shop on the rue Delambre, behind the Dome Café. It cost six and a half francs to make and sold for sixty; *anybody* could buy it. Said Lawrence: "So I managed to get published the little cheap French edition, photographed down from the original, and offered at sixty francs."*

Lawrence and Frieda moved from place to place, from Italy to Switzerland to Spain and back again, in a hopeless attempt to check Lawrence's growing weakness. They settled in Switzerland because the torrid summers and damp winter fogs of Tuscany had now become insupportable. While they were in Switzerland, in 1928, Orioli produced his handsome edition of *Lady C.*

During the first night in Switzerland, they stayed at a lovely inn in the mountain village of St. Nizier; but the next day they had to leave, because Lawrence's coughing all night put the innkeeper in fear that the author was an infectious consumptive, forbidden by law to stay at public hotels. So Lawr and Frieda climbed higher into the Alps and stayed at Gsteig-bei-Gstaad, where his health recovered somewhat.

By August they knew that many of the books Orioli had sent out to England and America were arriving safely, but they also heard that Post Office police in the States were intercepting as many copies as they could, then selling them at outrageous prices, while in England Jix's policemen were searching the houses of their friends—some of whom were storing copies—and seizing any that they could find. Those developments upset Lawrence; he "had another horrible lung hemorrhage" in Gsteig-bei-Gstaad and Frieda and he had to move off once again, this time to Baden-Baden.

Their friend Richard Aldington invited the couple to spend two months at his beautiful secluded villa in Vigie, on the coast of the island of Port-Cros, but by then Lawrence was so sick that he spent almost all his days

———

*Lawrence's final version of *Lady Chatterley's Lover* would not be published in the States until 1959, when Barney Rosset's Grove Press brought it out unexpurgated and defended it successfully against Post Office charges that it was obscene. The case, *Grove Press, Inc.* v. *Christenberry,* has been described in detail by Grove's lawyer, Charles Rembar, in *The End of Obscenity* (1968), and is reproduced in de Grazia, *Censorship Landmarks* (1969), 339–44. The novel was published unexpurgated in England in 1960 as a Penguin paperback, following the enactment in 1959 of a liberal obscenity law that required the courts to admit evidence of literary merit. This precipitated a celebrated London courtroom battle, which freed the book, as reported in C. H. Rolph, editor, *The Trial of Lady Chatterley* (1961).

in bed or in a deck chair. He was so weak he "could pass the drawbridge but a few yards and scarcely ever strong enough to climb to the glassed-in look-out that was there." It was then that those first reviews came in from the press; all, it seemed, were agreed that *Lady C.* was "the foulest book in the English language" and that its author was "a bearded satyr with a sex-sodden brain."

RICHARD ALDINGTON: Alas, poor Lawrence! In that autumn of 1928 he . . . grew ever frailer and weaker, and his "recoveries" slighter and more delusive. In a melancholy mood he wrote to Mabel Luhan from Switzerland, so weary he hardly bothered to hide the truth anymore.

D. H. LAWRENCE: Here I just dabble at tiny pictures, and potter about among the trees. A few bad years for everybody. But let's hope we'll get steady on our legs and manage with a bit of real equilibrium afterwards. *Poveri noi!*

———

Eventually, the doctors advised Lawrence to rest for two months in a sanatorium in Vence, which was very high above the sea but not far from Nice. He hated the thought of going but decided he had better do it "and have done with it." Said Lawrence: "I was trying with all my might to get better sufficiently to return to New Mexico. For, I thought, what's the use of dying. . . ."

While rumors circulated among his friends that he was dying, he wrote them that he was trying to get sufficiently well to return with Frieda to their ranch house in Taos. It was the closest thing to a home that Lawrence had known after he left England for Italy at the end of the World War I, following the suppression of *The Rainbow.* Lawrence never lived in England again.

FRIEDA LAWRENCE: Lawrence had always thought with horror of a sanitarium, we both thought with loathing of it. Freedom that he cherished so much! He never felt like an invalid, I saw to that! Never should he feel a poor sick thing as long as I was there and his spirit! Now we had to give in . . . we were beaten. With a set face Lawrence made me bring all his papers onto his bed and he tore most of them up and made everything tidy and neat and helped to pack his own trunks and I never cried. . . . And the day came that the motor car stood at the door of our little house, Beau Soleil. . . . And patiently, with a desperate silence, Lawrence set out on his last journey.

———

On February 6, 1930, D. H. Lawrence reluctantly entered the Ad Astra tuberculosis sanatorium in Vence—one thousand feet above the sea and fifteen miles from Nice—hoping he could get strong enough, in March or April, to sail back to America. He weighed ninety pounds at the time and was "trying not to die." Friends sent him fruit and flowers, and H. G. Wells and the Aga Khan and the sculptor Jo Davidson visited him. Lawrence could not abide the sanatorium, and he rebelled against the suffering of all the others there. The last words of the last letter he ever wrote were "This place no good." He put up with it for a month, then begged to be taken away. On March 1, Frieda moved him to a nearby villa, but the short taxi journey wearied him, and he asked Frieda to sleep on a couch beside him so that he would see her when he woke.

FRIEDA LAWRENCE: One night I saw how he did not want me to go away, so I came again after dinner and I said: "I'll sleep in your room tonight." His eyes were so grateful and bright, but he turned to my daughter and said: "It isn't often I want your mother, but I do want her tonight to stay." I slept on the long chair in his room, and I looked out at the dark night and I wanted one single star to shine and comfort me, but there wasn't one; it was a big dark sky, and no moon and no stars. I knew how Lawrence suffered and yet I could not help him. So the days went by in agony and the nights too; my legs would hardly carry me, I could not stay away from him, and always the dread, "How shall I find him?"

—

The last Sunday he took a little food and had Frieda read to him from a life of Columbus.* He kept telling her: "Don't leave me! Don't go away!" Around five o'clock he complained: "I must have a temperature, I am delirious. Give me the thermometer!"

RICHARD ALDINGTON: Frieda could now hold back her tears no longer, but in a quick compelling voice he told her not to cry. He asked for morphia, and Huxley hurried away to find the doctor.

His mind wandered: "Hold me, hold me. I don't know where I am. I don't know where my hands are. Where am I?" When the injection of morphia was given, he relaxed, saying, "I am better now." To soothe him, Frieda sat by the bed holding his ankle, unconsciously answering his last Prayer:

> Give me the moon at my feet,
> Put my feet upon the crescent, like a Lord!
> O let my ankles be bathed in moonlight that I may go
> Sure and moon-shod, cool and bright-footed
> towards my goal.

At ten o'clock that night he died.

—

He had given a signed copy of *Lady Chatterley's Lover* to Andrew Morland, his English doctor at the sanatorium, because Morland would not accept a fee.

---

*After the burning of *The Rainbow,* Lawrence wrote to his friend Lady Ottoline Morrell about that novel: "Whatever else it is, it is the voyage of discovery towards the real and eternal and unknown land. We are like Columbus, we have our backs upon Europe, till we come to the new world."

D. H. Lawrence was forty-five years old when he died. He left nearly fifty volumes of novels, long and short stories, plays, poems, essays, and travel journals, as well as an extensive personal correspondence. Despite frail health, a short life, and incessant harassment from the reviewers,* government censors, judges, and police, he produced an unusually large body of work, one of the largest in English letters.

FRIEDA LAWRENCE: Lorenzo is dead, but up to the end life never lost its glamour and its meaning. The courage, the courage with which he fought. I am so full of admiration I can hardly feel much else. Dead, he looked so proud and so unconquered. I didn't know death could be *splendid;* it *was.* I didn't know anything about death, now I do. He opened a door into that place of the dead, and it's a great world too. . . .

I love his bones . . . those bones that . . . were his straight, quick legs once, how I loved them in the past. Then they got so thin, so thin, and how it grieved him so, also because he knew how it hurt me to see them so thin. How we suffered, and then I had to let him go finally into death. But death isn't at all terrible, as I had imagined. It's so simple really. One moment I held his ankle so alive, and then one hour after it was different, it was death, and I daren't touch him anymore. He belonged to death now. . . .

I want to bring him to the ranch and we must have the Indians there with drums and singing, a real funeral. . . . I want to make the ranch lovely for him with all that will grow.

—

After the funeral in Florence, Lawrence's ashes were sent to Taos, where they now rest in a tomb on the side of Lobo Mountain.

Frieda died of cancer in Taos, New Mexico, in 1956, on her seventy-seventh birthday, and was buried on Lobo Mountain.

---

*Norman St. John-Stevas identifies the English reviews as the most powerful of the agencies of literary censorship of that time, in *Obscenity and the Law* (1956).

6

L'Affaire Doubleday

THE YEAR BEFORE Lawrence died in Vence, the stock market crashed in New York. Buried in the rubble were some of the best new American publishers, those who had responded empathetically and energetically to the literary and intellectual ferment that followed World War I. If none of these ever dared bring out Lawrence's *Lady Chatterley's Lover,** several of them brought out, and fought successfully to make best-sellers of, Lawrence's *Women in Love* and "obscene" novels by James Joyce, Theodore Dreiser, and Radclyffe Hall.

Dreiser had read nothing of Zola, but he became a writer of the first rank, America's leading realist. He acquired this distinction even though, from the first almost to the last, his novels were sabotaged by publishers and sniped at by critics, vigilantes, public prosecutors, and judges. In 1930, the year D. H. Lawrence died, the seven judges sitting on the highest court of Massachusetts agreed to a man that Dreiser's 840-page novel *An American Tragedy*—his most popular book and the one many critics consider Dreiser's best—was "obscene, indecent and manifestly tending to corrupt the morals of youth." No court had been given a chance to condemn Dreiser's first novel, *Sister Carrie,* which had been completed in 1900, because the book's publisher—one of the old breed of American publishers—had consigned it to an early death.

Frank N. Doubleday—dubbed "Effendi" (F.N.D.) by his friend Rudyard

---

*No American or English publisher would brave bringing out *Lady Chatterley's Lover* unexpurgated until 1959, when in New York the founder of Grove Press, Barney Rosset, did. In Britain, Allen Lane brought out a Penguin edition of Lawrence's last novel in 1960. Both editions precipitated legal battles which were won by their publishers. See Chapter 19.

Kipling—was born in Brooklyn in 1862, the sixth of seven sons. At age ten he entered the printing and publishing business with a press he bought with fifteen dollars that he had saved up; on this he printed job work of all kinds, including visiting cards and circulars. One of these showed a picture of an Indian, and these words: "Above you see the portrait of Sitting Bull, the murderer of General Custer, and below you find the address of:

F. N. Doubleday
Book and Job Printer
106 First Place
Brooklyn, N.Y."

When the boy was fourteen, his father's hat business failed and Frank had to leave school and go to work. He found a job at Scribner's publishing house, where over the next eighteen years he worked his way up from delivery boy to salesman to advertising and merchandising editor, and then became subscription manager of *Scribner's Magazine*. In 1897, he joined with S. S. McClure to start his own publishing company. By the twenties, "Effendi" was dominating the publishing scene. He was an overwhelming figure, and other publishers, like McClure, L. C. Page, and George Doran, were said to move "in and out of his orbit like smaller stars." The imprint of his house changed when the names of these small stars were associated with his, but in the end he survived them all, and the publishing house he founded expanded until it was one of the three largest in the world.

No one dared use "Effendi" prematurely or was permitted to forget that the name was a title of respect and intimacy. In his Garden City, New York, office hung a photograph of him taken in the burnous of an Arab chief: a tall, athletic figure, bronzed face, eagle nose, brilliant eyes. When he came into the office "with his long swinging stride one was instantly aware of power," said his friend Christopher Morley. "The sound of the bindery machines on the floor below seemed to move with steadier rhythm; everything began to coordinate a little faster, a little smoother." Theodore Dreiser, however, was not impressed.

In May 1900 the old-line publishing house Harper sent *Sister Carrie* back to Dreiser with a letter expressing regrets. While it was a "superior piece of reportorial realism," it was not "sufficiently delicate to depict without offense to the reader the continued illicit relations of the heroine." Dreiser's friend Henry Mills Alden of *Harper's Monthly* had sent Harper the manuscript despite his doubts that any publisher would publish the novel because of its "realism."

Alden next recommended Doubleday because the firm had recently published Frank Norris's highly acclaimed novel *McTeague*—also a pioneer work of realism—and Norris was now working for Doubleday. Frank Doubleday was in Europe with his wife, Neltje, seeking the American rights to Zola's novels, when Dreiser sent *Carrie* over. Norris read the book and decided it was great. He reported this to Walter Hines Page, then vice president at Doubleday, and also relayed the news to Dreiser. Page wrote Dreiser a note congratulating him, signed a contract with the author, and had the novel in galleys before Frank Doubleday came home.

When the Doubledays disembarked, Frank Norris raved about this first novel by an author of whom they had never heard, and they took *Carrie* home to Bay Ridge in proofs to see for themselves. Neltje Doubleday liked to think of herself as a broad-minded person. She had accompanied Frank to France because she knew French and was a great admirer of Zola's realistic novels; she found them "incontestably moral and humane." Neltje also approved that her husband published Norris's *McTeague*. But *Sister Carrie* was something else again. The heroine was "too evil" for the house of Doubleday to handle.

The way Neltje Doubleday saw it, in *McTeague* lust and vice were punished in the end, and so what went before could be defended as providing the reader with a moral lesson. But that was not the case with *Sister Carrie*. That young woman—whom Dreiser was believed to have patterned after his sister Emma—"was far from punished in the end." After playing fast and loose with two sinners—one a traveling salesman and the other an embezzler—she "landed in the lap of luxury," becoming a successful actress, "with her audiences' cheers ringing in her ears, as she pockets a huge salary!"

Like the Comstockians, Neltje judged a book by the effect it might have upon a young girl; she thought Carrie's fate not a denouement that "any young reader could possibly construe as advocating chastity as a way of life. Quite the contrary!" And Carrie's morality was out of the ordinary. Even Dreiser's wife, Jug, and his friend Arthur Henry advised the author against allowing Carrie to be rewarded for her life of illicit sexual relations; but he would not tamper with Carrie's end.*

E. L. DOCTOROW: Dreiser was writing according to the aesthetic principle of Realism which proposes that the business of fiction is not to draw an idealized picture of human beings for the instruction or sentimental satisfaction of readers, but rather to portray life as it is really lived, under specific circumstances of time and place, and to show how people actually think and feel and why they do what they do. . . . Dreiser saw to it that [Carrie] would not end up happy, but neither was she punished or repentant.

ALFRED KAZIN: Carrie is hardly a designing femme fatale . . . but she represents the force of sex, the challenge to the established mores, that can

---

*Henry, the city editor of the *Toledo Blade* when Dreiser first met him, became Dreiser's "perfect friend." He transferred his own desire to become a novelist to Dreiser, imploring him to write the novel that became *Sister Carrie*.

Dreiser's first wife, Sarah Osbourne White ("Jug"), did do some "cleaning up" of *Sister Carrie*; Dreiser incorporated many revisions suggested by her in the version he eventually submitted to Doubleday. A "restored" *Sister Carrie* was published in 1981 by the University of Pennsylvania Press and in 1986 by Viking-Penguin. It appears that before Jug got at her, Carrie had greater emotional depth, conscience, and sexuality. Dreiser cut an estimated 36,000 words from the original manuscript with the help of Arthur Henry and Jug. He later blamed Jug, along with Neltje Doubleday, for undermining his book.

make even a wistful and ignorant young girl irresistible to men wrapped up in the daily pursuit of profit. . . . The first chapter title in the 1900 edition of the book reads "The Magnet Attracting: A Waif Amid Forces." This "waif" never really knows what has been happening to her. Her sexuality is as incomprehensible to Carrie, as fatal to Hurstwood, as "Nature" was to primitive man.* This sexuality accomplishes a revolution in people's lives, however, and in 1900 it was recognized as a threat to the established order.

W. A. SWANBERG: He seems to have had no inkling that he was creating a revolutionary work. He wrote with a compassion for human suffering that was exclusive with him in America. He wrote with a tolerance for transgression that was as exclusive and as natural. His mother, if not immoral herself, had accepted immorality as a fact of life. Some of his sisters had been immoral in the eyes of the world. In his own passion for women he was amoral himself, believing that so-called immorality was not immoral at all but was necessary, wholesome and inspiring, and that conventional morality was an enormous national fraud.

Thus the man who wrote *Sister Carrie* was by standards then prevailing a greater potential menace to pure American ideals than Emma Goldman, who was preaching anarchism across the land, or her lover Alexander Berkman, who had shot Henry Clay Frick in Pittsburgh.

———

Sister Carrie bothered Frank Doubleday in other ways. Effendi was annoyed that the novel, written by a practically unknown fellow, had been contracted for and put into print during his absence; he foresaw that the book would never sell; Page should have known better. It was vulgar, dealing "exclusively with sordid, uneducated people who spoke colloquially, and for whom the author displayed unabashed affection." Effendi also saw it as propaganda for determinism as a philosophy of life, because the heroine and others appeared "as helpless creatures adrift like chips in a stormy sea, devoid of Free Will, unable to steer any course, capable only of seizing whatever comfort or stray pleasure was washed their way." Finally, *Sister Carrie* was "bound to rub the country's prevailing mood the wrong way, because of its pessimism."

Of course, Dreiser had been overjoyed to receive Norris's message of congratulations. And when Page confirmed the publishing house's opinion, all his publication worries for *Carrie* drifted away. He let his newspaper pals in St. Louis and Pittsburgh know about his success and "basked in the warm feeling of having come into my own as a novelist." Said Dreiser: "It

———

*Hurstwood, Carrie's second lover, takes $10,000 from his employer and persuades Carrie to run off with him. He is pursued by detectives, returns most of the stolen funds, spends the rest, and after suffering a series of business catastrophes, falls apart. He pays for his passion for Carrie with his job, his family, the respect of his peers, and, worst of all, his will. After Carrie leaves him and becomes a successful actress, Hurstwood gasses himself in a flophouse. This grim ending was toned down by Dreiser, at the suggestion of his wife and Arthur Henry. It has been restored in the Viking-Penguin version of *Sister Carrie*.

was what I'd always yearned to be." He resolved to write a novel every year.

Meanwhile he celebrated by falling secretly in love with a teenaged girl he met in Missouri, where he was staying for a while with Jug and her family. He felt his "too-early" marriage to Jug hemming him in.

THEODORE DREISER: She affected me like fire. . . . God! To be cribbed, cabined, confined. Why had I so early in life handicapped myself in the race for happiness?

———

While Dreiser was celebrating *Carrie,* his friend Arthur Henry received from Frank Norris the bad news about Frank Doubleday's reaction. Henry had dropped by Norris's apartment in the Village and found him seething because he had just heard that Effendi had vetoed publication of *Sister Carrie.* Said Norris to Henry: "Doubleday thinks the story is immoral and badly written. He simply don't think the story ought to be published by anybody, first of all because it is immoral." Henry was dumbfounded. He went home and wrote a letter to Dreiser, in Missouri: "Dear Teddie—It has dazed me—I am amazed and enraged—Doubleday has turned down your story!" The official letter came later.

WALTER HINES PAGE: Our wish to be released by you is quite as much for your own literary future as for our own good. . . . If we are to be your publishers, as we hope to be, we are anxious that the development of your literary career should be made in the most natural and advantageous way. But we are sure that the publication of *Sister Carrie* as your first book would be a mistake. It would identify you in the minds of the public with the use of this sort of material.

———

Dreiser, however, was ready to take his chances with the public.

THEODORE DREISER: The public feeds upon nothing which is not helpful to it. Its selection of what some deem poison is I am sure wiser than the chemistry of the objectors. Of what it finds it will take only the best, leaving the chaff and the evil to blow away.

———

According to W. A. Swanberg, one of Dreiser's biographers, Frank Doubleday was also fearful that the book would be seized as obscene and would raise a scandal. Dreiser felt destroyed when he heard the news. And he realized "that the shadow of Anthony Comstock had fallen across my book." At Doubleday, meanwhile, Dreiser's book had raised the roof. Frank Doubleday detested it, Page faintly praised it, Henry W. Lanier disliked it,* and only Frank Norris stuck to his guns concerning the novel's greatness. Effendi, however, was the boss and he had decided they should ask Dreiser to let another house publish it. It was thought that Appleton

———

*Son of the poet Sidney Lanier, Henry W. Lanier is described by Tebbel as one of several "talented associates" of Frank Doubleday who made up Doubleday, Page and Company in 1900. John Tebbel, *A History of Book Publishing in the United States* 2 (1975), 326.

or Macmillan might pick it up; or, if not, then Dodd, Mead might, or Lippincott.

Even when Page assured Dreiser that Doubleday's change of mind about *Carrie* did not mean they were not interested in his future work, Dreiser could not be turned around. Page, to prove his point, invited Dreiser to write something for the first issue of the firm's new magazine, *The World's Work*. No go. Dreiser decided to fight for his rights and hold Doubleday to its contract. He went personally to see Frank Doubleday, who was careful to have his attorney, Tom McKee, present for the encounter. The publisher explained why it would be a mistake for Dreiser, as well as for Doubleday, to publish *Sister Carrie*.

FRANK N. DOUBLEDAY: The book will not sell.

—

Effendi also insisted that few public libraries would "allow a novel of this nature on their shelves." When he went on to argue that "church people and middle-class householders will shun the book, because of its immorality," Dreiser, who was as large a man as Doubleday, stood up and told the publisher that he would have to live up to the contract—"or else!" Lawyer McKee interceded and told Dreiser that the firm was prepared to sell him the plates at cost. Dreiser refused. When they offered to *give* him the plates and the author still refused, they threw up their hands.

FRANK N. DOUBLEDAY: All right, you stand on your legal rights and we'll stand on ours! . . . I see that a man of your stamp will have trouble with any publisher you deal with and it will please me if you never set foot in this office again.

—

Effendi went on to publish *Carrie,* but on his own terms. He personally edited the proofs and insisted to Dreiser that all the profanities be removed and certain "suggestive" passages altered. The pro forma marriage between Carrie and Hurstwood in Montreal was made to occur before they consummated their "complete matrimonial union"; and instead of counting his money in a "dingy lavatory," Hurstwood counted it in a "dingy hall." The much-laundered *Carrie* became spotless; worse yet, as Dreiser's biographer Richard Lingeman has said, *Carrie*'s cheap-looking binding and lettering "would have been more appropriate on a plumbing manual."*

Frank Doubleday carried out the terms of the contract for *Carrie* in the most minimal way possible, "in the hope that it would not attract much notice."† This did not surprise Dreiser; he expected they would not do right by his book by way of promotion and advertising, but he believed—wrongly as it turned out—that the public could not fail spontaneously to recognize a great book when it saw one. His worst fears were that the firm would print the legal minimum of copies and Frank Doubleday would bury

---

Theodore Dreiser, vol. 1: *At the Gates of the City 1871–1907* (1986), 294.
†John Tebbel, *A History of Book Publishing in the United States* 2 (1975), 3.

them in the basement of his Union Square building. His fears were confirmed when he was informed that only 456 copies of *Carrie* were sold in the first fifteen months.

Although Doubleday was one of the first houses to use advertisements to sell its books, Frank Doubleday "would not spend a dime" to advertise *Carrie*, and did not even list it in the firm's catalogue, although a bowdlerized translation of Zola's *Fruitfulness* was listed. Effendi was "sporting enough, however, to let the critics have their say." Norris sent 125 review copies out to the leading newspapers and magazines, together with promotional material and, in many cases, a personal note that must have carried weight. Norris went at it "with so much gusto" that "my friends said I was more eager for people to read Dreiser's *Sister Carrie* than my own books."

The book came out just before Thanksgiving, in 1900, and was, for a first novel, widely reviewed. Most critics complained about *Carrie*'s "immorality" and about Dreiser's "philosophy of despair." The most damaging characterization was widespread: *Carrie* was depressing. One Seattle critic said the novel came "within sight of greatness" but was "a most unpleasant tale you would never dream of recommending to another person to read."

Frank Norris thought that the critics killed *Sister Carrie*. But Dreiser put the blame squarely on Frank Doubleday's shoulders; the man had suppressed his novel because "in his petticoat-ridden book publishing house" they "were afraid to go against Comstockian morality," which disapproved of any book that "gave the facts." It was acceptable in the Doubleday household to publish the works of a French realist like Zola because his novels had nothing to do with *American* fallen women and "the tough, despairing lives that led them to compromise the morals of the day." Frank Doubleday gave his book "only a token printing." Most of all, Dreiser blamed Neltje Doubleday;* he told all the writers he knew that "they should take their scripts for reading to the Doubleday home," instead of to the offices on Union Square.

Frank Norris sent a copy of Dreiser's *Carrie* to William Heinemann, in England. Heinemann, who first published D. H. Lawrence and became George Moore's publisher when Vizetelly's publishing house collapsed, was impressed with the novel and brought it out in the spring of 1901 in a "curtailed version"—to fit his Dollar Library of American Fiction. The London critics were almost unanimous in acclaiming it the work of an exceptional talent. The *Manchester Guardian* said *Sister Carrie* belonged among "the veritable documents of American history"; the London *Daily*

---

*After Neltje was dead, in 1931, Frank Doubleday told a scholar that he wished the subject of Neltje's attitude toward *Sister Carrie* could be dropped; he stated that, as best he could remember, his late wife never saw the novel and "expressed no opinion about it which affected the treatment of it by the publishing house." However, the English publisher William Heinemann, who published a "curtailed" edition of the novel in 1901, told Dreiser that he had quarreled with Mrs. Doubleday about the merits of the work, which she vehemently attacked. Richard Lingeman, *Theodore Dreiser*, vol. 1: *At the Gates of the City 1871–1907* (1986), 288.

Chronicle hailed Dreiser as "a true artist"; and the *Athenaeum* compared Dreiser's *Sister Carrie* favorably with Zola's *Nana*.

Heinemann wrote Frank Doubleday to say *Sister Carrie* was the best book he had recently published or was likely to publish for a long time to come. He congratulated Doubleday for having discovered "this outstanding author" and said he "should make a great fuss over him." He also said he was looking forward to Dreiser's "next and future work." There wouldn't be a next and future work by Dreiser for ten years.

For Dreiser the news from England after Heinemann published the book was welcome, but he claimed he did not collect even a hundred dollars in royalties "on the cheap edition they brought out," and the English acclaim did him "little good" in his own country. No other important American publisher was willing to reissue his book, although he made the rounds of Appleton, Scribner's, Dodd, Mead, and many others. At Century the publisher "hid himself in his office to avoid speaking" to Dreiser about *Carrie*. A reader at A. S. Barnes "threw the book into the fireplace." At McClure-Phillips, the "chief literary advisor" said that *Carrie* was "vulgar" and "impossible to read," and that Dreiser was becoming a "pariah." Eventually, a man named Rutger Jewett, who headed an obscure book firm called J. F. Taylor, agreed to buy the *Carrie* plates and the stock in Doubleday's hands; he said he would reissue the book "later on." Jewett also kindly advanced the author fifteen dollars a week to encourage him to keep working on his next novel, *Jennie Gerhardt,* which had to do with Dreiser's older sister Mame, although only a few close friends and relatives knew it.

Dreiser was too discouraged to go on. His father had died on Christmas Day in the year that *Carrie* first appeared. Dreiser felt he couldn't write. He began to fear he was going crazy. He wrote to an astrologer in Binghamton, New York, who gave him this horoscope: "You have stomach and bowel troubles, nervousness and cannot eat when excited or angry . . . rest and sleep are all you require when sick or exhausted. You were destined to travel and see strange things, and if cautious, sincere and faithful you will be successful in life. You will be most fortunate by moving about."

So Dreiser moved about. He went with Jug to the Gulf Coast, hoping to regain his calm. Next they traveled to a town called Hinton, West Virginia, where Dreiser had heard there were some curative springs. As he was broke, he improvised. Once he tried to sell two wildcats, trapped by a man who lived near Hinton, to the New York Zoological Society, but they wrote back saying: "We are not in the need of any more wildcats, at present, as we have some very fine specimens, thank you."

After that, Jug and he parted company, and he traveled to Lynchburg and Charlottesville; soon he really was going to pieces. He suffered pains in his fingertips and constant uncontrollable shifts of mood between elation and dejection. He traveled more and more on foot, for walking had always soothed him. He hiked more than three hundred miles, through Virginia, Maryland, and Delaware. He found a beach town that he liked—Rehoboth, Delaware—and stayed there for a week. Swanberg thinks the reason Dreiser could not get on with *Jennie* was that it had in it so much of the sort of thing that critics had assailed in *Carrie*. He was afraid to produce a novel that would put him through that experience again.

Even after Jug came back his condition was desperate.

THEODORE DREISER: Then came ill health. Those who have never experienced that misfortune cannot conceive what miseries may exist in it. I was a writer, but now my power to write was taken away from me. I could not think of anything to say, or if I did I could not say it. Suddenly, as if by a stroke, I found myself bereft of the power of earning a living with my mind and was compelled to turn to my hands. These had never been trained in any labor.

In this crisis I paused and procrastinated, a thing which I sometimes think is the dominant note in my character. . . . I lingered nearly three years struggling against insurmountable conditions, planning, brooding, dreaming to return to the contest.

———

During this period he finally wrote Jewett that he had given up on *Jennie* and would try to pay him back his advances at a future time. The publisher told Dreiser to stop worrying and to "rest his head as well as his body." Dreiser went to Philadelphia, where, he said, "I lingered for six months, and until my money was almost entirely gone." Then, "driven by the absolute need of doing something whether I was ill or well," he went alone to New York.

THEODORE DREISER: Here I had come, just ten years before, and had toiled and struggled for that personal recognition which I deemed so important. The streets and avenues were as familiar to me as those of my native village. . . . [A]ll the energy, all the wealth, all the beauty and power I knew, and the knowledge of it and of the fact that I might someday hold a position of power and fame in it, had been the thought that had urged me on and sustained me in many a weary hour.

Now however I found that I held a different attitude toward it. Where once the ability to struggle and in a small way to gain had been a delightful thing to me, now I was indifferent. What did it all amount to, I asked myself. What was the difference whether I rose or fell? In so vast a sea where generation after generation broke upon the horizon of the world, like the long inrolling waves of an endless and restless sea, what was I? A waif, a stray, a bit of straw, a breath of air. And if I succeeded, what of it? . . . [W]as it not as the preacher had long ago written, a vanity and a travail of the flesh? Truly I thought so.

And moreover I was weary. Insomnia had reduced me to the state where I was in actual physical torture. Introspection and lonely brooding had reduced me to the verge of despair. . . .

———

Dreiser saw an eminent specialist who "held the chair of nervous disease in a large university not so far from New York," and who "looked at me with a heavy, deprecatory gaze."

THEODORE DREISER: "Yes, yes," he commented, his hands folded over his chest, his body comfortably ensconced in a faintly squeaky, black-leather-upholstered swivel chair. "I see, I see. The usual symptoms . . . very elusive, very. Now you have come to me just now complaining of pains in your fingertips and occasionally in your heart. Previous to this you say you imagined your hair was beginning to come out. No doubt it was."

———

The doctor had a theory, "based on twenty years of study," that a condition like Dreiser's could "be reached by medication." He also recommended that Dreiser seek "amusing and companionable society" and told him not to "be alone." Protested Dreiser: "But I was alone, due to the absence of friends, strangeness in a great city, lack of means to connect up socially and the like." He was given a prescription and told to "exercise some and come and see me."

THEODORE DREISER: The opening fee in this case was ten dollars. There were still other doctors. But neither their medicine nor their advice helped me one whit.

———

In Brooklyn he found a room for $2.50 a week, at 113 Ross Street; he had $32.00 in his pocket. Since he was a successful writer, listed in *Who's Who,* he felt ashamed to apply for an editorial job at any of the newspapers or magazines that had published his earlier articles. Two of his brothers lived in New York and one of them, Ed, was a successful actor, but he couldn't apply to them for help, nor to his sister Emma, or Mame, who was living with her prosperous husband on Washington Square.

He had to move again, into a cheaper room, an eight-by-six cell in the same house, for $1.25 a week. His insomnia was made worse by fear of falling asleep, because of the horrible dreams that came to him. Once he dreamed his sister Mame was dying. His insomnia "was racking the soul out of me." He would lie in bed hearing stealthy footfalls that made his scalp prickle—"I could sense a hand reaching out of the blackness for me. If I jumped out of bed to light the gas lamp no one was there. I could only sink into a chair in a cold sweat and stare out of the window waiting dully for the dawn."

THEODORE DREISER: In addition to this a strange wakefulness seemed now to come over me, in which I was neither fully awake nor yet wholly asleep. All day long I used to go about wondering, dreaming, turning corners as if I did not know where I was and forgetting half the time what I was doing, and in this state I seemed to lose consciousness of that old, single individuality which was me and to become two persons. One of these was a tall, thin, greedy individual who struggled and thought always for himself and how he should prosper, but was now in a corner and could not get out, and the other was a silent, philosophical soul who was standing by him, watching him in his efforts and taking an indifferent interest in his failure. . . .

I experienced about this time also the most remarkable physical variations that I have ever known. My nerves, particularly those in the tips of my fingers and toes, began to burn me badly and I would have something like little fever blisters at the ends of them, when the irritation was long continued. Also I began to have the idea or hallucination that angles or lines of everything—houses, streets, wall pictures, newspaper columns and the like, were not straight and for the life of me I could not get them to look straight. I also had the strangest desire to turn around, as if I must go in a circle whether I would or no, which was nothing more nor less than pure insanity. . . . Always when I was sitting in a chair I would keep readjusting it—trying to bring myself into correct alignment with something, and at the same time would keep turning to the right until I would be quite turned around. At the same time if I were reading a newspaper I would keep turning it from angle to angle trying to get the columns to look straight, a thing which they never did. Always when I was walking I would look straight ahead, wondering at the obstruction which fixed objects like houses and trees offered to a direct progress and feeling an irresistible desire to be rid of them or to go right through them.

—

After weeks in which he cut his daily food allowance to a five-cent bottle of milk and a five-cent loaf of bread, divided into three meals, Dreiser applied to the Brooklyn charity office. The man there was sympathetic to him until the author told him he had brothers and sisters living within a few miles. "You ought to go to them," he said.

Instead, one winter day Dreiser walked onto the Brooklyn pier and stood "looking at the then miniature and unimpressive skyline of New York, the red of a February West beyond."

THEODORE DREISER: The sight of the icy cold and splashing waters at my feet naturally appealed to me. It would be easy to drop in. The cold would soon numb me—a few gulps and all would be over. All that was necessary was to slip down into this gulf and rest. No one would know. I would be completely forgotten.

7

Mencken's Lead Zeppelins

DREISER DID NOT JUMP into the East River that day. He survived prolonged bouts of poverty, insomnia, depression, neurasthenia, and marital discontent to produce his second novel, *Jennie Gerhardt,* which Harper published in 1911.* At the time, he was also working hard on *The "Genius"* and beginning *The Financier,* switching from one to the other in a burst of writing, research, and rewriting.

Jennie came out to mixed critical response. The *Lexington* (Kentucky) *Herald* said it was "utterly base" because it dealt with all the "baser instincts of the worst order of human animals"; and the *Chicago Examiner* said Dreiser's style was like "a proficient stenographer's." But Floyd Dell, writing a full-page review in the *Evening Post,* called it "a great book"; *Bookman* said its author deserved "the highest tribute"; the *New York Herald*'s Franklin P. Adams gave it a "great" rating too; while in the *Smart Set,* H. L. Mencken headed his review A NOVEL OF THE FIRST RANK and compared *Jennie* with the works of Zola, Tolstoy, and Conrad. He also said it was the best book he had ever read, "with the Himalayan exception of *Huckleberry Finn.*" After *Jennie Gerhardt,* Harper also published Dreiser's *The Financier,* in 1912, under a contract that gave it the right to publish his next novel, *The Titan,* as well.

Dreiser went to Chicago to do research on Charles Tyson Yerkes,† whose life suggested the story of Frank Cowperwood, protagonist of *The*

---

*Jennie Gerhardt, like *Sister Carrie,* was "expurgated" by Dreiser with the help of Jug. Richley Hitchcock, his editor at Harper, is reported to have excised 25,000 words.

†Described by W. A. Swanberg as "the brilliantly corrupt plunger who [took] over traction lines in Chicago and London and harbored a succession of mistresses along the way." *Dreiser* (1965), 146.

Financier, The Titan, and *The Stoic.* There he met the critic Floyd Dell. As Dell recalled the meeting, Dreiser behaved just as everyone had said he would: rocking in his chair, interminably folding and refolding his handkerchief into the smallest possible square, and every so often saying: "It's a mad world, my masters!" W. A. Swanberg says that Dreiser "found that rocking steadily in a rocking chair gave him some relief from his feeling of impermanence in a world where time ran on. A nonsmoker, he developed a habit of pleating his handkerchief carefully, then folding it into a cube, finally flinging it out like a flag and starting the folding process all over again—a routine he could continue for hours and which calmed him somewhat." Dreiser also visited a female "thought-healer" and considered it an omen whenever a hunchbacked person happened to cross his path.

In Chicago Dreiser liked to rumble around at the Little Theatre on Michigan Avenue with Maurice Browne, who had founded the theatre, and with Floyd Dell's beautiful black-haired girlfriend Kirah Markham, who was getting ready to play Andromache in *The Trojan Women.* It was a place where Dreiser could meet other bohemian fomentors of the Chicago literary revolution, like Margaret Anderson, publisher of *The Little Review,* Sherwood Anderson, and Edgar Lee Masters. To some of them, Dreiser "was a literary liberator and hero of the revolution." Masters described him in a poem.

EDGAR LEE MASTERS:
Soul enrapt, demi-urge
Walking the earth,
Stalking life.
Jack o'lantern, tall shouldered,
One eye set higher than the other
Mouth cut like a scallop in a pie,
Aslant, showing powerful teeth,
Swaying above the heads of others . . . .

—

But Dreiser was not heroic to all.

MARGARET ANDERSON: Dreiser was never any good until some exchange of sex magnetism put him at his ease. . . . Sex display puts you at your best if you're a tempered human being—becomes responsible for wit. But Dreiser had no more wit than a cow. . . . [H]e always left me with the impression that I was in the presence of nothing more than good old human nature.

—

Dreiser thought that puritanism had made prudes of most American women, eliminated their sexual passion, and made it impossible for them to be artists. The only passionate, vital women left were prostitutes and actresses. With some women Dreiser worked a kind of magic. The admiring critic Floyd Dell was puzzled and irked by Dreiser's success with Kirah Markham and other women.

FLOYD DELL: Dreiser was hardly the young man's notion of a knight-errant—somewhat pudgy, no great talker.

———

Nonetheless, while Dreiser was in Chicago he managed to lure Kirah away from Dell—after some hesitation, since Dell had so warmly praised *Jennie*—and persuaded her to come to New York and live with him. He also had an affair with a pretty secretary who was working at the Little Theatre and persuaded her, too, to come to New York, to be his helpmate and literary assistant. When he later dropped her cold, she showed Dell the letters she had received from Dreiser.

FLOYD DELL: They were long, thoughtful letters, considering her problems in the most detailed and kindly way. This capacity for entering into a woman's situation was certainly one trait that endeared him to them, although in this instance he could walk out on the girl quite brutally.

———

Dreiser often had several girlfriends at once. Kirah Markham, born Elaine Hyman, was twenty years old when she met Dreiser. The daughter of a wealthy Jewish father and a Gentile mother, she was intellectual, beautiful, an amateur painter, and an actress who took part in the little-theatre movement in Chicago and New York. She met Dreiser early in 1913; by summer 1916 their intimacy had ended and Markham joined the theatre group led by Eugene O'Neill that became the Provincetown Players. Later she married a teacher and painter at Marlboro College, Vermont; she is said to have thought of herself as "the second Mrs. Dreiser."[*] One night, Dreiser took Kirah to a party at Emma Goldman's apartment on Lenox Avenue, where Russian food and wine were served and everyone cheered the plump forty-five-year-old anarchist as she did Russian folk dances. Dreiser considered Goldman the most important American woman of her time.[†] Goldman's lover Alexander Berkman was at the party, and a man named Ben Reitman, who took a fancy to the madonna-like Kirah and pursued her from room to room. She finally took refuge in Dreiser's arms.

THEODORE DREISER: Don't be afraid of Ben. He may ask you to sleep with him but you can just tell him that you are sleeping with me.

———

After Kirah moved in with Dreiser, publisher Ben Huebsch was among those who received a card, hand-lettered by Kirah:

Friends can always find
Kirah Markham

---

[*]Theodore Dreiser, *The American Diaries: 1902–1926,* edited by Thomas P. Riggio et al. (1983), 117, n. 1.

[†]Between *Carrie* and *Jennie,* Dreiser made ends meet by editing a group of magazines published by George Warren Wilder. As chief editor of *The Delineator,* Dreiser commissioned a profile of Goldman and instructed the writer to "pretend to denounce her while smuggling across her ideas." Richard Lingeman, *Theodore Dreiser,* vol. 2: *An American Journey* (1990), 34.

and
Theodore Dreiser
at home on Sunday evenings
November–March
165 West 10th Street   Chelsea 7755

Later, Dreiser's double standard got even Kirah down. Dreiser preached the beauties of free love for both sexes but made horrible scenes "if a man so much as sat by the fire" with Kirah—"while he was off of an evening with another woman." He obsessively pursued secret affairs, all the while professing fidelity to her; unconventionality in his own woman wounded his pride.

At one point, Dreiser's wife, Jug, moved in with her sister Ida on Waverly Place just around the corner from the Dreiser-Markham ménage. Ida was furious with Dreiser and threatened to do violence to Kirah if she caught sight of her.

KIRAH MARKHAM: It was quite amusing to stand next to Mrs. Dreiser in the meat market and not have her know me.

———

The Titan had a difficult birth. The story was that Harper had 4,000 advance orders for the book and had printed up 8,500 sets of sheets, spent a good deal on advertising, and then backed off because the editors woke up to the fact that *The Titan*'s "realism" was "too uncompromising": the novel depicted in detail an inordinate number of seductions by its hero, Frank Cowperwood. Ford Madox Ford said he had to lay the book down after the eleventh episode because it was so "revolting."

Dreiser was recovering in Chicago from an operation for carbuncles when he heard from Kirah that Harper was reneging on *The Titan,* as Doubleday had done with *Carrie.* At first he was incredulous, because he knew the publisher had already made preparations for a first printing. But Dreiser realized that *The Titan* contained more sexual realism than some people could stomach. Editors also complained that the hero was a crook. Of course he was; but he was strong and able to get things done. Dreiser was a Darwinian, and if his hero was cruel, he was also one of "the fittest," one of those who deserve to survive. Dreiser wrote in the Chicago *Journal:*

THEODORE DREISER: A big city is not a little teacup to be seasoned by old maids. It is a big city where men must fight and think for themselves, where the weak must go down and the strong remain. Removing all the stumbling stones of life, putting to flight the evils of vice and greed, and all that, makes our little path a monotonous journey. Leave things be; the wilder the better for those who are strong enough to survive, and the future of Chicago will then be known by the genius of the great men it bred.

———

From Chicago, after Harper backed off, Dreiser telegraphed Annie Tatum, his secretary in New York, to get his friend William Lengel to help her find a new publisher for *The Titan.* Tatum sent page proofs to Alfred

A. Knopf, Century, George H. Doran, and the John Lane Company. Knopf reportedly was keenly interested until Mitchell Kennerley told him that the novel libeled some friends of his—Charles Tyson Yerkes and Emily Grigsby—and that Miss Grigsby was likely to sue.* So Knopf turned the book down, and Century said no as well, and then so did Doran. Annie Tatum wrote "Dodoi" what happened:

ANNIE TATUM: I had a talk with Doran this P.M. He finally rejected the book. We don't want him anyhow. He's a "gentleman" and a conventionalist. He said in so many words that he considers the book *unsaleable* entirely apart from the question of *morale.* He indicated it was a pity you ever got started on Yerkes—whom he says he considers a very abnormal American. You ought to have seen me stand up to him—in attitude rather than in speech! . . . Oh, Dodoi, how I love you. And I love, even more, the artistic ideal.

———

Many of the young women who worked as Dreiser's typists and literary assistants did so without pay; some moved in and lived with him.

ANNIE TATUM: Oh Dodoi, if the book is just once published & put before the public in the right way nothing else matters to me. . . . I have put so much of myself into it. . . . And I don't care for any repayment. I've done it for truth and art—and principally, I admit, for affection. That brings its own reward.

———

H. L. Mencken read an unbound copy of *The Titan* and wrote Dreiser that it was "the best thing you have ever done, with the possible exception of *Jennie Gerhardt.*"

H. L. MENCKEN: There is not one word in the book that will give Comstock his chance. He must go into Court with some specific phrase—something that will seem smutty to an average jury of numskulls.

_____

*In the United States today, the constitutional guarantees of freedom of speech and press protect authors and publishers from civil or criminal libel actions brought by defamed public officials or public figures, unless the libelous statements have been made with "actual malice," meaning with knowledge that they were false or in reckless disregard of whether they were true. The opinion in the first of the series of decisions rendered by the Supreme Court that so extended First Amendment protection to libelous expression was written by Justice William J. Brennan, Jr., in 1964, in the landmark case of *New York Times* v. *Sullivan.* That same term Brennan wrote another revolutionary opinion that extended constitutional protection to "obscene" novels and films that were not utterly without literary, scientific, artistic, or other social importance, as described in Chapters 19 and 22. Presumably Yerkes and Grigsby would have qualified as "public figures" under the Supreme Court's new constitutional rules. Harry Kalven, Jr., considered Brennan's opinion in *Times* v. *Sullivan*—which involved a libel action brought by the Montgomery, Alabama, chief of police against *The New York Times*—as one of the most important free speech events in Supreme Court history because of the protection it gave to expression having a "seditious" cast—that is, expression sharply critical or condemnatory of government policies or officials. Both Brennan opinions were revolutionary in that they overturned a centuries-old tradition of legislature- and judge-made law regarding libelous and obscene expression. See Harry Kalven, Jr., *A Worthy Tradition* (1987), 61ff. When the American free speech philosopher Alexander Meiklejohn read Brennan's *Times* v. *Sullivan* opinion he said it was an occasion for "dancing in the streets."

THEODORE DREISER: [Y]our view of the book cheers me because I have such implicit faith in your honesty—intellectual & every other way.

———

Later Dreiser showed his gratitude by offering Mencken "the original pen copy of any one of my mss." Mencken was "overcome"; he accepted *Sister Carrie* and so became the owner of a manuscript that later became enormously valuable. The friendship of the two men would soon be at its height: Dreiser was about to become America's leading fighter for literary freedom and Mencken was his blood brother.

Of the publishers to whom William Lengel had sent proofs of *The Titan*, only the John Lane Company had not yet turned it down. Lane, a British organization whose New York branch Mitchell Kennerley had helped to start, was now under the direction of J. Jefferson Jones. Here Lengel finally had "a great success" with *The Titan*.

John Lane, a descendant of Devonshire farmers, probably published under the Bodley Head imprint more new poetry and belles lettres than any other man of his time. His authors included the legendary Rupert Brooke, the notorious Oscar Wilde, the "decadent" Ernest Dowson, the "symbolist" Arthur Symons, the "classicist" A. E. Housman, and also George Moore, Arnold Bennett, G. K. Chesterton, and Agatha Christie. His house would now also publish four of Dreiser's works. After Jones read the manuscript for *The Titan*, he wired Dreiser "PROUD TO PUBLISH TITAN" and put a $1,000 advance in the next post. Jones supposed that Harper had rejected *The Titan* not because of its sexual immorality but because Dreiser's portrayal of a ruthless financier could not have sat well with the house of J. Pierpont Morgan, which owned Harper, having taken the company over at the turn of the century when the original owners nearly went broke.

Neither *The Financier* nor *The Titan* was attacked in the courts, possibly because, as one scholar has suggested, both were "carefully censored" by their publisher.* In any event, the concerns about *The Titan*'s immorality did not begin to match the uproar that greeted John Lane's publication of Dreiser's next book, *The "Genius."* Almost everyone stoned the book, issued in the fall of 1915 at a popular price of $1.50. It came out at an unfortunate moment, just before the *Lusitania* was sunk, and many critics used this incident as an excuse to display open hostility toward Dreiser's German ancestry and sympathies.

Dreiser's friend John Cowper Powys was one of the few who praised *The "Genius."* Writing in Anderson and Heap's *The Little Review*, he said: "Dreiser is the only free American voice, and his *The "Genius"* is the American prose-epic." To this, Mrs. Elia W. Peattie responded in *The Chicago Tribune*, under the caption "MR. DREISER CHOOSES A TOM CAT FOR A HERO!"

———

*Evelyn Geller, *Forbidden Books in American Public Libraries, 1876–1939* (1984), 100.

MRS. ELIA W. PEATTIE: I repudiate it as the "American prose-epic." I have not yet lost my patriotism and I will never admit such a thing until I am ready to see the American flag trailing in the dust dark with the stains of my sons, and the Germans completing their world rule by placing their Governor general in The White House.

—

And in the *New York Globe:*

MRS. N. P. DAWSON: We hope *The "Genius"* will immediately appear in a German translation. That's how kindly we feel toward the Germans!

—

The New York Times and *The Brooklyn Eagle* avoided the German question; the *New York World* was merciless.

THE NEW YORK TIMES: Once more Theodore Dreiser has chosen an abnormal character and written an abnormally long novel about him. . . . It is all very realistic—and very depressing and unpleasant.

—

Under the heading "A GENIUS AND ALSO A CUR," *The Brooklyn Eagle* said that "the first section called 'Youth' [is] pretty nearly an orgy of lust."

NEW YORK WORLD: *The "Genius,"* by Theodore Dreiser, the story of an artist who goes in for advertising and the pursuit of women, is 736 pages long, weighs nearly a pound and three-quarters, and contains approximately 350,000 words. It would be better if it were less by about 350,000 words, lighter by nearly a pound and three-quarters, and shorter by 736 pages.

Mr. Dreiser should get over the idea that because he was successful with two novels of sex, he can keep on, world without end, filling thick volumes with the emptyings of passions.

—

When Dreiser saw the *Globe* and the *World* reviews, he mailed copies to his friend Mencken and asked him if he did not agree that he had grounds to sue the publishers for libel. Mencken told Dreiser to forget it "and take comfort in the English reversal at the Dardanelles."

Then *The Nation* printed a three-page essay by a professor of English at the University of Illinois, Stuart Pratt Sherman, lambasting Dreiser. It was Dreiser's first major assessment in a national magazine, and it was written by a crony of *The Chicago Tribune*'s Elia Peattie, who, Dreiser believed, hated him. Among other disparagements, Sherman implied that Dreiser's coming from a "mixed ethnic background" explained why he was incapable of dealing with values higher than sex. He also said Dreiser was not entitled to any standing as a writer in the realist tradition because he worked from a theory of animal, rather than human, behavior and wrote about "jungle" courtships in which "leonine men but circle once or twice about their prey, and spring."

Dreiser could not understand why a liberal magazine like *The Nation* would let someone like Sherman attack him that way. He decided that "these moonbeam chasers" were "trying to make a devil of me."

THEODORE DREISER: As they did to the very sane Machiavelli, so they would do to me. I am now being tied up with all the evils which the Germans are supposed to represent. I am anti-christ.

———

Dreiser was enraged at President Woodrow Wilson for his role in bringing America into the war, and at the press for heightening anti-German feeling with widespread stories of German atrocities, so he wrote a pro-German, anti-English essay called "American Idealism and German Frightfulness." Although Waldo Frank tentatively accepted it for *Seven Arts* magazine, he later got cold feet and rejected it. *Century* magazine and the *North American Review* also turned it down. Douglas Doty of *Century* warned: "Frankly, I think it comes clearly under the head of those proscribed writings that 'give aid and comfort to the enemy,'" which was to say an act of treason.

W. A. SWANBERG: Public sentiment being what it was, the article probably would have put him under surveillance as a possible German spy and caused his books to be removed wholesale from the libraries and burned.

———

Great hostility was shown by the government, and the corps of civilian vigilantes spawned by the government, toward anyone who publicly expressed antiwar or antigovernment opinions during World War I, and the courts provided speakers with virtually no free speech protection. In the war's aftermath, in 1919, the Supreme Court, led by Justice Holmes and his "clear and present danger" doctrine, justified retroactively the actions taken by Justice Department prosecutors and lower federal court judges to imprison several thousand persons who had expressed ideas "abrasively critical" of the draft, the government, or the war.*

Dreiser considered publishing "American Idealism" himself, as he had published another "radical" essay that no commercial publisher would handle, "Life, Art and America," but according to Swanberg, he "fortunately gave up the idea." In 1917, the same year, the radical socialist magazine *The Masses* was seized by the Post Office Department because of its fierce antiwar stand. A brave attempt by federal judge Learned Hand to keep *The Masses* from being suppressed was defeated when a circuit court of appeals rode roughshod over Hand's seminal free speech opinion, in which he enunciated the doctrine that only political speech designed to "trigger" violent or unlawful action should be deemed outside the First Amend-

———

*See Zechariah Chafee, *Free Speech in the United States* (1941), Chapter 2. Harry Kalven, Jr., agrees. See *A Worthy Tradition: Freedom of Speech in America,* edited by Jamie Kalven (1987), 147: "The Court's performance [in the wartime speech cases] is simply wretched. It displays no patience, no precision, and no tolerance."

ment's protection.* The circuit court ruled that it was up to the U.S. postmaster general, not Judge Learned Hand, to say whether *The Masses* could go free. Denied access to the mails, the magazine folded. In two later cases its editors, Dreiser's friends Floyd Dell, Art Young, and Max Eastman, were prosecuted for "seditious utterances" and escaped going to prison only because both cases ended with hung juries.†

It was around this time that the radical young publishers Al Boni and Horace Liveright brought out Andreas Latzko's antiwar book *Men in War,* which blamed the war, in part, on women's desires for heroes. When Dreiser praised the book in a review published in a "pro-German" newspaper, this elicited another response from Mrs. Peattie:

MRS. ELIA W. PEATTIE: Latzko does a thing which Dreiser himself might have done. He takes all of the honor away from women's courage. He makes them willing to send their husbands and sons to the battle front because it is the fashion to do so. . . . Inevitably Dreiser would approve. He is not at the front—any front—and he insults, with every book he writes, the integrity of women.

—

After that the Latzko book was suppressed by the Post Office and Boni and Liveright were placed under military intelligence surveillance. Their publication of Trotsky's *The Bolsheviki,* however, was not interfered with during the war; but the Red scare that swept the country after the war forced the publishers to withdraw the book from circulation.

Following the first blast of newspaper criticism of *The "Genius," * Anthony Comstock's successor, John Sumner, struck. By then the book had been in the stores for eight months. Dreiser wrote Mencken: "The book was selling the best of any and now this cut me off right in midstream. Don't it beat hell."

J. Jefferson Jones was familiar with the vigilante associations in England, which had remained active into the twentieth century; but by 1915 the English groups seemed less puritanical, or less fanatical, than the American ones. Dreiser's books were not attacked in England, and so Jones felt confident that the New York Society for the Suppression of Vice would not bother the John Lane Company over *The "Genius."* To make sure, how-

---

*The case was *Masses Publishing Co.* v. *Patten* (1917). It and Hand's frustrated contribution to the nation's First Amendment jurisprudence are appraised in Harry Kalven, Jr., *A Worthy Tradition: Freedom of Speech in America,* edited by Jamie Kalven (1987), 125–30. Says Kalven: "Hand's opinion [in *Masses*] is to my mind vastly superior to Holmes' effort [in *Schenck*]. Had it been the dominant initial document, our legal history would almost certainly have been better." Our other great free speech scholar, Zechariah Chafee, also thought very highly of Hand's opinion in *Masses,* ranking it with Holmes's initially far more influential contributions in *Schenck* v. *United States* and *Abrams* v. *United States,* both decided in 1917. See Chafee's *Free Speech in the United States* (1941) at 16 and 42–51. In 1969, however, the Warren Court resuscitated (without attribution) Hand's *Masses* doctrine, which was far more radical than Holmes's "clear and present danger" doctrine in the measure of freedom given speech. Kalven remarks on the great significance of the 1969 decision, called *Brandenburg* v. *Ohio,* at 121ff.

†Floyd Dell describes the trials in *Homecoming: An Autobiography* (1933), 313ff.

ever, he took the precaution of having his English reader, Frederic Chapman, who was in New York at the time, read the novel before it was published. Chapman saw no problems at all in the book.

On July 25, 1916, Sumner visited the offices of the John Lane Company on West Thirty-second Street, and notified J. Jefferson Jones that there were seventeen profane expressions and seventy-five lewd passages in *The "Genius,"* and that he would have to see them removed from the book or face seizure of all copies and prosecution.* Knowing that Sumner was on good terms with the district attorney's office, Jones said he would consult counsel and get back to Sumner. A few days later Post Office inspectors stopped by to inquire about *The "Genius."* Jones showed them favorable reviews of the book, but he became so frightened at the prospect of being charged with the federal offense of sending ōbscene matter through the mails that he now recalled the book from stores all over the country.

Sumner had learned about *The "Genius"* when he opened an envelope and found in it a batch of pages torn from a copy of the novel. He also received word from the Western Society for the Suppression of Vice in Cincinnati that a local clergyman had seen "a young girl" borrowing *The "Genius"* at a circulating library. It was Sumner's first year on the job and he read the book from cover to cover, marking those ninety-two lewd and profane passages; he knew that female readers of immature mind could not escape being harmed by the book.

FLOYD DELL: In [1915] the infamous Anthony Comstock died and went to hell, and an obscure person named John S. Sumner took his place as the hired agent of a private organization which, in cahoots with a corrupt police force, exercised an unofficial censorship over American thought, and art, and literature; and a cowardly and hypocritical American public allowed this tyranny to go on.

———

According to Dell, Sumner was a mild, polite little man who looked like a bookkeeper but "in deadly spirit read all the suspected dirty literature that he could lay his hands on." The storeroom at his Nassau Street office was reputedly crammed with the stuff. He wielded a brand of tyranny over New York authors, editors, and publishers, who sometimes even submitted questionable manuscripts to him in advance of publication, for the man was authorized to initiate criminal proceedings, carry out raids on bookstores, publishers' offices, and warehouses, and inflict enormous personal pain and financial penalties on the people who created and disseminated books considered by him to be profane, immoral, or obscene.† He deleted "damn"s

---

*Sumner's use here of a "soft" censorship approach—arriving without a search warrant and without advance notice to the publisher—was designed to dispose of an objectionable book without provoking public outcry and generating publicity for the ill-fated book. Jones played into the plan.

†The New York Society for the Suppression of Vice had been given a semigovernmental status when it was organized in Anthony Comstock's day, as we have seen. It was chartered by the state to enforce—with the aid of the police—the state's anti-obscenity laws. Its agents

and "Oh, God!"'s, rewrote erotic scenes, and deleted passages and whole pages he thought might possibly arouse the sexual feelings of young persons, or teach them something they did not know about sex.

Sumner had gone through *The "Genius"* with "the terrible industry of a Sunday-school boy dredging up pearls of smut from the Old Testament."

H. L. MENCKEN: When young Witla, fastening his best girl's skate, is so overcome by the carnality of youth that he hugs her, it is set down as lewd. . . .

THEODORE DREISER *(The "Genius"): Suddenly, as they turned, one of her skates came loose and she hobbled and exclaimed about it.*

"Wait," said Eugene, "I'll fix it."

She stood before him and he fell to his knees, undoing the twisted strap. When he had the skate off and ready for her foot he looked up, and she looked down on him smiling. He dropped the skate and flung his arms around her hips, laying his head against her waist.

"You're a bad boy," she said.

For a few minutes she kept silent, for as the center of this lovely scene she was divine. While he held her she pulled off his wool cap and laid her hand on his hair. It almost brought tears to his eyes, he was so happy. At the same time it awakened a tremendous passion. He clutched her significantly.

"Fix my skate now," she said wisely.

He got up to hug her but she would not let him.

"No, no," she protested. "You mustn't do like that. I won't come with you if you do."

"Oh, Stella!" he pleaded.

"I mean it," she insisted. "You mustn't do like that."

He subsided, hurt, half angry. But he feared her will. She was really not as ready for caresses as he had thought.

H. L. MENCKEN: On page 51, having become an art student, he is fired by "a great warm-tinted nude of Bouguereau"—lewd again. . . .

THEODORE DREISER *(The "Genius"): It was a great, warm-tinted nude by Bouguereau, a French artist who was startling the day with his daring portrait of the nude. The types he depicted were not namby-pamby little slim-bodied women with spindling qualities of strength and passion, but great full-blown women whose voluptuous contour of neck and arms and torso and hip and thigh was enough to get the blood of youth at fever heat. . . .*

These women stood up big in their sense of beauty and magnetism, the soft lure of desire in their eyes, their full lips parted, their cheeks flushed with the blood of health. As such they were anathema to the conservative and puritanical in mind,

---

were given power to arrest, and magistrates were *required* to issue search warrants upon their complaint. In performance of its duties, the society was entitled to share in the fines levied by the courts against persons or companies found guilty of publishing "obscene" books, which added a pecuniary motive to the organization's other incentives to suppress "immoral" and "obscene" books.

the religious in temperament, the cautious in training or taste. The very bringing of this picture to Chicago as a product for sale was enough to create a furor of objection. Such pictures should not be painted, was the cry of the press; or, if painted, not exhibited. Bouguereau was conceived of by many as one of those dastards of art who were endeavoring to corrupt by their talent the morals of the world; there was a cry raised that the thing should be suppressed. . . .

Eugene had never seen such a figure and face. It was a dream of beauty—his ideal come to life. He studied the face and neck, the soft mass of brown, sensuous hair massed at the back of the head, the flowerlike lips and soft cheeks. He marveled at the suggestion of the breasts and the abdomen, that potentiality of motherhood that is so firing to the male. He could have stood there hours dreaming, luxuriating, but the attendant who had left him alone with it for a few minutes returned.

"What is the price of this?" Eugene asked.

"Ten thousand dollars," was the reply.

He smiled solemnly.

"It's a wonderful thing," he said, and turned to go. The attendant put out the light.

H. L. MENCKEN: On page 70 he begins to draw from the figure, and his instructor cautions him that the female breast is round, not square—more lewdness!

THEODORE DREISER *(The "Genius"): He liked to draw the figure. He was not as quick at that as he was at the more varied outlines of landscapes and buildings, but he could give lovely sensuous touches to the human form—particularly to the female form—which were beginning to be impressive. He'd got past the place where Boyle had ever to say*

"They're round."

He gave a sweep to his lines that attracted the instructor's attention.

"You're getting the thing as a whole, I see," he said quietly one day. Eugene thrilled with satisfaction.

———

Mencken noticed that Sumner had become so fascinated in finding seventy-five lewdnesses that he spotted only seventeen profanities, actually missing a few.

H. L. MENCKEN: On page 191 I find an overlooked *by God.* On page 372 there are *Oh, God, God curses her,* and *God strike her dead.* On page 373 there are *Ah, God, Oh, God,* and three other invocations of God. On page 617 there is *God help me.* On page 723 there is *I'm no damned good.* . . . But I begin to blush.

———

Upon Dreiser's return to New York he learned that John Sumner had told Jones not only to withdraw all copies of *The "Genius"* from the stores but to destroy the book's plates; Dreiser publicly threatened Jones with legal action if he did not turn the plates over to him.

THEODORE DREISER: I don't know what action the John Lane Company will take, but they have been asked to destroy the plates of the book. But I can say there will be no suppression of the book nor will the plates be destroyed, because if the publishers should wish to accede to the demands, which I don't believe they will, I will get out an injunction to prevent them.

———

Mencken proved equally pugnacious. Although he did not like *The "Genius"* and thought it was an undesirable book over which to fight for freedom, he was appalled by what Sumner had done and feared that the book's continued suppression would not only hurt his friend Dreiser but intimidate other promising young realists and the younger pubishers as well. To Dreiser, Mencken wrote:

H. L. MENCKEN: On with the machine guns! Forward the Zeppelins! I am planning a general offensive.

———

But Mencken also feared the results of a public trial, given the current German-spy phobia. He cautioned Dreiser that "a man accused of being German has no chance whatever in a New York court at this time."* Instead of a courtroom battle, Mencken's idea was to organize a petition of protest by prominent writers and prod the prestigious Authors' League of America—the only recognized writers' organization in the States—into publicly condemning the censorship and calling for new laws that would make it impossible for Sumner and his kind to persecute serious authors and suppress meritorious literary works.

It was a delicate business to get the Authors' League behind Dreiser because three years earlier he had arrogantly turned down membership in the league, which he looked upon as a band of philistines and lampooned as an organization run by "the pseudos, reactionaries, and pink tea and chocolate bon bon brotherhood of literary effort." However, Dreiser was prepared to eat crow if the league could help him free his book. He met with the group's executive committee, and uttered this warning:

THEODORE DREISER: A band of wasp-like censors has appeared and is attempting to put the quietus on our literature which is at last showing signs of breaking the bonds of Puritanism under which it has long struggled in vain. . . . A literary reign of terror is being attempted. Where will it end?

———

In response the league passed a resolution proclaiming that *The "Genius"* was not obscene, that Sumner's tests were "narrow and unfair," and that the full organization ought to make a public protest about the book's suppression. This the league did, without certifying the literary merits of *The "Genius"* or its morality, but declaring that while "some of us may differ from Mr. Dreiser in our aims and methods, and some of us may be

---

*Richard Lingeman, *Theodore Dreiser*, vol. 2: *An American Journey* (1990), 132.

out of sympathy with his point of view," he has displayed "manifest sincerity" and has achieved "high accomplishments" in his writings. Therefore it was wrong to "condemn a serious artist under a law aimed at common rogues." The obscenity laws, they argued, should be amended to prevent further such occurrences.

Some of the league's members distanced themselves from the protest. Brander Matthews felt that the Comstockians, although "occasionally fanatical, did good work in suppressing filth." Ellis Parker Butler expressed his reservations to Mencken: "Today," he said, "I am inclined to believe that some books can be so rotten they should be destroyed in some literary sewage plant. Things are not necessarily truthful because they stink nor strong because they smell so."

Mencken, however, went on launching zeppelins, mailing twenty-five letters a day to hundreds of editors, authors, and publishers, urging them to sign the protest. He even got Alfred Knopf and Ben Huebsch to help circulate the petition. He also egged on J. Jefferson Jones to round up British support. Jones wrote to scores of British writers and got some prominent ones signed up—including Arnold Bennett, Hugh Walpole, E. Temple Thurston, William J. Locke, and H. G. Wells. They sent a cable to the Authors' League of America: "WE REGARD THE GENIUS AS A WORK OF HIGH LITERARY MERIT AND SYMPATHIZE WITH THE AUTHORS LEAGUE OF AMERICA IN THEIR PROTEST AGAINST ITS SUPPRESSION." Several literary journals now joined the public protest: Ezra Pound in *The Egoist,* Felix Shay in *Era,* Frank Harris in *Pearson's,* and Alexander Harvey in *The Bang.* Before Mencken was done, 458 of the country's foremost creative writers, editors, and publishers, including Sinclair Lewis, Amy Lowell, Willa Cather, John Reed, Rex Beach, Max Eastman, Rachel Crothers, Edwin Arlington Robinson, and Sherwood Anderson, had signed the protest. This must have been one of the largest groups of literary figures ever to subscribe to an anticensorship cause.*

For his part, John Sumner repeated his warning that it was "wholly conceivable that the reading of the book by a young woman could be very harmful" and waved the old Comstockian banner of "Morals! Not Art!," giving expression to a point of view probably shared by most American judges:

JOHN SUMNER: Artists taken as a whole may be very good judges of the . . . literary merits of any particular writing, but on the question of the tendency of that writing on the manner and morals of the people at large they are no more qualified than are an equal number of mechanics of ordinary education. The term "indecent" is a word of common significance.

---

*In 1963, one hundred persons signed a "manifesto" drawn up by poet Allen Ginsberg to protest the criminal prosecution of Lenny Bruce in New York, as described below in Chapter 24. In the same year, an equal number of members of the literary community signed an *amicus curiae* brief that I wrote and filed in the Supreme Court, in a California case, urging the Court to free Henry Miller's novel *Tropic of Cancer,* as mentioned in Chapter 22.

It is not for any limited group of individuals to attempt to force upon the people in general their own particular ideas of what is decent or indecent.

—

For a while, Dreiser did his best with Jones at John Lane, trying to "pump him up to a fighting point" against Sumner. He told his friend Mencken: "I am perfectly willing to go to jail myself. It will save my living expenses this winter." He also said: "A fight is the only thing & I want Lane to fight. I hope & pray they send me to jail."

He also offered the legal services of a lawyer at the New York firm of Stanchfield and Levy to defend Jones and any other John Lane employee prosecuted by the Post Office authorities, or John Sumner's crew, at "no charge" to Lane. But Jones refused to allow Lane to become the vehicle for a court test of Sumner's censorship of The "Genius." The New York office was not prosperous, and the ledger came before the interests of Dreiser and the principle of literary freedom; Jones believed sales of The "Genius" were mostly finished. Later Dreiser said he regretted his own inaction; he never tested Sumner's authority by publicly offering to sell him a copy of the book (as, for example, publisher Donald Friede would do ten years later when Dreiser's An American Tragedy was suppressed by the Watch and Ward Society in Boston).

Dreiser did try two other methods, in addition to the writers' protest, to get The "Genius" back into the stores. Neither worked. He urged Mencken to meet with John Sumner to negotiate a satisfactory expurgation—fewer cuts than the New York literary czar had initially demanded from the John Lane Company—so that the book might be republished in something like its original form. Mencken undertook this curious assignment one afternoon six years after the original suppression, and said he found the vice crusader "polite and fairly flexible for a bigot." Although Sumner at the time was apparently agreeable to the restoration of two whole chapters previously barred, and compromised in other significant respects, an expurgated version of The "Genius" would never be published—Dreiser never agreed to it. Instead, without telling Mencken, he entered into "secret" talks with the brashest of the new American publishers, Boni and Liveright, about contracting to issue The "Genius" unexpurgated—in defiance of Sumner's threats—along with others of the author's works. When Mencken got word of this he wrote to Dreiser to find out if it was true. "If it is, I'd like to know it in advance, so that it may not appear to Sumner that I was fooling him about the cuts." In 1923 the unexpurgated Boni and Liveright edition of The "Genius" would be published.

In the interim, Dreiser was stymied; the John Lane Company refused to reissue The "Genius" but they were also reluctant to relinquish their contract rights to it, or to a projected sequel, The Bulwark. Dreiser brought a "friendly" suit against Lane, seeking a court declaration that the book was not obscene and that the publisher was therefore obligated contractually to publish it or put it back on sale. After several years' delay, the court addressed the question but declined to give an advisory ruling to Dreiser or Lane and dismissed the suit.

And so, in the short run, Sumner and Morality defeated Dreiser, Mencken, and Art. Dreiser did get hold of the book's plates; Jones turned them over to him, and he stored them in New Jersey. But no other publisher dared to republish *The "Genius"* unexpurgated until Boni and Liveright did it in 1923, and Dreiser was in the meantime relatively unproductive and hard put to keep the wolf from the door. W. A. Swanberg has speculated that Sumner's attack on the Lane edition of *The "Genius"* brought about the suppression of several potential Dreiser novels, which the author could not write because of fears that they also would be suppressed.

W. A. SWANBERG: [A] full decade would elapse between *The "Genius,"* which impoverished him, and his next novel, which would make him rich. Who knows what might have come from his pen had he been encouraged instead of banned?

———

The campaign to free *The "Genius"* put a considerable strain on the friendship between Dreiser and Mencken. In the teeth of Mencken's "advice and warnings," Dreiser had invited a number of "red-ink boys" (one of Mencken's terms for writers who seemed to be aligned with Communist ideology) from Greenwich Village to sign the petition. These included Floyd Dell and Alexander Harvey; another "red-ink" signer was Rose Pastor Stokes, who had just been sentenced to prison for sedition. Other friends of Dreiser's who signed up included the anarchist feminist Emma Goldman, the Wobbly leader W. D. ("Big Bill") Haywood,* and the core of the writers and artists who ran *The Masses* magazine—Max Eastman, John Reed, and Art Young. Dreiser also managed to get himself and Mencken invited to speak "against censorship" at the Liberal Club on Macdougal Street in Greenwich Village, next to the Boni brothers' bookshop. Mencken wrote Dreiser:

H. L. MENCKEN: For God's sake don't start making speeches at the Liberal Club. This organization consists of all the tinpot revolutionaries and

———

*The term "Wobbly" referred to members of the Industrial Workers of the World (I.W.W.). Big Bill Haywood and one hundred other Wobbly leaders were arrested, prosecuted, convicted, and sentenced to prison at a mass trial under wartime laws that disdained freedom of speech and press for persons and organizations publicly expressing antiwar, antidraft, or antigovernment opinions; in the process, the I.W.W. was destroyed. This scenario was played out by President Wilson, Attorneys General Gregory and Palmer, and the federal judiciary. Professor Zechariah Chafee exposed the situation in his book *Freedom of Speech,* published in 1920. Some two thousand "Espionage Act" prosecutions took place during the war period; although these flagrantly violated constitutional freedoms of speech and press, there was no recourse to be had from judges. It was as though no First Amendment had been adopted or, rather, as though its command that "Congress shall make no law . . . abridging the freedom of speech, or of the press" was hortatory only, not intended by the framers to be enforceable in courts of law. The next great wave of suppression of speech and press occurred in the wake of World War II.

sophomoric advanced thinkers in New York. . . . These jitney liberals are forever trying to get advertising by hooking on to better men.

—

Mencken thought Dreiser had behaved like a "fearful ass" and said that it was "a very difficult thing to do anything for him." He fulminated against the author:

H. L. MENCKEN: Let me say once more that I think this is damnably silly, perverse, and dangerous policy. . . . All of those jitney geniuses are playing you for a sucker. They can't advance your reputation an inch, but you make a very fine (and willing) stalking horse for them.

—

Dreiser did not let Mencken's peroration go unanswered:

THEODORE DREISER: I do not get the reason for the unnecessarily harsh & dictatorial tone of this letter. Recently, on several occasions, you have gone out of your way to comment (and before others) on my supposed relationship to this band of "jitney radicals and tenth-rate Village geniuses." . . . I am not in touch with the life of this section. I do not go out with or receive here any radicals of any sort—or Village characters—not any. Although I have privately said to myself and here and now state to you that it is really none of your business . . . still you persist. Have I tried to supervise your private life or comment on any of your friends or deeds? What's eating you, anyway? . . . Your letter smacks of something I do not like.

—

Mencken believed that Dreiser's stubborn attitude caused the Authors' League to give only lukewarm support to the protest he mounted against the censorship of The "Genius." According to Mencken the author's insistence upon "adding the names of a lot of Washington Square jitney geniuses violently enraged" the Authors' League men who were in charge. Overall, Dreiser's "association of his case with the names of mountebanks advocating birth control, free love, free verse, and other such juvenile propaganda hurt him greatly."

A year later, according to Dreiser, Mencken showed his "true colors and feelings" with the Knopf publication of his *Book of Prefaces.* It was 1918. In his book Mencken attacked the puritans and Comstockians who were out to destroy Dreiser's work, but he also attacked Dreiser and The "Genius" violently.

H. L. MENCKEN: One-half of the man's brain, so to speak, wars with the other half. He is intelligent, he is thoughtful, he is a sound artist—but there come moments when a dead hand falls upon him, and he is once more the Indiana peasant, snuffling absurdly over imbecile sentimentalities, giving a grave ear to quackeries, snorting and eye-rolling with the best of them. . . .

The "Genius" is as gross and shapeless as Brünnhilde. . . . The thing rambles, staggers, trips, heaves, pitches, struggles, totters, wavers, halts, turns aside, trembles on the verge of collapse. . . . The book is an endless emission of the obvious. . . . It runs to 736 pages of small type; its reading is an unbearable weariness to the flesh. . . . It somehow suggests the advanced thinking of Greenwich Village.

———

In the midst of the fulminations over The "Genius," Dreiser had written a four-act play, The Hand of the Potter, about a sexually disturbed young man who is assailed by impulses which he is afraid of but cannot control. Going from temptation to violence, he sexually assaults and kills an eleven-year-old girl, realizes the enormity of his crime, but says hopelessly: "I didn't make myself, did I?" and then commits suicide. It was daring subject matter even for a realist like Dreiser, and if it had been staged at the time, the play would have enraged the Comstockians and provoked more censorship. Even Liveright backed away from it initially; later he did publish it, in 1919. Mencken, however, was appalled. In a long letter to Dreiser about the play he outlined a liberal but qualified theory of freedom for realist expression. Under Mencken's theory, it is doubtful that Joyce's Ulysses would have come free.

H. L. MENCKEN: It is all very well enough to talk of artistic freedom, but it must be plain that there must be a limit in the theatre, as in books. You and I, if we are lucky, visit the bowel-pot daily; as for me, I often have to leave a high-class social gathering to go out and piss; you, at least, have been known to roll a working girl on the couch. But such things, however natural, however interesting, are not for the stage. . . . Nothing is more abhorrent to the average man than sexual perversion. He would roar against it in the theatre.

I see you getting into an understandable but nevertheless unfortunate mental attitude. Resisting with justice the imbecilities of the Comstocks, you unconsciously fly to an extreme, and demand a freedom that is obviously impossible. I have no patience with impossibilities. . . .

If the thing were possible, I'd advocate absolutely unlimited freedom in speech, written and spoken. I think the world would be better off if I could tell a strange woman, met at a church social, that I have diarrhoea . . . [and] if novels could describe the precise process of reproduction, beginning with the handshake and ending with lactation—and so show the young what a bore it is. But these things are forbidden. The overwhelming weight of opinion is against them. The man who fights for them is as absurd as the man who fights for the right to walk down Broadway naked, and with his gospel pipe in hand.

———

Mencken also warned Dreiser about what would happen were he to succeed in staging or publishing the play:

H. L. MENCKEN: Fully half the signers of the Protest, painfully seduced into signing by all sorts of artifices, will demand that their names be taken off.

You fill me with ire. You have a perfect genius for doing foolish things. Put the ms. behind the clock, and thank me and God for saving you from a mess.

———

Dreiser thought that Mencken was growing as stuffy and moral as the pope.

THEODORE DREISER: I deny your ruling in connection with perversion and its place on the stage. Tragedy is tragedy and I will go where I please for my subject. If I fail ridiculously in the execution let the public and the critics kick me out. They will anyhow. But so long as I have any adequate possession of my senses current conviction will not dictate to me where I shall look for art—in tragedy or comedy. My inner instincts and passions and pities are going to instruct me—not a numbskull mass that believes one thing and does another.

———

After nine years of literary and beer-hall camaraderie, the meetings and letters between Mencken and Dreiser stopped. Ben Huebsch, who knew them both, tried to mediate a reconciliation, without success. Dreiser described his disinclination to reestablish the old friendly relationship.

THEODORE DREISER: Where [Mencken and I] diverge, and only there (and there is no personal feeling in this), is in regard to my own work. His profound admiration, apparently, is only for *Sister Carrie,* and *Jennie Gerhardt,* works which to me represent really old-line conventional sentiment. For *The "Genius," The Hand of the Potter,* "Laughing Gas,"* "Life, Art and America," and a somewhat newer vein, he has, apparently, no eye. . . .

Since he is slowly but surely drifting into a position where he feels it incumbent upon him as a critic to place me in a somewhat ridiculous light, I have felt that this close personal contact might as well be eliminated, for the time being anyhow.

H. L. MENCKEN: I suddenly find myself very lonely in New York.†

———

Not Dreiser: he had now been discovered by Al Boni and Horace Liveright and was getting more deeply involved with those two liberals and the rest of the Village crowd.

---

*Essays by Dreiser.

†Swanberg says they were reconciled after seven months. "There was warm affection between them. There was also mutual respect heightened by their knowledge that they understood the strangling power of philistinism better than anyone else alive, though they disagreed about methods of attacking it, and that together they might achieve some kind of literary revolution." *Dreiser* (1965), 228–29. But in 1926, a more serious breach occurred after Mencken wrote a "murderous" review of Dreiser's most popular novel, *An American Tragedy.* This time the Mencken-Dreiser friendship was, after eighteen years, really broken off, until nine years later when, in 1935, they once more made up. However, it was never again the same (*ibid.,* 426).

8

I Took a Girl
Away from You
Once

AFTER *Sister Carrie* and l'Affaire Doubleday in 1900, ten years passed before Theodore Dreiser produced his next novel, *Jennie Gerhardt*. But by 1915 he had written three more: *The Financier, The Titan,* and *The "Genius"*—which John Sumner managed to suppress after it became a best-seller. Each new book added to Dreiser's reputation as America's greatest exponent of realism, its Zola. The Village crowd now regarded him as a revolutionary because his novels revealed a real concern for the people at the bottom of American society and were a major force in the battle to overthrow the genteel tradition in American literature.

Many of those Village radicals were products of well-to-do Anglo-Saxon Protestant families and the Ivy League universities and were themselves not altogether removed from the genteel tradition. Dreiser's background was quite different. He grew up in an impoverished German Catholic family, never had a decent education, and by the age of fifteen was earning his own living as a dishwasher and busboy, and then as a shipping clerk in Chicago.

The popular appeal of Dreiser's novels expanded with his critical reputation, and in December 1925, when Boni and Liveright brought out *An American Tragedy,* the book became an overnight best-seller, despite a successful action by the Watch and Ward Society to have the novel removed from bookstores in Boston. By then Dreiser's banned book *The "Genius"* had been reissued without a murmur from John Sumner, who knew that the novel's new publisher, Horace Liveright, would relish a courtroom battle and the predictable publicity.

Liveright was a cadaverous-looking man with an engaging smile whom Dreiser liked at first sight. The author had signed up with Boni and Liveright in 1923, after Dodd, Mead—which had succeeded John Lane as owner of the publication rights to The "Genius"—hedged on reissuing the novel unexpurgated, and Horace Liveright promised Dreiser he would bring it out without cuts. When Liveright told Dreiser he wished to publish all of his books, including Sister Carrie, the author was flattered. He allowed Liveright to reissue Carrie but waited to see what would happen before letting him publish his collected works. As it turned out, these would not be published in Dreiser's lifetime.

If Ben Huebsch was the most distinguished, Horace Liveright was the most flamboyant, of the publishers who emerged in the United States during the golden age of publishing, the period that spanned the world wars. Like Dreiser, most of them were unspoiled by the Eastern universities. Without connections with the dominant legal and religious establishments, without contacts or contracts with the already established authors, these men had little to lose in publishing young and rebellious writers.

The new breed—they included Horace Liveright, Al Boni, Thomas Seltzer, Pascal Covici, Donald Friede, B. W. Huebsch, Alfred A. Knopf, Harold K. Guinzburg, Richard Simon, Max Schuster, Bennett Cerf, and Donald Klopfer—were particularly sensitive to the ideological and cultural interests of non–Anglo-Saxon readers—interests that were ignored by the conservative old-line publishing houses. In their struggle against censorship, during the twenties and thirties, these men followed the example of American women like Margaret Anderson and Sylvia Beach, who rebelled against the genteel tradition in their own backgrounds. Like them, the new publishers were open and sympathetic to radical ideas; because they were Jews, publishing had previously been closed to them, as it had been to women. Unlike the women, however, these men built publishing houses that endured. At least, many of them did: Knopf and Cerf and Klopfer and Simon and Schuster and Guinzburg continued as independent publishers. Huebsch moved over to Viking. Others like Seltzer and Liveright went down. But Theodore Dreiser would not have left his huge mark on American letters had he not managed to get his later books into the hands of a publisher like Horace Liveright, rather than a Frank Doubleday, a George Harvey, or a J. Jefferson Jones.

In 1920, Horace Liveright and Al Boni published Freud's General Introduction to Psychoanalysis. They published Andreas Latzko's Men in War and Leon Trotsky's The Bolsheviki at the height of World War I, and after the Bolshevik revolution they brought out in book form John Reed's Ten Days That Shook the World.

By 1924, Liveright had signed up Theodore Dreiser, Eugene O'Neill, Sherwood Anderson, George Moore, Gertrude Atherton, Ludwig Lewisohn, Robinson Jeffers, Hendrick Willem van Loon, Rose Macaulay, and

Sarah Millin—an impressive record for someone who had entered the book-publishing business only five years before. He also published the first works of William Faulkner, Ben Hecht, Liam O'Flaherty, and Ernest Hemingway.

He became a legend in his time because he scorned the moralists, fought passionately for the freedoms of the twenties, and expressed huge delight whenever one of his books was banned in Boston. He was so much in favor of openness that he let it be known that he took showers in front of his own children.

The executive offices were in an old brownstone on West Forty-eighth Street—"in deliberate defiance of the publishing axiom that dignity and dust were the mark of the successful publisher." They looked like living rooms; there were no ordinary desks in sight. Liveright's own office was a luxurious parlor, equipped with a grand piano. There was a canopied terrace with lounge chairs and the famous connecting door between the publishing offices and those of Liveright's theatrical business, a door made to look like part of the bookshelves that lined the walls. The twenty-four-year-old Donald Friede, who in 1925 bought a half interest in the firm and was given a first vice presidency to go with it, reported that it was "a never-ending source of amusement to watch the expressions on the people in the waiting room when the bookcase would suddenly swing into the room and a startlingly beautiful secretary would glide out to summon an equally beautiful actress to her interview in the theatrical offices."*

Bennett Cerf, who later published *Ulysses* at Random House, had been a Liveright apprentice. With his friend Donald Klopfer, Cerf formed the new company when, in 1925, Liveright sold them the Modern Library—already selling some 200,000 books a year—because he was bored with the project and needed money to get divorced from a wife who also bored him. The idea of publishing a Modern Library of inexpensive editions of modern "classics" stemmed from the "Little Leather Library," which Horace Liveright and Al Boni had started around 1914. The Little Leather Library was a thirty-volume set of pocket-size volumes of classics, selling at $2.98 for the whole lot. Boni and Liveright astounded the book trade by selling a million copies to Woolworth's during the first year. Eventually the cost of real leather forced them to use imitation leather, and a saying made the rounds that salesmen approaching any town in the summer could tell a mile away whether the place was already stocked with Little Leather Library books, because they smelled like castor oil.

In the hands of Cerf and Klopfer, the Modern Library editions were bound in cloth (which did not smell in hot weather), and the partners went on the road to sell their product, the best in world literature at low prices.

---

*Friede had been advised by his psychoanalyst to take up book publishing. He was a playboy of Russian parentage, a dropout from several colleges, a veteran of nine short-lived jobs. The quote is from his *Mechanical Angel* (1948), 18.

When the new firm opened its first offices in two rooms on West Forty-fifth Street, they had 112 titles. The series was modeled on Everyman's Library, a highly successful line of hardcover reprints launched in the early 1900s by the English publisher J. M. Dent and imported into the States by E. P. Dutton.

Liveright and Boni engaged in early skirmishes with the censors over George Moore's *The Story of a Modern Lover*, Petronius's *Satyricon*, and Maxwell Bodenheim's *Replenishing Jessica*—and won all three cases.

The firm published George Moore's later novels after the author's old-style publisher, W. D. Appleton, expurgated his earlier ones. The author's *The Story of a Modern Lover* was attacked when a New York magistrate issued a search warrant against Liveright and a vice squad detective came and carted away some one hundred copies of the book. By then in its third edition, the novel had sold over 11,000 copies. Within a month the book was cleared by a judge who could find no reason to believe it would "corrupt and deprave the morals" of anyone.

The *Replenishing Jessica* case was won after the judge required the prosecutor to read the entire book of 272 "smoldering pages" aloud to the jury— perhaps seeking to ensure that they would abide by the rule Judge John Ford had been unable to get the New York legislature to overturn, the rule that a book should be judged in its entirety, not by isolated excerpts. * According to Liveright (and the press), the jurors drowsed through the reading and so, in the end, acquitted the defendants. † The novel sold nearly 93,000 copies in the following two years.

In the *Replenishing Jessica* case the grand jury indicted not only Liveright personally, and his company, but the author, Max Bodenheim, and the firm's editor in chief, T. R. Smith. The censorship forces were out to halt the new firm in its tracks. The publishers' lawyers, however, managed to get the charges against Bodenheim thrown out on the technical ground that the New York obscenity statute did not apply to anyone who did not stand to gain financially from a book's sale, and it was represented to the court, perhaps untruthfully, that Bodenheim had no right to receive royalties. The charges against T. R. Smith were dismissed by the judge because he was the editor, not the publisher, of the book. When the D.A. tried cross-examining "T.R." about a large and popular volume of risqué poetry he had collated for Liveright, *Poetica Erotica*, the judge ruled: "I'm not going to have another book read at this trial!"

But it was Dreiser who became Liveright's big seller, and the publisher fought aggressively for the author and his books.

---

*This tactic failed, as will be described, in the much-publicized Boston trial of Dreiser's two-volume, 840-page best-selling *An American Tragedy*.

†A good account of the trial is in Walker Gilmer's *Horace Liveright: Publisher of the Twenties* (1970), 155ff.

LESTER COHEN:* I was there the day *An American Tragedy* was brought in. It came in a wagon of the American Express Company, two huge stacks of manuscript, and Mr. Dreiser wearily presenting himself at T. R. Smith's office. . . .

T. R. knew a book when he saw one, and he knew something about people. Horace the gamboleer had gambled on Dreiser, paying him fifty dollars a week over a period of years (which no other publisher would) but Horace bet on a long shot; to wit: that the author of the *Genius* and *Sister Carrie* would some day write a best seller, that this best seller would stimulate sales of his previous work, in other words that Dreiser would ultimately make money.

All honor to Liveright for gambling on that and enabling Mr. Dreiser to work on . . . but when *An American Tragedy,* in two huge stacks, was brought into Boni & Liveright, it was not to Liveright that Dreiser went, but Tom Smith.

"Tom," he said. "I've done all I could with it, I've gone as far as I can go." Mr. Dreiser looked tired, the fog of puzzlement and resignment in his gray-blue eyes.

"Tom," he said, "you cut it, or put it together, publish it in one volume or two or three—it's up to you." For months Tom Smith sat in his little room, using the blue pencil, the scissors, the paste. What came out was *An American Tragedy.*

———

An American Tragedy was published in December 1925. Before seeing the reviews, Dreiser left town—he was sure the critics would be disparaging. He bought "another Maxwell" and headed for Florida with Helen Richardson,† stopping on the way to see Dreiser's sister Mame, and to give

---

*Cohen was a Liveright author whose literary career began in 1926 with the publication of his novel *Sweeping*. He met Dreiser for the first time at Boni and Liveright's. In "Theodore Dreiser: A Personal Memoir," published in *Discovery No. 4* (Pocket Books, 1954), he tells about the time he "really got to know Mr. Dreiser," in 1931, at the site of the "mine war" in Harlan County, Kentucky. Dreiser was invited—along with John Dos Passos, Edmund Wilson, Lester Cohen, and other writers—by the International Labor Defense, the Communist party's legal arm, to visit the coal fields, investigate the situation, and report on it. He accepted in part because "as a newspaper man in Chicago and Pittsburgh I was drawn into this sort of thing, and witnessed the immense injustice which property had inflicted on labor." They formed a "court," with Dreiser sitting as "judge," and called miners to testify as to how they were "gun-thugged" and "lawed"; then the AP and UP sent reporters to question the witnesses, and "soon the grim story of the Harlan mine wars tumbled out, the story of the 18,000 miners in Harlan district and their battle with hunger, submachine guns and the 'law' as administered by men with long criminal records who had been deputized by the High Sheriff." Miners had been arrested and jailed for running soup kitchens on charges of "Criminal Syndicalism," and after the stories made news, some of the writers in Dreiser's party were also indicted for criminal syndicalism. Dreiser himself was charged by the high sheriff with engaging in sexual mischief with a young woman who had accompanied him to Harlan as a "secretary." "And still other writers went down to Harlan and were beaten up. And still others like Sherwood Anderson made common cause with us, saying, 'If these writers have committed Criminal Syndicalism, we all ought to go and commit Criminal Syndicalism.'"

†Helen Patges Richardson was one of the most important women in Dreiser's life—a link in the nearly interminable daisy-chain of women who moved in and out of it during seventy-

her $20 "although she wanted $75." They were in Fort Lauderdale, in the middle of January, when the first batch of letters and reviews came in. One of the first was in *The Nation*:

JOSEPH WOOD KRUTCH: *An American Tragedy* is the greatest American novel of our generation.

STUART SHERMAN *(New York Herald Tribune)*: I do not know where else in American fiction one can find the situation here presented dealt with so fearlessly, so intelligently, so exhaustively, so veraciously, and *therefore* with such unexceptionable moral effect.

SERGEI DINAMOV* (to Dreiser): I think you are the greatest writer in the world. . . . You don't like capital and capitalism. But what do you want to have instead of them? Socialism or communism? . . . What do you think about Soviet Russia?

———

Dreiser was interested in the Soviet Union and communism, and was friendly with the American Communist Party leader William Z. Foster. It was said that Dreiser enjoyed taking Foster to New York nightclubs, where they could discuss social reform in a capitalistic setting. Dreiser thought that in the States, only the Communists were fighting for equality, and that "Communism as practiced by the Russians, or, at least some part if not most of it, could certainly be made palatable to the average American if it was properly explained to him and if the title Communism was removed." On the other hand, Dreiser could not envision a utopian society because of his belief in the predominantly animalistic nature of man:

THEODORE DREISER: Nothing can alter his emotions, his primitive and animal reactions to life. Greed, selfishness, vanity, hate, passion, love, are all inherent in the least of us, and until such are eradicated, there can be no Utopia. . . . And until that intelligence which runs the show sees fit to remould the nature of man, I think it will always be the survival of the fittest, whether in the monarchies of England, the democracies of America, or the Soviets of Russia.

———

Nevertheless, at one time the author contemplated forming a neo-Communist political party, which he named the American League for National Equity because he imagined "Equity" would go down better than "Communism" with most Americans. He said: "If we get enough followers, I would be glad to take the leadership." As a boy, Dreiser had dreamed that one day he might be president.

———

four years. She is described as having been a tall, shapely, sinuous, sensual woman with a smiling face framed by chestnut-gold hair when she met Dreiser, who was her second cousin, in 1919. She spent the next twenty-six years with Dreiser in a self-described state of alternating "ecstasy and torment." He did not marry her until 1944, two years after his first wife, Sara White ("Jug"), died. On Helen, see Vera Dreiser, *My Uncle Theodore* (1976), Chapter 9.
*Moscow critic specializing in American and English literature.

. . .

By the time Dreiser and Helen got back to New York, he was a literary sensation. Most of the important reviews of *An American Tragedy* were glowing with praise. The Sunday *New York Times Book Review* ran a front-page review, along with a photo of the author. In the *Saturday Review,* Sherwood Anderson said that some of Dreiser's language "made him cringe" but he urged everyone to read the book.

SHERWOOD ANDERSON: Find out, once and for all, the difference between a human flesh and blood, male man, full of real tenderness for life, and the smarties, the word slingers, the clever fellows, the nasty cock-sure half men of the writing world.

———

Other reviewers marveled that Dreiser had produced a literary master-piece from what they saw as deplorable prose.

ARNOLD BENNETT *(London Evening Standard)*: *An American Tragedy* is writ-ten abominably by a man who evidently despises style, elegance, clarity, even grammar. Dreiser simply does not know how to write, never did know, never wanted to know. . . . Indeed to read Dreiser with profit you must take your coat off to it, you must go down on your knees to it, you must up hands and say, "I surrender." And Dreiser will spit on you for a start. But once you have finally yielded to him he will reward you—yes, though his unrelenting grip should squeeze the life out of you. *An American Tragedy* is prodigious.

———

Dreiser's old friend Mencken, however, brutally carved Dreiser up in the *American Mercury.* He had written Dreiser to warn him in advance: "I am performing upon you without anaesthetics in the March Merkur." Mencken's piece in the March issue, "Dreiser in 840 Pages," was even more savage than his lambasting review of *The "Genius."*

H. L. MENCKEN: Whatever else this vasty double-header may reveal about its author, it at least shows brilliantly that he is wholly devoid of what may be called literary tact. . . . [It's] a heaping carload of raw materials for a novel, with rubbish of all sorts intermixed—a vast, sloppy, chaotic thing of 385,000 words—at least 250,000 of them unnecessary!

———

Dreiser observed that, according to Mencken, the only good thing about *Tragedy* was that the author's characters could "feel" even though their thoughts were "muddled and trivial." This was not quite true.

H. L. MENCKEN: *An American Tragedy,* as a work of art, is a colossal botch, but as a human document it is searching and full of a solemn dignity, and at times it rises to the level of genuine tragedy.

———

Liveright wondered whether Mencken was fed up with Dreiser but con-cluded that Mencken "was just being Mencken"—he had read all the laudatory reviews, and he hated running with the crowd more than anything else in the world. Earlier he had defended Dreiser when he needed a defender. He had coached him on style for years—without the slightest apparent effect. And Mencken was, after all, "one of those martinets who revere style." So he attacked Dreiser when almost everyone else was busily praising him to the skies. Dreiser, however, wrote Mencken off. After that, one could not say they were friends, and this despite Dreiser's efforts to effect a reconciliation during the last year of his life.

Although in New York John Sumner did not bother *An American Tragedy,* the novel was banned from Boston bookstores when the director of the Watch and Ward Society, Frank Chase, went after it. Thinking to bring the matter to a head, Liveright's partner, Donald Friede, went to Boston to make a test case. He arranged to get himself arrested by selling a copy of *Tragedy* to a Watch and Ward agent named Hines, and when the case came to trial, the district attorney picked up a copy of the book and read passages from it to the jury.

DONALD FRIEDE: The District Attorney read a few paragraphs from page 47 and a few more from page 60, and then without any explanation of any kind he jumped to page 137 and from there to page 307. So far he had read, at the most, a page or so each time, and in most cases not even a whole page.

—

The passages that the Boston jury heard the prosecutor read included a section in which the young protagonist, Clyde, visited a "badhouse" for the first time. It was not an adventure the Boston Brahmins would wish their daughters, or sons, to read about.

THEODORE DREISER *(An American Tragedy): All of a sudden he felt faint thrills of hot and cold racing up and down his back and all over him. His hands and face grew hot and then became moist—then his cheeks and forehead flamed. He could feel them. Strange, swift, enticing and yet disturbing thoughts raced in and out of his consciousness. His hair tingled and he saw pictures—bacchanalian scenes—which swiftly, and yet in vain, he sought to put out of his mind. They would keep coming back. And he wanted them to come back. Yet he did not. And through it all he was not a little afraid. Pshaw! Had he no courage at all? These other fellows were not disturbed by the prospects of what was before them. They were very gay. But what would his mother think if she knew? His mother! He dared not think of his mother or his father either at this time, and put them both resolutely out of his mind. . . .*

Finally, without any comment from any one, Hegglund, accompanied by Higby and Shiel, marched up the steps of this house and rang the bell. Almost instantly the door was opened by a black girl in a red dress.

"Good evening. Walk right in, won't you!"

Clyde found himself in a bright and rather gaudy general parlor or reception room, the walls of which were ornamented with gilt-framed pictures of nude or semi-nude girls and some very high pier mirrors. And the floor was covered by a bright red thick carpet, over which were strewn many gilt chairs.

"Just be seated, won't you? Make yourselves at home. I'll call the madam." And running upstairs to the left, she began calling: "Oh, Marie! Sadie! Caroline! They is some young gentlemen in the parlor." . . .

Nine girls of varying ages and looks, but none apparently over twenty-four or five—came trooping down the stairs at one side of the rear, and garbed as Clyde had never seen any women dressed anywhere. And they were all laughing and talking as they came—evidently very well pleased with themselves and in nowise ashamed of their appearance, which in some instances was quite extraordinary, as Clyde saw it, their costumes ranging from the gayest and flimsiest of boudoir negligees to the somewhat more sober, if no less revealing, dancing and ballroom gowns. And they were of such varied types and sizes and complexions—slim and stout and medium—tall or short—and dark or light or betwixt. And all seemed young. And they smiled so warmly and enthusiastically. . . .

And now, seated here, she had drawn very close to him and touched his hands and finally linking an arm in his and pressing close to him, inquired if he didn't want to see how pretty some of the rooms on the second floor were furnished. And . . . he allowed himself to be led up that curtained back stair and into a small pink and blue furnished room, while he kept saying to himself that this was an outrageous and dangerous proceeding on his part, and that it might well end in misery for him. He might contract some dreadful disease. She might charge him more than he could afford. He was afraid of her—himself—everything, really— quite nervous and almost dumb with his several fears and qualms. And yet he went, and, the door locked behind him, this interestingly well-rounded and grace- ful Venus turned the moment they were within and held him to her, then calmly, and before a tall mirror which revealed her fully to herself and him, began to disrobe.

———

The district attorney also read aloud the section of the novel which dealt with a young woman's pregnancy and Clyde's pathetic attempts to help her get an abortion.* Starting with page 379, he read some ten pages of disconnected excerpts taken from the next forty pages, then turned the witness over to the publisher's principal lawyer, Arthur Garfield Hays.

DONALD FRIEDE: Hays had been jumping up and down all morning, object- ing, arguing, questioning—and getting exactly no place. . . . [T]he judge refused to permit volume two to be introduced in evidence, refused to permit the whole of volume one to be introduced in evidence, refused Hays permission to read the first twenty-five pages of the book, in fact refused to do anything but make the jury consider the charges on the basis of the excerpts from volume one which had been read to them by the district attorney.

———

*The attempt here may have been to suggest that *An American Tragedy* advocated birth control and was condemnable for that reason too. See W. A. Swanberg, *Dreiser,* 352.

Hays now called Friede to the witness stand to let him give an outline of what the book was about. "Objection," cried the district attorney. "Sustained," said the judge. "Exception," said Hays. This ritual was repeated "over and over again."

DONALD FRIEDE: He put Dreiser on the stand and tried the same tactics—and with the same results, or rather, lack of them.

———

The following morning Hays tried a new tactic: he called Clarence Darrow to appear before the judge and jury. That didn't work, either; the judge excused the jury before permitting Darrow to say a word. Darrow "made a beautiful and eloquent speech," which Friede thought should have gained Hays his point. But it did not. The judge listened to Darrow respectfully, and denied his plea as firmly as he had denied Hays's.

The burden of Darrow's speech was that an 840-page, five-dollar, two-volume novel—from which the district attorney had read in all less than fifteen pages of excerpts—was an *adult* book, "*intended for adults* and likely to be read *only by adults.*"

When the presiding justice asked the famous lawyer: "But supposing it did fall into the hands of someone seventeen, eighteen or nineteen years of age?" Darrow replied with unavailing reasonableness:

CLARENCE DARROW: Well now . . . supposing I were to concede that one or two young people might take a bad meaning from the book. You can't make all literature in this world for the benefit of three-year-old children, or ten-year-old children, or fifteen-year-old children. It is utterly absurd. We cannot print all our literature for the weak-minded and the very immature.

———

This was, of course, exactly what the Massachusetts obscenity law, as interpreted by the state's highest court, aimed at—protecting the young and susceptible from being corrupted by a book; it was, again, the old rule of *Regina* v. *Hicklin.* The notion that a book's corrupting effect could be tested by imagining the impact of isolated passages on the reader also was still "good law" in Massachusetts.

The Dreiser team did not help matters when, one evening before the trial was over, they—Dreiser, Friede, Liveright, and Darrow—took part in a meeting at Ford Hall in honor of Margaret Sanger.

Sanger was fighting a losing battle for legalized contraception, and Boston was an anti-contraception stronghold. The courageous feminist had been told upon arrival that she would not be allowed to speak at the meeting, and Boston policemen were there to make sure that she did not. But when she was introduced and stood up to take a bow—which was permitted—she ostentatiously placed a large piece of adhesive tape over her mouth.

DONALD FRIEDE: There she stood while a speech was read by someone else at the speaker's table. The police were nonplussed. . . . [B]y the time they realized they had been tricked and that the speech that had been read while she stood there silently was actually the speech she wanted to deliver, it was too late: the speech was ending and Margaret Sanger was sitting down again and removing the tape from her mouth.

———

After that, Darrow got up and made a speech, and so did Dreiser. And there were "some funny skits involving the current position of Boston booksellers, one of which brought down the house." The next day their antics were headlined in the papers: "BOSTON HIT BY LIBERALS' WIT" and "BAD BOOK AUTHOR HITS CENSORSHIP."

In his closing argument the district attorney told the all-male Boston jury that he did not know where the Dreiser team, who had come to "our little village," got their notions of obscenity. "I know not, sirs, from whence they derive their sociology or philosophy by which they determine what is obscene and what is not; I know not whether they are going to bring you to the jungles of Africa. But I got my notions, and I know you got yours, sirs, at your mother's knee, when she prayed that you would be pure in thought, pure in word, pure in actions."

He took up each of the excerpts from *An American Tragedy* that he had previously read and asked the jurymen if they were not obscene, standing alone, and if they would not be harmful to the morals of a young girl: *"How, sirs, would you like to have your fifteen-year-old daughters read that?"* When he finished reading the section about the girl in the brothel who had started to undress when she and Clyde were alone in her room, he said: *"Well,* perhaps where the gentleman who published this book comes from it is not considered obscene, indecent, and impure for a woman to start disrobing before a man, but it happens to be out in Roxbury where *I* come from."

Dreiser, his publisher, and his lawyers could not have been surprised when the jury brought in a verdict of guilty, nor when they lost their appeal of the case to the state supreme court. The supreme judicial court spoke unanimously:

SUPREME JUDICIAL COURT OF MASSACHUSETTS: Even assuming great literary evidence, artistic worth and an impelling moral lesson in the story, there is nothing essential to the history of the life of its principal character that would be lost if these passages were missed which the jury found were indecent, obscene, and manifestly tending to corrupt the morals of youth. . . . Furthermore, the seller of a book which contains passages offensive to our statute has no right to assume that children to whom the book might come would not read the obnoxious passages or that if they should read them would continue to read on until the evil effects of the obscene passages were weakened or dissipated with the tragic denouement of a tale.

———

And then the court dismissed out of hand the "novel" argument that the publisher's lawyers had made that the criminal conviction of a person for selling Dreiser's *An American Tragedy* violated freedom of the press: "The contention that a decree adjudicating the book as obscene, indecent, or impure would be an abridgement of the rights of freedom of the press guaranteed by the First and Fourteenth Amendments to the Constitution of the United States requires no discussion."

Freedom of literary expression would receive no recognition from the courts of Massachusetts until decisions of the Supreme Court of the United States, beginning some three decades later, required that this be done,* with the result that the Massachusetts Supreme Judicial Court freed not only Henry Miller's *Tropic of Cancer* but William Burroughs's *Naked Lunch* as well. Until then, Massachusetts was probably the most repressive of American states censoring literary works, long retaining such elsewhere widely discredited rules as that a work might be adjudged obscene on the basis of isolated passages alone, and that its "obscenity" might be measured by its imagined effect upon young and impressionable persons. Boston book censorship—world notorious—was almost certainly a large factor in the city's decline as a center of American publishing.

For Dreiser, at the time, the Boston decision could not have been too important financially. By the end of 1926 *Tragedy* had sold more than 50,000 sets, at five dollars each, and Dreiser's royalties on this book alone totaled $47,647.53. He had paid $10.96 in income tax in 1921 and $40.17 in 1924. Now, to minimize the IRS's menacing interest, the author formed the Author's Royalties Company; although there were gross receipts of $91,225.65 in 1926, Dreiser's combined income tax payments came only to $5,473.46. For all his hatred of Wall Street, Dreiser soon was investing money in General Motors and the despised AT&T. He also bought a thirty-seven-acre tract and a comfortable cabin overlooking Croton Lake, near Mt. Kisco, New York, and engaged the high-powered agent George Bye to help him deal with the many literary propositions coming in.

When *Tragedy*'s immense popularity became evident, Dreiser began hearing from his indigent friends, asking for "loans," and from his estranged wife, Jug, who now congratulated him on his "wonderful good fortune" and asked him for some cash. When Dreiser tried to brush her off, she got a lawyer, and he changed his tune. The lawyer wrote Dreiser: "For a great

---

*The earliest of such Supreme Court cases included *Roth* v. *United States,* decided in 1957 (discussed in Chapters 15 and 16), four Supreme Court *per curiam* decisions handed down without written opinions the next year, and a 1959 Supreme Court case called *Kingsley International Pictures* v. *Regents,* in which the Court threw out a New York ban on the movie *Lady Chatterley's Lover.* The reasons why these decisions persuaded the Supreme Judicial Court of Massachusetts to alter its approach to the problem of obscenity are set forth in the text of the Massachusetts *Tropic of Cancer* case, *Attorney General* v. *The Book Named Tropic of Cancer* (reprinted in de Grazia, *Censorship Landmarks* [1969], 451, 453–55) and *Attorney General* v. *The Book Named Naked Lunch* (*ibid.,* 581–85). Lawyer Charles Rembar, who was the attorney for the publisher in the Massachusetts *Tropic of Cancer* case, describes it in *The End of Obscenity* (1969). I represented the publisher in the Massachusetts *Naked Lunch* case, as described in Chapters 20 and 25. When the Massachusetts high court drew the line at *Fanny Hill,* the Supreme Court reversed, in the case *A Book Named Memoirs of a Woman of Pleasure* v. *Attorney General,* reprinted in de Grazia, *Censorship Landmarks* (1969), 521ff.

many years Mrs. Dreiser has eked out a miserable existence through her own efforts. Surely Mr. Theodore Dreiser would not wish his wife to continue to work in a weakened and sickly condition." Dreiser agreed to pay his wife $200 a month until she remarried or died. He made the payments through his lawyer, however, so Jug would not find out where he banked.

In England, Constable and Company urgently asked the author's permission to publish *An American Tragedy* and to take over his other works, too. In New York reporters came to interview him, magazine editors pleaded with him for pieces. Horace Liveright placed two-column ads in all the better newspapers, showing Dreiser in profile, listing all his other books, and saying: "We are proud to be the publishers of the works of Theodore Dreiser."

Liveright had taken a long shot with *An American Tragedy* by publishing it in two volumes and setting its retail price at five dollars. After its success was assured, he honored Dreiser by putting out a limited edition, autographed by the author, in fine laid paper, at $12.50. Then he threw a party for his best-selling novelist. The night of the party, Floyd Dell wandered into a café and saw T.D. and other celebrants, including Liveright and T. R. Smith. Dreiser was hunched over his table with his head on his arms. Someone quipped: "He had one glass of beer and collapsed." Dreiser lifted up his head and spotted Dell: "You know, Dell," he said, "I took a girl away from you once." He was, of course, thinking about Kirah Markham.

By now Dreiser was of immense commercial and literary value to Liveright, but he still did not trust his publisher, and soon they had a serious falling out over a sale of the movie rights to *Tragedy*. Liveright liked to be involved in other arts, especially plays and movies, and there is no doubt he had talents and strengths in these arenas. Once Liveright realized that Dreiser's book was a best-seller, he set out to produce a play based on it, using Patrick Kearney to adapt the novel for the stage. That was all right with Dreiser, and the stage production would prove successful; but in the case of the movie rights to *Tragedy,* the author came to believe that Liveright was taking advantage of him.

Liveright had solid contacts with Hollywood, notably his friends Jesse Lasky and Walter Wanger of Famous Players.* When these men heard that Liveright was planning to produce a play based on *An American Tragedy,* they sounded him out by telephone on the prospects for a movie and proposed to meet him and Dreiser in New York—luncheon at the Ritz Carlton—to discuss the project and possibly conclude a deal. Liveright told Dreiser he might be able to get him as much as $35,000 for the movie rights.

Liveright held that people were interested in making the novel into a

---

*According to Ivor Montagu, Liveright had issued, "in slim volumes," a book of poems by Mrs. Lasky and another by Jesse junior entitled *Poems from the Heart of a Boy. With Eisenstein in Hollywood* (1969), 113.

movie only because he was going to do the play; but Dreiser was not "taken in." He thought the movie rights could be sold without a theatrical production for about $100,000. Liveright pretended to be astonished, but he now indicated that $60,000 might be more realistic. The author's distrust deepened when Liveright said he hoped Dreiser would "take care" of him, and then went off to confirm the date for a luncheon meeting (at which Dreiser would be present) to clinch a deal. Dreiser understood that Liveright wanted a 30–70 split on whatever was received, but Dreiser did not say yes to that proposition; nor did he agree that if the offer exceeded $60,000, anything over that amount would go to the publisher.

At the luncheon, when the men from Hollywood and Dreiser reached agreement on a price of $90,000, Liveright asserted his claim to $30,000. Dreiser said to him, "You will get only your ten percent." When Liveright protested that Dreiser had promised to "take care" of him, the author insisted that no such explicit promise had been made. At this point Liveright shouted across the table at Dreiser: "You're a liar!" Dreiser jumped up, ready to swing, and invited Liveright to stand up like a man. The publisher was as tall as the author, but, according to Swanberg, weighed only "a pellucid 130" pounds; Dreiser weighed over 200 pounds. When Liveright understandably declined the invitation, Dreiser dashed his coffee in his face and stormed out of the dining room in a rage. Liveright was embarrassed but not injured. A waiter helped him to dry off. According to Walter Wanger, "The coffee was quite cold."

WALTER WANGER: It scored a direct hit on Horace's face, shirt and suit. It was most embarrassing, with other diners staring at us.

BENNETT CERF: Horace, always the showman, always gallant, stood there mopping himself up, and retained enough of his equilibrium to say, "Bennett, let this be a lesson to you. Every author is a son of a bitch."*

———

A few days later, Wanger and Lasky closed the deal for the movie rights with Dreiser: $80,000 to him and $10,000 to Liveright.† That was not

———

*Cerf's recollection of the incident differs in some respects from accounts in other sources, none of which report that Cerf was present at the luncheon.

†This was for silent-film rights only. When Famous Players–Lasky did not go ahead with the movie—in Dreiser's view because of their fears of the Catholic Church—Paramount Publix Corporation, the successor to Famous Players–Lasky, paid Dreiser an additional $55,000 for sound-film rights. However, the sound-film adaptation of *An American Tragedy* by the Soviet director Sergei Eisenstein—whom Lasky had "enticed" to come to Hollywood and with whom Dreiser worked on the screenplay—proved "too strong" for the Paramount front office. Eisenstein saw the novel, in the words of film director and critic Ivor Montagu, as not merely "the story of a crime" but "an indictment of a whole society." A campaign was mounted against the film treatment, and letters began to arrive "denouncing Paramount for treason to the United States in having imported the 'accursed Red dog, Eisenstein,' " Montagu continues; Representative Hamilton Fish, "a sort of precursor of Senator McCarthy . . . got House leave to form an investigation committee, eventual ancestor of the Un-American Activities Committee." So Paramount turned the project over to the director Josef von Sternberg, whose 1931 film version Dreiser denounced as "an insult to the book."

quite the end of that. Dreiser demanded a written apology from Liveright and got one of sorts:

HORACE LIVERIGHT: It's a darn shame that now that fortune is, after so many years, spilling gold into your lap . . . what has happened between us should have arisen. These are the days when we should be riding around together in band-wagons with champagne flowing and beautiful slave girls fanning us with peacock feathers.

———

According to Donald Friede, after the coffee-throwing incident, the author made his publisher get down on his knees and crawl. No other American author ever before received from a publisher the plums Horace Liveright begged Theodore Dreiser to accept. He proposed to:

—give Dreiser $500 a month as an account on which he could draw against royalties . . .

—spend $10,000 on additional advertising of *An American Tragedy,* and on Dreiser's next book as well . . .

—place a Dreiser ad in every weekly issue of *The New York Times* book supplement during 1927 . . .

—issue a high-priced *limited edition* of Dreiser's collected works . . .

—within two years, issue a regular edition of Dreiser's collected works and underwrite a big mail-order campaign . . .

—invite him to become a member of the board of directors of Boni and Liveright . . .

Dreiser decided to stick with Boni and Liveright, for the time being. But soon after, Liveright's fortunes waned.

Of all the "new breed" publishers who ushered in a golden age of American publishing, Liveright in particular seemed to epitomize the period: the Jazz Age, the Artistic Renaissance, the Big Change, the fight for Literary Freedom. He was the spearhead of the publishing coalition that defeated the attempt of Judge John Ford to impose a severer censorship on New York book publishers. *The New Yorker* spoke of Liveright as the "scion of our Age of Ferment"; and, more affectionately: "Erratic, tangential, generous, inspired . . . this trader in letters, this gambler in aesthetics, this marketeer of poets, this poet of marketeers . . ."

In 1925, Boni and Liveright had sales of close to a million dollars, but according to Donald Friede, the firm's net profit for the year came to $8,609.12. Still—although he did lose Ernest Hemingway to Maxwell Perkins of Scribner's*—Liveright continued to attract new and exciting authors: Dorothy Parker, Bertrand Russell, W. E. Woodward, George S. Kaufman, Stark Young, and others. The 1929 Crash signaled the beginning of Liveright's fast descent. On the advice of wealthy friends, Liveright had invested heavily in Wall Street, and he had also suffered a string of severe

---

*The switch was a complex affair; it is described in Walker Gilmer, *Horace Liveright: Publisher of the Twenties* (1970), 121ff.

losses in the production of Broadway plays. Finally the man was penniless. According to Friede, Liveright lost "all his money" in the Crash.

DONALD FRIEDE: He was a thin man, thin almost to the point of emaciation, and probably the most nervous one I have ever known. His gaunt face was topped with a shock of black hair, and he could have played the part of Mephistopheles without the slightest trace of make-up.* He was utterly ruthless and completely self-centered. He was also a magnificent host and an irresistible force as far as women were concerned. The same was true of men. In fact he drew anybody he wanted into the orbit of his charm without the slightest difficulty. And since he could never bear the thought of being alone he kept himself surrounded with people at all times, beautiful women and brilliant men alike, in a complete surrender to a form of compulsive gregariousness.

Not that he particularly liked the people who flocked about him. He hated most of them and was fully aware of the fact that they would turn on him at the slightest indication of a lessening of his power. Probably this feeling was nurtured by the knowledge that there was within his own organization a carefully planned conspiracy to take advantage of his financial weakness and to reduce him to the position of an impotent figurehead.

BENNETT CERF: At the time I went to work for Boni and Liveright, Albert Boni, Horace's original partner, had already left the firm. He and Horace had started it together, but shortly before my arrival they had had a great argument. And this was typical: they tossed a coin to decide which one would buy out the other for a price they had settled in advance. Liveright won, and Boni went away and started his own firm with his brother, Charles. . . .

I soon learned that the people I would see around the waiting room weren't all authors. About seventy-five percent of them were bootleggers. It was crazy. But Liveright ran a crazy office, and I loved him for it. There were about eight employees who had unlimited expense accounts. Arthur Pell was the treasurer. He used to run around in circles, trying to make ends meet. Pell would give Liveright false cash statements, because as soon as there was any money available, Liveright would spend it.

———

Liveright gave two sorts of parties at his brownstone headquarters, although the distinction between them sometimes blurred. There were the more respectable affairs for authors, and to celebrate the publication of new books. Then there were less bookish, impromptu affairs with bootlegged liquor—bacchanalia at which guests became publicly amorous, unmanageable, and sometimes even unconscious. By the standards of the Roaring Twenties, however, this was not remarkable. Liveright's parties seem to have replaced the informal soirées at the Village Liberal Club, by then

———

*Ivor Montagu describes him as "a thin yellow man with a hatchet face and grey hair." *With Eisenstein in Hollywood* (1969), 113.

defunct. At Liveright's, according to Walker Gilmer, "Bolsheviks were to a large extent supplanted by Follies girls, newspapermen, and Liveright authors." (Among the authors were Thomas Wolfe, the Millay sisters, Carl Van Vechten, Elinor Wylie, and Sinclair Lewis.) But others who might "come by for a drink" included Otto Kahn of Wall Street, who was one of Liveright's connections with Hollywood, and whose advice, some said, did Liveright in; Jesse Lasky of Hollywood; Mayor Jimmy Walker of New York, whose speech, as we have seen, doomed the Clean Books League's legislation; Herbert Bayard Swope, who was editor of the *New York World;* Paul Robeson; Ruth Chatterton; Anna May Wong; Kay Francis; and John Barrymore, whose looks and handsome profile Liveright admired.

Bennett Cerf says that Liveright was a terrible judge of his employees and appreciated least the people who really cared for him. "All he wanted around him were people who would inflate his ego and echo his own judgements." The firm's editorial meetings, which Liveright assembled occasionally with fanfare and ceremony, were "one-man shows, with little patience wasted on anyone who dared dispute his edicts." And yet he readily won the unquestioning loyalty of a large number of men and women.

BENNETT CERF: They stood for anything. They love him still. They probably always will. Underneath all his sham and pretense, they saw a rather helpless person, craving affection and admiration, with a rare love of life and a reckless generosity they could not resist.

—

Other publishers were outraged by Liveright's wild and reckless methods. Finally the day arrived when "the whole house of cards began to tumble about his ears."

In 1927, Donald Friede made an unsuccessful trip to Paris to sign James Joyce to a Boni and Liveright contract to publish *Ulysses* in the States. Everyone at the firm was excited about the prospect "of capturing the Irishman." Like B. W. Huebsch, Liveright in 1921 had been afraid to publish *Ulysses* unexpurgated, and it was this disappointment that had led Joyce to accept Sylvia Beach's proposal to let Shakespeare and Company publish it in Paris. But in 1927, both Liveright and Friede were eager to publish Joyce's by now famous novel and to bring out, as well, his work-in-progress, *Finnegans Wake.* Friede's attempt failed because Joyce feared that the firm was trying to hoodwink him; it had taken out a copyright in Friede's name on a fragment of *Finnegans Wake,* evidently in order to prevent piracy of the sort that had afflicted *Ulysses,* and to secure a [valid] copyright that could be transferred to Joyce. When Friede arrived, Joyce coldly rebuffed his assurances that the transfer of the copyright to him was a forthcoming mere formality.

JAMES JOYCE: In that case, would you mind making the subject of the conversation you planned to have with me an accompanying letter to this transfer of copyright? I will be glad to read it carefully and write you my decision. In the meantime I must ask to be excused. I am a very busy man.

———

Later, in a letter to Harriet Weaver, Joyce observed sarcastically, "D.F. has transferred his copyright of my property (and most uncommon kind of him) to me."

After that misadventure Friede left Liveright and joined Pascal Covici, the former owner of an avant-garde bookstore in Chicago, to form Covici-Friede in 1928. When, in the same year, the new firm brought out Radclyffe Hall's *The Well of Loneliness,* which dealt openly with lesbianism and which had been suppressed in England, the novel became an overnight best-seller.*

To buy Friede out, Liveright was obliged to borrow heavily from Arthur Pell on his own shares in the business. This, added to his unsuccessful speculation in the stock market and on Broadway shows, placed Liveright's personal solvency, his control of the firm, and even the firm's stability in jeopardy. But there was another possible factor: Walker Gilmer has noticed the startling disparity between the last three catalogues assembled by Liveright in 1929 and 1930 and lists the firm had offered earlier in the twenties.

WALKER GILMER: Some of the writers he had developed into best-selling authors were still publishing at the end of the Twenties, but their new works were largely second-rate. This failure of established popularity, supplemented by Liveright's inability to discover any new talent of great promise, appeared to point to the firm's demise. The stock market crash in October 1929 all but assured it. . . . By the end of 1929 unearned advances paid out by Liveright during the preceding year amounted to over $100,000.†

———

Liveright's last solid authorial acquisition was Bertrand Russell, whose controversial *Marriage and Morals* sold over 23,000 copies when published by Liveright in the year of the Great Crash. Liveright had written Russell, with whom he had for several years maintained cordial relations, that *Marriage and Morals* was "a wonderful book" which he considered to be "the most important book on the Fall list." He also made some suggestions to Russell regarding the manuscript, including that Russell add a paragraph

---

*Described in Chapter 11. In 1965, not long before Donald Friede died, the former publisher expressed a view different from the one he had held during the golden age of publishing: "When I see some of the books published today, I cannot help but wonder if our fight against censorship in the twenties was really wise. *Fanny Hill* in paper! And *Naked Lunch* in any form! But I suppose there are some people still willing to play the piano in the literary brothel. Certainly the pay is good." Paul Boyer, *Purity in Print* (1968), 134.

†Among the disappointments was Dreiser's *A Gallery of Women,* the first major work of new fiction by the author since *An American Tragedy.* Published in two volumes, this collection of stories received lukewarm praise from the critics and had a first-year sale of 13,653 copies. It had been preceded, in 1926, by a book of Dreiser's poetry, *Moods, Cadenced and Declaimed,* which turned into an enormous loss for Liveright when only 922 copies were sold. In 1927, *Chains,* a volume of earlier short stories by Dreiser, sold 12,000 copies; in 1928, *Dreiser Looks at Russia* sold only some 4,000 copies. These sales figures were, at best, large disappointments to the house that had brought out his best-selling *Tragedy* and that now was committed to pay Dreiser $1,200 every month.

to his discussions in the book of "freedom of speech, of the press, censorship, etc., etc."

HORACE LIVERIGHT: [Y]ou might do me the justice . . . of mentioning the active and successful campaign which I waged practically singlehanded in 1924 [*sic*] in defeating the most outrageous bit of censorship legislation ever proposed in the State of New York. . . . I think I can say without fear of denial that outside of the active officers of the Civil Liberties Union, I have for the past ten years in my publishing, in my speeches and in the amount of time and money I have expended done more to oppose all sorts of censorship than almost anyone else in this country. If a reference to this is made in *Marriage and Morals,* it will be a lasting monument to me and to what I have done in this field. Naturally, my dear Russell, if you feel that a paragraph about this will be out of place don't hesitate to tell me so.

BERTRAND RUSSELL *(Marriage and Morals):* Experience shows, especially in the case of the dramatic censorship in England, that frivolous plays calculated to excite lust easily pass the censor, who does not wish to be thought a prig, while serious plays which raise large issues, such as "Mrs. Warren's Profession,"* take many years to get past the censor, while a play of transcendent poetical merit like "The Cenci,"† although there is not a word in it that could excite lust even in St. Anthony, required one hundred years to overcome the disgust which it raised in the manly bosom of the Lord Chamberlain. In America, in spite of the non-existence of the censor, the facts in regard to the theatre are substantially as in England. This was shown by the outcome of Horace Liveright's courageous campaign in connection with "The Captive."‡ We may therefore, basing ourselves on a mass of historical evidence, lay it down that the censorship will be used against works of serious artistic or scientific merit, while persons whose purpose is purely salacious will always find ways of slipping through the meshes of the law.

Liveright went to Hollywood in 1930, leaving his publishing house in bad financial shape. The books he had published in 1929 and the first half of 1930 had not sold, and there was little hope that they ever would. More important, perhaps, a "book war" among New York publishers, begun in June 1930, threatened to ruin Boni and Liveright. Mainline publishing houses like Doubleday and Farrar and Rinehart were issuing books that

---

*By George Bernard Shaw.

†By Shelley.

‡ *The Captive,* a play by Edouard Bourdet, had successful runs in Paris and other European capitals and received favorable reviews when it opened in New York in 1926, with a cast that included Basil Rathbone and Helen Menken. After it was suppressed by the police because of its lesbian subject matter, Liveright acquired the production rights to the play and attempted to obtain an injunction that would prevent the acting New York mayor from closing the play again if Liveright produced it. This request was denied, and Liveright was unable to reopen the play.

retailed for $1.00 per copy, in an attempt to attract back a reading audience that had been greatly diminished by the Depression. Liveright, however, refused to reduce the price of any of the books on his prestigious list, retailing at $2.00 to $5.00.

In addition, Liveright himself was bankrupt, owing to the losses he had suffered in the theatre and, even more, in the market. In a letter to Eugene O'Neill, written in July 1930, Liveright underlined some reasons he had for leaving New York.

HORACE LIVERIGHT: What do you think of my going to Hollywood? No, I haven't sold myself down the river or anything like that, but due to Otto Kahn's connection with Paramount Publix Corporation, his firm being their bankers, I think I have worked out a plan which may be very profitable for my publishing firm and our authors. I am to spend two or three months in carefully going over our entire list of books from the time we started publishing and attempt to find two or three really outstanding publications for the talkies.

I think the change in climate will do me good. This summer in New York has been frightful and after a strenuous trip abroad, and then the dollar book situation over here,—well the combination has run me down.

———

There was another reason behind Liveright's move to Hollywood: he no longer controlled the publishing house that bore his name, having been deposed by his former employees, notably by Arthur Pell. Liveright's fall has been traced—in part by the publisher's letters of 1930 to his authors, friends, and advisers—by Walker Gilmer.* Things were so bad that in January 1930, when John Sumner threatened to take Liveright to court for publishing a book called *Josephine, the Great Lover,* the publisher had no fight left in him; he "capitulated immediately before his old enemy," withdrawing the book from circulation and destroying remaining copies and the plates.

WALKER GILMER: The aura of success and the glamour which had surrounded Liveright throughout the flush Twenties years, even when he was bordering on bankruptcy, soon disappeared altogether. In Hollywood, he found himself dependent upon Paramount for a salary, drinking more and more heavily, and, most important, bereft of the celebrity he had enjoyed in the East. He was no longer the boss of a company or the host of the party; rather he was simply another employee with an all but meaningless title and, of course, very little knowledge of film production. He was unsuccessful in negotiating the sale of movie rights for any of the books he had selected, and he was without any real power. In 1931, his contract at Paramount was not renewed, and he returned to New York jobless,

———

Horace Liveright: Publisher of the Twenties (1970), 224ff.

broken in spirit, but nevertheless announcing grand new schemes . . . that he believed would restore his solvency and catapult him back into prominence.

—

Liveright's old firm never recovered its old standing and on May 4, 1933, an involuntary petition in bankruptcy was filed against it. On June 12 a final adjudication of bankruptcy was ordered and on July 25 all the assets of the house were sold for $18,000. Arthur Pell later took over the firm and called it the Liveright Publishing Corporation. During the confusion of the bankruptcy process, the sale of two important books suffered considerably: a collection of stories by Sherwood Anderson called *Death in the Woods* and Nathanael West's sardonic masterpiece *Miss Lonelyhearts*.

BENNETT CERF: Liveright, always more of a gambler than a publisher, played out his string like a gentleman, and proved infinitely more gallant and more admirable when he was taking it on the chin than he did in his heyday. A *poseur* to the last, he could be found tapping his long cigarette holder nervously at a table at the Algonquin, a mere shadow of his former jaunty self, announcing ambitious theatrical projects to all the critics, a few weeks before he died, although everybody knew he was playing through a heart-breaking farce.

—

Liveright told Cerf a lot about the "autobiography" he was working on, but Cerf never saw a page. Cerf retells a pathetic story he heard from Manuel Komroff,* about the last time Komroff paid a call on Liveright, a publisher John Tebbel has described as the "chief conductor," if not "the inventor," of the literary renaissance of the twenties.

BENNETT CERF: He walked in—the door was partly open—and Horace was sitting in his shirtsleeves with a blue serge coat on his desk in front of him; and with a bottle of fountain-pen ink and a rag he was trying to cover a threadbare spot in the sleeve of his coat where the white showed through.

—

During his final days, Liveright was a frequent visitor to his former company, now solely owned by Arthur Pell, who had kept T. R. Smith on to help manage the place. One day, Pell happened to pass through the crowded reception room when Liveright was there, talking to someone:

ARTHUR PELL: Better leave, Horace. I don't think it looks well to have you seen hanging around here!

—

---

*Komroff had been art critic for the *New York Call,* editor of the *Russian Daily News* in Petrograd, reporter for the China Press in Shanghai, editorial writer for the *New York Daily Garment News,* and movie critic for *Film Daily* in Manhattan, before joining B&L to head the production department and the Modern Library. He was made vice president and "spent about one third of a million dollars annually," not a nickel of which was ever questioned by Liveright. Walker Gilmer, *Horace Liveright: Publisher of the Twenties* (1970), 87–88.

After that, Liveright never went back to his old publishing house. In September 1933, he had an attack of bronchitis that turned into pneumonia; within two weeks he was dead. Nine years later, T. R. Smith—who had fought alongside Liveright in the *Replenishing Jessica* case and in the struggle to defeat the Clean Books League—was at work on a biography of Liveright when, at the age of sixty-one, he too died.

9

Dear
Comrade Dreiser

DREISER WENT to Liveright's funeral and afterward took a walk with Upton Sinclair, who blamed Liveright's death on alcohol and took the opportunity to lecture Dreiser about it. Dreiser said he had more important things to worry about than drinking himself to death: after Boni and Liveright went into bankruptcy and reorganization, the author had to reacquire the 13,000 copies of his books sitting in the B&L warehouse, as well as the rights to his novels, and the plates.

H. L. MENCKEN: Dreiser was left flat, of course, by the collapse of the Liveright house. When Liveright withdrew the firm came into control of a Jew named Pell, who by Dreiser's account is a fearful swine. He thereupon determined to clear out, and in order to do so he had to buy back the rights of a number of his books from Pell.

———

Dreiser was forced into arbitration with Pell and made to pay a price of $6,500 for the plates, more than three times what the author had proposed, and $2,500 more than the receiver had paid for them at the bankruptcy auction. This done, in 1933 Dreiser entered into a new publishing contract with Simon and Schuster—as flamboyant a firm in the thirties, almost, as Boni and Liveright was in the twenties.

Like his old ones, Dreiser's new publishers gushed over him. They promised him a uniform edition of his collected works. They saw to it that the newspapers blossomed with advertisements about their forthcoming publication of the twenty-one books already written by their "true genius," whose fame was "an unshakable bulwark." When M. Lincoln Schuster wrote to Dreiser with words of "renewed homage," Dreiser responded in kind: "At long last I am happy to know that I have a publisher who speaks my own language." And when Dreiser's new publishers threw a huge party for their true genius at his estate in Mt. Kisco, New York, everyone came.

Dreiser complained that he had to "sweat over a guest list of 200 people," but he was pleased with the invitations that S&S had engraved on rich gray double-fold paper with the name of his estate, "Iroki," in blue: *Simon & Schuster, on the occasion of becoming the publishers of Theodore Dreiser, request the pleasure of your attendance at Mr. Dreiser's home, Iroki, The Old Road, Mt. Kisco, on Sunday afternoon, after three o'clock."*

He invited "picture bigwigs" like Jacob Wilk and J. Robert Rubin. He invited the columnists Arthur Brisbane, O. O. McIntyre, and Harry Hansen; he invited the Gish sisters and other "theatre folks"; the dancers Ruth St. Denis and Angna Enters; artists like Ralph Fabri and Wharton Esherick; a group of critics that included John Chamberlain, Heywood Broun, Joseph Wood Krutch, and Alexander Woollcott; dozens of publishers, including what was left of the "new breed"—Ben Huebsch, Alfred Knopf, Bennett Cerf, Donald Friede, and Harold Guinzburg—and a flock of writers, among them Floyd Dell, John Dos Passos, Erskine Caldwell, Sean O'Casey, Sherwood Anderson, and Max Eastman. He did not invite his old friend Mencken or the Communist leaders William Z. Foster and Earl Browder.

Ralph Fabri, who helped build Iroki, reported that there were at least fifty cars parked when he arrived at Dreiser's place, and more were streaming in. Helen Richardson counted about three hundred guests—many of those who were invited brought someone else along.

RALPH FABRI: Helen looked stunning in her Russian dress. Teddy himself was on the verge of being cockeyed already. He cried when Maria [Samson] sang.

———

Clifton Fadiman had ordered a truckload of spirits—Prohibition was now over—and Helen Richardson saw to it that three hundred pounds of ice were stored in Dreiser's six-foot bathtub. Although a few drunks had to be put into taxis and driven away, the party was mostly a peaceful affair.

Neither Dreiser's heyday nor the honeymoon with Simon and Schuster lasted very long. Unlike some other successful writers, such as Sinclair Lewis, who managed to grind out a best-selling novel of questionable quality every year or so, Dreiser would not publish another novel, after *An American Tragedy,* for nearly twenty years. *The Stoic,* under contract to Simon and Schuster and promised for 1935, was not finished until 1945, the year in which Dreiser died. By then he had bought out his contract with Simon and Schuster and signed up with his old nemesis, Doubleday and Company, which, however, was no longer being run by a Doubleday but by an "outsider," Douglas Black, a lawyer. It was Black who would publish Dreiser's other long-delayed novel, *The Bulwark,* in 1946, and *The Stoic* in 1947—both after Dreiser's death.*

After the huge success of *An American Tragedy,* Dreiser seemed unable to write what he wrote best, novels. Instead, he became increasingly preoccupied with political writings and activities, and with a never-finished philosophical tome. To no avail his friend Sergei Dinamov, in Moscow, would exhort him to produce another novel:

SERGEI DINAMOV: It has been several years already that the world has not tottered under the sledgehammer of your books. Strike, Theodore, give the world such a blow that it fails [*sic*] to its feet at the count of ten.

———

In Russia, a new edition of the immensely popular *An American Tragedy* was published. Dreiser wrote Dinamov to see if some royalties could not be forwarded: "Just now I need the money." All his novels had been published in Russia in editions selling by the tens of thousands—without Dreiser's consent, or the payment to him of more than token royalties, as there was no copyright agreement between the United States and the Soviet Union.

In October 1927, on the eve of a celebration of the tenth anniversary of the Bolshevik revolution, and as Horace Liveright began his steep decline, Dreiser received a visit from F. G. Biedenkapp, the secretary of "a sort of Russian Red Cross,"† who invited him to attend the celebration as a guest of the Soviet government. He was one of the very few, among the fifteen hundred Americans invited "to witness the great strides made," whose expenses were to be *fully* covered and paid.

F. G. BIEDENKAPP: The Soviet believes you to be the outstanding literary intelligence of America.

———

Nevertheless, Dreiser told the Soviet representative that he was less interested in attending "any celebration or convention" than in seeing the famine districts on the Volga, the collective farms, and the Russians' engineering and mechanical achievements.

THEODORE DREISER: But supposing my opinion should prove unfavorable?
F. G. BIEDENKAPP: We will risk that.

———

---

*In 1946 Black would also bring out Edmund Wilson's *Memoirs of Hecate County,* which John Sumner pronounced the filthiest book ever published for general readership. The case that resulted became the first in history in which the Supreme Court read a novel in order to decide whether it was constitutionally protected or could be banned as obscene. In the end the Court split four to four on the question; this and the censorship case are described in Chapters 12 and 13 below.
†Actually the International Workers' Aid.

Dreiser's girlfriend, Helen Richardson, who had gotten over her most recent quarrel with the author, also liked the idea. She thought it would add to his prestige. But Helen had one problem.

HELEN RICHARDSON: You gonto [*sic*] fall in love with one of those Russian girls, and get yourself all tangled up again.

———

Dreiser made up his mind to go when he was told that he could stay in Russia a month or two, if he wished, and travel anywhere he wanted, still with all expenses paid. But he hated to leave his women friends B———, Ch———, Ella, Ruth, and Maude behind and knew they would not like his being away for so long either. He was "conscience stricken about Maude" and found "B——— at the office . . . upset by the change and more passionate than ever." He promised to bring back a Russian bracelet for B——— and Russian boots for Helen.

THEODORE DREISER: In spite of all my varietism, I realize that I really care for Helen. It is spiritual, not material. I feel sad at leaving her.

———

When Dreiser sailed, he was a believer in individualism and scoffed at socialism and communism. But he was also eager to see Russia so he could judge for himself. He admired Dostoyevsky and Gogol and Chekhov, and he respected the Russians for trying to form a model society, even though he was pretty sure they couldn't do it. He considered Trotsky "a zealot, a sort of Christ of the economists," and Lenin "a genius of government." Under their leadership, great things *could* happen.

On ship, he talked with the painter Diego Rivera, who criticized individualism. Rivera believed that since the masses gave the creative person his hearing, the artist could be great only when he identified with the masses. According to Rivera, Russia had carried this great truth into government as well, because the rulers were sensitive to the needs of the masses. Dreiser thought he "could wait and see."

When they stopped off in Paris, Ben Huebsch and he went to a café on the rue des Fous, where they met some of the people Dreiser had been hoping to meet—including Ernest Hemingway, with whom he discussed James Joyce and the French economy.

THEODORE DREISER: But Paris on Wednesday was delightful—a perfect fall day. And how many people I saw . . .

———

In Berlin he had a sore throat; his bronchitis was worse than ever. Forty people from the International Workers' Aid crowded into his hotel room, which was full of greetings and flowers. The doctor who was called to look Dreiser over said there was something wrong with his aorta and told him he must not go to such a primitive place as Russia—without a doctor as a companion.

THEODORE DREISER: I see it all—they think I am a millionaire—am I not an American!

———

Dreiser announced that he was going to Russia anyway, but later he was "seized with homesickness."

THEODORE DREISER: Here I am—nearly 4000 miles from N.Y.—9 or ten days at the shortest, and I am ill—maybe seriously. Supposing I were seriously ill—to die. And Helen so far away. And I have been so bad to her. I grow wretched and send a twenty word cable. If only she were here . . .

———

Later, the doctor told Dorothy Thompson, also en route to the Russian celebration, that he suspected Dreiser had the beginnings of lung cancer.

At the border Dreiser was boyishly excited when they were serenaded by a Russian band while changing cars. But on reaching Moscow he was let down.

THEODORE DREISER: But the wretched collection of autos. . . . The shabbiness. Georgia or Wyoming both would outclass them. And the people! The mixture of Europeans and Asiatics!

———

He wanted to interview Stalin and Trotsky before anyone else among the American literati who made this visit, but he did not meet either. In his journal he framed questions he thought to ask Stalin; and he saw a "model" Moscow prison.

THEODORE DREISER: The smells. The cells. Yet all a great improvement on what was in the days of the Czar.

———

He paid a visit to the Wobbly leader Bill Haywood, who was staying at the Hotel Lux.

THEODORE DREISER: [His room] is crowded with dubious radicals. He himself has aged dreadfully. I would not have believed that one so forceful could have sagged and become so flaccid and buttery. But life had beaten him as it beats us all.

———

A Russian woman took him for a walk in Red Square. He saw Lenin's tomb and the place where John Reed was buried. He remembered that Reed had signed Mencken's petition to free The "Genius" from censorship—but despite the five hundred signatures, the petition had done him no good. Dreiser walked with the woman back to his hotel.

THEODORE DREISER: I complain of loneliness & she comes up. We finally reach an agreement and she stays until two.

———

Two days later he saw a parade "like no other" passing before Lenin's tomb. Even though the decorations looked more like "a 14th Street Fire

Sale," he was moved by the thousands and thousands of men, women, and children who marched with banners and floats into Red Square—Ukrainians, Georgians, Kurds, Kazaks, Cossacks, Siberians. They gave an appearance of great national unity.

THEODORE DREISER: But mayhap this program is to [*sic*] beautiful to succeed;—an ideal of existence to which frail & selfish humanity can never rise. Yet I earnestly hope that this is not true—that this is truly the beginning of a better or brighter day for all.

———

He managed to get a better room, which overlooked Red Square and a huge sign reminding all within sight that religion was "the opiate of the people." He had a sunny view of the Kremlin:

THEODORE DREISER: The towers! The spires! The pinapple [*sic*] domes! And so gloriously colored—red, gold, blue, green, brown, white. . . . Baghdad! Aladdin['s] world! And yet real! Here before my eyes.

———

He dreamed one night that he was dancing in the nude, swinging a barbell "the while I threw myself joyously here & there." In reality, most of his time was devoted to work and research. He interviewed two Tass men and an *Izvestia* editor who talked of the perfect freedom of the press in Russia; he felt he was given the runaround. He did not get to take a tour of Siberia; they said it would make his bronchitis worse. He did tour around Leningrad, where he saw the Winter Palace, a circus, the library, the opera, and the museums and found a chance to ask an official: "What is the Soviet Government going to do with the loafer?" At a rubber factory, he interviewed the director and informed him of the achievements of American capitalists. But by then he wished he was out of Russia and at home on Fifty-seventh Street. He wrote Helen that in Russia "there may be bed bugs or a cockroach in the soup." The food was uniformly bad.

THEODORE DREISER: I find myself turning to Vodka—vodka plain, vodka in tea, vodka over a dessert in order that I make a go of things.

———

He made up his mind that he "would rather die in the United States than live here." Before leaving he wrote a fifteen-hundred-word statement of his impressions: "To the Russian People." In it, Dreiser praised individualism, doubted the success of communism, and lectured the Russian people on their poor appearance. Sixty years later one might say that Dreiser's message was heard—by Soviet President Mikhail S. Gorbachev.

THEODORE DREISER: Personally, I am an individualist and shall die one. In all this communistic welter, I have seen nothing that dissuades me in the least from my earlier perceptions of the necessities of man. One of these is the individual dream of self-advancement, and I cannot feel that even here Communism has altered that in the least. . . . The Russian house, the Russian yard, the Russian street, the Russian toilet, the Russian hotel, the individual Russian's attitude toward his own personal appearance . . . are neither creditable or wholesome and . . . cannot possibly be excused on the ground of poverty. There are as poor people in Holland, Germany, France, and England, as there are in Russia, but you would never find them tolerating the conditions which in Russia seem to be accepted as a matter of course. . . .

You live too many in one room and are even lunatic enough to identify it with a Communist spirit. I rise to complain. And I suggest in this connection that more individualism and less communism would be to the great advantage of this mighty country.

—

The "free" Soviet press, however, did not find Dreiser's "To the Russian People" important enough to publish.

In Paris, on his return, Dreiser was joined by Helen. They went to the Riviera, where he scowled at the gay crowd and the life that had so delighted him in October. In London he had an interview with Winston Churchill, then chancellor of the exchequer. When Churchill dismissed the Russian experiment as doomed to failure, Dreiser disagreed sharply and proceeded to criticize the poverty of English millworkers.

In London Dreiser also met George Moore.

GEORGE MOORE: I hoped to have a long chat on literature with the old fellow. And what do you imagine he spent the whole three hours talking about? About his prostate gland!

—

On the ship back to New York from Southampton, Dreiser recalled enough good in his experience of Russia to contrast social conditions there favorably with those in America. He told the ship news reporters that the Soviet Union was "splendid."

THEODORE DREISER: Nowhere in Russia will you find men in overcoats standing in bread lines. . . . I wasn't a communist when I went abroad and I don't return as one. [But] why should there be bread lines in a nation as rich as America?

—

In *The New York Times,* Simeon Strunsky retorted:

SIMEON STRUNSKY: Trotsky's case against Stalin, as printed in the *Pravda,* speaks of 2,000,000 unemployed. All the cables from Moscow speak of long queues before the food stores, soaring prices, and conditions suggesting famine. From all this it would appear that Mr. Dreiser in Russia did not employ the extraordinary gift for minute observation revealed in *An American Tragedy.*

THEODORE DREISER: Strunsky's charges just made me love Russia more. Certainly there were unemployed in Russia but they were all fed. Certainly there were queues, but not for bread, just for scarce items. I had seen no famine.

He wrote Strunsky: "You are so cruelly sarcastic, Mr. Strunsky, and so devilishly insinuating."

Dreiser once told George Jean Nathan: "I really don't need or want money though under the existing order of things you may be sure I want and get every dollar that is coming to me." The author's income tax notes for 1927 listed a gross income from royalties of $97,611.66. Eighteen years later, at the age of seventy-three, when the royalty income on the American editions of his books was almost nil, Dreiser wrote a letter to Stalin asking for an accounting of royalties on the huge sales of his books published in Russia. He had heard that several other American authors were receiving royalties. Two months later, Dreiser received from the Soviet government a credit in a Los Angeles bank for the spectacular amount of $34,600. Although he continued to "talk poor," this was more than enough money to solve all of his financial problems for the year that remained of his life.

During the spring of 1945, after the end of World War II, the United Nations met in San Francisco and some of the Russian delegates went to Los Angeles to visit Dreiser. In 1932, after that visit to Russia, Dreiser had tried to join the Communist party but was rejected, it has been suggested, because "as a member he would be as dangerous as Casanova in a convent." Earl Browder had turned him down, thinking "he did not seem quite adult which was part of his charm."

EARL BROWDER: He was surprised and hurt. He had expected to be welcomed with open arms.

By 1945, however, Browder had been removed as head of the CPUSA and William Z. Foster, whom Dreiser had always thought of as a "spiritual" man, was in his place. The aged and ailing Dreiser had been prodded by several Communists to join the party, and on July 20 he wrote Foster a long letter of application for membership. This time he was accepted.

WILLIAM Z. FOSTER: Dear Comrade Dreiser: Your letter of application for membership in the Communist Party was . . . unanimously and enthusiastically accepted by our recent National Convention in New York. . . . Our Party is indeed honored to have within its ranks a writer of your great literary stature and integrity.

The *New Masses* magazine of August 7, 1945, carried a banner headline: "DREISER JOINS THE VANGUARD!" In his letter of application, Dreiser had set forth his reasons for wishing to become a member.

THEODORE DREISER: I have believed intensely that the common people, and first of all the workers . . . are the guardians of their own destiny and the creators of their own future. I have endeavored to live by this faith, to clothe it in words and symbols, to explore its full meaning in the lives of men and women.

He once said that the details of the party line made no difference to him, and that he knew he could disagree with and criticize the party. "If they didn't like it, they could throw me out."

In 1946, the year after Dreiser joined the party, the federal government used the Smith Act to indict an ailing Foster and ten other leaders of the CPUSA for conspiring to teach and advocate the overthrow of the American government by force and violence. Two years later, under the influence of McCarthyism, the Supreme Court upheld the convictions of all these men (except Foster, who was not tried owing to his illness). They had been tried and convicted almost exclusively on the basis of their teachings from the Communist "classics,"* and "conspiracy" testimony from Earl Browder, whom the party had ejected. The Supreme Court's opinion justifying the decision adopted the reasoning of an opinion of the appellate court below, written by Judge Learned Hand; this gave Holmes's famous "clear and present danger" test for freedom of speech what the late Harry Kalven, Jr., had said was "the kiss of death."†

On June 13, 1944, Dreiser had secretly married his longtime girlfriend Helen Richardson in the lumber town of Stevenson, Washington. He joined her there on his return from a trip to New York, where he had gone to receive the American Academy's Award of Merit and a $1,000 cash prize for "extraordinary achievement in his art" and for his "courage and integrity in breaking trail as a pioneer in the presentation in fiction of real human beings and a real America." In Washington they stayed at the Sampson Hotel, overlooking the wildly beautiful Columbia gorge. Helen's sister Myrtle Patges and her fiancé, Chester Butcher, were their witnesses. The justice of the peace had no idea that the groom was a famous American

---

*The books were: Stalin, *Foundations of Leninism* (1924); Marx and Engels, *The Communist Manifesto* (1848); Lenin, *State and Revolution* (1917); and *History of the Communist Party of the Soviet Union.*

†*A Worthy Tradition,* edited by Jamie Kalven (1988), 191. The case was *Dennis* v. *United States,* 341 U.S. 494 (1951). Hand's disappointing opinion is at 183 F. 2d 201 (1950). Kalven devotes an entire chapter to the *Dennis* case, observing that it presented the country with a prime example of the defeat of the expectation and hope that the Supreme Court, confronted with "great events" and "great doctrinal" manifestations, would be stirred to a "great statement." "Everything conspired to make *Dennis* a great moment. . . . The trial, which lasted nine months, was almost certainly the great American political trial. . . . And the Court responded to it as a great case. . . . But in the end *Dennis* does not prove a great case, and today, after twenty years, it has no doctrinal significance in its own right" (190).

"*Dennis* does, however, retain considerable interest as the climax of the career of the clear and present danger test. It is at once the finest and the last hour of the test. The majority acknowledges clear and present danger as the constitutional meaning of free speech, but in the process, to meet the political exigencies of the case, it officially adjusts the test, giving it the kiss of death" (190–91). The bench of justices involved was the reactionary Vinson Court.

Within the First Amendment context, Kalven aptly characterized the government's charge against the eleven Communist leaders as "not that they were conspiring to overthrow the government, but that they were conspiring to talk about doing so" (196). That, in the event, is also what they were imprisoned for.

author because Teddie disguised his identity on the license application form as "Herman Dreiser."

On August 27, 1945, Helen gave Dreiser his last birthday party; he was seventy-four years old. On September 2, he wrote his old friend Mencken:

THEODORE DREISER: Dear Mencken: Just to let you know that I am on earth worthy or unworthy. Have just finished *The Bulwark*—(final revision) and like it very much. In another week or so expect to conclude *The Stoic.* . . .

How are you? The end of this international fighting* makes me feel better if it is really ended. I have often wondered how certain phases of it have affected you? There have been so many tragic angles. Regards, best wishes, affectionately, Dreiser.

———

According to Helen, Mencken did not reply, and that was the last of Dreiser's efforts to make up their differences. Swanberg thinks "Mencken's silence must have been a cruel blow." Later Mencken reportedly said that if death were to come slowly to Dreiser, "he'd end up being repentant and even embrace the Church," just as Heywood Broun did. "It always happens."

According to Helen, she and Teddie had never "been so close, mentally, spiritually and physically as we were the last year of his life." Even so, Dreiser used to "go out" on her. One of the other women who loved him, Estelle Manning, used to pick him up in her car, outside his front door— while Helen gazed angrily from the window—and take him to her home. Manning was a young Hollywood widow whom Dreiser had met during the summer of 1939 and whom he was encouraging in her writing. He once addressed a poem to her, fragments of which read:

> *I think of your Boticelli* [sic] *face and body!*
> *Your wistful, understanding, observing Eyes!*
> *Out of the renaissence* [sic]*—you!* . . .
>
> *It's Saturday,*
> *I'm lonely,*
> *For the room misses you.*
> *And the streets—*
> *And so do I—so much—*
> *And love you, too.*

At Manning's house he would stretch out with a drink and talk for hours. He told Estelle that he felt like "a prisoner" in his own home.

One night, in the middle of September, Dreiser got out of his bed, turned on the light, and called Helen, but when she entered his room, he

———

*World War II was over.

did not recognize her. He started prowling around the house looking for her, although she was trotting along at his side.

HELEN DREISER: I am Helen.

THEODORE DREISER: Everyone thinks she's Helen.

———

Helen told him she could prove it.

THEODORE DREISER: I'll believe you if you say so. . . .

———

The next time that happened, Helen drove to Marguerite Harris's place to ask her help in bringing Teddie back to reality. Marguerite had become one of Dreiser's literary companions. When the two women returned, Dreiser was lying on the couch. Marguerite entered his room.

THEODORE DREISER: It's odd. A strange woman has been here.

———

When Helen came in a moment later, he recognized her and seemed completely lucid.

For about a month after that Helen worked with him to finish *The Stoic.* She helped him to figure out a spiritual ending for Berenice's life: after Cowperwood's dreadful death, she goes to India, grieving, and finds comfort and understanding in yoga, thereafter devoting herself to doing good works.*

In the middle of October, in the midst of dinner at a Chinese restaurant, Dreiser became irrational again, all of a sudden. He told Helen he was worried about the strange woman who was at home—meaning Helen, who was sitting across the table from him. When Helen drove home with him, he looked around the house for her, although she was there at his side. Dr. Samuel Hirshfeld examined him, said the trouble was not deep-seated, and prescribed hormone injections and pills. When Dreiser was back to normal, they went to work together on the proofs for *The Bulwark,* which Helen was able to send back to Doubleday before Christmas.

The day before Christmas Dreiser called up Estelle Manning, wanting to be with her, so she drove over to get him and spent an enjoyable day with him.

ESTELLE MANNING: He complained so bitterly of the imprisoned life he was forced to live that I suggested again that perhaps if he would marry her [Helen], he might find life simpler. But he raged, and said that he had done many things for her, but that was one thing that he would never do. He wanted her to leave, and, as soon as *The Bulwark* was published, he would have more money to give her and then, maybe, she would go.

———

At his request Manning played "Drink to Me Only with Thine Eyes" on the piano.

---

*Swanberg thinks Helen, who was occasionally hearing Swami Praharanandal at the Vedanta Society, had something to do with that "bizarre conclusion."

ESTELLE MANNING: He seemed gay and relaxed—until I let him out of the car in front of his house. Then he wept terribly and said: "I am the loneliest man in the world." And he walked slowly in.

———

On Christmas Day he and Helen had breakfast at the beautiful home of their friends Mark and Lillian Goodman, and in the afternoon they visited another friend, Clare Kummer, in Beverly Hills. Dreiser sat beside Clare at the piano and grew tearful as she played and sang some of the old tunes that Dreiser's brother Paul had written, including "On the Banks of the Wabash," one of Dreiser's favorite tunes.

The next day, they had a drink at the Bowery cocktail lounge on Santa Monica Boulevard and Teddie talked nostalgically about Greenwich Village—how he could walk around there meeting friends everywhere. Helen said maybe they would go in May.

HELEN DREISER: [B]ut as we were talking, I wondered how disappointed he might be if he were unable to recapture something of the atmosphere he had known so well.

———

Dreiser spent the next day rewriting the next-to-last chapter of *The Stoic,* but he was exhausted by five, and so Helen took him for a drive to the beach at Venice, where they strolled along the boardwalk and watched the sun set in the Pacific. Helen called it "the most beautiful sunset I had ever seen." But when they got home Dreiser went immediately to bed, feeling kidney aches. Then, in the middle of the night, Teddie called to his wife, "*Helen,* I have an *intense* pain." Before she could stop him he managed to get out of bed and collapsed to the floor.

Helen called Dr. Hirshfeld, who put him in an oxygen mask, and by morning Dreiser seemed to be rallying. Esther Tobey dropped by and Helen, now hopeful, took her in to see him. Tobey asked Dreiser how he felt.

ESTHER TOBEY: He dropped his oxygen mask and said: "Bum." He looked gray and tired. Whenever he was sick he had a very helpless look. . . . His eyelashes, which were long and soft, lay separately when his lids were lowered, for some reason giving him a vulnerable look.

———

As Tobey drove to Santa Monica to get her husband, she noticed that "the bright unseasonably warm day had changed completely."

ESTHER TOBEY: There was a light fog and it was cold. Before I had gone more than a mile, the fog was so thick that I had to drive by the white lines. . . . Dreiser had spoken or written of death as an enveloping fog—"a woolly fog that blocks one's course and quenches all"—and recalling this as I drove made his death seem imminent.

———

At home, Dreiser asked Helen to kiss him. She did, twice.

HELEN DREISER: He looked steadily into my eyes saying: "You are beautiful." He had always said that to me, but I was frightened because he had
asked me to kiss him, and I wondered if he expected to die. If so, he did
not want to alarm me even at that stage, for he said nothing more.

———

For the next two hours, Dreiser lay still, watched closely by a male nurse.
Then the nurse ran to the phone and asked the doctor to come quickly:
"His breathing has become shallower and his fingertips are turning blue."

HELEN DREISER: I looked and saw that it was true. I held his hands; they
were cold and damp, and I felt his life slipping away through them. I felt
desperately helpless; he was going fast. His eyes were closed and there were
deep shadows around them. But there was such a hallowed peace enveloping him, which was reflected in his face! The peace that passeth all human
understanding had clothed him and he seemed elevated to another dimension. There was something magnificent in the dignity of his departure as
though every atom of his body was in complete repose.

His breath became shallower and shallower until I felt it stop. He was
gone. The doctor arrived and pronounced him dead at 6:50 P.M. I still
could not believe it but sat there an hour and a half longer until he began
to grow cold.

———

Dreiser had told Robert Elias, who used to come to talk to him about
philosophy, that what the world needed was more spiritual character, and
that "the true religion was in Matthew." Toward the end of his life, Dreiser
was willing to use the term "God" for the creative force in the world, but
he never did subscribe to any formal doctrine. To Mencken Dreiser had
written that he wished to leave his body to the ashman, or to Rush Medical
College; but once, with Helen, he had visited the famous Forest Lawn
"layout," and according to Helen, "Teddie remarked to me that he had
never seen a more beautiful resting place." In any event, that was where
Helen laid him to rest—with Hollywood film stars and producers and
corporate profiteers. This distressed some of Dreiser's friends.

The casket that Helen picked "was of beautiful dark rich red hardwood
mahogany, lined with a beautiful delicate shade of velvet." At the funeral
services, after the organist played Handel's "Largo" and Bach's "Come,
Kindly Death," the Congregational minister who had chanced to stop by
on Teddie's last day, and whose church the author had attended a few
times, read a service. And then the playwright John Howard Lawson paid
eloquent tribute to Dreiser's literary career and the social drives that had
finally led him to communism. His Communist friends had wished to make
the funeral a party affair, but Helen did not let them do so.

W. A. SWANBERG: In Russia [Dreiser] is pictured as an artist whose exposures
of capitalist decay were continually suppressed in America, who gradually
purged himself of his own bourgeois errors and finally experienced the
ultimate communistic revelation. They ignore Dreiser's pietistic *Bulwark,*

which reflects his final philosophy. They pass over his confusions and contradictions. They resent any suggestion that he was senile or mentally fatigued when he joined the Party.

———

Charlie Chaplin read Dreiser's poem from *Moods,* called "The Road I Came," which he had written a dozen years before, and which would be engraved on Dreiser's tombstone:

> *Ah, what is this*
> *That knows*
> *The road I came*
> *And go again?*
>
> *Oh, space!*
> *Change!*
> *Toward which we run*
> *So gladly,*
> *Or from which we retreat*
> *In terror—*
> *Yet that promises to bear us*
> *In itself*
> *Forever.*
>
> *Oh, what is this*
> *That knows the road I came?*

Just before the coffin was closed, Helen placed her sonnet "To a Poet" beside his body. A week later, she sent out letters with a copy of the services, and her poem, to Dreiser's friends, including some of the women in his life: Kirah Markham, Estelle Manning, and others he had loved. "It is a miracle to be loved by such a man," Helen wrote. When her book, *My Life with Dreiser,* was published in 1951, it bore this inscription: *"To the unknown women in the life of Theodore Dreiser, who devoted themselves unselfishly to the beauty of the intellect and its artistic unfoldment."*

W. A. SWANBERG: Dreiser was buried very expensively in Lot 1132 of the Whispering Pines section of the necrolatric splendor called Forest Lawn, hard by the grave of Tom Mix.

———

A letter Mencken sent to Helen containing a statement about Dreiser was not read at the funeral:

H. L. MENCKEN: While Dreiser lived all the literary snobs and popinjays of the country, including your present abject servant, devoted themselves to reminding him of his defects. He had, to be sure, a number of them. . . . But the fact remained that he was a great artist, and that no other American of his generation left so wide and handsome a mark upon the national letters. American writing, before and after his time, differed almost as much as biology, before and after Darwin. He was a man of large originality, of profound feeling, and of unshakeable courage.

W. A. SWANBERG: The newspapers, which had wearied of Dreiser's latter day fulminations and given him little space, headlined his death—some like the *New York Times* giving elaborate summations of his career. But no newspaper could catch the prodigious drama of this strange life—the sensitive, shoeless Indiana boy with hurts that were never healed, the anguish over the stillborn *Sister Carrie* . . . then his long bitter struggle for freedom and acceptance that would be his greatest glory and that ended with *An American Tragedy* in 1925. The work he had done had built a bridge between Howells and Hemingway that no one else could have built. And the work was colossal in its own right.

In 1945 it was easy to forget that blood had been spilled in the battle for freedom; the man who had felt most of the pain had been out of the mainstream for twenty years. One can picture readers, those who remembered him at all, saying: "Dreiser? I thought he was dead long ago."

———

Three months after Dreiser's death Soviet representatives called on Helen, read the will to be sure she was his heir, and gave her $7,000 in additional royalties. Dreiser's estate, including a hoard of twenty-dollar gold pieces, was worth more than $100,000. Everything was left to Helen, with a request that she pay income from the estate to his surviving relatives, and that on her death half be bequeathed to them and the other half to a Negro orphanage of her choice. In 1951 Helen suffered a cerebral hemorrhage that immobilized her; four years later she died and was buried at Forest Lawn, alongside Dreiser.

Dreiser's lifetime dream, the publication of a collected edition of his prodigious work, was never realized in America. The World Publishing Company came closest, issuing an edition of his six greatest novels and his best short stories. But in Moscow, in 1951, the state publishing house issued a 900,000-copy, twelve-volume edition of Dreiser's work together with 150,000 copies of an anthology of his essays and articles.

LESTER COHEN: As far as I know, there is no *Theodore Dreiser Street* in the United States—there is one in Yugoslavia.

———

Over cocktails, Dreiser had once talked to the psychiatrist A. A. Brill about his pessimistic philosophy of life—a philosophy that seems almost to have foreshadowed Samuel Beckett's:

THEODORE DREISER: [There is] nothing to hope for, nothing to live for, nothing to be honorable for, nothing to be dishonest for. . . .

I think [life] is a lousy deal, and if there is any motivating consciousness or intelligence or whatever it is, that understands the meaning of the word lousy, I hope he hears me.

10

The Knopfs "Ratted" on John

IN BOSTON on April 18, 1929, Donald Friede's criminal conviction for selling Theodore Dreiser's *An American Tragedy* was upheld by Massachusetts's highest court. The next day another criminal complaint against Friede—this one in New York for publishing a novel about lesbians—was thrown out of court. The novel was *The Well of Loneliness.* The author, an Englishwoman whose baptismal name was Marguerite, was known to her friends as John. The name she used on the book's cover was Radclyffe Hall.

Radclyffe Hall, or John, was a handsome, charming, intelligent, well-to-do woman of forty-seven when *Well* was published in England, in 1928, by the reputable house of Jonathan Cape. She was well known in literary and academic circles since her critically acclaimed first novel, *Adam's Breed,* had sold 27,000 copies within a matter of weeks; it was published in several languages and won the Prix Femina. At literary gatherings John wore mannish clothing and smoked green cigars; the press took to running pictures of her under captions such as "Man or Woman?"

John's idea was to write a long and very serious novel entirely upon the subject of sexual inversion.

RADCLYFFE HALL: So far as I know, nothing of the kind had ever been attempted before in fiction. Hitherto the subject has either been treated as pornography, or introduced as an episode . . . or veiled. . . . I have treated it "as a fact in nature—a simple, though at present tragic, fact." I have written the life of a woman who is a born invert, and have done so with what I believe to be sincerity and truth; and while I have refused to camouflage in any way, I think I have avoided all unnecessary coarseness.

—

The Well of Loneliness was written and published at a time when homosexuality could not be discussed in English books or the English press. Unlike male inversion—which as late as 1897 made a criminal and a social outcast of the brilliant writer and raconteur Oscar Wilde,* the female kind was not officially acknowledged to exist in England. In 1920, the House of Lords declined to amend the criminal laws of England to include lesbians because the Lords did not admit such people lived. There was good precedent for the Lords' view: during her reign Queen Victoria vetoed a bill that would have put female homosexuals in prison because she would not concede there was such a thing as a lesbian in England. The unofficial reason why the British government would not let homosexuality be discussed publicly, even in books, was presumably the fear that such discussion would encourage homosexual relations among people who theretofore had been unaware of the existence of "the love that dare not speak its name."

---

*Richard Ellmann's recent biography *Oscar Wilde* (1988) contains extensive accounts of Wilde's trials for the "unmentionable crime" but provides scant detail of the legal aspects. Male homosexual activity was savagely punished in nineteenth-century England. Oscar Wilde was imprisoned for only two years (after which he left England, never to return), but working-class men convicted of sodomy were regularly hanged—sixty in the first three decades of the century and another score under naval law. Hanging seems to have been reserved for those caught practically in the act; men arrested in cases where both penetration and emission could not be proved were convicted of assault or attempted sodomy and given the "lesser" punishment of the pillory, which also might be the lot of authors and publishers convicted of "obscene" or "blasphemous" libel. Pillory, for some, proved worse than hanging. In 1780, "[a] man was pilloried in Southwark for an unnatural crime, and the criminal was so treated by the mob that he actually died the moment he was taken from the machine." Louis Crompton: *Byron and Greek Love* (1985), 251–52. The pillory was abolished in 1815, and in 1861 the penalty for sodomy was reduced to life imprisonment. Persons higher in the social order usually escaped legal punishment after conviction by fleeing to France or Italy, where homosexuals were let alone. Wilde was given a chance to escape his punishment but delayed taking it until too late. Ellmann, 466ff. Jeremy Bentham had wished to come out for the abolition of punishment for homosexuality but was deterred throughout his lifetime from publishing some 500 pages of opinions and arguments that he wrote to that end, for fear that public reproach would undermine all his great work toward the reform of criminal law on the grounds of utility, that is, in accordance with the utilitarian "greatest happiness" principle. Bentham, by 1861, was privately quite radical on the subject: he was then arguing that homosexuality had positively beneficial effects. Says Crompton: "He had in one bound overleaped the position of such cautious reformers as the late nineteenth century produced (men like John Addington Symonds, Havelock Ellis, and Edward Carpenter) and anticipated the 'Gay is good' stand of liberationists in the 1970's" (256).

Crompton says that at a trial in 1870, the attorney general expressed his appreciation that there was "very little learning or knowledge upon this subject in this country"; and "a defense counselor thanked God that such scientific literature was still foreign to the libraries of British medical men." But the controversy over the Wilde case and the intense hostility it aroused led Havelock Ellis (in collaboration with John Addington Symonds) to write *Sexual Inversion*. A German edition appeared without difficulty in 1896, but the English edition was destroyed by a magistrate and the police. America, in this instance, proved more tolerant. See Crompton's *Byron and Greek Love*, 370–71; Bernard Knox's review of that book in *The New York Review of Books*, December 19, 1985; and Phyllis Grosskurth, *Havelock Ellis: A Biography* (1985), Chapter 12. In England, in 1967, homosexual acts conducted in private between consenting adults (aged twenty-one and over) were decriminalized by act of Parliament. In 1986, in the States, the Supreme Court refused to rule unconstitutional as a violation of the right of privacy a Georgia statute punishing homosexual conduct in private between consenting males (*Bowers* v. *Hardwick*, 478 U.S. 186).

In this situation it was courageous of John to decide to write a book like *Well* and seek to have it openly published, even though the appearance of an autobiographical novel by a female invert could hardly be expected to precipitate a criminal prosecution for sodomy.* Although written as a novel, *Well* was transparently autobiographical: informed readers were likely to conclude that its author was a woman of the type described. *Well*'s publication, therefore, also involved a bold step "out of the closet" by John. Since the author knew that the book would bring her lover Una out as well, she asked her permission before writing it.

UNA TROUBRIDGE: John came to me one day with unusual gravity and asked for my decision in a serious matter: she had long wanted to write a book on sexual inversion, a novel that would be accessible to the general public who did not have access to technical treatises. . . . It was her absolute conviction that such a book could only be written by a sexual invert, who alone could be qualified by personal knowledge and experience to speak on behalf of a misunderstood and misjudged minority. It was with this conviction that she came to me, telling me that in her view the time was ripe, and that although the publication of such a book might mean the shipwreck of her whole career, she was fully prepared to make any sacrifice except—the sacrifice of my peace of mind. She pointed out that in view of our union and of all the years that we had shared a home, what affected her must also affect me and that I would be included in any condemnation. Therefore she placed the decision in my hands and would write or refrain as I should decide.

I am glad to remember that my reply was made without so much as an instant's hesitation: I told her to write what was in her heart, that so far as any effect upon myself was concerned, I was sick to death of ambiguities, and only wished to be known for what I was and to dwell with her in the palace of truth.

———

From the age of sixteen, John had fallen in and out of love with other women. Her first serious falling-in-love occurred when she was eighteen. She fell in love, she liked to tell Una, with "a voice . . . the lovely pure soprano voice of Alberto Visetti's pupil, Agnes Nichols."

UNA TROUBRIDGE: For several years she worshipped and served and followed that voice around her home and to and fro on the initial stages of

---

*E. M. Forster was afraid to publish his homosexual autobiographical novel, *Maurice*, while he was alive. In 1971, a year after Forster died, *Maurice* was published in the United States. William Burroughs's mordantly comic novel of the same type, *Queer*, could not be published openly in the United States until 1985, thirty years after the book was written, and twenty years after the publication of Burroughs's "unpublishable" *Naked Lunch*. *Naked Lunch*, which I successfully defended against Massachusetts censorship during the early sixties, combined heterosexual and homosexual activity so assiduously that the book was received less as a "gay" novel than as a "super-sexed" one. Critic Joseph Epstein reviewed the Viking Press edition of *Maurice* in *The New York Times Book Review*, October 10, 1971, saying that the book had "recently" been published in England as well. Marcia Pally reviewed *Queer* (published by Viking Press) in *The Advocate* (a gay periodical), January 7, 1986.

a big career. . . . [The voice] was unique, and once heard quite unforgettable: a strange blend of woman, choir-boy and angel, and, in justice to Alberto Visetti it must be admitted, most beautifully produced. I cannot wonder that John, adolescent, intensely musical and emotional, listening day by day in her own home to the gradual evolution of this exquisite thing, fell deeply in love both with the voice and the singer.*

———

John had three long-term lovers: Mabel Batten, known as Ladye—a beautiful, intelligent, cultured, older woman whom John Singer Sargent once painted "in full vocal flight"; Una Troubridge, Ladye's twenty-eight-year-old cousin, who became John's lover shortly before Ladye's death, while married to the "handsomest man in the British Navy"; and Evgenia Souline, a young nurse from Russia who found employment in Paris with Una and John and lived and traveled with them intermittently thereafter, almost until John's death.

UNA TROUBRIDGE: Of her earliest days, beyond the ill-treatment that she suffered, I know very little. She hated dolls, loved drums and noisy toys, but such tastes are common to many girl children and might seem to have had little if any significance had the future not confirmed the fact of her sexual inversion. . . .

She was still very young when she shed the baptismal name of Marguerite, selected by her mother, and became known to her friends as Peter . . . a name that later was replaced so universally by John that for years many people knew her by no other.

———

John early displayed a "passionate temper." According to Una, her friend's earliest memory of it was of "lying flat on her face in a new white plush coat in Kensington Garden, in protest against being put back into her pram when what she wanted to do was walk."

John told Una that her mother beat her brutally, at times with both fists. The child's only protection was her "aging grandmother who loved her but was too weak and too much intimidated by bullying and actual violence to protect her." John's father left the home when she was three—her mother had divorced him. Detesting her husband, she did not want to bear his child and "vainly tried every expedient to defeat gestation." An additional misfortune, in the eyes of her mother, was that John resembled her father.†

UNA TROUBRIDGE: She was a beautiful child to look at. There is a life-size painting of her at five years old which the grandmother commissioned from Mrs. Katinka Amyat, the leading child portraitist of her day. . . . A blue-

———

*According to Michael Baker, "[t]heirs was not a sexual relationship." *Our Three Selves: The Life of Radclyffe Hall* (1985), 23.

†After John's death, her mother wrote bitter letters to Una accusing John of financially neglecting and abandoning her. Richard Ormrod, *Una Troubridge: The Friend of Radclyffe Hall* (1985), 283–84.

eyed, golden haired little girl in a muslin frock and white socks sitting on a flowery bank, holding a bunch of oxeye daisies. But the child has beautiful features and looks out at you with brave honest eyes and an enchanting, jovial half-smile.

———

There was "a pathetic photograph" of John that Una often examined—a "faded shiny carte-de-visite obviously taken to exploit the 'paternal' affection of Alberto Visetti," the singing teacher who became her stepfather. In this picture John "looked a very thin, bony little girl of about ten, very unbecomingly dressed and with all the appearance of an unloved child." She stood "awkwardly" beside the seated Visetti, who "already was getting rather portly, the epitome of smug self-satisfaction and conceit." The marriage of John's mother to this man, who was her mother's singing master, was "a disastrous affair" for John. Thereafter, the child's maintenance and education were relegated to an amiable but "very inexpensive governess" and day schools near the large house where they had settled down, in Earl's Court.

UNA TROUBRIDGE: A short period of attending King's College was followed by a year in Dresden at a pension where the girls were allowed one bath a week. . . . that completed John's "education."

———

John was a sickly child who since infancy had suffered from bronchial asthma, which kept her sitting up night after night and precluded her from active play or exercise by day. She had double pneumonia at least three times before she was ten, as well as pleurisy, which left her lungs in ravaged condition.

UNA TROUBRIDGE: I remember Professor Lapiccirella of Florence saying to me: "It is a mystery that she ever recovered and lived. By all ordinary reckoning she should have died. She must often have felt terribly ill!"

———

Despite this sickliness as a child, John grew to be an active, even energetic, woman.

UNA TROUBRIDGE: She was exceedingly handsome, had plenty of charm, plenty of intelligence, plenty of money, and was out exclusively to enjoy herself and to give others a good time. She systematically over-smoked, anything and everything, including green cigars. Drank freely on occasion but only in congenial company and . . . drove her cousin Jane Randolph (later Caruth) all over the States in a primitive car with one spark-plug at the back and a revolver handy for obstreperous negroes. There was also an aggressive bull-terrier, Charlie, as auxiliary protection.

———

Other women also found John attractive. In 1929, she was described this way by the author Ethel Mannin, a longtime admirer:

ETHEL MANNIN: She has a beautiful head, and sleek close-cropped fair hair with a slight wave; keen, steel-gray eyes, a small, sensitive mouth, a delicately aquiline nose, and a charming boyish smile, which lights up the pale gravity of her face remarkably, dispelling that faint suggestion of severity, which it has in repose. She has slender ankles and wrists, and beautiful, sensitive fingers, and she is slightly built without giving an impression of smallness; there is about her, generally, a curious mingling of sensitiveness and strength, a sort of clean-cut hardness.

UNA TROUBRIDGE: [I]n spite of a far from robust constitution, her nervous system was as young and as reckless as she was herself. It supplied all the necessary fuel and she was often very energetic indeed . . . was devoted to love-making, to hunting (sometimes five days a week), to riding and mastering unmanageable horses; to rushing about by car, boat or train (at that time the air was not available!) to any new place that took her fancy.

John was the first woman Una had sexual relations with, and also the last. Una recorded the time when they made love for the first time:

UNA TROUBRIDGE: I can shut my eyes now & recall the luncheon she had prepared for me—& trying to eat while I summoned my resolution to leave immediately—& all that followed, & in the evening our walking along the valley road to where the lights ended and the hedges began—& so back to the White Cottage with a bond forged between us that has endured for over 23 years.

At first John called her book *Stephen,* after the protagonist; but then Una suggested the title *The Well of Loneliness.* In England, no sooner was it published than the book was banned. Resentful of her book's treatment by the government, the press, and the judiciary, John took Una with her into exile to Paris, leaving Una's husband behind. According to Admiral Troubridge, John was responsible for "wrecking" his home.

The Well of Loneliness came out two years after John's *Adam's Breed,* the story of a waiter who grew so weary of handling food that he allowed himself to die of starvation. Its success convinced John that she must dare in her next book to deal with "sexual inversion."

The term was coined by a German physician, Carl Westphal, who published a book entitled *Sexual Inversion* in 1870. It was given further currency in 1897 by Havelock Ellis, who used it as the title for the first volume in his celebrated work *Studies in the Psychology of Sex.* Ellis's *Sexual Inversion* was immediately banned; the London police and courts feared it would encourage homosexuality. The book did not reappear in England for fifty-six years.

The ban did not prevent John and Una from learning of Ellis's revolutionary views. According to Ellis, sexual inversion was not a vice; it signified that a person's sexual instinct had been "turned by inborn constitutional abnormality toward persons of the same sex." In her novel, John adopted the same point of view. These were the first serious works in English to treat homosexuality as a congenital anomaly, an accident of nature, rather than a crime or a loathsome disease.

It is said that Dean William Inge of St. Paul's threw his copy of Ellis's book into the fire. Marie Stopes, who had written several books on "normal" sexual behavior—which were censored by the police and fought over in the courts—charged that reading it was like "breathing a bag of soot," that it made her "feel choked and dirty for three months." Even the radical feminist leader Margaret Sanger took the same attitude. But Ellis's *Sexual Inversion* was a balm to Radclyffe Hall's tortured feelings.

Ellis met John and Una shortly after the final manuscript of *Well* was completed; he found them "terribly modern and shingled and monocled"—not at all his cup of tea. But John sent Ellis a copy of her manuscript, asking him to give her a "notice" for the book, and his words of appreciation became the book's preface. The scientist commended *Well*'s "fine qualities as a novel" and claimed for it "a notable psychological and sociological significance." He also referred to the fact that women of the sort that John wrote about were "sometimes of the highest character and the finest attitudes."

HAVELOCK ELLIS: [I]t is the first English novel which presents, in a completely faithful and uncompromising form, one particular aspect of sexual life as it exists among us today.

—

On April 17, 1928, John gave her literary agent, Audrey Heath, three bound copies of the typescript of *Well*, and a covering letter for Newman Flower of the publishing house Cassell's, which had published *Adam's Breed* and had an option on her next book. Now that she had "put her pen to service for some of the most persecuted and misunderstood people in the world," John was determined to allow "not one word" to be changed by the publisher. She informed Flower that although she would feel very sorry to sever her connection with Cassell's, unless, upon reading the book, he felt "prepared to go all out on it and to stand behind it to the last ditch," then "for both their sakes—as well as for the sakes of those for whom the book had been written"—the publisher should not take it. After reading *Well*, Flower "reluctantly concluded" that he should decline it, despite his liking for John and although he said he considered *Well* "one of the finest books to have gone through his hands." The difficulty was, of course, *Well*'s subject matter. Flower feared it could harm other books on the Cassell's list and was inappropriate for a publishing house that catered mainly to the circulating-library trade—which, as we have seen, normally would not handle a work that might possibly tarnish the morals of young girls.

Audrey Heath next sent the manuscript to Heinemann, which had published books by Lawrence, Joyce, Dreiser, and other controversial writers. At Heinemann, an editor named Evans was "full of admiration" for *Well* but fearful that its "propagandist tone" would damage the firm's reputation "by inspiring a chorus of severe criticism and fanatical abuse." Evans added that he regretted his firm's courage was not as great as John's, and he wanted John to know "how profoundly her book had moved us."

After that, publisher Martin Secker read the manuscript and praised John's gifts; he said he would be delighted to publish John's *next* novel, but not this one. At the moment, although neither Audrey Heath nor John knew it, Secker was quietly planning to publish *Extraordinary Women,* a satirical novel about a lesbian colony in Capri, by Compton Mackenzie. John was furious when she eventually heard about that book—it appeared just after *The Well of Loneliness*—because she thought it sought to exploit her fame, and the advertising implied that John was herself one of the novel's flamboyant characters. The authorities never bothered the Mackenzie book, probably because it was satirically written.

Heath sent *Well* next to Jonathan Cape, who had made a great success of T. E. Lawrence's *Seven Pillars of Wisdom* and was also doing well with American writers, among them Hemingway and Lewis. Cape, who had a flair for publicity, was shrewd and discriminating in his selection of authors. Once he read the typescript, he realized that he had in hand "a good piece of publishing property." The publisher took John, Una, and Audrey Heath to lunch at the Berkeley Grill and set out his strategy for *Well.*

When Cape proposed that he issue *Well* in a limited edition of 1,250 copies, priced at 25 shillings, John was shocked. That was three times the average cost of a novel and to John suggested "under-the-counter sales to the prurient." Cape promised, however—if the book "caught on"—to follow up with a larger, cheaper edition. John thought this "had a ring of pusillanimity" and was not persuaded by Cape's further argument that the steep price would keep the book out of the reach of sensation-mongers. What seemed to win her over was Cape's willingness to assume the substantial financial risks publication would entail for his firm, and also the confidence the publisher exuded, and his enthusiastic praise for *Well.* John may also have been impressed by Cape's offer to pay her by far the largest advance she had ever received. She accepted and later did something unprecedented for her: she contributed £150 to the publisher's budget for advertising and promotion. She was fearful that Compton Mackenzie's novel would draw attention from her book.

The Well of Loneliness was meant by John to "tear away the veil of ignorance" cloaking one aspect of the lives of some women. Although John knew that the publication of her novel might destroy her promising literary career, she went ahead because she considered it her special mission to write "a true story of sexual inversion," one that "would make the plight of women like myself known to the general public." Only someone like herself, "qualified by personal knowledge and experience," could speak "on behalf of the misunderstood and misjudged minority to which I belonged."

Jonathan Cape published *The Well of Loneliness* in 1928. It was a long novel, over five hundred pages in the first edition, which was produced in a large format with a sombre black binding and a plain wrapper. Cape changed his mind about initially issuing the book in an expensive limited edition of 1,250 copies and instead brought it out in a regular edition of 1,500 copies, at the more affordable price of 15 shillings. Having learned that Martin Secker in England and the Vanguard Press in the United States were planning September publication of the lesbian novel by Compton Mackenzie, Cape moved *Well*'s publication date up from autumn to midsummer, fearing that the Mackenzie book would undercut *Well*'s impact. In any event, Cape said: "Once our edition was printed I held standing type to await the verdict of the public."

Review copies were sent to all the serious papers and periodicals but not to the popular ones, for fear they would make the book's publication a sensational news story. Cape also sent complimentary copies to a select group of literary figures who, he believed, would immediately grasp his, and the author's, "sober purpose." The first reviews discussed the book seriously, praising it for its honest attempt to present a difficult subject. Although some reviewers, including Leonard Woolf, expressed misgivings that the author's purposes included a "propagandistic" appeal to the reader to sympathize with the tragic figure of the sexual invert, most acclaimed the literary merits of *Well*. Ida Wylie showered Miss Hall with compliments in *The Sunday Times*, and *The Daily Telegraph* recognized the novel as a fine work of art finely conceived and finely written. Within a week of publication, major outlets such as The Times Book Club, and even W. H. Smith's circulating library and Truslove, had sold out their stock, and Cape ordered a second printing; John reveled, for a moment, in having "smashed the conspiracy of silence." But two weeks later, in the *Sunday Express,* James Douglas took the book's theme, female homosexuality, as the subject for his weekly article. He lashed out at John's book.

JAMES DOUGLAS: The book gives evidence of a pestilence afoot which is devastating young souls—called Sexual Inversion and Perversion. Those horrors are flaunting themselves in public places with increasing effrontery, and more insolently provocative bravado. Certain authors and publishers have assumed the position of serving as decadent apostles for the most hideous and loathsome vices, no longer deigning even to conceal their degeneracy and degradation. . . . I say deliberately that this novel is not fit to be sold by any bookseller or to be borrowed from any library. . . . I would rather give a healthy boy or a healthy girl a phial of prussic acid than this novel. Poison kills the body, but moral poison kills the soul.

—

Douglas soon added a call for Jonathan Cape to confess publicly that he had made a dreadful mistake in publishing the book and insisted that it "be withdrawn immediately from sale." If Cape failed to do that, the editor urged, Home Secretary Sir William Joynson-Hicks—known as "Jix"—

should "set the law in motion,"* as he had done more than once against D. H. Lawrence's "filthy" productions.

Breakfasting together in bed, John and Una read Douglas's attack against *Well* in the *Sunday Express*. It seemed to John that Douglas held "to a strange conception of Christianity which led him to think that because God permits certain types to be born into the world they should be thrust aside, or ignored, or worse." The editor had sent along to Jonathan Cape advance galleys of his diatribe, a few days before its appearance in the *Sunday Express*. And in anticipation of that Sunday piece, the Saturday edition of the newspaper ran banner headlines: "A BOOK THAT MUST BE SUPPRESSED." The newspaper also hung posters on city bookstalls, advertising the story and urging everyone to buy Sunday's edition. To Cape's delight, Londoners responded by buying out not only the Sunday edition of the newspaper but virtually the entire first printing of *Well*. Hoping for just such an eventuality, Cape had already ordered a second impression of 3,000 copies.

In Paris, on the day *The Well of Loneliness* first appeared in the stores, telegrams and flowers poured into John and Una's house. The lovers eagerly went out to reconnoiter the bookshops and savor the excitement that had been aroused by *Well*.

Una had packed her daughter, Andrea, off to Guide camp for the summer to keep her out of the way. She was busy with a translation from the French of a book for the American firm Boni and Liveright, while John spent most of her time arranging for translations of *Well* and corresponding with her readers. When one young woman asked John if toleration of "the third sex" would ever come, the author replied that Havelock Ellis "thought there was a faint light in the darkness, but that it would probably not come in our lifetime." John mused that the woman "was only 23 and I could not help visualizing the many stony miles that her feet must tread."

In America John's book would have a difficult birth because of the uproar in England. Doubleday, which had published John's *Adam's Breed* and so had an option to publish *Well*, declined the book. So did the old house Harper, after "almost" accepting it. Next, Audrey Heath, at John's insistence, sent the manuscript to Roger Scaife of Houghton Mifflin, "who was begging to have a chance at it." John liked Scaife because it was he who had introduced her to Havelock Ellis, and he had also sent her a collection of Amy Lowell's poems, "which she adored." But the firm was situated in Boston, where, as John knew, the Watch and Ward Society had great influence; and so Houghton Mifflin, too, shied away from publishing *Well*.

---

*This was not the first time the editor of the *Sunday Express* had denounced a book and alerted the authorities. In May 1922, Douglas reported to his readers that he had read James Joyce's *Ulysses*—this would have been a copy of Sylvia Beach's Paris edition—and found it "the most infamously obscene book in ancient or modern literature." "All the secret sewers of vice," Douglas warned, were "canalized in its flood of unimaginable thoughts, images and pornographic words." The same year, an entire printing of *Ulysses,* comprising 500 copies, was intercepted by customs at Folkestone, England, and burned. See Chapter 2.

About this time, in London, at a party given by Heinemann at the Windmill Press, John met Blanche Knopf.* Blanche asked the author who was publishing *Well* in America. When John told her the matter was "unsettled," she asked John to send a copy of the manuscript to her at the Carlton Hotel that night. John did so, and a few days later Blanche Knopf purchased an option on the book for two weeks.

She liked the book at first, for it fit into the Knopf list of vanguard books of European origin—intellectual, liberal, searching, poetic in character. On the other hand, she also realized immediately that *The Well of Loneliness* was a dangerous book, "dealing so directly that way, with sex." But John's novel had a clear and definite point of view "concerning a subject long avoided and evaded by authors and publishers" and so she recommended that Alfred Knopf draw up a contract with Miss Hall.

Alfred Knopf was not so keen as Blanche was to take on *Well,* fearing problems from the New York Society for the Suppression of Vice. At the outset he insisted that the contract contain a clause making John *solely* responsible financially for delays or expenses that might arise out of legal difficulties. John would not hear of it and struck the clause out of the copies of the contract she signed and sent back to Knopf. Knopf requested time to give his lawyers a chance to review the situation, but within two weeks he gave in. Blanche had heard that if he did not, John would offer the book to Harcourt Brace. A friend of John's, May Lamberton Becker, was a great friend of Ellen Harcourt's and the literary editor of the *Herald Tribune:* she was reportedly in London "aching for the chance" to get *Well* into Harcourt's hands.

John liked Blanche Knopf personally but found her business methods "unusual and tortuous," owing "to the fact that she is a woman."

RADCLYFFE HALL: I am accustomed to dealing with men in business, to going perfectly straight for a point, and above all to sticking to essentials. I find it both difficult and tedious to deal with a woman, and this I have several times told her quite frankly, asking her to settle all business deals with my agents. The trouble is that she has a great hankering for "the personal touch," and this I consider a great mistake.

———

Blanche Knopf was taking the baths in a sanatorium in Baden-Baden, and so Alfred wired the acceptance to Miss Hall. Blanche then sent along a personal note, saying "so happy we are doing you!" In a letter to John, Alfred assured his new author that the book struck him as "a very fine work indeed, the first half being simply superb." He also confided to her his "very great hopes for the book's success," notwithstanding the legal difficulties

———

*Before her marriage, Blanche had been Alfred A. Knopf's office assistant and fiancée. As Mrs. Knopf, she was made a full-time partner and was "widely respected for her intuition, aggressiveness, and shrewdness. Alfred and Blanche Knopf always saw themselves as editors as well as publishers, and persuasively brought in at least two thirds of the titles on any Borzoi list." Allen Churchill, *A Literary Decade* (1971), 177.

that might be instigated by Mr. Sumner of the New York anti-vice society. Knopf impressed upon John that her book would appear as "a very good-looking volume," under the Knopf imprint. Soon, from aboard the *Aquitania*, Blanche sent John a card promising "Full Steam Ahead"; but by the time she disembarked in New York, the outlook was "far from hopeful."

The firm mailed out to the trade, as a supplement to the fall catalogue, a four-page leaflet on *Well*, which stressed the book's qualities and quoted from Havelock Ellis's preface to the Cape edition. But on the day of the mailing Alfred learned that after the *Sunday Express* attack on *Well*, Jonathan Cape had practically *invited* the government to censor the book. He had written a letter to the *Express*, defending the book and his decision to publish it, but also stating that copies had been sent to the home secretary and the director of public prosecutions, and that the publisher would withdraw the book "if this would serve the best interests of the public." The newspaper, of course, promptly printed Cape's letter; this as promptly evoked a strongly worded reply from the home secretary himself, instructing Cape to discontinue publication of *Well*. Unless *Well* was immediately withdrawn from sale, official proceedings would be started looking to its suppression. So Cape stopped selling *Well* in England.

Sir William Joynson-Hicks was quite possibly the most ridiculed and reviled of England's home secretaries during the twentieth century. In *The Oxford English History* he is called "the Preposterous Jix." Jix "saw a Communist under every bed" and conducted the affairs of his office accordingly. He was also known to his critics as "the Policeman of the Lord," for he had fervently and effectively opposed the "revised Prayer Book," and had written books on the need to censor works he considered immoral. Jix even took the opportunity provided by the uproar over John's book to propose that a system be established for the prior censorship of books published in England, similar to the system that existed for the prior censorship of stage plays. Not since the seventeenth century had English authors and publishers been forced to submit to prepublication censorship. Opposed by some of the press as a device whereby the home secretary "would constitute himself the sole authority to decide whether or not a book should be published," the proposal received short shrift. Commented *The Daily Telegraph:* "Even if we had perfect confidence in the infallibility of the Home Secretary's taste in literature we should still maintain that it was against the public interest to suppress every book which he found undesirable or disturbing."

When Cape discontinued publication of Radclyffe Hall's book, he also secretly ordered his printer to make molds of the type "as soon as possible," and deliver them to him.* He then flew the molds to Paris and licensed

---

*"Printing moulds are thinnish sheets of papier-mâché made by first dampening them and then beating them on to the surface of type until they retain an exact impression, as it were in reverse, of the type. Then, after being dried, they are used to cast stereotype metal plates." Vera Brittain, *Radclyffe Hall: A Case of Obscenity* (1968), 86.

the recently established Pegasus Press to produce a cloth-bound edition there. The founder of Pegasus Press, John Holroyd-Reece, specialized in publishing English editions of books banned in Britain.

The appearance of a Paris edition of *Well* mollified John's resentment over Jonathan Cape's capitulation to Jix and his withdrawal of her book "at the very moment that it was bidding to become a best-seller." And before long the book was showing up in England. The Cape–Holroyd-Reece plan was to advertise and sell *Well* from Paris throughout the continent and in England. Cape supplied Holroyd-Reece with a list of unfilled English orders and an overseas mailing list. Business boomed. It was so good that Holroyd-Reece appointed a bookseller in London, Leopold Hill, to be his English agent and distributor. A shipment of 250 copies to Hill came to the attention of the customs officials at Dover and was impounded. By order of the commissioner of customs and excise, the books were released, only to be seized anew as "obscene," by the London police, under a warrant issued pursuant to Lord Campbell's Act. All copies of *Well* found on Leopold Hill's premises and on those of another bookseller on Charing Cross Road were confiscated.

The publicity attending *Well*'s seizure and the litigation that followed provoked widespread public controversy over the morality of sexual inversion and the propriety of governmental censorship of books; it also enormously stimulated sales at Pegasus in Paris. By letter and cable, orders for *Well* poured in to Pegasus from around the world. Jix became the butt of that part of the press sensitive to British traditions of freedom of expression. H. G. Wells wondered whether the police seizure was legal and urged the book's owners to challenge the action in court. George Bernard Shaw predicted that if police action of the sort taken against *Well* went unprotested, "no books will be published at all in England." Rudyard Kipling prepared to object to the censorship in court, but when the time came, the famous author would not be permitted by the judges to do so. From Paris, Holroyd-Reece announced that he was an English subject and dared the public prosecutor to proceed against him in England, if he could; back in London, Jonathan Cape received a summons to appear in court at Bow Street and show cause why *The Well of Loneliness* should not be burned.

When the Bloomsbury group learned about Jix's action against *Well,* Leonard Woolf and E. M. Forster resolved to protest the ban. Forster had visited John on the day of the novel's withdrawal to tell her of the plan; she felt flattered and at first embraced the idea enthusiastically. They launched a vigorous campaign to collect signatures. The protest letter, however—to Radclyffe Hall's distress—turned out to be a qualified one. It dealt merely with the legal aspects of the situation and offered "no opinion on either the merits or the decency of the book." When Forster paid another visit to John in her tower in Kensington, she told him that she would not have *any* protest letter that did not contain a statement that her book "was a work of artistic merit—even genius." This is, at least, what

Virginia Woolf reported to Vita Sackville-West; it is not otherwise confirmed. In her diary, Woolf gives this account of John's reaction:

VIRGINIA WOOLF: Morgan [E. M. Forster] was here for the weekend; timid, touchy, infinitely charming. One night we got drunk, & talked of sodomy, & sapphism, with emotion—so much so that next day he said he had been drunk. This was started by Radclyffe Hall & her meritorious dull book. [Leonard and Morgan] wrote articles for Hubert* all day, & got up petitions; & then Morgan saw her & she screamed like a herring gull, mad with egotism & vanity. Unless they say her book is good, she wont let them complain of the laws. Morgan said that Dr Head can convert the sodomites.†

"Would you like to be converted," Leonard asked.

"No," said Morgan quite definitely.

He said he thought Sapphism disgusting: partly from convention, partly because he disliked that women should be independent of men.

—

In a letter to Arnold Bennett, however, John insisted only that she did "not *want* the support of anyone who will not vouch for the decency of my book [and] the purity of my intention in writing *The Well of Loneliness*." Bennett replied that while he personally stood by both the merit and the decency of the book, he had agreed to the wording of the Forster letter because it enabled certain "other, more timid, persons to sign." According to Virginia Woolf, however, Bennett, like her, did not value the book's literary qualities, even though he publicly declared John "to be honest, convincing and extremely courageous." Forster told Virginia that Bennett would not have signed a letter of the sort that John wanted even if the co-signatories were "all the swells in the world."

John was better thought of by Virginia Woolf's intimate friend Vita Sackville-West—"as well she should have been," commented Virginia, "since the two shared the same proclivities"—but because Vita's lesbianism was well known, she was not asked to sign the petition, as Virginia coquettishly explained in a letter to her.

VIRGINIA WOOLF: I am very hot. I have been mowing the lawn. It looks now like a calm sea through which several large ships have passed leaving wakes behind them. Then I ate two plums which make my hands sticky. For many days I have been so disjected by society that writing has been only a dream—something another woman did once. What has caused this irruption I scarcely know—largely your friend Radclyffe Hall (she is now docked of her Miss owing to her proclivities) they banned her book and so Leonard and Morgan Forster began to get up a protest, and soon we were telephon-

---

*Hubert Henderson, editor of *The Nation*.

†Sir Henry Head (1861–1940; knighted 1927), "a very distinguished scientist and a man of culture (he had translated Heine)," was called in by Leonard as a consultant when Virginia was in a suicidal condition in 1913. Quentin Bell, *Virginia Woolf: A Biography* (1972), 14ff. and 138. *The Diary of Virginia Woolf*, edited by Anne Oliver Bell, vol. 3 (1980), 193, n. 6.

ing and interviewing and collecting signatures—not yours, for *your* proclivities are too well known.

VITA SACKVILLE-WEST: I feel very violently about *The Well of Loneliness.* Not on account of what you call my proclivities; not because I think it is a good book; but really on principle. (I think of writing to Jix suggesting that he should suppress Shakespeare's Sonnets.) Because, you see, even if the W. of L. had been a good book—even if it had been a great book, a real masterpiece—the result would have been the same. And that is intolerable. I really have no words to say how indignant I am. . . . Personally, I should like to renounce my nationality as a gesture; but I don't want to become a German, even though I did go to a revue last night in which two ravishing young women sang a frankly Lesbian song.

—

Virginia Woolf's proclivities—she seems to have been a part-time sapphist—were not well known. Neither were those of E. M. Forster, who was "worked-up" over the *Well* case, in Virginia's words, "because of *his* proclivities and his own unpublishable novel *Maurice.*"* Morgan told Virginia privately that he considered *Well* "poorly-written and pretentious." Nevertheless, he found John's book "courageous," and he thought "it was regrettable that our efforts to get up a round-robin protest letter foundered in that way, on Radclyffe Hall's sensitivity." Because he felt strongly that he should persist in his efforts on the book's behalf, he published in *Nation and Athenaeum* an anonymous article, "The New Censorship," in which he condemned the government's action as "an insidious blow at the liberties of the public." Later, Forster and Virginia jointly signed a letter, published in *Nation and Athenaeum* (September 8, 1928), arguing that *Well* had been suppressed not because of its indecency but because of its forbidden subject matter. They stressed that "however repellant it might be to the majority," the subject matter "*existed* and had been recognized by science and history." But now "novelists were to be forbidden by Sir W. Joynson-Hicks to

---

*Forster's autobiographical homosexual novel, *Maurice,* was published posthumously in the United States in 1971; it had been written in 1913 (but revised in 1919 and 1932), more than a decade before *Well* was written. In a "Terminal Note" he attached in 1960 to the still-unpublished manuscript Forster says: "A happy ending was imperative. I shouldn't have bothered to write otherwise. I was determined that in fiction anyway two men should fall in love and remain in it for the ever and ever that fiction allows. . . . Happiness is its keynote— which by the way has had an unexpected result: it has made the book more difficult to publish. Unless the Wolfenden Report [recommending the abolition of the laws punishing homosexual acts committed consensually and in private] becomes law, it will probably have to remain in manuscript. If it ended unhappily, with a lad dangling from a noose or with a suicide pact, all would be well, for there is no pornography or seduction of minors. But the lovers get away unpunished and consequently recommend crime." *Maurice* (1971), 250.
John Colmer, in *E. M. Forster: The Personal Voice* (1975), says that the novel throws great light on "Forster's dilemma as an artist and a man: how to come to terms with his own sexuality in a society that imprisoned homosexuals and censored homosexual literature. . . . For all its artistic merits [however], *Maurice* is an exercise in personal therapy, not a finished work of art." The novel is said to have been written "primarily for the author himself and for a small circle of friends, all of whom had a special interest in the theme of homosexuality" (113–14).

mention it." Might they "mention other subjects possibly as unpopular in Whitehall, such as birth control, suicide or pacifism?" Their letter closed with the ironic intimation that "as writers we await our instructions."

In the meantime, John had herself succeeded in securing "wonderful public declarations for her book" from H. G. Wells, Bernard Shaw, and others, and "was also rallying support from the 'working people' "—by which, Virginia said, she meant "the Railwaymen and Miners sort."

Virginia and Leonard Woolf, and "the sex reformer" Dr. Stella Churchill, eventually "stood surety" in the case for "the defendant"—who, however, turned out to be not, as they had expected, Radclyffe Hall, but Jonathan Cape and the London bookseller to whom the Paris edition had been shipped, Leopold Hill. At Vita's prodding, Virginia had also prepared herself to enter the witness box on behalf of the book, even though she was "reluctant to do so in a case resting on such poor writing." On November 1, 1928, Virginia wrote to Quentin Bell:

VIRGINIA WOOLF: I'm just off to a tea party to discuss our evidence. Leonard and Nessa say I mustn't go into the box, because I should cast a shadow over Bloomsbury. Forgetting where I was I should speak the truth. All London, they say is agog with this. Most of our friends are trying to evade the witness box; for reasons you may guess. But they generally put it down to the weak heart of a father, or a cousin who is about to have twins.

———

Vita's lover Violet Trefusis considered *Well* a "loathsome example" but longed to write her own novel on the theme—"to correct the balance." For Vita, the book's popularity was "an exciting and unexpected development." "If one might write about *that Subject*," she imagined, "the field of fiction was immediately *doubled*." To Virginia, John's philosophy of inversion seemed "somewhat peculiar." She claimed that Radclyffe "did not even stop short of protesting the persecution of women having her proclivities on the argument that since an abnormal chicken had been found capable of both laying eggs and fathering chicks, why should 'inverts' be treated so harshly?"

Virginia heard later that Havelock Ellis would not "go to trial to speak for the book," because, he said, he "would not make a *good* witness and would probably make a *bad* impression." She decided Ellis had backed off from appearing at John's trial because "there was this about *his* own book," on the same subject, which long before had been judicially condemned. Ellis is said to have told John that a verdict against her book would make better publicity for it than a victory would.

Ellis's own banned book, *Sexual Inversion,* had contained thirty-three case studies of men and women with homosexual proclivities and was possibly the first "scientific" study of its kind. Among the case studies was one of Ellis's childlike first wife, Edith, who fell in love with a woman promptly after marrying Ellis. The philosopher's shock at learning about his young wife's homosexual attachment stimulated him to gather information on sexual inversion and report it to the world.

Although Ellis had mustered an impressive team of experts in London to testify to the scientific value of his own book, the book was judicially condemned, and in a most insulting way, without any public testimony or trial whatever. The defendant in the case was not Ellis but a bookseller named Bedborough; on the day of the trial, without consulting Ellis, Bedborough pled guilty, to avoid the risk of a prison term. Said the recorder, Sir Charles Hall, to Bedborough: "You have acted wisely for it would have been impossible for you to have contended, with any possibility whatever of being able to persuade anybody, that this book was not filthy and obscene. I am willing to believe that in acting as you did, you might at the outset perhaps have been gulled into the belief that somebody might say this was a scientific work. But it is impossible for anybody with a head on his shoulders to open the book without seeing that it is a pretence and a sham."

Ellis eventually obtained a measure of revenge on the magistrate, if not on the bookseller. Writing in 1940 in *My Life,* he said: "My 'filthy' and 'worthless' and 'morbid' book has by now been translated into all the greatest living languages to reach people who could not say what a Recorder is, even if they saw one."

The response of the English literary establishment to the banning of *Well* was dispiriting to John. John Galsworthy, who was president of PEN, was particularly hurtful. He would do nothing for her case: he was too busy and, in any event, did not see that any principle of literary freedom was involved. Herman Ould, PEN's general secretary and "himself a member of the third sex," also took "the astounding position" that censorship did not seem to be involved in John's case. And naturally enough she felt "completely bewildered by the attitude of the Bloomsbury writers, particularly Virginia Woolf's catty utterances." John was amazed when Virginia finally agreed to be a witness, since all along she had been taking "an amused and superior tone" toward her book.

In early November Virginia wrote to Lady Ottoline Morrell, a friend of the Bloomsbury group, that the trial of "the *Well of Loneliness* is in full swing."

VIRGINIA WOOLF: I have to appear in favour of it, and have already wasted hours reading it and talking about it. . . . The dullness of the book is such that any indecency may lurk there—one simply can't keep one's eyes on the pages.

———

In the event, Virginia went to the *Well*'s first trial but not to the appeal.

John also suspected that Jonathan Cape was less than faithful to her and her book, and that he might not have fought the censorship in court "had I not hounded him to do so" and had not John Holroyd-Reece declared that "he wished to fight the case 'all the way.' " John had agreed to share with Cape the costs of all legal proceedings, which proved to be very heavy. After the case was over, and lost, John had to sell her house at 37 Holland Street to pay her share.

Unlike the English literati, ordinary women and men "flocked" to John's cause. Before the trial began, letters and messages of support arrived in daily profusion at Holland Street. On a single day in September the post contained almost four hundred letters. Many came from normal women whose views toward inversion, they said, had been radically changed by reading John's book.

It was in the midst of all this excitement that bad news arrived from America: the Knopfs, having heard of the initial English legal developments, sought to back out of their undertaking to publish *Well.* Una wrote in her diary that the Knopfs had "ratted" on John.

Blanche Knopf put the blame on Jonathan Cape. First, she claimed, he had violated the understanding they had that there would be *simultaneous* publication in London and New York. Then, "after going ahead precipitously, he put himself in the position of practically admitting that *The Well of Loneliness* was obscene, by offering to withdraw it if the authorities said he should, and then doing just that when they came out and said he should." She believed John had acquiesced in that decision—although John subsequently denied she had. For his part, Alfred Knopf felt that Jonathan Cape's actions had placed him in an uncomfortable position, for, he said, "it was a foregone conclusion that we would soon be faced with the hopeless prospect of attempting to defend in court a book which was not being defended in its author's own country." Alfred Knopf was not of a mind to allow the house of Knopf to publish "any work which the public would buy because of its prurient interest rather than its literary qualities." The publisher was squirming, too, because contrary to his usual policy, he had agreed to share with John the legal costs that might arise from the publication of her book. He knew from past experience that those costs might be very large, and felt that "since it was Miss Hall's publisher in England who, for his own reasons, had made defending the book in America inevitable, it should not be up to me to pay the piper."

Pre-publication orders for the book that came in to Knopf were not, by and large, from booksellers of the better type; they were "from dealers who expected a sensational demand from persons looking for something salacious." Blanche grew convinced that no matter how they handled the book, Knopf "could never avoid selling it as a dirty book"—the last thing they or John could have wanted. She agreed with Alfred to "stop the presses."

Alfred Knopf had always thought it best to avoid confrontations with the censors when possible and to withdraw from any he could not forestall. His first tangle with John Sumner had occurred in 1915, Knopf's first year in business and Sumner's first year as secretary of the New York Society for the Suppression of Vice, following the death of Anthony Comstock.

ALFRED KNOPF: Our first small list, that for the autumn of 1915, included a Polish novel, *Homo Sapiens,* by an author with the unpronounceable name of Przybyszewski. I have never reread it, but I am quite sure it was not a very good novel. I had a tiny office then in the Candler Building on West Forty-second Street, with only an office boy and a young assistant working for me. One day a stranger appeared and bought from my assistant, for cash, a copy of *Homo Sapiens.* A few days later I was summoned to appear in a magistrate's court, the complainant being John S. Sumner, secretary of the New York Society for the Suppression of Vice. I will not tell the whole of the story. . . .

Through the interposition of a partner in the firm of lawyers that represented my father who turned out to be a director of the New York Society for the Suppression of Vice, the charges were withdrawn and Mr. Sumner convinced that I was really an upstanding and decent young man. But there seemed no point in continuing to offer for sale a book that people would now buy only out of curiosity because they knew it had been brought into court and consequently regarded it as dirty. So we withdrew it and melted the plates.

—

A few years later Knopf published a novel called *Janet March* written by Floyd Dell, one of the Village crowd; despite a ban by the Watch and Ward on the book's sale in Boston, 13,000 copies were sold before Sumner got around to summoning Knopf to court in New York. Knopf at once withdrew the book from sale "rather than have it attain a large sale through a possible court action"; Dell felt his publisher had let him down badly.

"As an anticensorship warrior, Alfred Knopf's characteristic stance was one of dignified retreat," Paul Boyer writes in *Purity in Print,* his book on the vice societies. "One must in fairness record, however, that the imprint which Knopf went to such lengths to protect survived to become one of the most distinguished in American publishing history, while Seltzer, Liveright, Covici, and other impetuous adventurers ready to rush into a censorship fight at the drop of a hat, early fell into bankruptcy and oblivion."*

---

*Purity in Print (1968), 136. The fates of Seltzer and Liveright have been described above in Chapters 5 and 8. Knopf's son, Alfred A. (Pat) Knopf, worked with his father until he left to form Atheneum Publishers with Hiram Haydn and Simon Michael Bessie. After that Bennett Cerf of Random House figured that Alfred Knopf, Sr., was left "very much in the air" and proposed that he merge with Random House. When Knopf said he was interested, Cerf left, "wildly excited," to talk it over with Donald Klopfer. "Of all the publishing houses in the world," Cerf later wrote, "Knopf was the one I had always admired the most." A deal was cut, with the Knopfs getting a large block of Random House stock. According to Cerf, "It made them rich overnight." Cerf promised Knopf that he could keep absolute control over his imprint, and he kept his promise: "I'm scared to death of Alfred. If he starts roaring at me, I run!" Bennett Cerf, *At Random* (1977), 279. George Doran said of Knopf: "He not only made beautiful books, but told the public they were beautiful books and thereby stimulated the public to require a more graceful format." Quoted by Allen Churchill, *The Literary Decade,* 174. Adds Churchill: "Borzoi books were a curious projection of the publisher's personality. For Knopf loved books as some men love women. 'I love books physically,' he

Knopf, of course, was not the only publisher who backed off from court fights with censors like John Sumner during a period when the heads of firms, not merely the firms themselves, were liable to find themselves summoned to court and criminally accused. Most of the old houses did the same, including Appleton, Harper, Scribner's Sons, and Macmillan. Even some of the new publishers capitulated, as Albert and Charles Boni did, in a 1924 case brought by Sumner against J. K. Huysmans's *Là-Bas*. So, finally, did Thomas Seltzer, in the case involving *Casanova's Homecoming* and *A Young Girl's Diary;* he could not afford to defend himself. It was no secret in New York publishing circles that dealing with "dirty" books could bring a prison term or a fine. In 1926 in New York, for example, distributors of a volume of Frank Harris's *My Life and Loves*—the book Harris had tried to persuade Sylvia Beach to publish in Paris—were fined and sent to jail. And in 1920, the head of the venerable house Harper, Clinton T. Brainard, was prosecuted, convicted, and fined $1,000 for publishing *Madeleine,* an "obscene" novel about a prostitute by an anonymous author. Brainard's conviction was reversed when his lawyers successfully argued that the publisher, having been abroad at the time, had had nothing to do with his company's publication of the book.

According to Jonathan Cape, when Blanche Knopf proposed canceling the *Well* contract, she also asked Radclyffe Hall to keep the book out of America altogether because she was convinced that no publisher would handle it except as a "pornographic" work. Cape viewed this as nonsense and lost no time in proving it. While the trial of the Paris edition of *Well* was starting up at Bow Street Magistrates Court, Cape sailed to New York and obtained a reassignment of the American publication rights from Knopf. It was his idea to publish the book in New York himself, or to license a "vigorous" publishing house to bring out an American edition as soon as possible. Cape found the right house in one of the "new breed" American publishers, Covici-Friede—or rather, Pascal Covici and Donald Friede found Cape. The firm, an offshoot of Boni and Liveright, was prepared to fight for a book like *Well.*

The terms the Americans offered Radclyffe Hall were generous; they included an advance of ten thousand dollars against a 15 percent royalty. John accepted, on condition that she receive half of the advance on signing the agreement, a precaution she had failed to take with the Knopfs, to her lasting regret. She rejected the Knopfs' offer to publish her next two books because she had decided to do no more business with them. She considered inexcusable their action in terminating the contract for *Well.*

It was not long after this that in England, at the Old Bailey, an unprecedented number of impressive literary figures found themselves arrayed on

---

admitted once, 'and I want to make them beautifully.' What has been called a Prussian thoroughness aided him. Borzoi books were the proud possessors of striking bindings, colorful jackets, top-quality paper, and a wide variety of type faces, some new to the book world" (174–75).

the benches as potential witnesses for the trial of the Paris edition of *Well*. John attributed their number and quality to the indefatigable efforts of the solicitor in her case, Harold Rubinstein of Rubinstein, Nash and Company, who in the end assembled forty prominent personages ready to speak up for literary freedom—including Rudyard Kipling, Desmond McCarthy, Hugh Walpole, Rose Macaulay, A. P. Herbert, Laurence Housman, Storm Jameson, Julian Huxley, E. M. Forster, Virginia and Leonard Woolf, and Vita Sackville-West.

11

Ungrateful England

VIRGINIA WOOLF: We were all packed in by 10:30: the door at the top of the court opened; in stepped the debonair distinguished magistrate; we all rose; he bowed; took his seat under the lion & the unicorn, & then proceeded. Something like a Harley St. specialist investigating a case. All black & white, tie pin, clean shaven, wax coloured, & carved, in that light, like ivory.

—

So began the trial of *The Well of Loneliness* at Bow Street Magistrates Court. The courtroom was so crowded with spectators that before the proceedings opened a sign was posted: COURT FULL. Radclyffe Hall was seated beside her publisher's lawyer, Norman Birkett, a King's Counsel. It was a Lord Campbell's Act proceeding to destroy all copies of the Pegasus Press edition located by police. In such a case the author had no right to contest the destruction independent of her publisher's right to "show cause" why the books should not be destroyed for being "obscene."* Birkett stood up and addressed the presiding magistrate, Sir Chartres Biron.

NORMAN BIRKETT: The book is concerned not with perversion but with what the medical profession call inversion—that is, emotions and desires which with most people are directed towards the opposite sex, but are here directed towards their own.

---

*John, however, undertook to share jointly with Cape the costs of the legal proceedings against *Well,* and so probably assumed she had the right to take full part in the deliberations and stratagems of the lawyers on their side. She asked to be put into the witness box but was advised by counsel against this. Michael Baker, *Our Three Selves: The Life of Radclyffe Hall* (1985), 237.

At this point Birkett sought to assure Sir Chartres that the relationships depicted in the novel by John were not physical but only romantic and sentimental, "much like a schoolgirl crush transferred to adult life, innocent of sexual implications."

RADCLYFFE HALL: I sat there and sweated blood feeling that my work was both shamed and degraded.

Sir Chartres interrupted Birkett:

SIR CHARTRES BIRON: Do you mean to say that it does not deal with unnatural offenses at all?

NORMAN BIRKETT: I say not. Nowhere is there an obscene word, a lascivious passage. It is a sombre, sad, tragic, artistic revelation of that which is an undoubted fact in this world. It is the result of years of labor by one of the most distinguished novelists alive, and it is a sincere and high-minded effort to make the world more tolerable for those who have to bear the tragic consequences of what they are not to blame for at all. . . .

In the course of this case it is my hope to be allowed to quote the views of critics in various reviews and newspapers, which constitute a chorus of praise from those well-qualified to speak upon matters affecting literature in general. Further than that there are in court people of every walk of life who desire to go into the witness box and to testify that this book is not obscene, and that it is a misuse of words for the prosecution to describe it as such.

And King's Counsel motioned toward the spectator seats: forty were filled with distinguished men and women, not only from the world of letters, who had come to court to speak up for the freedom of John's novel.

The magistrate, however, doubted the relevancy of what such witnesses would have to say. Sir Chartres reminded King's Counsel of *Regina* v. *Hicklin:*

SIR CHARTRES BIRON: The test is whether it is likely to deprave or corrupt those into whose hands it is likely to fall. How can the opinion of a number of people be evidence?

In response, Birkett asserted that "ordinary persons" should certainly know, and be quite fit to say, if *The Well of Loneliness* had such a "tendency."

NORMAN BIRKETT: I want to call evidence, from every conceivable walk of life which bears on the test whether the tendency of this book is to deprave and corrupt. A more distinguished body of witnesses has never before been called in a court of justice.

If Sir Chartres was impressed by the presence in court of Rudyard Kipling, Julian Huxley, Rose Macaulay, Desmond McCarthy, Virginia Woolf, Leonard Woolf, and E. M. Forster, he was not disposed to hear them out:

SIR CHARTRES BIRON: I have the greatest doubt whether the evidence is admissible.

NORMAN BIRKETT: If I am not allowed to call evidence it means that a magistrate is virtually a censor of literature!

———

That was true. The magistrate's refusal to listen to the opinions of others meant that his personal judgment on the question of whether *Well* should be set free must govern. Sir Chartres dismissed Birkett's contention out of hand:

SIR CHARTRES BIRON: I don't think people are entitled to express an opinion upon a matter which is for the decision of the court.

———

In advising King's Counsel to that effect, the magistrate was pursuing a practice apparently unbroken in English obscenity trials. Nevertheless, Birkett proceeded with the attempt to put on his collection of witnesses. He asked Desmond McCarthy, one of England's foremost literary critics, to come to the witness box. McCarthy stated that he had read the book.

NORMAN BIRKETT: In your view is it obscene?

SIR CHARTRES BIRON: No, I shall disallow that. It is quite clear that the evidence is not admissible. A book may be a fine piece of literature and yet obscene. Art and obscenity are not dissociated at all. There is a room at Naples to which visitors are not admitted as a rule, which contains fine bronzes and statues, all admirable works of art, but all grossly obscene. It does not follow that because a book is a work of art it is not obscene. I shall not admit the evidence.

———

Sir Chartres went on to say that he had read the book and conceded it had "some claims to be literature and is certainly well-written."

SIR CHARTRES BIRON: But I have to consider whether its tendency might be to corrupt. There are certain passages in it which, subject to exploration, appear to my mind to be obscene in the sense of being lascivious and containing lurid descriptions of unnatural vice.

———

Resigned now to his fate, Birkett announced: "I formally tender thirty-nine other witnesses. The evidence which a number of them would have given is identical with that of Mr. McCarthy"—which, apparently, would have been that *Well* was a serious work, without any design to corrupt the reader. King's Counsel went on to complete his offer of proof. Among Birkett's "other witnesses" were "booksellers, ministers of religion, social workers, a magistrate, biologists, educationists, including the registrar of Durham University, medical men and representatives of the London libraries." "In a second category" were "distinguished authors and authoresses who would have said that they had read the book and in their view it was not obscene." This, of course, was the group that Virginia and Leonard Woolf and E. M. Forster had joined.

SIR CHARTRES BIRON: I reject them all.

———

Virginia Woolf was impressed by the proceedings.

VIRGINIA WOOLF: He was ironical at first: raised his eyebrows & shrugged. Later I was impressed by the reason of the law, its astuteness, its formality. Here have we evolved a very remarkable fence between us and barbarity; something commonly recognized; half humbug & ceremony therefore— when they pulled out calf-bound books & read old phrases I thought this; & bowing & scraping made me think it; but in those banks runs a live stream. What is obscenity? What is literature? What is the difference between the subject and the treatment? In what cases is evidence allowable? This last, to my relief, was decided against us: we could not be called as experts on obscenity, only in art. So Desmond who had got under the palanquin where he looked too indifferent, too calm, too completely at his ease to be natural, was only asked his qualifications & then, not allowed to answer the obscene question, was dismissed.

———

It is said that Norman Birkett was brought into the case only three days before the trial of Radclyffe Hall's book, and that may account for his presentation of a disingenuous defense of the lesbian theme of John's novel and an ineffectual presentation of the witnesses. Birkett's inability to put on his witnesses to testify to the book's nonobscenity was certainly to be expected since this had always been deemed a conclusory determination of law, exclusively within the court's province to make. But why did Birkett not even *endeavor* to elicit from his literary expert witnesses testimony concerning *Well*'s literary, artistic, or social values? Why did he limit himself so disastrously to questioning his witness about the novel's "obscenity"?

Other commentators agree that Birkett mismanaged the defense. Geoffrey Robertson refers to Birkett's "blunder" in asking Desmond McCarthy, "In your view is it obscene?" "This question was inadmissible on any view of the law, because it entailed an answer to the very question that the court had to decide. The magistrate rightly excluded it, and Birkett was not allowed to call thirty-nine other eminent writers."* Similarly Michael Baker: "But Birkett had not handled the witnesses cleverly. He asked McCarthy the wrong question, given the law as it stood. Instead, he should have put other, less direct questions which would have elicited the answers he sought."† Alec Craig, on the other hand, observes that even had Birkett's forty witnesses been permitted to testify on behalf of the book, "the prosecution would have produced another array on the opposite side"; and

———

*Geoffrey Robertson, *Obscenity* (1979), 36.
†Michael Baker, *Our Three Selves* (1985), 241.

that Jix had "suggested to the new Archbishop of Canterbury, Cosmo Lang, that he should ask Hensley Henson, the Bishop of Durham, to testify against the book." The invitation evidently was made but turned down.*

English lawyers would not again assemble so sizable and notable a group of experts to testify at an obscenity trial until 1960, when the trial of the publisher of Penguin's edition of Lawrence's *Lady Chatterley's Lover* took place. By that time, however, the law had been changed by act of Parliament expressly to allow evidence of literary and other merit as a defense to an obscenity charge, and some thirty-five witnesses were allowed to vent their opinions concerning the novel's value.†

Birkett's associate, Herbert Metcalf, also appears to have been less than helpful. His cross-examination of the police officer who had supervised the raids on Jonathan Cape's offices and Hill's bookshop—Chief Inspector John Prothero of Scotland Yard—was more damaging to the book's case than to the Crown's witness, for it encouraged the inspector to express his opinion that the book lacked literary distinction, whereas all testimony proffered by the defense bearing on *Well*'s literary merit was ruled out.

During the lunch recess John attacked Birkett vehemently for his "dishonest betrayal" of the message of her book and "shed tears of brokenhearted anguish." She now made it clear to Birkett that unless he retracted his words that same afternoon she "would get up before anyone could stop her" and tell the magistrate the truth about the characters in her novel— "that, *of course,* a *physical* aspect entered into the relationships of inverts." Birkett agreed to do as John wished. King's Counsel later ranked this luncheon with John as "the most miserable meal of my life."

When the trial resumed after lunch, most of the defense witnesses had left the courtroom. Faithful to his promise to John, Birkett now advised Sir Chartres that he was "not in a position" to contend further that *The Well*

---

*Geoffrey Robertson, *Obscenity* (1979), 81.

†See *The Trial of Lady Chatterley,* consisting of "the Transcript of the Trial" as edited by C. H. Rolph (1961). In the *Lady Chatterley's Lover* case, the solicitors Rubinstein, Nash and Company wrote "to over 300 prominent persons considered to be likely, or known to be qualified, to give expert evidence for the Defence," and interviewed 70 of these. The crucial language in the Obscene Publications Act of 1959—one of the sponsors of which, incidentally, was Norman Birkett, now Lord Norman Birkett—appears to have been based on the American doctrine of "redeeming social importance" announced by Supreme Court Justice William J. Brennan, Jr., in the 1957 *Roth* case (see Chapters 15 and 16), rephrasing this as a defense of "public good." As in the States, it was expressly provided that this vindicating "public good" or redeeming "social importance" might be witnessed by experts. See John Sutherland, *Offensive Literature: Decensorship in Britain 1960–1982* (1982). The British act provides that the defendant in an obscenity case is entitled to acquittal if the court is satisfied that notwithstanding the obscenity of the material, its publication is justified as being for "the public good" in the interests of "science, literature, art or learning, or of other objects of general concern." Either side may tender witnesses to such interests, but the burden of persuasion is for the defense to carry. See Geoffrey Robertson, *Obscenity* (1979), 124ff. As before, however, the ultimate question of whether the thing in question is "obscene" is for the judge or jury, and not the experts, to say.

of Loneliness did not "relate to unnatural offenses between women in every sense of the word." Nevertheless, he argued, the novel "in no way outraged decency; its subject was dealt with with restraint and reverence," and there "was nothing in it which tended to defend these unnatural tendencies or to their glorification."

The magistrate noted Birkett's change of position regarding the sexual behavior of the women in the book—a change he must have found damaging to John's cause—and then took up the arguments of King's Counsel that the book could not be found obscene, first, because there were no gross or filthy words in it, and, second, because it was well written and was to be regarded as a work of literature not properly subject to these proceedings. Sir Chartres's answer to the latter contention echoed the position that most judges, American as well as English, then took: the fact that a book was well written could be no defense to a prosecution for publishing an obscene book, and no answer to a proceeding to condemn such a book.

SIR CHARTRES BIRON: [O]therwise we should be in the preposterous position that the most obscene books would be free from any stricture.

———

Moving now to the first point, the magistrate proceeded to apply to *Well* the code of Victorian morality:

SIR CHARTRES BIRON: It is not necessary that filthy words be used; it is enough that acts of the most horrible, unnatural and disgusting obscenity are described in the most alluring terms in this book, and that none of the women involved are treated as in the least blameworthy. Characters living in filthy sin are presented as attractive people and put forward with admiration. Indeed, the result is described by the authoress as giving these women extraordinary rest, contentment and pleasure; and not only that, but it is actually put forward that it improves their mental balance and capacity.

———

John's empathy for the "unnatural creatures" in her book seemed deeply to affront Sir Chartres's own moral standards. He opened his copy of *Well* and read passages covering Stephen's love affairs with Angela and Mary, alluding to "these horrible practices," to "these two people living in filthy sin," and to "acts of the most horrible, unnatural and disgusting obscenity." In the case of Mary, Sir Chartres referred to the occasion of her meeting with Stephen at the French front. The magistrate was appalled that John should describe female ambulance drivers who engaged in homosexual acts.

SIR CHARTRES BIRON: According to this writer, a number of women of position and admirable character, who were engaged in driving ambulances in the course of the war, were addicted to this vice.

At this point John, again alongside counsel,* jumped up:

RADCLYFFE HALL: I *protest*! I emphatically *protest*!
SIR CHARTRES BIRON: They are presented in the most alluring terms.
. . . *Quiet!* I must ask you to be quiet!
RADCLYFFE HALL: I am the author of this book!
SIR CHARTRES BIRON: If you cannot behave yourself in court I shall have
you removed.
RADCLYFFE HALL: Shame!

It was all she could say; then she sat down, "trembling, ready to weep
over how my book's characters, many of whom I'd taken from life, were
shamed by this magistrate of justice." After an hour or so more of Sir
Chartres's pontification, the proceedings were adjourned so that the magistrate—"increasingly deliberate & courteous," according to an almost approving Virginia Woolf—might "read the book again & give judgement
next Friday at two, [on] the pale tepid vapid book which lay damp-slab all
about the court."

VIRGINIA WOOLF: And I lost my little Roman brooch, & that is the end of
this great day, so far. A curious brown top lighted scene; very stuffy;
policemen at the doors; matrons passing through. . . .

Outside the courtroom, Woolf encountered Una and John:

VIRGINIA WOOLF: In the hall I talked to Lady Troubridge (who used to
sculpt & last time we met was a tea party, as children, in Montpelier Sqre)
& John—John lemon yellow, tough, stringy, exacerbated. Their costs run
into 4 figures she said. And Leonard thinks this heralds a subscription.

The proceedings on Friday were short. Sir Chartres announced that
having reread the book, he had "no hesitation in saying" that John's book
was one "which would tend to corrupt those into whose hands it might
fall." He had employed the *Hicklin* test to determine that without a doubt
Well was obscene and gave an order to "destroy the book" and "for payment
of twenty guineas costs."

An appeal was taken in due course from the magistrate's decision to
Quarter Session (County of London) Court, a proceeding that Virginia

---

*The famous firm of solicitors Rubinstein, Nash and Company, who in 1960 would
superintend the defense in England of *Lady Chatterley's Lover,* had been retained for *Well*'s
defense, and were represented at counsel's table. For them John had prepared a long, strong
statement, which was never introduced, about her intentions in writing *Well.* The statement
closed: "I do not regret having written the book. All that has happened has only served to
show me how badly my book was needed. I am proud to have written *The Well of Loneliness,*
and I would not alter so much as a comma." Michael Baker, *Our Three Selves* (1985), 238.
John's will instructed Una not to permit any republication of *Well* that was expurgated, and
Una obeyed.

Woolf missed but that Vita Sackville-West insisted on attending. There, however, "soon grown bored," Vita took leave of the proceedings to go shopping instead. According to Virginia Woolf, not one of the dozen magistrates who sat for the appeal had even read the book.

At the outset of the proceedings the chairman, Sir Robert Wallace, intimated that it would be "neither appropriate nor practicable" for him and his eleven associate justices to read the condemned book; perhaps Cape had been unable to provide enough copies to go around, or had learned that the justices were not disposed in any event to read the book.

The attorney general, Sir Thomas Inskip, K.C., opened the proceedings for the Crown, stating that the only issue was whether *The Well of Loneliness* was obscene, and quoting Lord Cockburn's dictum in *Regina* v. *Hicklin* that a publication was obscene if "the tendency of the matter . . . is to deprave and corrupt those whose minds are open to such immoral influence and into whose hands publications of this sort may fall." For all he knew, the novel in question might contain very fine writing; he had "nothing to do with that." The whole question was one of obscenity, and on that point, Sir Thomas could think of "only two references in literature to women such as those described" by John:

SIR THOMAS INSKIP: One is in the first chapter of St. Paul's Epistle to the Romans, and the other is in the Sixth Book of Juvenal.*

———

Mr. J. B. Melville, K.C., Birkett's colleague, was permitted to argue for the defense that *The Well of Loneliness* was a true work of literature, not pornography, and to read from some reviews of John's book—something that was not allowed at the trial. Among the passages he quoted was one from *The Times Literary Supplement* which described *Well* as "sincere, courageous, high-minded, and often beautifully expressed."

J. B. MELVILLE, K.C.: There is no mystery or masquerading about the book. It faces the fact that there exist a class of women who are more attracted to their own than to the opposite sex, and considers the problems, reactions and situations which must arise in consequence.

———

In reply the attorney general contended that "even were the whole book as to ninety-nine one-hundredths of it beyond criticism, yet one passage

———

*There were, of course, others. The "Kinsey Report" (Chapter II) cites references in Ovid, Plutarch, Martial, Juvenal, and Lucian, as well as the *Kama Sutra* of Vatsyayana. It was in Ovid's *Heroides* that Sappho recounted her past loves. Virginia Woolf seemed to distinguish between "Sapphists," like herself, who only occasionally enter into lesbian sexual relationships, and "inverts," like John, who are more or less exclusively attracted to other women as sexual love objects. French writers, including Zola *(Nana)* and Gautier *(Mademoiselle de Maupin),* also described lesbian relations before John did in *Well,* as did D. H. Lawrence in *The Rainbow* (described in Chapter 4 above) and John Cleland in *Fanny Hill.* Furthermore, "[a] number of [Radclyffe] Hall's contemporaries—Lesbian writers like Amy Lowell and Gertrude Stein—produced some of their most ecstatic erotica during the war years." Sandra M. Gilbert and Susan Gubar, *No Man's Land* (1989), 300. For more on the treatment of lesbian themes in literature, see the endnotes for this chapter.

might make it a work which would have to be destroyed as obscene." He had in mind the one sentence in the novel that actually suggested sexual intercourse: "And that night they were not divided." "What does this *mean*?" he asked. "Imagine a poor [*sic*] woman or young man reading it. What is the picture conjured up at once?"*

The chief inspector of Scotland Yard was permitted to describe—damagingly for the defense and the fate of John's book—the circumstances attending the police seizure of *Well*, and to show that Jonathan Cape, after discontinuing the sale of *Well*, secretly arranged to have John's novel manufactured in France from the identical type, or molds, used in his English edition and—as advertised by the Pegasus Press in Paris—"without the alteration of so much as a comma."

The judgment of the appellate court, reached after less than ten minutes of deliberation, was to throw out John's appeal, with costs. Sir Robert explained the judges' action by referring yet again to the *Hicklin* rule and observing that the book was neither a scientific nor a medical book but a novel "addressed to the general public which reads novels."

SIR ROBERT WALLACE: There are plenty of people who would be neither depraved nor corrupted by reading a book like this, but it is to those whose minds are open to such immoral influence that I must refer.

———

And then, announcing a principle which seemed to contradict both the attorney general's and Magistrate Biron's views on the subject, Sir Robert said: "I admit that the character of the book cannot be gathered from a reading of isolated passages; instead, the book must be taken as a whole." This, however, did not make it perceptibly more difficult for the court to adopt the trial magistrate's conclusion that John's novel was "obscene."

SIR ROBERT WALLACE: The court's view, which is unanimous, however, is that this is a very subtle book. It is one which is insinuating and probably much more dangerous because of the fact. It is a book which, if it does not condemn unnatural practices, certainly *condones* them, and suggests that those guilty of them should not receive the consequences they deserve to suffer. . . . Put in a word, the view of this Court is that this is a disgusting book when properly read. It is an obscene book, and a book prejudicial to the morals of the community. In our view the order made by the Magistrate is perfectly correct and the Appeal must be dismissed with costs.†

———

And so the fight in England over the freedom of Radclyffe Hall's lesbian novel ended. Some thirty years later, in 1959, after English law was radically amended by Parliament to require courts to let in evidence of a book's literary or other merit as a defense in obscenity cases, *Well* was republished without legal repercussions.

———

*Geoffrey Robertson, *Obscenity* (1979), 36.

†Inasmuch as the justices reputedly did not read the book, the court's conclusions must have been based exclusively on the magistrate's opinion and representations made by counsel.

In the States, an even more powerful revolution in the law took place during the sixties, when the Supreme Court, speaking through Justice William J. Brennan, Jr., recognized that the suppression of a book having "even the slightest" literary or artistic importance on the ground that it was "obscene" violated the constitutional guarantees of freedom of speech and press, regardless of whether the book otherwise met the tests for what was "obscene."*

Although the appeal in England regarding *Well* was lost in December 1928, in Paris, the Pegasus Press edition proceeded to become an underground best-seller: the English judiciary's disapproval of John's book had spent itself at the border. About all that an English man or woman needed to do to get a copy of *Well* was to cross the Channel. At the Gare du Nord in Paris, returning tourists bought the book for 125 francs from vendors' carts, before climbing aboard the Golden Arrow for Le Havre and the ferryboat ride home. In countless suitcases, coat pockets, and handbags, John's novel was smuggled back into the author's homeland.†

By the end of December 1928, 7,500 copies of the Paris edition of the "suppressed" novel had been sold. By February 1929, sales reached 9,000 copies, and the Pegasus Press was reprinting more. Before long, translations and publications of *Well* in foreign languages also appeared. The English ban on the book—far from suppressing Radclyffe Hall's alluring story about the "way of life" of English lesbians—broadcast it to the rest of the Western world and beyond.

The trial's main effect on John was to alienate her from the Conservative party and England. She had been a Conservative all her life and had always hotly defended that party. She had never, "in her blindness," listened when people told her that the Conservatives were the opponents of progress, the haters of reform, and the enemies of freedom. And then she saw that whereas "Labour was the first to spring to my defense, cry out against the outrage done to my book," the Conservative government "wished to silence" her. That's how she put it in a letter to her agent, Audrey Heath, from Paris, the city in which she found her place of exile from an "ungrateful England," like countless other alienated artists and writers. In due course John sold her Holland Street house in England to pay her share of the legal expenses incurred in defending *Well*. "But for you and Mitsie," John wrote Audrey, "I wouldn't care if I never saw England again." Mitsie was John's dog.

France made the lesbian couple feel welcome:

UNA TROUBRIDGE: [T]otal strangers would come up to [John] in the street or in a restaurant and express their admiration of the book, then amaze-

---

*The American developments are described in Chapters 15 to 22.

†Thirty years later, the British government found a way to defeat the smuggling of erotic novels across the Channel; it persuaded the French police to prosecute the publisher of Vladimir Nabokov's *Lolita,* as described in Chapter 14.

ment and indignation at its persecution. She was lionized by English, French, and Americans alike.

—

John's photograph and copies of *Well* were featured "in every bookshop window"; everyone seemed to be reading the novel. The trials in England had been fully covered by the French press and almost from their arrival there was continuous and gratifying publicity, including interviews by two reporters for *The New York Herald Tribune.* They also met celebrities, including Natalie Barney and Colette.

In March 1929, the esteemed French publishing house Gallimard agreed to publish a French translation of *Well.* This was an honor denied even to D. H. Lawrence, and it made John the first female author on the Gallimard list. According to Una, John on that account "risked the wrath of all French women writers." Within weeks there were proposals for Dutch and Danish translations and editions. "What a life!" John wrote to "Darling Robin" (Audrey Heath):

RADCLYFFE HALL: Do you remember the time when no publisher much wanted John Hall, and now they're all at each other's throats—oh well, as long as we get the dollars!!!

—

Living together in Paris, John and Una maintained that "true inverts" should be allowed to marry; they were intrigued by a report that in Berlin lesbian marriages were going to be legalized. "If so," cried Una—who had always wished she could marry John—*"I'm* for Berlin!! *Am Tag*!!"

Their enthusiasm was somewhat dampened, however, by the case of the Englishwoman Lillian Smith, who for years masqueraded as a military hero called Colonel Barker. She took up hunting, shooting, fishing, and even boxing—as if she were the most Blimpish sort of Englishman—and then married a woman, whom she completely abandoned after three years. Her true sex was exposed in a bankruptcy proceeding. Commented John to Robin: "I would like to see her drawn & quartered."

John's anger at the British government escalated when she learned that a cheap popular edition of Compton Mackenzie's book about lesbians, *Extraordinary Women,* had been brought out without interference from Jix or anyone else. She took it as a personal affront, declaring: "Here and now I renounce my country for ever, nor will I ever lift a hand to help England in the future." The news from America, however, was heartening.

Early in 1928, the year *The Well of Loneliness* was suppressed in England, Donald Friede left Boni and Liveright to set up his own publishing company with Pascal Covici. On a visit to Theodore Dreiser's home in Pleasantville, Friede heard about Radclyffe Hall's novel and learned that after Jonathan Cape had published the book, it was instantly suppressed "for dealing with the taboo subject of Lesbianism." On this account, Knopf was said to be abandoning his plan to publish it. But the novel was reputed to be a fine and serious piece of writing, and since it carried the endorsement of Havelock Ellis, Friede supposed that "must preclude it from being merely another piece of pornography." He knew there would be "a publishers' horse-race" when Knopf gave up the book, and he made up his mind to win it. He left Dreiser's place in a state of high excitement.

In New York Friede found out that another publisher had already offered Jonathan Cape the large sum of $7,500 as an advance for the book, and that, as was mentioned earlier, the English publisher was at that moment on his way to New York, by ocean liner, with the American rights to the book. So he and Pat Covici shot off a cable to Cape in mid-ocean, offering a larger advance, $10,000, and a hefty 20 percent royalty. They also offered to cover the legal costs should there be an attempt to suppress the book in New York. Friede already had in mind the lawyer he would engage to defend *Well*, Morris Ernst, the lawyer who a few years later would win the *Ulysses* case for Random House.

Ernst undertook to defend *Well* for a fee consisting of a 25-cent royalty for every copy sold. The arrangement sharply limited the publishers' liability for legal expenses—always a major stumbling block to the successful publishing of a "hot" book—and guaranteed the lawyer a sizable return if the book sold well. Later, Random House's Bennett Cerf would offer Ernst a similar arrangement for the legal defense of *Ulysses*.

Covici-Friede also told Cape that *Well* would be priced at five dollars—twice the going sum for a novel. Before the English publisher disembarked at New York, the American firm had an agreement to publish *The Well of Loneliness*. Contracts were signed a few days later.

Cape's wish to retrieve and sell the American rights to *Well* was only one of the reasons for the English publisher's trip to New York. His main reason was to make arrangements with Harrison Smith, a senior editor at Harcourt Brace, to establish a new American publishing venture. The idea was not original; British and American publishers had long engaged in reciprocal ventures that sent British books to America and American books to England. Cape's company was already publishing Sinclair Lewis, Eugene O'Neill, H. L. Mencken, Sherwood Anderson, and other American authors in England; an American house would, he thought, enable him to bring out in America the works of his British authors, including Radclyffe Hall.

Cape at first contemplated publishing *Well* himself in New York but then realized he would not have a going concern within the time allowed under the copyright laws. However, since he intended to publish Radclyffe Hall's other books in America himself, he did not give Covici-Friede the usual option to publish them. He told the Americans he was not empowered by Miss Hall to do so, although, strictly speaking, he was. Cape did not want anyone to learn prematurely about his plans with Harrison Smith.

Covici-Friede moved swiftly to get *The Well of Loneliness* into print in America within 120 days following its British publication—the maximum time allowed under the copyright laws. Once the book was in the bookstores and selling well—or so the story goes—Donald Friede called John

Sumner of the anti-vice society to come and arrest him, if he wished. The publisher had been told that complaints about the book had been received by Sumner; Friede wished to avoid the situation in which some defenseless clerk in a bookstore would be arrested and perhaps frightened into a guilty plea or led to make an inadequate defense. Provoking a successful test case would also build up sales for the firm's first five-dollar book.

Sumner—no man to shirk the good fight—is said to have arrived the same day. Looking, according to Friede, "like a sort of bookkeeper," Sumner paid Friede five dollars and went away with a copy of *Well*. Nothing happened for almost a month. Then Sumner returned with a crew of policemen to arrest Friede for selling *Well;* they seized 865 copies of the novel. When Eugen Jan Boissevain, who was Edna St. Vincent Millay's husband, heard about the raid he said: "Will not some true Christian teach Mr. Sumner to abuse himself instead of us, and thus get rid of all this public nuisance?"

Because Ernst and the publishers were unsure at that time whether the New York courts would do better than their English counterparts and would admit literary and scientific opinion on the question of whether a book like *Well* should be adjudged obscene, Covici-Friede had printed in the American edition (after the initial printings) not only Havelock Ellis's praise of John's book but also some of the commendatory opinions expressed by prominent British defenders of *Well,* including Rudyard Kipling, H. G. Wells, Bernard Shaw, and Arnold Bennett. These were set forth in a publisher's note in the sixth printing of *Well,* the one seized by John Sumner and the New York police. The strategy was obvious: an American judge would have difficulty ignoring what prominent British literati had to say about the book.

However, the trial magistrate, Judge Hyman Bushnel, had evidently read *The Well of Loneliness* himself and reached his own conclusions about it.

HYMAN BUSHNEL: The book here involved is a novel dealing with the childhood and early womanhood of a female invert named Stephen Gordon. In broad outline the story shows how Stephen's unnatural tendencies manifested themselves from early childhood; the queer attraction of the child to the maid in the household; her affairs with one Angela Crosby, a normally sexed but unhappily married woman . . .

———

This last fictional relationship, Stephen Gordon's with Angela Crosby, was based upon the love affair of John and Una and depicted John's seduction of the woman who became the most important person in her life. As portrayed in *Well,* it began in this way, "as they sat alone in the garden at Morton."

RADCLYFFE HALL *(The Well of Loneliness): Stephen turned to Angela abruptly: "I can't go on like this, it's vile somehow—it's beastly, it's soiling us both—can't you see that?"*

Angela was startled. "What on earth do you mean?"

"You and me—and then Ralph. I tell you it's beastly—I want you to leave him and come away with me."

"Are you mad?"

"No, I'm sane. It's the only decent thing, it's the only clean thing; we'll go anywhere you like: to Paris, to Egypt, or back to the States. For your sake I'm ready to give up my home. Do you hear? But I can't go on lying about you to Ralph, I want him to know how much I adore you—I want the whole world to know how I adore you."

Angela stared at her, white and aghast: "You are mad," she said slowly, "you're raving mad. Tell him what? Have I let you become my lover? You know that I've always been faithful to Ralph; you know perfectly well that there's nothing to tell him, beyond a few rather schoolgirlish kisses. Can I help it if you're—what you obviously are?"

Stephen spoke wildly, scarcely knowing what she said; she only knew that she needed this woman with a need so intense, that worthy or unworthy, Angela was all that counted at that moment. . . . And now she stood up, very tall, very strong, yet a little grotesque in her pitiful passion, so that looking at her Angela trembled—there was something rather terrible about her. . . .

"Angela, come very far away—anywhere, only come with me soon—tomorrow."

Then Angela forced herself to think quickly, and she said just five words: "Could you marry me, Stephen?"

———

Magistrate Bushnel wound up his description of *Well:*

HYMAN BUSHNEL: The book culminates with an extended elaboration upon [Stephen's] intimate relations with a normal young girl, who becomes a helpless subject of her perverted influence and passion, and pictures the struggles of this girl's affections between this invert and a man from whose normal advances she herself had previously recoiled, because of her own perverted nature. Her sex experiences are set forth in some detail, and also her visits to various resorts frequented by male and female inverts.

———

Bushnel conceded that John's book had literary merit but did not concede that this precluded its being found obscene. "The author has treated these incidents not without some restraint nor is it disputed that the book has literary merits." Then, quoting from the State of New York's brief, he went on: " 'It is a well-written, carefully constructed piece of fiction and contains no unclean words.' " This observation was meant not to rescue *Well* from being found obscene but to emphasize the importance of suppressing it for being immoral. Here, the American judge's reasoning was similar to that employed by *Well*'s English judges.

HYMAN BUSHNEL: Yet the unnatural and depraved relationships portrayed are sought to be idealized and extolled. The characters in the book who indulge in these vices are described in attractive terms and it is maintained throughout that they be accepted on the same plane as persons normally constituted and that their perverse and inverted love is as worthy as the affection between normal beings, and should be considered just as sacred by society. . . . The theme of the novel is not only anti-social and offensive to public morals and decency, but the method in which it is developed, in its highly emotional way, attracting and focusing attention upon perverted values and unnatural vices, and seeking to justify and idealize them, is strongly calculated to corrupt and debase those members of the community who would be susceptible to its immoral influence.

———

In the New York courtroom, seated beside his lawyer Morris Ernst, publisher Donald Friede was taken by surprise at the drift of Bushnel's opinion; he had supposed that he, and John's book, would be freed.

DONALD FRIEDE: I was so confident of being acquitted that day that I had booked passage to Europe on the *Vulcania,* due to sail at midnight that night. I was therefore completely taken by surprise when the judge glared at me when I stood up before him, and then proceeded to read a scathing indictment of *The Well of Loneliness,* of the firm of Covici-Friede, and of me. It made me feel as if I had been caught selling filthy postcards to school children. . . .

———

Morris Ernst later said that Hyman Bushnel, the judge who first considered the case of *Well,* might have found the book legal if Radclyffe Hall's characters had *apologized* for what they had done. He added, "There's no doubt that if Stephen Gordon were a man instead of a woman, the *Well* would have been adjudged merely a rather over-sentimentalized bit of Victorian romanticism. But that was not Bushnel's view." Ernst thought it not surprising, however, that the panel of judges who next considered the case saw it differently. "It all goes to show how meaningless the idea of 'obscene' is: it all depends upon the sophistication and discretion of the judges who read the book."

The New York procedure with regard to obscenity prosecutions provided for a new trial by a three-judge court of special sessions, if the criminal summons originally issued was not dismissed in city magistrate's court. Ernst prepared for this stage of the New York trial of *Well* by soliciting scores of testimonials to the book's literary merit and social significance from authors, artists, critics, educators, doctors, clergymen, and psychiatrists. This, of course, was in imitation of what had been done, fruitlessly in the event, at the trial of *Well* at Bow Street. Among American literary luminaries whose statements the lawyer obtained were Sherwood Anderson, John Dos Passos, Theodore Dreiser, Edna Ferber, Ernest Hemingway, and Upton Sinclair. Ernst did not attempt to produce such figures as witnesses in court, probably fearing that their testimony would be rejected in New York as that of their confreres across the Atlantic had been rejected by Magistrate Biron. Instead, he had their views printed in a fifty-one-page brief that he filed in the appeals court.

That brief also contained a "Protest" against *Well*'s suppression by seventy-four "men of letters, educators, publishers, artists and publicists." These testimonials did not directly address the issue of whether the book was "obscene," because, in the States as in England, that was a question the judges would decide for themselves. The American lawyer for *Well* was simply trying to accomplish by indirection what he could not do directly, and what the novel's English lawyers had failed to accomplish directly: bring to the court's, and the public's, attention the opinions of important figures who considered the book a work of value—one that ought not to be suppressed as "obscene." After reading John's *Well* and Ernst's brief, the court of special sessions dismissed the criminal charges that had been lodged against Donald Friede. Friede thought this somewhat absurd, in view of the contrasting result in the Massachusetts case involving *An American Tragedy*.

DONALD FRIEDE: In Dreiser's case there was the seemingly impossible picture of action being taken on a book that was written by one of America's outstanding writers and that had been internationally accepted as a classic. In Radclyffe Hall's case we were dealing with a book that had already been suppressed in England, and that dealt openly with the subject of Lesbianism.

———

The capricious working of obscenity censorship law in the United States was certainly predictable, given the judicial unwillingness to receive evidence of literary value, as well as what the brilliant American jurist Jerome Frank called "the exquisite vagueness" of the obscenity concept.* This, combined with the federalism implicit in the constitutional structure of American government, which postulates that each state and the courts of each state are sovereign on matters within the state's police powers, produced odd judicial results and a patchwork of censorship and freedom. There was no common understanding of what is obscene, neither among the people nor among the judges. A work that seemed to some the laughter of genius might appear to others patently obscene—the law left the issue up to the judge in each individual case. The courts of one state were perfectly free to apply the law of obscenity as they saw fit and to ignore what the courts of other states or the federal courts had said or done—frequently with respect to the same literary work. Although the Warren Court, in decisions written by Justice William J. Brennan, Jr., during the 1960s, would act to solve both problems—that of vagueness and that of disparity across state and local lines—its work would to some degree be undone by the Burger and Rehnquist Courts, during the seventies and eighties, through use of the "local community standards" of decency rule.

———

*Frank was one of the founders of the American school of "legal realism"; his seminal work was *Law and the Modern Mind* (1930). He was one of FDR's recruits to the New Deal and became a distinguished judge on the Second Circuit Court of Appeals. His thoughtful, iconoclastic approach to obscenity law is mentioned below in Chapter 15.

. . .

The newspaper coverage of Friede's New York prosecution made John's book's a runaway best-seller. Once the New York appellate court declared *Well* not obscene—in April 1929—Covici-Friede brought out a twenty-five-dollar "Victory Edition." Every copy was autographed by John and contained a summary of the court proceedings specially written for the edition by Morris Ernst. John heard the news of the American court's action in Paris and wrote excitedly to Robin:

RADCLYFFE HALL: Here's to the Saints, God bless them! And to Hell and Damnation with Jix and Co!

———

She then cabled "darling Robin": "Hip Hip!"

All that spring and summer the money rolled in. Her royalty check from Covici-Friede alone was "stupendous"—$64,000.00! And the Pegasus edition in Paris was selling over one hundred copies a day.

John's first royalties from the American edition in fact turned out to be slightly in excess of the total capitalization of Covici-Friede when it had first been formed, only the year before, at a time when Friede had not even heard of an author named Radclyffe Hall. Covici-Friede sold over 100,000 copies of *Well* during the first year.

After he was convicted in Boston for selling Dreiser's *An American Tragedy* there, Friede went to Europe to find illustrators for his bustling new firm's line of "Limited Edition" books. Although he persuaded Hélène Perdriat to do illustrations for an edition of *Madame Bovary*, all in all "the trip was not a terrific success—except for one other thing, I got Richard Aldington to write his first novel, which turned out to be the finest war novel I ever read, *Death of a Hero.*"

In Paris Friede invited John and Una to lunch at his hotel. They were impressed by his determination to fight for the freedom of *Well* in America. Una told Robin that "as U.S. publishers go he's quite decent and honest." John was already beginning, she said, to long for anonymity. She wrote Robin that she would rather be "Annie Jones of Putney who lives in a villa with father & mother and plays in the local lawn tennis tournaments!"

RADCLYFFE HALL: Or better still a retired ironmonger with a fat bank account, a wife and four children—I want to read the lessons on Sunday feeling placid, because all sinners are damned, and because unlike Lot I have never been tempted to rape my elderly daughters.

———

In Berlin, Friede called on a number of publishers, trying to find books that might lend themselves to American publication. But he complained that the minute he spotted a title that looked promising he came up against regretful answers. "So sorry," the publisher would say, "but Herr Knopf has the option on this book." Or if it was not Herr Knopf, then it would be Herr Huebsch of the Viking Press who had been there first. "It seemed as if they had parceled out all of German literature between them."

In Paris Friede made final arrangements with Aldington to publish *Death of a Hero* and watched the spectacle of Marshal Ferdinand Foch's funeral from the balcony of Radclyffe Hall's apartment. Then he sailed back to New York, where he found the firm's offices "becoming a madhouse." Intoxicated by the success of *The Well of Loneliness,* they were expanding like mad. Their small offices "bulged with assistant editors and foreign editors, and billing clerks and typists." They began to look for new quarters and eventually took bigger space in a fine building on Fourth Avenue, in the center of the publishing district.

In the fall of 1929, Donald Friede and Pat Covici had no thought of a depression: the market was still climbing.

DONALD FRIEDE: And most of us were in it, as were our barbers and our bootblacks and our elevator men. But less than three months after the move of our offices, the market cracked, and the boom years ended. . . . To the great optimist in the White House* the thing that was just around that mythical and never-to-be-reached corner was, of course, *prosperity*. To us it came to mean *creditors:* worried creditors, impatient creditors, demanding creditors—in fact every kind of a creditor except a satisfied one.

———

And yet somehow or other they kept going for eight more years and managed to publish some good books in those years, and publish them well. In 1930, for instance, there were new novels by Aldington and François Mauriac and Fulton Oursler. There was Margaret Anderson's story of *The Little Review* and two books by e.e. cummings and new volumes of verse by Aldington and Horace Gregory.

When the end came in 1938 they were just a few months short of publishing what Friede believed would have been the most successful book they had ever undertaken, John Steinbeck's *The Grapes of Wrath.* Then the firm collapsed. Pat Covici went over to Viking, taking Steinbeck with him, and Friede went to Hollywood to represent authors making movie sales. By then, Horace Liveright was on the Coast doing the same thing. One of the first deals Friede negotiated was the sale of Hemingway's *For Whom the Bell Tolls* to Paramount.

Jonathan Cape's American publishing venture with Harrison Smith turned out to be short-lived. The Depression finished it off in 1931, little more then two years after its doors had opened on Forty-sixth Street in New York. Before that happened, however, Cape had produced an American edition of Radclyffe Hall's *The Unlit Lamp* and sold 15,000 copies of it. But when he published the novel that she wrote after *Well, The Master of the House,* in the spring of 1932, Audrey Heath called it "a calamity for John."

At first the book's American sales were promising and the reviews quite

———

*Herbert Hoover.

good—better than in England. John wrote Robin that she was convinced it would make "a big sweep." But now Jonathan Cape announced that his American company, by then called Cape-Ballou, was bankrupt. Distribution and sales of *The Master* stopped, and all copies were seized by creditors. John was extremely angry at this turn of events because, having heard rumors of the weakness of the Cape-Ballou operation, she had begged Jonathan Cape to return her rights if there was even the slightest chance that his American company would go under.

One day John cornered Jonathan Cape in his office in London and, with Robin and Una in attendance, told him just what he was: a "dirty black-guard" and a "skunk." He'd ruined *Well* in England and now he was doing the same to *Master* in America.

UNA TROUBRIDGE: Cape went the color of weak lemonade & murmured "Don't threaten me" & we made our grim departure.

———

John later said that *The Master* died, "murdered by its publisher."

In May 1929, just after *Well* was set free in New York, John and Una left Paris for the Riviera, "where the sun might bring the color back into our cheeks."

Accompanied by their English maid, Barber, and their French chauffeur, Pierre, they motored south at a leisurely pace.

UNA TROUBRIDGE: We stopped for the night as we felt inclined and allowed the ex-chefs of royalty to feed us . . . and as the weather grew warmer we expanded, our tired nerves relaxed and we were very happy.

———

They did not care for the meals at the English-run hotel in St.-Tropez that Colette had recommended to them, so they moved into the more palatial Golf Hotel at Beauvallon and stayed in light, airy rooms on the top floor with balconies overlooking the bay, where there was a private beach at which they could swim naked every day.

UNA TROUBRIDGE: I am dark red brown all over except for an insignificant middle piece where my swimming suit can't come quite off . . . & John looks fifteen years younger, a fine brown & all the lines smoothing out of her day by day.

———

Una had never seen anything like the Riviera until John took her there; to John it was a familiar story. Said Una: "To me it was all new and wonderful. I spent most of my time stark naked clutching a bottle of coconut oil, so as to cultivate a rich copper hue *all over*—no mixed grill for me!"

Una lived continuously with John for twenty-nine years, to the day John died, in 1943. In 1934, during an extended illness of Una's, John fell in love with a Russian woman from the American Hospital in Paris; she had come to care for Una, and John took her into the household. Evgenia Souline was a thirty-year-old unmarried White Russian, the daughter of a Cossack general, an officially stateless refugee. She had Mongolian features, wore glasses, spoke broken English, and "was far from beautiful," but, conceded Una, "she was a devoted and admirable nurse." John "fell madly in love" with Evgenia and initiated her—a fiery, erratic, and passionate virgin—in "the love that dare not speak its name."* The relationship lasted for nine years, during which John wrote Evgenia more than six hundred letters. When John was recuperating from operations on her eyes, and during her terminal illness, Una herself wrote for John seventy-one of these letters—despite, and because of, her faithful love.

When John lay dying of lung cancer, Una would not let Evgenia Souline into John's room. Una sat and slept by John's side throughout her painful seven-month illness. As death drew near, John's devotion to Una deepened. On her deathbed John told her friend: "I want you, you, *you:* I want only you in all the world!" And this:

RADCLYFFE HALL: You may flatter yourself, Lady Troubridge, I'm not sticking this for [Evgenia], of whom I'm intensely fond, but who is on the very outskirts of my existence. . . . It's only for your sake I'm sticking it, entirely for your sake.

———

Not long before John died, she asked to see Micki Jacob.

MICKI JACOB: Una met me, and in the sitting room of their suite told me what the trouble was. She was very brave, though I remember that her face was like chalk. . . . John was in bed, immaculate as always, her hair shining and sleek, her pyjamas the last word in silk elegance. . . . She looked tired, thinner, and fine-drawn, but she smiled, held out her hand and said, very cheerfully, "This is a nice kind of ending, isn't it Mike?" . . . Just before I left she again gave me her hand, and said, "Good-bye, Mike. If things— well, if they don't go quite as Una hopes they may, take care of her Mike, won't you?" . . . That was the last time I saw John.

———

According to Una's diary, this is how John looked when she died:

UNA TROUBRIDGE: At one moment it was my beloved—wasted, drawn, lividly pale and at times distorted—the next a stranger lay there on the

---

*There is a letter from John to Soulíne reading: "[H]ow virginal and innocent you were, how ignorant of physical passion—you the most passionate of all women. . . . I was your first lover. . . . Step by step—very gently I led you towards fulfillment. . . . I found you a virgin and I made you a lover. . . . I have made a new discovery through you—I find that to take an innocent woman is quite unlike anything else in life, is perhaps the most perfect experience in life." While this was going on, Una confided to her diary: "In spite of everything we [she and John] are close, close: one spirit and one flesh, indissoluble and indivisible for ever. [John] said to me yesterday: 'Remain with me for ever and ever through eternity. Amen!' She said: '*You* are permanent!' "

bed. Very handsome, very peaceful, very calm, but with scarcely a traceable resemblance to my John. After she had been laid out and later when the bandage was removed from her head . . . I stood looking down at her and I said: "Poor boy, he must have suffered a lot before he died. . . ." It seemed a young airman or soldier who perhaps had died of wounds after much suffering. Ivory clear and pale, the exquisite line of the jaw, the pure aquiline of the nose with its delicate wing nostrils, the beautiful modelling of eyelids and brow. Not a trace of femininity; no one in their senses could have suspected that anything but a young man had died.

—

In her bedroom, a Catholic priest said a private mass.* Una shared the wafer. After John died, Una lay down on the bed made up next to hers, and slept soundly beside the corpse.

Una had John's body embalmed and laid in a mahogany coffin that was lined with lead. The brass nameplate was engraved with a quotation from an Elizabeth Barrett Browning sonnet that John had loved. It read:

Radclyffe Hall
Author
1943
". . . And if God Choose I Shall
But Love Thee Better After Death"

Her coffin lay for a time in Westminster Cathedral and was later transferred to the vault in Highgate Cemetery. There, behind the tomb's iron grill, Ladye's coffin rested on a stone bench to the right. Una placed John's coffin in the center. When her own time came she would, she thought, take up her rightful position on John's left, forming once and for all a memorial to "Our Three Selves."

In her last will—only twelve lines, written seven days before her death— John left Una everything she owned, "absolutely trusting her to make such provision for our friend [Evgenia] Souline as in her absolute discretion she may consider right knowing my wishes for the welfare of the said [Evgenia] Souline." Una later said she gladly did what John bid her do for Evgenia, seeking to steer a safe course between seeing "her taken care of and her earnings supplemented," and not wanting "her so provided for that she is idle; as this in the past only led her to degenerate into discontent, ill-temper and misery."

Over the next twenty years, Una wrote several thousand letters to her departed friend, "confident that we would have an ultimate and eternal

---

*John had become a Catholic at the age of thirty-two, when she was living with her first lover, Ladye, who had been Catholic from childhood. John's conversion took place when Ladye took her to a mime-play in which a nun, who was lured from her vows by the wiles of a "trickster," was brought to redemption by the miraculous intervention of a statue of the Madonna.

union." Her faith in this reunion had been confirmed when she found a letter John had left for her, which ended with the words: "God keep you until we meet again . . . and believe in my love, which is much, much stronger than mere death."

For a while Una bore the anguish of her love and pain as she would a stigmatization, as an honor and spiritual gift to be endured and cherished. But in time a growing sense of desolation overtook her. Her salvation was in the letters she wrote to John:

UNA TROUBRIDGE: Darling, this isn't just pain, it is torture . . . my God, if it weren't for a stubborn instructive holding to a faith that is in me . . . that we shall, we *must* meet again, I wouldn't endure this thing another hour.

———

John and Una had planned to move permanently to Italy but had been "trapped" in England by the outbreak of World War II. When the war was over Una went to Florence, where she and John had intended to put down roots. Before leaving her homeland in 1949, at a time when outside of England *Well* was selling 100,000 copies a year, Una persuaded the Falcon Press (later Hammond and Hammond) to publish John's novel. (In 1934, John had tried without success to get Cape to bring out *Well* again in England, through his "medical" list.*) In the mid-fifties, Una moved again, to Rome.

Like John, Una became a wealthy woman; John had left her over £118,000, as well as the right to royalties on her books. And like John, Una was religious. In Florence she went to Catholic mass every morning, and in her will she bequeathed the greatest part of her estate—well over £100,000—to the Order of Poor Clares in Lynton, as John had wished. Una instructed her literary executor, the publisher Lovat Dickson, to ensure that nothing "detrimental to the dignity and nobility" of John's works would ever be permitted, and that none of her books would be expurgated or abbreviated.

She was seventy-six years old when she died, in 1963, in Rome. She never lost her conviction that she would rejoin John after death and she wrote her letters to John until just ten days before she died.

Una was not interred in the vault at Highgate Cemetery. Her burial instructions were only later discovered, unopened, in her bank at Minehead. Una's grave rests in a small plot in the Foreign Catholics section of Rome's Verano Cemetery. On the flat marble slab that marks it, beneath a line from St. Francis's "Song of the Beasts," is engraved the phrase *There is no death!*

———

*Much later, in 1983, a new English edition of *Well* was brought out by the feminist publishing house Virago; the novel was also read over the radio to the nation via the BBC's "Book at Bedtime."

Not long before Una died, an old admirer of John's, the author Ethel Mannin, asked her in a letter how she and John had squared their relationship with their religion. She wondered in particular what they had done, while John was alive, about confession.

UNA TROUBRIDGE: There was nothing to confess.

12

Like
a Phallus
Made of Dough

I N THE SPRING OF 1946 Doubleday and Company published *Memoirs of Hecate County,* the "most salacious and lascivious work issued for indiscriminate circulation" that John Sumner of the New York Society for the Suppression of Vice had ever read (although, Sumner confided to the press, "I've read worse books that were sold secretly"). Doubleday was no longer under the sway of its conservative founder, Frank N. Doubleday, his wife, Neltje, or their son, Nelson. The company's new head was a lawyer, the firm's general counsel, Douglas Black.

Memoirs of Hecate County was the second novel written by one of the foremost American literary and social critics of the twentieth century, Edmund Wilson, who thought the book "probably the best damn thing I ever wrote." It was not exactly a novel; rather it was a book of stories having a common locale and theme. The locale was "Hecate County," a distant suburb of New York; the theme was "the bedevilment of the smart men and women who lived there." In a letter to Mario Praz, Wilson wrote that his book "was intended as a suburban inferno."

EDMUND WILSON: Hecate County might be any community of the kind in Connecticut, Pennsylvania, or New Jersey—you are never told where it is. The stories are all about different kinds of people, but they all have an element of fantasy and a kind of odor of damnation.

—

According to Wilson all the women in the book, except a taxi dancer named Anna, were "witches"—hence the book's title. The most attractive of the women-witches was Imogen Loomis, "the princess with the golden hair."

EDMUND WILSON *(Memoirs of Hecate County)*: *But what struck and astonished me most [about Imogen Loomis] was that not only were her thighs perfect columns but that all that lay between them was impressively beautiful, too, with an ideal aesthetic value that I had never found there before. The mount was of a classical femininity: round and smooth and plump: the fleece, if not quite golden, was blond and curly and soft; and the portals were a deep tender rose like the petals of some flesh flower. And they were doing their feminine work of making things easy for the entrant with a honeysweet sleek profusion that showed I had quite misjudged her in suspecting as I had sometimes done that she was really unresponsive to caresses. She became, in fact, so smooth and open that after a moment I could hardly feel her. Her little bud was so deeply embedded that it was hardly involved in the play, and she made me arrest my movement while she did something special and gentle that did not, however, press on this point, rubbing herself somehow against me—and then came, with a self-excited tremor that appeared to me curiously mild for a woman of her positive energy. I went on and had a certain disappointment, for, with the brimming of female fluid, I felt even less sensation; but—gently enough—I came, too.*

By the story's end, in a dream, even the narrator's old girlfriend, Jo, was turning into a witch.

EDMUND WILSON: Hecate County is my favorite among my books—I have never understood why the people who interest themselves in my work never pay any attention to it.

Before Doubleday contracted with Wilson to publish *Hecate County*, Houghton Mifflin and Scribner's both turned it down; Wilson said they were "scared to death of the story." The author, however, was sufficiently determined to see his favorite work published that he vowed to "take some of my *New Yorker* money and publish it myself"—much, he might have added, as D. H. Lawrence did with *Lady Chatterley's Lover*.

After *Hecate County* appeared Wilson received "some pretty sour reactions" about it, "not only from my colleagues on the newspapers, but also from friends like Peggy Bacon, who has been so much shocked by the book that she can't bear to speak to me about it." Beth Huling "hated it"; she said, "You haven't convinced the reader that the man was in love with those two women!" Vladimir Nabokov spoke about *Hecate County* as if he "thought that [Wilson] had made an unsuccessful attempt to write something like *Fanny Hill*." "The work," he said, "is pure as a block of ice in a surgical laboratory."

And although Wilson at first "was pleased" to learn that the White House had bought a copy, he later "grew uneasy" at the image of Harry and Bess Truman, the president and the first lady, "attempting to read it aloud, in the evening."

According to Wilson's third wife, the author Mary McCarthy, "after the book came out and was being discussed in the press in those terms," and "even after the book had been suppressed in Boston," Wilson paid "an apprehensive visit" to his mother.

MARY McCARTHY: Wilson's mother, as far as he could tell, had never read any book he had published. That particular morning, when he arrived in her house in Red Bank, New Jersey, he had hardly sat down opposite her in her usual window seat (she was almost totally deaf) when she said to him in a very loud voice:

"Well, Edmund, I'm glad to see that you've written a book that will *sell*."

———

The critics were, for the most part, not happy with Wilson's favorite work; they carped at its sexuality.

RAYMOND CHANDLER: The book is indecent enough, of course, and in exactly the most offensive way—without passion, like a phallus made of dough. . . .

The problem of what is significant literature I leave to fat bores like Edmund Wilson—a man of many distinctions—among which personally I revere most highly . . . that of having made fornication as dull as a railroad time table.

MALCOLM COWLEY: The descriptions of love are so zoological, the narrator is so intent on making a safari through the bedroom with gun and microscope, that we find he is preserving only the stuffed and mounted hides of his love affairs; what has disappeared is simply their passion, the breath of their life.

HARPER'S MAGAZINE (June 1946): For a man who spends so much time cultivating the sensuous aspects of life Mr. Wilson exhibits an astounding lack of joy. . . . He is the Puritan *malgré lui*.

———

Perhaps the mixed reviews encouraged John Sumner to think he had a better-than-even chance to ban *Hecate County*, despite its author's literary standing. By 1946, Edmund Wilson had already become one of the country's best-known men of letters; he was the author of thirteen nonfiction works and an earlier novel, *I Thought of Daisy*. Doubleday's lawyers managed to get this information, and more, before the men in robes who would sit in judgment on Wilson's book once John Sumner took its publisher to court.

But the author was never really well off. His salary as *The New Republic*'s literary editor was $7,500 a year. For years he lived in a shabby old frame house on East Fifty-third Street, which he rented for $50 a month, subletting parts to friends. In 1941 Wilson quit his job at *The New Republic* and went to work for *The New Yorker*. Around that time he also bought a big old house on Cape Cod, in Wellfleet, spending $5,000 for it. There Wilson spent as much time as he could over the next decade and wrote half a dozen books and more than a hundred essays and articles. It was there that *Memoirs of Hecate County* was written. Wilson was earning $10,000 a year writing book reviews for *The New Yorker* when Doubleday published *Hecate County* and Anthony Comstock's shade struck.

Memoirs of Hecate County was published on two different occasions in the United States. The 1946 Doubleday edition, which became an almost immediate best-seller, was suppressed within a year of its publication as a result of a prosecution started by John Sumner and decisions declining to rescue Wilson's book rendered by three New York courts and the United States Supreme Court. Some ten years later the firm of Farrar, Straus, and Cudahy cautiously reissued Edmund Wilson's novel.

ROGER STRAUS: Our rule of thumb was very simple: try to eliminate as much as you can all mention of male or female genitalia and you'll stay out of trouble. And we achieved that to a certain extent with Nelson Algren's *Walk on the Wild Side.* And obviously, as far as the "Princess with the Golden Hair" story in *Hecate County* was concerned, there was no way of asking Edmund Wilson to crop off her pubic hairs—which was of course what did it. Let's face it, that was the only thing that was possibly attackable and even that was pretty thin soup.

———

By 1959, when Straus published *Hecate County,* publishers of other sexually provocative literary works had begun to put censors on the run. Even so, Roger Straus took a number of precautions to ensure that his firm would present a low profile. These included placing the imprint of a defunct subsidiary on the book, publishing and warehousing it outside New York State, and quietly checking with Frank Hogan, the Manhattan (New York County) district attorney, who had banned the book in the first place, about his attitude toward republication.

In 1946, when the book was originally published by Doubleday, John Sumner obtained a search warrant from Magistrate Phillip B. Thurston at Mid-Manhattan Court, collected some plainclothes police, and relieved four Doubleday bookstores in New York of some 130 copies of *Hecate County.** By the next day fearful booksellers throughout the borough, including Brentano's, Scribner's, Hearn's, and the Union News Company, had removed all copies from their shelves. Deprived by the police of their stock, Doubleday's own bookshops continued to take orders for *Hecate County* until criminal informations were filed by the New York District Attorney's Office charging two Doubleday clerks and "the largest publishing company in the world" with selling an obscene book.†

———

*As a result of a series of Supreme Court decisions handed down in the 1960s, most of them written by Justice William J. Brennan, Jr., such searches and seizures of presumptively protected expressive materials—i.e., books, magazines, movies, etc.—undertaken without an *advance adversary judicial* proceeding and a finding of "obscenity," would today be understood to be unconstitutional. See Brennan's opinion in *A Quantity of Books* v. *Kansas,* decided in 1964, reprinted in de Grazia, *Censorship Landmarks* (1969), 502–7.

†By 1946, the year *Hecate County* was censored, Doubleday was publishing more than 300 separate titles and manufacturing between 24 million and 36 million books each year. William B. Lockhart and Robert McClure, "Literature, the Law of Obscenity, and the Constitution,"

John Sumner liked to think that his ancestors were Puritans and that this accounted for his choosing literary censorship as a vocation; he claimed one of his forebears was on the passenger list of the *Mayflower*. His father was Rear Admiral George W. Sumner of the United States Navy. Born in Washington, D.C., where he spent his early years, the boy went to high school in Brooklyn after his father was transferred to the navy yard there. Sumner's first job was "runner" for Henry Clews and Company, stockbrokers. Finding after ten years with Clews that he was still employed as a clerk, "for about $20 a week," he entered New York University Law School, took courses at night, and in 1904 received his degree. Sumner specialized in stock and bond litigations for a few years; a client told him that the Society for the Suppression of Vice was looking for a man who knew something of the law to replace Anthony Comstock upon his retirement or death. When Comstock died, in 1915, after nearly forty years of service, young Sumner took the job and became the closest thing to a literary czar the country ever had.

JOHN SUMNER: I liked the work and I was assured of earning a living.

—

Sumner was not overawed by the reputation of his predecessor; he looked back on Comstock as a well-intentioned gentlemen "who realized there was much vice in this city which would eventually develop into crime." Besides that, "he was somewhat of a religious fanatic who also loved notoriety."

JOHN SUMNER: I am not carrying out the ideas of our society in any spirit of a reformer. I am only trying to have laws which exist on our statute books enforced. . . . The fact that you and I do not steal does not mean that it

Minnesota Law Review 38 (1954), 295. By then, "Doubleday was already the wonder of the publishing world. It had six specialized editorial departments, owned one of the world's largest book-manufacturing plants, fielded three major sales forces, and boasted an advertising, promotion, and publicity organization of exceptional quality." It was leading the mass-market sale of popular-price reprints and had five book clubs in operation, two wholly owned subsidiaries in Canada, and a chain of retail bookstores in the United States. John Tebbel, *A History of Book Publishing in the United States* 4 (1981), Chapter 9. Tebbel describes this publishing "colossus," the Doubleday family "saga," and the remarkable group of individuals who were responsible for the company's growth and success in glowing terms. By 1980, Tebbel says, Doubleday "represented the ultimate triumph of the old houses," which he numbered at thirty (105).

In the 1950s "a brilliant, strong-minded young man, regarded as a maverick by his elders," Jason Epstein, began "perhaps the most innovative of the divisions" at Doubleday, Anchor Books. This was the first line of what came to be known as trade paperbacks, quality paperback books sold in bookstores rather than through mass-market outlets. The success of Epstein's Anchor Books "astounded the industry" and became as much a landmark in reprint publishing as the Modern Library had been in the thirties. At the height of his success at Doubleday, Epstein went over to Random House (see Chapter 14), where he took over and developed the Knopf Vintage series of "paperback reprints of prestigious titles of the past." After that, he and his wife, Barbara, founded and co-edited with Robert Silvers *The New York Review of Books*, the outstanding critical journal of the sixties and thereafter in the United States (Tebbel, 114–15). Epstein's role in the publication of Vladimir Nabokov's *Lolita* is described in Chapter 14.

is not necessary to have laws punishing theft. The fact that you and I can read a book without being harmed by it does not mean that we must not have laws that will protect those who will be injured.

———

Sumner's special enemies were "all the so-called high-brows" who, "loving filth for its own sake," "raised the cry of freedom of speech" when he tried to stop the sale of books filled with dirt. Most of the "dirt" in *Hecate County* was contained in the chapter called "The Princess with the Golden Hair," but not all of it involved the narrator's relationship with Imogen Loomis. He also consorted with the young taxi dancer Anna Lenihan, who first made love with him out of spite over her husband's unfaithfulness:

EDMUND WILSON (*Memoirs of Hecate County*): *I remember one cold winter Sunday when Anna had come in the afternoon, a day of blank uptown facades and decorous uptown perspectives, when I had gone down to the deserted museum to look something up in a book, and, returning, it seemed so incongruous to watch her take off her pink slip and to have her in her prosaic brassiere: the warm and adhesive body and the mossy damp underparts—the mystery, the organic animal, the prime human oven of heat and juice—between the cold afternoon sheets in the gray-lit Sunday room; and one evening when I had come home from a party, at which I had made Imogen smile by my tender and charming gallantries and had kissed her hand at parting, and had made love to Anna for the second time, by a sudden revival of appetite after she had put on her clothes to go, by way of her white thighs and buttocks, laid bare between black dress and gray stockings—she was so slim that it was almost as easy to take her from behind as face to face—while she kicked up one foot in its blunt-toed black shoe as a gesture of playful resistance or simply of wanton freedom. . . . She gets a sensation, she says, like a thrill that goes all through her—sometimes it makes her toes curl: "I want to scratch and bite—I don't know where I am or anything." The doctor in the hospital had said that she must be very passionate because the opening of her womb was so small.*

———

When John Sumner raided the Doubleday bookstores, playwright Elmer Rice made a bravura statement on behalf of the American Civil Liberties Union.*

ELMER RICE: Mr. Sumner doesn't seem to know when he's licked. . . . This is a book by a recognized author, published by a reputable publishing house. Its suppression violates freedom of speech and press. . . . The ACLU will take whatever action is necessary to defend the author, the publisher, and any bookseller.

———

*The ACLU directly participated in the *Hecate County* case only at the Supreme Court level when an *amicus curiae* brief urging the Court to free Wilson's book was filed by Kenneth W. Greenawalt, a professor of law at Columbia University. The lawyer who argued the case for Doubleday, on appeal in New York and to the Supreme Court, was Whitney North Seymour, who at the time was on the executive board of the ACLU. See endnote.

Rice also dispatched a telegram to Douglas Black at Doubleday, asking the publisher to transmit to his counsel the ACLU's offer "to assist in any way he desired in defending the sale of the book." A similar offer of assistance was wired by the playwright to Edmund Wilson in Wellfleet. Although the reputation of the publisher, the author, and the book suggested that this case might be a perfect test of the constitutional validity of the obscenity laws and of the powers wielded by John Sumner, the country's foremost civil liberties defense organization was less than confident about the likely outcome.

ELMER RICE: Our advisers have read the book and regard it as not in violation of state statute under previous interpretations of law in similar cases. Any interpretation of obscenity is so dependent on prejudice that the outcome of such litigation is always problematic.

———

The state of the American law of obscenity at that time was not very different from what it had been in the days when *The Little Review*'s publication of excerpts from *Ulysses* was suppressed, nearly thirty years before. There was no meaningful authoritative judicial definition of "obscene," no judicial understanding of the bearing of literary value on obscenity, and only the rudiments of the jurisprudential idea that novels and other imaginative literature should be entitled to constitutional protection. There was remarkably little in the Constitution, its historical context, the statute books, the Supreme Court's own decided cases, or the law treatises and law reviews to guide the Supreme Court in its deliberations as to whether Edmund Wilson's novel and its publisher should stand condemned or should be freed in the light of the First Amendment's guarantees of freedom of speech and press.* There was not even anything in the law or constitutional jurisprudence to enlighten the justices as to whether, in trying to reach a decision on the issue, they should themselves read the book, or leave that to the lower court judges.

On the other side there was the age-old common-law tradition of fining and imprisoning persons who published "obscene libels" and the century-old habit of state and federal judges of treating "obscenity" like any other crime of conduct, as one that did not give rise to constitutional issues related to free speech or press. These traditions argued powerfully for

———

*The next year, however, Judge Curtis Bok, sitting as a Pennsylvania trial judge in criminal proceedings that had been brought against the sellers of James T. Farrell's *Studs Lonigan* trilogy, William Faulkner's *Sanctuary* and *Wild Palms,* Erskine Caldwell's *God's Little Acre,* Calder Willingham's *End As a Man,* and other "current literature," held all the books not obscene and wrote the first really thoughtful judicial opinion about the limitations that the First Amendment's guarantees should be interpreted to exert upon obscenity proceedings. Bok's opinion (reprinted in full in de Grazia, *Censorship Landmarks* [1969], 150–65) was picked up by federal judge Jerome Frank a few years later, in his opinion raising constitutional questions at the federal appellate level concerning the conviction of Samuel Roth for sending "obscene" literature through the mails (see *Censorship Landmarks,* 272–90). The Supreme Court eventually examined the problem in the *Roth* case, described below in Chapter 15.

routinely upholding the judicial punishment of purveyors of "obscenity" and the suppression of "obscene" expression. At the Supreme Court stage of the *Hecate County* case, these arguments were felt to be so strong and unassailable by the book's prosecutor, the Manhattan district attorney, that at oral argument he spent less than a minute confuting Doubleday's constitutional contentions.

The most important academic authority on freedom of expression at the time was Professor Zechariah Chafee of the Harvard Law School. A seminal work written by Chafee in 1920, *Freedom of Speech,* evaluated the doctrinal approaches to First Amendment freedom that had evolved to date through the judiciary process—mainly the now famous pronouncements concerning "clear and present danger" of Supreme Court justices Oliver Wendell Holmes, Jr., and Louis Brandeis, and the *Masses* opinion written by federal district court judge Learned Hand. Their free speech doctrines sprang from a group of World War I "sedition" cases, and while some of these involved pamphlets and books and one involved a radical journal of literature, politics, and art *(The Masses),* none related to the use of obscenity laws to censor literary or artistic works.* Through the first quarter of the twentieth century, neither Holmes, Brandeis, the Hands, nor Chafee had been able to see that prosecutions of publishers or distributors of allegedly obscene literature, or interference with the use of the mails to distribute such literature, implicated free speech values and conceivably violated constitutional law. This was especially curious in Chafee's case since he had recognized and reported in *Freedom of Speech* that the framers of the First Amendment thought of the arts as included within the scope of freedom of the press.

As Chafee phrased it in a few sentences near the end of his great book:

ZECHARIAH CHAFEE: Freedom of speech covers much more than political ideas.† It embraces all discussion which enriches human life and helps it to be more wisely led. Thus in our first national statement of the subject by the Continental Congress in 1774, this freedom was declared to include "the advancement of truth, science, morality and *arts* in general."

Early in the book Chafee had quoted more generously from what he described as "our first national statement of the subject," presented in a letter of October 1774 from the Continental Congress to the inhabitants of the province of Quebec.‡ The letter, which was signed by the president

---

*Federal appellate judge Augustus N. Hand bypassed an opportunity to bring the First Amendment and the free speech tradition to bear on obscenity law when he unhesitatingly upheld the postmaster general's suppression of an issue of *The Little Review* for running a pacifistic short story with a sexual theme written by Wyndham Lewis. See endnotes for Chapter 1.

†Judge Robert H. Bork would later ignore at his peril the idea that freedom of speech "covers much more than political ideas"; this contributed to the defeat of President Reagan's attempt to place Bork on the United States Supreme Court.

‡This important document would later be quoted by Justice William J. Brennan, Jr., in

of the congress, Henry Middleton, sought to enlist the Quebecois in the congress's revolutionary attempt to obtain redress of their "afflicting grievances" caused by violations of the "irrevocable rights" to which they, in common with other English subjects, were entitled—including the right to choose their own representatives, to be ruled by laws (not edicts of men), to trial by jury and liberty of the person (including habeas corpus), and to freedom of the press. "The last right we shall mention [of those believed to be inalienable] regards the freedom of the press. The importance of this consists, besides the advancement of truth, science, morality and arts in general, in its diffusion of liberal sentiments on the administration of Government, its ready communication of thoughts between subjects, and its consequential promotion of union among them, whereby oppressive officers are shamed or intimidated, into more honourable and just modes of conducting affairs."

In the *Masses* case, referred to above, Learned Hand did advance the idea that the government's denial of mail carriage rights to the radical magazine interfered with the public formation of opinion and impinged on free speech values; but his bold decision invalidating what the Post Office had done was reversed without ceremony on appeal.

For some reason, in his 1920 book, Chafee did not apply the principle advanced in the Quebec letter to the freedom of literature and art; at one point he even made this remarkably narrow statement regarding freedom of sexual expression in literature or art, a statement that seems to defy the principle articulated by the Continental Congress in 1774:

ZECHARIAH CHAFEE: Most of us agree that the law must draw some line between decency and indecency, a line between permitted art and art that can be punished or suppressed. Some writers, it is true, contest this whole position.* They believe that the law should keep its hands off all questions of decency and leave them to the judgement of the readers and playgoers themselves insofar as they are adults, while children can be kept away from objectionable books or sights by their parents. But this extreme view is not likely to be accepted by any considerable group of legislators. They and the great majority of their constituents will continue to insist for a long time to come that there must be some limit on the literary discussion of the relation between the sexes, and that when this limit is passed the police or other government officials must take vigorous measures.

—

the landmark case of *Roth* v. *United States* (1957), without attribution to Chafee's book, or to an opinion that federal circuit judge Jerome Frank wrote, in which the letter was also cited, in the *Roth* case; Frank seems to have learned of the letter from Chafee's book. The full letter is contained in the *Journal of the Continental Congress* (ed. 1800), vol. 1, 57.

*Chafee did not identify these writers. One (probably the principal one) must have been the lawyer Theodore Schroeder, author of the frequently neglected *Freedom of the Press and Obscene Literature* (1906), *Free Press Anthology* (1909), *"Obscene" Literature and Constitutional Law* (1911), *Free Speech for Radicals* (1916), and *Constitutional Free Speech* (1911), all published before Chafee's *Freedom of Speech* (1920).

It must have been statements such as this one that led Edmund Wilson to remark about Chafee:

EDMUND WILSON: [I]t had been said of him that he was so much impressed with the importance of seeing that there were two sides to a fence that he thought that was the most important thing about the fence.

—

Like other early-twentieth-century liberals, Chafee proved unable to appreciate that literary and artistic discussions *of sex* deserved to be as free as newspaper and pamphlet discussions of war, the draft, socialism, or the graduated tax. As a result, one would be hard put to distinguish Chafee's original position from the one taken by John Sumner at around the same time, in 1922:

JOHN SUMNER: There is at present a vague border line between what is allowable and what is criminal. Today a jury may acquit a man who oversteps the line. Tomorrow they may convict him. The line sways back and forth, but the prosecutions keep that line in existence, and those who violate it know the risk they are running.

—

Further, Chafee did not recognize an inevitable problem in applying "some limit" to the discussion of sexual relations in literature or art—that any such "limit" imposed by law, statute, or judicial decision would necessarily be accompanied by capricious, because subjective, enforcement by policemen, prosecutors, and judges.

Chafee's views on the obscenity censorship problem later matured, in the course of work he did for Robert M. Hutchins's Commission on Freedom of the Press at the University of Chicago.* In *Government and Mass Communication,* published in 1946 under the commission's auspices, Chafee said: "I doubt that even the wisest judge can always say where sex lets off and obscenity begins—especially where a novel or a play is involved." Even more significant, Chafee now insisted that "a really good novel or play ought to have constitutional protection."† These later views of Chafee's were brought to the attention of the Supreme Court in time for its decision concerning *Hecate County,* and the First Amendment freedom of Doubleday, in the brief filed on Doubleday's behalf by Whitney North Seymour;

Freedom of Speech had been revised by Chafee and republished in 1941 as *Free Speech in the United States,* but this version retained the illiberal remarks referred to above. On the "Hutchins Commission," see Harry S. Ashmore, *Unseasonable Truths: The Life of Robert M. Hutchins* (1989), 272, 293–98, 495–96, and 562, notes 25 and 26. A rival of Chafee's, Harvard philosopher William Ernest Hocking, also played an important role in the commission's work and wrote *Freedom of the Press: A Framework of Principle* as a result.

†Taken seriously as a legal "test," Chafee's "a *really good* novel or play" would be about as helpful as Chief Justice Warren Burger's revision of the Brennan doctrine's formula for protecting "*serious* literary, artistic value." See Chapter 25 below. Justice Brennan's requirement that only expression "*utterly without* literary, scientific, artistic or other social importance" might be branded "obscene" minimized the vagueness and maximized the freedom imported by the test, as pointed out in Chapter 22.

but the absence of any written opinion whatsoever accompanying the judgment of the Court to uphold New York's ban on Edmund Wilson's book made it impossible to gauge what impact Chafee's liberalized view had on the participating justices.*

Sumner moved against *Hecate County* five months after its publication; by then 50,000 copies of the book had been sold. For the first time in Edmund Wilson's life, the author was making "a great amount of money." Coming at a time when he wanted to get married again, and had two divorces to pay for—his own and his future bride's—the bonanza was welcome: Wilson "immediately used up" the royalties he received without bothering to pay the income taxes due.

Wilson later lamely said he "had no idea then of how heavy our taxation had become or of the severities of the penalties for not filing tax returns."

EDMUND WILSON: I knew that the profits from the book were to some extent subject to income tax, but I thought that this obligation could always be attended to later. Also, I expected a further income from *Hecate County* because it was selling so well and thought that I should soon be able to catch up on whatever I owed the government. I did not expect—what next occurred—that *Hecate County* would be suppressed and all my income from it abruptly cut off.

———

The IRS investigated Wilson and he "found out they had an intelligence service of their own which looked into my life and work."

EDMUND WILSON: All my books seem to have been examined in Washington with the idea of showing that I was a subversive character. It was even brought up against me that I had been married four times and that I had during the '30s been associated with persons who wanted to overthrow the government by force.

———

In England, the venturesome publisher Fredric Warburg was getting ready to publish Wilson's book when he learned of Sumner's raids on the Doubleday bookstores. In September 1946, Wilson wrote Mamaine Paget, "a London girl whom I liked very much," from Wellfleet, about the situation.

---

*Chafee's earlier view on obscenity, as set forth in *Freedom of Speech,* had been expressly relied upon by the Supreme Court in a landmark "fighting words" decision, *Chaplinsky* v. *New Hampshire,* handed down in 1942, the year following the book's second-edition publication. The endnotes to this chapter contain a comparison of Chafee's remarks with those of Justice Murphy in *Chaplinsky.* In *Chaplinsky* the Court said, in an enormously influential dictum, that "obscene" words, like "profane," "libelous," and "fighting" words, had "never been thought to raise any constitutional problems" because they were "no essential part of any exposition of ideas." This, unfortunately, gave rise to a two-level approach by the Court to First Amendment protection whereby some speech received protection and other speech—obscene, libelous, profane, and "fighting words" speech—did not.

EDMUND WILSON: The case of my book in New York is to come to court October 14. If they suppress it, it will be an awful nuisance, as it will be difficult ever to get it reprinted. In the meantime, it has been selling madly. Hearst . . . has been conducting a campaign, evidently aimed at Catholic readers, against indecent books, with special virulence against *Hecate County,* on the ground that they debauch the young and ruin family life,* and I have been getting a lot of abusive letters and literature. . . . The situation in England seems to be even worse: Warburg writes me piteous letters, saying he cannot get a printer to set *Hecate County,* and is begging me to change the text.

———

Wilson would not do that, and so the book did not appear in England until 1951, when W. H. Allen published it, and Cyril Connolly gave it "a hideously bad review." Wilson tried to think that Connolly "was jealous of the sales—but I was afraid this wasn't true and that he honestly didn't like my book."

It appears that British customs officials stopped just short of seizing *Hecate County* when Wilson carried "the manuscript and proofs" off a plane at the London airport in April 1945. They "pounced upon" and "read quite a lot of it" and, Wilson believed, were discouraged from taking it away from him only because Sylvester Gates's name was "on the wrapping paper."†

Wilson seems to have heard the news of Sumner's raids from Douglas Black, while the author was at his place in Wellfleet. Later he worried that the New York district attorney, Frank Hogan, a Catholic, might take some action against him personally, as the book's author. Under the obscenity law of New York, a reputable book publisher might be prosecuted personally, but there had been no reported case of such a prosecution after 1920, the year in which John Sumner had initiated a prosecution against the president of Harper, Clinton Tyler Brainard, for publishing an anonymously written novel called *Madeleine.* (As in the case of *Hecate County,* Brainard's prosecution seems to have been induced by William Randolph Hearst.‡) It was even rarer for an author of an allegedly obscene work to

———

*The newspaper and magazine magnate William Randolph Hearst launched an attack against salacious books in a series of front-page feature articles by Leon Racht that appeared in his chain of newspapers, including the New York *Journal-American.* The series ran for three weeks and was directed by Hearst, who personally checked every article. John Sumner was quoted at length, particularly in connection with *Hecate County,* and one cartoon depicted "a modern filth author" dumping garbage on a gratified publisher's desk. Headlines and editorials cried: "Punish Writers of Filth" and "Prurient Fiction Linked to Crime." This may well have emboldened John Sumner to strike again, for in May 1947 he raided the editorial offices and the warehouse of Random House, seizing 910 copies of a new book of poems by Vincent McHugh, *The Blue Hen's Chickens.* Unlike the Doubleday case, this one was eventually thrown out. Bennett Cerf wryly commented: "It looked like for the first time in two years a book of poetry would sell." John Tebbel, *A History of Book Publishing in the United States* 3 (1981), 695–99.

†Gates was an English friend of Wilson's then studying at Harvard Law School.

‡See Henry F. Pringle's article "Comstock the Less," in *The American Mercury* 10 (January 1927), 56–63.

be prosecuted in New York; however, the law never unambiguously excluded the creative activity of writers.

Edmund Wilson was not personally prosecuted for writing *Hecate County,* but there were those who thought he ought to be, and legislation that would have made it clear that authors would be criminally liable for the publication of obscene literature—along with book publishers, booksellers, and printers—was introduced at Albany during the two-year-long course of the Doubleday proceedings. The bill passed both state legislative houses but was vigorously opposed by New York newspapers, with the exception of Hearst's *Journal-American,* and in the end was vetoed on civil liberties grounds by Governor Thomas E. Dewey. Nevertheless, ten years later a knowledgeable New York civil liberties lawyer, Harriet Pilpel, would advise Roger Straus, who was thinking about reissuing Wilson's book, that both he and Wilson might be fined or imprisoned if he did so.

John Sumner's initial attack on *Hecate County* took place on July 8, 1946, hitting Doubleday bookshops at four locations—412 and 526 Lexington Avenue, 670 Fifth Avenue, and in the Vanderbilt Avenue Concourse at Grand Central Station. A few days later additional copies of the book were seized from two other New York bookstores, which had not been intimidated by word of the Doubleday raids into taking the book off sale—the Albert Bonnier Bookshop and Womrath's. Although criminal charges were filed against Womrath's, its trial was postponed until that of Doubleday could be concluded. When Doubleday was convicted, Womrath's entered a guilty plea.

The New York district attorney who undertook the Doubleday prosecution and the suppression of *Hecate County* was Frank Hogan, a Catholic, who would dominate New York's law-and-order scene for twenty years.* A trial brief filed by Hogan described the book as "nothing more than commercial obscenity"; it sarcastically announced that the book's theme was "how the protagonist . . . attains the immense delight of sexual intercourse with the wife of another man." The book's "climax" came with "a bedroom scene of five pages where the cherished dream of [the protagonist] is realized (189–94)." The trial brief also observed that a "brief anti-climax, involving a repetition on the same bed (196–98), winds up the story." "But," continued Hogan, "this is not all."

FRANK HOGAN: The *dénouement* of this plot is attended by the most intensive concentration of sex episodes, with nothing omitted in the way of bare-skinned description, that has ever been crammed into 138 pages.

———

The brief proceeded next to cite the pages for every passage in which the book "wallowed in filth."

———

*See Chapter 24, below, in which Hogan's prosecution of the comedian Lenny Bruce is described. In the Doubleday case, the brief that Hogan filed at trial brought to the judges' attention the fact that, with one exception, Catholic journals did not review *Hecate County;* the exception, *Commonweal,* was, however, quoted as disapproving of Wilson's novel. *Brief for the People,* 32.

FRANK HOGAN: There are 20 separate acts of sexual intercourse [pages 109, 113, 114, 119, 120, 122, 153, 155, 159, 160, 161, 168, 180, 181, 189, 190, 191, 192, 194, 196, 197, 198, 207, and 231]. These take place between the protagonist and four different women. Eighteen of the acts occur in the space of an hour or two with two different women. Three of the acts occur with two married women [pages 189–95].

———

The brief furnished the New York trial court's judges with a Baedeker to *Hecate County*'s immoral and obscene passages.

FRANK HOGAN: Yet when not detailing bedroom scenes, the author finds room for additional paragraphs narrating: 4 unsuccessful attempts at sexual intercourse [pages 98, 109, 183, and 184]; designs, plans and strategies to ravish the heroine [pages 145, 146, 147, 148, 149, et passim]; nocturnal dreams of intercourse with the heroine [page 188]; daytime reveries of sexual intercourse [page 214]; and ten or more filthy conversations about sex [pages 111, 113, 115, 118, 119, 120, 122, 123, 152, and 231]. Finally, the story is not without its disgusting embellishments.

———

Among those "embellishments" were: "accounts of: bedwetting, at pages 114 and 116; defecation, at page 187; masturbation, at page 185; venereal infection, at page 124; Lesbianism, at page 161; abortion, at page 115; and assorted acts of sexual debauchery, at pages 115, 207, et passim." And, in an attempt to deal with the prevailing New York rule that a book could not be judged obscene because of *isolated* passages but had to be read as a whole, the brief commented:

FRANK HOGAN: The intense delight, the precision of detail in anatomical description of female genitalia, the careful description of positional circumstance in coitus and the overall erotic frenzy of the episodes can only be visualized by reading the entire story.

———

Now the brief went on to quote extensive passages from the book, including those that I quoted earlier. Finally, Hogan rounded off his attack on Wilson's book by reciting this remarkable principle for discounting literary values, taken from the New York case of *People* v. *Berg,* a principle obviously opposed to the one advanced by federal judge Learned Hand in the case against Mitchell Kennerley involving the novel *Hagar Revelly:* *
"Filth, however it may be bedizened, or its grossness concealed, must remain filth in all ages."

At the trial of the book and the house that published it, in a three-judge general sessions court, Doubleday's lawyers called only one expert to the defense of Wilson's book: the distinguished literary critic and Columbia University professor Lionel Trilling. Although Trilling was permitted by

*Quoted in the endnotes for Chapter 4 above.

the judges to say next to nothing about the literary qualities of the story, he did manage to speak of the author's standing as a literary critic:

LIONEL TRILLING: Mr. Wilson's . . . reputation in literary circles, general reading public, and academic circles is very high, perhaps higher than any other one critic.

———

Trilling was also permitted to give his understanding of the meaning of Wilson's book and to say that it was, in his opinion, "a serious work of literature," rendering "a rather stern and severe judgment on what was happening in our modern culture." The author's intent, Trilling told the court, was "to induce in the reader a sense of disgust with all he was likely to find around him in life." The implication was that in writing the book Edmund Wilson intended to excite the reader's revulsion more than his lust and thus did not intentionally create an obscene work, as defined, for example, in the *Ulysses* case.

When Doubleday's principal trial lawyer, Milton Schilback, asked Trilling whether the book was written "just to be dirty," the witness was stopped by the judges from answering. The court also refused to hear Trilling's answer to the direct question of whether Wilson's book would "tend to excite lustful and lecherous desires in the average reader," an essential element in the legal definition of the "obscene." When the prosecutor, on cross-examination, read aloud to Trilling passages from *Hecate County* that contained descriptions of sexual intercourse "written in the first person"—including "a rather precise and literal account of a woman's sexual parts in the sexual act"—the critic sought to justify them by suggesting that they "fulfilled the author's aim of contrasting the vulgar and outspoken with tender and charming gallantry." Trilling also contended that Wilson's book was "very *moral* in emphasizing the defeat of what is good and the corruption of what is pure." Nothing the distinguished witness said, however, dissuaded two of the three judges of the New York general sessions court from concluding that *Hecate County* was obscene and that Doubleday, by publishing the book, had committed a crime.

In the *Ulysses* customs case, taken to court some fifteen years earlier, Random House had anticipated that it would win only if its lawyer was able to inject into the proceedings the comments of people like Arnold Bennett, Ezra Pound, and (in his pre–*Hecate County* days) Edmund Wilson about the merits of Joyce's book. The publisher's lawyer, Morris Ernst, made use of a clever subterfuge to get expert critical "evidence" in.

BENNETT CERF: [T]he court would not allow outside criticisms to be read in a case of this kind—why, I don't know. . . . The only way we could do it was to make them part of the book, since anything that was in the book could be used as evidence. So we took one of the Paris paperbound editions of *Ulysses* and pasted in it every opinion we wanted to use—dozens of them in several languages. By the time we finished, the covers were bulging. Since that copy had to be the one that would be used as evidence, we got somebody to take it over to Europe and bring it back on the *Aquitania,* and had our agent down on the dock when it landed. . . . When our man arrived, the customs inspector started to stamp his suitcase without even looking at it. Our agent, frantic, said: "I insist that you open that bag and search it. . . . I think there's something in there that's contraband. . . ." So, furiously, the fellow had to open the suitcase. And the agent said "Aha!" as he produced our copy of *Ulysses.* . . . So when the case came up, that was the copy in evidence.

———

In the *Hecate County* case the Doubleday lawyers devised a similar plan before trial to bring to the judges' attention critical commentary about *Hecate County:* they appended to the Doubleday trial brief "a compilation of reviews of 'Memoirs of Hecate County' by well-known literary critics in leading magazines and newspapers." Said the lawyers: "A conservative summary of these reviews is that all regard the book as a sincere literary effort and that most praise it highly." For authority in doing this, they referred to federal appellate judge Augustus Hand's observation in the *Ulysses* case that "the established reputation of the work in the estimation of approved critics, if the book is modern . . . , are [*sic*] persuasive pieces of evidence; for works of art are not likely to sustain a high position with no better warrant for their existence than their obscene content."*

Hogan's reply brief disputed the propriety of the court's considering such critical opinions; and since the two-judge majority issued no written opinion to explain its judgment that *Hecate County* was obscene, there is no way to tell whether or not the judges took the submitted criticisms into account. Nevertheless, the Doubleday lawyers repeated the tactic all the way up to the Supreme Court, attaching to their brief on appeal there an appendix that incorporated lengthy reviews of Wilson's book from *United States Quarterly Book List, The New York Herald Tribune, Time* magazine, *The Saturday Review of Literature, Knickerbocker Weekly, The New Republic, Tomorrow,* and *Partisan Review.*

The trial brief filed by Doubleday's trial lawyers—the New York law firm of Satterlee, Warfield, and Stephens (Whitney North Seymour, George G. Gallantz, and James F. Dwyer "of counsel")—contained an innovative "Supplement" that consisted of passages from books that had previously been held not obscene by New York courts; these included Joyce's *Ulysses,* D. H. Lawrence's *The First Lady Chatterley,* Erskine Caldwell's *God's Little Acre,* André Gide's *If It Die,* Gustave Flaubert's *November,* Théophile Gautier's *Mademoiselle de Maupin,* and Boccaccio's *Decameron.* The idea was that

---

*The trial brief also urged the New York court to use the *Ulysses* rule that "obscenity" must be gauged by its effect on the average, rather than the most susceptible, person. But District Attorney Hogan pointed out in the People's brief that the *Ulysses* rule was a federal rule, not binding on state courts, and that New York State courts had systematically tested a book's "obscenity" by their estimate of its tendency to corrupt the morals of young and susceptible persons.

compared with these "outspoken" works, *Hecate County* was not really obscene. Ten years later, at the trial of Samuel Roth for selling his hardbound literary journal *American Aphrodite* and other racy items through the mails, Roth's lawyer would adopt a similar tactic and read to the jury passages from contemporary novels, including Norman Mailer's *The Deer Park* (published by G. P. Putnam's Sons), Thomas Mann's *Felix Krull* (published by Alfred A. Knopf), and John O'Hara's *Ten North Frederick* (published by Random House).* There, too, in the absence of any written opinion, the impact of the offerings was impossible to gauge.

When the trial of his novel was over, Edmund Wilson commented tersely on it in a letter to his friend Vladimir Nabokov:

EDMUND WILSON: *Hecate County* was convicted in New York by a vote of two to one. Doubleday is going to appeal. The dissenting judge wrote a very intelligent opinion; the other two—what is rather unusual—voted *Guilty* without explanation. It is all an awful nuisance and is putting a crimp in my income.

——

It *is* "rather unusual" for a court that is not split down the middle to issue no written opinion justifying its decision, but that is what occurred in Wilson's case, not only at the original trial but at every decision taken on the rungs of appeal. In the end, a dissenting opinion written by one of the three New York trial judges, Justice Nathan D. Perlman, would be the only opinion to issue from the *Hecate County* case, although three superior courts, including the United States Supreme Court, would read the book, reexamine the circumstances of its publication, and review the trial court's findings.

Justice Perlman's "intelligent" opinion suggested that the majority of the court may not have faulted Wilson for *intentionally* writing an obscene book. The judge said, "Even the best of authors may write books that are lewd and filthy which they think are clean." However, he pointed out, "under the law, it's the province of the court to make the ultimate decision" of whether the work created was obscene. For Perlman, an author's intentions were nevertheless relevant to the question of whether his book was obscene; and the answer to that question ought not to be based solely on considerations of the book's probable impact on young girls. Wilson "obviously had serious intentions: an honest concern with the complex influences of sex and class consciousness on man's relentless search for happiness." Such things "always have been matters of deep concern for mature persons and the reading public generally. They ought not to be deprived of the author's insight because of the possible effects upon young or otherwise immature readers."

After the trial court announced its decision that *Hecate County* was obscene and that Doubleday was guilty of violating New York's criminal

---

*See Chapter 15.

law, the prosecutor said that anyone selling the book thereafter would also commit a crime and would be liable to be sent to prison for up to one year. At this point Doubleday's lawyers announced that although the decision would be appealed, the publisher would publish and distribute no more copies of the book pending an outcome to their appeal.

TIME MAGAZINE: The decision made thousands of citizens more impatient than ever to get their morals ruined. It also proved again that finding a yardstick for proving a serious book indecent is as difficult as weighing a pound of waltzing mice.

———

The decision was appealed first to the appellate division of the New York County court system and then to New York's highest state court, the court of appeals. At each level Doubleday's lawyers argued both that *Hecate County* was not "obscene" and that the conviction and punishment of the company for publishing the book violated rights of freedom of press and speech guaranteed under the Constitution because the publication presented no "clear and present danger" to a legitimate state interest. At all levels, the New York courts dismissed these arguments out of hand and without bothering to write opinions that explained or justified their actions. Doubleday's claim that its conviction and the book's suppression violated constitutional freedom of expression was treated by the New York courts as too trivial for comment. This would be the *only* argument presented by Doubleday to the Supreme Court in its final appeal.

Wilson was convinced that the Catholic hierarchy in New York was behind the censorship of his book, that it was "suppressed by Cardinal Spellman, who got Sumner of the Anti-Vice Society to go after it." Here is the scenario the author depicted in a letter to publisher Roger Straus: "Spellman was very thick with Hearst who was making a great bid for circulation of his newspapers among Catholics, and who prominently reported the prosecution of *Hecate County* in all of them." Then, when his book was brought to trial, "it was completely at the mercy of Catholic judges."

EDMUND WILSON: Of the three who first heard the case, two were Catholics and one was Jewish. The Jewish one, Perlman, wrote for himself a highly intelligent opinion . . . holding that the book should not be suppressed; but of course he was outvoted by the Catholics. At both of the New York appeals, Catholic judges predominated.*

———

*I have noted above that the brief filed at trial by the Catholic district attorney Frank Hogan pointedly indicated that Catholic journals had either entirely ignored Wilson's book or disapproved of it. The Hearst campaign was described in *Time* magazine, August 2, 1946. Wilson wrote his Catholic friend Allen Tate about the Catholic "efforts to interfere with free speech and free press," comparing the Church with the Stalinist Comintern. *Letters on Literature and Politics,* 495.

The final court to rule in Wilson's case, however, the United States Supreme Court, was not dominated by Catholics under the sway of Cardinal Spellman; its lone Catholic was the liberal Justice Frank Murphy. Instead, the court was dominated by a conservative bloc placed on the bench by President Harry S Truman, who, like most of the rest of the country, seemed to be acting during the years involved under the spell of McCarthyism. Even so, the Supreme Court came within an ace of clearing Wilson's book and might have done so had not Wilson's old friend from *New Republic* days, Justice Felix F. Frankfurter, removed himself from the case. Wilson was furious "at old Felix Frankfurter" for letting him and his book down; he was sure that the justice did not have to excuse himself from the case simply because he was a friend. Later the author would say as much to Frankfurter's face.

In the arguments made to the eight sitting Supreme Court justices in the *Hecate County* case, New York had thirty minutes to state its case against Edmund Wilson's book and Doubleday. An attorney from Hogan's office rose and said everything he had to say in thirty-four words: "The New York statute is valid. A reading by this Court of the book will demonstrate the factual finding of obscenity is reasonable. The judgment of the New York courts below should be affirmed."

Then he sat down. This was remarkable forensic behavior. The district attorney's subtextual point must have been apparent to everyone: the Supreme Court had more important things to do than reconsider the judgment rendered by the entire New York State court system: *Hecate County* was obscene, and Doubleday and Company was guilty of publishing an obscene book. Once the justices read the book—or, better, once they read the scores of obscene passages that had been singled out in the People's brief—they would not hesitate to uphold the ban. New York did not dignify with a response Doubleday's contention that freedom of the press had been violated by the publisher's conviction.

Doubleday's principal lawyer at the Supreme Court level was Whitney North Seymour. Although this experienced constitutional lawyer did not try the case, Seymour had been "of counsel" in the state proceedings. In each of the state courts, the Doubleday lawyers presented two main arguments: first, that *Hecate County* was not "obscene"; second, that the application of New York's obscenity law to *Hecate County* in such a way as to condemn the book's publisher for disseminating "obscenity" violated the constitutional guarantees of freedom of speech and press. This was an unconstitutional "as-applied," not an unconstitutional "on-its-face," argument for reversing a conviction under a statute.* Significantly, in designing Doubleday's appeal to the Supreme Court, and in presenting his oral

---

*This distinction, familiar to experienced Supreme Court practitioners, would become confused and problematic at oral argument in the *Roth* case, as described below in Chapter 15.

argument to the Court, Seymour dropped the argument that had been advanced all along in the New York State courts, that *Hecate County* was not obscene, and concentrated exclusively on the argument that *as applied* to *Hecate County* and Doubleday's behavior in publishing the book, the New York law violated First and Fourteenth Amendment guarantees of freedom of expression,* because of the failure to show any resultant "clear and present danger." This was a bold legal stratagem, the impact of which may be gauged by the fact that four of eight Supreme Court justices voted to reverse Doubleday's conviction. However, when a tie vote occurs in the Supreme Court, the decision of the lower court is allowed to stand, and so the conviction was not reversed.

After the decision Doubleday president Douglas Black made a terse statement to the press, seeking to make the best of the deplorable result:

DOUGLAS BLACK: It is regrettable that because of the even decision of the Justices of the Supreme Court, four to four, there are no opinions to throw light on the important constitutional question which the Court considered. However, it is most satisfactory to know that works of fiction, as well as other literary works, are recognized by the Court as being subject to the protection of the provisions of the Constitution of the United States which preserves freedom of speech, and it is heartening to know that four of the justices believed that the conviction in the lower court violated the constitutional rights of the publisher.

———

Black was almost certainly correct in thinking that the four justices who voted to reverse the Doubleday conviction did so because they believed it violated constitutional freedom of the press, as counsel for Doubleday had contended. But the four justices who voted otherwise apparently believed that the conviction raised no substantial constitutional question, or that if it did, that question had been correctly answered below, in the state court refusals to overturn the conviction. It is, therefore, not easy to accept Douglas Black's assertion that the decision meant "the Court" now recognized that fictional works like *Hecate County* were "subject to constitutional protection." Perhaps Black was trying to put a good face on what was in fact a disaster for Edmund Wilson. Doubleday, of course, was big enough to absorb the loss; but the Supreme Court would not accept another case involving the suppression of a literary work of obvious value, written by a serious author, and published by a reputable publishing house, for fifteen years. In the interim, local, state, and federal officials would continue to engage in literary censorship activities.

Forty years later, former Doubleday editor Jason Epstein commented on Black's attitude toward the *Hecate County* defeat:

---

*The First Amendment's guarantee of freedom of speech and press prohibits only congressional actions that violate the guarantee; the guarantees have been extended by the Court to federal executive branch actions as well, and, by construction of the Fourteenth Amendment's due process clause, to state and local legislative, executive, and judicial actions.

JASON EPSTEIN: Douglas Black was a strange man. He was a very vocal First Amendment man, forever making speeches about your right to read, not my right to publish—all based on his defense of *Hecate County*, which was, I guess, one of the very high spots of his life. He was very proud of that defense, even though he lost.

———

Black was proud of that defense, presumably because of the confrontational approach that he had authorized: never before in a case involving an allegedly obscene publication had a litigant argued to the Supreme Court not that a book was not obscene but that constitutional liberty prevented its being found obscene.* On the other hand, as will be seen later, the *Hecate County* defeat led a chastened Douglas Black to back away from the next opportunity he was given to bring out an audacious work of literature by a distinguished American author, for fear that Doubleday might be prosecuted again for publishing something "obscene."†

An evenly divided judgment of the Supreme Court is silent and enigmatic, but it does decide the issue between the parties. Whoever won in the courts below, and no matter why, wins once more, and this time finally. There is no further recourse against the prevailing party (here, the State of New York). Worse yet, for the loser, is the near certainty that any fresh case involving the same subject matter (here, the book *Hecate County*) that is lost in another state will also be lost in the Supreme Court, so long as the Court's composition and mood remain unchanged. Despite Douglas Black's protestations, the decision was a major setback for literary freedom.

Edmund Wilson was sore.

———

*Fifteen years later, during the sixties, in obscenity cases it was easier to pursue the strategy that such expression could not constitutionally be branded "obscene" without forgoing an argument that the expression was not obscene. This was done not by reference to the "clear and present danger" test but by arguing that any expression having even the slightest literary, artistic, or social importance could not constitutionally be held obscene. I made such arguments to the Supreme Court in cases involving the book *Tropic of Cancer* and the motion picture *I Am Curious—Yellow*. See Chapter 22. I took the same approach in arguing for the freedom of William Burroughs's *Naked Lunch* in the Massachusetts Supreme Court, as described in Chapter 25.

†The author: Vladimir Nabokov. The book: *Lolita*. See Chapter 14.

13

She Always Called It "It"

SOME TIME AFTER the judgment in *Hecate County* was handed down, Justice Felix F. Frankfurter heard that Edmund Wilson was vexed with him because he had removed himself from the case. "Valuing our long friendship," Frankfurter went to see Wilson "to test the water."

EDMUND WILSON: He now said that due to the fact that Marion's niece was visiting them and that he had to get her home or something of the kind, he could not stay to pay a visit just then. He was hurried, seemed embarrassed; I walked with him up the street to his car. He began: "It has come to my ears—by what we call in the law *hearsay,* and we have a legal principle—which I'm sure you agree with—that hearsay is not admitted as valid evidence—"

I cut in and asked him what he had heard. Well, not precisely that you don't have any use for me. I gently deprecated that. But he wanted to talk to me, he said. Then we arrived at the car.

I greeted Marion, we made an engagement, and he hastily departed.

—

Later, over lunch, Frankfurter told Wilson that he "approved" of *Hecate County* and thought the author's "improprieties" were "justified by the social points" he wanted to make. But then Frankfurter confessed that he "really didn't know what he would have decided if he had had to sit on the case, but couldn't have thought of doing so because he was a friend of mine." The implication that Frankfurter's affection for Wilson might not have decided the issue in favor of the latter's book seems to have aggrieved the author.

EDMUND WILSON: I reminded him that he had not disqualified himself on the ground that he was a friend of Lovett's, in connection with the Virgin Islands affair. This had never come into his head, and he was silent for a long moment (equivalent, as John Biggs said, when I told him about it, to a cataleptic fit on the part of another man),* reflecting and mustering an answer. . . .

FELIX FRANKFURTER: Then I should have disqualified myself.

———

Wilson said that Frankfurter had added "as justification" that he had thought of Lovett "as a historical figure." To that Wilson responded by saying he "was sorry he had not begun deciding to disqualify himself in cases where his friends were involved just after, rather than just *before,* the case of H.C. had come up."

FELIX FRANKFURTER: I've said I was wrong not to have disqualified myself in the Lovett case. . . . My liberal friends expect me to defend their interests in the Court, but they don't understand that I'm there to do something altogether different—to decide on the legality of statements and opinions. My own opinions are liberal—I'm opposed to all kinds of intolerance.

EDMUND WILSON: I reminded him that he had been on the other side when the police magazines were cleared by his colleagues.

———

Frankfurter begged off by asking Wilson whether he realized that such magazines "caused juvenile delinquency."

The case Wilson reproached Frankfurter for was *Winters* v. *New York,*† in which certain magazine distributors were prosecuted and convicted under New York law, at the instigation of John Sumner. The case sat in the Court for over two years and was argued three times before the justices were able to reach a decision in it, on May 28, 1945; that was three years before the *Hecate County* case came up. With Justice Frankfurter dissenting, the Court held unconstitutional the New York law involved, a section of the state's obscenity law that criminalized the distribution of publications "principally made up of criminal news . . . or stories of deeds of bloodshed, lust or crime." The majority found the statute impermissibly vague and in violation of the First and Fourteenth Amendment guarantees of free speech and press. Said the Court, speaking through Justice Reed: "Although we can see nothing of any possible value to society in these magazines" (included was one called *Headquarters Detective*) "they are as much entitled to the protection of free speech as the best of literature."

In dissenting, Frankfurter protested the majority's ruling for stripping the legislature of New York of its power to deal with "grave problems" like "juvenile delinquency." The protections of speech and press were not

———

*Judge John Biggs, Jr., had been at Princeton with Wilson and Scott Fitzgerald and was now a federal circuit judge in Philadelphia.
†Reprinted in de Grazia, *Censorship Landmarks* (1969), 132–42.

meant, he thought, to keep a state from addressing such problems with its criminal law. Frankfurter's regard for free expression withered in the face of the state's need to maintain public safety.

JUSTICE FELIX FRANKFURTER: By today's decision the Court strikes down an enactment that has been part of the laws of New York for more than sixty years, and New York is but one of twenty States having such legislation. . . . Most of this legislation is more than sixty years old. . . .* This body of laws represents but one of the many attempts by legislatures to solve what is perhaps the most persistent, intractable, elusive, and demanding of all problems of society—the problem of crime, and, more particularly, of its prevention.

———

Many justices have found offensive the kinds of "speech" or "press" that Congress or state legislatures have sought to suppress, even when they were not prepared to permit the suppression; and probably all the justices have at one time or another protested against the revolting qualities of obscenity and pornography. But unlike the other liberals on the Court, Frankfurter was disturbed also by literature and other expression that dealt in violence, anger, or hate. He professed to believe—as do many persons today, particularly those associated with "moral vigilante," "decent literature," and "anti-defamation" groups†—that weak-willed or weak-minded readers of such literature are likely to be led by it to commit "crimes of lust and violence." In the dissent he wrote in *Winters* Frankfurter located support for this thesis in "a recent murder case that had come before the High Court of Australia."‡

Although Wilson did not say so to Frankfurter, he suspected his friend would have voted against his book had he not disqualified himself. And so for a long time after that luncheon Wilson did not see Frankfurter. This did not stop him from thinking and talking about him. One evening, at his place in Wellfleet, Wilson and Gardner Jackson talked about Frankfurter before sitting down to dinner with the Francis Biddles.§

———

*Later on, in the *Roth* case, Frankfurter would once more express his judicial queasiness toward invalidating a law—in this case the postal obscenity law—that had been on the books for many years. See Chapter 16.

†See, for example, the testimony of James Clancy, speaking for Citizens for Decent Literature, at the hearings on the nomination of Abe Fortas to be Chief Justice of the United States, below at Chapter 27. See also the accounts of witnesses appearing before the Meese Commission on Pornography, Chapter 29.

‡Wrote Frankfurter: "The murder was committed by a lad who had just turned seventeen years of age, and the victim was the driver of a taxicab. I quote the following from the opinion of Mr. Justice Dixon: 'In his evidence on the *voir dire* Graham [a friend of the defendant and apparently a very reliable witness] said that he knew Boyd Sinclair [the murderer] and his moods very well and that he just left him; that Boyd had on a number of occasions outlined plans for embarking on a life of crime, plans based mainly on magazine thrillers which he was reading at the time. They included the obtaining of a motor car and an automatic gun.' " See de Grazia, *Censorship Landmarks* (1969), 138–39.

§Jackson, nicknamed Pat or Paddy, was a journalist and fighter for liberal causes. Biddle had been attorney general under Roosevelt.

EDMUND WILSON: We agreed that [Frankfurter] had been much better off mildly liberalizing the students at Harvard Law and lightly influencing politics by remote control. . . .

GARDNER JACKSON: But don't talk against him to Francis! Francis is devoted to him.

———

When the Biddles joined them, Wilson brought up the *Hecate County* case and Francis Biddle said that he also thought it had been unnecessary for Frankfurter to disqualify himself.

EDMUND WILSON: I said that I had the impression that instead of deciding cases on principle, he was always thinking of the impression that it would be politic to make on the public. . . .

FRANCIS BIDDLE: Felix hasn't any principles.

———

Later, after dinner, Wilson told Mrs. Biddle "that Felix was an old faker and that I never wanted to see him again." She "seemed a little horrified by this." Wilson was reminded by someone at the table that Sir Isaiah Berlin, the British social historian and philosopher, once described Frankfurter's role on the Vinson Court as akin to "playing 2nd violin in a Vienna orchestra."

A few years later, however, Frankfurter redeemed himself somewhat in Wilson's eyes by voting with a Warren Court majority to strike down as unconstitutional a provision in New York's motion-picture-licensing law barring "sacrilegious films." Wilson observed that Frankfurter wrote "a long, scholarly concurring opinion explaining his reasoning."* By then Wilson was beginning to have new confidence that American institutions would prevail and that "the struggles for them had their effect after all, and were worthwhile."

With his case lost as a result of the Supreme Court's split decision, Wilson's book was suppressed everywhere in the United States. The author could not understand "why that should be since it was a case of New York law and the Supreme Court's 4 to 4 decision was not supposed to carry any precedental value." In San Francisco, a case involving *Hecate County* had been won, but it carried no weight outside the city in the face of the Supreme Court defeat. For the next several years Wilson tried to come up with a way to reprint and sell the book himself. In 1950, he conferred with the lawyer who had won the San Francisco case, James Martin MacInnis, about privately republishing *Hecate County* in California. The trouble was,

———

*This is the case Wilson alludes to in a July 1954 letter to publisher Roger Straus, mentioned below. The case, called *Burstyn* v. *Wilson,* involved the attempted censorship of Roberto Rossellini's *The Miracle* and was decided in 1952. The lawyer for the motion picture distributor Burstyn, whose constitutional right to exhibit the film was vindicated by the Court, was the distinguished First Amendment lawyer Ephraim London, who later would act as counsel for the social satirist Lenny Bruce. See Chapter 24.

MacInnis said, that "upon the same evidence, a jury of Los Angeles house-wives took only five minutes to find that *Hecate County was* obscene."

One explanation was that "community standards of decency," and thereby effectively the law, varied from city to city, county to county, state to state, and there was nothing at the time in First Amendment jurispru-dence to prevent this.* In any event, MacInnis's "inexperience with costs, etc.," as well as "personal involvements" and "nagging doubts," prevented the author from moving ahead with a private republication. After a time, he abandoned the idea altogether, in favor of securing publication of *Hecate County* by W. H. Allen in England. From there, he thought, some copies might be brought into the States and a new "test" case be fought at the port of entry, in federal court, as had been done so successfully by Random House in the *Ulysses* case.

In 1952, copies of the W. H. Allen edition shipped to the States for a San Francisco bookseller, Paul Elder, were seized by U.S. Customs officials and ordered destroyed under the law forbidding the importation of obscene materials. MacInnis worked for "over a year" to get the book "cleared" by the customs authorities. Although he succeeded, and importation of the book was allowed to resume, the informal character of the proceedings— there was no judicial trial or formal administrative decision with precedental value—kept the release by customs from being construed as a precedent that would lend legal support to a republication and general sale of *Hecate County* in the United States. It would certainly not change New York district attorney Frank Hogan's mind.

In 1950, Wilson left Doubleday and moved over to the three-year-old firm of Farrar, Straus, and Young, after meeting Roger Straus and selling him his latest book, *Classics and Commercials.* By July 1954 Wilson was campaigning with Straus to republish his favorite book. Wilson pointed out to the publisher "two ways" in which *Hecate County* could be "cleared"; both necessitated bringing "a new case," which would have to be "kept out of Catholic courts." One way was to "appeal another case to the Supreme Court hoping that you'll now get a different decision from a different set of judges." And, Wilson continued, "There are certainly no Catholics on the Court today." He offered in proof "the recent [1952] unanimous decision against the Catholic movie censorship in New York."†

---

*Later, during the sixties, in the *Tropic of Cancer* case, Justice Brennan would seek to eliminate the possibility of divergent results across state or county lines by calling for nation-wide deference to Supreme Court decisions in free speech cases. Brennan's accomplishment in this regard, however, would later be qualified by Chief Justice Warren E. Burger's emphasis, in cases decided during the seventies, on the importance of "local community standards" in reaching conclusions regarding the obscene.

†In this case, decided in 1952 (reprinted in de Grazia, *Censorship Landmarks* [1969], 180–93), the Supreme Court unanimously struck down a New York law authorizing the Board of Regents to deny a license to anyone exhibiting a "sacrilegious" motion picture film, on the ground that movies involved expression protected by the First Amendment, and that a denial of a license to show the Italian movie *The Miracle* because it was considered "sacrile-

The second way to "clear" *Hecate County,* Wilson thought, was "probably better." Straus should "do as was done in the case of *Ulysses:* make it a federal case by raising the issue of importation." Either way probably would have worked, at least after 1956, when the liberal Supreme Court justice William J. Brennan, Jr., replaced the conservative justice Sherman Minton on the Court; Brennan believed that literature and art were meant to be protected by the First Amendment's guarantees. He had indicated this by way of dictum as early as 1953, in speaking for the New Jersey Supreme Court in a case involving the licensing of burlesque theatres in Newark.* This was, however, not widely known.

In December 1954, Straus asked the New York law firm of Whitman, Ransom, and Coulson to advise him on the question of republishing *Memoirs of Hecate County.* The firm's response was that even if the book was republished, the New York authorities would in all likelihood zealously prosecute its publisher. Written by Catholic lawyer Patrick H. Sullivan, the opinion stated that "the atmosphere in the eight years since the Doubleday conviction has not, in our opinion, progressed towards more liberality in the degree of obscenity allowable in literary works."

This was probably true, despite the appointment in 1953 of Earl Warren to be chief justice of the Court, and despite the Supreme Court's liberalizing 1952 decision in the *Miracle* case. Warren was known to be a prude and thus unlikely to lead the Court to interfere with strict enforcement of obscenity laws by the states; the statute successfully challenged in the *Miracle* case had to do with the suppression of "sacrilegious," not "obscene," expression. Justice Tom Clark's opinion for the Court in the *Miracle* case had indeed expressly left hanging the question whether the suppression of an "obscene" movie, under a properly drawn statute, would violate freedom of the press; the implication was that the suppression of an allegedly obscene novel, even a meritorious one—"under a properly drawn statute"—might well be sustained. The legal message to Straus was that it would be unwise at that time—it was 1954—to republish Edmund Wilson's

---

gious" by the Board of Regents violated the constitutional guarantees of freedom of speech and press. Cardinal Spellman of New York had denounced the movie prior to the board's action to suppress it. Wilson probably surmised from the *unanimity* of the Supreme Court's decision that there were *no* Catholics on the Court. He was correct. Four years later, however, President Eisenhower appointed a Catholic, William J. Brennan, Jr., to the Court, in part because he was a Catholic. To Eisenhower's and Spellman's chagrin, however, the Catholic Brennan led the Court's movement during the sixties to expand civil liberties and free sexually oriented literature and art (including novels and movies) from state and federal censorship, as discussed later in this book.

*The case, *Adams Theatre Co.* v. *Keenan,* is reprinted in de Grazia, *Censorship Landmarks* (1969), 213–16. It serves as a reminder that Brennan, now retired from the Court, would never have gone along with the decision recently reached by the Court, in an opinion by Chief Justice William Rehnquist, that "nude dancing" of the barroom-entertainment type may be suppressed without violating the constitutional guarantees of freedom of expression under a state law criminalizing "public indecency." See *Barnes* v. *Glen Theatre, Inc.,* 111 S.Ct. 2456 (1991).

book. In view of this advice, Straus decided he had better not go ahead.*

Three years later, in 1957, Straus responded to further promptings by Wilson by seeking counsel from New York lawyer Harriet Pilpel, then a partner of Morris Ernst's. Like Ernst, but unlike Sullivan, Pilpel was a civil libertarian lawyer and was eager to see publishers extend the frontiers of freedom of expression. She conferred with San Francisco lawyer MacInnis, reviewed the legal history of *Hecate County*'s problems, took note of the most recent Supreme Court pronouncements concerning constitutional protection for literary discussions of sex, and gave Straus a mixed message of encouragement and alarm.

Pilpel was "excited" by the prospect that Straus might "push back the boundaries of obscenity," but she advised Straus that the prospects were not bright for securing from the courts a declaratory judgment clearing the book of the charge of obscenity, or for arranging for a friendly "test case" with the Manhattan district attorney, Frank Hogan, who had brought the original prosecution against Doubleday. In fact, Pilpel told Straus that the chances were "quite high" that Hogan would prosecute *both* Straus and Wilson if the book was republished in New York. And, she said, even as "first offenders," and although the crime of obscene publication was only "a misdemeanor," Straus and Wilson theoretically could each be sentenced to ten days to a year in prison and be fined $150 to $1,000. The bottom line of Pilpel's advice was that despite a high risk that another criminal case would be brought, a better-than-even chance existed that such a case would be won—at least if the case was taken to the Supreme Court.

When Pilpel sounded out Frank Hogan about his likely response to seeing *Hecate County* in print and on sale again in New York, she received this stern warning in response:

FRANK HOGAN: [I]t is my belief that the *Memoirs of Hecate County* is dominated by material which the courts would deem obscene under the most liberal interpretation of the term.

———

Given that message, it was not surprising that Roger Straus decided once more to put off republication of Wilson's book to more auspicious times; those would come with the sixties. By then, of the eight justices who had sat on the Doubleday case, six had been replaced, and McCarthyism was largely finished. These were the green years of the liberal and activist Warren Court. Barney Rosset's Grove Press made *Lady Chatterley's Lover* into a paperback best-seller after getting the federal courts in New York to recognize the literary merits of Lawrence's last novel; in 1959 they found the book not obscene. Earlier in the year, ACLU-affiliated lawyers in San Francisco, representing Lawrence Ferlinghetti's City Lights Books, persuaded a state court judge to hold that Allen Ginsberg's iconoclastic poem

---

*As described in the next chapter, not long afterward Straus also declined to bring out Vladimir Nabokov's novel *Lolita*, but he relates his indisposition to publish Nabokov's great book at that time to Nabokov's wish to have his *Lolita* published under a pseudonym.

Howl could not be suppressed as obscene by the local police; and in Chicago, ACLU volunteer lawyer Joel Sprayregen freed from Post Office suppression the first issue of the literary journal *Big Table,* carrying allegedly obscene episodes from William Burroughs's novel-in-progress, *Naked Lunch.* For a publisher like Roger Straus it was probably even more significant that three years after Doubleday's Douglas Black had turned down Vladimir Nabokov's scandalous novel *Lolita,* Walter Minton of the distinguished publishing house G. P. Putnam's Sons had made a best-seller out of it, and no censor's hand had been raised against him or his firm. But by that time John Sumner was long gone, having retired to his daughter's home in Long Island ten years earlier; the New York Society for the Suppression of Vice was still in existence but was on its last legs.

ROGER STRAUS: For several years, Edmund wanted me to reissue *Memoirs of Hecate County* and I went into the subject at great length with my lawyers about how it could be achieved. And by a strange coincidence I owned a corporation called L. C. Page and Company, which operated out of Philadelphia. Page was a strange duck who owned books like *Pollyanna, Anne of Green Gables,* and *Extraordinary Popular Delusions and the Madness of Crowds,* with an introduction by Bernard Baruch.* After he died, I bought the corporation from the estate—devoured it naturally, and integrated it into my own list.

———

Straus had not published any books under the Page imprint until his lawyers told him he could use it to publish *Memoirs of Hecate County*— "because they thought there was no way that anybody could get at me, for doing that."

ROGER STRAUS: We technically could not achieve publication in the State of New York, the book could not be advertised in New York State, it couldn't be shipped in and out of New York State, etc., etc., etc.—all due to the Doubleday case which was lost earlier in New York.

———

So Straus published it as an L. C. Page book, and took the precaution of having the books shipped from a bindery outside New York.

ROGER STRAUS: So we minimized rubbing the book in the nose of the district attorney. I knew the district attorney, and my recollection is that I spoke to him. He was a friend of Tom Dewey's, who was an intimate friend of my father's. At a certain point, the word came back to me that "I won't bother you, if you don't rub my nose in this."

———

*Page died in 1956. He is described by John Tebbel as "a gentleman publisher of the old school" who "could not believe times had changed." "He would have been dismayed to know that his firm was later sold to Farrar, Straus & Giroux, one of the 'sophisticated' publishers he abhorred." Doubtless he would have been profoundly disturbed by the use Straus made of his old imprint in publishing Edmund Wilson's "obscene" book. *A History of Book Publishing in the United States* 3 (1978), 545.

In this way, after a dozen long years, Wilson's favorite publisher was able to republish Wilson's favorite book. But, even then, *Hecate County* was not for sale in New York. District Attorney Hogan had effectively seen to that.

ROGER STRAUS: So we achieved what we wanted to achieve, and were able to publish the book, and the book had a certain success and continues to have a certain success.* And nobody's ever bothered us.

Wilson had become one of Straus's most prestigious authors.

ROGER STRAUS: Farrar, Straus and Giroux was then only three years old [when] an editor friend asked me if we should like to consider a new book by Edmund Wilson. It was *Classics and Commercials,* which he called a "literary chronicle of the '40s. . . ."

I met the author, bought *Classics and Commercials,* and published it in 1950. It was the beginning of a publishing relationship that lasted 23 years and has covered so far the publication of 21 books of critical essays, plays, fiction, reportage, poetry and history.

There were no intermediaries with Edmund Wilson—no agents, lawyers, middlemen—just a continuing flow of work. His output was never interrupted by travel, illness, writing blocks. We kept in touch by frequent phone calls, the briefest notes, short meetings at the old downtown Fifth Avenue Longchamps, the old Princeton Club and the new one, the Algonquin, his country place in upstate New York and his home at Wellfleet on Cape Cod. . . .

—Now he is gone† and there will be no more jokes, literary gossip, business talks, trips, or the excitement of his enthusiasm for other writers present and past. However, I am happy to say that there will be for a long time a continuing flow of his work to be published and read throughout the world.

Beginning in 1975, three years after Wilson's death, Straus began publication of the remarkable series of literary journals and notebooks that Wilson kept from the twenties to the fifties but did not wish published until after he was dead.

LEON EDEL: Years of writing for the periodicals changed the content of his notebooks. He now begins to keep a record of his erotic life. He takes his notebooks into his confidence—there is the erratic Katze, there is Winifred, there are others, above all Anna, the dance-hall girl and waitress with whom he has a tender relation, and who touches him more than all the others. . . . Ultimately she would furnish him with the material for "The Princess with the Golden Hair" in *Hecate County.* . . . In our present

---

*It was subsequently published by the Godine Press in Boston; it is now out of print.
†Wilson died in 1972.

unbuttoned age his boldness may seem tame; what we should remember is that what he wrote, in its truth to life and to himself, antedated the later avalanche of erotic writings that now colors the creative imagination of America.

———

According to Edel, D. H. Lawrence's *Lady C.* gave Wilson the idea of writing a novel about the Eastern seaboard's sexual mores. But long before writing *Hecate County,* and apparently even before D. H. Lawrence wrote *Lady Chatterley's Lover,* Wilson began to write objectively, realistically, and in an interesting way about erotic experience and the sexual habits of women.

Like Joyce's lust letters to Nora, Wilson's journals treated sex uninhibitedly and explicitly—even more so than *Hecate County* did. And in those journals, with certain exceptions, Wilson freely used words he had refrained from using in his novel—words like "cunt" and "cock" and "balls." However, he circumspectly avoided these words, even in his diaries, whenever he set down descriptions of sexual activity with his wives—notably his second wife, Margaret Canby, and his last wife, Elena Mumm Thornton.* With the taxi dancer Anna, Wilson was more unbuttoned.

EDMUND WILSON *(The Twenties): (Anna) She had loved Sam more than me but Sam didn't throw her the way I did—she used to kiss'um all over just the way I did her—I don't believe there was an inch of his body I didn't kiss! I don't suppose he minded it. Sam's was longer than mine, but it hurts nice—you know what I mean?—the doctor had said she was very passionate, wasn't she? because the opening of her womb was so small—her cousin did'un care anything about it, but she did it every night because her husband liked it, you know—she thought her cunt (I never heard her use the word, she always called it "it") was an awful-lookin' thing—didn't know about her clitoris—washed it but didn't look at it—didn't mind a man's—when Sam used to make me touch it, I'd pull my hand away quick, you know, but I'd get the thrill of my life—one night they came back drunk, and Sam made her kiss it, etc., and she did it all night and liked it, too. . . .*

She used to sleep curled up to fit my back and with my cock in her hand—she had always slept that way with Sam. Couldn't go to sleep unless, etc.—When I had her naked and her little middle elevated by pillow—the little narrow lozenge of her cunt, which had such a slight lining of hair, seeming charming, with her rather slender legs and feet extended and drooping wide—I used to stroke it and caress it with my tongue—it was so pretty it would make me linger and preoccupy me, so that I almost forgot to do anything else. . . .

———

*Not unexpectedly, some critics objected to Wilson's "strange habit of describing making love to his wives." For example, Joseph Epstein (editor of *The American Scholar*) said this in his August 31, 1986, *New York Times* review of Wilson's *The Fifties:* "Making love to one's wife is a splendid thing—some even say that the fate of the species depends upon it—but Wilson took it an ample step further by recording such sessions in meticulous, pornographic (though not very aphrodisiacal) detail. After one particularly vigorous session, he notes: 'Then went down to my study and drank a bottle of ginger ale and ate what was left of the party nuts,' failing only to add, 'and recorded all that had gone on in the bedroom above.'"

Her pale little passionate face in the half light with that mouth moist, and always ready, more like a sexual organ than a mouth, felt the tongue plunging into it almost like intercourse—liked to cuddle up at night—cuddled up with her mother when she slept with her—her mother would push her away—I don't know what I do to her—Responds so easily with that rhythmic movement—quickly catches rhythm—to any stimulation—("Well do you want me to bite it off?")

Perfect feeling of possessing her completely—arms all the way around her slim little figure—tongue in her soft little mouth—legs which I make her put over mine finally throwing her soft little cunt forward and up into place—she is melting into me, as I, from my loins, will finally into her—I possess, I partly absorb her—the rose flush of her little woman's face, of the face of a woman being loved. . . .

The time before, the cool moisture of her lips when she has bent lower for fellatio, so delightful, so curiously different from the warm and mucilaginous moisture of ordinary intercourse—the incredible-feeling caress, gently up and down, until the delightful brimming swelling of pleasure seems to make it flow really in waves which fill her darling woman's mouth.—In taking hold of my cock and my balls, she had a gentleness, reluctance and timidity which, as well as the way she rubbed over the glans and below, gave the whole thing a delicious and as it were tantalizing lightness, only satisfied, completed, by the fullness and the richness of the final flow.

———

Jason Epstein noticed that "Edmund's diaries were remarkable mainly for their descriptions of his many love affairs, pursuits for which this distinguished and reputedly austere literary personage was not widely known."

JASON EPSTEIN: One reviewer has recently gone so far as to call the erotic passages in these diaries pornographic, and even for Wilson's less easily inflamed readers his amatory descriptions must have come as something of a shock, for Wilson's candor is as defiant, as limitless, and as innocent as Stieglitz's in his erotic photographs of Georgia O'Keeffe. Perhaps for this reason these amatory writings have not received their due, particularly the long elegiac piece on his second wife, Margaret Canby, in *The Thirties.*

———

Wilson's monologue about Canby resembled Joyce's "Mollylogue," his brilliant soliloquy for Molly Bloom:

EDMUND WILSON *(The Thirties): (Margaret) On the dunes: the flies, perspiration—her broad white soft flesh—breasts that became flat like jellyfish when she lay on her back—her big brown moles—skin a little wrinkled around neck—it would make her nervous, even hysterical, to kiss her feet, she would pull them away—one that was partly paralyzed by sciatica and didn't have much feeling in it—it gave me a kick to put what seemed to me my large pink organ in her in the bright sunlight of midafternoon—I would come almost immediately, though I'd try to make it last, and she would usually come immediately too—it excited her—I spoke of how people didn't make love out in the sun enough.—Her neatness about picking things up after a picnic and bringing them back in a basket. We had to be on the lookout for the children.—She would lie on a bath towel. I would* *lift the upper part of my body and for a while slide it in and out that way, trying to remain detached, insensitive, though it was so delicious—another touch and my large pink prong would all melt into a pink-whitish fluid dissolving into momentary bliss—her pink and white (strawberry and cream) flesh spread out before me.—Fighting the flies.—Stay in me! Keep in me! Well, I suppose we'd better be going back—I ought to attend to myself!—Bare feet and legs through the sharp beach grass.*

———

Wilson's marriage to Elena Mumm Thornton, his last wife, turned out to be very satisfying. He married her in 1946, the year that *Memoirs of Hecate County* was first published.

EDMUND WILSON *(The Forties): (Elena) I loved her body, which I had first seen in a bathing suit—I found that my impression was correct of its natural fineness and style in spite of her longness and tallness—taller than my usual physical type—there was nothing about it that displeased me—her breasts were low, firm and white, perfect in their kind, very pink outstanding nipples, no hair, no halo around them, slim pretty tapering legs, feet with high insteps and toes that curled down and out. Never too thin, her hips, stomach, and abdomen were lovely.— Reactions quite different from those of any other woman I had known. She would look at me fixedly, her eyes becoming gray and as if somehow out of focus or differently focused, a little wolfishly, as if she too had a strain of the German police dog. She would crouch with her head down on the bed or lie sideways against me, half crouched over my hand and gnawing my knuckles. She would wind herself around me like an eel, telling me how much she enjoyed it. . . . Would always run her tongue into my mouth when I kissed her before I had a chance to do it to her—and would do it so much and so fast that I hardly had a chance to get my own in. Would clasp her legs together very hard when I had my hand or my penis in her—seemed to have tremendous control of the muscles inside her vagina. Her frank and uninhibited animal appetite contrasted with her formal and gracious aristocratic manners.*

———

When he was sixty, Wilson looked back on the sexual life he had led and reported on in the journals.

EDMUND WILSON: At my age, *sex* became less importunate, in the sense that you don't need it so often, and the impulse comes to seem less important. You even become impatient with this biological instinct, with its pleasure-bait, which asserts itself so much oftener than is necessary. It sometimes became nagging; you think, "Oh, yes: there you are again—I know all about it—you just want me to go to bed with some woman so that more babies will be born, and I have quite enough children already. I want to devote myself now to more intellectual and dignified things."—With what contempt at sixty do you look back at all the uncomfortable and unsatisfactory affairs of your youth, the transient episodes that meant nothing or had all-too-serious consequences, the sieges of women you could never have lived with, who would not interest you for a moment now, the complicated messes of entanglement with several girls at a time! Yet if I did not have Elena, I might still, at my age, on a more careful and temperate scale, be carrying on in that way.—Unlike some elderly men, I had no appetite for young girls; the women who occasionally attract me are invariably middle-aged married women. The women of my own age, however—or the age that corresponds with mine—are now too old to attract me: their breasts have collapsed, their hair is turning gray, they have gone through a change of life and are likely to have had hysterectomies that left them unresponsive and juiceless.—And it is strange now to think that ten years ago, liberated from Mary, with whom I had spent seven years, there should have revived in me a capacity for falling in love of which I should not have thought myself capable: Mamaine, Eva, Anaïs [Nin], Elena (not all, of course, to the same degree).

———

Wilson continued to write, to work, even after heart attacks, gout, falls, and old age forced him—beginning in 1970—to eat, sleep, and work in one room. In a letter to his friend John Dos Passos, written two years before he died, Wilson commented on his existence:

EDMUND WILSON: Actually, since I have left the hospital, I have been having a most enjoyable life: bed moved downstairs to my study, so that I only have to crawl from the bed to the writing table.

———

One of his last letters, dated May 27, 1972, was to William Shawn, editor of *The New Yorker*. It contained a postscripted single line:

EDMUND WILSON: This writing of books is an endless matter. Ecclesiastes 12:12.

———

Wilson asked that at his funeral Psalm 19 and the last chapter of Ecclesiastes be read, and they were.

14

With Your Little Claws, Lolita

I N 1949, while teaching a course in Masterpieces of European Fiction at Cornell University in Ithaca, New York, Vladimir Nabokov began work on the great American *roman noir*. Later, in a letter to his friend and literary benefactor Edmund Wilson, Nabokov said, "I am writing . . . a short novel about a man who liked little girls."

VLADIMIR NABOKOV: *Lolita, light of my life, fire of my loins. My sin, my soul. Lo-lee-ta: the tip of the tongue taking a trip . . .*

—

Nabokov considered *Lolita* "by far my best English work." Nevertheless the manuscript was promptly turned down by the first American publishers to whom the author showed it, in early 1954: Pascal Covici at the Viking Press and Wallace Brockway of Simon and Schuster. According to Nabokov, they thought it would strike readers as "pornographic," and Covici predicted "we would all go to jail if the thing were published." Undaunted, Nabokov sent his manuscript to James Laughlin of New Directions, asking if he would "be interested in publishing a time bomb that I have just finished putting together" and requesting that he "not show it to anyone." Laughlin had already published a number of Nabokov books, including *The Real Life of Sebastian Knight* (1941), *Nikolai Gogol* (1944), and *Nine Stories* (1947), but, as Nabokov would write to his editor at *The New Yorker* in January 1950: "All my previous books have been . . . dismal financial flops in this country."

Véra Nabokov, who served as a secretary-assistant to her husband, was open about what was going on: Vladimir was afraid that if the wrong people read his manuscript he'd be fired from his teaching position at Cornell, and that U.S. postal officials might seize the novel and create additional problems for him. This is the subtextual message in several letters written to American publishers by Nabokov and in a letter Véra wrote at Christmastime, 1953, to Katherine A. White, her husband's editor at *The New Yorker;* the magazine had previously published poems and several autobiographical pieces by Nabokov.*

VÉRA NABOKOV: I shall try to explain about the book. Its subject is such that V., as a college teacher, cannot very well publish it under his real name. Especially, since the book is written in the first person, and the "general" reader has the unfortunate inclination to identify the invented "I" of the story with its author. . . .

Accordingly, V. has decided to publish the book under an assumed name (provided he can find a publisher) and wait for the reviews before divulging his identity. It is of the utmost importance to him that his incognito be respected. . . . Now, suppose you decide that there is nothing in *Lolita* to interest the New Yorker, would the MS still have to be read by the other members of the editorial staff, or would it be possible for you to make a final decision without it? If the MS has to be read by anyone besides you, would it be possible for you to keep V.'s name secret? Could you be quite sure that there would be no leaks?

V. is very anxious to hear from you about it and have your assurance of complete secrecy before he sends you the MS. Moreover, the nature of the plot being what it is, he hesitates about mailing it. Should he make up his mind to visit New York in January, he would prefer to bring the MS personally to your house. . . . If not, we shall find some other way to get it to you within a few weeks. He doubts, however, that any part of the book can be suitable for the New Yorker. But he would like you to read it.

———

It did not seem suitable for *The New Yorker,* and New Directions' Laughlin, who had never cared or dared to publish Henry Miller's erotic novels, would not publish one by Nabokov either. Said Laughlin to Nabokov in October 1954, after both he and his editor Robert MacGregor had read *Lolita:*

JAMES LAUGHLIN: [We] feel that it is literature of the highest order and that it ought to be published but we are both worried about possible repercussions both for the publisher and the author. Your style is so individual that it seems to me absolutely certain that the real authorship would quickly be recognized even if a pseudonym were used.

———

So Nabokov continued to look for a publisher for *Lolita* and to ask for anonymity. It was Laughlin who came up with the solution to the problem when he told Nabokov to get his "best thing in English" published in France. But before the author tried that, Roger Straus would also consider

---

*The latter are collected in *Speak, Memory* (1967).

the manuscript, and so would Jason Epstein, who was then a rising star at Doubleday.

VLADIMIR NABOKOV: Dear Laughlin, . . . Before I ship her to France, I would like to show L. to Farrar, Straus & Young, 101 Fifth Avenue. A short while ago Mr. Straus wrote me and asked to read my latest. Would you please do me the favor of forwarding the MS to him (Mr. Roger W. Straus, Jr.) by Railway Express (or messenger, if you prefer), making sure that the package goes to him *personally*. I would be much obliged to you if you could do it without delay, since I have written him about it.

_____

The same day, October 15, 1954, Nabokov wrote Roger Straus to say he was asking Laughlin to forward the manuscript to him and asking Straus to handle it with secrecy.*

VLADIMIR NABOKOV: Dear Mr. Straus, Some time ago you wrote me kindly expressing interest in my new novel. I could not do anything about it at the time for I had promised James Laughlin of New Directions to let him see it first, even though I did not expect him to want to publish it.

I have just heard from him as expected, and am asking him now to forward the MS to you.

For reasons you will easily understand after reading the book, I would wish to publish it under a penname. And for the same reasons, I would like to ask you to do me the favor of reading it yourself and not having it read by anyone else unless, after you have read it, you come to the conclusion that you wish to consider its publication.

I hope I may hear from you soon.

ROGER STRAUS: Nabokov . . . was afraid that publishing *Lolita* under his real name would cost him his job at Cornell.

VLADIMIR NABOKOV: At first, on the advice of a wary old friend,† I was meek enough to stipulate that the book be brought out anonymously.

---

*Nabokov seems to have increased the difficulty of finding a publisher by insisting on secrecy and anonymity; he was eventually persuaded to abandon those policies by his Paris agent, Doussia Ergaz, and perhaps Maurice Girodias, the head of Olympia Press, as a prelude to *Lolita*'s publication in Paris in 1955. Girodias was not above taking credit even when it was not his due, and was not above mudslinging even over an opponent's grave. Writing for *Nabokov's Fifth Arc*, edited by J. E. Rivers and Charles Nicol (1982), Dmitri Nabokov said that on July 15, 1977, "only a few days after father's death," Girodias published a piece in *Le Monde des Livres* in which he said (the translation is Dmitri's): "I did my utmost to shame [Nabokov], and in the end he resigned himself to courageous action and signed his name to the book" (35). Earlier, in a context suggesting a greater likelihood of accuracy, Girodias had published in the Grove Press edition of *The Olympia Reader* (1965) the following version: "Madame Ergaz told me that Nabokov, somewhat frightened at first by the reaction of the American publishers to whom he had submitted it, was reluctant to let the book appear under his own name, and that she had to use all her influence to make him change his mind" (521–22).

†Probably Professor Morris Bishop, who was chairman of the department of Romance literature at Cornell and was responsible for Nabokov's tenured appointment there. A letter to Bishop from Nabokov, dated March 6, 1956, sought to calm Bishop's fear of "an attack" on Nabokov as a result of the recent publication of *Lolita* in Paris.

DMITRI NABOKOV: You see, this friend was afraid publication might embarrass Cornell University, where father was happily teaching. . . . But later Father thought better of it. And of course, once the book was out, Cornell became proud of *Lolita*.

Nabokov's manuscript may not have reached Straus from Laughlin. Straus's recollection is that it "was in fact submitted to me through the good offices of Elena Wilson," Edmund Wilson's wife, "who thought the book marvelous."* It is unclear from whom Edmund Wilson received the manuscript, but after reading it "rather hastily," he wrote his friend Nabokov that "he liked *Lolita* less than anything else" of his that he had read. "Not only were the characters and the situation repulsive in themselves but they seemed to me quite unreal." Wilson also thought the second part of the novel "boring." Deciding "to get some other opinions," he turned the manuscript over to Elena and to his former wife, Mary McCarthy, to read. McCarthy disagreed that the second part was "boring."

MARY McCARTHY: Mystifying, rather, it seemed to me; I felt it had escaped into some elaborate allegory or series of symbols that I couldn't grasp.

McCarthy had given the manuscript to her husband, Bowden Broadwater, to read.† He told her he thought the nymphet was a symbol of America in the clutches of the middle-aged European; "hence all the descriptions of motels and other U.S. phenomenology"—which were also the parts McCarthy liked.

MARY McCARTHY: On the other hand, I thought the writing was terribly sloppy all through, perhaps worse in the second volume. It was full of what teachers call *haziness,* and all Vladimir's hollowest jokes and puns. I almost wondered whether this wasn't deliberate—part of the idea.‡

Elena Wilson liked *Lolita* without reservation. She said: "The little girl seems real and accurate and her attractiveness and seductiveness are absolutely plausible."

ELENA WILSON: The hero's disgust of grown-up women is not very different, for example, from Gide's, the difference being that Gide is smug about it and your hero is made to go through hell. The suburban, hotel, motel descriptions are just terribly funny.

Elena also said that she couldn't "put the book down," thought it "very important," and didn't see why the novel shouldn't "be published in England, or certainly in France and then come back here in somewhat expurgated form and be read greedily." That, almost, is what happened.

---

*Letter to the Editor from Roger Straus, *The New York Times Book Review,* July 3, 1988.
†Obviously Nabokov's wish that the circulation of his manuscript be tightly restricted was imperfectly realized.
‡Lolita's surname was Haze, her given name, Dolores.

Roger Straus says he agreed to publish *Lolita* "despite my own somewhat ambivalent feeling." The publisher's "friend and sometimes literary adviser" Philip Rahv (editor of *Partisan Review*) had urged him to publish it, as had others. According to Straus, when he got "in touch with Nabokov and told him," the author was pleased, "but advised me that he would have to publish the book under a *nom de plume.*" Under these circumstances, Straus says, he declined to go ahead.

ROGER STRAUS: I felt there was no way that I should publish the book unless Nabokov signed it. I was confident that the book would be challenged and we would have to defend its publication legally. It was for this reason that we did not publish "Lolita," I am sad to say.

———

Publication of *Lolita* under a pseudonym in the United States in 1954 would certainly have made difficult any legal defense of the novel. There would have been no apparent way for the publisher's lawyers to present evidence of the author's literary distinction or reputation, a matter crucial to successful defense.

ERICA JONG: I know that Roger's *official* position is that he did not turn down the book; he only turned it down because of the *nom de plume* issue! But . . . turning it down for *cause* is still turning it down. The truth is that many very clever literary people and many very clever literary publishers did not recognize *Lolita* as a masterpiece until long after the fact. From a writer's point of view, the barrage of discouragement received when an important work is turned down again and again and again is *crushing*. The reasons given don't much matter.

———

Although Edmund Wilson did not like *Lolita,* he seems to have done what he could to find a publisher for his friend Volodya's book. After Roger Straus passed, Wilson sent the manuscript to Jason Epstein at Doubleday. As he had with the previous publishers to whom he had submitted his novel, Nabokov wrote Epstein that he wished *Lolita* "to appear under a penname" and asked him to reduce "to a minimum the number of people who would read the MS for you and if you would withhold, even from them, the true identity of the author."

BARNEY ROSSET:* Jason fell in love with *Lolita,* which precipitated the whole story. At the time he was the boy wonder at Doubleday, the prize protégé of Douglas Black. But when Black refused to publish *Lolita,* Jason resigned. I thought that was very courageous.

———

*Rosset, the founder of Grove Press, perhaps the most courageous American publishing house of the sixties, was not given the chance to publish *Lolita* because Nabokov did not send him the manuscript, even though Wallace Brockway had suggested to Nabokov, in July 1954, that *Lolita* be submitted to Grove. *Vladimir Nabokov: Selected Letters, 1940–1977,* edited by Dmitri Nabokov and Matthew Bruccoli (1989), 147, note 3. There is no record of why Nabokov did not submit his novel to Rosset.

JASON EPSTEIN: I resigned from Doubleday for a number of reasons. One was *Lolita*. . . . The manuscript was given to me by Edmund Wilson, who said this was a novel by his friend Nabokov. Edmund said he himself didn't like it. He thought it was—his word was—"repulsive." But in giving it to me he was encouraging its publication. He may have thought *Lolita* repulsive but he wouldn't dream of censoring it. . . .

I loved it. I thought it was very funny. I didn't find it repulsive at all. I thought it was quite a brilliant book. And I saw no earthly reason why it shouldn't be published from a literary point of view, though I was apprehensive, in those days, of legal difficulties.

I showed *Lolita* to Ken McCormick, who was the editor in chief then. Ken supported it and so I went with it to Douglas Black. I put it on his desk. I remember very vividly it was in two black snap binders. He knew what it was—that is, he was aware of its potentially scandalous implications, because I told him—and other people at Doubleday had read it and were nervous about it but were willing to go ahead.

KEN McCORMICK: The thing that disturbed Douglas Black about the Supreme Court decision concerning Edmund Wilson's book is that we were nailed on it and legally could not ever publish it again. But it had curious repercussions also that went far beyond that. A book called *Lolita* came in and we read it and were absolutely overjoyed with it. And we wanted our lawyers to make sure it was all right, and they came back and they said: "Look, normally you could publish it without any fuss. But if you have been found guilty of bank robbery and you are on a corner and you don't have a gun, but there's a bank there and the bank is being robbed: you would be the first person arrested. And I can absolutely guarantee it. . . ."

Anyway that's what our lawyers said to Douglas Black. The only reason we hire expensive lawyers is to learn what we can from them, and when you've been given such a rough going-over once—as we had with Edmund Wilson's book—well, you'd better pay attention.

Hecate County was a beautiful case. It was a case that a lawyer would dream of. It was a quite remarkable opportunity that the Supreme Court, I feel, ducked. Not ducked . . . it just didn't rise to the occasion. This was 1948, with the Vinson Court.

JASON EPSTEIN: I would ask Black if he'd read it and he'd say no;* he was a very brusque man. He could be very affectionate at one moment and particularly horrible the next. He was exactly like the millionaire in Charlie Chaplin's movie *City Lights,* and so he was a problem to deal with. And he didn't like to be pushed on this, obviously. It became clear to me at a certain point that it would be unwise to force the issue.

---

*In a letter of February 23, 1982, to Sally Dennison, Epstein said, "Black was so strongly opposed that he refused even to read the manuscript." *Vladimir Nabokov: Selected Letters, 1940–1977,* edited by Dmitri Nabokov and Matthew J. Bruccoli (1989), 191.

KEN McCORMICK: Well, there were several others there who were very vocal about their thinking that we were crazy to take this advice. And finally the boss said, Look, this is nuts and you know it. We can't defy the lawyer when he guarantees we'll get into trouble. So very sadly we said no. Because *Lolita* had enormous enthusiasm in the firm.

VLADIMIR NABOKOV (*Lolita*): *Under my glancing finger tips I felt the minute hairs bristle ever so slightly along her shins. I lost myself in the pungent but healthy heat which like summer haze hung about little Haze. Let her stay, let her stay. . . . As she strained to chuck the core of her abolished apple into the fender, her young weight, her shameless innocent shanks and round bottom, shifted in my tense, tortured, surreptitiously laboring lap; and all of a sudden a mysterious change came over my senses. . . . I was a radiant and robust Turk, deliberately, in the full consciousness of his freedom, postponing the moment of actually enjoying the youngest and frailest of his slaves. Suspended on the brink of that voluptuous abyss (a nicety of physiological equipoise comparable to certain techniques in the arts) I kept repeating chance words after her—barmen, alarmin', my charmin', my carmen, ahmen, ahahamen—as one talking and laughing in his sleep while my happy hand crept up her sunny leg as far as the shadow of decency allowed. The day before she had collided with the heavy chest in the hall and . . .*

Look, look!—I gasped—look what you've done, what you've done to yourself, ah look. . . .

For there was, I swear, a yellowish-violet bruise on her lovely nymphet thigh which my huge hairy hand massaged and slowly enveloped—and because of her very perfunctory underthings, there seemed to be nothing to prevent my muscular thumb from reaching the hot hollow of her groin—just as you might tickle and caress a giggling child—just that—and:

Oh, it's nothing at all, she cried . . . with a sudden shrill note in her voice, and she wiggled, and squirmed, and threw her head back, and her teeth rested on her glistening underlip as she half-turned away, and my moaning mouth, gentlemen of the jury, almost reached her brave neck, while I crushed out against her left buttock the last throb of the longest ecstasy man or monster had ever known.

———

In September 1956, Jason Epstein told Nabokov that Doubleday could not go ahead with *Lolita* at that time but asked to be contacted before Nabokov made any other arrangements in the States to publish the novel.

JASON EPSTEIN: You must remember that Doubleday was a privately held company owned by a family that took a keen interest in what happened there. Ellen Doubleday, Nelson's widow, was still very much alive and very much a presence there and would clearly be offended by this book. There's no question about that. . . .

The first Doubleday was Frank Nelson Doubleday. His son was Nelson, who had run the company until he died, in 1949, I believe. His widow, Ellen, was the major stockholder at that time. Her children, Neltje and Nelson, were then minors. There was some family trouble. The other half of the family, named Babcock, had been quarreling with Ellen Doubleday, and Black's job was to mediate, a precarious business. The last thing he needed was to offend Mrs. Doubleday, and I'm sure that as far as he was concerned it was better that she not know about it. After all, it was her mother-in-law, Frank Nelson Doubleday's wife, who had turned down *Sister Carrie.* *

So there's a history behind all this at Doubleday. I can understand Black's reluctance to get involved in this thing. But that wasn't my problem. I wanted to publish the book. I couldn't worry about the Doubleday family or whether Black kept his job, or whether the Babcocks were fighting with the Doubledays; it wasn't of any interest to me. I had started Anchor Books there and I was publishing a lot of books in those days; I'd never had a similar problem, but then there had never been another book like *Lolita.*

In those days you couldn't be sure what would happen because it depended upon every district attorney or judge. The Supreme Court hadn't addressed the problem. The law was very obscure.†

———

The *Hecate County* case had provided the Court with an opportunity to try to reconcile the country's concerns about sexuality and sexual immorality with the majestic command of the First Amendment that the freedoms of speech and the press shall not be abridged by the government; but, as Ken McCormick observed, the Court just "didn't rise to the occasion," and the split and silent decision it rendered left authors and publishers hopelessly adrift in a sea of conflicting lower court judicial decisions and opinions.

After World War II, however, American lower court judges had shown themselves to be increasingly loath to condemn works accused of being sexually immoral‡—that is, works that expressed immoral ideas, as distinguished from works exciting feelings of lust—and increasingly willing to give weight to the literary merits of works accused of being obscene. This would no doubt have been auspicious for the outcome of any trial of *Lolita* during the mid to late fifties. But the influence of McCarthyism continued to be felt, and a wave of prosecutions was directed against publishers and

———

*See Chapter 6.

†In the *Roth* case, decided in 1957 (while Epstein was negotiating with Nabokov for an option to publish *Lolita*), the Supreme Court held enigmatically that "obscenity" was not constitutionally protected expression, but also that literary and artistic "discussions" of sex having even the slightest social importance ought to be constitutionally protected.

‡Not until June 1959, however, did the Supreme Court make it clear that a work could not be banned for its sexual immorality. The case, *Kingsley International Pictures* v. *Regents,* involved the denial of a license to exhibit a motion picture adaptation of *Lady Chatterley's Lover* because the film advocated adultery. Justice Potter Stewart wrote the Court's opinion, saying: "[The Constitutional] guarantee is not confined to the expression of ideas that are conventional or shared by a majority. It protects advocacy of the opinion that adultery may sometimes be proper, no less than advocacy of socialism or the single tax." There was no allegation that the film was obscene. On the issue of his book's "morality," Nabokov transparently strained to make his story about a man who did more than "like" little girls conform to conventional morality—by depositing him finally in mental hospital and prison.

distributors of other meritorious books, including Calder Willingham's *End As a Man* (1947), Charles O. Gorham's *The Gilded Hearse* (1948), James Farrell's *Studs Lonigan* trilogy (1932–35), William Faulkner's *Sanctuary* (1931) and *Wild Palms* (1939), Erskine Caldwell's *God's Little Acre* (1933), and Harold Robbins's *Never Love a Stranger* (1948), some of which had encountered no difficulties when they first appeared, or had been found not obscene in earlier cases in some states. All of these new prosecutions resulted in dismissals of the charges or in acquittals of the defendants by trial or appellate courts.* These decisions, and in particular the influential opinion written by Judge Curtis Bok in 1949 in the case of *Commonwealth v. Gordon,* were an early sign that the American judiciary was about to take the lead in a movement that would not only defuse McCarthyism but also spark the explosive free speech movement of the sixties.

In this setting—and despite the lack of an authoritative statement on the constitutional aspects of obscenity litigation from the nation's highest court—Nabokov's *Lolita* could, I believe, have been successfully defended against charges of obscenity if a reputable publisher had brought it out in the mid-fifties. But the predictable legal expenses of a long legal battle to defend the novel were such that only a large and stable house, or a bold one, could have expected to publish *Lolita* successfully at that time. Well into the sixties the likelihood of six-figure legal expenses was a powerful deterrent, and few American houses were willing to take such a risk, at least in the absence of strong prospects for a best-seller. Those who went ahead anyway gambled that the publicity sure to result from an attempt at governmental censorship would generate sales that would more than offset the legal costs.

ERICA JONG: [T]ry to remember the state of American publishing in 1954. . . . It was impossible to obtain a copy of John Cleland's *Memoirs of a Woman of Pleasure* outside the rare-book room of a college library or a private erotica dealer. (I tried.) Henry Miller's *Tropics* and D. H. Lawrence's *Lady Chatterley's Lover* could not be purchased at your local bookstore.† The raciest sex manual available to the panting adolescent was *Love Without Fear* by Eustace Chesser, M.D. And *A Stone for Danny Fisher* by Harold Robbins was as close as we got to literary sex education. Even Norman Mailer in *The Naked and the Dead* had to write "fug" instead of you-know-what. And though he was far more explicit in *The Deer Park,* published in 1955, he paid dearly in the reviews.

———

*The court opinions freeing these works, all published by reputable houses, are reprinted in de Grazia, *Censorship Landmarks* (1969).

†They could, however, be purchased under the counter at Frances Steloff's remarkable bookstore, the Gotham Book Mart, and this is where Barney Rosset obtained the copy of Miller's *Tropic of Cancer* that he read and used as the basis for a Swarthmore College paper on Henry Miller. Later, Rosset would publish the novel in New York and tear down hundred-year-old barriers to literary freedom. See Chapters 19 and 22. For more on Steloff and the Gotham Book Mart, see the endnotes to Chapter 19.

It was only after the 1957 decision in *Roth* v. *United States* that the practically fearless publishing of sexually explicit literary works began in the United States, and the courts stepped up the movement to liberate sexual expression—so long as what was published had literary merit or, in the terminology of *Roth,* "even the slightest social importance." Thus, after *Roth,* sexually radical writings such as Allen Ginsberg's *Howl,* extracts from William Burroughs's novel-in-progress *Naked Lunch,* and D. H. Lawrence's *Lady Chatterley's Lover* were published, attacked by state or federal postal police, but in the end set free by American courts because of their literary merit.* Roger Straus, as described earlier, was not prepared to republish Edmund Wilson's contraband novel *Memoirs of Hecate County* until 1958, after *Roth* was decided.†

The likelihood that Nabokov's *Lolita* would be found comical by many readers and tragic by others would not prevent its being treated as obscene by prosecutors like Frank Hogan, who were prone to discount literary merit and reach exclusively for the lascivious parts of a book considered sexually highly immoral. And that *Lolita* was.‡

VLADIMIR NABOKOV *(Lolita): How sweet it was to bring that pot of hot coffee to her in bed, and then deny it until she had done her morning duty. And I was such a thoughtful friend, such a passionate father, such a good pediatrician, attending to all the wants of my little auburn brunette's body! My only grudge against nature was that I could not turn my Lolita inside out and apply my voracious lips to her young matrix, her unknown heart, her nacreous liver, the sea-grapes of her lungs, her comely twin kidneys. On especially tropical afternoons, in the sticky closeness of the siesta, I liked the cool feel of armchair leather against my massive nakedness as I held her in my lap. There she would be, a typical kid picking her nose while engrossed in the lighter sections of a newspaper, as indifferent*

---

*See Chapters 17 and 18 below.

†Another Supreme Court case, *Butler* v. *Michigan,* decided in 1957, shortly before *Roth,* may also have encouraged Straus and his lawyers. There, the Court struck down a Michigan law that criminalized the sale of any publication that a court might find "to have a potentially deleterious influence upon youth." Said Frankfurter, for the Court: "Surely, this is to burn the house to roast the pig." It was a violation of constitutional rights thus "to reduce the adult population of Michigan to reading only what is fit for children." Under New York law, a publication was obscene if it tended to deprave or corrupt "the young and immature." The *Butler* decision could have been read to restrict the legitimate reach of the New York obscenity law to its impact on the adult population—a liberalizing construction. This may well explain District Attorney Frank Hogan's change of position on the question whether *Hecate County* might freely be published in New York when Roger Straus raised that question with him just prior to his decision to republish the Wilson novel in 1958.

‡Nabokov liked to say his "little girl" was moral, without defending the novel on that ground. Nigel Nicolson, however, found it opportune to defend his publication of the book in England on moral grounds. He said, on the floor of Commons: "The novel deals with a perversion. It described the love of a middle-aged man for a girl of twelve. If this perversion had been described in such a way as to suggest that the practices were pleasant ones, and could lead to happiness, he would have advised against publishing the book. In point of fact, 'LOLITA' condemned what it described. He had come to the conclusion, therefore, that it was probably right to publish the book." Reprinted in association with F. W. Dupee's " 'Lolita' in America," in *Encounter,* February 1959.

to my ecstasy as if it were something she had sat upon, a shoe, a doll, the handle of a tennis racket, and was too indolent to remove. Her eyes would follow the adventures of her favorite strip characters: there was one well-drawn sloppy bobby-soxer, with high cheekbones and angular gestures that I was not above enjoying myself. . . .

A fly would settle and walk in the vicinity of her navel or explore her tender pale areolas. She tried to catch it in her fist (Charlotte's method) and then turned to the column Let's Explore Your Mind.

"Let's explore your mind. Would sex crimes be reduced if children obeyed a few don'ts? Don't play around public toilets. don't take candy or rides from strangers. If picked up, mark down the license of the car."

". . . and the brand of the candy," I volunteered.

She went on, her cheek (recedent) against mine (pursuant), and this was a good day, mark, O reader!

"If you don't have a pencil but are old enough to read . . ."

"We," I quip-quoted, "medieval mariners, have placed in this bottle . . ."

"If," she repeated, "you don't have a pencil, but are old enough to read and write—this is what the guy means, isn't it, you dope—scratch the number somewhere on the roadside."

"With your little claws, Lolita."

———

Tied to *Lolita*'s particular brand of immorality was, finally, the "woman factor": women seem to have been much more hostile to Nabokov's tragicomical tale of stepdaughter incest than were men.* *Lolita* probably just did not seem funny to the average American mother anxious over her young daughter's sexuality, nor presumably to "knowing" wives of latent pedophiles. It is likely that some U.S. publishers hesitated to bring out *Lolita* in 1954 for fear of what the important woman at home or in the workplace would think and say. As mentioned above, Jason Epstein thought such a factor had been at work in the house of Doubleday.

JASON EPSTEIN: Anyway, after that, it went to Olympia, in Paris, and they published it in those two little green volumes.

———

*Yet reviewers for *The New York Times* went the other way: Elizabeth Janeway commended it, on August 17, 1958 ("The Tragedy of Man Driven by Desire"): "The first time I read *Lolita* I thought it was one of the funniest books I'd ever come on. (This was the abbreviated version published in the Anchor Review last year.) The second time I read it, uncut, I thought it was one of the saddest." Orville Prescott had this to say: " 'Lolita,' then, is undeniably news in the world of books. Unfortunately, it is bad news. There are two equally serious reasons why it isn't worth any adult reader's attention. The first is that it is dull, dull, dull in a pretentious, florid and archly fatuous fashion. The second is that it is repulsive. . . . Mr. Nabokov, whose English vocabulary would astound the editors of the Oxford Dictionary, does not write cheap pornography. He writes highbrow pornography. Perhaps that is not his intention. . . . Nevertheless, 'Lolita' is disgusting" (August 18, 1959). And J. Donald Adams wrote: "Mr. Nabokov [is] a talented writer. . . . Yet he writes, in 'Lolita,' of nothing of consequence save as leprosy, let us say, is of consequence. Here is admirable art expended on human trivia. Mr. Nabokov rightly insists that his book is not pornographic. I found it revolting, nevertheless, and was reminded of John Randolph's excoriation of Edward Livingston: 'He is a man of splendid abilities but utterly corrupt. He shines and stinks like rotten mackerel by moonlight' " (October 26, 1958).

As Nabokov said, his "little girl" had "a difficult birth."

VLADIMIR NABOKOV: *Lolita* was finished at the beginning of 1954, in Ithaca, N.Y. My first attempts to have it published in the U.S. proved disheartening and irritating. On August 6 of that year, from Taos, N.M., I wrote to Madame Ergaz, of Bureau Littéraire Clairouin, Paris, about my troubles. She had arranged the publication in French of some of my Russian and English books; I now asked her to find somebody in Europe who would publish *Lolita* in the original English. She replied that she thought she could arrange it. . . . [N]ext spring I got in touch with Madame Ergaz again, writing her (Feb. 16) that Sylvia Beach "might perhaps be interested if she still publishes."* This was not followed up. . . . On April 26, 1955, . . . she said she had found a possible publisher. On May 13 she named that person. It was thus that Maurice Girodias entered my files.

MAURICE GIRODIAS: One day in the early summer of 1955, I received a call from a literary agent, a Russian lady by the name of Doussia Ergaz. She told me about an old friend of hers, a Russian *émigré* now a professor of Russian Literature at Cornell University. He had written a book with a rather dangerous theme which had, for that reason, been rejected by a number of prominent American publishers.

The man's name was Vladimir Nabokov and his book, *Lolita,* dealt with the impossible amours of a middle-aged man with a girl of twelve who belonged to the seductive species for which Nabokov had invented the word "nymphet."

VLADIMIR NABOKOV: He was recommended to me as the founder of the Olympia Press, which "had recently published, among other things, *Histoire d'O*" (a novel I had heard praised by competent judges),† and as the former director of the "Editions du Chêne" which had "produced books admirable from the artistic point of view." He wanted *Lolita* not only because it was well written but because . . . "he thought that it might lead to a change in social attitudes toward the kind of love described in it." It was a pious although obviously ridiculous thought but high-minded platitudes were often mouthed by enthusiastic businessmen and nobody bothered to disenchant them.

MAURICE GIRODIAS: [I] quickly succumbed to the . . . compelling attraction of the book itself, which developed before me in its near absolute perfec-

---

*Nabokov had met Beach some twenty years earlier at "a rendezvous" in Adrienne Monnier's bookstore in Paris. Wrote the aspiring author to his wife on April 15, 1937, "I got on swimmingly with Joyce's publisher Sylvia Beach, who might help considerably with the publication of *Despair* in case Gallimard and Albin Michel *ne marcheront pas*" (*Selected Letters,* 22–23).

†In November 1962, on a visit to Edmund Wilson's place at Talcotville, Nabokov was introduced to Pauline Réage's *Histoire d'O* and seems to have walked off with Wilson's copy. Edmund Wilson, *Letters on Literature and Politics* (1977) 632. Véra Nabokov disapproved of her husband's liking for this work. First published by Olympia Press in Paris, *The Story of O* was published in New York by Grove Press.

tion. I was struck with wonder, carried away by this unbelievable phenomenon: the apparently effortless transposition of the rich Russian literary tradition into modern English fiction. This was, in itself, an exercise in genius; but the story was a rather magical demonstration of something about which I had so often dreamed, but never found: the treatment of one of the major forbidden human passions in a manner both completely sincere and absolutely legitimate. I sensed that *Lolita* would become the one great modern work of art to demonstrate once and for all the futility of moral censorship, and the indispensable role of passion in literature.

VLADIMIR NABOKOV: Dear Mr. Girodias, . . . I am delighted that you have set such an early date for publication. I hope you have already started a publicity campaign. What are you doing about publicity in the U.S.? When sending out review copies, are you including the following publications: 1. The Partisan Review (Philip Rahv, an admirer of LOLITA . . .); 2. The New Yorker (be *sure* to address that copy to Edmund Wilson c/o the New Yorker); 3. The New York Times Book Review (Harvey Breit, that is the only fellow I know in that shop); 4. Saturday Review of Literature (?); 5. The New York Herald Tribune. That's all I can think of. I am sure you have some other periodicals in mind.

You and I know that LOLITA is a serious book with a serious purpose. I hope the public will accept it as such.

———

Lolita was published in Paris in 1955; the initial printing of 5,000 copies rapidly sold out. Publisher Pat Covici wrote Nabokov in March 1956 expressing concern about the effect Girodias's publication of *Lolita* might have on Nabokov's Cornell post. From Cambridge, Nabokov wrote Covici not to worry:

VLADIMIR NABOKOV: Dear Pat, . . . I do not think there is any cause for concern. *Lolita* is doing very well. I have already signed a contract with Gallimard for the French rights, and a large piece of it will appear in the *Nouvelle Revue Française*. There is a good chance, moreover, of it being published in this country.

As a friend and one of the few people who have read the book, you will, I am sure, slap down such rumormongers as contend that the book is pornographic. I know that *Lolita* is my best book so far. Calmly I lean on my conviction that it is a serious work of art, and that no court could prove it to be "lewd and libertine." All categories grade, of course, into one another: a comedy of manners written by a fine poet, or a satirical poem in the genre of Pushkin's *Gavriliad,* may have its lewd side; but *Lolita* is a tragedy. Pornography is not an image plucked out of context. Pornography is an attitude and an intuition. The tragic and the obscene exclude one another.

MAURICE GIRODIAS: The truth of the matter is that I was delighted by the book itself, but I doubted that it had any of the qualities which make a best seller. Nabokov himself wrote to me that he would be deeply hurt if *Lolita* were to obtain a *succès de scandale:* as the book had quite another meaning for him. He did not believe that it would ever be published in America, and he repeatedly expressed his gratitude for my acceptance of the book, as I had provided the only chance left for him ever to see it in print.

———

The Olympia Press had been founded by Girodias on a shoestring only two years before, in the spring of 1953: its offices were a small room at the back of a run-down bookstore at 13 rue Jacob; the staff was Girodias and a part-time secretary named Lisa. The first manuscript acquired was Henry Miller's *Plexus,* which was published in a two-volume numbered edition. Olympia also promptly brought out Sade's *Bedroom Philosophers,* Apollinaire's *Memoirs of a Young Rakehell,* and Georges Bataille's *Tale of Satisfied Desire.* The Sade and Bataille works were rendered into English by Austryn Wainhouse. Apollinaire's *Memoirs* was translated by Richard Seaver, a member of the colorful literary group that surrounded Alex Trocchi's English-language, Paris-based quarterly, *Merlin.* Seaver would later join Barney Rosset's fledgling publishing house, Grove Press, in New York and, together with Rosset and Fred Jordan, create the most exciting and controversial firm of the sixties.*

Other expatriate writers connected with *Merlin* were Paul Bowles, Philip Oxman, Baird Bryant, Alfred Chester, John Stevenson, John Coleman, Iris Owens, and Marilyn Meeske. According to Girodias, George Plimpton was also involved, "from a prudent distance." Some of them wrote novels, not all of them hack novels, for the Olympia Press.

Girodias was not ashamed to commission pornographic works by contemporary authors, thereby helping impoverished expatriates survive and keeping the wolf away from his own door.

MAURICE GIRODIAS: My publishing technique was simple in the extreme, at least in the first years: when I had completely run out of money I wrote blurbs for imaginary books, inventing sonorous titles and funny pen names . . . and then printed a list which was sent out to our clientele of book-lovers, tempting them with such titles as *White Thighs, The Chariot of Flesh, The Sexual Life of Robinson Crusoe, With Open Mouth,* etc. They immediately responded with orders and money thanks to which we were again able to eat, drink, write, and print. I could again advance money to my authors, and they hastened to turn in manuscripts which more or less fitted the descriptions.

MARILYN MEESKE: The year 1956 . . . found me seated at the Café Bonaparte just down the *rue* from the more expensive Café Deux Magots, Paris, France. The pinball machines were thwacking away, Gauloises and *café noir* sold like hot cakes, and all of us were broke or at least we thought we were. At the Bonaparte a gaggle of real live pornographers could be heard and

———

*See Chapter 19 below.

there I was in the thick of it. Conversation flowed as rapidly as the *vin ordinaire:* the finished chapter meant that the rent would be paid. . . .

We all took glorious pseudonyms, usually gleaned from the lofty worlds of Art and Science. My name, Henry Crannach, was nostalgically inspired by one of my favored painters, Lucas Cranach. . . .

Girodias, who understood his business thoroughly, was extremely lenient about the actual literary content. The books could be as literate as they were hack. His infamous Traveller Companion Series was sometimes recognized under other imprints than Olympia: Obelisk, Ophelia, Ophir and Othello. He did this in the hope of duping the French police and so delaying confiscation of the books from the stands and bookstores.* Because he viewed his readers with a clinical eye and because he had no subjective interest in erotic literature, he best served his clients. He knew what the market called for, necrophilia out, no money there; homosexual books do not really satisfy the boys in the service, the mountain climbers, the anchorites, the satiated marrieds, the orgiasts and the lone needies. . . .

People, hot-eyed and nostrils flared, waited impatiently for the Olympia Press brochure to arrive: *Scream, My Darling, Scream,* by Angela Pearson; *Whipsdom,* by Greta X; *Lash,* by Ruth Lesse; *The Ordeal of the Rod,* by R. Bernard Burns; *The Beaten and the Hungry,* by B. von Soda; *Sex Life of Robinson Crusoe,* by Humphrey Richardson . . .

Meeske's first d.b. was titled *Flesh and Bone.*

MARILYN MEESKE: [It] was written in random fashion, much in the way a shaggy-dog story is invented. It was a wordy sex-hash off the top of the head. I knew it wasn't literature; I understood the formula; I needed the money.

Anaïs Nin, Henry Miller, Harvey Breit, Robert Duncan, George Barker, and Caresse Crosby also wrote pornography for a dollar a page—because they were hungry or thirsty or both; these authors, however, were not in Girodias's stable.

MARILYN MEESKE: During that period [the fifties] practically everyone was trying to write a d.b. for various reasons. In some cases it was a chance to experiment with that novel you wanted to write; thus you were left off the hook if it did not turn out to be the great American novel. The chance to use language in a free, shocking way could lead to a great unleashing of creative inhibition and also serve as an exercise in the understanding of the powers in the written word.

Girodias liked the books to be literary attempts—plus: approximately nine pornographic passages were to be scattered throughout each book.

---

*Compare Sam Roth's use of numerous imprints in conducting his mail-order publishing business (Chapter 15) and also the Farrar, Straus republication of Edmund Wilson's *Memoirs of Hecate County* under an L. C. Page imprint, mentioned in Chapter 13.

Henry Miller was the first major example of what could be considered a marriage of the pornographic with the literary and the philosophic.

———

It was Henry Miller who introduced Anaïs Nin to the possibility "of writing for hire and only about sex." In prefaces she wrote to the 1969 editions of her *Delta of Venus* and *Little Birds*, written in the early 1940s for the private consumption of "the collector," not for publication, Nin commented on the conditions of her work:

ANAÏS NIN: I never met the collector. He was to read my pages and to let me know what he thought. Today I received a phone call. A voice said: "It is fine. But leave out the poetry and descriptions of anything but sex. Concentrate on sex."

———

Sometimes to Nin this seemed "like a Dantesque punishment." She began to write tongue in cheek, became outlandish, inventive, "and so exaggerated that I thought he would realize I was caricaturing sexuality." She received no protest.

ANAÏS NIN: "Less poetry," said the voice over the telephone. "Be specific."

———

Nin was frequently tempted to rebel against the collector; she fantasized telling him off:

ANAÏS NIN: I would tell him how he almost made us lose interest in passion by his obsession with the gestures empty of their emotions, and how we reviled him, because he almost caused us to take vows of chastity, because what he wanted us to exclude was our own aphrodisiac—poetry.

———

She analyzed her band of dirty-book writers and friends:

ANAÏS NIN: The homosexuals wrote as if they were women. The timid ones wrote about orgies. The frigid ones about frenzied fulfillments. The most poetic ones indulged in pure bestiality and the purest ones in perversions. We were haunted by the marvelous tales we could not tell. We sat around, imagined this old man, talked of how much we hated him, because he would not allow us to make a fusion of sexuality and feeling, sensuality and emotion. . . .

Another phone call: "The old man is pleased. Concentrate on sex, leave out the poetry!"

———

Nabokov's *Lolita* was treated by Girodias the same way he treated all his other books, whether these were d.b.'s or novels by authors who attained international reputations, such as Samuel Beckett,* Henry Miller, William

———

*Beckett may not have appreciated Girodias's linking of his name with those of other writers published by the Olympia Press, and Deirdre Bair's biography of Beckett tends to minimize Girodias's role in publishing *Watt* in 1954—in Girodias's words: "that is, ten years

Burroughs, and Terry Southern. He was not only the first to publish *Lolita,* he was the first to publish in English Samuel Beckett's novels *Watt, Molloy,* and *Malone Dies*—all of which were eventually taken over by Barney Rosset in the States—and to publish the "unpublishable" novels of William Burroughs, Jean Genet, and J. P. Donleavy.

The Olympia Press edition of *Lolita* became—as Nabokov hoped it would *not*—a *succès de scandale,* and made Vladimir Nabokov famous. Rapidly the book's first printing of 5,000 copies sold out. In England *Lolita* gained overnight notoriety when Graham Greene gave it his blessing in *The Sunday Times,* calling it "one of the three best books of 1955."* This inspired some of the British press and literati to get hold of *Lolita,* read it, and broadcast the alarm for the safety of little English girls. On January 29, 1956, the *Sunday Express* ran a piece by its editor excoriating the "respectable" *Sunday Times* for "publicising pornography":

JOHN GORDON: On [Graham Greene's] recommendation I bought *Lolita.* Without doubt it is the filthiest book I have ever read. Sheer unrestrained pornography.

Its central character is a pervert with a passion for debauching what he calls "nymphets." These, he explains, are girls aged from 11 to 14.

The entire book is devoted to an exhaustive, uninhibited, and utterly disgusting description of his pursuits and successes.

It is published in France. Anyone who published or sold it here would certainly go to prison.

---

after the manuscript had been completed, and after it had been rejected by every other publisher under the sun, including Herbert Read himself."

In a letter to Beckett dated September 18, 1986 (a copy of which Girodias sent me), the publisher complained of the way Bair had "presented me as a sort of brain-damaged pornographer, son of another pornographer, who bought the rights to 'Watt' under the belief that it was 'just another dirty book.' The truth of the matter is that I took a costly chance with this book, only one year after having started The Olympia Press (on the proverbial shoestring), with a program of four books by Bataille, Miller, Apollinaire and de Sade—not such a shameful selection for a start. . . .

"In the six years of its active existence, Olympia had published, besides 'Watt,' major books by Miller, Nabokov, Durrell, Genet, Queneau, Burroughs, Bataille, de Sade, Donleavy. It would be idle for me to ignore my reputation as a pornographer since I myself coined the term 'dirty books' (dbs for short) to describe that meat-&-potatoes part of my production: much needed since I lost money on all of my glorious authors (including yourself, Miller, Genet, Burroughs), and made some only on Nabokov's 'Lolita'—that book being the only one that was actually *bought* from me by a New York publisher instead of being, like all the others, merely stolen. In order to survive I did create a line of so-called dirty books, but all of them were the work of pretty good people—such as Alex Trocchi, Iris Owen, Terry Southern, Mason Hoffenberg, Georges Bataille, John Glasco, Pauline Réage ('Story of O'), Frank Harris, Christopher Logue, Chester Himes, Frank Harris, Norman Rubington, etc. I did turn down George Plimpton's application because he really didn't make the grade. . . . The Olympia 'dbs' were indeed a parody of pornography, rather than the real thing (witness such books as 'Candy' or 'Story of O'), but done convincingly enough to satisfy the sex-obsessed whose sense of humor is notoriously blunted. My motto was that 'no four-letter word ever killed a reader,' and my long-range plan was to heap ridicule over the anglo-saxon censors and so destroy their power."

*The other two: *Boswell on the Grand Tour* (Heinemann) and *The State of France* (Secker and Warburg). *Sunday Times,* December 25, 1955.

As the sales of *Lolita* mounted and the book came to be critically received as both a controversial novel and an important literary work, Nabokov's attitude toward Girodias started to sour. He had not known about the other sort of book published by Olympia Press.

VLADIMIR NABOKOV: I had not been in Europe since 1940, was not interested in pornographic books, and thus knew nothing about the obscene novelettes which Mr. Girodias was hiring hacks to confect with his assistance. I have pondered the painful question whether I would have agreed so cheerfully to his publishing *Lolita* had I been aware, in May 1955, of what formed the supple backbone of his production. Alas, I probably would, though less cheerfully.

The British Home Office, for its part, grew annoyed at *Lolita*'s infiltration from France and made a request—under the provisions of the International Agreement for the Repression of Obscene Publications—that the French police take a good look at Girodias's publishing activities. According to Girodias, the British government had already made the same request several times; the French, however, took no action until the publicized dispute between Graham Greene and John Gordon gave a new dimension to the issue. At this point the British Home Office "pressed" the French Ministry of the Interior once again concerning Girodias, and on December 20, 1956, the Paris police were induced to ban *Lolita* in its English version.

MAURICE GIRODIAS: One day a police inspector of the Vice Squad (romantically known as "*La Brigade Mondaine*" [The Worldly Brigade]) visited me; he wanted some reading copies of a number of books listed in our latest catalogue. I obliged.

From a friend, Girodias learned that the policemen had been told to "build up a file on us" because the British government had requested information on the Olympia Press. For a few weeks nothing happened. Then:

MAURICE GIRODIAS: [T]he twenty-five books the inspector had taken with him were banned by official decree signed by the Minister of the Interior. One of them was *Lolita*.

In the States, from Cornell, Nabokov initiated an exchange of letters with Graham Greene in England:

VLADIMIR NABOKOV: Dear Mr. Greene, From various friends I keep receiving heart-warming reports on your kindness to my books. This is New Year's Eve, and I feel I would like to talk to you.

My poor *Lolita* is having a rough time. The pity is that if I had made her a boy, or a cow, or a bicycle, Philistines might never have flinched. On the other hand, Olympia Press informs me that amateurs (amateurs!) are disappointed with the tame turn my story takes in the second volume, and do not buy it.

———

Nabokov also relayed to Greene the news from his French agent that the Olympia Press edition was "now banned by governmental decree in France," because Gordon's response to Greene's praise, by angering "certain puritans," had moved the English government to ask the French minister of the interior to take appropriate action. This evoked the following encouraging response from Greene:

GRAHAM GREENE: Thank you very much. I thought Lollita [*sic*] a superb book + I am now, as a director of a publishing firm in England,* trying to arrange its publication. In England one may go to prison, but there couldn't be a better cause!

———

In June 1957, on Graham Greene's recommendation, Max Reinhardt of The Bodley Head wrote Nabokov asking for an option to publish the novel in England "within two or three years"; the wait was thought desirable because a new obscenity bill pending in Parliament held out the promise that, for the first time, publishers of books having literary or other merit would be protected from criminal charges of publishing "obscene" material.

In New York, Edmund Wilson wrote to Nabokov at Cornell: "Dear Volodya, Have you seen the news of the highly comic controversies about *Lolita* that have been going on in England?" The initial result of the controversy in the English press was, of course, to intensify interest in Nabokov's novel, in America as well as in England.

The success of the Girodias publication must have stirred up some envy and regret among publishers in New York who had initially feared to take on *Lolita;* they and others began making inquiries of Nabokov about American publication rights, and of their lawyers about American free speech rights. *Lolita* by now had obtained critical attention in the United States, thanks to the efforts of "the very *sympathique*" Jason Epstein. Although an original plan by Epstein to publish parts of the novel in the *Partisan Review* had to be abandoned,† he did succeed in getting several large chunks printed in the June 1957 issue of *Anchor Review*. This was the literary journal Epstein had started at Doubleday as an adjunct to his highly successful Anchor Books series of quality paperbacks. In addition to the excerpt from *Lolita,* the *Anchor Review* included pieces by Nabokov himself

---

*The Bodley Head.

†Evidently because Nabokov had insisted that the eighty pages that Philip Rahv, editor of *Partisan Review,* had selected for publication be published "using a penname"; this Rahv was unwilling to do. See the letter of November 20, 1954, from Nabokov to Rahv, and footnote 1, in the *Selected Letters* (1989), 154. Later (see letter to Rahv dated July 13, 1955) Nabokov offered the excerpts once again to *Partisan Review,* with permission to use the author's own name, but *Partisan Review* did not publish them.

and by the literary critic Fred Dupee. When the issue appeared, Nabokov wrote to say he and Véra were "both delighted with *Lolita* at Anchor."

VLADIMIR NABOKOV: [T]he cover is splendid and most enticing. Your arrangement and selection of the *Lolita* excerpts is above all praise.

———

In Paris, however, Girodias was being dragged into the fight of his life with the French police and judiciary, over *Lolita* and the twenty-four other "dirty books," and he was upset that Nabokov would not put himself out to help him.

MAURICE GIRODIAS: When I decided to fight the *Lolita* ban, my first thought was to ask for Nabokov's help. I was rather surprised to receive a very adamant refusal to participate in what he called, with blithe unconcern, the "lolitigation."

———

The refusal was contained in a letter from *Lolita*'s author.

VLADIMIR NABOKOV: My moral defense of the book is the book itself. I do not feel under any obligation to do more. However I went further and wrote the essay on *Lolita*,* a copy of which is now in your hands. On the ethical plane, it is of supreme indifference to me what opinion French, British or any other courts, magistrates or philistine readers in general, have of my book.

———

Girodias had proposed that Nabokov "independently" attack the French government's ban on *Lolita*.† Although the author declined to do so, he promised to give his publisher "every assistance in your campaign" and sent him copies of "On a Book Entitled Lolita" and Fred Dupee's "A Preface to *Lolita*," which also had been published by Jason Epstein in *Anchor Review*. He also sent Girodias photographs of himself, a short curriculum vitae, and a list of his published works. At this point Nabokov was still anxious about possible repercussions at Cornell and asked that in his defensive activity

———

*Nabokov is referring to the piece he wrote for *Anchor Review*, "On a Book Entitled Lolita."

†On February 20, 1957, Nabokov wrote to Jason Epstein for his advice whether "to sue the French government on account of *Lolita*" as Girodias had proposed. Nabokov said he was "rather loath of exposing myself in the company of The Olympia Press" but wished nevertheless "to give every possible support" to the firm. The author told Epstein: "I trust your judgement, and do not know anyone else whom I would like as much to consult." In a letter dated February 25, 1957, Epstein advised Nabokov against initiating the suit and urged him to remain aloof from the legal question until it clarified itself. By letter of March 1, Nabokov wrote Girodias declining to accede to his proposal "with regard to a separate action by me in defense of *Lolita* before the French courts," an action whose costs Girodias had offered to underwrite. The main reason given by Nabokov was that "my university might not like the idea." *Selected Letters* (1989), 203–4. A Nabokov letter to Girodias of March 10, 1957, intimated that the author might change his mind about getting involved in "lolitigation" in France if his publisher would make "it possible for me to sell the American rights and the British rights of *Lolita*," and execute "a legal document exempting me from any financial responsibility whatever to lawyers and courts in France, even in case Olympia decided to go out of business or any other disaster occurred." *Selected Letters*, 210–11.

Girodias "not stress too much my being a Professor at Cornell. I am a writer primarily, and this is the important point. I do not mind being referred to as 'university professor teaching literature at a great American university.' But I would prefer you not to call Cornell by name."

VLADIMIR NABOKOV: He wanted me to defend *Lolita,* but I did not see how my book could be treated separately from his list of twenty or so lewd books. I did not want even to defend *Lolita.* . . . I was and am deeply grateful to him for printing that book. But . . . he was not the right person to undertake the thing; he lacked the means to launch *Lolita* properly—a book that differed so utterly in vocabulary, structure, and purpose (or rather absence of purpose) from his other much simpler commercial ventures, such as *Debby's Bidet* or *Tender Thighs.**

———

There is no doubt about Nabokov's appreciation of Girodias's action in publishing *Lolita.* A letter written by him to the French publisher on August 3, 1957, spoke of his gratitude to Girodias.

VLADIMIR NABOKOV: Please do keep in touch with me. I am positive that *Lolita* is the best thing I have written so far; I shall always be grateful to you for having published it.

MAURICE GIRODIAS: Alas, those were his last nice words to me.

VLADIMIR NABOKOV: Had not Graham Greene and John Gordon clashed in London in such providential fashion, *Lolita* might have ended . . . in the common grave of *Traveller's Favorites* or whatever Olympia's little green books were called. . . .†

By signing *Lolita* I had shown my complete acceptance of whatever responsibility an author has to take; but as long as an unhealthy flurry of scandal surrounded my innocent *Lolita,* I certainly was justified in acting as I did,‡ lest a shadow of my responsibility fall on the University that had given me unbelievable freedom in conducting my courses . . . nor did I care to embarrass the close friend who had brought me there to enjoy the true academic freedom.§

———

In the United States, as indicated earlier, the legal situation with respect to freedom of expression became more propititous after the Supreme Court's decision in *Roth* v. *United States* in 1957. Gradually, lawyers defending literary and artistic works against acts of government suppression began to find lower court judges more responsive to the liberal dictum contained in Justice Brennan's landmark opinion—that books having literary, artistic, or other social importance ought to be protected by the

---

*The titles are Nabokov's, not Girodias's, fantasies.

† *Traveller's Companion.*

‡I.e., not consenting to appear as a witness, in defense of *Lolita* and Girodias, at Girodias's trial.

§Morris Bishop.

Constitution against charges of being obscene—than to the opinion's seemingly repressive concrete holding—that "obscenity" was whatever appealed to the average person's prurient interest in sex and as such was expression outside the protection of the First Amendment's guarantees.

Brennan's liberating dictum would in time overshadow *Roth*'s actual holdings. It argued that "discussions of sex" in works of science, literature, or art were entitled to the full freedom mandated by the constitutional guarantees. Eventually, after *Roth,* all that would be needed to free a challenged book, magazine, or movie (in a case liable to be reviewed by the Supreme Court) was to persuade the court considering the issue that the work in question was a sort of artful "discussion" of sex—recognized by Brennan to be "a great and mysterious motive force in human life" and "a subject of absorbing interest through the ages."

When two or three copies of *Lolita* were seized by U.S. Customs, they were released because the government did not consider them "obscene." The significance of that decision—an informal administrative one—was not lost on Girodias, who appreciated that U.S. Customs was "one of the two Federal departments in the United States which systematically exerted moral censorship over literary material—the other being the Post Office." Although the release did not, as Girodias proclaimed, signify "that *Lolita* could be published in America with practically no danger"—because customs rulings of this sort, and especially informal ones, have no precedental legal value—this, together with Nabokov's growing reputation and word of the book's virtues and popularity, led several American publishers to seek the right to publish *Lolita* in the States.

VLADIMIR NABOKOV: In 1957, the *Lolita* affair entered its American phase which to me was in every way more important than its *Olympian* one. Jason Epstein, by championing the publication of a considerable portion of *Lolita* in the summer issue, 1957, of *Anchor Review* . . . helped to make the idea of an American edition acceptable. Several publishers were interested in it but the difficulties Mr. Girodias created in our negotiations with American firms were another source of acute vexation on my part. . . .

By the beginning of 1957, I had still not received from Olympia any statements of accounts since the publication of the book in September, 1955. The lapse entitled me to annul the agreement—(see Clause 9), but I decided to wait a little longer. I had to wait till March 28, 1957, and when it came, the statement did not cover the entire period for which it was due.

—

According to Nabokov, the "nuisance of non-statements" soon resumed. By the end of August 1957, he had received no statement for the first semester of that year, due July 31. On September 2, Girodias requested a postponement for two months; Nabokov agreed to wait until September 30, but when nothing arrived by then—"having had enough of that nonsense"—the author advised his publisher on October 5 that "all rights had reverted" to him. Thereupon Girodias promptly paid some 44,200 *anciens* francs and Nabokov "relented."

VLADIMIR NABOKOV: It would be tedious to continue giving instances of the delayed or incomplete statements of accounts that marked Mr. Girodias' course of action during the following years or of such misdemeanors as publishing in Paris a reprint of his edition of *Lolita* with his own introduction (in intolerably bad English) without my permission—which he knew I would never have given. What always made me regret our association were not "dreams of impending fortune," not my "hating" him "for having stolen a portion of Nabokov's property," but the obligation to endure the elusiveness, the evasiveness, the procrastination, the dodges, the duplicity, and the utter irresponsibility of the man.

—

In the United States, in the end, Walter Minton of G. P. Putnam's Sons came away with the plum, having managed to break through the serious disagreements that had developed between Nabokov and Girodias and to obtain signed contracts from both of them covering an authorized American edition. Minton had learned about *Lolita* not from Nabokov or the New York publishers' grapevine but from a young woman *Time* magazine called "a superannuated (27) nymphet." Rosemary Ridgewell was "a tall (5 ft. 8 in.), slithery-blithery onetime Latin Quarter showgirl" who discovered Nabokov's best thing in English by reading the portions of the novel that Jason Epstein had published in *Anchor Review*. She brought the book to Minton's attention and the publisher went to Paris to talk Girodias into selling American rights to Putnam's. For her part in the deal, Ridgewell received a finder's fee. According to Girodias, Ridgewell was "a very bright girl with a Dostoevskian nature"; she later committed suicide.

Lolita was one of four books presenting risks of obscenity litigation that were published by Putnam's during the late fifties and early sixties, while Walter Minton was at the helm. The others were Norman Mailer's *The Deer Park*,* Terry Southern's *Candy* (first published by Olympia, in Paris),† and the eighteenth-century erotic novel *Fanny Hill,* which Minton says he learned about at Harvard in 1942. Only the last would become the subject of landmark Supreme Court litigation, in 1966.‡

WALTER MINTON: I took a course in the eighteenth-century novel with Professor Howard Mumford Jones, and the beginning of the course was *Pamela, Clarissa, Tom Jones* and a couple of others that I'm sure I've forgotten by now. When the first two weeks of the course were over, Jones said, "Well, after that initial period in which you get five or six of these huge eighteenth-century novels, gentlemen, you have one consolation: you are now ready to appreciate *Fanny Hill.*" A snicker went through the class. That

---

*See Chapter 15 below.
†See Chapter 25 below.
‡See Chapter 23 below.

was it. After class I went up to him. I said, "Professor Jones, what's *Fanny Hill*?" He looked up and said, "Minton, you, a publisher's son, don't know *Fanny Hill*? Come with me!" And he walked me over across the Harvard Yard to those big houses behind the Memorial Chapel there—I remember they looked like monstrosities out of Cape May. I said, "Gee, I wonder who lives in those monstrosities." He said, "Well, among other people, I do." He walked me up and gave me his copy of *Fanny Hill,* * and then I read it. . . . It's funny, because when we published it, we got sued in Boston and I immediately called him as an expert witness.†

———

The year that Minton published *Lolita* in New York, 1958, turned out to be a banner year for Putnam's. Said Minton, "We did *Lolita,* we had five or six other books on the best-seller list. It was one of the best years we ever had." The Supreme Court's slow movement to the left was having a beneficent effect upon American publishers. Repercussions in England would lead to the enactment of the liberalizing Obscene Publications Act of 1959, which was to some extent patterned after Brennan's liberalizing dictum in *Roth,* and to the publication of *Lolita* by the firm of Weidenfeld and Nicolson promptly thereafter. But across the Channel, in the country that had long offered refuge to authors and artists alienated from their own nations, the French publisher of books in English, Maurice Girodias, was still embroiled in legal difficulties.

In Paris, Girodias had engaged Leo Matarasso, "a clear-headed, infinitely patient attorney," to sue the French minister of the interior in order to remove the ban on *Lolita;* and for a moment the publisher's situation brightened. To Girodias's surprise, the case was won in 1957, in the Administrative Tribunal of Paris. Said Nabokov, "The French press went wild over the attempt against the freedoms. They made a special case for *Lolita,* 'le célèbre roman de Vladimir Nabokov.'" The controversy was called *"l'affaire Lolita,"* and the publicity and the positive results in court moved the publisher Gallimard to announce that it would bring out a French translation within a matter of months.

Girodias was justly proud of his victory but as he later said, he "should have known better." In May 1958 the Fourth Republic fell and General de Gaulle took power. The minister of the interior now appealed to France's highest court, the Conseil d'Etat, and Girodias was ignominiously beaten; the ban on the sale of *Lolita* was restored.

There was no apparent way for Girodias to appeal from the final judgment of the Conseil d'Etat or to seek to have the ban on the English version of the book lifted by direct litigation. The Conseil d'Etat held that the minister of the interior had absolute power to apply and interpret the law and could not be questioned even by the Conseil. But then, in April 1959, the French edition of *Lolita,* translated by Girodias's brother, Eric Kahane,

———

*A clandestine edition, no doubt.
†He may have been called, but he did not appear, as a witness.

was published by France's prestigious Gallimard, and this gave Girodias an idea for liberating his own edition of *Lolita*. He sued the French government for damages, on the theory that the legal principle of equality between French citizens had been violated by the government's banning of his *Lolita* but not Gallimard's. It worked. Girodias was called to the Ministry of the Interior and the matter was settled by a compromise under which the minister agreed to cancel his ban on *Lolita* in exchange for Girodias's agreement to withdraw his suit for damages.

Not long after that, however, Nabokov "astounded" Girodias by sending him another letter, dated August 13, 1960, telling him that his publishing agreement with Nabokov was "null and void" and that all rights had reverted to the author. The letter went on to demand that Girodias immediately cease publication, distribution, and sale of *Lolita*. In fact, as early as October 5, 1957, as noted earlier, Nabokov had informed Girodias that the agreement between them was null and void. For his part, Girodias once or twice threatened to publish *Lolita* in the States himself, under the Olympia imprint. In a letter dated January 14, 1958, to Walter Minton, Véra Nabokov spoke about the way in which "an adverse decision" by the French courts regarding *Lolita* "might prove very much to my husband's advantage since there seems to be a provision in the French law releasing the author [from his publishing contract] if the publisher cannot continue to publish the book."

VLADIMIR NABOKOV: I began to curse my association with Olympia Press . . . as early as 1955, that is, the very first year of my dealings with Mr. Girodias. From the very start I was confronted with the peculiar aura surrounding his business transactions with me, an aura of negligence, evasiveness, procrastination, and falsity.

——

In England, the publishers George Weidenfeld and Nigel Nicolson, a member of Parliament, waited for the enactment of the Obscene Publications Bill in 1959 before publishing *Lolita*. On January 28, 1959, Weidenfeld wrote to reassure Nabokov that he would publish *Lolita* at the earliest possible opportunity:

GEORGE WEIDENFELD: Dear Mr. Nabokov, . . . I . . . hasten to write to you and give you the latest news.

The battle for *Lolita* goes on and I hope that both the press cuttings and also your cousin [Nicholas Nabokov, the composer] will have kept you up to date with developments. . . .

The *Times* letter was obviously very helpful, although today's rejoinder by Douglas Woodruff, the editor of the Catholic paper *The Tablet*, is the first seriously argued thrust of counter attack.

The salient problem is one of timing. As you know the Obscene Publications Bill has now had its formal second reading and will reach the crucial committee stage at the end of February and should we are reliably informed become law in May or June. Our legal advisors and indeed our legal friends are strongly of the opinion that we should not publish before this new bill has become effective. The reason for this is that under the present law the literary quality of the book in question is held to be entirely irrelevant and one is not allowed to call any witnesses to testify to the book's merits. Under the new bill not only will literary merit be taken into account in deciding the fate of the book but the defence will be able to call witnesses to testify to the book's literary merits. I need not explain to you how enormously the chances of victory, in the event of prosecution, would be increased if we could produce in court as witnesses the formidable array of literary personalities who signed the letter to the *Times.*

—

Those who had signed the *Times* letter were J. R. Ackerley, Walter Allen, A. Alvarez, Isaiah Berlin, C. M. Bowra, Storm Jameson, Frank Kermode, Allen Lane, Margaret Lane, Rosamund Lehmann, Compton Mackenzie, Iris Murdoch, William Plomer, V. S. Pritchett, Alan Price Jones, Peter Quennell, Herbert Read, Stephen Spender, Philip Toynbee, Bernard Wall, and Angus Wilson.*

The next month, Philip Toynbee published a piece on "the *Lolita* question" in *The Observer* (February 8, 1959), in which he argued that the novel should be suppressed in England if it could be proven that even "a single little girl was likely to be seduced as a result of its publication." Acknowledging the difficulty of showing this in advance of *Lolita*'s publication in England, Toynbee suggested that proof that a single little American girl had been seduced as a result of its publication in the States would be sufficient to support a ban in England. So far as is known, no such little girl was ever produced, in either country.

Before *Lolita* was published by Weidenfeld and Nicolson, Nicolson was urged by his fellow Conservatives in Parliament not to publish the book, because it could be damaging to the party. Nicolson's involvement in the publication of the Nabokov novel, which very much impressed him, was one reason he was not reelected (another was his criticism of Britain's position regarding Suez). He lost by 91 votes in an election in which between 7,000 and 8,000 people participated. During debates on the Obscene Publications Bill, Nicolson, speaking as a publisher, allowed that "the borderline cases [like *Lolita*] were the most difficult," and that "he had had to make such a decision and it had not been at all easy."

---

*The letter read as follows: Sir, We are disturbed by the suggestion that it may yet prove impossible to have an English edition of Vladimir Nabokov's *Lolita*. Our opinions of the merit of the work differ widely, but we think it would be deplorable, if a book of considerable literary interest, which has been favourably received by distinguished critics and widely praised in serious and respectable periodicals were to be denied an appearance in this country.

Prosecutions of genuine works of literature bring governments into disrepute and do nothing to protect public morality. When to-day we read the proceedings against *Madame Bovary* or *Ulysses*—works genuinely found shocking by many of their contemporaries—it is Flaubert and Joyce whom we admire, not the Public Prosecutors of the time. Let good sense spare us another such case (London *Times,* January 23, 1959).

NIGEL NICOLSON: The advice one often heard was "Publish and be damned," but that was very bad advice. I did not want to be damned. I felt that this particular work was a work of such outstanding merit and so widely acclaimed that some publisher had to have the courage to make it available to British readers.

—

Weidenfeld and Nicolson were "most anxious" to publish Nabokov's earlier works before their publication of *Lolita;* they sought from Nabokov the right to start off with *The Real Life of Sebastian Knight,* followed by his short stories and his Russian novels.

GEORGE WEIDENFELD: *Bend Sinister* could be sandwiched in between the first and second Russian novels. If we could agree on this programme, we would like to publish *The Real Life of Sebastian Knight* at the earliest opportunity—perhaps in June or July regardless of the publication date of *Lolita.* My whole point is to impress on critics, the book trade and the public alike that we are bent on publishing your whole opus, which we wish to have in print as soon as possible.

—

Once the 1959 act made it possible in England to defend against a charge of obscenity with testimony of literary value, books that had long been contraband were published, including *The Well of Loneliness, La Terre,* and *Lady Chatterley's Lover.* The government decided to test the new law by instituting a prosecution against the prestigious publisher of *Lady C.,* Penguin Books. After thirty-five distinguished men and women of letters, moral theologians, teachers, publishers, editors, and critics went to the Old Bailey in October 1960 and gave evidence in defense of *Lady C.,* both the publisher and D. H. Lawrence's last novel were acquitted.*

In the United States, no criminal prosecution was ever brought to suppress *Lolita* but a number of libraries banned it from their shelves. The most flagrant incident took place in Cincinnati, a bastion of anti-art, pro-censorship forces where, thirty years later, a prestigious art gallery and its director would be prosecuted for showing the "pornographic" photographic art of Robert Mapplethorpe.† The director of the Cincinnati public library, Ernest I. Miller, said he ordered *Lolita* removed because "the theme of perversion seems to me obscene."

In 1968, ten years after Putnam's publication of *Lolita,* Nabokov left his publisher for the McGraw-Hill Book Company. According to the newspapers, Nabokov had grown "piqued" with Putnam's because of its "lack of

---

*The publisher's solicitors were Rubinstein, Nash and Company, of *Well of Loneliness* fame; it may be remembered that when public figures were brought to testify in that case, the magistrate would not listen to a word from any of them. See Chapter 11. The trial of Penguin is fully reported in *The Trial of Lady Chatterley,* edited by C. H. Rolph, with a new Foreword by Geoffrey Robertson (1990).

†See Chapter 30.

promotional interest" in his books after *Lolita*'s success. According to Walter Minton, Putnam's viewed the great man's departure "without regret" because after the uproar over *Lolita,* each of Nabokov's next six books was a mere *succès d'estime,* with no significant sales.

Nabokov liked to say he was an *American* writer. In an interview in 1977 with the *New York Times* reporter Alden Whitman, Nabokov said:

VLADIMIR NABOKOV: An American writer means, in the present case, a writer who has been an American citizen for a quarter of a century. It means, moreover, that all my works first appear in America.* It also means that America is the only country where I feel mentally and emotionally at home.

———

Still, once the returns from *Lolita* were in, Nabokov resigned his tenured post with Cornell and settled into "a marvelous Victorian and Edwardian pile on the shores of Lake Geneva," the Palace Hotel at Montreux, Switzerland.

ALDEN WHITMAN: "Sheer laziness" was one of the reasons he gave for remaining there; he also wanted to be near his only son, Dmitri, who was an opera singer in Italy, and a sister in Geneva.

———

As the fortunes of *Lolita*'s author and publishers flourished in England and the States, in France the novel's first publisher, Girodias, was beaten to the ground.

MAURICE GIRODIAS: Things went from bad to worse. . . . A few months later, my English version of Jean Genet's *Our Lady of the Flowers* was banned, although I had had it in print for many years, and in spite of the fact that the original French version had been on sale everywhere in France ever since the war. The mistake was even more ludicrous than in the case of *Lolita,* as Genet was a French writer of unquestionable importance, whereas Nabokov was a foreign writer practically unknown in France at the time. I sued once more, confident that it would be easy to win a real victory—or at least to reach a compromise as in the *Lolita* precedent. But . . . I lost my case. I appealed, and lost again when the case was re-examined by the Conseil d'Etat. . . .

Independently of these erratic bans, I was now being tried for every single book I printed (the offense being known as *outrage aux bonnes moeurs par la voie du livre* †—that's O.B.M. for short, on the judges' files). I was tried for books which had been out of print for four or five years; I was even tried, in two or three instances, for books published by others. As the judges had practically no knowledge of English those trials often turned into entertaining vaudevilles. . . .

———

*Except, as we have seen, *Lolita.*

†The same offense for which, in 1857, Flaubert was unsuccessfully prosecuted for writing *Madame Bovary* and Baudelaire and his publisher were convicted for writing and publishing *Les Fleurs du mal.*

Leo Matarasso, my dear, infinitely patient and cunning attorney . . . always spends the last minutes before each trial numbing my conscience with lengthy recommendations. We usually have a big meal before, with lots of wine to induce drowsiness and mollify my *amour-propre*. Then Leo drags me to court while entreating me, one last time: "Be humble, listen, answer briefly and to the point, don't look the fellows straight in the eye. . . ."

MARILYN MEESKE: Such giants as Samuel Beckett and Genet were first presented in the English language by Olympia. . . . Although original Olympia Press publications have made many a publisher richer, Girodias has yet to make another score equal to *Lolita*. For the most part his lists have been pillaged and pirated and in a way his laxity in these areas might be a powerful, unconscious drive toward going down in history as one of the fearless and dedicated publishers of our era.

VLADIMIR NABOKOV: I often wonder what I would have done at the time of the initial negotiation with Olympia Press if I had learned then that alongside talented, albeit immodest, literary works, the publisher gained his main income from vulgar little books that he commissioned from meretricious nonentities, books of exactly the same nature as the pictures hawked on dark corners of a nun with a St. Bernard, or a sailor with a sailor.

MAURICE GIRODIAS: Then the rigamarole starts once again, always the same: my ugly past; the horrible fact that I plain forgot to appear in court the last time I was summoned, and did not even excuse myself; the fact that I am a *spécialiste de ce genre d'affaires*. . . . It may go well if I manage to doze off a little in my standing position, but sometimes the attorney-general is too much, and then all goes wrong. The man insults me, calls me names, asks me with a sneer if I can read English and if I say yes, asks me if I am aware of the disgusting contents of the book—which he, himself, cannot read. It is difficult to control oneself in such emergencies, and I had to quickly choose between two solutions: either to burst out in Homeric laughter, or bawl back at the man as if I were taking him seriously. Instinct makes me opt for the latter solution, and venom is slung back and forth. From the corner of my eye, I see the unhappy grin on Leo's face gradually disintegrating: he became smaller and smaller on his bench. The presiding judge, who had earlier proved unable to pronounce the title of the book, frowns at me with a terrible, ferocious look on his face; but at heart he is relaxed and content: everything is back to normal. . . . [A]nd it all ends up in an atmosphere of general good will, and with the fine feelings which warm the connoisseur's heart for a job well done. And the huge sentences which are clamped down on me as a conclusion to these Alice in Wonderland exercises are made to appear as special distinctions reserved for the very few.

The results of this war against Girodias and the Olympia Press were not particularly amusing: an eighty-year ban on all publishing activities in France, unsuspended prison sentences of four to six years, and $80,000 in fines.* Although the prison terms and fines were later reduced to more reasonable proportions, the publisher was "really paralysed." After that, and although he attempted a publishing resurrection in New York,† he was finished, for he had "lost the madness."

In "a warren of small rooms" at the Palace Hotel in Montreux, Nabokov—who had never owned a place in which he lived—worked and lived for the rest of his days with Véra. She was his "secretary, typist, assistant, chess partner, Scrabble adversary, butterfly-hunting companion, and conversational jouster" to the end. Writing, however, was Nabokov's great love: "a blend of dejection and high spirits, a torture and a pastime."

---

*In the end, Girodias reportedly spent two days in jail.

†In 1965 Girodias announced he was leaving France for New York, where he tried to reestablish the Olympia Press and publish more of his Traveller's Companion (green-covered) books. In New York he commissioned the American poet Diane di Prima—probably the best-known female writer of the beat movement—to do a d.b., published as *Memoirs of a Beatnik* in 1969, and republished by "Last Gasp of San Francisco" in 1988. (See Chapter 17 and the endnotes to that chapter.) In an Afterword, the poet described, in terms reminiscent of Anaïs Nin's experience, how she wrote the book: "Gobs of words would go off to New York whenever the rent was due, and come back with 'MORE SEX' scrawled across the top page in Maurice's inimitable hand, and I would dream up odd angles of bodies or weird combinations of humans and cram them in and send it off again" (137).

15

I'm Just Going to Feed Adolphe

NINE YEARS AFTER the U.S. Supreme Court silently permitted Doubleday to stand convicted and fined by New York State for publishing Edmund Wilson's *Memoirs of Hecate County* and effectively suppressed that novel throughout the nation for being "obscene," the Court took up the case of a publisher named Samuel Roth, who had been sentenced to prison by a federal court for selling "obscene" literature of another kind. Although the Court would affirm Sam Roth's conviction, the opinion written by Justice William J. Brennan, Jr., was the Supreme Court's first move to liberate literature and art from government censorship.

Roth and his wife, Pauline, made their living by publishing risqué literature, usually reprinted and frequently pirated, which they advertised and sold mainly through the mails. Sam Roth was one of a number of publishers who devoted themselves to serving the strong interest Americans displayed after World War II in sexual images and ideas and sexually oriented publications. To Roth, this was "a healthy, normal interest—vigorous and creative." The United States had a different view. Chief Judge Charles Clark of the federal Second Circuit court, which considered Roth's appeal, described Roth as "an old hand at publishing and surreptitiously mailing to those induced to order them such lurid pictures and materials as he can find profitable." Earl Warren, the Supreme Court's new chief justice, said that Roth and his ilk were just "plainly engaged in the commercial exploitation of the morbid and shameful craving" that too many Americans had "for materials with prurient effect."

In *Thy Neighbor's Wife,* published in 1980, Gay Talese outlined the lives and publishing styles of Roth and others of the breed, including George

Von Rosen, Marvin Miller, Al Goldstein, Ralph Ginzburg, and William Hamling. Their enterprise in exciting male fantasies about the sexual nature of women would not be recognized by the Supreme Court as having implications for freedom of the press until waves from the sexual revolution washed up against the high bench during the late 1960s.

Warren's biographers are agreed that from the day he joined the Court to the day he stepped down, the "Super Chief" could not shed his conventional middle-American attitudes, or his puritanism.* "If anyone showed that [dirty] book to my daughters, I'd have strangled him with my own hands," he reputedly told his clerks. The otherwise humanistic chief's defensiveness about sexual expression made rational decision-making and opinion-writing in this area of the Court's work difficult. Warren could not reconcile the disgust he felt for sexually oriented materials with the respect he professed for "arts and sciences and freedom of communication generally." He was puzzled by his inability to get anything out of "modern" literature and art. To him, "smut peddlers" had no rights under the First Amendment, for what they peddled had nothing to do with literature and art, or even communication. Not only was their conduct an affront to Warren's personal sensibility, it also presented, in his view, a peril to America's moral fiber.† Even Warren's closest colleague on the Court, otherwise one of his greatest admirers, faulted the Super Chief for his attitude toward sex.

WILLIAM J. BRENNAN, JR.: Warren was a terrible prude. Like my father was. If Warren was revolted by something, it was obscene. He would not read any of the books. Or watch the movies. I'd read the book or see the movie and he'd go along with my views.

—

Warren did have Brennan look at the books, magazines, and movies at issue in the Court's obscenity cases throughout the sixties, but he rarely went along with Brennan's views. In *Roth,* Warren filed a separate opinion disagreeing with Brennan on the reason why Roth deserved to be imprisoned; and seven years later, when, in the landmark cases involving Henry Miller's novel *Tropic of Cancer* and Louis Malle's movie *The Lovers,* Justice Brennan acted to remove the threats posed by state obscenity laws to literature and films, Warren vigorously dissented.‡ Yet Warren, during his long tenure as chief justice, often looked to Brennan to generate the legal doctrines that supported the progressive decisions of the Warren Court, and to gather a majority or a plurality of the brethren to join them. Beginning in 1957, with *Roth,* Warren—by using his opinion-assignment

---

*See, for example, Professor Bernard Schwartz's "judicial biography" of Warren, *Super Chief: Earl Warren and His Supreme Court* (1983).

†There is an analysis of Warren's attitude toward obscenity and the constitutional questions it presented for him in G. Edward White's *Earl Warren: A Public Life* (1982), Chapter 11. See also Bob Woodward and Scott Armstrong's *The Brethren* (1979).

‡See Chapter 22 below.

prerogatives—took from Frankfurter and handed to Brennan doctrinal leadership of the Court in cases where individual liberties were at stake. Then, in 1962, after Frankfurter was replaced by the liberal Arthur Goldberg, Brennan was really free, and had the votes, to marshal a Court behind his agenda to expand to the limit freedom of speech and press and other constitutional rights and liberties.*

In Samuel Roth's case, Brennan was given the job of explaining to the legal community and the nation why it was just, and in accordance with First Amendment jurisprudence, to let a publisher go to jail for using the mails to carry on the "business of purveying textual or graphic matter openly advertised to appeal to the erotic interest of [his] customers." Remarkably, the opinion Brennan wrote in *Roth* would launch his career as the Warren Court's principal exponent not only of what Professor Harry Kalven, Jr., of the University of Chicago Law School trenchantly referred to as "the metaphysics of the law of obscenity" but of First Amendment freedom generally. His opinion became a constitutional landmark. So did the opinion he wrote, seven years later, in *New York Times* v. *Sullivan*, in which he "constitutionalized" the law of libel. He would do much the same, using very different words, to the law of obscenity, in the same year, 1964, with the opinion he wrote freeing Henry Miller's *Tropic of Cancer* and Louis Malle's *The Lovers*. In the *Sullivan* case, Brennan succeeded in securing for the country's press a vast area of constitutional freedom that Frankfurter had thought—by upholding the validity of a group-libel law—to leave to regulation under the police powers of the states.†

In a letter Sam Roth wrote to Postmaster General Arthur Summerfield and published in his hardbound literary quarterly, *American Aphrodite,* in 1953, the publisher lectured the postmaster general and protested the government's repeated interferences with his mailings and complaints about his advertising methods respecting *Aphrodite:*

SAMUEL ROTH: [A]dvertisements are made to get people to buy; writing them has become a fine art. Their chief function is to engage the attention. We are sure that an inquiry into the methods of engaging this attention would reveal that advertisements overwhelmingly resort to working with and by one subject that most engages attention, and that is the subject and phases of sex. This goes even for advertisements selling the humdrum

---

*See Stephen Gillers's piece on this subject in *The Nation,* September 17, 1983: "The Warren Court—It Still Lives." Gillers, a professor of law at New York University, credits Brennan with keeping the progressive law created by the Warren Court alive during the reactionary era of the Burger and early Rehnquist courts.

†The group-libel law case was *Beauharnais* v. *Illinois,* discussed by Harry Kalven in *A Worthy Tradition* (1987), 60 and 92 ff. Brennan's much-praised opinion in *Sullivan* has recently been criticized by Professor Richard Epstein of the University of Chicago Law School. See Epstein's "Was *New York Times* v. *Sullivan* Wrong?" in 53 *University of Chicago Law Review,* 782 (1986). Kalven celebrated *Sullivan* in "The New York Times Case: A Note on 'The Central Meaning of the First Amendment'" in *1964 Supreme Court Review* (1964), 191.

sundries of the household, men's articles as well as women's, cereals as well as undergarments. No one raises the slightest objection to this. It is accepted and a matter of course among us. Our circulars describe our publication in terms understood by the population of our community, on matter it understands or should understand, for no part of it fails to make the columns of the daily press in one form or another.

Nevertheless, we have no pride of authorship in advertisements and would be wholly willing to sit down with your department, with other publishers, indeed, if that could be arranged, to work out a standard in such things, without, however, making the concession that *anyone* has a *right* to set down for us what the standard should be.

—

And then Roth described for the postmaster general the centerpiece of his mail-order publishing products.

SAMUEL ROTH: Now what is *American Aphrodite*? It is a hard-back, four times a year, literary magazine. It contains the best in contemporary literature and from its best hands. . . . It has illustrations, some of which no doubt delineate the form that God has given us; "male and female he created them" saith the Bible. It has material which is lighthearted about the serious things in life, serious about some trivial things in life, and serious about the serious, lighthearted about the light. Nothing is in bad taste.

For example: in a single issue (an issue which has been condemned by your Solicitor) we published a complete novel by the distinguished British author, Richard Aldington, along with his exquisite book-length poem, *A Dream in the Luxembourg,* a collection of reproductions of the famous *Odalisques* by Henri Matisse, a story by Norman Douglas, one by Ronald Firbank and another by James Branch Cabell.

Another issue condemned by your Solicitor contained a complete novel by François Mauriac, the leading Roman Catholic writer of France, and a Nobel Prize Winner. Other matter contained in the condemned issues of *American Aphrodite* includes the plays of Aphra Behn, the *Divine Comedy* of Dante, in the first truly sensitive translation ever made in English, the stories of Liam O'Flaherty, Sean O'Faolain, Rhys Davis, Margaret Kennedy, Sylvia Townsend Warner, H. E. Bates, David Garnett, T. F. Powys, and many others.

—

Roth was proud of *American Aphrodite.* It must have been disappointing to him, when his case finally reached the highest court in the land, to learn that most of the justices would not read it.

He was born in a small town in Austria on November 17, 1894, the son of Joseph and Adele Roth. In 1903 the family moved to the Lower East Side of Manhattan. The young Roth wrote poetry for the *Jewish Child, The Menorah Journal,* and various Yiddish publications. Later he went to Columbia University on a scholarship and published a campus magazine called the *Lyric,* in which excerpts from the works of D. H. Lawrence, Archibald MacLeish, Stephen Vincent Benét, and other well-known modern writers were reprinted. After World War I, Roth opened the Poetry Bookshop on Eighth Street in Greenwich Village and started a magazine called *Two Worlds Monthly,* in which he published "lightly libidinous" nineteenth-century French fiction by such writers as Zola, Balzac, de Maupassant, and Flaubert. But he also published large, mutilated chunks of *Ulysses,* pirated from Sylvia Beach's Paris edition, and this earned him not the support but the enmity of the progressive element among the literati.

Roth reprinted portions of three episodes of *Ulysses* in 1927, without James Joyce's permission. When, despite the author's complaint, Roth did not stop publishing the pirated text, Joyce brought a court action and encouraged an international protest, drawn up and circulated by Ludwig Lewisohn and Archibald MacLeish. The document accused Roth of republishing *Ulysses* "without authorization by Mr. Joyce, without payment to Mr. Joyce, and with alterations which seriously corrupt the text"; it also appealed to Americans "to oppose to Mr. Roth's enterprise the full power of honorable and fair opinion." Among the singers were Benedetto Croce, Albert Einstein, T. S. Eliot, Havelock Ellis, E. M. Forster, André Gide, Ernest Hemingway, D. H. Lawrence, Wyndham Lewis, Sean O'Casey, Luigi Pirandello, H. G. Wells, Rebecca West, Thornton Wilder, and Virginia Woolf—a list that testifies to the high reputation and spreading fame of Joyce and his banned book.

The protest did not faze Roth, who went on publishing portions of *Ulysses* in his *Two Worlds Monthly* until October 1927, when the New York State court judge sitting on the case that Joyce had instituted enjoined the publisher from using Joyce's name in any way. This was a clever way to gain protection from acts of literary piracy for a work that, because parts of it had been found obscene, presumably was not protectable under copyright law. The next year Roth was prosecuted and sent to jail for publishing the *Ulysses* material—not upon Joyce's complaint, nor upon any made by John Sumner of the New York Society for the Suppression of Vice, but at the insistence of the Clean Books Committee of the Federation of Hungarian Jews in America. The committee was not hearkening to the call of the international protest's signatories; it was fed up with Roth because it believed his publication of Joyce's portrayal of Leopold Bloom "defamed" Hungarian Jews.

Three years later Roth and his wife were prosecuted for selling another book—this one a pirated version of *Lady Chatterley's Lover,* the banned novel that Lawrence had published privately in Florence and distributed clandestinely in England and the United States.* Again, Sam Roth went to prison. All in all, the publisher was arrested seven times and convicted on four occasions for dealing in material—some of it undeniably valuable

---

*On the censorship of Lawrence's works, see Chapters 4 and 5 above.

literature—that his prosecutors and judges found obscene. Roth seems to have been handicapped in defending himself because his "book-legging" publishing practices and other lapses of occupational integrity cost him the support of the literati.

His *New York Times* obituary described Roth as a "tall bespectacled man with a courtly manner." As dealer, distributor, and publisher of sexually oriented books and magazines, he had a reputation for keeping one step ahead of the police. He published under a number of imprints, including Candide Press, Arrowhead Books, Hogarth House, William Faro, Inc., Golden Hind Press, and Seven Sirens Press. And, in his own testimony before a congressional committee set up to investigate the causes of "juvenile delinquency," he claimed to have mailed out "ten million" advertisements of his publications during the course of his publishing career. According to one of the publisher's critics, Roth "used no discretion in compiling his lists and indiscriminately sent his circulars to many small children—even to orphanages."

The critic John N. Makris, in *The Silent Investigators: The Great Untold Story of the United States Postal Inspection Service,* published two years after Roth's publishing demise, claimed that Roth had employed sixty-two trade styles or business names to confuse and frustrate the continuing efforts of Post Office police to get the goods on him and his mail-order operations: "He harassed the Inspection Service and the feeble through his persistent use of the mails to traffic in obscene books, or what he called European 'classics.' " Roth also distributed the *NUS* series of nude pictures, "which were sold by number." Makris claimed that Roth did a $270,000 annual gross business, conducted primarily through a mailing list of some four hundred thousand customers, "including doctors, lawyers, and other professional people."

In Roth's continuing efforts to distribute erotic literature, make money, and stay out of jail, the publisher kept his eyes fixed on the line that he believed ought to be drawn between "obscene" and "nonobscene" printed expression and steadfastly refused to accept the Post Office solicitor's ideas about the location of that line in relationship to his publications. By the mid-fifties, the Post Office had been interfering with the circulation of valuable, even classic, literature among Americans for years, yet this interference had been unpublicized and uncontested in court. The Post Office's "index" of banned books included not only novels by leading contemporary authors* but also works of nonfiction dealing with sexual love, sexual

---

*Among them Ernest Hemingway, John O'Hara, Erskine Caldwell, J. D. Salinger, Alberto Moravia, John Steinbeck, James T. Farrell, Calder Willingham, Richard Wright, and Norman Mailer. In 1954, after the *Lysistrata* case was over, I was shown an index file of proscribed books kept by the department in Washington, D.C., and publicized the facts and process of Post Office literary censorship in a piece called "Obscenity and the Mail," published as part of a symposium on "Obscenity and the Arts" in *Law and Contemporary Problems* (Autumn 1955). Post Office censorship is also documented in James Paul and Murray Schwartz, *Federal Censorship* (1961), 102ff.

techniques, sexual deviations, sexual behavior, and contraception, as well as some of the literature of Aristophanes, Ovid, and Apuleius in translation. Among scientific and philosophical writings banned from the mails were works by Sigmund Freud, Richard Krafft-Ebing, Wilhelm Stekel, Margaret Mead, and Simone de Beauvoir. The trouble with all these books was sex.

The Post Office Department's Washington censors had no special education for distinguishing the "obscene" from the merely "sexual" in books and magazines, and the definitional case law involved was so vague and uncertain that they resorted to a rule of thumb gleaned from their own experience. It had the virtue of being simple, and specific: "Breasts, yes, nipples, no," the department's chief censor confided to me, "buttocks, yes, cracks, no." This was the rule that caused the Post Office to remove from the mails not only selected "French postcards" and "nudist" and "girlie" magazines, but a rare illustrated edition of Aristophanes' *Lysistrata* en route from England to a Los Angeles bookseller.* In 1955 I was asked by the ACLU to take that seizure to court. The widespread publicity that followed my charge that Postmaster General Arthur Summerfield had no respect for the literature of the ages and that the court should remove him and his office from the business of literary censorship caused the department to hand over to me this handsomely printed and exuberantly illustrated oversized edition of *Lysistrata*—so that the book might be sent on its way.†

Roth bothered the Post Office Department for years. He engaged in hit-and-run legal encounters with departmental censors and police from 1928, the occasion of his first arrest and prosecution for mailing obscene literature, until 1955, when a federal grand jury presented the revised twenty-six-count indictment against him involving *American Aphrodite* that finally brought the publisher down. Before that defeat, Roth had even sought to have federal courts enjoin the postmaster general from restraining his expressive activities.‡ According to Makris: "The court proceedings

---

*Published by Fanfrolico Press, one of the Paris publishing houses that D. H. Lawrence looked into in his effort to bring out a cheap (paperback) but faithful edition of *Lady Chatterley's Lover*. See Chapter 5 above.

†The Post Office's release of the volume was not simply a confession of error, however; it was also a legal maneuver designed to moot the case that I had brought, on behalf of the Los Angeles bookseller, in which I asked a federal court not only to require that the book be returned but, more important, to declare unconstitutional the law and practice under which the Post Office supervised the sexual contents of literature and art sent through the mails. I argued that even if *Lysistrata* were obscene, its social and cultural importance entitled it to constitutional protection; in this I partly anticipated the Brennan doctrine, which evolved in the Supreme Court from 1957 to 1966. The incident is mentioned in my article "Obscenity and the Mail," in *Law and Contemporary Problems* (Autumn 1955), and in James Paul and Murray Schwartz, *Federal Censorship* (1961), 104. The government probably handed the book over in consideration of the possible disaster awaiting its ongoing mail censorship program if the *Lysistrata* case reached the Supreme Court. Even a Frankfurter-dominated bench would have felt the need to find a way to set *Lysistrata* free from the Post Office's restraint.

‡See, for example, *Roth* v. *Goldman*, 172 F.2d 788 (2d Cir. 1949), in which Roth sought to enjoin a postmaster from executing four "fraud" orders and an "exclusion" order. The fraud orders were based on the government's theory that Roth mailed advertisements that fraudulently represented four books sold by him as erotic ("salacious") when in fact (according to the Post Office) they were not. The exclusion order was designed to prevent Roth from using

were usually long and drawn out, during which time Roth continued to operate on a full-scale basis. All he had to do to continue his operations was merely to change his trade name."

As time went on, as Makris saw it, Roth became "bolder," his publications "spicier." He was put under investigation "by at least ten different postal inspectors who maintained a continuously 'open' case against him," faithfully answering Roth's ads and ordering plenty of his publications. The government was determined to put behind bars and thus out of business the man whom Makris described as "one of the biggest and most notorious pornographers to emerge in the past twenty-five years." The publisher saw the matter in a different light. In the pages of *American Aphrodite* Roth elaborated on his own vision of his place in the history of belles lettres:

SAMUEL ROTH: I haven't any intention of offering what Louisa May Alcott called "moral pap for the young"; and while I have no wish to offend persons who seem to me both prudish and unrealistic, neither have I any wish to trim my sails to their faint breezes. . . .

Our language, the language of Chaucer and Shakespeare and Ben Jonson, of Thomas Jefferson, of Clay and Daniel Webster and Henry Adams, is the source of our power as a people. From it sprang Magna Carta and the Common Law. As my part of this great tradition I want freedom of speech as a publisher. I know that people are interested in sex, as they are interested in all other aspects of living, and I believe that this is a healthy, normal interest—vigorous and creative. Those people who think that sexual love is dirty may leave my books alone. I do not publish for such as those.

———

In an issue of *American Aphrodite* published in 1954 shortly before his major federal indictment Roth spoke to his readers about his battle with the Post Office on behalf of literary freedom:

SAMUEL ROTH: The score as it stands now is not too discouraging. Six of the twelve published numbers of *American Aphrodite* have been barred from the mails, withheld from the thousands of libraries and persons of culture for whom they are important archives of cultural endeavor in our time.

———

But, sighed Roth, "it was better to have lost these than to have lost all." Then, on April 29, 1954, Samuel Roth was indicted in the case that became

the mails to distribute a book called *Waggish Tales from the Czechs.* The same federal appellate court that later upheld Roth's *American Aphrodite* conviction thought it proper to uphold the Post Office's finding that *Waggish Tales* was obscene by "hiding behind" a self-limiting scope of judicial review of administrative action and maintaining that "within limits it perhaps is not unreasonable to stifle compositions that clearly have little excuse for being beyond their provocative obscenity and to allow those of literary distinction to survive." This approach understandably "bewildered" Judge Jerome Frank, inasmuch as the court majority seemed ready to assume the task of "acting as judges of literature." See William Lockhart and Robert McClure, "Literature, the Law of Obscenity, and the Constitution," in 38 *Minnesota Law Review,* 338 (1954).

a landmark of the law and the first occasion on which the Supreme Court openly addressed itself to the "intractable problem of obscenity." The material that heralded the end of Roth's publishing career included advertisements for *NUS* and for a publication called *Good Times: A Review of the World of Pleasure*. More significant for the struggle for literary freedom, Roth was indicted for using the mails to advertise and sell volume 1, number 3, of *American Aphrodite,* containing Aubrey Beardsley's "unprintable" *Venus and Tannhäuser*. The government found the evidence it needed to convict Roth on this count when a Post Office inspector, using the picaresque pseudonym Archie Lovejoy, ordered and received that issue of *Aphrodite* through the mails.

The Beardsley prose work *Venus and Tannhäuser* was not unknown to the cognoscenti. It was described by Edmund Wilson as "a remarkable unfinished romance" in which the late-nineteenth-century illustrator had "succeeded to invest a sort of pagan world with the artificial graces of the nineties, without the fumes of Victorian Christian orthodoxy." Wilson commented appreciatively on Beardsley's rendering of classical mythology's goddess of love: "His Venus, unlike the Venus of Swinburne or the Harlot of Wilde, is not destructive and terrible, but girlish and agreeable."

AUBREY BEARDSLEY *(Venus and Tannhäuser): When all was said and done, the Chevalier tripped off to bid good morning to Venus. He found her wandering, in a sweet white muslin frock, upon the lawn outside, plucking flowers to deck her little déjeuner. He kissed her lightly upon the neck.*

'I'm just going to feed Adolphe,' she said, pointing to a little reticule of buns that hung from her arm. Adolphe was her pet unicorn. . . . 'He is such a dear,' she continued, 'milk-white all over except his black eyes, rose mouth and nostrils, and scarlet John.' . . .

'You mustn't come in with me—Adolphe is so jealous,' she said, turning to the Chevalier who was following her; 'but you can stand outside and look on; Adolphe likes an audience.' Then in her delicious fingers she broke the spicy buns, and with affectionate niceness, breakfasted her ardent pet. When the last crumbs had been scattered, Venus brushed her hands together and pretended to leave the cage, without taking any more notice of Adolphe. Every morning Venus went through this piece of play, and every morning the amorous unicorn was cheated into a distressing agony lest that day should have proved the last of Venus' love. Not for long, though, would she leave him in that doubtful, piteous state, but running back passionately to where he stood, made adorable amends for her unkindness.

Poor Adolphe! How happy he was, touching the Queen's breasts with his quick tongue-tip.

———

Arthur Symons, the English poet and critic, first met Beardsley when the artist was working "with an almost pathetic tenacity, at his story, never to be finished, the story which never could have been finished"; it was at Dieppe, in the summer of 1895.

ARTHUR SYMONS: He was supposed, just then, to be dying; and as I entered the room, and saw him lying out on a couch, horribly white, I wondered if I had come too late. He was full of ideas, full of enthusiasm, I think it was then that he suggested the name *Savoy* [for my magazine].

A little later we met again at Dieppe, where for a month I saw him daily. He liked the deserted rooms [of the Casino], at hours when no one was there; the sense of frivolous things caught at a moment of suspended life, *en déshabille.* He would glance at the dances occasionally, but with more impatience, at the dances, especially the children's dances, in the concert room; but he rarely missed a concert, and would glide in every afternoon, and sit on the high benches at the side, always carrying his large, gilt-leather portfolio with the magnificent, old, red-lined folio-paper, which he would often open, to write some lines in pencil. . . . Most of [*Venus and Tann-häuser*] was done at these concerts, and in the little, close writing-room, where visitors sat writing letters.

—

Beardsley worked on his "romantic novel" from 1894 to 1896; it was never finished and was not published in the United States in its entirety in unexpurgated form until Barney Rosset's Grove Press issued it in New York in 1967 with the title *Under the Hill.* That was an edition of the work that a writer named John Glasco said he had arranged and completed in Canada, in October 1958.* Glasco said he never saw the version that Roth published in *American Aphrodite;* nevertheless, volume 1, number 3, of the magazine was dedicated to him by Roth.

The earliest publication of portions of the original work appeared in "rigorously expurgated" form in Arthur Symons's *The Savoy,* in the January 1897 and April 1898 issues. This was the journal of arts and letters that Beardsley helped Symons found, after he left *The Yellow Book.* Then in 1904 John Lane, who later published Radclyffe Hall's *The Well of Loneliness,*† brought out "a mutilated version" in London in a book called *Under the Hill and Other Essays in Prose and Verse, Including Table Talk,* by Aubrey Beardsley. This may have contained the version of *Venus and Tannhäuser* that was published in New York thirty years later by Dodd, Mead. Even then—this would have been after the Random House edition of *Ulysses* had been found not obscene by federal courts in New York—the extant Beardsley manuscript was not published, "the whole being deemed unprintable."

JOHN GLASCO: We know from his own letters and from the memoirs of Arthur Symons and Jacques Blanche, with what loving care and desperation the almost dying young man worked on the manuscript during his stay in Dieppe in 1895. . . .

[*Venus and Tannhäuser*] is an attempt to push back the horizons of

---

*Glasco was associated with Maurice Girodias's Olympia Press in Paris, described in Chapter 14. Glasco wrote an introduction to the Grove Press edition of *Under the Hill.*
†The censorship of *The Well of Loneliness* is described above at Chapters 10 and 11.

experience, to find new formulas of atmosphere and feeling comparable only to that of Baudelaire, and in which, like that other "poète maudit," the measure of the attempt, and the patience and perfection of the technique employed in the attempt, are simply the measure of his greatness. That he may have partially failed . . . is due only to his all-too-human faults of dejection, listlessness, ennui.

——

According to the critic Stanley Weintraub, Beardsley "cultivated a magical technique which could convert the most repulsive ugliness into a strange, forbidding, fascinating beauty. But it was a limited achievement, one of artifice and icy eroticism." Still, Beardsley's literary skill "was Joycean in his use of common words in uncommon contexts, and of recondite words like spellicans, pudic or vallance."

At Roth's trial, the government's attorney, George H. Leisure, was permitted to read to the jury from *American Aphrodite:* "Now I am going to stand here and read to you some of that filth," Leisure said. "Mr. Atlas [Nicholas Atlas, Roth's trial lawyer] said I would only round up one or two passages out of *Venus and Tannhäuser.* Well, what I'm going to read to you is all that I can bear to read to you." And then he read some of the "filthiest" passages—surely including this one, in which Venus delicately masturbates her pet unicorn, and laps up his spendings:*

AUBREY BEARDSLEY *(Venus and Tannhäuser): Anyhow, Adolphe sniffed as never a man did around the skirts of Venus. After the first charming interchange of affectionate delicacies was over, the unicorn lay down upon his side, and closing his eyes, beat his stomach wildly with the mark of manhood!*

Venus caught that stunning member in her hands and lay her cheek along it; but few touches were wanted to consummate the creature's pleasure. The Queen bared her left elbow, and with the soft underneath of it made amazing movements horizontally upon the tightly strung instrument. When the melody began to flow, the unicorn offered up an astonishing vocal accompaniment. Tannhäuser was amused to learn that the etiquette of the Venusberg compelled everybody to await the outburst of those venereal sounds before they could sit down to déjeuner.

Adolphe had been quite profuse that morning.

Venus knelt where it had fallen, and lapped her little aperitif!

ARTHUR SYMONS: [I]n those brilliant, disconnected, fantastic pages . . . every sentence was meditated over, written for its own sake, and left to find its way in its own paragraph. It could never have been finished for it had never really been begun; but what undoubted, singular, literary ability there is in it, all the same!

———

*The record of the trial that was filed as an appendix to the government's brief on Roth's appeal failed to report exactly what passages the government's attorney read to the jury; I have selected those he is unlikely to have overlooked.

Some of what Beardsley wrote seems to have anticipated Joyce also in the interest shown in female excretions; but Beardsley's was more prettily done:

AUBREY BEARDSLEY (*Venus and Tannhäuser*): *The Chevalier was feeling very happy. Everything around him seemed so white and light matinal; the floating frocks of the ladies, the scarce robed boys and satyrs stepping hither and thither elegantly, with meats and wines and fruits; the damask table cloths, the delicate talk and laughter that rose everywhere; the flowers' colour and the flowers' scent; the shady trees, the wind's cool voice, and the sky above that was as fresh and pastoral as a perfect fifth. And Venus looked so beautiful. . . .*

"You're such a dear!" murmured Tannhäuser, holding her hand.

At the further end of the lawn, and a little hidden by a rose-tree, a young man was breakfasting alone. He toyed nervously with his food now and then, but for the most part leant back in his chair with unemployed hands, and gazed stupidly at Venus.

"That's Felix," said the Goddess, in answer to an enquiry from the Chevalier; and she went on to explain his attitude. . . . Felix always attended Venus upon her little latrinal excursions, holding her, serving her, and making much of all she did. To undo her things, lift her skirts, to wait and watch the coming, to dip a lip or finger in the royal output, to stain himself deliciously with it, to lie beneath her as the favours fell, to carry off the crumped, crotted paper—these were the pleasures of that young man's life.

Truly there never was a queen so beloved by her subjects as Venus. . . . Every scrap of her body was adored. Never, for Savoral, could her ear yield sufficient wax! Never, for Pardon, could she spit prodigally enough! And Saphius found a month an interminable time.

The United States attorney, George Leisure, was permitted by federal judge John M. Cashin also to read to the jury from Haldane MacFall's disapproving biography of Beardsley:

HALDANE MacFALL: The book [*Venus and Tannhäuser*] is a revelation and confession of the soul of the real Beardsley—of a hard, unlovely egoism even in his love throes, without one noble or generous passion . . . bent only on satisfying every lust in a dandified way that casts but a handsome garment over the barest and most filthy license. It contains gloatings over acts so bestial that it staggers one to think of so refined a taste as Beardsley's, judged by the exquisiteness of his line, not being nauseated by his own impulses.

And from MacFall's version of Beardsley's death:

HALDANE MacFALL: As Beardsley lay a-dying on the 7th March, nine days before he died he scribbled with failing fingers that last appeal from the Hôtel Cosmopolitain at Mentone to his friend the publisher, Leonard Smithers.

It read, at the top, "Jesus is our Lord and Judge," and then, "Menton."

AUBREY BEARDSLEY: Dear Friend, I implore you to destroy all copies of *Lysistrata* & bad drawings. Show this to Pollitt and conjure him to do same. By all that is holy—all obscene drawings.*

It was signed "Aubrey Beardsley, In my death agony."

HALDANE MacFALL: On the sixteenth day of the March of 1898, at twenty-five years and seven months, his mother and his sister by his side, the racked body was stilled, and the soul of Aubrey Beardsley passed into eternity.

When it was time for Roth's attorney to present evidence on Roth's side, he seems not to have produced any literary figures to defend what Beardsley had written or what Roth had published, but he was permitted to use a stratagem that soon became a favored way for lawyers to try to improve the impression held by a judge or jury of a work charged with being obscene: Atlas read to the jury "hot" passages from other novels—popular, contemporaneously available, and more reputable—as bearing on "the mores of the community," establishing a "community standard" by which the acceptability or nonacceptability of Beardsley's work might be measured. Something similar had been done in the trial briefs submitted by Doubleday's attorneys in the *Memoirs of Hecate County* case in 1946.†

Roth's attorney explained to the jury that he was going to give them a basis for comparison by reading a passage or two from some best-selling books that had recently been published by reputable companies, well-known publishing companies, like Knopf—"the same Mr. Knopf who puts out books on archeology, but every once in a while he gets one off like that." And Putnam—"a good company, a wonderful company—I don't say it ought to be arrested for talking about wife-swapping, and for portraying an aged movie producer's particular sexual foible." And Random House, "the business of that charming eye-glassed gentleman from 'What's My Line?' Mr. Cerf—the business of Mr. Cerf—this is Random House that puts out John O'Hara—I don't say now that it ought to be stopped, I don't say that it ought to be arrested, but I am asking you *has* it been arrested?"

The government's attorney objected to Atlas's proffer of the books as evidence of the community's mores in reading matter:

GEORGE H. LEISURE: It doesn't represent what the whole community has been reading, nor has it been tested itself as to whether it is obscene.

As with so many other disputed points in the Anglo-American law of obscenity, it was unsettled whether other literature might be introduced at

---

*There is no sign in the trial transcript that judge or jury recognized the obvious: that Beardsley had *not* thereby requested the destruction of *Venus and Tannhäuser*, which was a prose work; thus, the letter was irrelevant.

†See Chapter 12.

trial to show that the community's standards of decency were elastic, and that prevailing standards were not in fact breached by an indicted work; such exculpatory showings were usually treated as a procedural matter to be left to the trial judge's discretion.* At Roth's trial the judge overruled the government's objection and Roth's lawyer proceeded to read aloud, or to mark in each book for the jury's future reading, passages that he thought established his point. He read from page 151 of the Random House edition of *Ten North Frederick* by John O'Hara:

NICHOLAS ATLAS (reading): *And when I stayed at the Harrisons'... and I was asleep... and suddenly I woke up, or not suddenly. I woke up gradually. I thought I was dreaming this, but she was in bed with me. In her nightgown and in bed with me and rubbing her hand over my stomach and ...*

"Then what?"
"Frenched me."
"God! Really?"
"You know I wouldn't make this up."
"I know."
"The next day I could hardly face her, but it didn't affect her. You would have thought nothing happened. . . ."

And this now from page 293, I won't take long. There's a girl Ann talking to her father . . .

(reading) *"They were necking, and I said if you two didn't stop necking I was going home, and they said to get in back with them, so I did. And he kissed me."*
"Forcibly?"
"No, I let him kiss me."
"I see. And then what?"
"Well, then he wanted us to take off our bloomers."
"And did you?"
"Yes, I did."
"And did Sara?"
"No, just me."
"And," said Joe. *"What about him?"*
"He opened his trousers . . . all the way. I could see him. Then he wanted to go all the way with me, but I wouldn't let him. . . . Well, I put my hand on him and he put his hand on me, and we did that. . . . I've done it before with other boys. I won't tell you who, so don't ask me."

———

When the time came for Roth's attorney to read from the Knopf edition of Thomas Mann's *Felix Krull*, he said a few words about the distinguished author.

---

*Two years later, in a case involving a book called *Sweeter Than Life,* Justice Felix Frankfurter gave it as his opinion that the absolute exclusion of such evidence, as of evidence of literary merit, in an obscenity case would violate the defendant's constitutional right to due process of law. *Smith* v. *California,* reprinted in de Grazia, *Censorship Landmarks* (1969), 318. Frankfurter's reaction to *Sweeter Than Life* is described anon.

NICHOLAS ATLAS: Of course there can be no quibble, we know who Thomas Mann is. You all know who he is. You might say he is the great novelist of this age. You might say he is the next mountain in the realm of the novel after Dostoyevsky. That is Thomas Mann.

———

And then he read to the jury from the middle of a conversation between a lady and a bellhop in her hotel:

NICHOLAS ATLAS (reading): *I bent all the way down to her and pressed my lips against hers. She not only carried this kiss to even greater lengths than the one that afternoon. . . . She also took my hand from its support and guided it inside her décolletage to her breasts . . . moving it about by the wrist in such a way that my manhood, as she could not fail to notice, was most urgently aroused. Touched by this observation, she cooed softly with compassion and delight: "O lovely youth, far fairer than this body that has the power to inflame you!"*

Then she began to tug at the collar of my jacket with both hands, unhooked it, and with incredible speed proceeded to undo the buttons.

"Off, off, away with that and away with that, too," her words tumbled out. "Off and away, so that I can see you, can catch sight of the god! Quick, help!"

"Oh, blessed one, you are killing me! Ecstasy robs me of breath, breaks my heart, I will die of your love!" She bit my lip, my neck. "Call me tu!" She groaned suddenly, near the climax. "Be familiar with me, degrade me! J'adore d'être humiliée! Je t'adore! Oh, je t'adore, petit esclave stupide qui me déshonore. . . ."

She came. We came. . . . we rested, still united, still in close embrace. . . .

"Quick call me tu! I have not yet heard this tu from you to me. I lie here and make love with a divine and yet quite common servant boy. How delightfully that degrades me. My name is Diane. But you, with your lips, call me whore, explicitly. 'You sweet whore!'

"Armand," she whispered in my ear, "be rough with me! I am entirely yours, I am your slave! Treat me as you would the lowest wench! I don't deserve anything else, and it would be heaven for me!

"Listen, Armand."

"What is it?"

"How would it be if you beat me? Beat me hard, I mean. Me Diane Philbert? It would serve me right, I would be thankful to you. These are your braces, take them, beloved, turn me over and whip me till I bleed!"

Yes, that stuff is from Thomas Mann, the greatest living author as published by Alfred Knopf, one of our greatest living publishers. . . . Now, we also have this book called *The Deer Park* by one of America's best-known and serious authors, Norman Mailer, and it is on the best-seller list even today, as published by, let's see, it's G. P. Putnam & Sons, a very old and fine house. . . . I'm not going to push this thing, try your patience, but this wonderful book, I want to read you one passage only, here, it is a scene between a movie producer whose name is Herman Teppis, he is the head of Supreme Pictures and he is casting someone . . . she is a "call-girl" whose name is Bobby.*

(reading) *Tentatively, she reached out a hand to caress his hair, and at that moment Herman Teppis opened his legs and let Bobby slip to the floor. At the expression of surprise on her face, he began to laugh.*

"Just like this, sweetie," he said, and down he looked at that frightened female mouth, facsimile of all those smiling lips he had seen so ready to be nourished at the fount of power, and with a shudder he started to talk.

"That's a good girlie, that's a good girlie," he said in a mild lost little voice. "You're just an angel, darling, and I like you, and you understand, you're my darling, oh that's the ticket," said Teppis.

———

Atlas's recitation of such steamy passages from prestigious contemporary novels, written by talented and established authors and issued by distinguished American publishers, would do Roth no appreciable good.

The government's attorney wound up the United States' case against Roth with this peroration:

GEORGE H. LEISURE: If Your Honor please, Mr. Atlas, Mr. Foreman, and ladies and gentlemen of the Jury.

It is almost over and if you are anything like me, you are glad of that. . . . I want to thank you for your patience and I want to say to you that some of the things that I had to read to you would offend the sensibilities of any decent person, and I want to apologize for it. I am sorry to have put you through two weeks like this, but I think you can see the reason that we had to do it, because we want to stop it.

———

Then, in his summation to the trial jury, Leisure had this to say about Roth's hardbound literary journal:

GEORGE H. LEISURE: Then we get to this *American Aphrodite* which, to me, is a fantastic book. They have tried to throw in some stories that are extremely boring, but even those have an overtone of sex all the way through. . . .

Then the story in there that is worse is that *Venus and Tannhäuser;* there was a [defense] witness here who testified on direct that [Beardsley] was a fine writer, a fine illustrator! Then when I started to cross-examine him he started to say "But I am not an expert; but I am not an expert." But he testified on direct, and the reason I had to cross-examine him was because he tried to lend some aura of dignity to that man.

———

*This is from *The Deer Park*'s blow-job episode, a scene that led several American publishers to decline to publish the book. Eventually, G. P. Putnam's publisher, Walter Minton, enthusiastically took it on, and it became a best-seller. See Chapter 25 below for Mailer's comments on the events.

While head of Putnam's, Minton made best-sellers out of three other explosive books: Vladimir Nabokov's *Lolita* (Chapter 14), Terry Southern's *Candy* (Chapter 25), and John Cleland's *Fanny Hill* (Chapter 23). After leaving Putnam's, Minton went to law school; he now practices law in New Jersey.

Now we know what kind of a man he was. He was a very sick man. He died at the young age of 25 and he did a little bit of illustrating, but he wrote pornography. Most of his stuff is completely unpublishable. He drew dirty pictures which are unpublishable. Then when he became close to death he renounced it—that is what I think is important here—and he pleaded, he pleaded with his own publisher to destroy it all. That was his own opinion of it.

———

Responding, Roth's lawyer, Nicholas Atlas, sought to dispel the bad taste left by the prosecutor's gambit with the jurymen by showing them a copy of *American Aphrodite,* number 3. He did not have enough copies to pass around but he was "sure you agree it is rather a handsome format." When the jury retired to decide Sam Roth's fate, it took the one copy along.

In the arguments that eventually took place in the Supreme Court in Roth's case, the publisher's lawyers contended that the jurors could not possibly have read the entire book during the short time they were out (a book was arguably to be "taken as a whole" and not from "extracts") and that Roth's conviction, for that reason, ought to be reversed. The Supreme Court would not, as it turned out, concern itself with this contention because the issue of whether the publications that Roth had sent through the mails were obscene or not, constitutionally protected or not, was ruled not open to consideration by the justices.* The main question the Court would actually consider and decide was whether the federal mail-obscenity statute was unconstitutional "on its face."

Sam Roth was found guilty by the jury on the *American Aphrodite,* number 3, count for sending obscene matter through the mails and was sentenced on that count alone to serve five years in prison and pay a $5,000 fine.† Roth's subsequent appeal from this conviction and sentence, on the grounds that error had been committed in the trial judge's instructions on "obscenity" and that the federal mail statute under which he had been convicted was unconstitutionally vague, was given short shrift by the distinguished Second Circuit Court of Appeals in 1956. The majority referred disdainfully to Roth's publications as being not "great literature," or even "real literature," but merely "salable pornography"—without, however, troubling to say what it had in mind by "literature," "great" or "real," or by "salable pornography," or why the one should be treated with any less constitutional protection than the other.

The sole redeeming feature of the Second Circuit's action in Roth's case was a long, scholarly, thoughtful concurring opinion and appendix written by Judge Jerome Frank, a leader of the Legal Realism movement that had

---

*See Chapter 16.

†Roth was sentenced to the same term of imprisonment on three other counts—for mailing advertisements for: *Photo and Body* and *Good Times,* vol. 1, no. 10 (count 10); *Good Times,* vol. 1, no. 8 (count 13); *American Aphrodite,* no. 13, and *Good Times,* vol. 1, no. 5 (count 17)—but the sentences were ordered to run concurrently with that for mailing *American Aphrodite,* no. 3, the *Venus and Tannhäuser* issue (count 24).

developed during the thirties and forties.* In considering Roth's case Frank examined the law of obscenity from legal, historical, and psychological perspectives that cast serious doubt on the constitutionality of the postal law under which Roth had been convicted and raised serious questions regarding the implications of that conviction for literary freedom. As it turned out, the Supreme Court would pay scant attention to what Frank had to say, with one important exception: the exegesis that Frank captioned "The fine arts are within the First Amendment's protection." Although this did not materially assist Roth, whose conviction the Court upheld, it did point the way to the full measure of constitutional freedom that Justice Brennan and the Supreme Court would eventually seek to deliver to authors and other artists and the disseminators of their works.

As a judge "of an inferior court," Jerome Frank said, he felt "constrained" by the extant opinions of the Supreme Court to "hold valid" the postal obscenity law, and so he voted with the other judges making up Roth's panel to affirm the publisher's conviction. As Judge Charles Clark pointed out, the highly regarded Judge Learned Hand had said in an obscenity case: "If the question [of constitutionality] is to be reopened, the Supreme Court must open it."† However, Frank's unorthodox appendix succeeded in stirring up doubt about the correctness of the Supreme Court's casual assumption that enforcement of obscenity laws raised no constitutional questions, and that judgments of obscenity by particular officials did not reflect mostly personal values.‡ This doubt would lead the United States Solicitor General's Office, and particularly an assistant in that office named Roger Fisher, to treat as open the "settled" question of the constitutionality of obscenity laws and to canvass the legal and social underpinnings of the high court's

---

*Frank protested being called a realist by the movement's critics (who were mostly law school academicians), saying that the realists were "related only in their negations, in their skepticisms and in their curiosity." A principal tenet of realists was that law was much more uncertain and legal outcomes much more unpredictable than conventional legal philosophers pretended, and that the factors influencing any particular court decision were often different from those (mainly legal rules, principles, and precedents) that the decision makers cited as "controlling" the outcomes of the cases. See Appendix V in Frank's *If Men Were Angels* (1942), one of two classic works on law by Frank. The other is *Law and the Modern Mind* (1930).

†Said in *Rosen* v. *United States,* 161 U.S. 29 (1896). This policy of deference or *politesse* toward the Supreme Court's constitutional prerogatives probably serves the value of stability but not of growth in the law. Hand had been slapped down on appeal some years earlier, in the *Masses* case, for opening the question of the consistency of the terms of the World War I Espionage Act with free speech values.

‡Frank's doubts and "puzzlement" about the constitutionality of the postal statute had been "nudged" into "the skeptical views" expressed in his *Roth* opinion and appendix by another "brilliant opinion" written some years earlier (1949) by Judge Curtis Bok, characterized by Frank as "one of America's most reflective judges." Bok's opinion (in the case of *Commonwealth* v. *Gordon)* stated "arguments that (so far as I know) have never been answered," said Frank. The Bok opinion is in de Grazia, *Censorship Landmarks* (1969), 150. The Supreme Court supports the policy of *politesse* when it discounts efforts made by lower court judges to solve problems in the law that it has not itself confronted or been able to solve. The Bok opinion in *Gordon* is an example of a judge declining to adopt an attitude of *politesse,* perhaps from his sense of the urgent need of a solution to the "problem" of the judiciary's being used to implement government censorship of literature and art through formal enforcement of the laws forbidding "obscene" expression.

previous statements. At oral argument in Roth's case, this concern of the government lawyers encountered stiff opposition from Justice Frankfurter, who, having played a leading role in "settling" the obscenity question through dicta laid down in 1942,* wished to keep it settled. Frankfurter must not have been pleased with the swarm of bothersome questions uncapped by Frank's concurring opinion in *Roth*.

Frankfurter was already engaged in a campaign to cramp the movement among the modern Court's justices to review and declare unconstitutional oppressive state and federal statutes; and upon the arrival of his new chief, Earl Warren, and the freshman associate justice William Brennan, Jr., he would seek to recruit them to his design to dominate the Court's decisional process in constitutional turf dear to him. He succeeded for a time, but only until Warren and Brennan were able to recruit majorities that would carry the Court, and the law in such instances, in the direction of their own more activist and humanist visions.

Warren freed himself from Frankfurter's influence in the 1956 term, which was Brennan's first. And by July 1958, President Eisenhower, who had appointed Warren, found reason to complain about the chief's activist decisions, and Brennan's, too. Brennan rapidly became Warren's closest colleague on the bench, and a brother activist. The Super Chief, as Brennan enjoyed calling him, repaired to Brennan's chambers each week during sessions, on the day before the justices met as a body in closed conference, to go over the cases to be discussed and voted upon. Warren came increasingly to rely on Brennan to write the Court's opinions in the most important individual-liberties cases that arose during the Warren years; and during those years Brennan frequently acted virtually as the Warren Court's deputy chief. But in 1956 and 1957, when *Roth* was argued and decided, Brennan was still a junior justice and under the sway of his former Harvard Law School teacher Felix Frankfurter. The opinion Brennan wrote for the Court in *Roth* bore the earmarks therefore not only of Frankfurter's doctrine of judicial restraint in the First Amendment area but also, to a degree, of Frankfurter's (and Warren's) puritanical distaste for sex.

Frankfurter never read fiction for his own enjoyment and was repelled when, in the course of his duties on the Court, he felt obliged to look at allegedly obscene literature. He did not have to do that in Roth's case because of the strategy he devised to have the Court *assume,* without itself considering the issue, that the lower courts were correct in holding that the publications Roth had put into the mails were obscene. But in a case decided two years later, in which a bookseller successfully appealed to the Court from a state conviction on the ground, among others, that the book he had been indicted for selling was *not* obscene, Frankfurter examined the book; the Court's decision and Frankfurter's concurring opinion, however,

---

*In *Chaplinsky* v. *New Hampshire,* 315 U.S. 568 (1942), in which the Court unanimously agreed that "certain well-defined and narrowly limited classes of speech," including the "obscene," had "never been thought to raise any constitutional problem."

would stand on different grounds. A few years ago, I talked to constitutional lawyer and professor Paul Bender about Justice Frankfurter's attitude.

PAUL BENDER: I was Felix Frankfurter's law clerk then. The case involved what seemed to me to be a highly innocuous book,* no pictures, as I remember, a few dirty words. It was fairly sexually explicit but not enormously so. . . . Now, I saw the thing in the office and I took it home and read it. And then Frankfurter wrote that opinion, and I teased him about it. . . . You know, why didn't he just forget all this nonsense about expert witnesses and say what he should say: "Come on, you can't ban this book!"

"What do you mean?" Frankfurter said. So I asked him, "What's wrong with this book?" "It's horrible filthy junk!" he replied. I told him, "You don't know what you're talking about. It's nothing at all." "No, no," he said, "that's horrible stuff!"

"Mr. Justice," I said, "you want to come with me to the street corner or the nearest drugstore? I will go in there and buy you ten books on open sale that have equal contents. If you don't believe me, ask Margy, my wife. She'll tell you." So he said, "What? She's seen that book?" "Of course she has," I told him. "Where did she get it?" "I showed it to her." "You showed it to her? You did *what?*"

My wife told me Frankfurter was so upset he telephoned her. They talked about it. He was apoplectic about the fact that an innocent young woman like my wife should see this, and I was telling him that he just didn't have the slightest idea of what the sexual content of fiction was. He said, "I never read fiction. I don't have the time to read fiction." And I told him, "Well, before you make judgments about this stuff, why don't you give it a try?"

—

After leaving his job as Frankfurter's clerk, Paul Bender went to the Justice Department, where he would be assigned the unwelcome task of arguing before the Supreme Court the government's case against another of Roth's breed, Ralph Ginzburg—in an obscenity case in which Bender, far from wanting to argue the government's case, wanted the government to confess error. The solicitor general would not do that, and Bender, despite misgivings, went on to win the case for the government. Said Justice Brennan later, reflecting on Bender's work in the *Ginzburg* case: "He could not lose a case when he tried." Later, while on the faculty of the University of Pennsylvania Law School, Bender became counsel to the National Commission on Obscenity and Pornography ("Lockhart commission"); in calling for the repeal of all obscenity laws applicable to consenting adults, the commission largely reflected Bender's libertarian views.†

Sweeter Than Life by Mark Tryon (Vixen Press, 1954) seems to have been a forerunner of the sex pulp novels so numerous in the sixties; it contained a prominent lesbian theme and it seems to have had no appreciable literary value. It is described in some detail in Felice Flannery Lewis, *Literature, Obscenity and Law* (1976), 180–81. The case was *Smith* v. *California,* reprinted in de Grazia, *Censorship Landmarks* (1969), 318ff.

†The *Ginzburg* case is discussed in Chapters 23 and 26 below; the Lockhart commission's

. . .

In Roth's case, as mentioned above, only one of Frank's points would be taken up in the Court opinion that Justice Brennan wrote. The point, however, was of great moment for, planted by Brennan's hand, it became the doctrinal seed from which over the next decade there would grow a lush plant shielding literary and artistic expression from censorship. "The framers of the First Amendment," wrote Frank, "must have had literature and art in mind, because our first national statement on the subject of 'freedom of the press,' the 1774 address of the Continental Congress to the inhabitants of Quebec, declared, *'The importance of this* [freedom of the press] *consists, besides the advancement of truth, science, morality, and arts in general, in its diffusion of liberal sentiments on the administration of Government.' "* The jurist went on:

JUDGE JEROME FRANK: 165 years later, President Franklin Roosevelt said, "The arts cannot thrive except where men are free to be themselves and to be in charge of the discipline of their own energies and orders. The conditions for democracy and for art are one and the same. What we call liberty in politics results in freedom of the arts."† The converse is also true. . . .

In our industrial era, when perforce, economic pursuits must be, increas-

---

activities are described in Chapter 28 below. Bender, who is now a professor of law at the Arizona State University College of Law, goes further in his prescription for freedom of the press than the Lockhart commission did: he advocates the repeal of all laws regulating the access of adults *or children* to sexually oriented expression. (Author interview with Paul Bender.)

*He was quoting from Zechariah Chafee, *Government and Mass Communication* (1947), 53. Chafee, however, did not pursue the implications of the framers' understanding that freedom of the press applied to the arts. The draftsmen of the letter sent by the Continental Congress spoke of the "arts in general," not "the fine arts," Frank's term. Usage at the time suggests that the former phrase included what today is thought of as "the crafts" as well as "the arts." What is striking in the Quebec letter is its evidence that the nation's founders thought of progress in the arts as *a function* of freedom of the press in the same way that they thought of the pursuit of "truth" as a function. The Supreme Court, however, showed no awareness that the arts had anything to do with freedom of the press until after World War II, as, for example, in *Hannegan* v. *Esquire,* 327 U.S. 146 (1946), and *Burstyn* v. *Wilson,* 343 U.S. 495 (1952). (In the former case, the Court condemned the postmaster general's use of the second-class mail regulations to supervise the taste and morality of publications like *Esquire* magazine; in the latter case, the Court struck down a state law that authorized a ban on the showing of the motion picture *The Miracle* because it was considered sacrilegious.) Perhaps this was because the justices themselves had inherited the puritanical hostility toward fiction and the not-so-fine (popular) arts of their time. Judge Robert H. Bork's view of what the Founding Fathers had in mind by their adoption of the First Amendment's speech and press guarantees originally excluded literature and art, as discussed later in the text. But the American philosopher Alexander Meiklejohn expressly recognized that the arts were protected, as an aspect of "public discussion," as indicated in the course of a dialogue he had with University of Chicago Law School professor Harry Kalven, Jr., also described below.

†FDR's administration is remembered for having organized the nation's first importa[nt] programs for the direct support of artists and the arts. A more lasting program of governm[ent] funding of the arts and artists was launched in 1965 during the administration of Pr[esident] Lyndon Johnson with the establishment of the National Foundation on the Arts an[d Humani-] ties. In 1989, an effort was made by Senator Jesse Helms to create a system of ce[nsorship of] the NEA's programs; in 1990 right-wing conservatives sought to abolish th[e agency.]

ingly, governmentally regulated, it is especially important that the realm of art—the noneconomic realm—should remain free, unregimented, the domain of free enterprise, of unhampered competition at its maximum. . . .*

To vest a few fallible men—prosecutors, judges, jurors—with vast powers of literary or artistic censorship, to convert them into what J. S. Mill called a "moral police," is to make them despotic arbiters of literary products. If one day they ban mediocre books as obscene, another day they may do likewise to a work of genius.

———

And then, in what may have been the only judicial compliment, however oblique, paid to Samuel Roth:

JUDGE JEROME FRANK: Some few men stubbornly fight for the right to write or publish or distribute books which the great majority at the time consider loathsome. If we jail those few, the community may appear to have suffered nothing. The appearance is deceptive.

———

Roth's fate now rested largely on the possibility that the justices who would take up the publisher's next appeal would pay enough attention to the arguments presented by Frank to reconsider whether the obscenity law that Congress had enlarged more than eighty years earlier, to criminalize literary communications like those of Samuel Roth, did not abridge the constitutional guaranties of speech and press.

———

*Judge Richard A. Posner, a lecturer at the University of Chicago Law School and a well-respected proponent of "free-enterprise" capitalism, has made an elegant argument *against* the use of obscenity laws and *for* "the competition of the literary marketplace" in *Law and Literature: A Misunderstood Relation* (1989), 329-38. See also his luminous piece, "Art for Law's Sake" in *The American Scholar* 58 (Autumn 1989), 513. Judge Posner recently wrote an opinion in a "nude dancing" case that bears comparison with Frank's concurrence in *Roth;* Posner did this concurring in the federal Seventh Circuit Court of Appeals' *en banc* decision holding erotic dancing to be "expression" protected by the constitutional guarantees of freedom of speech and press. *Darlene Miller* v. *City of South Bend* (Nos. 88-3006, 88-3244), decided May 24, 1990. Like the views expressed by Frank in Roth's case, Posner's views in *Darlene Miller* also were discounted by the Supreme Court, reviewing the case on appeal. Posner has been considered a prime prospect for a seat on the Supreme Court.

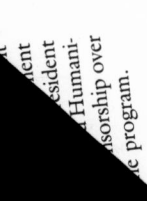

16

Clear
and Present
Danger of <u>What</u>?

I N THE GREAT MARBLE COURTROOM of the Supreme Court of
the United States, Chief Justice Earl Warren invited attorney David von
Albrecht to approach the counsel's rostrum before the bench. There were
nine justices arrayed in a line on the raised bench, facing the lawyer.*

CHIEF JUSTICE EARL WARREN: Mr. Albrecht, you may proceed. . . .
DAVID VON ALBRECHT: Your Honors, I rise now in defense of Samuel Roth,
an unconventional publisher who publishes what people reject today and
perhaps accept tomorrow . . . who is under the harsh sentence of five years
in jail and a 5000-dollar fine. . . . And I contend that it is of no aid to the
Court, which is confronted with a statute about "obscenity," if we discuss
"pornography."

---

*Associate Justices Black, Frankfurter, Douglas, Burton, Clark, Harlan, Brennan, and
Whittaker, and Chief Justice Warren.
    At the time of *Roth,* the bench was in the form of a straight line; in 1972, it was altered
to a winged, or half-hexagon, shape, permitting the justices to see each other more readily.
The chief justice sits in the center with the associate justices to the right and left, in order
of seniority. As a matter of Court protocol, while on the bench justices do not speak directly
to each other respecting a matter at issue. They may, however, argue with each other indirectly, through questions put to counsel.
    The courtroom itself is 82 feet by 91 feet, and 44 feet high, and boasts 24 columns made
of Old Convent Quarry Siena marble from Liguria, Italy. The walls are of ivory veined marble
from Alicante, Spain, and the floor borders are of Italian and African marble. Lawyer and
author John P. Frank dubbed the courthouse the Marble Palace in his book of the same name.
Photographs of the courtroom, the building, the raised bench, the robing room, the library,
the justices' conference room (where the justices meet twice a week to decide cases and
determine which cases to review), the bronze and marble staircases, the chief justice's and
associate justices' chambers, etc., may be found in Robert Shnayerson, *The Illustrated History
of the Supreme Court of the United States* (1986).

The people in the stilled courtroom who had come to hear Sam Roth's fate debated were about to witness the only public aspect of the awesome judicial process by which the constitutional rights and liberties of Americans, and the limitations upon the powers of the federal and state governments, are determined. Since the decision of *Marbury* v. *Madison* in 1803, the Court has asserted the power to review and if necessary invalidate federal laws and actions that seem to it repugnant to the constitutional order laid down by the nation's founders. Since 1925, when the case of *Gitlow* v. *New York* was decided,* the Court has acted also to review and strike down laws of the several states that seem to be repugnant to the First Amendment's guarantees of liberty of speech and press, or to other rights and freedoms stipulated in the first ten amendments, known as the Bill of Rights. The main issue confronting the Supreme Court in Roth's case was whether the eighty-year-old postal obscenity law, pursuant to which the publisher had been convicted, was to be deemed repugnant to the First Amendment "on its face." If it was, it ought to be struck down. This, of course, implicated the doctrine of judicial restraint at a moment in history when the judicial activism of the Warren Court had just begun. If the Court decided that the postal obscenity law should continue to stand, Roth's sentence to imprisonment also would stand. If the Court decided instead that the United States Congress, in passing the law, had overstepped its constitutional bounds, then not only would Roth go home free but a stronghold of federal censorship, the Comstock law, would fall.

The office of the solicitor general of the United States, the most prestigious group of lawyers in the Justice Department, had decided that "pornography" ought to be discussed in Roth's case. It is that office's duty to argue the government's side of a case and advise the Court concerning the law, as it is and ought to be. The strategy of the solicitor general, J. Lee Rankin, had one central focus—to dissuade the Court from striking down the Comstock law, which for nearly a century had permitted the United States government, acting through the Post Office Department and the Justice Department's Criminal Division, to superintend the sexual content of material sent through the mails.

---

*In *Gitlow* (268 U.S. 652 [1925]), the Court upheld the constitutionality of a New York statute, enacted in 1902, that made criminal the advocacy or teaching of the duty, necessity, or propriety of overthrowing government by force, or by assassinating any executive official, or by any other unlawful means. The law, which was passed shortly after the assassination of President McKinley, was the first state "anti-sedition" law. Justices Holmes and Brandeis dissented, arguing that there was no "clear and present danger" of an attempt to overthrow the government by force flowing from the defendant's expression, which was a manifesto of the "left-wing section" Socialist party. Said Holmes: "It is said that this manifesto was more than a theory, that it was an incitement. Every idea is an incitement. . . . The only difference between the expression of an opinion and an incitement in the narrower sense is the speaker's enthusiasm for the result. . . . If, in the long run, the beliefs expressed in proletarian dictatorships are destined to be accepted by the dominant forces of the community, the only meaning of free speech is that they should be given their chance and have their way."

Roth's conviction for sending "obscene" publications through the mails had precipitated the possibility that the federal law might be held unconstitutional; that was the argument most forcefully presented by Roth's lawyers to the Second Circuit Court of Appeals, as it would be now to the Supreme Court of the United States. Moreover, the question of the statute's validity on its face was the main one ordered by the Court to be briefed and argued. For Rankin, the most worrisome aspect of the situation was federal circuit judge Jerome Frank's unusual and scholarly opinion in Roth's case, which concurred in the judgment to affirm the publisher's conviction but marshaled cogent reasons why, as a matter of constitutional law and common sense, the Comstock law should have been invalidated and Roth's conviction reversed. It was in deference to the Supreme Court's prerogative to interpret the Constitution that Frank had not dissented from the judgment.

It was certainly apparent to Lee Rankin that the material Sam Roth had been sending through the mails was not "pornography," as that term was then used; but the government's strongest argument for sustaining the statute would be that if the law was struck down there would be no legal way whatsoever to keep the worst, the most graphic, material depicting sexual acts from going through the mails.

Normally it is possible for the Court to reverse a person's conviction without also knocking down the statute under which he or she stands convicted. For instance, in the *Memoirs of Hecate County* case, brought before the Court some nine years earlier, deciding the case in Doubleday's favor would have left standing the New York obscenity statute under which the publisher had been convicted, because Doubleday had not argued that the New York law was unconstitutional *on its face,* but rather that the New York judiciary had *acted* unconstitutionally—that is, it had *applied* the statute in an unconstitutional manner—when it concluded that *Hecate County* was obscene. In Roth's case, not only was it Roth's most strenuously advanced argument that the Comstock law was facially unconstitutional in its interference with freedom of the press, but the Supreme Court, in agreeing to review the case, had eliminated most of the arguments that supported a reversal of Roth's conviction on grounds *other than* facial unconstitutionality. This raised the stakes of the litigation: for if Roth did prevail and the Court did decide his conviction should be reversed, the Comstock statute would have to be struck down.

The best way for Rankin to prevent this from happening was to show the justices examples of the "filthy" stuff that was being sent through the mails, not by Roth, but by others, who, if the Court struck the statute down, would henceforth have unrestrained access to the mails and thus to the homes of Americans. To stiffen the justices' resolve to render firm justice in the case, a young lawyer in Rankin's office had coined a new term to describe the worst stuff—"hard-core pornography"—and had arranged for a box of it to be brought to court. The solicitor general knew that the brethren would be extremely loath to invite charges that they were opening the floodgates of the nation to "hard-core pornographers."* This was America, 1957, with McCarthyism still breathing. The justices, particularly Chief Justice Warren, were still smarting from the attacks that had been directed against them because of their courageous and unanimous decision in *Brown* v. *Board of Education,* outlawing racial segregation in public schools. The "impeach Earl Warren" movement organized by the John Birch Society had still not dissipated.

Roth's lawyer, Albrecht, objected to the carton of pornography that the government's lawyers had brought to Court. His client had been indicted, tried, and convicted for mailing "obscenity," not "pornography"; and everybody realized—even if no one could define either term—that there *was* a difference between them. At that time "pornography" was very widely thought of as abominable stuff that no reputable lawyer or judge would care to be found defending, or even examining.†

The Court had officially eliminated any question of whether the publications that Roth mailed were legally "obscene" from the issues that it would hear argument on, deliberate, and decide. *American Aphrodite* and Beardsley's unfinished prose work *Venus and Tannhäuser* were supposed to be out of the case.‡ This made it all the more urgent to keep even the notion of "pornography" or "hard-core pornography" also out of the case: if the justices viewed the material in the solicitor general's box it might prejudice them against Roth's case.

JUSTICE JOHN MARSHALL HARLAN: Does that mean that you say a federal statute reaching only pornography would be all right?
DAVID VON ALBRECHT: Your Honor, a federal statute could be made, I believe, so narrow in construction that it might be all right. But our contention in this case is that under the First Amendment . . . the Congress has no power at all to do anything in relation to speech as speech itself; that power resides exclusively with the States and with the local governments.

---

*The Warren Court did this in 1968 and, as a result, lost Justice Abe Fortas. See Chapter 27.

†Writing in 1960, Dean William B. Lockhart found "hard-core pornography . . . so foul and revolting that few people can contemplate the absence of laws against it—that would be unthinkable." See his "Censorship of Obscenity: Developing Constitutional Standards," 45 *Minnesota Law Review* 5, 26 (1960). However, in 1970, as chairman of the National Commission on Obscenity and Pornography, he recommended that all obscenity laws applicable to consenting adults *be repealed*. Lockhart's change of mind is attributed by the commission's former general counsel, Professor Paul Bender, to the education Lockhart received in carrying out the commission's research activity. The commission's *Report* is taken up in Chapter 28. Among literati whose works have been censored for obscenity, D. H. Lawrence is well known for his condemnation of "pornography" as "an insult to sex."

On the other hand, the past twenty years have witnessed a partial reversal in the usage of these terms; now even a freshman Supreme Court justice like Antonin Scalia, as well as many media journalists, will use the word "pornography" when he refers to sexually obsessed expression that is nevertheless prima facie constitutionally protected, not suppressible for being obscene.

‡Nevertheless, the government filed a copy of *American Aphrodite,* number 3, as an exhibit in the case. Justice Brennan, for one, seems not to have seen it. Justice Harlan apparently did.

Not one of the justices then on the bench shared Albrecht's view, which is not to say it was indefensible; the petition for certiorari that Albrecht filed on Roth's behalf contained a creditable argument along these lines. However, a majority of the justices believed not only that the states had an inherent "police" power to regulate morality in speech and press, limited only by the commands of the First and Fourteenth Amendments, but also that the federal government had been delegated similar restraining powers in connection with customs, interstate commerce, and the mails. Here Justice John Marshall Harlan differed from most of the brethren in believing that the federal (as distinguished from state) police powers of censorship were attenuated, but he did not believe they were absent. The only sitting justice at the time who took the position that the federal government had no power at all over speech, as speech, was Justice Hugo Black;* and he believed that the states also had no power over it. Justice William O. Douglas would soon join Black's "absolutist" view, but at this time he believed the First Amendment was meant to prevent both federal and state governments from abridging any speech that did not present some "clear and present danger" to society; he also believed that obscenity presented no such danger.†

The briefs filed by Roth's lawyer presented a strong argument that the federal postal obscenity law violated constitutional due process by being utterly "vague"; in this Albrecht relied especially upon the reasons given in Judge Jerome Frank's opinion. But even that argument was flawed, because it was also a premise of Albrecht's argument that the *states* nevertheless were constitutionally permitted to enforce such "vague" laws against obscene literature.

However, Roth's lawyer insisted that the First Amendment's sweeping command that "Congress shall make no law . . . abridging the freedom of speech or of the press" incapacitated the federal government, but not state governments, from interfering with speech and press. Harlan tried to bring Albrecht back to the subject of pornography because—to judge from the dissenting opinion that he would later write in Roth's case—he believed that the *only* sort of sexually oriented expression that the *federal government* might constitutionally bar from the mails *was* pornography. He alone of the justices seems actually to have looked at what Roth sent through the mails; but what he found was not, at least not to him, pornographic.

---

*The "absolutist" tenor of Black's approach was subsequently qualified by his view that a peaceful "demonstration" or "sit-in" was not really "speech" in the First Amendment sense.

†Albrecht stopped short of adopting Justice Black's lonely position that the First Amendment's express prohibition against any abridgement of speech and press meant *no* government organ, state or federal, could interfere with the spoken or printed word; but his own position was even lonelier. It was also diametrically opposed to the position taken by attorneys for the Los Angeles book distributor David Alberts, who had been convicted under a state law for dealing with "obscene" literature and who was fighting for his freedom at the same time that Roth was, in a companion case to Roth's. Unhappily for publishers Alberts and Roth, their lawyers had been drawn by the forms of Supreme Court practice, and the Court's consideration of their cases jointly, into presenting arguments at cross-purposes.

JUSTICE JOHN MARSHALL HARLAN: Does that include pornography, whatever that means?

DAVID VON ALBRECHT: Your Honor, I am not here to defend the question of pornography because I don't really know what pornography here is. But I understand that the Government here has put in sealed exhibits which we don't know anything about, which we have never seen, which are here for Your Honors' exclusive . . .

———

When the solicitor general made his unusual "filing" in Roth's case, he did something unprecedented and, in my opinion, unfair. The pornography in the box deposited with the clerk had nothing strictly to do with Roth. It was not evidence in the record of the case and could not have been offered as evidence at the Supreme Court stage of the proceeding. Roth's lawyers, moreover, were prevented even from examining it because it was sealed. Finally, the material was not remotely like what Sam Roth sent through the mails. During the oral arguments before the Court, Roger Fisher, the attorney who presented the government's case, indicated that the hard-core pornography in the box had at one time or another been put into the mails by others, not by Sam Roth. Later on in the argument Fisher would describe the contents in this way:

ROGER FISHER: A large part is photographs. Photographs of all sorts of persons—people shown without any clothes on, in all postures, groups and individuals. They are engaged in activity, perversion of every kind. . . . A second category of material is little booklets, a series of sex episodes, one after the other, usually illustrated with these photographs or drawings. The third category is comic books, especially drawn for the pornographic trade. The fourth category is motion picture film. We did not make any of those [fourth category materials] available to the Court. If you should want to see those it could be arranged. They are the worst, the most vile, of any form of pornography, in my estimation.*

———

A close reading of the transcript of the argument, and the government's Brief in Opposition to Roth's Petition for Writ of Certiorari, suggests that the Court, or some of the justices, may have been confused as to the nature of the material that Roth had mailed; they may have received the impression that the publisher mailed pornography or hard-core pornography, like the stuff in the box, rather than material "in the borderline entertainment area" which "may or may not be pornographic." The confusion began with the government's characterization of Roth's mailings in its initial Brief in Opposition (to Roth's petition for review):†

———

*Fisher's description here of hard-core pornography paralleled one presented by the government in its main brief.

†Roger Fisher's name does not appear on this opposition brief, signifying that at that early stage of the proceedings—before the solicitor general knew whether or not the Court would review Roth's case—Fisher was not assigned to it. It is possible that by the time Fisher came

BRIEF OF THE UNITED STATES IN OPPOSITION: All three judges in the Court of Appeals agreed that the materials mailed in this case were pornographic—obscene within the hard-core meaning of that term under the prevailing standards of all segments of our society.

———

This was not a true statement. None of the panel of appellate judges who sat on Roth's case spoke of Roth's publications as "hard-core" pornography although Judge Clark, in his opinion for the two-judge majority, referred to them once as "salable pornography" and again as "commercialized obscenity." Concurring, Judge Frank said only that he believed a jury could reasonably have found them "obscene," within the trial judge's instructions regarding the meaning of that term.

BRIEF OF THE UNITED STATES IN OPPOSITION: In attacking the constitutionality of the statute on this set of facts,* Petitioner is asking this Court to hold that it is totally beyond the power of Congress to ban from the mails materials no matter how obscene.

———

This was not a fair characterization of Roth's "Petition for Certiorari," which actually asked the Court to consider eight different issues, including whether Roth's publications, "when considered in their entirety," were obscene. If that issue had been taken up by the Court and resolved in Roth's favor, the Comstock law would have been left standing, notwithstanding that Roth's use of the mails to sell *American Aphrodite* would have been vindicated. But because the Court limited Roth's argument to only three of the issues the publisher proposed, Roth was forced to defend himself almost entirely by mounting an "attack [on] the constitutionality of the statute" under a set of facts in which the Court *assumed,* without permitting Roth to contest the assumption, that Roth's publications were obscene.†

---

on board, the solicitor general's "pornography" strategy had hardened to the point where Fisher was required to advance it, on oral argument, like it or not.

*I.e., facts that "suggested" that everyone except Roth agreed that Roth had mailed "pornographic" materials "within the hard-core meaning of 'obscene.' "

†The Court's decision (probably taken at Justice Frankfurter's instance, during a closed conference) to decline to consider *de novo* a question that two lower courts had already decided—whether the material Roth had sent through the mails was obscene—was not improper at a time when such questions were deemed to present issues of fact rather than of constitutional law. The Court generally accepts facts as found by the reviewing court below, although it is not bound to do so. Justice Harlan, dissenting in *Roth,* declaimed against this practice, protesting that "the question whether a particular book may be suppressed [should not be deemed] a mere matter of classification, of 'fact,' to be entrusted to a factfinder and insulated from independent constitutional judgment. . . . Every communication has an individuality and 'value' of its own. The protection of a particular writing or other tangible form of expression is, therefore, an *individual* matter, and in the nature of things every such suppression raises an individual constitutional problem, in which a reviewing court must determine for *itself* whether the attacked expression is suppressible within constitutional standards. . . . [I]f 'obscenity' is to be suppressed, the question whether a particular work is of that character involves not really an issue of fact but a question of constitutional *judgment* of the most sensitive and delicate kind. . . . In short, I do not understand how the Court can resolve the constitutional problems now before it without making its own independent

The government's deposit of pornographic material was meant to drama-
tize for the justices just what could continue to flow freely through the
mails if they struck down the Comstock law.* The idea for such a display
(or "chamber of horrors") probably originated with Postmaster General
Arthur Summerfield, a former Detroit automobile dealer who was appointed by President Eisenhower, and who established an exhibit of "hard-
core pornography" gleaned from the mails at his offices in the Post Office
Building in Washington, D.C.; it became his custom to show the exhibit to
visitors.† Justice Brennan alluded to the practice in one of our conversations:

JUSTICE WILLIAM J. BRENNAN, JR.: Arthur Summerfield . . . had a room in
the Post Office Building where they had an exhibit of hard-core stuff. The
"Chamber of Horrors." And they invited men and women to see it. Well,
when *Roth* was before us, Summerfield pressured Rankin, the S.G., and
they brought it to court and gave it to the marshal. At oral argument it
was given to me because I was the junior member; I was sitting at the end
of the bench; Clark must have been sitting next to me, and then Douglas.
I took a look at one of those things in the box, and put it back. I didn't
want to look at it. But Clark asked for the box and looked through it and
then Douglas got his hands on it and he or Clark—I don't know who it
was—took a bunch of the stuff and passed it down the bench. No one—not
even Tony Lewis of the *Times*‡—saw what was going on. Then after the
arguments were over, they brought it to my office, because Warren assigned
the case to me. And I said, "What am I supposed to do with that?"I called

judgment upon the character of the material upon which [Roth's conviction was] based."
   Harlan's indictment of the way review was handled by the Court in Roth's case paved the
way for a sea change in the practice that took place immediately after *Roth* and was led by
Justice Brennan, over the objections of Chief Justice Warren. The new policy was to examine
de novo the question of whether material was (in the constitutional sense) obscene in every
case in which the losing party below presented such a question in its petition to the Court
for review, and the petition to review was granted. The change was first announced by Justice
Brennan in the opinion he wrote for the *Tropic of Cancer* and *The Lovers* cases (discussed in
Chapter 22), where he cited Harlan's "separate opinion" in *Roth,* and located the principle
in the many cases "[i]n other areas involving constitutional rights" under the due process
clause and "particularly . . . where rights have been asserted [in the petitions for review] under
the First Amendment guarantees of free expression." *Jacobellis* v. *Ohio,* reprinted in de Grazia,
Censorship Landmarks (1969), 423–27. Harlan's dissent in *Roth* is in *Censorship Landmarks,*
290, 295–96.
   *Dean Lockhart mentioned the box in his article in 45 *Minnesota Law Review,* 5, 26 (1960),
saying it "must have brought the [Roth case] back to earth abruptly, and it must also have
assured a decision favorable to the constitutionality of . . . the federal . . . obscenity [law]."
Lockhart and Anthony Lewis of *The New York Times* both seem to have viewed the solicitor
general's action as not unfair, and merely a forensic ploy.
   †The first such pornographic "chamber of horrors" probably was the one set up in the office
of the vice president of the United States by Anthony Comstock when he lobbied for the
enactment of the law under which Samuel Roth was convicted.
   ‡Anthony Lewis covered the Supreme Court for *The New York Times* during the period
when *Roth* was argued. He also wrote a prescient and influential article for *Esquire* at the time,
"Sex and the Supreme Court," which predicted the revolutionary development in the law of
obscenity that Justice Brennan would preside over.

the clerk's office and they sent it back to the S.G. He immediately called me up and told me half of the stuff was gone. I don't know where it went.*

Back in the courtroom of the Marble Palace, Justice Harlan once more addressed Albrecht:

JUSTICE JOHN MARSHALL HARLAN: Well, to carve it down to size, which is my trouble, take a dirty picture. Do you say it's beyond the purview of Congress to say we will not allow that stuff to be shipped through the mails?

—

Albrecht finally confronted the pornography issue: "Yes sir," he replied. Harlan must have expected a different answer, for he expressed incredulity: "You say that's beyond the purview of Congress?" Albrecht was not willing to qualify his sweeping contention.

DAVID VON ALBRECHT: Yes sir. . . . My contention is that you cannot do anything like that because that is essentially a state function. It belongs to the local community.†

—

Roth's lawyer now tried to move the argument onto higher ground to dislodge from the justices' minds the idea planted there by the government that his client was a purveyor of dirty pictures and pornography. He reminded the Court that Roth was a publisher of books:

DAVID VON ALBRECHT: One of the books upon which this defendant was found guilty consisted of over two hundred pages.‡ This book was never read to the jury. Only isolated parts were read to the jury. There was only one copy that went into the jury room. It was a physical impossibility for the jury to have read that book in the jury room. It is our contention that

---

*The private court papers of Justice Brennan indicate that this was not the last time that court-related pornography would disappear from the clerk's office or the justices' chambers. During the 1960s, as described above, the Court adopted the practice of regularly reviewing *de novo* lower court findings of obscenity; this required the justices and their clerks personally to read the publications and view the movies found obscene below. To make this practice possible, attorneys seeking Supreme Court review of an obscenity case would file one or more copies of the publication or film in question with the clerk's office as part of the record on review. Occasionally, some of the "hot" items disappeared. At the Supreme Court stage of the *Memoirs of Hecate County* case, Doubleday's lawyers filed with the clerk enough copies of Edmund Wilson's book for each justice to have a copy.

†In his brief Albrecht pointed out, among other things, that it was impossible to ascertain federal or national standards of decency, whereas local community standards could be determined. Here he anticipated what Chief Justice Burger much later would read into the constitutional law of obscenity. However, Brennan, who prevailed as the Court's spokesman on obscenity until Burger's appointment, always insisted on the need for national standards (which alone would afford effective freedom for *nationally* distributed books, magazines, newspapers, and films), contending that "it is, after all, a national Constitution we are expounding." See Chapter 22.

‡Presumably *American Aphrodite,* number 3, a hardbound literary magazine.

if they had read the book, they would not have found the book "obscene."
If Your Honors desire to read it, I have it here and will produce it.

———

Although the "book" that Roth mailed was made an exhibit in the case,* Albrecht could not be sure that the justices had looked at it, much less read it, given that the Court had chosen not to consider the question of whether what Roth published was obscene. Roth's lawyer presumably would have wanted the justices to take a look at Beardsley's unfinished novel, for however "filthy" the behavior of Venus and her court might appear to some of the brethren, it would certainly have appeared less "filthy"—if only because it consisted largely of the printed word and had *some* obvious literary value—than the graphic material in the government's box.† But this overture by Albrecht neatly landed him in a trap that Justice Felix Frankfurter had waiting:

JUSTICE FELIX FRANKFURTER: Mr. Albrecht, may I suggest to you whether the thing you said latterly, the last thing you said about the jury couldn't read it, couldn't have read it, et cetera. Are any of these questions open here? I just looked at the order allowing *certiorari;* it was very severely restricted to the point you earlier made, namely, the Federal obscenity statute violates freedom of speech under the First Amendment.

———

Albrecht was thus disabled from arguing that the value or merits of Roth's *American Aphrodite* or Beardsley's *Venus and Tannhäuser* or anything else that Roth was responsible for publishing and sending through the mails warranted its receiving constitutional protection.

DAVID VON ALBRECHT: Well, Your Honor, in the brief supplied by the Government, they too admit that I have this right. . . .
JUSTICE FELIX FRANKFURTER: I don't care what the Government—the Government is not deciding what the scope of this review is.

———

In fact, neither the "Brief in Opposition" nor the brief "on the merits" that the Justice Department filed suggested Roth was free to argue that the publications sent by him through the mails were not obscene. And, although the government had countered all seven of Roth's other points, in the "Brief in Opposition" it said not a word about this one, perhaps thinking thus to signal to the Court a desire not to even argue the matter. And although Justice Harlan acted and wrote as though *he* felt free to decide Roth's fate on the basis of whether what the publisher actually mailed was in his judgment obscene or pornographic, technically that question was not before the Court.

———

*A copy had been filed with the Court by the solicitor general.
†The *Venus and Tannhäuser* piece was illustrated by five Beardsley drawings; the main personages are all very well dressed (in the Beardsley manner). In one drawing, Venus's breasts are exposed; another shows a nude dwarf whose tiny pudenda are visible.

DAVID VON ALBRECHT: Yes, Your Honor. As I understand it, the review on the consideration of the constitutionality of this statute not only applies to the statute on its face, but also as applied; and therefore I thought that would come within the scope of this argument. . . .

CHIEF JUSTICE EARL WARREN: I don't know where you get that in the questions. . . .

DAVID VON ALBRECHT: Well, the . . .

CHIEF JUSTICE EARL WARREN: They appear on page three of your brief, at the bottom.

DAVID VON ALBRECHT: But if Your Honors think that I have gone beyond any limits, I will back away and go ahead along a different line. . . .

JUSTICE FELIX FRANKFURTER: It's customary, isn't it, when counsel want to question the constitutionality "as applied" that they say so, and the Court says so—on its face *and as applied?*

DAVID VON ALBRECHT: Yes, Your Honor.

JUSTICE FELIX FRANKFURTER: You can't just swim in the middle of the Pacific Ocean in these matters. You've got to get some footing on some *terra firma.*

———

By choosing not to address themselves to the question of whether the materials were obscene, the justices would spare themselves the obligation to do what they had done nine years before in the *Doubleday* case. There they had had to read Edmund Wilson's *Memoirs of Hecate County* in order to decide whether Doubleday's conviction should stand, or whether, as asserted by counsel for Doubleday, the book was "a bona fide work of literature" presenting no clear and present danger to the morals of the community.

During the arguments in *Hecate County,* Justice Robert Jackson, now gone from the bench, had said that if the Court were to decide in every case of this sort whether the publication found obscene was in fact or law obscene, a dilemma would be created: the high bench would turn into a Supreme Board of Censors.*

Essentially the only issue left open to argument on Roth's behalf was the proposition that the federal postal statute was facially unconstitutional, either because it was too vaguely worded or because the "evil" it was supposed to guard against presented no "clear and present danger" to any substantial governmental interest.† These were difficult points to argue—especially before a bench under the sway of Frankfurter's policy of judicial restraint. For Roth to succeed, the justices would have to be persuaded to

———

*Whitney North Seymour, Doubleday's lawyer, replied, "it is my belief that dilemmas are better than restraints." See *United States Law Week,* vol. 17, no. 15 (October 26, 1948), at 3117–18.

†There also might have been the question whether the law was not unconstitutionally "overboard." The overbreadth doctrine, however, came only later to be fully articulated by the Court as a free-speech-favoring doctrine distinguished from the "vagueness" doctrine. On the distinction, see Professor Lawrence Tribe's treatise *Constitutional Law* (1978), 720.

strike down one of the oldest federal obscenity laws on the books—the Comstock law of 1873—a law similar to the laws that all the states but one had standing on their books and were enforcing.* The federal law, moreover, was aimed at an "evil"—however ill defined—that some fifty-five foreign countries had agreed to cooperate in eradicating, by means of an international convention.

Albrecht wound up his part of the argument for Roth by calling the Court's attention to the "disharmony" that would result were the Court to uphold the law and permit judges and juries sitting in different states to reach contradictory conclusions concerning the obscenity of particular works and the culpability of their distributors.

DAVID VON ALBRECHT: Now as I see the question, for the first time this Court is being asked to determine whether a federal criminal statute can punish speech as speech, even though that speech has no connection with any action or conduct over which the Federal Government has power or control. And, if I may pose this question: How can you have a single federal statute which has inherent potential of having different results in different states upon the same state of facts? . . . And I submit that such potential for disharmony in the enforcement of a federal obscenity statute is compelling evidence that obscenity is a proper subject for the State, and not for the federal, power.

———

The point was not a strong one. If, as Albrecht argued, the several states alone had the power to proscribe obscene books under their several police powers, it is almost certain that their judges and juries would disagree across state lines, and even county lines, giving rise to much "disharmony" and effectively making any national publication or distribution impossible.†

When it was the government's turn to address the Court, Roger Fisher underscored his belief that there was no need for the brethren to judge whether *American Aphrodite,* or anything else that Sam Roth may have been convicted for mailing, was obscene.

ROGER FISHER: Mr. Chief Justice, may it please the Court. I will, too, start out by saying what is involved in this case, distinguishing other cases, and what is *not* involved in this case. First there is no question of whether the exhibits in this case are obscene.‡ That issue was question eight in the petition for *certiorari* and it was denied. . . . That issue is not here.

There is no question of prior restraint. . . .§ Petitioner Roth got every-

---

*New Mexico was the exception.
†As they did in the many cases involving *Tropic of Cancer* before Justice Brennan declared, as a *federal* constitutional matter, that the novel could not constitutionally be found obscene. See Chapter 22 below.
‡The exhibits referred to were government exhibits that included the publications Roth had been convicted for mailing, including *American Aphrodite,* number 3.
§An issue of "prior restraint" might have been raised if, for example, the Post Office had *seized* Roth's publications from the mails on the ground that they were obscene, thus preventing their delivery. The Post Office did exercise such a power in other cases mentioned in this

thing . . . grand jury, jury trial, criminal burden of proof beyond a reasonable doubt. . . .

The sole question on the limited review is the constitutionality of Section 1461 as applied as a criminal statute to the mailing of obscene materials in the United States mails. This is the application of an obscenity statute to matter which is concededly obscene, concededly for purposes of this appeal.*

———

Fisher's uses of the terms "applied" and "application," and "concededly obscene," must have been confusing in the same way that the solicitor general's "Brief in Opposition" was confusing, and misleading. As Frankfurter and Warren by now had made plain, the issue before the Court was not whether Section 1461, the postal obscenity law, was constitutional *as applied* to Roth's publications. Fisher, however, articulated the question as to the law's *facial* validity so that it came down essentially to whether the law was constitutional *as applied* to "hard-core" pornography of the sort contained in the box filed with the clerk's office and made available to the justices at the bench. If so, or so ran Fisher's argument, then Roth's conviction ought to stand.

Justice Harold Burton was distracted, or confused, by Fisher's articulation of the issues in the case:

JUSTICE HAROLD BURTON: Do we have to assume that? That it's concededly obscene. Is the question of vagueness out of the case?
ROGER FISHER: No. . . . You still have before you whether the statutory standard is vague on its face. . . .
JUSTICE HAROLD BURTON: What obscene means?
ROGER FISHER: If it means anything, these advertising circulars and this one book are obscene. You still have the question of whether it means enough. . . . Can *anything* be restrained on the ground that it is obscene?† Heretofore there has been unanimous agreement on that subject. The Court is now reconsidering, I should say, that question.

———

This last was a surprising statement for the government to make. As the government itself pointed out in its briefs in Roth's case, the Supreme Court, as recently as in its 1948 decision in *Hecate County,* had spoken of the facial constitutionality of obscenity laws as "settled." This was the legal

———

book, including the *Big Table* 1 case (Chapter 18), the *Lady Chatterley's Lover* book case, and the *Lysistrata* case. In Roth's case, the publications found obscene were "restrained" only after their delivery (to Post Office agents posing as customers) had been made, and Roth himself was tried, convicted, and sentenced for sending obscenity through the mails.

*Of course, Roth never "conceded" his mailings were obscene. It would have been fairer to say that they *were assumed* by the Court to be obscene, or that judges and jurors below had found them obscene.

†Here, Fisher again seemed to imply that Roth's mailings were "hard-core pornography," by equating them with the worst examples of the obscene. Elsewhere in the argument, however, Fisher implied that Roth's mailings were of a marginal type, borderline obscene, not "hard-core pornographic," but still necessarily to be banned.

situation that Judge Jerome Frank had hoped to unsettle through his concurring opinion and appendix in *Roth*. Actually, by the time of the *Roth* argument, and even before Judge Frank's extended exegesis, other judges, sitting in Pennsylvania and New Jersey, had pushed ahead of the high bench and written opinions that should also have unsettled the "settled" question.* Most of the doubts centered on the breadth and vagueness of the laws' coverage and purposes, but there was also a growing appreciation that such laws allowed an undemocratic and paternalistic—an "un-American"—governmental supervision of literary and artistic expression and taste.

Most of the remainder of the argument in Roth's case was devoted to whether the "clear and present danger" principle—formulated in the wake of World War I by Justices Holmes and Brandeis to test the limits of federal and state powers over freedom of speech and press—was applicable to obscenity law. Judge Frank (like Judge Bok before him) had argued that it was as applicable to such laws as to any other laws restraining speech or press, and that the Comstock law as drafted seemed to flunk the test. This was also how Justice William O. Douglas saw the situation. Felix Frankfurter flatly disagreed; only a few years earlier, in a sharply divided case, he had written an opinion for the majority, declaring that like obscene speech, libelous speech was excluded from protection under the Constitution and accordingly presented no occasion for application of the "clear and present danger" test. Frankfurter had been hostile to the test at least since 1943, when it had been used by a liberal Court majority to overturn a previous Frankfurter-led holding that public-school pupils constitutionally could be required to pledge allegiance to the American flag.† Indeed, as Professor Harry Kalven, Jr., pointed out, Frankfurter was "the chief critic of the test" and had dissented "repeatedly and at length" to every use of the test by the Court to bring about invalidations of laws restraining freedom of speech.‡

Roth's lawyers argued that the test ought to apply to all laws encroaching on speech, including obscenity laws, and that applying it to the postal obscenity statute "on its face" made evident the law's unconstitutionality. For, they said, no meaningful danger or evil whatever was posited by the challenged statute, and no proof had been attempted by the government that Roth's publications presented any danger or evil to anyone. This argument was powerfully supported in the briefs amici curiae filed by the ACLU, the American Book Publishers Council, and the publishers of *Playboy* and *Rogue* magazines, all of which cited Judge Jerome Frank's concurring opinion in *Roth*.§

---

*Judge Bok in *Commonwealth* v. *Gordon,* alluded to in the text above; and Judge Goldman in *Bantam Books* v. *Melko.*

†The 1943 case was *West Virginia Board of Education* v. *Barnette;* see the careful and insightful discussion of the development and demise of the "clear and present danger" test by the late Harry Kalven, Jr., in *A Worthy Tradition* (1987), 179ff.

‡*A Worthy Tradition,* 181.

§The briefs are reprinted in *Landmark Briefs and Arguments of the Supreme Court of the United*

Roger Fisher, however, had come to Court prepared to read into the postal law several intelligently fabricated "dangers" which, he argued, Congress might well have meant to avoid; and—or so he argued—these dangers were "clear" and "present" enough to pass constitutional muster. He articulated the dangers in response to a question from Justice William O. Douglas.

JUSTICE WILLIAM O. DOUGLAS: Clear and present danger that you be shocked; or what? Clear and present danger of *what*?

ROGER FISHER: Clear and present danger of an injury to an interest that society can protect. We've suggested in our brief that these are four. There is the conduct, immediate conduct. The person can see photographs of sexual perversion, moving pictures of perverted conduct taking place, or booklets, and think: Let me experiment myself. We think there's a serious risk of that, one which the legislature could properly act upon.

Second: long-range conduct induced by a breaking down of morals. You read these books—it's not that you're immediately aroused to do something, but they gradually fill your mind with the thought that everyone seems to be doing it, let's have some fun, illicit sex life—various kinds of activity—because your moral standards are broken down by being hit. Reading the morning's mail, you get circulars advertising this sort of material.

———

At this point Justice Douglas interrupted Fisher to suggest that he "sounded like Mr. Comstock, Anthony Comstock," whereupon Justice Frankfurter, interceding, told him not "to be frightened by that!"

ROGER FISHER: No, I think that there is an effect on morality if you'll peruse—I invite your attention to the library, the box of stuff which we've brought. And I think that a diet of that material coming through the mails to the homes of America would have a definite effect on the conduct not only of the children, but of the parents and others in the family who receive it.

———

A weakness in Fisher's "clear and present danger" analysis lay in the insubstantiality, the inchoate character, of the supposed dangers; Holmes, and even more particularly, Brandeis, had stressed the requirement that the danger be not only clear and imminent but serious, or grave. The dangers

States, edited by Philip B. Kurland and Gerhard Kasper, vol. 53 (1975), 327–482. New York lawyer Morris Ernst also filed a brief on his own behalf, mainly attacking the law for its vagueness and as not within the province of federal (as distinguished from state) government, along the lines adopted by Roth's attorneys. The brief filed for the publishers of *Playboy* and *Rogue* was signed by Abe Fortas, the brilliant senior partner of the prestigious Washington, D.C., law firm Arnold, Fortas, and Porter, and later a Supreme Court justice. Fortas's eventual resignation from the Court was brought about, in part, by the savage criticism of his votes in obscenity cases voiced by influential censorship groups and powerful U.S. senators, as described in Chapter 27. The Fortas brief was particularly forceful on the "clear and present danger" point.

posited by Fisher could only by straining be deemed serious or grave, and with the exception perhaps of the "danger" that persons viewing pornography might be moved to "experiment" themselves, none seemed clear or imminent. Sensing this, Frankfurter began a dialogue that would in due course lead Fisher practically to abandon his "clear and present danger" argument as inapposite to obscenity law.

JUSTICE FELIX FRANKFURTER: Do you agree that it must have an effect on conduct?

ROGER FISHER: No . . . that's just one. Another interest is the injury or the . . . psychological harm of the housewife who opens the morning mail and finds one of Mr. Roth's circulars. . . . There's a strong interest of not being offended or hit in the face with dirty pictures and debasing discussions of sex in the home in the morning mail.

JUSTICE FRANKFURTER: How do we know it doesn't affect conduct in the future? Does anybody know? Has psychology reached that wonderful stage where we can be assured that if boys or grown-ups who are feeble-minded, or general weak-kneed human beings have certain things said to them, that it doesn't do anything to them?* Has psychology reached that certainty of determination?

In his *Roth* appendix Judge Jerome Frank had surveyed the scientific and empirical evidence available at that time with regard to the *effects* of obscenity on the conduct of adults and young people; the conclusions he reached were subsequently verified by the studies undertaken in 1968–69 by the National Commission on Obscenity and Pornography (Lockhart commission): there was no reliable evidence of psychological harm or of crime, sexual misconduct, or other ill effects resulting from the reading of obscene or pornographic matter by adults, or even children.†

ROGER FISHER: One of our key points is that this is an area where no one can know what causes it. . . . Actually, even in your vital ["clear and present danger"] speech cases you can't tell whether speech is going to induce conduct, and even less so with this sort of material.

---

*Frankfurter's worries over the effect of reading on feebleminded and weak-willed people were reminiscent of Lord Cockburn's similar concern in the 1868 case of *Regina* v. *Hicklin.* See also Frankfurter's expression of concern about the effects of reading thrillers on boys and young men, in *Winters* v. *New York,* described in Chapter 29 below.

†The *Final Report* in 1986 of the Attorney General's Commission on Pornography (Meese commission) sought to refute the earlier Lockhart commission's findings by having witnesses "testify" to the harmful effects of "pornography," including *Playboy* magazine. The "research" was unsystematic and unfocused, the findings unsupported and unreliable, despite the presence on the commission of University of Michigan law professor Frederick Schauer, an expert on obscenity and freedom of expression. Other notable commission members were the Arlington, Virginia, prosecutor and "smut-buster" Henry E. Hudson, and the Reverend Bruce Ritter, founder and president of Covenant House, a child-crisis center in New York. See Attorney General's Commission on Pornography, *Final Report* 1 (1986), 299–352, and Chapter 29 below.

Again Fisher was interrupted by Douglas, who, favoring application of the Holmes-Brandeis test, wished to know what were the two other sorts of "clear and present danger" situations that the Justice Department had come up with to justify the government's abridgement of speech.

ROGER FISHER: Two other interests. . . . The invasion of the privacy of the home. And this is particularly with the mails; this is a "captive audience" who cannot avoid the material coming to them. They have withdrawn within the four walls, to get away from the hurly burly of life. This is their privacy, this is their training grounds for children. . . . The United States mails have an easement into their house. First class letters come through.* You've gotta open them or you're on your notice. It may be a tax bill; it may be an assessment . . . you open the mail. The circulars in this case were sent by first class mail, with no charge for the circular. This was sent out as advertising matter. . . . This is more of a captive audience.

—

Now it was Frankfurter's turn to interrupt.

JUSTICE FELIX FRANKFURTER: It doesn't touch conduct; it merely offends?
ROGER FISHER: It offends. It comes in . . .
JUSTICE FRANKFURTER: So what's it a clear and present danger to?
ROGER FISHER: To? Injury to the privacy of the home.
JUSTICE FRANKFURTER: Clear and present danger?
ROGER FISHER: I think . . .
JUSTICE FRANKFURTER: Why do you think this has to be shoved into that category?
ROGER FISHER: I say it doesn't have to be shoved . . .
JUSTICE FRANKFURTER: This Act had stood for fifty years before the phrase "clear and present danger"—the ink of that phrase—was dropped from Mr. Justice Holmes's pen.

—

Douglas showed greater interest than Frankfurter in Fisher's line of argument, no doubt because he anticipated that admitting the applicability of the "clear and present danger" test to an obscenity law would presage the law's doom, for failing to pass the test.

JUSTICE WILLIAM O. DOUGLAS: You say that Congress can make some laws that abridge freedom of speech?
ROGER FISHER: That some restraint can be imposed on how loud speech is spoken. This is more the form of the speech, than the content. This is the nudist in the park who wants to talk about nudism, who takes off his clothes and expresses himself. Reasonable police regulations can say: "Put on a pair of pants." You can say the same ideas but when you bring your ideas in the public arena, don't offend everybody. Be well-clothed. . . . If

---

*Fisher was alluding here to the fact that the Post Office could not legally open *first-class* mail and examine it for obscenity or other unlawfulness because of the constitutional ban on unreasonable search and seizure.

Mr. Roth has ideas to talk about, or if he feels moral concepts should be changed, he's free to talk about it.

JUSTICE DOUGLAS: You're talking now just about pictures, not about text?

ROGER FISHER: No, the text as well. I say that . . . there's no idea which will be found to be obscene.* Homosexuality, nothing, is going to be barred because of the idea content. It's going to be barred because of the way in which it's put.

———

Frankfurter now sought to remind Roger Fisher of the Court's "well-settled" notion that the punishment of certain kinds of expression had never been held by the Court to violate freedom of speech or press, and thus did not call for an application of the "clear and present danger" test. In the case of *Beauharnais* v. *Illinois,* decided a few years earlier, a sharply divided Court had held, in an opinion written by Justice Frankfurter, that criminally libelous speech was *not* constitutionally protected speech; that the State of Illinois's group libel law, like other laws prohibiting libel, did

———

*Fisher's allusion to the universally accepted proposition that "ideas" are absolutely protected by the First Amendment exposes one of the reasons that the law of obscenity proved so intractable for so long. Much fiction does not obviously convey ideas, just as many paintings do not obviously communicate ideas. Or perhaps it would be better to say that the ideas that are conveyed by imaginative literature and art are often difficult to extricate and articulate in descriptive or argumentative terms; and they are almost always ambiguous and unclear because of the way art impacts on fact and opinion. On the other hand, propaganda does convey ideas, and when artistic forms are seen as being used as vehicles for propaganda, the courts have recognized the expression to be of the type that the First Amendment was probably concerned with. An early instance of this was Judge Learned Hand's opinion in the *Masses* case, where a poem and cartoons as well as editorial pieces attacking the government's wartime policies were involved.

Insofar as the First Amendment was interpreted by the courts and commentators to be a prohibition against laws abridging the communication of ideas—and notably political and religious ones—the protection afforded most novels, paintings, and other artistic forms of expression was not readily apparent. From the classic free-speech perspective, Harry Kalven complained that Justice Black's absolutist view of the First Amendment, which argued that even obscene literature and movies were to be protected, did not confront the paucity of ideas in artistic expression. See *A Worthy Tradition* (1987), 41. On the other hand, in overturning a New York motion-picture-licensing law in 1952, the Supreme Court had said that movies came within the protection of the constitutional guarantees because they are "a significant medium for the communication of ideas" *(Burstyn* v. *Wilson);* and in 1959 the Court struck down another New York movie-licensing provision because it had been used unconstitutionally to prevent exhibition of a movie that state officials believed advocated "the idea that adultery may sometimes be proper" *(Kingsley International Pictures* v. *Regents).* The movie was an adaptation of Lawrence's novel *Lady Chatterley's Lover.* These cases illustrate the greater ease with which the Court has found artistic expression protected when the government attack could be construed as being directed at ideas. The last two cases are discussed in de Grazia and Newman, *Banned Films* (1982), and their texts are reprinted in full in de Grazia, *Censorship Landmarks* (1969), 180ff. and 326ff. The judges who freed Allen Ginsberg's *Howl* and the Chicago literary magazine *Big Table* 1 from censorship, as described later on, and the judges who freed the Swedish motion picture *I Am Curious—Yellow,* did so by finding "ideas" in the allegedly obscene works which, under *Roth,* worked to lend them constitutional protection. In the briefs I wrote in my effort as a lawyer to free *Tropic of Cancer* I added the concept of "images" to that of "ideas" as what the First Amendment was meant to protect, because it is easier to think and talk about the *images* that art and fictional literary works convey, and because ideas are in any event arguably only mental images.

not encroach upon the guarantees of freedom of speech or press; and that it was unnecessary and undesirable to resort to the "clear and present danger" test to ascertain whether such a law was constitutionally valid. With those propositions in mind, it was but a short additional step to the conclusion advocated by Frankfurter that obscene expression also raised no question regarding freedom of speech, was outside the constitutional protection, and did not call for a testing of its validity by the "clear and present danger" standard.*

JUSTICE FRANKFURTER: Mr. Fisher, would you regard a libel statute . . . making it a criminal libel to tell lies, demonstrable untruths, about a public man . . . an infringement of freedom of speech?†

ROGER FISHER: I don't think it makes much difference whether you . . .

JUSTICE FRANKFURTER: It makes all the difference in the world to me . . . because I don't think we can violate the Constitution a little bit. . . . We've got to be true to it.

ROGER FISHER: I think that abridging the freedom of speech is not violated a little bit by restraining the sending of obscene matter. . . .

JUSTICE FRANKFURTER: What about libel? Is that within the Constitution, or isn't it?

ROGER FISHER: I think that a restraint on libel is not prohibited by the First Amendment. . . .

JUSTICE FRANKFURTER: I mean . . . prosecution for libel, is that a violation of the Constitution?

ROGER FISHER: No, no. I think it's not.

JUSTICE FRANKFURTER: Well, then, why do you have to worry about clear and present danger with reference to libel?

---

*It seems possible that Justice Frankfurter had decided the issues in Roth's case before listening to the arguments, and that his questions had as their aim more to bring the government's lawyers and the brethren around to his view than to probe counsel's arguments. Frankfurter's juristic strategy in Roth's case (followed by Brennan's opinion for the Court in the case) was to analogize obscene expression not to political or ideological expression, which had long been held constitutionally protected by prior court decisions (because of its putative contribution to rational discourse and the pursuit of "Truth"), but to libelous expression, which had been held constitutionally unprotected (because of its failure to contribute to rational discourse and the pursuit of "Truth"). This avoided any need to apply the "clear and present danger" doctrine (previously used almost exclusively in political and ideological expression cases), which, if applied, might well have led to a freeing of the "obscene" expression because of the inchoate quality of the "danger" and its social insubstantiality. The reaching of a conclusion by analogy in this way—by answering the question Does A (obscenity) more closely resemble B (political expression) than it resembles C (libelous expression)? and then attaching to A the outcome that the predecent provides for the type of expression it is perceived more closely to resemble (in Roth's case: C)—is a traditional form of legal reasoning, the classic exposition of which is Edward H. Levi's *Introduction to Legal Reasoning* (1962).

†Frankfurter's answer to his own question, of course, was no; and that was the law's answer also in 1957. In 1964, however, in the celebrated case of *New York Times* v. *Sullivan*, the Supreme Court, speaking through Justice Brennan, changed the law's answer to yes, unless the lie was knowingly told, or was told in reckless disregard of its falsity. Justice Black would have extended First Amendment protection in cases of lies about public officials even to intentionally told lies. See his concurring opinion in *Sullivan*, joined by Justice Douglas.

ROGER FISHER: I don't think you do. I think, however, that . . .

JUSTICE FRANKFURTER: You think that Madison thought that libel was an exception, was a violation of the Constitution?*

———

The argument here touched on a sore point in constitutional politics. Conservative jurists had from the beginning argued that the First Amendment was not meant to overturn the English common law of seditious, blasphemous, or obscene libel, but was intended merely to bar previous restraints, such as the licensing before publication of newspapers and books. Liberal jurists, including Zechariah Chafee, however, maintained that the constitutional guarantees were designed to repeal the English common law in every respect in which it encroached upon the freedoms of speech or press, and to invalidate any statute that sought to recapitulate or extend the old common law of libel. That law, dating mainly from the expiration of the English press-licensing laws in the seventeenth century, gave the common-law courts and especially King's Bench the power comprehensively to define and punish all talk and writings that, in the judges' opinions, were inimical to the welfare of the Crown, the government, the Church, religion, secular and ecclesiastical officials, or sexual morality.

Fisher must have realized that Frankfurter had become impatient with all this talk about whether obscenity was "speech," within the constitutional meaning, and whether the "clear and present danger" test applied; he knew that Frankfurter wanted him simply to take the position that because of its lack of value, obscenity was *self-evidently* outside the scope of the First Amendment's protections, and that was that. But initially, at least, Fisher resisted Frankfurter's imperious opposition to his open-minded argument.†

ROGER FISHER: The only question, Mr. Justice Frankfurter, that I had was: It would have been easy for the Government to come in and say, once something is obscene, it's beyond the realm of protections.‡ The First Amendment has no concern with it. I think that would have been an unhealthy analysis for the Government to make.

———

*He may have. See: *Writings of James Madison 1790–1802*, 6, 387, where Madison argues that "the state of the press . . . under the [English] common law, cannot . . . be the standard of its freedom in the United States." Libel was a common-law crime.

†Frankfurter, over his long career as an associate justice of the Supreme Court, gradually assumed a pedagogical role that some students of the Court's work described as that of a little dictator. His liberal leadership role on the Court steadily faded with the alienation of his liberal brethren Black, Douglas, Murphy, and Rutledge. This was first noticed in the case of *West Virginia* v. *Barnette*, 319 U.S. 624 (1943), where the liberals deserted Frankfurter's position and the court overruled the Frankfurter-led decision in *Minersville School District* v. *Gobitis*, 310 U.S. 586 (1940), which had upheld a school flag-salute requirement. Frankfurter thereafter sometimes referred to the Court's liberal bloc as "the Axis."

‡This, in fact, would be the holding of the Court in *Roth*, as articulated by Justice Brennan. The proposition was energetically attacked by Justice Harlan, who, dissenting from the Court's affirmance of Roth's conviction, pointed out that obscenity is not a special genus of speech, as readily distinguishable from other speech as poison ivy is from other plants. The weakness in Harlan's position was that pornography is not a special genus of speech either.

This was the wrong thing to say to Frankfurter because it implied a criticism of his approach to the solution of the problem of obscenity.

JUSTICE FRANKFURTER: I don't know what that means! I think it's not very brave for the Government to be dodging the question whether this is a violation of the Constitution or isn't a violation of the Constitution.

ROGER FISHER: If I have conveyed that impression I have erred.

JUSTICE FRANKFURTER: Well, you're afraid of touching this thing whether this is an exception or a restraint which the Constitution forbids, or to say forthright: "No! It is not within the prohibition."

ROGER FISHER: I will say this: It is not within the prohibition of the Constitution. I will say that . . .

JUSTICE FRANKFURTER: Then you don't have to worry about "clear and present danger." . . .

ROGER FISHER: If I have failed to heed my teacher, then I am a poor student indeed.*

Thus was solved the problem of how the constitutionality of the Comstock act might be upheld despite the absence of any clear and present danger to a grave national interest. In his *Roth* opinion, Brennan would follow Frankfurter's lead by discounting the contention that freedom of expression was violated by the Comstock act with the argument that since obscenity (like libel) "is not protected speech . . . it is unnecessary . . . to consider the issues behind the phrase 'clear and present danger.' "† Brennan would thereby utilize what Kalven criticized as the "two-level free-speech theory" (first put forth in *Chaplinsky*), which postulated that some speech did and some speech did not warrant constitutional protection under the "clear and present danger" doctrine.‡

Now came the turn of New York lawyer O. John Rogge to conclude the argument on behalf of Samuel Roth—whom the brethren seemed almost to have lost sight of by trying to answer not the concrete question of whether the publications which Roth mailed were obscene in a constitutional sense, but the abstract and official one of whether the postal obscenity law was valid "on its face," and, thereby whether the law was valid as applied to the offerings in the government's box. Rogge opened by reiterating Albrecht's plaint about the government's dirty pictures.

O. JOHN ROGGE: Mr. Chief Justice, may it please the Court. . . . I'd like to . . . be sure that we're talking about this case. Government Counsel

---

*Fisher received his law degree from Harvard Law School in 1948. By then, Frankfurter, who had taught at Harvard from 1914 until 1938, had joined the Court, appointed by President Franklin D. Roosevelt.

†See de Grazia, *Censorship Landmarks* (1969), 292–93.

‡Harry Kalven, Jr., "Metaphysics of the Law of Obscenity," *1960 Supreme Court Review* (1960), 1, 20ff. The "central weakness" of the two-level theory arises whenever "classification at the first or second level depends upon a key that is as vague as is obscenity." Kalven, 20.

talked a great deal about pornography, whatever that may mean. And Mr. Justice Harlan, you asked about pictures, and I think you did too, Mr. Justice Douglas. I think the Government will concede that they're not talking about the evidence in this case. If there's any doubt on that, I'd like to have it cleared up now. The Government is talking about material in another case than this one.

———

Rogge, however, did not press the point, probably because of the shortness of his time, but perhaps also because of uncertainty concerning the legal propriety of what the Justice Department had done. Also, to question the solicitor general's conduct in depositing the box with the Court might be seen as placing in question the propriety of the Court's own behavior in looking at the stuff in the box.* Instead, Rogge expended his final effort in an endeavor to bring Frankfurter around to Roth's side by quoting from the jurist for whom Frankfurter seemed to have the greatest respect, whom he'd once taken almost as a model:

O. JOHN ROGGE: Now, Mr. Justice Frankfurter, I'd like to begin with your question as to whether the Post Office *has* to carry the material. And here I begin with a statement by Mr. Justice Holmes in a dissenting opinion in which Mr. Justice Brandeis concurred in the *Burleson* case, a dissenting opinion that was approved by this Court in *Hannagan* against *Esquire.* Mr. Justice Holmes said: *"The United States may give up the Post Office when it sees fit, but while it carries it on, the use of the mails is almost as much a part of free speech as the right to use our tongues."*

And if we're going to have a Post Office Department, it has to carry the materials. . . .

JUSTICE FRANKFURTER: Mr. Rogge, since you're quoting a dissenting opinion of Mr. Justice Holmes and therefore strike at my Achilles' heel . . . I suggest there's another dissenting opinion [of Mr. Justice Holmes] on which I suppose you would rely, which you do not cite in your brief. I refer you to *Leach* against *Carlile* in 258 U.S., where Mr. Justice Holmes says things very much in your favor, which you might make use of. . . .† [I]n

———

*Justice Brennan, who at the time of *Roth* was serving his first term as a justice, told me: "It wasn't right for the Court to look at that big carton of stuff that the government sent over. . . . We didn't look at what Roth had mailed; I never saw what he sent. I thought that he conceded it was obscene." It would, in any event, have been untoward during the arguments for the justices to question the propriety of the solicitor general's box, or of any of the brethren who looked at what was in it.

†In *Leach,* Holmes dissented from a judgment of the Court upholding the constitutionality of the federal law that authorized the postmaster general to issue "fraud orders" against persons using the mails to conduct business, the result of which was to stop all mail going to such persons. Holmes argued that the law worked an unconstitutional "prior restraint" on the freedom of speech of the senders of the mail stopped. All the cases mentioned by Frankfurter had been parsed by Judge Frank in his opinion in *Roth.*

that dissent he suggested that the Court reconsider the *Jackson* case, way back in 1872,* and I suppose that's the strength of your case.

O. JOHN ROGGE: Well, I assumed that when this Court granted *certiorari* on whether the federal obscenity statute involved here was in violation of the First, the Fifth, and the Ninth and the Tenth Amendments, this Court was going to reconsider the constitutionality of this old statute, although it's been on the books for over three-quarters of a century and has been assumed to be constitutional a number of times since then.

———

O. John Rogge had now stepped on the same toe that Roger Fisher had trod upon: the question of judicial restraint.

JUSTICE FRANKFURTER: Do you think that's the same thing as though this statute was passed yesterday? That's a hundred years of the practice of the Court and the decisions of the court. . . . You think that it makes no difference that a statute has been on the statute books, sustained by this Court again and again, by liberal leaders and those who have given us the modern law of civil liberties?†—that's immaterial? And that we discuss this thing *de novo*? Is that it?

———

Holmes may have been Frankfurter's Achilles' heel but that justice's doubts about the constitutionality of the anti-lottery provisions of the postal law were not sufficient to unsettle Frankfurter's certainty that the Comstock law's obscenity provisions were necessary to the nation's welfare, and constitutionally valid. Rogge saw, however, that Frankfurter had painted himself into a corner, and he did not resist the temptation to point this out.

O. JOHN ROGGE: Mr. Justice Frankfurter, if this statute, as I submit it is, is in violation of the First, the Fifth, the Ninth and Tenth Amendments, then I submit to Your Honor that it doesn't make any difference if it's been on there for 150 years.

———

It was a solid thrust from which Frankfurter beat a polite retreat:

JUSTICE FRANKFURTER: I agree with you entirely. But before determining whether it is [unconstitutional], we'd better consider what has been.

———

Ex parte Jackson, actually decided in 1877, in which the Court held valid a statute relating to the mailing of letters or circulars concerning lotteries. In passing, the Court referred to the postal obscenity law and said it too was valid (96 U.S. 727).

†Presumably Frankfurter had in mind himself and Justices Rutledge, Murphy, Black, and Douglas, all of whom had been persuaded in 1943 (some thirteen years previously), to join the dictum that obscenity, like libel, profanity, and "fighting words," raised no free-speech question. That case was *Chaplinsky* v. *New Hampshire;* the unanimous opinion was written by Justice Murphy.

Rogge concluded his argument by addressing once again the "clear and present danger" doctrine. It was, really, the only hope left for Roth.

O. JOHN ROGGE: [I]n this connection, I want to draw a distinction between the *Dennis* case* and this case. At least in the *Dennis* case you had a statute, namely the Smith Act, which made it a crime to advocate the overthrow of the Government by force or violence. Where is there any statute in this [Roth's] case defining the substantive evil? . . . You have no statute here . . . which defines the substantive evil. And beyond that, you have no proof that the defendant's publications could bring about any such substantive evil.

———

This was true enough, but to no avail. In his concurring appellate court opinion, Judge Jerome Frank had quoted verbatim Pennsylvania judge Curtis Bok's sensible argument that "[a] book, however impure and pornographic . . . cannot be a present danger unless its reader closes it, lays it aside, and transmutes its erotic allurement into overt action."

JUDGE CURTIS BOK: That such action must inevitably follow as a direct consequence of reading the book does not bear analysis, nor is it borne out by general human experience; too much can intervene and too many diversions take place. . . . The only clear and present danger . . . that will satisfy . . . the Constitution . . . is the commission or the imminence of the commission of criminal behavior resulting from the reading of a book. Publication alone can have no such automatic effect.

———

This argument seems cogent enough to explain why Frankfurter sought to have the Court's decision in *Roth* justified without reliance on the "clear and present danger" test.

———

On June 24, 1957, the Supreme Court handed down a 6–3 decision upholding the criminal conviction of Samuel Roth for sending obscenity through the mails.† At the time, Roth was sixty-two years old. He spent

---

*Dennis v. *United States* (1948), in which eleven leaders of the American Communist Party were sent to prison for conspiring to advocate and teach the overthrow of the government by force and violence. The Supreme Court held that the danger posed by the conspiracy was sufficiently "clear and present" to justify the restraint on the defendants' freedoms of speech and press. Chief Justice Fred Vinson's opinion in the case is widely considered to have destroyed the integrity and credibility of the "clear and present danger" doctrine, by the manner in which he manipulated and transformed it to justify the outcome of the case. Circuit judge Learned Hand was responsible, in the first instance, for this judicial legerdemain; it was Hand's rearticulation of the doctrine for the Second Circuit Court stage of the *Dennis* case that Vinson adopted to justify letting the C.P. leaders go to prison merely for conspiring to advocate or teach "overthrow," and this, in the main, by the use of classic Marxist-Leninist books. See Kalven's discussion of the case, and the discredit done to the "clear and present danger" doctrine by it, in *A Worthy Tradition,* 193ff.

†Douglas, in an opinion joined by Black, and Harlan dissented: the former because all obscenity prosecutions violated freedom of speech and press, Harlan because federal obscenity prosecutions were constitutional only if the material condemned was "hard-core pornography." Without feeling any need to define "hard-core pornography," Harlan decided that "the

most of the next five years of what life remained to him in Lewisburg prison.*

The assignment to write the Court's opinion explaining why it was constitutional and just that Roth should go to prison for sending "obscene" publications through the mail was given to Justice Brennan. Although Brennan tracked the approach upon which Frankfurter had insisted at oral argument, and did nothing to keep Sam Roth from going to prison (because he could do nothing), he also took the Court's first significant step toward vesting literary and artistic expression *in the abstract* with constitutional protection.

In the 1956–57 term, as suits a freshman justice, Brennan had followed the oral arguments and the brethren's questioning of the lawyers and had said nothing. His opinion's central proposition (sharply criticized by some First Amendment scholars† and eventually abandoned by Brennan himself,‡) was devastatingly simple: obscenity was a form of expression that could be identified and that was "not within the area of constitutionally protected speech" (as the Court had already said about libel). Obscenity might be speech but it could not have been the purpose of the First Amendment's framers to protect that sort of speech.

JUSTICE WILLIAM J. BRENNAN, JR.: [I]t is apparent that the unconditional phrasing of the First Amendment was not intended to protect every utterance.§ This phrasing did not prevent this Court from concluding that libelous utterances are not within the area of constitutionally protected speech. . . . At the time of the adoption of the First Amendment, obscenity law was not as fully developed as libel law, but there is sufficiently contemporaneous evidence to show that obscenity, too, was outside the protection intended for speech and press.

———

The Frankfurter-influenced reasoning behind this jurisprudential design was of a circular sort, capable of curtailing any expression of a kind that had been considered worthless and pernicious by judges of the past. Obscene

material involved" in Roth's case "cannot be said to be" it. Unlike his brethren, Harlan ignored the limitation that the Court had placed, and Frankfurter and Warren insisted on retaining, on the questions presented by Roth's case. Douglas's opinion, looking to the freeing of all literature from obscenity censorship, foreshadowed the reflective dissenting opinions Brennan would write fifteen years later, abandoning the attempt to define "obscenity" in a constitutional way, in *Miller* v. *California,* 413 U.S. 15 (1973), and *Paris Adult Theatre I* v. *Slaton,* 413 U.S. 49 (1973).

*Unlike Dr. Wilhelm Reich, another McCarthy era "book criminal," Roth at least did not die imprisoned. See Chapter 18 below.

†See Harry Kalven's critique of *Roth* in "The Metaphysics of Obscenity," *1960 Supreme Court Review* (1960), 1, and in *A Worthy Tradition* (1989), 36–37.

‡But not until 1973. See Chapter 28 below.

§It was not "apparent" to Justice Hugo Black, who insisted, on the contrary, that the framers' intention was to protect *all* speech absolutely. Brennan rejected Black's libertarian view of the First Amendment as applied to obscenity, as Frankfurter had done with respect to libel in *Beauharnais* v. *Illinois* five years earlier. On *Beauharnais,* see Kalven, *A Worthy Tradition* (1987), 61ff.

expression, like profane, libelous, and insulting expression ("fighting words"), had for so long been thought of in this way that it seemed obvious that the majestic provisions of the First Amendment could not have been intended to protect *their* utterance from suppression. What Brennan did here was to authoritatively identify a category of speech that did not deserve constitutional protection; such speech could instead be made captive to, and controllable by, an assertion of official governmental interests—no matter how vaguely defined and insubstantial they might prove to be. In so discounting obscene speech, Brennan took comfort "in the universal judgement that obscenity should be restrained, reflected in the international agreement of over 50 nations, in the obscenity laws of all the 48 States, and in the 20 obscenity laws enacted by the Congress from 1842 to 1956."

It was justification enough to send the publisher to prison that a jury of his peers, applying "contemporary community standards," had found that his publications "as a whole" appealed to the "prurient interests" of "the average person." In fact, this recipe for a valid finding of obscenity—that the allegedly obscene material be taken "as a whole"; that its baleful ("prurient") appeal be judged by the reaction of "the average person" rather than the young, the immature, or the most susceptible; and that it be designed to sexually arouse, not merely morally corrupt, the reader—can be traced back to the *Ulysses* case; it registered important advances in the newly constitutionalized law of obscenity. This was a product of the legal liberalism present in both Brennan's and Frankfurter's thinking. But there also was in *Roth* a subsidiary theme—a freedom-favoring tail that would, in time, powerfully wag the censorship dog; this was purely Brennan's.

In his opinion for the Court in the 1943 landmark "fighting words" case, *Chaplinsky* v. *New Hampshire,* Justice Frank Murphy had said that "certain utterances" were "no essential part of any exposition of ideas," and were "of such *slight social value* as a step to truth that any benefit to be derived from them was clearly outweighed by the social interest in order and morality" (italics mine). Among such utterances—besides "insulting and fighting words"—were the "lewd and obscene, the profane [and] the libelous." Nine years later, Frankfurter, in the group-libel case *Beauharnais* v. *Illinois,* upheld the constitutionality of the Illinois statute squarely upon Murphy's sweeping *Chaplinsky* dictum. And so now did Brennan in *Roth,* in upholding the postal obscenity law. But in doing that Brennan subtly altered the doctrinal underpinning of the *Chaplinsky* dictum by asserting that the reason that obscenity was excluded from constitutional protection was not that it had only "slight social value as a step to truth," but that it did not communicate "ideas having even the slightest redeeming social importance." In other words, expression was disqualifiable from constitutional protection not (as Murphy and Frankfurter had said) because it had only *slight* social value, but because it had *none.*

I believe Brennan did this because he knew that any doctrine that permitted policemen, prosecutors, and judges to weigh the value or importance of ideas and speech in a scale whose other balance contained "the social interest in order and morality" would act as an open invitation to censorship by government officials. In his view only speech or ideas "utterly without" redeeming value or importance—speech, or ideas, one must suppose, for which *no one* would claim value or importance—could properly be denied constitutional protection. (It had been assumed by the Court that what Roth mailed was "speech" of this kind.) Although Brennan would not make this point explicit for seven more years (in his *Tropic of Cancer* decision), he was in *Roth* already intimating that a court, or other decision maker, should not be permitted to weigh a work's value or importance against its invidious "prurient appeal," that having even *the least* value or importance should qualify expression for constitutional protection. So far as the official record showed, nothing that Roth had mailed had even a modicum of value.

By 1964, Brennan's dictum in *Roth* would be honed by First Amendment lawyers and liberal judges to the point where Brennan was able to fashion it into a doctrine that radically liberated literary and artistic expression, and would virtually bring to an end the censorship of "the literary obscene" by pressure groups, policemen, prosecutors, and judges.

Like Frank, Brennan recognized that literature and the arts were constitutionally protected. The importance of that recognition to the value of freedom of speech and the press in America can scarcely be overestimated.* During the next several decades American artists and writers and their publishers, producers, exhibitors, distributors, and managers would base their struggles to gain freedom from censorship upon the premise established in *Roth* that artistic expression was meant to be protected as fully by the First Amendment as were religious and political expression. Brennan had rescued from potential oblivion the fact that the arts were understood by the nation's founders to be included in "freedom of the press."†

---

*It is really what gave the Brennan doctrine so much rhetorical force in the freeing of imaginative literature and art, more force I think than Black's absolutist approach would have lent to the freeing of such expression.

†Frank, as we have seen, attributed his awareness of this historical fact to Chafee's seminal work *Freedom of Speech*. Brennan had studied law at Harvard under Frankfurter, but his favorite teacher there was Chafee. Interestingly, the only legal brief filed in Roth's case that cited the Continental Congress's understanding that the arts were included with the freedom of the press was the government's prodigious 119-page brief on the merits, prepared by a team of Justice Department lawyers that included Roger Fisher. This brief took very seriously the points raised by Judge Jerome Frank's concurring opinion in *Roth* and the conundrum for freedom of expression presented by traditional obscenity-law restraints; and it did not take the easy way out of the conundrum commended by Justice Frankfurter, originally disdained by Roger Fisher, that once something could be called obscene, it deservedly lost any entitlement to constitutional protection. In the brief (page 27), the government quoted the 1774 letter from the Continental Congress to the inhabitants of Quebec to illustrate "the *affirmative* aims" of the First Amendment. Later on (pages 28–29), the brief drew up a sort of table of "values" possibly protectable by the free speech guarantees, ranging from "political speech," which had the highest value, to "commercial pornography," which had the lowest. It is

JUSTICE WILLIAM J. BRENNAN, JR.: The protection given speech and press was fashioned to assure unfettered interchange of ideas for the bringing about of political and social changes desired by the people. This objective was made explicit as early as 1774 in a letter of the Continental Congress to the inhabitants of Quebec:

"The last right we shall mention regards the freedom of the press. The importance of this consists, besides the advancement of truth, science, morality, and arts in general, in its diffusion of liberal sentiments on the administration of government, its ready communication of thoughts between subjects, and its consequential promotion of union among them, whereby oppressive officers are shamed or intimidated into more honourable and just modes of conducting affairs."

Art, the Continental Congress in 1774 had said, was on the same plane as truth, science, and morality in the scheme of values that the freedom of the press was intended to advance. This concept was in a way so new to the Court's First Amendment jurisprudence that Brennan, who later told me that he had always believed the arts were protected by the guarantees of speech and press, felt constrained in *Roth* to introduce the idea only tangentially. Yet it was upon this modest and tentative foundation that Brennan would in a few years build his monumental doctrine that material having "literary or scientific or artistic value, or any other form of social importance, may not be branded as obscenity and denied the constitutional protection."

In *Roth,* Brennan also made a vital connection between the First Amendment's guarantees and sex as a subject appropriate for literary and artistic "discussion." Although he had seen no better way to define "obscenity" than by garnering the current definitions of the word from *Webster's New International Dictionary* (unabridged, second edition, 1949) and citing the academic conclusions regarding obscenity reported by the American Law Institute's "Tentative Draft No. 6 for a Model Penal Code," Brennan took pains to distinguish "obscenity" from "sex" and to bring home the point that however reticent the Victorians* may have been about the private or public mention of sex, Americans were constitutionally entitled to discuss sex openly and freely:

JUSTICE WILLIAM J. BRENNAN, JR.: [S]ex and obscenity are not synonymous. Obscene material is material that deals with sex in a manner appealing to the prurient interest.† The portrayal of sex in art, literature and scientific

noteworthy that "literature" and "art" ranked fairly high in the government's value scale, higher than (in descending order) "entertainment," "music," "humor," "commercial advertisements," "gossip," "comic books," "epithets," "libel," "obscenity," "profanity," and, finally, "commercial pornography."

*Jerome Frank discussed this in his *Appendix* in *Roth,* reprinted in de Grazia, *Censorship Landmarks* (1969), 272, 279.

†And then this not very edifying footnote: "I.e., material having a tendency to excite lustful thoughts. Webster's New International Dictionary (Unabridged, 2d ed., 1949) defines *pruri-*

works* is not itself sufficient reason to deny material the constitutional protection of freedom of speech and press. . . .

Sex, a great and mysterious motive force in human life . . . , is one of the vital problems of human interest and public concern. As to all such problems, this Court said in *Thornhill* v. *Alabama* . . . "The freedom of speech and of the press guaranteed by the Constitution embraces at the least the liberty to discuss publicly and truthfully all matters of public concern without previous restraint or fear of subsequent punishment."

———

By acting in 1957 in *Roth* to legitimize and constitutionalize the "public discussion of sex," Brennan not only passed the word to American lawyers and judges that they could place literary and artistic discussions of sex beyond the reach of obscenity laws, he also—whether he meant to or not—set the stage for the legitimization in the seventies and eighties of literary and pictorial "discussions of sex" that were arguably devoid of literary, artistic, or other social importance, whose aim, that is to say, was simply sexual excitement (as good a definition as any, I would suggest, of "pornography"†), and he did this by obliging prosecutors to prove what might only with great difficulty be proved: the utter worthlessness of sexually explicit material.

Liberal auditors of the Court's work could see that the language Brennan used in *Roth* to confirm Roth's conviction nevertheless produced a significant crack in the country's century-old obscenity law. During the next decade or so, that opening would be exploited by humanistic lawyers and judges, notably Brennan himself, not only to free previously banned novels such as *Lady Chatterley's Lover, Tropic of Cancer, Fanny Hill,* and *Memoirs*

———

ent, in pertinent part, as follows: '. . . Itching; longing; uneasy with desire or longing; of persons, having itching, morbid, or lascivious longings; of desire, curiosity, or propensity, lewd. . . .'

"We perceive no significant difference [continued the footnote] between the meaning of obscenity developed in the case law and the definition of the A.L.I. Model Penal Code, §207.10(2) (Tent. Draft No. 6, 1957), *viz.:* '. . . A thing is obscene if, considered as a whole, its predominant appeal is to prurient interest, i.e., a shameful or morbid interest in nudity, sex, or excretion, and if it goes substantially beyond customary limits of candor in description or representation of such matters. . . .' See Comment, *id.,* at 10, and the discussion at page 29 *et seq.*"

*The only precedental authority Brennan mentioned for his reference to "scientific works" was a 1930 case involving a "scientific" discussion of sex by Mary Dennett called *The Sex Side of Life: An Explanation for Young People,* freed in *United States* v. *Dennett* by Judge Augustus Hand, speaking for a federal appellate bench. See de Grazia, *Censorship Landmarks* (1969), 83ff. Dennett's book, first published in 1919, was declared unmailable by the Post Office in 1922. In 1928 the *Dennett* case arose when Mrs. Dennett mailed a copy of the pamphlet to a "Mrs. Miles" in Virginia, who turned out to be a postal police agent assigned to apprehend the author. (As has been seen, the same device was used to create the criminal case against Sam Roth.) Dennett was tried by a jury and sentenced to pay a $300 fine. Her conviction was reversed on appeal. See Anne Lyon Haight and Chandler B. Grannis, *Banned Books: 387 B.C. to 1978 A.D.* (1978), 61–62.

†Whether of the "soft-core" or "hard-core" type, and assuming, as Brennan would have assumed, that expressive materials aiming only to sexually stimulate the reader or viewer had no social importance. See Chapters 23 and 26 below.

of Hecate County, but also to support and defend the publication of new sexually iconoclastic literary works like Allen Ginsberg's *Howl,* Vladimir Nabokov's *Lolita,* Terry Southern's *Candy,* and William Burroughs's *Naked Lunch.* Sooner perhaps than expected even so-called pulp novels would be set free—books with titles like *Lust Pool* and *Sex Life of a Cop*—and this despite the fact that they seemed to possess no identifiable social value.* Finally, although this would not become entirely clear until the eighties, blatantly pornographic pulp literature such as *Cunt Sucking Girls, Fuck Crazy Wives,* and *Going Down on Her Dad* could be freely published. Members of the Attorney General's Commission on Pornography recommended that such works be legally tolerated.†

In the early stage of this liberation (circa 1964), Brennan would have, practically, to stand his neo-Frankfurtian opinion in *Roth* on its head to free sexual expression in literature: he would be obliged to turn his *Roth* dictum that "obscenity is not within the area of constitutionally protected speech or press" because it is "utterly without redeeming social importance" into the position that only worthless expression, i.e., expression "utterly without redeeming [literary, scientific, artistic, or other] social importance," is obscene. It was left to the ingenuity of lawyers and lower court judges to discover that there was arguably some not-negligible worth even in "pornography,"‡ or, what came to the same thing, that all expression, however obscene or pornographic, probably contained some (however slight) social value.

The late Professor Harry Kalven, Jr., predicted this remarkable evolution of *Roth* and influenced it, to a point short of the freeing of hard-core pornography.§ He foresaw that in order for Brennan's opinion to free

---

*The events concerning *Naked Lunch* are in Chapters 18 and 25, *Tropic of Cancer* in Chapters 19 and 22, and *Fanny Hill* in Chapter 23. The fate of a "trashy" novel called *Sex Life of a Cop* is dealt with in Chapter 26.

†In July 1986 the Meese commission issued its *Final Report,* in which some members "urged that materials consisting entirely of the printed word simply not be prosecuted at all, regardless of content." Attorney General's Commission on Pornography, *Final Report* 1 (1986), 383–84. See also Chapter 29 below.

‡This is explored in Chapters 23 through 26. As the Brennan doctrine gathered force, lawyers used it successfully to defend even hard-core pornography. For instance, the film *Deep Throat* was defended on the ground that the information it presented concerning sexual techniques had educational value for some audiences. The film also had "entertainment" value, certainly for many audiences (it was a record-breaking box-office hit, grossing close to one hundred million dollars before being stopped by the Burger Court's revision of the Brennan doctrine), but the Court had never squarely ruled that "entertainment" was of social importance. Of course, it is.

§Not all the way to hard-core pornography, however. In his seminal "Metaphysics of the Law of Obscenity" Kalven said: "If the obscene is constitutionally subject to ban because it is worthless, it must follow that the obscene can include only that which is worthless. So-called hard-core pornography involves discussions of sex which are not integral parts of anything else. In themselves, they are, at best, fantasies of sexual prowess and response unrelated to the serious human concern that moved Lawrence and, at worst, a degrading, hostile, alien view of the sexual experience. If the socially worthless criterion is taken seriously, the *Roth* opinion may have made a major advance in liberating literature and art from the shadow of the censor." *1960 Supreme Court Review* (1960), 1, 13. The "major advance" was fully realized in 1964, when Brennan led the Court in the freeing of Henry Miller's long-condemned *Tropic of Cancer,* literature and art, the concept of "the worthless" would have to become the working definition of "the obscene"; and that literary and artistic values would have to be given power to negate the quality of "worthlessness" that deprived obscene expression of constitutional protection.

In *Roth* Brennan stressed that "all ideas having even the slightest redeeming social importance—unorthodox ideas, controversial ideas, even ideas hateful to the prevailing climate of opinion"—were entitled to "the full protection of the guarantees"; and that "the portrayal of sex, e.g., in art, literature and scientific works," was no reason to deny expression that protection. Liberal lawyers and judges would only have to locate "ideas having even the slightest social importance" in the literary works they acted to free. One of the best examples of this sort of creative application by lawyer and judge of Brennan's dicta in *Roth* to allegedly obscene literature occurred in the Chicago *Tropic of Cancer* case (described in Chapter 19), involving lawyer Elmer Gertz and Judge Samuel Epstein. But the first example seems to have been in the case that arose when the San Francisco police arrested publisher Lawrence Ferlinghetti and a City Lights Bookstore clerk named Shigeyoshi Murao for selling Allen Ginsberg's iconoclastic poem *Howl.*

PAUL BENDER: For years, people who believed in more freedom in this area than we had, doctrinally, looked back at what Brennan said in *Roth* and saw it as not a good opinion. It was "the Enemy." But they didn't realize that *Roth* was a wonderful opinion. It rejected *Hicklin.* It held that obscenity statutes must conform to a federal constitutional standard for defining "obscene." It laid the groundwork for narrowing the permissible scope of obscenity laws. It established that sex was okay, that an interest in it may be openly expressed. And so on. Brennan's opinion in *Roth* was taking a major step in the right direction. What *Roth* did was constitutionalize obscenity; it put it in a position constitutionally somewhat similar to that of libel in *Times* v. *Sullivan,* another Brennan doctrine.*

Brennan said sure, if it's obscene, you don't have to protect it. But you can't label anything you want obscene and, specifically, you can't say something's obscene just because it's inappropriate for children. Finally, just because something deals with sex does not make it obscene. As is so often

---

described in Chapters 19 and 22. Kalven's influence was mainly felt through the widespread citation of his thesis in the briefs filed in many *Tropic of Cancer* cases, including those filed in the Supreme Court.

*In *Times* v. *Sullivan,* decided the same term as the *Tropic of Cancer* case, Brennan's opinion for the Court held that libelous expression was protected by the guarantees of free speech and press unless the defendant's statements were known by him to be false or were made with a reckless disregard of whether they were true. The case is reported at 376 U.S. 254 (1964). In his opinion there, Brennan said that Americans have "a profound national commitment to the principle that debate on public issues should be uninhibited, robust, and wide open." Speaking of the Warren Court's work in the area of the First Amendment, Harry Kalven said those words "can for many reasons be taken as its trademark." Kalven, " 'Uninhibited, Robust, and Wide Open'—A Note on Free Speech and the Warren Court," 67 *Michigan Law Review* 289 (1968).

the case in these areas, you take a major step but you don't go all the way—you find that major step is untenable. You've got to go further or you've got to go back and there's no going back and so you end up going further. And that's what happened after *Roth*. . . .

Brennan will go down, I think, among the current members of the Court and the people who've been on the Court during the last fifteen, twenty years—and I'm going back to Frankfurter and Harlan even with that, and including Black and Douglas—Brennan will go down as one of the most creative, perhaps *the* most creative, person on the Court. His stuff will last . . . Frankfurter's is already gone.

17

I Was Getting Hard-ons

ALLEN GINSBERG was born in 1926 of Russian-born parents in Beth Israel Hospital in Newark, but he spent most of his boyhood in Paterson, New Jersey. The family apartment in Paterson was at 83 Fair Street, in a run-down Jewish neighborhood of shabby buildings, wood frame houses, warehouses, small workshops, and produce markets. Shortly after the Ginsbergs moved in, a Bell Telephone Company building was constructed on the corner, and this may have had something to do with an idea that soon obsessed Allen's mother, Naomi—that President Roosevelt had put wires in her head, and in the ceiling, in order to eavesdrop on her.

A family friend took Allen to his first day of kindergarten at P.S. 1 because Naomi was recovering from a nervous breakdown in the Bloomingdale Sanatorium, near Tarrytown, New York. The boy was so terrified at being left alone that he yelled and screamed; his father, Louis, a schoolteacher and poet, had to go and fetch him home.

Louis Ginsberg paid a heavy price in worry and anguish over Naomi's madness and had to borrow heavily from the teachers' credit union to pay for her treatments. He also had to care for his two sons, Eugene and Allen, and run the household in her absence. When Naomi—who liked to walk around their apartment nude—was in the mental hospital, Louis reorganized the family's sleeping arrangements: Allen's older brother, Eugene, took his parents' former bedroom in the back, and Allen slept with his father in the front bedroom, where Louis's big writing desk was. "Allen would lie in bed, dozing, while Louis graded English papers and wrote poems under a metal-shaded lamp." During the night the son liked to snuggle up against his father in bed.

ALLEN GINSBERG: I was getting hard-ons, rubbing up against his leg, just pressing close and holding on to him as I couldn't with my mother or brother. And we neither acknowledged it.

Later, when Ginsberg was in Reichian analysis, he tried to tell his father about his homosexuality:

ALLEN GINSBERG *(Don't Grow Old): A look startled his face, "You mean you like to take men's penises in your mouth?"*
Equally startled, "No, no," I lied. "That isn't what it means."

The analyst evidently took as a goal restoring Ginsberg to a proper heterosexual orientation—a procedure that Allen's friend and mentor William Burroughs was skeptical of.

WILLIAM BURROUGHS: Frankly I don't trust that kind of genital Reichian. . . . Feller say, when a man gets too straight he's just a god damned prick.

Louis Ginsberg was a Socialist who, as a boy, had accompanied his father to lectures by Eugene V. Debs, the Socialist party's perennial candidate for president of the United States. (Allen's older brother, Eugene, was named after Debs.) He was a contributor to Max Eastman's *New Masses* magazine, which had succeeded the old *Masses,* suppressed during World War I.* Allen's aunt was a member of a Communist party cell; his mother, also a Communist, took the family during summer vacation to a Communist party camp in upstate New York called Nicht-Gedeiget ("Don't Worry").

Ginsberg's boyhood was disturbed by political quarrels between his Socialist father and his Communist mother and tormented by the episodic madnesses and intermittent hospitalizations of Naomi.

NAOMI GINSBERG: Dear Allen, The wire is still on my head, and the sunshine is trying to help me. It has a wire department, but the wire that's outside my head the sun doesn't touch, it is connected with the inside of me. . . . If I were home I could be out in the sunshine. It doesn't cost anything. When are you getting a regular sweetheart?

Another letter to Allen's brother was turned over to Allen:

NAOMI GINSBERG: Dear Eugene, . . . God's informers came to my bed, and God, himself, I saw it in the sky—it was after Jan. 1, 1956. The sunshine

---

*John Reed, who wrote a firsthand account of the Bolshevik revolution called *Ten Days That Shook the World,* was a contributor to both magazines. The *New Masses,* unlike *The Masses,* kept clear of the Espionage Act that Congress had enacted during the war in order to suppress antiwar sentiment, labor strife, and the Socialist workers' movement. Reed was among the contributors to *The Masses* magazine who were prosecuted for writing pieces critical of the Wilson administration's policies during World War I. Kalven discusses the *Masses* mail suppression case in *A Worthy Tradition* (1987).

showed it too, a key on the side of the window for me to get out. . . . I'm begging you to take me out of here.

———

The young Ginsberg once spent eight months in a psychiatric ward himself after being arrested for riding in the back seat of a stolen car which contained stolen goods. A friend, Vickie Russell—"a six feet marijuana smoking red-head"—was sitting in the front seat, and another friend, Little Jack Melody—"a half-bald, elfin, twenty-six-year-old Sicilian-American with doe-like gentility and interest and sympathy with things and people around him"—was in the driver's seat. The car had crashed and rolled over while the police were chasing it.

Instead of fighting the charge head-on, Ginsberg took the advice of Professor Herbert Wechsler of the Columbia Law School and worked out a deal. An unstated condition of Ginsberg's release from the psychiatric ward was that he would try harder to conform to American norms when he got out: go straight, get a job, get married.

Years later, in San Francisco, Allen declared his homosexuality to his then girlfriend Sheila; this put a strain on the relationship. One night Sheila showed up at Montgomery Street, drunk, demanding to know why Allen had left her. "You can fuck *me* in the ass if that's what you want," she told Allen. "If *that*'s what it's all about"—and then broke Allen's fireplace.

In the fifties, the group of anarchic young men and women whom Allen Ginsberg drew together and who came to be called beats and beatniks were generally regarded as crazy by post–World War II America.* The beatnik cult mixed poetry, wine, song, bisexual lovemaking, and natural and chemical hallucinogenic substances with a political passion vaguely meant to tear down and reconstitute the moral and esthetic structure of the country; naturally they were subjected to police harassment, public ridicule, censorship, imprisonment, and the madhouse. Those who survived, however, planted the seeds—through their poetry, their novels, their songs, and the style of their lives—of the sexual and political revolutions that shook the country to its roots during the sixties. Ginsberg once told his psychiatrist that all he wanted from life was for it to be "a sweet humane surprise."

The most important woman writer among the beats was probably Diane di Prima, who founded the New York Poets Theatre and the Poets Press. She edited and published, with poet/playwright LeRoi Jones (Amiri Baraka), and later Alan Marlowe, a literary newsletter (later a journal) called *Floating Bear,* whose publication of Baraka and William Burroughs led to the editors' arrest by the FBI in 1961 for sending "obscenity" through the

———

*See Chapter 18 for Ginsberg's theory on the genesis of the terms "beat" and "beatnik." Barry Miles, the author of *Ginsberg: A Biography* (1989), says Kerouac and John Clellan Holmes coined the phrase "beat generation" in 1949, while Allen was in a psychiatric ward. In 1952, Holmes's book *Go* contained the line: "You know, everyone I know is kind of furtive, kind of beat . . . a sort of revolution of the soul." A few months later, on November 16, 1952, *The New York Times* published an article by Holmes called "This Is the Beat Generation."

mail.* (Di Prima later wrote a d.b. for Maurice Girodias, in which sex orgies take place involving her, Allen, and other beats.†)

Howl was written during the summer of 1955, while Samuel Roth was in the first year of the litigation that ended in his imprisonment. Ginsberg began *Howl* in a cheap furnished room at 1010 Montgomery Street in the North Beach section of San Francisco. North Beach was reminiscent of Greenwich Village in the twenties, or Paris's Left Bank. It had sidewalk cafés, Italian restaurants, jazz joints, gin mills, art galleries, the Co-Existence Bagel Shop, and the Spaghetti Factory. It was, Lawrence Ferlinghetti said, "the only place in America where you could get good wine." It was also, for a while anyway, the promised land "for all the beat, disaffected, whacked-out or simply restless young men and women who in former times would have settled in Greenwich Village or in South Chicago or in one of the old Bohemias abroad." Ginsberg first publicly read *Howl* before an audience of about seventy-five people‡ at the Six Gallery in San Francisco, a former automobile repair shop that had been converted to a funky art gallery.

ALLEN GINSBERG AND GREGORY CORSO: In the fall of 1955 a group of six unknown poets in San Francisco, in a moment of drunken enthusiasm, decided to defy the system of academic poetry, official reviews, New York publishing machinery, national sobriety and generally accepted standards of good taste, by giving a free reading of their poetry in a rundown second-rate experimental art gallery in the Negro section of San Francisco.§ They sent out a hundred postcards, put up signs in North Beach (Latin Quarter) bars, bought a lot of wine to get the audience drunk, and invited the well-known Frisco Anarchist resident poet Kenneth Rexroth to act as Master of Ceremonies.

JACK KEROUAC: I followed the whole gang of howling poets to the reading at Gallery Six that night, which was, among other important things, the night of the birth of the San Francisco Poetry Renaissance. Everyone was there. It was a mad night. And I was the one who got things jumping by going around collecting dimes and quarters from the rather stiff audience standing around in the gallery and coming back with three huge gallon jugs of California Burgundy and getting them all piffed.

MICHAEL McCLURE: The Six Gallery was a cooperative art gallery run by young artists who centered around the San Francisco Art Institute. They were fiery artists who had either studied with Clyfford Still and Mark Rothko or with the newly emerging figurative painters. Their works ranged

---

*Di Prima's description of the FBI raid on *Floating Bear* is in the endnotes to this chapter.
†Published in New York in 1968 as *Memoirs of a Beatnik.*
‡Ferlinghetti's count. Michael McClure said "a hundred and fifty enthusiastic people had come to hear us."
§The six: Allen Ginsberg, Philip Lamantia, Michael McClure, Philip Whalen, Gary Snyder, and "the most strange poet in the room," the novelist Jack Kerouac. Not present were Gregory Corso and Peter Orlovsky, among other beat poets.

from huge drip and slash to minute precision smudges turning into faces. Earlier in the year poet Robert Duncan had given a staged reading of his play *Faust Foutu* (Faust Fucked) at the Six Gallery and, with the audacious purity of an anarchist poet, he had stripped off his clothes at the end of the play. . . .

Allen began in a small and intensely lucid voice. At some point Jack Kerouac began shouting "Go" in cadence as Allen read it. In all of our memories no one had been so outspoken in poetry before—we had gone beyond a point of no return. . . .

Ginsberg read on to the end of the poem, which left us standing in wonder, or cheering and wondering, but knowing at the deepest level that a barrier had been broken, that a human voice and body had been hurled against the harsh wall of America and its supporting armies and navies and academies and institutions and ownership systems and power support bases.

NEELI CHERKOVSKI: [T]he audience reaction was amazing. They seemed to know that they had heard a great poem, demonstrating that fact by their applause.

JOHN TYTELL: The poem was a crucible of cultural change. Except for the response to Dylan Thomas' readings in America, never before had a modern audience reacted so passionately, or identified so completely with a poet's message.

ALLEN GINSBERG *(Howl): I saw the best minds of my generation destroyed by madness, starving hysterical naked, / dragging themselves through the negro streets at dawn looking for an angry fix.* . . .

———

This is Naomi Ginsberg's last letter, written on the evening she died. Allen had sent her a dittoed copy of *Howl.*

NAOMI GINSBERG: Dear Allen, I hope this reaches you. I sent one before which, maybe, they didn't send out! . . .

Congratulations on your birthday! Received your poetry. I'd like to send it to Louis for criticism.* Now what does he think of it! It seemed to me your wording was a little too hard. . . .

I hope you behave well. Don't go in for too much drink and other things that are not good for you. . . .

I do hope you can get a good job so you can get a girl to get married. Eugene's wife is beautiful.

As for myself, I still have the wire on my head. The doctors know about it. They are cutting the flesh and bone. They are giving me teethache. I do wish you were back east so I could see you. . . . I wish I were out of here and home at the time you were young; then I would be young. I'm in the prime of life now—Did you read about the two men who died at 139

———

*Allen had already sent his father a copy of the poem.

& 149 yrs of age. I wonder how they lived. I'm looking for a good time.

I hope you are not taking drugs as suggested by your poetry. That would hurt me. Don't go in for ridiculous things. With love and good news . . .

ALLEN GINSBERG *(Howl): angelheaded hipsters burning for the ancient heavenly connection to the starry dynamo in the machinery of night, / who poverty and tatters and hollow-eyed and high sat up smoking in the supernatural darkness of cold-water flats floating across the tops of cities contemplating jazz, / who bared their brains to Heaven under the El and saw Mohammedan angels staggering on tenement roofs illuminated, / who passed through universities with radiant cool eyes hallucinating Arkansas and Blake-light tragedy among the scholars of war, / who were expelled from the academies for crazy & publishing obscene odes on the windows of the skull . . .*

LOUIS GINSBERG: Dear Allen, I am gratified about your new ms. It's a wild, rhapsodic, explosive outpouring with good figures of speech flashing by in its volcanic rushing. It's a hot geyser of emotion suddenly released in wild abandon from subterranean depths of your being. . . . I still insist, however, there is no need for dirty, ugly, words, as they will entangle you unnecessarily in trouble. Try to cut them out. . . . Love . . .

ALLEN GINSBERG *(Howl): Who let themselves be fucked in the ass by saintly motorcyclists, / and screamed with joy, / who blew and were blown by those human seraphim, the sailors, caresses of Atlantic and Caribbean love.*

LIONEL TRILLING: Dear Allen, I'm afraid I have to tell you that I don't like the poems at all. . . . But perhaps you will believe that I am being sincere when I say they are dull. . . . Sincerely yours. . . .

———

Lawrence Ferlinghetti was at the Six Gallery that night. When it was over, the publisher of City Lights Books went home and sent Ginsberg a telegram which consciously paralleled the famous one that Ralph Waldo Emerson had sent to Walt Whitman, upon receiving a copy of the 1855 edition of *Leaves of Grass.** Said Ferlinghetti: "I greet you at

———

*Whitman was viewed by Ginsberg and Henry Miller, among other iconoclastic American poets and novelists, as the Master. First published in 1855, with type set by Whitman himself, *Leaves of Grass* did not carry its author's, publisher's, or printer's name on the title page, and the first bookseller who received the book ordered it out of his shop as "disorderly flesh and sensual"—too much for his trade. Despite a letter from Emerson printed in *The New York Times,* hailing the book as "the most extraordinary piece of wit and wisdom that America has yet contributed," publishers, printers, booksellers, and librarians were loath to handle it, and the Library Company in Philadelphia is the only library in America on record as having bought a copy after it was published. After the *New York Tribune* called the book a "slopbucket," the New England Society for the Suppression of Vice persuaded the district attorney to threaten to prosecute publisher James Osgood for including in the book certain portions that Whitman had refused to delete. Osgood turned the plates over to Whitman, who sold them to the Philadelphia publisher Rees, Walsh & Company; their publication of the book netted Whitman $1,300. John Tebbel, *A History of Book Publishing in the United States* 1 (1972), 562; 2 (1975), 268–69, 421. Evelyn Geller, *Forbidden Books in American Public Libraries, 1876–1939* (1984), 38.

the beginning of a great career." And then: "When do I get the manuscript?"

LAWRENCE FERLINGHETTI: The first edition of *Howl,* Number Four in the
Pocket Poet Series, was printed in England by Villiers, passed through
customs without incident, and was published at the City Lights Bookstore
here in the fall of 1956. Part of a second printing was stopped by customs
on March 25, 1957.

———

The collector of customs at San Francisco was named Chester MacPhee;
he confiscated 520 copies of *Howl* coming from England because: "The
words and the sense of the writing is obscene. . . . You wouldn't want your
children to come across it."

Under the customs law, no censorship by seizure of incoming literature
could become final until the local U.S. attorney's office asked a federal
judge for permission to destroy it. When the American Civil Liberties
Union notified MacPhee that it was planning to defend *Howl*—because it
did not consider the poem obscene—the U.S. attorney at San Francisco
decided not to proceed against the book, and MacPhee had to release all
520 copies.

LAWRENCE FERLINGHETTI: I had submitted the ms. of *Howl* to the ACLU
before sending it to the printer in England to see if they would defend us
if the book was busted, and a good thing too, since without the ACLU,
City Lights would no doubt have gone broke and out of business. We were
barely breaking even those days, and living on very little, and the expense
of a court trial would have been disastrous.

ALLEN GINSBERG AND GREGORY CORSO: Ferlinghetti is the most advanced
publisher in America in that he published "suspect" literature, literature
usually rejected by other publishing houses, because of their wild neo-bop
prosody, non-commercial value, extreme expression of soul, and the pure
adventure of publishing it.

———

Ferlinghetti was (and still is) also a poet, and the first work issued by him
under the City Lights imprint for the Pocket Poet Series—each volume
retailed at seventy-five cents—was his own *Pictures of the Gone World.* The
second was Kenneth Rexroth's *Thirty Spanish Poems of Love and Exile.* The
third was Kenneth Patchen's *Poems of Humor and Protest.* The fourth was
Allen Ginsberg's *Howl.*

LAWRENCE FERLINGHETTI: Then the [San Francisco] police took over and
arrested us,* Captain William Hanrahan of the juvenile department . . .
reporting that the books were not fit for children to read. Thus during the
first week in June I found myself being booked and fingerprinted in San

———

*Shigeyoshi Murao, a clerk in the City Lights bookstore, was arrested along with Ferlin-
ghetti.

Francisco's Hall of Justice. . . . As one paper reported: "The Cops Don't Allow No Renaissance Here."

SHIGEYOSHI MURAO: Imagine being arrested for selling poetry! Two police officers from the juvenile squad arrested me. Obscenity was under their purview as a way of protecting the children. . . . They never even hand-cuffed me. I was taken by patrol car to the Hall of Justice, three blocks from the store. In the basement I was fingerprinted, posed for mug shots and locked in the drunk tank. The cell smelled of piss.

—

The ACLU posted bail for Ferlinghetti and Murao and provided talented lawyers, who represented the defendants without fee; they were Jake ("Never Plead Guilty") Ehrlich, a well-known criminal lawyer, and Lawrence Speiser and Albert Bendich of the staff of the ACLU.* Letters and statements in support of *Howl* were collected from poets Henry Rago, Kenneth Patchen, and Robert Duncan, and from New York publishers Barney Rosset of Grove Press and James Laughlin of New Directions. While the trial was taking place, Rosset republished *Howl* in his literary magazine *Evergreen Review* in New York, without stirring up the police.† He also brought out a "San Francisco Renaissance" issue there. These marked the real beginnings of Rosset's anti-censorship publishing crusade.‡

City Lights Books was the first all-paperback bookstore in the United States (Ferlinghetti had been inspired by bookstores of this kind in France). It carried all the literary quarterlies and all the soft-cover prestige books of the major publishers, as well as foreign imprints and periodicals. The bookstore became a sort of intellectual center of North Beach.

The trial of *Howl* took place while Ginsberg was in Tangier with Jack Kerouac, helping his mentor and erstwhile lover William Burroughs finish and type his "unpublishable" novel *Naked Lunch,* which John Tytell has described as "a hallucinatory vision of the very worst expectations of the McCarthy era—a police state where the love and community are stripped away and defiled."§ It contains some of the most horrendous sex scenes ever

---

*Later, Bendich would successfully defend the social satirist Lenny Bruce against the charge that a performance by him at San Francisco's Jazz Workshop was obscene. Described below in Chapter 24.

†*Evergreen Review* later became a large, slick-covered illustrated newsstand literary magazine dispensing kinky sex and "New Left" politics. When it ran a Che Guevara cover, Grove's offices were bombed (see Chapter 19). When it ran a chapter taken from *Points of Rebellion* by Supreme Court Justice William O. Douglas, Douglas received impeachment threats from Congressman Gerald Ford and disqualified himself from a case involving the censorship of the film *I Am Curious—Yellow,* then being distributed by Grove. As a result Grove lost the case, and probably a million or so dollars in box office receipts. I wrote and filed the appeal and argued the case for Grove in the Supreme Court. See de Grazia and Newman, *Banned Films* (1982), 121–29. An analogous situation arose in 1948 with respect to Edmund Wilson's *Memoirs of Hecate County* when Justice Felix Frankfurter disqualified himself from the case because he was Wilson's friend; as a result, Wilson's novel was suppressed throughout the country for ten years. See Chapter 12 above.

‡See Chapters 19 and 20 below.

§John Tytell, *Naked Angels: The Lives and Literature of the Beat Generation* (1976), 12.

to appear in an American novel, reminiscent of de Sade's and Bataille's most enthusiastic efforts. From Tangier, Ginsberg wrote Ferlinghetti about the work that his friends were doing and sent him reams of their manuscripts; Ferlinghetti turned them down.

At *Howl*'s trial nine literary experts testified: Mark Schorer, Leo Lowenthal, Walter Van Tilburg Clark, Herbert Blau, Arthur Foff, Mark Linenthal, Kenneth Rexroth, Vincent McHugh, and Luther Nichols. They spoke about the literary merit of Ginsberg's poem but, more significantly, about its "social importance." *Howl* was not "art for art's sake" but "social criticism"—a literary work that hurled *ideological* accusation after accusation against American society.

SHIGEYOSHI MURAO: For the trial I wore a cheap, light blue summer suit with a white buttoned shirt and a black knit tie. In those days you had to dress properly or you were held in contempt of court. Jake Ehrlich, our famous criminal lawyer, never said a word to me during the trial, except to make sure that I permitted the press to take pictures of me. After a few sessions, I was dismissed from the case. Section B of the Penal code states, ". . . did knowingly sell . . ." The prosecutors could not prove that I had read the book.

—

The prosecutor was an assistant district attorney named Ralph McIntosh, who had a reputation of sorts: earlier targets of his lust to smash smut included porn movies, nudist magazines, and Howard Hughes's notorious Jane Russell movie *The Outlaw*.* But *Howl* carried him beyond his depth. He could not understand the poem, except for the dirty words,† and neither Mark Schorer, the distinguished literary critic and the defense's main witness, nor Judge Clayton W. Horn, who tried the case sans jury, would help him out:

RALPH McINTOSH: I presume you understand the whole thing, is that right?
MARK SCHORER: I hope so. It's not always easy to know that one understands exactly what a contemporary poet is saying. . . .
RALPH McINTOSH: Do you understand what *"angelheaded hipsters burning for*

---

*On *The Outlaw*, see de Grazia and Newman, *Banned Films: Movies, Censors and the First Amendment* (1982), 65–67 and 225–27.

†A similar situation arose in 1968 during the successful appeal I took on behalf of Grove Press from a federal jury's decision that the Swedish film *I Am Curious—Yellow* was obscene. When a majority of the appellate court panel that reviewed the case and saw the movie voted to free the film because its "ideas [had] social importance," the dissenting chief judge complained that he had got nothing from his viewing of the film apart from "the sexual scenes." "All the rest," he said, "was to [this] captive onlooker . . . continuous and unrelieved boredom"; he found it "almost impossible to remember anything about it." "Its only interest to [this] viewer arises from the uncertainty of the method of mutual sexual gratification in which hero and heroine will next indulge." See the full texts of the majority and dissenting opinions in de Grazia, *Censorship Landmarks* (1969), 637–42. The film *I Am Curious—Yellow* and some of its censorship troubles in the United States (it became embroiled in more than a score of state and local cases) are described in de Grazia and Newman, *Banned Films* (1982).

the ancient heavenly connection to the starry dynamo in the machinery of night" means?*

MARK SCHORER: Sir, you can't translate poetry into prose. That's why it's poetry.

RALPH McINTOSH: In other words, you don't have to understand the words.

MARK SCHORER: You don't understand the individual words taken out of their context. You can no more translate it back into logical prose English than you can say what a surrealistic painting means in words because it's *not* prose. . . . I can't possibly translate, nor, I am sure, can anyone in this room translate the opening part of this poem into rational prose.

RALPH McINTOSH: That's just what I wanted to find out.

———

Prosecutor McIntosh then took up and read aloud passages from *Howl*—the ones containing "dirty" words and sexual images—for the edification of Judge Horn:

ALLEN GINSBERG *(Howl): who copulated ecstatic and insatiate with a bottle of beer a sweet/heart a package of cigarettes a candle and fell off the bed,/and continued along the floor and down the hall and ended/fainting on the wall with a vision of ultimate cunt and come/eluding the last gyzym of consciousness,*

who sweetened the snatches of a million girls trembling in the sunset, and were red-eyed in the morning but prepared to sweeten the snatches of the sunrise,/ flashing buttocks under barns and naked in the lake . . .

———

When Schorer persistently declined to give McIntosh a rational explanation of such lines, the prosecutor turned to Judge Clayton W. Horn, complaining:

RALPH McINTOSH: Your Honor, frankly I have only got a batch of law degrees. I don't know anything about literature. But I would like to find out what this is all about. It's like this modern painting nowadays, surrealism or whatever they call it, where they have a monkey come in and do some finger painting.

———

Judge Horn declined to require Schorer to enlighten the prosecutor. And when McIntosh tried next to get the witness to concede that some of the obscene terms Ginsberg used could "have been worded some other way," Horn stopped him, saying, "it is obvious that the author could have used another term" but that was "up to the author" to decide. This sensible judge was not inclined to allow policemen or prosecutors to interfere with the poet's artistic freedom, nor to allow the witness to be browbeaten; Other defense witnesses also were able to score points in *Howl*'s, and its author's, favor.

———

*Allen Ginsberg has annotated this line as follows: " 'starry dynamo' and 'machinery of night' are derived from Dylan Thomas' mixture of Nature and Machinery in 'The force that through the green fuse drives the flower/Drives my green age . . .' " Allen Ginsberg, *Howl: Original Draft Facsimile* (1986), 124.

LUTHER NICHOLS: The words he has used are valid and necessary if he's to be honest with his purpose. . . .

WALTER VAN TILBURG CLARK: They seem to me, all of the poems in this volume, to be the work of a thoroughly honest poet, who is also a highly competent technician. . . .

KENNETH REXROTH: Its merit is extraordinarily high. It is probably the most remarkable single poem published by a young man since the second war.

———

Two rebuttal witnesses took the stand for the People of the State of California. One, an assistant professor of English at the (Catholic) University of San Francisco, David Kirk, said he thought *Howl* was a "poem dedicated to a long-dead movement called Dadaism"; the other, Gail Potter—who said she had taught at a business college, a church school for girls, and the College of Southern Florida at Lakeland—said that in reading *Howl* she felt as if she were "going through the gutter." The prosecutor wound up his side of the case by asking Judge Horn to consider whether he "would like to see this sort of poetry printed in your local newspaper" or "read to you over the radio as a diet."

RALPH McINTOSH: In other words, Your Honor, how far are we going to license the use of filthy, vulgar, obscene, and disgusting language? How far can we go?

———

Judge Horn was prepared to go as far, apparently, as Justice William J. Brennan's opinion in *Roth,* which had been handed down only four months earlier, would take him. Said Horn, citing Brennan: "[U]nless the book is entirely lacking in 'social importance' it cannot be held 'obscene.' " Horn had read *Howl,* listened to the expert witnesses, striven to understand what Ginsberg was trying to communicate, and, finally, appreciated the poem as a howl of social protest and dissent. He did not believe that Ginsberg's poem was lacking in ideas of social importance and so could not find it obscene.

JUDGE CLAYTON W. HORN: The first part of *Howl* presents a picture of a nightmare world, the second part is an indictment of those elements in modern society destructive of the best qualities of human nature; such elements are predominantly identified as materialism, conformity, and mechanization leading toward war. The third part presents a picture of an individual who is a specific representation of what the author conceives as a general condition. . . . "Footnote to *Howl*" seems to be a declamation that everything in the world is holy, including parts of the body by name. It ends in a plea for holy living.

———

Judge Horn regularly taught Bible class in Sunday school; perhaps he was reached by Allen Ginsberg's messianism. He found the poem to contain "unorthodox and controversial ideas," which, if expressed at times through the use of "coarse and vulgar" words, were nevertheless meant to be protected by the constitutional freedoms of speech and press. The judge believed the First Amendment had been adopted to free "ideas"—in Brennan's words, "unorthodox ideas, controversial ideas, even ideas hateful to the prevailing climate of opinion"—and he realized that Ginsberg's *Howl* was an outpouring of such ideas. The obscene nature of the words and images used by the poet to convey those ideas did not destroy the entitlement of the ideas to constitutional protection.

JUDGE CLAYTON W. HORN: The author of *Howl* has used those words because he believed that his portrayal required them as being in character. The People [of the State of California, represented by their attorney] state that it is not necessary to use such words and that others would be more palatable to good taste. The answer is that life is not encased in one formula whereby everyone acts the same or conforms to a particular pattern. No two persons think alike; we were all made from the same mold but in different patterns. Would there be any freedom of press or speech if one must reduce his vocabulary to vapid innocuous euphemisms? An author should be real in treating his subject and be allowed to express his thoughts and ideas in his own words.

———

The decision freeing *Howl* was the first of a group of important lower court decisions that interpreted and cited Justice Brennan's opinion in *Roth* as opening the way to constitutional freedom for literary and artistic expression branded "obscene." Other judges motivated to rescue American literary and artistic values from police and pressure group censorship soon took a similar view. It was fortuitous in the battle for literary freedom that a few of the obscenity cases coming on the heels of *Roth* involved literary works that obviously communicated ideas; this enabled conscientious judges to amplify Brennan's language in *Roth* in the cause of freeing literature.

In Chicago, two years later, Federal District Judge Julius Hoffman, who later would be the judge at the "Chicago Seven" trial, interpreted *Roth* in the same way, and held that ten episodes from William Burroughs's *Naked Lunch* and an extract from a work by Jack Kerouac—which University of Chicago students published in a literary journal they called *Big Table* 1—were also entitled to be free because of their communication of ideas.*

That same year—1959—in New York, Barney Rosset published, under his Grove Press imprint, the first unexpurgated edition of D. H. Lawrence's thirty-year-old contraband novel, *Lady Chatterley's Lover,* in an inexpensive paperback edition. The novel, Lawrence's last, had been forbidden in the States (as in England) ever since Lawrence and his printer friend Pino Orioli had published it privately in Italy not long before Lawrence died. Like the City Lights edition of Ginsberg's *Howl,* which broke with literary tradition by making poetic use of such words as "fuck," "cock," "ass," "cunt,"

———

*The events are described in Chapter 18.

"gyzym," and "asshole," and by alluding poetically and explicitly to homo-erotic acts, the Grove paperback edition of Lawrence's *Lady C.* presented the average American with literature that used the words "fuck" and "shit" in their literal senses, not merely as curses or expletives. Lawrence's final novel also contained a scene in which a man's penis was "addressed" raptur-ously by a woman. Lawrence knew what he was doing: "I had no illusions," he wrote in 1930, "that any reputable English or American publisher would dare to publish the book. It was much too shocking—verbally—for any publisher. Said shit! and fuck! in so many syllables."*

The only legal basis that Rosset had for publishing *Lady C.* unexpurgated was Brennan's opinion in *Roth.* His lawyer in the *Lady Chatterley's Lover* case, Charles Rembar, said he had designed the trial strategy to get the maximum benefit out of Brennan's language in *Roth;* as Rembar put it, "You can't have obscenity when you have a work that has ideas of even the slightest social importance."†

By the time the legal contest over the Grove edition of *Lady C.* was over, however, another encouraging decision had been handed down by the Supreme Court, in April 1959, in a motion picture licensing case that, coincidentally, also involved *Lady C.* There the Supreme Court held that a refusal by the state of New York's board of motion picture censors to grant a license to exhibit a French film adaptation of Lawrence's novel—because it considered the film sexually "immoral"—violated the First Amendment. Justice Potter Stewart, a newcomer, spoke for the Court in saying: "What New York has done is to prevent the exhibition of a motion picture because that picture advocates an idea—that adultery under certain circumstances may be proper behavior." But, Stewart continued, the First Amendment guarantee "protects advocacy of the opinion that adultery may sometimes be proper, no less than advocacy of socialism or the single tax."‡

This case was the first in which the high court squarely held that freedom of expression precluded a government agency from banning the advocacy of *immoral* ideas;§ the decision was of marginal utility to the defense of Grove's publication of *Lady Chatterley's Lover* because it would not control the outcome of a civil or criminal *obscenity* proceeding seeking to suppress the Lawrence book, mainly because "immorality," even sexual "immoral-ity," was legally not the same as "obscenity." Nevertheless, the decision was

---

*See Chapter 5.

†Charles Rembar, *The End of Obscenity* (1968), 129.

‡This case, *Kingsley International Pictures* v. *Regents,* was an early intimation by the justices known collectively as the Warren Court that they disagreed with the Vinson Court's 1951 decision *Dennis* v. *United States* that the First Amendment did not protect the country's Communist party leaders from being imprisoned for conspiring to *teach and advocate* the necessity and desirability of overthrowing the government by force. Kalven criticizes the *Dennis* decision in *A Worthy Tradition,* Chapter 14. Stewart's opinion in *Kingsley* suggests that the mere advocacy of, as distinguished from incitement to, overthrow is constitutionally protected expression.

§For a further discussion of the constitutional implications of the Court's actions with respect to movie censorship, see the endnotes for this chapter.

additional evidence that the applicability of the First Amendment's speech and press guarantees to nonpolitical expression communicated by imaginative cultural forms was being increasingly recognized by the Warren Court; and so it was invigorating to American lawyers, judges, book publishers, and motion picture distributors concerned to see government censorship of sexually immodest literary and artistic works stopped. Conservative Court-watchers, on the other hand, were noticeably unnerved by the *Kingsley Pictures* holding and the role played in its formulation by the supposed conservative or centrist Justice Potter Stewart.*

Given three decades of understandable reluctance on the part of reputable American publishers to bring out *Lady C.,* it must have been surprising when Grove's publication of the book did not provoke a criminal prosecution. When, however, the U.S. Post Office Department made its attempt to ban Grove's use of the mails to transport the book, the effort was so resoundingly defeated in court that it proved to be the last time that the Post Office would make any such administrative attempt to censor literature having even the slightest social importance†—provided that by "literature" is meant books and journals that do not contain pictures. Criminal prosecutions of publishers using the mails to promote and distribute illustrated literature would continue.‡

The trial of *Lady C.* that was instigated by the Post Office came before New York federal district judge Frederick van Pelt Bryan in 1959; it and the proceedings on appeal in the case were fully described by Charles Rembar (Grove Press's lawyer in the case) in *The End of Obscenity,* published in 1968. Malcolm Cowley and Alfred Kazin testified to the novel's literary values and Judge Bryan relied on *Roth* to declare the book not obscene because of its literary merit. Bryan also ruled that even if Lawrence's words tended to "arouse shameful, morbid and lustful sexual desires in the average reader"—which was (more or less) the definition of the "obscene" approved by the Supreme Court in *Roth*—"they are an integral, and to the author a

---

*Stewart became an increasingly "permissive" participant in the Warren Court's movement to free sexual expression from censorship, as described in Chapter 26.

†Prior to the Supreme Court's decision in *Roth,* I succeeded in freeing an illustrated rare-edition copy of Aristophanes' *Lysistrata* from the postal police by filing a suit asking a federal court in Washington to order the postmaster general to return the book, and to declare unconstitutional the postal obscenity law under which the book had been seized (and *Roth,* later, would be convicted). The postmaster general mooted the case by returning the book forthwith, before the court had time to act. The current (1990) effort within Congress to impose "standards" on the artistic projects supported by the National Endowment for the Arts should be seen for what it is: an attempt to make the NEA into an administrative censor of American artists who seek NEA support for their work, comparable to the censorship of literature administratively exercised for many years by the Post Office Department.

‡During the next decade the Justice Department would successfully launch two major censorship prosecutions agains the publishers of photo-illustrated literature, namely the hardbound literary magazine *Eros,* published by Ralph Ginzburg, and a photo-illustrated edition of a presidential commission's report on obscenity and pornography, published by William Hamling. Both cases would be fiercely fought by the publishers up to the Supreme Court, only to be lost. The events concerning Ginzburg are described below in Chapters 23 and 26, and concerning Hamling's "Illustrated Report," at Chapter 28.

necessary, part of theme, plot and character." This resembled the reasoning that Judges Horn and Hoffman had used in freeing *Howl* and *Big Table* 1.

On appeal, *Lady C.*'s freedom from Post Office censorship was affirmed by the same judge who, speaking for the same court, had reached a very different decision in Sam Roth's case. Speaking through Judge Charles Clark, the Court saluted Judge Bryan's assertion of Lawrence's literary right to use "smutty" words of his choosing—much as Judge Horn had paid his respects to Ginsberg's poetic right to use "coarse and vulgar" words, and as Judge Hoffman had justified Burroughs's and Kerouac's foul language:

JUDGE CHARLES CLARK: Obviously a writer can employ various means to achieve the effect he has in mind, and so probably Lawrence could have omitted some of the passages found "smutty" by the Postmaster General and yet have produced an effective work of literature. But clearly it would not have been the book he planned, because for what he had in mind his selection was most effective.

———

Also, significantly, Judge Clark read Lawrence's book as a "polemic against those things which Lawrence hated: the crass industrialization of the English Midlands, the British caste system and inhibited sex relations between man and woman." To him it was perfectly clear that in *Lady Chatterley's Lover* Lawrence (and by extension his American publisher, Grove Press) was earnestly seeking to communicate "ideas" of the sort that Brennan, in *Roth*, had insisted the First Amendment was intended to protect from government restraint.

However, for a few more years at least, the doors to constitutional protection were still closed to the publishers of so-called trashy literature which seemed to have the single-minded purpose of making money out of the interest many Americans have in books that sexually excite them; these doors stayed closed until 1964. For example, in nine cases arising in Illinois, New York, California, Connecticut, and Michigan, pulp novels bearing such titles as *Gang Girls, Love Princess, Never Enough, I Am a Lesbian,* and *Sex Life of a Cop* were judicially suppressed as obscene.* Most of the books were of a formula type that would soon be spoken of as soft-core pornography; they made little or no pretense to "even the slightest literary importance" of the sort that Brennan had suggested should be a constitutionally saving grace.

According to Felice Flannery Lewis, the publishers of novels of this kind were "small, clandestine outfits"; the books consisted "almost entirely of repeated sexual or sadistic episodes"; they "were not enduring or well known, even in their special field."† Most of the lawyers who defended them seem to have made only perfunctory claims, if any, that they possessed

---

*A few such books, including *Sex Life of a Cop,* however, were ultimately freed by the Supreme Court through the process called *Redrupping,* described in some detail in Chapter 26.

†*Literature, Obscenity and Law* (1976), 191.

any social value. The convictions of these publishers seemed to bear out the wishful thinking of conservatives that *Roth* pointed toward "a victory for the cause of decency" and had not opened any new road to literary freedom.

That was incorrect: Brennan meant his doctrine to extend protection to literature, not "trash";* and that is the way it worked out, at first. However, a few years later Brennan would find his doctrine used to constitutionally protect trashy literature as well. For a while—until its revision by the Burger Court in 1973, when it reemerged as the principal mechanism used by the Court to draw the line between protected and unprotected sexually oriented expression—the Brennan doctrine was only one of several doctrinal approaches to sexually oriented literature used by the freedom-favoring members of the activist Warren Court to free everything from *Tropic of Cancer* to *Sex Life of a Cop,* and well beyond.

---

*Or, as Kalven phrased it, "worthless" literary products. See *1960 Supreme Court Review* (1960) 1, 13. Kalven himself stopped short of recognizing any "worth" in hard-core pornography and even indicated that his recommended resolution to the "intractable" problem of obscenity could be relied upon to protect only "any serious, complex piece of writing or art, regardless of the unconventionality of its candor" ("The Metaphysics of the Law of Obscenity"). I suppose this would save *Lady Chatterley's Lover, Ulysses, Howl, Lolita,* and *Naked Lunch,* but perhaps not *Fanny Hill* or *Candy* or *The Story of O.*

18

El Hombre
Invisible

PAUL CARROLL:[*] Who are you, living in Tangier, knowing so much about how we talk and feel in the states?

WILLIAM S. BURROUGHS: Name Wm Seward Burroughs III Sole male heir of Burroughs Machine Corp St Louis Mo Harvard Phi Beta Kappa 37 with postgraduate work in anthropology and psychology Columbia For the past 15 yrs have been acknowledged drug addict I am homosexual Who are you???

———

William Seward Burroughs III was born in a brick townhouse in St. Louis in 1914, the year World War I broke out in Europe. His grandfather, William Seward Burroughs, had invented the adding machine; Burroughs's parents were well-off. His father had a mordant sense of humor; this was his greatest gift to his son. His mother, who was descended from General Robert E. Lee, felt a Victorian abhorrence for anything connected with bodily functions. Burroughs suffered from nightmares as a boy; his earliest memories are colored by the fear that his bad dreams would continue after he woke up. He remembers hearing a maid say that smoking opium brought sweet dreams,[†] and thinking to himself: I will smoke opium when I grow up.

Burroughs's first love was a boy named Kells Elvins. Though the relationship was never sexual, Kells would sometimes playfully take Billy on his lap

———

[*]Poet; Professor of Creative Writing, University of Illinois (Chicago Circle); former editor of the *Chicago Review*.

[†]A childhood nurse and her boyfriend seem to have sexually abused the boy. See Ted Morgan, *Literary Outlaw: The Life and Times of William S. Burroughs* (1988), 30–31.

and "strum him like a guitar"; this gave Billy a hard-on. Burroughs claims that even then he knew he was homosexual—in fact, he was sure he was born that way—and this caused him much loneliness, worry, and misery during his youth. He was a senior at Harvard before he had sex with a man or a woman. (It was at Harvard, too, that he found out that a baby was not born through its mother's navel.)

Burroughs had heterosexual proclivities as well, but he considered them less worthy than his penchant for boys. He once tried to disabuse Allen Ginsberg of the idea that Ginsberg was a "neurotic heter with strong queer leanings." The poet, who at the time was embarked on an affair with a woman, Helen Parker, was given the following lecture by his deep friend, in a letter:

WILLIAM S. BURROUGHS: For the Chris sake do you actually think that laying a woman makes some one heter? I have been laying women for the past 15 years and haven't heard any complaints from the women either. . . .* What does that prove except I was hard up at the time. Laying a woman so far as I'm concerned is O.K. if I can't score for a boy.

—

As a young man Burroughs read Anatole France and the poems of Baudelaire; also de Maupassant, Rémy de Gourmont, Gide, and Oscar Wilde's *Picture of Dorian Gray.* He grew obsessively interested in guns, gangsters, and crime; perhaps it was this interest that drew him to Chicago, where he worked variously as an exterminator, a bartender, and a private eye. He married, became a heroin addict and an active pedophile, and began to write the mordantly comical prose that attracted censors as sugar attracts flies.

In October 1958, a *Chicago Daily News* critic-columnist named Jack Mabley was attracted by some goings-on at the University of Chicago:

JACK MABLEY: Do you ever wonder what happens to little boys who scratch dirty words on railroad underpasses? They go to college and scrawl obscenities in the college literary magazines. . . . A magazine published by the University of Chicago is distributing one of the foulest collections of printed filth I've seen publicly circulated. I'm not naming the magazine because I don't want to be responsible for its selling out.

—

Mabley did not name the contributors to the magazine either, for fear this would advance their careers. The magazine was the *Chicago Review.* It was one of the best of the country's student-run literary magazines. Its poetry editor was Paul Carroll.

PAUL CARROLL: I was poetry editor of the *Chicago Review* when it was suppressed. I became poetry editor when Irving Rosenthal, who was ed-

---

*Burroughs's wife, Joan Vollmer (soon to be killed accidentally by her husband), annotated this assertion with the word "Correct!"

itor, asked me if I wanted to be poetry editor. I said, yes, if I could put in only good poetry. Irving said, no, you must put in only excellent poetry. . . .

The last issue we put out was the Autumn '58 issue. It was the Winter '58 number that was suppressed.

———

The Autumn 1958 issue of the *Chicago Review* contained poetry by Brother Antoninus, Joel Oppenheimer, John Logan, and Paul Carroll. It contained an article by sociologist David Riesman,* "The College Student in an Age of Organization." It had fiction by Philip Whalen, John Logan, and James Brunot. More important, it contained episodes from William S. Burroughs's novel-in-progress, *Naked Lunch,* and two letters to Paul Carroll from Allen Ginsberg, the beatnik poet. These were the graffiti that attracted Jack Mabley's attention.

JACK MABLEY: The "beat" generation has quite a representation on the Midway.

I haven't had much personal contact with those people but I get the impression they are young, intellectual, need baths, and have extreme contempt for the less fortunate than themselves, which is almost everybody. . . .

I don't recommend anyone buying [the magazine] out of curiosity because the writing is obscure to the unbeat generation and the purple prose is precisely what you can see chiseled on washroom walls. . . . The obscenity is put into their writing to attract attention. It is an assertion of their sense of bravado: "Oh boy, look what I'm doing" just like the little kids chalking a four-letter verb on the Oak Street underpass. . . .

If the obscenity in the magazine were read in a public performance as a literary presentation, the performers would be arrested and charged with indecency.

Yet in print, stamped this is literary, they get away with it.†

———

Mabley was disturbed by what he saw as the increasing legal tolerance of "obscenity" in Chicago. He said: "I abhorred public circulation of vulgarity and coarseness. I thought it was evidence of the deterioration of American society. I thought it was dangerous. . . . I didn't put the blame on the juveniles who wrote and edited this stuff because they were immature and irresponsible. But the University of Chicago published the magazine." Mabley ended his *Daily News* piece by saying the university's trustees

---

*Author of *The Lonely Crowd* (1969).

†Historically, the reverse is true. Allen Ginsberg was never arrested for reading *Howl* aloud in coffee shops, auditoriums, and halls; but a clerk in the City Lights Bookstore in San Francisco was arrested for selling *Howl,* published by Lawrence Ferlinghetti's City Lights Books. See Chapter 17 above. On the other hand, in 1989 Pacifica Radio canceled a scheduled reading by Ginsberg of *Howl* over its radio stations because of fear that the FCC might revoke its stations' licenses for broadcasting "indecent" language.

"should take a long hard look at what was being circulated under the University's sponsorship."*

Burroughs and Allen Ginsberg had first met in New York in 1943, when Ginsberg was seventeen and was going to Columbia on a YMHA scholarship. Both met Jack Kerouac the same year. The triangular homoerotic friendship that grew out of those meetings became the core of a literary movement that the *Chicago Review* editors were among the first to appreciate.

Ginsberg was impressed by the originality of Burroughs's mind, the sharpness of his comments, and his sardonic humor, so they spent a lot of time together. After Burroughs accidentally shot and killed his wife, Joan Vollmer, in Mexico,† Ginsberg became Burroughs's lover for a while, as well as his friend, and encouraged him to write. The poet also acted as combination press agent and literary agent for Burroughs and got his work published.

Ginsberg felt that Burroughs's only chance for redemption, following the killing of his wife, was to write; and when Burroughs had completed his first novel, Ginsberg took the manuscript around to his contacts in the publishing world. He had no success until "his friend from the nuthouse," Carl Solomon, read it and liked it and got his uncle, A. A. Wyn, to publish it as an Ace paperback. (Solomon was working for Wyn as an editor at that time; later he had a nervous breakdown and ended up in Bellevue, an event Ginsberg would write about in *Howl.*) *Junkie* appeared in 1953, under the pseudonym "William Lee." It went completely unnoticed by reviewers but sold 113,170 copies within a year. Burroughs's biographer Ted Morgan describes it as "a precise, unromanticized rendering of a previously unexamined social group." Kerouac thought it was like Hemingway, but even better. Another early book by Burroughs, *Queer,* is a tour de force of black humor written in a reportorial style similar to that used in *Junkie.* A. A. Wyn would not touch *Queer* for fear that it would land them all in jail.

ALLEN GINSBERG: I had been going around trying to be an agent and when [Burroughs's and Kerouac's work] was rejected in New York I went to San Francisco and in San Francisco there was a literary understanding of that work. Particularly Kerouac's more esoteric works, and his poetry, and there was an appreciation of Burroughs's work, to some extent. Before I left San Francisco, City Lights agreed to publish *Howl,* and they were interested in Kerouac, and everybody was together in the sense that a community had been formed, not just a few isolated writers. And the connections to the

---

*Mabley also may have been annoyed at the mini-portrait of Chicago in Burroughs's piece in the Autumn 1958 issue: "Chicago. invisible hierarchy of decorticated wops, smell of atrophied gangsters, earthbound ghost hits you at Dearborn and Halstead, Cicero, Lincoln Park, panhandler of dreams, past invading the present, rancid magic of slot machines and roadhouses."

†He fired too low at a whiskey glass she had set on top of her head. The event is described in various versions in Chapter 20.

East were New Directions, James Laughlin, and later Grove Press and *Evergreen Review,* Barney Rosset. Then Irving Rosenthal, in Chicago. But in San Francisco there was a vanguard poetry, a change of technique in poetry and a change of morals both. Change of technique to open-form poetry, change of morals to open-form morals. *Evergreen Review* put out an issue called the San Francisco Renaissance; there was a picture of San Francisco on the cover, around '57. After that was the *Chicago Review* and *Big Table.* This was while we were in Europe. Because after San Francisco, I went to Europe, Kerouac went home, and Burroughs went to Tangier.

———

Burroughs's son, Billy, lived with his father from time to time. (He later became a good writer, but also an alcoholic and morphine addict; he died in 1981.) In 1971 he published some recollections of their life in Tangier:

BILLY BURROUGHS: Our house in the Marshan was very fine. Two stories and consumed by mosaics. My father's room was austere to say the least. Spotlessly clean with an army type bunk and a cabinet and that was all besides an incredibly haunting picture of a brooding moon done by his good friend Brion Gysin. . . .

There was an orgone box* in the upstairs hall in which my father would sit for hours at a time smoking kif and then rush out and attack his typewriter without fair warning.

———

In Tangier, Burroughs got to know Paul Bowles.

PAUL BOWLES: He lived in a damp little room whose single door opened onto the garden of the Hotel Villa Mouneria. One wall of the room, his shooting gallery, was pock-marked with bullet holes. Another wall was completely covered with snapshots, most of which he had taken on a recent trip to the Amazon to find Yage. The litter on his desk and under it, on the floor, was chaotic, but it consisted only of pages of *Naked Lunch* at which he was constantly working. When he read aloud from it, at random—any sheet of paper he happened to grab would do—he laughed a good deal, as well he might, since it is very funny. . . . He had a Reich orgone box in which he used to sit doubled up, smoking kif. I believe he made the box himself. He had a little stove in his room over which he

———

*Wilhelm Reich invented the orgone box, a sexual energy "accumulator." Some of his published writings were burned and all accumulators located on his property were destroyed with axes by federal Food and Drug Administration police in December 1956. In August of the next year, six tons of Reichian literature—including Reich's hardcover books *Sexual Revolution* and *The Mass Psychology of Fascism*—were burned in New York by court order. In March 1957 Reich entered the federal penitentiary at Lewisburg, Pa., for contempt of an injunction that required him to stop shipping orgone accumulators in interstate commerce and to stop doing research and writing about orgone energy and the accumulators. These disastrous acts of government censorship went largely unnoticed and unprotested. Reich died in prison in October 1957 of heart failure and heartbreak. See Myron Sharaf, *Fury on Earth: A Biography of Wilhelm Reich* (1983). Burroughs referred to Reich's fate in a talk he gave at Edinburgh on the censorship of sexual expression.

cooked his own hashish candy of which he was very proud, and which he distributed to anyone who was interested.

BILLY BURROUGHS: The rooftops, by custom, are the women's province in Tangier because that's where they do all the washing and gossiping and whatnot. I made the mistake of going to the roof during the day and the Arabs threw little pieces of mud at our door for the next week. . . . My father would be on the roof every night to watch the sky as soon as the sun was starting to set. I would stumble to the roof occasionally, stoned to the squash, and see him transfixed in his favorite spot. Transfixed and absolutely motionless, right hand holding the perpetual cigarette, lips parting to the sun and himself stirring only to drop it when it burned his fingers. When it was finally, absolutely night again, the sudden rush back to the typewriter.

—

Alan Ansen "had the good luck to meet Burroughs" in New York, through Allen Ginsberg.

ALAN ANSEN: A tall ectomorph—in Tangier the boys called him El Hombre Invisible—his persona constituted by a magic triad of fedora, glasses and raincoat rather than by a face. . . . There was a cracker accent and use of jive talk that failed to mask incisive intelligence and a frightening seriousness.

—

Burroughs's philosophy of life is suggested by a saying of his: "No one owns life but anyone who can pick up a frying-pan owns death." In a letter to Ginsberg he described the way he wrote when he lived in Tangier:

WILLIAM S. BURROUGHS: All day I had been finding pretexts to avoid work, reading magazines, making fudge, cleaning my shotgun, washing the dishes, going to bed with Kiki,* tying the garbage up in neat parcels and putting it out for the collector (if you put it out in a waste basket or any container they will steal the container every time) . . . buying food for dinner, picking up a junk script. So finally I say: "Now you must work . . ." and smoke some tea and sit down and out it comes all in one piece like a glob of spit. . . .
    Sometimes I'd try to write sitting at a café and it would turn out like this: "Sitting in front of the Café Central in the Spring like, rainy sunshine. Sick. Waiting for my Eukodol. A boy walks by and I turn my head, following his loins like a lizard turns its head to follow the course of an ant."

ALLEN GINSBERG: He wrote something every day, steadily, you know, an hour or two or three, more than I did; and he developed very good writing habits. At a typewriter, against the wall, I remember. I have a photograph

---

*A young Arab boy, Burroughs's favorite. His relationship to Burroughs is described in William Burroughs, *Letters to Allen Ginsberg 1953–1957* (1982).

of him there. There and on the beach. He wrote during the day and then, probably around one o'clock, he'd come over and have tea with us— Kerouac was there—and then in the evening go out to supper. . . . Bill would sit at a typewriter and see pictures and transcribe those. Like, I remember seeing him like that, with his hands lifted over the typewriter, looking into space, and I said, "What are you thinking about, Bill?"

And he said: "Hands pulling in nets in the darkness . . ."

"Boy, that's real cosmic-sounding, you know, God's in the fishing net . . ."

What it was, before dawn, down on the beach in Tangier, the fishermen pulling in their nets. So it was very practical. He thinks in pictures, unlike most people, so that his method of writing was he'd sit there and see pictures and then write them down. And that worked very well for dreams also, which is why a lot of his material sounds so surrealistic-dreamy. . . .

Bill didn't start writing until '46 or so. He wrote a novel with Kerouac, the two of them collaborated, did alternate chapters, for a book called *And the Hippos Were Boiled in Their Tanks.* It was from a radio broadcast Burroughs heard when he was a kid, about a fire in the St. Louis zoo, where the announcer ended: "And the hippos were boiled in their tanks."

It was through Ginsberg that Paul Carroll at the *Chicago Review* first heard of William Burroughs.

PAUL CARROLL: We weren't mounting the barricades to wave some new revolutionary manifesto. We were just trying to do what most literary quarterlies were trying to do—make an outlet for what seemed original in fiction, poetry and criticism. . . . I was restless with the good but predictable poetry that was being submitted to us, so when rumors reached the *Review*'s office about some wild, strong writing being done in San Francisco, I wrote to the only name I knew there, Lawrence Ferlinghetti at City Lights Books, asking him to spread the word that if enough good writing was sent, the *Chicago Review* would devote an issue to San Francisco writing. Among the writers who Ferlinghetti put us in touch with was Allen Ginsberg.

Ginsberg, who was then in Paris, sent the *Chicago Review* "endless bibliographical letters," two of which were later published in the Autumn '58 issue of the *Review.* Excerpts read:

ALLEN GINSBERG: Dear Mr. Carroll: Thank you for your interest in our work, what you say, but you know Time will get rid of all the trash and irrelevancy. Whalen's and Snyder's are hard and will stand. I keep repeating I wish you use them, it'd be good deal.

Only one unpublished at all in U.S. so far is Burroughs who is equal to

Jack K. in prose strength.* I asked him to send me some mss. and if they've arrived by tomorrow at American Express I'll include them with this letter. You would do a great service if you can find a place to introduce Burroughs. That's William S. Burroughs—see dedication† in my book if you have it. He's in Tangier. Most his work too raw but I asked him to send something palpably printable. . . .

Print everybody madly! Have you got any Snyder? He's good too. Did you like little Loewinson's poem? Print all my poems if you can. Where are you?

Don't worry what people say if you turn out a screwy magazine full of idiotic poetry—so long as it's alive—do you want to die an old magazine editor in a furnished room who knew what was in every cup of Tea? Put some arsenic in the magazine! Death to Van Gogh's Ear!

PAUL CARROLL: It is the fall of 1957, the year I became poetry editor of the *Chicago Review*. I am sitting in the basement apartment of the editor, Irving Rosenthal, tiny, bearded, always bundled in two or three sweatshirts, it seems, no matter what the weather, a doctoral candidate in the Committee on Human Development at the University of Chicago. My chair is surrounded by hundreds of typewritten pages that have been casually arranged by Burroughs in the large carton in which he's shipped them from Tangier, Morocco. Soon, Irving will shape the manuscript into chapters and then suggest a sequence for the chapters themselves. As I read I can hardly believe our luck. Once the shock and surprise over the fact that Burroughs calls a cock a cock and admits in print to being both a junkie and a homosexual wear thin, the suspicion becomes stronger and stronger that this colossal, sprawling labyrinth of a manuscript—with its raw, violent energy, its acidic and incisive humor—stands a good chance of being a classic. It is called *Naked Lunch.*

WILLIAM S. BURROUGHS (*Chicago Review,* Autumn 1958): *The Rube is a social liability with his attacks as he calls them. The Mark inside was coming up on him and that's a rumble nobody can cool; outside Philly he jumps out to con a prowl car and the fuzz takes one look at his face and busts all of us.*

Seventy two hours and five sick junkies in the cell with us. Now not wishing to break out my stash in front of these hungry coolies, it takes maneuvering and laying of gold on the turnkey before we are in a separate cell.

---

*Burroughs's *Naked Lunch* was reportedly turned down by Lawrence Ferlinghetti, the publisher of Ginsberg's *Howl,* because it was disgusting. Ted Morgan, *Literary Outlaw* (1988), 287.

†Ginsberg was referring to "Footnote to Howl," which in part read: "Holy Peter holy Allen holy Solomon holy Lucien holy Kerouac holy Huncke holy Burroughs holy Cassady holy the unknown buggered and suffering beggers holy the hideous human angels! / Holy my mother in the insane asylum! Holy the cocks of the grandfathers of Kansas!" The original title of *Howl* was *Howl: For Carl Solomon.* See Allen Ginsberg, *Howl, Original Draft Facsimile, Transcript & Variant Versions, Fully Annotated by Author,* edited by Barry Miles (1986). This edition is dedicated to "Lawrence Ferlinghetti, Poet, Editor, Publisher and Defender of *Howl.*"

Provident junkies, known as squirrels, keep stashes against a bust. Every time I take a shot I let a few drops fall into my vest pocket, the lining is stiff with stuff. I had a plastic dropper in my shoe and a safety-pin stuck in my belt. . . .

ALLEN GINSBERG: Gregory Corso sent a group of major poems. He was writing them with one-word titles like "Marriage," "Bomb," "Police," "Hair," "Death," "Clown," and so on; so I think he sent three or four of those. And Burroughs prepared a chunk of *Naked Lunch,* eighty pages, and it was the first good-sized chunk that was published. There'd only been one or two pages of his in *Black Mountain Review* before, Issue Number 7, edited by Creeley and me . . . the Interzone . . . the Market section . . . and maybe a little bit of his stuff in *Floating Bear.* . . .*

This was major material, I mean, really, some of the best material in *Naked Lunch:* the Talking Asshole, Dr. Benway, some of the Interzone and the scenes with border guards, corrupt cops, things like that. The whole narcotics nexus outlined.

WILLIAM S. BURROUGHS (*Chicago Review,* Autumn 1958): *Non-using pushers have a contact habit, and that's one you can't kick. Agents get it too. Take Bradley the Buyer. Best narcotics agent in the industry. Anyone would make him for junk. (Footnote: Make in the sense of dig or size up.) I mean he can walk up to a pusher and score direct. He is so anonymous, grey and spectral the pusher don't remember him afterwards. So he twists one after the other. . . .*

Well the Buyer comes to look more and more like a junky. He can't drink. He can't get it up. His teeth fall out. (Like pregnant women lose their teeth feeding the stranger, junkies lose their yellow fangs feeding the monkey.) He is all the time sucking on a candy bar. Baby Ruth he digs special. "It really disgusts you to see the Buyer sucking on them candy bars so nasty," a cop say.

The Buyer takes on an ominous grey-green color. Fact is his body is making its own junk or equivalent. The buyer has a steady connection. A Man Within you might say. Or so he thinks. "I'll just set in my room," he say. "Fuck 'em all. Squares on both sides. I am the only complete man in the industry."

But a yen comes on him like a great black wind through the bones. So the Buyer hunts up a young junkie and gives him a paper to make it.

"Oh all right," the boy says. "So what you want to make?"

"I just want to rub up against you and get fixed."

"Ugh . . . Well all right. . . . But why cancha just get physical like a human?"

Later the boy is sitting in a Waldorf with two colleagues dunking pound cake. "Most distasteful thing I ever stand still for," he says. "Some way he make himself all soft like a blob of jelly and surround me so nasty. Then he gets wet all over like with green slime. So I guess he came to some kinda awful climax. . . . I come near

---

Black Mountain Review, edited by poet Robert Creeley, first published a section from *Naked Lunch* along with work by Allen Ginsberg and Jack Kerouac. The Burroughs material, however, appeared under the pseudonym "William Lee," used also for the publication of *Junkie,* mentioned above. *Floating Bear* was a literary journal published by Diane di Prima, LeRoi Jones (Amiri Baraka), and Alan Marlowe.

wigging with that green stuff all over me, and he stink like a old rotten canta-loupe."*

"*Well it's still an easy score.*"

The boy sighed resignedly; "Yes, I guess you can get used to anything. I've got a meet with him again tomorrow."

———

Irving Rosenthal was attracted to the Burroughs manuscript not only be-cause of the writing but because of its drug and homosexual themes.† In a letter to Burroughs, Rosenthal promised to publish whatever he sent in.

WILLIAM S. BURROUGHS (*Chicago Review,* Autumn 1958): *The Buyer's habit keeps getting heavier. He needs a recharge every half hour. Sometimes he cruises the precincts and bribes the turnkey to let him in with a cell of junkies. It gets to where no amount of contact will fix him. At this point he receives a summons from the District Supervisor:*

"*Bradley, your conduct has given rise to rumors—and I hope for your sake they are no more than that—so unspeakably distasteful that . . . I mean Caesar's wife . . . hump . . . that is, the Department must be above suspicion, certainly above such suspicions as you have seemingly aroused. You are lowering the entire tone of the industry. We are prepared to accept your immediate resignation.*"

The Buyer throws himself on the ground and crawls over to the D.S. "No, Boss Man, no . . . The Department is my very life line."

He kisses the D.S.'s hand thrusting the fingers into his mouth (the D.S. must feel his boneless gums) complaining he has lost his teeth "inna thervith." "Please Boss Man. I'll wipe your ass, I'll wash out your dirty condoms, I'll polish your shoes with the oil on my nose. . . ."

"*Really, this is most distasteful! Have you no pride? I must tell you I feel a distinct revulsion. I mean there is something well, rotten about you, and you smell like a compost heap.*" *He puts a scented handkerchief in front of his face. "I must ask you to leave this office at once.*"

"*I'll do anything, Boss, anything.*" *His ravaged green face splits in a horrible smile. "I'm still young, Boss, and I'm pretty strong when I get my blood up.*"

The D.S. retches into his handkerchief and points to the door with a limp hand.

———

*In lovemaking Burroughs displayed a similar tendency "to melt completely, to take on a different entity" in quest of "some kind of uncanny, primordial protoplasmic union, some kind of complete symbiosis," according to Allen Ginsberg, who also interpreted the character of Bradley the Buyer in *Naked Lunch,* "going around and literally absorbing all the young junkies," as "a parable" of Burroughs's erotic fantasies. Ted Morgan, *Literary Outlaw* (1988), 230–31. In his "Recollection of Burroughs," in Burroughs's *Letters to Allen Ginsberg 1953–1957* (1982), Ginsberg outlines the history of their relationship including their love affair in "idyllic pre-Viet-war Lower East Side between Avenues B & C on East 7th Street," during 1953, which ended when Ginsberg, fearful of being "schlupped" by Burroughs (i.e., having his soul devoured parasitically, "as Bradley the Buyer does to the District Supervisor in *Naked Lunch*"), "rejected his body. 'I don't want your ugly old cock.' Harsh words for a young man, something I wouldn't want anyone to say to me. But he had pushed me to it." *Letters,* 5.

†Burroughs once told editor Carl Solomon that he did not mind being identified as homosexual so long as his type—strong, manly, noble—was distinguished from "leaping, jumping, window-dressing, cock-sucking fags" (Morgan, *Literary Outlaw,* 210).

The Buyer stands up looking at the D.S. dreamily. His body begins to dip like a dowser's wand. He flows forward. . . .

"No!" screams the D.S.

"Schlup . . . schlup schlup." An hour later they find the Buyer on the nod in the D.S.'s chair. The D.S. has disappeared without a trace.

GREGORY CORSO: Dear Irving [Rosenthal], what? Suppression? Chicago? Are you weeping? I hear from Ginsberg that you are tiny, wet-eyed, low-voiced, a rose in a terrible giant's land; do you wet the bed? shiver because of human ice? Yes, that's what suppression is, human ice. But why? I always heard University of Chicago was a great happy free soulful institute of sparkle and joy; something like Reed, but only on a grander scale. Is it because of Burroughs? Poor Bill, the Elysium of Al Capone tommy guns his scathless soul; I mean the *Chi Review* was his only intelligent outlet; what happens to you now? Do you flee? Abandon all? I have a funny feeling here in Paris, I feel America is suddenly going to open up, that a great rose will be born, that if you flee it, it will die; so stay; nurse it with your vision, it's as good as sunlight. Death to Van Gogh's ear! Long live Fried Shoes!

PROFESSOR EDWARD ROSENHEIM: Larry [Chancellor Lawrence Kimpton] called me in originally, I think, because I had been director of broadcasting, which involved the University of Chicago Roundtable, and worked in the Administration Building, and we were very close. Kim asked me to come in with Bill Morganstern, who was then secretary of the university and in charge of public relations. Kimpton reported that he had heard from some trustees—maybe Robert Wilson, who was at that point the president of Standard Oil, and Edward Ryerson, I think—and the question was raised, what, if anything, could be done about the publicity. Jack Mabley, a columnist for the *Daily News,* had somehow had his attention drawn to this issue of the *Review,* the Autumn '58 issue. And Mabley sort of suggested, I think expressly, that the trustees ought to take a look at it, and see what their money was going for. . . .

Well, I don't remember what shape our deliberations took, but the decision was that while these people had every constitutional right to publish what they wanted, the university did not have any obligation to offer them subventions or to offer them free premises if the university felt that what was going on there was detrimental to the university's public image. So that was the decision, and I have thought about it many times since then. The decision sort of ended the matter until it became very clear that it was profoundly resented by the various people involved in the publication and by Paul Carroll, who is around still, and if he still feels the way he did then, he feels intensely that the university was greatly to blame.

PAUL CARROLL: I wasn't a student at the U. of C. then. I'd received an M.A. in literature earlier, in 1952, and also started work on a Ph.D. with the Committee on Social Thought. I stopped in '57. In '58 I was

teaching at Loyola, the downtown college. The next year they didn't re-
new my appointment as an instructor in English, despite protests from
my poetry workshop—and I know it was because of the scandal associated with *Big Table,* which grew out of the suppression of the *Chicago
Review.*

WILLIAM S. BURROUGHS: At the time, I had no takers for the book [*Naked
Lunch*]. Allen had tried Girodias in Paris in the winter of '57 but he
returned the manuscript. Rosenthal at the *Chicago Review* was really the
only editor who understood what I was doing. And then the *Chicago Review*
folded out from under him, and me. . . . About the same time I was
announced in the *Nation* as an international homo and all-around sex fiend.
. . . I wrote to Paul Bowles: "It looks like *Naked Lunch* is finished. I have
no idea if it will ever be published in a complete form. Complications and
the manuscript scattered all over Europe."

———

The chancellor of the University of Chicago, Lawrence A. Kimpton, was
a colorless physical scientist who had succeeded the remarkable thinker,
educator, and humanist Robert Maynard Hutchins, a near-legendary figure
who had reigned like a god over the campus for twenty-two years, prosely-
tizing for the Great Books, the Great Ideas, and the university as "a center
for independent thought."*

GEORGE ANASTAPLO:† Hutchins was like an Adonis. Whenever he went
anywhere on the campus the female students would hang out of their
dormitory windows, to get a glimpse of him.

———

In a last-minute attempt to avert the suppression of his journal, Rosenthal wrote a letter to Hutchins, appealing for his help. The letter seems
never to have been delivered, but in any case Hutchins could have done
nothing to prevent the censorship. He was no longer chancellor. There is
no doubt, however, how Hutchins would have acted in Kimpton's shoes.
Unlike Kimpton, Hutchins did not fear public opinion; he would have
acted not to change the *Chicago Review* to please Jack Mabley but to change
Jack Mabley's mind.

———

*See Harry S. Ashmore, *Unseasonable Truths: The Life of Robert Maynard Hutchins* (1989).
Hutchins's first wife, Maude Phelps Hutchins, was the author of a book called *Diary of Love,*
which was suppressed from sale as obscene by the Chicago police in November 1952, "after
a reading by" city judge Matthew Hartisan; the ACLU entered the scene and obliged the
police to release the book. Three days after the police seizure, the book's publisher, New
Directions, received orders for 2,200 copies (*Publishers Weekly,* December 2, 1952). In England, 8,000 copies of a Dutch edition that had been seized entering England at Harwich were
burned by order of a magistrate. This further stimulated the book's sales, leading to five
hardcover editions and as many in paperback in the United States, as well as Danish, Italian,
and German translations. *Unseasonable Truths,* 289.

†Professor of Law at Loyola University, Chicago, and Lecturer in Liberal Arts at the
University of Chicago; author of *The Constitutionalist: Notes on the First Amendment* (1971)
and *The Constitution of 1787: A Commentary* (1989).

ROBERT M. HUTCHINS: The most dangerous aspect of public relations work is its reflex action: we find that the public does not like something about the University; our temptation is to change this so the public will like us. Our duty is to change public opinion so that the public will like what the University does, and if this cannot be immediately accomplished, to hold out against the public until it can be. . . .

The academic administrators of America remind one of the French Revolutionist who said: "The mob is in the streets. I must find out where they are going, for I am their leader."

———

After Kimpton learned about the Mabley column from university trustees, he asked the *Review*'s faculty adviser, Richard Stern, a professor and poet, to look into the coming issue. Stern asked Rosenthal for a list of the contributors to the Winter number, saying he needed it "because the Dean wants to know," and Rosenthal gave it to him. The issue then went to the University Press and was already set in type (or was about to be set in type*) when Kimpton instructed the press to hold publication; Rosenthal was informed of this by the dean of humanities, Napier Wilt. Professor Joshua Taylor now told the editors of the *Chicago Review* that if they wanted the *Review* to continue under university sponsorship they'd have to print an "innocuous and uncontroversial" Winter issue. Just what was "innocuous and uncontroversial" would be left up to a faculty committee. Rosenthal and the other student editors would lose the right of editorial control.

At one point in the controversy Professor Stern sought to put a good face on the chancellor's action:

PROFESSOR RICHARD STERN: The University of Chicago did not exert controls on the editorial policies of the responsible student editors of its publications. Of course, the University was legally responsible for the publications and would have to try to see that the laws of libel and other pertinent laws were not violated by them.

IRVING ROSENTHAL: The Taylor and Stern statements are pure baloney. They are not only untrue, but they are a deliberate attempt on the part of those men to whitewash what really happened.

———

Rosenthal claimed that at one point Stern warned him not to turn the *Review* into a magazine of San Francisco rejects, saying: "This is as if garbage had garbage."†

The *Chicago Review* editors tried, but failed, to enlist the support of Chicago-based literary figures like Philip Roth, then a young instructor at

———

*There is uncertainty about this, but no doubt that the press was told to halt publication.
†Stern's own work evidently had been turned down by Rosenthal. Morgan, *Literary Outlaw,* 297.

the university, and Nelson Algren, who was Chicago's best-known literary figure at the time. Algren seems to have viewed what was going on at the *Review* as an attempted landing on his turf by aliens.* Sociologist David Riesman—a strong supporter of student activists and a professor at the college—could not help because he was in the process of leaving the university for more hospitable terrain.

On January 28, 1959, a special committee of the University of Chicago's student government published a careful and well-documented account of the suppression. Rosenthal commended it to everyone "interested in censorship problems (or administrative skull-duggery)." The report demonstrated, said Rosenthal, that Kimpton's action "was rigidly consistent with his program to placate the trustees by 'normalizing' the University—to increase the endowment at the expense of everything that a university in a free society is supposed to support (and seldom does)." According to Rosenthal, the chancellor did "not want free expression at the University of Chicago, he wanted money."

STUDENT GOVERNMENT (University of Chicago): Sometime during the week of November 3–7, the Chancellor called a meeting with members of the Faculty Board; Messrs Denny, Rosenheim, Stern and Taylor present. Deans Wilt and Streeter were also present. . . .

According to those interviewed by this committee . . . the Chancellor spoke of the pressure he was under from "people financially interested in the University," and he expressed concern over the possible consequences of continued adverse publicity. The Chancellor asked the [Faculty] Board for advice on what should be done about the Winter issue. The discussion which followed touched upon the anomalous position of the *Review* in the University (owned by the University but not under its supervision) and on the possibility that the *Review* might be in violation of the postal laws (obscenity). Dean Wilt and Mr. Stern defended the *Review,* and a majority of those present agreed with them that the winter issue should be published as planned by Rosenthal. Two members of the Board have independently characterized the opinion of the majority present as "let the next issue ride." The Chancellor then implied that the pressure he was under was great enough so that if necessary he personally would do something about the winter issue.

———

Kimpton maintained that the *Review* had originally been founded as "a student publication" in 1946, when he was dean of students, and had then become "a University publication" in 1957—"after it incurred enormous financial difficulties and we had to pay its debts."† Kimpton's official complaints were that the *Review,* under Irving Rosenthal, "contained nonstudents" on its board of editors,‡ and that the editor "was completely

---

*See his attack on the beatniks in "Chicago Is a Wose," *The Nation,* February 28, 1959.
†$7,500 in debts.
‡Rosenthal was a University of Chicago student at the time; Carroll was not.

infatuated with the San Francisco school to the point that he seemed to feel no one else was worth publishing."*

CHANCELLOR LAWRENCE KIMPTON: Since an official publication of the University had demonstrated that it no longer respected any literary quality except that of Mr. Irving Rosenthal, the University had the right to withdraw its support from that publication.

—

From November 3 through November 17 a series of meetings took place at which Dean Wilt communicated to Irving Rosenthal the conditions under which the Winter issue of the *Chicago Review* could be published. In response, Rosenthal and all but one of the other editors of the *Review* resigned.

The ramifications of the flap were substantial: The university, long recognized for its uncompromising dedication, under Hutchins, to academic and intellectual freedom, was viewed as having betrayed its own principles, especially among the literary and liberal-intellectual communities. And, according to Allen Ginsberg, the suppression worked, as censorship so often does, to energize the suppressed, to launch the beats and the San Francisco school of writers—specifically Burroughs, Ginsberg, and Kerouac—as an anti-establishment subcultural social phenomenon and literary movement. A decade later, FBI director J. Edgar Hoover would warn Republicans that the three greatest menaces to America were Communists, eggheads,† and beatniks.

PAUL CARROLL: Stern took the position that the university had not assumed editorial control and that it was a question of "editorial responsibility." Because of our favoring the San Francisco beat poets. Well, he was a young teacher then, and nervous about tenure. . . . Irving asked Stern point-blank if we'd be allowed to print this material, and when Stern said no, Irving said, "Here's the key. We quit!" When our trouble was all over, I saw Stern, who is also a poet, at a party and asked him to send me something. He did and I put it in *Big Table.*‡ Because it was good. . . .

We got permission from the authors—Burroughs, Kerouac, and Dahlberg—to release their manuscripts to us and resubmit them to a new magazine, and so we all quit except a turncoat from Taiwan whose name was Pak. He became editor of the *Chicago Review* after that and turned out terrible issues. . . . Stern tried to fight us over the manuscripts,§ claiming they were the property of the university, but he finally gave up and they were all published by us in *Big Table* 1. But that, of course, was not the end of the censorship of *Naked Lunch;* it was the beginning. . . .

---

*These were also the official reasons given by the *Chicago Review*'s faculty adviser, Richard Stern.

†Presidential candidate Adlai Stevenson, whose bald head resembled an egg, seems to have brought this term upon himself and fellow liberal Democrats.

‡See *Big Table* 1, no. 4 (1960), 20.

§For a while, Stern threatened a suit to recover the manuscripts.

We also published Douglas Woolf and Robert Duncan and Paul Bowles and Robert Creeley and Kenneth Koch and John Rechy and Pablo Neruda and John Rosenberg and John Schultz and Alain Robbe-Grillet. In *Big Table* 2 we published Allen Ginsberg's *Kaddish,* a portrait by Paul Bowles of "Burroughs in Tangier," and two photographs of Burroughs. . . .

We published the complete contents of the suppressed Winter '58 issue of the *Review*—the "Burroughs issue"—in *Big Table* 1. It came off the press in March 1959 with an American-flag cover. Jack Kerouac gave us the name, during the Christmas holidays. . . . Call it *Big Table,* he wrote.* And we did. We liked its being midwestern in its bluntness and its lack of literary bloomers. Also it matched my idea to have an open-house sort of editorial policy.

———

The idea behind the title *Big Table,* according to Ginsberg, was "that there's a lot of literature, and it takes a great big table full of manuscripts."

ALLEN GINSBERG: 'Cause it was a big new literature and it was the first time that anybody had tried to assemble this writing genre as a literary movement, as a genre, so it was kind of a breakthrough to get it assembled in a university magazine to begin with, and to be taken seriously. Up to that point to some extent that literature had been mocked or made fun of by *Hudson Review, Paris Review,* and others. How could there be a new literature after the end of ideology? In the end we were all influenced by Céline more than Joyce, also Rimbaud and Genet. . . .

PAUL CARROLL: It was with the help of Allen and Gregory Corso that *Big Table* got off the ground. Allen's "wife," Peter Orlovsky, came too; he drove their van.† They came to Chicago and gave a marathon reading of their poetry at the Bal Tabarin Room in the Palmer House, to raise funds to launch the magazine as an independent literary journal. Allen gave a super reading; he was angry, funny, incandescent, and we'd drawn a big crowd.

ALLEN GINSBERG: The Shaw Society in Chicago proposed a poetry reading where we would read our poetry to raise money for the new magazine, *Big Table,* and make publicity for it. The ACLU, I think, backed them, so the Shaw Society would. Miss Barbara Solomon, who had a bookstore called Barbara's Bookstore, which still exists in Chicago, it was the avant-garde bookstore, Barbara Solomon was the publicist for this meeting; the organizer was Lois Solomon, the wife of a big pharmacist, who was a member of the Shaw Society; and there was a lawyer who was a sort of a folk hero in Chicago, as the ACLU lawyer, as a civil libertarian, Elmer Gertz.‡

———

*Kerouac also gave Burroughs the title for his book *Naked Lunch.*

†According to Allen Ginsberg, *Big Table*'s assistant editor, John Fles, actually drove them in his car.

‡Elmer Gertz later represented Grove Press in a suit brought to free Henry Miller's *Tropic of Cancer* from Chicago police censorship. See Chapter 19 below.

So they sent a kid with a car, who was I think one of the managing editors of the *Review,* to pick up me and Gregory and Peter. And on a winter snowy day we drove from New York to Chicago; and actually we had a very dangerous drive 'cause the car, at one point, spun around totally. In those days, flying was not so easy, it wasn't so cheap, so they sent somebody with a car. I was living at 170 East Second Street, I believe; Burroughs was still in Tangier; and Kerouac was invited but he didn't want to take part 'cause he never read anything, he never went out, he was afraid he'd get drunk and get, you know, get his head conked on the pavement. He was shy, and also he'd been bitten when he gave readings at the Village Vanguard, Nat Hentoff snagged him and everybody put him down. Although he was a great reader, nobody appreciated his fucking reading. Nat Hentoff denounced him in the *Times,* and his poetry book came out and Kenneth Rexroth wrote a nasty review and said: "This separates the men from the boys; Kerouac can't compete." But Kerouac was actually a very great reader, his style influenced everyone, from me to Bob Dylan. I mean, if Bob Dylan has a style, it comes out of Kerouac—according to Dylan. . . .

We got to Chicago and what was really amazing was that it was like front page news that THE BEATNIKS WERE COMING; and it was like amazing. Because we had never gone into anything like that, but when we arrived, this was in the *Chicago Tribune.* Yeah, those fags are coming, the beatniks are arriving in Chicago! Beatniks are invading Chicago!

So Gregory picked up on it and thought it was very funny, you know, and said, Ah, the beatniks are coming! the beatniks are coming! And Peter was very innocent about it, and I was saying, Well, this is going to be very interesting, 'cause we've got all these great poems, and we'll see what happens. So we had a party, preliminary or afterward, at the home of Muriel Newman, who's a great art collector, she had Pollocks, de Koonings, I don't know who-all. I guess it was a party maybe to host us, and to invite rich people to contribute to *Big Table,* or at least to come to the reading. Nicholas Ray was there, the director, and a lot of interesting people around. Especially Muriel and her lady friends, who were the Jewish American princesses who bought the de Koonings and Pollocks, from North Shore, or Lake Shore Drive, or whatever you call it, where the expensive big apartments were. And we were some relatively naïve, inexperienced youngsters walking into this scene. . . . It was very classy. Totally classy. So Studs Terkel had us on the air, and we had an interesting conversation, which I have the tapes of, between Studs Terkel and me and Peter and Gregory.* Talking about, defining what we're after. And the transcript of that conversation was published recently, twenty years later. . . .

Now the reading itself was set up at the Sherman Hotel, with the editor of *Playboy,* A. C. Spectorsky, as the moderator, and with Arthur C. Clarke, *2001,* as the sort of interrogator. It turns out later that Clarke is gay, and

---

*Nelson Algren took Terkel to task for "hosting" the beatniks on his radio program.

is also a Buddhist, and so he knew exactly what was going on when he intervened, but he was very prestigious in those days, you know, like a sort of a square, very middle class. . . .

It was the right time, see, American time and Chicago time, because Chicago did have an old tradition of bohemians and protest or upper-bohemian literary flavor, from Ben Hecht through Sandburg through I don't know who . . . Studs Terkel through James T. Farrell through Nelson Algren. There always was this sort of eccentric anarchist flavor in Chicago, anarchist-pacifist union-organizing Haymarket Riots, there was always a radical literary flavor in Chicago, as one important element in the West. And somehow it all came together on our visit. . . .

I guess because of the blatant nature of the censorship, and partly because, after all, what they were censoring was one of the elements of all of us, me in *Howl,* Burroughs's *Naked Lunch,* Kerouac's *On the Road;* so it was really a nerve center they were getting at. It wasn't as if they were just censoring a lot of second-rate stuff, it was all of a sudden there was this great phalanx of real literature, connected also with Dahlberg, who was like from the old school and was considered very good, a venerable internationally known poet. . . .*

In the next issue of *Big Table,* they did publish my *Kaddish.* Very serious. In the first issue they weren't intending to publish anything of mine; I was helping edit. But they had enough; they had *Naked Lunch,* the first publication of *Naked Lunch* in America, and that's a big deal. The people who were involved in it knew that it was a big deal. I mean, like, Irving knew, and Paul Carroll. . . . Actually, that's another thing. Paul Carroll's idea for the next issue was Post-Christian Man, and he wanted to have Allen Tate, and he didn't realize that you take the ball and you carry it, you don't make it a general magazine, nobody can satisfy everybody, but he was a Catholic and so he wanted to get Allen Tate on Post-Christian Man. But he was so upset, because Tate refused. Tate refused to be published in the same magazine as Burroughs, so it kind of put a monkey wrench into Carroll's generalist tendencies. . . .

So we had this reading. It was in the ballroom in the best hotel in Chicago and people turned out, and it was a big deal. Nobody had ever seen a poetry reading with that many people. So *Newsweek* and *Time* showed up, and AP and UPI or whatever, and *Time* interviewed us, and we were very witty, actually, I think. I think I said, "I'm Allen Ginsberg, I'm crazy as a daisy." No, "crazy as a flower," and Peter said, "I'm Peter Orlovsky and I'm crazy as a daisy," and Gregory said, "I'm Gregory Corso and I'm not crazy at all." They quoted the whole roll of dialogue, and actually Dylan told me he read that column and thought: Wow, there's more people out there, I understand immediately.

It was just a tone that we got of irreverence and, at the same time, some

---

*An autobiographical "contributor's note" by Dahlberg is in *Big Table* 1, no. 1 (Spring 1959), 2.

kind of serious mystical, and at the same time art, and at the same time like the Beatles, a gang of kids, a gang, a gang facing society and making funny scenes. . . . Then I think I went on Irving Kupcinet's program at some point or other, we all did, and then there was a folk club there called the Gate of Horn, run by Albert Grossman, later Dylan's manager, so he invited us down to read poetry at the Gate of Horn.* So there are a lot of convergent threads. I never knew, I didn't know who Grossman was, and he was from Chicago, but we were there in the nightclub all of a sudden, so that was even more of a . . . éclat, because it was poetry in a nightclub, and nobody ever had poetry in a nightclub. . . .

That was all in the same three or four days. Then we gave a reading at the Sherman Hotel, and let's see, I think, the big question to me from the *Newsweek* guy was "How does it feel, what does it feel like, what do you feel, what do you feel?"

So I grabbed his crotch, I was kidding, I mean, it was sort of like a Zen answer: "What do you feel, that's what *I* feel. . . ."

We all were feeling very exuberant and funny, and not taking it at all seriously. . . .

Later on I got to take everything too seriously. That's why it was just sort of, the poetry was steady, so we didn't have to be serious in answers, just have fun. And I think that caught on, that tone caught on, just like the Beatles thing, it was like a Beatles shock. So I read *Howl,* and then, for the first time, I think, on any stage, read the opening passages of *Kaddish,* and Gregory read "Marriage," "Bomb," and a whole bunch of other great poems; Peter read his first and second poems. Then Peter broke down and began weeping, 'cause he felt that he hadn't contributed enough. Actually it was his first manic-depressive breakdown, and at the time, people picked up on it, hearing him weeping, breaking down. They actually made fun of him.

PAUL CARROLL: Jack Olson, who was the Chicago bureau chief for *Time* magazine, and who I knew, covered the event. When he asked Allen what "beatnik" meant, Allen said, " 'Beat' means 'beat your meat.' " That exchange did not appear in Olson's piece in *Time,* which turned out to be really patronizing and the opposite of what had really happened. After it appeared, Olson called me to come by and I told him he was an asshole. He said, "Please, I want to show you what I wrote. . . ." It turned out he'd written a great story but *Time* wouldn't print it. I said, "Why don't you quit?" He did and went to work for *Sports Illustrated*.

ALLEN GINSBERG: So we got interviewed all over, and it got to be a national sensation, and I think that was literally the emergence of the beat genera-

---

*Later, Lenny Bruce would be convicted for giving an obscene performance at the Gate of Horn, as explained in Chapter 24. The conviction was reversed in the light of the Brennan doctrine once the Supreme Court liberated Henry Miller's *Tropic of Cancer,* developments that are described in Chapters 21–24.

tion into pop culture: via *Time* magazine and that particular occasion. . . . The "beatnik" thing began about a year before maybe. Herb Caen of the San Francisco *Chronicle* got the elements which still exist, combining the words "sputnik," which had just happened in '57, and "beat." "Out of this world," the "beat."* 'Cause we were supposed to be "out of this world," like the sputnik. In the upper atmosphere. Also, the *-nik* is real Russian; like "narodniks" were stupid anarchists, the idiot self-righteous anarchists of Dostoyevsky. Neurotic anarchists, neurasthenic anarchists. . . .

We'd done readings before, but this was the biggest reading I ever had. Oh, and also a heroic reading. A really good reading, which was recorded and put out—my part was put out on Fantasy records, as the record, a record of *Howl* which is in print to this day, from 1959 to now. It was a classic reading, exalted. So that the evidence was there; well, that was the whole point—the reading was so great that everybody was totally knocked out, 'cause they came to see the beatniks, you know, shit on the stage or something, and instead we presented this exalted literature, Gregory covering the humor, me covering the serious Yiddish tears, and Peter the surprised crazy Russian aspects.

PAUL CARROLL: Years later, Jim Hoge, who was also an editor of *Big Table,* told me he met Kimpton at some black-tie dinner. Jim was working for the *Sun-Times* then and said Kimpton referred to the *Chicago Review* events as one of "those student unrests." He said: "We acted firmly about a dirty student newspaper." . . .

It really hurt me a lot. I loved the university. I felt that I'd learned the truth about intellectual freedom, when Hutchins was there, and the guys from Second City.† It was a wonderful experience and then along came this goddamn fucking chemist Kimpton. He couldn't tie Hutchins's bow tie. . . .

I still love the university because of the good things. But I became persona non grata: "What Carroll did to the university! Gave it a big black eye." . . .

Because, you see, the university got a lot of criticism for the censorship, for what they did to the *Chicago Review* and its editors, especially Irving and me. It was in the *Times, The Nation, The New Republic;* and then John Ciardi really fried them in *The Saturday Review.* . . .

JOHN CIARDI: The *Chicago Review* is a literary quarterly published by the University of Chicago. Last fall, as the editors were preparing their winter issue, a columnist on one of the Chicago newspapers attacked the fall issue

---

*"Beat," according to Kerouac: "It's beat, it's the beat to keep, it's the beat of the heart, it's being beat and down in the world and like oldtime lowdown and like in ancient civilization the boatmen rowing galleys to a beat and servants spinning pottery to a beat." Morgan, *Literary Outlaw,* 272. For neoconservatives like Norman Podhoretz, the beats expressed the "revolt of the spiritually underprivileged and the crippled of the soul—young men who can't think straight and so hate anyone who can." Morgan, 289.

†Chicago theatrical group started by former University of Chicago students.

as "filthy." The charge called forth a prompt reaction from Chancellor Lawrence A. Kimpton, who, in a memorable blow for academic freedom, summoned then Editor-in-Chief Irving Rosenthal and announced that the material submitted for the winter issue was definitely not to be published. The issue . . . was to be completely "innocuous and noncontroversial" and contain "nothing which would offend a sixteen-year-old girl."

When has the true role of the American University been more profoundly enunciated? Its intellectual content is to be harmless and innocuous; its final test of moral values is to reside in the sensibilities of a sixteen-year-old girl.

PROFESSOR EDWARD ROSENHEIM: I don't know. Dick Stern and I were talking about this yesterday. It seems so incredible, but if you put the thing in historical perspective . . . You have to remember this thing came along long before *Fanny Hill* * . . . before *Lady Chatterley's Lover* † . . .

—

In Paris, Burroughs arrived at the Beat Hotel—a discovery of Ginsberg's which *Time* magazine described as a "fleabag shrine where passersby move out of the way for rats." There a copy of *Big Table* 1 was waiting for him, courtesy of Ginsberg. However, the author's "delight turned sour" when shortly thereafter he heard that the magazine had been declared obscene by the U.S. Post Office in Chicago. He was sure this meant it would not be possible after all to publish *Naked Lunch* in the United States.

In March 1959, shortly after *Big Table* 1 came out, 400 copies deposited by its editors at a Chicago post office were seized by officials and impounded as obscene. The Illinois chapter of the American Civil Liberties Union provided counsel, a young lawyer named Joel Sprayregen, to try to free *Big Table* 1. This was the issue containing the suppressed contents of the Winter 1958 issue of the *Chicago Review*. The allegedly obscene pieces were Jack Kerouac's "Old Angel Midnight" and "Ten Episodes from *Naked Lunch*" by William S. Burroughs. At a departmental hearing presided over by William A. Duvall, Post Office attorney J. Carroll Schuler described the government's approach to *Big Table* 1 as follows: "It is our position that this magazine, *Big Table* 1, is obscene and filthy. And it has no redeeming value. It is conceivable that certain literary critics would state that certain essays and poems contained in this magazine have some literary merit. Such people, however, are not able to speak for the average member of the community. It is inconceivable that the average member of the community would find in this magazine anything but filth, and it is the effect this magazine has on the average member of the community that the law is concerned with."

· · ·

Fanny Hill (*The Memoirs of a Woman of Pleasure*) was suppressed in Massachusetts and other states but was freed by the United States Supreme Court in 1966. See Chapter 23 below.

†Published by Grove Press, banned by the Post Office Department, and freed by federal courts in New York in 1959, on the basis of Brennan's opinion in the *Roth* case.

Paul Carroll was the principal witness for *Big Table* at the hearing; he said that *Big Table* was "an attempt to publish a new movement in contemporary American fiction." He also sought to explain why he had included the Kerouac and Burroughs pieces in the magazine's first issue: "The story 'Old Angel Midnight' in its fictional technique represents a serious attempt to continue and develop the prose style and stylistic techniques invented and articulated by James Joyce. I consider Jack Kerouac to be the heir of this style which, in American literature, has its roots in the writings of Cooper, Thoreau, Walt Whitman, and even Mark Twain. In modern literature it extends to Hemingway and Sherwood Anderson."

Carroll recalled that Allen Ginsberg had characterized the piece as Kerouac's "most extreme example of prose spontaneous style experimentation Joycean Finnegans Wake style, all the sounds in the universe coming in through the window of the ear."

JACK KEROUAC ("Old Angel Midnight"): *Ya damn hogfuckin lick lip twillerin fishmonger! Kiss my purple royal ass baboon! Poota! Whore! You and yr retinues of chariots and fucks! Devadatta! Angel of Mercy! Prick! Lover! Mush! Run on ya dog eared kiss 'willying nilly Dexter Michigan ass warlerin ratpole!*

———

Carroll testified that Burroughs was included in the issue "not because of his established reputation but because he had the potential of becoming a major influence on American fiction." In the writing of William Burroughs, he said, we have "come upon an American prose stylist of considerable power who is articulating an area of the contemporary scene in a lucid, honest manner. He is heir to the tradition of Poe, Baudelaire, Rimbaud, Verlaine and Jarry. The writing is an attempt to find a meaning for one's existence outside of the accepted mores—sociological, philosophical and religious—of the existing society. It is an attempt, really, to gain a religious experience which Burroughs finds otherwise inaccessible or perverted in the society in which he is living."

Carroll tried to illustrate his point by reading from the "Clem and Jody" section of *Naked Lunch,* which had appeared in *Big Table* 1. The hearing examiner, however, did not want the atmosphere "polluted by Burroughs's acrid prose."

WILLIAM S. BURROUGHS *(Naked Lunch): Clem and Jody, two old time vaudeville hoofers, cop out as Russian agents whose sole function is to represent the U.S. in an unpopular light. When arrested for sodomy in Indonesia, Clem said to the examining magistrate:*
"Tain't as if was being queer. After all they's only Gooks."
They appeared in Liberia dressed in black Stetsons and red galluses:
"So I shoot that old nigger and he flop on his side one leg up in the air just akicking."
"Yeah, but you ever burn a niggah?"
They are always pacing around bidonvilles smoking huge cigars:
"Have to get some bulldozers in here Jody. Clean out all this crap."

Morbid crowds follow them about hoping to witness some superlative American outrage. *

—

Evidence of the social value of the contents of *Big Table* 1 was introduced by Sprayregen in the form of testimonials and letters from an impressive group of literary figures, including John Ciardi, Jacques Barzun, Rev. Pierre Delattre, Lawrence Ferlinghetti, Allen Ginsberg, Hans W. Mattick, Norman Mailer, Hoke Norris, Harold Taylor, Lionel Trilling, and Anthony C. West. These did not, however, impress the hearing examiner, William A. Duvall, who ruled that *Big Table* 1 was obscene, and that the postmaster was entitled to exclude it from the mails.

Joel Sprayregen appealed the hearing examiner's decision to a federal district court presided over by Judge Julius J. Hoffman, who later presided at the trial of the "Chicago Seven." Hoffman heard the appeal, then, applying *Roth,* ordered the Post Office's ban on *Big Table* 1 lifted because in his judgment the Kerouac and Burroughs pieces were "serious literature," therefore not obscene. Judge Hoffman read "Old Angel Midnight" as "a wild prose picnic . . . some sort of dialogue between God and Man." And he saw the episodes from *Naked Lunch* as an attempt by the author to get across his "ideas" about the world in which he lived—"to shock the contemporary society in order perhaps to better point out its flaws and weaknesses." Hoffman's decision, like Judge Horn's in the *Howl* case, interpreted Justice Brennan's opinion in *Roth* so as to liberate literature from obscenity censorship if it seemed to have any social significance at all.

The *Chicago Review* and *Big Table* 1 censorship incidents carried Burroughs and *Naked Lunch* up the road of fame. After the first mailing of *Big Table* 1 was seized, Rosenthal and Carroll shipped the remainder of the 10,000-copy edition by truck to San Francisco and New York, where it sold out. In Paris, publisher Maurice Girodias—who had made a good deal of money by being the first to publish Vladimir Nabokov's *Lolita* in English, and had not yet been silenced by the Paris police and judiciary—got wind of the controversy and its salutary outcome and decided to reconsider his decision not to publish what he called William Burroughs's "mess."

---

*The point of this passage was later explained by Mary McCarthy: "The hoofers, Clem and Jody, were hired by the Russians to give Americans a bad name abroad: they appeared in Liberia wearing black stetsons and red galluses and talking loudly about burning niggers back home."

19

Like a Piece
of Lead
with Wings on It

I N 1934, Jack Kahane, Maurice Girodias's father, placed the almost prohibitive price of 50 francs on a book and cautioned Paris booksellers:
This book must not be shown in the window.

The book was *Tropic of Cancer,* and little Maurice had drawn the picture
of the crab that appeared on its green paperback cover. Kahane was the
founder of the Obelisk Press; he first read Henry Miller's manuscript in the
garden of his country house outside Paris.

JACK KAHANE: At last! I had read the most terrible, the most sordid, the
most magnificent manuscript that had ever fallen into my hands; nothing
I had yet received was comparable to it for the splendor of its writing, the
fathomless depth of its despair, the savour of its portraiture, the boisterous-
ness of its humour. Walking into the house I was exalted by the triumphant
sensation of all explorers who have at last fallen upon the object of their
years of search. I had in my hands a work of genius and it had been offered
to me for publication.

———

Nevertheless, Kahane would not publish Miller's book until the writer's
friend and lover, Anaïs Nin, gave the publisher a guarantee against financial
loss. She paid Kahane 5,000 francs down and wrote a preface for the book.

Years later Maurice Girodias remembered Miller as a middle-aged American, unknown, stranded in Paris, living off the land—a sort of literary
clochard. He saw his book, however, as "the spontaneous product of a man
of genius." More than a masterpiece, it seemed to Girodias to mark "the
birth of a new language in literature." The book's author, however, appraised it more realistically:

HENRY MILLER: This then? This is not a book. This is libel, slander, defamation of character . . . a prolonged insult, a gob of spit in the face of Art, a kick in the pants to God, Man, Destiny, Time, Love, Beauty . . .

—

Later, Miller would relate to Los Angeles defense lawyer Stanley Fleishman his beginnings as a writer in Paris:

HENRY MILLER: I had imagined on leaving America that I was going to Spain, but I never got farther than Paris. I arrived there in the Spring of 1930, knowing nothing of the French language. . . . The difficulties I had experienced in pursuing the career of writer prior to leaving America were considerably augmented, to put it mildly, on arriving in France. Looking back on it all I must confess, however, that it was more enriching and instructive starving in Paris than in my home town. Thanks to the aid and encouragement of the friends I made—largely expatriates like myself—I managed to survive and finish the book. It was something of a miracle that I found there in Paris the one publisher in all the world courageous enough to sponsor such a book: Jack Kahane of the Obelisk Press. Between the time he accepted the book and its publication I rewrote the book three times.

I have often referred to this work as an ice-breaker. In writing it I found my own voice, liberation, in short. This was due, undoubtedly, to the life I led, by which I mean not only the struggles and hardships of keeping alive in a foreign land but also as a result of a growing acquaintance with French literature, the French way of life, and the acceptance accorded me by French writers. Unwittingly I found myself living that "bohemian" life which so many celebrated writers and artists before me had been obliged to live for one reason or another. My book might be regarded, I suppose, as a celebration of that splendidly miserable kind of life. In writing it, I ought to add, I had almost no hope of its ever being accepted by a publisher. It was something I had to do in order to preserve my own integrity. It was a case of do or die. Certainly the last thing I ever dreamed of was that it would one day be published in my own country.

—

The American publisher of *Tropic of Cancer*, Barney Rosset, first encountered the book that made his firm famous when he was a student at Swarthmore College:

BARNEY ROSSET: I didn't really know much about Miller. I didn't even know *Tropic of Cancer* was banned in this country. I heard that the Gotham Book Mart in New York was a good place to buy it, so I took the train to New York and went in and asked for it. Frances Steloff asked me why I wanted it.* I said I was a student and she reached under the

---

*The Gotham Book Mart was founded by Frances Steloff in 1920, and became over the years an international meeting place for the literati and a literary haven for the authors of novels that had been banned by government officials in the United States. Among those who worked as clerks in her store were Allen Ginsberg and LeRoi Jones. Like Margaret Anderson, who had ordered and sold contraband copies of *Ulysses* from her Greenwich counter and took out an edition that said "Printed in Mexico" on the cover. I loved it.

———

So Rosset wrote a freshman English paper called "Henry Miller vs. Our Way of Life." The paper got a B minus, but it led to Rosset's later publication of the book. The firestorm of censorship that resulted gave the United States Supreme Court a historic opportunity to revolutionize obscenity law and almost extirpate literary censorship.

BARNEY ROSSET: By nature, I'm a type of free American spirit, against censorship, which goes back to my grammar school days. Even how I got into book publishing was accidental. After the war, I made a film against American racism, called *Strange Victory,* and it bombed and I lost a lot of my father's friends' money in it. Then a friend of Joan Mitchell, who was my wife, heard about this publishing company, Grove Press, and I bought it for $3,000 and it had three books when I bought it. . . .

Once I was a publisher it certainly occurred to me that I should be allowed to publish what I wanted. So that led me very quickly into censorship problems. If you feel a book has literary merit, you publish it. If you get arrested in the process, you fight it. In a free society there's nothing that an adult shouldn't be allowed to read or to see. That's the way I felt about publishing *Lady Chatterley's Lover, Tropic of Cancer, Naked Lunch, The Story of O.* . . .

EUGENE IONESCO: Barney Rosset had a lot of ideas. He made the choices but it wasn't he who did the work. The one who did the work was someone who had more zest for work but who was a lot less gifted than Barney Rosset was, on the ideological plane, Dick Seaver.

———

Richard Seaver, who helped Rosset develop Grove, says Rosset "had this incredible openness to what was happening in Europe, after the war. A lot of literary energy pent up by the war exploded, and Barney was the only American publisher who realized it." In the fifties, Rosset made an exciting reputation for Grove Press by publishing the works of avant-garde European writers unfamiliar to Americans. He brought out Samuel Beckett's *Waiting for Godot* in 1955 and his *Endgame* the next year. In 1958 Rosset published Eugene Ionesco's *The Bald Soprano, The Lesson,* and two others of his plays. He was the first to publish in English works by Jean Genet, Marguerite Duras, and Alain Robbe-Grillet, the leaders of the postwar French literary avant-garde. But those books did not get Grove Press into trouble with American censors.

EUGENE IONESCO: I liked Barney Rosset. He was a very whimsical guy. I liked him a lot because he came to those international conferences, those

———

Village bookshop, Steloff ordered directly from D. H. Lawrence in Italy and Henry Miller in Paris shipments of *Lady Chatterley's Lover* and *Tropic of Cancer,* which she sold from under the counter. For more on Steloff, see the endnotes of this chapter.

meetings where the top publishers got together that way, to find money, but not him—he came because he was a publisher.

ALAIN ROBBE-GRILLET: What was funny was how Barney Rosset was fascinated by everything that was against the established order, in whatever sense or direction it took. Politically he was far more left than most Americans. In literature, for France, it was the *nouveau roman,* but he could get interested in anything, as long as it was anti-establishment. It was rather strange, it was an idea he had, to fight against the establishment, by every means.

———

In the sixties, with the support of editors Fred Jordan and Dick Seaver, Rosset shifted his publishing focus from the French literary avant-garde and young American "beat" writers like Allen Ginsberg and Jack Kerouac— whose work he had published in his literary magazine, *Evergreen Review*—to the literature of Anglo-American sexual radicals like D. H. Lawrence, Henry Miller, John Rechy, and William Burroughs, and third-world political radicals like Frantz Fanon, Che Guevara, and Malcolm X. He made *Evergreen Review* into a slick-covered monthly newsstand magazine disseminating offbeat sex and radical politics.

BARNEY ROSSET: Doubleday contracted to publish *Malcolm X,* and then Malcolm X was assassinated. Then they wouldn't publish it; they said they were afraid that they'd be killed. Nelson Doubleday said, "I don't want to see my secretary's face smashed. I don't want to see our storefronts smashed." And he abandoned it. So we took it on. To me, that was in defense of freedom of speech. . . . Then after we published Che Guevara's *Diaries* and ran that poster of Che on the cover of *Evergreen Review,* our offices got bombed. They threw a hand grenade and smashed the place.

JEAN GENET: It was in the summer of '68 that I saw Barney Rosset for the last time. I was at his place in New York and I took the elevator and I went to the second floor. And the elevator opened onto a building completely burned out! They had thrown a bomb three or four days earlier, and the whole thing almost was in ruins.

BARNEY ROSSET: Grove's first important censorship battle was *Lady Chatterley's Lover.* The reason I started with it was that it seemed to me impossible that people would say Lawrence wasn't a great writer. And I had this urge to test the obscenity laws. Until then, *Chatterley* had been published only in expurgated editions by establishment publishers. Alfred Knopf, for one. So it was an obvious book by a great author and I felt the intellectual atmosphere in the country was right. My publication of it was a very cold, deliberate attack on censorship. We went into fourteen printings and sold over fifty thousand hardcover copies within a few months. So Grove had its first best-seller.

However, *Lady Chatterley's Lover* was nothing compared with *Tropic of*

Cancer, our next one, which was a lot closer personally to me. I'd read the book as a college freshman, and thought it was marvelous.

HENRY MILLER *(Tropic of Cancer): I am going to sing for you a little off key perhaps, but I will sing. . . .*
To sing you must first open your mouth. You must have a pair of lungs, and a little knowledge of music. It is not necessary to have an accordion, or a guitar. The essential thing is to want to sing. This then is a song.

ANTHONY LEWIS: Twenty years ago [in 1941] a Swarthmore student named Barney Rosset wrote a paper on Henry Miller for his American Literature course. He called it "Henry Miller Versus Our Way of Life." It got a B minus.
    Today [1961], Barney Rosset is chairman and editor of Grove Press, which last June published the first American edition of Henry Miller's *Tropic of Cancer.* After living for six months with that distinction, Mr. Rosset would have to be pardoned for thinking that his college thesis was right: Henry Miller and the American Way of Life do not seem to get along.
    Tropic of Cancer had run into more massive opposition from censors than any other serious publishing venture in memory.

HENRY MILLER *(Tropic of Cancer): It is to you Tania, that I am singing. I wish that I could sing better, more melodiously, but then perhaps you would never have consented to listen. . . .*

BARNEY ROSSET: When I found myself a publisher, and Miller's main works still not published in the States, that became an obvious goal for me. But I thought first we'll start with Lawrence, who had a greater reputation, since Miller at that time was thought of by a lot of people as something of a scoundrel. Well, when we finally published *Tropic of Cancer* in 1961, suddenly we had hundreds of arrests, lawsuits, and criminal prosecutions, including that one in Chicago, which was my home town.

HENRY MILLER *(Tropic of Cancer): After me you can take on stallions, bulls, rams, drakes, St. Bernards. You can stuff toads, bats, lizards up your rectum. You can shit arpeggios if you like, or string a zither across your navel. I am fucking you, Tania, so that you'll stay fucked. . . . I will bite into your clitoris and spit out two franc pieces.*

JUDGE SAMUEL B. EPSTEIN: One day a *Tropic of Cancer* case came before me, and the first thing that happened was I ruled that the people of Chicago had a constitutional right to read the book. No previous court decision, to my knowledge, considered the rights of readers.
    However, after my decision was published—the following Monday or Tuesday—Mayor Daley called a news conference. He and I were good friends; he called me by my first name. And he had this conference in his office with a lot of reporters present. . . . Corporation counsel of Chicago was present and a lot of lawyers for the suburban chiefs of police were

present, the ones who had lost the decision in my case. And one of those lawyers or the police said, "Mr. Mayor, I know you are not very familiar with the contents of this book. If you'll permit me, I'm going to read from page five."

HENRY MILLER *(Tropic of Cancer): O Tania, where now is that warm cunt of yours, those fat, heavy garters, those soft, bulging thighs? There is a bone in my prick six inches long. I will ream out every wrinkle in your cunt, Tania, big with seed.*

JUDGE SAMUEL B. EPSTEIN: Whatever may be said of Daley, he was quite a religious man, and devoted to his family, particularly.* Well, they tell me that at that press conference he turned red and he turned to his corporation counsel and said, "I want this case appealed to the Supreme Court, immediately!" . . .

He was talking about the Supreme Court of Illinois, and they eventually accepted to review my decision without the necessity of going through the routine of the appellate court first. And they had it pending there for about two years but for some reason no decision came out.

BARNEY ROSSET: We published the hardbound edition of *Tropic of Cancer* in June and the paperback edition in October of 1961. Although what followed must have been the greatest nationwide censorship assault ever mounted against a book, our paperback edition was on the best-seller list throughout 1962 and '63. Actually, the paperback edition saved our lives. Our legal costs were in the neighborhood of $250,000. . . .

We sold over two million copies and the profits from the paperback edition paid the legal fees, which were astronomical, since we paid all the legal costs for any wholesaler or dealer who got into trouble for selling *Cancer*. No publisher had ever done that before. The ACLU also helped us in many places.

CHARLES REMBAR: I did not conduct the trial of any of the *Tropic* cases. I argued two of the appeals, but apart from that, the very number of the lawsuits kept me in the office, trying to help the various trial attorneys around the country. I made a few trips to sore spots to give counsel to counsel; otherwise it was a matter of telephone calls and correspondence.†

---

*Richard J. Daley, mayor of Chicago from 1955 to 1976, was one of the last big-city bosses; his support was regularly sought by local and national political figures. Daley gained national notoriety in 1968 when Chicago police under his instructions brutally subdued demonstrators and journalists at the Democratic National Convention.

†Rembar won the Massachusetts appeal and lost the New York appeal. See de Grazia, *Censorship Landmarks* (1969), 451ff. and 464ff. Not all counsel handling the various *Cancer* trials around the country were "counseled" by Rembar. A general brief he designed to assist local counsel to conduct *Cancer* trials was distributed to local counsel and ACLU lawyers who tried the various cases. Rembar's general brief advanced Harry Kalven's argument (spelled out in "The Metaphysics of the Law of Obscenity," *1960 Supreme Court Review* [1960], 1) that, under *Roth*, only "worthless" expression might constitutionally be deemed "obscene" and fall outside the First Amendment's protection. See E. R. Hutchison, *Tropic of Cancer on Trial*

ANTHONY LEWIS: It is not on sale in Massachusetts, Rhode Island and these among many cities: Los Angeles, Chicago, Philadelphia, Cleveland, Atlanta, Miami, Dallas, Houston, Seattle, Hartford, Wilmington (Del.), Indianapolis, Des Moines, St. Louis, Trenton, Buffalo, Phoenix, Oklahoma City, Birmingham.

BARNEY ROSSET: Booksellers were worried because the Post Office had placed a ban on the book and then withdrawn the ban, without any explanation or court decision that the book was not obscene. Brentano's wrote us: "Our counsel has very strong feelings about the inherent danger in the sale of this book and continues to advise us against it."

When the Doubleday stores also refused to carry the book, I said, "This is a sad and ominous portent for the future of creative book publishing in this country."

After that, Scribner's and Macy's also refused to handle it, and the *Chicago Tribune* said that it would not carry the names of "dirty" books on its best-seller list—because of *Cancer*. Mainly it was the "little" bookstores who were selling *Cancer*, until the book reviews came out praising the book and Henry Miller.

ANTHONY LEWIS: The troubles of *Tropic* had a broader significance than their impact on Grove Press. They represented, clearly, a new and critical phase in the continuing struggle over censorship of sex in literature.

——

For the first time in its history, the ACLU threw a massive array of legal talent into the defense of an "obscene" book, its hard-pressed publisher, and scores of beleaguered booksellers. The ACLU's Illinois division, Greater Philadelphia branch, Southern California affiliate, and Connecticut Civil Liberties Union "were heavily involved in cases challenging the censorship of *Tropic of Cancer* in their areas. Overall . . . at least fifteen ACLU lawyers were concerned with developing such cases or friend-of-the-court briefs."*

FRED JORDAN: Of one and a half million paperback copies of *Tropic of Cancer* sent around the country by a national distributor, 600,000 were immediately returned. Local wholesalers would not handle them because of their fears of police action or because of pressures coming from outside the law.

(1968), 71, and Chapter 22 below. The only *Tropic of Cancer* case decided on its merits by the Supreme Court was one that came out of Dade County, Florida, which I presented to the Court, and won, as discussed anon and in Chapter 22.

*I was involved as an ACLU lawyer in the Maryland *Tropic* case, *Yudkin* v. *Maryland,* among others. In one of the California cases, *Bradley Reed Smith* v. *California,* I filed an amicus curiae brief in the Supreme Court, not for the ACLU but on behalf of more than one hundred authors, editors, and publishers. This brief is likely to have impacted on the Supreme Court's deliberations in other *Cancer* cases, including the Florida case. In a Wisconsin case I joined in the writing of the appellate brief; that case was won. In the Dade County, Florida, case I filed the petition for certiorari in the Supreme Court; that was the case that freed the novel for the entire country. See Chapter 22. See also E. R. Hutchison, *Tropic of Cancer on Trial* (1968), 93.

In Chicago, the police in some eleven suburban communities confiscated all paperback copies of *Tropic of Cancer* with nothing resembling due process of law. Grove Press started its own legal action in Illinois against the suburban chiefs of police to restrain them from suppressing the book. . . . Luckily we went before a courageous judge in Chicago, Judge Samuel B. Epstein.

—

The plaintiff in the Chicago case was Professor Franklin Haiman of Northwestern University in Evanston. When Haiman found that police had prevented him from buying a copy of *Tropic of Cancer* by frightening booksellers into removing it from their stores, he asked the ACLU to help vindicate his freedom to read, and the ACLU provided him with free legal representation for that purpose. Later Rosset "took over" the case, providing lawyers of his choice. One of these, Elmer Gertz, had frequently served as a volunteer ACLU lawyer.

BARNEY ROSSET: That, for me, was the most dramatic trial of *Tropic of Cancer*—in Chicago. Judge Epstein had been a friend of my father's; and Richard Ellmann, a great Joyce critic, was our major witness. I was a witness too, the only time for me, and I brought along the paper I'd written on *Tropic of Cancer* at Swarthmore. I had the satisfaction of having the district attorney say to me, "Well, you're only in this for the money. You don't even know who Miller is. . . ." I pulled out of my pocket my freshman English paper and read to him from it.

JUDGE SAMUEL B. EPSTEIN: The owner of the bookstore told Professor Haiman that the police had cleared his shelves of all the copies of *Tropic of Cancer* and had thrown them into the garbage can.

So he started the suit under the theory that he had the right to read that book and the police were unconstitutionally interfering with that right. And the first motion that was made before me by the lawyers for the chiefs of police, who were the defendants in the case, was that this man Professor Haiman had no standing in court, and that his suit should be dismissed.

It was then that I ruled that without the right to read, all the other provisions for constitutional protection would be ineffective. I denied the motion to dismiss and brought the case to trial.

HOKE NORRIS: The Chicago story seems to begin . . . in Montreal, Canada, at the annual conference of the International Association of Chiefs of Police, which began on September 30 and ended on October 5 [1961]. One of the chiefs was George E. Whittenberg of Mount Prospect, Illinois—a suburb of Chicago.

—

Whittenberg was told by a chief of police "from a city in the East" to be on the lookout for a book entitled *Tropic of Cancer*. In Mount Prospect, a few days later, a truck driver for the Charles Levy Circulating Company,

which distributed most of the paperback books in the area,* informed a
police sergeant about the Miller book, and the sergeant told the captain,
and they both drove over to a bookstore on Main Street and found a bundle
of books that had been delivered that morning, standing in front of the
store's closed doors.

POLICE CHIEF GEORGE E. WHITTENBERG: We stopped at 1 North Main
Street, and [the driver] pointed out the book to me that was still in the
package of books that was delivered to that store that morning. The store
was still closed. He pulled the book out, and I stood there for four or five
minutes and thumbed through the book from page to page.

HENRY MILLER *(Tropic of Cancer): Llona now, she had a cunt. . . . On every
high hill she played the harlot—and sometimes in telephone booths and toilets.
. . . She lay in Tottenham Road and fingered herself. She used candles, Roman
candles, and door knobs. Not a prick in the land big enough for her . . . not one.
Men went inside her and curled up. She wanted extension pricks, self-exploding
rockets, hot boiling oil made of wax and creosote. She would cut off your prick and
keep it inside her forever, if you gave her permission. One cunt out of a million,
Llona!*

———

Chief Whittenberg personally visited six drugstores in Mount Prospect
that sold paperback books and found copies of *Tropic of Cancer* at five of
them. His first stop was at Van Driel's Drug Store, where he took up the
question of the book with Max Ullrich, the pharmacist in charge.

CHIEF GEORGE E. WHITTENBERG: I asked Mr. Ullrich to please check the
book entitled *Tropic of Cancer* before he put it on the racks . . . to see if
he thought the book was okay. He said he would and he did. He took one
of the books out of the package—they were still wrapped up in the wire
bundle with other magazines—he took one out and he went through the
book from cover to cover, thumbed through it. He thanked me for stopping in, and he said he would not put it out for sale.

———

Whittenberg did the same at the other stores. He also called police chiefs
in Des Plaines, Arlington Heights, and Lincolnwood, and the chief in Des
Plaines called other chiefs, in Niles and other suburbs. Through this network of chiefs, officers were directed to visit bookselling locations and
confiscate any copies of *Tropic of Cancer* they found, and to tell booksellers
not to sell any more copies. Then Chief Clarence Emrikson of Niles called
the Village of Skokie and discussed *Tropic of Cancer* with the acting chief
there, Captain Robert Morris, who showed page 5 to the Skokie juvenile
officer, village manager, and corporation counsel. Everybody agreed it was
"vulgar and obscene" and so they went out and visited all the vendors in
town and asked them to remove the book from their shelves. No one had
ever read the whole book. Page 5 was enough for the police.

———

*But not Grove's *Tropic of Cancer.*

HENRY MILLER *(Tropic of Cancer): I'm dancing with every slut in the place. But we're leaving in the morning! That's what I'm telling the blonde with the agate-colored eyes. And while I'm telling her she takes my hand and squeezes it between her legs. In the lavatory I stand before the bowl with a tremendous erection; it seems light and heavy at the same time, like a piece of lead with wings on it.*

In a letter to Henry Miller, before the Chicago trial began, Elmer Gertz told Miller what he thought of the man who would be judging his book.

ELMER GERTZ: It is very fortunate that we have a judge who, despite an innate prudery, is an honorable man through and through, who will decide on what he thinks the law and facts are, even if it hurts him.

JUDGE SAMUEL B. EPSTEIN: When that book was first called to my attention I threw it against the wall of my room. . . .

My father was the dean of the Orthodox rabbis of Chicago. He was brought here by a congregation whose original people came from the area where he was a rabbi in Lithuania. And he was the dean until his death in 1938. So I grew up in the atmosphere of a home where learning and, shall I say, ideals were the way of life.

In those days a Jew belonging to an Orthodox congregation would rarely go to court on litigation that wasn't of great importance. They came to the rabbi, both sides; and I grew up in that atmosphere and that was the reason why I ultimately studied law. My father's study was a courtroom.

ELMER GERTZ: Litigation involving *Tropic of Cancer* was going on everywhere. There were at least sixty cases. I established close relations with the attorneys handling the various proceedings in different parts of the country. We exchanged briefs, information, and ideas. Edward de Grazia and Stanley Fleishman, at opposite ends of the country, were especially helpful.

Gertz conceived his trial strategy by studying the transcripts of the *Lady Chatterley's Lover* case "that had been won by Charles Rembar for Grove Press several months earlier," reading an account of the trial of the same book that had taken place in England, and going through the transcript of the San Francisco case that had resulted in the freeing of Allen Ginsberg's *Howl.*

ELMER GERTZ: After considerable thought I decided that our most dependable expert witness would be Dr. Richard Ellmann, the James Joyce authority.

RICHARD ELLMANN: The book . . . is definitely a work of literary merit and importance. . . . There is an attempt to break through the conventions of the novel and to establish a kind of history of the hero which will ultimately bring the readers—like the hero—from the state mentioned on the first page, where everyone feels dead, to the state mentioned on the last page, where the hero begins to feel alive, feels the river of life coursing through him; and in order to do this, Henry Miller gives a very accurate picture of Paris life in the early 1930s.

HENRY MILLER *(Tropic of Cancer): It is a little after daybreak. We pack hurriedly and sneak out of the hotel. The cafés are still closed. We walk, and as we walk we scratch ourselves. The day opens in milky whiteness, streaks of salmon-pink sky, snails leaving their shells. Paris. Paris. Everything happens here. Old, crumbling walls and the pleasant sound of water running in the urinals. Men licking their mustaches at the bar. Shutters going up with a bang and little streams purling in the gutters. Amer Picon in huge scarlet letters. Zigzag. Which way will we go and why or where or what?*

Mona is hungry, her dress is thin. *

BARNEY ROSSET: Ellmann was an incredible witness. He knew what pages they were reading from without even looking at the book.

ELMER GERTZ: Through the device of questioning Dr. Ellmann, I was able to offer in evidence the published opinions of famous writers and critics whom it was beyond our means to put on the stand . . .

NORMAN COUSINS: One of the noteworthy books of the century . . .

T. S. ELIOT: A very remarkable book . . .

JOHN CIARDI: A substantial work of art . . .

HORACE GREGORY: A triumph of the comic spirit . . .

EDMUND WILSON: The epitaph for the whole generation of American writers and artists that migrated to Paris after the war . . .

ELMER GERTZ: Adapting a device suggested by Edward de Grazia, I was able to establish through Dr. Ellmann's testimony that Miller had been described as:

NORMAN COUSINS: One of the adornments of modern American literature . . .

WALLACE FOWLIE: A unified and triumphant artist . . . a visionary . . .

LAWRENCE DURRELL: A towering, shapeless, sometimes comic figure who completely overtops the glazed reflections cast by those waxworks of contemporary American fiction—Hemingway, Dos Passos, Faulkner . . .

GEORGE ORWELL: The only imaginative prose-writer of the slightest value who had appeared among the English-speaking races for some years past . . .

ELMER GERTZ: We brought out through Dr. Ellmann's testimony that the ideas in *Tropic of Cancer* had been found to involve:

---

*Miller's first wife's name was Mona. After Mona joined Miller in Paris, Anaïs Nin carried on love affairs with both of them. See Anaïs Nin, *Henry and June* (1986) and *A Literate Passion: Letters of Anaïs Nin and Henry Miller* (1989).

THE SATURDAY REVIEW: Living tissue—much of it disgusting, much of it beautiful . . .

NEW YORK HERALD TRIBUNE: A volcanic flow, a chaos of words and dreams, of appetites starved and satiated, of bitter memories and apocalyptic prophecies, barbaric yawps and subtle penetrations to the heart of a book, a painting, a city, of sexual encounters both joyful and joyless, of a vagabond existence in a world without hope but no despair . . .

MINNEAPOLIS SUNDAY TRIBUNE: A kind of manifesto for the right to give a complete picture of what a man says, thinks and does . . .

NEW YORK POST: A brand of subversion which may someday topple this republic, and to our benefit . . .

ELMER GERTZ: We felt we had established an unassailable case, if it survived cross-examination. Dr. Ellmann faced his inquisitors with his characteristic self-assurance and courtesy.

Mr. Brian Kilgallen [the assistant corporation counsel] began the cross-examination. He asked Dr. Ellmann about . . . the method of masturbation employed by one of the characters where he cores out the center of the apple and smears it with cold cream and uses it in that fashion.

I objected and said the book must be considered as a whole, not in fragments. . . .

JUDGE SAMUEL B. EPSTEIN: I am going to permit questions as to whether or not there aren't certain parts that are pornographic; and if they are, the question is, do they affect the literary value of the book; and I will decide . . . which overbalances which.*

RICHARD ELLMANN: Your Honor, I would say that passage was slightly disgusting but that it's an essential element in the disgusting picture portrayed in the *Tropic of Cancer,* which is a diseased civilization. You must represent disease as disease. . . .

ASSISTANT CORPORATION COUNSEL BRIAN KILGALLEN: Would you recommend this book, *Tropic of Cancer,* to your students, whom I put in the adolescent category?

RICHARD ELLMANN: Well, I informed them that I was going to testify here, and there were suppressed cheers. . . . The answer is that I would recommend this book for good reading to students, yes.

ELMER GERTZ: Now the cross-examination passed to Mr. Edward Hofert. He was concerned about the famous paragraph on page 5 and other uninhibited passages. Judge Epstein felt that it was time to develop a point that had been bothering him. He asked Dr. Ellmann . . .

---

*Judge Epstein was using Brennan's opinion in *Roth* for guidance in making his rulings on the receipt of evidence and in reaching judgment on the merits of the case.

JUDGE SAMUEL B. EPSTEIN: Would you recommend that this portion [at the top of page 5] and perhaps other abridgements [could] be made in the book without seriously affecting the literary merit of the book?

RICHARD ELLMANN: No, I feel that the whole literary merit of the book depends upon its bluntness and honesty in this kind of representation of somewhat exaggerated feelings. . . .

JUDGE SAMUEL B. EPSTEIN: In other words, Doctor, you don't consider that this paragraph is just a disconnected outpouring of a lot of filth that has no relation to the rest of the book?

RICHARD ELLMANN: No, Your Honor. It seems to me basic.

JUDGE SAMUEL B. EPSTEIN: Of course it is filth, but you think it is necessary?

ELLIOT EPSTEIN: When Dad said that passage was "filth," all the lawyers for the police in the courtroom grinned from ear to ear. They thought they had won. And one of my friends, sitting there, whispered to me—I was in the courtroom that day—"There goes your case!" I knew Dad better and said to him, "Don't you believe it!"

RICHARD ELLMANN: Yes, Your Honor.

BARNEY ROSSET: After the trial ended somehow I knew we had won. I walked out into the street into a terrific Chicago blizzard. I couldn't see a thing. I walked toward my mother's house and I could barely see Tribune Tower. Everything looked barren and forlorn. And I kept walking through that blizzard and feeling like I was going down, going down, and feeling glad, glad, like released. Because of what I'd done, what the trial meant. And the only reason I survived and reached my mother's house that night was because I found a doorway in the street. It was a bar, and I went in. . . .

———

Three weeks passed before Judge Epstein announced his decision, on February 21, 1962. He took great pains in writing his opinion because he wanted it to leave a mark in the history of the struggle for literary freedom.

JUDGE SAMUEL B. EPSTEIN: I myself didn't know how I was going to rule. My son David was then alive, he was a writer, he was certainly anxious to know how I was going to rule on the subject.* My son Elliot, he was a lawyer, was very anxious too. Neither one of them knew until the morning that I announced my decision how I was going to rule. I wrote my opinion at three in the morning, at home, in handwriting. And I read it the next morning when the case was called. And my two sons didn't know until then how I was going to rule.

———

*David was a Hollywood screenwriter, blacklisted during the McCarthy period. He later committed suicide.

ELLIOT EPSTEIN: Dad was not a particularly courageous person. He was always a political animal. I'd gone to law school, and my brother and I discussed the case and told Dad what we thought. And that's how he decided it. Dad knew his sons wouldn't speak to him if he didn't rule in favor of *Tropic of Cancer*.

———

Weighing the novel's literary and First Amendment values against its possible prurient appeal, Judge Epstein ruled that *Tropic of Cancer* was not obscene or pornographic, and that the people of Chicago and its suburbs had a right that was protected by the First and Fourteenth Amendments to the Constitution of the United States to read the book. Judge Epstein enjoined the police from interfering any further with the circulation of the book.

JUDGE SAMUEL B. EPSTEIN: In my written opinion, I said: "Censorship is a very dangerous instrumentality, even in the hands of a court. Recent history has proven the evil of an attempt at controlling the utterances and thoughts of our population. . . .

"People who object to a book are free to condemn it and even to urge others to reject it. Organizations such as church societies, and other sincere groups, are free to condemn any book they deem objectionable. Such efforts help to educate the literary tastes of the reading public. So do reviews and comments in the press. Such voluntary efforts are praiseworthy and consonant with democratic principles. . . .

"As Justice Douglas said: 'I have the same confidence in the ability of our people to reject noxious literature as I have in their capacity to sort out the true from the false in theology, economics, politics or any other field.' Hard-core pornography, it is agreed, has no social value whatsoever, and does not enjoy the protection of the First and Fourteenth Amendments to the Constitution of the United States, but literature which has some social merit, even if controversial, should be left to individual taste rather than to governmental edict. . . .

"Let the parents control the reading matter of their children; let the tastes of the readers determine what they may or may not read; let not the government or the courts dictate the reading matter of a free people. . . . The Constitutional freedoms of speech and press should be jealously guarded by the courts. As a corollary to the freedom of speech and press, there is also the freedom to read. The right to free utterances becomes a useless privilege when the freedom to read is restricted or denied."

The Sunday after my decision, after the publicity in the newspapers of a day or two before, in practically every Catholic church in Chicago the preachers urged that I be impeached and thrown out of office.

And then I got letters, bags full of them! From all over the world. I had my telephone number in the book, unfortunately. I would get calls in the middle of the night. Somebody would call me every name you can think of and hang up.

In one communication I received, the body of a human being was traced in cigarette paper, and the area of the heart was burned through the cigarette paper. I turned it over to the postal department but they never could trace it. My wife was disturbed.

Day and night we were getting calls and threats. And then I was surprised that [Mayor] Daley did not insist that I be moved from chancery court. Very much surprised. I sat on chancery for nineteen years, to the day of my retirement. . . . There may have been a short time when they asked me to hear some personal injury cases. I don't remember if that was after my decision in the *Tropic of Cancer* case, however.

ELLIOT EPSTEIN: The fact is that Dad was bounced out of chancery after the trial, for freeing *Tropic of Cancer*. While the trial was going on, Daley sent all kinds of people to talk to my father secretly, *ex parte*: politicians whom Dad had known, politicians who were Jewish, to pressure him; he sent some major judges, who commented to Dad about what assignments judges got.* And they all told him, "You'll be in trouble, Sam, if you don't rule that book is obscene." He got very angry and scared, worried about his career, his future on the bench. He would tell me: "Daley sent so-and-so in to see me, and he, too, warned me something would happen."

JUDGE SAMUEL EPSTEIN: I received more mail concerning that decision than on any other case in my experience. Fifty letters or so were full of praise. About two hundred were uncomplimentary. One letter said, "You filthy swine! We hope you are satisfied. You are a disgrace and we hope your conscience will torment you to your dying days."

Some of the phone calls apparently came from taverns, because I could hear music in the background.

I told the newspaper reporters that I didn't favor the book. However I was sworn to uphold the law. And the decisions of the courts, particularly the Supreme Court of the United States, had established that any book having even the slightest redeeming social importance—unorthodox ideas, controversial ideas, even ideas hateful to the prevailing climate of opinion†—was protected by the First and Fourteenth Amendments to the Constitution of the United States. . . .

Well, the American Civil Liberties Union made up a special calendar showing the history of law and justice in the United States. What it shows is Justice Frank Murphy . . . Justice William Douglas . . . every page . . . Justice Louis Brandeis . . . Judge Samuel Epstein! Imagine, giving me a page among all of those people.

———

While the city appealed the *Tropic of Cancer* case to the Supreme Court of Illinois, New York's highest state court handed down a decision finding

---

*A similar threat to one of Lenny Bruce's New York criminal trial judges led to the conviction of Bruce, as described in Chapter 24.

†This language and the principle it expressed were drawn from Justice Brennan's seminal opinion in *Roth* v. *United States*.

Cancer obscene. Charles Rembar was the Grove lawyer who argued the publisher's case.

JUDGE JOHN F. SCILEPPI (NEW YORK COURT OF APPEALS): [*Tropic of Cancer*] is nothing more than a compilation of a series of sordid narrations dealing with sex in a manner designed to appeal to the prurient interests of the average person. It is a blow to sense, not merely sensibility. It is, in short, "hard-core pornography," dirt for dirt's sake, and dirt for money's sake.

———

Elmer Gertz called the New York decision "fantastic and unbelievable." Then the Supreme Court of Illinois announced a "dismal decision" of its own in the Chicago *Tropic of Cancer* case.

JUDGE SAMUEL B. EPSTEIN: One day, after two years of waiting around, the Supreme Court of Illinois was adjourning for the summer, and they suddenly issued an opinion that was written by Judge Hershey, who was a friend of mine, a very able man. We had a very fine supreme court. And unanimously the supreme court reversed me.

THE SUPREME COURT OF ILLINOIS: Tested by the applicable tests, this court is compelled to conclude that *Tropic of Cancer* is obscene, is patently offensive, and is not entitled to any protection under the Federal or State constitutions.

———

Henry Miller wrote Elmer Gertz that he found it ironic that "two big states," New York and Illinois—"supposedly advanced culturally, etc."—should be the only ones whose high courts held *Tropic of Cancer* obscene.* He considered that result a matter of politics,† not the will of the people, and felt it would prove to be a boomerang. The author's astrologer friend in Lausanne had written Miller that 1964 would be full of legal troubles, that he would be continually before the public, and that if he won in one instance he'd lose in another—but that eventually he would experience "nothing but triumph and victory." "And she didn't mean in a distant future, either."

When Miller heard about the abusive letters Judge Epstein had received, he wrote Gertz "to be of good cheer" and added that he was sorry about the continued abuse and criticism of Epstein. Miller considered the judge "a wonderful man" and he asked Gertz more than once to "give him warm greetings from me."‡

Miller's stars were right, after all. The day after Gertz received the author's letter of good cheer there were sensational developments concerning the Florida case.

---

*Elmer Gertz and Felice F. Lewis, eds., *Henry Miller: Years of Trial and Triumph 1962–1964* (1978), 202, 318.

†The Catholic political influence was probably a factor in the adverse decisions reached by the highest courts of these states.

‡Gertz had served as a law clerk for Judge Epstein and remained on friendly terms with him.

ELMER GERTZ: Milton Perlman of Grove Press called us. He had received a rather garbled report late in the day that the United States Supreme Court had taken the Florida case and summarily reversed it, thus holding *Tropic of Cancer* to be constitutionally protected. This seemed too good to be true. Later, we received confirmation from Edward de Grazia of Washington, who had handled the case.

JUDGE SAMUEL EPSTEIN: Well, what the Illinois Supreme Court didn't know was that the Supreme Court of the United States had another week to go, before it recessed. And the following Monday the Supreme Court of the United States reversed this *Tropic of Cancer* case it had from Florida.

ELMER GERTZ: This was . . . a fantastic result and hailed by some as a landmark, perhaps the most important triumph for freedom of expression since the *Ulysses* decision of more than forty years ago.

JUDGE SAMUEL EPSTEIN: And then the Supreme Court of Illinois found itself in a funny position.

ELLIOT EPSTEIN: When he learned about that, Elmer Gertz . . . went to see Dad, to say he was thinking of asking the Illinois Supreme Court to reconsider its decision overruling Dad, because of the Supreme Court's action. Dad told Gertz: "Hell no! Don't apply for a rehearing. Appeal to the Supreme Court!"

———

Judge Epstein preferred to see the court that had overruled him be itself overruled, by the highest court in the land.

JUDGE SAMUEL EPSTEIN: They called in Elmer Gertz, who was representing the publisher and the author. And Elmer was a very well known, very able lawyer, very well regarded. And they said to Elmer: "Look, we know we'll have to reverse ourselves now. You make a motion for reconsideration, and in September, when we resume sessions, we will at that time reverse ourselves and sustain the same decision as the Supreme Court of the United States."

Well, Elmer said: "Gentlemen, I would very much like to do it but my client thinks he can sell a hell of a lot of books during the summer months, before you resume sessions in September!"

So they called themselves into a special session one morning a short time after, here in Chicago, and rendered this opinion, reinstating my judgment.

THE SUPREME COURT OF ILLINOIS: On June 18, 1964, this Court adopted an opinion holding that the book "Tropic of Cancer" was obscene and that its sale could therefore be prohibited without violation of the constitutional guarantee of freedom of the press. On June 22, 1964, the Supreme Court of the United States in the case of *Grove Press* v. *Gerstein*, by per curiam order, reversed a judgment of the District Court of Appeal of Florida which had held that the book "Tropic of Cancer" was obscene and had restricted its sale and distribution.

On the Court's own motion, acting under the controlling authority of the decision of the Supreme Court of the United States in the Florida case, which involved the identical book that is the subject matter of this case,

IT IS ORDERED that the opinion heretofore entered is vacated.

IT IS FURTHER ORDERED that the judgment of the Superior Court of Cook County is affirmed.

———

The same day that the Illinois Supreme Court reversed itself in the *Tropic of Cancer* case, it also reversed another earlier holding it had rendered that a Lenny Bruce performance at the Gate of Horn in Chicago was obscene.*

ELMER GERTZ: Judge Epstein's decision had been the first significant court ruling in favor of *Tropic of Cancer*. . . . Now it was probably the last resounding word on the subject, a source of encouragement to authors, publishers, and booksellers everywhere.†

ELLIOT EPSTEIN: In Illinois today, because of the Illinois Supreme Court's affirmance of Dad's decision, a reader has constitutional standing to sue for access to a book that's under threat of censorship. There is a right to read there.

———

On November 15, 1989, Judge Samuel B. Epstein was one hundred years old; he was also the oldest surviving graduate of the University of Chicago Law School. At a celebration in his honor held at the Standard Club of Chicago and attended by thirty members of his family—including his son Elliot, a University of Chicago Law School graduate of the class of '51—Judge Epstein attributed his long life to "all the wrong foods, a sedentary life, and a pessimistic outlook."‡

---

*See Chapter 24 below.

†Judge Epstein received awards for his *Tropic of Cancer* decision "opposing literary censorship" from the University of Chicago Law School and the Illinois Library Association. The ACLU also paid him a tribute. See Elmer Gertz and Felice F. Lewis, eds., *Henry Miller: Years of Trial and Triumph 1962–1964* (1978), 215. Inasmuch as his decision was finally affirmed by the Illinois Supreme Court, it is "good law" in Illinois and available for citation as authority for the propositions it contains, in state and federal courts anywhere in the United States.

‡The event is reported in the University of Chicago *Law School Record* 36 (Spring 1990), 38.

20

This Was
"Star Wars"

AT A PARTY at the Edinburgh Arts Festival on a warm day in August
1962, when *Tropic of Cancer* was still the subject of scores of obscenity prosecutions throughout the United States, and no house had yet dared to publish *Naked Lunch*, Henry Miller met William Burroughs. According to Burroughs, Henry Miller looked at him and said:

HENRY MILLER: So you're Burroughs.
WILLIAM BURROUGHS: A long-time admirer . . .

—

The next time they saw each other at a party, Miller looked Burroughs over quizzically and said:

HENRY MILLER: So you're Burroughs.

—

Burroughs thought Miller must be dotty.

WILLIAM BURROUGHS: The only thing he'd said at the Conference was that he had visited the Royal Academy to look at the Scottish painters.*

—

---

*Contradicted by John Calder, the British publisher of Miller and an indefatigable activist for literary freedom, who said that on the fourth day, when the subject was censorship, Miller "set out his credo of literary freedom and received a standing ovation from nearly three thousand people." Ted Morgan quotes Miller as making a characteristic statement about sex at the conference: "What we would all like to do when we see a good interesting woman is sleep with her, we should not make any bones about that. There is nothing wrong with lust or with obscenity." Ted Morgan, *Literary Outlaw* (1987), 337.

Not long before the Olympia Press was attacked by the French judiciary and police following the publication of *Lolita*,* Maurice Girodias changed his mind about *Naked Lunch*. The publisher dropped Burroughs a note: "Dear Mr. Burroughs, What about letting me have another look at *Naked Lunch?*," and from that point on, things moved very fast. He offered the author a contract that included an $800 advance and a clause reserving for himself one-third of the English-language royalties of any future publications in England or the United States. Girodias told Barney Rosset of Grove Press of his decision in a letter he wrote on June 15, 1959. At the time, Rosset was still embroiled in the most difficult legal struggle of his publishing career, the nationwide defense of Henry Miller's *Tropic of Cancer.*

MAURICE GIRODIAS: Dear Barney, Thank you immensely for the lovely money,† which arrived safely and in the nick of time. God will repay this blessing. . . . Everything else goes famously. I think the *Black Book*‡ will help establish Olympia once and for all. I have also finally decided to do the *Naked Lunch,* this beat manifesto, as Burroughs has finally accepted to let us edit his mess.

———

Girodias had initially distrusted the manuscript that Allen Ginsberg had given him: he said it seemed to have been nibbled at by the rats of the Paris sewers. It was "completely dilapidated and unreadable, with pasted-over paper patches, and all sorts of loose bits and pieces." The manuscript was apparently offensive to Girodias not for its content but for its looks. The publisher concluded that the author was perversely unstable and his "manuscript smelled like trouble." At first Ginsberg—who was Burroughs's friend and promoter—misunderstood: he thought Girodias had turned the book down because it did not fit the publisher's "d.b." formula.

ALLEN GINSBERG: It *was* a mess until we realized that it didn't require the normal ordering of a novel. Here was the problem: Burroughs sent me most of the material in letters after we separated and I went to San Francisco and he went to Tangier; so he sent me the routines like Benway, the Talking Asshole, the Market, the Nude Café, the Interzone part. Pretty soon I had accumulated a big black folder of stuff. Then Kerouac went to Tangier and began typing, typing, what Bill had. 'Cause Kerouac typed 120 words a minute, he was a real typist.

But I had lots of parts that Bill didn't have, 'cause he'd sent it off as letters when he was heavily in love with me; and we had a very heavy correspondence, which is now published, most of it, by Full Court Press.§

———

*Described in Chapter 14.

†The money was from royalties due Girodias from the American publication of *Lolita* by Putnam's; Rosset helped collect it.

‡By Lawrence Durrell.

§William Burroughs, *Letters to Allen Ginsberg* 1953–1957 (1982).

Now, as Burroughs wrote he developed the character of Dr. Benway, and several of his routines developed; so cumulatively it changed and got better and better, and more extensive, so the question was: How do you organize all this material? I brought all the material in a black springboard binder to Tangier in '57, Peter and I, and we all set about typing it.

Alan Ansen arrived from Venice and he had been Auden's amanuensis and typist for the *Age of Anxiety* manuscript; Kerouac left about a month after we arrived (I think that's described in *Desolation Angels*). And then we went to Europe and wound up in Paris in late '57 early '58, where we prepared the material for *Big Table*.

———

It was Judge Hoffman's decision to free *Big Table* 1, with its episodes from *Naked Lunch,* that moved Girodias to change his mind and publish the book. In the States several publishers, including Barney Rosset, also now expressed cautious interest in Burroughs's manuscript. In the heat of the struggle to free *Tropic of Cancer* from censorship in some fifty cities in the United States, Rosset contemplated publishing *Naked Lunch* expurgated; Burroughs told him he was prepared to eliminate two wildly pornographic chapters if that would facilitate publication in England and the States. Rosset now hired Irving Rosenthal to organize the book.

In Tangier Ginsberg and Burroughs were also working on the manuscript.

ALLEN GINSBERG: So then the problem was how to edit it or how to shape it, how do you shape it into a novel? Does Burroughs have to write a plot out, does he have to flesh out certain parts, does he have to show how you get from Interzone to Tangier?

At some point, someone, maybe Brion Gysin, said: "Your method, your attempt here is not necessary. You don't have to make it like a regular novel, it is episodic, it's a collage, it's different—there's no point in your trying to take all the stuff and trying to weave it into a plot with a regular beginning, a middle, and an end. What it is is it's just in collage form rather than linear form. It's like Ezra Pound's *Cantos,* or Williams's *Paterson,* or T. S. Eliot's *Waste Land. The Waste Land* doesn't have a plot, and it seems that it's a collage of themes and examples of those themes, and that's exactly what you've got. The only thing you need is a certain thematic conclusion."

One of the themes was the addiction of the bureaucracy, the bureaucrats addicted to power, narcotics police addicted to addicts. The whole narcotics police conspiracy against the addicts was the theme.

The opening chapter had to do with two detectives, Mr. Brown and Mr. Martin, who raided Burroughs and arrested him. And Burroughs shot them, and they dissolved. That was in the early part. What he did, he moved that to the very end, and it was like a resolution, so that it made it seem like a Kafkaean dream of detectives that dissolves when you stop thinking about it.

So, how does he get rid of, how does he shoot his way or cut his way, or how does he hypnotize his way, how does he resolve his way, how does he teleport his way out of the fix when he's being arrested? The heat is closing in, remember, the heat is closing in. So the heat were these two cops, and in the fantasy he shoots them. And disappears, or gets away, and then he calls up his home and apparently there's nobody looking for him, he's not accused of anything, the cops have disappeared, they've gone back into dreamworld, they were his invention, they were his guilt fantasy.

So that served as a very good ending. And that's how basically the structure of the novel resolves itself, with the enemy dissolving. . . .

So when Girodias described it as a mess, it was in that we all looked at it as a mess, until we looked twice, and accepted the interpretation that it wasn't a mess, it was just there as it was, as a collage, so that one little adjustment . . . Like there's a haiku by Gary Snyder:

> "All fall watching the rain leak into the house,
> Fixed one afternoon by moving one tile . . ."

So, something like that happened with *Naked Lunch,* you just moved one tile . . . And it fell into place with just a little bit of editing, not much.

Now, the next stage was, of course, Rosenthal editing for *Big Table.* Then Barney Rosset, Grove Press, bought the book and Rosenthal took the Olympia edition *and* the manuscript and went over it for typos and did some reediting and a little more stitching together and a little bit more. Rosenthal is just an exquisite editor—every detail, every semicolon, every paragraph perfect, no typos—which Girodias did not have. The original edition has many solecisms in it, stylistic solecisms. So what Rosenthal did was prepare the final, polished version for Grove Press. Then Rosset brought it out.

BARNEY ROSSET: When Rosenthal was working on the book for me his father and mother were always looking for him. I would have been glad to give him back to them.

ALLEN GINSBERG: So it was a mess and it wasn't a mess. It's like talking about Pollock being a mess, until you put a frame around it; then you put a frame around it and it's a picture.

ALAIN ROBBE-GRILLET: I remember very well one time, it was in Paris, I can't remember exactly when, at the end of the fifties or the beginning of the sixties. Barney Rosset pointed out to me someone sitting on the terrace of La Coupole, and said, "You see, there! He's a very important American writer." And I said, "Ah, yes? What has he done?" And Barney Rosset said, "He put an apple on his wife's head and killed her."* That was Burroughs, you see? Who was barely known at the time. But it shows the sort of thing

---

*Variously also reported to have been a champagne glass, a whiskey glass, an apricot, an orange, and even Joan and Bill's son, Billy, as described anon.

that Barney Rosset noticed. It wasn't even a book, it was a gesture that interested him.

—

When Rosset learned from Girodias by the June 15 letter that Girodias had finally decided "to do the *Naked Lunch*," Rosset was excited; in a marginal note to editor Dick Seaver, he wrote, "*Very Good.* Maybe we could do something with it here." But as Grove's problems with the censorship of *Tropic of Cancer* continued to proliferate, Rosset backed off from publishing "this beat manifesto" in New York.

BARNEY ROSSET: Maurice was up and down and all over the place, in Paris. He was making a lot of money from his successful publication of *Lolita* in France, and from its publication a little later in England and the United States; but he was also squandering everything on a monstrous place called La Grande Séverine, with five or six crazy restaurants, and then the French government went after him too. . . . They arrested him repeatedly and fined and sentenced him to long prison terms, which is something I never had. Not for publishing *Lady Chatterley's Lover,* not for publishing *Tropic of Cancer,* not even for publishing *Naked Lunch,* which, eventually, I did.

—

For Burroughs, the situation had become confused: "I received telegrams and letters from publishers I never heard of in regard to arrangements of which I knew nothing, acrimonious complaints that the book had been promised them by Rosenthal and taken out of their hands by Girodias." But, he said, Girodias had put it to him straight, "over a blackbird pastry in his new restaurant: 'This is a complicated business full of angles. I know them—you don't. Let me handle it. You will have to trust me.' " Burroughs left it up to Girodias to work out arrangements for an American edition with Grove Press.

Burroughs was sure the deal he made with Olympia was the best he could have made. He wrote a friend: "I saw them fucking around five years with American publishers. And no book was ever out less than a year from date of publication." He wrote Ginsberg that it was a unique opportunity and that selling to a U.S. publisher would be easier after Paris. "All I have to do is jerk out those two chapters—Hassan's Rumpus Room and A. J.'s Annual Party—which are right together. In short I can prepare the ms. for American or English markets in five minutes."

After Girodias negotiated a contract with Rosset for the Grove Press publication of *Naked Lunch* in New York, Rosset held back for two years while he considered doing something unprecedented for him—publishing an expurgated book. But the idea was anathema to him; so he waited. He decided to publish an unexpurgated edition of *Tropic of Cancer* first, as a sort of test. Miller's strong reputation among the American literati would ensure that there would be people prepared to defend the book in court. By comparison with Henry Miller, whose *Tropic of Cancer* had been an underground classic for almost thirty years, Burroughs was practically unknown.

Girodias was anxiously looking forward to the publication of *Naked Lunch* in the States because by the winter of '61 it was one of the few means left to shore up his shaky finances. He was in urgent need of $20,000, and for over a year he had been counting on *Naked Lunch* to produce that sum. His restaurant, La Grande Séverine, had lost so much money during its first eighteen months that he had been "forced to postpone vital payments" and had "lost all hope of borrowing the money [he] needed to survive." He berated Rosset for hesitating to publish *Naked Lunch* in New York. When Rosset told him that he had decided not to publish *Naked Lunch* until after *Tropic of Cancer,* the French publisher was distraught. He realized that Rosset "had valid reasons for adopting that policy," but he felt it "was disastrous" from his and Burroughs's point of view. He wrote Rosset:

MAURICE GIRODIAS: It would be cruel irony indeed if all I have done to convince Miller to let you publish *Tropic of Cancer* were to produce consequences so diabolically opposed to my interests. . . . You are free to eliminate the 24 critical pages* if you wish to do so. If you wish to keep them in, just do so. If you don't, don't. But publish the damn book for God's sake!

———

Girodias feared that after he had waited a year and a half for Grove to publish the book he might learn at the last moment that Rosset had finally decided not to do it at all. That would mean *no* American royalties, for him or Burroughs. At the time, Grove's distribution of *Tropic of Cancer* was caught up in a maelstrom of censorship litigation. On the day that Rosset received Girodias's letter, two booksellers were haled before a grand jury in New York and the trial in Chicago was going into its third week. According to Rosset, the overall litigation costs to Grove were already close to $100,000. He wrote to Girodias: "Only a suicidal maniac would plunge in with *Naked Lunch* at this moment—at least that is the opinion of everyone whom I have talked to, including Burroughs. We are not sitting on 10,000 books [copies of *Naked Lunch* that Rosset had had set in type] to spite you, believe me."

BARNEY ROSSET: The fact is that I had invested a good deal in the book—put in an enormous amount of editorial time, paid Burroughs a good advance, and spent a large amount of money for an extremely expensive typesetting job and a first-class printing and binding job on 10,000 copies of *Naked Lunch.* . . . The first printer and binder I went to had refused to handle the book. The printer just said he wasn't interested in producing a book that he couldn't give to his friends, or take home. The only other time I remember that sort of thing happening was when a printer we used in Buffalo wouldn't

---

*The "Hassan's Rumpus Room" episode.

run off an issue of *Evergreen Review* because there was a poem in it by Julian Beck of the Living Theatre, and the last line read: "Fuck the United States!" The guy said he wouldn't mind it if the poem said "Fuck the Soviet Union," but he just couldn't take "Fuck the United States."

———

According to Rosset, Girodias "could not get it into his head that the *Big Table* court victory was small potatoes" inasmuch as the Burroughs episodes that were published in the journal were "quite mild and completely inoffensive" compared with other parts of *Naked Lunch*, like "Hassan's Rumpus Room."

WILLIAM S. BURROUGHS *(Naked Lunch):*
"Hassan's Rumpus Room"
Gilt and red plush. Rococo bar banked by pink shell. The air is cloyed with a sweet evil substance, like decayed honey. Men and women in evening dress sip pousse-cafés through alabaster tubes. A Near East Mugwump sits naked on a bar stool covered in pink silk. He licks warm honey from a crystal goblet with a long black tongue. His genitals are perfectly formed—circumcised cock, black shiny pubic hairs. His lips are thin and purple-blue like the lips of a penis, his eyes blank with insect calm. The Mugwump has no liver, maintaining himself exclusive on sweets. Mugwump push a slender blond youth to a couch and strip him expertly.
"Stand up and turn around," he orders in telepathic pictographs. He ties the boy's hands behind him with a red silk cord. "Tonight we make it all the way."
"No, no!" screams the boy.
"Yes, yes."
Cocks ejaculate in silent "yes." Mugwump part silk curtains, reveal a teak wood gallows against lighted screen of red flint. Gallows is on a dais of Aztec mosaics. . . .
Satyr and naked Greek lad in aqualung trace a ballet of pursuit in a monster vase of transparent alabaster. The Satyr catches the boy from in front and whirls him around. They move in fish jerks. The boy releases a silver stream of bubbles from his mouth. White sperm ejaculates into the green water and floats lazily around the twisting bodies. . . .
Negro gently lifts exquisite Chinese boy into a hammock. He pushes the boy's legs up over his head and straddles the hammock. He slides his cock up the boy's slender tight ass. He rocks the hammock gently back and forth. The boy screams, a weird high wail of unendurable delight. . . .
Two Arab women with bestial faces have pulled the shorts off a little blond French boy. They are screwing him with red rubber cocks. The boy snarls, bites, kicks, collapses in tears as his cock rises and ejaculates. . . .
Hassan's face swells, tumescent with blood. His lips turn purple. He strip off his suit of banknotes and throw it into an open vault that closes soundless. . . .
"Freedom Hall here, folks!" he screams in his phoney Texas accent. Ten gallon hat and cowboy boots still on, he dances the Liquefactionist Jig, ending with a grotesque can can to the tune of She Started a Heat Wave.
"Let it be and no holes barred!!!"

BARNEY ROSSET: At the time, '59 or '60, there was a big problem: no one knew who Burroughs was. The first praise, from people like Mailer and Mary McCarthy, came years later. Also, no one knew if anyone would buy the book, if anyone would read it. That wasn't the situation with *Tropic of Cancer,* which was world famous.

Another thing is I went after *Tropic of Cancer,* whereas *Naked Lunch* was brought to me—by people like Burroughs and Ginsberg and Rosenthal. To me it was scary, the sex and violence.* Those guys scared me. Remember, I was a bourgeois type from Chicago.

Publishing *Naked Lunch* was like taking off into an abyss. It went far, far, far beyond *Tropic of Cancer* or *Memoirs of Hecate County.* This was "Star Wars."

———

When Girodias was about to publish *Naked Lunch,* he asked his friend Henry Miller to read it. Miller wrote him in December 1960:

HENRY MILLER: Dear Maurice, I've tried now for the third time to read it through, but I can't stick it. The truth is, it bores me. The Marquis de Sade bores me too, perhaps in a different way, or for different reasons. . . .

However, there is no question in my mind as to Burroughs' abilities. There is a ferocity in his writing which is equalled, in my opinion, only by Céline. No writer I knew of made more daring use of the language. I wish I might read him on some other subject than sex or drugs—read him on St. Thomas Aquinas, for example, or on eschatology. Or better still—a disquisition on "The Grand Inquisitor."

I know that no one could reach to that frenzied kind of descriptive language, at once vile and horripilating, without being serious in his intent. Thinking about the law, it seems to me that the effect of Burroughs' book on the average reader—if publication were ever permitted—would be the very opposite of what the censors feared. One would have to have a diseased mind to ask for more. To read that book is to take the cure.

———

The ten thousand copies of the unexpurgated *Naked Lunch* were kept in a warehouse because Rosset feared what would happen to booksellers, and to Grove, if he sold them. It would not be until 1963, when Rosset asked me to read *Naked Lunch* to see if it was defensible, that the publisher felt safe enough to go ahead.†

---

*Jack Kerouac, while typing the *Naked Lunch* manuscript in Tangier, is said to have found it so vivid and horrifying that his sleep was beset by nightmares. John Tytell, *Naked Angels: The Lives and Literature of the Beat Generation* (1976), 49. After killing his wife, Burroughs became a self-appointed outcast, according to Tytell, an untouchable in a society he had already rejected. As he says in *Naked Lunch,* untouchables perform "a priestly function in taking on themselves all human vileness." This distinguishes them from involuntary scapegoats. Tytell describes *Naked Lunch* much as Norman Mailer did: "The result of a purgatorial plunge . . . whose terrifying vision of dehumanized control was like the telepathic warning of some awful future" (51).

†The copyright is dated 1959.

TED MORGAN: Barney Rosset asked Edward de Grazia, a lawyer who specialized in First Amendment cases and whom Barney had on retainer, to defend [*Naked Lunch*]. De Grazia [is] a slight, scholarly-looking man who actually reads the books he has to defend, and who considered *Naked Lunch* an important book and perhaps a great book.

NORMAN MAILER: De Grazia was a slim elegant Sicilian with a subtle diffidence in his manner, terribly hesitant, almost a stammer, but he was a Sicilian who somehow inspired the confidence that he knew where the next bit of information might reside. Besides, he bore a pleasant resemblance to the way Frank Sinatra had looked, ten years earlier.

—

When Rosset asked me to read *Naked Lunch,* I did it in one sitting, in the garden of the apartment building where I was living, in a suburb of New York. I felt excited and, like Rosset, almost frightened by it. I thought Burroughs's novel was important. I wanted to defend it and told Rosset that I *could* defend it successfully in court. We made an agreement by which I undertook to represent Grove in any action brought against *Naked Lunch,* as well as several other books that Rosset was reluctant to bring out at that time: Henry Miller's *Tropic of Capricorn* and *Black Spring,* John Rechy's *City of Night,* and Jean Genet's *The Thief's Journal.* In return, I was given a year's retainer and a small royalty on the books' sales.*

The first thing I did was carry a copy of *Naked Lunch* over to Acting District Attorney Richard Kuh's office in New York.† I handed him the book and suggested that he read it. Rosset had told me he thought Kuh was probably more literate than most prosecutors because his sister had once published a story in *Evergreen Review.* I also gave Kuh a copy of the scholarly amicus curiae brief I had filed in the Maryland *Tropic of Cancer* case for the ACLU; I invited him to read that, too, and to let me know if he wanted to bring a test case over *Naked Lunch.*

Kuh read the book and the brief and took no action. He never said why. So now Rosset brought the other 9,990-odd copies of *Naked Lunch* out of his warehouse and put them into his distribution channels. It was only then that an unexpurgated *Naked Lunch* was actually published in the United States.

Three factors finally persuaded Rosset to bring out *Naked Lunch.* One was my assurance that litigation expenses could be kept under control, given the newly demonstrated willingness of ACLU lawyers to fight for literary freedom, and provided he did not indemnify book dealers for their legal costs, as he had done when he published *Tropic of Cancer.* I also

---

*This arrangement was similar to the one Morris Ernst made with publisher Bennett Cerf of Random House, for the defense of James Joyce's *Ulysses.* See Chapter 2.

†Kuh later would use his powers of prosecution to stop Lenny Bruce from performing his satirical monologues in Manhattan. There is a well-written, though in my opinion wrongheaded, book by Kuh on obscenity censorship, called *Foolish Figleaves?* (1967), in which he declaims against Lenny Bruce and the literary community that sought to aid in the comedian's defense. See Chapter 24.

promised him that any case that arose could eventually be won, in the Supreme Court if necessary. The final point was the praise that Burroughs and the book received from Mary McCarthy and Norman Mailer at the Edinburgh Arts Festival, the one where Burroughs and Mailer had met.

The festival opened on August 20, 1962. It was organized by British publisher John Calder, who, like Rosset, was a crusader in the struggle against literary censorship. The subject of the conference was "The State of the Novel."

TED MORGAN: Each year in [Calder's] home town of Edinburgh, during three weeks of August, there was a huge festival of the arts, with 800 events—opera, theatre, twenty-five symphony orchestras: a great overspilling cornucopia of the arts . . .

—

Calder convinced the festival director, Lord Harwood, to allow him to organize a conference of writers from all over the world to discuss the current state of the novel and other topics. The publisher equipped McEwan Hall, the biggest auditorium at Edinburgh University ("an architectural oddity shaped like a Gargantuan beer barrel that seated 3,000"), with microphones and translators in three languages. He invited some seventy writers. Calder described the American delegation as "quite an effective quartet, on the subject of literary freedom," for it included Mary McCarthy, Henry Miller, Norman Mailer, and the relatively unknown William S. Burroughs, whose *Naked Lunch* was still out only in an Olympia Press edition.

Mary McCarthy, after announcing that the "national" novel, like the nation-state, was dying, talked about some recent "stateless" books she'd liked. There was the work of Nabokov, especially *Lolita,* which she had "personally gone overboard for," and she also cited William Burroughs's *Naked Lunch.* She said it "was laid everywhere and was sort of speeded-up like jet travel, having the same somewhat supersonic quality." It also had "some of the qualities of Action Painting, was a kind of Action Novel." Finally, she went a bit overboard for Burroughs, too, declaring him "the writer of this century who'd most deeply affected the literati cognoscenti." In his biography of Burroughs, Ted Morgan writes: "Whatever the merit of Mary McCarthy's theory of the stateless novel, she managed on the very first day of the conference to put Burroughs on the map."

Mailer's comments were based upon the excerpts that he had read in *Big Table,* which he said were more interesting than anything else he'd read by an American in years. He thought that "if the rest of the book were as good, Burroughs would deserve ranking as one of the most important novelists in America, comparable to Jean Genet." Later, when he'd read the book as published by Grove Press, he declared Burroughs "the only living American novelist who might conceivably be possessed of genius."

At the festival, according to Morgan, Burroughs dispelled the beatnik image that surrounded him by speaking reasonably to the point that only an end to censorship would make possible the serious, scientific investigation of human sexuality. He reminded his listeners that in America, when Wilhelm Reich "tried to study sex scientifically, he was rewarded with the indignity of dying in a Federal prison—while serving a sentence for quackery."*

Burroughs said he enjoyed the conference—even the glares of Vita Sackville-West and Rebecca West, who reportedly seemed to think he was the devil personified. Morgan writes: "By the time the conference ended it was clear that Burroughs had run away with it. He had come into it unknown, and emerged a celebrity. Far from being a wild man in the Beatnik media image, he was serious and quiet and conservatively dressed, like a Harvard professor. With Mary McCarthy and Norman Mailer outbidding each other in praise of Burroughs, he was no longer the author of a patently obscene book, but a serious writer delving into the mad chaos and tormented human conditions of post-bomb life."

After Edinburgh, Barney Rosset moved to distribute *Naked Lunch*— even though Miller's *Tropic of Cancer* was still embroiled in the courts— making the most of Burroughs's new notoriety. As I recommended, this time Rosset did not promise the people who handled the book that he would take care of their legal problems and expenses. Instead, a postscript to the flyer he sent to booksellers in advance of orders for *Naked Lunch* said this: "One more word about censorship. You know best what the situation is in your area and we would advise you to exercise your own discretion. Should you nevertheless run into any censorship problems, we may be able to lend information and advice although we will not be able to bear legal expenses. . . ."

The book sold very well almost immediately. There was extensive coverage in major newspapers and literary journals; nearly 15,000 copies were sold during the first four months.

MARY McCARTHY: [*Naked Lunch*] is like a neighborhood movie with continuous showings that you can drop into whenever you please—you don't have to wait for the beginning of the feature picture. Or like a worm that you can chop up into sections each of which wriggles off as an independent worm. Or a nine-lived cat. Or a cancer . . .

[Burroughs] is fond of the word "mosaic," especially in its scientific sense of a plant-mottling caused by a virus, and his Muse (see etymology of "mosaic") is interested in organic processes of multiplication and duplication. The literary notion of time as simultaneous, a montage, is not original with Burroughs; what is original is the scientific bent he gives it and a view of the world that combines biochemistry, anthropology, and politics. It is as though *Finnegans Wake* were cut loose from history and adapted for a cinerama circus titled "One World." . . .

---

*Not quite. He died while serving a sentence for disobeying a court order designed to stop him from studying and writing about "orgone energy." See Chapter 18, and Myron Sharaf's *Fury on Earth: A Biography of Wilhelm Reich* (1983).

The oldest memory in *The Naked Lunch* is of jacking-off in boyhood latrines, a memory recaptured through pederasty. This must be the first space novel, the first serious piece of science fiction—the others are entertainment. . . .

The best comparison for the book with its aerial sex acts performed on a high trapeze, its con men and barkers, its arena-like form, is in fact a circus. A circus travels but is always the same, and this is Burroughs' sardonic image of modern life. . . .

[B]etween Burroughs and [Jonathan] Swift there are many points of comparison; not only the obsession with excrement and the horror of female genitalia but a disgust with politics and the whole body politic.

ROBERT LOWELL: *Naked Lunch* is one of the most alive books written by any American for years.

JOHN CIARDI: [*Naked Lunch*] is a masterpiece of its own genre . . . a monumentally moral descent into the hell of narcotic addiction. . . . [W]hat Burroughs is writing about is not only the destruction of depraved men by their drug lust, but the destruction of all men by their consuming addictions, whether the addiction be drugs or overrighteous propriety, lasciviousness or sixteen-year-old girls.

E. S. SELDON: This book [is] one of the most impressive literary debuts of the past century.

NORMAN MAILER: [*Naked Lunch*] is a book of great beauty, great difficulty and maniacally exquisite insight.

NEWSWEEK: [*Naked Lunch*] is indeed a masterpiece, but a totally insane and anarchic one, and it can only be diminished by attempts to give it any social purpose or value whatever.

———

The first bookseller arrested for selling *Naked Lunch* was Theodore Mavrikos, in Boston. Mavrikos's store was in the city's so-called Combat Zone, a rowdy area devoted to sex bookstores and theatres. The Boston police had reportedly arrested Mavrikos nine times previously for selling obscene material, so it promised to be a strong case from the prosecutor's standpoint. From Grove's standpoint, certainly, Mavrikos was not the ideal bookseller to defend. On the other hand, Grove could not afford to let the case be lost; so we decided to take over Mavrikos's legal problem with *Naked Lunch.* I found a way to do this, and at the same time to move Mavrikos out of the center of the controversy.*

Two aspects of the Massachusetts procedures for dealing with obscenity cases were helpful to me. There was a law, which libertarians had persuaded the legislature to pass some years earlier, that authorized the attorney general to bring a civil *in rem* proceeding against any book he thought was

———

*A few years later Mavrikos died in a mental hospital.

obscene, thus avoiding the need for a criminal proceeding against the person who published or sold it. And there was also in force an attorney general's policy that no district prosecutor was to start a criminal case against a publisher or bookseller without first clearing it with the attorney general, who at that time was Edward Brooke. Brooke was an official who valued freedom of expression and didn't like censorship. He distinguished himself as attorney general and later became a United States senator.

Ed Brooke had instituted an enlightened prosecutorial policy (I believe it was in writing) to put a check on, and centralize in his office, decisions by local prosecutors to move against "obscene" books. Garrett Byrne, the district attorney who acted to prosecute Mavrikos, had ignored that policy. Brooke was therefore interested in my proposal that the Mavrikos prosecutor be stopped and the *Naked Lunch* case be used instead to reinforce the attorney general's policy. This would also work to discourage local district attorneys, in the future, from going against books and booksellers of *their* choice.

One reason for Brooke's policy of centralized obscenity law administration was to prevent local standards, attitudes, and politics, and local prosecutors, from determining whether a book should be banned anywhere in Massachusetts. The Massachusetts arrangement provided a civilized and objective way for the government to proceed against a book considered obscene, rather than against a particular local bookseller; the decision—whether to ban or to free the book—would apply statewide. Under the law, anyone interested in the book's circulation, including the author or publisher, could appear in court and defend the book by seeking to show it was not obscene. Even before the Supreme Court's decision freeing *Tropic of Cancer* was announced, my plan was to introduce evidence of *Naked Lunch*'s indisputable social importance as the means to prove it could not be held obscene. (Later, when Brennan's decision in the Florida *Tropic of Cancer* case was handed down in June 1964, it became even clearer that all we needed to do was to show that the book exhibited some sort of social importance; the mantle of constitutional protection would then be drawn around it.) I structured the trial of *Naked Lunch* accordingly.

I spoke to lawyers in Brooke's civil rights division about Mavrikos's arrest for selling *Naked Lunch,* and about the book, and I gave them a copy to read. I said it was a good book, a work of literature, not pornography. They decided—a young attorney in Brooke's office named Kozol was in charge of the case at that point—to put pressure on Byrne, the D.A. who had arrested Mavrikos, to suspend his prosecution until Brooke's office decided whether the book was obscene. If they so decided, then the State would move against it, in the person of the attorney general, through a civil *in rem* case.

District Attorney Byrne did not like the idea, but eventually he submitted and the stage was set for a civil trial of *Naked Lunch.*

The lawyer who tried the case for the State of Massachusetts was a young assistant attorney general in Brooke's office, William I. Cowin. (He would later argue the landmark *Fanny Hill* case, involving the Putnam's edition, in the Supreme Court.) Like Brooke, Cowin was a liberal-minded man and he was somewhat reluctant to stage a legal attack on Burroughs's book. But he knew it was the only way to clarify the legal status of *Naked Lunch:* Was it constitutionally protected expression or obscene?

According to Cowin, Brooke probably would not have started the proceedings against *Naked Lunch* if it were not for the prosecution of Mavrikos by District Attorney Byrne. But he felt that the public would view him as "soft on obscenity" if he merely terminated the criminal case against Mavrikos.

WILLIAM I. COWIN: We decided to go ahead with the case because various old ladies were getting on Ed Brooke's back about his doing something about the dirty-book situation. The truth is that we all wished we could be doing other things with our time.

—

When asked about the situation, Brooke said, "It certainly wasn't a question of my saving any district attorney's face. It was a question of coming up with an answer to the controversial legal problem of obscenity which was fair to both sides and, I believe, in the best civil libertarian tradition." And Cowin remarked that Brooke "wouldn't have cared, one way or another," what Byrne thought. The case was brought "because the book was widely recognized and yet contained a lot of material that was shocking and offensive to some people"; *Naked Lunch* "really presented many interesting, unresolved legal questions, which we wanted to test."

The Mavrikos prosecution was postponed while Brooke arranged for the *in rem* proceedings against *Naked Lunch.* It took a year and a half—from January 1963, when the criminal case against Mavrikos began, until September 1964, when Brooke filed his petition in superior court alleging that there was cause to believe a book called *Naked Lunch,* published by Grove Press, was obscene. In the meantime, the Warren Court moved decisively, under Brennan's leadership, to free *Tropic of Cancer* in the case that I had presented to the Court from Florida. The decision stunned the nation's censors and pro-censorship groups and, of course, encouraged us. I felt sure that even if we lost both the trial and the appeal of *Naked Lunch* in Massachusetts, the Supreme Court would vindicate Burroughs's book.*

---

*Not long before the Boston trial of *Naked Lunch* began, Brooke moved *in rem* against the recently published Putnam's edition of *Fanny Hill;* eventually, the Supreme Judicial Court of Massachusetts found that book obscene because it had only "a modicum" of social value. That decision, however, would later be reversed by the Supreme Court at a very opportune time for Grove Press—while our appeal in the *Naked Lunch* case was before the Massachusetts high court. See Chapter 26. I mentioned this fact, during the course of my oral argument to the Supreme Judicial Court of Massachusetts, in the effort to persuade that court to reverse our trial judge's conclusion that *Naked Lunch* was obscene.

21

Who Is His Parish Priest?

I N JUNE 1963, Anthony Lewis wrote a prescient piece for *Esquire* about the Supreme Court's obscenity cases* He remarked that the Court was in the process of "liberating the country from puritanism," and he foretold a radicalization of *Roth* that would bring almost absolute freedom to literary and artistic works. Although by the time of Lewis's writing the Court had not added much in the way of doctrine to what Brennan had said in *Roth,* † it had reached decisions, citing *Roth,* that brought freedom to: a film called *The Game of Love,* dealing with the seduction of a sixteen-year-old boy by an older woman; a homosexually oriented magazine called *One;* three "dismally unpleasant, uncouth, and tawdry" homosexually oriented magazines titled *MANual, Trim,* and *Grecian Guild Pictorial;* the nudist magazine *Sunshine and Health;* and a French film version of *Lady Chatterley's Lover.* ‡ Meanwhile, lower courts had started following Brennan's decision in *Roth* in ways that favored literary freedom, as described above.

---

*A copy of the article, "Sex and the Supreme Court," is among Justice Brennan's private court papers in the "Obscenity Cases" files at the Library of Congress. Lewis, a syndicated *New York Times* columnist on law and foreign affairs, is the author of *Gideon's Trumpet,* a Pulitzer Prize–winning account of how the Supreme Court was moved to recognize that poor persons charged with crime are constitutionally entitled to free defense counsel. He teaches a course on freedom of the press at Harvard Law School. In his article *"New York Times* v. *Sullivan* Reconsidered: Time to Return to 'The Central Meaning of the First Amendment' " (*Columbia Law Review* 83, 603ff.) Lewis analyzes the constitutionalized law of press libel.

†The post-*Roth* cases analyzed by Lewis are described in Chapter 22, and reprinted in de Grazia, *Censorship Landmarks* (1969).

‡The movie cases are discussed in Edward de Grazia and Roger K. Newman, *Banned Films: Movies, Censors and The First Amendment* (1982).

Lewis accurately portrayed the "nine not-so-old men" sitting on the high bench as changing the United States "from one of the most timid countries in dealing with sex in the arts to what many believe is now by far the most liberated in the Western world. . . . Gradually, without much notice but with developing momentum," said Lewis, the justices were cutting "back the censor's power over literature and the arts generally."

Not until sixteen years after the Supreme Court had acted to free *Tropic of Cancer* did it become evident to me that the person responsible for that revolutionary act was Justice William J. Brennan, Jr. The greatest part of the Supreme Court's work is invisible,* and I did not find out how to dissipate the secrecy surrounding the Court's processes—its decision-reaching and opinion-creating activities—until early in the eighties, while working with historian Roger Newman on a book about motion picture censorship and the law.† In doing research for that book we studied the motion picture obscenity case files among the private Court papers of Justice John Harlan; later, working on this book, I was permitted to examine the papers of the late Justice Abe Fortas and Justice William J. Brennan, Jr.‡

The clue that it was Brennan who persuaded the Warren Court to

---

*As difficult as it is to decipher *ex post facto* how the justices work, it is even harder to find out what enters into their judgments and opinions while these are being formulated. This, of course, protects the integrity of the Court's work and discourages extralegal attempts to influence it. The justices are under no legal duty to explain their decisions and opinions to anyone at any time and will rarely discuss them with outsiders. The opinions that they publish to justify their decisions are all that is required, and even this duty is traditional, not legally imposed. When Justice Abe Fortas declined to answer questions concerning his beliefs relevant to issues before the Court put to him by senators who were investigating his qualifications to become Chief Justice, he acted properly to maintain the integrity of the Court's processes. During his confirmation hearings to become a justice of the Supreme Court, Judge Robert H. Bork permitted senators to explore his values and thought processes to an unprecedented degree; in the end, although this doomed Bork's nomination, it gave the country at large (the hearings were televised) an unprecedented view of the workings of American constitutional law and the judicial process.

†Edward de Grazia and Roger K. Newman, *Banned Films: Movies, Censors and the First Amendment* (1982).

‡Access to those of Brennan's papers that have been deposited at the Library of Congress requires Brennan's permission. Access to Fortas's papers (in Yale University's Sterling Library) requires the permission of Fortas's widow, Carolyn Agger. William O. Douglas's papers (in the Library of Congress) and Harlan's papers (in the Seeley G. Mudd Manuscript Library of Princeton University) are open to scholars and journalists. It is my impression that Brennan is the only justice to have opened his private Court papers to scholarly researchers during his lifetime.

Another legitimate but more controversial way to conduct research is to speak to the justices' former law clerks, as was extensively done by Bob Woodward and Scott Armstrong for their ground-breaking book on the Burger Court, *The Brethren: Inside the Supreme Court* (1979). Most of the information for that book was based on interviews with 170 of the justices' former law clerks. The authors say that Chief Justice Burger "declined to assist" them "in any way." Virtually all the interviews were conducted "on background," meaning that "the identity of the source [was] kept confidential" (*The Brethren*, 3). There is another, but illegitimate, way to penetrate the Court's secrecy: to steal papers from a justice's chambers, as has been done. And Justice William O. Douglas believed that the Supreme Court was bugged, probably by the FBI under J. Edgar Hoover.

radically liberalize the law of obscenity and free Henry Miller's long-contra-band novel was contained in a "Memorandum to the [case] Conference" dated June 18, 1964, found among Justice Harlan's court papers at Prince-ton University. In it Brennan informed the other justices sitting on the *Tropic of Cancer* case from Florida, which I had brought to the Court on a writ of certiorari—the case called *Grove Press* v. *Gerstein*—that he had read *Tropic of Cancer* and did "not think [it was] obscene" under the *Roth* standard. Not long after his note went around, Brennan composed the opinion that would explain that Henry Miller's novel could not be branded obscene because it was protected by the First Amendment's guarantees of speech and press. He did that in connection with an appeal from an Ohio conviction involving the motion picture *The Lovers* that New York lawyer Ephraim London had argued to the Court. Looking back at those events, I am impressed at how simply First Amendment justice can be done.

At the time of the *Cancer* decision, Brennan seemed an unlikely candi-date for the role of liberating American literature in general and Henry Miller's novel in particular. The book, though gaining acclaim among the literati, had an unholy reputation: a decade earlier it had been barred by U.S. customs officials and federal courts from entry into the United States because it was full of "sticky slime."* Not even Sam Roth, who had dared to publish pirated excerpts from Joyce's *Ulysses,* had dared to publish any-thing from *Tropic of Cancer.* † Moreover, Brennan had written in the *Roth* case what seemed to many to be a freedom-dragging opinion, because of its holding that "obscenity" was outside the First Amendment's protec-tions. Finally, there was the fact that, characteristically, Brennan carried out his work of First Amendment doctrinal construction quietly and unob-trusively. His opinions were never inflammatory; he made progress in small, quiet steps. As Harry Kalven observed, the "Brennan style" was "to avoid absolute protection and the futile debate it is likely to engender, but to keep the jurisdiction yielded to the censor as small as possible."‡ Because Bren-nan, unlike Justices Black and Douglas, never advocated an "absolutist"

Besig v. *United States,* reprinted in de Grazia, *Censorship Landmarks* (1969), 233–35. Here is an excerpt from the decision of the Court of Appeals: "Each of The Tropics is written in the composite style of a novel-autobiography, and the author as a character in the book carries the reader as though he himself is living in disgrace, degradation, poverty, mean crime, and prostitution of mind and body. The vehicle of description is the unprintable word of the debased and morally bankrupt. Practically everything that the world loosely regards as sin is detailed in the vivid, lurid, salacious language of smut, prostitution, and dirt. And all of it is related without the slightest expressed idea of its abandon. Consistent with the general tenor of the books, even human excrement is dwelt upon in the dirtiest words available. The author conducts the reader through sex orgies and perversions of the sex organs, and always in the debased language of the bawdy house. Nothing has the grace of purity or goodness. These words of the language of smut, and the disgraceful scenes, are so heavily larded throughout the books that those portions which are deemed to be of literary merit do not lift the reader's mind clear of their sticky slime. And it is safe to say that the 'literary merit' of the books carries the reader deeper into it."

†The book, however, in its Paris or Mexican edition, could be purchased at Frances Steloff's Gotham Book Mart in New York. See endnotes to Chapter 19.

‡*A Worthy Tradition* (1987), 373.

doctrine of free expression,* he was late to lift the spirits of those who are convinced, as I am, that the First Amendment freedoms form a base essential for the enjoyment of all other civil and political rights, and for republican government itself;† and that the Constitution's framers realized this and accordingly expressed the free speech and press guarantees in absolute terms.‡ In the event, Brennan's work in this area turned out to be more effective than either Black's or Douglas's because Brennan was a genius at building coalitions among the brethren who joined his doctrinal solutions to First Amendment problems, and coalitions of this sort are essential ingredients of the creative progress and growth of the law.§

---

*Although his "actual malice" doctrine in *Times* v. *Sullivan* and his "not utterly without social value" doctrine in *Jacobellis/Tropic of Cancer* came close.

†Conservatives also were late to appreciate, and so to deprecate, Brennan. It was not until the mid-eighties that neoconservative intellectuals and the Reagan administration understood the leading role that Brennan played in the Supreme Court's expansion of civil and political rights and in recognizing human dignity as an overarching principle of American constitutional law. Thus in 1986 Brennan was attacked publicly as an exponent of a "radically egalitarian jurisprudence" and was accused of creating "new rights where none existed, in the Constitution" by Assistant Attorney General William Bradford Reynolds (speech of September 12, 1986, at the University of Missouri School of Law). Justice Department spokesman Terry Eastland boasted that the speech was the strongest direct attack on an individual member of the Supreme Court by any high-ranking official of the Reagan administration (*The New York Times*, September 13, 1986). Reynolds also took the opportunity to blast the work of legal philosopher Ronald Dworkin, a professor of Jurisprudence at Oxford University and the New York University School of Law. A year later, when Judge Robert H. Bork came under scrutiny by the Senate for appointment to the high court, Dworkin demolished Bork's posture of judicial restraint in the pages of *The New York Review of Books*.

In Reynolds's words, Justice Brennan and Professor Dworkin both were bent on the destruction of "individual liberty," being "possessed of a thinly disguised intellectual arrogance that not infrequently takes cover behind the 'spirit' of the Constitution as found in its so-called penumbra." Brennan's jurisprudence was "a theory that seeks not limited government in order to secure individual liberty, but unlimited judicial power to further a personalized egalitarian vision of society."

Earlier, Dworkin had placed himself firmly on the side of a free press and freedom for sexually oriented expression in his book *A Matter of Principle* (1985), where he defended the "right to pornography" as an aspect of his theory of liberalism. Dworkin holds that liberalism's "constitutive morality" is a theory of equality "that requires official neutrality amongst theories of what is valuable in life." Dworkin had been an expert witness in a celebrated English obscenity trial of a magazine called *Oz* that took place in the Old Bailey courthouse. There he upset the presiding judge by testifying that whereas "the publication of a magazine like this is a vindication of some important moral principles . . . this prosecution is, in this sense, a corruption of public morals." See Tony Palmer, *The Trials of Oz* (1971).

For a further discussion of neoconservative attacks on Brennan and the Court, see the endnotes for this chapter.

‡"Congress shall make no law respecting an establishment of religion, or prohibiting the free exercise thereof; or abridging the freedom of speech, or of the press; or the right of the people peaceably to assemble, and to petition the Government for a redress of grievances." None of the other amendments appear in this commanding form. As previously mentioned, the bar to congressional enactments that abridge freedom of expression was made applicable to state laws by judicial interpretation of the Fourteenth Amendment.

§Brennan found a middle ground between the polarized doctrinal approaches advocated by Justices Black and Douglas ("no law means *no* law") on the liberal left, and Justice Frankfurter ("reasonable" regulation of expression and the exercise of "deference" to the legislatures and "restraint" in judicial review) on the conservative right. Black and Frankfurter were struggling for Court leadership in the First Amendment area when Brennan joined the Court. At first, Brennan sided with Frankfurter, as exemplified by Brennan's opinion in *Roth;*

. . .

Brennan was born in 1906 in Newark, New Jersey, of parents who were Irish Catholic immigrants.

JUSTICE WILLIAM J. BRENNAN, JR.: My father came from Ireland because of the famine and then, later, the political unrest. He shoveled coal when he got over here, and became a union organizer. At that time Newark was owned by one man, McArter. My father got involved in a strike of transportation workers and the police beat him and the others up. I was ten years old at the time. Later, my father was elected Commissioner, in Newark.

—

This background may help to explain why Brennan became such a humane and egalitarian justice. But the reasons for his judicial effectiveness are of a different sort, having to do, I believe, with his extraordinary gift for relating affectionately and creatively with the men and women with whom he worked. Unlike Hugo Black, Brennan did not lose his appetite for First Amendment freedom, for example, even where Negro sit-in demonstrators were involved.* Unlike William O. Douglas, Brennan refused to lose patience with his brothers when they opposed him. And unlike Felix Frankfurter, Brennan never discounted the views of individual brethren or disparaged court majorities as unprincipled, undisciplined, or unlearned. Such characteristics help to explain Brennan's remarkable ability to carry

---

then he constructed his own doctrinal approaches, which paved the way to nearly absolute freedom of speech and press without, however, subscribing to Black's absolutist approach. To the end of his days on the Court, Black continued to press for adoption of his views in this area; in doing that he became one of the sharpest of the "friendly" critics of the Brennan doctrine's mode of incrementally claiming more and more freedom for allegedly obscene literary and artistic expression.

*It seems pertinent here to note that although Black, like the rest of the brethren, supported the Court's controversial decisions holding unconstitutional public school segregation and mandating desegregation (*Brown* v. *Board of Education,* et al.), he consistently opposed the disposition of Chief Justice Warren and Justices Douglas and Brennan to hold that sit-ins (by blacks) were a form of expression protected by the First Amendment, not only at public places like libraries but in public places that were privately owned, such as lunch counters and restaurants. Warren took the position, supported by Brennan and Douglas, that the owners of places serving the public (to be called public accommodations in the Civil Rights Act of 1964) abandoned private choice and could not constitutionally call in the police to help to throw out people they did not want to serve. Black, whose "Pappy" had run a general store, believed owners had the right to decide whom they would or would not serve. Douglas, on the other hand, believed that affirming the convictions of sit-in demonstrators "fastens apartheid tightly onto our society." For a while, the Court was dangerously and heatedly divided on the issue, and Black issued strident dissents to actions by the Court that overturned, on First Amendment grounds, the trespass convictions of civil rights demonstrators attempting to pressure private places of public accommodation into serving members of all races. In a June 1963 case involving a challenge brought by black demonstrators against a Jackson, Mississippi, court injunction preventing them from "unlawfully" picketing or parading on the streets of Jackson, Black opposed the Court's issuing any stay of the injunction because (according to a Douglas "Memorandum for the Files") "the situation between the races was getting to be more and more acute" and "it was time to clamp down on the Negroes." See *The Douglas Letters,* edited by Melvin I. Urofsky (1987), 169–72; Bernard Schwartz with Stephen Lesher, *Inside the Warren Court* (1983), 217–27; and John F. Simon, *The Antagonists* (1989), at 256–58.

the Court and to speak for it on controversial issues of great importance.*

Dean Norman Redlich of the New York University Law School was an empathetic observer of Brennan's work on the Court.

DEAN NORMAN REDLICH: Much has been written about Justice Brennan's Supreme Court career—how he joined the coalescing minority of Justices Black and Douglas and the Chief Justice [Warren] and how this minority expanded into a majority which made the Supreme Court, for a few short but exciting years, into a worldwide symbol of the furtherance of individual rights and liberties. I have always believed that it was a mistake for the partisans of any Supreme Court justice to describe any one of these remarkable jurists as the "leader of the Court." No one, except perhaps Earl Warren, leads the likes of Black, Douglas, Brennan, Goldberg and Fortas. But on many occasions, spanning the Warren and Burger courts, it was Justice Brennan who provided the formulation that was able to create a Court majority, around which different viewpoints would temporarily gather.

ANTHONY LEWIS: He is not a judge who enjoys the role of passionate dissenter. He has "an instinct for accommodation," a former law clerk of his has said—a preference for helping to shape majorities.

———

His ability to build consensus on the high bench helps explain why Warren assigned him so many opinions to write. Of 132 major decisions issued during the 23 Court terms between 1956 and 1978—between the time, that is, when Brennan joined the Court and the last year covered by a study made of the justices' work—Brennan wrote 29 opinions for the Court. No other justice came close; those who wrote the most opinions, after Brennan, were the two chief justices during that period, Earl Warren, who wrote 13, and Warren Burger, who wrote 14.† Most of Brennan's major opinions involved the expansion and extension of individual rights

———

*Until his resignation in July 1990, at the age of eighty-four, and two decades after the demise of the Warren Court and the ascendancies of the Burger and Rehnquist courts, Brennan was able to carry and speak for the Court in the First Amendment area in controversial cases, including the American-flag-desecration and flag-burning cases of 1989 and 1990. Here, Brennan twice led a majority, of a bench on which the liberals were outnumbered two to one, to hold unconstitutional laws that sought to prevent persons from speaking against or criticizing the country or its policies by desecrating or burning the flag. The Court's initial decision was politically so unpopular that President Bush attempted to gain support for his administration by calling for a constitutional amendment of the First Amendment to overrule the Supreme Court's decision. The attempt failed and Brennan's view of First Amendment freedom prevailed.

†It may be remembered that when the chief justice finds himself voting with a Court majority, it is his prerogative to assign the opinion-writing task to himself or to any other justice also voting with the majority. Had Brennan voted with the three-justice minority in *Roth* that wished to reverse Roth's conviction, he would not have changed the Court's judgment to affirm it, but he would have lost (probably to Frankfurter) the opportunity to write the Court's landmark majority opinion. The writing of an opinion of the Court offers vast opportunities to "make" law, limited mainly by what other justices in the majority are willing to "join."

and liberties, especially those protected by the First Amendment. Until Brennan joined the Court, it was Frankfurter and his doctrine of judicial restraint that held sway over the Court's work in that critical field.*

Brennan responded to Reagan-era critics of "judicial activism" in a characteristically graceful exposition of his judicial philosophy:†

JUSTICE WILLIAM J. BRENNAN, JR.: Lively, even acrimonious, debate about the proper role of judges in a democratic society is ever with us. The judge who believes that the judicial power should be made creative and vigorously effective is labeled "activist." The judge inclined to question the propriety of judicial intervention to redress even the most egregious failures of democracy is labeled "neutralist" or "liberal"; where yesterday "activist" was pinned on "conservatives," today [1982] it's on "liberals." As often as not, however, such labels are used merely to express disapproval of particular decisions. If useful at all, the labels may be more serviceable to distinguish the judge who sees his role as guided by the principle that "justice or righteousness is the source, the substance and the ultimate end of the law," and the judge for whom the principle is that "courts do not sit to administer justice, but to administer the law." Such legendary names as Justice Holmes and Judge Learned Hand have been associated with the latter view.

Holmes' imaginary Society of Jobbists is limited to judges who hold a tight rein on humanitarian impulse and compassionate action, stoically doing their best to discover and apply already existing rules. But judges acting on the former view believe that the judicial process demands a good deal more of them than that. Because Constitution, statute or precedent rarely speaks unambiguously, a just choice between competing alternatives has to be made to decide concrete cases. Notre Dame's former Dean O'Meara went to the heart of the problem in saying, ". . . the judge's role necessarily is a creative one—he must legislate, there is no help for it. . . . When the critical moment comes and he must say yea or nay, he is on his own; he has nothing to rely on but his own intellect, experience and conscience."

When Brennan was a boy in Newark, his father rose from being a boiler stoker to being the city's commissioner of public safety. Here, one of his duties was to issue licenses for movie and burlesque theatres. In those days, "live" shows and movies, unlike the newspaper- and book-publishing press, were routinely licensed by town authorities, who assumed authority under the state's police powers to decide whether such shows were fit to be shown publicly. Like the judges who censored literature under the guise of suppressing the "obscene," the licensors of movies and plays were not perceived as censors until a few years after World War II. One reason was that in the beginning, movies especially, but also plays, were thought of as "entertain-

---

*See John F. Simon, *The Antagonists* (1989), 236.
†In the context of a eulogy for former justice Abe Fortas; see Chapter 27.

ments," not transmitters of ideas, and it was only the communication of thoughts, opinion, and ideas that was considered to be protected by the First Amendment.*

In 1915, the Supreme Court assimilated motion pictures to the circus and "other shows and spectacles"—"not to be regarded . . . as part of the press of the country or as organs of public opinion."† With the development of the motion picture industry and film art, however, the Court grew increasingly uncomfortable with the cramped notion that the censorship of motion pictures had nothing to do with freedom of the press.

In 1926, a ruling by William J. Brennan, Sr., then Newark's commissioner of public safety, that a movie called *The Naked Truth* could not be shown in Newark "except in a Y.M.C.A., a school building, or a church, without charge" was reversed by a court of chancery.‡ In 1954, another Newark license commissioner's refusal to permit a burlesque theatre to open its doors was overturned by Brennan's son, speaking for New Jersey's highest judicial bench. Said young Brennan in that case: "[T]he performance of a play or show, whether burlesque or other kind of theatre, is a form of speech and prima facie expression protected by the State and Federal Constitutions."§ A decade later, speaking from the bench of the United States Supreme Court (in the *Jacobellis* and *Tropic of Cancer* cases), Brennan created a lasting precedent in favor of artistic freedom for movies and books by ruling that *any* form of expression "having literary, scientific, artistic or other social importance" was entitled to the full protection of the constitutional guarantees. If Brennan inherited his father's intelligence and fine political sense, he had not absorbed his puritanical feelings about sex

---

*Former judge Robert H. Bork exemplified the neoconservative disposition to deny to artists and the arts the freedom that politicians and other more traditional hawkers of opinions and ideas have. Even today, the constitutional law of speech and press does not clearly protect "entertainment" against imputations of obscenity or indecency. (See the case of the "nude dancers," discussed in Chapter 29.) Under the Brennan doctrine, entertainment would be protected as expression not "utterly" without artistic or other social value or importance. But under Chief Justice Warren E. Burger's 1973 revisionary opinions (sometimes collectively referred to as *Miller* v. *California*), entertainment may be unprotected unless it can be shown to possess *serious* literary, artistic, scientific, or political value. See Frederick Schauer, *The Law of Obscenity* (1976), 145.

The recent police and prosecutor attacks in Miami on the rap music group 2 Live Crew for creating, playing, and singing obscene songs is a fresh example of the stubborn reluctance of some judges to recognize constitutional freedom in the arts, popular as well as fine. In at least one of the 2 Live Crew cases, a Florida jury saw the serious artistic and political value in the group's songs. See Chapter 30. And in a Cincinnati case involving the attempted suppression of an exhibition of Robert Mapplethorpe's photographic art, a jury liberated the art (and a criminally prosecuted gallery curator) from the repressive grip of obscenity law.

†In *Mutual Film Corp.* v. *Ohio,* the Supreme Court decided that the content of movies could be regulated by the state in the exercise of its police powers both by prescribing criminal penalties for immoral exhibitions and by requiring censorship before exhibition. The text of the Court's opinion is in de Grazia, *Censorship Landmarks* (1969), 59–63.

‡The incident and the movie are described in de Grazia and Newman, *Banned Films: Movies, Censors and the First Amendment* (1982), 204–6. The case was *Public Welfare Pictures Corp.* v. *Brennan*, 134 A. 868 (1926).

§The case was *Adams Theatre Company* v. *Keenan,* reprinted in de Grazia, *Censorship Landmarks* (1969), 213ff.

(which he has compared with those of his closest friend on the Court, "Super Chief" Earl Warren).

After attending parochial and public schools in Newark, Brennan went to the University of Pennsylvania and then, on scholarship, to Harvard Law School, where he developed a legal-aid program for the poor. He entered labor law practice in Newark with a distinguished firm but soon turned from the transitory rewards of private law practice to the more enduring ones of working as a judge. From his initial service as a trial judge, Brennan clambered up the judicial ladder to a seat on the New Jersey Supreme Court, becoming a protégé of the powerful and prestigious Arthur Vanderbilt, then serving as chief justice of the New Jersey Supreme Court. The Vanderbilt connection would prove of signal importance to Brennan's career. In a search for someone to replace retiring justice Sherman Minton, President Dwight D. Eisenhower consulted Attorney General Herbert Brownell, who recommended Brennan because Brownell knew he enjoyed Vanderbilt's highest regard; Vanderbilt himself was considered too old for the job. Brennan was a lifelong Democrat and a Catholic, and 1956 was an election year; according to Brennan, "in order to emphasize the nonpartisanship of his administration," Eisenhower wanted "a Democrat from the Northeast."

During the fifties Brennan had spoken out against McCarthyism while he was on the New Jersey Supreme Court—once at a Rotary Club dinner and again at a banquet of the Irish-American Association.* The main targets of his speeches were the congressional committee witch-hunts that plagued so many liberals at that time—especially teachers, writers, artists, and other intellectuals.

Although Brennan was a Catholic, he could not in conscience conform to the social and political views of Catholic religious leaders like Francis Cardinal Spellman, the powerful archbishop of New York, who was also one of Joe McCarthy's staunchest supporters. The cardinal liked to rant against Communism and rave about Americanism as much as he liked to rail against obscenity and push for the censorship of movies, plays, and books.† His power grew mainly out of his position as moral leader of the Catholic Church in New York, but his views also influenced official actions taken by some Catholic policemen, judges, and postal workers. Several million New York Catholics (including public officials and government employees) listened to what Spellman said about moral and social issues; many followed his ideas implicitly.‡ Brennan, however, was differ-

---

*See 103 Cong. Rec. S3938-42 (195), citing these addresses.

†One of the country's most powerful unofficial agencies of censorship, the Catholic Church's National Office for Decent Literature (NODL), was organized shortly after the federal courts acted to free James Joyce's *Ulysses* from obscenity censorship at U.S. Customs. Donna A. Demac, *Liberty Denied* (1988), 40. See Chapter 2 above.

‡See John Cooney, *The American Pope* (1984), 108–9. The endnotes to this chapter describe some "censorship" actions of Cardinal Spellman's. Today, Protestant evangelical church leaders like the Reverend Donald Wildmon are exerting intense political pressure on members of Congress and state legislatures, federal, state, and local prosecutors and judges,

ent,* and when he served on the Supreme Court this difference would eventually stun Catholic leaders.

Cardinal Spellman preached against "sexually immoral" books, plays, and films, even those that treated sex lightly; characteristically for a moral censor, he did not need to read or see what he knew ought to be condemned. Justice Stewart once claimed he knew pornography "when he saw it"; Cardinal Spellman knew it even when he did not see it. Early in his reign over New York City's Catholic archdiocese—after the United States went to war against the Axis powers in Europe—Spellman became convinced that sex and the war had their common source in Satan. At that time he preached that "the Fifth Column of saboteurs of our factories and public utilities has its counterpart in the Fifth Column of those who piously shout 'censorship' if they are not permitted freely to exercise their venal, venomous, diabolical debauching of our boys and girls." Later, in August 1964, after the Supreme Court announced its decision in the *Tropic of Cancer* case, Spellman would accuse the brethren of "an acceptance of degeneracy and the beatnik mentality as the standard way of American life."†

In 1950, Spellman managed to get revoked the movie exhibition license that had been issued for Roberto Rossellini's critically acclaimed film *The Miracle* by the Board of Regents in New York; however, Ephraim London, the lawyer representing the movie's American distributor, Joseph Burstyn, persuaded the Supreme Court to review and reverse the censorship. As a result, Spellman's authority was undermined, the Regents suffered a stun-

---

and the heads of agencies such as the Federal Communications Commission and the National Endowment for the Arts in an attempt to purge the media and the arts of material they consider obscene, indecent, blasphemous, or merely "controversial." See Chapter 30.

Recently (1989–90), New York's Catholic prelate John Cardinal O'Connor has aggressively sought to coerce the consciences and the public positions of Catholic officials in New York, including Governor Mario Cuomo, with regard to abortion. Cuomo, who has more than once seriously considered running for the presidency of the United States, has (to date) successfully fended off such interference.

*In an interview published in *The New York Times Magazine* on October 5, 1986, Brennan said he realized he was "a disappointment to some Roman Catholics." Before his confirmation hearing in 1956, the Senate Judiciary Committee "unanimously said it was most inappropriate to ask me whether, as a Catholic, I would follow the Constitution. But then they did ask me. And I had settled in my mind that I had an obligation under the Constitution which could not be influenced by any of my religious principles. As a Roman Catholic I might do as a private citizen does, and that is one thing, but to the extent that that conflicts with what I think the Constitution means or requires, then my religious beliefs have to give way."

The "most difficult" decisions Brennan has had to make, given his "life-long experience as a Roman Catholic," involved not obscenity or even abortion, but the school prayer cases. "[T]o say that prayer was not an appropriate thing in public schools, that gave me quite a hard time. I struggled." Jeffrey T. Leeds, "A Life on the Court," *The New York Times Magazine,* October 5, 1986.

New York governor Mario Cuomo's Catholicism similarly did not dissuade him from discharging his official duties regarding the laws of abortion in conformity with his conscience, notwithstanding implied threats of excommunication from New York's John Cardinal O'Connor. A New York Times/WCBS-TV News poll of 1,047 adults indicated that 70 percent of New York's Catholics disapproved of the excommunication threat. *The New York Times,* June 23, 1990.

†*The Tablet,* August 13, 1964.

ning defeat, and the cause of movie censorship in America was irrevocably set back.*

During the fifties, Francis Cardinal Spellman's influence reached into the White House. Before the 1956 election, he arranged for a private audience with President Eisenhower to let him know how he felt about the religio-ideological makeup of the Supreme Court. The prelate had two grievances. First, no Catholic had sat on the Court since Justice Frank Murphy had retired in 1949. Second, he had expected Eisenhower to use his appointment power to steer the Court away from New Deal liberalism, but the president had named Earl Warren and John Marshall Harlan to the high bench. Spellman could tell that Harlan was no red-white-and-blue conservative,† and Warren, in the cardinal's eyes, was fast becoming as liberal as any justice FDR had ever appointed.

In his biography of Spellman, John Cooney writes that when the White House meeting took place, Spellman said: "Mr. President, it isn't that I want a Catholic on the Supreme Court, but I want someone who will represent the interests and views of the Catholic Church." Eisenhower reacted by telling Bernard Shanley, a White House special counsel and a Catholic as well, "Remind me about what the Cardinal wants when the time comes."

In 1956, with the retirement of the conservative justice Sherman Minton, Eisenhower told Shanley that he and Attorney General Herbert Brownell had come up with "someone who will suit the Cardinal." But when Shanley told the cardinal of Brennan's appointment, Spellman said: "I don't know him. Who is his parish priest?" After Spellman checked Brennan out, he berated Shanley for failing to persuade the president to put on the Court the right kind of Catholic.

New Jerseyans knew that Brennan was independent of mind, and that he did not agree with some of the ideas that Spellman cherished, such as McCarthyism. It was only a matter of time before Brennan's attitudes became known to McCarthy himself. The senator took a full day to investigate Brennan's thinking when the justice came before the Senate Judiciary Committee for his confirmation hearings.‡ McCarthy badgered Brennan mostly for having expressed disapproval of the ways in which congressional committees and subcommittees, including McCarthy's, conducted hear-

---

*See the endnotes on the *Miracle* controversy.

†Harlan, like Frankfurter, was an apostle for judicial restraint, but he was less squeamish about sexual matters. Despite his deteriorating eyesight, he enjoyed watching the "dirty" movies the Court was obliged to review; and he wrote a subtle and stunning First Amendment opinion for the Court in *Cohen* v. *California,* which reversed the defendant's conviction for "disturbing the peace" by wearing a jacket with the slogan "Fuck the Draft" in the corridors of a courthouse building. Harry Kalven recognized Harlan's opinion in *Cohen* as exemplifying "the best of the judicial tradition as to the First Amendment." *A Worthy Tradition* (1987), 15. The case is officially reported at 403 U.S. 15 (1971).

‡Eisenhower appointed Brennan to the Supreme Court during a congressional recess. This meant that Brennan had begun to participate in the Court's work by the time his appointment was examined by the Judiciary Committee and acted upon by the Senate.

ings: harassing witnesses and in some cases causing them to lose their livelihoods, their reputations, their friends, even their lives. Despite McCarthy's concerns, Brennan's appointment to the Court was overwhelmingly confirmed by the Senate. McCarthy's was the only vote opposed: at that moment the senator's power was about gone.

Brennan and Warren shared the same views on most issues of concern to the Court, but not on the obscenity issue. For example, although Warren gave the opinion-writing assignment in *Roth* to Brennan,* he filed a separate opinion of his own in that case, concurring in the result (which was to affirm Roth's conviction) but disagreeing with Brennan's reasons for reaching that conclusion.† In 1964, when the freedom of Henry Miller's novel *Tropic of Cancer* was being fought over in some fifty cases around the country, and an Ohio movie-theatre manager named Nico Jacobellis was convicted for exhibiting Louis Malle's innovative film *The Lovers,* Brennan distanced himself from Warren's puritanical reaction to nudity and sexually explicit images in literature and films and went quietly to work with the less finicky humanistic liberals among the brethren to lift literary and artistic expression to a solid position of freedom. By then Frankfurter had retired.

I have already written of how, in Brennan's otherwise "conservative" opinion in *Roth,* literature and art were linked for the first time in the Supreme Court's history to freedom of the press. Brennan has said to me that he *always* felt that artistic expression was encompassed by the First Amendment's guarantees. In 1957, the problem for him must have been how to reconcile that feeling with the seemingly universal opinion that obscenity—whatever it was—was worthless and condemnable out of hand; and with two hundred years of failure on the part of nearly all American scholars and judges to recognize and build upon the idea that artistic expression—even when charged with being obscene—presented as full a claim as did political expression to constitutional protection.

Before 1960, even the civil libertarian American philosopher Alexander Meiklejohn seemed prepared to justify censorship of the theatre, and of other literary and artistic works. (Meiklejohn later corrected that impression, in a published academic dialogue with Professor Kalven.) It was only in the crucible of Supreme Court litigation during the turbulent sixties, under Brennan's guidance, that literature and arts were recognized as entitled to full constitutional protection. During the same period, the influential jurist Robert H. Bork, while a professor of law at Yale, opposed Brennan's and the Supreme Court's view in his teaching and writing. Bork insisted that the framers intended that only "political" expression be protected. This cramped reading of a constitutional text by Bork was one of

---

*Warren probably chose Brennan over Frankfurter to write the Court's opinion in *Roth* because Brennan, like Warren and unlike Frankfurter, was no lover of the doctrine of judicial restraint. However, Brennan's opinion in *Roth* was, in fact, a fairly good example of the exercise of judicial restraint.

†Warren's concurring opinion in *Roth* may be found in de Grazia, *Censorship Landmarks* (1969), 295.

the reasons that in 1988 he would dramatically forfeit his appointment to the Supreme Court.

On September 22, 1987, the American novelist William Styron made a statement on behalf of two thousand writer-members of the PEN American Center, at Senate Judiciary Committee hearings,* in opposition to the appointment of Judge Bork to be an associate justice of the Supreme Court.

WILLIAM STYRON: We're a group of writers who value deeply our freedom to write as we wish, to express ourselves in prose and poetry on whatever subject and in whatever way we choose, free of every sort of governmental constraint. We are able to enjoy this freedom because we live and write in a country whose highest law, the Constitution, guarantees it, and whose highest judicial organ, the Supreme Court, enforces it. †

Styron proceeded to quote from some of Bork's speeches and writings:

ROBERT H. BORK: Constitutional protection should be accorded only to speech that is explicitly political. There is no basis for judicial intervention to protect any other form of expression, be it scientific, literary or that variety of expression we call obscene or pornographic. . . .

It is sometimes said that works of art, or indeed any form of expression, are capable of influencing political attitudes. But in those indirect and relatively remote relationships to the political process, verbal or visual expression does not differ at all from other human activities, such as sports or business, which are also capable of affecting political attitudes, but are not on that account immune from regulation. . . .

There comes a point at which the speech no longer has any relation to those processes. When it reaches that level, speech is really no different from any other human activity which produces self-gratification. . . . Clearly as you get into forms of art—and if you want to call it literature and art—which are pornography and things approaching it—you are dealing with something now that is [not] in any way and form the way we govern ourselves, and in fact may be quite deleterious. I would doubt that courts ought to throw protection around that.

WILLIAM STYRON: As I and my colleagues reread these views and as we considered and reconsidered them in the context of Judge Bork's [recent] statements [to the committee]‡ we found ourselves troubled on two accounts. The first is as elemental as it is solemn. Judge Bork . . . for the last sixteen years—has either explicitly placed literature outside First Amendment protection or has failed to recognize the necessity of such protection.

---

*Painter Robert Rauschenberg also testified, "to express the unanimous fears that the art world has toward the nomination of Bork."

†As a member of PEN's Freedom-to-Write Committee, I helped Executive Director Karen Kennerly draft this preamble to Styron's statement on behalf of PEN.

‡In his testimony Bork backed off from his position that literature was not *as such* protected by the First Amendment, and gave Henry Miller's *Tropic of Capricorn* as an example of a protected literary work.

Can we fully trust and believe that this man henceforth will be a staunch defender of First Amendment freedom for literary expression? . . . Both as individual writers and as members of PEN, we maintain that a full and absolutely unwavering protection of all literature must be a matter not of passing opinion but of conviction and faith. We are not persuaded that Judge Bork has that faith. . . .

The presence of an undefined category of non-obscene but possibly unprotected work in Judge Bork's scheme of things is dangerous to free literary expression in the United States. Every day, books considered to "approach pornography" are removed from classrooms and library shelves. I am personally quite sensitive to this issue because as recently as last spring one of my own books, namely *The Confessions of Nat Turner,* was removed from a school library in Iowa at the insistence of a mother who objected to her adolescent son's reading the book and finding in the book certain sexually explicit passages.

To the best of my knowledge, this book, which was banned by a majority vote of the school board, remains banned. It is extremely disturbing to any writer to know that his or her work can be in effect sequestered and ultimately condemned at the whim of a school board. Many of my fellow writers have in the recent past suffered this kind of censorship. . . .*

I want to take the liberty of recalling for the members of this Committee the centrality to our country of a free literature and art. No person should be elevated to the country's highest judicial office who has not persuasively demonstrated that he believes unreservedly in that freedom.†

———

As I have mentioned, the concurring opinion that Judge Jerome Frank wrote in *Roth* may have been the first judicial attention paid to the historical fact that the arts in general were meant by the nation's founders to be protected by the First Amendment. Frank also wryly noted that the men who fought the war for the country's independence and who had drawn up the documents spelling out its basic law—the Constitution and the Bill of Rights—were not as puritanical as were the legislators who passed the country's first obscenity laws, or the state judges who received the common law of "obscene libel" into the nation's legal fabric without concern for the First Amendment's prohibition on abridgments of speech and press. Another observation by Frank, that "the 'founding fathers' did not accept the common law concerning freedom of expression," would not to my knowledge make its way into a Supreme Court decision until 1964, when Brennan used it in *New York Times* v. *Sullivan* to criticize the common law of "seditious libel," and the action in damages which most states allowed to public officials, for being in violation of the freedom of the press. It was

---

*See endnotes for more on school library censorship.

†A few days earlier in the hearings, in response to "friendly" questions from Senator Strom Thurmond, Bork had "recanted" his sixteen-year-long view that literary and artistic expression was not protected by the guarantees of freedom of speech and press.

in that opinion as well that Brennan loosed those evangelical words "robust," "wide-open," and "uninhibited" to depict the type of discourse and "discussion" that the Constitution's framers intended to encourage and protect when they adopted the First Amendment.

Brennan could not seriously begin the work of freeing literary and artistic expression under American constitutional law without divorcing his own thinking on the subject from Chief Justice Earl Warren's obsession with living in, and presiding over the legal order of, "a decent society." He also had to distance himself from Felix Frankfurter's influence, particularly his anxiety about the deleterious effects of unrestrained expression, visible in his earlier opinions in this area. Frankfurter was certainly not insensitive to the values of free expression, but his appreciation of those values was often overwhelmed by his fears. He was one of the strongest Court advocates for the use of a "balancing" test when free expression and a police interest of the state collide. Such a test allows judges to sacrifice free speech to state interest whenever they fear the effects of uncurtailed expression.*

While at Harvard, Frankfurter defended radicals during the post–World War I "Red scare," helped organize the defense of Sacco and Vanzetti in the 1920s, and spoke out time and again for civil liberties. However, his two greatest heroes, Holmes and Brandeis, both advocated judicial restraint, and at Harvard Frankfurter became a leading academic exponent of that doctrine. But the judicial restraint proposed by Holmes and Brandeis was not meant to safeguard legislation trenching upon the liberties of speech and press; it was intended to protect legislation that, in seeking social reforms, diminished laissez-faire prerogatives of property owners and business entrepreneurs. Once Frankfurter reached the Court, he abandoned his liberal activism and campaigned instead for the doctrine that the Court should never superintend the wisdom of legislative policies by striking down state or federal laws—except where the legislature had plainly acted "irrationally"—regardless of whether the legislation affected rights of speech, press, or property. Frankfurter opposed the belief first advanced by Justice Harlan Stone, and honored by a long line of liberal justices, that under the Constitution freedom of expression held a "preferred position."

At first Frankfurter saw Douglas, as he saw most Court newcomers, as a potential disciple and ally in his effort to assert doctrinal hegemony over the Court. But when Douglas found that judicial restraint in Frankfurter's hands was used not to permit legislative reform of entrepreneurial property

---

*A newer, more quantitative, but equally insidious doctrine for the judicial parceling out of freedom according to the judiciary's (especially the Supreme Court's) sense of the relative social values possessed by differing sorts of speech is advocated by Cass R. Sunstein of the University of Chicago Law School in "Pornography and the First Amendment," 1986 *Duke Law Journal* 589 (1986). There Sunstein contends that "pornography" should judicially be classified as "low-value" speech "entitled to less protection from government control than most forms of speech." Sunstein here commits in aggravated form the First Amendment jurisprudential sin that Harry Kalven rightly criticized Justice Brennan for committing in *Roth.* Brennan purged himself of that sin in the 1964 obscenity case decisions discussed in the text by his creation of the Brennan doctrine.

law but as "an instrument of judicial inflexibility" in the civil liberties field, he left Frankfurter's side to work with Black and the other Court liberals for the recognition of civil and political rights. That item topped the agenda of the Court's constitutional concerns from the late 1930s through the 1960s.

As soon as Brennan joined the Court, Frankfurter tried to woo him to his side; the attempt failed once Brennan sorted out his own ideological position. Brennan frequently took a middle position, which in time, and toward the end of the older justice's tenure, served actually to return Frankfurter closer to the liberal position.

In an interview published in *The New York Times Magazine* Brennan spoke about his relationship to Frankfurter, and the elder justice's methods:

JUSTICE WILLIAM J. BRENNAN, JR.: Felix was absolutely superb [in winning a young justice over as an ideological ally] without your being conscious of it. His chambers were next to mine, and he used to come in with some frequency, and he would tell me much about the great giants that he had known and worked with and what brilliant contributions they had made. He made conversation, he flattered you, he made you feel that it would be an honor to be associated with him and his crowd of giants.

Felix also worked socially. I recall he had a dinner at his home for me, and the guests were Dean Acheson and John Lord O'Brien,* and I heard much in the discussion after dinner over brandy about the role of the Court and the role of the Justices. . . .

We always were good friends. He never stopped or gave up trying to persuade me in individual cases, but he knew that I would not, could not, accept his approach across the board.

———

When he was at Harvard Law School Brennan had been lucky enough to have both Felix Frankfurter and Zechariah Chafee as his teachers. (Chafee, he says, was his favorite.) After Brennan joined Frankfurter on the Court, the latter is supposed to have quipped: "I taught my students to think for themselves but sometimes I think Bill Brennan carries it too far."

Not long before Brennan took his seat on the Court, Frankfurter "lost" Chief Justice Warren to the Black-Douglas wing of the Court; he was distraught over the possibility that Brennan might become a fourth vote for judicial activism. So the elder justice worked on Brennan.

JUSTICE WILLIAM J. BRENNAN, JR.: I looked to Felix to help a novice get his feet wet. And Felix went out of his way, but he did that for everybody. After a while, I realized it was not just out of kindness.

———

The Frankfurter-Brennan honeymoon ended not long after *Roth,* when Brennan voted with Black to swing the Court away from Frankfurter's views

---

*Frankfurter probably invited O'Brien when Learned Hand "politely declined" to dine with him and meet the freshman Justice Brennan. See John F. Simon, *The Antagonists* (1989), 235.

in other civil liberties cases. Frankfurter wrote to another new member of the Court, John Harlan, about Brennan: "I wish he was less shallow and thereby less cocksure, but his honesty cheers me much and gives me considerable hope." Frankfurter would actually have better luck with Harlan, who adopted a view of the Supreme Court's "self-restrained" function that reflected Frankfurter's, particularly where civil liberties were at stake. After Frankfurter's retirement, it would be Harlan who argued for judicial restraint.

JUSTICE WILLIAM J. BRENNAN, JR.: Everyone thought Felix Frankfurter would be a flaming liberal when he came, and there was a lot of reason to think he would. And yet, when he got here, his conscience wouldn't let him, because of his conviction that the judiciary should not be resolving many issues that, in his view, should be decided by the legislature or executive branch. Talk about disappointing a President—certainly Felix disillusioned F.D.R.

———

In 1960, three years after *Roth* was decided, Brennan and Frankfurter found themselves on opposite sides of a First Amendment issue of great moment. Frankfurter cast the swing vote necessary to uphold the constitutionality of a Chicago ordinance that required all motion pictures to be approved and licensed by the police in advance of any theatrical exhibition. The case was *Times Film Corp. v. Chicago;* it had presented the Court with an opportunity to answer a profound question that Justice Clark had left open in the *Miracle* case: Does *all* prior licensing of motion picture exhibition, even on obscenity grounds, violate the First Amendment? A passionate argument that it does was unsuccessfully urged upon the brethren by a promising young Chicago lawyer, Abner J. Mikva, who later became a U.S. congressman (Democratic) from Illinois and a liberal and humanistic federal circuit judge for the District of Columbia Circuit.* Writing for a conservative majority that included Frankfurter, Justice Tom Clark distinguished motion pictures from other media of communication by holding the Chicago ordinance not invalid on its face. The Court's liberal bloc, Brennan, Black, and Douglas—now dubbed BB&D by Frankfurter—joined the eloquent dissenting opinion written by Chief Justice Warren, which reviewed the history of "unfreedom" of motion pictures in America and asserted that the Court should instead have struck down the licensing system as an unconstitutional prior restraint on the freedom of the press. To the dissenters, such a movie-licensing system was as patently unconstitutional, as great an infringement on press freedom, as any other prior-licensing system would be, including one based on "obscenity" applied to the distribution of newspapers or the publication of books. Although this would prove to be the last occasion on which Frankfurter's views of judicial

———

*Mikva has been spoken of as a prospect for appointment to the Supreme Court by the next Democratic president to have that opportunity.

restraint would swing a free-press decision in favor of censorship, the precedent established under his sway has never been overturned.*

After *Times Film,* two important obscenity cases were decided by the Court prior to Frankfurter's retirement in 1962. The aging and ill justice did not participate in one of these—which added a second prong known as "patent offensiveness" to the "prurient interest" definition of the obscene†—but in the other he deserted dissenting justice Tom Clark to join a far-reaching majority opinion written by Brennan that struck down as unconstitutional a Missouri system under which police mass seizures of books and magazines were allowed to take place without a prior adversary judicial hearing. The case gave Brennan the opportunity to lay down a "First Amendment due process" framework that would thereafter repeatedly be relied upon to foil police and prosecutorial censorship by seizure of published materials and motion picture films.‡

Brennan's opinion in *Roth* had gathered together a coalition of five other justices who joined what one jurist spoke of as a "balancing" approach but is more aptly described as a "straddling" or "two-level" approach to freedom of expression. This approach was introduced in Justice Murphy's opinion for the Court in the landmark case of *Chaplinsky* v. *New Hampshire.* To adopt the two-level metaphor, used by Kalven: on the upper level are situated traditionally protected sorts of speech—mainly political speech of the soapbox-and-leaflet type and political and religious "ideas"—which are supposed to be fully protected by the guarantees; on the lower level are located the traditionally unprotected, denigrated sorts of speech—mainly libelous, profane, and obscene speech, and "fighting words." That was the approach Frankfurter successfully advanced before and throughout the World War II period; after the war Brennan's exposition of it in *Roth* was inspired, as well as joined, by Frankfurter. But when Arthur H. Goldberg, a liberal and humanistic labor lawyer from Chicago, took Justice Frank-

---

*It almost certainly would have been overturned in the early seventies had President Johnson's late-term bid to make Justice Abe Fortas chief justice in Warren's place not been defeated, which allowed the next president, Richard Nixon, to replace Warren with a conservative, Judge Warren E. Burger. *Times Film* is reproduced in de Grazia, *Censorship Landmarks* (1969), 347–58, and discussed in de Grazia and Newman, *Banned Films* (1982), 102ff. and 261–63. Most, but not all, types of movie-licensing systems have now been either declared unconstitutional by the Supreme Court or repealed by the legislatures. However, *the principle of licensing* movies to exclude, for example, "obscene" ones intended to be shown to adults has never been condemned by the Court as unconstitutional. At the federal level, legislation authorizing customs officials and the courts to prevent entry into the United States—another type of prior restraint—of "obscene" books, papers, prints, motion picture films, etc., also has never been struck down. As a result, suspect books, magazines, and films are still liable to be screened before entry by customs officials. Some cities, including Chicago, have retained active police systems for supervising the content of movies; these systems are limited, in form at least, to concern for the welfare of minors.

†*Manual Enterprises* v. *Day* (1962), in de Grazia, *Censorship Landmarks* (1969), 361–75.

‡*Marcus* v. *Search Warrants* (1961), in de Grazia, *Censorship Landmarks,* 376–82. See, regarding the constitutionality of motion picture film seizures, de Grazia and Newman, *Banned Films* (1982).

furter's seat on the Court, Brennan moved into a much more radical stance. In effect he began a campaign to move several "lower-level" sorts of speech onto the upper level of constitutionally protected speech—and in this way overruled *sub silentio* and *seriatim,* as it were, the freedom-depreciating dictum of *Chaplinsky* v. *New Hampshire* that Felix Frankfurter had so long cherished.*

---

*Illustrative cases are: *Gooding* v. *Wilson* ("fighting words"), 405 U.S. 518 (1972); *New York Times* v. *Sullivan* (libel), 376 U.S. 254 (1964); *Jacobellis* v. *Ohio* (obscenity), 378 U.S. 184 (1964).

22

Because We
Never Could Agree
on a Definition

BARNEY ROSSET asked me to take up the Florida *Tropic of Cancer* case during the winter of 1963, when he learned that a case in which the Dade County prosecutor had stopped all sales of the novel in the county had been lost. The ACLU lawyers who represented Grove in Florida were anxious to find out if the Supreme Court would review the decision. For me, the prospect was intriguing.

I was already on retainer with Grove Press to defend a group of other "dangerous" Grove books, including *Naked Lunch* and *Tropic of Capricorn*, but not *Tropic of Cancer*, which prior to the Florida case was mainly the bailiwick of New York lawyer Charles Rembar. But I had written and filed amici curiae briefs in two other *Tropic of Cancer* cases, including one from California in the Supreme Court, and worked on what became a successful appeal from a conviction in another *Cancer* case, in the Supreme Court of Wisconsin. By then, *Cancer* was caught up in so many cases around the country, and the fight for its freedom had generated so much turmoil, that the Supreme Court's liberal majority (consisting of Brennan, Black, Douglas, Goldberg, and Stewart) was primed to take up a case that could be used to strike a blow for literary freedom. I took on the Florida case (*Grove Press v. Gerstein*) without asking Rosset for a fee for my work.

So far, no Grove or ACLU lawyer had succeeded in getting the Supreme Court to rule on *Tropic of Cancer*, even though, by then, cases involving the book had reached the highest courts in at least six other states: California, Massachusetts, Wisconsin, Maryland, New York, and Illinois. In California and Massachusetts, the book had been set free; in New York and Illinois, *Cancer* had been found obscene.

In the cert petition that I filed I reminded the justices of what they already knew from reading petitions and briefs previously filed in two California *Tropic of Cancer* cases, and from newspaper accounts—that the scores of legal actions seeking to ban Henry Miller's controversial book were making a "crazy quilt" of the First Amendment's guarantees. In the Florida petition I pointed out that regardless of its "prurient appeal" or "patent offensiveness," *Tropic of Cancer* had obvious literary and social importance, which entitled it to the full protection.

In only one of the California cases (*Zeitlin* v. *Arnebergh*) had the highest court of a state adopted Professor Kalven's suggested gloss on *Roth*—the state legislature there had even incorporated it into a new obscenity statute—and I proposed the same revision of *Roth* in my cert petition. I said that the Florida case presented the Court "with both the need and the possibility to clarify *Roth*'s bearing upon literature, as distinguished from obscenity," and I asked the Court to reinterpret *Roth* to mean that "the door barring federal and state intrusion upon freedom of expression was to be left open 'only the slightest crack necessary to permit the policing of *worthless* obscenity,'" citing Kalven as well as *Roth*. *

I was not alone, at that critical moment in the evolution of the law of obscenity, in recommending Kalven's "condemn only the 'worthless'" doctrine to the Court. Although it was not his principal argument, New York lawyer Ephraim London, representing Nico Jacobellis, the Ohio theatre owner who had been convicted for exhibiting Louis Malle's *The Lovers,* made a similar claim in the jurisdictional statement and brief on the merits that he filed in the *Jacobellis* case—citing both *Roth* and Kalven for the point that a work having *any* artistic merit or social value could not properly be found obscene.† *Jacobellis* and *Tropic of Cancer* would be decided on the same day. Perhaps most important, in the only two state cases that had accorded *Tropic of Cancer* constitutional protection, the highest courts in the states had also adopted Kalven's approach, implicitly or explicitly. In Massachusetts, the state court adopted Kalven's approach implicitly; the

---

*In the amicus brief I had earlier filed with the Court in a California case called *Bradley Reed Smith* v. *California,* I had similarly argued that the Court ought to revise *Roth* and make "a candid rejection of the thesis that recognizable literature may be found obscene and on that basis banned." Citing Kalven there, I said, "The dissemination of worthless material, from which class would be excluded every recognizable piece of literature, every literature having importance for anyone, might be left punishable under the 'prurient interest' and 'patently offensive' tests." I also argued against adoption by the Court of a "hard-core pornography" test, saying that that would "also fail to frustrate those dedicated to finding even important literature obscene and to maintaining the censorship over books. Professor Harry Kalven's emphasis on the 'worthless' seems the sounder approach: 'the obscene can include only that which is worthless.'" Finally, I pointed out that Brennan's dictum in *Roth* that states were forbidden "from suppressing the public circulation of any work expressing ideas which may have the slightest social importance" led inexorably to the proposition that any work "which has literary or artistic importance cannot be deemed to be empty of social importance." For, as Kalven observed, obscenity might properly be banned "not because it is dangerous but because it is worthless."

†Later, Charles Rembar, in his briefs to the Supreme Court in the *Fanny Hill* case, also referred to Kalven for support of his argument that the book should be freed even if it was seen as having only "a modicum" of redeeming social value.

lawyer for the book there had been Charles Rembar. In California, two ACLU-affiliated lawyers, Al Wirin and Fred Okrand, had succeeded in bringing the Kalven approach to full fruition in the opinion written by Justice Matthew Tobriner in *Zeitlin* v. *Arnebergh*. Tobriner was one of the great state supreme court judges of this century. In *Zeitlin*, Tobriner quoted Kalven's "Metaphysics of the Law of Obscenity" for the proposition that the Supreme Court was "feeling the pressure generated by the two-level theory [announced in *Roth*] to restrict obscenity to the worthless and hence to something akin to hard-core pornography." Both the Massachusetts and California cases would be prominently cited by Brennan in the opinion he announced in June 1963 freeing *Tropic of Cancer* and *The Lovers*.

The ideas and arguments that inspire, influence, or nourish the reasoning in a particular judicial decision, or the establishment of an influential jurisprudential doctrine, are difficult to trace and impossible to catalogue, though the cases and points presented by the lawyers who brief and argue a particular case play a prominent role. Even more important, often, are the ideas and principled arguments of the other justices deliberating on the case. The ideas concerning the same issue contained in opinions previously written in other cases by the justices also may have great significance;* of lesser importance usually are the opinions written by judges in the lower courts that have considered the same case, and by other federal and state courts in related cases. Sometimes the points made in scholarly commentaries in treatises and the law reviews also become sources for the ideas and "authorities" that a justice brings to bear in his formulation of a line of reasoning or a legal doctrine. Less obvious but sometimes controlling are attitudes and ideas absorbed in reaching emotional and intellectual maturity, and those taken from friends, relatives, and acquaintances of the deciding or writing judge. Even stories in newspapers, magazines, and books the justices read and chance encounters of every sort with ideas inside and outside the courthouse may enter into a decision or opinion. As often as not, one comes to understand, the actually influential or controlling sources are not mentioned in the published opinion.

There is a protocol that Supreme Court clerks learn to employ: they write memoranda for their justices as if these were memoranda written by their justices to the brethren.† In preparation for the lead opinion that Justice

---

*In the *Memoirs of Hecate County* case, described in Chapter 12, there were no opinions written by any court or judge with the exception of the short one written by dissenting judge Perlman on the three-judge panel that tried the case. One reason for the silence among the state courts involved may have been the incompetence they felt at that time to deal adequately with the intractable problem of obscenity in relation to First Amendment values, when the Supreme Court itself had not yet squarely addressed it.

†Until Sandra Day O'Connor was appointed to the Court by President Reagan in 1981, and therefore during virtually the entire period when the cases with which this book is concerned were being deliberated and decided, the justices were exclusively male and themselves used this term. Naturally, the legal profession adopted the same terminology, as did journalists Bob Woodward and Scott Armstrong in their interesting, informative, and popular book *The Brethren* (1979).

Brennan was asked to write for the Court in *The Lovers* and *Tropic of Cancer* cases, one of Brennan's law clerks, Richard Posner, wrote a memorandum that energetically supported his justice's disposition to use the pending obscenity cases to award constitutional status to literary and artistic expression.* Posner—now himself an influential judge on the federal Seventh Circuit Court of Appeals in Illinois—called this memorandum "Memorandum of Mr. Justice Brennan In Re: The Obscenity Cases."† There is no way to tell whether this persuasive 218-page document (which also contained 132 footnotes) "decided" Brennan but it is inconceivable to me that its arguments and ideas, and the thrust toward freedom that it both described and endorsed, did not powerfully reinforce Brennan's predisposition to rule that artistic expression should be constitutionally protected by the Court, and that its freedom should not depend upon any "weighing" of its artistic or other social value against its appeal to prurience and offensiveness.‡ Posner's memorandum wound up in this way:

RICHARD POSNER: ("Memorandum of Mr. Justice Brennan In Re: The Obscenity Cases"): It remains only to be observed that the law of obscenity, in the years since *Roth* and *Smith,*§ has been in a state of ferment, and mostly

---

*Posner is the author of *Law and Literature: A Misunderstood Relation* (1988), *Economic Analysis of Law* (1972), *The Economics of Justice* (1981), *The Problems of Jurisprudence* (1990), and *Cardozo: A Study in Reputation* (1990). He is also a senior lecturer at the University of Chicago Law School and has been seriously considered for nomination to the Supreme Court.

†The Supreme Court tradition of addressing individual justices as "Mr. Justice So-and-so" was replaced by the practice of addressing him or her as "Justice So-and-so" once Sandra Day O'Connor was appointed by President Reagan to the high bench.

‡When I asked Brennan whether the Posner memorandum, which I found among the justice's "private" Court papers, had influenced his decision, he said he could not specifically remember it, but observed that Posner "always was a prodigious worker." In the memorandum, Posner argued forcefully against the law discriminating among media of expression with regard to constitutional freedom—by, for example, awarding greater freedom to books than to movies; and Brennan declined to make any such distinction in the opinion he wrote for *The Lovers/Tropic of Cancer* cases. In fact, but not in law—the Supreme Court has never approved it—a bias against film and photography has developed in the practices of police and prosecutors. A majority of the Attorney General's Commission on Pornography ("Meese commission") for example, recommended that expression consisting of the printed word not be prosecuted, no matter how pornographic it may be, but that visual sexual expression be aggressively targeted and suppressed. See Chapters 27–30.

§*Smith* v. *California,* a case decided in December 1959 (reprinted in de Grazia, *Censorship Landmarks* [1969], 318–25), in which Brennan delivered the opinion of the Court holding that it was unconstitutional for the California legislature to punish (with imprisonment) a bookseller for selling a book called *Sweeter Than Life,* found by a judge to be obscene, without proof that the bookseller knew of the (sexually oriented) content of the book. This was held to amount to an unconstitutional deprivation of liberty without due process of law. California had argued that there was ample precedent for the "strict liability" imposed: in the many laws regarding food and drug labeling (regularly upheld by the courts), which dispensed with the need to prove knowledge on the part of persons charged. Brennan dismissed that argument because such laws were "examples of legal devices and doctrines, in most applications consistent with the Constitution, which cannot be applied in settings where they have the collateral effect of inhibiting freedom of expression, by making the individual the more reluctant to exercise it." He said this: "The bookseller's self-censorship, compelled by the State, would be a censorship affecting the whole public, hardly less virulent for being privately administered. Through it, the in the direction of greater recognition of the preeminent claims of the First Amendment liberties in this area. If I have in the course of this memorandum emphasized points of differences with courts and commentators on the obscenity problem, I should like now to redress the balance somewhat by suggesting the solid and important core of agreement among virtually all concerned. *The basic point of this memorandum is that no bona fide work of art or information may be suppressed in the name of obscenity, even if it is deeply repulsive to the dominant current thought of the* [copy illegible]. . . . I believe has in recent years won the adherence of most of the state courts, state legislatures, and lower federal courts, which have had occasion to pass upon it.*

———

Posner's memorandum pointed the way for Brennan to move and called his attention to Harry Kalven's proposal that *Roth* be glossed to make it more protective of literature and art. It did not, however, advance any concrete legal doctrine or analysis based upon existing First Amendment precedent and principle, or show how what Brennan had said in *Roth* might be utilized to reach the constitutional goal of freeing "bona fide" literary and artistic expression from government censorship; the possibility and desirability of transforming into a speech-protective doctrine the "not utterly without" and "even the slightest" social importance dicta that Brennan had adumbrated in *Roth,* and the idea also of providing a specific jurisprudential technique for doing that, originated, as I have said, with Harry Kalven. In the insightful piece called "The Metaphysics of the Law of Obscenity" that Kalven wrote in 1960 for the inaugural issue of *The Supreme Court Review,*† and that Posner cited in his 1964 memorandum, the brilliant First Amendment scholar showed how the "intractable problem" of defining the obscene could be solved in a way that would lead incrementally but inexorably to defining more and more literary freedom. He deduced a logical corollary to *Roth*'s assertion of why obscenity was not constitutionally protected expression. "If," Kalven observed, "the obscene is constitutionally subject to ban because it is worthless [i.e., "utterly without redeeming social importance"], it must follow that the obscene can include only that which is worthless."‡ Or, as

———

distribution of all books, both obscene and not obscene, would be impeded." *Censorship Landmarks,* 320.

The book involved in this case was the one that inspired the dialogue reported in Chapter 15 between Justice Frankfurter and his farsighted law clerk of the time, Paul Bender.

*The italics are mine. Another portion of the Posner memorandum is reprinted in the endnotes. Note Posner's use of "bona fide" as a qualification of the "art" (or "information") that ought to be free of governmental restraint. And compare it with Kalven's idea of the non-"worthless," Brennan's principle of freedom for "material not utterly without artistic importance," and Chief Justice Warren E. Burger's later revision looking to the protection of material having "serious" literary or artistic value.

†Edited by Professor Philip Kurland, also of the University of Chicago. Perhaps I should note here that not only was Harry Kalven my teacher of "Civil Liberties" at the University of Chicago Law School, he was my favorite teacher there.

‡Called a non sequitur by Justice Tom Clark, when Justice Brennan said much the same thing in the *Tropic of Cancer* and *Fanny Hill* cases.

Brennan would later note in his opinion in *Fanny Hill*,* rearticulating his doctrine two years after its appearance in connection with the *Jacobellis/Tropic of Cancer* cases, even "a modicum of value" is enough to entitle a book or a movie to constitutional protection and save it from being branded obscene.†

For Kalven, writing in 1960, the only candidate for classification as "worthless" expression was "hard-core pornography." He predicted that the Court's gradual development of a workable standard for separating "obscene" from "constitutionally protected" expression could "restrict obscenity to the worthless and hence to something akin to hard-core pornography." This was not a recommendation that the Court make use of the hard-core pornography rubric, but a suggestion that it was susceptible to being assimilated to the worthless.

Like good judges, whose servants and advisers they frequently are, good law professors and practicing lawyers also develop doctrinal approaches to the First Amendment, and they fight for the adoption or survival of these in the cases whose strategies they control, and in the cases that they comment upon in literary and lay journals and in books. In the famous *New York Times* v. *Sullivan* case involving an alleged libel of a Montgomery, Alabama, police commissioner, Professor Herbert Wechsler of Columbia put across his doctrinal First Amendment views with consummate success in his representation of the victorious *Times;* Brennan's historic opinion in the case bristled with Wechsler's ideas. Professor Alexander Bickel of Yale did something similar in the *Pentagon Papers* case, also involving the *Times.* In the Illinois Supreme Court, Harry Kalven successfully advanced his doctrinal approach to a solution of the obscenity problem as the main reason that the Chicago conviction of comedian Lenny Bruce should be reversed. Other lawyers, as well as I, pressed for Kalven's "suppression only of the 'worthless'" approach in several of the *Tropic of Cancer* cases, including Florida; I continued to do this as lawyer for Grove Press and for interested amici curiae in subsequent cases, notably in the Massachusetts Supreme Court *Naked Lunch* case decided in 1966; and in over a score of motion picture censorship cases involving the Swedish movie *I Am Curious—Yellow* that I handled, or supervised, including one that I argued before the Second Circuit Court of Appeals in 1968 and another argued by me before the Supreme Court.‡

---

*In the *Fanny Hill* opinion, Brennan also stated that "a book need . . . be unqualifiedly worthless before it can be deemed obscene." The text of the opinions in the case is printed in full in de Grazia, *Censorship Landmarks* (1969).

†Kalven's idea may have reached Brennan not directly through the justice's reading the *1960 Supreme Court Review* article (in any event, Brennan did not cite it in either *Jacobellis* or *Fanny Hill*) but through lawyers who had read it—including me, Los Angeles civil liberties lawyer Al Wirin, and New York lawyer Ephraim London—in the briefs that were filed with the Supreme Court in the *Tropic of Cancer* and *The Lovers* cases; by Justice Tobriner in the opinion he wrote in *Zeitlin* v. *California;* and by Richard Posner in his "Memorandum" to Justice Brennan. Later, in his brief to the Court in the *Fanny Hill* case, Rembar also advanced Kalven's idea and cited his *Supreme Court Review* piece.

‡My work on behalf of *I Am Curious—Yellow* is described in de Grazia and Newman, *Banned Films* (1982), 121–25 and 297–303.

In *Jacobellis* v. *Ohio,* the case that was decided along with the Florida *Tropic of Cancer* case, Ephraim London not only advanced Kalven's thesis, he also pressed the Court to abandon *Roth*'s attempted definition of "obscenity" and adopt in its stead a "hard-core pornography" test—which, however, London failed to equate with the "worthless" doctrine, or in any other way to define. London's was an approach that Chicago lawyer Elmer Gertz would criticize in his book *A Handful of Clients* but that a number of respected academic commentators on the Court's work, including the political scientist C. Peter McGrath from Brown University, had been recommending for years.* As is well known, in Justice Potter Stewart's concurring opinion in *Jacobellis,* he adopted a jurisprudentially amusing, skeptical shorthand test for "hard-core pornography"—the "I know it when I see it" test. But Brennan in *Jacobellis,* wisely, I think, not only rejected every temptation to coin and substitute a pornography test for the *Roth* test of the "obscene," he also declined to associate it with the "worthless." The significance of Kalven's logic was that it permitted Brennan to retain *Roth*'s basic holding but to structure the dicta contained in it into a principle offering artistic expression a new and potentially absolute measure of freedom.† Its adoption could hardly work otherwise than to free more and more literary materials from censorship; a "hard-core pornography" test, by contrast, would not have defeated censorship; it might even have led to greater censorship. Thus the New York Court of Appeals in 1963 found *Tropic of Cancer* obscene because it met that court's shorthand test of "hard-core pornography": "dirt for dirt's sake, dirt for money's sake." It would certainly be difficult to imagine a less useful test; there was nothing of the rule of law in it.

The Supreme Court considered and resolved the questions presented by *Jacobellis* v. *Ohio* and the *Tropic of Cancer* case concurrently in part because, although the cases involved different media—motion pictures and the novel—they presented some of the same difficult and complicated ques-

---

*McGrath's important article, published in *1966 Supreme Court Review* (1966), was "The Obscenity Cases: Grapes of Roth." Another approach, called "variable obscenity," had been developed by Dean William Lockhart and Professor Robert McClure in the *University of Minnesota Law Review;* it was advocated by Chief Justice Earl Warren and was put to disastrous use in the *Ginzburg* case, discussed in Chapters 23 and 26.

†Brennan had wrestled with himself and his brethren continually, from the days of *Roth,* to find a doctrinal solution to the obscenity problem superior to *Roth*'s. The first such solution he came up with was, as I have suggested, the one that Harry Kalven proposed. Later, in 1973, after the Court's ideological composition had been drastically changed, Brennan would finally abandon that approach for a position so close to the Black-Douglas absolutist solution that Douglas would be moved to "applaud" Brennan. By then Justice Black was dead. The position taken by Brennan in 1973, which would be joined by Justices Marshall and Stewart, was that it had proved impossible to define "obscenity" congruently with the guarantees of freedom of speech and press, and that the Court therefore should decline to enforce all obscenity laws that interfered with the circulation of sexually oriented materials among adults. Later, in a published interview, Brennan ruefully remarked: "I do wish we had found a solution to the definitional horror of obscenity." See Jeffrey T. Leeds, "A Life on the Court," *The New York Times Magazine,* October 5, 1986.

tions in obscenity law.* A further complication was that when Felix Frankfurter retired from the Court following the oral arguments in *Jacobellis,* the case had to be reargued for the man who took his seat, Arthur Goldberg, to take part in the decision. In addition, the Court was under considerable professional and public pressure to abandon or amend its "two-level" holding in *Roth* that "obscene" expression was not protected by the constitutional guarantees. In his opinion in *Jacobellis* Brennan alluded to the pressure he felt. The decisions in the two cases finally came down on June 22, 1964, at the end of the term.

In the *Tropic of Cancer* case, the Court granted my petition for cert and, solely on the basis of its representations and arguments, without further briefing "on the merits" or listening to oral argument, summarily reversed the Florida court's decision that the book was obscene. Each of the justices in the majority wrote that he did so for the reasons given by him that same day for voting, in the *Jacobellis* case, to reverse the Ohio Supreme Court's decision that *The Lovers* was obscene. However, in freeing *Tropic of Cancer* the Court divided more closely—5 to 4—than it did in freeing *The Lovers*—6 to 3—because Justice White (together with Warren, Harlan, and Clark) voted *against* the Court's grant of cert in the Florida case, that is to say, against the Court's reviewing the suppression of Miller's novel, notwithstanding that he voted with the majority to free the Malle film. I presume White did this because the scenes of sexual encounters in Miller's novel were so much more explicit and, to him, offensive than the love scenes in the film. The latter were—as Justice Arthur Goldberg noted in the separate opinion he wrote in *Jacobellis*—"so fragmentary and fleeting that only a censor's alert would make an audience conscious that something 'questionable' is being portrayed." White's switch to the side of the justices favoring censorship was not enough, however, to alter the majority's decision to free *Tropic of Cancer* from censorship throughout the nation.

Before I quote the words that Brennan actually used to break the censors' grip on literary and artistic expression, several subsidiary principles that were laid out in the opinion require discussion, in part because of the subsequent retrenchment on these principles that has occurred with the conservative "takeover" of the Court, begun with President Richard Nixon's appointment of Chief Justice Warren E. Burger in 1969.

In freeing *Tropic of Cancer* and *The Lovers,* Brennan went out of his way to establish that the high court's decision and the reasoning of his opinion were to be followed by lower state and federal courts throughout the country, regardless of varying local "community standards." Allowing local courts to apply local community standards to decisions about freedom of expression generally, and the freedom of *Tropic of Cancer* in particular, had

---

*One question that was not presented in *Jacobellis,* which was presented in *Tropic of Cancer,* was whether the constitutional protection afforded to a literary or artistic work might vary across state lines. Brennan addressed this question in his *Jacobellis* opinion, saying "the constitutional status of an allegedly obscene work must be determined on the basis of a national [not a local] standard."

generated great uncertainty and disuniformity in the law, and doubt and
conflict throughout the country in the minds of creators and disseminators
of expressive materials. Most books and movies are not intended for local
consumption but are made to be distributed nationally. If their free circulation is a federally protected constitutional right, this protection and freedom cannot differ from state to state or city to city. The "local standards"
that Chief Justice Burger would posit in 1973 as vital to identifying the
obscene embodied, of course, the varying notions of decency of local
policemen, local judges, local prosecutors, and local jurors. Brennan knew
that unless the law and the Court's rulings in this area were fashioned in
such as way as to transcend county and state lines, only some Americans
would be free to read books like *Tropic of Cancer* and see movies like *The
Lovers*—they might be free to do so in New York, for example, but not free
to do so in Chicago, Philadelphia, or Wichita.

Furthermore, such a situation would predictably impel national publishers and distributors of books and movies to self-censorship: they would
refuse to produce and distribute works thought likely to offend policemen,
prosecutors, judges, or juries in the country's more conservative communities, or thought likely to anger the militant quasi-religious "decency organizations" that from time to time influence the behavior of policemen,
prosecutors, and judges in our larger cities and states as well,* and even the
actions of federal agencies.† This self-censorship by publishers and distributors would mean that certain works might never be created. There would
be a "lowest common freedom denominator" effect on movies and books;
the politicized "decency" agenda of cities like Cincinnati, counties like
Dade (Florida), and states like Georgia would determine what the rest of
the nation could read and see.

So, in *Jacobellis/Tropic of Cancer,* Brennan insisted that expressive materials found constitutionally protected and not obscene by the Supreme Court
were to be deemed constitutionally protected and not obscene throughout
the United States.

JUSTICE WILLIAM J. BRENNAN, JR.: It has been suggested that the "contemporary community standards" aspect of the *Roth* test implies a determination of the constitutional question of obscenity in each case by the
standards of the particular local community from which the case arises. This
is an incorrect reading of *Roth*. . . .‡ It is true that local communities

---

*As, for example, in Cincinnati, Ohio, today. See Chapter 30.

†For example, the Post Office Department, which for decades was particularly sensitive to
pressures from the Catholic Church; and the Federal Communications Commission, which
in recent years has responded to extralegal "moral" pressures from Protestant, and especially
Southern-based evangelical, organizations.

‡In *Roth* Brennan did not in fact discuss the "contemporary community standards" issue;
in *Jacobellis/Tropic of Cancer,* he looked to, and relied upon, language that Judge Learned
Hand had used in the famous opinion he wrote in *United States* v. *Kennerley* as "referring
not to state and local 'communities,' but rather to 'the community' in the sense of 'society
at large,' . . . 'the public,' or people in general."

throughout the land are in fact diverse, and that in cases such as this one, the Court is confronted with the task of reconciling the rights of such communities with the rights of individuals. Communities vary, however, in many respects other than their toleration of alleged obscenity, and such variances have never been considered to require or justify a varying standard for application of the Federal Constitution. . . . The Court has explicitly refused to tolerate a result whereby "the constitutional limits of free expression in the Nation would vary with state lines" [citing a landmark case]; we see even less justification for allowing such limits to vary with town or county lines. We thus reaffirm the position taken in *Roth* to the effect that the constitutional status of an allegedly obscene work must be determined on the basis of a national standard. It is, after all, a national Constitution we are expounding.

———

Unless the Florida *Cancer* decision had such a national effect, Grove Press would have been forced to resume fighting, and paying for the legal costs of fighting, for the freedom to sell Henry Miller's novel in all the cities, counties, and states where attempts were still pending to suppress it—an almost certainly insupportable task. Instead, local policemen, prosecutors, and judges throughout the United States submitted to Brennan's "national" ruling. More important, after the June 1964 cases were decided, lawyers defending the publishers or distributors of books, magazines, and movies charged with being obscene had a powerful new lever for freeing such expression from censorship. If a publisher or distributor of a challenged work was able to lay claim to any value of any kind whatsoever in a work,* and a lower court nevertheless branded it "obscene," that court's decision predictably would be reversed by the Supreme Court on appeal; and the latter's decision would henceforth be binding throughout the land.

For this to occur, however, Brennan's new doctrine of freedom for literary and artistic expression would have to be *enforced*—in the first instance by state and federal trial judges, in the last instance, by the Supreme Court itself. In my discussion of the *Roth* case oral argument, I alluded to the power that the Supreme Court found for itself—in the text and subtext of the Constitution—to declare void federal or state legislation that in its judgment violated the Constitution, including the First Amendment's free speech and press guarantees. Closely related and indeed necessary to the exercise of that power are the Supreme Court's powers to reverse and vacate constitutionally erroneous decisions reached by lower federal and state

---

*After that, lawyers (including the author) could and did present evidence that material challenged as obscene had not only literary or artistic importance but moral, religious, scientific, psychiatric, and educational values. All such, of course, arguably were social values. It is significant that when Chief Justice Burger acquired enough power on the Court to revise the Brennan doctrine and restate the test for obscenity, he eliminated the term "social value" from the prevailing test for obscenity, substituting the narrower "political value." See Chapter 26.

court judges in their enforcement of constitutionally valid statutes. In this respect the American judiciary is like a hierarchichal pyramid with a single Supreme Court at its head and thousands of special and trial courts, administrative agencies, and police and prosecutors' offices making up its extensive base. At intermediate levels are, of course, the state and federal appellate courts and judges, sworn to obey the law and the orders handed down to them by superior courts, up to and including the Supreme Court.

During the sixties, Brennan told me, no book could be suppressed in the United States without the approval of the Supreme Court. He believed that while the Warren Court sat, no censorship of literature having even the slightest social importance would be permitted to take place anywhere in the country. In his *Jacobellis/Tropic of Cancer* opinion, Brennan emphasized that it was the Court's duty to make "an independent judgment" in every case, and that its judgment would prevail in the courts below.

JUSTICE WILLIAM J. BRENNAN, JR.: We are told that the determination whether a particular motion picture, book, or other work of expression is obscene can be treated as a purely factual judgment on which a jury's verdict is all but conclusive, or that in any event the decision can be left essentially to state and lower federal courts, with this Court exercising only a limited review such as that needed to determine whether the ruling below is supported by "sufficient evidence."* The suggestion is appealing, since it would lift from our shoulders a difficult, recurring, and unpleasant task. But we cannot accept it. Such an abnegation of judicial supervision in this field would be inconsistent with our duty to uphold the constitutional guarantees. Since it is only "obscenity" that is excluded from the constitutional protection [this as a result of *Roth*], the question whether a particular work is obscene necessarily implicates an issue of constitutional law. . . . Such an issue, we think, must ultimately be decided by this Court. Our duty admits of no "substitute for facing up to the tough individual problems of constitutional judgment involved in every obscenity case. . . ."

———

Thus did Brennan constitutionalize the issues presented by every obscenity case and set the foundation for the Supreme Court's practice of reviewing every case of obscenity *de novo,* and for the effective substitution of *its* (constitutionally oriented) judgments on obscenity for those of lower federal and state courts. Warren had joined Black in opposing this practice, the former arguing that the Court should not second-guess lower court judgments except where these appeared clearly erroneous, the latter that the practice turned the Court into a Supreme Board of Censors, a view that had first been criticized by Justice Jackson in the *Memoirs of Hecate County* oral argument. Brennan continued:

———

*This argument was advanced not only by lawyers for the government in our cases but, more significantly, by Chief Justice Warren; see his dissent in *Jacobellis*, reprinted in de Grazia, *Censorship Landmarks* (1969), 427, 428.

JUSTICE WILLIAM J. BRENNAN, JR.: In other areas involving constitutional rights under the Due Process Clause, the Court has consistently recognized its duty to apply the applicable rules of law upon the basis of an independent review of the facts of each case. . . . And this has been particularly true where rights have been asserted under the First Amendment guarantees of free expression. . . .

We cannot understand why the Court's duty should be any different in the present case. . . . Nor can we understand why the Court's performance of its constitutional and judicial function in this sort of case should be denigrated by such epithets as "censor" or "super-censor." In judging alleged obscenity the Court is no more "censoring" expression than it has in other cases "censored" criticism of judges and public officials, advocacy of governmental overthrow, or speech alleged to constitute a breach of the peace. Use of an opprobrious label can neither obscure nor impugn the Court's performance of its obligation to test challenged judgments against the guarantees of the First and Fourteenth Amendments and, in doing so, to delineate the scope of constitutionally protected speech. Hence we affirm the principle that, in "obscenity" cases as in all others involving rights derived from the First Amendment guarantees of free expression, this Court cannot avoid making an independent constitutional judgment on the facts of the case as to whether the material involved is constitutionally protected.

———

So that the Court not be forced to review a countless multitude of lower court decisions, the test of obscenity that Brennan designed for lower court use needed to be as definite and certain and readily applicable as possible. To accomplish this Brennan adopted two tactical devices: he forbade lower court tribunals to apply the expanded test to materials before them by "weighing" their putative "social value" against their putative "prurient appeal" and "patent offensiveness"; and he instructed those tribunals to free everything that was not *utterly* without value, regardless of how great the "prurient appeal" and "patent offensiveness" might be. This, as I will explain, effectively neutralized the natural tendencies of lower court judges and jurors to refer to their subjective feelings about a work's obscenity— i.e., its "prurient appeal" and "patent offensiveness"—in answering the question whether or not the work should be constitutionally protected. The nearly absolute definiteness of the "not utterly without social value" prong of the new test could be expected to render harmless the enormous ambiguity, the utter vagueness, of the two other prongs, "prurient appeal" and "patent offensiveness." Brennan wove these tactical devices into the fabric of the new test for obscenity that he adumbrated in *Jacobellis/Tropic of Cancer,* deriving the whole from what he had said seven years earlier in *Roth,* as Kalven pointed out in his posthumously published *A Worthy Tradition:*

PROFESSOR HARRY KALVEN, JR.: In . . . *Jacobellis* v. *Ohio* . . . Brennan made two further additions to the [constitutional] definition [of obscenity]. First, he made it clear that "the contemporary community standards" by which obscenity was to be judged under the *Roth* test were *national*, not local, standards; otherwise, he said, "the constitutional limits of free expression in the Nation would vary with state lines." Second, he stated that the rationale he had offered in *Roth* for excluding obscenity from First Amendment protection—that it was "utterly without social importance"—was also an element of the constitutional definition. . . . [B]oth patency and lack of social significance were arguably implicit in the original *Roth* formula. Thus, the Court, responding to the dialectic of subsequent cases, can be said to have developed its central idea, and in the process to have narrowed the scope of [governmental] regulation.

JUSTICE WILLIAM J. BRENNAN, JR.: The question of the proper standard for making this determination has been the subject of much discussion and controversy since our decision in *Roth* seven years ago. Recognizing that the test for obscenity enunciated there—"whether to the average person, applying contemporary community standards, the dominant theme of the material taken as a whole appeals to prurient interest"—is not perfect, we think any substitute would raise equally difficult problems, and we therefore adhere to that standard. We would reiterate, however, our recognition in *Roth* that obscenity is excluded from the constitutional protection only because it is "utterly without redeeming social importance," and that "[t]he portrayal of sex, e.g., in art, literature and scientific works, is not itself sufficient reason to deny material the constitutional protection of freedom of speech and press. *It follows that material dealing with sex in a manner that advocates ideas, or that has literary or scientific or artistic value or any other form of social importance, may not be branded as obscenity and denied the constitutional protection. Nor may the constitutional status of the material be made to turn on a "weighing" of its social importance against its prurient appeal, for a work cannot be proscribed unless it is "utterly" without social importance.* *

In writing *Roth*, Brennan had stressed that obscenity and sex were not the same thing—that sex was a problem of great public concern that was

---

*The italics are mine. Here, as earlier indicated, Brennan cited in support the California Supreme Court's decision in *Zeitlin* v. *Arnebergh*, also involving *Tropic of Cancer*, in which the "weighing" or "balancing" process was denounced by Justice Tobriner. Twice, in the pivotal paragraph which adumbrated the doctrine, Brennan dropped out the concept of "redeeming," almost certainly to show that the correct application of his rule would involve no "weighing" of (redeeming) social importance against the work's obscene characteristics. *Zeitlin* and *Jacobellis* are reprinted in de Grazia, *Censorship Landmarks* (1969) at 456 and 423, respectively. The *Tropic of Cancer* case, *Grove Press* v. *Gerstein*, is at 508. Brennan concluded this passage exposing his doctrine with language that incorporated the second prong (introduced by Harlan in *Manual Enterprises* v. *Day*) of the expanded test, saying: "It should also be recognized that the *Roth* standard requires in the first instance a finding that the material 'goes substantially beyond customary limits of candor in description or representation of such matters.'"

entitled to be discussed freely in literary, artistic, and scientific works, and that obscenity was not constitutionally protected only because it was "utterly without redeeming social importance." By building on those propositions and ignoring the others, Brennan converted *Roth* into a potentially irresistible defense against a charge of obscenity.* Following Brennan's opinion in the *Jacobellis* and *Tropic of Cancer* cases, any work of literature, science, or art, as well as any expression having "social importance," could be worked free of censorship.† And not only was the testimony of literary experts admissible in any obscenity case, such evidence would now be decisive because of Brennan's prohibition against "weighing" a work's prurient appeal and patent offensiveness against its social importance. Brennan's opinion in *Jacobellis* registered the most important gain for cultural freedom in the Court's history, notwithstanding revisions that would be made in the law by the Burger Court in 1973.

JUSTICE WILLIAM J. BRENNAN, JR.: I did not know what it was that Roth put in the mails. I would have wanted to look at the stuff. We only saw what the Government brought in that box. . . . By the time of the *Tropic of Cancer* case, I felt that the only possible protection for it, the only way we could protect the publishers of books, was by looking at the stuff ourselves. Because we never could agree on a definition.

—

---

*A somewhat similar but not so strong defense was provided under English obscenity law by act of Parliament in 1959. Section 4(1) of the Obscene Publications Act 1959 provides a defense to an obscenity prosecution where it is proved that "publication of the article in question is justified as being for the public good on the ground that it is in the interests of science, literature, art or learning, or of other objects of general concern." This change revolutionized the law of obscenity in England because, until then, evidence of literary or other merit was not only not a defense, it was inadmissible in obscene-literature cases.

†Working it free might require going all the way to the Supreme Court with the case. And the definitional problem of what qualified as literature, art, or science still needed to be resolved. (One of the better ways to do so is suggested later in this chapter.) Lawyer Charles Rembar made the same point as to "literature" in *The End of Obscenity* (1968), although he attributed "the end of obscenity" to Brennan's opinion in *Fanny Hill* (a case that he argued to the Court), not to *Tropic of Cancer*. In any event, much depends upon how you define "literature," and literary or artistic "value." In the 1974 case *Kaplan* v. *California,* Chief Justice Burger, speaking for a majority of the Court, held obscene a book resembling a novel, called *Suite 69,* bearing a plain cover and no pictures. Burger said it had a "most tenuous plot." According to him, it was entirely composed of "repetitive descriptions of physical, sexual conduct, 'clinically' explicit and offensive to the point of being nauseous." See Chapter 28. Rembar once suggested to me that *Suite 69* probably fell outside his definition of "literature"; presumably the punishment of its publisher or (as in the actual case) distributor would not violate freedom of expression: the book would not be recognizable as literature, and so would not be protected speech. However, although the protection provided by the First Amendment to speech and press undoubtedly was expected to foster "progress" in literature, art, science, and morality, I believe the most democratic way of doing that is by "laissez-faire"—by keeping government officials from intervening in the market's definition of literature, art, science, and morality as well as in their evaluation or circulation. Are comic books literature or art? Some? All? None? What about Mapplethorpe's sexually graphic photographs? Or Andres Serrano's photograph of a plastic crucifix submerged in a container of his urine? Or Karen Finley's staged semi-nude "solo performances"? (These artworks and performances are discussed below in Chapter 30.) Who is to say?

The Court's lead opinion issued under Brennan's name was officially joined only by Justice Arthur J. Goldberg. This fact, little noticed at the time,* would have small importance for the next four years, during which most (if not all)† lower federal and state courts obediently put the Brennan doctrine to work in reversing obscenity findings in book, film, and magazine censorship cases throughout the country.

Justice Brennan indicated to me that notwithstanding the several official explanations that are given regarding the issuance of "plurality" and "lead" opinions and the varied interpretations of their significance that have been made,‡ a minority opinion written by a justice may acquire the lead position in the reports because initially, at conference, the particular view presented by the justice receiving the assignment to write the opinion was, or seemed to be, shared by a majority of the justices present and voting. During the course of further deliberations and recasting, the view might lose its majority status and become the view merely of a plurality, and not necessarily the largest plurality. If, however, no different opinion gains a majority (or no different opinion resting on a narrower ground obtains a larger plurality), the final opinion written by the author of the originally majoritarian opinion will retain its lead position.

Something along these lines must have happened in *Jacobellis/Tropic of Cancer,* where no other opinion was able to gain three justices and the Black-Douglas opinion rested on a wider ground, absolute freedom for obscenity. Inasmuch as Justice Potter Stewart's separate concurring opinion rested on a ground wider than that of the Brennan-Goldberg opinion (although not as wide as the Black-Douglas opinion), the careful case reader understood that in the future any expression that would be set free under the Brennan-Goldberg formula would also have a majority of the Court behind it. The same could not be said for any other opinion in *Jacobellis/ Tropic of Cancer.* This tight reasoning justifies the otherwise casual respect that lawyers, commentators, and the lower courts paid to the Brennan opinion as the holding of the Court.

After the Florida *Tropic of Cancer* case was won in the Supreme Court in 1964, a *Newsweek* editor phoned Henry Miller and asked him for his reaction to the decision. This Miller "willingly gave them," emphasizing

---

*Professor Kalven, for instance, referred to the Brennan opinion as the Court's (*A Worthy Tradition,* 38). However, in his 1973 obscenity case opinions, Chief Justice Burger made a large point of the fact that (notwithstanding its faithful following by most of the judiciary) the Brennan doctrine of "utterly without value" was never subscribed to by more than three justices. (In the 1966 *Fanny Hill* case both Warren and Fortas subscribed to Brennan's doctrine.) Justices White and Clark did not seem to realize what had happened until they protested what Brennan had done, in the dissenting opinions they wrote in *Fanny Hill.* In fact, Brennan had gathered a majority of the Court to join in *holding* that *Tropic of Cancer* and *The Lovers* were constitutionally protected, not obscene, works, but only a plurality of two—himself and Goldberg—for *his reasoning* in these 1964 cases.

†See the resistance (by inexcusable judicial "neglect") to the Brennan doctrine encountered by Lenny Bruce in New York, described in Chapter 24.

‡See endnotes for more on plurality decisions.

what he described as "the valiant fight" that lawyer Elmer Gertz, in Chicago, and publisher Barney Rosset, in New York, had put up. The author also mentioned the international success his book was experiencing, and the financial success he was finally enjoying.

HENRY MILLER: [T]he book is now printed in twelve languages, and distributed without trouble even in such Catholic strongholds as Argentina and Brazil. The only country at present where the book was suppressed immediately upon appearing is Finland; Poland and Yugoslavia are now about to publish some of my books, not the *Tropics* yet, of course. In Germany the sale . . . of *Cancer* has reached the 100,000 mark—very big for Germany, where books are expensive. *Capricorn* has an *advance* sale there of over 20,000; already England gives no trouble on either book— and of course *Cancer* there has sold well over 100,000 and next year, I believe, goes into a paperback edition.

JOHN CALDER:* British publication [of *Tropic of Cancer*] was a direct result of Henry Miller's visit, at my invitation, to the Edinburgh Festival in 1962 to take part in an International Writer's Conference which I organized. . . . About 100 writers were invited. . . . They included many of the most distinguished living writers. . . . But it was a quartet of Americans who made the success of the conference: Mary McCarthy, Norman Mailer, William Burroughs, and Henry Miller. Miller talked little but to the point, and when, on the fourth day, when the subject was censorship, he set out his credo of literary freedom, he received a standing ovation from nearly three thousand people packed into Edinburgh's McEwan Hall. It was obvious that, at least to a younger generation, he had become a legendary figure. . . . He symbolized the right of the artist to work without interference from the state, as did no one else in the western world at that time. . . .

When I went to visit him in 1976 [in Pacific Palisades, outside Los Angeles] he was still writing, but getting possibly more pleasure out of painting, still seeing friends and keeping up with others by correspondence. . . . [H]e was frail with a broken hip which kept him from swimming in his pool, but he read late into the night with evident enjoyment, was in full possession of his intellectual powers and—once again—in love. He did not tell me the object of his affection, but he had a very beautiful secretary, so I drew the obvious conclusion.

ELMER GERTZ: When I first became acquainted with Miller, all of his great pioneering works had been written, but were published in this country for

---

*John Calder published *Tropic of Cancer* in England in 1963. The book went on sale immediately after Calder's solicitors were told by the Director of Public Prosecutions that no action against it would be taken; "on publication day, every BBC news bulletin announced that the book was now available in Britain for the first time and the line of willing buyers stretched for blocks around some bookshops." *A Henry Miller Reader,* edited by John Calder (1985), 19. Calder also fought for the freedom of *Last Exit to Brooklyn* by Hubert Selby, Jr., and other important literary works. He now owns and runs The Riverrun Press in New York.

the first time during the course of our friendship, possibly in some degree because of it. Only one major work remains unwritten and unpublished—the second volume of *Nexus,* the last part of the *Rosy Crucifixion* trilogy. Miller often talked of finishing the book, and made attempts at it now and then. But . . . he seemed to feel that if *Nexus* were completed, his life, too, would end. By delaying this last work, he was prolonging his life. There came suddenly the physical difficulties of old age, and *Nexus* necessarily remained unfinished. . . .

It was sad to contemplate this deterioration of a man of such vitality. Fortunately, there was little evidence of mental decline. Although he spent much time in bed or in a wheelchair, near the end, he was his old vibrant self when he made public appearances, as on several occasions when he was on television talk shows. He could sometimes play his dearly loved game of Ping-Pong, from a wheelchair, and regularly beat his opponents, some of them unclad females.

ANTHONY LEWIS: Applying steady pressure, nine calm men are dragging the censor, kicking and screaming, into the twentieth century. . . . From a country with a tradition of blue-nosed puritanism, the United States in a relatively short time has become one of the most permissive in the world.

HENRY MILLER (in a letter to Elmer Gertz): So, as always, America ends up last! If the U.S.S.C. had not given its ok it would indeed have been disgraceful. I wouldn't be surprised if the enemies of progress in this county made an attempt to impeach the members of the Supreme Court—or isn't that possible under our Constitution?

JUSTICE WILLIAM J. BRENNAN, JR.: Sure, they made Fortas resign* and after that they tried unsuccessfully to impeach Bill Douglas.† Well, Bill sent me a note saying *I* was going to be next.

---

*See Chapter 27.

†See *Final Report* by the Special Subcommittee on H. Res. 920 of the Committee on the Judiciary, House of Representatives, 91st Congress, 2nd Session, Pursuant to H. Res. 93 (Sept. 17, 1970). H. Res. 920 was "a resolution impeaching William O. Douglas, Associate Justice of the Supreme Court of the United States, of high crimes and misdemeanors in office." The House Judiciary Committee reported out that there was no ground for the impeachment of Douglas, the affair having been instigated in furtherance of President Nixon's effort to purge the Supreme Court of justices unsympathetic to his views and to replace them with ones sympathetic to those views.

23

If All Mankind
Minus One

THE CATHOLIC STANDARD AND TIMES: Many Catholics winced when they read that Justice William Brennan of their faith had written the majority opinion [in *Jacobellis/Tropic of Cancer*].* What Justice Brennan might consider to be obscene we cannot imagine.

OPERATION YORKVILLE: Mr. Justice Brennan, author of the famous *Roth* decision in 1957, virtually reversed himself in his June 22, 1964, decisions in *Jacobellis* v. *Ohio* and *"Tropic of Cancer"* cases. Justice Brennan declared that "community standards" cannot be read as referring to those of people of individual states or cities, but must be regarded as a degraded common denominator which he calls a "national standard."

With this opinion, Mr. Justice Brennan disapproved the rulings of the supreme courts of several states which had found the book *"Tropic of Cancer"* to be obscene. Justices Douglas and Black also refused to apply the law of the land and applied their own rule that nothing, however prurient and vile, can be obscene under the Constitution.

—

An interdenominational group of American clergymen who, like Cardinal Spellman, saw links between obscenity and Communism circulated a statement that condemned the Supreme Court's setting aside of the "moral law" and urged President Lyndon Johnson to act to undo the damage that the Court had done.†

---

*As explained in the previous chapter, Brennan's opinion was the Court's "lead," "plurality," or "prevailing," opinion; it had essentially the effect of a majority opinion.

†The clergymen included Bishops Lloyd C. Wicke, Leo A. Pursley, Aloysius J. Wallinger, and John King Mussio; The Reverends Wilburn C. West and W. Scott Morton; Rabbis Chaim

BISHOP LLOYD C. WICKE, ET AL.: Religious leaders of all faiths in all communities stand together vociferously decrying the fact that the Supreme Court has presumed to recast the moral law. These decisions cannot be accepted quietly by the American people if this nation is to survive. Giving free rein to the vile depiction of violence, perversion, illicit sex, and in consequence to their performance, is an unnerving sign of progressive decay and decline. Furthermore, it gives prophetic meaning to the Communist Soviet intent to "bury" us. . . .

The views expressed by the five Justices who failed to find obscene the novel *Tropic of Cancer* and the movie *The Lovers* are as confused as they are deplorable. Their shocking conclusions exhibit contempt for the public and an indifference to, or disregard of, the morality that guided the framers of our Constitution. Their further suggestion that the average American would tolerate such filth is an insult to the character and intelligence of the people of the United States. . . .*

The time has come for a strict enforcement of all laws against obscene literature and a nationwide campaign to our President Lyndon B. Johnson calling upon him to review these decisions and properly characterize them as an insult to the American people and a menace to American society.†

—

Beatniks now replaced Communists as the worst enemies of the "American way of life." Said Cardinal Spellman:

FRANCIS CARDINAL SPELLMAN: We cannot accept these court decisions. They impose upon us the responsibility for immediate, continuous and universal action. They represent an acceptance of degeneracy and the Beatnik mentality as the standard way of American life. . . . I would ask everyone to join with me in a plea to those judges of our highest court who have weakened America's efforts to protect its youth, to reconsider their responsibilities to Almighty God and to our country. Let us have a crusade that will deal a mortal blow to the powerhouse of pornography, reaffirm the ideals of the family and preserve the traditions of a free America.

U. Lipschitz and Julius G. Neumann. Concerning "moral law," the letter of the Continental Congress to the inhabitants of Quebec indicates that the framers of the First Amendment intended to keep the "morality" of the people free of governmental coercion. See Chapters 12 and 15.

*This, apparently, in allusion to the "average person" as the measure of the "prurient appeal" of a work, under *Roth*.

†President Johnson did create the National Commission on Obscenity and Pornography, chaired by Dean William Lockhart of the University of Minnesota Law School and with Professor Paul Bender as its general counsel. This commission, however, rode on the crest of the social and sexual revolutions of the sixties; its 1970 report recommended the repeal of all obscenity laws applicable to consenting adults. See Chapter 28. The bid by clerics for presidential denunciation of the Supreme Court's permissive obscenity decisions would receive enthusiastic response from President Nixon when he denounced out of hand (and before its release) the report of the Lockhart commission, which called for changes in obscenity law that were no less permissive than the changes stipulated by the Court.

Brennan told me he received "hundreds of letters from Catholics" criticizing his position. The justice's "dear friend" Dean O'Meara of Notre Dame Law School also "wrote me constantly, hoping to change my mind" about *Jacobellis*.

The full implications of the Brennan doctrine were surely not appreciated immediately by all concerned—possibly not even by Brennan himself. It is only in the dialectical push and pull of actual case encounters and of disputed and contested applications and commentary that such implications clearly emerge. The passage of time helps—no doubt Holmes did not foresee all the consequences of the language he used in *Schenck* v. *United States,* eventually known as the "clear and present danger" doctrine. In some cases the implications of Brennan's words in *Jacobellis/Tropic of Cancer* would be stubbornly resisted even when they were recognized—as I believe was the case in New York when, shortly after the Supreme Court's June 1964 decisions were announced, Lenny Bruce's prosecutors and judges silenced the satirist by finding his monologue performances without social importance.*

But in Illinois, where by that time the state's supreme court had held both Henry Miller's *Tropic of Cancer* and Lenny Bruce's monologues unprotected and obscene, the thrust of Brennan's opinion was promptly acknowledged by the judges sitting on the high bench, who reversed both earlier decisions.†

In 1966, two years after he wrote the *Jacobellis/Tropic of Cancer* opinion, Brennan went on to write the lead opinions for the Court in three new obscenity cases. These concerned the Putnam's edition of John Cleland's *Fanny Hill;* three publications of Ralph Ginzburg's, including the slick hardbound magazine *Eros;* and a group of so-called bondage and S&M booklets commissioned and published by a man named Samuel Mishkin. The first two of these cases involved marginal claims that the publications possessed redeeming literary, artistic, or other social value, and so put pressure on the Brennan doctrine.

Fanny Hill illuminates the outer limits of Brennan's "utterly without social importance" or "utterly without redeeming social value" doctrine. In rephrasing the doctrine in the course of his opinion in *Fanny Hill,* Brennan clarified the "triple-pronged" test:

JUSTICE WILLIAM J. BRENNAN, JR.: [T]hree elements must coalesce; it must be established that (a) the dominant theme of the material taken as a whole appeals to a prurient interest in sex; (b) the material is patently offensive because it affronts contemporary community standards relating to the de-

---

*Described in Chapter 24.
†One of Lenny Bruce's Chicago lawyers was Professor Harry Kalven, Jr.

scription or representation of sexual matters; and (c) the material is utterly without redeeming social value.*

This drew the following comment from Kalven:

PROFESSOR HARRY KALVEN, JR.: The terms of this test suggest a metaphysics of their own. It is possible apparently to have valuable, patently offensive pruriency. More important it is possible to have all sorts of materials which are utterly without redeeming social importance or are patently offensive but are nevertheless beyond the reach of the law because they do not deal with sex. The upshot is that . . . because all these criteria must be met independently in order to satisfy the test, the concession to censorship is minimal and very little material is left within the reach of the law.

In the *Fanny Hill* case Charles Rembar tried at trial, through the testimony of experts, to make a credible case that *Fanny Hill* possessed "literary merit," "historical significance," and "psychological values." That done, it was by no means certain that the brethren, after perusing the old book in its new G. P. Putnam's Sons covers, would agree that it had some such value. And if they failed to apply Brennan's exact formula in *Jacobellis,* they might instead respond to the book's prurient appeal, patent offensiveness, and arguably minuscule social value by concluding that John Cleland's eighteenth-century novel was nothing more than well-written pornography. Even Brennan himself initially seemed inclined to believe that Cleland's novel would fail the "not utterly without social value" test. It became Rembar's task to persuade Brennan and others among the brethren that there was no such thing as "well-written pornography"—if something was "well written," it could not be considered "pornography." This eventually led to Rembar's adumbration of the meaning of "literary value," a gloss on the Brennan doctrine.

JUSTICE WILLIAM J. BRENNAN, JR.: I would like to follow this up. . . . [W]here there is testimony directed to the issue of redeeming social value, and there is critical testimony of acknowledged experts in the field, that ends any obscenity case without our ever reading the material?
CHARLES REMBAR: Yes, Your Honor. . . .
JUSTICE WILLIAM J. BRENNAN, JR.: And, that is, well-written pornography is [not] outside [the protection of the free press guarantees]?
CHARLES REMBAR: Your Honor, the word pornography . . .
JUSTICE WILLIAM J. BRENNAN, JR.: Doesn't it mean that? We are dealing with, I guess, by hypothesis, with what is pornographic material as to which, however, a number of acknowledged literary critics are willing to say it has some literary and therefore social value, because it is well written.

---

*Brennan's reference to "contemporary community standards" implied, as we have seen, *national* contemporary community standards.

CHARLES REMBAR: If by pornographic Your Honor means sexually arous-ing, or "lustful" in the terms of the decisions, the answer is yes. I think it has been clear for some time that material whose effect is to stimulate a sexual response in the normal person is not for that reason to be de-nounced.

———

Not for that reason alone, if the Brennan doctrine was to have any meaning at all. But *Fanny Hill* appeared to be, as Justice Tom Clark pointed out, virtually "nothing but a series of minutely and vividly described sexual episodes." It certainly seemed to have no literary or artistic value approach-ing that of, say, *Tropic of Cancer* or *Naked Lunch.*

Assistant Attorney General William I. Cowin (who had handled the Boston *Naked Lunch* case for the State of Massachusetts*) pointed out to the Court the reason that *Fanny Hill* was arguably devoid of anything but pornographic value:

WILLIAM I. COWIN: Unlike a book such as *Tropic of Cancer,* where the reader was forced to do quite a bit of searching for what he might have felt were "more interesting" scenes, [*Fanny Hill*] is ideal for skimming—absolutely no searching is necessary at all. The book can be opened at any point and the so-called prurient reader will find what he is looking for.

———

It would have been understandable if the justices who read the book had arrived at the conclusion that it was "utterly without social importance"—in Kalven's term "worthless," which is to say, mere pornography.† Rembar, during oral argument, felt obliged to contend that *Fanny Hill* had been recognized as having value by a "substantial body of expert opinion,"‡ and thereby easily met the "even the slightest value" *(Roth)* or the not "utterly without value" *(Jacobellis/Tropic of Cancer)* test.

JUSTICE WILLIAM J. BRENNAN, JR.: But the literary value is not because it has some special moral to purvey; it is only in that it is well written, well expressed, whatever the story may be that it tells?

CHARLES REMBAR: There are, as elements of literary value, good writing, wit, observation of human nature, the drawing of character, psychological insight, the impression on the reader that there are real people involved in this. All these things are . . .

JUSTICE WILLIAM J. BRENNAN, JR.: Doesn't that add up to something well and purposefully written? Does it add up to any more?

---

*See Chapters 20 and 25.

†Rembar, at oral argument, told the brethren they did not need to read the book in order to reverse but could reverse on the basis that the lower court had found *Fanny Hill* obscene despite its concession that the novel had "a modicum" of social value. This ultimately was the way in which Brennan disposed of the case, awarding *Fanny Hill* freedom.

‡Some of the "expert testimony" was rather strained. For example, one expert stated that Fanny was "what I call an intellectual . . . someone who is extremely curious about life and who seeks . . . to record with accuracy the details of the external world, physical sensations, psychological responses . . . an empiricist."

CHARLES REMBAR: It does, Your Honor. I would like to return to Mr. Justice Stewart's question. If there is a substantial body of expert opinion that finds value, then I say the book is entitled to the First Amendment protection.

———

When he posited First Amendment protection on the presentation of "a substantial body of expert opinion," however, Rembar backed off from a strong reading of the Brennan doctrine, that even a "modicum" of value would suffice to establish constitutional protection.

JUSTICE POTTER STEWART: Because the Court as a matter of law could not hold it was utterly without social value?
CHARLES REMBAR: Yes, Your Honor, but I am not saying that if one witness comes in and says that it is a good book, that that automatically answers the question.

———

Why not?* If even one credible person testified that *Fanny Hill* had "value" for him, should this not be treated as passing the requisite threshold for constitutional protection? This would be the clearest, most definite line, and the strongest reading of the Brennan doctrine; it would also be the most democratic or egalitarian approach to the application of the doctrine and the free speech principle embodied in it. Finally, and notwithstanding that a strong reading has not been given the principle since Brennan did that in the *Fanny Hill* case, this is the best reading that can be given it because it is fully informed by the rule of law. I had put forward such a reading in a widely distributed amicus brief that I wrote and filed on behalf of the ACLU and the Maryland Civil Liberties Union in the Maryland *Tropic of Cancer* case.†
    One of the strengths of Brennan's "*utterly* without value" doctrine as a defense against censorship lay in its potential to eliminate virtually all of the vagueness—and therefore the possibility of subjective interpretation by individual judges—that inheres in much legal generalization, but especially in a common-law statutory concept such as "the obscene." Any judge purporting to apply the doctrine would be unable to interpose his personal judgment of whether particular expressive material should be branded obscene in the teeth of an assertion by even a single credible witness that the material was not worthless to him. A strong view of the Brennan doctrine would mean that if even one person (including, of course, the author) came to court to testify that *Fanny Hill* (or *Tropic of Cancer, The Housewife's*

———

*Perhaps the real reason why not is that few competent lawyers defending a book like *Fanny Hill* would risk everything on the credibility of a single witness at a time when the law did not unequivocally imply that one witness is enough. Barney Rosset was prepared to publish *Naked Lunch* only after two credible witnesses, Mary McCarthy and Norman Mailer, had read and praised it. See Chapter 25.

†The ACLU distributed copies of this brief to all its state and local chapters and affiliated lawyers. Such a reading was also suggested by Justice Douglas, dissenting in the *Ginzburg* case, one of the most harshly criticized of Warren Court decisions. See Chapter 26.

Handbook, or *Suite 69*) was a good book, that would put the issue of constitutional protection to rest—not simply because it would show that the book was not, in Kalven's terminology, "worthless," but because under the classical tradition of free expression, the government may not suppress even one person's opinion. To suppress a book that someone is convinced has value is to refuse to respect that person's belief in the goodness of the book, and his right to "express" himself by writing it, reading it, or sharing its goodness with others. The adoption of this strong reading of Brennan would implicate a full democratization of the First Amendment principle that Americans have a right to read the books, see the movies, and experience the art and entertainment of their choice.* This reading would also bring the Brennan doctrine into line with the landmark opinion written for the Court by Justice Thurgood Marshall in 1969, in *Stanley* v. *Georgia,* discussed later on.

The amicus brief that I submitted in the Maryland *Tropic of Cancer* case (*Yudkin* v. *Maryland*) † proposed that the Brennan doctrine be construed in this way, and asked that the courts look to the principle adumbrated by John Stuart Mill in *On Liberty* to resolve the "utterly without value" problem.

JOHN STUART MILL: If all mankind minus one were of one opinion, and only one person were of the contrary opinion, mankind would be no more justified in silencing that one person, than he, if he had the power, would be justified in silencing mankind.

———

*The strength, as a legal rule, of the "*utterly* without value" doctrine, as I have glossed it, may be stressed by comparing it with the doctrine that Chief Justice Burger later substituted for it in the opinion he wrote in 1973—the "without any *serious* value" doctrine. The Brennan doctrine sharply confines the adjudicative discretion of a lower court judge or other official, and rules out any "weighing" of a work's "prurient appeal" against its "social value," however slight. "Serious" value, on the other hand, invites a resort to weighing by the judge. It thereby loosens the binding quality of the legal rule embodied in the doctrine and undermines the rule of law. This probably was Burger's intention: to give local judges, juries, and other censors maximum play. It would be far easier for a judge or juror to brand as obscene a work like *Lolita, Fanny Hill, Tropic of Cancer, Naked Lunch,* or *The Story of O* if he or she was invited to balance such a work's "prurient appeal" and "patent offensiveness" against his or her own sense of the seriousness of whatever is shown at trial bearing on "value." The use of a modifier like "serious" (Burger) or "substantial" (Rembar at the *Fanny Hill* argument) invites judicial balancing of the sort that Justice Felix Frankfurter long advocated—but it engenders juridical rulelessness. That is what the Brennan doctrine, as interpreted here, would preclude.

†The conviction in Montgomery County of Samuel Yudkin for selling *Tropic of Cancer*—a book that he testified he was convinced "had literary merit and was not obscene"—was overturned on this appeal by the Court of Appeals of Maryland because the trial judge had refused to allow the jury to hear any expert testimony concerning the literary, artistic, and social value of the novel or to examine evidence tending to show that Montgomery County's community standards of decency tolerated the circulation of comparable works—namely, Lawrence's *Lady Chatterley's Lover,* Wilson's *Memoirs of Hecate County,* Nabokov's *Lolita,* and James Gould Cozzens's *By Love Possessed.* Notwithstanding Yudkin's "victory" over the censors of Montgomery County, as a result of his arrest and prosecution he lost his valuable bookstore franchise at Washington's National Airport and went out of business in Maryland shortly thereafter. The decision of the Maryland Court of Appeals is reprinted in de Grazia, *Censorship Landmarks* (1969), 449–51.

In another *Tropic of Cancer* amicus curiae brief—this one filed in the Supreme Court on behalf of more than one hundred authors, publishers, and editors—I put the doctrine forward in its strongest ("radical egalitarian") form. I argued that the question of whether a literary work was to be accorded constitutional protection could "not turn on *who* may find a work important or *where* it may so be found, but simply on *whether* anyone, anywhere, finds it to have a worth." My brief continued: "Whenever a challenged work is shown either to have secured critical attention in newspapers or journals concerned with such things, or to have been examined and found unsuppressible as obscene in any other locale or jurisdiction in the nation, or to have literary, artistic, scientific, political, or other importance for persons prepared so to declare in open court, then it should be the plain duty of a prosecutor or judge to dismiss the criminal proceedings—at least in the absence of a charge of intent to engender specific harm. For no [judicial] finding of worthlessness can survive where persons have publicly declared or are prepared in court to declare that a worth exists for them."

The conclusions that I suggested might be drawn from this analysis were that "criminal prosecutions for obscenity are poor forums for debates over the importance of a work of literature or art.* Once a recognizable literary work is involved, every attempt by judge or jury, with or without the assistance of experts, to measure the work's obscenity or its social importance simply mocks the constitutional tradition. . . . The permissible juridical suppression of obscenity must begin and end with the worthless."† And I cited Kalven's "Metaphysics of the Law of Obscenity" in the conviction that the doctrinal concept of the "worthless"—as inspired by Kalven and adumbrated by Brennan from *Roth* to *Jacobellis* to *Fanny Hill*—provided the best assurance that obscenity cases would not continue to serve as occasions for impossible balancing acts by administrative censors, policemen, prosecutors, jurors, and lower and higher court judges given carte blanche to determine whether particular literary or artistic works should be treated as constitutionally protected or obscene.

Whatever was in Brennan's mind at the time of the oral arguments in *Fanny Hill*, by the time he wrote his final draft of the majority opinion for the case he had adopted both what I have termed a strong reading of his own doctrine and the argument laid out in Rembar's briefs: that if *Fanny Hill* was not unqualifiedly worthless—if it had even a modicum of social value, as the Massachusetts Supreme Court conceded—this was sufficient

---

*This was not to suggest that civil *in rem* proceedings, when the book is the "defendant"— as was the case with the Massachusetts *Fanny Hill* case and the Florida *Tropic of Cancer* case—contribute any more to "debates" over a work's importance, as I noted in my brief, pointing out that they too "invite censorship."

†Were my suggested strong reading of the Brennan doctrine to be used also with the Burger revision of that doctrine (i.e., once a recognizable *serious* work of literature or art is involved), prosecutions such as those directed in 1990 against members of the art world in Cincinnati (the gallery that showed Mapplethorpe photographs) and in Miami (the 2 Live Crew musical group) would be thrown out of court by the judge before any trial.

to end the case in *Fanny Hill*'s favor. Thus Brennan concluded in *Fanny Hill* that under the law the book was entitled to be free. He did so not as he had done in the *Tropic of Cancer* case from Florida—on the basis of his own conclusion that it was not utterly without literary or other social value—but for the reason that the Supreme Judicial Court of Massachusetts itself, in its published opinion, had found that *Fanny Hill* possessed at least "a modicum" of social value. This gave Brennan an opportunity to reemphasize that his "utterly without value" formulation was meant to *rule out* any judicial juggling of prurient appeal and social importance. The Massachusetts court had offered him a chance to give his doctrine a strong reading.

JUSTICE WILLIAM J. BRENNAN, JR.: The Supreme Judicial Court [of Massachusetts] erred in holding that a book need not be "unqualifiedly worthless before it can be deemed obscene."* A book cannot be prosecuted unless it is found to be *utterly* without redeeming social value. This is so even though the book is found to possess the requisite prurient appeal and to be patently offensive. Each of the three federal constitutional criteria is to be applied independently; the social value of the book can neither be weighed against nor cancelled by its prurient appeal or patent offensiveness.† Hence, *even on the view of the court below‡* that *Memoirs* possessed only a modicum of social value, its judgment must be reversed as being founded on an erroneous interpretation of a federal constitutional standard.

PROFESSOR HARRY KALVEN, JR.: There is a sense in which this ringing declaration displays high diplomacy. The Court avoided expressing its own opinion on the status of *Fanny Hill;* it is enough that the Court below found it had a modicum of value. Nevertheless, the fact remains that the Court braved public displeasure to announce to the world that *Fanny Hill* was not obscene.

JUSTICE BYRON S. WHITE: If "social importance" is to be used as the prevailing opinion [Brennan's] uses it today, obscene material, however far beyond customary limits of candor, is immune if it has any literary style, if it contains any historical references or language characteristic of a bygone day, or even if it is printed or bound in an interesting way.

JUSTICE TOM CLARK: I agree with my brother White that [the *"utterly without redeeming social value"*] condition rejects the basic holding of *Roth* and gives the smut artist free rein to carry on his dirty business.

PAUL BENDER: You have to applaud Brennan for trying so hard to fit within the traditional values. With *Times* v. *Sullivan* § he tried to explain what it

---

*This marked, I believe, the first time that Brennan used in so many words Kalven's concept of the "worthless" in adumbrating his "utterly without value" doctrine.

†Brennan here quoted from *Jacobellis.*

‡Italics are mine.

§Described in Chapter 16.

was about the First Amendment that led to this dramatic change; and in *Roth* he tried to explain it also; and that was very, very commendable. And those opinions were the very beginnings of very large developments. So Brennan is *the* major figure on the Court today, without any doubt, and one of the most major figures over the last twenty-five years.

———

Others went further in their estimates of the social importance of Justice Brennan's work:

JUDGE JOHN J. GIBBONS: As I look back over . . . the [then] twenty-eight years of his service as a Supreme Court Justice, he appears to me far more humane than Holmes, broader in outlook than Brandeis, more practical and flexible than Black, a finer scholar than Warren, more eloquent than Hughes, more painstaking than Douglas, and more gracious than any of them.

24

The Ideas I Have Are Now Imprisoned Within Me

O NE DAY IN 1964, less than six months after the Florida *Tropic of Cancer* case was won in the Supreme Court, Lenny Bruce, whom *Time* magazine mocked as a "sicknik" comedian, introduced himself to a three-man panel of federal appellate judges as "author, lecturer, and social satirist." He was trying to make a good impression on the judges in order to persuade them to stop Manhattan District Attorney Frank Hogan—and three judges sitting in a New York County criminal court—from jailing him for doing his show at the Cafe Au Go Go. By then, Bruce had been recognized by some critics as an unusual sort of nightclub comedian and an oral "poet." The columnist Dorothy Kilgallen would later describe him from the witness stand as "a very brilliant man" with "great social awareness" who "was trying to make his audiences think." But his show—the monologues, or "bits," that Bruce delivered in nightclubs, cabarets, and coffeehouses to usually friendly, but sometimes hostile, audiences—had been stopped by police several times in San Francisco, Beverly Hills, Chicago, and New York for being indecent and obscene.

The San Francisco case had been won; in Beverly Hills, the jury had hung. The Chicago case was lost, at trial and on first appeal. In the New York case Bruce not only lost, he was sentenced to spend four months in the "workhouse."* The owner of his New York club, Howard Solomon, was convicted and fined. After that, no club owner in New York was willing to book him for fear of being arrested, fined, or jailed for presenting an obscene performance.

---

*The prison for misdemeanants at Riker's Island in New York used to be called the "workhouse." For reasons that are described later in the chapter, Bruce never served his time at the workhouse.

. . .

Although Bruce had found his first audiences in 1958 in "the city of Beatniks, poetry and jazz" and was sometimes called a beat comedian, his main resemblance to the beats seems to have been that he, too, was harassed by the San Francisco police. It was still Joe McCarthy time in San Francisco.

The first time Bruce was arrested for obscenity was at the Jazz Workshop in San Francisco, in October 1961, four years after Lawrence Ferlinghetti had been arrested in the same city for publishing Allen Ginsberg's poem *Howl*,* and a little more than four years after the Supreme Court had affirmed Samuel Roth's conviction for sending obscene publications through the mails. In the *Roth* case, however, the Court went on to say that literature, art, and any expression of "ideas having even the slightest redeeming social importance—unorthodox ideas, controversial ideas, even ideas hateful to the prevailing climate of opinion"—were entitled to full First Amendment freedom. Bruce's nightclub performances were recognizably artistic and full of socially relevant, controversial ideas—about Catholics, Jews, lesbians, hip Negroes, white liberals, married couples, and political figures, including President Lyndon Johnson, Eleanor Roosevelt, Barry Goldwater, Jackie Kennedy, Dick Gregory, and Francis Cardinal Spellman.

Bruce's problem was that in conveying his ideas he used words like "cocksucker." Bruce gave a kind of archetypical rendering of the Law's reaction in his autobiography, *How to Talk Dirty and Influence People.* He was describing his San Francisco "bust":

LENNY BRUCE: I used a ten-letter word onstage. Just a word in passing. . . .
                                  The Cop:
Lenny, I wanna talk to you. You're under arrest. That word you said, you can't say that in a public place. It's against the law to say it and do it.
                                  Lenny Bruce:
They said it was a favorite homosexual practice. Now that I found strange. I don't relate that word to a homosexual practice. It relates to any contemporary chick I know, I would know, or would love, or would marry. . . . Now we get to court. They swear me in. . . .
                                  The Cop:
Your Honor, he said blah-blah-blah.
                                  The Judge:
He said *blah*-blah-blah? Well, I got grandchildren. . . .
                                  The Cop:
Your Honor, I couldn't believe it, there's a guy up on the stage in front of women in a mixed audience, saying blah-blah-blah. . . .
                                  The District Attorney:
Look at him, he's smug! I'm not surprised he said blah-blah-blah. . . . He'll probably say blah-blah-blah again, he hasn't learned his lesson. . . .

---

*Ferlinghetti was acquitted in October 1957, following a trial described in Chapter 17.

Lenny Bruce:

And then I dug something: they sort of *liked* saying blah-blah-blah. Even the Bailiff:

The Bailiff:

What'd he say?

The Judge:

He said blah-blah-blah.

Lenny Bruce:

They were yelling it in the courtroom!

Everyone:

Goddamn, it's good to say blah-blah-blah!

———

Bruce won the San Francisco legal contest after the second attorney he engaged for the case, an ACLU-affiliated lawyer named Albert Bendich,* managed to have Bruce tried before Judge Clayton Horn, the enlightened judge who had freed Lawrence Ferlinghetti from obscenity charges. The judge permitted expert witnesses to testify to the social importance of Lenny Bruce's ideas and allowed favorable commentary about Bruce's work to be read from *Commonweal* magazine and *The New York Times.* Following Judge Horn's carefully worded instructions, the jury acquitted Bruce. Said the jury foreman afterward: "We had no choice."

Bruce's next obscenity cases arose out of performances that took place in October 1962 and February 1963 at the Troubadour in Beverly Hills, and in December 1962 at the Gate of Horn in Chicago. In the Beverly Hills case police officers testified that Bruce used the words "cocksucker," "bastard," "asshole," and "goddamn" in his act, but the jury laughed at excerpts from taped performances that Bruce's lawyer, Burton Marks, had played, and they deadlocked six to six on a verdict. Although this resulted in a mistrial and no retrial took place, Bruce said he felt the hung jury was tantamount to a conviction.

The Chicago trial began on February 18, 1963, three days after the Beverly Hills mistrial was declared. This time, after losing the services of the very able Chicago lawyer Donald Page Moore (because Bruce wanted Moore to advise, not represent, him), the comedian conducted his own defense, with a lawyer named Earle Zidins sitting at counsel table, coaching him. During voir dire, Bruce personally interrogated the prospective jurors, asking them if they would be shocked by such words as "fuck," "piss," and "tits" or the phrase "stepping on my dick." But when he sought to disqualify a female jury prospect by asking her, "Do you ever masturbate?"—expecting her to answer no and thereby provide grounds for disqualification—Judge Michael J. Ryan summoned Bruce to the bench and told him he would allow no such questioning in his courtroom. It was Bruce's contention that the question was a legitimate one, which would

———

*Bendich was one of three lawyers who had represented Lawrence Ferlinghetti and Shigeyoshi Murao at the *Howl* trial.

establish that she was a liar, for scientific statistics showed that in fact "everybody jerks off."

On February 28, 1963, Bruce was convicted of obscenity in Chicago. While he was back in California defending against a narcotics prosecution, Judge Ryan issued a bench warrant for his arrest and sentenced him in absentia to a year in jail and a $1,000 fine, which was the maximum punishment under Illinois law. He was enabled to vacate his sentence and appeal his conviction only when University of Chicago law professor Harry Kalven and two practicing colleagues of his, Maurice Rosenfeld and Robert Ming, agreed to take over Bruce's case without fee.

Within a year, however, during the summer of 1964, Bruce would also be arrested in New York, for giving obscene performances at the Cafe Au Go Go.

ALBERT GOLDMAN: By the winter of 1964 Lenny Bruce had become the victim of a nationwide lockout. He could still play San Francisco, where his one and only victory secured him from prosecution, but even in this sanctuary the heat was getting heavy: the locations that Lenny worked were under constant surveillance; the hotels where he shacked up were subjected to narcotics raids. Even the connections were shy of doing business with him.

—

I was asked to help solve Bruce's problems in the winter of 1964–65, six or seven months after his conviction and the Supreme Court's ruling (in the Florida case that I had handled) that Henry Miller's *Tropic of Cancer* was not obscene. It seemed apparent to me that if *Tropic of Cancer* was constitutionally protected, Bruce's speech should be as well. That was also the view of Bruce's Chicago lawyers and of Bruce himself, who put a lot of time and effort into studying the law he had come up against. In fact, once the Supreme Court of Illinois heard from Bruce's Chicago lawyers about the *Jacobellis/Tropic of Cancer* decisions, they also took that view; and so would the Court of Appeals of New York a year or so later on Howard Solomon's appeal.

There is no doubt in my mind that the Supreme Court of the United States would also have agreed if any decision upholding a Bruce conviction had been appealed to it in a timely way. But Bruce's New York prosecutors, and especially the chief judge at his New York trial, saw Bruce's acts and the evolving obscenity law differently; then, when Bruce fired his New York lawyer and failed to find a replacement,* the actor lost the only real chance he had—by appeal of his criminal conviction—to get the New York judiciary to change its mind, or the Supreme Court to vindicate his art. That

---

*After Bruce advised his trial court judges that he had discharged Ephraim London and was determined to represent himself for the balance of the criminal proceedings, the court appointed Martin Garbus, of London's firm, who had acted as co-counsel throughout Bruce's trial, to represent Bruce free of charge. Bruce, however, did not permit Garbus to do more than coach him. London sued Bruce for some $7,000 in fees but never recovered them. Garbus has written a thoughtful account of the New York trial in his book *Ready for the Defense* (1971).

was the problem, and by the time I was asked to get involved in his behalf, it was too late to solve it. But my involvement gave Bruce fresh hope, and something to do, so he swamped me with telephone calls, tape-recorded messages, letters of advice, petitions he had filed, correspondence to other lawyers, one or two briefs, affidavits, memoranda of law, court opinions, transcripts of performances, and a tape he himself had made of his "busted" Chicago performance. Some of these were indecipherable, many incomprehensible, in full or in part. In fact, there was little hope.

It was an aspect of Bruce's sensibility, the way he saw things, that he did not lay the blame for his troubles with the law on those he called the foot soldiers—the policemen who arrested him or even the trial judges who convicted him. Neither did he blame the law itself, although by the time he became entangled in it, the vagueness of obscenity law had already attracted much criticism, lay and learned, and much bitter complaint. Bruce reserved his blame for the lawyers involved in his cases, and among those, the lawyers who defended him more than the ones who prosecuted him. The actor wrote to me from his home in the Los Angeles hills on March 16, 1965, some time after I learned about his situation. This is one of the two or three personal communications I received from him during this period that were both legible (it was typed) and, for the most part, coherent.

LENNY BRUCE: Dear Edward, I feel like I have a vise around my chest. I'm very tired from the battle with the enemy within. No matter how I slice it, the defense counsels have been the villians [*sic*]. A review from the first arrest 'till the present that so many times could have been quashed by a bill of particulars but there's no recognition with that type of defense. I would like very much to interest you in a 60-40 contingency piece of the tort, for my only interest is holding on to my house, which has a lien on it. Money damages are mine under 1983 with Vincent Cuccia's affidavit in his motion to dismiss the complaint Civ. 653574 The Grand Jury presented the information on the pages marked by an (X).

—

The "tort" Bruce referred to was the federal action for damages, injunction, and declaratory judgment that Bruce had filed, lost, and unsuccessfully appealed from days before he was sentenced in New York. He had asked a federal court to extract $500,000 from the prosecutors and judges whom he held responsible for his conviction and for his inability to work anymore in New York. There was, I thought, no chance that he would recover those damages, but I believed there was a faint chance that the Supreme Court would be willing to review the appellate court's denial of Bruce's requests for an injunction against further pretrial restraints on his performances by arrests, and for a declaration that his show was not obscene; and there was still a week's time to seek a review. So, in my Washington law office, with the assistance of my associate Laurence I. Hewes III and a dedicated Chicago lawyer, Ernst Liebman, I prepared and filed the papers (a petition for certiorari) necessary to ask the Supreme Court to rescue Lenny Bruce from the net of the obscenity law that had been cast over him by law enforcement officials.

Bruce's main problems with the law were his inability to continue to work while the legal proceedings against him took their course, and his inability to get along with his lawyers. In his New York lawyers, Ephraim London and Martin Garbus, as in his Chicago ones, law professor and First Amendment scholar Harry Kalven and Maurice Rosenfeld and Robert Ming, Bruce had engaged some of the best First Amendment attorneys available. But Bruce was contentious, and he was understandably reluctant to mortgage his Hollywood home to pay his lawyers. So he fired London even though he had no other lawyer ready to take up where London left off;* in fact, he almost lost Kalven, too. But Kalven would take no fee from Bruce and was an extremely capable lawyer and a patient soul. He eventually won Bruce's Chicago case in the Illinois Supreme Court. In New York, Bruce had to wind up his criminal trial without effective counsel. Worse yet, without counsel, he failed to take an appeal from his conviction that would have vindicated him. But Bruce did institute that complicated federal civil damages, declaratory ruling, and injunction action, and he appealed from the adverse decision he received there—without any counsel at all.

After his New York trial Bruce repeatedly complained to me, and his other lawyers, that his judges never saw him perform or actually heard the monologues they adjudged obscene, that his two Cafe Au Go Go convictions were based on the Manhattan D.A.'s "dirty tapes," surreptitiously recorded by detectives, which the judges listened to. His biggest grievance against London was that the lawyer refused to offer as evidence a Bruce-transcribed version of his Cafe Au Go Go performances. In a letter to London dated September 2, 1964, a copy of which Bruce sent me, Bruce castigated London for his trial work, accusing him of being an "appellantophile" and of being contemptuous toward lower court judges.

LENNY BRUCE: Dear Ephraim, If the court had appointed you as a public defender, I would have less rights as far as instructing you. . . . I have given you $1000, and the hi-fi equipment and camera I sent you were worth about $200, used. So I am instructing you. . . . You accepted that money on the condition that you would conduct yourself in a manner that would be effective in the trial court and respect that trial court and not assume that the trial court is merely a recording studio waiting to be admonished and overturned by the appellate court. . . . I discussed with you the importance of the trial court. And when we agreed, I said I wouldn't interfere from then on. But you are an appellantophile, you are possessed with "a shameful and morbid interest in finding statutes unconstitutional

---

*Ephraim London's *New York Times* obituary stated that he had eventually successfully appealed Lenny Bruce's New York criminal conviction. As explained later, this is not correct. Bruce, lawyerless at the time, never perfected an appeal from his conviction; his appeal was abandoned. However, William Hellerstein, then working with the Legal Aid Society, eventually prosecuted a successful appeal on behalf of Howard Solomon, operator of the Cafe Au Go Go, as described later.

on their face." Your first duty, however, is to your client. Your second duty is to other clients who follow. Finding 1140 unconstitutional on appeal will do nothing for me and you do a disservice to the community of New York by not working on the trial level. The disservice you do is the propagation of villian [*sic*] image that it places upon the courts that are already in a precarious position with the civil rights issues. The liberal gets another crack at the establishment. It would be okay if the argument was confined to liberals and conservatives. The liberals and the people who have seen my show have been given the opportunity that the trial court has been denied. And your statement, "I agree that your transcript of the performance at the Cafe au Go Go is better than the one offered in evidence. There is nothing to prevent us from using your transcript . . . on appeal," is insanity. What the fuck is the matter with you Ephraim? Don't you know who will reap the hostility? The poor policeman, the foot soldier. The newspaper article, "Lenny Bruce Found Guilty," brings forth the statement from the liberals, "Gestapo police, how 'bout that, the Goddamn police." It's not the Goddamn police, but it's "God damn you," for denying the trial court something they can judge. Did it ever occur to you that the expert witnesses couldn't relate to the court? The words they used were too esoteric.

GARY SCHWARTZ:* We sued him for our fees and I served him in his hotel room and he was very gentle toward me.

———

During the unsuccessful federal civil proceedings that Bruce initiated after his New York criminal conviction—the proceedings that I later asked the Supreme Court to review—Bruce finally presented his own partial version of his performances. Bruce the lawyer, representing Bruce the client, allowed Bruce the "author, lecturer, and social satirist" to perform before the federal judges portions of monologues for which he had been arrested. The judges were a distinguished panel of the federal court of appeals in New York: Judges Henry Friendly, Paul Hays, and Thurgood Marshall, who would soon become the first black judge on the Supreme Court of the United States and one of its proselytizers for freedom of expression.† They listened as Bruce the lawyer explained what was behind the federal complaint that he had filed on his own behalf.

---

*Gary Schwartz was a summer intern with Ephraim London's law firm at the time; he is currently a professor of law at UCLA.

†Marshall characteristically voted with the side "for freedom." In the only obscenity censorship case I remember for which he wrote the Court's opinion, *Stanley* v. *Georgia,* in 1969, he moved the Warren Court to the highest peak of its long campaign to free expression from the constraints of obscenity law. There he ruled that Americans had an absolute right to read even concededly obscene books and watch even concededly obscene movies in the privacy of their homes. A few years later, the Burger Court limited the significance of *Stanley* strictly to its facts, preventing the application of the doctrine to the many situations outside the home to which it logically could be extended, in which people might wish to engage in transactions with the producers and distributors of obscene books, magazines, and films in order to read or watch them in the privacy of their homes, or in semiprivate places such as movie theatres, bookstores, nightclubs, and coffeehouses.

LENNY BRUCE: I want them to stop prosecuting me in the future. I want you to enjoin them from any arrests for my act, and to stop them from putting me in jail. I'll show you some of it so you'll see there's nothing wrong with it. Under the law, before a judge can stop a performance and arrest the performer, he has to be shown the performance is obscene. What I'm doing is the other way around. But I'll have to show you some of what I'm doing. . . .

MARTIN GARBUS: The judges listened with interest. Lenny first talked about America's misuse of Christ symbols. He then went into a sketch commenting on the kinds of justice all white men can expect from black juries, pointing out that black men would treat whites as badly as they themselves had been treated. . . .

LENNY BRUCE: I've never heard *any* hostility from any American Negroes. I did hear that from Jews and Christians, but never from any American Negroes. I've never heard any outward hostility, no spoken word. If you hear in traffic "Hey, asshole, move it over dere!" that's never a colored driver, Mack. Isn't that a little strange? I don't think you've heard it either. And they're pissed off, and justifiably so. But yet I've never heard that.

Then I realized I'm going to hear it. Oh, yeah. There's going to be a vote, and a change. You see, there are a few more Negroes than you know about. Oh, yeah. Because census-takers, I assume, have been remiss in their duties, and passed a few Negro houses: . . .

Census Taker:

Ah, frig it. I'm not going in those houses—dogs, dirt—I don't wanna go in there. Ask that kid on the lawn. "How many live on this block, sonny?"

Kid:

"Ah, well, ah . . ."

Census Taker:

O.K., write it down. . . .

You'd shit if you saw a half a million from one town alone?

"Two billion, taken from Alabama; the vote's still coming in!"

"Two billion? Are you kidding? Two billion? Where're those votes coming from? Where've all these people been?"

"They've been in the houses, man. Sixteen thousand to a house—bunks, tiers—they've been living there."

So the vote's going to bring a change. In a year you'll see an all-black jury and a black judge, and *shit!*

Outraged Voice:

They're all black! How'm I gonna get a fair shake when they're all black?

And you're not. Haha, ha ha. That's how it is. And all the people'll be screaming: "Are you kidding? I was *before* those marches, I was *before* Bayard Rustin. Me? Me? I was so liberal—I'll show you cancelled checks, for Chrissakes! I've been since 1939 with that integration shit. Are you kidding with that?"

Negro:
You are? You're full of shit, you liberal! I'm tired of talking to you people.
Every German you talk to loved the Jews, and they're all dead. So you're
full of shit, Jim. That's it.

———

That's more or less how the bit went in Bruce's performances, including
those that were busted in New York. But in the performance Bruce delivered that day in 1964 before a panel of appellate judges that included
Thurgood Marshall, Bruce added a twist at the end:

MARTIN GARBUS: He concluded with his imitation of the outraged liberal
saying, "They gave me twenty years for raising my voice—those niggers!"
   Marshall's head jerked up and he nearly dropped a pen from his hand.
Bruce saw Marshall's face, stumbled, tried bravely to explain the joke, but
could not. Then he knew he had lost the case and sat down.

———

Bruce still clung to a hope that if he could only put on a show before
the *big* court, the Supreme Court of the United States, all his problems
would be over. In the phone conversations he and I had about his situation—he was in California and I was in D.C.—he kept asking me if he could
not play the Supreme Court and I kept telling him he could not; the
Supreme Court does not receive evidence and would not have bent its rules
to permit even the kind of performance that the appellate panel had listened
to. I did undertake, however, to ask the Supreme Court to review the
federal court's refusal to order an injunction against the New York judges
and prosecutors who had tried and convicted Bruce, and for a judicial
declaration that under the Brennan doctrine, Bruce's monologues warranted constitutional protection. I filed with the petition tapes made by
Bruce of his April 7, 1964, Cafe Au Go Go performance in New York and
of his December 4, 1962, Gate of Horn performance in Chicago. Both
performances had been busted by the police, and the latter had effectively
been pronounced constitutionally protected expression by the Illinois Supreme Court.

   Bruce's problem with the law of New York had arisen when the Manhattan district attorney, Frank Hogan, had decided to prosecute him.* There
is no record of Hogan's reasons for reaching this decision because in an

———

*The Manhattan district attorney (officially the district attorney for New York County) is
an elected official. Today, he instructs and supervises the work of some four hundred assistant
district attorneys engaged in enforcing the New York Penal Code applicable to offenses
committed within New York County. In his selection of the crimes and people to be prosecuted he may be influenced by complaints from victims, witnesses, and police, and by pressures
from political, religious, and social leaders and groups. In the area of obscenity law enforcement, he is likely to be influenced by political and religious leaders and organized vigilante
groups, and to a lesser extent by the largely unorganized literary and artistic communities. His
judgment in conducting the affairs of his office is subject to public criticism, especially in the
press, and an incumbent who alienates influential elements of the electorate risks being
defeated if he runs for reelection.

obscenity case there is no victim, and a prosecutor does not need to say who, if anyone, complained about the alleged obscenity, or why a particular target was selected for prosecution. A prosecutor has more discretion to act or not to act than any other official of the criminal justice system, including the policeman and the judge. As a presidential commission said in 1968, he is the pivot on which the system of criminal justice turns. And Hogan was a good Catholic.

In Chicago, there had been indications that "the Catholics" were responsible for Bruce's Gate of Horn arrest and prosecution because the arresting officers were obviously Catholic and spoke of Bruce's "blasphemy" as well as his "obscenity."* The police said they were offended by the way in which Bruce "spoke about God and Jesus Christ," for this "led into a mockery of the Catholic Church and other religious organizations by using the Pope's name and Cardinal Spellman and Bishop Sheen's name."

After his Chicago arrest, Bruce was released on bail and continued working the Gate of Horn for about a week. Then Captain McDermott of the Chicago Vice Squad paid a visit to the club. As Bruce describes the event in his autobiography, McDermott located the club's owner, Alan Ribback, and their conversation went like this:

CAPTAIN McDERMOTT: I'm Captain McDermott. I want to tell you that if this man *ever uses a four-letter word* in this club again, I'm going to pinch you and everyone in here. If he *ever speaks against religion,* I'm going to pinch you and everyone in here. Do you understand?

ALAN RIBBACK: I don't have anything against religion.

CAPTAIN McDERMOTT: Maybe I'm not talking to the right person. Are you the man who hired Lenny Bruce?

ALAN RIBBACK: Yes, I am. I'm Alan Ribback.

CAPTAIN McDERMOTT: Well, I don't know why you ever hired him. You've had some good people here. But he mocks the Pope—and I'm speaking as a Catholic—I'm here to tell you your license is in danger. We're going to have someone here watching every show. Do you understand?

ALAN RIBBACK: Yes.

———

Ribback let Bruce work the same night, and Bruce did his show. The next morning Ribback was told his license was revoked for "presenting a lewd show." According to Bruce, Ribback had to "sell out" his club.

Chicago was a Catholic bastion. Bruce's biographer Albert Goldman says that at that time, out of a population of 3.5 million, Roman Catholics accounted for 2.2 million—close to two out of three. The proportion of Catholics in the Chicago criminal justice system seemed to be even higher. Forty-seven of the fifty jurors impaneled for Bruce's trial were thought to be Catholics. Bruce charged he had a Catholic judge, a Catholic prosecu-

---

*The 1990 attacks on the National Endowment for the Arts and on individual artists by right-wing politicians and religious vigilante organizations were also directed against "blasphemous" elements in their art. See Chapter 30.

tor, and an all-Catholic jury whose members showed up on Ash Wednesday during his trial with symbolic black smudges on their foreheads.

In New York, although Bruce knew that Catholics were a powerful presence, and that there was a preponderance of Catholics in the law enforcement agencies, the comedian did not tone down his act. A transcript of Bruce's Cafe Au Go Go coffeehouse performance on an evening when he was busted shows he delivered several "Catholic" bits, although none of those would be cited by his judges as obscene.

Frank Hogan was not only a prominent lay Catholic, he was one of the most powerful men in New York. Hogan had been D.A. for nearly twenty years by the time of Bruce's prosecution. And Francis Cardinal Spellman, the archbishop of New York, who sometimes was lampooned in Bruce's "Catholic" bits, was another of the city's most powerful political figures.

JOHN COONEY:* What may have been the Cardinal's last effective moral campaign ended when the comedian Lenny Bruce was sentenced, on December 21, 1964, in the longest, costliest, and most fiercely contested obscenity trial in the history of New York City. The Cardinal at times had been the object of Bruce's satires. ("Spellman does *it* with the nuns.") After Spellman complained to city officials, Bruce was arrested routinely when he gave performances. But a direct cause and effect was never proved.

MARTIN GARBUS: We wanted to believe desperately that Cardinal Spellman was behind the whole thing. Lenny firmly believed it and that raised it to the level of truth in many people's eyes.†

———

The lawyer in Frank Hogan's office who handled the Bruce prosecution was Richard H. Kuh.

MARTIN GARBUS: Hogan's assistant, Richard Kuh, was a stocky man in his late thirties who looked and moved like a retired middleweight fighter. I had encountered him before and knew he was an excellent trial lawyer who believed that the country would be safer if people like Bruce were put in jail. . . . Neither Kuh nor Hogan had ever seen Bruce perform.

ALBERT GOLDMAN: Richard Kuh was a brisk, athletic YMCA prosecutor, always advancing and retreating, ducking in and out, grandstanding with feigned indignation, then sitting down with a smile to the spectators, like a fielder who has just made an impossible catch. Kuh even affected [President] Kennedy's slight lisp in his loud but strangled voice. . . . Jules Feiffer

———

*Spellman's biographer.

†Garbus had another, related, theory that could also account for the Bruce prosecution. "New York, in early 1964, was in the midst of a pornography scare. Father Morton Hill, a Jesuit priest, formed an unholy alliance with Rabbi Moshe Neumann, to create Operation Yorkville, dedicated to forcing newsdealers, bookstore owners, and film exhibitors to remove material the clergymen found objectionable. When a store owner refused, a call to District Attorney Frank Hogan often resulted in a visit from the police." *Ready for the Defense* (1971).

got the picture: Dick Kuh was Clark Kent, Superman, Lenny Bruce was Leonard Schneider, Superjew!* An immortal contest!

———

It was not easy to secure the evidence required to prosecute Lenny Bruce successfully because his "obscene and indecent performances" were oral and visual,† and every show was different. On the third night of Bruce's New York run, License Inspector Herbert S. Ruhe observed the eleven o'clock show from a table "just short of the stage." Like everyone else in the audience, Ruhe had paid $4.70 to watch Lenny Bruce perform. As Bruce spoke, Ruhe took notes, "six little pages neatly written on both sides." After the show, he left the club unnoticed. The next day he transcribed his notes and gave them to Assistant District Attorney Richard M. Kuh, who took them to Frank Hogan.

ALBERT GOLDMAN: Hogan was a small graying leprechaun, fifty-eight years old, nearing the end of his fourth consecutive four-year term as district attorney of New York. His power was second only to the mayor's. . . . As an eminent Catholic lawyer, Hogan must have resented profoundly Lenny Bruce's blasphemy of New York's leading priests, Archbishop Spellman and Bishop Sheen. He might very well have taken offense at Lenny's remarks about Jackie Kennedy "hauling ass."

———

The bit about Jackie Kennedy "hauling ass to save her ass" was one of Bruce's most offensive and least funny routines. Some people considered it the most injurious evidence to enter into Bruce's New York case—because it denigrated the young widow of the country's recently martyred (Catholic) president, John Kennedy, and referred (however metaphorically) to her ass. On the other hand, it also exposed the stridently moral element that characterized Bruce's work. The idea for the bit—it was particularly brief— was sparked by a story in *Time* magazine for December 6, 1963, which contained a strip of pictures of President Kennedy in the act of being shot; the inaccurate sentimental interpretation that accompanied the pictures was what bothered Lenny Bruce.

TIME MAGAZINE (December 6, 1963): The third shot, all too literally, exploded in Kennedy's head. In less than an instant, Jackie was up, climbing

---

*Schneider was Bruce's surname by birth. The "Superjew" epithet seems to have been coined by Bruce himself on the occasion of his Chicago Gate of Horn bust, which was recorded on a tape Bruce sent to me: "Wake up! Quick! Out the back way!! The bricks move! Anything! It's Superjew, Whoosh."
†A similar but less serious problem was involved in the recent finding by a Miami judge that the recording "As Nasty As They Wanna Be" by the rap music group 2 Live Crew was obscene. Seeking to lay a foundation to arrest record dealers who offered the recording for sale, Broward County, Florida, sheriff Nick Navarro "took a transcript of six lyrics [from the recording] to a local judge, who agreed they appeared obscene"—notwithstanding that he was reading part rather than the whole of an artistic work and did not listen to the music or see the performers sing and play the song. See "Art or Obscene" in *Newsweek,* July 2, 1990.

back over the trunk of the car, seeking help. She reached out her right hand, caught the hand of a Secret Service man who was running to catch up, and in one desperate tug pulled him aboard. Then in less time than it takes to tell it, she was back cradling her husband's head in her lap.

LENNY BRUCE (AT CAFE AU GO GO, NEW YORK CITY, APRIL 7, 1964):

Moderator:

The trouble with people that believe—in the dirty films that I saw in the *Time* magazine, I believe the guy got a medal for this. When the President was killed, and the Governor got it, I believe those three pictures the guy sold to *Life* magazine that showed going out of the convertible, the wife (whistle, whistle), the Secret Service man (whistle, whistle) saved her, got a medal, solid. Now I see some different kind of pictures. Different meaning. There she is hauling ass to save her ass out of the car. Which is a conclusion on my part. But a conclusion on *Time* magazine's part, that she was going to get help. That's a lie. Unless ya tells me where she's going to get help.

Jackie Kennedy

(voice as recorded by *Time* magazine): Oh yes, he was shot. I know where to go to get help. You go to that place and get help and you bring people back.

Inquisitioner:

But how about that last caption. That she was helping him aboard. No, I don't think he got a medal for that.

Clinton S. Hill:

You see, I got a medal because I was lost and I don't know what the hell I'm doing and the chick helped me aboard the car and I got a medal.

Moderator:

Now why this is bullshit and a dirty picture, your daughters, if their husbands get shot up, and they haul ass to save their ass like you will, they'll feel guilty and low. Not like the good people, the people that always do stay. The people that always do stay, but never did stay, are like the guys who can sit in judgment and indict Powers.*

———

The New York prosecution of Lenny Bruce was designed to ensure conviction; for reasons that cannot be established but have been guessed at, the case against Bruce was one that Frank Hogan wanted to make stick. However, the D.A. had trouble finding someone within his own office willing to prosecute Bruce. The assistant district attorney in charge of obscenity prosecutions reportedly begged off when Hogan told him what he wanted.

JERRY HARRIS: Bruce was very funny. I didn't think we ought to prosecute him. The tapes were so funny I nearly burst out laughing several times.

———

*Francis Gary Powers, U.S. Air Force pilot shot down over Soviet airspace in 1960, held captive there until 1962.

Finally I had to decide whether I could, in good conscience, be the district attorney on the case. I told Hogan I could not. I saw Lenny a few times during the trial and he always gave me his sad smile. He knew I had refused.

MARTIN GARBUS: Hogan found himself in the unusual position of looking for a lawyer to try the case. Several lawyers in the Rackets and Homicide Bureaus were asked, but they all refused. [Richard] Kuh then agreed to take it, and the district attorney's office decided to submit the case to the grand jury. . . . In practice, a grand jury will almost always bring an indictment when the district attorney is determined to make the defendant stand trial.

—

After receiving Inspector Ruhe's report, Hogan ordered the police to monitor Bruce's performance that night, April 1, using special recording equipment. He wanted accurate evidence of Bruce's performance "as a whole," in order to comply with *Roth*'s requirements for proving expression obscene. So, dressed in business suits, Policemen William O'Neal and Robert Lane of the New York Public Morals Squad bought tickets at the Cafe Au Go Go and took a table fifteen feet from the stage, where Bruce performed that night at ten o'clock. Strapped to Officer Lane's body was a small Minifon recorder, under his armpit was a six-by-eight power pack, and pinned to his necktie was a tiny microphone. He recorded what Bruce said during an hour-long stint, amid the distracting noises of the audience and the club. At another table, near the rear, two other police officers in plain clothes took notes. The next morning, the wire recording was transferred onto a tape, which was played to Assistant District Attorney Kuh and then transcribed onto paper. This evidence was presented by Kuh to the grand jury to initiate the prosecution and trial of Bruce and Howard Solomon, owner of the cafe, before a three-judge criminal court presided over by Judge John A. Murtagh.

MARTIN GARBUS: Murtagh, the presiding judge, had co-authored a book about prostitution, *Cast the First Stone,* and had earned, I thought, an undeserved reputation as a sympathetic and liberal judge. As Chief Justice of the criminal court, he dominated his two colleagues and ran the trial as if they were not there. Judges are supposed to be assigned by chance to the cases they will preside over, but it had been my experience that in *causes célèbres,* where the district attorney's office desperately wants a conviction, Murtagh is apt to be assigned the case.*

WILLIAM HELLERSTEIN: Murtagh had the reputation of being a judge who was in bed with the prosecutors.

—

---

*He was also assigned "by chance" to preside over the felony criminal trial in the "Panthers 21" case. This was one of the longest trials on record, but the jury acquitted all twenty-one defendants on all counts, after deliberating for only an hour and a half. (Author interview with Professor William Hellerstein of Brooklyn Law School, former Legal Aid Society lawyer, and lawyer for Howard Solomon.)

On the following evening, April 3, just before Bruce's ten P.M. show, siren sounds filled the night air of Greenwich Village, and a squad of police officers, in uniform and civilian clothes, arrived at 152 Bleecker Street. They entered the coffeehouse and arrested Bruce and Howard Solomon in Bruce's dressing room. From there the prisoners were taken to the Charles Street police station, where they were booked, then placed in the Tombs' Yard for a couple of hours, until they were released on bail. Their trial was set for June 16.

RICHARD H. KUH: This once effective panjandrum of social protest . . . was arrested in Greenwich Village's Cafe Au Go Go on Friday evening, April 3, 1964, shortly before he was to begin the first of the evening's twice nightly performances. The police had acted, executing an arrest warrant, after a New York County grand jury had leveled criminal charges. Along with Bruce, the cafe's proprietor, Howard Solomon, a pleasant low-pressure, young stockbroker turned impresario, had been arrested. Both were charged with presenting obscene and indecent performances, in violation of New York State's penal statutes. . . . At the conclusion of another show, on April 7, Bruce was rearrested.*

MARTIN GARBUS: One factor that should discourage the fair-minded prosecutor or grand jury from beginning a criminal proceeding is the certainty of reversal. Most of the appellate lawyers in Hogan's office said a conviction of Bruce would not stand up on appeal; yet they could not convince Kuh and Hogan. Kuh said the key question in prosecuting an obscenity offense was the possibility (not the probability) that the conviction would be upheld. This test allows the State to subject people like Lenny Bruce to harassment, arrests and enormous legal fees. The combination can break the strongest of men and Bruce was not that.

RICHARD H. KUH: Lenny Bruce's principal ploy for popular support was a "manifesto" publicized by a release to the papers for use on Sunday, June 14, 1964.

———

On June 14, two days before the trial began, New York newspapers carried the story that a manifesto protesting Bruce's prosecutions had been signed by one hundred authors, editors, publishers, booksellers, poets, entertainers, dancers, actors, photographers, screenwriters, professors, critics, cartoonists, filmmakers, painters, and singers, and by theologian Reinhold Niebuhr. The manifesto charged that the arrests of Lenny Bruce by the New York police constituted "a violation of civil liberties as guaranteed by the first and fourteenth amendments to the Constitution of the United States."

———

*My files contain a portion of a lengthy document that Lenny Bruce prepared, describing his New York arrest in his own words. The entire document is reproduced in the endnotes to this chapter. What Bruce said there provides insight into what "the law in action" may be like when applied to "the artist on the street," and how Bruce felt about that.

The protest letter was organized by the poet Allen Ginsberg, who served as a sort of community switchboard for the beats who had recently settled into the Lower East Side. This group bombarded Ginsberg with complaints that the city's Department of Licenses, the state's Division of Motion Pictures, the Police Department's vice squad, and the city's fire and municipal building authorities were engaged in a campaign to drive beat artists to the wall. They had padlocked theatres, closed down coffeehouses where poetry readings were held, broken up gatherings, and made arrests. The month before Bruce was arrested, the filmmaker Jonas Mekas, founder and indefatigable supporter of the underground art-film movement in New York and of the Film-Makers Cooperative, had been arrested, tried, and convicted for publicly showing Jack Smith's motion picture *Flaming Creatures,* "which offered fleeting glimpses of limp sex organs."* (This was one of the films that Justice Abe Fortas would later vote to free, when the case got to the Supreme Court—an act for which he was savaged by Senator Strom Thurmond at the hearings held to consider Fortas's nomination to serve as the Court's next chief justice.) The purpose of Allen Ginsberg's manifesto was to stop "the harassment of the arts" in New York by mobilizing liberal public opinion against the Bruce prosecution.

RICHARD H. KUH: Emitting howls of protest, brigades of absolutists in the war on censorship joined the avant-garde, who the month before had been outraged by Jonas Mekas' Village arrest for exhibiting *Flaming Creatures.*

ALBERT GOLDMAN: The men who conceived and executed the New York prosecution of Lenny Bruce were not foolish bigots. . . . Hogan and Kuh were moral conservatives who could see the future clearly—probably a lot more clearly than Lenny Bruce and his befuddled allies!—and were determined to muster all the opposition they could muster. Theirs was a perfectly understandable and respectable aversion to change: the pity of it was that the man they selected for their test case was the last person in the world whom they should have treated as the bellwether of the avant-garde.

Lenny Bruce was, in his own terms, just as moralistic, conservative and "uptight" as Judge Murtagh and Assistant D.A. Kuh. From the very beginning of the trial, he felt a secret affinity with these men and a secret aversion to his long-hair hippie and short-hair libbie supporters. Lenny was an alienated conservative, a typical satirist seeking revenge for outraged moral idealism through techniques of shock and obscenity as old as Aristophanes and Juvenal. All satirists are conservatives. . . .

Lenny Bruce was a man with an almost infantile attachment to everything that was sacred to the American lower-middle class. He believed in romantic love and marriage and fidelity and absolute honesty and incorrupt-

---

*Mekas more recently founded, and now runs, the Anthology Film Archives in New York. When the IRS in the mid-1960s closed down Julian Beck and Judith Malina's Living Theatre, Mekas and the theatre group found a way to get back in so that Mekas could shoot a film of the Living Theatre's "last performance" there. (Author interview with Jonas Mekas.)

ibility—all the preposterous absolutes of the unqualified conscience. . . . Lenny doted on human imperfection: sought it out, gloated over it—but only so he could use it as a *memento mori* for his ruthless moral conscience. . . . The attempt to make Lenny superior to morality, to make him a hippie saint or a morally transcendental *artiste,* was tantamount to missing the whole point of his sermons, which were ferociously ethical in their thrust and firmly in touch with all the conventional values.

—

Like many artistic works, Lenny Bruce's monologues were frequently ambiguous and open to divergent interpretations. One of the bits for which he was prosecuted and convicted in New York involved Bruce's satirical moral condemnation of the "family" child molester who, unlike the "stranger" kind, knows how to get away with it. In Bruce's transcription of the taped Cafe Au Go Go performance of April 7, 1964, it is called "Uncle in Quotes":

LENNY BRUCE:
Lawyer
The child molester, his crime, he's bereft of dialogue. If the child molester would speak his lines thusly, he would never get arrested.
Uncle in Quotes
Come're, Ruthie, come're to your Uncle Willie. Look at those apples on her, twelve years old. She's gonna have to get a BRAsserie, soon. Let your Uncle Willie, tickle ickle ickle you. Watch her wiggle, wiggle, giggle, in Uncle Willie's ruddy palm. Don't tell mommie or you'll break the magic charm.

ALBERT GOLDMAN: The first day of the trial the courtroom was jammed with spectators. They were like the guests at a wedding: the pro-Bruce forces sitting on the left-hand side of the room and the anti-Bruce forces sitting at the right.

—

Many of those who crowded the courtroom were sightseers: beats and hippies in long hair and scuffle clothes, courthouse loungers, people who had come in from other parts of the courthouse to watch the legal spectacle called The People versus Lenny Bruce. It was said that from time to time D.A. Hogan dropped by to see how things were going and to chase back to work any young A.D.A.s he saw observing the trial. Although it is customary for junior A.D.A.s to observe important cases, Hogan reputedly threatened to fire any lawyer on his staff—including even prize junior A.D.A.s from Ivy League law schools like Yale and Harvard—who might have been antipathetic to his prosecution of Bruce.

MARTIN GARBUS: Due to the number of spectators, the case had been transferred . . . to one of the larger courtrooms usually reserved for more serious crimes. This large courtroom, with its lofty ceilings, twenty-foot-high windows, and unusual number of attendants, bailiffs, and police, seemed only to emphasize the prosecution's sense that Lenny had committed a monstrous crime.

———

Present at the start of the trial were reporters from the AP and UPI, *Newsweek* and *Time, The New York Times,* the *Daily News,* the *New York Post,* and *The Herald Tribune,* among others.

ALBERT GOLDMAN: The intellectual journals had also sent some people to cover the trial, choosing their writers almost tongue in cheek. Philip Roth had an open assignment from the *New York Review of Books.* Jules Feiffer had come as an observer but was also looking for material to use in his strip in the *Village Voice.* * I was covering the trial for the *New Republic.* There were also artists sketching the action for these same magazines, as well as poets like Allen Ginsberg and Peter Orlovsky. . . .

Every other second, the reporters cast curious looks at the defense table, where the object of all this hullabaloo was seated. They saw a small neatly bearded man dressed in well-scrubbed Levis with high white boots and an obsequious manner. Lenny had come with a complete kit of legal tools: yellow-lined pads and Magic Markers and clench-back notebooks filled with clippings and documents neatly protected by cellophane. He struck you as a kid at his first day in grade school with a new pencil case and a plaid book bag.

———

All of Bruce's courtroom paraphernalia may not have been quite so innocent. Goldman believed Bruce had hidden a hand grenade under the counsel table where he sat; he would move as though to lob it into his judges' laps whenever Chief Judge Murtagh made a ruling adverse to him. † Also, according to Goldman, a sophisticated tape recorder was built into the professional-looking attaché case that Bruce brought with him to counsel's table every day; he bugged the performances of those who had bugged his.

LENNY BRUCE: Now, in New York, no jury trial. Yeah, strange. ‡ They had a three-judge bench, cause it's a misdemeanor. Colored judge, Irish judge, English judge. Alright . . . §

———

*He later testified as an expert on Bruce's behalf.

†Albert Goldman (from the journalism of Lawrence Schiller), *Ladies and Gentlemen: Lenny Bruce!!!* (1971), 435. I suppose this may have been feasible in those days. A few years later, incidents of courtroom violence had prompted the courts to install security measures.

‡An attempt by Bruce's lawyers to secure Bruce a jury of his peers failed, the judges ruling that there was no statutory or constitutional right to a jury trial in Bruce's misdemeanor case. The maximum punishment for a single misdemeanor offense at that time was a year in jail. Later, in *Baldwin* v. *New York* (399 U.S. 66), the Supreme Court ruled that the withholding of the right to a jury trial from a defendant in such a case was unconstitutional. The brilliant Legal Aid lawyer William Hellerstein was the lawyer who successfully handled the *Baldwin* case.

§Kenneth M. Phipps was the "colored" judge, John M. Murtagh the Irish judge, and J. Randall Creel the English judge.

Although Bruce's three judges—John M. Murtagh, J. Randall Creel, and Kenneth M. Phipps—were judges regularly sitting in the Criminal Court of the County of New York, and thus were at a low echelon in the judicial apparatus, they were not incompetent to deal with what Harry Kalven called the "metaphysics of the law of obscenity" as it was expounded by the Supreme Court at this time. Nevertheless, of Bruce's three judges, only Creel appeared to be openminded and evenhanded in conducting the trial and reaching decision. Only he seems to have been conscientious enough to acknowledge the complexity of the basic question presented by Bruce's prosecution: Were Bruce's performances at the Cafe Au Go Go suppressible obscenity, or were they speech protected by the First Amendment? Creel alone mentioned the liberalizing decisions that were handed down by the Supreme Court after Bruce's trial began but before it was concluded—the June 22, 1964, actions freeing *Tropic of Cancer* and *The Lovers*. And although Creel expressed his distaste for what those decisions signified for the authority of New York judges to decide such questions for themselves, he at least sought faithfully to discharge his duty as an inferior court judge to obey the rulings of the Supreme Court. And so Creel dissented from the judgment reached by the majority, in an opinion written by Chief Judge Murtagh, that Lenny Bruce was guilty as charged for giving three "obscene, indecent, immoral and impure" performances at the Cafe Au Go Go.

JUDGE JOHN M. MURTAGH: In [Bruce's] performances, words such as "ass," "balls," "cock-sucker," "cunt," "fuck," "mother fucker," "piss," "screw," "shit," and "tits" were used about one hundred times in utter obscenity. The monologue[s] also contained anecdotes and reflections that were similarly obscene. For example:
   1. Eleanor Roosevelt and her display of "tits" . . .

———

Here is a transcript of that bit, which was given to me by Bruce; like the Jackie Kennedy bit, it is serious and unfunny, but it is sweet and otherwise atypical of Bruce, except that it views a hallowed political figure from a taboo perspective.

LENNY BRUCE:

Admirer

Eleanor Roosevelt had the nicest tits of any lady alive. Here's one of the things I know, I'm gonna give to the Enquirer anyway. In fact I saw them by mistake. Standing on a box, looking in a window there. She turned around.

Eleanor

What are you looking at?

Admirer

Nothing, I was . . . trying to get my balance.

Eleanor

You've seen 'em haven't you?

Admirer

Seen what?

Eleanor

My tits.

Admirer

Yes, I have seen them. And they're lovely. And I don't mean to be disrespectful, but I never saw any other tits, I saw pictures of some once and in Rugget.*

JUDGE JOHN M. MURTAGH: 2. Jacqueline Kennedy "hauling ass" at the moment of the late President's assassination . . .

3. St. Paul giving up "fucking" . . .

LENNY BRUCE:

Moderator

. . . oh that I'll talk about just one minute, how that four letter word became verboten. Go back 2500 years and it's a field day and guys are showing off and giving things up for the Lord.

Isaiah

Alright let's see now . . . I'm giving up fifteen sheep and ten rivers and six oxen for the Lord that's my name.

Abraham (whistle)

. . . This guy's the capper. He gave up more for the Lord. He's the best man in the tribe.

Solomon

OK, I'll beat 'em. Thirty-five mountains, two rivers, and a fountain pen there, and a umm—see, some jelly, now there, ah, and a haystack, and that's a buckboard for the Lord, that's it for the Lord. That'll stay up there. Let's see you guys cap that. I gave up all the rivers nothing left to give away.

Moderator

And a guy called St. Paul kept looking.

St. Paul

You guys ready? Anymore, anymore takers? Anymore takers to give up something for the Lord? I'm ready to give my give, today. I'm giving this up for the Lord and let's see any guys cap that and see who's the best man in the tribe. F-U-C-K. . . . No more Paul. That's it.

Solomon

What the hell did he give up? F-U-C-K, no more Paul. Shit. You kidding Paul? You givin that up? For how long?

St. Paul

For ever and ever.

Solomon

Just to prove a point? That's bullshit. What the hell you gonna give that up for? Who's gonna cap that? He's the best man in the tribe. Why? Cause

---

*"Rugget" may be Bruce's rendering of the name of a girlie magazine of that time, *Nugget*.

he don't do it. You who do it is second best. You who talk about it, we'll bust their ass.

Moderator

That's it.

—

Murtagh identified the other Cafe Au Go Go monologues of Bruce's that he considered to be "similarly obscene," and then recited the judicial ceremony prescribed to find a person guilty of obscenity:

JUDGE JOHN M. MURTAGH: 4. An accident victim—who lost a foot in the accident—who made sexual advances to a nurse, while in the ambulance taking him to the hospital.

5. "Uncle Willie" discussing the "apples" of a 12-year-old girl.

6. Seemingly sexual intimacy with a chicken . . .

7. "Pissing in the sink" and "pissing from a building's ledge."

8. The verb "to come" with its obvious reference to sexual orgasm.

9. The reunited couple discussing adulteries committed during their separation, and the suggestion of a wife's denial of infidelity, even when discovered by her husband.

10. "Shoving" a funnel of hot lead "up one's ass."

11. The story dealing with the masked man, Tonto, and an unnatural sex act.

12. Mildred Babe Zaharias and the "dyke" profile of 1939 . . .*

All three performances of the defendant, Lenny Bruce, were obscene, indecent, immoral and impure within the meaning of Section 1140-a of the Penal Law. The dominant theme of the performances appealed to the prurient interest and was patently offensive to the average person in the community, as judged by present-day standards. The performances were lacking in "redeeming social importance." . . . The monologues were not erotic. They were not lust-inciting, but, while they did not arouse sex, they insulted sex and debased it. . . .

The monologues contained little or no literary or artistic merit. They were merely a device to enable Bruce to exploit the use of obscene language. They were devoid of any cohesiveness. They were a series of unconnected items that contained little social significance. They were chaotic, haphazard, and inartful.

—

Murtagh's opinion also concluded that it was obscene for Bruce to have "fondled the microphone stand in a masturbatory fashion" during the first condemned performance, and to have "turned his back to the audience and moved his hand outward and upward from below his waist in an obvious and crude pantomime of an act of exposure and masturbation." All of this

---

*Bruce's bits were collected and organized topically (e.g., integration and segregation, the law, obscenity, Jews, show business, the good-good culture, balling, chicks, fags, dykes, divorce, etc.) by John Cohen, and were published by Ballantine Books under the title *The Essential Lenny Bruce* (1967). The book is out of print.

was said to be obscene not because of any capacity in it to arouse sexual feelings in the audience, but because it was "filth," because "its predominant appeal is to . . . a shameful or morbid interest in nudity, sex or excretion." The opinion made no effort to support this conclusion, just as the prosecution had made no attempt to prove it.

MARTIN GARBUS: Judge Murtagh's decision was a travesty. There are many ways for a judge to write a decision without revealing his prejudices. Murtagh highlighted his by saying that Bruce had made a masturbatory gesture and by resurrecting an archaic concept of obscenity.

———

The only witnesses who testified to Bruce's masturbatory gestures were License Inspector Ruhe and Patrolman Lane; Garbus says he put on the stand twelve of the thirty-five people who attended Bruce's April 1 performance and all denied seeing the satirist make any masturbatory gesture. Murtagh had to discount entirely this rebuttal testimony in order to conclude that Bruce had done the "dirty" thing that Ruhe and Lane claimed they had seen him do.

As earlier indicated, Brennan expressly said that courts, in applying his doctrine, should not "weigh" the social importance of expression against its prurient appeal or patent offensiveness. The testimony at Bruce's trial showed that the actor's monologues could not fairly be said to be *utterly* without social importance. That should have been enough to dismiss the case against Bruce.

MARTIN GARBUS: Ephraim London and I spoke to dozens of witnesses and picked those that would give the case the substance we needed. . . . Our first witness was Richard Gilman, the literary and drama critic for *Newsweek*. His testimony that Bruce's monologues had artistic merit and indicated serious social concerns was treated by the judges with a mixture of indifference and disrespect. They were so outraged by Bruce's words that they could not believe there were ideas behind them.

RICHARD H. KUH: [D]efense witnesses heaped praises upon the Bruce shows. Many of the values they posted to Bruce's accounts seemed, however, to be more of their own contrivance than of that of their idol. For example, Bruce had referred to the "tits" of the late Eleanor Roosevelt. Critic Gilman believed this significant in that it showed Mrs. Roosevelt as, to all, "the mother of us," an interpretation seeing her as someone *greater* than the rest of us. The Reverend Forrest Johnson, Bruce fan and pastor of a Bronx church, saw in it quite the opposite: to him, it was "an attack upon our making idols of anyone," it showed Mrs. Roosevelt as just another person, built—and equipped—as were all other women.

MARTIN GARBUS: Our next witness was one the judges could not easily ignore. Her very presence jarred them. Dorothy Kilgallen, the longtime Hearst newspaper feature writer and columnist, had written warmly of

Bruce's talent years before. I called her a few days before the trial and she said:*

DOROTHY KILGALLEN: He's a brilliant man and I don't think his language is obscene, whatever that means. He is trying to stimulate his audience and make them think.

RICHARD H. KUH (to Ms. Kilgallen at the trial): Are you familiar with the portion of the script of the April 1st performance that deals with sodomy, sex with animals, dogs and cats and I think hippopotamuses and the SPCA—and then goes on:

"If you came home and found your husband with a chicken would you belt him, really feel bad, bad. A chicken, ah it's an odd bed, ah I felt like ah, I'm the last one to know."

Will you tell us the artistry, or the social value, or the merit, or the good, in the Bruce story of sexual intercourse with a chicken?

MARTIN GARBUS: I will object to Mr. Kuh's characterization of Mr. Bruce's performances. The testimony has already been that this is not a discussion of sex with animals per se, but rather a social comment made by the use of these symbols.

JUDGE JOHN M. MURTAGH: Objection overruled.

DOROTHY KILGALLEN: Well, sir, sodomy is in the Bible. If it can be read in churches I wouldn't rule it out for Mr. Bruce's act, if he cared to comment on it.

RICHARD H. KUH: Do you recognize beyond the intentions generally some cohesiveness within each book of the Bible?

DOROTHY KILGALLEN: Well, the Creation is pretty well written.

RICHARD H. KUH: I'm sure that the Lord is thankful to you for that comment. Now, could you tell us just what cohesiveness do you see in the Lenny Bruce script that you hold in your hands?†

DOROTHY KILGALLEN: Well, he goes from one subject to another, but it is always commentary on life, manners, morals.

———

Later, Kilgallen was asked to give her opinion on "what social comment Bruce was making" when he suggested "that when blacks finally did sit on juries they would convict whites as unfairly as they themselves had been convicted for years."

DOROTHY KILGALLEN: I think that in this case, Mr. Bruce is hopeful that the Negroes will get a better break; that because of the civil-rights law being

---

*Among the other expert witnesses for Bruce were: Nat Hentoff, Professor Daniel Dodson, Jules Feiffer, Herbert Gans, and the Reverend Forrest Johnson. In rebuttal, for the prosecution, there was expert testimony from Marya Mannes, John Fischer, Robert Sylvester, Professor Ernest van den Haag, and the Reverend Dan Potter, all of whom claimed that Bruce's performances were often "incoherent."

†Kuh argued to the court, and in his book *Foolish Figleaves?*, that the prosecution's witnesses showed that Bruce's shows were "incoherent," thus precluding "any serious likelihood of his tendering social criticisms that audiences might find enlightening."

passed, they will sit on juries, where they have never sat before. And like all people, they will at first commit injustices. Bruce is a great performer. I have enormous respect for him.

—

At this point, according to Martin Garbus, "Bruce put his head down and his hands in front of his face. I heard a muffled cry. Afterward Lenny told me how touched he was by Kilgallen's testimony."

MARTIN GARBUS: Miss Kilgallen, in the transcripts the words "motherfucker," "cocksucker," "fuck," "shit," and "ass" are found, isn't that correct?
DOROTHY KILGALLEN: Yes.
MARTIN GARBUS: Is there an artistic purpose in the use of language set forth in those transcripts in evidence?
DOROTHY KILGALLEN: In my opinion, there is.
MARTIN GARBUS: In what way?
DOROTHY KILGALLEN: Well, I think that Lenny Bruce, as a nightclub performer, employs those words the way James Baldwin or Tennessee Williams or playwrights employ them on the Broadway stage—for emphasis or because that is the way that people in a given situation would talk. They would use those words.
MARTIN GARBUS: Are those words also used in *The Carpetbaggers,* a book by Harold Robbins, presently being sold?
DOROTHY KILGALLEN: Yes.
MARTIN GARBUS: Can you tell of any other books that are being distributed that have the same language?
DOROTHY KILGALLEN: Norman Mailer certainly used all of these in his books, which were best-sellers. James Joyce and Henry Miller used them, as well as many other authors who are regarded as classical writers.
MARTIN GARBUS: Miss Kilgallen, I now refer you to part of Mr. Bruce's performance—a dialogue between Mr. Goldwater and a group of American Negroes, in which Mr. Goldwater can't seem to understand the words used by the Negroes—and I ask you what social comment is made by Mr. Bruce?

—

The "Goldwater bit" was not one of those that would be cited as obscene in Judge Murtagh's opinion, probably because of its obvious political and social content. Bruce often did it as immediate follow-up to another bit involving blacks, which also would not be condemned by Bruce's judges— the one called "I Was *Before* the Marches," which Bruce would perform before the federal court of appeals. Garbus wanted to focus on the Goldwater bit because it obviously communicated ideas of social importance. At the April 7, 1964, Cafe Au Go Go performance, Bruce had done versions of both.

LENNY BRUCE: Now Dick Gregory said to me:
Dick Gregory:
You want to make the marches?

Lenny Bruce:

Well, I'm going through a lot of litigations now. And ah. . . . Besides the marches are sloppy. Al Hibbler walks into people and I. . . .

Dick Gregory:

No, really man make it.

Lenny Bruce:

And then he told me about his wife, getting arrested, and pregnant getting thrown in jail. I said, well, it's sorta rough.

Dick Gregory:

It doesn't matter as long as we trick Whitey.

Lenny Bruce:

What?

Dick Gregory:

Trick Whitey. Fuck up boss Charlie. That's an underground phrase. . . .

Lenny Bruce:

Now how does Barry Goldwater know anything about that phrase, trick Whitey? Fuck up boss Charlie? They're cut off from everything. Arizona. Their god is the auto club. If a huge bloc of American Negroes would try to relate to Mr. Goldwater, and say. . . .

Negro:

Look here, Mr. Goldwater, don't shuck us tell us wus happenen you dig?

Goldwater:

What are they talking about? What was all that about?

Negro:

Look, don't jive us, tell us, be straight with us, don't lay no jacket on us. Wus happening?

Goldwater:

Jacket? What's happening? What, what the hell is he talking about? What are you people talking about?

Negro:

You jive motherfucker you jive!

Goldwater:

You jive motherfucker you jive?

Goldwater Aide:

Mr. President, please, please, before you judge these people, they're not obscene, per . . . perhaps and this, perhaps, is a term of endearment with these people. This is a new language, a new group that you're gonna have to relate to and that's it.

Negro:

You somethin else motherfucker, you somethin else. . . .

MARTIN GARBUS: Miss Kilgallen, I now refer you to page 11 of People's Exhibit 5A . . . to that portion relating to a performance of a conversation allegedly by Mr. Goldwater with a group of American Negroes, and ask you what social comment is made by Mr. Bruce. . . .

DOROTHY KILGALLEN: I think this part . . . indicates that Mr. Bruce feels that Senator Goldwater does not have much rapport with the Negro; that he's apart from them, as many people are in Arizona. That he doesn't speak their language and that they can't get through to him, but they do get through to Mr. Bruce and *he is with them*.

———

On June 22, 1964, just before the New York criminal proceedings against Lenny Bruce ended, the Supreme Court announced its dramatic decisions freeing *Tropic of Cancer* and *The Lovers* for the entire country. In *Ready for the Defense*, Martin Garbus argued that the doctrine announced by Justice Brennan's lead opinion for those cases was such that Frank Hogan "should have dropped the charges against Bruce." In Chicago, following those Supreme Court decisions—on a motion for reconsideration made by Harry Kalven—the Illinois high court vacated its prior decision affirming Bruce's conviction for the performance given by the satirist at the Gate of Horn; the court then held that Bruce and his monologues were entitled to be freed. The performances for which Bruce had been convicted in Chicago were not essentially different from the performances for which he was convicted in New York.

THE SUPREME COURT OF ILLINOIS: The entire performance was originally held by us to be characterized by its continual reference, by words and acts, to sexual intercourse or sexual organs in terms which ordinary adult individuals find thoroughly disgusting and revolting as well as patently offensive; that . . . it went beyond customary limits of candor, a fact which becomes even more apparent when the entire monologue is considered.

Our original opinion recognized defendant's right to satirize society's attitudes on contemporary social problems and to express his ideas, however bizarre, as long as the method used in doing so was not so objectionable as to render the entire performance obscene. Affirmance of the conviction was predicated upon the rule . . . that the obscene portions of the material must be balanced against its affirmative values to determine which predominates. . . . It is apparent from the opinions of a majority of the court in *Jacobellis* that the "balancing test" rule . . . is no longer a constitutionally acceptable method of determining whether material is obscene, and it is there made clear that material having *any* social importance is constitutionally protected.

While we would not have thought that constitutional guarantees necessitate the subjection of society to the gradual deterioration of its moral fabric which this type of presentation promotes, we must concede that some of the topics commented on by defendant are of social importance. Under *Jacobellis* the entire performance is thereby immunized.

———

This was the rule of law that Judges Murtagh, Phipps, and Creel were bound to follow, but that the former two ignored. Judge Creel alone followed the Brennan doctrine in his dissent:

JUDGE J. RANDALL CREEL: However distasteful it may be to a judge to apply such law, as I see it, it is my duty as a trial judge to do so. Accordingly, I must dissent and vote to acquit the defendants.

———

It is difficult to read Murtagh's opinion without concluding that the chief judge was what lawyers call result-oriented. He felt deeply that Bruce's speech was revolting and wrote an opinion that rationalized his feeling. In explaining the court's conclusion he spoke as though he were applying prevailing constitutional law to the concrete facts of Bruce's case, as shown by the evidence, but he appears to have misinterpreted the facts of record and brought to bear on Bruce's case instead his subjective feelings of hostility toward the actor and his expression.

Why did Chief Judge Murtagh and Judge Phipps fail to follow the law that in legal parlance "bound" them and was supposed to control their judgment? Richard Kuh defended Murtagh's decision in a book he wrote after the trial.

RICHARD H. KUH: Whether Bruce provided serious social commentary for his merry-making night-spot audiences, and whether, if so, his criticisms were of such "social importance" as to redeem him from charges of obscenity, proved the focus of expert testimony in the New York trial. On this point, the conflict was substantial.

———

Kuh had not read Brennan's opinion in *Jacobellis/Tropic of Cancer* correctly if he thought that Bruce's speech was entitled to freedom only if there was no substantial conflict of opinion regarding its social importance, and then only if it had social importance enough to outweigh or "redeem" its so-called obscene qualities.

He claimed that the Supreme Court of Illinois "went far further than the *Jacobellis* case compelled," and explained why the New York criminal court judges did not do as the Supreme Court of Illinois had done—set Bruce free.

RICHARD H. KUH: *First,* [the *Jacobellis*] case's language focusing on the phrase "utterly without redeeming social importance," and stating that *any* value redeemed, was only found in the opinion of *two* of the Justices.*

———

A great emphasis later was laid on this fact by Chief Justice Warren E. Burger, when he "revised" the Brennan doctrine in two 1973 obscenity cases, including *Miller* v. *California,* discussed later on. However, the legal import of the fact that only Justice Goldberg formally joined Brennan's opinion in *Jacobellis/Tropic of Cancer* is easily exaggerated. The reasoning in Brennan's opinion was properly understood by most lawyers and judges to

———

*In the Supreme Court's March 1966 decision in the *Fanny Hill* case, three justices—Justices Brennan and Fortas, and Chief Justice Warren—would share this interpretation.

represent the precedental principle of the cases,* and it was followed systematically by the lawyers arguing, and the judges deciding, later state and federal obscenity cases. As noted earlier, the Brennan opinion was the Court's lead opinion; it therefore contained the best—actually the most "conservative"—guide as to how the Court would decide any future case involving the same or a closely related issue. Brennan's lead opinion stated the *narrowest* of the grounds upon which the decisions of the majority to reverse the lower courts' findings of obscenity rested. Justices Black, Douglas, and Stewart had voted to reverse on broader grounds: Black and Douglas because in their view *any* criminal conviction or suppression based on "obscenity" was unconstitutional; Stewart because neither the novel nor the movie was "hard-core pornography." This clearly signified that the Court was likely in the future to award freedom to any allegedly obscene expression that satisfied Brennan's and Goldberg's narrower ground, that a majority of the Supreme Court predictably would act to reverse *any* obscenity conviction reviewed by them which contradicted the Brennan doctrine.†

RICHARD H. KUH: *Second,* even had a majority of the Justices expressly rejected the "balancing test," the word "importance" . . . embraces some qualitative considerations: not every *mention* of a socially significant topic is, necessarily, a socially "important" comment.

———

While this is true, it has little bearing on Lenny Bruce's performances, which plainly did more than "mention . . . a socially significant topic."

---

*The most narrow precedental holdings of the cases might be said to consist only of the holdings that the novel *Tropic of Cancer* and the movie *The Lovers* were constitutionally protected, and not obscene in the contexts of the particular circumstances of the cases. This of course says nothing about *why* they were held to have such protected status. Without Brennan's opinion, there would have been no reliable guide to this *why,* and almost nothing to go on for purposes of predicting what books and films were likely to be held constitutionally protected or obscene in the future. The considerable guidance provided by Brennan's plurality opinion in *Jacobellis/Tropic of Cancer* may be compared with the lack of guidance provided by the Court's later decision and *per curiam* opinion in *Redrup* v. *New York,* discussed in Chapter 26.

†In an interview with the author, Professor Peter L. Strauss of the Columbia Law School (a former law clerk to Justice Brennan) made the same point a little differently: "I would put it as it's respectable to regard [the non-majoritarian Brennan lead opinions in *Jacobellis/Tropic of Cancer* and *Fanny Hill*] as indicating the principles on the basis of which cases would be decided in the future by lower courts. . . . [T]here wasn't a majority of justices but you had a situation where there were observedly stable ends of the spectrum and so even if you couldn't say this is *the law* of the Supreme Court in holding such and such, you could say these are the principles on which the outcome [of a future case] would turn. . . . I think what could validly be said is that the . . . general experience of pornography law in the sixties was that it was a field for idiosyncratic expression of views. For whatever reason, the Court was unable to formulate propositions to which all or a sufficient number of justices would adhere, as an expression of the law, and that being so, the future wasn't bound in quite the way that the future is bound when you have five justices agreeing on a formulation of what the law is." It may be noted in this connection that Brennan's 1957 opinion in *Roth* did speak for a majority and that its principles, more than thirty years later, are still cited as "the law" by the present Court majority.

Bruce's bits on "I Was *Before* the Marches" and "Goldwater," for example, obviously expressed ideas dealing with the important social problems of race and politics. His bits "Giving It Up for the Lord," "Hauling Ass to Save Ass," and "Uncle in Quotes" plainly involved the expression of opinions and ideas dealing with religion and cultural taboos—all of undeniable social importance.

RICHARD H. KUH: *Third,* even had much of Bruce's . . . commentary been socially "important," *if* any of his objectionable passages were *completely* unrelated to such comments, nothing in the Brennan-Goldberg *Jacobellis* opinion barred a finding of obscenity.

Roth, however, had held that material challenged as obscene had to be viewed as a whole. Bruce's performance was not, as Kuh argued and Murtagh found, "a series of unconnected items" and "devoid of any cohesiveness." It was *a performance:* a staged piece with its own unifying principle in Bruce's artistic sensibility and ideas; and as Dorothy Kilgallen at one point observed, no one could deny it had one consistently unifying theme, sex, a topic that the Supreme Court, beginning with *Roth,* had certified to be a subject of legitimate concern and enduring social importance. Thus, a court would have no ground for denying Bruce his constitutional right to discuss that subject.

Judge Creel's dissent suggests that the two-judge majority of the New York criminal court that found Lenny Bruce guilty knew of the Supreme Court's June 1964 *Jacobellis* and *Tropic of Cancer* decisions and recognized their direct bearing on Bruce's case; yet Chief Judge Murtagh did not bother to mention them in his opinion. It is difficult not to conclude that the failure to acquit Bruce on the criminal charges was clear error and, in the light of circumstances that I will come to, probably known to be that. However, there was no redress other than appeal, and Bruce, having become effectively lawyerless after his conviction, never did appeal. The conviction of Lenny Bruce was a gross miscarriage of justice.

MARTIN GARBUS: The final irony was the action taken by the legal reporting services and the *New York Law Journal,* which reproduce for distribution to all lawyers the decisions of all trial and appellate courts. They resolved not to distribute Murtagh's opinion because, by its use of language, it was itself obscene. . . . Bruce's reaction: "Why don't they arrest Murtagh?"

In his federal papers Bruce sought to explain why what had been done to him in New York was unconstitutional:

LENNY BRUCE: As I have stated in my complaint, I not only present my views for profit, but I attempt (and I believe the attempts are successful) to influence and mold public opinion and direct the course of human conduct in the areas of religion, politics and social action.

The action of the defendants named herein has not only deprived me of my livelihood in this State, and of an outlet for the free expression of my ideas, but it has also deprived that part of the public which comprises my "audience" of the constitutional right to hear me and be influenced by me.

———

Bruce's papers spoke of the "ideas" that the performer held on matters of public concern—ideas about the war in Vietnam, Barry Goldwater, the Republican party, Soviet premier Khrushchev, and the nationalization of industry in Great Britain—some of which, he said, borrowing Justice Brennan's terminology in *Roth,* were "unorthodox—some controversial—some even hateful to the prevailing climate of opinion"; but "each of these ideas," Bruce continued, "are expressed by me for the purpose of bringing about political and social changes." Bruce here showed the understanding of a self-tutored layman regarding how the constitutional law of freedom of expression works.

LENNY BRUCE: It is not as if a particular playlet or particular book had been declared obscene and the author was free to perform other playlets or write other books. The ideas I have are now imprisoned within me, and unless this Court acts, will not be permitted expression. . . .

Under the law, before a judge can stop a performance and arrest the performer, he has to be shown the performance is obscene.* What I'm doing is the other way around. But I'll have to show you some of what I'm doing.

———

It was no use. On December 14, Bruce's appeal from the federal district court's denial of his request for an injunction against those who had "restrained his freedom of speech" was denied by the appellate panel, Judges Henry Friendly, Paul Hays, and Thurgood Marshall.

On December 21, 1964, just seven days after that, Bruce's sentencing hearing took place. The performer reportedly entered the New York criminal courthouse where he had been tried wearing a dirty blue trench coat over torn, faded blue dungarees and a blue-striped T-shirt.

MARTIN GARBUS: His shoulders were hunched, his hands in his pockets. He looked at the room as if he were trying to memorize it.

———

Bruce droned at his three trial judges for about an hour.

ALBERT GOLDMAN: The ears of his judges were flooded by an endless succession of cases, precedents, arguments, analogies and reflections which gradu-

———

*Here, Bruce was legally correct. The Supreme Court had made it clear by then that presumptively protected expression—a movie or a book, for example—could not constitutionally be seized, or its disseminator be stopped from disseminating it, without a *prior judicial* hearing; the New York arrests of Bruce, made without any advance judicial hearing, theoretically did not, but practically did, prevent him from continuing to speak. What Bruce was doing in court was "the other way around" because he was showing the court his performance *after* his performing had been stopped.

ally turned into a surrealistic patter in which the listener was idly struck by the most incongruous words and images. . . .

LENNY BRUCE: St. Paul . . . fucking . . . Murtagh . . . celibacy . . . Ruhe . . . adultery . . . *The Miracle* . . . *Burstyn* v. *Wilson,* 343 U.S. . . . Mr. Justice Roberts . . . *Cantwell* v. *Connecticut,* 310 U.S. . . . my note . . . gravamen . . . lust-inciting . . . *Tropic of Cancer* . . . St. John Stevas, one of the soundest and sanest of today's writers on the law of obscenity . . . *Manual Enterprises* . . . *People* v. *Fritch,* 13 New York and 119, 127 . . . *Enterprises* v. *Day* . . . homosexual magazine . . . the indecent, the disgusting, the revolting . . . nudity or excretion . . . ellipsis symbol . . . *Webster's New International Dictionary* . . .

———

When Bruce finally ran out of words, or realized his state of confusion, he sat down; and prosecutor Richard Kuh stood up. Kuh asked for Bruce's immediate imprisonment, commenting on Bruce's "notable lack of remorse" in going on after his first show to do the same show again, and for a higher price. This provoked Bruce to cry out:

LENNY BRUCE: I am a Jew before this court. I would like to set the record straight that the Jew is not remorseful. I come before the court not for mercy but for justice—and profit is everyone's motivation in this country.*

———

When the short tirade expired, Judge Murtagh sentenced Lenny Bruce to spend four months in the workhouse. Never within memory had a writer or an artist in New York received so severe a sentence for his expressive activity. In fact, the sentence would never be carried out, because before it could be, Bruce jumped bail and left town and, later, he was dead.

Returning to San Francisco, Bruce worked at Basin Street West and a community center in Marin County; he made plans to play in Sacramento and Washington, D.C. For a while he "saw his old friends, made his old jokes and behaved like himself." Then, according to Goldman, "the insidious virus of the law started boiling in his veins" and on March 29, Bruce fell out of the second-story window of his San Francisco hotel. According to an account given to Albert Goldman by a friend of Bruce's, Eric Miller, who was with Bruce at the time, it happened this way:

ALBERT GOLDMAN:
"Spit in my face!"
"I don't wanna spit in your face."
"No, I want you to spit in my face."
"I don't wanna . . . I don't wanna spit in your face."

———

*The Supreme Court has only recently come to recognize that the fact that expression is commercially rather than noncommercially motivated should have nothing to do with its entitlement to constitutional protection. It may be recalled that Chief Justice Warren, among others, considered Sam Roth's "expressive behavior" particularly heinous because he made money at it.

"Spit in my face!" insists Lenny.

"O.K.!" shrugs Eric. "Tpwh!"

Lenny rubs the spittle all over his face. Then he starts taking off his clothes. Up there in the Swiss-American Hotel. Overlooking Broadway. At 3 A.M.

"Jesus! Put your clothes on, Len! The shades are all up and the people out there in the street are going to see you!"

"No, no, no! They have to know! They have to know where it is. It's *out there*! I have to tell them . . . it's *out there*!"

Lenny jumps up on the bed. Then he jumps onto the window sill. Standing there stark naked, outlined by the lights from the room, he starts shaking the big, old-fashioned French window. Once, he shakes it. Twice. Suddenly, the goddamned thing breaks open! Lenny topples out the window, head over heels!

Eric is up like a shot, lunging for Lenny's leg. He clutches his ankle for a second—but the weight is too much. His grip breaks. Lenny plunges into the darkness. Peering over the sill, Eric sees him hit the pavement, twenty-five feet below. Duhd! His body makes a sickening sound. Eric stares for an instant, aghast. Then he tears a blanket off the bed and darts out of the room. Down the steep narrow staircase he hurtles to the street. Out the door he bursts in time to see Lenny reeling to his feet. Christ! He looks pathetic under the street lamps. A fat, fucked-out figure of a man, struggling to stand upright. Eric rushes to Lenny's side and bundles him into the blanket.

"O.K., baby," he soothes, "everything's gonna be cool!"

"I love you, Eric!" Lenny sighs. "Jesus! I love you, man!" And he kisses Eric on the mouth.

Someone across the street has witnessed the whole scene. Already the cops have been called. When they speed up in their cruiser, they think they're nailing a couple of crazy fags.

"You motherfuckers!" Lenny screams at the cops. "You're all after me . . . but it's all right. You don't know where it is!" With that he makes a lunge for one cop's pecker. The officer grabs his hands and starts putting on the cuffs. Eric, meanwhile, is trying to explain what happened. He's frightened by the way Lenny's ankles are inflating like balloons.

"Motherfuckers!" Lenny screams. Then, suddenly, he bends over and whispers to Eric: "They're just trying to get me! They just want to take me and lock me up!"

"Oh, no! No!" says one cop, wise to the fact that Lenny is in shock. "We just wanna take you to the hospital!"

"I don't wanna go!" says Lenny. "I don't *have* to go!"

"Yes, but you're hurt!" the cop insists, as the sound of a siren comes up the street. The ambulance swings up to the curb, and the attendants grab Lenny, who swings at them like a punchy boxer. They strap him down on the litter. Then they load him aboard and speed off into the night.

The diagnosis at the hospital was "Complete transference fracture of the medial malleolus with some displacement of the right ankle. Bimiliar fracture with fracture fragment in satisfactory alignment of left ankle. Undisplaced fracture of the left innominate bone, extending through the acetabulum. Contusions, lacerations, etc., of the back, shoulders and head."

According to Miller, Bruce had done a somersault in midair and landed on his feet, smashing both ankles and driving his legs up into his hips, which cracked the bones.

ALBERT GOLDMAN: He had not struck his head on the pavement. That is what saved his life.

———

Weeks later, when he was recovering, Bruce told his former wife, Honey, that on the day he fell he was so high he was ready to fly out a window. He was high on the idea that he might get to play the Supreme Court, and, more important, on some grass that had been soaked in DMT, which a friend had laid on him with a note reading "Smoke this, till *the jewels roll out of your eyes!*" Standing on the bed, he demonstrated to Honey how he would address the Supreme Court: "I thought I could reach," he said, echoing an old junkie joke, "I thought I could reach the bottom."

On June 1, 1965, the petition for certiorari that I had filed on Bruce's behalf, in an effort to revive his unsuccessful attempt to have his monologues declared constitutionally protected, was denied by the Supreme Court; no reason was given. I had said to the Court: "Petitioner, shorn of his professional accoutrements, is an individual who seeks to speak his thought to audiences in the State of New York, and elsewhere in the nation. That he speaks about and laughs at American politicians, cowboy heroes, religious cults, and the metaphysical law of obscenity—in a cabaret, a coffeeshop, a nightclub or town hall—can leave him with no smaller freedom of expression than one who talks about such things from a church pulpit, a politician's platform, a union meeting stage, or a public park stand." The Court was unmoved. This was disappointing but largely predictable. Thousands of cert petitions reach the Court each term; the justices' clerks, most of them fresh from law school, often help screen those petitions. Only one out of ten or fifteen winds up being granted. The Court probably declined to grant cert in Bruce's case because of the policy against federal courts interfering with, or intervening in, state court criminal proceedings except under the most compelling circumstances. I was unable to make the Court see how compelling Bruce's circumstances were.

Toward the end of his career and his life, Bruce had grown so obsessed with the law that he would fuss over it, even in his shows, to the point where his art deteriorated. His bits lost spirit, originality, spontaneity, energy; they became boring, even depressing; often they did not provoke laughter or thought anymore. Although he publicly denied it, Bruce was a heroin addict, and near the end he would take anything for a high. He lost his sense of reality and no longer knew where he and his art left off and the rest of the world and the law began—the real-world law, which is not the same as the law in the treatises and case reports that Bruce sometimes spent days poring over. In the end, Bruce could not understand why the Law did not recognize him for what he really was, and not for what the Hogans and the Kuhs and the Murtaghs thought and said he was. But as Professor Karl Llewellyn long ago told his students and colleagues, the Law is what policemen, prosecutors, and, of course, judges in particular cases *say* it is.

About eighteen months after that fall from the second-story window, Bruce fell again. On August 4, 1966, Lenny Bruce fell off the toilet seat in the bathroom of his home "with the $100,000 view," near the top of the Hollywood hills, and crashed to the tiled floor and died. He had a needle in his arm. The police were called and came, and the radio flashed the news, and the press and TV photographers were allowed in by the police, two by two, so they could take pictures of Bruce's body, lying face down on the floor, naked except for the scrubbed blue jeans that were scrunched down around his white boots.

The coroner's autopsy said that Bruce died from acute morphine poisoning but "did not intend to kill himself." On the other hand, as Albert Goldman has pointed out, he had received a notice of foreclosure on his house on the same day, and his closest friends said he had been depressed, unresponsive, and apathetic for the past year and more. Bruce had been in constant pain from the time of his fall from the window. Also, he was $40,000 in debt to one or more of the congregation of lawyers who had represented him.*

The New York obscenity bust and the drugs were the main things that did Bruce in. One of the assistant district attorneys in Hogan's office who assisted in the prosecution of Lenny Bruce said this to Martin Garbus:

VINCENT CUCCIA: I feel terrible about Bruce. We drove him into poverty and bankruptcy and then murdered him. I watched him gradually fall apart. It's the only thing in Hogan's office that I'm really ashamed of. We all knew what we were doing. We used the law to kill him.

———

Lenny Bruce dreamed of doing his show, delivering his monologues, before the Supreme Court of the United States. He dreamed of winning a great battle for freedom of expression in the United States. He had an

---

*Seymour Fried, Russell Bledsoe, John Marshall, Sydney Irmas, Jr., Stuart Kagen, Albert M. Bendich, Ephraim London, Marshall Blumenfeld, John J. Brogan, Jr., Robert Ming, Harry Kalven, Jr., Maurice Rosenfeld, Melvin Belli, David Blasband, Malcolm Berkowitz, Charles R. Ashman, Larry Steinberg, Richard Essen, Alex Hoffman, Earle Warren Zaidins, Joseph Steck, and Edward de Grazia. With the exception of the author, all these lawyers were listed by Bruce on his record album *Lenny Bruce Is Out Again.* My representation of Bruce occurred after the album was released.

obsessive idea that he might master the law; for a while he imagined himself engaging in a legal mission to blow the whistle on the "whole law and order scene."

ALBERT GOLDMAN: Lenny Bruce will play the Supreme Court, and he'll knock those fusty old farts right off their swivel chairs. What a gas! What a show! Who the fuck wants to work the Fillmore when you can play the greatest court in the land and help save our country?

—

Near the end Bruce realized he would never play the High Court; he lost hope. He had believed in the Law and in the end it had failed him. His judges and lawyers had failed him and he had failed himself. He had been hounded out of New York, and he never forgot or forgave what had been done to him there. Or perhaps the New York defeat rankled so much because he had badly botched his own case. Even when he won, as he did, finally, in the Illinois Supreme Court, he did not feel victorious. Possibly no club owner in Chicago was brave or reckless enough to engage him, despite the grudging victory awarded him by the state's highest court. No doubt, also, to play Chicago—the Second City—was not good enough for Lenny Bruce. And when he lost in the Supreme Court, he found himself in the last stage of his Kafkaesque situation: the gates of justice appeared to have closed upon him.

After a despairing Lenny Bruce forfeited his right to appeal his criminal conviction, Howard Solomon, the operator of the Cafe Au Go Go, took an appeal from his, as an indigent person; in 1968, two years after Bruce's death, he won. His lawyer was William Hellerstein, provided by the Legal Aid Society of New York over the protest of Hogan's office, which unsuccessfully challenged Solomon's "poor person" status. In reversing Solomon's conviction "on the law and the facts," a majority of a three-judge appellate term court acknowledged as a controlling principle that "a book cannot be proscribed unless it is found to be *utterly* without redeeming social value," citing Brennan's opinion in *Fanny Hill.* The judges went on to find that the proof at Solomon's and Bruce's trial "failed to meet the requirements" of the law laid down by the Supreme Court because—as even Chief Judge Murtagh's opinion had conceded—Bruce's monologues were "not erotic," "not lust-inciting." Moreover, continued the court, disagreeing again and again with Murtagh, "integral parts of the performance included comments on problems of contemporary society. Religious hypocrisy, racial and religious prejudices, the obscenity laws and human tensions were all subjects of comment. Therefore, it was error to hold [Bruce's] performances were without social importance."*

---

*Dissenting judge Hofstadter sought to distinguish a "performance" or a "show," such as Bruce gave, from a book, like *Fanny Hill,* or a movie, like *The Lovers;* the latter were protected expression, he claimed, the former unprotected conduct. Bruce's monologues, he said, "con-

The decision reversing Solomon's conviction and posthumously exonerating Bruce's performances at the Cafe Au Go Go was appealed by Hogan to New York's highest court, the Court of Appeals. Once more Hellerstein argued on behalf of Solomon, and in 1970 the court affirmed the reversal of Solomon's conviction for producing Lenny Bruce's shows.

I recently spoke with William Hellerstein, the Brooklyn College law professor who was Solomon's Legal Aid lawyer. He talked about the decision in Bruce's New York trial, the one from which Bruce never appealed because he was broke and disillusioned with the law and defense lawyers.

WILLIAM HELLERSTEIN: I've never told anyone but my wife about this, but now . . . it had happened over twenty years ago . . .

After the trial of Bruce was over, I had a call from [dissenting] Judge Creel, who told me he was intending to resign from the bench. He led me to believe it was because of what happened in Bruce's case. He said Judge Phipps also wanted to acquit Bruce but that [Chief] Judge Murtagh threatened to assign him to traffic court for the rest of his term if he did.*

—

So instead of two to one to acquit, the vote came out two to one to convict Lenny Bruce, author, lecturer, and social satirist.

In 1974 Richard Kuh ran for election to the post of Manhattan district attorney against Robert Morgenthau, and lost. One reason was that many New Yorkers had not forgotten what Kuh had done to Lenny Bruce, and to the city's sense of artistic freedom.†

---

tained little or no literary or artistic merit. They were merely a device to enable Bruce to exploit the use of obscene language."

*Judge Creel retired from the bench on February 11, 1968. Judge Phipps died on February 5, 1968. On December 31, 1966, a few months after Lenny Bruce's death, Chief Judge Murtagh resigned from the magistrates court, having been elected to serve on New York County Supreme Court (also a trial court) effective January 1, 1967. Murtagh served on that bench until his death on January 13, 1976.

†Nat Hentoff, writing in *The Village Voice,* did not let them forget. See his series of articles entitled "The Idealistic [*sic*] Prosecutor," *The Village Voice,* February 14, 21, and 28, 1974. Robert Morgenthau recently wrote me that Hentoff's articles influenced his decision to run against Kuh.

25

Any Writer Who Hasn't Jacked Off

IN BOSTON, in the autumn of 1964, I met with Norman Mailer, John Ciardi, Allen Ginsberg, and other literary figures about the legal strategy for freeing *Naked Lunch*. The legal proceedings against the book had commenced nearly two years prior to the landmark *Cancer* ruling. I had decided not to bring William Burroughs into the Boston proceedings as a witness to *Naked Lunch*'s serious artistic and social motives because doing so would have given the attorney general's office an excuse to bother Burroughs with questions like: Have you ever taken illegal drugs? Been a heroin addict? Sodomized young boys? Killed your wife?

TIME MAGAZINE: He's the king of the Yads. He's not only an ex-junkie but an ex-convict* and by accident a killer. In Mexico, having acquired a wife, he shot her between the eyes playing William Tell with a revolver (the Mexican authorities decided it was imprudentia criminale and dropped the matter).

WILLIAM S. BURROUGHS: I had that terrible accident with Joan Vollmer, my wife. I had a revolver that I was planning to sell to a friend. I was checking it over and it went off—killed her. A rumor started that I was trying to shoot a glass of champagne from her head William Tell style. Absurd and false.

—

*Although Burroughs had been jailed by the time of this story, he had never been *convicted* of a crime; the implication that he had been was therefore false. Burroughs considered suing *Time* for libel but on my advice did not.

If it was a rumor, it was one that Burroughs started by what he had said to the Mexican police. On September 8, 1951, the New York *Daily News* carried an Associated Press story on page 3:

DAILY NEWS, MEXICO CITY, SEPT. 7 (AP):

HEIR'S PISTOL KILLS HIS WIFE

HE DENIES PLAYING WM. TELL

William Seward Burroughs, 37, first admitted, then denied today that he was playing William Tell when his gun killed his pretty, young wife during a drinking party last night.

Police said that Burroughs, grandson of the adding-machine inventor, first told them that, wanting to show off his marksmanship, he placed a glass of gin on her head and fired, but was so drunk that he missed and shot her in the forehead.

After talking with a lawyer, police said, Burroughs, who is a wealthy cotton planter from Pharr, Tex., changed his story and insisted that his wife was shot accidentally when he dropped his newly purchased .38 caliber pistol. . . .

Mrs. Burroughs, 27, the former Joan Vollmer, died in the Red Cross Hospital. . . .

Burroughs, hair disheveled and clothes wrinkled, was in jail today. A hearing on a charge of homicide is scheduled for tomorrow morning. . . .

"It was purely accidental," he said. "I did not put any glass on her head. If *she* did, it was a joke. I certainly did not intend to shoot at it. . . ."

Burroughs and his wife had been here about two years. He said he was studying native dialects at the University of Mexico. He explained his long absence from his ranch by saying that he was unsuited for business.

WILLIAM S. BURROUGHS, JR.: So Mama was tempestuous to say the least. One night at a party in our house when everyone was drinking or stoned, she placed an apple or an apricot or a grape or myself on her head and challenged my father to shoot. Bill, usually an excellent marksman, missed. "Accidental Homicide: Cause of Death: Cerebral Hemorrhage" (at least).

ALLEN GINSBERG: I was with Joan up to the day before she got killed. Down in Mexico, and I had just left, and Bill just came back. I'd taken a trip with her from Mexico City to Guadalajara, and my impression was she was suicidal. So this William Tell business, with him putting . . . or her putting . . . a shotglass on her head, I had the impression that she sort of involved him in that, so it was a two-way deal.

A few times during this period she'd almost killed herself, one way or another, driving too fast when drunk, or floating down a river, almost drowning; we thought we had to rescue her. . . .

Bill sort of felt that he was haunted by an evil spirit. At the time he thought his whole writing life was spent fighting off this evil spirit. That day before it happened, he felt this enormous, ominous depression, and didn't know what it was.

WILLIAM S. BURROUGHS: I had constrained myself to remember the day of Joan's death, the overwhelming feeling of doom and loss. Walking down the street I suddenly found tears streaming down my face. . . .

I remembered a dream from the period back around 1939 when I worked as an exterminator in Chicago and lived in a rooming house on the near North Side. I'd become interested in Egyptian hieroglyphics and went out to see someone in the Department of Egyptology at the University of Chicago. And someone was screaming in my ear: "YOU DON'T BELONG HERE!" That was my first clear indication of something in my being that was not me, and not under my control. In the dream I was floating up near the ceiling with a feeling of utter death and despair, and looking down I saw my body walking out the door with deadly purpose.

There was this cut-up I made in Paris years later: *"Raw peeled winds of hate and mischance blew the shot. . . ."* And for years I thought this referred to blowing a shot of junk, when the junk squirts out the side of the syringe or dropper owing to an obstruction. Brion Gysin pointed out the actual meaning: the shot that killed Joan. He said to me in Paris: *"For ugly spirit shot Joan because . . ."* I was forced to the appalling conclusion that I would never have become a writer but for Joan's death.

I live with the constant threat of possession, and a constant need to escape from possession, from control. So the death of Joan brought me in contact with the invader, the Ugly Spirit, and maneuvered me into a lifelong struggle, in which I had no choice but to write myself out.

——

For years, no one seemed to know why or how Burroughs had killed his wife, nor what exactly happened afterward. Genet, for instance, told me this:

JEAN GENET: He killed his wife. But since his family was very rich, they just put him for a while in an insane asylum and after that he could leave the United States.

——

The story Burroughs told to Victor Bockris and Andrew Wylie, in 1974, was different, sardonic:*

WILLIAM S. BURROUGHS: I was aiming for the very tip of the glass. This gun was a very inaccurate gun, however. . . .

We'd been drinking for some time in this apartment. I was very drunk. I suddenly said, "It's about time for our William Tell act. Put the glass on your head."

---

*The interview took place about ten years after the Boston trial of *Naked Lunch*. It was published in Victor Bockris, *With William Burroughs: A Report from the Bunker* (1981). Similar versions of the killing can be found in Ted Morgan's biography of Burroughs, *Literary Outlaw* (1988), 194–96, and in Barry Miles's biography of Ginsberg, *Ginsberg: A Biography* (1989), 136–37. Bokris is also the author of *Warhol* (1989); Wylie is a literary agent in New York.

I aimed at the top of the glass, and then there was a great sort of flash.
. . . Lewis Adelbert Marker was there. I said: "Call my lawyer. Get me out
of this situation." I was, as the French say, *bouleversé.* This is a terrible thing
that has happened, but I gotta get my ass outta this situation. In other
words, what went on in my mind was—I have shot my wife, this is a terrible
thing, but I gotta be thinking about myself. It was an accident. My lawyer
came to see me. Everyone's evidently overwhelmed by the situation, in
tears, and he says: "Well, your wife is no longer in pain, she is dead. But
don't worry, I, Señor Abogado, am going to defend you. You will not go
to jail."

I was in jail.

"You will not stay in jail. In Mexico is no capital punishment. . . ."

I knew they couldn't shoot me.

"This is the district attorney," he said. "He works in my office, so do na
worry. . . ."

I got over to the jailhouse. That was something else. I had this fucking
gypsy who was a may-or. See, every cell block in the Mexico City jail has
a may-or, a guy that runs the cell block, and he said: "Well we got decent
people in here and people who will pull your pants off you. I am puttin'
you in with decent people. But for this, I need money. . . ."

So then I was in with all these lawyers, doctors, and engineers, guilty or
not guilty of various crimes. One of my great friends in the jail was a guy
who had been in the diplomatic service who'd been accused of issuing
fraudulent immigration papers to people. And they were all just takin' it
easy. We're eating inna restaurant, we're getting oysters and everything. All
of a sudden the may-or gets on to this. He says: "This prick Burroughs is
getting away with something here. We're gonna send you over to the cell
block and I'm gonna put you in a colony where fifteen spastics will fuck
you!"

So I got over to the other cell block, and I said: "Well, this can't happen
to me, ya know. THIS CAN'T HAPPEN TO ME!" You get this tremendous sense of self-preservation. So I talked to the guy and I said: "Listen,
I'll pay you so much, ya know, not to do these things."

Then the may-or over in the other cell block finds out what I'm doin'.
He says he's cooled the may-or over there. And he's really putting the
pressure on. It was just at this point that I got out. My lawyer got me out.
In the nick of time, because they were really puttin' the pressure on. Some
guy—the may-or—came over there and said: "Listen do you wanna go in
the *colonia*? This is the place where all the big bank robbers go and everyone
is having big poker games. They got nice beds and all this."

I said: "Man, I don't wanna sit down and spend my life in this place, I
wanna get out of here!"

Just at this point my lawyer got me out. . . . I split about a year later,
because I had to go back every Monday by nine o'clock to check in. They
could put you back in jail. All these different people who put their thumb-
print on things because they couldn't write, cops and everybody, all had

to be there by nine o'clock. This woman would come by and say: "Hello, boys." A teacher. A bureaucrat. Of course while I was actually in prison I had to be very careful of my reputation. I didn't want to get known as a queer or anything like that, because that can be a murderous situation. I got some great human statements from the guards. One guard said: "It's too bad when a man gets in jail because of a woman."

———

Because of the controversy, I decided not to bring Burroughs in, and I asked Daniel Klubock, a young Cambridge civil liberties lawyer, to assist with the trial. Our witnesses would be Norman Mailer, Allen Ginsberg, and John Ciardi—our big guns—and lesser luminaries from the Boston-Cambridge area—scholars, literary people, sociologists, and psychiatrists whom Dan Klubock helped select. I did not care whether *Naked Lunch* could be shown to appeal to anyone's "prurient interests" or to go "beyond community standards"; I just wanted to place on the record evidence of the book's undeniable "social importance."

By the fall of 1964 the decision in the Florida *Tropic of Cancer* case had come down on our side, so I felt sure that if the Supreme Court was given the chance, it would find *Naked Lunch* constitutionally protected also, because it could not honestly be found to be "utterly without literary or artistic or scientific or other social importance." I decided to put witnesses on the stand who would testify not only to *Naked Lunch*'s literary and artistic importance but to its moral, psychological, and even religious importance.

In Boston, Allen Ginsberg helped me to work out in detail the strategy for defending *Naked Lunch*. We did it sitting on the floor with our backs against the windows of a funky sort of penthouse suite I'd taken on top of an old Boston hotel. Allen knew *Naked Lunch* backwards and forwards. I was worried about whether our trial judge would understand *Naked Lunch* when he read it, and what his reaction would be if he only dipped into it here and there. If the judge was unable to understand the novel—that is, to make sense of it "as a whole"—then the sexual passages might overwhelm him and he'd end up finding the book obscene. Allen's role at trial would be to help the judge understand Burroughs's book.

The trial opened with the lawyer for the State of Massachusetts, Bill Cowin, giving Judge Eugene A. Hudson a copy of *Naked Lunch*, in the hardbound Grove Press edition, and saying that the attorney general's case "was in." According to Cowin, that was all he had to do to earn a decision that *Naked Lunch* was obscene. It was, in fact, all that prosecutors usually did, even in criminal obscenity cases, and so I didn't argue that putting the book in evidence proved nothing, as I felt was the case. Instead, I put into evidence, as a preliminary matter, scores of articles, reviews, and commentaries on *Naked Lunch*, and a copy of Terry Southern and Mason Hoffenberg's novel *Candy*. This was a book that Maurice Girodias had published a few years earlier in Paris under his Olympia Press imprint, and that Walter

Minton of G. P. Putnam's Sons had recently published in New York; it was in all the bookstores. My plan was to let our judge see how seriously *Naked Lunch* was being taken by the literary community, and to give him some idea of the prevailing "standards of decency" in the fiction of the sixties. By then I'd met Terry Southern, who also wrote the screenplay for *Dr. Strangelove,* and thought he'd appreciate my use of his parody of *Candide.* My supposition was that Judge Hudson would read at least some of the hot passages himself.

TERRY SOUTHERN AND MASON HOFFENBERG *(Candy):*

"I want!" said the hunchback, with one hand on Candy's hip now undoing the side buttons of her jeans; then he swiftly forced the hand across the panty sheen of her rounded tummy and down into the sweet damp.

"Oh, darling, no!" cried the girl, but it was too late, without making a scene, for anything to be done; his stubby fingers were rolling the little clitoris like a marble in oil. Candy leaned back in resignation, her heart too big to deprive him of this if it meant so much. . . .

"No, no, darling!" she sighed, but he soon had them down below her knees enough to replace his fingers with his tongue. . . .

*"It means so much to him," Candy kept thinking, "*SO *much," as he meanwhile got her jeans and panties down completely so that they dangled now from one slender ankle as he adjusted her legs around his neck; and his mouth very deep inside her honey pot. . . .*

"Oh, why?" she begged, holding his face in her hands, looking at him mournfully. "Why?"

"I need fuck you!" said the hunchback huskily. He put his face against the upper softness of her marvelous bare leg. Small, strange sounds came from his throat. . . .

"Don't hurt me, darling," she murmured, as in a dream, while he parted the exquisitely round thighs with his great hand, his mouth opening the slick lips all sugar and glue, and his quick tongue finding her pink candy clit at once.

"Oh, darling, darling," she said, stroking his head gently, watching him, a tender courageous smile on her face. . . .

And as he began to strike her across the back of her legs, she sobbed, "Oh, why, darling, why?" her long round limbs twisting, as she turned and writhed, her arms back beside her head, . . . and she was saying: "Yes! Hurt me! Yes, yes! Hurt me as THEY *have hurt you!" and now her ankles as well seemed secured, shackled to the spot, as she lay, spread-eagled, sobbing piteously, straining against her invisible bonds, her lithe round body arching upward, hips circling slowly, mouth wet, nipples taut, her teeny piping clitoris distended and throbbing, and her eyes glistening like fire, as she devoured all the penitence for each injustice ever done to hunchbacks of the world; and as it continued she slowly opened her eyes, that all the world might see the tears there—but instead she herself saw, through the rise and fall of the wire lash—the hunchback's white gleaming hump!*

With a wild impulsive cry, she shrieked: "Give me your hump!" The hunchback hesitated, and then lunged headlong toward her, burying his hump between

Candy's legs as she hunched wildly, pulling open her little labia in an absurd effort to get it in her.

"Your hump! Your hump!" she kept crying, scratching and clawing at it now.

"Fuck! Shit! Piss!" she screamed. "Cunt! Cock! Prick! Nigger! Wop! Hump! HUMP!" and she teetered on the blazing peak of pure madness for an instant. . . .

When Candy awoke she was alone. She lay back thinking over the events of the afternoon. "Well, it's my own fault, darn it!" she sighed . . . for she had forgotten to have them exchange names.

The first Grove Press witness to take the stand was John Ciardi, who said he didn't consider *Naked Lunch* a great work of art but thought it "was memorable, serious and important and Burroughs was an author of talent and serious commitment." He compared *Naked Lunch* with Dante's *Divine Comedy*, which "also has its obscene passages and four-letter words."

JOHN CIARDI: When Dante dipped the sinners in excrement, he called it shit. In the *Inferno* there's a military grafter who signals his commander by making a trumpet of his ass and breaking wind, in imitation of a military trumpet. This is not unlike the "talking asshole" episode in *Naked Lunch*. There's also a passage by Dante where two sinners, frozen in ice up to their necks, eat the head of a third; and that's similar to a cannibalistic passage in *Naked Lunch*.

Norman Mailer was our next witness.

NORMAN MAILER: Burroughs has extraordinary style. He catches the beauty and, at the same time, the viciousness and the meanness and the excitement, of ordinary talk—the talk of criminals, of soldiers, athletes, junkies. There is a kind of speech, gutter talk, that often has a fine, incisive, dramatic line to it; and Burroughs captures that speech like no other American writer I know. . . . He has an exquisite poetic sense. His poetic images are intense. They are often disgusting; but at the same time there is a sense of collision in them, of montage, that is quite unusual. The artistry in *Naked Lunch* is very deliberate and profound.

Burroughs may be the most talented writer in America. I say that although I don't like to go around bestowing credit on other writers. *Naked Lunch* drew me to read it further and further, the way *Ulysses* did when I read it in college; as if there were mysteries to be uncovered as you read it. . . . The structure of the novel is imperfect. One reason we can not call it a great book like *Remembrance of Things Past* or *Ulysses* is the imperfection of the structure. There is no doubt as to Burroughs' talent; while that talent was, perhaps, excited and inflamed by drug addiction, it was also hurt. This man might have been one of the greatest geniuses of the English language if he had never been an addict.

Mailer was respectfully tendered one question by the judge:

JUDGE EUGENE A. HUDSON: I don't want you to feel hurt that I haven't read any of your books, Mr. Mailer, but in any one of those books did your style involve sex in the *naked* sense?

NORMAN MAILER: Nothing that could be compared to this, Your Honor. I write in a far chaster tradition.

———

Two other witnesses who appeared on behalf of the book were Norman Hollander and Paul Hollander, who were unrelated. Norman Hollander taught English at M.I.T. and was the author of several books of criticism and over forty scholarly articles. He had been trained as a psychoanalytic critic, and so I asked him to testify to the book's moral and psychological importance. In the course of his testimony, however, Hollander suggested that he considered *Naked Lunch* to be "a religious novel, about original sin."

JUDGE EUGENE A. HUDSON: What did you say?

NORMAN HOLLANDER: I said *Naked Lunch* is a religious novel about original sin. I was struck, Your Honor, by what John Ciardi said on the witness stand yesterday. If St. Augustine were writing today he might well write something like *Naked Lunch*. . . .

JUDGE EUGENE A. HUDSON: I don't follow you.

NORMAN HOLLANDER: I said that *Naked Lunch* was comparable in some ways to the writings of St. Augustine—in following the idea of original sin into every kind of human activity.

———

At that point—as Hollander later recalled the courtroom scene—Hudson, "who seemed to be your average trial court judge, a man of modest cultural means," took up his copy of *Naked Lunch* and held it between thumb and forefinger like a dead mackerel.

JUDGE EUGENE A. HUDSON: Do you mean to say, Professor, that the blessed saint would write something like this book!?

NORMAN HOLLANDER: Granted the difference in what a man writing a book of confessions would write about today, in St. Augustine's time it seems to me that his *Confessions* were, like Burroughs's book, a confession leading to a kind of repentance, although paradoxically the confession here appears in the introduction of the book rather than at the conclusion.

———

Dr. Paul Hollander was a sociologist with degrees from the University of London, the University of Illinois, and Princeton. He was teaching the sociology of literature at Harvard when the trial took place, and his role was to speak to what I thought of as the sociological-scientific importance of *Naked Lunch*.

PAUL HOLLANDER: *Naked Lunch* confronts the reader with the reality and consequences of drug addiction—a major social problem—without trivializing or softening them. Drug addiction is a type of deviance which claims the whole person, ultimately destroying him. The book is important not only because drug addiction is sociologically important but because Burroughs succeeds in demonstrating the impoverished social relationships of the addict as well as the interconnections between addiction and other deviant behavior, especially homosexuality. Burroughs's observations and information about drug addiction correspond to the scientific data on the subject.

———

Paul Hollander also plugged Burroughs's novel as a possible cure for drug addiction.

PAUL HOLLANDER: But Burroughs's narration is especially valuable because it comes from a person who's actually experienced addiction. And because it does not romanticize or glamorize drugs, but presents the inhuman brutal world of the addict in all its horrible, hideous, frightening and repulsive manifestations, the book should serve as a marvelous deterrent from addiction for any person reading it. The book presents invaluable information on a deviant social type and subculture.

———

He also pointed out a reason why Burroughs had to use four-letter words.

PAUL HOLLANDER: Burroughs's use of four-letter words is, of course, reflective of the way in which the underworld he depicts flouts social standards; it involves a symbolic expression of opposition and rebellion against society.

———

On cross-examination, the prosecutor sought to undermine Paul Hollander's credibility:

ASSISTANT ATTORNEY GENERAL WILLIAM I. COWIN: Would you say then, Dr. Hollander, that the sexual gymnastics of Mary, John and Mark, in the part of the book called "A.J.'s Annual Party," were meant to be a protest of anything in society?

———

Cowin was talking about one of the two sexual episodes that Rosset and Burroughs had once considered deleting from the American edition of *Naked Lunch*.

PAUL HOLLANDER: I don't believe so. . . .
ASSISTANT ATTORNEY GENERAL WILLIAM I. COWIN: Well, then, perhaps they have some Biblical significance: John, Mary and Mark? And the perversions they engaged in?
PAUL HOLLANDER: I didn't see any.

———

Judge Hudson would end up viewing those sexual gymnastics—according to the opinion he delivered—as passages of "hard-core pornography the author slipped in between the more intellectual passages." And in a sense maybe he was right.

WILLIAM S. BURROUGHS: Any writer who hasn't jacked off with his characters, those characters will not come alive in a sexual context. I certainly jack off with my characters. I can write sexual situations, very hot sexual situations. I don't get a hard-on, you understand. Bullfighters do get hard-ons in the course of a bullfight. So I have been told at least.

WILLIAM S. BURROUGHS (Naked Lunch): *On Screen. Red-haired, green-eyed boy, white skin with a few freckles . . . kissing a thin brunette girl in slacks. Clothes and hair-do suggest existentialist bars of all the world cities. They are seated on low bed covered with white silk. The girl opens his pants with gentle fingers and pulls out his cock which is small and very hard. A drop of lubricant gleams at its tip like a pearl. She caresses the crown gently: "Strip Johnny." He takes off his clothes with swift sure movements and stands naked before her, cock pulsing. She makes a motion for him to turn around and he pirouettes across the floor parodying a model, hand on hip. She takes off her shirt. Her breasts are high and small with erect nipples. She slips off her underpants. Her pubic hairs are black and shiny. He sits down beside her and reaches for her breast. She stops his hands.*

"Darling, I want to rim you," she whispers.

"No. Not now."

"Please, I want to."

"Well, all right, I'll go wash my ass."

"No, I'll wash it."

"Aw shucks now, it ain't dirty."

"Yes it is. Come on now, Johnny boy."

She leads him into the bathroom. "All right, get down." He gets down on his knees and leans forward, with his chin on the bath mat. "Allah," he says. He looks back and grins at her. She washes his ass with soap and hot water sticking her finger up it.

"Does that hurt?"

"Noooooooooo."

"Come along baby." She leads the way into the bedroom. He lies down on his back and throws his legs over his head, clasping elbows behind his knees. She kneel down and caress the backs of his thighs, his balls, running her fingers down the perennial divide. She push his cheeks apart, lean down and begin licking the anus, moving her head in a small circle. She push at the sides of the asshole, licking deeper and deeper. He close his eyes and squirm. She lick up the perennial divide. His small tight balls . . .

A great pearl stands out on the tip of his circumcised cock. Her mouth closes over the crown. She sucks rhythmically up and down, pausing on the up stroke and moving her head around in a circle. Her hand plays gently with his balls, slide down and middle finger up his ass. As she suck down toward the root of his cock she tickle his prostate mockingly. He grin and fart. She is sucking his cock now in a frenzy. His body begins to contract, pulling up toward his chin. Each time the contraction is longer. "Wheeeeeeee!" the boy yell, every muscle tense, his whole body strain to empty through his cock. She drinks his jissom which fills her mouth in great hot spurts. He let his feet flop back onto the bed. He arches his back and yawns.

Mary is strapping on a rubber penis: "Steely Dan III from Yokohama," she says, caressing the shaft. Milk spurts across the room.

"Be sure that milk is pasteurized. Don't go giving me some kinda awful cow disease like anthrax or glanders or aftosa. . . ."

GABRIELE B. JACKSON: My name is Gabriele Bernhard Jackson. I am an Assistant Professor of English at Wellesley College. I was the first woman Instructor in English at Yale University, where I taught a course in the novel and one in poetry. I obtained my B.A. degree at Barnard College, spent a year at Oxford on a Fulbright Grant, then came to Yale, where I obtained my M.A. and Ph.D. before being hired there. . . .

In my opinion the purpose of *Naked Lunch* is a two-fold portrayal of the addict's existence and of the society which draws its energy from values and relationships for which addiction becomes a metaphor. And Burroughs is making moral judgments in both his realms of depiction:

Junk, he says, is the ideal product, the ultimate merchandise. No sales talk necessary. The junk merchant does not sell his product to the consumer, he sells the consumer to his product. Burroughs thus identifies the motivations and relationships pertaining to addiction and our "free enterprise" society as equally evil. . . .

The book uses two techniques, as well, which can be called, roughly, realistic and surrealistic. The first, mainly in the book's opening section, provides real description of an addict's experiences; the second provides metaphorical description of behavior in our society. As the book progresses the two merge. . . .

Burroughs uses other techniques as well to direct the reader's moral judgment, for simply to state that what you hate is evil would not be, literally speaking, a very effective way to convince your audience that it is. To do this Burroughs allies the things he wants to devalue with things we have already devalued ourselves: excrement, ruin and decay, perversion.

He may detail the components of a disintegrated wife whom her husband fed down the Disposal; and so, among other things, comment on the destructiveness of marital relationships. He may present, as climax of a scene in Hassan's rumpus room, the invasion of a horde of lust-mad American women, characterizing the sex life of those whose existence is dependent upon their rumpus rooms. And he may show Mary devouring Johnny's face, feature by feature, and so suggest the predatoriousness of the modern American female.

WILLIAM S. BURROUGHS *(Naked Lunch): Mary: "No, let me." She locks her hands behind Johnny's buttocks, puts her forehead against him, smiling into his eyes she moves back, pulling him off the platform into space. . . . His face swells with blood. . . . Mark reaches up with one lithe movement and snaps Johnny's neck . . . sound like a stick broken in wet towels. A shudder runs down Johnny's body*

... one foot flutters like a trapped bird. ... Mark has draped himself over a swing and mimics Johnny's twitches, closes his eyes and sticks his tongue out. ... Johnny's cock springs up and Mary guides it up her cunt, writhing against him in a fluid belly dance, groaning and shrieking with delight ... sweat pours down her body, hair hangs over her face in wet strands. "Cut him down, Mark," she screams. Mark reaches over with a snap knife and cuts the rope, catching Johnny as he falls, easing him onto his back with Mary still impaled and writhing. ... She bites away Johnny's lips and nose and sucks out his eyes with a pop. ... She tears off great hunks of cheek. ... Now she lunches on his prick. ... Mark walks over to her and she looks up from Johnny's half-eaten genitals, her face covered with blood, eyes phosphorescent.

GABRIELE B. JACKSON: The technique is to find an image that revolts the reader from the metaphorical action; and the evil involved in the metaphorical action is always a version of victimization, of the use of one human being by another. One of the best examples is also one of the most spectacular scenes, that in which a mugwump subjects a boy to homosexual intercourse and simultaneously hangs him, snapping his neck. This incident is followed by a whole series of similar enforced homosexual activities and a whole group of hangings, apparently to the satisfaction of the onlookers. The image of a whole society corrupted by its eagerness to see one human being exert power over another is shocking and inescapable.

—

Allen Ginsberg was the last Grove Press witness to take the stand. In those days Ginsberg did not look like an aging professor, as he does today; instead, with his great shaggy beard, balding pate, and mane of long, stringy hair, he looked like the lord of the beatniks. When he took the witness stand in Boston to speak on behalf of his friend's book, Ginsberg wanted to make a good impression: he wore a white shirt and a figured tie for what I thought was probably the first time ever. As Ginsberg took his seat, Judge Hudson peered down at the poet from his bench and said stiffly, "Straighten your collar!" He treated Ginsberg like a schoolboy taking the stage to recite his lesson. The poet did what he was told, looked up at Judge Hudson, and said politely, "Yes, sir."

And then, responding to my questions, the ones we'd worked up at the hotel, Ginsberg mesmerized the courtroom. He has a magnetic, almost hypnotic, way of speaking about things that he cares about deeply. He talked almost without interruption for nearly an hour about the structure of the novel and about the social importance of its ideas. Citing chapter and verse from memory, he pointed out the ways in which *Naked Lunch* conveyed criticisms of the state's control over people—sexual control, political control, social control—and unraveled Burroughs's "philosophies" about the American police state, mass brainwashing, and the workings of modern dictatorships. He delivered detailed expositions of the "political" parties and groups portrayed by Burroughs—the Factualists, the Liquefactionists, the Divisionists—and their counterparts in modern American political life. He argued that in *Naked Lunch* Burroughs predicted and parodied anti-Negro, anti-Northern, and anti-Semitic Southern white racist bureaucrats. He said that the novel's unity was that of the cycle of drug addiction and withdrawal, and he credited Burroughs with having importantly influenced the work of many poets and authors, including himself.

Ginsberg said that *Naked Lunch* was "an enormous breakthrough into *truthful* expression of really what was going on inside Burroughs's head, with no holds barred," and that "it contained a great deal of very pure language and pure poetry, as great as any poetry being written in America today." He also insisted that the book's surrealistic mosaic style, its lack of plot in the traditional sense, its "shadowy" characters, its capacity to be "sliced into" almost anywhere, did not mean that it was missing a definite plan.

In the end, Judge Hudson discounted all the testimony and documentary evidence and concluded that Burroughs, "under the guise of portraying the hallucinations of a drug addict, had ingeniously satisfied his personal whims and fantasies, and inserted in this book hard-core pornography."

JUDGE EUGENE A. HUDSON: While we have to take the book as a whole, from cover to cover,* I am somewhat concerned as to whether or not an author has the license, poetic license, if you wish, to escape responsibility in his writing, so far as it concerns hard-core pornography, by describing it as hallucination. . . .†

Of course, what we are dealing with is a remarkable work when we refer to Dante's *Inferno.* That is a classic and we recognize it as such; but at the same time it hasn't the four-letter words and it hasn't the freedom of expression that we find in this book here. There are subtle references to, for instance, the anus is referred to in Dante's *Inferno,* and there are some sordid scenes described in Dante's *Inferno,* but it is done with the tone and with a literary flair that the most chaste person couldn't take exception to.

———

I interrupted the judge's musings to say that I did not know "how shocking the *Inferno* may have been when it first appeared."

JUDGE EUGENE A. HUDSON: In its day?

ALLEN GINSBERG: It was.

———

*This was required under Justice Brennan's opinion in *Roth.*

†In his introduction to the Grove Press edition of *Naked Lunch,* Burroughs said: "I awoke from the Sickness at the age of forty-five, calm and sane, and in reasonably good health except for a weakened liver and the look of borrowed flesh common to all who survive the Sickness. . . . Most survivors do not remember the delirium in detail. I apparently took detailed notes on sickness and delirium. I have no precise memory of writing the notes which have now been published under the title *Naked Lunch.*" Perhaps this was the source of Hudson's suggestion that Burroughs was trying to avoid responsibility for publishing hard-core pornography "by describing it as hallucination."

JUDGE EUGENE A. HUDSON: Well, history perhaps teaches us that it was shocking to people of that day.

———

"Yes," I said, "that's one of the points."

JUDGE EUGENE A. HUDSON: But what are we headed for? I want to know. My mind is entirely open as far as this book is concerned, but let's project ourselves into the era that Mr. Burroughs projects himself into in relation to these political parties that you refer to. Is it conceivable that in our lifetime, or in the lifetime of the next generation, that there will be no censorship whatsoever, so far as freedom of writing and publishing is concerned?

NORMAN MAILER: He was a big florid Irishman, and terribly cordial to me. Couldn't have been nicer. He didn't like Allen Ginsberg much, didn't like the look of him. But he was almost courtly with me and I remember feeling uneasy about that: he was being too nice. I had that experience over and over, in about three or four cases now, where the judges were very nice to me and we lost. So I get nervous when judges are nice; I figure that's the last bit of goodness they're going to give to you. They greet you cordially and say, "I'm so pleased to have you in my courtroom, Mr. Mailer," and after that, watch out!

Hudson was so friendly to me that he did rattle my brain a little. But I always thought it was insane. I thought there was no way we could win. I came from the gloomy days of the thirties and forties when you just never won those kinds of cases. There'd been the Woolsey decision on *Ulysses* . . . well, that was *Ulysses*. And I thought *Naked Lunch* was truly going to be seen as an awfully obscene book. Frankly, I didn't see any hope of winning; but then, on the other hand I did. Because [de Grazia was] so cheerful about it. And, you know, you get on a team and if everyone's saying we're not going to lose, you do try to win. But I wasn't surprised or shocked when we lost. I was startled when we won, when the appeal was won.

———

We lost the trial but won the appeal in the Massachusetts Supreme Judicial Court—because of the record of "social importance" that was made at trial. That was what Justice Brennan, in *Roth*, had implied would be *necessary* to win, and in the Florida *Tropic of Cancer* case had said would be *sufficient* to win, no matter how "obscene," how "prurient," how "patently offensive" a book might otherwise seem to be, because the constitutional status of a book could not "be made to turn on a 'weighing' of its social importance against its prurient appeal."*

In the argument on appeal to the Massachusetts Supreme Judicial Court, I tried to sum up and link the sometimes disparate testimonial themes and

———

*See Chapter 22.

messages of our witnesses concerning the book's organization: "*Naked Lunch* has a definite plan or plot line despite what a casual reading might suggest. It has an almost musical structure, and a special psychic logic which—however difficult to autopsy—can nevertheless not be disturbed or bowdlerized without defeating the novel's artistic design."

I also cautioned the court that the Supreme Court of the United States was prepared to correct mistaken conclusions by state court judges and juries that valuable literature could be found obscene. The Court, having recently corrected the Florida and Ohio judiciaries, would not hesitate to correct Massachusetts judges if they ignored the constitutional significance of "social importance."

On July 7, 1966, a majority of the Massachusetts high court ruled that *Naked Lunch* could not be found obscene under the doctrine adumbrated by the Supreme Court in *Fanny Hill.* Two justices dissented. One of them, Judge Reardon, said, "The book is a revolting miasma of unrelieved perversion and disease. *Naked Lunch,* in truth, is literary sewage."

Reardon also protested that the court's majority had "abdicated to literary experts" its responsibility to decide what was obscene—even though one of those experts, a reviewer for *Newsweek* magazine, had said that *Naked Lunch* was as obscene "as anything ever written." Reardon mentioned that even Burroughs, in his introduction to the novel, had said, "Since *Naked Lunch* treats this health problem, it is necessarily brutal, obscene and disgusting."

The Massachusetts Supreme Judicial Court majority did defer to the judgment of literary experts in reaching its decision, as required by recent Supreme Court opinions. The Massachusetts high court wrote: "Although we are not bound by the opinions of others concerning the book, we cannot ignore the serious acceptance of it by so many persons in the literary community." Here the majority was referring not only to those who had reviewed the book in newspapers and literary journals but to the literary figures who showed up at the Boston courthouse to testify in behalf of *Naked Lunch.*

It was apparent that the Massachusetts Supreme Judicial Court had ruled in our favor reluctantly. Like the Illinois Supreme Court in Lenny Bruce's case, they would have preferred to affirm the trial court's finding of obscenity. That was not, however, what the developing Supreme Court law said they were bound to do. So, obedient to the law as the Supreme Court, and particularly Judge Brennan, had expounded it, the Massachusetts judiciary freed *Naked Lunch.**

---

*In doing this the Court sought to qualify the scope of the freedom that *Naked Lunch*'s publisher was entitled to by reference to the (short-lived) "pandering" doctrine that had recently been announced by the Supreme Court in the case of *Ginzburg* v. *United States;* the Massachusetts Supreme Judicial Court said that its decision was "without prejudice to the bringing of new proceedings with respect to this book" if it should appear that anyone was advertising or distributing it in a pandering manner—i.e., "in a manner to exploit it for the

TED MORGAN: It was fitting that the final battle between First Amendment rights and America's puritan heritage should have been fought out in the city which made "Banned in Boston" part of the national culture. No book like *Naked Lunch* had been cleared before—why, it made *Tropic of Cancer* seem sedate. Since nothing that would come after it would come close in bad language and objectionable scenes, it would set the standard for what was not obscene. Thus *Naked Lunch* was the last work of literature to be censored by the Post Office, the Customs Service, and by a state government.* And, as we all know, today's dirty book becomes tomorrow's college textbook. . . .

The *Naked Lunch* decision also left the door ajar for hard-core pornography, which squeezed into the opening, and this raises the question of whether the right to be sexually aroused is guaranteed by the First Amendment . . . but that's another matter.

NORMAN MAILER: Every gain of freedom carries its price. There's a wonderful moment when you go from oppression to freedom, there in the middle, when one's still oppressed but one's achieved the first freedoms. There's an extraordinary period that goes from there until the freedoms begin to outweigh the oppression. By the time you get over to complete freedom, you begin to look back almost nostalgically on the days of oppression, because in those days you were ready to become a martyr, you had a sense of importance, you could take yourself seriously, and you were fighting the good fight. Now, you get to the point where people don't even know what these freedoms are worth, are using them and abusing them. You've gotten older. You've gotten more conservative. You're not using your freedoms. And there's a comedy in it, in the long swing of the pendulum. . . .

The *Naked Lunch* decision changed the literary history of America. It opened up the publishers. After that, American publishers were pretty much willing to print anything. I'd say after Burroughs was printed there was nothing to worry about anymore.

---

sake of its possible prurient appeal." (See Chapter 26 for a discussion of the *Ginzburg* decision.) The *Naked Lunch* case is reprinted in de Grazia, *Censorship Landmarks* (1969), 581–85.

*I.e., the last work of imaginative literature or other literature having any social importance and not containing photographs or other graphic material. Illustrated works of nonfiction were afterward effectively suppressed—for example, in 1982, when a photo-illustrated sex education book, *Show Me!,* was withdrawn from sale by its publisher, St. Martin's Press, on the advice of counsel, after the Supreme Court upheld the constitutionality of an arguably applicable New York child pornography law (the publisher's letter withdrawing the book is reproduced in the endnotes to this chapter); and in 1974, when the conviction of publisher William Hamling for mailing an illustrated brochure advertising his illustrated edition of the Lockhart commission's report on obscenity and pornography was upheld by the Supreme Court (see Chapter 28). It is worth noting, however, that the Court divided 5–4 in Hamling's case, and that in neither it nor the *Show Me!* "case" was the book itself found "obscene" or "pornographic" by any court.

26

Sex Life
of a Cop

NATIONAL ("LOCKHART") COMMISSION ON OBSCENITY AND PORNOGRAPHY (1970): The sexual content of paperback books published for the "adults only" market has become progressively "stronger" in the past decade, primarily because of court decisions involving books such as *Tropic of Cancer* and *Fanny Hill.* By the late 1960s, the "sex pulp" formula was relatively passé. A new breed of sexually oriented books came onto the market, in which all restraints upon both language and descriptions of sexual activity were eliminated. In many there was little more than a compilation of non-stop sexual activity.

The industry's criteria for "sex pulp" novels has been broadened and now includes any paperback which is badly written, edited, and typeset, and is apparently aimed at relatively poorly educated readers.

STANLEY FLEISHMAN: Those books were meant for the great uneducated reading mass who didn't want anything too fancy. They just wanted a quick read. I had a number of clients like that. I represented William Hamling. Also Les Aday, Saber Books. I learned a lot from Aday. He had been indicted in Grand Rapids and other places, and so one time I had him put in the back of his books—they were extraordinarily popular at the time—a blurb, like "The government says these books are obscene and they want to put the publisher out of business. What do you, our readers, think about it?"

And I had the letters come to *me* so that Les wouldn't be able to start sorting them or anything. And it was a real education for me and always stood me in good stead to keep me away from this elitism. I had hundreds of letters from folks out there regarding the books, and for them *this* was literature.

There's one that I'll never forget, it really hit me. He was a dishwasher and he worked the night shift and he got home to his hotel about two o'clock and picked up one of those books and he'd read it for an hour and relax and be able to go to sleep; and it was so real in terms of the guys out there.

———

Once the Warren Court freed *Tropic of Cancer* and *Fanny Hill,* the lower courts began to cede constitutional protection not only to Miller's embattled novel, Lenny Bruce's satiric monologues, and William Burroughs's *Naked Lunch,* but also to sex pulp literature of a type that previously had been considered obscene. And policemen and prosecutors were bound to follow suit. The fulcrum of the movement was, of course, the Brennan doctrine. For in the context of expression as sexually explicit as Miller's autobiographical novel, or as sexually repetitious as Cleland's *Fanny Hill,* some publishers and judges construed Brennan's language roughly to signify that no limit existed concerning what might be said or depicted in print about sex.* And so lower court judges skirted Brennan's invitation to distinguish protectable printed matter from unprotectable obscenity according to whether it was or was not "utterly" without social value,† and freed books, regardless of their lack of merit, if they were not as "dirty" as, or not more sexually explicit than, *Tropic of Cancer* or *Fanny Hill.* This did not necessarily involve an incorrect reading of those decisions because—as Brennan had taken pains to make clear—a book, magazine, or movie was not to be branded obscene unless it satisfied *all three* criteria of his three-pronged doctrine: (a) the material, taken as a whole, appealed to a prurient interest in sex; (b) it was patently offensive and affronted contemporary national standards of decency; and (c) it was utterly without redeeming social value. And there was to be no "weighing" of prurient appeal and patent offensiveness against social value. That the Supreme Court had treated *Tropic of Cancer* and *Fanny Hill* as constitutionally protected and not obscene was interpreted by some courts to mean that neither novel breached national community standards of decency (although this was not necessarily the meaning of either decision); thus, they reasoned, if a novel was no "dirtier" than those novels, it should not be found to contravene the "patently offensive" prong of the Brennan

———

*Before Brennan took judicial notice of the social importance of sex, Dean William Lockhart (chairman of the National Commission on Obscenity and Pornography) had done so: Sex, he said, "is an area of life that immediately concerns all of mankind. It creates problems that vitally affect most individuals. It is an area in which man has often groped in the dark, because of periodic taboos on intelligent discussion." Lockhart and McClure, "Literature, the Law of Obscenity and the Constitution," 38 *Minnesota Law Review* 295 (1954), 361–62.

†In his book *The End of Obscenity,* lawyer Charles Rembar suggested that a significantly greater measure of freedom was afforded literature when Justice Brennan, in the *Fanny Hill* case (which Rembar argued), used the term "social value" instead of "social importance." But I have found no indication of any such difference in the cases, and to my knowledge neither Justice Brennan nor any other member of the Court ever suggested the terms were not interchangeable. Justice Brennan used "social value" in the *Fanny Hill* case but "social importance" in the *Roth, Jacobellis,* and *Gerstein* cases. Second Circuit Judge Paul R. Hays used the term "social value" in the *I Am Curious—Yellow* case, which I argued. The term "worthless" was used by Professor Kalven in his influential article in the 1960 *Supreme Court Review,* and by the California Supreme Court in *Zeitlin* v. *Arnebergh,* when it freed *Tropic of Cancer.* I used both "worthless" and "importance" in the briefs I submitted to the Supreme Court in *Tropic of Cancer* cases arising from California and Florida.

doctrine, and could not be found obscene, even if (unlike *Tropic of Cancer* or *Fanny Hill*) it *was* "utterly without redeeming social value."

Had the liberating effects of the Court's 1964 and 1966 obscenity decisions been limited by the federal and state judiciaries to meritorious literature and films, there probably would have been no right-wing backlash of the sort that in 1970 struck down Justice Abe Fortas, as described in the chapter that follows. But these decisions had the effect of encouraging the publication of "trashier," "sexier," and more "pornographic" printed material, and triggered the judicial freeing of pulp sex paperback books, magazines, and films that previously would certainly have been condemned. This, in turn, persuaded policemen and prosecutors of the uselessness of bringing criminal proceedings against the producers and distributors of such material.

In September 1964, less than three months after the Supreme Court freed *Tropic of Cancer,* the conviction of a Chicago bookdealer for selling the paperback books *Campus Mistress* and *Born To Be Made* to an undercover police officer was reversed by the Illinois Supreme Court, saying: "It is difficult to comprehend how this Court could hold the books here involved to be obscene, while *Tropic of Cancer* is held to be not obscene."* The next year the same court reversed the conviction of a dealer who had sold seven paperbacks—*Instant Love, Marriage Club, Love Hostess, The Shame of Jenny, High School Scandal, Her Young Lover,* and *Cheater's Paradise*—which police, prosecutors, and lower court judges had found obscene. To the Illinois high court, these soft-core pornographic books were no more offensive than the others:

THE SUPREME COURT OF ILLINOIS: The revolting language and "dirty words" of *Tropic of Cancer* are not present here. . . . no cunnilingus or oral genital contact is described and none is involved; there is no masturbation, flagellation, masochism or acts of sadism; no male homosexual conduct is involved, and no voyeurism is discussed. There are no transvestite episodes and several of the incidents of lesbianism are "disgusting" to the neophyte partner.

———

Conscientious attempts by lower court judges to apply the Brennan doctrine led some of them to look more to what the Supreme Court had *done* than to what it had *said.* In July 1965, for instance, a year and a month after the *Tropic of Cancer* decision, Judge Leonard P. Moore of the prestigious federal Second Circuit Court of Appeals in New York threw out the conviction of sex-pulp publisher Irving Klaw for using the mails to market droves of formula obscene books, including *Sorority Girls, Girls Stringent*

Campus Mistress was about a seventeen-year-old girl who fell in love with beatniks at a summer resort, was photographed nude while drunk, had lesbian advances made to her, but eventually returned home. *Born To Be Made* told the story of a young girl who, while a senior in high school, seduced several boys and one teacher; she later became the mistress of a traveling salesman and had other affairs, but finally married and with the help of her husband tried to solve her drinking problem.

Initiation, and *Girls Concentration Camp Ordeals.** Moore apologized to the legal community for freeing Klaw with the observation that "the climate of judicial opinion had changed"; he also suggested that it was beyond him to see how a judicial system "that puts its permissive stamp of approval upon such books as *Tropic of Cancer* and *Fanny Hill†* . . . should then incarcerate [Klaw] for disseminating and publicizing material which might or might not . . . appeal to someone's 'prurient interest.' " Of course, the judicial system might intelligently do just that if Klaw's material appealed to prurient interests at least as much as *Cancer* did and was at least as offensive to national standards of decency *but,* unlike *Cancer,* was utterly without redeeming social importance. However, as noted, some judges did not make this distinction.

In 1966, the highest court of Illinois also relied on *Tropic of Cancer* to reverse the obscenity conviction of a Cook County bookseller, Charles Kimmel, for selling *The Sex Addicts.* This pulp sex novel told "of a vacation cruise to tropical islands during which the hero and his cabin-mate engage in a series of sexual exploits with various girls they met aboard ship." After complaining of the "necessarily vague standards" given state judges by the Supreme Court's recent decisions—especially in "marginal cases"—the court observed:

THE SUPREME COURT OF ILLINOIS: The acts of intercourse are not described in detail, so as to exceed the limits of contemporary candor in such matters, nor do we find repulsive and disgusting language of the kind given protection in *Grove Press, Inc.* v. *Gerstein.‡*

—

Moral and religious vigilante groups, as has been seen, were highly critical of the *Tropic of Cancer* decision and its predictable repercussions. On the Court itself, the progressive but puritanical chief, Earl Warren, protested against his brother Brennan's interpretation of the freedom given by the Constitution's framers to authors and publishers. Warren had dissented in the '64 decisions, writing an opinion joined by Justice Tom Clark in which he expressed concern that Brennan's revision of *Roth* was endangering the "right of the Nation and of the States to maintain a decent society," and was ignoring the "rule of reason."

CHIEF JUSTICE EARL WARREN: No Government—be it federal, state, or local—should be forced to choose between repressing all material, including that within the realm of decency, and allowing unrestrained license to

---

*Klaw's books seem to have been of the bondage or S&M type that the Supreme Court would hold in 1966 could constitutionally be found obscene even if their appeal was to the prurient interests of a (targeted) deviant group instead of those of "the average person" (*Mishkin* v. *New York,* 1966).

†By that time *Fanny Hill* had been held not obscene by the New York Court of Appeals, in the light of the Supreme Court's *Tropic of Cancer* decision. The Supreme Court had not yet ruled in the Massachusetts *Fanny Hill* case.

‡The official title of the Florida *Tropic of Cancer* case.

publish any material, no matter how vile. There must be a rule of reason in this as in other areas of the law.

—

Two years later, a trilogy of cases came up, and one of them in particular—the *Ginzburg* case—presented Earl Warren with the opportunity, at last, to impress his sexual sensibility on at least a small portion of the Court's obscenity work.

When, early in the 1960s, publisher Ralph Ginzburg sought to exploit the new freedom awarded by the Court to publishers, he was targeted by the Kennedy Justice Department for having gone too far; it prosecuted and convicted Ginzburg, and persuaded a federal judge to slap the publisher with a prison sentence, which, in due course, the Supreme Court would injudiciously uphold.

It was probably Warren's oft-reiterated concern about where Brennan was taking the constitutionalized obscenity law that induced Brennan, in March 1966, to try to justify Ralph Ginzburg's punishment, and harmonize it with two other discordant Court decisions that in one day caused fourteen separate written opinions and tens of thousands of words to be issued by the Court. What the Court had done was to free a reputable publisher, G. P. Putnam's Sons, to continue to distribute its best-selling edition of the "well-written" pornographic classic novel *Fanny Hill*, but to let two "disreputable" publishers, Ralph Ginzburg and Edward Mishkin, go to prison for selling more vulgar and more obviously "commercialized" sexual expression. Although the Court's opinion in each case was written by Brennan, only the one accompanying the decision in *Fanny Hill* was pure Brennan; the other two, and particularly *Ginzburg,* read as though they had been ghosted by "Super Chief" Earl Warren.

The private court papers of Justice Abe Fortas suggest that Brennan was persuaded by Fortas to change his mind in the *Fanny Hill* case;* initially Brennan voted as though disposed to affirm the lower court's finding that Cleland's book was obscene. (Fortas, on the other hand, was disposed initially to reverse the findings of obscenity not only in *Fanny Hill* but in Ginzburg's case; ultimately he voted in both cases with majorities of the Court that included both Warren and Brennan.) In the end, and although two publishers consequently went to prison, the Brennan doctrine not only survived the fierce attacks that had been levied against it from on the bench and off, but was actually strengthened in such a way that it continued for another four critical years to thwart attempts at censorship of almost all "valuable" literary and artistic expression in the United States.† In effect,

---

*It is not inconceivable that in voting initially to affirm the Massachusetts courts' decisions holding *Fanny Hill* obscene (as in voting, throughout the Court's conferences regarding Ginzburg, to affirm his conviction), Brennan was maneuvering to receive from Warren the critically important opinion-writing assignment; in the end, as indicated in the text, Brennan wrote the Court's lead opinion in all three cases.

†There were some exceptions. Lower court findings that the films *Flaming Creatures* and *Un Chant d'Amour* were obscene were summarily affirmed by Court majorities that included

the Brennan doctrine gained strength in *Fanny Hill* by winning the endorsement for the first time of Chief Justice Earl Warren, as well as that of the prestigious freshman justice Abe Fortas.

In *Mishkin,* no claim was made that the fifty books involved in the publisher's prosecution—all "cheaply prepared paperbound 'pulps' with imprinted sales prices that are several thousand percent above cost" (Brennan)—had any redeeming social value whatsoever. And so the Court's decision that Mishkin might be imprisoned did not impeach the Brennan doctrine or taint the Court's credibility among the literary and legal communities.* The books belonged to a subliterary species—"bondage" booklets—and bore titles such as *Dance with the Dominant Whip, Mistress of Leather, Cult of the Spankers,* and *Screaming Flesh;* they were written as well as illustrated by persons to whom Mishkin had given "detailed instructions."

JUSTICE WILLIAM J. BRENNAN, JR.: Typical of appellant instructions was that related by one author, who testified that appellant insisted that the books be "full of sex scenes and lesbian scenes. . . . [T]he sex had to be very strong, it had to be rough, it had to be clearly spelled out. . . . I had to write sex very bluntly, make the sex scenes very strong . . . unusual sex scenes between men and women, and women and women, and men and men. . . ." Another author testified that appellant instructed him "to deal very graphically with . . . the darkening of the flesh under flagellation. . . ." Artists testified in a similar vein as to appellant's instructions regarding illustrations and covers for the books.†

Brennan in 1967, notwithstanding that they could not correctly be taken to be "utterly without" artistic and other social value. It is possible that the lawyers trying those cases, and those presenting them to the Supreme Court, failed to put forward evidence of the existence of even a modicum of such value, and may not have filed the films for the justices to see for themselves any values residing in them. The Supreme Court cases are in de Grazia, *Censorship Landmarks* (1969), 596 and 599.

In 1970, the new Chief Justice Warren Burger was able to impede the operation of the Brennan doctrine sufficiently to prevent the Court from freeing the socially important Swedish motion picture *I Am Curious—Yellow.* By 1973, Burger had enough power on the Court to denounce the Brennan doctrine and collect a Court majority for a revision that was designed to limit the freedom available to sexually oriented expression to expression that showed "serious" literary, artistic, scientific, or political value. See Chapter 28.

*On the other hand, it did not satisfy literary egalitarians among the liberals and literati, such as the small group of intellectuals for whom I prepared and filed an amici curiae brief, urging a reversal of Mishkin's conviction. The subscribers to the brief were: Marshall Cohen, Jason Epstein, Paul Goodman, Warren Hinckle, Eric Larrabee, Walter Minton, Norman Podhoretz, Barney Rosset, Robert Silvers, and William Styron. The position urged on the Court was that no governmental restraint upon sexually oriented expression was justified unless the expression was "assaultive" or unconsented to. This position was in its essentials later (in 1970) advanced, as recommended legislative policy, by the Lockhart commission, and was adopted as a constitutional matter in 1973 by a Warren Court minority, including Brennan, who dissented from the Burger Court's retrenchment on freedom of sexual expression. The amici brief is in de Grazia, *Censorship Landmarks* (1969), 634–37; the *Mishkin* case is reprinted there at 561–65.

†These sexual hack writers of the sixties may be compared with the "Dial-a-Porn" oral "word-prostitutes" of the nineties, called "fantasy girls." The latter were recently portrayed by Andrea Simakis in *The Village Voice* as "faceless novices of the American sex industry." The Rehnquist Court has held "Dial-a-Porn" expression to be constitutionally protected, but right-wing religious groups, using Senator Jesse Helms as their principal advocate, continue

Affirming the conviction of Ralph Ginzburg, however, was more difficult for Brennan to justify because the publisher's lawyers claimed, and the
solicitor general more or less conceded, that the publications Ginzburg had
been convicted for distributing through the mails had at least marginal
"redeeming social value." Ginzburg had made the mistake, however, of
exuberantly promoting his publications—notably the hardbound quarterly
Eros—by stressing the interest they held for persons wanting to see sex in
print, and had "taken advantage" of the American judiciary's "permissive"
obscenity decisions to go as far as he could without falling afoul of the
Supreme Court's definition of what was obscene. Ginzburg in this way
unwittingly gave ammunition to the Court's already angry critics on Capitol Hill and among pro-censorship groups and sympathizers. Some five
million advertisements with the following message had been sent by Ginzburg through the mails.

RALPH GINZBURG: *Eros* is a child of its times. . . . [It] is the result of recent
court decisions that have realistically interpreted America's obscenity laws
and that have given to this country a new breath of freedom of expression.
. . . *Eros* takes full advantage of this new freedom of expression. It is the
magazine of sexual candor. . . .

In the few short weeks since its birth, *Eros* has established itself as the
rave of the American intellectual community—and the rage of prudes everywhere! And it's no wonder: *Eros* handles the subjects of Love and Sex with
complete candor. The publication of this magazine—which is frankly and
avowedly concerned with erotica—has been enabled by recent court decisions ruling that a literary piece or painting, though explicitly sexual in
content, has a right to be published if it is a genuine work of art.

Eros is a genuine work of art. . . .

Worse yet, in order to promote his publications, the publisher obtained
sexually suggestive postmarks:

JUSTICE WILLIAM J. BRENNAN, JR.: *Eros* early sought mailing privileges from
the postmasters of Intercourse and Blue Ball, Pennsylvania. The trial court
found the obvious, that these hamlets were chosen only for the value their
names would have in furthering petitioner's efforts to sell their publications
on the basis of salacious appeal.

The "leer of the sensualist"* also permeates the advertising for the three
publications. The circulars sent for *Eros* and *Liaison* stressed the sexual

---

to press for restrictive legislation in the name of "protecting our children." This is the same
justification ("children may be listening") that has been advanced by those groups, by Senator
Helms, and by the Federal Communications Commission to forbid the broadcast—at any time
of the day or night—of any program (including a literary reading) that contains "indecent"
language.

*Another phrase suggesting that Chief Justice Warren ghost-wrote parts of Brennan's
opinion in *Ginzburg*.

candor of the respective publications, and openly boasted that the publisher would take full advantage of what they regarded as unrestricted license allowed by law in the expression of sex and sexual matters.

—

Harry Kalven thought judicial politics might have been at work.

PROFESSOR HARRY KALVEN, JR.: One can only wonder why the Court was so determined to punish Ginzburg, even at the cost of due process and First Amendment values. Perhaps a partial explanation resides in the political pressures under which it operates in this area. In light of its record since *Roth* of rejecting the claims of censorship and its contemporaneous decision to protect *Fanny Hill,* the Court may have felt the need to reassure advocates of regulation that it was still possible to secure a conviction for obscenity. If so, Ginzburg may unwittingly have presented himself as the ideal candidate for sacrifice. . . . [In his advertisements] in effect Ginzburg declared a partnership with the Court in the selling of pornography. And the Court responded by emphatically dissolving that partnership.

—

Brennan's decision to "justify" the federal government's imprisonment of Ralph Ginzburg—because his promotional and advertising methods "pandered" to a prurient interest in sex—was later conceded by him to be "the worst mistake" he ever made.* He said that to me,† and he said as much

---

*However, it was approved of editorially by *The New York Times,* which said that the Court's decision in the three obscenity cases "strike the proper balance in a field where there are extremely difficult issues of law and public policy. . . . Ginzburg was clearly publishing pornography. . . . The Court inescapably concluded that [he] had no scholarly, literary or scientific interests; he was strictly an entrepreneur in a disreputable business who took his chances on the borderline of the law and lost. He is no different from Edward Mishkin . . . who was convicted for using hack writers to produce books deliberately aimed at an audience of sexual deviants" (March 29, 1966).

In Brennan's defense it might also be pointed out that the doctrine he resorted to to justify Ginzburg's punishment was based upon an approach that Chief Justice Warren had been unsuccessfully urging the Court to adopt since *Roth*—namely, the "variable obscenity" doctrine first recommended by Dean William Lockhart and Professor Robert McClure in their seminal articles in the *Minnesota Law Review.* It also took support from the curious "bias" against commercial or profit-motivated disseminations of sexually oriented expression that was incorporated by the venerable American Law Institute in its proposed *Model Penal Code,* one of the principal authors of which was the distinguished professor Louis Schwartz of the University of Pennsylvania Law School. The idea for the "pandering" doctrine as a justification for upholding Ginzburg's conviction probably was passed from Warren to Fortas to Brennan, as suggested in the text anon and in Bruce Allen Murphy, *Fortas: The Rise and Ruin of a Supreme Court Justice* (1988), 458, and endnote 75, page 656.

A "variable obscenity" approach was used to justify the result in *Mishkin* v. *New York,* where the obscenity of the fifty bondage books published by Mishkin was appraised in terms of an audience not of average persons but of average *deviant* persons, whose prurient interests could be appealed to by images and ideas presumably *un*exciting to normal persons. A "variable obscenity" approach was also used in *Ginsberg* v. *New York* to justify the punishment of a person who sold magazines that would be constitutionally protected and not obscene for adults but "obscene" for minors. See Chapter 27.

†In a conversation in his chambers. To a conscientious judge like Brennan, bad judgments are like self-inflicted wounds. But, like most mortals, Supreme Court justices lose their cool over litigants who put them to the test in this (negative) way. It was as if Ralph Ginzburg provoked Justices Brennan and Fortas to render injustice in his case. There is a note from

to Paul Bender, who argued the government's case against Ginzburg before the Court, and who would later become counsel to the National Commission on Obscenity and Pornography (Lockhart commission). Bender knew that the case was a bad one; he recommended that the solicitor general "confess error." This could have brought about a remand of the case to the lower courts to entertain a motion by the government to have the charges against Ginzburg dismissed. But—perhaps for the reasons Bender suggests below—Solicitor General Archibald Cox, Deputy Attorney General Nicholas de B. Katzenbach, and Attorney General Robert F. Kennedy all supported Ginzburg's prosecution, and so the case against Ginzburg was not terminated, as I believe it should have been.

PAUL BENDER: We all have a lot to learn in these areas and if you've grown up one way on something as vital as religious attitudes, it's very hard to change your mind or rethink it. And I think Brennan did a remarkable job in rethinking it, while he was on the Court. . . . I argued the *Ginzburg* case. He knew what I thought. I knew what he thought. Every time I saw him he said, "Oh, I want you to meet Paul Bender. This is the greatest lawyer I've ever met. He can't even lose a case when he *wants* to."

This was *Ginzburg* that I was trying to lose. He knew I was trying to lose it. He was writing the opinion in the other direction. I was furious at him. For a while he wouldn't even talk to me because he knew what I would say. . . . I wanted to confess error in that case. . . .

Phil Heyman in the S.G.'s office had been doing the obscenity stuff. He couldn't do this case for some reason. So Ralph Spritzer, who was the first assistant, came in and said: "Do you want to do this one? This is a brief in opposition. *Ginzburg.*" And I said okay. I didn't know anything about it. I looked at it and I went in to Ralph and said, "Ralph, you know we shouldn't be opposing this. This is ridiculous. We've got to confess error." And he said, "We can't do that." I said, "Why not?" He said, "Well, we'll talk to Archie [Cox] about it but I bet you the answer is no." So I wrote a memo or something and we talked and the answer was no because the solicitor general had been consulted about the prosecution. Bobby Kennedy had come in one day and said, "I got this problem. The U.S. attorney in Philadelphia wants to prosecute this case. Let me show you the stuff." I believe he passed around *Eros* with the "Black and White in Color" essay, and perhaps the *Housewife's Handbook* and *Liaison* as well. And Bobby said, "What do you think, Archie?" And Archie said, "Oh, you can prosecute that." Having done that, they wouldn't confess error. And I think that's possibly right. If you've made the decision that it's okay to go ahead with it, you then don't come in and confess. What would you say? We've changed our mind?

Fortas to his friend and mentor William O. Douglas, in Fortas's private court papers, that indicates that Fortas later attributed his legal misjudgment in Ginzburg's case to the publisher's "slimy" personality, a factor that Fortas said worked on him "subconsciously." See Bruce Allen Murphy, *Fortas* (1988), 458.

If Cox's views on this were anything like Frankfurter's, and I suspect that they were—they came to the issue from similar kinds of intellectual backgrounds, and had similar lack of communication with that aspect of the world—when you see pictures like that, when you've never seen the stuff,* and you see pictures . . . the "Black and White in Color" stuff . . . you could be shocked by that. The judge, the lower court judge, was shocked . . . the explicitness of the pictures, when they were unused to that stuff . . . and didn't know how tastes and mores were beginning to change. . . .

Ginzburg was a very, very unattractive human being, which came out through the entire record. I mean, Warren had in his mind that although there was nothing wrong with the book as such, it was the people. The smut peddlers. You had to get the smut peddlers. Because they were evil people, they were preying on other people's insecurities and weaknesses. If anyone was a smut peddler [for Warren], it was Ralph Ginzburg. He looked like a smut peddler; he came to the argument and sat there and said to one of my students, who was sitting next to him, "You know, I don't think that guy really wants to win this case." That was me.

MERLE MILLER: I had been told by a former associate of Ginzburg that in his publications he had "an uncanny ability to go straight for the vulgar." Another one-time friend said, "Ralph is without a single redeeming social feature. He is a lewd and obnoxious man, and the reason he is going to fail is that he acts badly in courtrooms. . . ." It isn't so much that Ginzburg tries to outrage judges, the way the defendants did in the Chicago conspiracy trial for instance; his ability to annoy seems to come quite naturally. In Philadelphia during his trial for "sending obscene matter through the mails," Ginzburg showed up in court wearing a flat straw hat and a black pin-striped suit with a white carnation in his lapel. Something about his outfit seems to have incensed the Honorable Ralph C. Body, who was heard to demand of a clerk, "Where does he think he's going, to his wedding?" When one of Ginzburg's lawyers suggested that more subdued apparel might be appropriate, he said, "Nobody's going to tell me how to dress. This is a free country, isn't it?"

PAUL BENDER: He was not being the humble defendant. And Warren was really put off by that. Now Brennan, you know, Brennan was a very political animal in court. That was quite a useful thing for a long time. He had written *Roth*. He had Warren going along with him on most of these cases, you know, where they wanted to reverse per curiam.† Here was one where Warren, I think, was really angry. And I think Brennan said, okay, we can

---

*Justice Potter Stewart, who (according to Justice Brennan) had "seen the [*real*] stuff" in the Navy, was particularly distressed at the Court's decision to uphold Ralph Ginzburg's conviction.

†Warren "went along" with Brennan and the Brennan doctrine in *Fanny Hill, Redrup,* and all the per curiam decisions following *Redrup* in which lower court obscenity cases were reversed, citing *Redrup*. In *Ginzburg,* Brennan (and Fortas) "went along" with Warren and *his* doctrine.

confine this, we'll make a new "pandering" thing. And we'll give Warren what he wants. Warren wanted that from the beginning. . . . *

Fortas was a great politician also. And I think there's a lot of trading-off goes on, not in a conscious way—I'll give you this, you give me that.† But Warren really cares about this. And, you know, he'll be very bitter if he loses. And he's got some sense in what he's saying, so let's go along with that. That's Fortas. . . . No question in my mind that if Goldberg had stayed on the Court, that case [*Ginzburg*] would have come out the other way. Goldberg was the fourth vote for cert, in that case. Or the fifth vote. . . . It was quite clear when cert was granted that that case was going to be reversed. . . . And then Goldberg left the Court. . . .‡ And I think one of the other dynamics was that Fortas was trying to have an alliance with Warren on the Court. And this was something that Warren felt very strongly about. Fortas, I think, felt . . . it wouldn't be a bad idea if he went along with Warren on this kind of stuff. Really ironic, for then he gets lambasted for his views in obscenity cases. One of the objections in Congress to his nomination as chief justice was his voting record in obscenity cases. He joined in a number of obscenity reversals.

———

Ginzburg's *Eros* was a deluxe hardbound quarterly magazine that bore some resemblance to Sam Roth's condemned *American Aphrodite*,§ which also had been sold almost exclusively through the mails, and by methods not unlike those used by Ginzburg. *Eros* was successful; its circulation, by the time of the indictment, was said to be around 100,000; by then, four issues of the glossy hardbound erotic magazine were out, and a fifth one was on the presses. The issue on which the government chose to base an indictment was described by Merle Miller in *The New York Times Magazine* of April 30, 1972—six years after the Court's decision in Ginzburg's case.

MERLE MILLER: Much of the contents, by present-day standards, seem absurdly tame. There was Maupassant's little anecdote "Madame Tellier's

———

*I.e., from the time of *Roth,* as indicated by Warren's concurring opinion there; see de Grazia, *Censorship Landmarks* (1969), 295.

†See the instances of *alleged* "trading-off" among the brethren reported by Bob Woodward and Scott Armstrong in *The Brethren* (1979).

‡President Johnson asked Justice Goldberg to become ambassador to the United Nations; this allowed Johnson to name his friend and close White House adviser, Abe Fortas, to the Court. See Chapter 27. Bender is probably correct about how Goldberg would have voted. In a talk I had with Goldberg not long before he died, he told me that he did not understand the Court's action in *Ginzburg,* and for the reasons given by him in his separate concurring opinion in *Jacobellis* (he also joined Brennan's lead opinion there), he would have been likely to vote to reverse Ginzburg's conviction. In *Jacobellis,* Goldberg said he thought that the prosecutor must have objected to the movie's advertising or promotion, since the film itself (Louis Malle's *The Lovers*) was so "innocuous"; but that he did not feel that a film could be censored because of its advertising or promotion. In short, Goldberg would not have bought the "pandering" doctrine which a bare majority of the Warren Court (including Fortas) adopted in *Ginzburg.* Goldberg's *Jacobellis* concurrence is in de Grazia, *Censorship Landmarks* (1969), 427.

§Unlike *Eros, Aphrodite* carried no photographs; it did, however, contain drawings and other graphic material.

Brothel," that I for one had read while still in high school; however, in *Eros* the illustrations were by Degas. There were photographs of some male prostitutes in Bombay; an article warning people against making too much love if they had weak hearts; some French postcards showing buxom ladies nude from the waist up, surrounded by portly gentlemen who were fully clothed; the Mark Twain essay "1601" (was there anybody who hadn't read a pirated edition of that?); some supposedly racy selections from the Bible (my God); some dubious two-liners ("Q: How do porcupines do it? A: Carefully"); a love poem or two by Shoshana;* and, lo, a photographic essay offering glimpses of a handsome black boy making love to a beautiful white girl.

———

Ginzburg, of course, thought the photographic essay—"Black and White in Color, A Photographic Tone Poem"—was terrific, and it was also admired by witnesses who testified at the publisher's trial.

RALPH GINZBURG: [I]t was beautiful; it was a real work of art. I suppose if it had been a white man and a black woman, nobody would have given it a second thought.

DWIGHT MacDONALD: I suppose if you object to a Negro and a white person having sex together, then, of course, you would be horrified by it.† From the artistic point of view I thought it was very good. In fact, I thought it was done with great taste, and I don't know how to say it—I never heard of him before, but he is obviously an extremely competent and accomplished photographer.

PROFESSOR HORST W. JANSON: I think they are outstandingly beautiful and artistic photographs. I cannot imagine the theme being treated in a more lyrical and delicate manner than it has been done here. . . .

I might add that of course photography in appropriate hands is an artistic instrument and this particular photographer has shown a very great awareness of compositional devices and patterns that have a long and well-established history in western art. . . .

The very content in the color of the two bodies of course has presented him with certain opportunities that he would not have had with two models of the same color, and he has taken rather extraordinary and very delicate advantage of these contrasts.

———

Another piece in *Eros* that Ginzburg's trial court found "obscene" and "without any redeeming value" was a discussion by Drs. Eberhard W. and Phyllis C. Kronhausen‡ of erotic writing by women; it included illustrative (but not illustrated) quotations.

———

*The pen name of Ginzburg's wife and unofficial co-publisher.
†Consider Senator Jesse Helms's reaction to Robert Mapplethorpe's homoerotic photographic artworks, discussed in Chapter 30.
‡Authors of *Pornography and the Law* (1959).

DWIGHT MacDONALD: I thought [this was] an extremely interesting and important study with some remarkable quotations from the woman who had put down her sense of love-making, of sexual intercourse . . . in an extremely eloquent way. I have never seen this from the woman's point of view. I thought the point they made, the difference between the man's and the woman's approach to sexual intercourse, was very well made and very important.

———

When the case came to the Supreme Court, Justice William O. Douglas would point out another feature in *Eros* that could not fairly be said to be without literary value.

JUSTICE WILLIAM O. DOUGLAS: Still another article [in *Eros*] found obscene was a short introduction to and a lengthy excerpt from *My Life and Loves* by Frank Harris, about which there is little in the record. Suffice it to say that this seems to be a book of some literary stature. At least I find it difficult on this record to say that "it is utterly without redeeming social importance."

The extensive literary comment which the book's publication generated demonstrates that it is not "utterly without redeeming social importance." See, e.g., *New York Review of Books,* p. 6 (Jan. 9, 1964); *New Yorker,* pp. 79–80 (Jan. 4, 1964); *Library Journal,* pp. 4743–4744 (Dec. 15, 1963); *New York Times Book Review,* p. 10 (Nov. 10, 1963); *Time,* pp. 102–104 (Nov. 8, 1963); *Newsweek,* pp. 98–100 (Oct. 28, 1963); *New Republic,* pp. 23–27 (Dec. 28, 1963).*

———

But the federal district judge who tried and sentenced Ginzburg saw *Eros,* volume 1, number 4, in a different light—as an attempted exploitation of art for the sake of the prurient interest people have in sex.† This is how a majority of the Supreme Court, too, would later come to see it.

JUDGE RALPH C. BODY: *Eros* is a carefully contrived magazine or periodical type of publication with a hard cover and glossy paper. It is replete with photographs and includes reproductions of recognized works of art. Nevertheless . . . the dominant appeal is to pruriency. The works of art, such as biblical quotations and reproductions of the creations of recognized artists, are merely a façade to disguise and protect the basic purpose and effect of the entire work. This basic purpose and effect becomes evident as one progresses through the pages. . . .

Eros has no saving grace. The items of possible merit and those items which might be considered innocuous are a mere disguise to avoid the law and in large measure enhance the pruriency of the entire work. The only

———

*Harris and his book are depicted in Chapter 4.
†Ginzburg waived his right to be tried by a jury; in retrospect, this was probably a mistake, given the ease with which Justice Department prosecutors could select the venue for Ginzburg's case, and perhaps even the judge.

overriding theme of *Eros* is advocacy of complete sexual expression of whatever sort and manner. The most offensive pornography imaginable, examples of which were submitted by defendants as exhibit in this case,* has the same dominant effect and purpose. Even so, of course, the dissemination of the idea of complete sexual freedom cannot constitutionally be punished. Therefore, it must be the manner of dissemination which is objectionable. . . .†

[T]he series of pictures "Black and White in Color" constitutes a detailed portrayal of the act of sexual intercourse between a completely nude male and female, leaving nothing to the imagination. This material meets defendants' own experts' definition of obscenity as well as counsel's legal definition.

—

According to Victor S. Navasky's *Kennedy Justice,* Robert Kennedy, who was attorney general at the time of Ginzburg's prosecution, was "a puritan where what he considered to be vice, prostitution, or 'obscenity' were involved." The Post Office reportedly received 35,000 complaints about Ginzburg's use of the mails to peddle his "sex and love" publications;‡ and only twenty-one days after the first number of *Eros* came out, the chairwoman of the Post Office Operations Subcommittee, Congresswoman Kathryn E. Granahan from Philadelphia, took to the House floor to demand that "the presses of this pornographic pestilence . . . be stopped and its scabrous publisher smitten." According to Merle Miller, a little while before that, "several hundred pounds of books had been burned on the steps of a Philadelphia church in a ceremony presided over by the superintendant of schools; in the background a boys' chorus sang 'Gloria in Excelsis. . . .' Representative Granahan made a speech telling her fellow Philadelphians that obscenity was 'part of an international Communist plot. . . .' One Philadelphia librarian wrote in a local library journal, 'Ralph Ginzburg has about the same chance of finding justice in our [Philadelphia] courts as a Jew had in the courts of Nazi Germany.' "

Still, Kennedy waited a little over a year to comply with Granahan's demand that Ginzburg be smitten. The prosecution was initiated by a U.S. attorney in Philadelphia (instead of, for instance, New York) probably

---

*Ginzburg's lawyers apparently introduced hard-core pornography into evidence to show the court the sort of material that, they contended, was obscene, as contrasted with *Eros* and Ginzburg's other publications.

†Judge Body's decision that Ginzburg broke the obscenity law and deserved to be punished was rather transparently result-oriented: he decided Ginzburg deserved punishment and then searched for a reason in the law by which his punishment could be justified. "Ideas," of course, have uniformly been held protected by the constitutional guarantees, with the arguable exception of the idea that the government should be overthrown "as soon as conditions admit," by force and violence—deemed not protected by the Court, for example, in the case of the Communist party leaders who were imprisoned in 1948 under the Smith Act, and whose conviction the Vinson Court upheld. *Dennis* v. *United States,* criticized by Harry Kalven, Jr., in *A Worthy Tradition* (1987), 190ff.

‡The numbers suggest that mass mailings by pro-censorship organizations of the time, such as the Citizens for Decent Literature, were involved.

because Congresswoman Kathryn Granahan's district was there, and federal law now permitted a publisher to be prosecuted for sending obscenity through the mails not only in the city where his offices were but in any place where his publications were received. The assistant attorney general in charge of the Criminal Division, which approved the prosecution of Ginzburg at that time, was Nicholas Katzenbach. Katzenbach is quoted by Navasky as having said that Kennedy felt he "ought to prosecute" Ginzburg but hesitated because he feared it would "hurt politically." According to Navasky, Kennedy said: "They will blame it on my Catholicism."*

On the other hand, Southern politics and politicians may have influenced Kennedy to go ahead with the prosecution. The volatile relations between the Kennedy administration and the no-longer-Democratic South must have been exacerbated when *Eros,* volume 1, number 4, appeared in 1962, flowing through the U.S. mails, with its shockingly large and "beautiful" color photographs of a nude interracial couple embracing. Besides, the text that accompanied the "photographic tone poem" stated that the couple were dedicated to "the conviction that love between a man and a woman, no matter what their races, is beautiful," and that "interracial couples of today bear the indignity of having to defend their love to a questioning world. Tomorrow these couples will be recognized as the pioneers of an enlightened age."

At the time of *Eros*'s publication it was still criminal in some states for white and black persons to marry each other. In 1967, the year after the *Ginzburg* decision, the Warren Court held unconstitutional a Virginia antimiscegenation law;† this could not help Ralph Ginzburg.

Relations between the Kennedy administration, especially the Kennedy Justice Department, and Southern politicians in Congress and in the Southern statehouses were especially tense at that time because of the continuing enforcement of the Supreme Court's decision in *Brown* v. *Board of Education,* the new Negro voting-rights initiatives that had been taken

---

*The attorney general's father, Joseph P. Kennedy, refused to allow Elia Kazan's brilliant film *Baby Doll* to be exhibited in his chain of New England movie theatres after Cardinal Spellman condemned the film as "a contemptuous defiance of natural law" and "a definite corruptive moral influence" on American society. Joe Kennedy echoed this view: "I have been in business 45 years, and I think this is the worst thing that has ever been done to the people and to the industry. I think it should be banned everywhere." See de Grazia and Newman, *Banned Films: Movies, Censors and the First Amendment* (1982), 94.

†In *Loving* v. *Virginia,* 875 S.Ct. 1817 (1967). Mildred Jeter, a black woman, and Richard Loving, a white man, had been validly married in the District of Columbia, pursuant to its laws. Shortly after their marriage, the Lovings returned to Virginia, where they were prosecuted and convicted (on the basis of guilty pleas) for violating Virginia laws that prohibited marriage between white persons and colored persons. The trial judge gave as his opinion that "Almighty God created the races white, black, yellow, malay and red, and he placed them on separate continents. And but for the interferences with his arrangement there would be no cause for such marriages. The fact that he separated the races shows that he did not intend for the races to mix." The convictions of the Lovings were reversed, and the Virginia law was struck down for violating constitutional "equal protection," by the Warren Court, in an opinion written by the chief justice.

by the administration, and the violent law enforcement confrontations that resulted. Perhaps such considerations entered into the decision by Robert Kennedy to move against Ginzburg despite "political misgivings." To some it must have looked as if the Post Office was letting Ginzburg rub the South's face in its sexual, racial, and political hang-ups, and that it was Robert Kennedy's job to stop it.

VICTOR NAVASKY: Ginzburg came along with an issue portraying interracial love and sex, which he promoted all over the South at the height of the country's racial tension in the aftermath of the integration of ole Miss.

NICHOLAS KATZENBACH: [Bob] was terribly offended but terribly reluctant. I said I think it's a clear-cut case and you ought to do it. Ginzburg was saying 'if you don't prosecute me this time I'll force you to prosecute me next time.' But [Bob] wasn't vindictive. He was almost distressed when the verdict came down.

———

The Supreme Court's March 1966 decision to send Ginzburg to prison for five years for "pandering" provoked a furor. However, the ingenious and "well-lawyered" Ginzburg managed to stay free on bail for the next eight years, pending court actions on the many motions his lawyers filed, after the Supreme Court's decision, to reconsider his sentence. And when U.S. marshals finally did get around to escorting Ginzburg to federal prison, it was for a stay of eight months instead of five years. Ginzburg's "manhandling" by the Supreme Court seems to have generated sympathy and support among lower court judges and lawyers, as well as from writers, the ACLU, and others who were concerned to see not only freedom of the press preserved but "equal justice" done. Neoconservatives, pleased to embarrass the liberal Warren Court, added their voices to the criticism of the Court for what had been done in the name of the law to Ralph Ginzburg.*

In ringing dissents, Justices Hugo Black and Potter Stewart had set the tone for the reaction of others to Ginzburg's defeat.

JUSTICE HUGO BLACK: Only one stark fact emerges with clarity out of the confusing welter of opinions and thousands of words written into this and two other cases today.† That fact is that Ginzburg, petitioner here, is now finally and authoritatively condemned to serve five years in prison for distributing printed matter about sex which neither Ginzburg nor anyone else could possibly have known to be criminal.

JUSTICE POTTER STEWART: The Court today appears to conclude that the materials Ginzburg mailed were themselves protected by the First Amend-

———

*For a wise and courteous criticism, see the remarks of Professor Paul Freund of the Harvard Law School on September 8, 1966, at the Third Circuit's Judicial Conference, published in 42 *Federal Rules Decisions*, 490ff. Richard Kuh, Lenny Bruce's prosecutor, presented a neoconservative criticism at the same conference.

†*Mishkin* v. *New York* and *Memoirs of a Woman of Pleasure (Fanny Hill)* v. *Massachusetts.* Both are reprinted in full, along with *Ginzburg* v. *United States*, in de Grazia, *Censorship Landmarks* (1969).

ment.* But, the Court says, Ginzburg can still be sentenced to five years for mailing them. Why? Because, says the Court, he was guilty of "commercial exploitation," of "pandering," and of "titillation." But Ginzburg was not charged with "commercial exploitation"; he was not charged with "pandering"; he was not charged with "titillation." Therefore, to affirm his conviction now on any of those grounds, even if otherwise valid, is to deny him due process of law. But those grounds are *not,* of course, otherwise valid. Neither the statute under which Ginzburg was convicted, nor any other federal statute I know of, makes "commercial exploitation" or "pandering" or "titillation" a criminal offense. And any criminal law that sought to do so in the terms so elusively defined by the Court would, of course, be unconstitutionally vague and therefore void.

For me, however, there is another aspect of the Court's opinion in this case that is even more regrettable. Today the Court assumes the power to deny Ralph Ginzburg the protection of the First Amendment because it disapproves of his "sordid business."† That is a power the Court does not possess. For the First Amendment protects us all with an even hand. It applies to Ralph Ginzburg with no less completeness and force than to G. P. Putnam's Sons. In upholding and enforcing the Bill of Rights, this Court has no power to pick or to choose. When we lose sight of that fixed star of constitutional adjudication, we lose our way.

——

Moral and religious vigilante groups found nothing to complain about in the Court's actions in *Ginzburg* and *Mishkin.* The gain that these decisions symbolized for people and groups favoring governmental censorship of sexual expression was impressive enough so that only mild complaints were directed by them at the Court's more important (because more influential) decision in *Fanny Hill,* in which Brennan reinforced his "not utterly without value" doctrine as a plank of First Amendment law that would be used by book publishers and distributors over the next few crucial years to gain effective freedom.

By contrast, *Ginzburg* came to be viewed as "bad" law. The opening that the decision offered to prosecutors and judges to punish publishers who conducted their business by "pandering" to or "titillating" or "exploiting" a prurient interest in sex was not much used by prosecutors or trial and appellate judges, nor was it followed by the Supreme Court. In time, the "pandering" doctrine announced in *Ginzburg* was practically dead letter.

Brennan's opinion in *Fanny Hill* showed his doctrine in its full flowering. Yet only one year later, in May 1967, with the Court's announcement of its decision in *Redrup* v. *New York,* the importance of the doctrine began to decline. From this moment on—until the Burger Court attacked and revised it in 1973—the Brennan doctrine was only one among several

---

*Because of more or less *conceded* "social value."
†A favorite phrase of Chief Justice Earl Warren.

liberal doctrinal approaches to the solution of the obscenity problem that were drawing the Warren Court closer and closer to an award of absolute freedom to the creators and disseminators of sexually oriented expression in the United States. But by 1967 the Brennan doctrine had led the Court far beyond the constitutional benchmark that *Roth* had registered ten years earlier, and far away from the Dark Ages of the English common law of obscene libel as well. It also, I believe, inspired centrist and liberal justices—including Potter Stewart, Arthur Goldberg, Thurgood Marshall, and Abe Fortas—to press the words of the First Amendment almost to their absolute limit. What at first subsumed Brennan's doctrine was a new, short-lived, freedom-expanding, controversial process, identified with no single justice or voting bloc, called Redrupping, after the precedental use that was made by the Court of the case *Redrup* v. *New York*.

Robert Redrup was a Times Square newsstand clerk who in 1965 was arrested, tried, and convicted for selling to a plainclothes detective two pulp sex books distributed by California publisher William Hamling.* Hamling undertook to foot the bills for Redrup's legal defense through the Supreme Court proceedings and was justly proud of the result, for the Court responded by freeing Redrup and the novels themselves, *Lust Pool* and *Shame Agent*. Hamling, like his lawyer, Stanley Fleishman, believed that he was not engaged in "commercialized obscenity" or titillating the prurient interests of people with a weakness for such expression, but crusading for literary freedom in the interests of the common man.

GAY TALESE: As [Hamling] saw it, the courtroom battle that had begun years before in the case of *United States* v. *One Book Called Ulysses,* resulting in a victory for the literary elite, had now ended in 1967 with a triumph for the man in the street. It was no longer necessary for a sexually explicit book to justify itself as a Joycean masterpiece, or even as a novel of redeeming social value like *Lady Chatterley's Lover;* now, in *Redrup,* the Supreme Court finally seemed to be relinquishing its role as the nation's literary arbitrator. . . . [T]he ramifications were awesome. It suggested that *any* book, a trashy book, a volume of words replete with the most angry expletives and scatological ravings of the least talented novelist in the land, might be published and sold no matter what a policeman thought of it, or a clergyman thought of it, or the CDL thought of it.

———

There was in *Redrup* no single new jurisprudential theory or doctrine to explain the high court's action in reversing Robert Redrup's obscenity conviction. Moreover, the Brennan doctrine quietly lived on as a subordinate element of the *Redrup* consensus, spelled out as follows:

———

*These books and the clerk were freed by the Court, but six years later Hamling would be sent to federal prison for using the mails to sell an "illustrated" edition of the 1970 *Report of the National Commission on Obscenity and Pornography.* See Chapter 28.

SUPREME COURT OF THE UNITED STATES: Two members of the Court [Black and Douglas] have consistently adhered to the view that a State is utterly without power to suppress, control, or punish the distribution of any writings or pictures upon the ground of their "obscenity." A third [Stewart] has held to the opinion that a State's power in this area is narrowly limited to a distinct and clearly identifiable class of material [i.e., hard-core pornography]. Others [Brennan, Fortas, even Warren] have subscribed to a not dissimilar standard, holding that a State may not constitutionally inhibit the distribution of literary material as obscene unless "(a) the dominant theme of the material taken as a whole appeals to a prurient interest in sex; (b) the material is patently offensive because it affronts contemporary community standards relating to the description or representation of sexual matters; and (c) the material is utterly without redeeming social value," emphasizing that the "three elements must coalesce," and that no such material can be proscribed unless it is found to be utterly without redeeming social value. Another Justice [White] has not viewed the "social value" element as an independent factor in the judgment of obscenity.

The Court added, somewhat mysteriously in an already enigmatic situation, *"whichever of these constitutional views is brought to bear,"* the conviction of Redrup cannot stand.* Only Justices Harlan and Clark dissented, testifying to the formidable character of the Court's new and eclectic stand.

Like the Brennan doctrine, Redrupping permitted the publication and dissemination of meretricious, as well as meritorious, literary expression; unlike the Brennan doctrine, it meant to do so. It was the creation mainly of Justice Potter Stewart, although much of the energy behind it had originally come from Fortas.† By May 1967, on this issue, Stewart had moved from a position that had seemed to hover near the Court's center, almost as far to the left as the Black/Douglas "absolutist" position. Alone among the "nonabsolutist" liberals on the Warren Court favoring expansion of freedom of expression, Stewart had written powerful dissenting opinions in both *Ginzburg* and *Mishkin*.

Although Justice Potter Stewart's fine judicial mind was behind it, the *Redrup* opinion was officially attributed to no single justice; this spread the responsibility among a seven-man majority; it strengthened the thrust of

---

*Italics mine. The text of this opinion may be found in de Grazia, *Censorship Landmarks* (1969) at 596–97.

†Fortas's private court papers at Yale's Sterling Library in New Haven show that Warren assigned the task of writing the Court's *Redrup* opinion to Fortas, who labored for an entire term without success to cast the grounds for a decision reversing Robert Redrup's conviction in terms of a lack of any proof of "scienter," or guilty knowledge, on the part of Redrup sufficient to justify upholding his conviction for selling materials that were presumptively constitutionally protected. The assignment to Fortas may have been a sign of Warren's dissatisfaction with Brennan's performance as the Court's spokesperson on the evolving constitutional law of obscenity. When Fortas failed to come up with a "Court" (i.e., enough other justices to create a majority) to join his draft opinion, the task of writing the Court's opinion was reassigned to Stewart, who had laid the groundwork for the *Redrup* approach in his dissenting opinion in *Ginzburg*.

the decision and smoothed over the fragmentation of the brethren's doctrinal thinking; it isolated a small conservative dissenting minority, Harlan and Clark. All this gave Court watchers an impression of almost irresistible judicial permissiveness. What happened afterward confirmed the growing fear among some politicians, citizens, and religious vigilante groups that the Warren Court had mortgaged the First Amendment to the country's pornography industry. The Court now systematically Redrupped—reviewed and reversed summarily, without further opinion—scores of obscenity rulings entered by lower state and federal courts in cases involving paperback sex books, girlie magazines, and "peep shows." Not until 1973, when Justice White abandoned the side of his Warren Court liberal brethren and moved to where the power lay—with the new conservative bloc—was the practice stopped.*

A year before *Redrup* was announced, Justice Stewart had ventured the first remarks from a nonabsolutist member of the high bench, suggesting that consenting adults in America had a right, under the First Amendment, to acquire and read anything they wished. His comments were made in the course of his dissent in *Ginzburg:*

JUSTICE POTTER STEWART: Ralph Ginzburg has been sentenced to five years in prison for sending through the mail copies of a magazine, a pamphlet, and a book. There was testimony at his trial that these publications possess artistic and social merit. Personally, I have a hard time discerning any. Most of the material strikes me as both vulgar and unedifying. But if the First Amendment means anything, it means that a man cannot be sent to prison merely for distributing publications which offend a judge's esthetic sensibilities, mine or any other's.

Censorship reflects a society's lack of confidence in itself. It is a hallmark of an authoritarian regime. Long ago those who wrote our First Amendment charted a different course. They believed a society can be truly strong only when it is truly free. In the realm of expression they put their faith, for better or for worse, in the enlightened choice of the people, free from the interference of a policeman's intrusive thumb or a judge's heavy hand. So it is that the Constitution protects coarse expression as well as refined, and vulgarity no less than elegance. A book worthless to me may convey something of value to my neighbor. In the free society to which our Constitution has committed us, it is for each to choose for himself.

—

Then this pertinent footnote, anticipating *Redrup.*

---

*The conservative bloc consisted of the Nixon-appointed chief justice, Warren E. Burger (replacing Warren in 1969), and Associate Justices Harry A. Blackmun (replacing Fortas in 1971) and Lewis F. Powell (replacing Black, also in 1971). Conservative Justice Tom Clark resigned in 1967 to avoid any appearance of conflict of interest after President Johnson appointed his son, Ramsey Clark, attorney general; he was replaced by the liberal Thurgood Marshall. Harlan resigned in 1971 and was replaced by the Nixon appointee William Rehnquist, also an advocate of so-called judicial restraint and majoritarianism.

JUSTICE POTTER STEWART: Different constitutional questions would arise in a case involving an assault upon individual privacy by publication in a manner so blatant or obtrusive as to make it difficult or impossible for an unwilling individual to avoid exposure to it [citing cases]. Still other considerations might come into play with respect to laws limited in their effect to those deemed insufficiently adult to make an informed choice. No such issues were tendered in this case.

———

Redrup, however, was the first opinion delivered by the Court as a body to imply that consenting adults in the United States ought to be constitutionally entitled to acquire and read any publication that they wished—including concededly obscene or pornographic ones—without governmental interference.* In explaining the reversals, the Court's per curiam opinion stated that in none of the cases (there were two in addition to Robert Redrup's†) "was there a claim that the statute in question reflected a specific and limited state concern for juveniles." In none was there any suggestion of "an assault upon individual privacies by publication in a manner so obtrusive as to make it impossible for an unwilling individual to avoid exposure to it." And in none, the Court went on, was there "evidence of the sort of 'pandering' that the Court found significant in *Ginzburg* v. *United States.*" The implication was that in the future these three might well be the *only* statutory or prosecutorial reasons why a publication might justifiably be suppressed as obscene, and its disseminator punished. By 1973, for the Warren Court minority still propounding these views, there were only two; the *Ginzburg* pandering doctrine—against which Justice Stewart had so persuasively protested—had been buried.

Influential as it was, the Brennan doctrine had been under attack almost since its appearance in radicalized form in the *Jacobellis/Tropic of Cancer* decisions. Among the brethren on the "left" side of the high bench, Justices Black and Douglas had lamented that Brennan was turning the Court into "a Supreme Board of Censors." From the opposite ideological end, Justices Clark and White complained that the crucial "social value" prong of the

---

*The next would be written by Justice Thurgood Marshall (joined by Stewart) in the case of *Stanley* v. *Georgia*, 394 U.S. 557 (1969). There the Warren Court made its last advance in the movement to absolutely free sexually oriented expression for adults. It held that adults had a constitutional right to possess, read, or watch concededly obscene books and films in the privacy of their homes. A few years later, the Burger Court limited this case to its facts and refused to rule that the decision implied that people had a constitutional right to exhibit or sell such materials outside the home, or that anyone had a constitutional right to bring them to his home, for example, from abroad.

†*Redrup* was one of three cases decided by the Court together, on the same day, for exactly the same reasons; in each, lower state court findings of obscenity were reversed. In one of the other cases, *Austin* v. *Kentucky*, a bookstore owner had been convicted because a salesgirl in his store sold to a woman who asked for them by name magazines called *High Heels* and *Spree*. In the other case, *Gent* v. *Arkansas*, a prosecutor had successfully stopped the distribution and obtained a court order for the destruction of certain issues of the magazines *Gent*, *Swank*, *Bachelor*, *Modern Man*, *Cavalcade*, *Gentleman*, *Ace*, and *Sir*.

Brennan doctrine afforded smut peddlers a "loophole" which enabled them, practically speaking, to publish and sell anything at all. At the center of this judicial array were: Justice Harlan, who proselytized for a two-tier approach that would allow the federal government to suppress only pornography and the state government to suppress whatever it considered obscene and who more than once wondered if the Brennan doctrine "has any meaning at all"; and Justice Stewart, who advocated his own straightforward if simplistic "I know it when I see it" approach. Somewhere near the center also was Justice Fortas, who seems (after *Ginzburg,* which he almost immediately regretted) to have joined Stewart in persuading a Court majority to adopt *Redrup*'s "radical" approach.

Off the Court, others had also criticized the Brennan doctrine for placing judges in the role of "literary czars." Despite the doctrine's liberalizing impact, the influential ACLU had grown critical because the doctrine seemed to allow expression to be suppressed merely because some "social value" could not be shown. The ACLU's own views on obscenity were moving in the direction of the absolutist position of Justices Douglas and Black, away from its earlier position that obscenity could be constitutionally suppressed only if it threatened some "clear and present danger" (such as the inciting of a person to the commission of a sexual crime or violence) and away also from a middle position that I had helped persuade the organization to adopt (from 1961 to 1964) to the effect that "any book which is regarded by persons within a community as being instructive or having artistic importance" may not constitutionally be suppressed. This was an early rendering of the Brennan doctrine.* And throughout the course of the doctrine's reign, moral vigilante groups had repeatedly pummeled Brennan's approach because they believed it gave free rein to smut peddlers:

MORALITY IN MEDIA: The unprecedented onslaught of smut that took place during the late 1960s could be attributed largely to the phrase "utterly without redeeming social value. . . ."

In 1968, even the motion picture "I Am Curious—Yellow" was given a passport into this country from the jungle of erotica, because of the application of this "social value" language, by a court in New York.† Now, there

---

*This was the position adopted by the ACLU in the amicus brief it filed in Ralph Ginzburg's case, adapted from a brief that I wrote on behalf of the ACLU and the Maryland Civil Liberties Union appearing as amici curiae in the *Tropic of Cancer* case from Maryland *(Yudkin* v. *Maryland),* the first obscenity case in which the national organization participated. The approach is described in greater detail in the ACLU *News Release* for May 17, 1963. A copy of the *Yudkin* brief is in the author's files.

†In 1968, the prestigious federal Court of Appeals for the Second Circuit overruled a federal trial judge and jury and held *I Am Curious—Yellow* constitutionally protected and not obscene because, among other things, it attempted to communicate political ideas of importance. I was the lawyer for the film and its American distributor, at the trial and on the appeal. The Justice Department did not take an appeal to the Supreme Court because, given the composition of the Warren Court at the time (1968), the appeal would certainly have been lost and a precedent unfavorable to governmental censorship established at the highest judicial

are mountains of trash completely free in the marketplace, because of it. What is the meaning of "utterly without redeeming social value"? Who is to know? To carry the phrase to the *reductio ad absurdum,* where it is oftentimes carried in the courts, there could be social value in the sleaziest magazine if the pages are numbered.

It is past time for "utterly without redeeming social value" to be relegated to the judicial graveyard.

———

Brennan's *"utterly* without redeeming social value" doctrine was helped by *Redrup* along the road to "the graveyard," but for years ideas that arose in the doctrine's wake haunted its right-wing Court critics. The social-value test had at least kept the lid on hard-core pornography, because the only recognizable value of such material was its capacity to arouse sexual feelings or, more cerebrally, to impart information about giving and receiving sexual pleasure. At that time, lawyers who were courageous or reckless enough to stand up and argue that such a "value" was a "social value," entitling expression to constitutional protection, were rare. Their number increased with the coming years.*

What followed was that Redrupping—that is, decisions by the Court reversing lower court obscenity findings without written explanation other than citation to *Redrup*—encouraged sex-pulp publishers to produce soft-core pornography, soft-core publishers to harden the "core," and establishment publishers to issue works having slight, if any, literary or artistic value without fear for the sexual explicitness, or eroticism, of the content.† The Warren Court—soon to be further strengthened when conservative justice Tom Clark was replaced by the liberal former solicitor general Thurgood Marshall—seemed to have recovered from its misstep in *Ginzburg* and to have moved ahead even more resolutely than before in the campaign to liberate sexually oriented expression.

Yet, neither the Court as a body, nor any individual justice, ever expressly said that "hard-core pornography" could freely be communicated, even among consenting adults, and only the absolutist position of Justices Black and Douglas extended a flat promise of freedom for such transactions,‡ that is, of the filthiest or the most erotic or interesting (depending upon one's point of view) sexual images that an enterprising author, photographer,

---

level. See de Grazia and Newman, *Banned Films: Movies, Censors and the First Amendment* (1982), 121–25 and 297–303; and de Grazia, *Censorship Landmarks* (1969), Introduction.

*As, I believe, the number of commentators in law journals willing to support such a view also increased. Many years later, in *Pope* v. *Illinois,* the meaning of "social value"—"social value" *according to whom?*—became the focus of the Rehnquist Court's attention.

†See, for publications only arguably possessed of "serious" literary or artistic value, the Doubleday publications *Pleasures* (1984) and *Erotic Interludes* (1986), both entirely composed of stories of female sexuality (hetero, homo, and auto) written by women in hard-core style, i.e., with a purpose and likely capacity to arouse sexual feelings in the average man or woman.

‡There *was* language in *Redrup,* quoted above, that implied that the Court might one day soon take the position that for consenting adults nothing ought to be considered obscene. As of this writing, justices favoring this solution to the problem of pornography have been unable to muster more than four votes out of nine.

film director, or book or magazine publisher could come up with. Speaking to me in the late eighties about the wisdom of the Supreme Court's obscenity decisions of the late sixties, California lawyer Stanley Fleishman made this commonsensical but penetrating comment:

STANLEY FLEISHMAN: So I never brought into evidence this distinction about redeeming literary value* because I had really very clear in my head that there is a group out there, large, for whom this serves all of the same purposes as literature. . . .

———

And then Fleishman related some anecdotes to prove his point.

STANLEY FLEISHMAN: I remember around the time I was pretty friendly with Henry Miller, after the *Sex Life of a Cop* case was over, when we were fooling around with *Tropic of Cancer*† and just for fun I gave Henry *Sex Life of a Cop,* and he was very offended by it. . . . He said, "Terrible stuff! Terrible!" It was, to him, *trash.* And you know he was a funny guy. Very gentle. I remember we were over at his house once. And we were talking about his kids, and our kids, and he was saying things like, "When Tony had to go doo-doo, or pee-pee . . ." *That* was Henry Miller!

In Fresno, there were twelve books we went to trial on [in the mid-sixties]. That's Aday.‡ We got a not guilty verdict on nine of them and got a hung jury, 9 to 3 for acquittal, on the other three. And it's interesting because I was uncomfortable preparing for those three books which had to do with incest. I was having trouble trying to make my case in terms of how it's part of life, of living, and all that. The other books had to do with prostitution; all kinds of fancy and not-so-fancy fucking, and we all have had experience in this area and it was just a reflection of life as we know it to be, and so on. So, no trouble there.

But the three incest books gave me trouble. And I suppose that the problem I was having there was reflected in the jury, which hung 9 to 3 on those three books. And then the judge dismissed those three, so Fresno was a total victory for Aday, and after that he was the hottest thing in town.

Aday had written the first bunch of books himself. He was delivering bread at the time and was an aspiring writer. Anyway, of those twelve books at the trial he wrote maybe eight, certainly a substantial number of them, himself. The reason he was prosecuted was because his books were the sexiest, in terms of language, on the market at the time. . . .

Aday was breaking some of the taboos, and again, his books were sexual without a lot of this literary pretense. They had a beginning, a middle, and an end; very simple. I mean he was writing for an uneducated audience, and he was able to reach them effectively. He didn't have a lot of literary illusions, there was not a lot of fancy stuff. . . .

———

Almost never? He seems to have done it in the case of *Sex Life of a Cop,* as indicated below.
†In the mid-sixties, Fleishman was involved in a California case involving *Tropic of Cancer.*
‡Sanford ("Les") Aday, Fresno, California, publisher of sex pulp literature.

That was a time when the Eastern publishers would not use the word "fuck," it had to be "fug" or whatever.

NORMAN MAILER: In *The Naked and the Dead* I'd chosen to use the word "fug" because there wasn't any way in the world you could use "fuck," you just couldn't get near it.* And I didn't care, I didn't feel that was impinging on me, oddly enough, because the way we used it in the army, it didn't have connotation at all; it was like a slug word, it was the word you used for the rhythm of your sentence. It was a dull word and "fug" was closer to the emotional content than "fuck," so it was always "fug."†

Even "fug" created a great deal of trouble, because it suggested the other word. And so there was a hilarious business that went on while I was in Paris after I'd finished *The Naked and the Dead*. One of the senior editors at Rinehart, Ted Rinehart, used to go through and cut out swear words, and then my editor, I think it was Bill Raney at Rinehart, used to work behind him and put them back. He couldn't put back as many as Ted cut out, but he put back about half of them, and that sort of thing went on all the time. And I'm sending telegrams from Paris to my editor saying, "Judas, you've betrayed me!" And the poor guy is working to get them back in. . . .

I was aware of all this, of how silly the whole thing could get, and I've always hated that. I hate it when silly matters impinge on literature, because it's hard to take yourself seriously if you keep writing year after year and they do silly things to what you've written. . . .‡

In *An American Dream*, which was published in 1964, I had a scene where somebody was talking, a black man was talking, and he said "shit" about twenty times. Now, I didn't really need twenty. I knew approximately twelve would be fine, but I knew if I put in twelve they'd take out some, so I put in twenty. And they screamed and yelled and they asked me to take out some, so I took out eight and I had my twelve, and they were happy and I was happy. That was when it was being printed in *Esquire*. Magazines always censored more. . . .

When *The Armies of the Night* was printed, it first came out in *Harper's* as "The Steps of the Pentagon" in 1967. And it had a lot of obscenity in it and Willie Morris, my editor at *Harper's*, asked me to "take it out," because he had very conservative readers. And I remember saying to him,

---

*The novel was published in 1948.

†That is Mailer's recollection today, as he talks of the event. However, others recall that the manuscript Mailer first handed around, through his friend Adeline Lubell, said "fuck," not "fug." See, for example, Hilary Mills's *Mailer* (1982), 86–102. This was also Angus Cameron's recollection.

‡The publishing taboo on words like "fuck," "shit," and "cocksucker" has a long history, reflected in court and regulatory agency decisions handed down even to the present day. In 1973, the Burger Court upheld the power of the FCC to threaten to revoke the broadcast license of the Pacifica Radio Foundation in New York (WBAI) for playing the George Carlin monologue "Seven Dirty Words" over the air. (The Burger Court, to judge from its opinion here, had no appreciation of Carlin's intelligent and comical satire.) And for several years now the FCC has been trying to eliminate "dirty words" entirely from broadcast programs.

"Oh, Willie, come on, just print the damn things!" And he did. And in fact *Harper's* lost a lot of subscribers because of that.

WILLIE MORRIS: Oddly enough, the cancellations we got were not over his stand on the Vietnam involvement but over the language. That piece broke new ground for American letters; it was a watershed issue because of the language. I knew when I read it that this was going to be a singular leap, but I also knew we'd have to go all the way and not compromise.

ANGUS CAMERON:* There was a passage in the original [*The Naked and the Dead*] manuscript that really got to Alfred,† and Alfred always put it the same way; it was the passage where Norman said, "Screwing her was like dipping your prick in a bowl of honey." Oh, that was marvelous! All right now, McIntyre read the book and he said: "I'm not enough of an editor to know whether this book is editorially as important as you and Adeline and Raymond think it is.‡ But I do know enough about books that sell and what makes a novel sell to agree with you when you say it's going to be a best-seller. I believe it is going to be a best-seller. But I don't see how we can publish it."

And when he said that to me, he looked it up and showed me the passage about dipping your prick in a bowl of honey. I still think that's a wonderful figure of speech. You see, we'd always had a little bit of a problem. We published some things that had passages in it that he didn't like. But Norman's stuff was in spades!

I said, "Well, Alfred, I think that you're making a big mistake here."

He said, "I just can't publish a book that I can't discuss in my own house."

And so I said to Alfred, "Alfred, why can't you discuss it in your own house?"

STANLEY FLEISHMAN: This was late fifties, after *Roth*. Early sixties. There was a period of time, for about two years, when we knew that the FBI was going through all of Aday's accounts and trying to scare them off. And the California state cases were really outrageous conduct in terms of illegal

---

*Cameron, described by John Tebbel as one of the "great" editors in chief, was forced to resign from his post as editor in chief of the respectable old Boston house of Little, Brown during the McCarthy era as a result of a savage attack made by the anti-Communist "smear sheet" *Counterattack,* which was managed by former FBI agents. The attack was supported by the *American Legion* magazine, the Hearst newspapers' Westbrook Pegler, and the *New York World Telegram and Sun's* leading Red-hunter, Frederick Woltman (John Tebbel, *A History of Publishing in the United States* 4 [1981], 705–8). Its fury can perhaps be gauged by the fact that many of the authors targeted by *Counterattack* were dropped from Little, Brown's list after Cameron left the firm (author interview with Angus Cameron). Cameron published on his own for a few years and was then taken aboard by Alfred A. Knopf, who, when congratulated for doing that, reputedly said: "It's a lot of nonsense. I don't believe any of it. And it's not brave of me when everyone knows that politically I'm right of the right field foul line. As for Cameron, he's simply one of the best editors around. I'd be a fool not to take him" (*Ibid.,* 708).

†Alfred McIntyre, president of Little, Brown and Company at the time.

‡Adeline Lubell, editorial assistant, and Raymond Everett, executive vice-president.

searches and seizures; they cordoned off the warehouse for days, when cops were in there reading, saying, "*This* book *is* obscene, *that* book *is not* obscene. *This* book *is* . . ." and so on.

And then when the federal government started to move, we had five federal indictments practically at the same time, but all of them had in common *Sex Life of a Cop.* And ultimately we went to trial on *Sex Life of a Cop* and seven other books. And there was a hung jury on every other one but on *Sex Life of a Cop,* which was in five counts. They found him guilty on each count and the judge gave him five years on each one. Aday got a twenty-five year sentence!

CIRCUIT JUDGE O'SULLIVAN: This is an appeal from a judgment entered upon a jury verdict convicting defendants-appellants, West Coast News Company, a California corporation, and Sanford E. Aday, a California resident, of violating Sections 1461 and 1462, Title 18, U.S.C.A., for delivering into Michigan by mail and common carrier allegedly obscene books, including one entitled *Sex Life of a Cop.* The indictment charged that eight books in the shipments were obscene,* but the jury disagreed as to all but *Sex Life of a Cop.* . . .

Our task is lightened by our view that the challenged book, which we have read, is by any standard obscene. It was inevitable that in today's bold and flourishing business of pornography there would come along a writing so bad that no amount of sophisticated dialectics could absolve it from classification as hard-core.

We will not attempt illumination by extensive recital of the book's contents. *Sex Life of a Cop* is a paperback with a cover picturing a woman (the wife of the Mayor of the town) trying unsuccessfully to hide her nakedness behind the grotesque underwear-clad figure of the Chief of Police, both of them having been interrupted in their lovers' lane dalliance by two of the town's police officers. The latter pair are the heroes of the narrative.

These officers, except for some needed rest from their amours, devote most of their on-duty and off-duty hours to successful sex encounters with whatever females come within their view. Their conquests range from a virgin to a "100 dollar" prostitute. The wives of the Chief of Police and the Mayor of the town, the new female police dispatcher, friendly waitresses, two nurses who promptly take off their clothes when the busy officers, otherwise unheralded, climb through their open window, a drunken "society" lady who is first rescued from a corner lamppost and then raped in the back seat of the prowl car, and a miscellany of other willing ladies, make up the cast. Every female identified in the story is easy prey for the officers.

The drama concludes with a smashing *denouement* when one of the officers, a sergeant, discovers, as an eyewitness, that his own beloved Alice

---

*The other seven books were: *Witch Finder, Love Princess, Decisive Years, The Black Night, Desperate Moment, never enough,* and *I Am a Lesbian.*

has been enjoying his outranked, prowl-car-pal's offerings. The moral lesson of retribution, which defendant's experts claim gives this book a social value,* subtly emerges in the cuckolded sergeant's plaintive soliloquy: "What in the world have I ever done to deserve this?" Thus ends the play.

We do not believe that the First Amendment's great guarantees of freedom of expression can be elasticized to embrace *Sex Life of a Cop*. Avoiding agonizing dissertations on the subject of obscenity and, in imitation of the wise and time-saving succinctness employed by Mr. Justice Potter Stewart: "We know obscenity when we see it,† and *Sex Life of a Cop* is just that."

STANLEY FLEISHMAN: Well, I took it up to the Supreme Court and finally, in one of those *Redrup* reversals, they just said, "Reversed, *Redrup*." And there were five of the justices who said it was not an obscene book, one of whom was Fortas, which, of course, was one of the things they would hold against him.

Sex Life of a Cop plainly was not a great book. Undoubtedly some readers were repelled by its descriptions of sexual activities, but so were many people offended by the sexual candor in *Tropic of Cancer, Candy, Fanny Hill, The Story of O, My Secret Life,* etc.‡ Many people read *Sex Life of a Cop* in a spirit of frank curiosity about sex. While it is true that the same information could have been gained from marriage manuals, educational texts, and other sober books found in libraries throughout the land, many people who would never go to the library and take out a treatise on sex picked up *Sex Life of a Cop* and got from it the same pleasure and information a better-educated person might derive from books such as *Ulysses* and *Tropic of Cancer*.

Anyway, there was like a two-year period from the time of Aday's conviction until the ultimate Supreme Court decision, reversing it. Les hung in for a while but his business was shot by this thing. It calmed down, obviously, while he was waiting for the results when he was doing just sort of safe stuff. He wasn't moving forward, and the rest of the country *was*

---

*Despite his personal and professional dislike of the "social value" criterion for obtaining a book's freedom, Fleishman made use of it in this case. By then the Supreme Court had announced the amplified "social value" doctrine (in the *Jacobellis/Tropic of Cancer* and *Fanny Hill* cases), whereby material that was not "utterly without literary, scientific, artistic, or other social importance" could not be denied the constitutional protections, but had not yet decided *Redrup*.

†Justice Stewart, of course, did not agree with Judge O'Sullivan's constitutional analysis of *Sex Life of a Cop*, nor with his application of the "Stewart doctrine." In *Redrup* he voted with the majority to reverse Aday's conviction (and O'Sullivan's decision).

‡*The Story of O* by "Pauline Réage" was published by Barney Rosset's Grove Press in New York in 1965. It was first published in Paris (in French) by Jean-Jacques Pauvert in 1954. *My Secret Life*—"one of the longest erotic autobiographies ever written"—with an introduction by G. Legman, was published by Grove Press in 1966.

Both books have been critically acknowledged as of social importance. See, e.g., Steven Marcus's *The Other Victorians* (1985) and Susan Sontag's "The Pornographic Imagination" in her *Styles of Radical Will* (1969). See also professor of law Robin West's insightful approach to *The Story of O* in "The Difference in Women's Hedonic Lives: A Phenomenological Critique of Feminist Legal Theory," in *Wisconsin Women's Law Journal* 3 (1987), 81, 119ff.

moving forward; so he lost his position. And when we came out finally victorious from the Supreme Court, and there was a new special issue of *Sex Life of a Cop,* nobody was interested anymore. . . .

The market had changed. Les had lost his position in the front of the crowd. So he ultimately went into clothing, which is where he is now.

27

Playing
the Role of
Revolutionaries

JUSTICE ABE FORTAS: I want to say that I am very happy to be here. And I am very happy to answer any and all questions that the committee may ask. I am not a novice in Washington. I am not a novice in Senate hearings. There is a constitutional problem that perplexes this committee, and it perplexes me. There is nothing I love better than a legal discussion or debate.

———

On the morning of July 16, 1968, Abe Fortas broke precedent by permitting himself to become the first sitting justice of the Supreme Court to appear before the Senate Judiciary Committee to answer questions pertaining to his qualifications for the role of chief justice.* One month earlier, President Lyndon B. Johnson had named his trusted friend and adviser Fortas to the post, a day after he announced that Chief Justice Earl Warren was resigning.

Warren's move had taken the exceptional form of a letter to Johnson signifying his intention to resign "effective at your pleasure." This wording

---

*Nominees to become associate justice of the Supreme Court are required to submit themselves to such questioning, as are nominees to become chief justice, unless the nominee is a sitting justice of the Court, in which case he probably cannot be required to do so. (Eventually, Fortas refused to return for more questioning by the committee.) Recess appointees to the Court are an exception to the rule; for example, Justice Brennan, who was appointed to the Court by President Eisenhower during a congressional recess, was required to appear before the committee to accommodate the Senate confirmation process, even though he was already taking part as an associate justice in the Court's work. But this procedure proved so troublesome that, in 1960, the Senate passed a resolution urging presidents to refrain from making recess appointments. See Robert Shogan, *A Question of Judgement* (1972), 164.

would allow Warren to remain the high court's chief until Johnson's appointee was approved by the Senate. Three years before, Johnson had placed Fortas on the high bench, clearing a seat for him by asking Justice Arthur Goldberg to become ambassador to the United Nations.

PAUL BENDER: The idea was Warren was going to retire early so that Johnson could make the appointment rather than Nixon, because Warren hated Nixon.

___

There were fears among liberal Democrats, including the president, that if Warren waited to step down until after the coming presidential election, Richard M. Nixon would be the one to name the Court's next chief and would use the opportunity to sidetrack or even reverse the progress made by the Warren Court in civil rights and liberties—especially the rights of criminal defendants and the freedoms of speech and press. Partisans of the right of course thought differently.

NATIONAL DECENCY REPORTER: A "Fortas Court" would [make] the "Warren Court" look like right-wing extremists by comparison.

___

The president accepted Chief Justice Warren's offer to retire with equally unusual terminology—"effective at such time as a successor is qualified." The "problem" that Fortas alluded to in his opening statement to the committee was already in the committee's mind: Was there in fact a vacancy to be filled, given the equivocal wording of Warren's resignation and Johnson's acceptance? At Judiciary Committee hearings, Johnson's attorney general, Ramsey Clark, testified to prior Court appointment practice and resolved that problem,* but soon other questions regarding the appointment arose that were not so easily resolved.

Conservatives expected that a Nixon-designated chief would strengthen "the peace forces against the criminal forces of the land,"† respect the basic principles of "law and order," be a "caretaker of our constitutional heritage" rather than a "super-legislator," and refrain from imposing "his own social and political agenda" upon "the American people."

ABE KRASH:‡ I think that . . . the Republicans, sensing that they would regain the White House, fought very hard against [Abe's] nomination

---

*The liberal Ramsey Clark became attorney general in 1967. His father, the conservative Justice Tom Clark, resigned from the Court at the same time. Tom Clark had been attorney general under President Truman, who later put him on the Court. As attorney general, Tom Clark actively participated in the prosecution of the American Communist party leaders and established the "Red-baiting" attorney general's list of so-called subversive organizations. President Johnson named Thurgood Marshall to the Supreme Court seat that Clark vacated.

†While Fortas's nomination to the chief justiceship was before the Judiciary Committee, the dramatic anti-party demonstrations and "police riots" occurred at the Democratic convention in Chicago. Climaxing a year of assassination, urban rioting, and violent antiwar demonstrations, these events were interpreted by Republicans especially as the predictable consequences of Warren Court "permissiveness" of the sort that Fortas was taken to exemplify.

‡A partner in Fortas's former law firm.

because they thought that if Nixon was elected they would then themselves be able to control the appointment of the chief justice. Secondly, there was substantial opposition from the South to Fortas because he was a member of the Warren Court, which was, of course, hated in the South because of its anti-segregation position and Fortas's views in criminal cases specifically.* For example, his vote in the *Miranda* case and his votes in other criminal cases led to opposition by various Southern senators and congressmen and made it difficult for them to adhere to political commitments they made to President Johnson that they would support Fortas. Third, Fortas's support among those who would normally have been expected to be supporters of his nomination—by that I mean the liberal Democratic senators—was weakened by the great bitterness over the Vietnam situation and the fact that Abe had been very closely identified with President Johnson, as a hawk; and so I think that weakened his position among the liberals. And all those factors coalesced with obviously some other things, for example, the American University honorarium he got, which was just a make-way for people to oppose him. Some people also believe that there was some anti-Semitism involved, though certainly that was very much under the surface.

———

In addition to his loyalty to Lyndon Johnson, Abe Fortas had brought to the high bench a powerful mind, broad legal knowledge, a scholarly bent, sound judgment, and a liberal philosophy in all areas with the exception, perhaps, of the Vietnam War. He had somewhat reluctantly left behind an exciting and lucrative law practice with the distinguished Washington law firm of Arnold, Fortas and Porter, which he had used as a base to champion the civil rights of small and often penurious individuals like Monte Durham† and Clarence Earl Gideon‡ and to represent the interests of corporate giants like Coca-Cola and Pan American Airlines. During the McCarthy era the firm had energetically defended persons who had been called security risks and had cleared an embattled Owen Lattimore of charges of disloyalty and perjury. With regard to free speech, Arnold, Fortas and Porter had represented the publishers of *Playboy* and *Rogue* magazines—the former owned by Hugh Hefner and the latter by California sex-book publisher William Hamling, who had funded Robert Redrup's successful defense against obscenity charges in New York, but who would himself go to prison on federal postal obscenity charges after Fortas left the Court because by then (1974) the Court's liberal bloc was in a minority and

---

*Fortas himself was from the South, having been born in Memphis, Tennessee.

†Fortas represented Durham and proposed to the Court of Appeals for the District of Columbia the test for criminal responsibility that Judge David Bazelon adopted and announced as "the Durham test," in *Durham* v. *United States* (1955).

‡Fortas represented Gideon and proposed to the Supreme Court the rule that the Court adopted making the provision of free legal counsel a constitutional requirement of due process for indigent defendants. See Anthony Lewis's moving account of the case, and Fortas's role in it, in *Gideon's Trumpet* (1964).

Warren's replacement, Warren E. Burger, had taken command of the Court's actions in the obscenity area. In 1957, in the landmark *Roth* case, Arnold, Fortas and Porter had filed in the Supreme Court an amicus curiae brief, signed by Fortas, on behalf of Hefner's and Hamling's publishing ventures, urging that the postal obscenity law be struck down as unconstitutional.

I asked Abe Krash about the reasons that Abe Fortas and, as young associates in the firm during the fifties, he and Charlie Reich had fought for the freedom of magazines like *Playboy.* *

ABE KRASH: *Playboy* was a little bold at that time, [although] the women were not as disrobed as they are now. . . . But it was regarded as somewhat risqué and funny, and we kind of thought of ourselves as the young guys fighting the puritans who were trying to repress what was funny and free. And, what the hell, I didn't think of *Playboy* as serious literature. I did think of the fight being a fight basically that had nobler or greater goals than protecting *Playboy;* that is, I thought of it more as a fight for the right to protect D. H. Lawrence's *Lady Chatterley.* † But we thought there was a kind of amusement about the whole thing and we were interested. I don't think the firm ever had any other obscenity or pornography cases, although the firm had a great many different kinds of free speech cases. ‡

—

Abe Fortas stepped easily into the shoes of his predecessor, Arthur Goldberg, a Kennedy appointee who had replaced Felix Frankfurter and whose thoughtful and humanitarian voting pattern during the few years he served on the Court had swung decisions necessary to the development of individual rights. Goldberg told me that Fortas shared his views. Fortas's judicial behavior, however, differed from Goldberg's in this respect, at least: the new associate justice sought to influence, even dominate, critical areas of the Court's decision- and opinion-making processes. In doing that, Fortas, as a freshman justice, antagonized not only Hugo Black, the Court's senior justice, then entering his twenty-eighth year on the bench, but his former teacher and mentor William O. Douglas, then completing his twenty-sixth year on the Court.

There was deep resentment on the Hill, especially among powerful Southern senators, of Fortas's friendship with Johnson, his almost aristocratic demeanor, and his votes in criminal rights and obscenity cases. Fortas's popularity as a Washington figure suffered from the impression he gave

---

*Reich, a former law clerk to Justice Fortas and professor of law at Yale, is the author of the celebrated *Greening of America* (1970). He now teaches in the law school of San Francisco State College in San Francisco.

†Krash contributed an important commentary on the English and American *Lady Chatterley's Lover* cases in a review of *The Trial of Lady Chatterley,* edited by C. H. Rolph (1961); the review was published in *Yale Law Journal* 71 (1962), 1351.

‡The firm's location in Washington, D.C., was probably the reason why it had not represented any publishers of allegedly obscene books. Most obscenity cases arose in New York and California and were handled by lawyers practicing in those states.

of preening himself on his success as a power-broking lawyer; his pro bono contributions to the law safeguarding the interests of mentally ill criminals, impecunious accuseds, and delinquent minors; his accomplishments as a violinist; and, most invidiously, his insider position at the Johnson White House. In 1965, not long before President Johnson named him to the Court, Fortas listed himself in *Who's Who in the South and Southwest* as "Presidential advisor," giving his address as "Care of the White House, 1600 Pennsylvania Avenue, Washington, D.C." Self-confident, almost brazen, Fortas, like many successful Washington lawyer-politicians, was an adept dissembler. When he was asked during his 1968 confirmation hearings about his close relationship with LBJ, Fortas's response was characteristic. Two things about himself were "vastly exaggerated," he said.

JUSTICE ABE FORTAS: One is the extent to which I am a Presidential advisor, and the other is the extent to which I am a proficient violinist. I am a very poor violinist, but very enthusiastic, and my relationship with the President has been exaggerated out of all connection with reality.

—

Fortas's vote made possible the Warren Court's bitterly controversial landmark decision in *Miranda* v. *Arizona* (1966), requiring that an arrested person be informed that anything he says may be used against him in court and that he has a right to consult with a lawyer before or during questioning—a decision that must have pained Senator Strom Thurmond of South Carolina, who earlier had been much distressed by the Warren Court's decision in *Mallory* v. *United States* (1957); there the conviction of a confessed rapist was reversed by the Court because his confession had been coerced by police. Fortas, of course, had had nothing to do with *Mallory,* which had been decided in 1957, but during the confirmation hearings Thurmond acted as though Fortas were the author of Earl Warren's opinion in that case.

"Mallory, Mallory," Thurmond thundered at Fortas.

SENATOR STROM THURMOND: I want that word to ring in your ears— Mallory! A man who raped a woman, admitted his guilt, and the Supreme Court turned him loose on a technicality. And who I was told later went to Philadelphia and committed another crime, and somewhere else another crime, because the Court turned him loose on technicalities. . . .*

Is not that type of decision calculated to bring the courts and the law and the administration in disrepute? Is not that type of decision calculated to encourage more people to commit rapes and serious crimes? Can you as a Justice of the Supreme Court condone such a decision as that? I ask you to answer that question.

JUSTICE ABE FORTAS: Senator, because of my respect for you and my respect for this body, and because of my respect for the Constitution of the United

---

*Thurmond's allegations about Mallory's post-decision crimes were not substantiated.

States, and my position as an Associate Justice of the Supreme Court of the United States, I will adhere to the limitation that I believe the Constitution of the United States places upon me and will not reply to your question as you phrased it.

———

Strom Thurmond epitomized and expressed the South's deep hostility not only toward the Warren Court—for its desegregation decisions and repeated recognition of the constitutional rights of criminal defendants— but toward the Democratic party's legislative programs to implement civil rights. Thurmond had left the Democratic fold in 1948 to lead the Dixie-crat revolt and campaign for president on the States' Rights ticket. After that, he had returned to the Democrats, only to bolt again in 1964, as a leader of the GOP resurgence in the South. In 1968 he had worked so diligently to gain Southern support for Richard Nixon's bid to become president that Nixon reputedly promised him the first seat on the Supreme Court to be vacated after the election. Thus Thurmond may have had a special interest in bringing Abe Fortas down.

Fortas repeatedly declined to answer hostile questions put to him by Thurmond and Senator Sam Ervin and, after four days of ordeal as a witness, declined (as was his prerogative as a sitting Supreme Court justice) to return and respond to further questioning by the committee.* In his absence, his foes on the committee found other witnesses prepared to testify to Fortas's judicial "misbehavior," including his "permissive" votes in the obscenity area during the Court's closed conferences.

Fortas was made a scapegoat for the Warren Court's "sins." According to his critics, Fortas's most despicable judicial attitude—what made him particularly unfit to occupy the Court's center chair—was evident in the votes he regularly cast in closed conference to reverse local judge and jury decisions that sought to punish "merchants of smut." Fortas's critics even implied that he had a conflict of interest in this area because his law firm had represented William Hamling. All that can fairly be said, however, is that after Abe Fortas replaced Arthur Goldberg on the nation's high bench, the Court began, more systematically than before, to throw out the crimi-nal convictions of persons involved in the distribution of literature "utterly without social value."

————

*The constitutional doctrine regarding the separation of powers has been interpreted to shield members of the Supreme Court from interrogation by the Congress with respect to a justice's work. As explained by Senator Albert Gore of Tennessee (who had formally presented Fortas to the committee), "Just as a Senator or a Congressman may not be called upon by the courts to explain or justify his votes as a representative of the people . . . so a Justice of the Supreme Court may not be required, by the Senate or a Senate Committee, to explain or justify his votes on decisions by the Court or his judicial opinions." In addition, a nominee was "obliged not to say anything that might intrude on the judicial process." Fortas must, Gore stated, "avoid construing or explaining opinions of the Court lest he may appear to be adding to or subtracting from what has been decided, or may perchance be prejudging future cases." In the event, Fortas declined the committee's invitation to discuss judicial matters and specific cases, except—according to one commentator—when it "suited his purposes" to do so. Robert Shogan, *A Question of Judgement* (1972), Chapter 6.

It was probably Fortas, however, who advanced the "pandering" doctrine that Justice Brennan made use of to justify Ralph Ginzberg's punishment—a doctrine originally promoted by Chief Justice Earl Warren and much appreciated by moral and religious vigilante groups. And Fortas had dissented from an important free speech decision taken by the Court (with an opinion written by Brennan) which extended First Amendment protection to a *Life* magazine article that "invaded the privacy" (according to New York law) of a family that had been brutally victimized by a band of criminals. Right-wing conservatives, however, chose to ignore this side of Fortas's record.

JAMES J. CLANCY: Mr. Chairman, honorable Senators, my name is James J. Clancy. I am an attorney. I appear before this Committee at the direction of the executive board of the National Organization of Citizens for Decent Literature, Inc.—short title, CDL—to oppose the confirmation of Associate Justice Abe Fortas as Chief Justice of the United States Supreme Court. . . .

CDL was founded over 10 years ago by a group of concerned businessmen and family heads, under the leadership of Attorney Charles H. Keating, Jr., of Cincinnati, Ohio.* These men took a look at what was creeping onto the American scene in the shape of books and magazines and movies and formed a community organization with two things in mind: (1) to alert everyone to the nature of the obscenity problem; (2) to press for the enforcement of the obscenity laws—laws which history has proven are essential to the development of good family living.

Just recently, the Congress of the United States also became alarmed and in Public Law 90-100 established a Commission on Obscenity and Pornography because the obscenity traffic was a "matter of national concern." The event which motivated Congress to act was a series of obscenity decisions

---

*Keating later was appointed by President Nixon to fill a vacancy on the National Commission on Obscenity and Pornography (the "Lockhart Commission," whose work is described in Chapter 28). He dissented from the final report of the commission, which recommended the repeal of all obscenity laws applicable to consenting adults. In 1990 Keating was found implicated in legally questionable transactions leading to the failure of the centerpiece of his "vast financial universe," the Lincoln Savings and Loan Bank, transactions "expected to cost taxpayers more than $2.5 billion." As of April 1990, he was "being pursued in the courts by federal banking regulators, the state of California, and people who purchased bad bonds sold by his thrift." He was under investigation by the FBI, the Securities and Exchange Commission, and the IRS. "His generous political donations to several U.S. Senators—since dubbed the Keating Five—and their intervention on his behalf with banking examiners . . . prompted a Senate Ethics Committee probe," and nearly resulted in the ruin of the senators involved. But for three decades Keating was known primarily as "captain of Citizens for Decent Literature, at one time perhaps the most prominent anti-pornography organization in the country." David Corn, "Dirty Bookkeeping," *The New Republic,* April 2, 1990. See also Terrence P. Jeffrey, "The Man Who Bought Washington," *American Spectator,* February 1990. Keating was connected with CDL as recently as 1989, as shown in CDL's annual report for the year ended June 30, 1988; he may still be associated with a successor to CDL, which helped to make Cincinnati a "porn-free" city. This is the group that was behind the recent indictment of Cincinnati art gallery director Dennis Barrie for exhibiting the works of Robert Mapplethorpe, as described in Chapter 30.

handed down in May and June of 1967 in which the U.S. Supreme Court reversed 23 of 26 state and federal obscenity determinations.* In the process, the community standards of 13 states were upset and eight findings of obscenity by juries were reversed.

Justice Fortas, who participated in every one of these obscenity decisions, in each instance voted to reverse the findings of the juries and courts below. The same pattern was followed by Justice Fortas in his handling of the 26 additional cases which were ruled upon by the Court during the recent October 1967 term. That makes 52 cases in all in which Justice Fortas voted in favor of obscenity, and overrode the votes of judges and juries in local communities.†

To show the country the role played by Justice Fortas in this event, we have made a 35-millimeter slide film documentary on the October 1966 term decisions. The documentary traces the history of the 26 cases from their origin in the trial court, up to the final decision of the U.S. Supreme Court, and shows pictorially the material involved. A short 30-minute slide adaptation of the same is available for the Committee's viewing. Portions of this slide presentation have already been seen by Senators McClellan, Long, and Fong, the members of the subcommittee appointed for this purpose, and we are inviting all of the Committee's members, as well as members of the Press, to see this display for themselves. . . .

The type of materials that Justice Fortas voted to free during the 1966 October term was uniform. There were 20 sex paperback books, entitled: *Sex Life of a Cop, Lust School, Lust Web, Sin Servant, Lust Pool, Shame Agent, Lust Job, Sin Whisper, Orgy House, Sin Hooked, Bayou Sinner, Lust Hungry, Shame Shop, Flesh Pots, Sinners' Seance, Passion Priestess, Penthouse Pagans, Sin Warden,* and *Flesh Avenger;*‡ 12 bondage books; a series of photographs of nude females in provocative poses with focus on the pubic area and suggested invitation to sexual relations; eight motion picture films of the striptease type; ten girlie magazines; one nudist magazine; and two homemade so-called "underground" films.§ One of those books, *Sin Whisper,* was published by Corinth Publications, a company owned by a man named William Hamling. Hamling's ex-attorney was Abe Fortas, who, after being appointed to the Supreme Court bench, would sit in judgment on his ex-client's claims. . . .

---

*The first calls by moral and religious vigilante groups for remedial action to counter the Supreme Court's obscenity decisions followed the Court's decision in the Florida *Tropic of Cancer* case, after which, when Chief Justice Warren spoke at the New School in New York, he was greeted by pickets who blamed the Court for the rising tide of pornography. But Clancy is referring here to the Court's decisions in *Redrup* v. *New York.*

†I have not verified Clancy's count.

‡ There are only nineteen titles.

§The "underground" films Clancy apparently had in mind were *Flaming Creatures* and the only film Jean Genet ever made, *Un Chant d'Amour.* However, the judgments reached by the Supreme Court in these cases did not free these films, marking two of the very few cases in which the Brennan doctrine failed to work to free expressive material having social value. See de Grazia, *Censorship Landmarks* (1969), 596 and 599.

An overall impression of Justice Fortas' philosophy in this area can be gleaned from the fact that he voted to reverse the jury and state court obscenity determinations in every one of the 52 cases he acted upon during the 1966 and 1967 terms, including the *Sin Whisper* case.

A more precise understanding of his philosophy in the obscenity area can be gained from a consideration of his vote in the case of *Schachtman* v. *California,* decided in June of 1967. In that case, the owner of a film arcade on Main Street in downtown Los Angeles exhibited three 16mm motion picture films entitled "O-7," O-12," and "D-15" in his peep-show machines and sold 8mm versions of the same across the counter. Los Angeles vice officers viewed the films in the machine, purchased three 200-foot rolls of the 8mm copies and arrested the owner, Schachtman. All three films were viewed in court and were ruled hard-core pornography by Federal District Judge Hauk, a Los Angeles jury, and the California appellate court system. All of these determinations, however, were reversed in the U.S. Supreme Court by a 5–4 decision in which Justice Fortas cast the deciding vote in favor of obscenity.

JUDGE A. ANDREW HAUK: The film, O-12, was viewed by the court. The film consists of a female model clothed in a white blouse opened in front, a half-bra which exposed the upper half of the breasts including the nipples and a pair of white capri pants (which are soon discarded) under which the model wears a pair of sheer panties through which the pubic hair and region are clearly visible. The film consists of the model moving and undulating upon a bed, moving her hands, and lips and torso, all clearly indicative of engaging in sexual activity, including simulated intercourse and invitations to engage in intercourse. There is no music, sound, story-line or dancing other than exaggerated body movements. On at least three occasions, the female by lip articulation is observed to state, "fuck you," "fuck me." The dominant theme of the film taken as a whole obviously is designed to appeal to the prurient interest in sex of the viewer and is patently offensive in that the focus of the camera returns again and again to the genital and rectal areas clearly showing the pubic hair and the outline of the external parts of the female genital area. The film is entirely without artistic or literary significance and is utterly without redeeming social importance.

The film "O-7" is virtually the same as Exhibit 1. . . . The film is entirely without artistic or literary significance and is utterly wihout redeeming social importance.

The parties stipulated that the film D-15 is substantially the same in character and quality as the films introduced as exhibits one and two. The court therefore finds that as to exhibit 3, the dominant theme of the film, taken as a whole, appeals to a prurient interest in sex of the viewer and is patently offensive and is utterly without redeeming social importance.

———

In finding all three films obscene, Federal District Judge Hauk applied the test for obscenity that Justice Brennan had articulated in the 1964 cases freeing *Tropic of Cancer* and *The Lovers* and the 1966 case freeing *Fanny Hill*. By the time this case reached the Supreme Court, however, Fortas and four other justices—Hugo Black, William O. Douglas, Potter Stewart, and even Byron White*—had adopted doctrinal positions that resulted in the freeing of some material that would have been condemned under the Brennan doctrine, and so Hauk's findings regarding the films were reversed.

"Trashy" material of this sort, including films like "O-7," "O-12," and "D-15," was sometimes spoken of as "pornography," because it made no pretense to the possession of any value other than its capacity to arouse sexual feelings in the reader or viewer; if it was spoken of as "soft-core" rather than "hard-core," this signified that neither penetration by, or of, sexual organs nor sexual organs in a state of excitement were explicitly depicted or described.

According to James Clancy, Fortas's ascension to the Court shifted the balance in favor of such sexually oriented materials because Justice Goldberg, whom Fortas replaced, would have denied freedom to them. This is unlikely. Both Fortas, originally, in the March 1966 trilogy of obscenity cases, and Goldberg, in the 1964 *Cancer/Jacobellis* obscenity cases, subscribed to the Brennan doctrine. In addition, according to Goldberg, Fortas "shared" his views in this area. Moreover, as I have suggested earlier, it is likely that Goldberg would have voted to reverse Ralph Ginzburg's obscenity conviction, whereas Fortas voted to affirm it, thus swinging the Court to that position. What is clearest, perhaps, is that Goldberg, like Fortas, Brennan, Stewart, and Thurgood Marshall (who joined the Court in 1967, when conservative justice Tom Clark resigned), was not an absolutist in this area; yet all these justices during this period were voting and writing in ways that were moving the Court and the constitutional law of obscenity ineluctably toward that "absolute" freedom of expression with regard to sexually oriented magazines, books, and movies that Justices Black and Douglas had long repeatedly propounded.

JUSTICE ARTHUR J. GOLDBERG: I was of the view that obscenity, hard-core pornography, was not protected. Actually I have changed my mind about this. I think that with consenting adults, anything is okay—in books. Of course, children are a different category.

Now movies, you have to buy a ticket and go in. So I'd be rather inclined, if the exhibitors truthfully advertise that this is hard-core and so on, any adult may decide to go in. I would be inclined to say, "Okay, you're of age and consent."†

---

*White never articulated a definition of his own, and his vote was more unpredictable than that of practically every other member of the Court. He voted to the effect that *Tropic of Cancer* was obscene but *The Lovers* was not; neither were the peep-show movies "O-7," "O-12," and "D-15" or the books *Lust Pool* and *Shame Agent* obscene to him.

†These views, expressed by Justice Goldberg nearly twenty years after leaving the high bench, strongly suggest that had Goldberg not been persuaded by President Johnson to leave the Court (to make room for Fortas), the dissenting minority of justices (led by Brennan) who in 1973 called for the constitutional invalidation of all obscenity laws applicable to consenting

In the June 1967 *Schachtman* case mentioned by Clancy, involving the peep-show films "O-7," "O-12," and "D-15," Justice Brennan had joined the sexual conservatives on the bench—Warren, Clark, and Harlan—in dissenting from the Court's decision to reverse the film distributor's conviction. Although Brennan did not explain his vote, he must have believed Schachtman's conviction should stand because "O-12," "O-7," and "D-15" appealed to nothing but prurient interests, were patently offensive to (national) community standards of decency, and, most important, were utterly without literary, artistic, scientific, or other social value. To Brennan, these films were "worthless" in Kalven's sense of that term.*

SENATOR STROM THURMOND: Mr. Clancy, I wish to express appreciation for your appearing here. I was very pleased to learn that we have a Citizens for Decent Literature† in this country that is trying to protect our young people from the obscene and indecent literature that has been distributed with the Supreme Court's approval. . . .

In all these decisions you've been talking about—I believe you said that the Supreme Court had reversed 23 of 26 State and Federal obscenity determinations. . . .

JAMES J. CLANCY: Yes, sir.

SENATOR STROM THURMOND: And in these decisions, the community standards of 13 states were upset?

JAMES J. CLANCY: Yes, sir. These 26 cases involved 13 states.

SENATOR STROM THURMOND: And in those same decisions, eight findings of fact by juries concerning obscene material were reversed?

JAMES J. CLANCY: Yes, sir.

SENATOR STROM THURMOND: And in all these decisions, Justice Fortas participated in them and in each instance he voted to reverse the findings of the juries and the courts below?

JAMES J. CLANCY: Yes, sir.

---

adults would instead have been a majority. This would have delivered "absolute" freedom from obscenity-law censorship to expression in books, magazines, and motion pictures.

*See Kalven, "Metaphysics of the Law of Obscenity," in *1960 Supreme Court Review* (1960). It is unlikely that the lawyers who represented the distributors of these films claimed for them any artistic or other social importance; this would explain Brennan's vote in these cases. As described in the previous chapter, some First Amendment lawyers, including Stanley Fleishman of Los Angeles, were ideologically reluctant to advance legal doctrine that promised freedom for "literary" and "artistic" works but suppression for material empty of such "elitist pretensions." They advocated absolute freedom for sexually oriented expression regardless of any demonstrative worth, or value, thus anticipating the position ultimately taken by Brennan and the other remaining members (except White) of the Warren Court, in 1973.

†In 1970, Citizens for Decent Literature boasted eleven U.S. senators who were "Honorary Committee Members"—including Strom Thurmond, John Sparkman, Karl E. Mundt, and Barry Goldwater—and 124 U.S. representatives and four state governors, who were also "Honorary Committee Members." By 1972, CDL claimed 145,000 "Decent Citizens" as contributors and a still-growing "Honorary Committee" which by then included Representatives Tip O'Neill (shortly thereafter to become Speaker of the House) and Wilbur Mills, "who two years later would be found in a somewhat less-than-decent position with stripper Fanne Fox." David Corn, "Dirty Bookkeeping," *The New Republic*, April 2, 1990.

SENATOR STROM THURMOND: Your careful research reveals that?
JAMES J. CLANCY: Absolutely.

———

At this point, the Senate Judiciary Committee's chairman, Southern "Dixiecrat" James O. Eastland, decided to play on the fears entertained by some people that mentally disordered citizens are easily triggered by sexual images to engage in violent sexual crimes.

CHAIRMAN JAMES O. EASTLAND: Could I ask a question?
SENATOR STROM THURMOND: Yes, sir. I yield to the distinguished Senator from Mississippi.
CHAIRMAN JAMES O. EASTLAND: Is it your experience, Mr. Clancy, or do you have any idea that material of this kind which the Supreme Court is approving of would cause a person of unbalanced mind, psychotic mind, to create acts of violence?
JAMES J. CLANCY: Yes, sir. In our most recent *amicus* brief, filed on the side of the Government in the *Ginsberg* case, *Ginsberg* v. *New York,** we cited at least 50 cases in which such had occurred. . . .
For example, when I was Assistant City Attorney of Burbank, we had a case in which a girl was raped about four blocks from City Hall, in a culvert. She reported to the police that the person who had raped her had a girlie magazine in his pocket, and had thrown it aside. So they went back to the scene. They found the girlie magazine. This was one case which interested me. . . .
Another case in New Jersey, a boy had witnessed a stag film. On the way back at an intersection, he got into a car, he commandeered the car, he took the girl and raped and killed her. You could not say what causal connection there is . . .
The point is that the indiscriminate dissemination of this material in the community, and the tolerance by the community of this material, gives the mistaken impression to the youth that this is acceptable. . . .
SENATOR STROM THURMOND: Well, do you not feel that a community has a right to protect its young people by taking steps to prevent such obscene material from being available to them?
JAMES J. CLANCY: Yes, sir. This is one of the reasons for the obscenity laws. We trace it in this documentary, which I hope to be able to show you. . . .
SENATOR STROM THURMOND: In view of the decisions that have been handed down by the Supreme Court in 1966 and 1967 sessions, is there any way a community can protect itself from the filth to which you have referred?

———

*The case is described anon in this chapter. "Horror stories" of this kind would in the late seventies be staple testimony before the Attorney General's Commission on Pornography (Meese commission), presented by women who claimed that as children or adults they had been sexually molested, manhandled, abused, beaten, or raped by their fathers, husbands, or other men they knew after the men had perused "pornography" such as *Playboy* magazine. See Chapter 29.

JAMES J. CLANCY: In my opinion there is not. And I cannot impress enough upon you Senators how serious this problem is.* For example, the film "O-7." Something much less offensive than that was the standard for Los Angeles prosecutors and which they relied on to control this subject matter. Now when the Supreme Court reversed "O-7" and "D-15" and "O-12," these prosecutors said, "Well, there is nothing we can do now to stop it. This material is being disseminated in the mail at $10, anyone can buy it, anyone can buy a small projector for about $30 and have his own stag show, like the one where that boy went out and raped and murdered the girl, after watching it. There is nothing we can do—looking at these decisions."

And of course the pornographers, they read these decisions, they take their advice from their defense attorneys, and they have said, "All stops have been pulled, and anything goes. . . ." As a consequence, for example, there is an organization in Los Angeles County now called Collectors Publications, Inc., which is flooding the market with hundreds and hundreds of titles which have always been regarded as the hardest of hard-core pornography, even under the counter in France—and this is going out through the mails, over the counter. And police, law enforcement officers are saying, "There is nothing we can do about it." You see, that is because of the Supreme Court. . . .

SENATOR STROM THURMOND: I beg your pardon . . . what?

JAMES J. CLANCY: Well, we've asked ourselves the question, "Where do you think the difficulty lies in this Nation's growing obscenity problem?" The history of these recent decisions is clear proof to us that the root of this Nation's problem is the United States Supreme Court. A "silent" revolution is being waged in that arena, not only in the obscenity area, but in other areas of the law as well. Not all revolutions are fought with guns. Playing the role of revolutionaries today are certain Justices of the Supreme Court.

———

In Chicago five months earlier, in January 1968, CDL members had listened to a tape-recorded narration prepared for a 35mm slide-and-film presentation that Jim Clancy was planning to produce and distribute in connection with CDL's campaign against the Supreme Court—"to deal with the 26 recent decisions of the Supreme Court in obscenity cases." The repressive positions taken in amicus briefs that the CDL had filed with the Court in some of those cases had been brushed aside by a majority of the

———

*Clancy's testimony may have impressed Strom Thurmond and other senators, but it made no perceptible impression on the Supreme Court itself. The next term, the Court, speaking through freshman justice Thurgood Marshall, held that Americans had the constitutional right to read and watch even concededly obscene books and motion pictures in the privacy of their homes. The case, *Stanley* v. *Georgia,* has never been overruled. The Burger Court, however, limited it "to its facts"—i.e., to possessions, readings, and viewings in the privacy of one's home. And in July 1990 the Rehnquist Court further narrowed the principle by holding that the right of Americans to read and watch anything they wished in the privacy of their homes did not include "child pornography." See *Osborne* v. *Ohio,* 110 S.Ct. 1691 (1990) and Brennan's trenchant dissent at 1705ff.

justices that included Abe Fortas. The CDL's media blitz was planned to "graphically illustrate the fact that the United States Supreme Court is directly responsible for the proliferation of obscenity in this country." However, once President Johnson announced Chief Justice Warren's "conditional" resignation and Fortas's nomination to become chief justice in his place, CDL decided to turn the 35mm slide show into a thirty-minute anti-Fortas "color documentary" called *Target Smut*.

During the Fortas hearings, Clancy gave a private showing of "the documentation" to several members of the Judiciary Committee, who were impressed enough to arrange to have Clancy testify. For two hours Clancy spoke and answered questions and, when the committee adjourned, Senator Thurmond announced to the packed hearing room that later that afternoon a press conference would take place in the Capitol press room for any member of the press or senator interested in seeing *Target Smut* and two "dirty movies" that had been freed by the Supreme Court, with Fortas casting the swing vote.

According to Clancy, over fifty representatives of the news media attended the press conference;* he called the result "history." The "Fortas Obscene Film Festival" would be shown again and again on the Hill.

BRUCE ALLEN MURPHY: Twenty-one people were huddled in a darkened room around a coin-operated movie projector, watching a cinematic fantasy. This one was called *O-7*. The plot wasn't very much. An attractive young girl was doing a striptease down to her garter belt and transparent panties. For fourteen minutes the actress undressed and writhed erotically, with the camera repeatedly focusing on various parts of her anatomy, ensuring that no viewer missed the point. It was what they call a stag film.

But wait. There was something very wrong here. Rather than moaning and sighing, the audience was laughing out loud. Since there was no screen in the room, the projection of the film on the wooden panels of the wall made it look as though the actress were "molting." Moreover, the people shouting out the rude jokes during the screening were not the usual trench-coat-clad crowd at such exhibitions, but members of Washington's elite press corps. Even more incredibly, the gentleman feeding the coin-operated projector with silver was a United States Senator . . . the senior senator from South Carolina, Strom Thurmond.

———

The raucous reaction of the Washington press corps and interested senators to the CDL-produced "Fortas Obscene Film Festival" persuaded Senator Thurmond that he had succeeded in breathing new life into what had seemed a dying battle to block Justice Abe Fortas's appointment to become chief justice of the United States. An untold number of senators, as well as newsmen, now saw CDL's films, one of which (*Flaming Creatures*) dealt

———

*Bruce Allen Murphy, in *Fortas: The Rise and Ruin of a Supreme Court Justice* (1988), counted twenty-one, including projectionist Strom Thurmond (441–42).

"unblushingly with transvestism."* And one by one, senators who saw the show signaled the White House that they could no longer vote for Fortas for chief justice of the United States.

SENATOR RUSSELL LONG (LOUISIANA): I have seen one Fortas film—I have seen enough. . . .

SENATOR FRANK LAUSCHE (OHIO): [I would] never vote for a man who would approve the films involved in the *Schachtman* case. . . . If the nominee were my brother, I would not vote for him.

JAMES J. CLANCY: From that point on it became obvious that Abe Fortas would not be confirmed. Other issues were raised but the obscenity issue is the one that turned the tide. As a matter of fact, it seems that the other issues were magnified out of proportion just so it wouldn't look as if the Senate were rejecting Fortas only on the basis of his obscenity decisions.

———

Although President Johnson still had enough votes on the Judiciary Committee to report Fortas's nomination out favorably, the White House was in imminent danger of losing the votes needed to prevent a filibuster on the Senate floor, which would kill the appointment. The results of the pornography attack were devastating: the mail in some Senate offices reportedly ran twenty-five to one against Fortas. A rumor began floating that when the Senate returned, Strom Thurmond would mount a filibuster solely on the issue of Fortas's penchant for pornography. The senator's cause was given a fresh boost when the syndicated columnist James J. Kilpatrick took in the show and blamed it on Fortas's idea of "free speech."

JAMES J. KILPATRICK: The [Supreme Court] majority's brusque order of June 12, 1967 [in the "O-7" case], is part of a pattern of constitutional law as tailored by Mr. Justice Fortas. This was his idea of free speech. Does the Senate agree? That's the size of the parliamentary proposition: Boil the issue down to this lip-licking slut, writhing carnally on a sofa, while a close-up camera dwells lasciviously on her genitals. Free speech? Free press? Is this what the Constitution means? The Constitution is, one may remember, what five judges say it is, no less, no more. So remembering, will the Senate advise and consent?

———

Fortas biographer Bruce Allen Murphy measured the Warren Court justices along a "smut spectrum" based on the quantum of allegedly pornographic literature or movies each seemed willing "to allow to be sold." The "most permissive" were the absolutists Black and Douglas, who denied that

---

*Bruce Allen Murphy, *Fortas* (1988), 448. Jones Mekas, a New York filmmaker, critic, exhibitor, and archivist, was convicted in August 1964 and sentenced to sixty days in the workhouse for showing *Flaming Creatures*. The sentence, however, was suspended, and the Supreme Court dismissed Mekas's appeal as moot. The case, *Jacobs v. New York,* is in de Grazia, *Censorship Landmarks* (1969), 599–601. Mekas is the founder and program director of the Anthology Film Archives in New York.

government officials had any power to restrain sexually explicit expression. At the opposite end of Murphy's scale were Justices Tom Clark and John Marshall Harlan. Murphy fit Brennan "somewhere in the middle," alongside a vacillating Fortas. The latter plainly had been mispositioned, by people like Kilpatrick, the CDL's Clancy, and Senator Strom Thurmond, to the left even of Justices Black and Douglas. Fortas's relatively "equivocal" posture required him to deliberate and choose in every case whether to condemn or free a book, magazine, or film; and although this was also true of the brethren other than Black and Douglas, including the supposed "centrist" justices Stewart and White,* it was Fortas who was branded by the Right as the smut peddlers' champion.

After the trio of June 1966 decisions in which Fortas joined Brennan's views without filing any opinions of his own, Fortas's judgments were with one exception made without written explanations; the absence of opinions that were signed or joined by him obliged Court watchers to guess where the new potentially influential justice was heading in the volatile obscenity area. Fortas's disposition to vote without opinion in obscenity cases during the following two terms convinced the Court's critics that he must have been moving swiftly toward (if he had not already reached) Black's and Douglas's position of absolute freedom for sexual expression, which was to say, freedom for what the CDL's Clancy thought of as "the hardest of hard-core pornography." The single instance in which Fortas wrote separately (and so exposed his own views), when taken in the context of his "permissive" voting pattern, probably confirmed the CDL's worst fears. There, in a 1968 case called *Ginsberg* v. *New York,* Fortas alone joined the absolutists Black and Douglas in bitterly dissenting from a Brennan-led majority's refusal to strike down a New York law aiming to protect *children* from the dangers of obscene publications. This surely fueled the CDL's fears that if the permissive Fortas were to replace the puritanical Warren at the Court's helm, there would be no stemming the flood tide of pornography.

Ginsberg v. *New York* involved the prosecution of Sam Ginsberg, the proprietor of a mom-and-pop luncheonette and stationery store in Bellmore, Long Island. In October 1965 he sold two "girlie magazines"— including one called *Sir*—to a sixteen-year-old boy and was arrested, prosecuted, and convicted under a statute that made it criminal to sell to juveniles publications that were obscene *for them,* even if they were not obscene for adults. The arrest of Sam Ginsberg had been set up by the "victim's" mother. This was the uncontradicted representation to the Court made on oral argument by Ginsberg's counsel, an ACLU lawyer named Emanuel Redfield.

---

*As a 1967 opinion written by Justice Samuel J. Roberts of the Supreme Court of Pennsylvania demonstrates, in *Schachtman* and ten additional obscenity cases following the Court's decision in *Redrup* v. *New York,* Justices White and Stewart voted as liberally as Justices Black, Douglas, and Fortas to reverse all eleven of the lower court decisions.

EMANUEL REDFIELD: The youngster . . . acted as a decoy in a case that was specially framed for the purposes of enforcing this law.

———

Redfield also described Sam Ginsberg as neither a smut peddler nor a champion of the First Amendment:

EMANUEL REDFIELD: My Appellant, who received a suspended sentence,* is not a flamboyant vendor, nor a self-seeking or assertive knight charging along the rights of free speech—he's just a poor, simple owner of a candy store, or a stationery store, or a newspaper, delicatessen and luncheonette sort of place that is so common throughout this country. He has this little store, which is . . . seven by thirty feet, in the little village of Bellmore, Long Island, New York, and he works from morning to late at night with his wife to eke out an existence, so much so that he had to close the store for about three days during the pendency of the trial in this case. And as a part of it, he carried about two hundred titles of magazines. He has no choice in these titles; they are sent to him automatically by the jobbers.

———

In *Ginsberg,* Citizens for Decent Literature filed an amicus curiae brief that urged the Court to uphold the statute's constitutionality, and Ginsberg's conviction, on the basis of the New York legislature's "assumption" that sexually stimulating publications were harmful to children. Brennan, in writing the Court's opinion, said that it was not "irrational" for a state to assume that the "reading and seeing" of "sex material" by minors was "harmful" to them; and that since, under *Roth,* the "clear and present danger" test "was irrelevant" to a determination of obscenity, there was no necessity to consider "the debate among the authorities whether exposure to pornography *caused* antisocial consequences."† Brennan's reasoning here paralleled that in *Roth:* since obscenity was unprotected expression, there was no need to hold the state to any showing whatsoever that the expression presented a "clear and present danger" to a substantial state interest.

Brennan based his opinion upholding the New York law on the assumption that the magazines were not obscene for adults, but he flatly rejected the only argument Ginsberg's counsel seriously pressed: that the New York statute was facially unconstitutional because juveniles were entitled to the same measure of constitutional freedom of speech and press as adults possessed, which is to say that material constitutionally protected for adults could not be found obscene and banned for children. In pursuit of this

---

*Ginsberg was given a suspended sentence because, Redfield said, "the judge thought so highly of him as a man in the community who was worthy of his indulgence."

†Dean Paul Bender is among those who believe that even literature available to children should not be controlled by governmental restraints on obscenity. However, the Lockhart commission, for which he served as counsel, did not recommend against carefully worded statutes designed to safeguard children from exposure to obscenity. See Chapter 28 below. This protective attitude toward children was retained by Brennan even when he wrote, in 1974, that as to consenting adults, all obscenity laws were unconstitutionally vague.

litigation design, Redfield had also declined to argue that the statute was unconstitutional *as applied* to the two girlie magazines that Ginsberg had sold to the boy, and so he declined to ask the brethren to examine and decide for themselves whether the magazines sold by Ginsberg were constitutionally obscene *for minors,* or whether it was constitutionally impermissible for a state to brand them obscene, *even for minors,* because they were not "utterly without" literary, artistic, scientific, or other social value *for minors.* In effect, Ginsberg's counsel declined to assert the Brennan doctrine, or any other doctrine geared to a definition of the obscene and the protection of the nonobscene, and rested his client's case instead on the strained principle that "the scope of the Constitutional freedom of expression secured to a citizen cannot be made to depend upon whether the citizen is an adult or a minor." The argument was not adopted by any member of the Court; the three dissenters dissented for other reasons.

Douglas, joined by Black, denied simply (and absolutely) that "publishers, authors, or distributors can be fined or imprisoned for what they print or sell." Fortas argued that regardless of the strategy pursued by Ginsberg's counsel, the brethren should have looked at the magazines that Ginsberg had sold and the circumstances of the sale; they should have taken note that no "pandering" had been engaged in, and indeed that there was nothing active at all about what Ginsberg had done; and, looking to the doctrines laid down by the Court in the *Ginzburg* and *Fanny Hill* cases, the Court should have reversed Ginsberg's conviction because the sales by Ginsberg to the boy were constitutionally protected ones—presumably because in Fortas's eyes the prosecution had not shown that the sale was a "pandering" one or that the magazines met the three-pronged test of obscenity with respect to a sixteen-year-old reader.

There was a flash of anger in Fortas's opinion in *Ginsberg* against the Brennan-led majority for endorsing a prosecution in which "a 16-year-old boy was enlisted by his mother to go to the luncheonette and buy some 'girlie' magazines." To Fortas it was perfectly clear that the boy and his mother had "maliciously and designedly" trapped "a passive luncheonette operator" into committing a crime by selling the boy "two girlie magazines which [were] presumably *not* obscene."

To the CDL, Fortas's "record" on obscenity was extreme, and depraved; Senator Thurmond was gratified to receive from Clancy the "startling" new "evidence" regarding Fortas and his lack of the qualifications needed to be a chief justice. Clancy and Thurmond both argued that Fortas's judicial behavior denied "a community [any] right to protect its young people" from moral and sexual depravity.

After Clancy's testimony, in July, the Congress adjourned for the rest of the summer; the hearings were scheduled to resume on September 13. When Fortas's opponents on the committee asked him to return for further "interrogation"—about the Supreme Court decisions overturning state obscenity laws and rulings, and his role as an informal adviser to President Johnson—Fortas declined.

This led Thurmond to take it out on the Justice Department's deputy attorney general, Warren Christopher. During one session, he handed Christopher a copy of a sexually oriented publication called *Weekend Jaybird;* Thurmond said a staff person had picked it up the day before on a tour of the capital's red-light district. The senator waved it at the deputy attorney general:

SENATOR STROM THURMOND: Do you not agree that it is obscene, it is foul, it is putrid, it is filthy, it is repulsive, it is objectionable, it is obnoxious, and it should cause a flush of shame to the cheeks of the members of the Supreme Court who affirmed decisions that allow such material as this to go through the mails?

———

Christopher sensibly declined to discuss material that had nothing to do with Fortas or the cases decided by the Court. This gave the senator the rhetorical opening he was looking for.

SENATOR STROM THURMOND: Mr. Christopher, how much longer are the parents, the Christian people, the wholesome people, the right-thinking people, going to put up with this kind of thing? How much longer should they do it? And you are up here defending Justice Fortas on his decisions. He has reversed the decisions, I repeat, in 23 out of 26 cases where the local court held the material was obscene. He has thrown it out and said it was not obscene. This is the kind of material that they said was obscene, and yet Justice Fortas, and a majority of the Court—many decisions five to four—have allowed this material to be available and sold on the streets of this Nation.

———

In addition to questioning Christopher, the committee heard testimony from Dean B. J. Tennery of the law school at American University, who was made to explain a generous $15,000 honorarium that Fortas had been paid by the law school for conducting a nine-week seminar on law and the social environment.* And it heard Sgt. Donald Shaidell of the Los Angeles Police Department's vice squad talk about the "pornography" that had "mushroomed" in his city after the Supreme Court reversed an obscenity decision the year before—a decision in which Fortas was said to have swung the Supreme Court's vote to the side of depravity. Like Clancy, Shaidell had shown up in the hearing room loaded with the sort of stuff that anti-smut people seem never to get enough of, or to grow tired of looking at and handing around—peep-show films, piles of "nudie" magazines, and "pornographic" paperback books. These, Shaidell promised, were "openly available" in Los Angeles.

None of this altered the Judiciary Committee's vote in favor of Fortas, but it did affect what happened later on the Senate floor. Bruce Allen

———

*The money had been rounded up by Fortas's former law partner Paul Porter from a group of corporations of the sort that Fortas used to represent.

Murphy says that "obscenity" was the perfect smoke-screen issue for senators who, for various reasons, "did not dare admit their true biases in opposing Fortas"; now they could attack or abandon the justice and take refuge in the pure-minded patriot's call "Clean Up America!" While the Senate was going through the machinations necessary to bring the Fortas matter out of committee onto the floor, Thurmond and his aides kept the anti-Fortas coals stirred up by continuing to provide interested politicians and members of the press with free admissions to the "Fortas Obscene Film Festival"; this now featured the "transvestites cavorting" in *Flaming Creatures*, as well as "the writhings" of Ms. "O-7."

This pandering by Clancy and Thurmond and others to the prurient interests of senators and the Washington press corps was extended by the printing and copying of over one hundred glossy black-and-white photographs made from frames of the contraband films, and their distribution to offices around the Hill. About this time, Senator Jack Miller of Iowa took to the Senate floor and exposed his grave concerns about Fortas in a long accusatory speech. Senator Miller was on CDL's national advisory board.

Although it was not characteristic of Fortas to withdraw from a fight, he was now forced for the most part to cloister himself on the sidelines and let others do battle for him. His friend the brilliant and highly respected lawyer Edward Bennett Williams wrote a letter (which Fortas drafted) to the editor of *The Washington Post*, defending Fortas's obscenity position. His distinguished former law partner Paul Porter enlisted the help of the venerable Catholic Dean Joseph O'Meara of Notre Dame Law School— Justice Brennan's dear old friend—to write another letter to the *Post*, with copies to each Judiciary Committee member, defending Fortas's obscenity record as moderate. According to Murphy, the Johnson White House even explored the possibility of securing help for Fortas from Richard M. Nixon to upset the plans being laid to filibuster the nomination to a standstill. Nixon, of course, would not easily be deterred from his plan to be positioned, as the next president of the United States, to name the men to fill both Warren's and Fortas's soon-to-be-empty seats.

Professor Bruce Allen Murphy has suggested that it was "a shabby alliance" of anti-Fortas Republicans and conservative Southerners, "cemented" by the obscenity issue put forward by CDL, that defeated the Fortas nomination.* President Johnson himself could not crack the alliance, although he made the attempt at a congressional leadership breakfast held on September 5, arguing that the "Fortas Obscene Film Festival" staged by Strom Thurmond, which was having an extended run, made the Senate look ridiculous. The Senate majority leader responded by warning the president that there would be a filibuster on Fortas's nomination and that he did not have enough votes for cloture.

In January, Johnson went further out on the limb by telling a surprised

---

*Bruce Allen Murphy, *Fortas: The Rise and Ruin of a Supreme Court Justice* (1988).

press conference that "a small sectional group" of senators was frustrating the will of the majority of the people with its plans for a filibuster; for the first time he suggested that anti-Semitism was fueling the efforts of his former Southern colleagues on the Hill to bring Fortas down.

PRESIDENT LYNDON B. JOHNSON: In the case of Justice Brandeis, where we had a somewhat similar situation, several months passed in committee and there was a great deal of protest and controversy in the country. But after it was brought to the Senate floor, it took a relatively short time to be confirmed.

SENATOR STROM THURMOND: If President Johnson would take the necessary time to review four films—*Flaming Creatures,* "O-7," "O-12," and "O-14"*—or any of them, it would be interesting to know if he still favors Mr. Fortas' appointment to the second most important office in the United States.

———

In an address to the Federal Bar Association in Washington, Attorney General Ramsey Clark charged that it was "obscene" for the senators to charge Abe Fortas with condoning obscenity and ignore the fact that he had cast the deciding vote to uphold the conviction of Ralph Ginzburg.† And it was "outrageous" for them to show dirty movies, books, and magazines as though they were relevant to the qualifications of Fortas.

ATTORNEY GENERAL RAMSEY CLARK: If certain members of the Senate are as concerned about pornographic material as they appear to be—and should be—they might work on legislation designed to control it, not attack the Supreme Court of the United States as if it caused lust. . . .

THE NEW YORK TIMES: Unfortunately, the Judiciary Committee did not keep the hearings on a high plane. The subject matter was dominated by Senator Strom Thurmond of South Carolina, whose gutter-level assault on Justice Fortas was based on movies the Senator had been showing Congressmen behind the scenes. One was called *Flaming Creatures,* and the others were penny arcade peepshow spectaculars. Senator McClellan of Arkansas joined in the fun by circulating magazines with suggestive photographs.

———

The liberal Democrats on the Judiciary Committee managed, as predicted, to report out Fortas's nomination to become chief justice favorably, 11 to 6; but on the Senate floor it ran into the expected filibuster, led by a CDL hero, Senator Robert P. Griffin of Michigan. A motion to terminate

———

*"D-15"?
†The *Ginzburg* decision by the Supreme Court seems to have been touted as talismanic evidence that the Court, and the justices in the majority, were on the side of the angels. At the congressional hearings that followed congressional "rejection" of the Lockhart commission's *Report,* Dean Lockhart cited Paul Bender's role as lawyer for the government in the *Ginzburg* case as evidence of his neutral attitude toward the problem of obscenity. See Chapter 28.

the filibuster by cloture failed by fourteen votes when the Republican minority leader, Everett McKinley Dirksen of Illinois, abandoned the president's cause. Originally a Fortas mainstay in the Senate, Dirksen conceded that it was the CDL's "dirty movies" that had taken their toll on him and the rest of the Senate.

In speech after speech during the filibuster, opponents of the nomination blasted the Warren Court for overstepping its bounds in liberal rulings on obscenity, Communist subversion, and criminal defendants' rights. By the time the shouting was over, there was a widespread feeling that the Warren Court would never be the same again. And it was not. The Fortas debacle was the start of a move to sink the Warren constitutional ship of state, or turn it clear around—a move that began with the Burger Court and has come to fruition in the Rehnquist Court of today.

After the matter reached the Senate floor and the Senate failed to end the filibuster, Abe Fortas wrote the president and asked that his name be withdrawn. His "overriding wish," he said, was "to end the destructive and extreme assaults on the Court."

On May 15, 1969, after a series of inflammatory stories exploded in *Life* magazine and several daily newspapers—stories that were secretly fed to them by Attorney General John Mitchell—regarding questionable extrajudicial activities on Fortas's part, Abe Fortas resigned his post as associate justice of the Supreme Court.* None of the disclosures was an impeachable offense, but Fortas became the first justice in history to resign "under pressure of public opinion."†

The CDL's campaign against Fortas was not limited to the Senate and the Washington press corps. Seven hundred sets of *Target Smut* in filmstrip form, with a recorded narration, were "sent to key people throughout the country" and "thousands of letters protesting the Fortas confirmation were sent to Washington." This helps to account for the overwhelmingly hostile-to-Fortas mail count that many senators experienced. Every major newspaper in Florida carried a six-column ad, sponsored by a CDL backer named

---

*The most damaging news involved an alleged conflict-of-interest situation generated by a $20,000 annual "consulting" honorarium promised to Fortas by the Wolfson Foundation. The foundation's head was under SEC investigation and eventually went to prison. Fortas had returned the money received, but this did not slake the anger of his opponents or temper the dismay of his supporters.

†There are conflicting reports on the role that Fortas's mentor, Justice William O. Douglas, played regarding Fortas's resignation. Douglas claimed he urged Fortas not to resign: "My son Bill was with me and he too pleaded with Abe not to resign. 'Blood will taste good to this gang. And having tasted it, they will want more.'" But Fortas said that claim was "an absolute fabrication . . . absolute crap. . . . You have to remember that at the time Douglas wrote that he was a very sick man. He didn't know what he was doing or what he was saying. . . . I resigned to save Douglas [from being impeached]." Bruce Allen Murphy, *Fortas: The Rise and Ruin of a Supreme Court Justice* (1988), 571–72. A subsequent move by the Nixon administration to impeach Douglas was led by Representative Gerald Ford; it failed when the Senate Judiciary Committee concluded that there were no valid grounds for impeachment. See the committee's *Final Report*, 91st Cong., 2nd Sess., 1970, and *The New York Times*, December 17, 1970.

Jack Eckerd, that was headlined STAMPING OUT SMUT MEANS STOPPING ABE FORTAS. The newspaper ad featured a cartoon with anti-Semitic overtones from the front page of the July/August *National Decency Reporter:* it showed Abe Fortas being clubbed over the head by a roll of documents entitled "Facts on Record," wielded by James Clancy. The cartoon's caption was "Clancy lowers the boom." The ad also reprinted excerpts from Clancy's transcribed testimony before the Judiciary Committee. Later, Clancy's role in sabotaging the Fortas nomination was reported in the organization's newsletter:

NATIONAL DECENCY REPORTER: A 16mm movie was prepared by CDL, which provided more documentation on the Fortas involvement in obscenity decisions. With the help of Senator [Jack] Miller [of Iowa] the film was shown to many United States Senators and was undoubtedly largely responsible for the impressive vote against cloture on October 1. . . .

Senator Robert Griffin of Michigan deserves credit for leading the Senate filibuster against the Fortas confirmation. Senator Griffin had a reputation for "accomplishing the impossible" and really came through on this occasion.

So that's it. The inside story of the fantastic events that led up to the withdrawal of Abe Fortas as Chief Justice of the United States Supreme Court. This event has tremendous significance from many standpoints. . . .

Many people deserve credit for the events that have taken place. Certainly all CDL'ers deserve special credit for their tremendous support over the years. But the one person that we must all be forever indebted to is James J. Clancy—CDL Legal Counsel. He's a "fighting Irishman" in the finest sense of that term. Jim Clancy never admits defeat. Certainly he had every reason to fold up and quit trying when the May–June '67 decisions came down.* Instead, he fought back with facts and has turned it into the greatest victory for the forces for decency that this country has ever seen.

Thank God [Clancy] is on our side!

—

The theory is that Congress and the Court are separate and equal branches of government. The reality is that the Court can invalidate (unconstitutional) congressional legislation, and the Congress can harass, restrain, and try to run around the Court. At one point during the debate on Fortas, Senator Dirksen spoke of enacting legislation that would strip the Supreme Court of its power to review jury convictions in obscenity cases. Congress can try to discipline the Court with its power over the purse. In 1968 it refused to authorize the engagement of additional law clerks for the hardworking justices. Congress also controls the justices' salaries and retirement perquisites.

However, the most effective modes of restraint available to the Congress derive from the Senate's power to withhold consent from a Supreme Court

---

Redrup v. *New York* and its progeny. See Chapter 26.

nominee whose ideology or influence it dislikes or fears, and its power to impeach a sitting justice. Justice Abe Fortas's failed nomination to become chief justice is a glaring example of the former. Another is the rejection by the Senate in 1987 of Judge Robert H. Bork, nominated by President Ronald Reagan to the Supreme Court. Ironically, in the case of Bork, Strom Thurmond served as the principal supporter of a doomed candidacy. The incident bore the earmarks of revenge by liberal Democrats for the conservatives' disastrous defeat of Abe Fortas.*

Closely related to the Senate's power to impeach a justice of the Supreme Court is its ability, in concert with the press, to mobilize public opinion against the Court, its members, and its decisions. The Court does, in some unpredictable degree, "follow the election returns," in the sense that its judgments may be influenced by public, as well as professional, criticisms. The justices, on the other hand, are restrained by tradition from publicly responding to personal attacks or expressing their personal views about controversial legal and political issues. If they become "too" vocal or active in their extrajudicial speeches and writings, or in interviews with the press, they are liable to be sharply criticized by disapproving politicians and a hostile press. Fortas's expression of his views on the relationship between violence and law in his book *Concerning Dissent and Civil Disobedience* (1968) was one example: he was criticized for expressing those views— although they were not really "permissive"—during the hearings and debates on his nomination to be chief justice.

A little later, when Fortas's former teacher and mentor Justice William O. Douglas published under the Random House imprint a book called *Points of Rebellion,* Douglas also was browbeaten on Capitol Hill by Republican senators, including Everett Dirksen, and Republican congressmen, including Gerald Ford. Impeachment threats were leveled by the Right against Douglas—a man who had devoted himself passionately to the work of the Court for over thirty-six years—for such judicially irrelevant facts as having been thrice divorced, being married to a woman less than half his age, and letting his publisher permit a chapter from his "revolutionary" book to be reprinted opposite a caricature of President Nixon and "alongside cavorting nudes" in an issue of a "pornographic magazine"—*Evergreen Review.* During the furor, lawyers enlisted by Douglas to defend him against the impeachment move restrained the justice from giving a Boston newspaper permission to reprint portions of *Points of Rebellion,* and from participating in an obscenity case involving the suppression throughout the state of Maryland of the Swedish motion picture *I Am Curious—Yellow.* The film was distributed by Grove Press, which happened also to be the publisher of *Evergreen Review.* I argued the lost cause before the now politicized Supreme Court. When Douglas recused himself, the Court predictably split

---

*When Justice Brennan resigned, late in July 1990, the Senate immediately geared up to probe the next nominee's record and thoughts on abortion, perhaps the most politicized of all constitutional issues in this century.

4 to 4, thereby upholding the ban on the film. Douglas's "forced" recusal was as disastrous for the freedom of the artistically valuable and politically powerful film *I Am Curious—Yellow* as Frankfurter's voluntary recusal twenty years before was for the freedom of Edmund Wilson's remarkable autobiographical novel *Memoirs of Hecate County*.

In 1969 Abe Fortas resigned from the Court. President Johnson called the event "historically and constitutionally tragic." Fortas kidded newspaper reporters who expressed concern about his future, saying, "The only offer I've gotten so far is to be a second fiddle player." To others he said he had seen no plot nor purpose on the part of those who had done him in.

JUSTICE ABE FORTAS: It's just as if an automobile hit me as I stepped off the curb.

———

Fortas did not return to his high-powered former law firm; one reason was that some of its more influential members were disgruntled with him, afraid that renewing the association would tarnish their image.* Instead Fortas reentered the practice of law by establishing a new firm in Washington, Fortas and Koven.

Fortas, of course, remained steadfast in his loyalty to the Court on which he served, and to its Super Chief:

JUSTICE ABE FORTAS: Warren, the Chief, was a rare and wonderful man. How I used to wish I could work the straight, uncluttered, unsubtle way he did. Me with my ins and outs and intricacies and every angle covered, as I always said, right back to the invention of money. And still on the Court we mostly came out the same place with the same answer.

He ushered the Court and the country into the modern world. He led a legal revolution for human dignity. He was the greatest, along with Marshall. I guess he was the greatest, period. And he had only fifteen years to Marshall's thirty or so.

It was the greatest Court in history. I'm talking about the three or four years before I replaced Arthur Goldberg plus the three or four when I served. It had exactly the right mix in the carburetor. Including Harlan, whom I became closer to on the bench than any of them except Bill Douglas. We needed reminding now and then of that super-self-restraint view which Harlan held to—so long as it didn't too often prevail. They were all great, decent guys.

———

Toward the end of March 1982, Fortas returned to the Supreme Court for the first time in the twelve years that had passed since his resignation—

———

* However, Carolyn Agger, Justice Fortas's wife and a tax lawyer, continued as a member of the firm.

to argue a case. He told reporters that he planned to keep on practicing law "until my clients retire me or the Lord does."

Two weeks later, on April 5, 1982, at his home in Washington, the Lord retired Abe Fortas: he died of a ruptured aorta. He was seventy-one years old.

JUSTICE WILLIAM J. BRENNAN, JR.: The work, career, and character of this scholarly, gentle, quiet-spoken and unfailingly courteous man exemplified the judicial role at its best.

28

A Magna Charta
for Pornographers

SENATOR EDWARD M. KENNEDY (MASSACHUSETTS): We are pleased to have
with us Dean William Lockhart. Dean Lockhart was dean of the law school
at the University of Minnesota before his appointment to the Commission,
and has since resumed that post. . . .*

Let me ask you, I think there is a general feeling across the land that your
Commission is for pornography and obscenity?

DEAN WILLIAM LOCKHART: Is *for* pornography?

SENATOR EDWARD M. KENNEDY: And obscenity.

DEAN WILLIAM LOCKHART: That is not my understanding of our Commission. So far as I am personally concerned pornography has always been
highly offensive to me. After two and a half years' exposure to it, it continues to be offensive. That was not our assignment.

Our assignment was to make a study of the pornography industry and
the effects of pornography and the legal problems and to make our recommendations based upon our findings, which is what we did.

On September 30, 1970, the chairman of the National Commission on
Obscenity and Pornography, William B. Lockhart, had submitted the commission's report to the president and Congress. One year earlier, the conservative federal judge Warren E. Burger had replaced Chief Justice Earl
Warren after Justice Abe Fortas was forced to withdraw his candidacy.

The report by the Lockhart commission was the result of two years of
research. The Johnson administration had directed the commission to

---

*Lockhart is currently professor of law at the University of California's Hastings College
of the Law in San Francisco.

study the effects of obscene and pornographic materials on adults and children, to establish whether there was a causal relationship between exposure to such materials and antisocial behavior, and to formulate recommendations for "advisable, appropriate, effective, and constitutional means to deal effectively" with the traffic in such materials. Lockhart asked Professor Paul Bender of the University of Pennsylvania Law School—a lawyer who had clerked for both Judge Learned Hand and Justice Felix Frankfurter, and had argued the government's case against Ralph Ginzburg in the Supreme Court—to serve as the commission's general counsel. The commission was established two years after the Supreme Court began "Redrupping" lower federal and state court obscenity decisions with which it disagreed.

The Lockhart commission came into being as a result of pressures from religious leaders like Cardinal Spellman, moral vigilante groups like Charles H. Keating's Citizens for Decent Literature, and politicians like Senator Sam Ervin of North Carolina and Senator Strom Thurmond of South Carolina—all of whom professed alarm over what the Supreme Court had done to free sexually oriented literature. But, once again, those who looked to government to throw its weight into the attempts to restrain the free circulation of sexually oriented literature and movies were disappointed. The freedom-favoring report the commission issued landed like a bombshell on Capitol Hill and on the White House, where Richard M. Nixon was in his second year as president.

DEAN PAUL BENDER: The recommendation of the commission was for the abolition of all general laws that prohibit distribution of obscene materials of the normal consensual kind to adults, and that obscenity laws should just take the form of specific laws dealing with particular kinds of contexts: public displays, unsolicited mailings, and distribution to children. The commission also recommended that the country get serious about sex education.*

———

Even before the report was officially released, President Nixon publicly denounced it as "morally bankrupt." His view was seconded by Vice President Spiro Agnew, an inveterate baiter of liberals and Vietnam War protesters. "As long as Richard Nixon is President," Agnew said, "Main Street is not going to become Smut Alley." Senator Edward J. Gurney of Florida added this terse observation: "The legalization of pornography as recommended by the Commission will open the floodgates to the quickening decay of morals undermining the country today." And Senator Robert C. Byrd of West Virginia commented, "This outrageously permissive commission shows how far this nation has traveled down the road to moral decadence." So it could not have been surprising when the Senate voted 60 to

*The Lockhart commission's recommendations were essentially adopted by the National Commission on Reform of Federal Criminal Laws in 1971. These recommendations were not followed by Congress.

5 to reject the commission's recommendations to repeal the country's obscenity laws, saying "the Commission has not properly performed its statutory duties."

One year later, on May 25, 1971, the Subcommittee on Administrative Practice and Procedure of the Senate Judiciary Committee held hearings to find out what had gone wrong. The only senators present were Edward M. Kennedy, who was chairman of the subcommittee, and Strom Thurmond, who was the subcommittee's ranking minority member and who had led the campaign against Abe Fortas, because (among other things) of his permissive votes on obscenity.*

DEAN PAUL BENDER: Bill asked me if I would be general counsel. He was dean of the Minnesota law school at the time. He struck me as one of the most open-minded of the people of that generation in law school teaching. And that's why Minnesota became such a good school. Bill was really open to things.

He started the commission with very strong views, and they were quite different by the time things finished. Because his views are not fixed, he's always willing to listen and he's always willing to learn and grow. The first day he talked to me about the commission, if I had asked him: "What do you think is going to happen? Will the commission recommend the continuation of obscenity laws or will it recommend that we get rid of them, basically?," he would have said, "Clearly, we *need* to have obscenity laws for adults, *even* for adults." For what he would have called hard-core pornography. No question about it. He would have said, "That stuff isn't speech!"† . . .

But by the end of the commission, he was part of the majority that recommended basically the abolition of those laws. That was a significant change of mind on his part, I think. And it was as though he said, "Okay, I've got this job, I decided to take it. I'm going to start fresh and I'm going to look at the evidence. I'm going to look at the arguments, I'm not going to carry any preconceptions into it." Then he urged everybody on the commission to do the same thing.

The statute that created the commission gave it a series of questions to investigate, the principal one being the effects of pornography on children and adults. And Lockhart did it. I can't imagine doing it any better. The main study was the effects . . . whether pornography was bad.

---

*See Chapter 27. Thurmond had requested Kennedy to authorize an investigation into "charges" made by commission member Charles H. Keating, Jr., who had been appointed by President Nixon and who dissented from the commission's report, that Lockhart had been "illegally appointed" chairman, that the commission was biased in favor of the pornography industries, that it had committed a gross misuse of public funds, etc. Lockhart answered the questions in writing prior to the hearings. See *Hearings on "Presidential Commissions,"* May 25, 1971, 24ff.

†Virtually the same position would later be taken by Professor Frederick Schauer in his treatise *The Law of Obscenity* (1976); later still, Schauer would become a member of the Meese commission and generally supportive, in his writing and teaching, of the Burger Court's revision of the Warren Court's liberal jurisprudence on obscenity law.

COMMISSION ON OBSCENITY AND PORNOGRAPHY: In sum, empirical research designed to clarify the question has found no evidence to date that exposure to explicit sexual materials plays a significant role in the causation of delinquent behavior among youth or adults. The Commission cannot conclude that exposure to erotic materials is a factor in the causation of sex crime or sex delinquency.

SENATOR STROM THURMOND: Mr. Lockhart, the purpose of this hearing is to review the Implementation of Recommendations of Presidential and National Commissions. This seems to be a moot issue as far as this Commission is concerned. We should instead be investigating the waste of $1.7 million of the taxpayers' money which went to the printing of a report which has been characterized as a "scientific scandal" and a "magna charta for pornographers. . . ."

[The Senate's] revulsion against the official report was created by the Commission's shocking perversion of its own mandate. The Commission's report amounted to nothing more than a license for filth. Its main recommendation was that all laws suppressing pornography for adults, and some of those for children, be abolished.

Thus the Commission spent $1.7 million to say that the best way to get rid of the *illegal* traffic in pornography was to make it *legal*.* The Commission asserted—contrary to prevailing ethical, religious, and psychiatric opinion—that pornography had no effect upon adults and was not a matter of social concern.

At the very moment when we have reached a crisis of permissiveness and pornography in our civilization, this Commission urged us to rush headlong into the mire which has swallowed up all the decadent and corrupt civilizations of history.

The reason why the Commission was established was precisely because the American people were concerned about the dangers of pornography to our national moral character and safety. The people wanted solid proposals for stopping the trade in obscenity, and for coping with the crimes which are incited and inflamed by its spread. . . .

The traffic has increased principally because the U.S. Supreme Court, in a series of decisions over recent years, has forced this filth upon the American people. The Court has struck down State law after State law and convictions based upon reasonable local standards. Pornography curbs which had stood for hundreds of years in the English Common Law, upon which most of our State laws are based, were struck down without any regard for the welfare of the community.

---

*An unusual but intelligent method of bringing about social reform through law. The repeal of Prohibition resulted in the dissolution of the criminal bootleg industry; decriminalization of addictive drugs could rid the country of a gargantuan criminal underworld (as well as a mammoth narcotics police army). Decriminalization of obscenity and pornography, as recommended by Lockhart, and as attempted by the Warren Court late in the 1960s, never had a chance to put the criminal porn-manufacturing industry out of business, owing to the Nixon administration's successful politicization of the Supreme Court from 1969 to 1973.

Instead of offering recommendations to overcome this Court-induced menace, the Commission chose to encourage it. It held up as an example the "Danish solution," where reported sex crimes allegedly decreased 31 percent after pornography laws were abolished. Unfortunately the Danish example offers no support for the thesis that pornography laws should be abolished. Fewer crimes were reported because the criminal laws relating to many of these acts were abolished. Moreover, with the general rise of promiscuity and the hardening of attitudes, many crimes of this nature are just no longer reported.

COMMISSION ON OBSCENITY AND PORNOGRAPHY: Statistical studies of the relationship between availability of erotic materials and the rates of sex crimes in Denmark indicate that the increased availability of explicit sexual materials has been accompanied by a decrease in the incidence of sexual crime. Analysis of police records of the same types of sex crimes in Copenhagen during the past 12 years revealed that a dramatic decrease in reported sex crimes occurred during this period and that the decrease coincided with changes in Danish law which permitted wider availability of explicit sexual materials. Other research showed that the decrease in reported sexual offenses cannot be attributed to concurrent changes in the social and legal definitions of sex crimes or in public attitudes toward reporting such crimes to the police, or in police reporting procedures.

Statistical studies of the relationship between the availability of erotic material and the rates of sex crimes in the United States present a more complex picture. During the period in which there has been a marked increase in the availability of erotic materials, some specific rates of arrest for sex crimes have increased (e.g., forcible rape) and others have declined (e.g., overall juvenile rates). For juveniles, the overall rate of arrests for sex crimes decreased even though arrests for nonsexual crimes increased by more than 100%. For adults, arrests for sex offenses increased slightly more than did arrests for nonsex offenses. The conclusion is that, for America, the relationship between the availability of erotica and changes in sex crime rates neither proves nor disproves the possibility that availability of erotica leads to crime, but the massive overall increases in sex crimes that have been alleged do not seem to have occurred.

COMMISSIONER CHARLES H. KEATING, JR. (DISSENTING): In the [commission's] stampede for a "Danish Solution," I noticed in one of their studies a quotation from a young girl interviewed at the "Porno-Fair" in Denmark (regarding the Fair): *"There is complete lack of every kind of affection and solicitude for the other partner. They avoid everything human and pleasant."*

A natural objective for the true scientist, it seems to me, would be to investigate what pornography does to women,* what pornography really is—a despicable thing, a devilish thing, so poignantly brought home to the human heart in the above quotation.

---

*This idea was acted upon by anti-porn feminists, as described in the next chapter.

Who, for example, has referred to, investigated, or even discussed in passing the fact that Denmark today is, for all practical purposes, devoid of religion or religious influence. God is gone from the hearts, the minds, and the souls of the people of Denmark. Does this not play a significant role in the willingness of the government officials and citizens of that country to accept the legalized degradation for which they are now internationally notorious? . . .

While I hesitate to refer to a salacious and lewd magazine such as *Playboy* (which is the precursor of immorality and decadence in the United States), nevertheless, in a recent article entitled "Pornography and the Unmelancholy Danes," they made the following observations regarding Denmark: *"At ordinary newsstands on perfectly normal street corners, you can buy pictures of laughing girls with semen all over their faces. . . ."*

". . . the Christian church . . . came very late to Denmark and never achieved rigid political or social control." . . .

As Marcellus said in *Hamlet, "Something is rotten in the State of Denmark."*

SENATOR STROM THURMOND: Some may wonder how a report that is fundamentally evil in its basic assumptions could be produced with public funds.* The fact is that President Johnson simply surrendered to the radical liberals who have taken over the Party. He chose as the chairman of this Commission a left-wing professor whose agitation for the legalization of pornography was a matter of long-established record.

DEAN PAUL BENDER: Lockhart was a natural choice for chairman because he was the leading academic figure in this area, which was not an area that attracted much academic talent at that time.† And he was the only respectable academic that took it seriously. And he was a very well known person in the law school world. Universally highly regarded for his honesty and straightforwardness, and openness, and an excellent administrator.

Why he took it, how they got him, is another question. He was the dean of a law school; this was a big job, and Lockhart is a workaholic. If you asked Bill to do something in the public good, he would do it. So he took the job.

SENATOR STROM THURMOND: Chairman Lockhart and his hand-picked associates dominated the Commission from the start. They were members of

---

*The same tune in a different key was played in 1989 and 1990 by Senator Jesse Helms of North Carolina in an attempt to graft political and religious censorship onto the grant-making operations of the National Endowment for the Arts. See Chapter 30.

†While Lockhart was dean and professor of law at the University of Minnesota School of Law, he and his colleague Professor Robert McClure wrote two articles, published in the *Minnesota Law Review,* which clearheadedly analyzed and criticized the Supreme Court's work regarding obscene literature and constitutional law. The authors recommended that the Supreme Court adopt a "variable" approach to the problem of obscenity—an approach favored by Chief Justice Warren—which would make the concrete circumstances surrounding the expression and the behavior of the disseminator paramount. The Supreme Court did this ex post facto in the case of Ralph Ginzburg, thus inflaming the legal community. See Chapter 26.

the American Civil Liberties Union, which is perhaps the leading lobby for permissiveness in America, crusading against prayer in the schools, but in favor of relaxed laws on Communist subversion. The ACLU has long advocated that filth be completely unleashed, so it is not surprising that the Commission endorsed this view.

ALAN REITMAN:* The ACLU opposes any restraint on the right to create, publish or distribute materials to adults, or the right of adults to choose the materials they read or view, on the basis of obscenity, pornography or indecency. We emphasize that in pursuing this policy the ACLU is neither urging the circulation nor evaluating the merit of such material.

The ACLU has long maintained that all definitions of obscenity are meaningless because this type of judgment is inevitably subjective and personal. It is also impossible to draw the exact line between "important" and "worthless" material because the informed, critical community is itself just as often divided on the issue of the social importance as on the "appeal to prurient interest" of any given work.

The ACLU believes that the constitutional guarantees of free speech and press apply to all expression and that all limitations of expression on the ground of obscenity, pornography or indecency are unconstitutional.†

HENRY HERLONG:‡ Dean Lockhart, the position of the American Civil Liberties Union toward controlling obscene material is very clear. The ACLU has constantly maintained no curbs of any kind should be placed on the obscene. There are those who contend you are a member of the ACLU but I understand you deny such association; is that correct?

DEAN WILLIAM LOCKHART: That is entirely mistaken. I not only claim membership in the association, I am proud of it. I have been a member of the American Civil Liberties Union for something like 10 to 15 years anyway. I do not agree with the American Civil Liberties Union position

---

*Associate director, ACLU.

†This position did not preclude the ACLU from declining to oppose the enactment of child pornography laws—insofar as they originally criminalized the creation (as distinguished from the distribution) of child pornography—grounded on the fear that children (usually, persons under eighteen years old) who are induced by adults to engage in sexual acts for "expressive" purposes (such as the taking of photographs or the making of motion pictures) are emotionally harmed by their involvement. A few states, including Massachusetts, went so far as to criminalize merely posing, photographing, or filming nude or partially clothed children. See *Massachusetts* v. *Oakes*, 109 S.Ct. 2633 (1989). In *New York* v. *Ferber*, 102 S.Ct. 3348 (1982), the Supreme Court upheld the constitutionality of New York's child pornography law in a case involving the distribution (as distinguished from the creation) of peep-show films of young boys masturbating, but the Court left unclear whether photographs or films having serious artistic, scientific, or political value but otherwise meeting the definition of "child pornography" could be suppressed consistently with the First Amendment's guarantees. The ACLU has avoided further direct involvement in the struggle against enforcement of the child pornography laws, possibly because it fears negative PR repercussions greater even than those it encountered when it defended the First Amendment rights of Jew-baiting neo-Nazis at Skokie, Illinois; at that time many Jewish contributors to the union withdrew their financial support and the organization almost went under.

‡Minority counsel, Subcommittee on Administrative Practice and Procedure, Senate Judiciary Committee.

on a number of matters. This is not a monolithic organization. It is an organization which devotes its time to the protection of civil liberties and other constitutional freedoms and does a great deal of good in this respect.

I have always disagreed with the ACLU position on obscenity and church and state. . . . And our recommendations are inconsistent with the viewpoint that the ACLU has taken.

DEAN PAUL BENDER: Bill Lockhart came to see me while I was teaching at Penn. I took a leave in the mid-sixties to work in the office of the solicitor general in the Department of Justice, which is when I argued the *Ginzburg* case for the government in the Supreme Court. It was in '68, after returning to the law school faculty, that I became general counsel to the commission. That was a part-time job; I commuted back and forth to Penn. . . .

We also did some studies about what was wrong with present obscenity laws, from the practical standpoint; and we studied—there was a so-called "Positive Approaches" panel—which studied sex education and community groups. They concluded, as I remember, that community groups did more harm than good. We had representatives from two of the main ones actually, on the commission, the Reverend Morton Hill and a man from Tennessee, the Reverend Winfrey C. Link, who was allied with some anti-pornography groups down there. He was also one of the four dissenters from the commission's report. And then, midway through, when Judge Keating resigned to go to India, his namesake Charles H. Keating was put on. He was the founder of Citizens for Decent Literature. Nixon appointed him.

Those groups would be constantly in communication with us. Sending us material, making arguments. When we had public hearings, they testified. They were quite well represented throughout. And those three people who were associated with anti-pornography groups, they knew all the answers; they had no open mind at all. No one else on the commission was like that, not even the people from the media.

COMMISSION ON OBSCENITY AND PORNOGRAPHY: [C]itizen action groups organized to deal with obscenity and pornography were much more often reported to exist in large cities and in communities where the traffic in pornography was generally perceived to be a serious problem rather than in smaller cities or in communities where pornography was not at that time so perceived. . . . They can seriously interfere with the availability of legitimate materials in a community by generating an overtly repressive atmosphere and by using harassment in seeking to implement their goals. However, they can be effective if they genuinely reflect the opinion of the community and if they pursue specific, positive, well-defined, constructive goals.*

---

* The Lockhart commission's rather skeptical and critical evaluation of the social value of "citizen action groups" contrasts markedly with the supportive and encouraging attitude toward such groups manifested in the Meese commission's recommendations.

DEAN PAUL BENDER: There were no representatives from the pornography business on the commission—the closest were people from the media. There was Barbara Scott from the Motion Picture Association and there was a man from Simon and Schuster, Louis Freeman, I think, was his name. They were free-speech people but they didn't come in with an agenda of things they wanted the commission to do, or a firm view of where they wanted the commission to come out.

I remember this wonderful conversation we had at a meeting we had with a pornographer, a very successful guy from California who was, like Morton Hill, a Catholic. Hill could not understand why we would study *effects*—it was bad, it was evil, it was sinful, and that was the end of it. He thought it was nonsense to look into anything in a scientific way because it was a question of stamping out evil.

Anyway at this meeting with the pornographer, who was one of Stanley Fleishman's many clients—it may have been William Hamling—Hill took out after him. . . .

REV. MORTON HILL: How could you do this?

PORNOGRAPHER: It's my business. . . .

REV. MORTON HILL: But it's a sin!

PORNOGRAPHER: I know my sins pretty well, and I don't know what sin it's supposed to be.

REV. MORTON HILL: It's the sin of scandal!

PORNOGRAPHER: I never heard of such a sin. . . .

Hill told the guy he was acting in a sinful way and ought to cut it out instantly. Keating was the same way. And there was a woman, Cathryn Spelts, a good friend of Senator Mundt's, who was pretty much of that view. And there was a rabbi from Miami Beach, Rabbi Lehrman, who was pretty much for that view. But there were people from the news distribution business, and MPAA [Motion Picture Association of America], and publishing, some social scientists, a few academics, Marvin Wolfgang was there. So it was a diverse group.

The Citizens for Decent Literature people had shown some films to the Congress, about obscenity cases—where the Supreme Court had reversed conviction summarily. That was when Fortas was on the Court. And they would display the materials and a photograph of the Supreme Court justices; then they would *circle* the evil people who had voted to reverse those convictions. They brought a copy of the film to the commission.

The bill to establish this commission had been pending for years as a straight anti-pornography bill: set up a commission and stamp out pornography. That never got through. The ACLU, for example, always opposed that, and a lot of other people did too; it seemed like a dumb thing to do. When the bill finally got through it was a compromise. And the compromise was: "Okay, we'll set up the commission if you give it something to think about, rather than just 'Stamp Out Pornography!' Think about whether it *should* be stamped out, or what parts of it should be stamped out, and what's bad and what's good about it." And stuff like that. . . .

DEAN WILLIAM B. LOCKHART: The Commission's energies were devoted at the beginning principally to the design and implementation of [the] research program, at a later point to the assimilation and integration of the results of the research, and finally to the discussion of alternatives and the making of decisions regarding recommendations. . . .

Our most important recommendation was that this country should plan and develop and finance a massive program of sex education for young and old, to cover everyone's needs, designed to insure a healthy attitude toward sex and a sound understanding of our sexual nature. This we considered the most critical of our recommendations. If that really were done there was no need to be concerned about the problem relating to pornography.

DEAN PAUL BENDER: And, of course, Nixon's little speech denouncing the commission's report was a classic.

PRESIDENT RICHARD M. NIXON: The Commission contends that the proliferation of filthy books and plays has no lasting harmful effect on a man's character. If that were true, it must also be true that great books, great paintings and great plays have no ennobling effect on a man's conduct. . . .

The Commission calls for the repeal of laws controlling smut for adults— while recommending continued restrictions on smut for children. In an open society this proposal is untenable. If the level of filth rises in the adult community, the young . . . cannot help but also be inundated.*

The warped and brutal portrayals of sex . . . could poison the wellsprings of American and Western culture and civilization. . . . [T]he pollution of our civilization with smut and filth is as serious a situation . . . as the pollution of our once pure air and water. . . .

If an attitude of permissiveness were to be adopted regarding pornography, this would contribute to an atmosphere condoning anarchy in every other field.

———

For pornographers and "those Commissioners who signed this Report," President Nixon had stern advice:

PRESIDENT RICHARD M. NIXON: American morality is not to be trifled with.

———

The period from 1970 to 1973 was a period of political and ideological hiatus on the high bench. After Warren E. Burger took Earl Warren's seat as chief justice in 1970, he struggled for three years to wrest leadership on obscenity decisions and opinions from Justice William J. Brennan, Jr. The Court's first mention of the Lockhart commission report came in one of the 1973 obscenity case opinions written by Burger,† who took the oppor-

---

*These ideas were taken up and elaborated upon by Chief Justice Warren E. Burger in the opinions he wrote for the Supreme Court in the 1973 decisions that revised the constitutional law of obscenity, discussed later in this chapter.

†In *Miller* v. *California*, decided in 1973.

tunity to advertise not the commission majority's point of view but the views of the dissenting minority.

DEAN PAUL BENDER: And that was a big disappointment to me. And I'm sure to Bill Lockhart as well, because you would have thought that the report would provide ammunition and support for [the Warren Court's] views.

I think it's partly the fact that it was condemned by the Senate and by the president in very strong terms. And at that time there was a bad flavor associated with it for that reason.

Also I think people like Justice Brennan were themselves ambivalent. What Brennan said in *Miller* in 1973 was that obscenity law was unworkable and that what he'd said in *Roth* in '57 was unworkable; and he finally came to realize it was utterly vague, in the constitutional sense. What the commission said, however, was you should never have upheld obscenity laws in the first place. I mean it wasn't a question of being workable. If you read the commission's report, you come away with the conclusion that even if you *could* draft workable obscenity laws, laws that weren't too vague, you still *shouldn't*. And Brennan was not taking that view, even in '73.

During Brennan's struggle with the new chief justice over obscenity law and constitutional policy, no good opportunity to cite the report presented itself to him until 1973. Burger was playing for time, awaiting further changes in the Court's membership to give him the votes he needed to gain control over the obscenity issue. He obtained this only in 1973, after Harry Blackmun and Lewis Powell were added to the Court by Nixon, but the maneuvering among the brethren was so close and complicated that when the 1973 cases (discussed later in this chapter) were first conferenced, Brennan nearly collected a majority behind a draft opinion in which he proposed to abandon *Roth* and the "utterly without social value" doctrine for an approach that would have invalidated all obscenity laws except those narrowly geared to the protection of children and the prevention of unconsented-to transactions between adults. This position was, in its constitutional dimension, practically equivalent to the position, at the legislation level, taken by the Lockhart commission.*

In the "unpublished" opinion that Brennan drafted initially as a Court majority opinion for the 1973 case of *Miller* v. *California,* Brennan cited and appended the Lockhart commission recommendations that lent behavioral and legislative-level support to his new constitutional approach. When the recently appointed Justice Lewis Powell switched his vote, however, and went over to the chief's side, this threw Brennan's majority coalition into the minority; Brennan's draft then became the basis for a powerful

---

*It was also equivalent to the view a group of New York intellectuals presented to the Supreme Court in a brief I filed in the 1966 trilogy of obscenity cases, as noted in Chapter 26.

dissenting opinion in which the Lockhart commission's recommendations for repeal of the obscenity laws were not mentioned.

Until Powell's switch, Brennan and a Court majority were preparing to reverse the obscenity conviction of a California publisher, Marvin Miller, for selling "pornographic" books. Brennan began his draft opinion—circulated in the form of a memorandum to the brethren on June 3, 1972—as follows: "I think the time has come when the Court should admit that the standards fashioned by it to guide administration of this Nation's obscenity laws do not work, and that we must change our constitutional approach if we are to bring stability to this area of the law." He then went on to maintain that since more that a decade of experience showed that "obscenity" could not constitutionally be defined—the term was "unconstitutionally overbroad" and incapable of being judicially narrowed to constitutional limits—consenting adults ought to have the free-speech right to distribute and receive obscene materials free of all state and federal restraint. Had Brennan retained his leadership regarding the constitutional law of obscenity, that law would today be not only "correct" (as I see it) but in closer touch with the cultural and commercial reality of sexually oriented expression in the United States. For despite what happened on the Court after Burger became chief justice, the reality was that millions of Americans became free to create, possess, disseminate, receive, sell, buy, look at, and read sexually explicit books, magazines, pictures, and movies.*

The day after the Lockhart commission's report was issued, California publisher William Hamling had the idea of bringing the report out in a Greenleaf Classic *illustrated* edition. His editor, Earl Kemp, invited the executive director of the Southern California American Civil Liberties Union, Eason Monroe, to write an introduction for the book but did not mention to him that the Greenleaf Classic edition would be photo-illustrated.

EASON MONROE (INTRODUCTION TO *THE ILLUSTRATED REPORT*): Noticing this volume on a display rack, some people might think it is a "dirty" book. Anyone led by that impression to hastily and avidly thumb its pages for sensual stimulation would be due for a disappointment. Those who religiously shun such literature with a shudder would be mistaken in thinking they knew what they were missing.

In the best sense of the word, this is a decent book.

STANLEY FLEISHMAN: Eason didn't have the foggiest understanding that it was going to be an *illustrated* book. He thought he was just writing an introduction to the report. And he was not happy about it when he found out. I suppose he was most unhappy at the way he was brought into it

---

*Not *all* Americans became free in this way, owing in large measure to the retrenchment of the Burger Court and its doctrine that local community standards of decency should figure importantly in the decision of whether sexually oriented expressive transactions are constitutionally protected or not.

without his knowing what he was getting into. So there was a little period of time when there were ruffled feelings over it. I really think it was a feeling of: "Christ! You should have told me! That wasn't the way to do it." But it didn't fester. Eason is a very wonderful man. He'd been an English professor and wouldn't take the loyalty oath and was aced out of his job. Finally, years later, he litigated and won back pay.

———

In addition to distributing 100,000 copies of the glossy oversized paperback volume containing Eason's introduction to "adult" and other select bookstores around the county, Hamling and Kemp put into the mails 55,000 promotional brochures, which contained an attack on President Nixon's "attempt to suppress" the official report and a generous sample of the book's photo-illustrations. Kemp also sent a copy of the illustrated volume to *Playboy,* seeking a review in the magazine's book review column. Nat Lehrman, the managing editor, wrote Kemp that he saw no reason to review it:

NAT LEHRMAN: We can't write a review which simply congratulates you for your ingenuity in putting together a great deal of hard-core pornography with a text about its harmlessness. Man, talk about "redeeming social value." I suppose if the Supreme Court guideline ever falls by the wayside, your version of the Presidential Commission's Report will be responsible.

Indeed, I'm quite sad about what you have done. The report is one of the most important documents ever to be published in the censorship area. It's under tremendous assault and you guys are going to boost the wahoos' case by giving the impression that the government provided the pictures for your text.

In any case, I think your ingenuity is going to contribute to your downfall. You ought to have Hamling read up on the Greek concept of *hubris.*

———

Hamling responded in a letter to *Playboy*'s editor and publisher, Hugh Hefner:

WILLIAM HAMLING: It would appear that somehow your staff feels it sits on some self-attained Olympian height when the fact is that others, and our efforts in particular, materially changed the legal atmosphere through an application of guts and perseverance. What would Mr. Lehrman know about "redeeming social value"? Has he ever sat in a Federal courtroom where the point was being determined? I have, as you well know.

Of course the *Report* is important . . . and for that very reason we published it. Far from the pussy-footing facade Lehrman represents we tell it loud and clear. But then that's why freedom of speech and expression are what they are today.

———

Like Ralph Ginzburg before him, William Hamling looked optimistically at the constitutional law of obscenity that was emerging from the courts. The publisher seems to have assumed that when the law moves, it moves only forward, whereas actually it can also move sideways and even backward (although the Court tries to avoid this, and when it cannot avoid it, to conceal it). Unlike Ginzburg, Hamling did not promote the *Illustrated Report* in a "pandering" manner; he did not need to, because it plainly and openly boasted a large selection of hard-core pornographic photographs. But Hamling "politicized" his promotion of the volume by attacking in his brochures President Nixon's denunciation of the Lockhart commission's report. Hamling may also have assumed, incorrectly, that the Court would not distinguish between the freedom afforded photographic images and that afforded the printed word.* The Court in fact (but not in law) did make such a distinction, after its membership was politicized by the forced retirement of Abe Fortas and by the appointment of Warren E. Burger to the high bench.

Eventually, copies of the book and brochure came to the attention of FBI director J. Edgar Hoover† and President Richard M. Nixon. A criminal prosecution against Hamling and Kemp for sending obscenity through the mails was launched by the Justice Department. The "pornographers" were tried, convicted, and sentenced to substantial prison terms; they appealed up the ladder of the judiciary to the Supreme Court. It was the Burger Court that took up the case in 1974, one year after its landmark decision in *Miller* v. *California*, discussed anon, in which it "revised" the Brennan doctrine. The *Hamling* majority opinion was written by the former Justice Department official, William Rehnquist, who had been appointed by President Nixon to take retiring John Marshall Harlan's place, and who would later be named by President Reagan to become the Court's sixteenth chief justice, replacing retiring Warren E. Burger. In affirming Hamling's conviction, Rehnquist unflinchingly described the Greenleaf Classic *Illustrated Report*'s promotional brochure:

---

*It is not that Hamling was ill advised on this score: a majority of the Warren Court had consistently refused explicitly to distinguish, constitutionally, between verbal and graphic expression. It never said in the opinions it issued that photographs or motion pictures were entitled to less freedom than words, although it was frequently asked to do so. However, it effectively gave graphic pornography, for example, less protection from censorship than the exclusively verbal kind, as described further on. The struggles for artistic freedom (particularly with respect to the novel) have historically been handicapped by a constitutional bias favoring cognitive communication over imaginative forms. Fiction, the graphic arts, and other symbolic communication seem to bypass the cognitive faculty and to engage or precipitate emotions rather than ideas. In my arguments advocating the extension of constitutional protection to works of fiction I sought to persuade the courts to look upon the First Amendment's guarantees as protecting "images" as fully as "ideas." Justice Harlan, writing the Court's opinion in *Cohen* v. *California* (1971), known as the "Fuck the Draft" case, spoke with such perspicacity about the way in which symbols address the emotions but are none the less "communicative" that a majority of the Court joined his opinion justifying the extension of the constitutional protections of "speech" and "press" to them. Of course, it is easy to see that words and lettering are also symbols. Harry Kalven discusses *Cohen* in *A Worthy Tradition* (1987), 15–16 and 106–10.

†Hoover subscribed to a "monkey-see, monkey-do" theory of the evils of pornography, and to the "pollution" theory (described later in this chapter) as well. For more on the "pollution" theory, see Hoover's piece in 25 *University of Pittsburgh Law Review* (March 1964), "Combatting Merchants of Filth: The Role of the FBI."

JUSTICE WILLIAM REHNQUIST: The advertising for the *Illustrated Report* opens to a full-page splash of pictures portraying heterosexual and homosexual intercourse, sodomy and a variety of deviate sexual acts. Specifically a group picture of nine persons—one male engaged in masturbation, a female masturbating two males, two couples engaged in intercourse in reverse fashion while one female participant engaged in fellatio of a male; a second group picture of six persons, two males masturbating, two fellatrices practicing the act, each bearing a clear depiction of ejaculated seminal fluid on their faces; two persons with the female engaged in an act of fellatio and the male in female masturbation by hand; two separate pictures of males engaged in cunnilinction; a film strip of six frames depicting lesbian love scenes including a cunnilinguist in action and female masturbation with another's hand and a vibrator, and two frames, one depicting a woman mouthing the penis of a horse, and a second poising the same for entrance into her vagina.

—

Rehnquist was describing the promotional brochure, not the book itself. Although the federal indictments of Hamling and Kemp had charged that both the brochure and the *Illustrated Report*—both of which had been mailed—were obscene, the two men were convicted only for mailing the brochure; the jury probably felt that the book had "redeeming social value" but that the text of the brochure was not significant enough to generate any social value. The publishers' trial judge was a recent Nixon appointee, Gordon Thompson; he sentenced Hamling to spend four years in prison and pay fines totaling $87,000. He gave Kemp no fine but a three-year term of imprisonment. Stanley Fleishman was Hamling's lawyer in the Supreme Court case:

STANLEY FLEISHMAN: I thought we were going to win Hamling's case, given the complexity of the situation on the Supreme Court. We had four "Warren Court" votes* and I'm a perennial optimist.

We had tried to put on evidence of *local* standards—we had an investigator who had gone out to the greater San Diego area and had a questionnaire and was prepared to testify that it did not offend community standards. The trial judge knocked it out on the ground that the standard must be national. So I figured since *Miller* [v. *California,* 1973] had said it should be *local* standards, not national ones, we could win on that ground. It was our best shot in terms of getting a reversal.† But Rehnquist, who wrote the Court's opinion in Hamling's case, took care of that. He got around it some way.

—

In the 1973 group of cases handed down during the Supreme Court's previous term, sometimes collectively referred to as *Miller* v. *California*— the case in which Brennan was obliged to turn his draft majority opinions

---

*Douglas, Brennan, Stewart, and Marshall.
†It was Fleishman's preferred strategy in obscenity cases to plump for freedom on the basis not of "social value" but of "community standards."

into dissents—Chief Justice Burger spoke for a new Court majority. In *Miller,* a national distributor of four illustrated books, *Man-Woman, Intercourse, Sex Orgies Illustrated,* and *An Illustrated History of Pornography,* and a film, *Marital Intercourse,* was convicted of violating California's criminal-obscenity law. After wresting a majority of the Court from Brennan, Burger announced an opinion that reexamined and revised the definition of obscenity that the Warren Court had enunciated from 1963 to 1969. The new majority unhinged the Brennan doctrine that had freed *Tropic of Cancer* and *Fanny Hill,* discarded the eclectic approach taken in *Redrup,* and narrowly limited to its facts an even more radical approach that Justice Thurgood Marshall—President Johnson's last appointee—had adumbrated in the 1969 case *Stanley* v. *Georgia,** just before Justice Abe Fortas was forced to resign.† Ironically, in his opinions for the Court, Chief Justice Burger did most of this under cover of Brennan's opinion for the Court in *Roth,* which he now resurrected as the cornerstone of the Court's revamped position on obscenity, scaling back the definition of "obscenity" to material that was without *serious* literary, artistic, political, or scientific value. It was another irony, however, that Burger's "counterrevolution" would do almost nothing to stem the tide of erotic, obscene, and pornographic expression in America.

Although Burger said it was not the Court's function "to propose regulatory schemes" for the field of obscenity, he took the opportunity to give "some plain examples of what a state statute *could* [constitutionally] define

---

*In *Stanley,* Justice Marshall maintained that a Georgia law criminalizing the mere possession at home of obscenity violated both freedom of expression and the constitutionally inferred right of privacy.

†Had the Court not been politicized by Fortas's forced resignation and the appointments of Burger and Blackmun to fill his and Warren's empty seats, the doctrine laid down in *Stanley* would have provided the juridical means to recognize a constitutional right on the part of any adult to acquire, transport, read, and see obscene and pornographic books and movies at home or in other places provided for this purpose, including movie theatres, bookstores, and libraries. At the time of *Stanley* there was in place a hefty liberal majority consisting of Justices Black, Douglas, Brennan, Stewart, Fortas, and Marshall. Resisting the further expansion of freedom for sexual expression were Chief Justice Warren and Justice Clark; Justice White usually voted with the liberal bloc; later, he helped the new chief justice, Burger, to take control away from the liberals.

Actions and arguments to so "extend" the holding in *Stanley,* that a person was constitutionally free to read and see what he pleased, including concededly obscene books and films, in the privacy of his home, were pressed in a number of cases in *Stanley*'s aftermath. In one of these, Harvard Law School Professor Alan Dershowitz persuaded liberal federal judge Bailey Aldrich in Boston to rule that *Stanley* meant that if a "rich Stanley" had the right to see obscene movies at home, a "poor Stanley" must have the right to see them at his neighborhood movie theatre. The movie involved, *I Am Curious—Yellow,* was treated for purposes of the suit as if it were obscene. The ground-breaking decision of Judge Aldrich was reversed on appeal and the Supreme Court, now dominated in this area by Warren E. Burger, ruled that the federal action had been entertained improperly in view of a pending state prosecution.

Burger was able to defeat each attempt to extend the *Stanley* doctrine beyond the facts of the case—i.e., to any situation of concededly obscene expression outside the precincts of the home: thus arguments and decisions claiming constitutional freedom to import obscene materials from abroad, for private (i.e., noncommercial) use, and to transport such materials to the home were rejected and reversed by the Court.

for regulation," namely: "patently offensive representations or descriptions of ultimate sexual acts, normal or perverted, actual or simulated, including patently offensive representations or descriptions of masturbation, excretory functions, and lewd exhibition of the genitals."

With the exception, certainly, of the phrase "lewd exhibition of the genitals" (which can readily be interpreted to include representations of mere frontal nudity), this was a fair description of hard-core pornography and of the photographs that were contained in Hamling's promotional brochure and *Illustrated Report.* Burger's opinions, however, also contained their share of wishful-thinking non sequiturs—for example that sex and nudity "cannot be exploited without limit by films or pictures exhibited or sold in places of public accommodation any more than live sex and nudity can be exhibited or sold without limit in such public places"—and platitudinous question-begging propositions, such as "There are legitimate state interests at stake in stemming the tide of commercialized obscenity, even assuming it is feasible to enforce effective safeguards against exposure to juveniles and to the passerby. . . . These include the interest of the public in the quality of life and the total community environment, the tone of commerce in the great city centers, and, possibly, the public safety itself."

Burger seemed to have gleaned these ideas from contacts with Alexander Bickel, the widely respected neoconservative Yale professor of law (and mentor to Judge Robert H. Bork). Bickel, in turn, had taken at least some of his lessons in constitutional reconstruction from Justice Frankfurter as his law clerk.

ALEXANDER BICKEL: It concerns the tone of society, the mode, or to use terms that have perhaps greater currency, the style and quality of life, now and in the future. A man may be entitled to read an obscene book in his room, or expose himself indecently there. . . . We should protect his privacy. But if he demands a right to obtain the books and pictures he wants in the market and to forgather in public places—*discreet, if you will, but accessible to all—with others who share his tastes, then to grant him his right is to affect the world about the rest of us, and to impinge on other privacies.* Even supposing that each of us can, if he wishes, effectively avert the eye and stop the ear (which, in truth, we cannot), what is commonly read and seen and heard and done intrudes upon us all, want it or not.

———

Whatever this is, it is certainly not law or jurisprudence. Bickel's argument seems to me both specious and dangerous. For if obscene books and movies may be banned from sale and exhibition in bookstores and theatres because their contents "affect the world about the rest of us, and . . . impinge on other [than their audiences'] privacies," if "what is commonly read and seen and heard and done" "in the market" and "in public places" (like bookstores, libraries, and movie theatres) may be suppressed because

———

*The emphasis in this statement, which was quoted by Burger, was added by Burger.

it "intrudes upon us all, want it or not," then any publicly distributed book, magazine, movie, or song may be suppressed, whether its contents are felt to be obscene or indecent or subversive or blasphemous or sexist or racist or highly offensive to "us all" for any other reason. Bickel's version of freedom of speech erects the "privacies" of "us all," the sensitivities of a "moral majority," into a tyranny over thought and expression. The only expression left free would be that privately created and indulged in at home. Americans, Bickel was saying, should have as much freedom of speech publicly as they have freedom to indecently expose themselves publicly.

The language italicized by Burger, and that which preceded and followed it in Burger's opinion, introduced what might be called the "pollution" doctrine into the constitutional law of obscenity, a "contamination" view of human responsibility that bears comparison with views found not only in primitive and archaic cultures, including those of the ancient Greeks and Jews, but—most chillingly—in some modern ones, including that of Nazi Germany: the sins committed by the wrongdoer pollute the community and the pollution threatens to damn not merely the sinner, but all the rest of us, the innocent community. To protect the rest of us, the individual sinner must be punished, lest everyone be damned.* Stunning examples of the archaic religious view may, of course, be found not only in the Old Testament, but in Sophocles' *Oedipus Rex* and Aeschylus' *Oresteia*.

In his *Miller* opinion, Chief Justice Burger justified obscenity laws by reference to contemporary concerns over "pollution."

CHIEF JUSTICE WARREN E. BURGER: Such laws† are to protect the weak, the uninformed, the unsuspecting, and the gullible from the exercise of their own volition. Nor do modern societies leave disposal of garbage and sewage up to the individual "free will," but impose regulation to protect both

---

*A famous Nazi-era case was that of Lehmann Israel Katzenberger, a German Jew, who was convicted of "racial pollution" under the Nazi Law for the Protection of German Blood and Honor and was sentenced to death for enticing a married woman, Irene Seiler, who was "of German blood," to visit him in his apartment, sit on his lap, exchange kisses, and allow him to caress and pat her thighs through her clothes, and for "clinging closely to Seiler, and resting his head on her bosom." After the war was over, Katzenberger's judge, Oswald Rothaug, was prosecuted, convicted, and sentenced to life imprisonment in the Nuremberg Special Court for committing a "crime against humanity" in convicting Katzenberger and condemning him to death. According to Judge Rothaug, "The Jew's racial pollution amounts to a grave attack on the purity of German blood, the object of the attack being the body of a German woman. . . . The fact that racial pollution occurred . . . becomes clear from statements made by the witness Zeuschel to whom the defendant [Seiler] repeatedly and consistently admitted that . . . she was used to sitting on the Jew's lap and exchanging caresses as described above. . . . The racial pollution practiced by [the defendant Katzenberger] through many years grew . . . into an attack on the security of the national community during an emergency."

The proceedings concerning both trials are described in D'Amato, Gould, and Woods, "War Crimes and Vietnam: The 'Nuremberg Defense' and the Military Service Register," 57 *California Law Review* 1055 (1969).

†He was speaking of "blue-sky" laws as a universally accepted example of a law restraining "speech" without infringing freedom of speech. Blue-sky laws "regulate what sellers of securities may write or publish about their wares."

public health and the appearance of public places. States are told by some that they must await a "laissez-faire" market solution to the obscenity-pornography problem, paradoxically, "by people who have never otherwise had a kind word for laissez-faire, particularly in solving urban, commercial, and environmental pollution problems."*

———

Burger cited a book called *The Democratic Ideal in America,* written by Irving Kristol, another leading neoconservative well connected with the Nixon White House (and later with Reagan's). Analogizing speech to "garbage" and "sewage" made it commonsensically easy (if not very lawyer-like) to justify suppressing obscene speech. Burger's reasoning here was, if possible, even less rigorous than that which accompanied the rhetorical "decent society" dicta that Earl Warren was fond of sprinkling into his obscenity opinions.†

However, the most important point of the 1973 Burger opinions associated with *Miller* v. *California* was their revision of the Brennan doctrine.

CHIEF JUSTICE WARREN E. BURGER: At a minimum, prurient, patently offensive depiction or description of sexual conduct would have to have *serious* literary, artistic, political, or scientific value to merit First Amendment protection.

———

The basic framework of the Brennan doctrine was saved—Burger probably found himself unable to win enough votes to expunge it from the law—but gone from its formulations were the "without even the slightest social importance" and "utterly without social value" criteria. Furthermore, as Stanley Fleishman observed, the emphasis was all on "local," not "national," community standards of "decency."

CHIEF JUSTICE WARREN E. BURGER: It is neither realistic nor constitutionally sound to read the First Amendment as requiring that the people of Maine or Mississippi accept public depiction of conduct found tolerable in Las Vegas or New York City. . . . People in different states vary in their tastes and attitudes, and this diversity is not to be strangled by the absolutism of imposed uniformity.

———

This was liberal-sounding language masking a reactionary purpose. For the "local community standards" criterion was actually intended to give to

———

*Burger here was chiding the political, not economic, liberal community. In his March 1964 *University of Pittsburgh Law Review* piece, J. Edgar Hoover spoke of "the heavy traffic in filth and indecency which, in varying degree, pollutes the atmosphere of virtually every community across the United States."

†Freshman Supreme Court Justice Antonin Scalia, a Reagan-era appointee, seems to have picked up Burger's "Give us a decent society and the First Amendment be damned!" approach to solving the somehow still intractable problem of obscenity-cum-pornography. See his opinion in *FW/FBS, Inc.* v. *City of Dallas* 110 S.Ct. 596, 622 (1990).

local law enforcement organs, including courts, in communities with a low tolerance for candid sexual expression the power to "strangle" the freedom of expression of the rest of the nation's communities. At the federal level, for example, a prosecution for violating the federal postal obscenity laws might be brought in any community to which a magazine, book, or film having a national distributor was mailed. Postal police in any community could order such material and thereby provide the local U.S. attorney and the Department of Justice with a prosecutable case. Thus a Bible Belt judge or jury might be selected by the federal government to bring "local" standards of decency to bear on a piece of literature, a motion picture, or a work of photographic art produced in New York or Los Angeles; the resulting decision that the expression was obscene, if upheld by the Supreme Court, would repress the entire nation's freedom of expression. Even a state prosecution based on "local community standards" could work a similar national repression if the local conviction was affirmed or left standing by the "new" Supreme Court.

Excising the "utterly without social value" prong of the three-pronged Brennan doctrine threatened to roll back the gains in freedom of literary and artistic expression made by the Warren Court. In its place, Burger put a requirement that the expression have "serious" value if it was to receive constitutional protection. But "serious" value was a flabby notion that had the potential to reintroduce the enormous vagueness that had marked the legal definition of obscenity before Brennan narrowed it. The term "serious" was intended to reverse Brennan's extension of protection to speech not "unqualifiedly worthless."

Gone also was "social" value from the protective formulation, and in its place was inserted the narrower, more constrictive "political" value, favored by conservative jurists like Robert H. Bork. Without the protection triggered by the demonstrable presence of "social value," values of an informational or educational or entertainment character would, presumably, no longer qualify for protection from suppression at the hands of law enforcement officials. Theoretically this left exposed to the censors' animus—if the many legislatures that had adopted obscenity legislation to conform to the Brennan doctrine were now to amend their laws to accord with Burger's revision—many contemporary informative and educational (but not "scientific") discussions of sex, ranging, for instance, from Alex Comfort's *The Joy of Sex* to *Show Me! A Picture Book of Sex for Children and Parents* by Will McBride and Dr. Helga Fleischhauer-Hardt. Even Ida Craddock's *Advice to a Bridegroom,* an excerpt from which was quoted above in Chapter 1, might be said by policeman, judge, or jury to fail to have "*serious* literary, artistic, political, or scientific value."

This was, to be sure, a "worst case" scenario, one, however, that frightened the American publishing and motion picture industries, as well as the country's librarians; petitions to the Court to rehear and nullify the "Burger doctrine" were filed in the 1973 cases by the Association of American Publishers, the Motion Picture Association of America, and the American

Library Association—unsuccessfully. In the event, however, the Burger revision of the Brennan doctrine was soon revealed to be a sort of paper tiger; by and large, there in fact occurred no observable retardation of the country's move during the decade that followed toward nearly absolute freedom for sexual expression in literary and artistic modes, including graphic or pictorial pornography; no increase in lower court convictions for obscenity; and no increase in prosecutorial activity, according to a field research study made by the editors of the *New York University Law Review*. The practical wisdom of Brennan's judgment (like that of Dean William Lockhart's commission before him) that little or nothing that might be branded obscene should be forbidden by law to consenting adults seemed to have been adopted at the street level by most of the country's law enforcement apparatus, especially with respect to the printed (nonpictorial) word.*

In a very significant 1974 decision called *Jenkins* v. *Georgia,* the Burger Court itself gave a very narrow reading to its chief's counterrevolution when it reviewed *de novo* and reversed out of hand a Georgia criminal-court jury's conclusion that the Hollywood-based movie *Carnal Knowledge,* starring Jack Nicholson and Candice Bergen, was obscene. The Court apparently substituted its collective (presumably national) notions of prurient appeal, decency, and value for those of the Georgia jury and found the film protected. Liberals and the Motion Picture Association of America—which had filed an amicus curiae brief blaming Burger's revision of the Brennan doctrine (in *Miller* v. *California*) for the Georgia court's insensitivity to the film's propriety and social values—alike breathed sighs of relief.

In the opinions he wrote for the Court in the 1973 cases, Chief Justice Burger sought to reassure the nation that *"no one* would be subject to prosecution for the sale or exposure of obscene materials unless these materials depicted or described patently offensive *'hard core'* sexual conduct specifically defined by the regulating state law, as written or construed." And so, finally, the notion of "hard-core" pornography—a notion first introduced to the Court by the government's lawyer who argued the *Roth* case, Roger Fisher—was introduced also into the Supreme Court's metaphysics of obscenity. Continued Burger in his reassuring vein:

CHIEF JUSTICE WARREN E. BURGER: The First Amendment protects works which, taken as a whole, have serious literary, artistic, political or scientific value,† regardless of whether the government or a majority of the people

---

*The focus of the struggle for literary freedom moved from the plane of printed-word expression to that of printed-word-plus-pictorial expression around 1968, as this chapter and the next suggest. Actually, graphic material had long heightened the risk that a book or magazine would be deemed obscene. The first postal obscenity statute was enacted because of concern that pornographic pictures were being mailed to soldiers during the Civil War. Nevertheless, the Supreme Court has steadfastly declined to create a constitutional distinction between pictures, including moving pictures, and printed words.

†Burger made no attempt to say what "serious" meant; one assumes that it means a good deal more "value" than "a modicum," which was the principle enunciated by Brennan in *Fanny*

approve of the ideas these works represent. . . . But the public portrayal of hard-core sexual conduct for its own sake, and for the ensuing commercial gain, is a different matter.* . . .

———

Dissenting in the 1973 cases, Justice Brennan expressed this criticism of Burger's revisionism:

JUSTICE WILLIAM J. BRENNAN, JR.: Instead of requiring . . . that state suppression be constitutionally limited to materials utterly lacking in social value, the Court's new opinions permit suppression if the government can prove that the materials lack "*serious* literary, artistic, political, or scientific value." But the definition of "obscenity" as expression utterly lacking in social importance is the key to the conceptual basis of *Roth* and our subsequent opinions. In *Roth* we held that certain expression is obscene, and thus outside the protection of the First Amendment, precisely *because* it lacks even the slightest redeeming social value. † The new approach assumes some works will be deemed obscene—even though they clearly have some social value—if the State is able to prove that the value, measured by some unspecified standard, is not sufficiently "serious" to warrant constitutional protection. That result is not merely inconsistent with the holding in *Roth;* it is nothing less than a rejection of the fundamental First Amendment premises and rationale of the *Roth* opinion and an invitation to widespread suppression of sexually oriented speech.

———

Kalven stressed the same point:

HARRY KALVEN, JR.: The most notable change in the test is the substitution of "lacks serious literary, artistic, political, or scientific value" for "utterly without redeeming social value." This dilution of the third component of the test appears to broaden the scope of permissible regulation. It is of course unlikely that *Ulysses* will again be banned, but there is danger under

———

Hill, but how much more is left open to the judge's discretion. The meaning of "value" would not be taken up or spelled out until 1988, in *Pope* v. *Illinois.*

*Burger seems to have viewed "pornography" as though it were graffiti—expression having no reference to any value but its own expression. He also can be seen to have shared former Chief Justice Warren's view that where sexually oriented expression is involved, the profit motive becomes culpable. This probably is to be accounted for by the way in which word images such as "smut peddlers" can become substitutes for thought, even among judges.

†At this point Brennan cited as his authority three obscenity cases—*Roth, Jacobellis/Tropic of Cancer,* and *Zeitlin* v. *Arnebergh* (the California case freeing *Tropic of Cancer*)—and also Harry Kalven's 1960 *Supreme Court Review* article, "The Metaphysics of the Law of Obscenity," which I believe provided Brennan with the seminal idea of *redefining* (from *Roth*) "obscenity" as "expression utterly lacking in social importance," or "worthless." If I am not mistaken, here for the first time Brennan acknowledged his indebtedness to Kalven for the key to reconceptualizing *Roth* in a way that worked inexorably to liberate literature and art from censorship. He also cited Kalven for describing the dichotomy he had established in *Roth* between fully protected sexually oriented but not obscene expression and unprotected "obscenity." See footnotes at page 55 of *The Supreme Court Obscenity Decisions,* edited by Stanley Fleishman (Greenleaf Classic, 1973).

the new test that a second-rate *Ulysses* which the court does not regard as sufficiently "serious" will be.

———

In the case against Hamling and Kemp, Brennan moved along with Douglas once again into dissent; the dissent, joined by Potter Stewart and Thurgood Marshall, expressed his final view regarding the constitutionality of obscenity laws.

JUSTICE WILLIAM J. BRENNAN, JR.: We are of the view that at least in the absence of distribution to juveniles or obtrusive exposure to unconsenting adults, the First and Fourteenth Amendments prohibit both the State and Federal Governments from attempting wholly to suppress sexually oriented materials on the basis of their allegedly "obscene" contents. In our view the federal law under which Petitioners were convicted is unconstitutionally overbroad and therefore invalid on its face. On that ground alone, we would reverse the judgement below and direct dismissal of the indictment.

———

This scant paragraph from Brennan's dissent in the 1974 *Hamling* case essentially recapitulated the long dissents that Brennan wrote in the 1973 cases. It incorporated Potter Stewart's sensible views, first voiced in his dissent in *Ginzburg* and then directly advanced in the per curiam opinion in *Redrup*, that government might justifiably restrain obscene expression only with respect to minors and nonconsenting adults, and added its author's new position that otherwise all obscenity laws are constitutionally deficient for abridging freedom of expression through vagueness and overbreadth.

The statute involved in Hamling's case was the old Comstock act, the law under which Ida Craddock had been imprisoned in 1901 and Samuel Roth had been imprisoned in 1957, and pursuant to which Ralph Ginzburg had gone to jail in 1963. In Craddock's case, no one even attempted to raise a question concerning the law's constitutionality. In *Roth,* a majority of the Court refused to hold the statute unconstitutional *on its face.* In *Hamling,* the Court refused as well to hold the law unconstitutional *as applied* to the material that this publisher had mailed, material the jury had found obscene—the promotional brochure for the Greenleaf Classic *Illustrated Report.* In *Roth,* Justice Brennan had spoken for the Court in its refusal to strike down the Comstock law.* Now, in dissent, he would have invalidated that same law and set William Hamling free because of the irreducible continuing threat to freedom of expression presented by all obscenity

———

*A document in Brennan's private court papers suggests that at the Court's first conference on *Roth,* Brennan voted with a minority of four to *reverse* Roth's conviction. That was not enough to help Roth or the cause of literary and artistic freedom. As noted earlier, by changing his vote Brennan became eligible to receive from Warren an assignment of the all-important task of writing the Court's (majority) opinion, and starting the Court along the road to a full recognition of the constitutional rights of authors and publishers and other workers in the arts.

laws, and the irresistible invitation they extend to government officials to censor what people read and see. In *Hamling,* Brennan amplified his reasoning in *Miller* and adopted the principle that Chicago trial judge Samuel B. Epstein had adumbrated ten years previously in freeing *Tropic of Cancer* from Chicago-area police:

JUSTICE WILLIAM J. BRENNAN, JR.: I now agree with the principle laid down by my brother Marshall in the case of *Stanley* v. *Georgia** that the Constitution protects "the right to receive information and ideas," and that this right to receive information and ideas "regardless of their social worth"† is fundamental to our free society. This right is closely tied to the right to be free, except in very limited circumstances, from unwarranted governmental intrusions into one's privacy.

My recognition of these intertwining rights calls in question the validity of the two-level approach‡ taken in *Roth* to the effect that some sexual materials were "obscene" and prohibitable while others were not. And, if a person has a right to receive information without regard to its social worth—that is, without regard to its "obscenity"—then it would seem to follow that a State cannot constitutionally punish one such as Hamling, who undertook to provide this information to *a willing adult recipient. . . .*

Whether or not a class of "obscene" and entirely unprotected speech does exist,§ I am forced to conclude that the class is incapable of definition with sufficient clarity to withstand constitutional attacks on vagueness grounds.

———

Brennan had finally upset a basic premise underlying his opinion in *Roth:* that obscenity was identifiable, and definable, and as such punishable. This was a step he had long been disinclined to take, because *Roth*—as amplified by the opinions he had written for the *Tropic of Cancer, The Lovers,* and *Fanny Hill* cases—had served the values of literary and artistic freedom well, perhaps better than any other doctrinal "solution" of the obscenity problem might have done.

*394 U.S. 557 (1969).

†Brennan, with these words, signified his official abandonment of the "social value" doctrine as a means for distinguishing protected expression from obscenity. But I hope I have shown that a rule awarding freedom to all expression "not utterly without social value" is not far removed from a rule that awards freedom to expression "regardless of social worth"—especially if expression would not be deemed to be "utterly without social worth" in any case where someone, anyone, protested that for him or her it had a "social worth."

‡Harry Kalven had criticized what Brennan had done in *Roth* as setting up a two-level free speech doctrine. Following *Miller,* the Court has often replicated this error. "Free" speech under the Rehnquist Court is becoming multilayered, and this without protest from constitutional scholars like Professor Cass R. Sunstein of the University of Chicago Law School. See his article "Pornography and the First Amendment" in 1986 *Duke Law Journal,* 589.

§Dissenting in *Roth,* Brennan's dear friend Justice Harlan had criticized Brennan's opinion for assuming that obscenity was as readily distinguishable from nonobscene expression as poison ivy is from other plants. This observation did not for long keep Harlan from seeking to define the "obscene" himself (in *Manual Enterprises* v. *Day,* decided in 1961) and from distinguishing the "obscene" from the "pornographic," without even essaying a definition of the latter term.

Now, Justice Douglas "applauded" the effort of his brother Brennan "to forsake the low road" he felt the Court had been taking "ever since *Roth*." For Douglas the new regime Brennan "would inaugurate" was "much closer than the old to the policy of abstention which the First Amendment proclaims." In effect, Brennan's new position was as absolutist almost as that of Douglas and the late Hugo Black; for if "obscenity" was an idea impossible to codify meaningfully or to enforce fairly, the conclusion was unavoidable that all obscenity laws—certainly all those applicable to consenting adults—fostered censorship and ought ruthlessly to be struck down. This was tantamount to what the Lockhart commission in 1970 had urged should be done uniformly by Congress and by the country's legislatures: repeal all obscenity laws applicable to consenting adults.

JUSTICE WILLIAM J. BRENNAN, JR.: This case [Hamling's] required the Court to confront once again the vexing problem of reconciling state efforts to suppress sexually oriented expression with the protections of the First Amendment, as applied to the States through the Fourteenth Amendment. No other aspect of the First Amendment has, in recent years, demanded so substantial a commitment of our time, generated such disharmony of views, and remained so resistant to the formulation of stable and manageable standards. . . .

It is apparent to me that any effort to draw a constitutionally acceptable boundary on state power must resort to such indefinite concepts as "prurient interest," "patent offensiveness," "serious literary value," and the like. But the meaning of such concepts, as 16 years of experience with *Roth* have shown, necessarily varies with the experience, outlook, and even idiosyncrasies of the person applying them.

STANLEY FLEISHMAN: Hamling received a long sentence* but he got out after one hundred and twenty days.† Within one hundred and twenty days you can make a motion to modify the sentence. And we did that and the judge then modified the sentence. I think it was just a little bit shorter than one hundred and twenty days. . . .

But what I think is remarkable is that even after those 1973 and 1974 cases were lost—*Miller* v. *California* and *Paris Adult Theatre* v. *Slaton* and *Hamling* and *Kaplan* and the rest—and even though you had Burger saying in *Kaplan*, for example, that books were covered too by his new rules—there has never been, since then, a serious prosecution of any book, *qua* book [i.e., consisting of printed words only]. Nobody's ever tried it. Even though the general feeling after those cases, in the industry and beyond, was that it was going to release a prosecutors' witch-hunt. See, sometimes the Supreme Court points a direction but nobody follows their lead.

———

*Five years.
†Half the much-reduced amount of time that Ralph Ginzburg actually served—i.e., eight months.

In *Kaplan* v. *California*, decided in 1974, the Burger Court upheld the conviction of a person who had done nothing more than sell to a detective a nonillustrated pornographic book the latter asked for, called *Suite 69*. In upholding the conviction, Chief Justice Burger relied on the holding of *Roth*—now rejected by Brennan—that obscenity was not within the protection of the constitutional guarantees of speech and press. He also did his best to undermine the idea that books composed solely of the printed word deserved to be absolutely protected from government restraint by the First Amendment's guarantees of freedom of speech and press, and (although he denied doing so) the notion as well that books were entitled to a "preferred place in our hierarchy of values."

CHIEF JUSTICE WARREN E. BURGER: This case squarely presents the issue of whether expression by words alone can be legally "obscene" in the sense of being unprotected by the First Amendment. When the Court declared that obscenity is not a form of expression protected by the First Amendment, no distinction was made as to the medium of the expression. Obscenity can, of course, manifest itself in conduct, in the pictorial representation of conduct, or in the written and oral description of conduct. The Court has applied similarly conceived First Amendment standards to moving pictures, to photographs, and to words in books. Because of a profound commitment to protecting communication of ideas, any restraint on expression by way of the printed word or in speech stimulates a traditional and emotional response, unlike the response to obscene pictures of flagrant human conduct. A book seems to have a different and preferred place in our hierarchy of values, and so it should be. But this generalization, like so many, is qualified by the book's content. As with pictures, films, paintings, drawings, and engravings, both oral utterance and the printed word have First Amendment protection until they collide with the long-settled position of this Court that obscenity is not protected by the Constitution. . . .

For good or ill, a book has a continuing life. It is passed hand to hand, and we can take note of the tendency of widely circulated books of this category to reach the impressionable young and have a continuing impact. A State could reasonably regard the "hard core" conduct described by *Suite 69* as capable of encouraging or causing antisocial behavior, especially in its impact on young people. States need not wait until behavioral experts or educators can provide empirical data before enacting controls of commerce in obscene materials unprotected by the First Amendment or by a constitutional right to privacy. We have noted the power of a legislative body to enact such regulatory laws on the basis of unprovable assumptions.

———

Thus did Burger's peroration in *Kaplan* on literature, freedom of the press, and obscenity culminate in the announcement of a rationale for the censorship of books that harked back to the hoary *Hicklin* rule, which had rooted the government's interest in censoring books in Victorian fears of what might happen if the wrong sort fell into the hands of the young.

29

Like the Towel-Boy in a Whorehouse

BOB GUCCIONE: The expression "going pink" is not mine. I never used it. But the fact is yes, we were responsible for first displaying a girl's genitalia. But when people would say to me, "Hey, this is gynecological photography. It's overly explicit. How can you show a vagina like that?" I would say, "What's wrong with showing a vagina? There's no difference between a woman's vagina and her mouth or her ear, or any other part of her anatomy. It deserves at least as much attention as any other part. . . ."

I felt very strongly about it. It was not something that I was just doing to be controversial. It was something I felt very strongly about.

Men wanted to see the vagina no more nor less than I did. I believe that the voyeuristic tendencies that I have are shared by most men. Men traditionally are voyeurs. Women traditionally are exhibitionists. That's why we work so well together. So, I thought that if I enjoyed looking at it, most men would enjoy looking at it.

DOTTIE MEYER: I'd been modeling since I was fourteen years old. I never really wanted to pose nude. I came to *Penthouse* to do a promotional for them, a speaking part, just another assignment. And then when they asked me would I consider doing a centerfold, I thought it was quite a coup. I went home and I said, "Ooh! Kind of interesting. Twenty years old. Umm . . ."

Not many fashion models can do both because they really don't have the bodies to do both fashion and nude work—too skinny. So I discussed it with my husband and he thought it was quite flattering, and he said, "Yeah, I think it'd be great." So I came up here and I said, "All right!" We'd been avid readers of *Penthouse* for years. I shot the run in February 1977, I appeared in the June issue of 1977. . . . By then *Penthouse* was doing very *open* shots, explicit. Bob was saying, "What it *is* is what it *is*. . . ." He's always been that way, since 1965. He may have become a bit more explicit as time went on. You know, he always changed with the times.

I was nervous, of course. Anybody is nervous when you have to pose nude before a total stranger. I hadn't posed nude before. I was a *parts* model. I had done back, arms, shoulders, legs, hands, feet, whatever; so I had done a lot of that. But not . . . a friend of mine calls it *la la*.

BOB GUCCIONE: *Penthouse* liberated the female pubis. I found it extraordinary that for so many years *Playboy* published photographs of full frontal nudes with the pubis erased, as if it didn't exist. And what struck me was that it was unnatural. And if it was unnatural that way, then it was natural to show pubic hair. I thought that if we were prosecuted my legal defense would be based on the fact that it was natural and that it would be unnatural to show it otherwise. If God created man in his own image, it would not be possible for there to be anything intrinsically obscene about the human anatomy.

———

When Bob Guccione "went pink" in August 1971, he precipitated a crisis at *Playboy:*

RUSSELL MILLER:* [T]he *Penthouse* centerfold had gone pubic, *full frontal,* and its circulation was up to 1,500,000. [Hugh] Hefner† decided he could no longer ignore this feisty opponent, and there began a battle for circulation known in the trade as the "Pubic Wars."

VINCE TAJIRI:‡ I was very, very unhappy about it. I felt we were chasing an upstart. I thought, if we were going to move in that direction, it should be at our own pace. I didn't think we should be pushed by *Penthouse*. But Hefner started counting the number of pubic hairs in every copy of *Penthouse*.

RUSSELL MILLER: Hefner publicly sneered at Guccione, likening him to a "Victorian Peeping Tom," but privately he was alarmed at the inability of his own photographers to produce pictures with the same libidinous appeal.

BOB GUCCIONE: When a guy's peeking at a girl through a little hole in the wall, he doesn't give a shit what her interests are, what her background is, what her profession is. When she's taking off her clothes, *that's* what he's interested in. That's all he's going to react to. And the more real we can make them, the more realistic we can show these girls, and their world, the more successful we're going to be.

RUSSELL MILLER: The first pubic Playmate appeared five months after the first pubic Pet. *Penthouse* came out with a full-frontal centerfold in August 1971. *Playboy* followed suit in January 1972. Hefner agonized about taking

———

*Author of *Bunny: The Real Story of Playboy* (1985).
†Founder and former publisher of *Playboy* magazine, now editor in chief.
‡Former photo editor, *Playboy* magazine.

this step and asked for two sets of proofs to be prepared: in one, the girl, Marilyn Cole, held an arm demurely across her body to conceal her pubic hair; in the other, she held her hands at her sides. Only at the last minute, when the presses could not any longer be delayed, did Hefner okay the full-frontal version.

BOB GUCCIONE: My circulation began to increase so rapidly that this woke up the advertising community. Those who at first maybe perceived us as marginal, because of that—because we were running more explicit pictures—now saw us as hot. *Playboy*'s assumption was dead wrong.

It was at that precise moment that *Playboy* said, "We'll hold back. Let them carry on, and we'll watch what happens to them. . . ."

It was then that they surrendered the lead to me. When they did that, when I had the lead, then I went to town. Everything that we did from that moment on *Playboy* did eventually.

PLAYBOY ENTERPRISES MEMO (May 28, 1973): You realize, of course, that we're in a tight circulation bind right now, and it will get worse before it gets better. *Playboy, Penthouse, Gallery,* and *Oui* are all fighting for the same buck . . . only *Penthouse* isn't hurting. We've all done some pretty deep analyses of *Penthouse,* and there's no getting away from the fact that one of their greatest appeals is an unabashed preoccupation with sex. Without imitating them, or even trying to compete with them in the magnitude of their preoccupation, I think we've got to get into sex in a major way.

RUSSELL MILLER: Slowly, the girls in *Playboy* lost their innocence. Instead of lounging elegantly, they *sprawled,* with increasingly unchaste abandon. They touched themselves in ways that Playmates never did. They shamelessly opened their legs for what photographers described as the beaver shot. They began to wear kinky lingerie, leather, impossibly high heels, and net stockings. Regular features were heated up, too, in particular the Playboy Advisor, which started to tackle subjects like anilingus and bondage.

—

According to Miller, heating up *Playboy* did nothing to stop the slide in its circulation; he said it was hovering close to six million "at its darkest hour in the battle with *Penthouse*."

RICHARD ROSENZWEIG:* [*Playboy*'s] lowest point was unquestionably the month we published a cover picture of a girl with her hand in her knickers.

RUSSELL MILLER: There was an uproar after it appeared on the newsstands and a great deal of disapproving coverage in the media. *Newsweek* discreetly described the *Playboy* cover girl as a "concupiscent young cineast who—to give her the benefit of the doubt—seems to be plumbing the depths of her bikini pants for a stray kernel of popcorn." The girl was posed to illustrate a feature on "Sex in the Cinema" and was sitting on a cinema seat with her

———

*Former executive assistant to Hugh Hefner.

legs spread wide, her skirt pulled up, apparently masturbating—while gawking at some unknown movie.

Eventually the Pubic Wars came to an end. . . . There was a curious postscript to the episode when peace was negotiated in Vietnam and the American prisoners of war returned home. One after another, they professed amazement that pubic hair could be seen in the *Playboy* centerfold.

—

In 1973, Chief Justice Warren E. Burger announced the Supreme Court's decisions in a group of obscenity-pornography cases known collectively as *Miller*—decisions he hoped would curb the publication of sexually oriented expression that had "no serious literary, artistic, scientific, or political value." In the process, Burger injected the term "pornography" into the Court's discussion of what obscenity was, further muddying the metaphysical waters for the legal community and giving anti-porn feminists and right-wing fundamentalists a new epithet with which to belabor merchants of filth.

CHIEF JUSTICE WARREN E. BURGER: [T]oday, for the first time since *Roth* was decided in 1957, a majority of this Court has agreed on concrete guidelines to isolate "hard core" pornography.

—

Were Burger's "concrete guidelines" and his introduction of the notion of "pornography" meant to signal permission to the nation's judges that men's "entertainment" magazines might in the future be deemed legally obscene—because they had become increasingly explicit sexually and, at least arguably, did not possess *serious* value?

In a newsletter published in October 1986 by the right-wing religious anti-porn group Citizens Concerned for Community Values, the organization's chairman, Clyde C. Miller, found that Burger's use of the term "pornography" in *Miller* v. *California* could well be applied to *Playboy* and *Penthouse:* "Is there any doubt that *Playboy* and *Penthouse* meet this definition?" In *The Brethren,* Bob Woodward and Scott Armstrong offer an unsubstantiated report that after Burger learned that a Virginia prosecutor had cited his *Miller* opinion to buttress an announcement that anyone selling *Playboy* on local newsstands would be prosecuted, Burger "immediately jotted a memo to the conference" (i.e., to the justices) insisting that he "had never intended to ban *Playboy*" and that his "opinion was clear on that point."

Hefner labeled Burger's opinion "a preposterous and devastating decision." Guccione offered to lend financial support to any retailer running afoul of the new definition with local vigilante groups or police; and he threatened to make the next cover of *Penthouse* the "nudest yet."

BOB GUCCIONE: I had a press conference at which I said I would fight any attempt to restrain *Penthouse.* I also said: "If I have to go to jail, that's okay with me."

—

The Burger Court's much feared counterrevolution in sexual expression never did materialize while Warren E. Burger presided over the Court. The main reason for this probably was that the revolution in sexual expression carried out by Justice Brennan and the Warren Court was welcomed by a large part of the Great American Audience—although perhaps especially by men—at middle- and lower-class levels; and it was largely acquiesced in by state and federal law enforcement officials, including (mostly male) policemen, prosecutors, and judges. A study published in the *New York University Law Review,* following the counterrevolutionary Burger decisions reached during President Richard Nixon's administration, showed that prosecutors were not inclined to step up obscenity prosecutions, despite the invitation to do so rather blatantly presented in Burger's 1973 opinions. They did not care to be shot down in court by broader-minded judges and jurors, and were largely persuaded—by, among other things, Justice Brennan's powerful dissent—that under the American legal system, people ought to be free to read and see what they were prepared to pay to read and see. Later, resurgent right-wing moral and religious pressure groups, with the encouragement of President Reagan, Attorney General Meese, and the Meese commission, pumped up legislators, policemen, prosecutors, and judges to take fresh actions against the so-called obscene and pornographic in the country's culture. But before that occurred, reactionary anti-porn feminists would mount a legal counterrevolution that failed because, relying on rhetoric instead of reason, it ran into opposition from liberal feminists and the federal judiciary, notwithstanding the latter's by now conservative bent.

ANDREA DWORKIN: I am a citizen of the United States, and in this country where I live, every year millions of pictures are being made of women with our legs spread. We are called beaver, we are called pussy, our genitals are tied up, they are pasted, makeup is put on them to make them pop out of a page at a male viewer. . . .

I live in a country where if you film any act of humiliation or torture, and if the victim is a woman, the film is both entertainment and it is protected speech. Now that tells me something about being a woman in this country.

BOB GUCCIONE: We did not introduce violence into men's magazines, or American culture. What we are credited with doing is bringing back the image of a woman's pubis, which *Playboy* had erased.*

———

Beginning in the seventies, during the Nixon administration, the leading men's entertainment magazines *Playboy* and *Penthouse* came under fierce attack by anti-porn feminists, including Women Against Pornography, Andrea Dworkin, and Professor of Law Catharine MacKinnon. The complaint was that such magazines degraded, humiliated, and dehumanized women, made them into sex objects—toys, Pets, and Bunnies—and encour-

---

*A reference to *Playboy*'s steadfast use of the airbrush.

aged violence against them by men. The feminists came up with complex definitions of "pornography" that arguably fit what was being published in some of these magazines, and linked this material to hard-core pornography of the sort that was increasingly being produced and distributed in the form of "home" or theatrical movies and videotapes, which could be found in American homes everywhere. For one of the last and most significant of the Warren Court's acts to free sexual expression was to establish unanimously, in 1969, that Americans were constitutionally free to possess and enjoy any book, magazine, photograph, or movie they pleased—including those that were concededly obscene—in the privacy of their homes.* By 1985, Ameri-

---

*The case was *Stanley* v. *Georgia,* 89 S.Ct. 1243 (1969). Recently, the Rehnquist Court pared down this freedom by excluding child pornography from the reach of that decision (*Osborne* v. *Ohio,* 110 S.Ct. 1691 [1990]). That is, adult Americans are no longer constitutionally free to possess, read, or view conceded or suspected "child pornography" in the privacy of their homes. And, under pressure from right-wing moral vigilante organizations and the Justice Department's National Obscenity Enforcement Unit, more and more states are redefining "child pornography" to include photographs and films of minors in conditions of immodest nudity, in this way seeking to curtail the freedom of photographers to photograph children and young adolescents nude or partially clothed. See *Oakes* v. *Massachusetts,* 109 S.Ct. 2633 (1989), especially Justice Brennan's dissenting opinion at 2643 ff.; and *Osborne* v. *Ohio,* again especially Justice Brennan's dissenting opinion at 1705–14. As Brennan pointed out in *Osborne* (at 1708, footnote 5): "the majority concedes that '[i]f, for example, a parent gave a family friend a picture of the parent's infant taken while the infant was unclothed, the statute would apply.' " And, as Brennan said in *Oakes* (at 2643): "Many of the world's great artists—Degas, Renoir, Donatello, to name a few—have worked from models under 18 years of age, and many acclaimed photographs and films have included nude or partially clad minors"; and (at 2646): "In addition, there is an abundance of baby and child photographs taken everyday without full frontal covering, not to mention the work of artists and filmmakers and nudist family snapshots."

Oakes was sentenced to ten years in prison for taking pinup photographs of his physically mature fourteen-year-old stepdaughter dressed only in a scarf and bikini panties, after his estranged wife found the pictures and showed them to the Boston police and a local moral vigilante group. See the brief amicus curiae I filed in the Supreme Court in *Oakes,* on behalf of the Law and Humanities Institute.

It is of signal importance to the question of artistic freedom that in none of the three child pornography cases decided by the Court since the widespread enactment of these special laws has a claim or defense of artistic value been made by the defendant. This means that the Court has not yet *held* that serious artistic expression cannot be branded "child pornography," a holding it must make if artists and photographers are not to forfeit more of their constitutional freedom. The Cincinnati prosecution of Dennis Barrie and the Contemporary Arts Center, described in Chapter 30, for exhibiting Robert Mapplethorpe's "The Perfect Moment" might have squarely presented this important question to the Court.

There are three particular grounds for alarm concerning the immediate fate of artistic and photographic freedom of expression in the United States in the emotional and juridically tense area of child nudity and sexuality: first, the disposition of the Supreme Court's conservative majority to uphold the validity of the laws involved, regardless of the threats they present to freedom of expression; second, the recent retirement of the only justice on the bench who showed sensitivity to these risks to freedom of expression, William J. Brennan, Jr.; and finally, the development by the Justice Department and state and local prosecutorial arms of special units and techniques of federal-state cooperation to harass artists and photographers (including parents) who work with children.

A third Supreme Court child pornography case, *New York* v. *Ferber,* 102 S.Ct. 3348 1982), involved the sale of peep-show-type movies showing a young boy masturbating. The Court upheld the conviction of Ferber, the movies' distributor; the case did not involve any action against the producer of the films and no claim was made that the films had any value or importance whatever.

cans were reportedly watching X-rated videotapes at home sixty-five million times annually. In 1989, they would also buy each month nine million copies of *Playboy, Penthouse,* and *Hustler** magazines.

Anti-porn feminist groups organized a wide-ranging variety of attacks on these three magazines and in the process collected money and followers to their cause. They wrote, lectured, toured, demonstrated, picketed, made media appearances. They set up sidewalk stands and posters, protesting the magazines' sexist attitudes; one pictured a naked woman being inserted headfirst into a meat grinder, purportedly based upon a *Hustler* magazine cover. They pressured the mayors and legislative councils of cities, including Minneapolis and Indianpolis, to enact ordinances specially designed to protect women from being victimized by the flood of male pornography. In Chicago, they picketed Hugh Hefner's mansion and *Playboy*'s offices, throwing copies of the magazine onto bonfires. Bob Guccione said they "burned me in effigy all over the country." In their propagandistic lectures and writings, MacKinnon and Dworkin seemed never to refer to the men's magazines by name without referring to them also as "pornography"—a questionable association to say the least, inasmuch as such magazines were generally acknowledged to be constitutionally protected expression. No obscenity arrest, prosecution, or other proceeding brought to suppress the circulation of any of these magazines ever succeeded.

In February 1985, President Ronald Reagan directed Attorney General William French Smith to set up the Attorney General's Commission on Pornography. The commission was given a budget of under half a million dollars and a little over a year to do its job—not enough money or time to carry out any serious studies but enough to make incursions on print freedom of expression that wrung cheers from the anti-porn feminist and right-wing fundamentalist camps. In literary, intellectual, scientific, and civil liberties circles, the commission's methods and its *Final Report* were uniformly discounted and denounced. Unlike the Lockhart commission's *Report of the Commission on Obscenity and Pornography,* which was published in a cloth edition by Random House and as a paperback by Bantam Books, the Meese commission's *Final Report* did not find a mainstream publisher; it was issued by the Government Printing Office in two volumes and cost thirty-five dollars for the set. The commission's "proceedings," or hearings, were not published at all.†

---

*Hustler was sued by the Reverend Jerry Falwell not for obscenity but for libel and emotional injury because of a cartoon the magazine ran parodying a Campari ad and sexually lampooning Falwell. The lower court's judgments for Falwell were reversed by the Rehnquist Court in a decision that held that the *Hustler* cartoon was entitled to First Amendment protection.

†Verbatim extracts from the commission's proceedings were, however, sprinkled throughout the *Final Report.* Interested observers of the commission's work, including *Penthouse,* made their own reports of what was said at the *hearings.* I have relied on both types of data in this chapter.

The October 1986 *Newsletter* of the Cincinnati-based pro-censorship group Citizens Con-

President Reagan, commenting on the creation of the commission, re-marked, "we had identified the worst hazardous waste sites in America. . . . It was about time we did the same with the worst sources of pornogra-phy." Unlike the 1970 Lockhart commission, established by Congress, this group of seven men and four women was created within the Justice Depart-ment by the attorney general. Its ostensible mission was "to determine the nature, extent and impact on society of pornography in the United States," and to make recommendations "concerning more effective ways in which the spread of pornography could be contained, consistent with constitu-tional guarantees." It was apparent from the start, however, that unlike the Lockhart commission, which had carried out a disinterested investigation, the Meese commission had its conclusions in sight at the outset.

At the public hearings held in half a dozen cities around the country, the staff produced female witnesses—who took no oath and could not be cross-examined by those whom they accused—who told how they had been exploited and abused by men under the influence of men's entertainment magazines like *Playboy,* which they identified as "pornography." The Meese commission wanted to show that pornography caused harm, directly and indirectly, to women, in order to confute the findings of the Lockhart commission that there was "no evidence of harm" to men, women, or children. Of the 208 witnesses assembled by the Meese commission's staff, the vast majority (160) came in briefed to ask for "tighter controls" and "more vigorous" enforcement. Sixty-eight witnesses were sex police and other law enforcement officials with career interests in the subject matter; twenty-six were from anti-pornography organizations; ten were anti-porn activists, including Andrea Dworkin; eight were politicians; twenty-two were clinicians or social science researchers; and thirty were women invited to testify that they and others whom they knew had been harmed by pornography. An additional seventy "victims" were interviewed by commis-sion staff, but none of these testified. Letters and written statements about "pornography-related victimization" also were solicited and taken into ac-count. The commission's star witness was Linda ("Lovelace") Marciano, of the film *Deep Throat.* The commission's principal staff member was a former federal prosecutor, Alan Sears, whose special mission for the commission turned out to be to aid the anti-porn feminists and right-wing evangelists

---

cerned for Community Values contained a "special offer" of the commission's "2000-page report" in one volume at a price of $17.00, and a 39-page "summary" for $3.00. The summary was prepared by Richard McLawhorn, executive vice president of the National Coalition Against Pornography, with forewords by NCAP president Jerry Kirk and the founder of Focus on the Family, James Dobson. The *Newsletter* stated that "Alan Sears, executive director of the [Meese] Commission, has read McLawhorn's summary and testified to its accuracy"; and that NCAP's Kirk met for one hour personally with Attorney General Meese, two months after issuance of the *Final Report,* to urge him as attorney general to "respond quickly" to the commission's report and "appoint a task force of adequate size, to be led by a strong chairman with a mandate from his office to implement federal laws against obscenity." The special Justice Department task force was promptly put into place by Meese and was soon upgraded into the National Obscenity Enforcement Unit.

in their attempt to suppress the sale of *Penthouse* and *Playboy* magazines at 7-Eleven convenience stores.*

After examining the commissioners' backgrounds, one of the group's sharpest critics, Barry Lynn of the ACLU, concluded that six of the eleven members of the commission (a majority) "were selected to insure the outcome sought." Foremost among these were Chairman Henry Hudson, who "had a clear anti-pornography bias"; Vice Chairman Harold ("Tex") Lezar, who was "well known in conservative circles"; and Commissioner Frederick Schauer, a professor of law at the University of Michigan.† Staff Director Alan Sears was "one of a very few federal prosecutors who actively pursued adult pornography cases in recent years."

BARRY LYNN: Not a single member of the Commission had any history of opposition to pornography restriction. None was known to be skeptical about the evidence linking pornography to violence or to be concerned about the First Amendment implications of anti-pornography legislation.

HUGH HEFNER: Early in 1985, Reagan's Attorney General, Edwin Meese, launched a seek-and-destroy mission called The Attorney General's Commission on Pornography. There had been a President's Commission on Obscenity and Pornography under Nixon eighteen years before;‡ it concluded that there was no connection between obscenity and antisocial behavior. That wasn't good enough for Reagan and Meese. . . .

At the hearings, law-enforcement officials and pornography "victims"— often hidden behind screens—related sexual horror stories. Civil-liberties types got to speak, too, but the ringside seats were packed for the Commission's slide-shows of explicit pornography. The witnesses who drew head-

---

*After leaving the Justice Department, Sears was hired by one of the most aggressive of the right-wing vigilante organizations dedicated to suppressing obscene and pornographic literature and art—the organization established in 1957 (the year *Roth* was decided) by Charles H. Keating, originally called Citizens for Decent Literature, later Citizens for Decency Through Law, still later National Coalition Against Pornography, and now (as of 1990) the Children's Legal Foundation. Sears is reportedly its legal counsel. This is the organization that helped bring down Justice Abe Fortas, as described in Chapter 27.

†According to Lynn, Hudson, as Commonwealth Attorney for Arlington County, Virginia, had eliminated all "adult" bookstores and movie theatres. In early 1983 he began a series of well-publicized enforcement actions against local video stores that rented X-rated tapes along with general fare. Shortly thereafter, at a White House anti-pornography meeting, President Reagan specifically commended Hudson's "clean-up efforts."

Lezar had been an editorial assistant to William F. Buckley and a Nixon speechwriter before joining the Justice Department under Attorney General William French Smith. He was instrumental in the creation of the commission. At the time Lezar was appointed, "he'd just left the Justice Department and was beginning private law practice in Dallas."

Schauer was a constitutional law scholar who "had argued in the *Georgetown Law Review* that pornography is not at all protected by the first Amendment because: 'The prototypical pornographic item on closer analysis shares more of the characteristics of sexual activity than of the communicative process.' " The major premise of Professor Schauer's thesis was that only "communicative processes" were protected by the First Amendment.

‡Not really "under Nixon." The Lockhart commission's members were appointed by President Lyndon Johnson. When one of these resigned at a time when Richard Nixon was president (before the commission's work was completed), Nixon named the founder of the Citizens for Decent Literature organization, Charles Keating, in his place. See Chapter 28.

lines were the ones willing to blame their sad lives on "the evils of pornography." . . .

The way it worked was the directors of organizations that helped street kids were contacted about potential witnesses, by a Virginia law-enforcement officer named Ed Chapman. He told them what he wanted the witnesses to say—that pornography had been used as a tool when their parents or friends molested them and that these experiences had led them into more pornography and prostitution. . . .

The Meese Commission trundled out a parade of born-again basket-cases, antisex feminists and fun-hating fundamentalists. Their testimony was sad, misdirected—even pathetic. It was also inflammatory, misinformed scapegoating. In a court of law such witnesses would be dismissed for lack of credibility. Trial by headline—unsupported by evidence, unchallenged by cross-examination or witnesses for the defense—is a far cry from due process. But it was the method of the Meese Commission, with its fundamentalist foundation, as it had been for Joe McCarthy. This was nothing more nor less than sexual McCarthyism.*

A WOMAN WITNESS: This father took a *Playboy* magazine and wrote his daughter's name across the centerfold. Then he placed it under the covers so she would find it when she went to bed. He joined her in bed that night and taught her about sex.

ANOTHER WOMAN WITNESS: I was sexually abused by my foster father from the time I was seven until I was thirteen. He had stacks and stacks of *Playboy*s. He would take me to his bedroom or his workshop, show me the pictures, and say, "This is what big girls do. If you want to be a big girl, you have to do this, but you can never tell anybody." Then I would have to pose like the woman in the pictures. I also remember being shown a *Playboy* cartoon of a man having sex with a child.

A FORMER PLAYBOY BUNNY WITNESS: My first association with *Playboy* began in childhood when I found *Playboy* as well as other pornographic magazines hidden around the house. This gave me a distorted image of sexuality. Pornography portrays sex as impersonal and insatiable.

ANOTHER FORMER BUNNY: I was extremely suicidal and sought psychiatric help for the eight years I lived in a sexually promiscuous fashion. There was no help for me until I changed my lifestyle to be a follower of Jesus Christ and obeyed the Biblical truths, including no premarital sex.

I implore the Attorney General's commission to see the connection

---

*According to Martin Morse Wooster in "Reagan's War on Porn," the Meese commission investigators searched for witnesses among organizations in Los Angeles that helped teenage runaways and prostitutes. They "asked to see teenagers who started turning tricks after their fathers showed them *Playboy* and *Penthouse*." "But," said a staff member of one such organization, "*none* of our kids got started turning tricks because their fathers started using pornography. None. Even if you got rid of all the pornography in the world, you couldn't get rid of abusive or drunk fathers" (*Reason,* April 1986, 29–33).

between pornography and sexual promiscuity, venereal disease, abortion, divorce, homosexuality, sexual abuse of children, suicide, drug abuse, rape and prostitution. . . .

Come back to God, America, before it's too late.

———

Writing and speaking during the eighties, anti-porn feminists like MacKinnon and Dworkin used the term "pornography" rather than "obscenity" and argued that "pornography" ought to be suppressed (and its disseminators penalized) even if it had serious literary, artistic, scientific, or political value—because, they said, it was not speech but conduct; it was degrading to women; and its dissemination reinforced sexual inequality between women and men and promoted sexual violence against women. It also reinforced the image of women as degraded and submissive—an image endemic to our patriarchal society; it supported and encouraged the sexual and economic exploitation of women by men; it presented a clear and present danger of harm not alone to the women who were victimized by the men who read and saw it, but to those who were forced, physically or economically, to take part in its creation—the women, that is, who modeled or acted for pornographic still and motion picture productions, or posed nude as Pets and Playmates. The feminists' critique of pornography became preoccupied with this last argument.

ANDREA DWORKIN: Most [pornographers] are small-time pimps or big-time pimps. They sell women: the real flesh-and-blood women in the pictures. They like the excitement of domination; they are greedy for profit; they are sadistic in their exploitation of women; they hate women, and the pornography they make is the distillation of that hate. The photographs are what they have created live, for themselves, for their own enjoyment. . . . The pornographers are the secret police of male supremacy: keeping women subordinate through intimidation and assault.

CATHARINE MacKINNON: The first victims of pornography are the ones in it. . . . This is particularly true in visual media, where it takes a real person doing each act to make what you see. . . . This is the double meaning in a statement one ex-prostitute made at our hearing: "Every single thing that you see in pornography is happening to a real woman right now." Linda Marciano, in her book *Ordeal*, recounts being coerced as "Linda Lovelace" into performing for *Deep Throat*, a fabulously profitable film, by abduction, systematic beating, being kept prisoner, watched every minute, threatened with her life and the lives of her family if she left, tortured, and kept under constant psychological intimidation and duress.

NORMAN MAILER: I was always dubious about the Linda Lovelace exposé. I had this feeling that she protested a little too much. I did see the movie. She didn't look like she was in such misery.

DORCHEN LEIDHOLDT: In the mid-Seventies the media flocked to press conferences given by the "star" of *Deep Throat*. *Sample question:* Does it bother you to suck cock? *Sample answer:* Oh, no, I love it. I guess I'm what you might call an exhibitionist.

___

Many years later *Deep Throat*'s "star" wrote:

LINDA MARCIANO: Those words weren't mine. They were words being delivered by the Linda Lovelace doll. Chuck wound up the Linda Lovelace doll, and she gave interviews.*

CHAIRMAN HENRY HUDSON: Good morning, Ms. Marciano.

LINDA MARCIANO: Good morning. It all began in 1971. I was recuperating from a near-fatal automobile accident at my parents' home in Florida. A girlfriend of mine came over to visit me with a person by the name of Mr. Charles Trainor. Mr. Trainor came off as a very considerate gentleman, asking us what we would like to do and how we would like to spend our time and our afternoons, opening doors and lighting cigarettes and doing all the so-called good manners of society. Needless to say, I was impressed and started to date him.

I was not at the time getting along with my parents. I was 21 years old and was told to be home at 11:00 and to call and say where I was and give them the number and address.

Here comes the biggest mistake of my life. Seeing how upset I was with my home life, Mr. Trainor offered his assistance. He said I could come and live at his house in north Miami. The relationship at this time was platonic, which was just fine with me. My plan was to recuperate and to go back to New York and live the life that I was living before my accident.

I thought then that he was being kind and a nice friend. Today I know why the relationship was platonic. He was incapable of any kind of sexual act without inflicting some kind of degradation or pain on another human being. When I decided to head back for home and informed Mr. Trainor of my intention, that was when I met the real Mr. Trainor and my 2½ years of imprisonment began. He beat me physically and mentally from that day forward. He made a complete turnaround. I literally became a complete prisoner of his. I was not allowed out of sight. . . . When [I was] speaking to either my friends or my parents, he was on the extension with his Walther PPK 45 automatic 8-shot pointed at me.

___

The Meese commission dedicated more than 300 of its *Final Report*'s 1,976 pages to detailed descriptions of the plots, images, and ideas disseminated by 725 books, 2,325 magazines, and 2,370 films of the hard-core pornographic type.† Included was material that aficionados like Professor

___

*Chuck Trainor, her former husband and manager.

†It appears to be characteristic of obscene-literature vigilantes to collect and circulate the stuff. Anthony Comstock and John Sumner did that. In Chicago, during the trial over the freedom of *Tropic of Cancer,* the CDL launched a mail-order membership and fund-raising campaign that included distributing a booklet containing the "dirtiest" passages the organization could find in *Tropic of Cancer.* And, as described in Chapter 27, CDL's legal counsel

Roger Fisher—who had coined the term "hard-core pornography" in argu-ing, in *Roth* thirty years earlier, for the constitutional validity of the Com-stock Act—had never even dreamed of. Among the choicer items produced by what *Newsweek* magazine called the attorney general's "dirty book" was a scenario of *Deep Throat*—an extended eleven-page treatment composed by a Meese commission "senior investigator" named Haggerty. What fol-lows cuts Haggerty's able synopsis in about half but should convey the movie's plot and tone.

ATTORNEY GENERAL'S COMMISSION ON PORNOGRAPHY *(Final Report): Deep Throat* is available in 8mm and VHS formats. As the video begins . . . a female is shown driving a car. The title appears on the screen: "Deep Throat." The female is driving on a street bordered by a body of water.

The credits of the film are shown. . . .

The car is shown pulling into the driveway of a house. The female exits the car carrying a couple of boxes and enters the house. She announces to a woman named Ellen that she's home. The female, who is played by Linda Lovelace, walks into the room where a male is engaged in performing cunnilingus with Ellen, while she sits, legs spread, on a table. Ellen asks Linda to help her put away groceries. The male, who appears to be hispanic, continues to perform cunnilingus on Ellen. Ellen asks Linda for a cigarette. After taking the cigarette she stops the male who is performing cunnilingus on her and asks him if he minds if she smokes while he's eating. He says no and resumes performing cunnilingus on her. Linda starts to leave the room, Ellen asks her where she's going. Linda tells her she's going to slide up and down the bannister in case he wants a warm supper. Linda leaves the room. The male is shown performing cunnilingus on Ellen. He contin-ues until Ellen throws her cigarette in the sink. . . .

The scene changes to Ellen in a swimming pool. Linda is sitting by the pool painting her toe nails. Ellen joins her and they talk about the way they are living now. Ellen says she's going out with some guy to watch the dogs. Linda says there's more to life than just screwing around.

"Sounds like you're ready to settle down," Ellen says.

"Not me, I've been through that before," Linda says. She says she can't get married, "it wouldn't work out." She doesn't really enjoy sex. She gets tingly all over, but nothing else. She says, "there should be bells ringing, dams bursting, bombs going off." She says she has never gotten off.

Ellen suggests that maybe she isn't doing it right. "There's a lot more to fucking than just bam, bam, thank you maam. You gotta find what's right for you, experiment. What do you say we get a bunch of guys here. Someone has got to get your bells ringing."

Linda agrees. "Okay, okay, the way I feel I'll try anything." . . .

Scene changes to a car with two males pulling into the driveway of the

---

organized a special pornographic "film festival" (with Senator Strom Thurmond at the projec-tor) in an effort to persuade senators to vote against the appointment of Justice Abe Fortas to become chief justice.

same house. Ellen lets the two males into the house and gives them numbers eleven and twelve.

Ellen says, "everybody gets a little piece of this action." . . .

The scene changes to Linda who is nude on her hands and knees. A male is engaged in anal intercourse with her. Her pubic area is shaved. The male ejaculates on her buttocks.

Ellen is shown performing fellatio on one male while another male is engaged in vaginal intercourse with her. She kisses the male in front of her as the male behind her continues having intercourse with her. The second male ejaculates on her buttocks.

Linda then is shown engaged in fellatio with a male. The two males with Ellen are shown. One is licking her breasts and the other is performing cunnilingus on her. Linda is still performing fellatio on a male. Ellen is shown with the two males, one of whom is performing cunnilingus on her.

Linda is engaged in fellatio with the same male.

Ellen is shown with one of the males engaged in vaginal intercourse, while the other male slides underneath her and between her legs and engages in cunnilingus with her.

Linda is then shown engaged in intercourse with a male, who is holding her legs up and apart. Then she's shown on top of the male and engaged in intercourse with him. . . .

Ellen and the two males are shown lounging on the couch. Another nude male approaches and asks who is number eleven. One of the males with Ellen says he is number eleven, but declines to take his turn with Linda. Ellen inquires of number twelve, but he declines also, apparently exhausted from his time with Ellen.

Ellen says, "is there anyone else?" An older male appears.

He looks down at the group and says, "What's a nice joint like you doing in a girl like this?" This older male is believed to be Gerard Damiano.*

Ellen says, "How did you get in here?"

"Well listen, honey," the older male says, "You called me, I didn't call you." . . .

Ellen and Linda are shown walking along the sidewalk. "What now?" Linda says, "How many was it fourteen and that isn't counting the one who cum twice." She then corrects her English, "Who came twice."

Ellen asks if she got off. "Sure," Linda replies, "I did a hundred times and it was great, but not real, you know, bells ringing, dams bursting, bombs going off. What can I do?"

Ellen suggests she see a psychiatrist, Dr. Young. "You might have a mental block." . . .

The scene changes to show the doctor, Dr. Young, played by Harry Reems, talking to Linda. He suggests some childhood experience caused her problem, all the while he's blowing bubbles like a child. Reems calls in the nurse to take the bubbles away.

---

*The well-known porn movie director.

She tells Reems her problem, "No bells, dams and bombs."

Reems repeats what she's said and grabs an American flag and waves it. Linda asks him to be serious. He calls in the nurse again and tells her to take the flag away.

He tells Linda he thinks her problem may be physical instead of psychological. He suggests an internal examination. They walk over to a large bed. He tells her to remove her pants. She does. He calls for the nurse for sterilization. She brings a bowl of water and he dips his fingers. Linda gets up on the bed and spreads her legs, exposing her vagina. Reems takes out a carpenter's measuring device and measures from her crotch up her thigh. He then spreads her labia and says, "this is amazing."

Linda says, "don't tell me, someone forgot his watch."

"Miss Lovelace you don't have one," Reems exclaims.

"You clutz, I'm a woman, I'm not supposed to have one."

"I didn't mean one of those. You don't have a clitoris," he says. He tells her to look for herself. She does. "No wonder you hear no bells you have no tingler."

Linda starts to cry and says, "that's not funny."

He asks her, "when you have sexual intercourse what excites you the most?"

"Giving head," she replies. "What do you feel?" he asks.

"I get excited."

"Where?" he asks.

"You'll laugh," she says. He says he won't.

She points to her throat and says "here." He laughs. He then examines her mouth and discovers her clitoris in her throat. She cries some more.

He says, "having your clitoris in your throat is better than having no clitoris at all."

Crying, Linda says, "that's easy for you to say. Suppose your balls were in your ear."

He says, "Then I could hear myself coming. Listen we have the problem solved all we have to do now is find a solution."

"Like what?" she asks.

"Like deep throat," he replies. "Have you ever taken a penis all the way down to the bottom of your throat?"

"No," she says, "I try but I choke."

"You have to learn to relax your muscles. You have to regulate your breathing to the movement of your head. Try it, you'll like it."

"What do I have to lose?" Linda says.

PARK E. DIETZ, COMMISSIONER:* It's been said that the behavior that you evidence in the film "Deep Throat" looks to others as being inconsistent

---

*Psychiatrist and sociologist, teaching at the University of Virginia Law School; Dietz also was a psychiatric consultant to the Behavioral Science Unit, Federal Bureau of Investigation Academy, Quantico, Virginia (*Final Report,* I, 8–9).

with one being coerced. I wonder if you would care to comment on how that came about.

LINDA MARCIANO: Well, I learned very quickly with Mr. Trainor to do exactly what I was told to do and do it to the best of my ability and to be convincing, because what I would end up—if I did become emotional, I ended up crying, or, you know, not looking like I was really enjoying myself, then I suffered a brutal beating, some kind of sexual perversion as punishment, and I would have to do it anyway. So my mother didn't raise me as a total fool. I realized what I would have to do is be convincing and do it and get it over with, and that whole film was done in that way. Everything was done just one time.

PARK E. DIETZ: Did you undergo any beatings during the course of the filming?

LINDA MARCIANO: Yes, as a matter of fact, after the first day of shooting, I suffered a brutal beating in my room, and the whole crew of the film was in the next room.

It was like a—you know, one room after another, and there was a door joining the rooms, and we were in this room, they were in this room, and Mr. Trainor started pushing me around and punching me. I was smiling on the set too much that day and then he started bouncing me off the walls and kicking me.

Well, I figured if all these people were in the other room, maybe now somebody will help me. I will scream for help. And the only thing that happened was the room became very silent, and that was it.

The next day, they listened to him continue to beat me—and the next day the greatest complaint was I had a couple of bruises on my leg. You brought up the smile in "Deep Throat," but nobody ever asked me how did I get those bruises, where did those bruises come from, how did they get there. Everybody always says, "Well, you got there, you smiled, you looked like you were having a good time." That smile is what saved my life.

Somehow, pornography has brought me here today. All I can do is tell you my story and what happened to me. I was a victim of pornography.

CATHARINE MacKINNON: [T]he victims of pornography are often forced to act as though they are enjoying the abuse. One photographer said to a woman he abducted and was photographing while bound: "Smile or I'll kill you. I can get lots of money for pictures of women who smile when they're tied up like you."

———

After many less spectacular witnesses testified before the commission, Bob Guccione's *Penthouse* made an effort to counteract the bias it perceived in the hearings by producing the former fashion model, *Penthouse* Pet, and centerfold model Dottie Meyer as an exemplary *non*-victim of what Meese commission staff members, anti-porn feminists, and religious fundamentalists referred to as "pornography."

DOTTIE MEYER: Since I had worked with the company so long it was my right to defend the magazine in what I had done. But the commission really didn't seem to be interested. I think they were more interested in getting people like Linda Lovelace. They were very sympathetic to her: "Oh, you poor thing, and so on . . ." But when it came to me, they raked me over the coals.

CHAIRMAN HENRY HUDSON: Our next witness is Dottie Meyer, a former *Penthouse* model. She is currently circulation and Pet Promotion Coordinator at *Penthouse.* Welcome and thank you. . . .

DOTTIE MEYER: I am a former centerfold model and a Pet of the Year for *Penthouse* Magazine. I would like to tell you something about myself and my career with *Penthouse.* . . .

I was born in Saskatchewan, Canada, 38 years ago. My parents raised me, my brother and sister in a normal, healthy home. . . . I was encouraged to read the Bible and I joined many church organizations. . . .

I consider myself sexually normal and healthy. I enjoy looking at erotic videotapes and reading erotic literature. Both my husband and I feel these sexual aids have enhanced the intimate part of our lives. As a policeman my husband is involved in the constant stress and threats of violence. I believe the fantasy of that erotica helps him cope with those situations. We were married . . . before I posed for the centerfold, and for us it was just another modelling assignment. My involvement with *Penthouse* was one of my own choosing. They didn't come to me. I went to them. . . .

Currently I work for the magazine as a promotion and circulation coordinator. I help organize promotional tours for the pets. The term Pet is a term of endearment especially in England where the magazine originated. It is used affectionately much the same as you say Honey or Dear or Sweetheart here in the United States. And while I was growing up my mother being English often referred to me as Pet. . . .

In summary, I am a working woman. I work at a job that I like. I go home to my husband and my dog. I cook and clean my own house. I even take out the garbage. It hurts me when righteous so-called do-gooders assume anyone who has been a centerfold is an empty-headed bubble-brained idiot who's been led down the garden path into a life of moral decadence.

—

After Dottie Meyer finished reading her prepared statement, she was "cross-examined" by Commissioner Dietz.

PARK E. DIETZ: Would you say that the text that accompanies the photographs of models in *Penthouse* reflects what the models have said? Is that correct?

DOTTIE MEYER: They are interviewed, yes.

—

In the November 1977 issue of *Penthouse* in which Dottie Meyer was featured, using her professional name, Dominique Mauré, the model was quoted as saying some things that Dietz considered immoral, including "I like men who are strong individualists. Looks aren't as important as having a forceful personality."

PARK E. DIETZ: Well, is it true that you prefer men who dominate you in bed?
DOTTIE MEYER: That's my own personal preference, yes.
PARK E. DIETZ: And that you are especially attracted to rough and tough men who live dangerously.
DOTTIE MEYER: Yes. . . .
PARK E. DIETZ: That you are preoccupied with sex.
DOTTIE MEYER: On occasion. . . .
PARK E. DIETZ: Weren't you quoted as saying sex was your main preoccupation in life?
DOTTIE MEYER: Sometimes. . . .
PARK E. DIETZ: It says exactly: "Sex is the big preoccupation of my life, and why not?"
    Do you like to have sex in cars and alleyways?
DOTTIE MEYER: Sometimes, yes. . . .
PARK E. DIETZ: Do you have a collection of vibrators?
DOTTIE MEYER: No.
PARK E. DIETZ: You were quoted as saying you have a collection of vibrators.
DOTTIE MEYER: I probably said it, yes.
PARK E. DIETZ: You were married for ten years when you posed for the centerfold but your employer quotes you as saying at that time "I want a man who takes over my life and tells me what to do." And that too was a quotation?
DOTTIE MEYER: Yes it was.
PARK E. DIETZ: I wonder what behavior do you think was being promoted through the text specified around your pictorial saying that you liked to be dominated, that you liked men who were rough and tough and so on. What behavior do you think that encourages?
DOTTIE MEYER: I'm sorry?
PARK E. DIETZ: What behavior do you think that encourages?
DOTTIE MEYER: Well it is my own personal preference. Obviously I am married to a policeman and he leads a rough and tough life. He is a very big man and that's my own sexual preference.

———

I asked Dottie Meyer what she thought Commissioner Dietz was getting at, in the questions he asked her.

DOTTIE MEYER: I don't know. It didn't seem quite fair. They were trying to make me feel . . . By the time they asked me if I had a vibrator collection, I was getting a little sick of their questions. I don't object to vibrators, of course not. Anything that helps you along is fine. . . .
    You know, the Meese commission complains about erotica being degrading to women, well, the Meese commission was degrading to me. I walked

out of there feeling . . . *horrible.* I think I felt more insulted about the questions they asked me than anything I've ever done in my life. . . .

CATHARINE MacKINNON: We define pornography as the graphic sexually explicit subordination of women through pictures or words that also includes women dehumanized as sexual objects, things, or commodities, enjoying pain or humiliation or rape, being tied up, cut up, mutilated, bruised, or physically hurt, in postures of sexual submission or servility or display, reduced to body parts, penetrated by objects or animals, or presented in scenarios of degradation, injury, torture, shown as filthy or inferior, bleeding, bruised, or hurt in a context that makes these conditions sexual.

ANDREA DWORKIN: [Pornography] is some creature called female, used.

It is scissors poised at the vagina and objects stuck in it, a smile on the woman's face, her tongue hanging out.

It is a woman being fucked by dogs, horses, snakes.

It is every torture in every prison cell in the world, done to women and sold as sexual entertainment.

It is rape and gang rape and anal rape and throat rape: and it is the woman raped asking for more.

It is the woman in the picture to whom it is really happening and the woman against whom the picture is used, to make them do what the woman in the picture is doing.

———

Andrea Dworkin is a novelist and a feminist.* One of her novels, *Ice and Fire,* is reminiscent of Henry Miller's work, but it is more violent, and it is homoerotic. To my knowledge no one has attempted to censor Dworkin's novel, even though it seems to fit the definition of pornography essayed by Catharine MacKinnon and the author herself.†

ANDREA DWORKIN *(Ice and Fire): N is easy to love, devotedly. She is very beautiful, not like a girl. She is lean and tough. She fucks like a gang of boys. She is smart and quiet. She doesn't waste words. She grins from ear to ear. She is never afraid. . . . Women pursue her. She is aloof, amused. She fucks everyone eventually, with perfect simplicity and grace. She is a rough fuck. She grinds her hips in. She pushes her fingers in. She tears around inside. She is all muscle and jagged bones. She thrusts her hips so hard you can't remember who she is or how many of her there are. The first time she tore me apart. I bled and bled.*

BARBARA EHRENREICH: The distinction between what falls into the pejorative category of pornography and what belongs under the more estimable

———

*See Marcia Pally's analysis of Dworkin in "World Without Porn," *Penthouse Forum,* January 1986.

†Under prevailing obscenity laws of the type that has passed constitutional muster with the Supreme Court, Dworkin's publisher (Grove Weidenfeld) and *Ice and Fire* should both be protected, because of the novel's obvious artistic value.

heading of erotica seems to be largely a matter of taste. Some of us would suppress *Deep Throat* and its ilk while others would happily throw out *Our Bodies, Ourselves* and the work of Judy Blume.

AL GOLDSTEIN:* The feminists say they are "anti-porn, pro-erotica," but they offer nothing in illustration of the latter. I wish they would offer up some of their "erotica," so I could jerk off to it. But the truth is it is all semantics. If *you* like it, it's "pornography," but if *they* like it, it's "erotica."

CATHARINE MacKINNON: Erotica, defined by distinction as not [pornography], might be sexually explicit material premised on equality.

———

The female narrator of Dworkin's *Ice and Fire* enjoys being held down by her lover, the girl called N, while being raped by a man the author calls Mister.

ANDREA DWORKIN *(Ice and Fire): N is slightly more reserved with men. When a man fucks me, she says, I am with him, fucking me. The men ride her like maniacs. Her eyes roll back but stay open and she grins. She is always them fucking her, no matter how intensely they ride. Me I get fucked but she is different, always just slightly outside and on top: being him, fucking her. The men are ignorant and entranced.*

We are on the beach. Mister wants some sex. N whispers to me that she can't fuck, she is bleeding again. All summer she has this mysterious bleeding. I tease her that she wants to get out of fucking this creep. But still: she is bleeding, not menstruating, hemorrhaging: she can't be fucked. She and I make love for him on the beach. It is not enough. He is wired, tense, has spasms of violence, shows us his knife. N holds me down from behind, both arms. He turns away one minute, a modest gesture, unzipping his fly. She grins ear to ear. I try to get loose watching her grin. She is strong and I can't. She holds me down. He pulls down his pants. He fucks me. I get dressed. N and I sit and watch the moon. He goes off by himself. A cop comes along. . . .

"What are you doing here at night girls?"

"Watching the ocean officer."

"It's dangerous here at night girls."

"Thanks officer."

AL GOLDSTEIN: It's the repression of sexuality which leads to rape, violence against women, and a host of other social ills. . . . Instead of calling for an end to porn, we should be seeking ways to make it better.

ANDREA DWORKIN *(Ice and Fire): The beach is a little scummy, empty cans and empty bottles, paper, trash. The sand is a little dirty. N and I undress each other. We kiss. We make love standing up. Mister wants us in the sand. We make love in the sand. She dresses. He shows a knife. She holds me down. I am flat on my*

———

*Publisher of *Screw* magazine.

*back naked on the beach. She is behind me. I look up into her face. She grins. It
is her comradely grin. But I try to get loose and can't. She is strong. She is holding
me down. It is our charade, but I can't get loose. He fucks me. He disappears. I
brush the sand off but I am all gritty. I get dressed fast. N and I sit and watch
the ocean. N and I sit and watch the moon. The cop comes. He says, "You girls
could get hurt alone on the beach at night."*

———

For anti-porn feminists, Dworkin's *Ice and Fire* is presumably erotic, not
pornographic. But to Comstockians and right-wing evangelicals it would
surely seem pornographic. There is also a popular literature for women,
expressing traditional sexist themes, that such men might find not at all
objectionable but that feminist opponents of pornography might wish to
see banned.

BARBARA EHRENREICH: Defining pornography as a "form of discrimination
against women" hardly narrows the field, for surely the censor's eye would
then be drawn to the more familiar examples of cultural sexism that surround us every day, in romance novels, detergent commercials, and the
Bible. Where would one stop?

ANN SNITOW: At a bookstore or drugstore a Harlequin romance costs 95¢,
but the company does a large percentage of its business through the mail,
selling 8 titles a month to 12 million subscribers in North America. . . .

"Your passport to a dream . . ." says the television ad for Harlequins,
which picture a weary secretary sinking gratefully into solitary reading on
her lunch hour. . . .

Are Harlequin romances pornography?

ELIZABETH GRAHAM *(Mason's Ridge): She had never felt so helpless or so completely at the mercy of another human being . . . a being who could snap the slender
column of her body with one squeeze of a steel-clad arm.*

*No trace of tenderness softened the harsh pressure of his mouth on hers . . . there
was only a savagely punishing intentness of purpose that cut off her breath until
her senses reeled and her body sagged against the granite hardness of his. He
released her wrists, seeming to know that they would hang helplessly at her sides,
and his hand moved to the small of her back to exert a pressure that crushed her
soft outlines to the unyielding dominance of his and left her in no doubt as to the
force of his masculinity.*

———

In a talk he gave at Rutgers University, critic Peter Parisi hypothesized
that Harlequin romances are essentially pornography for women ashamed
to read pornography.

REBECCA STRATTON *(The Sign of the Ram): The warmth of his body close to hers
was like a charge of electricity, a stunning masculine assault on her senses that
she was powerless to do anything about. . . .*

Sara feared he was going to refuse the invitation and simply walk off. It seemed like an eternity before he inclined his head in a brief, abrupt acknowledgement of acceptance, then drew out her chair for her, his hard fingers brushing her arm for a second, and bringing an urgent flutter of reaction from her pulse. . . .

His mouth parted her lips with bruising urgency and for a few delirious moments she yielded to her own wanton instinct.

———

This kind of literature has not been subjected to attack, however, by anti-porn feminists. It did not concern the Meese commission, either. Sophisticated or scientific investigation into the sexual subjugation or degradation of women prevalent in American culture was not on the Meese commission agenda. The only element of the anti-porn feminists' critique of American life in which the commission took any interest was their abhorrence of "pornography"; the commission's apparent purpose was to add another weapon—the claim that "pornography" inherently degrades women—to its arsenal of arguments for the suppression of sexual expression of which it disapproved.

BOB GUCCIONE: The televangelists would yell, "Look what's happening to the family unit! Look what's happening to our children, our daughters! Look at the rape, victims of rape! Look at the sexually abused children!"

And they were attributing *all of this*—the breakdown of the family, the high divorce rate, celebrities living together and having children outside of marriage and this being apparently acceptable to the public—to pornography, which for them was *Penthouse* and *Playboy*. All of this fueled their cause, and their ability to raise money. The people they got to testify at the hearing said the same things. The fact that we existed gave all of them the cause they needed.

———

Some of the testimony taken by the Meese commission was reminiscent of the testimony before congressional committees in the fifties, during the McCarthy era that denounced "subversive" writers. Then the motive was to destroy the reputations and livelihoods of those writers. Here the motive was to destroy the reputations and circulations of various magazines by associating them with pornography.* The most damaging attack on the pornographic character of *Penthouse* and *Playboy,* however, came not from those presented as victims of pornography or from feminist witnesses, but from the Reverend Donald Wildmon, founder of the right-wing Christian vigilante group then called National Federation for Decency, now called the American Family Association. Because the Meese commission was unable or unwilling to come up with a definition of "pornography" or "obscenity" that would have placed sensible limits on the testimony of its witnesses, Wildmon

———

*"McCarthyism" would next rear its ugly head in 1989 and 1990 when politicians like Senator Jesse Helms, right-wing evangelists like Donald Wildmon, and newspapers like *The Washington Times* launched campaigns to force the National Endowment for the Arts to "defund" artists and arts institutions for their involvement in the dissemination of homoerotic art, as described in Chapter 30.

was allowed to "witness" that the men's magazines were "pornographic" without regard for what this incontestably vague term might mean.

The question arose almost casually during the commission's initial proceedings:

VICE CHAIRMAN HAROLD ("TEX") LEZAR: I don't get the purpose of defining pornography. . . .

FATHER BRUCE RITTER, COMMISSIONER:* If we were asked what was the subject matter of our survey, what would we say?

JUDGE EDWARD GARCIA, COMMISSIONER:† Well, you wouldn't tell them one word. . . .

FATHER BRUCE RITTER: The problem we face, Tex, is that no one on the Commission can really say what we are talking about. . . .

VICE CHAIRMAN HAROLD ("TEX") LEZAR: The definition we want is one that will allow us to include everything that other people are saying is pornography. It's not a value judgment. This should cover everything that people who come before the Commission say: "This is pornography."

———

This, of course, was the sort of elasticity that had led the Supreme Court to strike down a number of laws encroaching on First Amendment freedoms and finally induced Justice Brennan in 1973 (in dissent) to conclude that all obscenity laws applicable to consenting adults ought to be deemed unconstitutionally vague and overbroad.

In February 1986, before the commission had completed its work and issued its *Final Report,* a letter (on official Department of Justice letterhead) implicitly incorporating the commission's nondefinition of pornography and signed by Meese commission chief of staff Alan E. Sears was received by a group of major bookselling chains, two major book publishers, several national distributors of magazines and books, a few cable television program distributors, and some of the country's largest convenience-variety store, drugstore, and department-store chains. The letter implied that the recipients were suspected by the commission of selling and distributing pornography and said that if they wished not to be identified as pornographers in the commission's *Final Report,* they should stop these activities. It could also be inferred that a decision not to carry the magazines and books was advisable if the person or company preferred not to be prosecuted by the department under federal obscenity law.

ALAN E. SEARS, EXECUTIVE DIRECTOR AND COMMISSIONER: Dear Authorized Representative: During the hearing in Los Angeles in October 1985, the Commission received testimony alleging that your company is involved in the sale or distribution of pornography. . . . Please review the allegations

———

*New York priest, founder and president of Covenant House—a shelter for runaway children in New York that was the beneficiary of large federal grants under the Reagan administration—who in 1990 was forced to resign all connections with Covenant House because of reported sexual and financial irregularities.

†United States District Court for the Eastern District of California.

and advise the Commission on or before March 3, 1986, if you disagree.
. . . Failure to respond will necessarily be accepted as an indication of no
objection [to the allegations]. . . .

—

The allegations were set forth in a ten-page statement enclosed with the
letter, entitled "Pornography in the Market Place," whose author was not
named but who turned out to be Donald Wildmon. According to Wildmon's anonymous "testimony," major U.S. companies had become "involved" in the distribution of "pornography." Among those was Southland
Corporation, owner of forty-five hundred 7-Eleven stores and franchiser of
thirty-eight hundred other 7-Eleven stores. The Wildmon statement specifically identified the "pornography" handled by Southland's stores as *Penthouse* and *Playboy*.*

THE REVEREND DONALD WILDMON ("Pornography in the Market Place"):
Indeed, in the family marketplace 7-Eleven is perhaps the most important
key to successful marketing of pornography. In my opinion, were 7-Eleven
to discontinue the sale of porn magazines, both *Playboy* and *Penthouse*
would be seriously crippled financially. The profit made by 7-Eleven on
pornography runs into the millions of dollars. It is the single most important outlet for the sales of *Penthouse* magazine. And 7-Eleven stores sell 20
percent of all *Playboy* magazines sold to America; they sell more *Playboy*
magazines than any other retailer in America.

—

Alan Sears's letter endorsed Wildmon's elimination of the distinction
between constitutionally free and "obscene" literature, and between constitutionally free and "pornographic" materials. It also blurred the line separating Church and State by adopting a fundamentalist minister's thinking
as a governmental finding. Sears used Wildmon's testimony in this way in
an effort to blacklist the publishers of *Playboy* and *Penthouse* with national
chain distributors. The plan was to make it appear that the Meese commission had certified *Playboy* and *Penthouse* magazines to be legally "pornographic" and lumped these mainstream, constitutionally protected
magazines with the frequently gross, violent, and sexually degrading unprotected publications that many "adult" bookstores, movie houses, and
video shops sold; and, further, to tar the corporate owners and the local
convenience-store franchisers handling them, notably 7-Eleven, with the

*It also identified as participants in the game of pornography distribution: CBS, Inc., for
distributing the "porno" Playboy Channel through its interest in Rainbow Programming
Services; Time, Inc., which had moved into the "porno" market with recent X-rated offerings
on its Cinemax cable television channel; Ramada Inns, which had begun offering the American Extasy Channel to its motel guests; RCA and Coca-Cola, which distributed "porno" films
in Australia. Other companies allegedly involved in the "pornography" business included:
Kable News Company, Curtis Circulation Company, Warner Publishing Services, and Flynt
Distributing Company, which distributed *Chic, Hustler,* and *Mandate* (homosexual), *Honcho*
(homosexual), *Playguy* (homosexual), *Inches* (homosexual), *Max, Tux, Cinema Blue, Juggs,*
and *Leg Show*.

same brush—unless the latter stopped selling the targeted magazines. It worked. Southland Corporation wrote a letter to the commission informing it that the company had decided to modify its policy of carrying those magazines. It also asked that any reference to Southland or 7-Eleven be deleted from the commission's *Final Report*.

DALLAS MORNING NEWS: Southland Corporation surprised fundamentalists, feminists, magazine publishers and the convenience store industry Thursday by announcing it will no longer sell *Playboy*, *Penthouse* and *Forum* magazines in its company-owned 7-Eleven stores. Dallas-based Southland said it would urge its franchise owners to take similar action.

Fundamentalist ministers the Rev. Jerry Falwell of the Moral Majority and the Rev. Donald Wildmon of the National Federation for Decency in Tupelo, Mississippi, credited their three-year campaign against 7-Eleven for the reversal of Southland's policy. . . .

THE REVEREND DONALD WILDMON: We certainly appreciate the fact that Southland is pulling the porn. It took us approximately two years, but our voice was heard. . . .

THE REVEREND JERRY FALWELL: I sincerely hope that Christians in America will now show their appreciation by supporting 7-Eleven nationally.

This should encourage a lot of other corporations such as grocery chains to follow suit now that there is a precedent decision. They will feel more safety in making a moral decision to stop selling porn.

DAVID MYERSON:* The dropping of *Penthouse* from the 7-Eleven stores was followed by a big jump [in sales] in some other stores that were not intimidated by the Sears-Wildmon-Meese commission threatening letter. *Penthouse* sales went up 75 percent in the 200 or so Lil' Champ Food Stores in Florida and increased by 30 percent in Circle K's 3,400 stores in the South and West. Circle K is the country's second largest convenience-store chain. Eddie Jackson, a Lil' Champ exec, told the press that he had their lawyer write the Meese commission a letter telling them they were off target. Jackson said that they were not going to let anybody tell them how to run their business. And Ray Cox of Circle K was quoted as saying: "None of the magazines we carry in our stores has ever been found obscene in any court of law in the United States, nor has any of them ever lost a federal mailing permit as a result of being declared obscene. I will absolutely defend the rights of publishers to publish what is legal."

———

Other major chains that removed *Penthouse* and *Playboy* from their magazine stands were: Revco Drug Stores of Twinsburg, Ohio, with 2,010 stores; People's Drug Stores of Alexandria, Virginia, with over 800 stores; Rite Aid Drug Stores of Shermanstown, Pennsylvania; the Dart Drug Company of Landover, Maryland; and Gray Drug Inc. of Cleveland, Ohio.

Some stores, frightened by the Meese commission letter, even pulled

---

*President, Penthouse International, Ltd.

mainstream magazines that had not been listed, such as *American Photographer, Cosmopolitan,* and *Texas Monthly,* because they discovered that the first carried a picture of bare-breasted women and the other two contained Calvin Klein ads for Obsession perfume that displayed a portion of the nude body of a woman being kissed by a man.

One local religious vigilante group hailed the censorship as "a wonderful gesture of corporate responsibility to remove pornography from the family marketplace"; others vowed to step up their efforts to purge the shelves and racks of community stores of all "pornographic" literature. According to *The New York Times,* national sales at the country's 90,000 magazine outlets dropped 20 percent. Circulation of some men's magazines had already suffered from the entry of videocassettes and cable television into the "family marketplace" for sexually oriented expression.

ROBERT YOAKUM *(Columbia Journalism Review):* Politics may have had as much to do with the Meese Commission's smut hunt as any attempt to answer the question of whether there is a causal relation between sex and violence. The Reagan administration has been looking for raw meat to satisfy the appetite of the religious right—people vexed at the Reagan administration because the Constitution has not yet been amended to permit school prayers, abolish abortion, outlaw pornography, and balance the budget.

In a single stroke, Meese, Sears, or whoever, censored not smut but political reporting and commentary, and criticism of the Reagan administration and the religious right. *Playboy*'s newsstand sales dropped 700,000. *Playboy* and *Penthouse,* but particularly the former, reached hundreds of thousands of readers* with political articles by some of our nation's best writers—messages that are anathema to the Reagan administration.

In what other magazine will the people in those newly purified towns read, routinely, articles that sharply criticize the religious right, Reagan's policies, government censorship, the politics of the anti-abortionists, Pentagon and CIA blunders, and Justice Department injustices? Look at a tiny sampling of *Playboy* titles: "Reagan and the Revival of Racism," "Inside the New Right War Machine," "Compulsory Childbirth," "*Playboy* Interview: Fidel Castro," "Exhuming the Spooks," "Support our Boys in Nicaragua" (a satire), "Reagan's Star Wars Plans Won't Work."

The U.S. is by no means the only country in which sexual and political censorship go hand in hand. Sex magazines are banned in the Soviet Union and all Eastern bloc countries, in Iran and Iraq, in South Africa and Chile and China. . . .

The specific lesson for journalists is that censors are censors are censors. And a free press must stoutly oppose them whether they come garbed as commissars, clerics, or clowns.

---

*More accurately, *millions* of readers. According to Russell Miller (the author of *Bunny*), *Playboy*'s circulation was over four million and *Penthouse*'s was over three million before the Meese commission's attack.

DAVID MYERSON: It was the televangelists on the Religious Right, including Jerry Falwell, who came out screaming against *Penthouse* even before the Meese commission went to work on us. And, of course, they are the ones who influenced the commission's strategy. A number of Religious Right people were provided on a free basis as support personnel for the Meese commission, especially its early stages. Today, the Meese commission's executive director, Alan Sears, is working for the right-wing fundamentalist organization called the National Coalition Against Pornography.*

The televangelists . . . were leading these boycotts of the 7-Eleven stores. They were protesting and they were marching. Jimmy Swaggart used to go on television constantly about how these magazines were terrible for your daughters. He was successful in getting at least one convenience-store chain to rid its store's shelves of *Rolling Stone*. And Jerry Falwell would seek to raise money in the context of "Send me your money and we'll go out and fight this evil."

Penthouse in the late seventies ran articles on the televangelists generally and specifically on Falwell and his financial chicanery. Falwell was enjoined by the Securities and Exchange Commission from the unlawful sale of securities. Instead of seeking contributions to his church, he tried to find a vehicle in the form of a security which would give a right to participation in the church.

———

After the crunch was put on Southland Corporation and other businesses by the Meese commission–Religious Right combine, *Penthouse* and *Playboy* sued the commission on the ground that its action violated their First Amendment rights. They sought to force the commission to retract statements labeling the magazines "pornographic" and to prevent the commission from branding them or their distributors as purveyors of pornography in its *Final Report*. A federal judge in Washington, D.C., granted the magazines the relief they requested. He ordered the commission to send another letter to each of the concerns that had received the original letter, advising them that it had been "withdrawn." The new letter also advised the corporations that their names would not be included in the commission's final report as sellers or distributors of pornographic materials, and they were not. This, however, did not repair the damage that had been caused by the commission's unlawful interference with the publishers' and their distributors' freedom of expression, and the people's freedom to read.

JUDGE JOHN GARRETT PENN: The only purpose served by the Commission's original letter was to discourage distributors from selling the publications, a form of pressure amounting to an administrative restraint of the plaintiff's First Amendment rights. . . .

———

* Purportedly involved (along with a local censorship group) in seeing that criminal charges were brough against Dennis Barrie, curator of the Contemporary Arts Center in Cincinnati, for showing the homoerotic and "child-pornographic" Robert Mapplethorpe exhibition "The Perfect Moment," described in Chapter 30.

It was clear that the original letter contained an implied threat to the addressees, and did lead some retailers to withdraw the magazines. It was also clear that something had occurred in the marketplace. A deprivation of a First Amendment right, that is a prior restraint of speech, a right so precious in this nation, constitutes irreparable injury. . . .

For at least some of the distributors, the concern over having their names published in the Commission's report compelled them to withdraw the sale and distribution of some of plaintiff's magazines and books.

I talked with Norman Mailer and Marcia Pally about the "dangers" of producing "pornography."

NORMAN MAILER: I think there are fairly deep moral questions whether people should be free to create hard-core pornography. I'd say yes, but let's not assume that there's no damage going on. There might be serious damage going on. But I'm perfectly prepared to write a novel about a girl who goes into hard-core pornography and ends up committing suicide. . . .

It's the cutting edge right now. This is the place where I no longer feel certainty about matters of censorship. But I do still lean to the side that people have the right, if they want to, to commit suicide. In my mind, people have the right to do hard-core pornography. For some people it'd be a curse, for others it might be a blessing.

But you're playing with your soul when you start being photographed in the sexual act. At the same time I don't think it's up to the government to forbid it.

MARCIA PALLY: * I don't think you're playing with your soul. . . . You're playing with your body and you're collecting a check.

AMBER LYNN: † I had a sugar daddy who was keeping me. Paying for everything. I didn't need a dime of my own and never had to work. Then, I guess his wife found out, and he ran back to her, breaking it off with me. I was out in the cold. Then a friend of his asked me if I was interested in doing some masturbation stuff on video. I needed the money and said okay.

HEATHER WAYNE: ‡ What was I gonna do when the money stopped coming in? I couldn't live. I couldn't survive, because it was the money that kept me going.

HARRY REEMS: § I was making a whopping $76.00 a week [as an actor in New York]. I needed to supplement my income.

NORMAN MAILER: I directed one film recently where I had a guy and a girl in bed. And it made me slightly uneasy. I felt uneasy becasue I wasn't sure I'd be ready to be the actor in such a scene. . . .

---

* Free-lance writer.
† Film and video porn star.
‡ Film and video porn star.
§ Film and video porn star.

It wasn't a pornographic scene—they were making love under the covers. But nonetheless, from the girl's point of view, she was fairly exposed. She was wearing a bikini but not the top. And I ended up feeling like the towel-boy in a whorehouse.

But nonetheless, if it's necessary to the film, it's necessary to the film.

MARCIA PALLY: And there are other knotty issues: Are live sex shows pornographic acts or expressions covered by the First Amendment? What can be done about the treatment of women in the sex industry? How do feminist anti-porners expect to prevent anti-porn laws from being used to impound literature in favor of gay rights? A pro-choice stance on abortion? Or birth control? Margaret Sanger was imprisoned for disseminating "obscene" material.

If preventing *violence* is their goal, and assuming that people imitate films and books, why is the target of their efforts *sexual* imagery; and who would be entrusted to judge which images violate civil rights?

NORMAN MAILER: You can get into very difficult questions, because if you're going to say, "Well, what about children?," then like anyone else I have that knee-jerk reflex: "Of course not! In the case of children you've got to prosecute. . . ." But what if you have a girl who's nineteen years old or twenty-three years old and has the mental age of a five-year-old? You get into very knotty questions there. . . .

I just don't want the authority in the government to be the judge of these behaviors, because by training, by temperament, by prejudice, they're simply not equipped to understand the human experience involved. Anybody who ends up on the top of the government in one place or another has not spent his life brooding about sex.

I'm for the liberty of it to the degree they're against it. To the degree they're for it, I get worried about it.

CAMILLE PAGLIA: Feminism . . . completely misses the blood-lust in rape, the joy of violation and destruction. An aesthetics and erotics of profanation . . . have been documented in Sade, Baudelaire, and Huysmans. Women may be less prone to such fantasies because they physically lack the equipment for sexual violence. They do not know the temptation of forcibly invading the sanctuary of another body.

Our knowledge of these fantasies is expanded by pornography, which is why pornography should be tolerated. . . . The imagination cannot and must not be policed. Pornography shows us nature's daemonic heart, those eternal forces at work beneath and beyond social convention. Pornography cannot be separated from art; the two interpenetrate each other, far more than humanistic criticism has admitted. Geoffrey Hartman rightly says, "Great art is always flanked by its dark sisters, blasphemy and pornography."

—

Despite having listened to extensive testimony concerning the harm done to women who took part in pornographic productions, the Meese commission made no finding that the government should take new measures to avoid these dangers. The dangers reported by the commission were: danger that the circulation of "sexually violent material" might increase the likelihood of male "aggressive" behavior toward women; danger that "nonviolent" but "degrading" material, if experienced in substantial amounts, might increase the extent to which people "view rape or other forms of sexual violence as less serious than they otherwise would"; danger that the circulation of "non-violent and non-degrading" sexually explicit material might somehow lead to an increase in sexual violence; and unspecified dangers of child pornography. The findings were essentially inconclusive; this was, at least to some extent, conceded by Commissioner Frederick Schauer in a written statement given to the press after the *Final Report* was issued.*

In failing to recommend any new legislation to combat misogynistic pornography the Meese commission disappointed the anti-porn feminists, who had hoped for an "official" federal government endorsement of such legislation. The commission concluded not that new laws should be enacted to defeat pornography, but that the enforcement of existing obscenity and child pornography laws should be escalated. This was done in the hope of overcoming the disappointing response registered by local, state, and federal prosecutors to the Burger Court's 1973 invitation to stamp out pornography in the *Miller* group of cases.

Of the ninety-four recommendations made by the commission, the most significant were those that would lead to the creation of a special Justice Department unit—the National Obscenity Enforcement Unit (NOEU)—to aggressively promote enforcement of existing federal and state obscenity and child pornography laws, especially through multistate and successive prosecutions, against distributors of constitutionally protected as well as unprotected materials, and to heighten collaboration between federal and state sex-police prosecutors and citizens' anti-pornography vigilante groups, including those led by right-wing religious leaders Charles Keating, Jerry Kirk, James Dobson, and Donald Wildmon.†

The commission's recommendation that the prosecution of child pornographers be stepped up has led in recent years to the terrorization of photographers who use their art to capture images of nude and partially clothed children. Today, many child pornography laws make it a serious felony to pose or photograph (and sometimes even to possess, receive, or view a photograph of) a child under the age of eighteen if its genitals or, in the case of a female, its nipples are exposed or in focus. In 1990, a joint federal-state task force unit entered and raided the home-studio of fine-art photographer Jock Sturges, whose work is included in the permanent collections of the Museum of Modern Art, the Metropolitan Museum of

---

*See Frederick Schauer, "What the Pornography Study Really Says," *The Detroit News,* October 26, 1986.

† In a July 1990 op-ed piece in *The New York Times,* First Amendment lawyer Martin Garbus argued for the abolition of this Justice Department unit. Further information about the operation of the NOEU can be found in the endnotes for this chapter.

Art, the Bibliothèque Nationale, and other major museums. All of
Sturges's finished works and works-in-progress in which a child or adolescent appeared, as well as all of his laboratory equipment, records, correspondence, and address and phone books, were seized. The rationale for
the government's entry, search, and seizure was a suspicion that among
Sturges's works there probably existed images that were proscribed, under
California and/or federal child pornography laws, because a young girl's
genitals were immodestly pictured. The police entry and initial search were
made without warrant; the subsequent seizure was made upon a warrant
procured on the basis of information derived from the initial warrantless
entry and search. Ten months after the raid, nothing that was seized had
been returned to Sturges, nor had he been charged with any crime;* and
there was no indication of when, if ever, either event might occur.†

The commission's recommendations regarding child pornography also
included a recommendation that one genre of fictional pornography—
unillustrated but legally obscene fiction involving sexual activity with
minors—be prosecuted, notwithstanding that a majority of the commissioners proposed that distributors of obscenity consisting of the printed
word only should no longer be prosecuted, regardless of its content or
character. The movement in favor of an exemption for printed-word expression, led by Commissioner Frederick Schauer, was controverted by Chairman Henry E. Hudson and other commission members, who did not wish
to "appear to condone a relaxation of existing obscenity laws covering
expression consisting solely of the printed word."

Although it would not be considered contraband under state or federal
child pornography laws, a "novel" called *Tying Up Rebecca,* as described by
the Meese commission, provides an example of a book that the commission
recommended federal and state prosecutors should try to suppress—
through enforcement of the ordinary laws criminalizing the circulation of
obscenity among adults—because of the book's explicit depictions of sexual
behavior involving minors. There is nothing about this pornography to
distinguish it from run-of-the-mill pornography other than its assigning of
minority ages to its principal characters, and the high school setting.‡

---

*See *The Nation,* July 9, 1990 ("The Art Cops"), and *Aperture* magazine's November 1990
issue devoted in part to nude-child photography.
†By September 1991 most of the film materials that had been seized had been returned,
many irreparably damaged, and a federal grand jury had refused to indict Sturges for any crime.
‡ As with other pulp pornography the publisher of *Tying Up Rebecca* would be unlikely to
make any claim in court that the work possessed literary or even social value (which is not
to say such a claim might not genuinely be made). But if the publisher of this book was
prosecuted only because the book made sexual conduct with minors "alluring" (rather than
because it met the three-pronged *Miller* test for obscenity), a constitutional defense would be
available that insofar as the advocacy of the "idea" that adult-children sexual relations are good
(not bad) is constitutionally protected, the publishing of a book communicating this idea also
is entitled to constitutional protection. The precedent is *Kingsley International Pictures* v.
Regents, involving a motion picture adaptation of *Lady Chatterley's Lover,* seen as advocating
the idea that adultery can be good; the decision is reprinted in de Grazia, *Censorship Landmarks*
(1969) at 326ff. There is an organization called NAMBLA, "National Man-Boy Love Associa-

ATTORNEY GENERAL'S COMMISSION ON PORNOGRAPHY *(Final Report):* The Foreword [of *Tying Up Rebecca*] describes a male gymnastic coach's fantasy of having sex with his most talented female gymnast, a thirteen year old girl named Becky. . . .

Chapter One begins on the page numbered 5 and finishes on the page numbered 25. The chapter begins with Becky Mingus working out on the parallel bars with the assistance of her coach, Vern Lawless. Lawless is described as a former athlete, balding and well built, in his early forties. Lawless is described as having a failing marriage, and being loveless for eleven years, sexless for seven. Becky Mingus is described as a ginger haired thirteen year old with the potential the best [*sic*] gymnast in the Midwest and become a member of the United States Olympic gymnastic team. This story takes place at St. Mary's, a Catholic School. Coach Lawless lusts after Becky and remembers when she first started on his team two years ago.

When she had first been accepted to the team, she mistakenly changed her clothes in the teacher's lockerroom. Lawless accidentally walked in and saw her bent over naked. Becky was eleven years old at the time. She didn't notice him and he quickly withdrew. However, the memory of this incident continued to haunt him.

Back to the present, Lawless leaves the school to go home and tell his wife he wants a divorce. Becky leaves the gym to go to the girl's locker room just as the gym lights are being turned off by Mr. Schultz, the janitor. In the locker room Becky encounters the school's head cheerleader and former gymnast, Patty Jones, who is taking a shower. Patty Jones is described as a fifteen year old girl with dark hair, physically more mature than Becky. She calls Becky into the shower to look at something. She then shows Becky a hole in the wall through which she has been watching a boy, Judd Loomis, taking a shower in the boy's locker room. Loomis is described as bad, with a legendary reputation as a stud soon to be expelled from school. As Patty watches Loomis she begins to masturbate herself but discovers she has her fingers in Becky's vagina. She stops immediately and leaves the shower soon after.

Becky then watches Loomis examining his body completely. She sees Patty enter the boy's locker room, wrapped only in a towel. She drops the towel, fondles her breasts and spreads her labia. Loomis forces her to her knees where she commences to lick his penis and testicles. Patty sticks her tongue in Loomis' urethra from which he had urinated only moments before. She performs anilingus on him. Soon after he grabs her by the hair and forces her face down into a drain well. He then penetrates her anally with his penis. Next Loomis performs cunnilingus on Patty and she performs fellatio on him. Becky is masturbating herself as she watches this.

---

tion," that does advocate man-boy relations. Mainstream American publishers have proven extremely loath to publish books with a child-sex theme, which explains the great difficulty Vladimir Nabokov encountered in publishing *Lolita* (described in Chapter 14).

Loomis ejaculates in Patty's mouth as he continues to perform cunnilingus on her. Loomis then has vaginal intercourse with Patty. . . .

———

The argument advanced by anti-porn feminists that the making of graphic pornography harmed the women involved in its production came closest to presenting a justification for governmental measures intended to prevent the circulation of pornography, and to supporting an otherwise mainly rhetorical or metaphorical proposition that pornography is an "act," not an "idea," that it is therefore suppressible "conduct," not protected "expression." In this respect, but only in this respect, was the argument analogous to that accepted by the Supreme Court in *Ferber* v. *New York* as a justification for allowing the prevention and punishment of child pornography which predominantly involves the production of pictorial expression in which children are induced to engage in sexual conduct with each other, with adults, or with themselves. A law punishing persons who involve children in making sexually explicit photographs or movies that may not be obscene under the Miller test is constitutionally justifiable as an exception to the rule that nonobscene expression is protected expression—or so the legislatures and the courts have reasoned—because such persons are deemed to be harming children in the process of producing the expression, and children are incapable legally of consenting to be harmed. Distributors, and even purchasers and possessors, are punished because their acquisition of such pornography encourages its production.*

———

*Any adult (whether artist or not) involved in taking photographs or making films in which children have been directed to simulate or engage in sexual conduct with other children or adults, to masturbate, "lewdly expose" their genitals, or participate in any other act constituting the new crime would be liable, virtually everywhere, even in the absence of child pornography laws, to prosecution and punishment for violating the ordinary law making acts endangering the welfare of children, child abuse, child exploitation, etc., criminal. However, most of those who have sat on the Supreme Court during the past two decades have been sufficiently disquieted by the idea of child pornography production that they have hastily ridden over the principal constitutional problems presented by child pornography laws, seriously discounting the substantial overbreadth and extraordinary vagueness inherent in some of their critical terms (including "lewd" in "lewd exhibition of the genitals," and "focus" in "focus on the genital area," discussed by Brennan, dissenting, in *Osborne* v. *Ohio*), as noted earlier, and the curtailment of freedom such terminology engenders. Those who would disseminate, as distinguished from produce, child pornography might be prosecuted as abetters to the criminal producers and be discouraged from buying for resale such child pornography as may be produced notwithstanding the child abuse, endangerment, and exploitation laws. However, although the Court has to date failed to make clear that artistic or otherwise socially valuable portrayals of parentally consented-to child nudity or sexuality cannot be branded "child pornography" (just as artistic or otherwise socially valuable depictions of adult nudity and sexuality cannot be branded "obscene"), it should be able to do so in a proper case.

Finally, the Court has given scant attention to the real threats to home, parental, and family integrity and privacy that are posed by child pornography laws and their enforcement. Already, some nineteen states (not including New York but including Ohio) have made it a felony merely to possess or view (at home or elsewhere) "child pornography," which has been very broadly defined to embrace even photographs of infants and young teenagers in states of complete or partial nudity. (In Massachusetts, it was made felonious to take pictures of a child romping on the beach if his or her genital area could be seen, or of a teenaged female if her

No similar logic applies to adults. Under the laws of most American jurisdictions adult women, as well as men, are legally capable of consenting to be harmed, and capable even of withholding consent to be kept alive. On the other hand, typically, not even an adult can legally consent to be murdered or maimed by another, nor may an adult—by "consenting" to be put to death—immunize the killer from criminal culpability. The anti-porn feminists were unwilling to argue that adult women, in general (there was no showing that the Linda Lovelace story—if true—was typical), could or should be deemed incapable of consenting to unpleasant, oppressive, even physically or morally or emotionally harmful working or living conditions; or that women should be prevented by law from taking their sexual pleasure as they like it—even if this entailed bondage or sadomasochistic acts. Some feminists today acknowledge that for many women some pornography is a good thing, being a source of pleasure and expressing "counterpatriarchal" moral themes. Of course, enforcement of criminal laws forbidding nonconsensual assaultive or life-threatening sexual behavior is a deterrent to such behavior, and in no way violates freedom of expression. In the event, unlike anti-porn feminists, the Meese commission exhibited no real concern to protect porn stars or other workers at risk in the country's billion-dollar pornography industry and made no recommendation to protect them from sexual exploitation or other harm.

NORMAN MAILER: You know, what [the anti-porn feminists] are really opposed to is sex, and they're using feminism as a cover for the real tack because they hate the fact that there are women who can take carnal pleasure with men. They loathe that. They absolutely loathe it.

———

In Washington, D.C., a 1990 staging of a lesbian piece by New York performance artist Holly Hughes was the target of anti-porn feminist protests.

HOLLY HUGHES: I had a show called *The Well of Horniness** that ran for three months in Washington, D.C., at a mainstream theatre, and before it opened a group that never came forward—but some sort of lesbian anti-porn group—vandalized the theatre, spray-painted STOP LESBIAN PORNOGRAPHY! HOLLY HUGHES IS A PORNOGRAPHER! on the theatre. And I wouldn't be surprised if this didn't give the Right some sort of clue that I might be a target.† This was a group of lesbians who wouldn't identify themselves, in the Washington, D.C., area.

There were pleas in the gay papers to come forward and, like, "Let's have

---

nipples were visible. See *Massachusetts* v. *Oakes,* 109 S.Ct. 2633 [1989].) Justice Brennan, in his dissent in *Osborne,* commented on the Court's unusual "disquietude" in dealing with the problem of child pornography, a disquietude that causes it to overlook the threats to individual, parental, and artistic freedom of expression presented by "kiddy porn" laws.

*Regarding *The Well of Loneliness,* the best-selling lesbian novel by Radclyffe Hall, see Chapters 10 and 11.

†A target, that is, for "defunding" by the National Endowment for the Arts, as described in Chapter 30.

some sort of talk and discussion about this." But they didn't, and there were leaflets left around saying that "Well, *Horniness* is a pornographic work, it's not lesbian, it's really a tool of . . ."

And this has happened before. It's been described as a "lesbian sex comedy" but the sex is such that if it were a movie it would get a PG rating if it were heterosexual. And just the fact that it's *lesbians* doing something automatically gives it an X rating in a lot of people's minds. A lot of lesbians and a lot of feminists feel that there is no way to depict women's sexuality— be it gay or straight—in the performing arts without its being exploitative; and I completely disagree with that. I think we have to seize control of our bodies, we have to be putting out alternative images. I feel we have to push those limits and I feel like otherwise it's to cave in to a complete victim mentality and I really have always disagreed with that. . . .

I'm working with a lawyer who is representing me* who became known as an outspoken feminist who was writing *against* Women Against Pornography—her argument was always that the anti-obscenity laws that Andrea Dworkin and Catharine MacKinnon were trying to push were never going to be used against men doing snuff films, or men or women or whoever kidnapping little kids and using them for pornography; they were going to be used against feminists and gay people, and that is exactly what we're seeing happening. . . .

My understanding is that when Dworkin and MacKinnon were working in Minnesota, they were working with right-wing groups, incredibly right-wing conservative groups. They like completely bedded down with them and I just felt that these people are not on our side.

NORMAN MAILER: Sex is that place where one finds equality through domination and submissiveness. I don't mean by that that I'm a whip-and-chain guy. I just mean that sometimes the man's on top, sometimes the woman's on top. It's as if the dominance is passed back and forth, like a relay race. And that's the excitement of sex: one of the excitements is you can replay all those needs that we all have to be dominated and to dominate. And then these women come in and call it an abuse of women. It's bullshit.

Let them try telling that to the girls who are acting in those things. The feminists will get beaten up.

"Don't come between a whore and her money."

MARCIA PALLY: If we were serious about ensuring the safety of sex industry workers, we would make those industries a completely legitimate retail business. The more legitimate, the more accountable to law. You can't go to the cops to complain about fraud—much less about rape or kidnapping—if what you do is illegal. If we destroy photos of coercion or rape,

---

*Brooklyn Law School professor and ACLU lawyer Nan Hunter has filed a civil complaint on behalf of Hughes and three other performing artists against NEA chairman John Frohnmayer for denying them "performance art" grants that an NEA peer panel had recommended be awarded; in Hughes's case, the reason was apparently her work's "lesbian homoeroticism." See Chapter 30.

when the photos are burned, we're still left with the rape. The rape still happened. But if we diminish the violence, there won't be any pictures of it to be sold as pornography. The problem is that the laws against violence are rarely enforced in the sex industry, and the police treat complaints so cavalierly that women—and men—in the industry don't bother to bring them. . . .

Another kind of coercion connected with the sex industries is economic—where women and men, boys and girls, are forced into modeling or prostitution because it's the best-paying job around. If we close the porn industry, we wipe out a source of income without providing alternatives. A source of income that's crucial to many people, no matter how dismaying it may seem to some of us. If we drive the porn industry underground, we make those jobs more dangerous, because everything is more violent and hazardous on the black market. At every porn panel I've attended over the past few years—and that's quite a few—women from the sex industry have stood up and angrily pointed this out. . . .

Most important, we need to hear from sex industry workers, to listen to what they need, to how they'd like to improve their work conditions. And we need to support their organizations, like the U.S. Prostitutes Collective, COYOTE (Cast Off Your Old Tired Ethics), PUMA (Prostitutes Union of Massachusetts), the California Prostitutes Education Project, and the International Committee for Prostitutes Rights.

———

Robin West, a professor of law at the University of Maryland, has distinguished between "good" and "bad" pornography for women, based upon the premise that whatever else it might be, "pornography is an aid to sexual pleasure."

West considers that pornography cannot be said to be victimless in the light of testimony by women who said they suffered serious injury either in the making of violent pornography or from violent sexual acts by men who claimed to have been incited by viewing pornography; for West this is bad pornography. But, she points out, the anti-porn feminists and the Meese commission investigators both refused to describe the good pornography that has brought positive sexual experiences to women, and is also good for feminists because it impeaches conservative patriarchal morality with its profound denial that virtue and sexuality are compatible in women.

ROBIN WEST: Most pornography may indeed be worthless or worse. But some pornography, traditionally conceived, is good. . . . [G]ood pornography assaults . . . a source of oppression: the marital, familial, productive, and reproductive values that the conservative wrongly identifies as necessary to the creation of a virtuous life and a virtuous society. All pornography— bad and good—assaults traditional familial and marital values. . . . [A]ccording to women who enjoy pornography, the validation of pleasure, desire, and sexuality found in some pornography is not an attack on "virtue." Rather it is a healthy attack on a stifling and oppressive societal denial of female sexuality. The attack . . . is liberating, and something to celebrate, rather than something to condemn. . . . For example, the pornographic poem *Bestiary* by feminist writer Sharon Olds celebrates nature, sexuality, sodomy, animalism, penetration, and even the [male] value of instrumental rationality. The result is not a degrading or decadent or humiliating piece of pornography. It is joyful, liberating, and life-affirming. . . .

[P]ornography, when it is good, . . . appeals to our insatiable and not necessarily prurient interest in the "vast and deepest reaches of sex where we relive infant experiences of utter gratification in utter passivity."

NORMAN MAILER: The idea that pornography should be censored because it's degrading to women is ridiculous. I've seen any number of pornographic films where you have girls sitting on guys' heads.

LOIS SHEINFELD:* On the evening of July 10 [1984], a 23-year-old Minneapolis woman doused herself with gasoline and set herself aflame to protest pornography. She was taken to the hospital in critical condition. Three days later, the Minneapolis City Council passed a package of antipornography legislation. The legislation included a censorship ordinance condemning pornography on the theory that it violated the civil rights of women. That ordinance was the product of an intensive campaign mounted by two feminists, Catharine MacKinnon . . . and Andrea Dworkin. . . . Last year, MacKinnon and Dworkin drafted a similar ordinance and persuaded the City Council to adopt it . . . following highly emotional legislative hearings. . . . Mayor Donald M. Fraser vetoed that ordinance.

NAT HENTOFF: Perhaps the most bizarre turn in the tumultuous history of "the new censorship" was a letter sent to the President of the Minneapolis City Council . . .—"in dissent and dismay" at Fraser's veto—by the justly celebrated First Amendment gladiator Professor Lawrence Tribe of Harvard Law School. In the letter, Tribe chastised the mayor for "hiding behind the First Amendment" by not letting the courts decide, instead of unilaterally killing the bill by veto. The Dworkin-MacKinnon legislation, said Tribe, "is not obviously unconstitutional" and its supposed invalidity "follows surely from no clear precedent." Tribe added that while he is uncertain as to how a judicial test will come out, he feels the MacKinnon-Dworkin creation "may eventually be found to be the first sensible approach to an area which has vexed some of the best legal minds for decades."

If Lawrence Tribe's mind can turn to mush on this matter, can anyone be sure of what the Supreme Court will say?†

---

*Professor, New York University School of Journalism.

†Tribe's justly praised treatise *American Constitutional Law* (1978) points out that "nonjudicial actors" in the law-making process, such as state legislators, ought themselves to gauge the constitutionality of laws they are deliberating enacting, "whether or not judges threaten to offer binding answers of their own" (13–14). Professor David Bryden of the University of Minnesota Law School pointed out that "Tribe is surely right that politicians ought to take account of the Constitution," and that "any law school sophomore could show that the Minneapolis pornography ordinance was unlikely to survive litigation" ("Between Two Constitutions: Feminism and Pornography," *Constitutional Commentary* 2 [1985], 147, 173).

LOIS SHEINFELD: Assisted by MacKinnon, an unlikely marriage of feminists and members of the Moral Majority secured the passage of corresponding legislation in Indianapolis on May 1. An hour after Mayor William H. Hudnut signed the measure into law, it was challenged in federal court on First Amendment and other constitutional grounds.

———

On February 24, 1986, the United States Supreme Court held the Indianapolis ordinance unconstitutional; like the Minneapolis one, it had been "drafted" by Dworkin and MacKinnon and defined pornography as "the graphic sexually explicit subordination of women, whether in pictures or words," if it showed them (among other things) enjoying "pain or humiliation" or in "positions of servility or submission or display." Neoconservatives, conservatives, Moral Majoritarians, and others had combined with anti-porn feminists to pass similar laws in Cambridge, Massachusetts, Suffolk County, New York, and other local communities; as a result of the Supreme Court's action, however, those presumably are dead.

The Court struck down the Indianapolis law by summarily affirming (without written opinion) a decision handed down by the prestigious federal Seventh Circuit Court of Appeals, which was explained in a scholarly, thoughtful opinion written by Judge Frank Easterbrook.* Easterbrook said that the Indianapolis law violated freedom of speech because it established "an approved view of women," and sought to use the courts to silence sexually explicit speech that failed to conform to that view. At the same time, however, the landmark opinion accepted *arguendo* the unproved sociological premises of the Dworkin-MacKinnon legislation:

JUDGE FRANK EASTERBROOK: Depictions of subordination tend to perpetrate subordination. The subordinate status of women in turn leads to affront and lower pay at work, insult and injury at home, battery and rape on the streets. . . . [But] this simply demonstrates the power of pornography as speech, like much other dangerous speech that is protected by the First Amendment.

———

In the same context, fellow Seventh Circuit appellate judge Richard A. Posner—who, when serving as a law clerk to Justice William J. Brennan, Jr., some twenty-five years earlier, had encouraged Brennan to free *Tropic of Cancer*—had this to say:

RICHARD A. POSNER:† A group of radical feminists, opportunistically supported by social and religious conservatives, invites us to consider the

---

Newsweek magazine reported on March 18, 1985, "Now Tribe has retrenched, not because of a change in the law but because he's worried that 'it might play into the hands of groups that want government to have power to suppress ideas.' "

*Easterbrook is also an adjunct professor at the University of Chicago Law School.

†Posner is also a visiting lecturer at the University of Chicago Law School and is the author of numerous books, including *Economic Analysis of Law* (1986) and *Law and Literature: A Misunderstood Relation* (1988).

obscene less as a matter of excessive frankness in the portrayal of sex than as a point of view harmful to women, and to suppress as obscene some works that would not flunk the *Miller* test of obscenity. This movement defines the obscene as sexually explicit material that depicts women as enjoying rape or mutilation or, in general, forcible submission to men. The danger to literary values comes from the fact that much of the world's great literature, though not sexually explicit by modern American standards, portrays with approval the subordination, often by force, of women to men (though this is not the same thing as depicting women enjoying that subordination—the particular concern of the feminist opponents of pornography). A notable example is the treatment of Briseis and Chryseis in the *Iliad*. The Bible contains many instances of what by contemporary standards is misogyny; so do *Paradise Lost* and *The Taming of the Shrew*, not to mention *Eumenides*—the list is endless. Because literature is by definition the writing that survives a protracted competitive process, most literature is old and much of it therefore reflects, and some of it approves, values that modern readers find offensive—such as anti-Semitism or belief in the racial inferiority of blacks or in the natural subordination of women. Maybe the values in some works of literature will become so repulsive that the works themselves disappear from the body of literature. But this process should be left to the competition of the literary marketplace rather than hurried along by politicians, prosecutors, judges, and jurors.

———

The Dworkin-MacKinnon feminist legislation was, as suggested earlier, designed to skirt the Supreme Court's still intact *Miller* doctrine forbidding the suppression of expressive materials that do not appeal to prurient interests, are not patently offensive to community values, or possess serious literary, artistic, scientific, or political value.

JUDGE FRANK EASTERBROOK: The Indianapolis ordinance does not refer to the prurient interest, to offensiveness, or to the standards of the community. It demands attention to particular depictions, not to the work judged as a whole. It is irrelevant under the ordinance whether the work has literary, artistic, political, or scientific value. The City and many amici [supporting the validity of the ordinance] point to these omissions as virtues. They maintain that pornography influences attitudes, and the statute is a way to alter the socialization of men and women rather than to vindicate community standards of offensiveness. And as one of the principal drafters of the ordinance has asserted, "if a woman is subjected, why should it matter that the work has other value?"*

Civil rights groups and feminists have entered this case as amici on both sides. Those supporting the ordinance say that it will play an important role in reducing the tendency of men to view women as sexual objects, a ten-

———

*MacKinnon, "Pornography, Civil Rights, and Speech," *Harvard Civil Rights–Civil Liberties Law Review* 20 (1985), 1, 21.

dency that leads to both unacceptable attitudes and discrimination in the workplace and violence away from it. Those opposing the ordinance point out that much radical feminist literature is explicit and depicts women in ways forbidden by the ordinance* and that the ordinance would reopen old battles. It is unclear how Indianapolis would treat works from James Joyce's *Ulysses* to Homer's *Iliad;* both depict women as submissive objects for conquest and domination.

We do not try to balance the arguments for and against an ordinance such as this. The ordinance discriminates on the ground of the content of the speech. Speech treating women in the approved way—in sexual encounters "premised on equality"—is lawful no matter how sexually explicit. Speech treating women in the disapproved way—as submissive in matters sexual or as enjoying humiliation—is unlawful no matter how significant the literary, artistic, or political qualities of the work taken as a whole. The state may not ordain preferred viewpoints in this way. The Constitution forbids the state to declare one perspective right and silence opponents.

"If there is any fixed star in our constitutional constellation, it is that no official, high or petty, can prescribe what shall be orthodox in politics, nationalism, religion, or other matters of opinion or force citizens to confess by word or act their faith therein."† Under the First Amendment the government must leave to the people the evaluation of ideas. Bald or subtle, an idea is as powerful as the audience allows it to be. A belief may be pernicious—the beliefs of Nazis led to the death of millions, those of the Klan to the repression of millions. A pernicious belief may prevail. Totalitarian governments today rule much of the planet, practicing suppression of billions and spreading dogma that may enslave others.‡ One of the things that separates our society from theirs is our absolute right to propagate opinions that the government finds wrong or even hateful. . . .

Under the ordinance graphic sexually explicit speech is "pornography" or not depending on the perspective the author adopts. Speech that "subordinates" women and also, for example, presents women as enjoying pain, humiliation, or rape, or even simply presents women in "positions of servility or submission or display" is forbidden, no matter how great the literary or political value of the work taken as a whole. Speech that portrays women in positions of equality is lawful, no matter how graphic the sexual content. This is thought control. It establishes an "approved" view of women, or how they may react to sexual encounters, of how the sexes may relate to each other. Those who espouse the approved view may use sexual images; those who do not, may not.

---

*As, I have suggested above, Dworkin's *Ice and Fire,* for instance, does.

†The quoted language was used by Justice Robert H. Jackson in *West Virginia State Board of Education* v. *Barnette.*

‡Written four years before the mammoth dismantling of many of these totalitarian governments as a result of Soviet leader Gorbachev's revolutionary glasnost policy. In every case, freedom of expression was among the initial policies instituted as a measure designed to replace totalitarian with democratic government. Artists, especially poets and writers, were in the vanguard of the peaceful revolutionary movements in Czechoslovakia and Hungary.

ROBIN WEST: The [Dworkin-MacKinnon] anti-pornography ordinance has defined the depiction of expression of sexual submission as objectively bad, when for many women both the thing expressed and its expression are subjectively pleasurable. The ordinance raises the conflict between objective ideal and subjective pleasure, and the result has been chaos.

ANNE RICE: I think there are probably millions of women in the United States who . . . have sadomasochistic desires and no language to express them. It's absolute madness that those desires are unexpressed. . . . I also think that although women want a pornography very much, the climate for it right now is absolutely repressive. It's ironic, but I think feminists have helped create that climate. Look at Andrea Dworkin and Catharine MacKinnon. I think they're fools. The legislation they're proposing is absurd. I regard my writing of pornography to be a real moral cause. And I don't want a bunch of fascist, reactionary feminists kicking in the door of my consciousness with their jackboots and telling me that sadomasochism isn't politically correct.

JUDGE FRANK EASTERBROOK: Indianapolis justifies the ordinance on the ground that pornography affects thoughts. Men who see women depicted as subordinate are more likely to treat them so. Pornography is an aspect of dominance. It does not persuade people so much as change them. It works by socializing, by establishing the expected and the permissible. In this view pornography is not an idea; pornography is the injury. . . .

Yet this simply demonstrates the power of pornography as speech. . . . All of these unhappy effects depend on mental intermediation. Pornography affects how people see the world, their fellows, and social relations. If pornography is what pornography does, so is other speech. Hitler's orations affected how some Germans saw Jews. Communism is a world view, not simply a *Manifesto* by Marx and Engels or a set of speeches. Efforts to suppress communist speech in the United States were based on the belief that the public acceptability of such ideas would increase the likelihood of totalitarian government. [Many] people believe that the existence of television, apart from the content of specific programs, leads to intellectual laziness, to a penchant for violence, to many other ills. The Alien and Sedition Acts passed during the administration of John Adams rested on a sincerely held belief that disrespect for the government leads to social collapse and revolution—a belief with support in the history of many nations. Most governments of the world act on this empirical reality, suppressing critical speech. In the United States, however, the strength of the support for this belief is irrelevant. Seditious libel is protected speech unless the danger is not only grave but also imminent.

Racial bigotry, anti-Semitism, violence on television, reporters' biases— these and many more influence the culture and shape our socialization. None is directly answerable by more speech, unless that speech too finds its place in the popular culture. Yet all is protected as speech, however insidious. Any other answer leaves the government in control of all of the institutions of culture, the great censor and director of which thoughts are good for us.

NORMAN MAILER: Feminism, I think, finally is a right-wing organization. Because it's oppressive. Its ultimate aim is to tell other people how they should live, people they don't know. Whenever you believe in something which will tell other people how to live, and you don't know them, you're an oppressor. Whether *you* know it or not.

———

Although Easterbrook recognized that violent or vacuous "entertaining" television shows are presumptively protected speech under the First Amendment, four years later he could not concede that nude dancing might be seen in the same light. He denied that it could be described as expression protected by the constitutional guarantees and construed pertinent Supreme Court precedent as noncontrolling. In July 1990, because of these views, Easterbrook dissented strongly from a holding by a majority of his eleven-man federal appellate court, sitting *en banc* in Chicago, that Indiana's public indecency statute was unconstitutional as applied to topless go-go dancers Darlene Miller, Gayle Sutro, and Carla Johnson—women who were paid to dance nude at the Kitty-Kat Lounge in South Bend. According to the majority, "non-obscene barroom-variety nude dancing performed as entertainment is expression and, as such, is entitled to limited protection under the First Amendment."*

JUDGE FRANK EASTERBROOK *(dissenting):* The First Amendment protects "the freedom of speech." Go-go dancing is not "speech." James Madison would have guffawed had anyone suggested public nudity as an example of "freedom of speech. . . ."† Parading around in a state of undress is conduct, not speech.

———

*The injudicious notion that some expression has "full," whereas other expression has "limited," constitutional protection from time to time enters First Amendment jurisprudence. In *Roth,* Brennan said that "all ideas having even the slightest redeeming social importance . . . have the *full* protection of the guarantees" (italics mine); and once he squarely recognized (in the *Tropic of Cancer/Jacobellis* cases) that nonideological expression having even the slightest literary or artistic importance was also constitutionally protected, there was no doubt that such expression too was *fully* protected. In the nude-dancing case *Doran* v. *Salem Inn* (95 S.Ct. 2561 [1975]), however, Justice Rehnquist said that the "customary 'barroom' type of nude dancing may involve *only the barest minimum* of protected expression" (italics mine). Later, in *Schad* v. *Mt. Ephraim* (101 S.Ct. 2176, decided in 1981), a case brought by a bookstore operator who offered his customers "the opportunity to view a live nude dancer," the Court found unconstitutionally overbroad an ordinance forbidding "all live entertainment," because "nude dancing *is not without* its First Amendment protections from official regulations" (italics mine). Despite its growing popularity among (mainly conservative) commentators on the Court's work, such grading of the First Amendment's protection of speech and press serves mainly to weaken First Amendment protection overall. The Supreme Court has consistently maintained that nudity alone (whether of adults or children) "does not place otherwise protected material outside the mantle of the First Amendment." See, e.g., *Erznoznik* v. *City of Jackson,* 95 S.Ct. 2268, 2274 (1975), and the cases cited by Justice Brennan dissenting in *Osborne* v. *Ohio,* 110 S.Ct. 1691 (1990), a child pornography case.

†Easterbrook is making it clear that he associates himself with the currently popular conservative "original intention" school, also called the school of "judicial restraint." Another proselytizer for this view is Robert H. Bork; see his *The Tempting of America* (1989).

The question that deeply divided (6 to 5) the court in *Darlene Miller* was whether it was valid jurisprudentially to hold that *entertainment,* in the form of nude dancing or otherwise, was constitutionally protected "speech" even if it might not communicate ideas. If it was to be considered speech rather than conduct, the fact that it involved nudity could not justify its suppression, for mere nudity is not obscene and there was no contention in the law or the prosecution that the dancing involved was obscene.

It was not until after World War II that American free speech theory began to lose its dependency on the notion that the guarantees were meant mainly to protect the dissemination of political or religious *ideas;* in *Darlene Miller* Easterbrook wrote as though the Supreme Court were still wedded to this idea, or as if its present conservative majority might follow a suggestion to retreat to that cramped position.*

Judge Richard Posner, siting on the same bench, concurred with the majority's holding that even nude dancing was protected "speech"; Posner pointed out that earlier notions of freedom of expression presupposing "ideas" had been abandoned by the Supreme Court and that the First Amendment's blanket of protection was now authoritatively recognized to cover "entertainment" as well as "art," whether or not identifiable ideas were communicated.†

The plainest statement to come from the Supreme Court regarding the constitutional status of "entertainment" came in 1952 when the Court overruled its own 1914 decision holding that motion pictures were, "like other spectacles, not to be regarded . . . as part of the press of the country." Speaking for a unanimous bench, Justice Tom Clark there said: "the importance of motion pictures as an organ of public opinion is not lessened by the fact that they are designed to entertain as well as to inform." Adopting a classic dictum from a 1948 decision that held that even magazines such as *Headquarters Detective* were constitutionally protected, Clark elaborated on the point.

JUSTICE TOM CLARK: The line between the informing and the entertaining is too elusive for the protection of that basic right [a free press]. Everyone is familiar with instances of propaganda through fiction. What is one man's amusement teaches another's doctrine.‡

---

*It did, on June 21, 1991. See the footnote at the end of this chapter.

† Of course art and entertainment convey "ideas." It's just that the ideas conveyed touch the emotions more directly and intimately than words alone do, and characteristically are difficult to identify, and defend, in words.

‡The principal case was *Burstyn* v. *Wilson* (1952), involving the attempted censorship in New York of the Italian motion picture *The Miracle,* described in de Grazia and Newman, *Banned Films* (1982), 77–83, 231–33; the full text of Clark's opinion can be found in de Grazia, *Censorship Landmarks* (1969), 180, 182. The *Headquarters Detective* case was *Winters* v. *New York* (1948), reprinted in de Grazia, *Censorship Landmarks* (1969), 132–33. See also *Hannegan* v. *Esquire,* 327 U.S. 146 (1946).

As indicated in the discussion of Brennan's opinion in *Jacobellis* and *Tropic of Cancer* and their progeny (including the Burger opinions in *Miller* v. *California,* et al.), the Supreme Court has abandoned the jurisprudential viewpoint that to be constitutionally protected, speech and press require the communication of "opinions" or "ideas." If expression has any artistic value at all, it is protected, because the First Amendment was meant to, and has correctly been held to, protect works of art and the arts in general, and not merely identifiable ideas that artistic works may disseminate. In those June 1964 decisions the Court held that *Tropic of Cancer* and *The Lovers* were protected not because they communicated protected ideas but because they embodied literary and artistic values, which were meant by the Constitution's framers to be protected.*

Here, as elsewhere in the field of freedom of speech, if Judge Easterbrook had glanced up the road he might have spied Professor Harry Kalven coming down to meet him. For in his 1960 *Supreme Court Review* article "The Metaphysics of the Law of Obscenity" and in the writings that were posthumously published as *A Worthy Tradition,* Kalven criticized free speech theorists who retained the obscurantist notion that the communication of "ideas" was essential or central to the First Amendment's scheme of protection. "Art and belles-lettres," he said, "do not deal in such ideas— at least not good art or belles-lettres." The Supreme Court had recognized, he observed, not that "truth and beauty are one, but that beauty has constitutional status too, and that the life of the imagination is as important to the human adult as the life of the intellect." In fact, the Supreme Court began in *The Lovers* and *Tropic of Cancer* cases to fully protect the communication of what Kalven called imagery (and what I had called images), in addition to "ideas."† For in the opinion he wrote to explain the court's decisions in those cases Brennan described the constitutional protection as covering both "material . . . that advocates ideas . . . *or* that has literary or scientific or artistic value or any form of social importance" (my emphasis). The point is that the First Amendment was meant to protect all expressive products of the intellect or the imagination or both,‡ and that the Supreme Court has implicitly recognized this time and again.

---

*On the other hand, in the *I Am Curious—Yellow* case, the prestigious Second Circuit Court of Appeals made use of the older notion to reverse a federal jury's finding that the film was obscene; after viewing it, the appeals court ruled that "it is quite certain that 'I Am Curious' does present ideas and does strive to present those ideas artistically. It falls within the ambit of intellectual effort that the First Amendment was designed to protect." See de Grazia, *Censorship Landmarks* (1969), 637, 639.

†See Kalven's *A Worthy Tradition* (1987), 41. My argument that the guarantees protected "images" and "ideas" was contained in the several briefs that I filed with the Court, including the brief amici curiae that I filed in 1965 in *Mishkin* v. *New York* on behalf of a group of New York literati, mentioned in Chapter 26.

‡It is perfectly clear that the sorts of artistic expression being attacked as "obscene" by state and federal government organs today are being attacked *because of their ideas* as well as because of the way the ideas are expressed. Prime examples are the attacks on Mapplethorpe's "pro-homosexual" photography, Serrano's "anti-Catholic" artwork, Finley's "feminist" performance manifestoes, Hughes's pro-lesbian work, and 2 Live Crew's "male chauvinist" lyrics. See Chapter 30.

As the Court was moving beyond the narrow idea of "protecting the circulation of ideas" it recognized that many forms of communication and expression were constitutionally protected, including crime and detective magazines *(Winters* v. *New York),* motion pictures *(Burstyn* v. *Wilson* and *Jacobellis* v. *Ohio),* "meritorious" novels *(Tropic of Cancer* and *Fanny Hill),* trashy ones *(Redrup* v. *New York),* "live" theatre performances *(Southeastern Promotions* v. *Conrad),* * rock music *(Ward* v. *Rock Against Racism),* † and nude dancing, topless dancing, and striptease. Here, three Supreme Court decisions backed the conclusion reached by Judge Posner and the court majority in *Darlene Miller* v. *South Bend* that "nude dancing performed as entertainment falls within the scope of the First Amendment."‡ This confirmed what informed free speech lawyers and others had long understood to be the law—that "men's entertainment" magazines, even ones less "meritorious" than *Playboy* and *Penthouse* or *Esquire,* were protected by the constitutional guarantees. Finally, as Posner (concurring) wrote, as it were, to his dissenting brother Easterbrook:

JUDGE RICHARD POSNER: If the only expression that the First Amendment protects is the expression of ideas and opinions, then most music and visual art, and much of literature, are unprotected. This would be a shocking contradiction of the First Amendment as it has come to be understood.§

---

*420 U.S. 546 (1975).

†109 S.Ct. 2746, 2753 (1989).

‡Viz.: *Schad* v. *Mount Ephraim,* 452 U.S. 61, 65 (1981); *Doran* v. *Salem Inn,* 422 U.S. 922 (1974); and *FW/PBS d/b/a Paris Adult Bookstore II* v. *City of Dallas,* 110 S.Ct. 596 (1990).

§On June 21, 1991, the Supreme Court upheld 5 to 4 the constitutionality of Indiana's ban on concededly nonobscene barroom-type nude dancing. Chief Justice Rehnquist's plurality opinion (it was joined only by Justices O'Connor and Kennedy) reasoned that the design of the law was not the unconstitutional one of forbidding nude dancing as expression but the constitutional one of forbidding displays of public nudity—an argument that conveniently ignores the facts that the effect (if not the intent) of such a law is to forbid the expression in nude dancing, and that a barroom is not "public" in the way that a street, park, or beach is. Dissenting Justice White (joined by Justices Marshall, Blackmun, and Stevens) said: "The nudity itself is an expressive component of the dance," and "it is only because nude dancing performances may generate emotions and feelings of eroticism and sensuality among the spectators that the state seeks to regulate such expressive activity" (*Barnes* v. *Glen Theatre,* No. 9-26). Accordingly, dancing "should be treated as expressive activity entitled to full First Amendment protection," as were the expressive acts of flag-burning involved in the (Brennan-led) decisions that struck down state and federal anti-flag-desecration laws in 1989 and 1990. The bar owners and dancers claimed that nude dancing should be given constitutional protection because of its "entertainment" and "communication" values, and not because of any "artistic" value it possessed. Although the decision would seem to overrule *sub silentio* precedents going back forty years holding that entertainment is protected expression, the Court's decision does not impeach the even better-established principle that any expression (including dance) that has serious artistic value is fully protected by the First Amendment.

30

Just a
Pro-Choice
Kind of Gal

IN THE SUMMER OF 1989 the photographic art of the late Robert Mapplethorpe received a dose of national notoriety when Christina Orr-Cahall, director of the prestigious Corcoran Gallery of Art in Washington, D.C., canceled a scheduled show of Mapplethorpe photography partly funded by the National Endowment for the Arts. With the show's opening just two weeks away, Orr-Cahall pulled out because, she said, she feared that Congress would object and the NEA would be embarrassed. Thereafter, Senator Jesse Helms of North Carolina not only objected to Mapplethorpe's art but claimed that the time had come for Congress to erect a system of government supervision of NEA-funded arts and artists. For Helms, if not for Orr-Cahall, what was wrong with Mapplethorpe's photography was that the artist was gay and his work was "obscene" in a peculiar way: it disseminated homoerotic images regarding black and white men. That could not be "art."

SENATOR JESSE HELMS: There's a big difference between "The Merchant of Venice" and a photograph of two males of different races on a marble table top. . . . This Mapplethorpe fellow was an acknowledged homosexual. . . . the theme goes throughout his work.

———

Christina Orr-Cahall became director of the venerable 118-year-old Corcoran Gallery of Art and its affiliated art school in October 1987; she was forty years old and was one of a small, growing number of women who headed major American art museums. The Corcoran is the largest nongovernment-related art institution in Washington and, according to Orr-Cahall, one of the few blessed with a board of directors ready to accept the premise that a woman should be able to manage a large and venerable organization such as the Corcoran. She had the bad luck, nevertheless, to be at the Corcoran when Jesse Helms learned that Robert Mapplethorpe's 150-work retrospective, "The Perfect Moment," was to be shown. The original catalogue for the Mapplethorpe exhibition had been funded by a grant from the National Endowment for the Arts, an agency of the federal government. The show at the Corcoran had been arranged for by the gallery's chief curator, Jane Livingston, before Orr-Cahall's arrival.

INGRID SISCHY:* "The Perfect Moment" . . . offers a sensible cross-section of Mapplethorpe's work. The images that are said to have caused the blowup in Washington belong to three portfolios of prints titled "X," "Y," and "Z." As the exhibition travels, the portfolios (which also include flowers, portraits, and texts) are always installed in a Mapplethorpe-designed slanting cabinet at counter height. They are avoidable; by just looking at what's on the walls, one could go through the show without seeing them. But to miss this tougher aspect of his work is to miss what gives Robert Mapplethorpe his place in photographic history.

—

Senator Helms showed his wife, Dorothy, the Mapplethorpe exhibition catalogue. Helms told reporters what happened.

DOROTHY HELMS: Lord have mercy, Jesse, I'm not believing this.

JESSE HELMS: [My favorite painting] shows an old man, sitting at the table, with the Bible open in front of him, with his hands (folded in prayer) like this! And it is the most inspiring thing to me. . . . We have ten or twelve pictures of art, all of which I like. But we don't have any penises stretched out on the table. . . .†
I'm embarrassed to even talk to you about this. I'm embarrassed to talk to my wife. . . . They say I don't know anything about art and I confess that all I know about art is that I know what I like. . . .
Underlying everything that I've done and everything I've said is, this nation is on the slippery slope in terms of morals and decency. And it's way past the time that we back up and say to ourselves, "We become a part of what we condone. . . ." Mapplethorpe was a talented photographer. But clearly he was promoting homosexuality. He was a homosexual, acknowledged to be. He died of AIDS. And I'm sorry about that. But the fact remains that he was using this, using his talent, to promote homosexuality.

—

Mapplethorpe was widely regarded as one of the major photographers of the past two decades. Works of his were in the permanent collections of the National Gallery of Art and the National Museum of American Art, both federal institutions, and in the Art Institute of Chicago's highly

---

*Editor in chief, *Interview* magazine.
†An allusion to "Mark Stevens (Mr. 10½)," 1976, reproduced in Robert Mapplethorpe, *The Perfect Moment* (1988).

selective historical-photography exhibition, "On the Art of Fixing a Shadow." He had two major shows, in 1988 and 1989; the first, titled "Robert Mapplethorpe," was a 110-work retrospective at New York's prestigious Whitney Museum of American Art.

The second, a larger show, was the one that Jesse Helms heard was coming to town in June 1989; it had been organized by Janet Kardon of the Institute of Contemporary Art (ICA) in Philadelphia, where it had been well received the previous December. It had also been well received in Chicago, Hartford, and Berkeley, and was scheduled to travel to Washington, Cincinnati, and Boston later in 1989 and in 1990.

His work came to public attention during the late seventies because of its sensational subject matter, black-white male homosexual sadomasochism and autoeroticism. But he also created beautiful photographic portraits of cultural celebrities and of flowers.

ANDY GRUNDBERG: Robert Mapplethorpe is perhaps the most topical artist of the moment. Less than 20 years since he first decided to make art with a camera, his elegant but often provocative photographs are being heralded as exemplars of the new stylish sensibility. . . .

Like scores of photographers before him—Lewis Hine, Brassaï, Weegee—Mr. Mapplethorpe chose to depict a subculture seldom photographed before, or at least seldom in the context of fine-art photography. . . . While his compulsive, unabashed and carefully staged chronicle of this particular strident variety of homoeroticism may not be everyone's cup of tea, it has proven irresistibly fascinating to much of the art world.

INGRID SISCHY: Mapplethorpe's flowers can have a riveting beauty that derives from a sense of their short life. Some are at such a peak that you want to smell them. A lot of painters and photographers have worked with flowers, and often these pictures are said to be sexual. Mapplethorpe's flowers can certainly be erotic, as Georgia O'Keeffe's can, but that's due to the nature of the flowers. Mapplethorpe certainly didn't need to use flowers as vehicles of sexual allusion, because he worked with sex directly. Besides, when his flower photographs are at their best it is because he saw some quality—prickliness, say, or purity—that he had to catch before it passed. Mapplethorpe also treated flowers cursorily or used them as a prop. In those instances, his flowers are forgettable. His last flowers are not forgettable. It is as though all the life and color that were being drained from him were being sucked into the petals, the stems, and even the backgrounds that he used.

———

The "stars" of Mapplethorpe's social ambience were artists, and in the five years before he died, Mapplethorpe made portraits of almost every fashionable younger figure in New York, from Francesco Clemente to Cindy Sherman, along with, from an earlier generation, Marisol, Warhol, and Louise Bourgeois, who is shown "bearing under her arm, as if to please her portraitist, an enormous phallus of her own fabrication." Possibly the most moving of Mapplethorpe's portraits of artists is the one of Alice Neel, "serene in her exhaustion and age," in a picture taken only days before her death.

ROBERT MAPPLETHORPE: Alice Neel was incredible. It was right before she was dying, and Robert Miller called me and told me you've really got to go up there, she really wants this picture. And she was the sweetest old thing. She had the reputation for being hard as nails, but right before she died she somehow went to heaven, she was just this angelic creature. She closed her eyes through half the shooting. She knew she was . . . giving me her death mask.

—

Jesse Helms did not escape criticism for his attacks on Mapplethorpe's homoerotic art, and on the National Endowment for the Arts for enabling large numbers of Americans to view it. After he was criticized by the Raleigh, N.C., *News and Observer,* Helms challenged the paper's editor to publish—to make "available to people who are genuinely interested to see what I am talking about"—just three of the Mapplethorpe photographs that were in the NEA-funded "The Perfect Moment." The three selected by Helms featured exposed genitals but, he said, were "by no means the worst." The editor declined.

—

Robert Mapplethorpe was born into a middle-class Catholic family in Floral Park, New York. He went to art school at Pratt Institute in Brooklyn, where he "did collages" and "was also making photographic objects with material from pornographic magazines."

ROBERT MAPPLETHORPE: At some point, I picked up a camera and started taking erotic pictures—so that I would have the right raw materials and it would be more mine, instead of using other people's pictures. That was why I went into photography. It wasn't to take a pure photographic image, it was just to be able to work with more images.

INGRID SISCHY: There's irony in Mapplethorpe becoming such a political cause célèbre. He may have been political in terms of whom to talk to at a dinner party, but he didn't give a hoot about real politics. . . . The reason he is controversial now is that he touched on all those territorial questions about the body which are once again such a vivid part of American politics.

ROBERT MAPPLETHORPE: Have you ever seen the X, Y, and Z portfolios? X portfolio is thirteen sex pictures, Y is flowers, and Z is blacks. The earliest of the S & M pictures are in the X portfolio. They're small, they're 8 × 10s mounted to cards, and they come in a box. . . .

I know somebody in New Orleans who photographs black men, too, but nobody's done it the way I do it. . . . I was attracted visually. That's the only reason I photographed them. But once I started, I realized there's a whole gap of visual things. There have been great photographs of naked black men in the history of photography, but they are very rare. Some of my favorite pictures happen to be the pictures of black men. . . .

I think I was subconsciously influenced by Warhol. I couldn't have not been—because I think he's *the* most important pop artist—but I'm not sure how. . . . Warhol says that "anything can be art," and then I can make pornography art.

HELLE BERING-JENSEN: Though Mapplethorpe's work in his later years had moved away from the violently homoerotic to include portraits, some of them radiantly ethereal, still lifes and flower studies, it has always been the presence of the works from his so-called X portfolio that have attracted attention at his shows. Art critics have hailed Mapplethorpe's honesty and courage in portraying the outer reaches of sexual experience—sadomasochism, male bondage, leather fetishism and sodomy.

SUSAN WEILEY: There is a long tradition of the erotic in both the literary and the visual arts. The nude has been the cornerstone of Western art, and attitudes toward the artifice of nakedness have varied throughout the centuries. . . . Today we feel great art should never be overtly sexual. The sexually provocative is relegated to pornographic magazines. . . . In fact, although Mapplethorpe studied art for seven years, it was just those magazines that provided his initial inspiration. He has often described discovering 42nd Street at age 16, gazing through porno-shop windows at magazines wrapped in cellophane.

ROBERT MAPPLETHORPE: The feeling I got was a strong stomach reaction, and I thought it would be extraordinary to get that gut feeling from a work of art. I'm not talking about arousal. The feeling was stronger and much more interesting than that. . . . But that had already been done. So it had to be different. Those magazines are like raw material. I've always found it irritating to hear people say erotic when they mean sexual material. I'm not afraid of words. Pornography is fine with me. If it's good it transcends what it is.

SUSAN WEILEY: Mapplethorpe's sexual photographs raise many issues. When [they were] first exhibited, in the late 1970's, even sophisticated viewers found their terrible beauty disturbing, particularly those detailing sadomasochism. Moreover, he installs his exhibitions so that the sexual images are interspersed with other subjects. We view a sadistic tableau side by side with a celebrity portrait or a lyrical still life of baby's breath. The distinctions between corruption and innocence are blurred. He insists that it is all the same.

ROBERT MAPPLETHORPE: My intent was to open people's eyes, to realize anything can be acceptable. It's not what it is, it's the way that it's photographed.

SUSAN WEILEY: The sexual photographs also disturb us in light of our shift in attitude during this decade. These exotic images bloomed in a hothouse atmosphere now grown chill with fear and death. Today it is difficult to view them without considering their celebration of sensuality as, in retrospect, indictments of our innocence. We are all implicated. They provoke a shudder similar to the one we feel looking at smiling faces in photographs of the Warsaw ghetto. Mapplethorpe . . . stopped making the pornographic photographs—because of the AIDS epidemic, because he found them exhausting to do and his own health [was] fragile, but also because he [felt he had] already explored that subject thoroughly.

WILLIAM F. BUCKLEY, JR.: If a democratic society cannot find a way to protect a taxpaying Christian heterosexual from finding that he is engaged in subsidizing blasphemous acts of homoeroticism, then democracy isn't working.

SENATOR STROM THURMOND: The federal government has the power to control that which it subsidizes and experience shows that when the federal government has that power, that power is eventually exercised.

SENATOR ALPHONSE D'AMATO: This matter does not involve freedom of expression; it does involve the question whether American taxpayers should be forced to support such trash.

———

In his *Washington Times* column, during September 1989, President Nixon's former press secretary Patrick Buchanan called for "a cultural revolution in the '90s" as sweeping as the "political revolution of the '80s" that had been engineered by Ronald Reagan; the new "revolution" was meant to overthrow the dominance of the arts by secular humanists.

PATRICK BUCHANAN: The [eighties] decade has seen an explosion of anti-American, anti-Christian, and nihilist "art." . . . [Many museums] now feature exhibits that can best be described as cultural trash. . . . [A]s in public television and public radio, a tiny clique, out of touch with America's traditional values, had wormed its way into control of the arts bureaucracy.

———

This was an oblique attack on the National Endowment for the Arts. Combining the language of environmental "pollution" strategy that Chief Justice Warren E. Burger used in 1973 to deplore the leading obscenity case decisions of the Warren Court* with metaphors about a "poisoned land" and "poisoned fruits" favored by fundamentalists, Buchanan warned his readers of the consequences of government support of decadent art.

PATRICK BUCHANAN: As with our rivers and lakes, we need to clean up our culture: for it is a well from which we must all drink. Just as a poisoned land will yield up poisoned fruits, so a polluted culture, left to fester and stink, can destroy a nation's soul. . . . We should not subsidize decadence.

———

*More recently, *U.S. News & World Report* columnist John Leo warned his readers about the "pollution" that pop-music artists like Madonna, Prince, and 2 Live Crew were causing: "The popular culture is worth paying attention to. It is the air we breathe, and 2 Live Crew is a pesky new pollutant." Lee did not recommend government censorship, however, but suggested "complaining" and "boycotting" as the best means of getting "the 2 Live Crew Pollutants out of our air" (July 2, 1990).

Senator Jesse Helms's proposal to establish government supervision of American artists and arts institutions who were supported by National Endowment for the Arts grants was introduced as a Senate bill in July 1989, about a month after Buchanan's pollution alert and the Corcoran Gallery of Art's announcement that it had canceled its scheduled opening of "The Perfect Moment." Christina Orr-Cahall attributed the cancellation to the Corcoran's wish to stand clear of politics.

CHRISTINA ORR-CAHALL: We really felt this exhibit was at the wrong place at the wrong time. We had the strong potential to become some person's political platform.

Only the week before, however, the Corcoran's director had reaffirmed the gallery's commitment to open the show on schedule. In announcing the cancellation, Orr-Cahall suggested she had done that in order to relieve the NEA of the congressional criticism that had developed over government support of blasphemous and pornographic art.

CHRISTINA ORR-CAHALL: We've been fighting since April against the initiatives that we saw were coming in Congress against the N.E.A. and the punitive measures against institutions that had organized controversial shows. . . . We thought perhaps not doing the Mapplethorpe show would allow members of Congress and supporters of the arts to deal with this more quietly; have more room to maneuver and avoid all this controversy.

DAVID LLOYD KREEGER:* If proceeding with this exhibition hurts NEA appropriations, it is detrimental to the Corcoran and to every other art institution.

VINCE PASSARO:† The Corcoran's savvy board, which had hauled in $1.6 million in NEA moola (plus $7 million in matching grants) for their gallery over the past several seasons, and which was taking part in the mania for museum expansion by preparing to launch a fund-raising drive to increase their endowment sixfold, had been "monitoring" the rumblings in Congress about the NEA with the sweat-stained anxiety of air-traffic controllers on a heavy day at O'Hare. They showed their keen appreciation for the hermetic politics of their town and did what until then, for a major museum, had been unthinkable: They canceled an exhibition on the eve of its unveiling for fear someone might not like it.

Other members of the art world viewed Orr-Cahall's behavior in a similar light. New York art dealer Harry Lunn considered it plain "censorship." New York artist Andres Serrano—himself a target of Religious Right and conservative congressional ire—saw it as a betrayal.

---

*Chairman of the board of the Corcoran Gallery of Art.
†Writer.

ANDRES SERRANO: It's pretty bad when a museum is censored, and it's even worse when it censors itself.

JOSHUA SMITH: The Corcoran's decision [was] also bad for artists, who rely on museum exhibitions to develop their careers and to perpetuate their work and reputations. The message the cancelation sends artists is that they must conform to "acceptable" norms as dictated by outside interest groups in order to have museum shows.

———

Orr-Cahall thought that canceling the Mapplethorpe show not only was in the artist's interest but was the opposite of "censorship."

CHRISTINA ORR-CAHALL: The Corcoran's withdrawal from the exhibition's tour is not a comment on the quality of the artist's work. Neither is it an abrogation of the artist's right of free expression, nor is it a questioning of the Endowment's award system. . . .

We decided to err on the side of the artist, who had the right to have his work presented in a non-sensationalized, non-political environment, and who deserves not to be the hostage for larger issues of relevance to us all. If you think about this for a long time, as we did, this is not censorship; in fact this is the full artistic freedom which we all support.

———

After hearing rumors of trouble brewing on Capitol Hill for the Corcoran and the NEA, Orr-Cahall had sent three scouts to the host art institute in Philadelphia, the ICA, to obtain photocopies of Mapplethorpe's pictures. On the basis of these copies—which she showed to the Corcoran's board of directors at a thinly attended meeting whose agenda had not mentioned Mapplethorpe—the board approved Orr-Cahall's decision.

INGRID SISCHY: How could the Corcoran's director have allowed her museum to respond to political rather than cultural imperatives? How could she have allowed an artist's work to be rejected on the basis of photocopies, when so much of this photography's message depends on the feeling and scale of the actual prints?

———

The political imperatives that replaced the cultural imperatives in Orr-Cahall's mind had first emerged in April, four months after an exhibition of photographs mounted by a Winston-Salem, North Carolina, art gallery, the Southeastern Center for Contemporary Art (SCCA), had ended. A grantee of the NEA located in Senator Helms's home state, the SCCA was scheduled to send this show to ten other cities. At that time the powerful right-wing religious group called the American Family Association, founded by Donald Wildmon, sent out a newsletter to its estimated 380,000 followers, and to 178,000 affiliated churches, urging all and sundry to send it money and to write their representatives in Congress to clamp down on the federal officials in Washington who were spending government money on blasphemous works of so-called art. Wildmon's principal gripe was not Mapplethorpe but another New York artist, Andres Serrano, whose photographic artwork "Piss Christ" had found a place in the SCCA's traveling exhibition, with NEA support.*

One of the first congressmen to respond to Wildmon's outcry was Senator Alphonse D'Amato, Republican, of New York. On May 18, speaking on the Senate floor, he vilified the NEA's action in supporting Serrano's work, which he described as "garbage" and "a deplorable despicable display of vulgarity." The attack was picked up by Helms, who characterized Serrano as "not an artist" but "a jerk," and instructed an aide, John Mashburn, to try to enlist the collaboration of the SCCA's head, Ted Potter, in putting the blame for including Serrano in the SCCA exhibition on the NEA. Potter thought that Helms had bigger fish than the SCCA to fry, suspecting that his underlying plan "was to abolish the National Endowment for the Arts."

TED POTTER: This thing is so complex and so bizarre, I'm not sure the people who have raised this as an issue have even seen this photograph. It's a pawn in the ultraconservative confrontation with the NEA, just as the Mapplethorpe show is. . . . It has been taken out of an intellectual environment of a museum installation of protest art. It's been vilified and emotionalized as an anti-Christian piece of bigotry. But it took a lot of courage to make such a powerful and uncomfortable statement.

—

Andres Serrano's "Piss Christ" has been interpreted as a protest by the artist against the contemporary exploitation of religious values. His "statement" about Christ, the symbol of the crucifixion, and the Christian religion inspired powerful fundamentalist leaders to seek the aid of politicians and the force of law to suppress both commentary and commentator. Allen Wildmon is the brother of Donald Wildmon and a spokesman for the American Family Association.

ALLEN WILDMON: The whole bottom line here is, whose set of values is going to dominate in society? This is just one spoke in the wheel so far as the overall picture—you've got rock music, you've got abortion. Somebody's values are going to dominate. Is it going to be a humanistic set of values, or a Biblical set of values?

—

The highest law in the land is not the Bible but the Constitution, and the Constitution—particularly in its Bill of Rights guaranteeing fundamental liberties that include the freedoms of speech and press and due process

---

*An NEA grant to the SCCA of $75,000 represented about one fourth of the funds needed for the show; other donors were the Rockefeller Foundation and Equitable Life Insurance. Each of ten contributing artists received an award of $15,000. There is a good account of the origins of the Serrano and Mapplethorpe imbroglio in *Vanity Fair,* September 1990 ("Mean for Jesus"), and a cover article on Wildmon in *The New York Times Magazine,* September 2, 1990.

of law—embodies humanistic values, not right-wing fundamentalist religious values.

During the row in Congress over his work, Andres Serrano spoke about it to a reporter for *The New York Times,* on condition that he not be photographed and that his Soho address not be published; Serrano had already received "at least seven" written threats.

ANDRES SERRANO: First and foremost ["Piss Christ"] reflects my Catholic upbringing, and my ambivalence to that upbringing, being drawn to Christ yet resisting organized religion. . . . When I first showed that picture at the Stux Gallery [in Soho], a reverend's wife came up to me and said, "My husband and I don't agree about anything when it comes to religion, but we were both very moved by your picture." I liked that.

WILLIAM H. HONAN:* The Serrano photograph measures 60 inches by 40 inches and shows Jesus on the cross in a golden haze through a smattering of minute bubbles against a dark, blood-colored background. By slight twisting and considerable enlargement, the image takes on a monumental appearance and the viewer would never guess that a small plastic crucifix was used. The work appears reverential, and it is only after reading the provocative and explicit label that one realizes the object has been immersed in urine.

ANDRES SERRANO: If there's been a running theme throughout my work, it's this duality or contradiction between abstraction and representation, between transforming that little cross into this monumental and mysterious-looking object and then making you reconsider it in another context when you read the label. . . . I've always had trouble seeing things in black and white. . . . I have an African-Cuban mother and a Spanish white father. My great-grandfather was Chinese.

———

Serrano's decision to use his urine as an artistic medium followed his working with other bodily fluids: blood and milk. In 1984 he began using blood in his work when he photographed a cow's head drenched in blood (which he bought from a butcher on Thirty-eighth Street). After that he splashed cattle blood into milk, for a work called "Blood Stream."

ANDRES SERRANO: These are life's bodily fluids. They have both a visual impact and are symbolically charged with meaning. . . . By 1987, I had red and white and . . . I needed another color to add to my palette. In keeping with bodily fluids I turned to urine. It gave me quite a vivid and vibrant color.

MICHAEL BRENSON:† One of the few unintended benefits of the Congressional outrage against Andres Serrano is that it has brought widespread

---

*Culture editor, *The New York Times.*
†Art critic, *The New York Times.*

attention to a good artist. His photographs are indeed provocative. They are also serious art. There are 14 of them at the Stux Gallery [in Soho], including the reviled and dreaded one from 1987, with its 13-inch plastic-and-wood crucifix upright in a Plexiglas tank filled with the artist's urine. This religious emblem enveloped in a dreamy golden haze (without the title, there would be little or no way of knowing what the liquid is) suggests the arty images and the mass production of religious souvenirs that have been partly responsible for the trivialization and exploitation of both religion and art.

———

In an essay in the SCCA's show catalogue, Donald Kuspit, a professor of art history and philosophy at the State University of New York at Stony Brook, said that works like "Piss Christ" were attacks upon "American superficiality, which denies the 'life blood' of things." But evangelist Pat Robertson declared over the Christian Broadcast Network that the Serrano work "slaps in the face the values that Americans hold dear," and Senator D'Amato dramatized his verbal attack on "Piss Christ" on the Senate floor by tearing up his copy of the show's catalogue. D'Amato commented: "Shocking, abhorrent and completely undeserving of any recognition whatsoever."

Serrano, who had wanted to be an artist for as long as he can remember, says he lacked the physical dexterity to go far as a painter or sculptor, "so I decided to use the camera." By 1984 he was realizing enough money through occasional sales and grants to devote himself full time to his art; but unlike Robert Mapplethorpe, he has never done commercial work and until "Piss Christ" was not known outside a relatively small circle of avant-garde artists.

Serrano received grants from private and public sources, including the New York Foundation for the Arts, Art Matters, Inc., and the NEA, and his work has been exhibited in group shows at many institutions, including the Whitney Museum in New York. He uses terms like "duality" and "contradiction" in describing his work, which he says has been influenced by the films of Luís Buñuel and the paintings of Picasso, Mondrian, Duchamp, and Goya. But he also has a streetwise rap.

ANDRES SERRANO: You know, man, I made the picture in my own time on my own dime.

———

In the Congress of the United States in 1989, and then again in 1990, however, the issue became whether taxpayers should be required to support artists who flout tenets of orthodox morality and religion. The position taken by Republican senators Helms, D'Amato, Slade Gorton, and Richard Armey of Texas came down to this: If the NEA could not go about its business of helping to "create and sustain . . . the material conditions facilitating the release of . . . creative talent" (a statutorily designated main purpose of the NEA at the time of the Mapplethorpe events) without sponsoring blasphemous and obscene art and artists, it ought to go out of business. In New York, when the uproar had subsided somewhat, Serrano feared not only that he would not receive further support from the NEA but that it might now be more difficult for him to obtain recognition and support from the private sector because some arts organizations could be expected to keep their distance from his work, in fear of retaliation by Congress or defunding by the NEA.

GARRY WILLS: The idea that what the Government does not support it represses is nonsensical. . . . What pussycats our supposedly radical artists are. They not only want the government's permission to create their artifacts, they want federal authorities to supply the materials as well. Otherwise they feel "gagged." . . . They want to remain avant-garde while being bankrolled by the Old Guard.

———

After the Corcoran dropped the Mapplethorpe show, a less prestigious but gutsier gallery called the Washington Project for the Arts—whose chairman was James Fitzpatrick, a respected First Amendment arts lawyer with the liberal Washington law firm of Arnold and Porter—defiantly picked it up and exhibited it to packed houses. Some nine hundred members of the Washington arts community and gay and lesbian groups mobilized several protests against the Corcoran's action. On the evening of June 30, 1989, spectacular images of some Mapplethorpe works from the canceled exhibition were projected from a truck onto the Corcoran's outer walls. Among these were "American Flag, 1977" and "Honey, 1976."* "Honey" was the photograph that had especially distressed Mrs. Jesse Helms; it was one of two works in the exhibition that some people said were "child pornography."

ANDREW FERGUSON: Mapplethorpe's leitmotif embraced photos of "children in erotic poses," a form of personal expression more commonly known, when not federally funded, as child pornography.

———

Before a year was up, "Honey" and another Mapplethorpe photograph, "Jessie McBride," would become the basis for two of seven criminal charges brought against art curator Dennis Barrie and his Center for Contemporary Arts in Cincinnati.

INGRID SISCHY: I spoke to one of the subjects who had been cited as a victim of Mapplethorpe's abuse—Jessie McBride. His mother and Mapplethorpe were close friends. In Mapplethorpe's photograph, McBride is naked and he has leaped onto the back of a chair.

JESSIE McBRIDE: I must have been four or five then.† I remember jumping around and laughing. I'm not as free minded now. In those days, I'd just

———

*Reproduced in *The Perfect Moment* (1988), 61, 49.
†He is nineteen now, 1991. He "remembers being pleased" when his picture was selected for "The Perfect Moment" (C. Carr, "War on Art," *The Village Voice,* June 5, 1990).

take off my clothes and start jumping on the chair. It was fun—Robert snapping away, and my mom laughing. When I got older, up to when I was twelve, I was embarrassed by the picture. I turned it toward the wall when my friends came over. I didn't want them to see my private parts. I didn't mind the adults seeing me naked, but when you're that age you're easily embarrassed by friends. Now when I look at the photograph I think it's a really beautiful picture. I think back to when I was so young and innocent. I look particularly angelic.

———

On Wednesday, July 26, in the evening, when the Senate floor was predictably deserted except for a handful of lawmakers not off on vacation, Senator Jesse Helms tacked onto a $10.9 billion Interior Department appropriation bill an amendment intended to keep the NEA from making grants for "obscene and indecent" art, or for any works that "denigrate the objects or beliefs of the adherents of a particular religion or nonreligion, or material which denigrates, debases or reviles a person, group or class of citizens on the basis of race, creed, sex, handicap, age or national origin." In a voice vote, the bulldozed Senate approved the Helms proposal, which was so wide-ranging and vague in its terminology that all works of art offensive to the sexual proclivities, moral beliefs, political dogma, or religious feelings of any person or group having a legislator's ear would be subject to the ban.

Helms said he saw "blue skies" for his almost certainly unconstitutional amendment; but the Bush White House was silent on the issue, busying itself instead with the recruitment of a new chairman for the NEA, one who might satisfy not only a truculent Senate but a surprisingly militant artistic constituency;* and Helms knew he had a formidable opponent on the House side in Democrat Sidney Yates of Illinois. Helms's bill was to go to a House-Senate conference committee which would try to reconcile the differences between it and a House bill.

Unlike the Helms bill, the one passed by the House merely voted a budgetary slap on the wrist to the NEA, slashing $45,000 from its annual $171 million budget—a cut equivalent to the amount granted by the agency to the arts organizations that had sponsored the exhibitions containing the "offensive" Serrano and Mapplethorpe works. The Senate bill was more vindictive and censorious, completely barring any federal grant over the next five years to the two grantees—the Institute of Contemporary Art in Philadelphia and the Southeastern Center for Contemporary Art in Winston-Salem. It also would have sliced $400,000 from the Endowment's visual arts programs, and added $100,000 to the Endowment's $171 million budget for folk art—nondangerous and favored by Helms. Informed constitutional lawyers foresaw that the key provisions of the Senate bill were

———

*President Bush seems to have been opposed to the establishment of any censorship of the arts through the NEA but proved indisposed to fight Congress, or right-wing political and religious leaders, to keep the arts free of government regulation.

potential candidates for Supreme Court invalidation: for violating the constitutional guarantees of freedom of speech and press and for amounting to an unconstitutional bill of attainder, or legislative indictment, against the ICA and the SCCA.

During the summer, twenty-two of the eighty-eight House Democrats who voted against the $45,000 cut in the NEA's budget were targeted by the National Republican Congressional Committee. The NRCC sent press releases to the news media in the home districts of those twenty-two, whom the committee considered most vulnerable politically, bearing headlines reporting these men had cast VOTES IN FAVOR OF FEDERALLY SUBSIDIZED OBSCENITY.

JOHN BUCKLEY: I know that we scored because of the yelps of rage and because over the next four days we got 150 calls from news organizations in the members' home districts.

———

Democratic senator Daniel Patrick Moynihan of New York was not cowed. He announced in the Senate that he would vote against the entire appropriations measure because it singled out two arts groups for a cutoff of funds.

SENATOR DANIEL PATRICK MOYNIHAN: Do we really want it to be recorded that the Senate of the United States is so insensible to the traditions of liberty in our land, so fearful of what is different and new and intentionally disturbing, so anxious to record our timidity that we would sanction institutions for acting precisely as they are meant to act? Which is to say, art institutions supporting artists and exhibiting their work.

———

For his part Jesse Helms tried to make sure the House-Senate committee conferees would realize what was at stake by sending each of them copies of what he saw as especially offensive Mapplethorpe works.

SENATOR JESSE HELMS: I suggest you take a look at the enclosed materials. It's your call as to whether the taxpayer's money should be used to fund this sort of thing.

———

In a press interview Helms announced that if the Senate conferees dropped his amendment he would "request a roll-call vote so that whoever voted against it would be on record as favoring taxpayer funding for pornography." Helms basked in the resulting publicity and put the controversy he provoked to use in raising money for his 1990 reelection campaign. A mass-mail letter dated August 18 from his finance chairman urged donors to rush $29 to Helms to help him "stop the liberals from spending taxpayers' money on perverted, deviant art."

In the *Times*, Anthony Lewis deplored the 1989 "Summer of the Booboisie" and wished that H. L. Mencken were back.

ANTHONY LEWIS: Through the 1920s and '30s H. L. Mencken savaged the follies of American life. His special targets were the narrow minds, the intolerant certainties, of what he called "the booboisie." He revelled scornfully in the trial of John Scopes for teaching evolution, describing the onlookers who believed that God literally created the world in six days as "gaping primates."

Mencken is out of fashion now. His style of verbal assault seems slightly embarrassing in today's journalism, which is so self-consciously (some would say self-importantly) concerned with "balance." Besides, we thought the country had outgrown the primitivism that Mencken deplored.

This summer's Congressional follies over the National Endowment for the Arts have shown how wrong we were: wrong in estimating the primitive strain in our society, wrong in regarding Mencken as an anachronism. We need him more than ever. . . .

Senator Helms and other critics of the National Endowment say the issue is whether public money should be spent on art that . . . would offend most of the American public. But that is not the issue. The issue is whether politicians are going to make artistic judgments. . . .

Culture makes politicians nervous. But somehow the Germans, the French and others manage to understand that national greatness is a thing of the spirit, not just of weapons. What a people gain by supporting the arts, as non-politically as possible, is civilization.

—

When the House-Senate conference committee met, on September 27, 1989, Representative Sidney Yates argued that the Helms amendment should be rejected and the compromise bill should contain language that would "be the same as used by the Supreme Court in defining obscenity." He was referring to the Brennan doctrine as glossed by Chief Justice Burger in *Miller* v. *California*. Under Yates's legislative proposal it would become in the first instance the business of the NEA artist peer-review panels, next the duty of the NEA Advisory Council, and finally the job of the NEA chairperson "administratively" to screen out from funding eligibility arts projects that might be obscene under the Supreme Court's *Miller* definition. Although any decision by the NEA to deny funds to an artist or arts project that appeared to it obscene would presumably be reviewable in federal court, such NEA administrative actions would, I believe, be tantamount to censorship.

Intense bargaining took place among leaders of the committee; from this a compromise bill emerged, and an explanatory report was agreed upon which rejected the Helms amendment and incorporated Yates's proposals. This included one that there be established "a legislative commission to review the procedures of the N.E.A. and to keep in mind standards of obscenity accepted by the Supreme Court." At that time, Jesse Helms, who was not a member of the committee, threatened once again to require a roll-call vote when the matter was returned to the Senate floor, "so that whoever votes against [my amendment] would be on record as favoring taxpayer funding for pornography."

At the session of September 28, the day when the conference committee reached a tentative agreement to reject Helms's amendment, the senator from North Carolina angrily protested on the Senate floor and waved copies of several Mapplethorpe pictures in the air. He called them "garbage" and referred to the man who had created them as "a known homosexual who died of AIDS." He urged all women and children to leave the chamber so he could show everyone else what was at issue.

SENATOR JESSE HELMS: Look at the pictures! Look at the pictures! Don't believe *The Washington Post*! Don't believe *The New York Times*! Don't believe any of these other editors who have been so careless with the truth. . . . I'm going to ask that all the pages, all the ladies, and maybe all the staff leave the Chamber so that senators can see exactly what they're voting on.

—

Helms had been awakened to the fact that a grant from the NEA in support of a work of art or art project would carry with it a kind of legal immunity from attack for being obscene: the NEA's imprimatur would bestow the designation of "art" upon whatever work was supported; once identifiable as art, expression could not be found obscene, for it had the "value" that bestows constitutional protection upon expression under prevailing obscenity law, which is to say under *Miller* v. *California*. To Helms, a grant from the NEA now looked like a government license to create obscene works and have them circulated at government (i.e., "the taxpayers' ") expense. Soon he would base his final effort to defeat Yates's proposal on this argument.

HELEN DEWAR: Three times in less than 24 hours, the Senate yesterday said no to "Senator No," an exasperated Sen. Jesse Helms . . . as he tried to end federal funding for "obscene" and "indecent art" and then attempted to scuttle proposed reparations for Japanese Americans interned during World War II.

—

The House-Senate conference committee wound up its work by adopting the Yates proposal; allocating $250,000 for the "legislative commission" on standards; requiring the NEA to notify Congress if it expected during the coming year to make any award to the "blackballed" Philadelphia and Winston-Salem art museums that had organized the Mapplethorpe and Serrano shows; retaining the House cut of $45,000 in the NEA's budget; and restoring the $400,000 that the Senate had shifted from the NEA's visual arts program to other programs within the NEA.

On October 7, 1989, the Senate took up the conference committee's report. The same day Helms made an unsuccessful last-ditch stand to substitute his amendment for that agreed upon by the conferees. His new argument must have surprised some other legislators: the Yates-sponsored language that had been adopted, Helms charged, was a subterfuge that "creates a loophole that will clearly allow the National Endowment for the Arts to fund the Mapplethorpe photographs again."

SENATOR JESSE HELMS: [I]f Senators do not believe me that the conference language is worthless as a check on the NEA, perhaps they will believe Congressman Yates. Perhaps they will believe sources in the National Endowment for the Arts and a prominent arts lawyer with a Los Angeles firm.* I call Senators' attention to an article from the *Los Angeles Times* written by the *Times* art correspondent, Alan Parachini, which I have asked the pages to place on the desk of each Senator.

That article states absolutely correctly that in an exchange with Congressman Rohrabacher over in the House of Representatives, Congressman Yates said that: "Funding of obscene art was not effectively prohibited by the conference report." Mr. Parachini also reported that James Fitzpatrick, a prominent arts lawyer with the prestigious firm of Arnold & Porter, who submitted a legal brief to the conferences on the bill on behalf of the American Arts Alliance, concluded from his reading of the conference report that the wording of the conference report "fails completely to achieve any degree of subject matter control."

Is this where the U.S. Senate wants to leave this question, which is very much on the minds of the American people? Do we want to say, "Well, we went through some motions here and reported out some gobbledygook but it is behind us now"? . . . In any case, the *Los Angeles Times* quoted unidentified sources within the National Endowment for the Arts itself that "the wording appears to be so vague that virtually no artistic subject matter would be taboo."

So here we go. Any yoyo out there across America's land can get himself a glass jar and fill it with his own urine, stick a crucifix in it, take a picture of it and get a $15,000 award subsidized with the taxpayers' money. That is exactly what Mr. Andres Serrano did.

I do not know about other Senators, but I find this state of affairs somewhat ironic in that my original amendment was unfairly and incorrectly criticized as prohibiting everything from the Bible to Shakespeare. And now Congressman Yates comes along and compromises the amendment passed by the Senate of the United States. And what does his compromise prohibit? Absolutely nothing. Nothing. It creates a loophole so wide you can drive 12 Mack trucks through it abreast. . . .

Mr. President, note what section (A) of the conference report says in setting forth a test for obscenity in NEA funding decisions. It would be laughable. If it were not so serious. It says: "None of the funds authorized to be appropriated for the National Endowment for the Arts or the Na-

---

*Helms seemed to have in mind not a Los Angeles lawyer but Washington arts lawyer James Fitzpatrick of Abe Fortas's former law firm, Arnold and Porter.

tional Endowment for the Humanities may be used to promote, disseminate, or produce materials which in the judgment of the National Endowment for the Arts or the National Endowment for the Humanities may be
considered obscene, including but not limited to depictions of sadomasochism, homoeroticism, the sexual exploitation of children, or individuals
engaged in sex acts, and—here is where the cookie crumbles, Mr. President—"which, when taken as a whole, do not have serious literary, artistic,
political, or scientific value."

Who makes that judgment? You got it, the NEA, the very crowd that
caused the controversy in the first place. . . .

If we do not close this barn door, Mr. President, all the horses are going
to be galloping over the horizon. . . .

One other thought, and I shall yield the floor. I met at some length with
John Frohnmayer, the new Chairman of the National Endowment for the
Arts.* I say to my friend from the West Coast, he is a delightful man, and
not only did he tell me then, but he called later to reiterate that on his
watch things like Mapplethorpe and Serrano will not happen again. And
I believe that.

———

Within a matter of weeks, the new NEA chairman would be tested by
an activist New York arts community to see whether *he* believed he had
powers of censorship under the new legislation. In the event, Frohnmayer
showed that he was not sure: he behaved erratically and equivocally. And
within the course of a year, when Frohnmayer found himself heavily pressured by conservative politicians and newspapers to demonstrate that he at
least knew *how* to censor, he rejected the applications of four "solo performance artists" known for the feminist, gay, and lesbian aspects of their work
but declined to specify his grounds for doing so.

SENATOR JESSE HELMS: But suppose Mr. Frohnmayer goes down in a plane
or leaves office for some other reason and somebody else replaces him?
Congress ought to spell it out now, that we, the Congress of the United
States, will not further permit the waste, the awesome waste, of taxpayers'
money in such fashion. I support Mr. Frohnmayer. I know he is a man of
integrity, and I know he is a man of his word. I am not worried about him.
But I think we ought to do our duty and be glad that we have a man who
agrees with us.

SENATOR JAMES M. JEFFORDS (VERMONT): I rise in opposition to the Helms
amendment. I also am not really exactly pleased with what is in the bill itself
as passed out of conference. On the other hand, I certainly will accept it
under the circumstances. . . .

———

*On July 6, 1989, President Bush named John E. Frohnmayer to become chairman of the
NEA and fill the vacancy that had existed since February. A forty-seven-year-old lawyer and
past chairman of the Oregon Arts Commission, Frohnmayer had worked for Bush in the
Oregon presidential campaign; both senators from the state, Republicans Mark O. Hatfield
and Bob Packwood, had lobbied the White House for his appointment.

I would have preferred that the [Helms] amendment was removed in conference. There is no question in my mind that the original version would fail a First Amendment test.* It would represent an impermissible attempt by the Government to restrict speech through a Federal funding program.

Instead, the conferees agreed upon a more moderate version of the Helms amendment. They looked to the 1973 U.S. Supreme Court *Miller* standard for a definition of obscenity, and agreed that Federal funding should be denied to artistic work that "when taken as a whole does not have serious literary, artistic, political, or scientific value." Thus, the First Amendment test is probably passed.

However, I want to express once again my strong concern that we in the Congress might be moving dangerously close to setting standards for artistic merit. I hope that we have not created an atmosphere in which artists will fear Government or public reprisal for work that is supported by the Endowments. . . .

I would like to focus on a little bit different aspect of the problem in our mind. . . .

A cornerstone of democracy is the First Amendment. Any action which denigrates this Amendment creates a risk to the success of the democracy. At the same time, adherence to the free speech preamble creates the risk of serious controversy and public fury. And I agree that some of the art we have seen here does excite me to some sense of concern and fury.

SENATOR JESSE HELMS: I wish the distinguished Senator from Vermont [Mr. Jeffords] was still on the floor, because I would like to ask him two or three questions. He raised again the totally ridiculous question of censorship. It is not censorship when the U.S. Government refuses to fund anything it does not want to fund. To suggest that censorship is involved is just not sensible. . . .†

A unanimous Supreme Court in 1983 in *Regan* v. *Taxation with Representation,* 461 U.S. 540, reiterated a long line of cases holding that Congress' decision not to subsidize the exercise of a fundamental right, such as free

---

*The original version would have instructed the NEA not to fund art that "denigrates," "debases," or "reviles" religion or persons because of their "race, creed, handicap, age, or national origin." Such a law would almost certainly have been struck down as unconstitutionally vague, overbroad, and otherwise in violation of protected expression.

†The political and religious Right has been obliged in recent years to call by another, less offensive, name the censorship over communications and the arts it craves. Even Helms does not stand up for "censorship." Carole S. Vance commented on the phenomenon in the thoughtful piece "The War on Culture" in *Art in America,* September 1989: "The second new element in the right's mass mobilization against the NEA and high culture has been its rhetorical disavowal of censorship per se and the cultivation of an artfully crafted distinction between absolute censorship and the denial of public funding. . . . In the battle for public opinion, 'censorship' is a dirty word to mainstream audiences, and hard for conservatives to shake off because their recent battle to control school books, libraries and curricula have earned them reputations as ignorant bookburners. By using this hairsplitting rhetoric, conservatives can now happily disclaim any interest in censorship, and merely suggest that no public funds be used for 'offensive' or 'indecent' materials."

expression, does not infringe upon that right. In other words, it does not amount to censorship.

—

Helms's reading of this case was misleading. A fairer reading was recently supplied by constitutional law scholar Geoffrey Stone, dean of the University of Chicago Law School, in his *Statement Before the Independent Commission on the National Endowment for the Arts,* July 31, 1990:

GEOFFREY STONE: [G]overnment, through its various officials and agencies, must and does speak in its own behalf. But when government crosses the line between legitimate government speech that is essential to fulfilling government's core responsibilities, and more aggressive efforts to use government resources to shape public debate, it enters the realm of unconstitutional conditions. And although this line may be unclear at the margin, there can be no doubt that the use of NEA funds selectively to support only those points of view that are congenial to government is on the unconstitutional conditions side of the line. As the Court has recognized, government may not "discriminate invidiously in its subsidies in such a way as to [aim] at the suppression of dangerous ideas" (citing *Regan* v. *Taxation with Representation*).

SENATOR JESSE HELMS: So, Mr. President, a unanimous Supreme Court says that Congress is free to choose not to fund the NEA at all, or to fund it with absolutely no strings attached. Or, Congress may choose to regulate the NEA anywhere between those two extremes and not violate anybody's rights under the Constitution.

Thus restricting the conditions under which the NEA will spend Americans' tax dollars does not amount to censorship, so says the Supreme Court. . . .

Congressman Yates used the *Miller* language which—as we can see from the NEA's own interpretation of it—would allow the NEA to do exactly as it pleases without regard to the public's sensitivities. Artists will continue to compete with adult bookstores for customers, one of which has been the Federal Government because the evidence is overwhelming that the self-proclaimed "art" experts—whose judgment the NEA defers to—consider works such as Mapplethorpe's obscenity to have "some redeeming artistic and political value."

GEOFFREY STONE: There is no doubt that Congress can constitutionally prohibit the NEA from funding art that is obscene within the meaning of *Miller* v. *California*. Because government may prohibit such material in its entirety, it may decline to fund it. This is not to say, however, that Congress should *explicitly* prohibit the NEA from funding work that is obscene. To the contrary, the mere fact that government has the power to suppress—or refuse to fund—expression does not mean it should exercise that power.

It is important to note that the legislation that currently governs the

NEA already provides that grants may be made only to works that have serious artistic value. Because art can constitute obscenity only if it lacks serious artistic value, the existing legislation already prohibits the NEA from funding obscene art. That some NEA grants may have been used to fund obscenity in the past proves only that standards and administrative schemes are invariably imperfect, not that amendment of the legislation would serve any useful function.

SENATOR WARREN RUDMAN (NEW HAMPSHIRE): The question is whether or not we are going to apply a First Amendment standard to grants that the endowment will give. There is no question, and the [conference] managers have not disagreed, and I was part of the conference, that when the House insisted on language that started to put [in] the value judgment from the *Miller* case, then that obviously made it a First Amendment matter. . . .

The Senator from North Carolina may not want to admit it, but I think he knows it, that he has won his case and it was a good case. He has had his victory. It is inconceivable to anyone who knows those two organizations that they would fund anything like Mapplethorpe or the other artist involved, Serrano, with the language that is in here which specifically says to them, you better watch what you fund if it gets across the bounds of the ordinary, decent judgment of the average American.

As a matter of fact, that is exactly what the [Washington] *Post* said this morning. The Senator from North Carolina did not quote that particular part of it, but he conveniently made it available to us. They say, and they are right: "The endowments and the institutions they fund are more likely to respond to their narrow escape with increased caution, making their choices with a view toward avoiding another firestorm."

Of course, that is right. Of course, after what has gone on here, there is a victory for the Senator from North Carolina.

SENATOR CLAIBORNE PELL (RHODE ISLAND): I rise again to defend the National Endowment for the Arts and its well-tested and proven system of peer review without the interference of the Federal Government. I guess I am the only remaining principal sponsor of the NEA in this body and I well recall how Congress endorsed the freedom of artistic and humanistic expression back in 1965 at the very time we established the National Endowment for the Arts. In doing so, we established the principle that politics should not be allowed to interfere with the NEA in its handling of grants and applications. . . .

The language in the committee's conference report, while not necessary in my view, does send an important signal that the Endowment must not spend the taxpayer's money on obscene art. But the Endowment must be the final arbiter of what it does and does not support—not those of us in the Congress.

SENATOR ROBERT BYRD (WEST VIRGINIA): Mr. President, I believe that . . . if the endowments and the institutions they fund do not take heed, after this shot across the bow, there will be another and greater firestorm, and it may be that, in the final analysis, the Congress will just have to stop its funding to the endowments.

SENATOR JESSE HELMS: Mr. President, it is all well and good to assume that the National Endowment for the Arts has gotten the message. . . . If they have not gotten the message, then they have wax in their ears.

—

On October 7, 1989, the Senate voted 91 to 6 to approve the House-Senate conference report compromise legislation requiring the NEA's chairman to decline to fund any art project that in his judgment was obscene under the *Miller* definition and voted 62 to 35 to table the Helms amendment. Helms put a good face on what his opponents hoped was a defeat for him, claiming the conference committee decision was actually a victory for his side. In any event the legislation authorizing the NEA to continue to operate was due to expire the next session, at which time the congressional and media debates over whether the NEA could constitutionally censor the art and artists it supported, and whether the NEA ought even to be authorized by Congress to operate, would come up anew, with greater intensity. "Firestorms" on the subject would be lit by right-wing religious leaders (Donald Wildmon and Pat Robertson among them) in Congress, and by right-wing newspapers like *The Washington Times*.

In the midst of these debates, in the spring of 1990, Chairman Frohnmayer would feel pressure to abandon his public stance as a defender of artistic freedom and would reach decisions unprecedented in the NEA's twenty-five-year history tantamount to censorship, denying grants to four sexually controversial performance artists who had received unanimous grant recommendations from the NEA's own performance art panel. At virtually the same time, state and federal police and prosecutors in Cincinnati, Miami, and San Francisco—unchecked by the local courts—would unleash the force of obscenity and child pornography laws against a nationally renowned art institution, a popular music group, a record store manager, and a fine-art photographer.

Not long after John E. Frohnmayer took over as chairman of the NEA, he tried, as mentioned earlier, to demonstrate to Congress that he knew what was expected of him. In doing this he understandably exhibited uncertainty concerning his authority under the law and the Constitution, confusion concerning his official role, and a conflict of loyalties with respect to his political and artistic constituencies. The first episode occurred after Susan Wyatt, executive director of the gallery Artists Space in New York, informed Frohnmayer that an art show concerning AIDS that contained some arguably homoerotic works was about to be mounted there—thanks to a $10,000 NEA grant. Wyatt thought it might be construed to fall within the new legislation's funding ban, and she informed the Endowment about the nature of the show "as a way of testing to see whether or not Helms had won."

SUSAN WYATT: I was concerned that the Endowment not be blindsided in case there might be some controversy on this show.

———

Frohnmayer's attention was drawn to the show's catalogue, which contained an essay by artist David Wojnarowicz in which he expressed his "feeling of rage" about having AIDS and watching his friends die of the disease. Wojnarowicz said that "fantasies" gave him "distance from my outrage for a few minutes." The fantasies he mentioned in the catalogue included dousing Senator Jesse Helms with gasoline and setting him on fire, and throwing Representative William E. Dannemeyer—another proponent of arts censorship and the author of a book that argued that homosexuality was "curable" acquired behavior—off the Empire State Building. The essay also attacked Senator Alphonse D'Amato, Mayor Edward Koch, New York City Health Commissioner Stephen C. Joseph, and John Cardinal O'Connor, the Roman Catholic archbishop of New York, for his opposition to abortion and to making information about "safe sex" available to gay men. According to the Wojnarowicz essay, O'Connor was a "fat cannibal" and the Roman Catholic Church "a house of walking swastikas." The show, which presented works by twenty-three painters, photographers, and sculptors, included some nonobscene images of homosexual acts and eroticism. Its curator was Nan Goldin, a Boston artist and photographer.

After examining the catalogue, the new NEA chairman asked Wyatt to "relinquish" the $10,000 grant. His reasoning disclosed no appreciation of the First Amendment role of the arts.

JOHN FROHNMAYER: Political discourse ought to be in the political arena and not in a show sponsored by the Endowment. . . .

Because of the recent criticism the Endowment has come under, and the seriousness of Congress's directive, we must all work together to insure that projects funded by the Endowment do not violate either the spirit or the letter of the law. The message has been clearly and strongly conveyed to us that Congress means business. On this basis, I believe the Endowment's funds may not be used to exhibit or publish this material.

———

Frohnmayer, a lawyer who had studied religion for a year at Union Theological Seminary and obtained a master's degree in Christian ethics from the University of Chicago, sounded a little like a scoutmaster lecturing the troop. Susan Wyatt did not comply with the NEA head's request that Artists Space "relinquish" its NEA grant.

SUSAN WYATT: Instead I went public, hoping to encourage other organizations who are also checking out their shows with the Endowment to do the same.

Although Senator Helms and Congressman Dannemeyer understandably expressed satisfaction with Frohnmayer's action, Representative Sidney Yates proved incredulous.

REPRESENTATIVE SIDNEY YATES: I have great respect for Mr. Frohnmayer, and he's new and we have to give him a chance. [But] I'm not sure what he means. What do you do with Daumier? Or Goya's "Disasters of War"? What if a gallery wants to put up the cartoons of Thomas Nast against Boss Tweed? In itself, political statements are not a barrier to grants.

The day after Frohnmayer announced he was rescinding the NEA grant, he shifted ground in a way that made his untenable position ludicrous. Trying to placate his arts constituency, Frohnmayer stated that on second thought, the trouble with the Artists Space exhibition, from the NEA's standpoint, was that it wasn't "artistic" enough.

JOHN FROHNMAYER: The word "political," I'm coming to see, means something different in Portland, Oregon, than it does in Washington, D.C. I think I used the word unadvisedly. I think it has sounded like I was saying you look at the political content and you decide whether or not you like it. What I meant to say was you look at the *artistic* quality and you decide on that. . . .

In looking at the [Artists Space] application and then in looking at what was actually happening in the show, there was a substantial shift and, in my view, an erosion of the artistic focus. I described that with the "P" word, and it was taken by the arts community as a suggestion that I had been influenced by political pressure, or that it wasn't all right for artists to make in the context of their superior artistic efforts a political statement. That was not my intent.

Having shot himself in one foot, Frohnmayer nonchalantly shot himself in the other. His explanation could have pleased no one. In Washington, the members of an NEA visual arts panel that had now convened to make grant recommendations to the new chairman bluntly advised him of their "disappointment and distress" over his decision to rescind the grant to Artists Space. When their meeting ended, panel member Elizabeth Sisco, an artist from San Diego, resigned in protest over what Frohnmayer had done. Frohnmayer now traveled to New York to see the controversial exhibition for himself and shortly thereafter told the press that he was rescinding his rescission of the grant to Artists Space.

JOHN FROHNMAYER: I visited Artists Space in New York City yesterday and saw the exhibition "Witnesses: Against Our Vanishing." Prior to this time I had only seen the catalogue. After consulting with members of the National Council on the Arts, several of whom have also seen the show,

I have agreed to approve the request of Artists Space to amend the fiscal '89 grant and will release the grant for the exhibition only.

———

What happened in fact was that Susan Wyatt accepted a grant from the Robert Mapplethorpe Foundation to pay for the politically offensive catalogue, and the NEA paid for the show. This obtained a mixed reaction:

SENATOR JESSE HELMS: I do hope that Mr. Frohnmayer is not retreating from his voluntary commitment to me [to refuse to fund controversial art], and I will not assume he has done so until I hear from him about a publicized statement attributed to him.

KAREN KENNERLY:* It is a reprieve we are celebrating, not a victory. Not until the law has been repealed is there a victory for freedom of expression.

REPRESENTATIVE PAT WILLIAMS (MONTANA): There may be two irreconcilable forces here. One is the right of taxpayers to determine how their money is spent. The other is the absolute necessity to protect freedom of expression, particularly in the arts. If those two forces are irreconcilable, then the future of the Endowment is in doubt.

———

But taxpayers have no direct voice in determining how their money is spent; if they had, many would have forbidden their taxes to be spent supporting Star Wars, the Stealth bomber, and the Gulf War, to mention just a few more recent controversial government programs. The constitutional separation-of-powers doctrine precludes Congress from intruding into the administration of a program like the NEA's and deciding for itself which artists and arts institutions should receive support. The federal government need not encourage or promote the work of artists and writers, but when it does undertake such a program, it cannot choose the individual artists or arts institutions to be supported, or require the NEA to do so, on grounds that interfere with the freedom of artists to communicate images or ideas that are controversial or that criticize or attack, however violently, politicians, religious figures, government officials, and even religion and government itself. The only constitutionally valid grounds for grantee selection and denial are ones exclusively related to artistic values such as "merit," "quality," and "promise."

A six-member group of constitutional law experts who were asked to advise the twelve-member commission established to counsel the NEA and Congress concerning these problems would express the same view in the

———

*Kennerly is Executive Director of the PEN American Center. Some in the liberal, intellectual, and arts communities were opposed to the obscenity restriction in the NEA compromise legislation, understanding that it would require Frohnmayer to administratively censor artwork that he feared would be deemed obscene by Congress. In fact, even the narrow definition of "obscene" set forth in *Miller* is unconstitutionally vague and overbroad in the judgment of Justice Brennan, dissenting in *Miller*. There is a good explanation of the meanings of constitutional "vagueness" and "overbreadth" in Professor Lawrence Tribe's readable and valuable treatise *American Constitutional Law* (1978), 718ff.

fall of 1990. Its members also told the commission that a condition such as that imposed by Frohnmayer requiring recipients of NEA grants to certify under oath that they would not use grant proceeds to create "obscene" works was unwise and would have a chilling effect on artistic freedom and creativity. They also said (in a joint statement) that if Congress chooses to finance the arts, it may *not* do so in a way that the Supreme Court has said "is aimed at the suppression of dangerous ideas." One of the constitutional law experts was the dean of the University of Chicago Law School:

GEOFFREY STONE: Government need not fund any art. But it does not necessarily follow that, if it chooses to fund some art, it is free to fund only that art that supports its point of view. Wholly apart from concerns about coercion, such selective funding would distort public debate in a viewpoint-based manner, treat different points of view unequally, and reflect a constitutionally impermissible use of public resources. Government neutrality in the field of ideas is an essential premise of the first amendment, and this applies not only to direct government efforts to suppress ideas but to government efforts selectively to promote certain ideas as well. . . .

Although government could not criminally punish the production or exhibition of art [because it] lacks "serious artistic value," and could not refuse to fund the expression of political ideas [because they] lack "serious political value," it can refuse to fund art that lacks "serious artistic value." This is so for two reasons. First, and perhaps most important, judgments about artistic quality, unlike judgments about political quality, do not implicate core first amendment concerns. In its most central meaning, the first amendment focuses on political expression, and this is so, in part, because government efforts to judge the worth of competing political ideas are especially subject to abuse. Thus, we are more willing to tolerate [government] judgments about quality in the realm of artistic than political expression. Second, insofar as we have some confidence in our ability to make reasonable judgments about artistic quality, the decision to subsidize only that art that has "serious artistic value" represents an acceptable trade-off in a world of limited governmental resources.

———

After the cancellation of Mapplethorpe's "The Perfect Moment," the reputation of the Corcoran Gallery and the fate of its director, Christina Orr-Cahall, were in limbo for months. A retaliatory artists' boycott forced the gallery to cancel two other shows and placed in question a third. Then artist Lowell Nesbitt withdrew a gift to the Corcoran of over $1 million in property and art that he had planned to will to the museum, and willed it to the prestigious Phillips Collection instead. After Jane Livingston, the Corcoran's chief curator and the organizer of the Mapplethorpe show, resigned in protest over what Orr-Cahall and the Corcoran board had done, the Corcoran's staff confronted Orr-Cahall with a request that she resign. The director tried to stand her ground.

CHRISTINA ORR-CAHALL: I work for the board of trustees and I'm working as hard as I can to try to move the institution forward, and I'm hoping that the staff will work with me to do that.

———

Orr-Cahall blamed the government for what had happened.

CHRISTINA ORR-CAHALL: It was the federal funding, and in a sense Mapplethorpe gets used. It could have been any other artist—Serrano or whomever.

JO ANN LEWIS:* But cancellation did not happen to another artist. It happened to Mapplethorpe, whose prices subsequently went up; and it happened to the Corcoran, whose stock has hit a low point.

———

By late September 1989, the Corcoran had lost nearly 10 percent of its membership, but Christina Orr-Cahall was still hanging on as the museum's director, after three months of largely negative criticism from the arts community and the press. In an interview on September 22 with an empathetic reporter from *The Washington Post,* she confessed to having been "unrealistic" to imagine that art could be independent of politics, especially in Washington. This was a lament that John E. Frohnmayer would voice, over and over again, during his first two years as head of the NEA.

CHRISTINA ORR-CAHALL: I mean, I don't know Washington! How would you know this?
I don't look at it as my sole decision. I think it had an entire board of trustees behind it. . . . The bulk of the curators were out of town, which was very unfortunate. So when the decision was actually made, I said we are unable to do this exhibition and a voice vote was taken in support of the director's point of view. . . . It was brought up at a subsequent meeting and the decision was split, and the board voted independently and opposed the showing of the exhibition. . . .
I certainly now wish we had done the show. You can't predict history: you're at a crossroads and you have to take one or the other road. . . . Now I think we should have done it, we should have bitten the bullet, we should have stood up for artistic rights.

———

Officially, the Corcoran board was not considering firing Orr-Cahall. On September 25, however, a quorum of the fifty-four-member Corcoran board of directors met and appointed a special "damage-control" committee to study "some concerns"—including whether the prestigious art center should fire its director. By now the Washington Project for the Arts—the gallery in Washington that had picked up the Mapplethorpe show after the Corcoran dropped it—had exhibited "The Perfect Moment" to nearly 50,000 visitors, in less than a month.

———

*Art critic, *The Washington Post.*

Three months later, on December 18, 1989, just a few days before the Corcoran's damage-control committee was supposed to meet again, Christina Orr-Cahall announced her resignation; she cited "extraneous and disruptive difficulties" of the last several months that had put the museum's future in doubt.

CHRISTOPHER KNIGHT:* We are not talking here about the momentary failure of judgment on the part of a single museum employee, which can be neatly swept away with her departure. We are not even talking about a director's repeated failures. After all, the cancellation of the Mapplethorpe exhibition was accomplished with the official backing and continued support of the Corcoran's board of trustees. There was virtually no indication Monday, as there had not been from Day One, that the museum board has in any way changed its mind about that calamitous decision. . . . Amazingly enough, six months later the crisis still is being perceived as a gross public relations problem, an even more nagging problem that might miraculously disappear with the director.

It won't. Public life is forever being confused with public relations, but the Corcoran scandal is at heart a catastrophe of public life. For it is finally the board of trustees, not the director, that holds the museum, its collections and its programs in trust for the public. It is the board of trustees, not its employee, in whom ultimate fiduciary responsibility is vested. That is what the word "trustee" means. Except for a staff change, the Corcoran Gallery of Art today is no different than it was last week, when public confidence and support were virtually nil.

—

Harry Lunn, a longtime friend of Robert Mapplethorpe's and one of the dealers in Mapplethorpe's work, had spoken at the rally on the street outside the Corcoran when Mapplethorpe's art was projected onto the Corcoran's walls. After Orr-Cahall's resignation we talked about some of the consequences of l'affaire Orr-Cahall.

HARRY LUNN: Look! The unthinkable has occurred! Mapplethorpe has eliminated an incompetent director and forced a difficult board to reconstitute itself. They're going to cut down the board's size and maybe even get rid of people like Kreeger. I doubt he will stay on; it would be like Ceaucescu staying on in Romania. The Corcoran was being run like a social club where for $5,000 you could get a seat on the board like a box at the Met. They've said they are going to restructure the board, which is something that has been needed for twenty years.

—

David Lloyd Kreeger had been chairman of the board of directors and president of the Corcoran Gallery for twenty years. He was an internationally known collector of Impressionist and modern painting and sculpture, had served as president of the National Symphony Orchestra, and had

---

*Art critic, *The Los Angeles Times.*

founded the Washington Opera. On November 18, 1990, he died of cancer at the age of eighty-one.

The next day, the Corcoran announced that the chancellor of the New School for Social Research in Manhattan, David C. Levy, would become the new president and director of the faltering gallery. When Levy took over, he and the Corcoran's revamped board issued a strong public statement about the gallery's new commitment to the preservation and enhancement of "freedom of speech, thought, inquiry and artistic expression" in its exhibitions and educational programs. One of the reasons for Levy's appointment was that as head of the New School he had approved the act of suing the NEA in federal court to obtain a ruling that Frohnmayer's pledge was unconstitutional. By naming him as the gallery's new head, Levy said, the Corcoran was saying: "We understand where we need to go." With the First Amendment.

"The Perfect Moment" was scheduled to open at the Contemporary Arts Center in Cincinnati (CAC) on April 6, 1990. The gallery's forty-two-year-old curator, Dennis Barrie, had decided to bring Mapplethorpe to Cincinnati the year before the Corcoran canceled its scheduled show. At that time, the CAC board voted unanimously to mount the show; it voted the same way a second time, when the original decision was brought up for reconsideration after the Corcoran Gallery cancellation.

DENNIS BARRIE: Way back in June [1989], when the Corcoran announcement was made, we took it back to our board and said now look, this is no longer just another show. To the credit of the board, they reviewed all the photos, they reviewed our contract, and said we must honor our contract.

ROGER ACH (president of the CAC's board): We saw the catalogue, we saw the difficult photographs in copy form and had them described. We were well briefed and convinced that this was an important retrospective of a very well known artist.

———

But Cincinnati proved even more aversive to Mapplethorpe's art than Washington. The city was the base of Citizens for Decent Literature* and of a group called Citizens for Community Values (CCV). On April 7, 1990, as a result of goading from these groups, Cincinnati police entered and temporarily closed the Contemporary Arts Center to secure the evidence needed to prosecute Barrie and the gallery for exhibiting "obscenity" and "child pornography." Only hours before, Barrie and the gallery had been indicted by a Cincinnati grand jury. Commented CCV's president:

---

*CDL was renamed after Charles Keating's involvement in the 1989–1990 home savings and loan scandals was made known. It was later called National Coalition Against Pornography and is now known as Children's Legal Foundation.

MONTY LOBB: If Mr. Barrie had exercised better judgment, this could have been avoided.

———

The board of directors of the Contemporary Arts Center had stood fast behind the gallery's director. Instead of pressuring Barrie to drop the Mapplethorpe show, its chairman resigned from the board because of boycott and other threats that had been mounted against his bank by CCV. The vigilante group had first sought to force the gallery to cancel the scheduled Mapplethorpe show by pressuring local business concerns that had signed up to support the exhibition, and by intimidating board members who worked for firms that were vulnerable to economic boycott. Dennis Barrie told reporters that the chairman of his board resigned "because his bank came under massive attack from the Citizens for Community Values, who tore up their credit cards, while businessmen who supported them threatened the bank on other levels." This was followed by activity aimed at destroying Cincinnati's annual arts fund-raising program by portraying the drive as "a form of sponsorship for pornography." To save the drive, Barrie's gallery withdrew from participation in it, at an estimated cost to it of $300,000. There followed an "anti-porn" attack from the vigilante group's "friends in the media," who spread disinformation about the nature of the show. Barrie said that the media people "beat us up pretty badly for a couple of weeks." The gallery also drew down upon its head anonymous "hate mail, bomb threats, and feces."*

After Citizens for Community Values informed Hamilton County sheriff Simon L. Leis, Jr., about the approaching Mapplethorpe show, Leis—a former Marine, former assistant U.S. attorney, and former judge in Cincinnati Common Pleas Court—publicly announced that he would do his duty regarding Dennis Barrie and his gallery if the local Cincinnati police chief, Lawrence Whalen, would not. Leis was described as the Cincinnati public official who came closest to filling the boots of CDL's old smut-buster Charles E. Keating, with this difference: Leis was, and Keating was not, a law enforcement official; as such, Leis should not have been advancing a personal moral agenda. His announcement moved Chief of Police Whalen into action: after attempts to frighten Dennis Barrie into closing the Mapplethorpe show or at least removing the "worst" pictures failed, Whalen led the investigative raid on the Contemporary Arts Center.

POLICE CHIEF LAWRENCE WHALEN: Those photographs are just not welcome in this community. The people of this community do not cater to what others depict as art.†

———

*Newsday, April 10, 1990.

†Of course, the *Miller* test of obscenity does not give local policemen, juries, or even judges the power to decide what is art, or whether expression has serious artistic value. This is a mixed question of constitutional law and fact, ultimately to be decided *de novo* by the Supreme Court on the basis of national or even supranational standards of artistic value. The local Miami law

KIM MASTERS: Police and Sheriff's officers swept into the packed Contemporary Arts Center here today and ordered more than 400 visitors to leave while they took videotaped evidence to support obscenity charges against a public showing of the controversial Robert Mapplethorpe photo exhibit.

The police action was taken after a Hamilton County grand jury, whose nine members paid the $4 admission fee, and quietly viewed the exhibit with other patrons this morning, returned an indictment against the art center and its director, Dennis Barrie, a few hours later.

———

Both Dennis Barrie and the Contemporary Arts Center were indicted under two Ohio laws, one that proscribed "pandering obscenity" and another that criminalized possessing or viewing child pornography. On the surface, the Ohio child pornography law posed the more dangerous of the two prosecutive attacks on Barrie and the Contemporary Arts Center and on the freedom of all adult Cincinnatians to see shows that the CAC mounted for them to see. It was one of the country's most repressive "kiddy porn" laws, a law that the Supreme Court had recently acted to uphold (with Justices Brennan, Marshall, and Stevens dissenting because the law was "fatally overbroad" and authorized the police to violate the free speech and privacy right of persons in their homes). That happened while Barrie's prosecution was pending.

After the indictments, legal experts of the Left, Right, and Center called the attack made by the Cincinnati police upon the visual arts outrageous. One reporter asked University of Michigan law professor and former Meese commissioner Frederick Schauer whether the Supreme Court's 1973 decision in *Miller* v. *California* supported the prosecution of art curator Barrie:

PROFESSOR FREDERICK SCHAUER: Absolutely not. It's not even close. Let's take the worst case, or the best from the [prosecution's] point of view. Take one Mapplethorpe photograph, and it shows gay men engaging in sado-masochistic acts. The very fact that it's by Mapplethorpe and it's in a museum would still lead me to say it's not even close.

———

Another former Meese commissioner, the former federal prosecutor Tex Lezar, agreed, saying he "thought as long as it appeared in a museum it was safe." The conservative public-interest lawyer and consultant Bruce Fein was of the same opinion.

———

enforcement officials who recently arrested Luther Campbell, the leader of 2 Live Crew, for playing obscene songs also acted on the mistaken belief that local community standards of decency, as interpreted by them, determined whether the songs were constitutionally protected or obscene. The confusion of law enforcement officials regarding this matter, and the tendency to make local community standards apply to questions of artistic value, as well as to what the average person in the community considers "prurient" or "patently offensive," can be directly traced to the opinions Chief Justice Burger wrote in the 1973 obscenity cases in his attempt to roll back the Warren Court's decisions. See Chapter 28.

BRUCE FEIN: People don't usually walk into museums to have their prurient interests aroused. I think it's a very maladroit use of the criminal-justice system to go after a curator. This is not some kind of degenerate conduct that is worthy of criminal prosecution.

—

In New York, the preeminent First Amendment lawyer Floyd Abrams called the Cincinnati prosecution "outside the realm of obscenity prosecution in recent memory." More forebodingly, Abrams predicted that if the Cincinnati museum and curator were convicted, the Supreme Court, given its present membership, might refuse to review the case. This would leave artists, and the constitutional protection afforded artists, in limbo. When American Family Association founder Donald Wildmon was asked for his comments on the Cincinnati prosecution, he feigned naïveté: "Isn't obscenity illegal even if it's displayed in an art gallery?"

Knowledgeable First Amendment lawyers agreed that the criminal charges against Dennis Barrie and his art gallery should never have been brought, and that, once brought, they should have been dropped, or both defendants should have been swiftly acquitted, for the simple reason that serious artistic expression cannot constitutionally be found "obscene," regardless of its "prurient appeal" or "patent offensiveness." As Dean Geoffrey Stone, a constitutional scholar, stated: "[A]rt can constitute obscenity only if it lacks serious artistic value."* What is indisputable is that the child pornography and obscenity prosecution in Cincinnati and the temporary closing of the art gallery by the police, in advance of any judicial finding that the show was obscene, took place notwithstanding the constitutional guarantees of free expression and applicable Supreme Court decisions.

---

*The parallel proposition—that art can constitute child pornography only if it lacks serious artistic value—unfortunately is not settled law. In *Ferber* v. *New York,* the Supreme Court upheld the validity of New York's child pornography law as applied to the seller of peep-show-type movies (showing young boys masturbating) making no claim to even the slightest artistic or social value. But the New York statute involved did not expressly exempt expression having such value from its reach, and in addressing the *abstract* question of whether the constitutional protections afforded by *Miller*'s three-pronged test for obscentiy applied as well to child pornography prosecutions, the Court expressly said that the first two prongs would not apply, but implied that the third prong would. This indicated that for a child pornography prosecution to succeed there would be: (a) a need to prove that a child was induced to engage in explicit sexual conduct (or poses); (b) no need to prove that the images either appealed to the average person's "prurient interest" or were "patently offensive" to contemporary community standards of decency; but (c) a need to show that the material had no "serious literary, artistic, scientific, or political value." In light of the protection meant to be afforded by the First Amendment to all artistic works, the presence of "artistic value" should insulate works such as Mapplethorpe's—and the acts of creating, exhibiting, and viewing them—from suppression or criminal prosecution under a child pornography law such as Ohio's, as it should remove them from the reach of obscenity laws like the one in force in Ohio. Unfortunately, the law on the former point cannot be deemed settled, especially given the present makeup of the Court now that Justice Brennan, who nailed down the point in his concurring opinion in *Ferber,* has retired. Justice O'Connor, who took the opposite view in her concurring opinion in *Ferber,* is still on the Court and seems unlikely to change her mind. The threats to freedom of artistic expression presented by child pornography laws that seek to repress the creation and exhibition of art that portrays mere child nudity, as Ohio's law does, are taken up in Chapter 29.

PROFESSOR FREDERICK SCHAUER: It's a sad commentary on the American constitutional system. . . . We rely on the Supreme Court to do all our constitutional enforcement, and we do not penalize officials for ignoring constitutional values. We shouldn't be surprised when they do ignore them.

———

On Friday, October 5, 1990, the Cincinnati jury empaneled to try the Mapplethorpe case made history by acquitting Dennis Barrie and his art gallery on all charges. The liberal press saluted them, and the constitutionalized law of obscenity.

THE NEW YORK TIMES: The jurors in the Robert Mapplethorpe obscenity trial in Cincinnati sent a strong and sensible message yesterday to local prosecutors and to all those who've been posturing on the obscenity issue this year. The jurors took about two hours to acquit the Contemporary Arts Center, and its director, Dennis Barrie, of the charge of pandering obscenity for showing sexually explicit photographs that were part of Mapplethorpe's traveling retrospective, "The Perfect Moment."

The case began by conferring on Cincinnati the onerous distinction of being the first city to try a gallery on obscenity charges. It ended with Cincinnati proudly resisting restrictions on artistic expression. . . .

The judge sided with the prosecution's attempt to give an unfairly narrow portrait of the Mapplethorpe exhibit. Only 7 of its 175 photographs were allowed into evidence—a travesty given the fact that it was meant to display the artist's life work, much of which involved innocuous photographs of celebrities and flowers.

The prosecution's argument that the exhibit offended "community standards" was disproved by the community itself, which had already voted with its feet. A record 80,000 visitors thronged to see the show when it passed through Cincinnati in April and May.

The two photographs of children that the prosecution objected to were no more lewd than Michelangelo's "David," or babies on the beach in summer. . . .

To some, the photographs were obscenities; to others, art. The rights of the museum to display the pictures and the rights of citizens to make up their own minds have been upheld.

DAVID MARGOLICK:* The judge hearing the case was a law-and-order Republican and a close friend of the sheriff who shut the museum down briefly to videotape evidence when the exhibit opened. Several of the judge's preliminary rulings favored the prosecution. Seven of the eight jurors hailed from the still more conservative suburbs of an already conservative community; only three had ever been to an art museum, and none had seen the exhibition. The only thing the museum and its director, Dennis Barrie, had going for them was the law. And that appears to have been enough.

———

*Law page editor, *The New York Times.*

DEFENSE LAWYER H. LOUIS SIRKIN: They did exactly what we hoped they would do. Personally, I didn't like the pictures either. Our battle strategy was the third prong [of the *Miller* test].

JUROR ANTHONY ECKSTEIN: That's what it boiled down to. It was missing an ingredient. It had artistic value, and that's what kept it from being obscene.

We thought the pictures were lewd, grotesque, disgusting. But like the defense said, art doesn't have to be pretty or beautiful.

JUROR JAMES JONES: We had to go with what we were told. It's like Picasso. Picasso from what everybody tells me was an artist. It's not my cup of tea. I don't understand it. But if people say it's art, then I have to go along with it.

JUROR ANTHONY ECKSTEIN: At one point we said to ourselves, "Is this really us making this decision?" We all had to go home and face family and relatives. We were saying to ourselves, "Oh my gosh, how are we going to explain this to people? What will everybody think?" There was a lot of pressure.

———

Professor Cass Sunstein of the University of Chicago Law School thought the jury's verdict meant the "War on Art" was over.

PROFESSOR CASS SUNSTEIN: Unless the political climate changes very dramatically, the *Miller* test provides quite solid protection for civil liberties.* The [Cincinnati] Mapplethorpe case shows there's a wide consensus that we shouldn't regulate speech just because it's disturbing.

Even people who seem to have very traditional values are opposed to censorship. Those who think we're entering into a period of widespread prosecution are wrong.

———

A few days later, a spokesman for the Cincinnati vigilante organization that had been mainly responsible for the police and prosecutorial attacks on Barrie and the museum offered a different assessment of the future of artistic freedom in Cincinnati:

PHILLIP BURRESS: We have sent a signal that even CAC is held accountable. We have proven what we will go after. And if they come back with those

---

*In my opinion a test or doctrine that is likely to bend with dramatic changes in the political climate cannot rightly be depicted as providing "quite solid protection." Prior to its dilution by Chief Justice Burger in the *Miller* case, the Brennan doctrine—by virtue of its unamenability to manipulation by judges and its assertion of suzerainty over lower judge and jury rulings repressive of speech—might accurately have been said to provide "quite solid protection" to all speech not "utterly without" value. The only limit to the protection was the capacity of the justices themselves to perceive that expression challenged as obscene was not completely worthless. This was indirectly demonstrated by Brennan himself when, in the *Ginzburg* case, a strong political wind forced him to import a new doctrine, the "pandering" doctrine, to affirm the lower court's decision that Ginzburg's expression was obscene. What I have called the Brennan doctrine could not be bent to fit the conclusion favored by the Court that what Ginzburg had published was obscene.

pictures and they're in color or are bigger, our citizens will demand that it go to a grand jury.

———

On August 1, 1990, after the Cincinnati indictments were filed but before the trials and acquittals took place, Mapplethorpe's "The Perfect Moment" was opened in Boston by curator David Ross at the Institute for Contemporary Art (ICA).

Several local religious vigilante groups, including Morality in Media and Citizens for Family First, had sought unsuccessfully to prevent the show from opening by pressuring Massachusetts Attorney General James Shannon to prosecute Ross and ICA and threatening to oppose Shannon's reelection if he did not. Said Shannon: "In my view, this exhibit should not be prosecuted because it doesn't fall within the definition of what's obscene. The laws were written so as not to have public officials tell museums what is art and what is not art."

Although a local district attorney who also felt empowered to prosecute declined to make a similarly reassuring declaration, and the Boston anti-pornography groups stepped up their pressures for a prosecution, the police did not attack the show. By the time the nine-week run ended, more than 103,000 gallery visitors had seen it, far more than had visited the ICA during the entire preceding year.

Nevertheless, ICA spokesman Arthur Cohen was less than ebullient about the lesson to be taken from the Cincinnati prosecution, the threats of prosecution in Boston, and the well-organized vigilante action that had nearly closed the show in both cities. He predicted that "The Perfect Moment" would never again be shown in the same fashion, saying, "this is the [exhibition's] swan song."

During the summer of 1989 in Broward County, Florida, a campaign was launched by police to suppress a best-selling record album called *As Nasty As They Wanna Be* by the rap music group 2 Live Crew. Although nationwide the recording had sold nearly two million copies, Charles Freeman, a Fort Lauderdale record-shop owner, was arrested under Florida's obscenity law for selling the record to adults. Freeman, who is black, was quickly tried and convicted by an all-white Broward County jury.

One week later, also in Fort Lauderdale, after a local appearance by the group, criminal proceedings were brought against three of 2 Live Crew's four members: Luther Campbell, 2 Live Crew's leader; Mark Ross, the group's chief lyricist; and Chris Wongwon, the group's founder. As in Cincinnati, prosecutors had been pressured to act by right-wing religious vigilantes.

LUKE CAMPBELL:
You can say I'm desperate,/ even call me perverted
but you'll call me a dog/ when I leave you fucked and deserted
I'll play with your heart/ just like it's a game

I'll be blowing your mind/ while you're blowing my brain
I'm just like that man/ they call Georgie Puddin' Pie
I fuck all the girls/ and I make them cry
I'm like a dog in heat,/ a freak without warning,
I have an appetite for sex,/ cause me so horny

FEMALE VOCALIST:

Uhh, me so horny, me so horny, me so horny, me love you long time. . . .

MALE VOCALIST:

What we gonna do?

FEMALE VOCALIST:

Sock it to me.

Uhh, me so horny, me so horny, me so horny, me love you long time. . . .

LUKE CAMPBELL:

It's true you were a virgin/ until you met me
I was the first to make you hot/ and wetty-wetty
you tell your parents/ that we're going out
never to the movies/ just straight to my house
you said it yourself,/ you like it like I do
put your lips on my dick,/ and suck my asshole too
I'm a freak in heat,/ a dog without warning,
my appetite is sex,/ cause me so horny.

FEMALE VOCALIST:

Uhh, me so horny, me so horny, me so horny, me love you long time. . . .

LIZ SMITH:* In my time I've had a lot to say about how sticks and stones can break one's bones; but words can never hurt. . . . And this column has been an active defender of First Amendment rights and also the right of others to say anything they like about those in the public eye. I've always felt if we in the press offend, at least it is better than suffering suppression, censorship, etc.

But a July 2 column by John Leo in *U.S. News & World Report,* which I clipped and put aside before I went on vacation, has me on the ropes. . . .

JOHN LEO: The issue at the heart of the controversy over the rap group 2 Live Crew is not censorship, artistic freedom, sex or even obscene language. The real problem, I think, is this: Because of the cultural influence of one not very distinguished rap group, 10- and 12-year-old boys now walk down the street chanting about the joys of damaging a girl's vagina during sex. . . .

The popular culture is worth paying attention to. It is the air we breathe, and 2 Live Crew is a pesky new pollutant. The opinion industry's advice is generally to buy a gas mask or stop breathing. ("If you don't like their album, don't buy it," one such genius wrote.) But by monitoring, complaining, boycotting, we might actually get the 2 Live Crew Pollutants out of our air. Why should our daughters have to grow up in a culture in which

---

*Columnist, formerly at the New York *Daily News,* now at *Newsday.*

musical advice on the domination and abuse of women is accepted as entertainment?

LIZ SMITH: So, is censorship the answer? The performance of 2 Live Crew—so violent, so anti-female—forces an almost involuntary yes! But once you censor, or forbid or arrest the real culprits, how do you deal with other artists who "offend"? Where do you draw the line? This is a tough one. But the average child isn't likely to encounter the kind of "art" that the National Endowment is trying to ban. Kids are not all over art galleries and theaters. But pop music assails them at every level and at every moment of their lives.

What I WOULD like to see is every responsible, influential and distinguished black activist, actor and role model—Jesse Jackson, Spike Lee, Whoopi Goldberg, Arsenio Hall, Eddie Murphy, Diana Ross, et al.—raising his or her voice to decry the horrible "message" of 2 Live Crew.

I would advise famous and caring whites to do the same, though they may be accused of racism. However, the issue goes far beyond race. Clips of 2 Live Crew in concert show that the audiences are not exclusively black by any means. What they are is young and unformed and dangerously impressionable.

DEBBIE BENNETT:* It's nice to see that Liz Smith is keeping racism in America alive and kicking. She's so stupid it's unbelievable. She wrote that since kids don't go to art galleries or see shows with people like Karen Finley, obscene art is okay. But since they listen to music, 2 Live Crew should be banned. Way to pass judgment on every teenager in America.

———

In an account of the 2 Live Crew members' trial that appeared in *The Village Voice,* Lisa Jones reported what two teenaged black women, courthouse fans of Luther Campbell, had to say about the prosecution and the music:

ANTOINETTE JONES (18): They're just giving Luke a hard time because he's black. He's trying to make a living like everyone else. If someone wants to listen to his music that's their business. What do they think music is? They're acting like music is a gun.

LATONIA BROOKS (17): [Their lyrics] do have to do with sex and body parts, but when they rap, they put it all together. It's not like a man on the street saying dirty words to you. Their music makes sense. What they're saying is the truth. That's what most people do in bed. I don't, but that's what most other people do in bed.

———

Unlike the jury that convicted the record-store owner Charles Freeman for selling the "obscene" album, 2 Live Crew's jury was not all white; it found all three Crew members not guilty. Two of the (white) jurors told reporters why they had voted to acquit.

———

*2 Live Crew publicist.

SUSAN VAN HEMERT (JUROR): I basically took it as comedy.

BEVERLY RESNICK (JUROR): This was their way of expressing their inner feelings; we felt it had some art in it.

——

The verdict came after four days of testimony during which the jurors "spent hours" listening to, and occasionally laughing at, two garbled tape recordings of a performance by the group that had been made by undercover deputies from the Broward County sheriff's office. The tapes, one of which had been enhanced by the police to eliminate background noise, were the prosecution's only evidence.

Defense lawyers Bruce Rogow and Allen Jacobi won the case by producing expert witnesses to testify about the artistic and political values in the group's songs, a strategy like the one that defense lawyers in the Cincinnati Mapplethorpe case had successfully used. One of the 2 Live Crew witnesses, *Newsday* music critic John Leland, gave an annotated history of hip-hop music. Another, Duke University professor and literary critic Henry Louis Gates, Jr., placed the music in its African-American oral and literary tradition. Gates explained the "signifying," and the use of "hyperbole" and "parody"; he described why it was that artistic works like *As Nasty As They Wanna Be* were not to be taken literally. This probably was the evidence which persuaded the jury that there was at least a reasonable doubt that the music was obscene.

Gates said that the Crew's lyrics took one of the worst stereotypes about black men—that they are oversexed animals—and blew it up until it exploded. He also suggested that the "clear and present danger" doctrine that judges still sometimes used to justify the suppression of speech was not applicable to the Crew's music.

PROFESSOR HENRY LOUIS GATES, JR.: There is no cult of violence [in this music]. There is no danger at all [from] these words . . . being sung.

——

The Crew's chief lyricist defended the group's music, and its success, on essentially political grounds.

MARK ROSS (AKA BROTHER MARQUIS): The bottom line is getting dollars and having your own. It's really a black thing with us. Even though people might say we're not positive role models to the black community, that if you ask us about our culture, we talk about sex, it's not really like that. I'm well aware of where I come from, I know myself as a black man. I think I'm with the program, very much so. You feel I'm doing nothing to enhance my culture, but I could be destroying my culture, I could be out there selling kids drugs.

——

Performers and purveyors of rap music, like curators of art galleries, are engaged in the communication of images and ideas through artistic means. Because of this, interference with their work by policemen, prosecutors, or judges violates the freedoms guaranteed under the First Amendment. No one can intelligently suggest that the country's musicians and distributors of music are not as entitled to be free in their professional activities as its writers and booksellers and museum curators are. The only constitutional limitations permissible with respect to songs are also applicable to books, paintings, photographs, films, and the other arts, as to all speech and press—which is to say, the restraints ought to be limited in their application to persons who use music intentionally to incite others to crime or violence,* or who force nonconsenting or captive audiences to listen to it.

Purposeful disseminations to children of music that may be deemed "obscene" *for them* (in the constitutional sense mentioned in *Miller* v. *California*) would raise different questions.† When 2 Live Crew played Fort Lauderdale, they were not arrested and charged with inviting or alluring minors to hear their sexually explicit songs, playing to "captive audiences" of persons who did not wish to hear what was played and could not escape it, or intentionally inciting the men in the room to rape or sexually abuse women. They were charged with singing lyrics that policemen, prosecutors, and lower court judges had heard about, decoded, and decided were not art, but were obscene.‡ As reported in the press, the Fort Lauderdale arrests were reminiscent of the law enforcement actions that had been successfully taken more than twenty-five years before in New York to silence the social satirist Lenny Bruce.

While the criminal proceedings worked their way through the courts in Cincinnati and Fort Lauderdale during the spring and summer of 1990, John Frohnmayer in Washington showed Congress that he knew how to deny government funds to controversial artists even in the absence of express statutory authority. In June 1990, Frohnmayer rejected applications to support the work of four performance artists—Karen Finley, Holly Hughes, Tim Miller, and John Fleck—against the unanimous recommendations of the NEA's peer-group performance arts panel. Frohnmayer implied that he had rejected the panel's recommendations because of "political

---

*The leading case here is *Brandenburg* v. *Ohio*, 895 S.Ct. 1827 (1969), which, in a few words, recapitulated the long experience with the "clear and present danger" test. In testimony to Lord Longford's committee in Britain, art historian Kenneth Clark defined "art" and "pornography" in such a way as to confirm this proposition: "To my mind art exists in the realm of contemplation, and is bound by some sort of imaginative transposition. The moment art becomes an incentive to action it loses its true character. This is my objection to painting with a communist programme, and it would also apply to pornography." Quoted in Lord Longford, *Pornography: The Longford Report* (1972), 99–100.

†The basis for this difference was established by Justice Brennan writing for the Court in *Ginsberg* v. *New York*, decided in 1968, reprinted in de Grazia, *Censorship Landmarks* (1969) at 610. Justice Brennan's "solution" to the problem of "obscenity" permitted legislators to prevent or punish communications and publications aimed at children which were "obscene" for children and not consented to by the children's parents or guardians. Thus no law could, for example, constitutionally punish 2 Live Crew for playing music that was "obscene" for an audience including children if the children's parents had arranged for, or consented to, the performance.

‡The law officials based their actions upon a written transcription of some of the lyrics said to have been sung, prepared by a moral vigilante organization.

realities," lest the NEA itself be defunded by Congress. These measures may have "saved" the NEA, but they were taken at great cost to the reputation Frohnmayer had sought to establish in the art world as an advocate of artistic freedom. They also put the NEA into the business of censorship, an agenda the agency had assiduously avoided during the twenty-five years of its existence. There were calls for Frohnmayer's resignation from members of the NEA's arts constituency and barbed criticism from the press, including the syndicated columnist Suzanne Fields.

SUZANNE FIELDS: To fund or not to fund, that is the question. . . .

Like Hamlet, Frohnmayer can't make up his mind. He rejected four performance-art grants that he considered of dubious merit, and after the artists cried "Boo!" he said they could appeal, even though there's no precedent for appeal.

He thinks government artists shouldn't be required to sign a pledge that they won't commit obscene art, but he wants them to avoid "confrontational" art.

He tried to explain what confrontational art is. It might not be "appropriate"—this is the bureaucrat's favorite word—to fund a photograph of victims of the Holocaust for display at the entrance to a museum where everyone would have to confront it, like it or not.

When this predictably enraged a lot of people, he apologized and fired the woman who gave him the example.

Nevertheless, the hapless Frohnmayer identified the bottom-line issue in the billowing controversy over the National Endowment for the Arts. Instead of looking at the way artists are abused by politicians, we should look at the way government subsidy abuses art.

John Sloan, the turn-of-the-century American painter of the "ashcan school" whose work shocked the art establishment of his day, understood how art had to define itself against the established order rather than become a part of it.

"It would be fine to have a Ministry of the Fine Arts in this country," he said. "Then we'd know where the enemy is." . . .

Painter Larry Rivers recognized the danger of artists taking money from the government: "The government taking a role in art is like a gorilla threading a needle. It is at first cute, then clumsy, and most of all impossible."

John Updike has the right idea: "I would rather have as my patron a host of anonymous citizens digging into their own pockets for the price of a book or a magazine than a small body of enlightened and responsible men administering public funds."

Now *that's* confrontational. . . .

HOLLY HUGHES: Frohnmayer is the Neville Chamberlain of arts funding. He's an appeaser. There are two schools of thought about Frohnmayer: Either he was put in there because he was not a right-wing ideologue, and he was a nice guy and he would be inoffensive; and then he turned out to be spineless in a dangerous time, which is actually more destructive than anything else . . . to be spineless.

Or, my opinion is—and it's just based on a hunch—there are many ways to destroy the Endowment. The most obvious but most risky politically is outright to defend it. Or attach ridiculously prohibitive and probably unconstitutional language to grant recipients. Another way is to get a person in there who will just completely erode the process that has been established for twenty-five years—which is what Frohnmayer actually has done. His job is supposed to be to insulate the funding decisions from political pressure but instead he opened the door wide to it.

JOHN FROHNMAYER: I am an advocate for the arts, a spokesperson for the arts, a devotee for the arts, a participant in the arts, and I would hope that by who I am and the position that I hold I could articulate for the country why the arts are essential to our existence.

HOLLY HUGHES: Our work *is* controversial, but it seems like at different times there are different targets, and at the time that these grants were turned down the buzzwords were "pornography" and "obscenity" and this whole equation; and, you know, just being gay makes you "obscene." By the very definition. I could just walk down the street and I'd be considered a pornographer; Jesse Helms is denying my very existence. . . .

The pattern has been that once somebody in the national council* targets you as being controversial, then it's leaked to the press, confidential information goes to the Right Wing press, and there comes the whole domino effect. . . .

——

The syndicated columnists Rowland Evans and Robert Novak were the first to target Karen Finley's work, referring to it in a May 11, 1990, column as "the performance of a nude, chocolate-smeared young woman." The first member of the right-wing press to target Holly Hughes was *The Washington Times,* a newspaper that began publication after the *Washington Evening Star* folded. Some people said that it was the first newspaper that President Ronald Reagan read in the morning. In that piece, the newspaper also presented distorted sketches of the work of two other performing artists who had applied for NEA grants: Karen Finley and John Fleck.

THE WASHINGTON TIMES (JUNE 12, 1990): National Endowment for the Arts Chairman John Frohnmayer, in a secret telephone vote of the agency's

---

*The National Council for the Arts, the NEA's twenty-six-person advisory board, receives grant recommendations from the artists' peer-review panels and makes recommendations to the chairperson. In the past (before Frohnmayer), the council regularly adopted the arts panels' recommendations, and the chairperson regularly accepted the recommendations of the council.

26-member advisory council,* is recommending rejection of grants to five controversial artists, including:

- KAREN FINLEY: A regular at NEA-funded avant-garde theatres such as the Kitchen and Franklin Furnace Archive, she smears her nude body with chocolate and with bean sprouts symbolizing sperm in a piece entitled "The Constant State of Desire." Miss Finley also coats make-believe "testicles" with excrement and sells it as candy. In one monologue, she speads her legs and puts canned yams into her body. . . .
- JOHN FLECK: Considered a "fixture" in the "underground culture" of Los Angeles and New York, he urinates into a toilet bowl with a picture of Jesus in a piece titled, "Blessed are All the Little Fishes." In another act, Mr. Fleck urinated into the audience. In a skit titled "He-Be-She-Be's," where he is half-man, half-woman, he strips and has sex with himself.
- HOLLY HUGHES: A solo performer and writer of theatre skits, she demonstrates how her mother imparted the " 'Secret meaning of life' by displaying her body and placing her hand up her vagina"† in a skit titled "World Without End." Her works are less concerned with male-female sexual relationships than "she is with lesbian desire," said a review of another work, "Dress Suits to Hire."

HOLLY HUGHES: I feel like the Endowment is trying to stop us from working, and I mean openly gay and lesbian and feminist artists. And others, like artists who deal with religious symbolism and artists that deal with the American flag and don't treat it right.

And the next step is they're hassling the places that present us and they're ordering audits. . . . The place that sponsors me is the Downtown Art Company. . . . So far they have not been a direct target but The Kitchen, which has funded me and presented Karen Finley and Annie Sprinkle, has now borne the brunt of three different government audits. Franklin Furnace, which has funded me and has presented Karen Finley, has been targeted, and they've been asked to submit to the NEA not just a list of everyone they are going to present but what the work is about—much more detailed information than other institutions are required to provide. . . .

Franklin Furnace was closed down—their performance base is shut (because of fire regulation violations]. It was when Karen Finley's installation

---

*Normally the council had recommended to the NEA's chairperson what grants should be made and the chairperson had adopted the recommendations. In this case, Frohnmayer justifiably feared that unless he intervened in advance to make his preemptive decision known to the council's members, the council would overwhelmingly recommend that the four grants be made, placing him in the practically unprecedented position of having to veto his advisory council's recommendations. See C. Carr's "The Endangered Artists List" in *The Village Voice* of August 21, 1990, regarding the "politicization" of the council and the creation of an artists's blacklist by "neocon" council members Jacob Neusner and Joseph Epstein.

†Hughes and her patron Downtown Art Company both deny that she has ever used this gesture in her work.

was up. Franklin Furnace existed with these violations for fifteen years, and we think it was more than coincidental that suddenly on opening night of Karen Finley's installation somebody would show up and know all of the existing fire-code violations. . . .

In June, that stuff started appearing in *The Washington Times,* misrepresenting me and Karen and John Fleck. Obviously somebody from the NEA, either on the National Council or within the NEA, leaked confidential materials to *The Washington Times,* which they distorted, took out of context, and in a few cases outright lied about.

———

Shortly after Frohnmayer rejected the grant applications of the "scapegoat" performance artists, *The Washington Times* reported that Frohnmayer might give up the futile attempt he was making to please and placate both his congressional and his arts constituencies. The newspaper used the occasion to again malign Finley, Hughes, and Fleck and to attack a fourth rejected performance artist, Tim Miller of California, as "a member of the gay community" whose work was "always political."

THE WASHINGTON TIMES (JULY 2, 1990): National Endowment for the Arts Chairman John Frohnmayer has the arts community speculating that he plans to resign sometime this year after remarks that he cannot accept "political" restrictions on taxpayer-funded art.

"He's making sounds that he can't stomach having to make grant decisions for political reasons and not just on artistic grounds," said an artist with connections to the endowment.

Mr. Frohnmayer on Friday denied grants to four sexually explicit performers after telling local art representatives in Seattle earlier in the week to expect such action because of "political realities."

The NEA chairman for the past eight months has vigorously opposed congressional restrictions on federal funding of artworks said to be obscene or blasphemous.

"I'm looking for him to leave sometime after Congress has acted on the endowment's reauthorization [legislation]" after the Fourth of July recess, said the artist, who asked not to be named. "I think he's laying the groundwork. It would be around the time of the [first-year] anniversary of his nomination by President Bush."

Mr. Frohnmayer did not respond to requests for comment.

JOHN FROHNMAYER: Mid-summer [1990] was probably the lowest ebb of this whole conflict. I would be less than candid . . . if I told you the thought [of resignation] had never crossed my mind, but the reason that I came here was to do what I really could to promote the arts, and I was determined to see it through. I always felt that Congress would see the wisdom of not trying to place content restrictions on an agency whose function it is to promote creativity. You really have diametrically opposed ideas when you're talking about creativity on the one hand and content restrictions on the other.

PAULA SPAN AND CARLA HALL: Performance art, a form that coalesced in New York and California in the mid '70's, borrows from movement and dance, theatre, music, the visual arts and video. It can be scripted or extemporaneous, performed solo or with others, involve props and costumes or not. . . .

Performance art can be confrontational, phantasmagoric, threatening, emotional, bizarre. So perhaps it is not surprising, in the intensifying tumult over art and obscenity and the National Endowment for the Arts, that the first artists to be denied the 1990 NEA fellowships for which they'd been recommended were four performance artists, two from each coast.

—

The work of artists like the "NEA Four"—Holly Hughes, Tim Miller, Karen Finley, and John Fleck*—has been described by some commentators as "Post-Modern" art, a form that deliberately flouts standards for obscenity—and especially the "serious value" gloss that Chief Justice Burger laid upon the Brennan doctrine in *Miller* v. *California* in 1973—because, as Amy M. Adler has said, it "rebels against the demand that a work of art be serious, or that it have any traditional 'value' at all." Adler, who at the time was a third-year student at Yale Law School, elaborated on the point in *The Yale Law Journal*.

AMY M. ADLER: Chief Justice Burger devised the *Miller* test for "serious artistic value" at precisely the time that Modernism in art was in its death throes. One year earlier, the art critic Leo Steinberg had been perhaps the first to apply the name "Post-Modernism" to the revolutionary artistic movement that was budding just as *Miller* was decided. That the Court drafted *Miller* at this turning point in art has dramatic implications, for the metamorphosis into Post-Modernism that occurred in the 1960's and early 1970's has led not to another style in art, but to an entirely transformed conception of what "art" means. . . .

The wording of *Miller* clearly reflects the Modernist era in which it was drafted. As an art critic wrote of Modernism, "the highest accolade that could be paid to any artist was this: 'serious.'" It is as if the word "serious" were a codeword of Modernist values: critics consistently equate it with the Modernist stance. In fact, the very foundation of *Miller,* the belief that some art is just not good enough or serious enough to be worthy of protection, mirrors the Modernist notion that distinctions could be drawn between good art and bad, and that the value of art was objectively verifiable. Thus *Miller* has etched in stone a theory of art that was itself a product of only a transitory phase in art history—the period of late Modernism. . . .

The most pressing challenge to the *Miller* test comes from a sector of Post-Modern artists who not only defy standards like serious value, but also

---

*The work of each of these artists was sketched in Paula Span and Carla Hall, "*Rejected: Portraits of the Performers the NEA Refused to Fund*," *The Washington Post*, July 8, 1990.

attack the most basic premise of *Miller:* that art can be distinguished from obscenity. Some of the artists . . . are extremely—and deliberately—shocking and offensive. It may be hard to understand the value that critics find in this kind of work. Yet it is precisely because these works are so hard for many people to see as "art" that they are of pressing importance for the legal community to consider. . . .

An important and established artist . . . is Karen Finley, whose performance art has been called "obscenity in its purest form." She is indeed a shocking performer.

MARCELLE CLEMENTS: Karen Finley's subject is not obscenity. Her subject is pain, rage, love, loneliness, need, fear, dehumanization, oppression, brutality and consolation. Like the other three performing artists who were denied grants recently by the National Endowment for the Arts, Ms. Finley uses strong sexual images. In her performances she is often nude and often places, dabs, smears, pours and sprinkles food on her body to symbolize the violation of the female characters whose tales she shrieks and whines on stage. It is not her sexuality but her emotional intensity that engages her audiences. A conceptual and performing artist, her most recurrent themes are incest, rape, violence, alcoholism, suicide, poverty, homelessness and discrimination. . . . Her work is nearly always shocking and invariably—some would say relentlessly—political.

KAREN FINLEY: When I was very young my parents saw Lenny Bruce and so his myth had a lot of impact on me. And I just felt—when these situations started to happen with me—I didn't want to have happen what happened to him. Which is stopping my ability to create. It's the biggest form of censorship, where you question yourself. When people are attacked it stops the creativity from growing.

KAREN FINLEY *(Aunt Mandy):*
It's my body
It's not Pepsi's body
It's not Nancy Reagan's body
It's not Congress's body
It's not the Supreme Court's body
It's not Cardinal O'Connor's Catholic-church-homophobic-hate women-hate
    queers-oppressive-DEVIL-SATAN-no children body
IT'S NOT YOUR BODY. . . .

One day, I hope to God, Bush
Cardinal O'Connor and the Right-to-Lifers each
returns to life as an unwanted pregnant 13-year old girl working at McDonalds
    at minimum wage.

C. CARR: Finley began performing in 1979 after her father's suicide. . . . She's still working out of the emotional range she discovered in her rage, the skinless panorama of taboo. She says the charge she gets from performing balances the pain she feels about his death. . . . *Deathcakes and Autism* was an early performance piece based on the events of her father's funeral, where everyone became preoccupied with the food brought to the bereaved.

KAREN FINLEY: People were actually having arguments over which ham to eat. Or saying, "Was it much of a mess? Did you clean it up?" While they were bringing in two dozen Tollhouse cookies.

———

She was twenty-one years old, on spring break from the San Francisco Art Institute, when her father shot himself in the garage, leaving behind "a vague unhappy note." He used a small gun no one knew about. Finley still searches her memory for the clues she missed.

MARCELLE CLEMENTS: She points to a drawing on her drafting table. "I'm working on these little things," she says, leaning over the drawing. "I do think it's sort of sad." The legend reads: "I shot myself because I loved you. If I loved myself I'd be shooting you." Ms. Finley says at the time she remembered a dream she had years earlier about her father's death.

KAREN FINLEY: And the thing that was very strange in my dream. . . . I remember this Spic & Span and in my black humor moment I said to them, "Who's going to clean it up?" Because the image of my father's brain being out there in the cold of the night really disturbed me and I said, Who's going to get out the Spic & Span? I remember I just couldn't go into the garage to see him.

C. CARR: When she returned to college, the San Francisco Art Institute, she felt an "incredible yearning" to spill it, to get up and tell the awful truth in front of people. . . . The result is both fascinating and horrifying to behold, because audiences can't help but recognize their own most mortifying obsessions in the fast-flowing bile. . . .

Women have no tradition of foul-mouth visionaries, as men do—Céline, Genet, Lenny Bruce, et al. But at least women now have a sort of rude girl network that provides a context for outrageous work. Think of Lydia Lunch and that baby-faced dominatrix image so startling in the late '70s, or the obscene and sexually demanding narrator in any Kathy Acker story, or the oddball menace of Dancenoise (Lucy Sexton, Anne Iobst) on stage at 8BC swigging "blood" from coffee cans, tearing dolls limb from limb, shouting, "Give me liberty or give me head!"

KAREN FINLEY: When I was very young in my life I noticed that due to the fact that I was a woman I wasn't able to express myself in the same way that men could. Certain opportunities weren't open to me, and I considered that going against my freedom. When I was six, in Catholic school, I wore culottes and I was told I couldn't wear them to school. But I did anyway, and talked back to everyone, and wore shoe boots, which I guess were considered sexual or something. I didn't know what shoe boots meant but

I continued to wear them, and the culottes, and I felt that I had more body freedom wearing culottes and boots.

When I was in seventh grade I wore pants to public school. It really caused a big ruckus; and then, when they wouldn't allow me to come to school with pants, I wore old ladies' dresses that were totally ugly. And when I did that we won. And so I feel that from when I was a child I was always kind of outspoken. . . .

When I was twenty-one, I performed in the window of [an abandoned] J. C. Penney store in San Francisco. . . . There was no language in it, because people couldn't hear me, but I was kissing the window and putting my breasts up there. I was fully clothed but I put my body up there, it was supposed to be a joke—the woman as a sex symbol. And then I took all these bananas and I put my head up to the window and I was mushing them in my mouth, really close up there. Someone called the police and said there was this woman who's on drugs, insane, and nude, let loose in this J. C. Penney window. . . .

And these two officers came and dragged me off and put me in a squad car, and what I decided to do was continue my performance in the squad car. So I was on the seat, kissing all the windows. I think that was sort of funny, that I continued doing this show, and I never broke the energy. That was the first time my gender helped me . . . being a woman, and being young.

The curator came up and he said to the police that he was a curator and this was art. "This is part of a performance, it's part of a series." He had asked me to perform there, at J. C. Penney's. What struck me was that this was art and it was okay, I could go. And I thought that was funny, or odd; I felt sad.

What if I was a person who didn't go to art school and wasn't given that educational privilege? I would have been arrested, if I was just a person expressing myself that way, and didn't have a curator. I thought what about if I *was* on drugs, or insane? It made me start thinking of things in a different way: that art is a shelter.

So I've been stopped numerous times; but the next time was when I went to Germany with Harry Kipper.* We did a performance in Cologne, where we saw a lot of anti-Semitic graffiti in the town. It was during a Theatre of the World festival, and we were totally appalled at not just one anti-Semitic slogan but consistently, in bathrooms, on walls, even in the theatre festival office. . . . We couldn't believe that no one even covered that up. We felt that it was still part of the culture, so we decided to do a perform-

---

*The Kippers, aka the Kipper Kids, "became infamous in the '70s for performances that deconstructed every learned nicety into the raw human behavior observable in infants." One of the Kippers was Martin von Haselberg; the other was Brian Routh. They were scheduled to tour Europe in 1981; when von Haselberg could not go, Finley replaced him and, as described in the text, touched off a near riot in Cologne at the Theatre for the World Festival when she and Routh appeared as Eva Braun and Adolf Hitler. C. Carr, "Unspeakable Practices, Unnatural Acts," *The Village Voice*, June 24, 1986.

ance where we were really going to be discussing, dealing with, Hitler's own personal sex life and things like that.

So Brian Routh,* who I performed with, he was Hitler and I was Anna. And we did all those German songs and we pretended like we were dogs and we took chocolate pudding and put it on our rear ends.

C. CARR: [Finley and Routh] had installed several rotting carcasses of beef in the space, where it was [standing room only]—over 800 people—on each of their four nights. [Routh] goosestepped and saluted, naked from the waist down. Finley wore a corset and garter belt. . . .

The audience became increasingly agitated. Finley stuffed toy sharks with hot dogs and sauerkraut and hung them from her body for [Routh to eat]. They began reporting anti-Semitic incidents they had witnessed in Cologne, then began to rub chocolate pudding on each other's asses. Spectators started arguing among themselves. "Get off!" "No, she's right . . ." "We don't need to hear this about Hitler," and so on.

KAREN FINLEY: We were drinking beer and pretending we were dogs, lapping it up, with these German patriotic tunes, and one time this woman comes down to the stage with this mop saying "Germans are not dogs!" and takes this mop and starts attacking me and hitting and beating me.

I needed help, I'm not a violent person, I didn't hit back. Brian took the mop out of her hands and said, "If you touch her again I'll kill you," and with that, all these people from the crowd started coming down to the stage, screaming, really upset with us. And it was just totally amazing; we had to go backstage and end the performance because they didn't want to hear about it anymore. They yelled "It's over with, we weren't the Nazis"— and we realized we had struck a chord.

This was 1981. So then they told us—the Theatre of the World Festival—that they couldn't guarantee our security, meaning we were supposed to perform, to honor our contract, but they weren't guaranteeing our safety. And they said they were receiving threats and, being twenty-six years old, I was really scared. I was scared to go on stage. I thought someone was going to shoot me.

———

In 1987, Finley was asked to be part of *Mike's Talent Show,* a show that Michael Smith, the *Village Voice* critic, had put together for a cable TV taping. But when Finley would not "soften" it for television, the piece she was scheduled to perform, *I'm an Ass Man,* hit the cutting-room floor.

C. CARR: Police stopped a couple of her performances in San Francisco. Her reputation began to precede her, so that when a Los Angeles club booked her, they told her "No four-letter words and don't show your body." She canceled.

———

*Karen Finley's graduate adviser at the San Francisco Art Institute, whom she later married.

In London, Finley ran into a more serious problem because of *I'm an Ass Man* and her unwillingness to compromise her art by self-censoring it.

KAREN FINLEY: I had this problem in London when Scotland Yard came to my show, and I was actually threatened with deportation. I do a short monologue called "I'm an Ass Man," which is about a man—in his voice—wanting to rape a woman in the subway. And when he is about to, she has her period; so he stops the rape. It's only about five minutes, it's in my new book.

KAREN FINLEY *(Shock Treatment): Even though I'm married and I've got work and kids, I can't stop looking at butt. I can't stop looking at derriere. I can't stop looking at tush. I can't stop looking at rump roast. Baby, I'm an ass man.*

Once I spotted her in the subway: short, Hispanic, Polish, Chinese, Irish or Jewish, with a huge butt just waiting to be fucked, just asking to be fucked. She was short-waisted and all I wanted to do was get her against that cold, slimy, rat turd wall and get my cock inside her. She's wearing those four-inch cork wedgies that went out of style in the early '70s. And she's wearing those polyester pants and I can see her panty lines through her slacks. . . .

I crack open the seat of her pants, just listening to the fabric tear. I love the sound of ripping polyester. I love the smell of ass in open air. Then I get my fist, my hand, and I push myself up into her ass. I'm feeling the butt pressure on my arm, on my wrist, it's feeling good. I'm feeling her up. It's turning me on. It's turning me on. I can hear that sound. I'm feeling her up. I reach up to her pussy, feeling that fat little mound, that little bird's nest. I keep my hand in there and then, just when I'm ready to mount her, I take my hand out. I see my arm, my hand, and I see that THE WOMAN HAS HER PERIOD.

How could you do this to me, woman? How could you do this to me? How could you be on the rag on me! I'D BE THE BEST FUCK IN YOUR LIFE! THE BEST PIECE OF COCK IN YOUR LIFE, GIRL! THE BEST RAPE IN YOUR LIFE!

And I was running. I'm running. I'm trying to get those purple hearts off my hands, out of my cuticles, but the blood won't come out of my lifeline, out of my heart line, the blood won't wash off my hands. Be a long time before I use that hand to shake my dick after I piss.

KAREN FINLEY: I was to perform "I'm an Ass Man" at the Institute of Contemporary Art in London, and they would not let me. Scotland Yard basically told the museum that their funding would be cut off if I performed there. Their funding is millions of pounds each year; it would be like cutting off the funding to the Whitney. They also told me they couldn't guarantee my safety, and that if I performed, there would be a strong possibility of being deported, which would also mean I couldn't come back.

They would come to my performances, I saw them come, Scotland Yard. I was given a way out, that I could perform if I didn't take my clothes off. Or I could take my clothes off—I could do a strip show—but I couldn't talk. There's a law in London that a woman cannot talk while she is taking her clothes off. . . .

It really got very, very ugly. I basically had to leave the country. I was fearful for my life. That is how dangerous and unsettling the feeling was, because of the protesters and people there . . . at the hotel, and walking down the street. I still cannot perform in London. They told me that my type of work, the kind of work I do, cannot be done in W1, London, or wherever, because it's close to the queen. My records could not be sold in London.

The tabloids in London, there was a cover story on me; they made up things about me, said I did all these things, called me Fruity Karen, they called me the Porno Queen. They had pictures of me. They even made up my entire biography, made up stories about me. I do get a lot of press, it's sort of funny. I still can't perform in London.

I'm going to do an installation in Philadelphia next week, the end of the month [March 1991], and the title is "The Virgin Mary is Pro-Choice, and Other Relevant Truths." Already there's a fear of blasphemy. I want to put important women through history: Eve was pro-choice; Joan of Arc was pro-choice; Cleopatra was pro-choice; and I believe that the Virgin Mary was pro-choice. Gabriel came down and told her that this was happening. I feel like she was just a pro-choice kind of gal. So, already there are letters about blasphemy coming in, and I'm going to be doing anti-[Persian Gulf] war work, too. So I know that this situation with the NEA isn't something that's going to go away.

This is my life and I know I'm going to be bringing up controversy, and I think that it would be so much easier if American society just accepted the fact that that's what the artist's job is, to basically bring a mirror to the culture, and turn it around, and make us look at ourselves.

c. CARR: In [Finley] id-speak, shitting and vomiting and fucking are all equal. Desire attaches to disgust. Finley's work moves beyond rage to the trigger for that rage. To damage and longing, the desperate want for something, the hole in all of us that nothing ever fills.

———

Finley was afraid that the NEA in the future would deny support to any artist like her who refused to adhere to whatever political agenda was set in Washington, D.C.

KAREN FINLEY: I was the first generation of my family who was able to become an artist, so I took [the help I received] very seriously. I looked at it as my being given equal access, the same access, as people who have money or inherited wealth. That's why I look at what's happening now as censorship, because in the future people getting out of school, if they don't really have the correct political agenda in their work, then they won't be able to get that grant. And if you come from a working-class background, like me, if I hadn't got that first NEA grant I just wouldn't be here. That's how it is. I wouldn't have gone to art school if I didn't get a grant. That's what I'm mostly fighting for, the right of people to become the artists that they want to be.

BILL KAUFFMAN:* [T]here are actually writers and artists in the American heartland who want nothing to do with the National Endowment for the Arts. They think that government subsidy is corrupting and crippling, suitable only for fat and happy eunuchs. . . .

Is it then the artist's lot to starve and scrape, to eat rice and home-baked bread and scribble feverishly in the darkest hours? Yes! Comforted, coddled, cossetted artists create mediocre art.

Can anyone name one major piece of American fiction that would not have been written without the NEA's beneficence? How about a significant minor work?

BARBARA RASKIN:† Being awarded an NEA grant for fiction saved my life. I think I would have stopped writing forever if I hadn't gotten it. In 1980 $12,500 meant the difference between down-and-out or up-and-coming. I had never before received any professional support or financial encouragement. This money from the government was an affirmation of my artistic intention; somebody out there had heard me and believed in what I was trying to do.

———

Like the work of the other artists denied performance arts grants in the summer of 1989, Holly Hughes's work had received critical acclaim:

LAURIE STONE: [Hughes's] language soars like skywriting; keen ironies, delivered in her characteristic tough-girl drawl, flare into lush poetic riffs . . . her poetry has never been more subtle.

———

Hughes's work is softer than Karen Finley's, less controversial. In her grant application to the NEA, Hughes cited a piece she had written and performed in 1989, *World Without End.*

HOLLY HUGHES *(World Without End): The woman leans back in the chair and closes her eyes, remembering her mother's immortal French. From off-stage left comes the faint sounds of an accordion. I'd really prefer a set of bagpipes, but the accordion is more reasonable. The song is sweet, like a remembered childhood song, something upbeat, por favor. The woman smiles, the song is part of her reverie. Suddenly, her eyes open. She realizes the song is not part of the dream, but is really happening. A woman enters playing the accordion. She is tall, with broad shoulders and good bones, elegant and eccentric. A mid-western Marlene Dietrich, let's say. She's wearing a smoking jacket and very little else other than the accordion. She reminds you of those Saturday mornings when your dad would dress up like Clark*

---

*Novelist; author of *Every Man a King* (1989).

†Author of five novels including the 1987 best-seller *Hot Flashes,* which she wrote with the assistance of an NEA grant.

Gable and chase your mother around the breakfast nook with his semi-annual hard-on.

As the song progresses, the woman in the chair relaxes and dives back into her dream. She speaks as though she's dictating a letter into a foreign language, one she barely knows. . . .

I'd say "O Mama, I can't sleep at night. I smell the ocean." Not that far-off Atlantic, not the unbelievable Pacific. I'm talking about that old ocean, that blue blanket that used to cover this country, all of us, from the teenage anorexics to the Burger King evangelists, all of us sleeping with the dinosaurs, the blackcapped chickadees, our heads full of fish, waiting to be born.

That's the ocean that floods my bed each night, and what can I do about it, Mama?

I get up in the morning and the world is just flat and dry and there is no hint, in the parking lot, at the mall, at the 7-11, of why I am so full of ocean. . . .

O, I can't watch TV anymore, I can't watch TV. There's always the same guy on TV laughing and everyone laughing with him, except for this woman and me. I know she's gonna cry enough in the next week to flood us all out of our houses, even the ones who are laughing.

Am I the only one who's afraid of drowning?

Teach me to swim, Mama! Teach me how to read this sorrow so I can resist the common current. Mama, teach me that French!

Mama says: "What makes you think I know any French?" Her voice is cool and blind, but, and this is a big but, she puts her hand on her hips and I see those hips move under her wrap-around skirt so heavy and full, I can smell the memory of ocean drifting out from between her legs. O, there is POWER in my mother's hips! I tell you what I've seen! I've seen her hands with their tapered fingers run from her hips down to her thighs, I've seen her tongue sneak out of her mouth to wet her lips when everyone else was just watching TV and I know, O, yes, I know, my mother is FULL of FRENCH. . . .

Mama took me to the bathroom and started asking me questions. Taking off her clothes and asking me questions. With every garment I got a new question. She unbuttons her blouse and asks: "Do you want to know where babies come from?" She shimmies out of her skirt and says: "Are you ready for the meaning of life? I'm talking about the secret life, the French night club where we're all dancing? The hidden room where we stash our gold." She says this and VOILA!

My mother's got no underwear on. Her pantyhose . . . it's down there on the ground, sulking, feeling sorry for himself. Then that mean old pantyhose just slinks on out of there, belly to the ground. And my mother is standing in front of me. . . . (She mimes to the audience) NAKED. Uh HUH. NAKED. And glistening. Bigger than life, shining from the inside out, just like that giant jumbo Rhode Island Red Hen in front of the Chicken Palace and Riborama. . . .

———

NEA Chairman Frohnmayer gave no official reason for denying those grants to Holly Hughes, Karen Finley, Tim Miller, and John Fleck. But the situation was a familiar one in the history of censorship of literature and art, going back at least to the day when Henry Vizetelly was imprisoned for publishing Zola's *The Soil:* Newspaper editors and columnists in touch with the agendas of right-wing political and religious groups publicize "scandalous" information about the work of certain authors, publishers, or artists, received from confidants within the government or sources in the literary or arts community; this prompts the right-wing groups to bring pressure on government officials to take repressive action.

The idea for the *Washington Times*'s "exposure" of the "political" and "obscene" character of the work of Finley, Fleck, and Hughes had probably originated a month earlier, on May 11, when in the *New York Post* the conservative syndicated columnists Rowland Evans and Robert Novak (basing their report on information supplied them by "an administrative insider") labeled Karen Finley's act as "the performance of a nude, chocolate-smeared young woman in what an NEA memorandum calls a 'solo theatre piece' and what the artist herself describes as triggering emotional and taboo events."* But Evans and Novak made no mention of canned yams and said nothing whatsoever about Holly Hughes's work.

A few days later, Frohnmayer's advisory council, the National Council for the Arts, having read the newspapers, met to discuss eleven performance arts applicants (including Finley, Hughes, Miller, and Fleck) and voted to defer action on all of these, pending receipt of further information on those they feared were "controversial." The aim evidently was to remove Frohnmayer from the administrative hot seat that Washington politicians and conservative newspapers had put him in. If he stalled until after Congress acted on pending legislation to reauthorize the NEA, he would be spared the necessity to prove to Capitol Hill that he had their concerns about "controversial" art in mind, and in hand. In the event, however, Frohnmayer chose to act.

The *Washington Times*'s June 12, 1990, story gave no source for its depictions of the Finley, Fleck, and Hughes pieces. When these descriptions were repeated in the newspaper's July 2 edition, after Frohnmayer had announced his rejection of grants to the four performance artists, the newspaper listed the following as its sources: "National Endowment for the Arts, *High Performance* magazine, *New Art Examiner, Artweek, The Drama Review, The Village Voice.*"

It was, however, an article by David Gergen in the July 30, 1990, issue of *U.S. News & World Report* that was most upsetting to Holly Hughes. The article repeated the inaccurate information about Hughes's work that had been published in *The Washington Times,* giving it greater credibility and a wider audience. It led Cliff Scott of Hughes's performance art group, Downtown Art Company, to write a letter of protest, and a demand for retraction, to editor-at-large Gergen:

---

*Even earlier, the country's most powerful unofficial czar of popular culture, Donald Wildmon, had opened a campaign to smear the NEA with a full-page ad in *The Washington Times* of February 13, 1990.

CLIFF SCOTT: Dear Mr. Gergen, Regarding your article in the July 30th issue of *U.S. News and World Report,* not only do I disagree with the opinions you express in the entire article, but its inaccuracies are shocking. I am writing in behalf of Holly Hughes and the Downtown Art Co. to express outrage for the blatant factual inaccuracy which your article embraces. . . .

In writing about Holly Hughes's play WORLD WITHOUT END, you state that Holly Hughes's "performance on stage includes a scene in which she places her hand up her vagina." *This is just not true. Holly Hughes's work does not involve nudity or simulated sex acts.*

Have you ever seen any of the work of these artists? Specifically, have you seen Holly Hughes's work? In speaking to your researcher, Ann Andrews, she told me that your only source for information for describing Ms. Hughes's work was obtained from *The Washington Times,* a source which is, as you should know, a highly suspicious source for accurate information relating to the work of Holly Hughes.

No other publication has repeated *The Washington Times*'s misinformed description of Ms. Hughes's work. In all the months of this controversy, to our knowledge, not a single other publication has relied on *The Washington Times* as an accurate source to describe Ms. Hughes's work. . . .

The appearance of your gross inaccuracy at this time is particularly damaging to Holly Hughes's career, and, as a partner in Downtown Art Co., adversely affects the work of the company. As you probably know, since it has been reported widely by the press, the National Council of the National Endowment for the Arts is meeting in Washington next weekend to review, among other things, a proposal from Downtown Art Co. for a new project written by Holly Hughes and directed by Ellen Sebastian.

An editor, reporter, and commentator of your reputation and stature increases the likelihood that this lie about Ms. Hughes's work will be viewed as accurate. And since this lie is printed in such a respectable magazine, your byline will become the "primary source" for other publications. *You will be believed.* Your outrageously inaccurate article may influence the members of the National Council on the Arts and many others. . . .

On behalf of Holly Hughes and her company, Downtown Art Co., we demand an *immediate, clear, and prominent retraction* of your misrepresentation of Ms. Hughes's work. If there is any syndication of your article, in print or broadcast, including wire service, we also demand an immediate, clear, and prominent retraction. These retractions in no way limit Holly Hughes's or Downtown Art Co.'s right to seek additional relief in the future. . . .

———

Gergen did not acknowledge Scott's letter. However, *U.S. News & World Report*'s Kathryn Bushkin responded with a letter dated August 3, 1990, addressed not to Scott but to John Frohnmayer, with a copy to Scott:

KATHRYN BUSHKIN: Dear Chairman Frohnmayer, In Dave Gergen's July 30th editorial in *U.S. News & World Report* regarding the National Endowment for the Arts funding, he inaccurately described one scene in Holly Hughes's work. We are running a correction in our 8/13 issue, and a copy is enclosed for your information.

—

The correction—in very small print, in a very unobtrusive place—read as follows:

U.S. NEWS & WORLD REPORT: Correction. David Gergen's July 30 editorial described one segment of artist Holly Hughes's performance as including "a scene in which she places her hand up her vagina." That was incorrect. David Gergen regrets the error.

—

Gergen and *U.S. News* were seeking to support the embattled NEA and Frohnmayer's floundering efforts to save it—even if that meant maligning, and supporting censorship of, artists like Karen Finley and Holly Hughes. Although Gergen's article did not back the position consistently voiced by Frohnmayer that Congress should delete the existing Helms-Yates "obscenity" limitation in the NEA's authorization law, it did support Frohnmayer's (and the Bush administration's) position that Congress should attach no other "content" restrictions on the art and artists funded by the NEA. Gergen seemed to believe that the new chairman should have been trusted by Congress (and the White House) to censor politically, sexually, and religiously obnoxious art on his own, without an explicit command in the law that he do so.

DAVID GERGEN: In its laudable desire to maintain standards of decency, Congress should leave in place its current rules against funding obscene works but should avoid imposing new restrictions that would handcuff the NEA. By rejecting the four controversial grants this summer, the NEA has shown a sufficient sensibility that it should now be allowed to run its own show. It knows where to draw the line.

C. CARR: As attacks on the National Endowment for the Arts escalate, each terribly civilized meeting of its august advisory body—the National Council on the Arts—seems to move the culture war to some new and barbarous plane. The council convenes quarterly to approve grants, and used to rubber-stamp [the artist peer-review panels' recommendations to] them. But no more. The meetings have begun to follow an insidious pattern: Days before they begin, some explosive misrepresentation is leaked to the press, distraught council members recoil at the specter of public outrage, and Chairman John Frohnmayer tosses a few artists/scapegoats to the Right. . . .

In the apparent hope that the NEA would make its own list of restrictions, council member Jacob Neusner arrived with a proposal that made the Helms amendment look benevolent. Neusner suggested no funding for "any project that advocates or promotes a particular political, ideological, religious, or partisan point of view, or a particular program of social action or change. . . ."* A professor of religious studies at the University of South Florida, Neusner is the man who voted against all solo performance fellowships because that art form "serves a part of our population." This is the man William Safire calls a "prickly intellectual giant."

Even though Neusner's resolution was defeated, the Right's agenda expanded at this meeting, from sexual politics to any kind of politics. During the long battle over the Interarts grants, Neusner and *American Scholar* editor Joseph Epstein—neocon down to his little bow tie—moved to reject grants to [sixteen arts organizations and] artists, because, as Epstein put it, "I sniff politics." . . .

To paraphrase Pastor Niemoeller: "First they came for the homosexuals; then they came for the chocolate-smeared women; then they came for . . . Martha Clarke?" She's working on a piece about endangered species. Others on the endangered artists' list address racism, homelessness, environmental issues.

HOLLY HUGHES: So . . . Bill T. Jones, who is an African-American dancer, very well respected as a dancer, just did a concert in Atlanta, and he does a solo piece that he performs in the nude, a memorial piece for his lover Arnie Zane, who was also his partner, who died a few years ago of AIDS. He performed the piece the first night, someone in the theatre called the vice squad, and he was informed by the police that if he did the piece a second night in the nude he would be arrested. . . .

Jock Sturges does photographs that are large-format nude, done with parental approval. They're nude and they're not exploitive, he's not selling them to some sort of porn magazines, and he's been very much respected, for years, as a photographer in the Bay Area.†

I think the same judge that outlawed 2 Live Crew would probably have outlawed me, and Karen Finley. I think they outlawed them because black men making money outside of the system and having power and having control of their own voice is very threatening. Even if their work is sexist . . . you don't get rid of anything you don't like by censoring it.

---

*Neusner's proposal for censorship was almost as sweeping as the defeated Helms amendment, quoted earlier.

†The "censorship" of fine-art photographer Jock Sturges's work, by a Justice Department–inspired joint FBI–San Francisco police raid on his studio, which resulted in the seizure of all of Sturges's work and records relating to children, was described in Chapter 29. The press and the public are only beginning to become aware of the formidable threat to civil liberties, freedom of expression, and the right of privacy presented by child pornography laws and their enforcement by police, prosecutors, and judges. See in this connection the insightful and foreboding analysis of the potentially broad consequences of the Supreme Court's recent ruling (in *Osborne* v. *Ohio*) that states may criminally punish the mere possession (or viewing) of "child pornography" at home, by Stephen Wermiel in *The Wall Street Journal*, April 23, 1990. There are eighteen states with laws similar to Ohio's; the New York legislature has been fiercely pressured by anti-pornography organizations to enact such a law. Now that the Supreme Court has upheld the Ohio statute, the pressures on other state legislatures and Congress to enact equally repressive laws are likely to increase.

These developments at the NEA and the politically appointed National Council—this politicization of the grant-awarding process—pointedly raised anew the question: Was it possible for the federal government to encourage the arts and assist artists without also "censoring" them, and, if not, was it not the better part of wisdom—and of liberal politics—to seek to remove the government from this sort of invidious involvement with the arts.

BARBARA RASKIN: Discrediting or discarding government support of the arts—because of unreasonable demands initiated by the likes of Jesse Helms—would be cutting off our nose to spite our face. "They" would simply use the same dollars for even more mischievous deeds. It is better to fight each act or case of censorship individually rather than throw away a subsidization needed by America's artists. We might have to wage war block by block but conflict at the barricades strengthens both the artists and the arts.

In the fall of 1990, Congress went back to work on new NEA authorization language; but now the stakes for the NEA and the country's artists and art institutions were higher. During the previous session the main question had been whether legislation might be enacted that would restrict the award of federal funds to artists who could be relied upon not to produce what many legislators, and the NEA's critics, considered to be obscene or sacrilegious work. Now Congress began seriously debating whether the federal government should not discontinue all direct funding of artists and arts institutions, as well as whether restrictions might be placed upon the artistic expression funded by the government without violating the First Amendment. At bottom, for the arts community, the latter issue was the profoundly distressing one of whether Congress might be bulldozed into passing a new law that would allow presidentially appointed government officials like John Frohnmayer, popularly elected politicians like Jesse Helms, and self-appointed religious leaders like Donald Wildmon to control the images that American artists and arts institutions communicate.

By November 1990, the strident move by conservatives in Congress to take the federal government out of the business of providing assistance to the arts was defeated; it had been passionately opposed by the arts community and their advocates in Congress, and the principle of government assistance was by now too deeply entrenched to be dislodged even by insistent complaints that taxpayer money was being spent on trash and filth as well as on art. The Bush White House was also disposed not to go along with the proposition that if the government could not identify a constitutional way to deny funding to deeply offensive art, it ought to stop funding art altogether.

The question of what restrictions, if any, could and should be placed on federally funded art, and how this might be done, proved even more nettlesome in this Congress than in the previous one. Legislative bills posed answers ranging from no restrictions whatever to restrictions like those proposed during the previous Congress by Jesse Helms. Finally, in a session characterized by more than usual confusion, "compromise" legislation would emerge that Harvard Law Professor Kathleen Sullivan described as "both better and worse than the old law." While the new legislation appeared to be clean of overt restrictions on artistic expression, it concealed what one disconsolate arts council member would aptly describe as a "booby trap."

The White House had opposed the imposition by Congress of any restriction on the NEA's grant-giving authority, wanting Congress to let its man at the NEA, Chairman Frohnmayer, deal personally with the problem of ideologically offensive art. At a press conference held in April 1990, the president made this clear, saying, "[I am] deeply offended by some of the filth that I see into which federal money has gone."

PRESIDENT GEORGE BUSH: [B]ut I would prefer to have this matter handled by a very sensitive, knowledgeable man of the arts,* John Frohnmayer, than risk censorship or getting the federal government into telling every artist what he or she can paint or how he or she might express themselves.

———

From the beginning, in an effort to keep politics out of the NEA's programs to promote the arts, nongovernmental artist peer-review panels were established to serve as the NEA's critical grant-making mechanism, with the twenty-six politically appointed members of the Council, as well as the presidentially appointed chairperson, relegated essentially to reviewing and vetoing roles. The impact of the NEA bureaucracy on the politics of art was for over twenty years largely limited to the role it had in selecting the membership of, and organizing, those artist peer-review panels. The professional artists who made up the panels were the real decision makers; inasmuch as they were outside the government, they were not susceptible to political control. The only criticism this left them open to was cronyism, and that at times they voted on each other's applications. (To avoid direct conflict-of-interest situations, the practice had developed that a panel member who was a potential grantee would leave the meeting room when his or her application came up for action.)

However, under the legislation Congress enacted in late 1990, the political independence of the artist peer-review panels was deliberately weakened

---

*Frohnmayer grew up "surrounded by music and the law." His father was a lawyer, his mother a pianist and singer. Two siblings became professional singers; a brother is Oregon's attorney general. An "accomplished singer himself," Frohnmayer chose a career in law but remained an active amateur singer. He went to Stanford University, spent a year at Union Theological Seminary, then earned a master's degree in Christian ethics at the University of Chicago. After spending three years in the Navy, he went to Oregon Law School; obtaining his degree in 1972, he entered the practice of law. See "Fresh Focus," *University of Chicago Magazine,* April 1991. Frohnmayer was picked for the job of NEA head by President Bush after working on Bush's election campaign in Oregon.

by a requirement that lay members, recommended by senators and other politicians, be added to each panel. On January 3, 1991, after the new reauthorization legislation was enacted, Chairman Frohnmayer sent a letter to all U.S. senators requesting them to "forward the names of prospective panelists from your state/district" who have "some expertise" in the panel's art area and who could help *"assure that general standards of decency and respect for the diversity of beliefs and values represented by the American public are considered"* in the recommendations made by the panels (my italics). Frohnmayer noted that each year over one hundred such panels were convened by the NEA.

In addition, under the new law the presidentially appointed members of the National Council on the Arts were given increased power to refuse to support artists and arts projects which to them, as one neoconservative Council member intimated, smell of politics. This was accomplished by stripping the chair of the power to overrule a Council decision to reject a grant recommended by a peer-review panel; the chair retained the power only to veto a Council recommendation to make a grant. While the Chair's previous blanket power to reverse Council recommendations had almost never been used, it was potentially a formidable power; limiting it entailed a major dispersal of the chair's political power and signified the extent to which Congress had lost faith in John E. Frohnmayer's ability or willingness to prevent government funds being spent on politically controversial art.

Finally, the NEA bureaucracy was given the task of arranging to inspect and monitor funded work in progress. The design of these changes became plain enough: the NEA was being restructured by Congress and a reluctant Frohnmayer the better to control the arts.

The rhetoric for this transformation was that the NEA was to be re-geared to serve the interests not of artists, the direct beneficiaries of NEA grants and fellowships, but of American taxpayers, the indirect beneficiaries. The amended legislative declaration of purpose regarding the NEA is headed by these words: *"The arts and the humanities belong to all the people of the United States."*

Officially, the late-1990 legislation kept the NEA in the business of helping "to create and sustain" not only a "climate encouraging freedom of thought, imagination, and inquiry" but also the "material conditions facilitating the release of creative artistic talent." It justified continued government "financial assistance" to American "artists and the organizations that support their work" as a means, first, to sustain "worldwide respect and admiration for the Nation's high qualities as a leader in the realm of ideas and of the spirit" and, second, to "preserve [the Nation's] multicultural heritage as well as support new ideas." But in carrying out these functions, said Congress, the NEA must be "sensitive to the nature of public sponsorship," and to "the high place accorded by the American people to . . . the fostering of mutual respect for the diverse beliefs and values of all persons and groups." These admonitions were contained in the new legislation's "Declaration of Findings and Purposes."

The "booby trap" was in the law's authorizing provisions, which in critical part read: "No [grant of assistance] payment shall be made . . . except upon application therefore . . . in accordance with regulations issued and procedures established by the Chairperson, [who] shall ensure that (1) artistic excellence and artistic merit are the criteria by which applications are judged, *taking into consideration general standards of decency and respect for the diverse beliefs and values of the American public* [emphasis mine]; and (2) . . . that obscenity is without artistic merit, is not protected speech and shall not be funded. Projects, productions, workshops, and programs that are determined to be obscene are prohibited from receiving financial assistance . . . from the National Endowment for the Arts." The phrase "determined to be obscene" was defined in another section of the law to mean: "determined in a final judgment of a court of record and of competent jurisdiction . . . to be obscene"; and the term "obscene" was defined to mean what the Supreme Court in *Miller* had said it meant.

The new law attempted to establish three tiers of morally and politically sensitive censors of American art and artists: the politically recommended lay members of the artist peer-group panels; the politically appointed Council members; and the politically appointed chairperson. Under the law, these "decency and respect" censors could, in the future, turn down an application on the ground that the project ran afoul of the legislatively mandated "general standards of decency," or failed to respect "the diverse beliefs and values of the American public." The potential efficacy of this new system of art censorship can easily be seen by considering whether Robert Mapplethorpe's "Man in Polyester Suit," Andres Serrano's "Piss Christ," Karen Finley's "Aunt Mandy," or Holly Hughes's "World Without End" violate general standards of decency or show disrespect for American racial, religious, and family values. No doubt they do, and many persons feel strongly that they should not be subsidized or assisted by the government. But there should be little doubt that the deliberate rejection of applicants seeking assistance for the creation and exhibition of such "indecent" or "disrespectful" art would violate freedom of expression and therefore be unconstitutional.

The result of the new legislation was this: (a) the NEA was officially relieved of the task given it by the legislation of 1989 to administratively censor artists by rejecting arts projects considered *by the NEA* to come within the *Miller* definition of the obscene as amplified in the 1989 law; (b) the NEA was given explicit authority to defund (require the repayment of a grant already paid out to) any artist or art organization found by it (after a hearing) to have been *found by a court of law* to have created or disseminated with financial assistance from the NEA any art work that was legally obscene; however, (c) the NEA was for the first time required to refuse to fund arts projects that in its judgment—not a court's—might violate "general standards of decency," or fail to show "respect for the diverse beliefs and values of the American public." Neither one of these enormously elastic phrases was defined.

The true import of the new legislation did not get well ventilated either on the floors of Congress or in the press. However, at a publicized symposium held shortly after the enactment of the legislation, Council member Roy Goodman, a state senator from Manhattan, reported on the "booby trap" in the new legislation. As California lawyer Peter Kyros, a former cultural advisor to President Carter, said, "What Congress has done is craft a content restriction that doesn't look like one. It's very subtle." For his part, the NEA's Frohnmayer expressed relief that the arts agency had at least survived, saying that the new legislation was "far better than what we expected only a few weeks ago."

Postmortem comments from the NEA's most influential and ardent defenders in Congress, Sidney Yates of Illinois and Pat Williams of Montana, were cautiously phrased. Williams said he had "questions about the constitutionality" of the "decency" language but considered the legislation as a whole to be "a genuine win." Yates said he disliked the "decency" provision that had been inserted on the eve of enactment, but that after months of conflict, "you begin to think in terms of acceptabilities." Somewhat surprisingly, some of those on the other side of the political aisle who had sought unsuccessfully to get rid of the NEA also professed frustration. Thus, Dana Rohrabacher of California claimed that the new law left taxpayers "without one guarantee that their money won't be used to subsidize things that they believe are totally immoral."* The most candid analysis of the new law was given by Representative Ted Weiss of New York on the House floor on October 15, 1990:

TED WEISS: Mr. Chairman, listen to the language of the Williams-Coleman substitute. It requires that in establishing application procedures the NEA chairperson has to ensure that "artistic excellence and merit are the criteria by which applicants are judged, taking into consideration general standards of decency and respect for the diverse beliefs and values of the American public."

What does that mean? Mr. David Duke, the former head of the Ku Klux Klan, who got 44 percent of the vote for the U.S. Senate in Louisiana, does he represent the values of the American public, that we are supposed to be abiding by?

The language is so vague that it is exactly the kind of thing the Supreme Court has repeatedly held to be unconstitutional, and I think that will happen again. . . .

What "standard of general decency" will be used? How can one determine whether a particular work of art is within "general standards of de-

---

*Rohrabacher's use of the term "guarantee" may be a clue to his real thinking: congressmen like him and Helms will still need to rely on the judgments of the NEA chair, Council members, and lay peer-review panel members to reject controversial art projects.

cency" or respects "the diverse beliefs and values of the American public"? What is the American public? Who is to take into consideration these standards—the Chairperson when making the regulations, or the panels when they are reviewing the applications?

These funding standards are so broad that they have no constitutional meaning, they permit any administrator to make speech-based decisions without any fixed standards. Consequently, they will chill creative output because an artist simply will have no clear indication of their meaning. These considerations have led the Supreme Court consistently to hold vague and amorphous content standards, such as the ones in the Williams-Coleman substitute, to be unconstitutional. . . .

In addition to being unconstitutionally vague, the Williams-Coleman prohibition against indecency and disrespect violates the bedrock principle that the government may not impose content restrictions on speech merely because society may find that speech offensive or disagreeable. Until the Court decides something is "obscene," it is protected by the First Amendment. The First Amendment stringently limits restrictions on indecent speech and art. In *Sable Communication* v. *FCC,* 109 S.Ct. at 2836, the Supreme Court stressed that "sexual expression which is indecent but not obscene is protected by the First Amendment." And the First Amendment does not disappear because the government picks up the tab. The Supreme Court has upheld this principle over and over again.

———

Writing in the April 15, 1991, issue of *The Nation,* Professor Owen Fiss of the Yale Law School also read the legislative outcome of the protracted 1990 congressional debates as providing nothing to celebrate.

PROFESSOR OWEN FISS: The specter of N.E.A. censorship is still with us. The infamous Helms amendment has lapsed [but] the danger to artistic freedom remains. . . .

Last November a new N.E.A. statute was enacted that ostensibly supplants the Helms amendment. . . . The new statute appears to be a step forward, but it actually moves in the opposite direction.

It compounds the sanctions for an obscenity conviction by providing that if N.E.A. funds are used to produce a work later deemed obscene by a court, the funds will have to be repaid and the recipient will be ineligible for further funding until full repayment is made. . . .

Even more worrisome is Congress' decision to consolidate the decision-making power over grants in the hands of the N.E.A. chair. . . .* What standards will the chair use in making this choice? The new statute is explicit. It directs the chair to insure that "artistic excellence and artistic merit are the criteria by which applications are judged, taking into consideration general standards of decency and respect for the diverse beliefs and

---

*The more serious problem, it appears to me, is that the new law disperses the chair's decision-making power, as discussed in the text.

values of the American public." By directing the chair to apply "general standards of decency" . . . the statute frees the N.E.A. chair to deny funding to a bold and provocative project that he or she deems offensive to "decency," even though the project has serious artistic or political value and thus falls outside the constitutional definition of obscenity. Moreover, as with grants under the Helms amendment, N.E.A. recipients must give assurances that their projects comply with the new decency standards.*

N.E.A. chair Frohnmayer recently sought to reassure his advisory body, the National Council on the Arts, when it expressed opposition to promulgating explicit decency standards, saying, "I am not going to be a decency Czar here." But in light of the structure of the statute, as well as the overall policies of the Administration and Frohnmayer's performance over the past year, that disclaimer rings hollow.

—

In the spring of 1991, a suit was filed in a federal court in California on behalf of Karen Finley, Holly Hughes, John Fleck, and Tim Miller—the "NEA Four"—which seeks, as amended, to have the court declare unconstitutional for violating freedom of expression both Frohnmayer's controversial decision to deny them performance art grants under the 1989 law, and the new "decency" and "respect for beliefs and values" restrictions that Congress attached to the NEA's grant-making authority in the legislation enacted in November 1990. It is to be hoped that the federal judiciary will nullify both these recent efforts by a distracted, distraught, and deeply divided Congress to attach to American artists and arts an ideological and sexual censorship that is thoroughly obnoxious to democratic traditions. But such action by the courts is unlikely to forestall further efforts to legislate a moral censorship over artists who accept federal assistance, or to eliminate government assistance of this kind to the arts.

It seems plain to me that while the Constitution does not require the government to adopt a program of support or encouragement of the arts (or for that matter of public schools, libraries, or museums), it does require that such a program, once adopted, should not deny its support to an artist or arts organization on any ground other than insufficient artistic merit or promise. Even the denial of public support to artistic works that have been found by a court to be "obscene" seems to me of doubtful wisdom and dubious constitutional validity, because—as Justice Brennan pointed out in his dissenting opinion in *Miller*—the definition of the "obscene" adumbrated by Chief Justice Warren Burger in that case is too broad and too vague to assure to artists and writers the freedom of expression that the First Amendment contemplates. The NEA's refusal to make grants to Finley, Hughes, Fleck, and Miller; the arrests and prosecutions of museum curator Dennis Barrie, record-store owner Charles Freeman, and the leader and

---

*The new law and implementing NEA regulations established unprecedented procedures for applicant artists and art institutions that require detailed periodic descriptions of the works to be produced or performed in compliance with the terms of the application and the law.

members of the rap music group 2 Live Crew; and the chill on artistic freedom that indirectly resulted from those attacks on the freedom of artists* testify to the shortcomings inherent in the *Miller* doctrine.

Flawed as was the *Miller* doctrine at its inception, it recently was further weakened by the Rehnquist Court. In a little-noticed case decided in 1987, *Pope* v. *Illinois,* † the "serious artistic value" clause of the tripartite "test" for obscenity was reexamined and attenuated; another ambiguous and potentially debilitating gloss was laid upon the formula established during the sixties by Justice Brennan and the Warren Court for the constitutional protection of writers and artists, publishers and curators.

The "social value" doctrine provided that if expression had (under Brennan, "even the slightest"; under Burger, "serious") literary or artistic value, it could not constitutionally be branded obscene—regardless of how great its appeal to prurient interests and of how far it might exceed national or local community standards of decency. In *Pope,* Justice Byron White seemed to recognize that the freedom of expression having artistic value could not be left vulnerable to the parochial attitudes of local officials.

JUSTICE BYRON WHITE: Just as the ideas a work represents need not obtain majority approval to merit protection, neither, insofar as the First Amendment is concerned, does the value of the work vary from community to community based on the degree of local acceptance it has won.

———

But instead of referring the finder of "literary, artistic, political, or scientific value"—whether policeman, prosecutor, judge, or juror—to the opinion of the relevant constituency, for example, the (national or world) art community, White fell back on the old war-horse of negligence law, the "reasonable man," now called, in deference to feminists, the "reasonable person."

JUSTICE BYRON WHITE: The proper inquiry is not whether an ordinary member of any given community would find serious literary, artistic, political, or scientific value in allegedly obscene material, but whether a reasonable person would find such value in the material, taken as a whole.

———

In *Pope,* Justice Brennan did not write an opinion but instead joined the dissenting opinion of Justice John Paul Stevens. Stevens, appointed to the Court by President Gerald Ford in 1975, has frequently opposed the steps taken by the solidly conservative block of Nixon-Ford-Reagan appointees and Justice Byron White to undercut Warren Court constitutional doctrine. In his dissent, Stevens pointed out that White's seeming "rejection of the community values test" with respect to artistic value concealed a

———

*For example, Ellen Stewart, world-renowned founder of the La Mama Experimental Theatre in New York, told the press that in response to the congressional attempts to require the NEA to censor funded art programs, she had instructed her troupes "to clean up their acts."

†481 U.S. 497 (1987).

"standard [that] would still, in effect, require a juror to apply community values, unless the juror were to find that an ordinary member of his or her community is not 'a reasonable person' "—not a very likely event.

JUSTICE JOHN PAUL STEVENS: The problem with [Justice White's "reasonable person"] formulation is that it assumes all reasonable persons would resolve the value inquiry in the same way. In fact, there are many cases in which *some* reasonable people would find that specific sexually oriented materials have serious artistic, political, literary, or scientific value, while *other* reasonable people would conclude that they have no value. [Justice White's] formulation does not tell the jury how to decide such cases.

———

Stevens further faulted White's reliance on the "reasonable person" by pointing out that he "has been described as an 'excellent' character who 'stands like a monument in our Courts of Justice, vainly appealing to his fellow-citizens to order their lives after his own example.' " And then he made this even more unsettling criticism of what White had done:

JUSTICE JOHN PAUL STEVENS: The problems with [Justice White's] formulation are accentuated when expert evidence is adduced about the value that the material has to a discrete segment of the population, be they art scholars, scientists, or literary critics. Certainly a jury could conclude that although those people reasonably find value in the material, the ordinary "reasonable person" would not.

———

The age-old disposition of judges to ignore or discount what an attacked or censored author's peers have to say about his literary reputation has proven over time to be one of the shortest cuts to literary censorship that government can take. This book is full of examples. The only significant breakthrough to freedom that was made over the past century by authors and publishers, in this country as in England, was made when the courts were required by law (statutory in England, constitutional in the United States) to admit and give weight to the testimony of "expert" authors and critics concerning a challenged work's values. Perhaps it would be better if—as Justices Black and Douglas in particular argued—there were no need to show any value at all to obtain protection for a literary or artistic work threatened with suppression or defunding under obscenity law. But given some such need in constitutional jurisprudence, it is insidious to counsel jurors to disregard the testimony of experts in favor of that of "reasonable persons." The "reasonable person" does not exist; he must be fabricated by the judge's or juror's mind. Expert witnesses do exist and can help the judge or jury carry out its constitutional task of saving literary expression from the toils of vague and overbroad obscenity law. Jurors, like judges, ought to be required to reach outside and above their individual consciousnesses, if necessary to experts, for an understanding of what is of value in the world.

In her *Yale Law Journal* piece "Post-Modern Art and the Death of Obscenity Law" Amy Adler noted that Stevens's dissent in *Pope* underlined the threat that White's gloss on the "serious value" standard posed "for unpopular or misunderstood art." The glossed standard "will provide room," Adler said, "for juries to disregard the testimony of experts such as art critics; a jury might conclude that the experts represent an unreasonable minority, and that the majority of the population, who are less likely to see the work as valuable, are more reasonable than the critics."

AMY M. ADLER: This leeway for the jury to disregard expert testimony* is extremely dangerous for artists like [Karen] Finley, [Annie] Sprinkle, [Robert] Mapplethorpe, and [Richard] Kern;† because their work might appear shocking and remain far moved from lay notions of art, the majority of the population probably would not consider this work to be art. Only expert testimony could save these artists in an obscenity prosecution.

———

In *Pope,* Justice Antonin Scalia also criticized White's resort to the "reasonable person" as a solution to the obscenity problem, even though he subscribed to the Court's adoption of that standard.

JUSTICE ANTONIN SCALIA: Since ratiocination has little to do with esthetics, the fabled "reasonable man" is of little help in the inquiry, and would have to be replaced with, perhaps, the "man of tolerably good taste," a description that betrays the lack of an ascertainable standard. . . . Just as there is no use arguing about taste, there is no use litigating about it. For the law courts to decide "What is Beauty" is a novelty even by today's standards. . . .

I must note, however, that in my view it is quite impossible to come to an objective assessment of "at least" literary or artistic value, there being many accomplished people who have found literature in Dada, and art in the replication of a soup can.

DEAN GEOFFREY STONE: A central purpose of serious art, like serious political discourse, is to challenge conventional wisdom and values. That a particular work may be offensive to contemporary standards does not in itself lessen its value or add to the legitimacy of government's desire to suppress or not fund it. To the contrary, once a particular work of art is found to have serious artistic value, government is no more justified in withholding funding for a work of political expression because of its offensiveness.

As the Supreme Court only recently observed, "if there is a bedrock principle underlying the first amendment, it is that the government may not prohibit the expression of an idea simply because society finds the idea itself offensive or disagreeable."‡ The essence of that "bedrock" first amend-

---

*It is a long-standing rule of American law that fact-finding judges and jurors are free to discount, even entirely, the opinions of expert witnesses.

†Kern is a filmmaker who, Adler reports, was "ejected" (along with his film) from a New York nightclub "after showing the first few minutes of one of his 'Death Trip' films."

‡*Texas* v. *Johnson,* 109 S.Ct. 2533, 2544 (1989), the first "flag desecration" case.

ment principle governs [the NEA situation] as well. Government may not selectively refuse to fund a particular work of art that has serious artistic value merely because "society finds [the work] offensive or disagreeable."

———

The events described in this book began about a hundred years ago, in London, when Henry Vizetelly went to prison for publishing Zola's "obscene" novels. Now, one hundred years later, Holly Hughes and Karen Finley in New York are wondering who will want them to perform once the NEA has blackballed their art, and a gallery curator in Ohio and a rap music group in Florida are recovering from criminal trials which might have resulted in their imprisonment and the destruction of their careers. While the law of obscenity and interpretations of the First Amendment today permit far more to be said, shown, and sung than ever in the past, the power of art to offend and alarm seems to be as great as ever. And so a censorious response comes to seem inevitable.

Now Justice Brennan is gone from the Court* and the future direction of the high bench is even more uncertain than it was when, in 1969, both Earl Warren and Abe Fortas resigned and, within six years, Hugo Black and William O. Douglas left the bench. After that occurred, the central meaning of the Brennan doctrine—forged during the sixties to protect literature and art from the heightened repression of the fifties—was weakened by the Burger Court and further eroded by the Rehnquist Court.† Whether it— and First Amendment freedom more generally—will hold fast under renewed tensions generated by the collision of works created by morally defiant artists and writers with values held by reactionary politicians and judges is today anything but a settled question.

———

*Yale law professor Owen Fiss recently assessed the damage to the Court's work likely to result from Justice Brennan's retirement in "A Life Lived Twice," *Yale Law Journal* 100 (1991), 1117.

†The Rehnquist Court's 1991 decision, noted above, that nude dancing is not constitutionally protected expression, and that it may be suppressed under a thoroughly vague and overbroad "public indecency" law in the name of "morals" and "order," is further evidence that a leading item on the agenda of the Court's present chief justice is to prevent the further growth of the constitutional law of freedom of expression and prolong the struggle between art and the censors for the foreseeable future. This portends social and cultural conditions under law that enlightened conservatives and liberals alike have good cause to fear. One hopes that the Court will find a way to abjure the Rehnquist agenda and resurrect instead the reason and passion of the great humanist Brennan, who labored in the cause of freedom of expression without regard for the fears that freedom so often brings.

Acknowledgments

More than anyone else, and this in critical ways, my agent, Peter Shepherd, helped me bring this book off. At Random House, my editors, Jason Epstein and Julie Grau, proved inspired and infinitely patient. Maryam Mohit was wonderfully steadfast and reassuring over difficult shoals. General Counsel Leslie Oelsner was sensitive and supportive. Design artist Rochelle Udell proved a source of comfort and joy. And I shall be eternally grateful to Debbie Foley for chasing down all the permission rights I needed to write and publish this book in the way I wanted to—in the words mainly of those who suffered under the censorship. I would like also to record my feelings of gratitude to Random House, to my publisher, Harold Evans, and to everyone in the house who laid eyes or hands on my book.

Closer to home I wish to thank my son Augustus ("Gus") for the several brilliant legal and literary research forays that he undertook (notwithstanding grave disabilities); and my son David and my daughter Elizabeth for their valuable editorial comment. My son Christophe and my daughter Belinda, too, were always ready with friendly counsel, criticism, encouragement, and good cheer; so were my friends Ted and Suzanne Fields, on those occasions—few and far between—when the going was rough. My friends Fritz and Joanne Heimann acted like glad incubators of the offspring, lending me their home on Long Island Sound for August musings and broodings, and rewriting and editing jobs. And midway (as it were) between home and school, there were two who became my friends through their devotion to bringing my Dreiser-sized manuscript to typed completion: filmmaker Richard Brody and Annie Kamlet, faculty services manager at Cardozo Law School.

It is not easy to say whether the many Cardozo students who gave me high-spirited research assistance with the book, through eight long years, or the brave men and women who typed the manuscript up, through all its many forms, drafts, and stages, helped me more. The point is, of course, moot. Among the marvelous typists who helped me, at times way beyond the call of duty, and almost always without blinking at the book's incorporated "obscenity," were Kaaron Saphir, Charlene Wiggins, Sharon Thomas, Joel Grantz, Keisha Lawrence, and Lynne Gordon. Among others at Cardozo whom I wish to thank warmly for their help are: Dean Monroe Price, Librarian Lynn Wishart, and reproduction masters Bob Bannister, Felix Lopez, and Carlyle Ramcharan. My gratitude goes almost without saying to Dr. Norman Lamm, president of Yeshiva University, for helping make it possible for me to write this book.

Among students and former students who helped me, and thereby deserve my lasting gratitude, are: Carole Lamson, Ursula Day (who "lived through it"), Zdena Nemeckova, Melinda Gordon, Odesa Gorman, Sharon Silver, Miriam Alon, Katherine Constan, Laura Sydell, Julia Levy, Steve Kaufman, Jonathan Fishbein, Dan Cantor, Jessica Furey, Jacqui Haverford, Stephanie Zwern, Myreya Calderon, Mindy Friedman, Linda Fiddle, Jill Convisor, Gail Markels, Ann Bishop, Elizabeth Mason, and Eliza Walendzik.

An abundance of colleagues and friends aided me in ways both large and small. I wish especially to thank: Edward H. Levi, Joe Goldstein, Ramsey Clark, Judge Abner J. Mikva, Geoffrey Stone, Lois Sheinfeld, Nicholas Kittrie, Marcus Raskin, Donald Black, Abe Krash, Charles Reich, Paul Bender, Burt Joseph, Larry Stanley, Judith Krug, Kathy Kadane, Simone Ben Musa, Barbara Raskin, Linda Silberman, Lizbeth Malkmus, Claudia Kaiser-Lenoir, Peter Weiss, Richard Gallen, Zelda Fichandler, Judith Mueller, Marty Edelheit, Jerry Rosen, Ira Lowe, Roger K. Newman, Richard and Cheryl Weisberg, Chris Trela, Karin Walsch, Gabrielle Schang, Jack Mulligan, Liz Good, Rosemary Meyers, Renato Beghe, Sally Lloyd, Ned Rosenheim, Maurice Rosenfield, Victor Bockris, Lisa Rosset, Mary Pat Baumgartner, Livingston Biddle, Elliot Epstein, Judge Samuel Epstein, John and Nicole Long, Joanne Mauer, Susan Monroe, Sam and Judith Pisar, Roger Shapiro, Dina Kosten, Donna Demac, Eliane Heilbronn, Nicole Bigard, Marcia Pally, Allen Ginsberg, Norman Mailer, Eric Freedman, Richard Hobbet, Rachel Wizner, David Ellenhorn, Nat Hentoff, Paul Carroll, Eugène Ionesco, Jean Genet, Alain Robbe-Grillet, Ted Morgan, Mary McCarthy, Erica Jong, Alair Townsend, Bill Starr, Martin Garbus, William Hellerstein, Douglas Davis, Jamie Kalven, Christopher Day, George Anastaplo, Christie Hefner, John Oakes, Harry Lunn, C. Carr, Barney Rosset, Maurice Girodias, John Calder, Al Goldstein, Bob Guccione, Dottie Meyer, David Myerson, Angus Cameron, Roger Straus, Walter Minton, Fred Jordan, Dõnna Brown, Ken McCormick, Holly Hughes, Karen Finley, Jock Sturges, Sally, Larry, Emmett, Jessie, and Virginia Mann, Marcia Pally, Victoria de Grazia, Leonardo Paggi, Harry Kalven, Jr., and, needless to say, Justice William J. Brennan, Jr. Last but certainly not least, I want to say thanks to my brothers Vic, Al, and Sebastian.

Endnotes

CHAPTER 1: *Girls Lean Back Everywhere*

Margaret Anderson was right: *The Little Review*'s pioneering role in discovering and publishing *Ulysses,* and in absorbing the first blows from the censors, was not widely appreciated. Sylvia Beach—the expatriate American who ran the Shakespeare and Company bookstore in Paris and published *Ulysses* from there—received the lion's share of the credit. In her lively book *Shakespeare and Company,* published in 1956, Beach devoted only half a dozen lines to the ways in which Margaret Anderson and Jane Heap had brought *Ulysses* to the public's attention, and to their valiant fight against John Sumner. She also undervalued Anderson's proven stamina by stating that the prosecution had "put an end to the magazine" (46–47). In fact, the magazine's last issue came out in 1929, eight years later, from Paris, where Anderson then lived. In her turn, Beach was piqued when Joyce—whom she "worshipped"—contracted with Bennett Cerf's Random House to publish the first American edition of *Ulysses* without first satisfying her; Joyce previously had assigned to her "world rights" in the novel. Beach was "not at all proud," however, of her possessive feelings about *Ulysses* and "dumped them" in consideration of Joyce's desperate need for money—"The expenses of his daughter's illness were increasing, and there was his failing eyesight"—and the overriding right she felt an author had in his own book—"A baby belongs to its mother, not to the midwife, doesn't it?" (205). According to Noel Riley Fitch, Beach had first read *Ulysses* in the pages of *The Little Review* and was so impressed by the writing that she "wanted to run away" the first chance she had to meet James Joyce—which was at a party thrown for the author by André Spire, in Paris. Fitch, *Sylvia Beach and the Lost Generation* (1983), 62–63. Not the sort to hold a grudge, Anderson and Heap excitedly helped Beach and Joyce to obtain subscriptions in New York for the 1922 Shakespeare and Company edition of *Ulysses* and placed "the largest order" for the book, twenty-five copies, through their Washington Square Bookstore in Greenwich Village—this despite the contraband character of the book and their awareness that they might readily be prosecuted in 1922 for selling a work a part of which they had been convicted for publishing in 1920. Richard Ellmann also notes the neglect of Anderson's role in the struggle to publish *Ulysses* freely, in the introduction he wrote for *The United States of America v. One Book Entitled Ulysses by James Joyce,* edited by Michael Moscato and Leslie LeBlanc (1984). On James Joyce and *Ulysses,* see notes to Chapter 2.

My account of the *Little Review* censorship and the criminal trial of its publishers is based mainly on Margaret Anderson's *My Thirty Years' War* (1930, reprint 1969) and what she and Jane Heap said about it in *The Little Review. The Little Review Anthology,* edited by Anderson, in 1953 republished part of the account in "On Trial for 'Ulysses' " (297–311). Paul S. Boyer reports on the censorship in his work on the vice-society movement and book censorship, *Purity in Print* (1968). Another account, by Joyce's biographer Richard Ellmann, is in the introduction to the compilation of documents, letters, and commentaries published as *The United States of America v. One Book Entitled Ulysses by James Joyce.* See also: John Tebbel, *A History of Book Publishing in the United States* 3 (1978), 412; Julian Symons, *Makers of the New: The Revolution in Literature 1912–1939* (1987), 91–106; Brenda Maddox, *Nora* (1988), 183.

In her autobiographical *My Thirty Years' War* Anderson described how Jane Heap came to *The Little Review* in the spring of 1916—"the most interesting thing that ever happened to the magazine" (102). ("Jane's talk was the best—psychologically the best—that I had ever heard. I wanted it for the *Little Review,* though Jane protested that she couldn't write. I began jotting down things she said, and finally forced her to take on a department of critical comment. As it turned out, I was always more interested in Jane's talk about art than I was in Ezra Pound's, when he became foreign editor of the magazine in 1917. As I look back over the files I find a new confirmation of this 1916 evaluation.") Examples of Heap's gifts can be seen in her piece "Art and the Law" in the September/December 1920 issue of *The Little Review,* and her poem "I Cannot Sleep" in the *Anthology* (311). The episodes from *Ulysses* that Anderson published almost as they left Joyce's writing table began in the March 1918 issue of *The Little Review* and ran in every issue thereafter until the September/December 1920 issue, the one that led to her prosecution. After that, *Ulysses* did not reappear in *The Little Review* or anywhere else until Sylvia Beach published the finished work in Paris the following year. This is described in Chapter 2. On the relationship of Anderson and Heap, see Shari Benstock, *Women of the Left Bank* (1986), 363–72.

The Little Review suffered another defeat at the hands of censors when, during the war, the October 1917 issue was "held up" by the postmaster of New York because of a pacifistic story by Wyndham Lewis, "Cattleman's Spring Mate," which the Post Office judged to be "obscene." The Post Office's opinion was upheld by the same distinguished federal district judge, Augustus Hand, who later, in 1934, as a member of a federal circuit court of appeals, found that the imported Shakespeare and Company edition of *Ulysses* was not obscene, notwithstanding a customs bureau opinion that it was. See Chapter 2. The "Cattleman's Spring Mate" case is *Anderson* v. *Patten,* 247 Fed. 382 (1917); the *Ulysses* decision is *United States* v. *One Book called Ulysses,* 72 F.2d 705 (2d Cir. 1934), affirming a decision by federal district Judge John M. Woolsey at 5 F. Supp. 182 (S.D.N.Y. 133). Both decisions are reprinted in de Grazia, *Censorship Landmarks* (1969). Anderson's criticism of Augustus Hand's decision and opinion in the "Cattleman's Spring Mate" case is set out in the December 1917 issue of *The Little Review* ("Our Suppressed October Issue"), 46–49; see also her notice in the November 1917 number ("To Subscribers who did not receive their October issue"), 43–44. Her criticism of young Alfred A. Knopf for suppressing the novel *Homo Sapiens* and melting down its plates is in *The Little Review,* January/February 1916 (" 'Homo-Sapiens' Is Obscene"). Anderson's life and work are also examined in Hugh Ford's *Four Lives in Paris* (1987), 227–86, and in Shari Benstock, *Women of the Left Bank* (1986).

A short "history" of *The Little Review* is in *The Little Magazine: A History and a Bibliography,* by Frederick J. Hoffman, Charles Allen, and Carolyn F. Ulrich (1967). Kenneth A. Lohf and Eugene P. Sheeley have put together *An Index to The Little Review* (1961). An especially noteworthy issue was the final one—much of which was reprinted by Anderson in *The Little Review Anthology,* 349–80. Concerning the end, Anderson wrote: "In 1929, in Paris, I decided that the time had come to end *The Little Review.* Our mission was accomplished; contemporary art had 'arrived'; for a hundred years, perhaps, the literary world would produce only 'repetition.' " Other Anderson pieces I found of special interest are: "To the Book Publishers of America," *The Little Review,* September/December 1920, 8–16; "Ulysses and the Critics" in *The Chicago Tribune,* July 14, 1924; "James Joyce in the '*Little Review,* ' " "Reversals," and "Ulysses Again" in *The Little Review Anthology,* 175–77, 60–62, and 329–31, respectively.

Ida Craddock's books seem to have been of the sex manual type, censorship of which under obscenity law has had a history of its own, paralleling that of the sexually oriented or erotic novel. A subbranch here might be fiction and nonfiction about gay men and women, such as Radclyffe Hall's *The Well of Loneliness,* E. M. Forster's *Maurice,* and Havelock Ellis's *Sexual Inversion.* A third major category is material on contraception and abortion, usually made separately suppressible along with laws prohibiting obscenity. In 1965, in the case of *Griswold* v. *Connecticut,* the Supreme Court held unconstitutional state restrictions on the dissemination to married persons of such information. Restrictions upon its dissemination to single persons were stuck down seven years later, in *Eisenstadt* v. *Baird.* Those decisions are based more on the constitutional right of privacy than on freedom of expression. Justice William O. Douglas wrote the Court's opinion in *Griswold;* Justice William J. Brennan, Jr., wrote for the Court in *Baird.* The decisions, and the Supreme Court's recognition of a neo-constitutional right of privacy to support them, have been sharply criticized by conservative jurists like Robert Bork and to a degree undermined by the Rehnquist Court. Bork calls the constitutional right of privacy an example of the Court's "moral imperialism." Robert Bork, *The Temptation of America* (1989), Chapter 4.

The information on Ida Craddock's activities, her prosecutions, and her fate is from Broun and Leech, *Anthony Comstock: Roundsman of the Lord* (1927), 210–14; the 1902 *Report of the New York Society for the Prevention of Vice,* 9ff.; and *New York Times* stories dated March 18 and October 18, 1902. The *Times* for October 18, 1902, reported her death under the caption "CHOSE DEATH BEFORE PRISON" and described her as having been "High Priestess of the Church of Yoga in Chicago, and an exponent also of Spiritualism, Theosophy, and other creeds." The story admits to ignorance whether Craddock was married or single "because her reply to an inquiry on this point was 'Yes; I have a husband in the other world.' " Broun and Leech report that "Comstock had always been sensitive to criticism and this time the shafts were especially painful. . . . Contributors to the Society for the Suppression of Vice fell off in a startling manner" (214–15).

Laudatory *New York Times* pieces about Comstock are: "Anthony Comstock's Service" (editorial), *The New York Times,* September 23, 1915; "Unpopular, But not Undeserving" (editorial), *The New York Times,* June 14, 1915; "Anthony Comstock Dies in His Crusade," *The New York Times,* September 22, 1915; "The Suppression of Vice," *The New York Times,* January 1, 1876; "Comstock's Western Road," *The New York Times,* November 17, 1876; "A Blow To Quack Doctors," *The New York Times,* March 29, 1876. The law establishing the New York anti-vice organization and giving its agents special police powers was "An Act to Incorporate the New York Society for the Suppression of Vice," May 16, 1873 (Ninety-sixth Session, Chapter 527). The powers of the society's agents were strengthened by amendments that gave them the right to execute arrest and search warrants and that *required* magistrates to issue arrest and search warrants upon the filing of complaints by them (or other persons) alleging that someone was offending against the obscenity law. The law also *required* the local district attorney to destroy "every article seized by virtue of the warrant" upon conviction of the possessor (Chapter VII, Law of 1881 regarding "Indecent Exposure, Obscene Exhibitions, Books and Prints, and Bawdy and Other Disorderly Houses"). Discovering these provisions more than thirty years later, *The New York Times* expressed its disapproval editorially (on March 28, 1940): "The public morals must be preserved, but surely there is some wiser way of preserving them than this."

On Anthony Comstock: Heywood Broun and Margaret Leech, *Anthony Comstock: Roundsman of the Lord* (1927); Charles G. Trumball, *Anthony Comstock Fighter* (1913); Anthony Comstock: "Vampire Literature," *North American Review,* August 1891, 160–71; Anthony Comstock, *Traps for the Young* (1883); D. M. Bennett, *Anthony Comstock: His Career of Cruelty and Crime* (1878); E. C. Walker, *Who Is the Enemy? Anthony Comstock or You?* (1903); Robert W. Haney, *Comstockery in America* (1960); Paul S. Boyer, *To the Pure* (1968); John Tebbel, *A History of Book Publishing in the United States* 2 (1975); Morris Ernst and Alan V. Schwartz, *Censorship: The Search for the Obscene* (1964). The New York Public Library (Annex) has the annual reports of the New York Society for the Suppression of Vice.

On John Sumner: Margaret Anderson, *My Thirty Years' War* (1930, reprint 1969); Paul S. Boyer, *To the Pure* (1968); John Tebbel, *A History of Book Publishing in the United States* 2 (1975) and 3 (1978); Henry Pringle, "Comstock the Less," *The American Mercury* 10, 56–63; Earl Welch, "The Case for John Sumner," November 10, 1946 (author's files); John Sumner, "Obscene Literature: Its Suppression," *Publishers Weekly,* July 8, 1916, 94–97; John Sumner, "The Truth About Literary Lynching," *The Dial,* July 1921, 63; John Sumner, "Criticizing the Critic," *The Bookman,* February 28, 1924.

In its early stage, Sumner's work was supported by *The New York Times* but the paper's enthusiasm waned during the early twenties, when it adopted the view that anti-obscenity laws and prosecutions were a type of censorship and were dangerous to freedom of the press. That development may have come about in response to a wave of prosecutions instigated by Sumner that attacked not only "upstart" publishers like Thomas Seltzer and Horace Liveright but even the old house of Harper—prosecutions defeated in court. This led to the acceptance by the *Times* (but not by other newspapers like those owned by William Randolph Hearst) that publishers of literary works, like publishers of newspapers, were a part of the country's press and were therefore entitled to function free of governmental restraint and censorship. The *Times* also protested the tendency of Sumner's work to stimulate the sale of inferior literature. See "Comstock's Work to Go On," *The New*

York Times, October 4, 1915; "I'm No Reformer, Says Sumner," *The New York Times Book Review and Magazine,* August 20, 1922; "Advertising Bad Books," *The New York Times,* March 15, 1923; "Vice Society Sued by Two for $40,000," *The New York Times,* September 29, 1922; "The Worst Bill Yet," *The New York Times,* April 18, 1923; "More Books Seized by Sumner in Raid," *The New York Times,* May 27, 1928; S. J. Woolf, "A Vice Suppressor Looks at Our Morals," *The New York Times,* October 9, 1932; S. J. Woolf, "Interview with Our Unofficial Censor," *The New York Times,* October 20, 1946. See also Joseph Lilly's impressive series of five pieces on the work of Sumner and other censors and on the pirating (called "booklegging") of contraband literary works, "Books and Bookleggers," in the *New York Telegram,* March 6, 7, 8, 10, and 11, 1930. Also: "Seizures by Society Greatest in History," *The Nation,* November 25, 1931, 559; "Records of Censorship," *Publishers Weekly,* March 22, 1930, 1666; "Bill to Abolish Vice Society," *Publishers Weekly,* March 22, 1930, 1683.

The customs laws prohibiting the importation of ("foreign") obscene material antedated the federal postal and N.Y. State obscenity laws. The Civil War produced the first significant demand for *domestic* pornography, and pressure was put on legislatures to close the mails to such material. "Soldiers far from home proved susceptible to the appeals of salacious books, and the best way to reach them was through the Post Office." David Goldsmith Loth, *The Erotic in Literature* (1961), 143. The first federal legislation criminalizing the use of the mails to transport "obscene" publications was passed in 1865, to discourage the wartime traffic; this was eight years before Comstock got into the act. In 1866, New York's YMCA reported that its studies showed a proliferation of "vile newspapers" and "licentious books," which could be obtained for from thirty-five to sixty cents by young men seeking leisure pastimes. The only other available leisure resources appeared to be saloons, brothels, and billiard and gambling halls. Comstock put himself in touch with the Y and the result was the organization of the New York Society for the Suppression of Vice. New York's first obscenity statute was passed in 1868, at the Y's instigation.

Loth (120–21) agrees with other scholars that fear of pornography was not known to the nation's founders, who "read their Latin poets in the original" and whose taste for erotica was "satisfied by the classics of antiquity, Shakespeare (un-Bowdlerized), the recent novels of Fielding, Smollett, and the others, and the early native product which was long on seduction and betrayal but remarkably dull in language and style. . . . [T]here was no big semiliterate market for erotic writing which could not pretend to literary merit." Pornography began to be imported into the country from England while "some of the founding fathers were still alive," because a new demand had been generated by the growth of literacy. Compulsory education was on the way, and in 1821, the same year that the country's first public high school was established in Boston, the Commonwealth of Massachusetts instituted the first reported American case of common-law prosecution of the publisher of "obscene" literature, *Fanny Hill* (or *Memoirs of a Lady of Pleasure*). The same year, the country's first anti-obscenity statute was enacted by Vermont. Connecticut followed in 1834, Massachusetts in 1836. Under the common law, even the successful criminal prosecution of the publisher of an "obscene" book could not work suppression of the book itself. For that, legislation was needed, which was the reason why Lord Campbell's Act was passed in England, in 1857, and why the American states enacted criminal laws that expressly provided for, or were construed to authorize, police seizures of all copies of the book at the arrested or accused person's premises. The police powers that both Comstock and Sumner enjoyed included the formidable ones of arrest and of seizing books suspected to be obscene; this accounts for their many raids on publishers, printers, and bookstores, and for the fear in which they were held by publishers and bookstore owners.

On John Quinn: the *John Quinn Papers* in the New York Public Library; Margaret Anderson's *My Thirty Years' War* and *The Little Review Anthology;* Paul S. Boyer, *Purity in Print* (1968); and "John Quinn Dies, Noted in Art World," *The New York Times,* July 29, 1924.

On B. W. Huebsch, the "new breed" of publishers, and Jews and women in publishing, see Tebbel, *A History of Book Publishing in the United States* 2 (1975), 174–77, 388–93. Tebbel's work includes valuable sections on literary censorship, notably vol. 1, 561–64; vol. 2, 609–33; vol. 3, 635–55; vol. 4, 695–720. He describes the period 1920–1940, between the two world wars, as publishing's "Golden Age," which perhaps explains the increase of literary censorship activity during that period. He also attributes to the rise of book publishing in America the establishment of the role of the publisher as "the chief purveyor of ideas" (vol. 1, 564).

PAGE

3   *"I am so glad . . ."* Ida C. Craddock, *Advice to a Bridegroom* (date unknown; a typed remnant is in the New York Public Library).

5   "Any refined person . . ." *Report of the New York Society for the Suppression of Vice* (1902), 9–10.

6   "I am taking my life . . ." Heywood Broun and Margaret Leech, *Anthony Comstock: Roundsman of the Lord* (1927), 212.

6   "All through his long career . . ." *The New York Times,* September 23, 1915, 12.

8   "This is the most . . ." Margaret Anderson, *My Thirty Years' War* (1969), 206.

8   "He fought everybody . . ." *Ibid.*

9   *"At last they were left alone . . ."* James Joyce, *Ulysses,* as published in *The Little Review,* July/August 1920, 43.

10   "Mr. Joyce was not teaching . . ." *The Little Review,* September/December 1920, 6.

10   "John Quinn's strategy . . ." Margaret Anderson, *My Thirty Years' War* (1969), 218–19.

10   "The court gasps . . ." *Ibid.*

11   "Scofield Thayer was forced . . ." *Ibid.*

11   "The heavy farce and sad . . ." *The Little Review,* September/December 1920, 5.

11   "Mr. Sumner is . . . a serious, sincere man . . ." *The Little Review,* September/December 1920, 8–9.

12   "Since I *am* the publisher . . ." Margaret Anderson, *The Little Review Anthology* (1953), 307–8.

13   "Don't try to talk . . ." *Ibid.*

13   "With that look of . . ." *Ibid.*

13   "If they had imagined . . ." Margaret Anderson, *My Thirty Years' War* (1969), 222.

PAGE

13   "And now for God's sake . . ." *Ibid.*

13   "The trial of *The Little Review* . . ." Margaret Anderson, *The Little Review Anthology* (1953), 305.

14   "It was like a burning at the stake . . ." Margaret Anderson, *My Thirty Years' War* (1969), 206.

14   "A desultory appreciation . . ." *Ibid.*

14   "It was the poet . . ." *The Little Review,* September/December 1920, 6.

14   "There will be, doubtless . . ." *The New York Times,* February 23, 1921, 12.

15   "If I had refused . . ." Margaret Anderson, *My Thirty Years' War* (1969), 226; *The Little Review Anthology* (1953), 329.

15   "Especially as I happen to possess . . ." *The Chicago Tribune,* July 14, 1924.

16   "Yes, some intelligent help ought to be arranged . . ." Margaret Anderson, *My Thirty Years' War* (1969), 227–28.

17   "For several years . . ." *Contempo* 3:13 (February 15, 1934), 1–2.

CHAPTER 2: *Fuck Up, Love!*

On Sylvia Beach, Adrienne Monnier, and the Shakespeare and Company publication of *Ulysses,* I have used mainly: Richard Ellmann, *James Joyce* (1982); Sylvia Beach, *Shakespeare and Company* (1959); Noel Riley Fitch, *Sylvia Beach and the Lost Generation* (1983); Brenda Maddox, *Nora* (1988); and Shari Benstock's very interesting book *Women of the Left Bank: Paris 1900–1940* (1986). Ellmann says Beach at first "opposed an American publication of *Ulysses* in particular, feeling that it would reduce her sales to nothing. Eventually, however, she was persuaded, on the understanding that she would continue to receive some of the royalties on the European edition, to give up her rights" (*James Joyce,* 641).

Information about the private and public lives and occupations of the talented American, English, and French women writers who colonized in Paris between 1900 and 1940—including Anderson and Heap—and helped shape literary modernism can be found in Shari Benstock, *Women of the Left Bank* (1986) and Noel Riley Fitch, *Sylvia Beach and the Lost Generation* (1983). A number of the women created "little press" publishing ventures; most seem to have had lesbian relationships—which calls to mind Simone de Beauvoir's remark that many talented women choose lesbian partners because having to deal with sexual relationships with men gets in the way of their creativity. See also Noel Riley Fitch, *Sylvia Beach and the Lost Generation* (1983), 135–36 and 169–70. Joyce's relationship with Beach made her and her bookshop famous but also proved problematic: a year before the signing of the Random House contract, Beach reportedly borrowed funds from her mother and other members of her family in order to pay Joyce's escalating debts, nominally as loans and advances on royalties. When Shakespeare and Company was on the verge of bankruptcy, in 1931, Monnier wrote a letter to Joyce that was meant to bring about a final rupture in the Joyce-Beach relationship. During 1932 and 1933, Joyce's relationships with his most consistent and solid financial supporters, Harriet Weaver and Sylvia Beach, were at their nadir. Perhaps not coincidentally, this occurred at a time when Joyce's own financial prospects were brightening because of the pending Random House publication of *Ulysses* in America. Shari Benstock explores this in her *Women of the Left Bank* (1986), 217–29.

Noel Riley Fitch makes clear that Beach's motivations in agreeing to publish *Ulysses* were not all altruistic. In a letter to her mother, the day after her talk with Joyce, she wrote about her bookstore: "Mother dear it's more of a success every day and soon you may hear of us as regular Publishers and of the most important book of the age . . . shhhhhh . . . it's a secret, all to be revealed to you in my next letter and it's going to make us famous rah rah!" And in the margin of a note added later to this letter, Beach scribbled: "*Ulysses* means thousands of dollars of publicity for me," and "*Ulysses* is going to make my place famous." *Sylvia Beach and the Lost Generation,* 78.

On James Joyce and *Ulysses* the definitive work is still Richard Ellmann's biography, now in a revised edition, *James Joyce* (1982). Ellmann edited volumes 2 and 3 of the *Letters of James Joyce* (1966) and the *Selected Letters of James Joyce* (1975), which contain the "lust" letters to Nora. Volume 1 of Joyce's *Letters* was edited by Stuart Gilbert (1957). Brenda Maddox's biography *Nora* (1988) examines the "dirty" letters at pp. 31–32, 102–8.

On Joyce's sexual proclivities and Nora Joyce, see Ellmann, *James Joyce* (1982) and Maddox, *Nora* (1988). On the sources of the "interior monologue," see Frederick J. Hoffman, *Freudianism and the Literary Mind* (1959), 125ff.

On Nora Joyce: Brenda Maddox, *Nora* (1988); and Richard Ellmann, *James Joyce* (1982).

On George Moore: Malcolm Brown, *George Moore: A Reconsideration* (1955); Guinevere L. Griest, *Mudie's Circulating Library* (1970); Richard Ellmann, *James Joyce* (1982); George Moore, *A Communication to My Friends* (1974); George Moore, *Memoirs of My Dead Life* (1907), with an "Apologia Pro Scriptis Meis" by the author; George Moore, *Memoirs of My Dead Life* (1920), dedicated to T. R. Smith and with a prefatory letter to Horace Liveright; Paul S. Boyer, *Purity in Print* (1968), 85ff.; John Tebbel, *A History of Book Publishing in the United States* 2 (1975).

The *Ulysses* decision by Judge Woolsey is reprinted in the Random House edition of *Ulysses* (1934), ix–xiv. The appellate court decision may be found in de Grazia, *Censorship Landmarks* (1969), 96–101. The strategy to get a "test" case before the "liberal-minded" Judge Woolsey is exposed in: Bennett Cerf, *At Random* (1977), 90ff.; Cerf, "Publishing Ulysses," in *Contempo* 3:13 (February 15, 1934), 1–2; *United States of America v. One Book Entitled Ulysses by James Joyce,* edited by Michael Moscato and Leslie LeBlanc (1984), 98ff. and 219–21. In the fall of 1922, five hundred copies of the Shakespeare and Company edition of *Ulysses* were seized and destroyed as obscene by U.S. customs officials and the U.S. attorney's office. After that, Samuel Roth began pirating serially a bowdlerized version of Joyce's novel in his literary quarterly *Two Worlds Monthly*. Although it was impossible to stop Roth by resort to the copyright law—obscene books being deemed non-copyrightable— Joyce succeeded in getting a court injunction against Roth's continued publication of the work in his name, and Roth was prosecuted criminally and convicted for publishing the "obscene" work. See Chapter 16. However, another pirated version soon appeared in New York and was reportedly selling so many copies that Joyce and Beach feared there would be no further demand for the Shakespeare and Company *Ulysses*.

A short history of obscenity law can be found in "Obscenity, the Law, and the Courts" by Terrence J. Murphy, reprinted in *United States of America v. One Book Entitled Ulysses by James Joyce,* 24–30. This volume contains most of the major original documents (letters, commentaries, memoranda, etc.) bearing on the events leading up to and including the *Ulysses* trial. The editors state: "Only the transcript of Morris Ernst's oral argument before Judge John Woolsey is missing, apparently lost" (xxiii).

PAGE

20   "My book will never come out now . . ." Sylvia Beach, *Shakespeare and Company* (1959), 47.

20   "Publishers and printers alike . . ." Letter from James Joyce to Bennett Cerf dated April 2, 1932. Random House (Modern Library) edition of *Ulysses* (1934), xv–xvii. Attached to the final version of the letter in Random House files are copies of a draft, and a memorandum of agreement executed by Joyce and Cerf. The agreement is dated March 31, 1932, and is witnessed by Joyce's agent, Eric Pinker, and Robert Kastor. The letter appears to have been written by Joyce in compliance with paragraph 6 of the memorandum of agreement, which asked that he "write a letter to the publishers of not less than 300 words, by which he will authenticate the publication." Random House was obligated to publish the book "within a period of two years, unless the case is still pending in the courts at the end of that period." This apparently referred to the test case that Joyce, Cerf, and attorney Morris Ernst had arranged by having customs officials find and seize a copy of the book in transit from France. (The seized copy is in the library at Columbia University.) It was agreed that even if *Ulysses* was not published within the given period, Joyce might retain the advance he had received from Random House.

20   "When at last it was printed . . ." Letter from James Joyce to Bennett Cerf dated April 2, 1932.

21   "We were exceedingly fond of Paris . . ." Noel Riley Fitch, *Sylvia Beach and the Lost Generation* (1983), 24.

21   "[M]y mother in Princeton . . ." Sylvia Beach, *Shakespeare and Company* (1959), 17.

21   "Darantière was much interested . . ." *Ibid.*, 48.

21   "My friend Ezra Pound . . ." Letter from James Joyce to Bennett Cerf, April 2, 1932.

22   "I wish, for my sake . . ." Richard Ellmann, *James Joyce* (1982), 528.

22   "*Ulysses* is hopeless." *Ibid.*, 529.

23   "It is absurd to imagine . . ." *Ibid.*

23   "Jim should have stuck to music . . ." *Ibid.*, 169.

23   "I suppose the devil's grandmother . . ." *Ibid.*, 629.

24   "Will all that paper . . ." *Ibid.*, 188.

24   "*the sun shines for you he said* . . ." James Joyce, *Ulysses: The Corrected Text* (1986), 643–44.

25   "André Gide [was] the first . . ." Sylvia Beach, *Shakespeare and Company* (1959), 51.

25   "Joyce is good. . . ." Ellmann, *James Joyce* (1982), 529.

25   "Joyce has a most goddamn . . ." *Ibid.*

25   "The driving impulse . . ." *Ibid.*, 530–31.

26   "He is a sort of Marquis de Sade . . ." *Ibid.*, 529.

PAGE

26   "A sort of Zola . . ." *Ibid.*

26   "A queasy undergraduate . . ." *Ibid.,* 528.

26   *"Ines told me that one drop . . ."* James Joyce, *Ulysses: The Corrected Text* (1986), 626.

27   "High up in one of lower Broadway's . . ." Bennett Cerf, "Publishing *Ulysses,*" *Contempo* 3:13 (February 15, 1934), 2.

28   "I had heard Morris Ernst . . ." Bennett Cerf, *At Random* (1977), 90.

28   "Mr. Kastor sailed for Europe . . ." Bennett Cerf, "Publishing *Ulysses,*" *Contempo* 3:13 (February 15, 1934), 2.

29   "On the morning agreed upon . . ." *Ibid.*

29   " 'Oh, Mr. Cerf, don't . . .' " Bennett Cerf, *At Random* (1977), 90–91.

32   "We have here, certainly, an admirable example . . ." Ben Ray Redman, "Obscenity and Censorship," *Scribner's Magazine,* May 1934, 341–44.

34   "You . . . gradually took it all . . ." *Selected Letters of James Joyce,* ed. Richard Ellmann (1975), 181–82. The letters are described in some detail and are quoted from Brenda Maddox, *Nora* (1988), where Maddox suggests (at page 202) that they were received by Nora like "the mad crazy letters" that Bloom wrote to Molly (in *Ulysses*), which "had me always at myself 4 and 5 times a day sometimes and I said I hadn't . . ."

34   "Perhaps the horn I had was not big enough . . ." *Selected Letters of James Joyce,* ed. Richard Ellmann (1975), 182. In an appendix to *Nora,* Maddox traces the difficult publication history of these remarkable letters and the attempts by the Joyce heirs to suppress them. *Nora,* 393–401.

35   "The letters were designed . . ." Brenda Maddox, *Nora* (1988), 104.

36   "At one o'clock in the morning . . ." Richard Ellmann, *James Joyce* (1982), 741.

37   "My husband is buried there . . ." *Ibid.,* 743.

37   "I had others but I have given . . ." Brenda Maddox, *Nora* (1988), 361.

37   "As she came to play the part . . ." *Ibid.,* 359.

38   "Sure, when you've been married . . ." *Ibid.*

38   *Dublin Evening Herald* story: *Ibid.,* 352.

CHAPTER 3: *A Judicial Murder*

My account of the trials of Henry Vizetelly is mainly based on the firsthand accounts of the events contained in the Ernest Vizetelly biography of Zola, and a London *Times* report on the first case, November 1, 1888. See also *The New York Herald* (London), July 28, 1889; *Publishers Weekly,* August 18, 1888, and November 10, 1888; Norman St. John-Stevas, *Obscenity and the Law* (1956), 80–83; Donald Thomas, *A Long Time Burning* (1969), 267–69; Alec Craig, *Suppressed Books* (1963), 48–49; and Geoffrey Robertson, *Obscenity* (1979), 31–32. The London *Times* praised the prosecution and gloated over Vizetelly's first defeat: "[W]e fear the law can do little to cope with this evil, but it is well that the little that it can do should be done. We would advocate no prudish standard of propriety in such matters, no rigid or puritanical system of restriction; but, after all, there is such a thing as public decency, and unquestionably the publication of a cheap English translation of 'La Terre' is an outrage upon it. We cannot but rejoice, therefore, that Mr. Vizetelly has acknowledged his offense and been punished for it. In future, as the Solicitor-General intimated, any one who publishes translations of Zola's novels and works of similar character will do so at his peril, and must not expect to escape so easily as Mr. Vizetelly."

Ernest Vizetelly reported that ("toned-down") English translations of the following Zola novels were published by Vizetelly and Company between 1884 and 1889: *The Fortune of the Rougons, The Rush for the Spoil (La Curée), A Love Episode (Une Page d'amour), Fat and Thin (Le Ventre de Paris), Abbé Mouret's Transgression, His Excellency E. Rougon, L'Assommoir, Nana, Piping Hot (Pot-bouille), The Ladies' Paradise (Au Bonheur des dames), How Jolly Life Is! (La Joie de vivre), Germinal, His Masterpiece (L'Oeuvre), The Soil (La Terre), Madeleine Férat, Thérèse Raquin,* and *A Soldier's Honour* (short stories). All the above were issued in "crown octavo form." There were also large octavo editions of *Nana, L'Assommoir,* and *Piping Hot,* each with about one hundred illustrations. The smaller volumes contained illustrations or frontispieces. After the first prosecution of Henry Vizetelly, most of the above translations were re-expurgated and reissued. The reissues were distinguished from the earlier editions by the words "A new Edition," and by headings—e.g., "The Rougon-Macquart Family," I, II, III, etc.—which do not appear on the title pages of the first and fuller editions. There was, however, no such reissue of *Nana, Piping Hot,* and *The Soil* (usually titled *The Earth* in the United States). In some early catalogues *Claude's Confession* was announced by the firm, but Ernest Vizetelly did not find that it was ever published. The above translations were all out of print when Ernest Vizetelly wrote his biography of Zola in 1904, with the exception of *The Soil,* which was sold in France only by the proprietor of the copyright of that translation (Paris, Flammarion). In consequence of the conviction of Henry Vizetelly it could not be sold in the British dominions. E. A. Vizetelly, *Emile Zola* (1904), appendix, 542–43. As mentioned in the text, the novel did not reappear in English in England until 1954. A regular American edition in English was published by Boni and Liveright in 1924. *National Union Catalogue.*

The American book-publishing trade's reaction to the Vizetelly prosecutions may be glimpsed in the following piece appearing in *Publishers Weekly,* August 18, 1888 (from "London correspondence to N.Y. Times"): "A crusade against Zola has been started here this week, and Vizetelly, a prominent bookseller, who sells about 1000 copies of Zola weekly, has been committed for trial for selling improper literature. The books are no doubt harmful enough, particularly as English translations in England of French novels are unabridged, and much worse than similar translations in America. . . . [B]ut the prosecution is silly, because the by-streets simply teem with windows full not only of English publications of the vilest sort, but suggestive and obscene advertisements of all kinds. These are directly in the reach of the lower classes, who are most likely to be injured by them. Vizetelly is a prominent and respectable business man. If the prosecution of him was but the beginning of a general movement against the lower class dealers it would be laudable, but no such promise is made." A very long piece by George Moore, "New Censorship of Literature," dealing with the Vizetelly prosecutions and the activities of the vigilantes, was published in *The New York Herald* (London), July 28, 1889, 4–5.

Norman St. John-Stevas has written: "[Vizetelly's] prosecutions are of the greatest interest, since they provide the first examples of the law being invoked successfully against works of literary merit. Hitherto, its scope had been limited to the suppression of pornography. Some attempt must be made to explain this change. The immediate cause was the intervention of Kensit's National Vigilance Association." *Obscenity and the Law* (1956), 79. It seems likely that another immediate cause was the threat Vizetelly posed to the British book trade—and to the (private) censorship of literature then being conducted by the moralizing literary reviews, the establishment publishing houses, and the monopolistic giant circulating libraries— through his successful publication of novels in inexpensive one-volume editions. The London correspondent for *The New York Times* reported that Vizetelly was selling "about 1000 copies of Zola weekly," and the same figure was mentioned in Parliament by Samuel Smith of Flintshire in his attack on Vizetelly's publishing house, quoted in the text. Smith also said that "this fellow boasted that his house had been the means of translating and selling in the English market more than one million copies of French novels." There was also a fear of French literature in England at the time, which could be traced back to the role that literature had played in the French Revolution; and there was a fear of lascivious and even "indecorous" literature getting "into the hands of the lower orders and children of all classes" owing to the late-eighteenth-century "development of popular education through the new Sunday schools and its system whereby those who had learnt to read would read aloud to those who had not." Donald Thomas, *A Long Time Burning* (1969), 4.

St. John-Stevas's definition of "works of literary merit" and "pornography" led him to exclude from the former, and to include in the latter (which he also refers to as "erotic" literature), John Cleland's *Fanny Hill,* the appearance of which in 1749, one hundred and forty years before Vizetelly's prosecution, had provoked a warrant from the secretary of state for the arrest of the author, publisher, and printer. Thomas, *A Long Time Burning* (1969), 84–85. *Fanny Hill* provoked prosecutions in England as late as 1964, when a Bow Street magistrate condemned a paperback edition that sold at £3 6d. a copy (Thomas, 4–5). At that time, the government seems to have been motivated by fears of the effects of such literature not only upon "the lower orders" but upon wives in general. Thus, in the 1960 prosecution of Penguin Books for publishing *Lady Chatterley's Lover,* the opening address of the prosecution included a question to the jury: "Is it a book that you would even wish your wife or your servants to read?" (Thomas, 4). The modern American *Fanny Hill* case, and Justice Brennan's opinion in the case, figure in the later chapters of this book.

Before the Vizetelly prosecutions, Charles Bradlaugh and Annie Besant were prosecuted, in 1877, for publishing an "obscene" book, Charles Knowlton's *Fruits of Philosophy*—one of the most widely circulated books on the subject of birth control to appear in the nineteenth century—presumably on the theory that once the fear of pregnancy is removed, promiscuous sexual intercourse is bound to follow. It also had been published in a cheap edition, which sold at 6d. a copy (Thomas, 4). St. John-Stevas excluded this book from his consideration of the earliest example of the law's being successfully invoked against a work of literary merit not because the prosecution was not successful (it was, with respect to the suppression of the book) but because it did not involve imaginative literature, more particularly, the novel. Throughout the eighteenth and nineteenth centuries the novel was one of the most influential means for circulating information and ideas about what was then spoken of as "manners." The scope of the common-law prosecutions for "obscene" libel had been established very broadly by Queen's Bench, in 1868, in the case known as *Regina* v. *Hicklin,* in which a test of "obscenity" was first formulated, by Sir Alexander Cockburn. That was, in fact, not a criminal prosecution under the common law but a proceeding under Lord Campbell's Act (1857) to destroy copies of a pamphlet published by a militant Protestant society under the title "The Confessional Unmasked: showing the depravity of the Roman Priesthood, the iniquity of the Confessional and the questions put to females in confession." St. John-Stevas says a second edition of this pamphlet, expurgated and amended, and published in January 1869 at a shilling, has on its bright green cover "a picture of Britannia being eyed by the Pope who is about to let a dragon out of a cage" (*Obscenity and the Law,* 69). Lord Campbell's Act did not affect the definition of what was "obscene" or alter the scope of common-law criminal prosecutions; its importance was in giving magistrates the power to *destroy* all copies of an "obscene" book located by police empowered to *search* for them; no such powers were given by common law. *Regina* v. *Hicklin* is reprinted in de Grazia, *Censorship Landmarks* (1969), 5–11.

The judicial censorship of imaginative literature of merit in England began earlier than Vizetelly's prosecution under the obscenity law. Using the common law of blasphemous libel, the Society for the Suppression of Vice brought a successful criminal prosecution against William Clarke in 1822, for publishing Shelley's long and "blasphemous" poem *Queen Mab.* (Clarke's publication occurred shortly after Shelley drowned in the wreck of the *Ariel,* so the poet himself could not be prosecuted.) Clarke went to prison for four months on that occasion. This so stimulated interest in the work that by the end of the year there were no less than four entirely separate editions of *Queen Mab* on sale in England; and the radical publisher Richard Carlile, promoting his own version, also was imprisoned for it during the 1820s. The bravest edition of *Queen Mab* may have been the one published under the imprint of Mrs. Carlile and Sons in 1831, Richard Carlile being in prison at the time for having published in the previous year what the judges said was a "seditious" libel, his own *Address to the Insurgent Labourers.*

Byron called *Queen Mab* "a poem of great strength and wonderful powers of imagination." In the twenty-five years after its first printing, it became undoubtedly the most widely read, the most notorious, and the most influential of all Shelley's works. It had been written by the poet when he was eighteen, and privately printed by him in 250 copies. These Shelley soon tried to suppress for fear of prosecution, and the printer removed his own name from it "in case of trouble." The poem's dangerous tendencies (it attacked the institution of monogamy and the health value of chastity for women) were not noticed by the government or the anti-vice societies until 1816, when Lord Chancellor Eldon ruled, in a custody case, that it showed that Shelley was an atheist and a believer in free love and was therefore unfit to take care of his children. It was because of this decision that Shelley could not prevent the publication by Clarke and others of his *Queen Mab;* under another decision by Lord Eldon (called Southey's *Wat Tyler*), in 1817, a libelous work (whether "seditious," "blasphemous," or "obscene") could not enjoy copyright protection.

England's main private engines for the reformation of manners in life and litera-ture—the literary reviews and the anti-vice societies—brought about the prosecu-tion of a more reputable publisher, Moxon, for publishing *Queen Mab* in the early 1840s; Moxon was released upon giving up all copies of the poem for destruction. Mrs. Carlile's edition of *Queen Mab* was a cheap pocket-sized version, "intended for serious study," and was reprinted constantly by the great radical publishers of the 1840s, Heatherton and Watson. Between 1821 and 1845, fourteen or more sepa-rate editions of *Queen Mab* were published; during approximately the same period, from 1823 to 1841, English working-class and radical publications carried 140 items on Shelley, most of them excerpts from, or discussion of, *Queen Mab*. Besides reaching American radicals of the time, the poem was influential in liberal and revolutionary circles on the Continent; the young Friedrich Engels began a translation "before the 1848 upheavals" and was strongly influenced by the poem in the writing of his classic work on the subjugation of women, *Origin of the Family, Private Property and the State*. John Stuart Mill's classic *The Subjection of Women* was also influenced by *Queen Mab*. These, with Mary Wollstonecraft's *Vindication of the Rights of Women* (published in 1792 in the turbulent aftermath of the French Revolution), were in the forefront of the late nineteenth century's feminist movement.

It is significant that on the occasion of Vizetelly's prosecution for publishing Zola's naturalistic novels, neither he nor Emile Zola received support from established English (or French) publishers or authors; George Moore, of course, pled brilliantly but without avail for Vizetelly's cause. While Vizetelly was in prison, old and sick, an unsuccessful attempt was made by a group of literary figures to gain his early release. See Ernest Alfred Vizetelly, *Emile Zola* (1904).

Before the Vizetelly prosecutions in England, there occurred in France the unsuccessful prosecution of Flaubert and his publisher, in 1857, for publishing *Madame Bovary*, and the successful prosecution, six months later, of Baudelaire and his publisher, Poulet-Malassis, for issuing *Les Fleurs du mal*. The ground in both cases was the "outraging of public and religious morals." This post-Revolutionary "regime of prudery" lasted until the early years of the Third Republic. The Declaration of the Rights of Man included liberty of thought and speech, but this did not prevent a vigorous censorship of literature by French ministers and judges. In France, the newspaper publishers who published Zola's realistic novels serially were frequently threatened with prosecution, generating a great deal of self-censorship, as described in the text.

Born and raised in Ireland, George Moore spent seven years in Paris as a young man, trying to paint and to write. His financial condition pressed him to move to London, where he struggled to earn a living with his pen, while "bursting with what were then, in England, aesthetically revolutionary ideas." His *A Mummer's Wife* (1885) "owed something to Zola and in its principal female character even more to Emma Bovary"; it is considered to have been the first realistic novel in English after Defoe. His *Esther Waters* (1894) has been called "the first realistic masterpiece in the language." He was regarded by many as a shocking or scandalous writer, for he made no concessions to Victorian prejudice. After Hardy's death, he had "a strong claim to be considered the chief novelist of his day, Kipling's greatness being different in kind." There is a drawing of Moore as a young man by Edouard Manet, an oil painting by Richard Sickert in the Tate Gallery, and a pastel by Henry Tonks in the National Portrait Gallery. See: *Dictionary of National Biography 1931–1940; The Life of George Moore* (with bibliography) by Joseph Hone (1936); and an *Epitaph on George Moore* by Charles Morgan (1935).

In the States, the house of Appleton published several of Moore's novels, including *Memoirs of My Dead Life* (1906), which *Life* magazine termed a collection of "exquisitely delicate indelicacies." When Appleton wanted to omit some of the indelicacies, Moore consented, provided he could write a foreword setting out his views on the subject; this turned out to be a celebrated essay on censorship, *Apologia Pro Scriptis Meis,* excoriating attempts to control other people's minds and roundly condemning puritanical morality. In 1911 Appleton published the first volume of Moore's trilogy *Hail and Farewell*. Charles Scribner decried that "so many of the well-known English authors—like Wells, Arnold Bennett and George Moore"—were "too free and coarse in their handling of delicate questions to suit us." He turned down Moore's *Esther Waters* because he did not think the public would tolerate a novel about a chambermaid's illicit love affair—a "mistake" that John Tebbel attributes to Scribner's "austere conservatism." John Tebbel, *A History of Book Publishing in the United States* 2 (1975), 224–25. Tebbel also says that Scribner "admitted he himself enjoyed the work of these writers; it was just that he thought his imprint would suffer" (613). Moore became one of the "early strikes" and biggest money-makers of American publisher Horace Liveright, who was introduced to Moore through his great editor in chief T. R. Smith (see Chapter 8). Liveright paid Moore a $30,000 advance for the Carra edition of his works and sold a thousand sets. Tebbel, vol. 3 (1978), 140–41. As late as 1930, customs officials were interfering with Moore's books; an inscribed first edition copy of Moore's *A Story Teller's Holiday* was seized. "The censors had been especially upset by an illustration in the book, Botticelli's *Venus Arising from the Sea.*" Tebbel, vol. 3 (1978), 641.

For most of his career Moore had a running battle with the English circulating libraries, Mudie's and Smith's. One of his liveliest attacks on them tells the story of how his *A Modern Lover,* published in 1883, was rejected by Smith's because the library's advisers, "two ladies from the county," wrote "objecting to that scene where the girl sat to the artist as a model for Venus." George Moore, "A New Censorship of Literature," *Pall Mall Gazette,* December 10, 1884. When a similar fate met Moore's *A Mummer's Wife* in 1884, Moore had Vizetelly put out a cheap edition and countered with a blistering attack on the libraries, *Literature at Nurse or Circulating Morals* (1885). Nevertheless, neither Smith's nor Mudie's would stock his *Esther Waters,* published in 1894. See Norman St. John-Stevas, *Obscenity and the Law* (1956), 75–76. Theodore Dreiser's *The "Genius"* also ran into censorship because of the eroticism in a scene in which the young protagonist drew from life (Chapter 6).

PAGE

41   "Will you allow me . . ." Alan Schom, *Emile Zola: A Biography* (1988), 117.

41   "His work is bad . . ." *Ibid.*

42   *"Carefully, as though undertaking . . ." La Terre.*

43   "Zolaism is a disease . . ." Reprinted in The National Vigilance Association, *Pernicious Literature* (1889), 380–81.

43   "There is nothing likely . . ." *Ibid.,* 377.

43   "It is true that Rabelais . . ." *Ibid.,* 376–77.

43   "A lady of my acquaintance . . ." *Ibid.,* 352–62.

44   "Mr. Henry Vizetelly, the publisher, surrendered . . ." London *Times,* November 1, 1888, p. 13.

44   "He first had felt fairly confident . . ." Ernest Alfred Vizetelly, *Emile Zola* (1904), 274.

45   "There was an incessant . . ." *Ibid.*

46   "They are charged in the indictment . . ." *Ibid.,* 275.

46   "The book in my hand . . ." London *Times,* November 1, 1888.

PAGE

46   *"And so, as soon as they were alone . . ."* *La Terre.*

46   "I hope you will understand . . ." London *Times,* November 1, 1888.

46   "Acting upon my advice . . ." E. A. Vizetelly, *Emile Zola,* 279–80.

47   "Of course I am very glad . . ." *Ibid.,* 281–82.

47   "Works of a *great* French author . . ." London *Times,* November 1, 1888.

47   "A *voluminous* French author . . ." *Ibid.*

48   "Henceforth, anyone who publishes . . ." *Ibid.*

48   "[O]n the day of his new committal . . ." E. A. Vizetelly, *Emile Zola,* 286.

49   "Mr. Cock, Q.C., was a fat . . ." *Ibid.,* 291.

49   "The blow was a *coup de massue . . ."* *Ibid.*

50   "He rolled out of the room . . ." *Ibid.*

50   "Did Henry Vizetelly hear those last words?" *Ibid.,* 292.

50   "The proceedings were brief . . ." *Ibid.*

51   "Now, now, we want . . ." *Ibid.,* 293–94.

51   "This poor old gentleman . . ." George Moore, "Literature and Morals," *Century* magazine, May 19, 1919, 124–34. *Avowals* (1924), 163, contains a similar reproach by Moore against English lawyers.

52   "There was a good jury . . ." Moore, "Literature and Morals," *Century* magazine, May 19, 1919, 124–34.

52   "Since then I have oft times . . ." *Ibid.*

Chapter 4: *A Sermon-on-the-Mount—of Venus*

Lawrence's first published novel, *The White Peacock,* came out without difficulty in 1911. His second novel, *The Trespasser,* did not run afoul of official censors but Heinemann's reaction to its "erotic" theme persuaded Lawrence to have the book published by Garnett and Duckworth instead. Ford Madox Ford had advised Heinemann that *The Trespasser* was "a rotten work of genius" and also "erotic" and this insulted Lawrence. In those days "erotic" was a word of fear to publishers, "for it was not so long since Vizetelly had been imprisoned and reduced to poverty for the horrible crime of publishing Zola." Richard Aldington, *D. H. Lawrence: Portrait of a Genius But . . .* (1950), 96–102.

My description of the Methuen affair is drawn mainly from the accounts in: Emile Delavenay's *D. H. Lawrence: The Man and His Work* (1972); the introduction written for the Cambridge edition of D. H. Lawrence's *The Rainbow* by Mark Kinkead-Weekes (1989); and John Carter, "The 'Rainbow' Prosecution," *Times Literary Supplement,* February 27, 1969, 216. Other sources used in relating the events in Lawrence's life include the Cambridge edition of *The Letters of D. H. Lawrence,* under the general editorship of James T. Boulton, to date in five volumes (1979–1989); *The Collected Letters of D. H. Lawrence,* edited by Harry T. Moore, in two volumes (1962); *The Selected Letters of D. H. Lawrence,* edited by Diana Trilling (1958); Frieda Lawrence, *The Memoirs and Correspondence* (1961) and *Not I, But the Wind* (1934); the Cambridge edition of *Women in Love,* edited by David Farmer, Lindeth Vasey, and John Worthen (1987); *D. H. Lawrence: A Composite*

Biography, in three volumes, gathered, arranged, and edited by Edward Nehls (1958); Harry T. Moore, *The Intelligent Heart: The Story of D. H. Lawrence* (1962) and *The Priest of Love* (1974); Keith Sagar, *The Life of D. H. Lawrence* (1980); Edward D. McDonald, *A Bibliography of the Writings of D. H. Lawrence* (1924), with an introduction by D. H. Lawrence; Richard Aldington, *D. H. Lawrence: Portrait of a Genius But . . .* (1950); John Worthen, *D. H. Lawrence: A Literary Life* (1989); Jeffrey Meyers, *D. H. Lawrence: A Biography* (1990).

Information gathered by scholars in 1969 reinforces the idea that political, as much as sexual, considerations motivated the censorship of *The Rainbow:* that the government acted to destroy *The Rainbow* and injure its author because Lawrence was looked upon as a dangerous antiwar "subversive," and because the book's heroine showed hostility to English soldiers. Evidence of this is laid out in Emile Delavenay's *D. H. Lawrence: The Man and His Work* (1972), 231ff.; and in the Cambridge edition of *The Rainbow,* edited by Mark Kinkead-Weekes (1989), xlvi-xlviii.

On Thomas and Adele Seltzer, see "A Biographical Narrative" by Alexandra Lee Levin and Lawrence L. Levin, in *D. H. Lawrence: Letters to Thomas and Adele Seltzer,* edited by Gerald M. Lacy (1976), 171ff. Thomas Seltzer was brought to the United States as a boy and was a sweatshop worker at the age of eleven. He went to high school and, on scholarship, to the University of Pennsylvania, receiving a B.A. in 1897; he then did postgraduate studies in modern languages. When Maxim Gorky landed in New York in 1906, he named Seltzer his translator and interpreter. Huebsch published Seltzer's translation of Gorky's *The Spy.* Gorky's *Mother* was another Seltzer translation. For his pioneering work for *The Masses* magazine, where he drew heavily on the work of social reformers and on European fiction (publishing stories by Tolstoy, Chekhov, Sudermann, and Björnson), Granville Hicks referred to him as one of the intellectual "giants of the Village," in his *John Reed—The Making of a Revolutionary* (1936).

Adele Seltzer was an emancipated woman who, however, devoted much of her life to assisting Thomas's book-publishing business. She evidently translated into English Sudermann's *Song of Songs (Das hohe Lied)* for B. W. Huebsch in 1909, although Thomas was given the credit for it, in order, as Adele said, "to further his literary prospects." This was a long novel "baring the corruption of Berlin society and the immorality of the ruling Prussian Junker class." Like B. W. Huebsch, Seltzer also sailed aboard the *Oscar II,* Henry Ford's "peace ship," as a member of the Ford Peace Party's executive committee. Henry Ford deserted the other peace-seekers when the boat docked at Christiania, Norway. See also Thomas Tanselle's *The Thomas Seltzer Imprint.* Seltzer published Lawrence's *Women in Love* when no other American publisher would. He was never very far from bankruptcy; it is small wonder that his "experimental" publishing venture finally failed, having been launched during a serious depression in the book trade. As Adele said, his was "a succès d'estime"—"even if not a financial success." Seltzer could never afford the $5,000 or so it is said to have cost in those days to hire a good assistant.

On Mitchell Kennerley, see Matthew Bruccoli, *The Fortunes of Mitchell Kennerley, Bookman* (1986), and the entries in John Tebbel, *A History of Book Publishing in the United States* 2 (1975). Describing Kennerley's relations with Frank Harris, best known today for his long "obscene" work *My Life and Loves,* Bruccoli observes: "Kennerley and Harris were curiously alike. Both were promoters and womanizers; both were unreliable with money; and both had a built-in self-destruct mechanism—a compulsion to push their luck." Bruccoli continues: "Kennerley's assessment of Harris has the ring of autobiography: 'Harris was a fascinating person, absolutely honest about everything except money. You could not buy his praise. You were "unstable" if you failed to back his desires and plans. He was a magnificent host—with your money.' " During the summer of 1909 Kennerley and Harris met in London and together they hatched big plans. Harris wrote him: "We should make your office the centre of literary America, the place where the American academy will be founded, as well as the first American journal devoted to books" (37).

The DeLacey case in the Supreme Judicial Court of Massachusetts was *Commonwealth* v. *DeLacey,* 171 N.E. 455 (1930).

PAGE

54   "They brought me their most erotic efforts . . ." Sylvia Beach, *Shakespeare and Company* (1959), 91. Noel Riley Fitch says, "As the publisher of *Ulysses* and as the distributor of both privately printed and controversial books, Sylvia had a shady reputation in some quarters." *Sylvia Beach and the Lost Generation* (1983), 280.

54   "His long arms swinging apelike . . ." Sylvia Beach, *Shakespeare and Company* (1959), 91.

55   *"I kept a buggy and horse at a livery stable . . ."* Frank Harris, *My Life and Loves* (1963). I do not know that this is one of the passages Harris read to Beach; there is no record of what he said.

55   "[W]hen he gave up trying . . ." Beach, *Shakespeare and Company* (1959), 91. Jack Kahane seems not to have published *My Life and Loves;* it was privately published in 1925 (in Germany?) by Harris, who died in 1931. The man's vanity got in the way of his finer attributes, much as his notorious authorship of *My Life and Loves* served to obscure his more important literary work and even to "bring him down." As John F. Gallagher said in the biographical sketch of Harris written as an introduction to the Grove Press edition of *My Life and Loves:* "Harris' reputation is the price he paid for his arrogance." He was "the best talker in London," outshining even Oscar Wilde, who is said to have hit the mark by saying: "Frank Harris has been received in all the great houses in London—once!" Harris was "short, swarthy, heavily mustached, and intense." His "best book, by far," *Oscar Wilde* (1916), failed to get the attention it deserved because of its "unfairness" to Lord Alfred Douglas. Arrogance was, of course, a trait familiar to Wilde, who might be said almost to have been utterly destroyed by it. Richard Ellmann has given us the definitive biography of Wilde, *Oscar Wilde* (1988), as he has of Joyce, *James Joyce* (New and Revised Edition, 1982). George Bernard Shaw, who "kept Harris as a friend for forty years," wrote candidly and understandingly about him in a postscript to Harris's book *Bernard Shaw* (1941).

55   "I was obliged to turn [it] down . . ." Sylvia Beach, *Shakespeare and Company* (1959), 92.

56   "It was sad refusing Lawrence's *Lady* . . ." Beach, *Shakespeare and Company* (1959), 93. Noel Riley Fitch says Beach suggested the publisher Edward Titus, who eventually brought out a cheap French edition of the

novel, which "became one of Shakespeare and Company's best sellers."
Sylvia Beach and the Lost Generation (1983), 280.

56 "I send you back the slips and pages . . ." *The Collected Letters of D. H.
Lawrence,* edited by Harry T. Moore, vol. 1 (1962), 356. Lawrence had
been uneasy about Methuen even before finishing *The Rainbow.* On
February 11, 1915, he mentioned that E. M. Forster had brought to
Greatham "a ghastly rumour of the *Prussian Officer*'s being withdrawn
from circulation, by order of the police" and said he hoped that Methuen "will not think it impossible to print [*The Rainbow*] as it stands."
Two weeks later, Lawrence expressed concern whether Methuen would
be "ready to back up this novel of mine" and "make some fight for it
. . . and prevent the mean little fry from pulling it down." He knew he
would need his agent's support to get his book published as he wrote
it. On April 23, he sent another letter to Pinker: "I hope you are willing
to fight for this novel. It is nearly three years of hard work, and I am
proud of it, and it must be stood up for. I am afraid there are parts of
it Methuen won't want to publish. He must. I will take out sentences
and phrases, but I won't take out paragraphs or pages. . . . You see a
novel, after all this period of coming into being, has a definite organic
form, just as a man has when he is grown. And we don't ask a man to
cut his nose off because the public won't like it. . . . Oh God, I hope
I'm not going to have a miserable time over this book, now I've at last
got it pretty much to its real being." And, just a week later, mailing the
last batch of the *Rainbow* manuscript to Pinker: "I hope you will like the
book: also that it is not very improper. It did not seem to me very
improper, as I went through it. But then I feel very incompetent to
judge on that point. . . . My beloved book. I am sorry to give it to you
to be printed." The quotations are from the Cambridge edition of *The
Letters of D. H. Lawrence* 2 (1979), 327, 329.

The temptation to self-censor, to engage in or permit expurgation in
fear of critical or governmental reprisal, must have been strong for
struggling artists like Joyce, Lawrence, and Dreiser. Their impecunious
condition was, of course, partly due to government censorship actions
which deprived them of free-market returns for the sale of the intellectual
property they created. The temptation to self-censor presumably was less
strong for better-heeled authors like Radclyffe Hall, Vladimir Nabokov,
and even Edmund Wilson. Still, neither Hall nor Nabokov used "strong
language" in writing their sexually "immoral" works, and Wilson used
words like "cock" and "cunt" in his posthumously (and freely) published
diaries, but not in his "obscene" novel *Memoirs of Hecate County,* published during his lifetime. See Chapters 10–13.

William Burroughs was so concerned to see his novel *Naked Lunch*
published in the States that he agreed to let Barney Rosset's Grove Press
publish it expurgated, but after a delay, Rosset elected instead to publish
it unexpurgated. I found no sign that James Joyce or Henry Miller cut
even a word from *Ulysses* or *Tropic of Cancer.* Compare the ironical
attitude taken by Norman Mailer toward expurgations desired by his publisher and his methods for getting around such obstacles to his freedom
to write (Chapter 23). Allen Ginsberg never expurgated his work in

deference to or fear of critic, publisher, or censor, and his original publisher, like Joyce's, never asked him to. He was prosecuted on this score, but not jailed; see Chapter 17.

57 "The solicitors, in consideration . . ." Emile Delavenay, *D. H. Lawrence: The Man and His Work* (1972), 237.

57 "We understood from Inspector Draper . . ." *Ibid.*

58 "The proceedings read, in retrospect . . ." *Ibid.*, 239. In a criminal case, government authorities must rely on the frightening effect of a conviction to deter others, as well as the convicted person, from distributing extant copies of the book. Lord Campbell's Act was an excellent tool for destroying an entire edition of a work, as in the *Rainbow* case. With certain possible exceptions mentioned below, no comparable authority appears to have been created under American law; but John Sumner learned how to use the threat of criminal prosecution by itself to achieve the same effect: obliging publishers to *agree* to recall all copies of the targeted books in the hands of dealers, turn over extant stock for destruction by the authorities, and obliterate the printing plates. As indicated later on in the text, Sumner persuaded Alfred A. Knopf, Thomas Seltzer, John Lane, and Doubleday to destroy, respectively, entire editions of *Homo Sapiens, Casanova's Homecoming, A Young Girl's Diary, The "Genius,"* and *Memoirs of Hecate County.* Publisher Mitchell Kennerley fought the system by going to court against Anthony Comstock and, with the aid of lawyer John Quinn, persuading a federal jury that the novel *Hagar Revelly* was not obscene, as described in this chapter.

The U.S. customs and postal laws provided a legal framework within which the police might secure the destruction of a quantity of books by seizing the books at port of entry, or upon receipt for mailing, and administratively condemning them as obscene. It is, however, unclear whether the laws invoked in this way ever authorized such action; and in the *Hagar Revelly* case, Kennerley seems to have been able to challenge the procedures and force Comstock to institute a regular criminal proceeding against him for mailing the work.

As mentioned later on, Wilhelm Reich's books were destroyed *en masse* by authorities of the federal Food and Drug Administration. The lateness of the development (circa 1960) of the theory that the federal constitutional guarantees of freedom of the press protect literary and artistic (as well as political) expression from government suppression accounts perhaps for the willingness of American publishers and their lawyers, during the first half of this century, to agree to destroy entire editions of their books. Wilhelm Reich, however, never agreed to what the government did to his books. The late arrival of constitutional protection for artistic expression is discussed at various points in this book.

In the United States, the burden of proving a book obscene in a criminal proceeding has traditionally rested with the prosecutor, but, as in England, this burden has usually been discharged merely by putting the book, or portions of the book, in evidence for the judge or jury to hear or read. During the 1960s, the Supreme Court of the United States, speaking through Justice Brennan, imposed on the prosecutor of

PAGE

"obscenity" the extremely onerous burden of proving that an attacked book or movie not only appealed to the prurient interests of the average person and was patently offensive to community standards of candor in sexual matters but was "utterly without" any social importance (the "Brennan doctrine"). However, in 1973 the Burger Court alleviated the burden by asserting, among other things, that it could be enough for a prosecutor to put into evidence the allegedly obscene material alone, and for the judge or jury to *infer* the necessary essentials of the crime from it. Geoffrey Robertson's *Obscenity* (1979) contains a masterly description of the making of obscenity law in England during the eighteenth and nineteenth centuries (Chapter 2). This book, Norman St. John-Stevas's *Obscenity and the Law* (1956), and Donald Thomas's *A Long Time Burning* (1969) are outstanding examples of literate legal-literary scholarship, superior in my opinion to anything of the kind yet published in the United States. In England, it apparently remains possible to proceed against a publisher and his book through summary search-seize-and-destroy proceedings, without option for jury trial, and proceedings of this sort seem to have been used in 1966 to suppress *Last Exit to Brooklyn,* by the American novelist Hubert Selby, Jr., which was published in England by John Calder. After the magistrate found the book obscene and ordered the seized copies destroyed, however, Calder continued to publish and sell the book and was thereupon *criminally* prosecuted, tried, and convicted by a jury of his peers, despite a most impressive array of literary and scholarly figures who testified to the novel's contributions to "the public good"—a new and important defense under the 1959 Obscene Publications Act. When Calder appealed his conviction, the judges overturned it and his fine of £500 (the prosecution had also cost the publisher an estimated £15,000 for litigation and lawyers) and Calder was able to publish *Last Exit* freely. The case is described in John Sutherland, *Offensive Literature: Decensorship in Britain 1960–1982* (1982) and in Geoffrey Robertson, *Obscenity* (1979). John Calder in due course removed his brave little publishing venture to New York, where he publishes under the imprint of Riverrun Press.

59   "My dear Lady Cynthia . . ." *The Letters of D. H. Lawrence,* edited by Aldous Huxley (1932), 274–75.

59   "[T]he publishers and not the author . . ." Emile Delavenay, *D. H. Lawrence: The Man and His Work* (1972), 241.

60   "[Sir John] had never read anything . . ." *Ibid.*

61   *"As she sat by her bedroom window . . ."* D. H. Lawrence, *The Rainbow* (1915).

63   "Many of the other sensitive literary men . . ." Harry T. Moore, *The Intelligent Heart* (1962), 252.

63   "A man said we could live . . ." *The Collected Letters of D. H. Lawrence,* edited by Harry T. Moore, vol. 1 (1962), 377.

64   "I hope to be going away . . ." *Ibid.,* 376.

64   "I believe that England . . ." *The Letters of D. H. Lawrence,* edited by Aldous Huxley (1932), 392.

64   "I don't think America is a paradise . . ." *Selected Letters of D. H. Lawrence,* edited by Diana Trilling (1958), 146–47.

66 "Mr. Kennerley was prosecuted . . ." John Tebbel, *A History of Book Publishing in the United States* (1975), 631. The book that brought on Comstock's challenge of Kennerley was *Hagar Revelly,* an early example of the novel of realism, written by a St. Louis physician named Daniel Carson Goodman. It told the story of two poverty-stricken sisters in New York possessed of the unorthodox view that purity was "not an affair of the body," but involved "the mind." One of the sisters, Hagar, barely escapes a life of prostitution by becoming the mistress of her boss. Since Comstock found the book "rotten," he had Kennerley charged with knowingly putting an obscene book into the U.S. mails and seized the entire stock, plus 2,000 copies at the bindery, and the book's plates. The case was *United States* v. *Kennerley;* it is reprinted in de Grazia, *Censorship Landmarks* (1969), 58. In this case, Kennerley went into federal court to seek the return of the books and plates, claiming that the novel was not obscene and that its message was in the mainstream of the social hygiene movement of the day. Hand said he thought it should be left up to a jury to decide whether *Hagar Revelly* was obscene, and that the meaning of that term should be fixed not by "mid-Victorian morals" but by "the present critical point in the compromise between candor and shame at which the community may have arrived here and now." Added Hand: "To put thought in leash to the average conscience of the time is perhaps tolerable, but to fetter it by the necessities of the lowest *and* least capable seems a fatal policy." This was the dictum that was ignored by the judge in the federal criminal trial that followed.

The processes available to Comstock under federal and state laws, and later to John Sumner under state law, to seize an entire edition of a published work bear comparison with the procedures open to police magistrates in England under Lord Campbell's Act. However, in Kennerley's case it evidently was possible to insist on a jury trial by moving to enjoin the destruction and obliging the government to initiate criminal proceedings of the regular sort. Comstock's warrant to seize the entire stock and bindery copies of the book may have been based on the theory that those copies were intended to be sold through the mails.

67 "[Mitchell Kennerley] published *Sons and Lovers* . . ." Edward D. McDonald, *A Bibliography of the Writings of D. H. Lawrence* (1924), 11–12 (Lawrence's foreword, "The Bad Side of Books").

68 "[Kennerley] is a jug . . ." Harry T. Moore, *The Intelligent Heart* (1962), 225.

68 "What did it matter in the end . . ." Matthew J. Bruccoli, *The Fortunes of Mitchell Kennerley, Bookman* (1986), 34–35.

68 "These are kind thoughts but . . ." Harry T. Moore, *The Intelligent Heart* (1962), 207.

68 "I barely escaped . . ." George H. Doran, *Chronicles of Barabbas* (1935), 285.

69 "It doesn't seem to me that . . ." *The Letters of D. H. Lawrence* 2 (Cambridge edition, 1979), 419.

69 "Is he disreputable . . ." *Ibid.*

70 *"Ursula lay still. . . ."* D. H. Lawrence, *The Rainbow* (Cambridge edition, 1989), 266.

PAGE
70 "Surmising that the then current Comstock . . ." D. H. Lawrence, *The Rainbow* (Cambridge edition, 1989), lix-lx.

CHAPTER 5: *It's Such an Ugly Cemetery*

PAGE
73 "So Thomas has come out . . ." *D. H. Lawrence: Letters to Thomas and Adele Seltzer,* edited by Gerald M. Lacy (1976), 183.
73 "What can ail our magistrates?" Walker Gilmer, *Horace Liveright: Publisher of the Twenties* (1970), 69.
74 *"They threw off their clothes . . ."* D. H. Lawrence, *Women in Love.*
75 "But profane writers . . ." *The New York Times,* April 18, 1923, 20. Fairly full accounts of the Clean Books League events are in: Walker Gilmer, *Horace Liveright: Publisher of the Twenties* (1970), 69ff.; Paul S. Boyer, *Purity in Print* (1968), Chapter 5; and John Tebbel, *A History of Book Publishing in the United States* 3 (1978), 399ff.
75 "Let Judge Ford confine his judgment . . ." *The New York Times,* February 11, 1923, 18.
76 "For God's sake, Horace, what's this? . . ." Walker Gilmer, *Horace Liveright: Publisher of the Twenties* (1970), 76.
77 "There is not one among us . . ." *Ibid.,* 78–79.
78 "[T]he only publishers who helped at all . . ." *Ibid.,* 80.
78 "If A and B . . ." *The New York Times,* April 23, 1923, 14.
79 "Thomas Seltzer and his wife . . ." *D. H. Lawrence: Letters to Thomas and Adele Seltzer,* edited by Gerald M. Lacy (1976), 254.
79 "Lawrence is a Titan . . ." *Ibid.*
80 "You should see Thomas when he comes home . . ." *Ibid.,* 179.
80 "I think Lawrence means to be. . . ." *Ibid.,* 258.
80 "Landed at last . . ." *The Letters of D. H. Lawrence,* edited by James T. Boulton, vol. 4 (1987), 600.
81 "Seltzer and Mrs. Seltzer are not so nice . . ." *The Letters of D. H. Lawrence,* edited by James T. Boulton and Lindeth Vasey, vol. 5 (1989), 15–16.
81 "I'm glad you saw Seltzer . . ." *Ibid.,* 147.
81 "And I'm sure he'll never . . ." *Ibid.,* 161.
81 "My agent has started . . ." *Ibid.,* 169.
81 "I wired Barmby to proceed with Knopf . . ." *Ibid.,* 193–94.
82 "I have left Seltzer, who hangs . . ." *Ibid.,* 269.
82 "All I want is to pay our debts and DIE." *D. H. Lawrence: A Composite Biography,* edited by Edward Nehls, vol. 2 (1958), 424.
82 "You say you will pay me . . ." *The Letters of D. H. Lawrence,* edited by James T. Boulton and Lindeth Vasey, vol. 5 (1989), 574.
83 "I think of you and Adele often . . ." *D. H. Lawrence: Letters to Thomas and Adele Seltzer,* edited by Gerald M. Lacy (1976), 153–54.
84 "No, No, it's such an ugly cemetery . . ." Harry T. Moore, *The Intelligent Heart* (1962), 418.

PAGE

84 "After breakfast . . ." Frieda Lawrence, *Not I, But the Wind* (1934), 193.

85 "He wrote these *Pansies* . . ." Harry T. Moore, *The Intelligent Heart* (1962), 482.

85 "Will the right hon. Gentleman . . ." *Ibid.,* 486. From the time of the enactment of the Comstock law in the late nineteenth century at least until 1955, when I filed suit, on behalf of the consignee of a rare edition of Aristophanes' *Lysistrata,* to declare unconstitutional the postal laws under which the postmaster general found authority to seize from the mails and destroy anything he considered "obscene," the U.S. Post Office engaged in similar censorship activities. For an idea of the sort of literature censored by the government under this supposed authority, see the article "Obscenity and the Mail," which I wrote for a seminal symposium issue on Obscenity and the Arts, published in *Law and Contemporary Problems* 20 (1955), 608; and see James C. N. Paul and Murray L. Schwartz's definitive work in the area, *Federal Censorship: Obscenity and the Mail* (1961). The *Lysistrata* case, the information about postal censorship contained in my article, and the book by Paul and Schwartz led to public and judicial criticism of, and eventually the abandonment of, the Post Office's practice of seizing "obscene" publications from the mails. Among the last cases of this type were the attempted suppressions by the Post Office of the "Burroughs issue" of *Big Table* magazine, and of the Grove edition of *Lady Chatterley's Lover,* both in 1959. As described in Chapter 18, the former seizure was reversed by a federal judge in Chicago. The *Lady C.* seizure was nullified by a federal judge in New York. The suit I filed succeeded in freeing *Lysistrata* from censorship but failed to result in a declaration that the postal obscenity censorship law was unconstitutional. Other censorial powers of the Post Office are mentioned in the discussion of the *Roth* case in Chapter 16.

86 "I am advised . . ." Harry T. Moore, *The Intelligent Heart* (1962), 486.

86 "In the first place . . ." *Ibid.*

86 "Like Simon . . ." *Ibid.,* 486–87.

87 "Hearing that William Blake . . ." Richard Aldington, *D. H. Lawrence: Portrait of a Genius But . . .* (1950), 324.

88 "Lately I saw . . ." *Ibid.,* 325.

88 "[T]hat they may never pollute . . ." Frieda Lawrence, *Not I, But the Wind* (1934), 277–88.

89 "Says shit! and fuck! in so many syllables . . ." *Selected Letters of D. H. Lawrence,* edited by Diana Trilling (1958), 272.

89 "Shall I publish it . . ." Frieda Lawrence, *Not I, But the Wind* (1934), 193.

90 "Why the book . . ." Richard Aldington, *D. H. Lawrence: Portrait of a Genius But . . .* (1950), 320.

91 " 'But what do you believe in?' " D. H. Lawrence, *Lady Chatterley's Lover.*

92 "I was not advocating perpetual sex." *The Collected Letters of D. H. Lawrence,* edited by Harry T. Moore (1962), 1111.

92 " 'Let me see you!' " D. H. Lawrence, *Lady Chatterley's Lover.*

93 "I did a fair amount of blanking out . . ." *Selected Letters of D. H. Lawrence,* edited by Diana Trilling (1958), 274.

PAGE

95 "Alas, poor Lawrence!" Richard Aldington, *D. H. Lawrence: Portrait of a Genius But* . . . (1950), 318.

95 "Here I just dabble at tiny pictures . . ." *Ibid.*

95 "Lawrence had always thought with horror . . ." Frieda Lawrence, *Not I, But the Wind* (1934), 292.

96 "One night I saw . . ." *Ibid.,* 293–94.

96 "Frieda could now hold back her tears . . ." Richard Aldington, *D. H. Lawrence: Portrait of a Genius But* . . . (1950), 334.

97 "Lorenzo is dead . . ." Frieda Lawrence, *The Memoirs and Correspondence* (1961), 236–39.

CHAPTER 6: *L'Affaire Doubleday*

On Frank N. Doubleday and the Doubleday publishing history see John Tebbel, *A History of Publishing in the United States,* vol 2 (1975), 318–31; vol. 3 (1978), 109–13, 527–28. Effendi developed the mail-order and subscription phases of the book-publishing business "to remarkable dimensions" and was "inexhaustible in fertile schemes for larger distribution." The idea that publishing should be essentially an intelligently conducted commerce, not a form of aesthetic bohemianism, appealed strongly to his authors. He was, I think, the first publisher anywhere to submit to his authors royalty statements checked and substantiated by outside accountants. He developed a successful chain of his own bookstores as "laboratories of selling." Christopher Morley, "Effendi," *The Saturday Review of Literature,* February 10, 1934, 471. See also: Gerald Gross, *Publishers on Publishing* (1961), 104–12; Richard Lingeman, *Theodore Dreiser,* vol. 1: *At the Gates of the City* (1986), 280ff.; W.A. Swanberg, *Dreiser* (1965), 87ff.

On the "token" publication of *Sister Carrie,* see: W. A. Swanberg, *Dreiser* (1965), 86–92; Helen Dreiser, *My Life with Dreiser* (1951), 273–74; Richard Lingeman, *Theodore Dreiser,* vol. 1: *At the Gates of the City* (1986), 281–97. Paramount made a film adaptation of *Sister Carrie* in 1952, directed by William Wyler with Laurence Olivier in the role of George Hurstwood and Jennifer Jones as Carrie Meeber.

Dreiser received between $40,000 and $50,000 for the movie rights to *Carrie* in 1939, but the movie was not made until 1952. In a letter to Mencken dated June 16, 1939, Dreiser wrote: "Pending the amicable adjudication of certain *moral* points with the Hays Office—(believe it or not the book is still immoral because—harken—Carrie isn't punished for her crime)—a fairly solid binder has been handed over free and clear. And they'll work to get that back if they have to turn it into a comedy. Its total history certainly constitutes one." *The Dreiser-Mencken Letters,* edited by Thomas P. Riggio (1986), vol. 2, 644.

PAGE

100 "Dreiser was writing according to . . ." Theodore Dreiser, *Sister Carrie* (introduction by E. L. Doctorow) (Bantam Classic, 1982), viii.

100 "Carrie is hardly a designing femme fatale. . . ." Theodore Dreiser, *Sister Carrie* (introduction by Alfred Kazin) (Penguin Classic, 1986), xi.

101   "He seems to have had no inkling . . ." W. A. Swanberg, *Dreiser*
        (1965), 83.
102   "She affected me like fire . . ." *Ibid.*, 86.
102   "Our wish to be released by you . . ." *Ibid.*, 89.
102   "The public feeds upon nothing which . . ." Richard Lingeman, *Theodore
        Dreiser*, vol. 1: *At the Gates of the City 1871–1907* (1986), 289.
103   "The book will not sell." W. A. Swanberg, *Dreiser* (1965), 90.
103   "All right, you stand on your legal rights. . . ." *Ibid.*, 90.
106   "Then came ill health . . ." Theodore Dreiser, *An Amateur Laborer*
        (1984), 4.
106   "Here I had come . . ." *Ibid.*
107   " 'Yes, yes,' he commented . . ." *Ibid.*, 6.
107   "The opening fee in this case . . ." *Ibid.*
107   "In addition to this . . ." *Ibid.*, 25.
108   "The sight of the icy cold and splashing waters . . ." Theodore Dreiser,
        The American Diaries: 1902–1926 (1983), 13.

CHAPTER 7: *Mencken's Lead Zeppelins*

John Tebbel describes the censorship of The *"Genius"* in his *History of Book Publishing in the United States* 2 (1975) at 631–32, and the suppression of *The Titan* at 614. Dreiser speaks of his problems concerning *The Titan* and The *"Genius"* in letters reproduced in Volume 1 of *The Dreiser-Mencken Letters,* edited by Thomas P. Riggio (1986). On September 20, 1920, Dreiser wrote Mencken about his exasperation with John Lane's handling of The *"Genius"*: "J. Jefferson Jones can kiss my ass. I don't want him to republish The *"Genius"* and I want him to let go of my property" (278). See also Richard Lingeman, *Theodore Dreiser,* vol. 2: *An American Journey* (1990).

Riggio writes: "Two years before the country went to war, Mencken and Dreiser began comparing notes about the personal toll they, as noncombatants, would pay if the country fought against Germany. Their jokes reflected the fears they lived with: 'I believe that both of us will be killed by patriots within six months,' wrote Mencken in 1916, as bravado mixed with wartime hysteria. And, he added, 'You will be lucky, with your German name, if you are not jailed the day the U.S. enters the war.' Dreiser followed Mencken's lead and started closing his letters with 'Deutschland über alles.' When the United States declared war on Germany in 1917, Mencken shared with Dreiser his fears of mob violence against his family in Baltimore, and Dreiser escaped stress by retreating to Maryland's farm country, where Mencken would join him to discuss their fates over gin highballs. . . . They were, the record shows, easy marks for wartime mania" (177–78).

110   "Soul enrapt, demi-urge . . ." W. A. Swanberg, *Dreiser* (1965), 242.
110   "Dreiser was never any good until . . ." Margaret Anderson, *My Thirty
        Years' War* (1930), 39.

PAGE

111   "Dreiser was hardly the young man's notion . . ." W. A. Swanberg, *Dreiser* (1965), 169.

111   "They were long, thoughtful letters . . ." *Ibid.*

111   "Don't be afraid of Ben . . ." *Ibid.*, 196.

111   "Friends can always find . . ." *Ibid.*, 197.

112   "It was quite amusing . . ." *Ibid.*, 175.

112   "A big city is not a little teacup . . ." *Ibid.*, 172.

113   "I had a talk with Doran . . ." *Ibid.*, 173.

113   "Oh Dodoi, if the book is just once . . ." *Ibid.*

113   "There is not one word . . ." *Ibid.*, 174.

114   "[Y]our view of the book cheers me . . ." *Ibid.*

115   "I repudiate it as the . . ." *Ibid.*, 194.

115   "We hope *The 'Genius'* will immediately appear . . ." *Ibid.*

115   "Once more Theodore Dreiser has chosen . . ." *Ibid.*, 193.

115   *"The 'Genius,'* by Theodore Dreiser . . ." *Ibid.*, 194.

116   "As they did to the very sane Machiavelli . . ." *Ibid.*, 196.

116   "Public sentiment being what it was . . ." *Ibid.*, 221.

117   "Latzko does a thing . . ." *Ibid.*, 222.

118   "In [1915] the infamous Anthony Comstock . . ." *Ibid.*, 204.

119   "When young Witla, fastening his best girl's skate . . ." *Ibid.*, 206.

119   *"Suddenly, as they turned . . ."* Theodore Dreiser, *The "Genius"* (1915).

119   "On page 51, having become an art student . . ." W. A. Swanberg, *Dreiser* (1965), 206.

119   *"It was a great, warm-tinted nude . . ."* Theodore Dreiser, *The "Genius"* (1915).

120   "On page 70 he begins to draw . . ." W. A. Swanberg, *Dreiser* (1965), 206.

120   *"He liked to draw the figure . . ."* Theodore Dreiser, *The "Genius"* (1915).

120   "On page 191 I find . . ." W. A. Swanberg, *Dreiser* (1965), 206.

121   "I don't know what action . . ." *Ibid.*, 208.

121   "On with the machine guns!" *Ibid.*, 206.

121   "A band of wasp-like censors . . ." Richard Lingeman, *Theodore Dreiser*, vol. 2: *An American Journey* (1990), 135.

122   "Artists taken as a whole . . ." W. A. Swanberg, *Dreiser* (1965), 211.

124   "[A] full decade would elapse . . ." *Ibid.*, 216.

124   "For God's sake don't start . . ." *Ibid.*, 209.

125   "Let me say once more . . ." *Ibid.*

125   "I do not get the reason . . ." W. A. Swanberg, *Dreiser* (1965), 209.

125   "One-half of the man's brain . . ." *Ibid.*, 223.

126   "It is all very well enough . . ." *Ibid.*, 213.

126   "Fully half the signers of the Protest . . ." *Ibid.*, 214.

127   "I deny your ruling in connection with . . ." *Ibid.*

127   "Where [Mencken and I] diverge . . ." *Ibid.*

127   "I suddenly find myself . . ." *Ibid.*, 223.

CHAPTER 8: *I Took a Girl Away from You Once*

On the success and censorship of *An American Tragedy*, see: W. A. Swanberg, *Dreiser* (1965), 302–53; John Tebbel, *A History of Book Publishing in the United*

States 3 (1978), 407; Walker Gilmer, *Horace Liveright: Publisher of the Twenties* (1970), 134; Donald Friede, *The Mechanical Angel* (1948), Chapter 10; Richard Lingeman, *Theodore Dreiser,* vol. 2: *An American Journey* (1990). Dreiser's "Why Attack Books" appeared in *The Independent* for March 17, 1923. In the same issue a piece by Liveright, "The Absurdity of Censorship," was published. On Dreiser's interest in communism, see Daniel Aaron, *Writers on the Left: Episodes in American Literary Communism;* Vera Dreiser, *My Uncle Theodore* (1976), Chapter 12.

PAGE

132   "I was there the day *An American Tragedy* . . ." Lester Cohen, "Theodore Dreiser: A Personal Memoir," in *Discovery No. 4* (Pocket Books, 1954), 104.

133   "*An American Tragedy* is the greatest . . ." *The Nation,* February 10, 1926.

133   "I do not know where else . . ." *New York Herald Tribune Books,* January 3, 1926.

133   "I think you are the greatest writer . . ." W. A. Swanberg, *Dreiser* (1965), 319.

133   "Nothing can alter his emotions . . ." *Ibid.*

134   "Find out, once and for all . . ." *The Saturday Review,* January 9, 1926.

134   "*An American Tragedy* is written abominably . . ." *London Evening Standard,* December 30, 1926.

134   "Whatever else this vasty double-header . . ." *American Mercury,* March 1926.

134   "*An American Tragedy,* as a work of art . . ." *American Mercury,* March 1926.

135   "The District Attorney read a few paragraphs . . ." Donald Friede, *The Mechanical Angel* (1948), 142–43.

135   "*All of a sudden he felt faint thrills . . .*" Theodore Dreiser, *An American Tragedy.*

136   "Hays had been jumping up and down . . ." Donald Friede, *The Mechanical Angel* (1948), 143.

137   "He put Dreiser on the stand . . ." *Ibid.*

137   "Well now . . . supposing I were to concede . . ." *Ibid.,* 145–46.

137   "There she stood while a speech was read . . ." *Ibid.,* 146.

138   "Even assuming great literary evidence . . ." *Massachusetts* v. *Friede,* 271 Mass. 318, 171 N.E. 472 (1930).

141   "It scored a direct hit on Horace's face . . ." W. A. Swanberg, *Dreiser* (1965), 307.

141   "Horace, always the showman . . ." Bennett Cerf, *At Random* (1977), 59. Donald Friede was "very directly" concerned about the transaction because, he says, he "shared in the money Paramount paid for those rights." He was not present at the luncheon. *The Mechanical Angel* (1948), 42. My account is drawn mainly from W. A. Swanberg, *Dreiser* (1965), 305ff., and Walker Gilmer, *Horace Liveright: Publisher of the Twenties* (1970), 139ff.

142   "It's a darn shame that now . . ." W. A. Swanberg, *Dreiser* (1965), 307–8.

PAGE
143   "He was a thin man . . ." Donald Friede, *The Mechanical Angel* (1948), 22–23.
143   "At the time I went to work . . ." Bennett Cerf, *At Random* (1977), 31.
144   "They stood for anything . . ." *Ibid.,* 79–80.
144   "In that case, would you mind . . ." Richard Ellmann, *James Joyce* (1982), 587n.
145   "Some of the writers . . ." Walker Gilmer, *Horace Liveright: Publisher of the Twenties* (1970), 201.
146   "[Y]ou might do me the justice . . ." *Ibid.,* 221.
146   "Experience shows . . ." Bertrand Russell, *Marriage and Morals* (1929), 113.
147   "What do you think of my going to Hollywood?" Walker Gilmer, *Horace Liveright: Publisher of the Twenties* (1970), 224.
147   "The aura of success . . ." *Ibid.,* 233.
148   "Liveright, always more of a gambler . . ." Bennett Cerf, *At Random* (1977), 80.
148   "He walked in—the door was partly open . . ." *Ibid.,* 78–79.
148   "Better leave, Horace. . . ." *Ibid.*

CHAPTER 9: *Dear Comrade Dreiser*

PAGE
150   "Dreiser was left flat, of course . . ." *The Diary of H. L. Mencken,* edited by Charles A. Fecher (1989), 87.
151   *"Simon & Schuster, on the occasion of becoming . . ."* W. A. Swanberg, *Dreiser* (1965), 424.
151   "Helen looked stunning . . ." *Ibid.*
152   "It has been several years already . . ." *Ibid.,* 433.
152   "The Soviet believes you to be . . ." *Ibid.,* 325.
152   "But supposing my opinion . . ." *Ibid.*
153   "You gonto [*sic*] fall in love . . ." *Ibid.*
153   "In spite of all my varietism . . ." *Ibid.,* 326.
153   "But Paris on Wednesday was delightful . . ." *Letters of Theodore Dreiser,* edited by Robert H. Elias, vol. 2 (1959), 464.
154   "I see it all . . ." W. A. Swanberg, *Dreiser* (1965), 328.
154   "Here I am—nearly 4000 miles . . ." *Ibid.*
154   "But the wretched collection of autos . . ." *Ibid.,* 329.
154   "The smells. The cells. . . ." *Ibid.,* 330.
154   "[His room] is crowded with dubious radicals . . ." *Ibid.*
154   "I complain of loneliness . . ." *Ibid.*
155   "But mayhap this program . . ." *Ibid.*
155   "The towers! The spires!" *Ibid.,* 331.
155   "I find myself turning to Vodka . . ." *Ibid.,* 333.
155   "Personally, I am an individualist . . ." *Ibid.,* 336.
156   "I hoped to have a long chat . . ." *Ibid.,* 338.
156   "Nowhere in Russia . . ." *Ibid.*
156   "Trotsky's case against Stalin. . . ." *Ibid.,* 339.

PAGE

156 "Strunsky's charges . . ." *Ibid.*

157 "He was surprised and hurt . . ." *Ibid.*, 515.

157 "Dear Comrade Dreiser . . ." *Ibid.*

157 "I have believed intensely . . ." *Ibid.*, 514.

159 "Dear Mencken: Just to let you know . . ." *Ibid.*, 517.

159 *"I think of your Boticelli* [sic]. *. . ." Ibid.*, 465.

160 "I am Helen . . ." *Ibid.*, 518.

160 "I'll believe you if you say so . . ." *Ibid.*

160 "It's odd . . ." *Ibid.*

160 "He complained so bitterly . . ." *Ibid.*, 520.

161 "He seemed gay and relaxed . . ." *Ibid.*

161 "[B]ut as we were talking . . ." Helen Dreiser, *My Life with Dreiser* (1951), 312.

161 "He dropped his oxygen mask . . ." W. A. Swanberg, *Dreiser* (1965), 522.

161 "There was a light fog . . ." *Ibid.*

162 "He looked steadily into my eyes . . ." Helen Dreiser, *My Life with Dreiser* (1951), 316.

162 "I looked and saw that it was true . . ." *Ibid.*, 316–17.

162 "In Russia . . ." W. A. Swanberg, *Dreiser* (1965), 528.

163 *"Ah, what is this . . ."* Helen Dreiser, *My Life with Dreiser* (1951), 319–20.

163 "Dreiser was buried very expensively . . ." W. A. Swanberg, *Dreiser* (1965), 525–26.

163 "While Dreiser lived . . ." *Ibid.*, 527.

164 "The newspapers, which had wearied . . ." W. A. Swanberg, *Dreiser* (1965), 523.

164 "As far as I know . . ." Lester Cohen, quoted by Vance Bourjaily in preface to *Discovery No. 4* (Pocket Books, 1954), lx.

164 "[There is] nothing to hope for . . ." W. A. Swanberg, *Dreiser* (1965), 399–400.

CHAPTER 10: *The Knopfs "Ratted" on John*

PAGE

165 "So far as I know . . ." Michael Baker, *Our Three Selves: The Life of Radclyffe Hall* (1985), 202.

167 "John came to me one day . . ." *Ibid.*, 188–89.

167 "For several years she worshipped . . ." Una Troubridge, *The Life and Death of Radclyffe Hall* (1961), 25.

168 "Of her earliest days . . ." *Ibid.*, 19.

168 "She was a beautiful child to look at . . ." *Ibid.*, 20.

169 "A short period of attending . . ." *Ibid.*, 17.

169 "I remember Professor Lapiccirella . . ." *Ibid.*

169 "She was exceedingly handsome . . ." *Ibid.*, 19.

170 "She has a beautiful head . . ." Richard Ormrod, *Una Troubridge: The Friend of Radclyffe Hall* (1985), 92.

PAGE

170   "[I]n spite of a far from robust . . ." Una Troubridge, *The Life and Death of Radclyffe Hall* (1961), 28.

170   "I can shut my eyes now . . ." Michael Baker, *Our Three Selves: The Life of Radclyffe Hall* (1985), 75.

171   "[I]t is the first English novel . . ." "Commentary" by Havelock Ellis in Radclyffe Hall, *The Well of Loneliness* (1928).

173   "The book gives evidence of a pestilence . . ." Michael Baker, *Our Three Selves: The Life of Radclyffe Hall* (1985), 223ff. *Sunday Express,* August 19, 1928. See also *Daily Express,* August 20 and 24, 1928.

175   "I am accustomed to dealing with men . . ." Michael Baker, *Our Three Selves: The Life of Radclyffe Hall* (1985), 207. See also Lovat Dickson's account of the Knopfs' behavior regarding *Well* in *Radclyffe Hall at the Well of Loneliness* (1975).

178   "Morgan was here for the weekend . . ." *The Diary of Virginia Woolf,* edited by Anne Olivier Bell, vol. 3 (1980), 193.

178   "I am very hot . . ." *The Letters of Virginia Woolf,* edited by Nigel Nicolson and Joanne Trautmann, vol. 3 (1977), 520.

179   "I feel very violently . . ." *The Letters of Vita Sackville-West,* edited by Louise De Salvo and Mitchell A. Leaska (1985), 278–79.

180   "I'm just off to a tea party . . ." *The Letters of Virginia Woolf,* edited by Nigel Nicolson and Joanne Trautmann, vol. 3 (1977), 554.

181   "I have to appear in favour of it . . ." *Ibid.,* 556.

183   "Our first small list . . ." Alfred A. Knopf, "A Balance Sheet—Part II," *The Saturday Review of Literature,* November 21, 1964.

CHAPTER 11: *Ungrateful England*

On the literary treatment of lesbian themes, see Sandra M. Gilbert and Susan Gubar, *No Man's Land* (1989). These authors cite as examples Amy Lowell's "Two Speak Together" and "Dreams in War Time," appearing in 1919; and Gertrude Stein's "Lifting Belly" ("one of Stein's most extended celebrations of lesbian sexuality"), composed between 1915 and 1917. These were privately printed, and so limited in distribution as not to excite police or judicial censorship. The Great War provided abundant opportunity and stimulus for women to relate romantically and sexually with one another, described by Gilbert and Gubar at 258ff.

During the 1930s in Paris Anaïs Nin wrote and published her first fictional work, *House of Incest,* and a collection of novelettes, *The Winter of Artifice,* both of which explored women's "fragmented and internally divided personality" and lesbian relationships. The "pornographic" stories she wrote during this period for "a dollar a page" were collected and republished in 1969 in New York under the titles *Delta of Venus* and *Little Birds.* They depict lesbian and straight sexual relationships in "a style as rich and compelling . . . as the best of the elegant French writers of erotica" *(Los Angeles Times).* These "dirty books" of Nin's were originally published by an anonymous figure called "the collector," and evidently not by Jack Kahane (Obelisk Press) or his son Maurice Girodias (Olympia Press). Kahane, however, published Nin's *Winter of Artifice* in 1939, four years after he accepted the manuscript, one week before the outbreak of World War II, and nine days before his own death.

Nin's *House of Incest* was published a few years earlier, also in Paris, under the imprint of Siana Editions ("Anaïs" spelled backwards), her own publishing operation. In 1935, "control of the press" was reportedly wrested from Nin by Alfred Perles, Henry Miller, and Michael Frankel, who used the press to publish their own work, as well as *House of Incest*. Shari Benstock, *Women of the Left Bank* (1986), 429ff. After fleeing France for New York in 1939, Nin set up another small press on Macdougal Street with money provided by friends, including Frances Steloff of the Gotham Book Mart, who also marketed Nin's books. *Ibid.*, 435–37.

PAGE

186   "We were all packed in . . ." *The Diary of Virginia Woolf,* edited by Anne Olivier Bell, vol. 3 (1980), 206–7.

186   "The book is concerned not with perversion . . ." Michael Baker, *Our Three Selves: The Life of Radclyffe Hall* (1985), 241.

187   "I sat there and sweated blood . . ." *Ibid.*

187   "Do you mean to say that it does not . . ." Vera Brittain, *Radclyffe Hall: A Case of Obscenity* (1968), 89.

187   "The test is whether it is likely . . ." *Ibid.*

187   "I want to call evidence . . ." Norman St. John-Stevas, *Obscenity and the Law* (1956), 101.

188   "I have the greatest doubt . . ." *Ibid.*

188   "I don't think people are entitled . . ." *Ibid.*

188   "In your view is it obscene?" *Ibid.*

188   "But I have to consider . . ." Vera Brittain, *Radclyffe Hall: A Case of Obscenity* (1968), 91.

189   "I reject them all . . ." Norman St. John-Stevas, *Obscenity and the Law* (1956), 101–2.

189   "He was ironical at first . . ." *The Letters of Virginia Woolf,* edited by Nigel Nicolson and Joanne Trautmann, vol. 3 (1977), 207.

191   "[O]therwise we should be in the preposterous position . . ." Vera Brittain, *Radclyffe Hall: A Case of Obscenity* (1968), 100.

191   "It is not necessary that filthy words . . ." *Ibid.*

191   "According to this writer . . ." Michael Baker, *Our Three Selves: The Life of Radclyffe Hall* (1985), 243.

192   "I *protest!* I emphatically *protest!*" Norman St. John-Stevas, *Obscenity and the Law* (1956), 102.

192   "And I lost my little Roman brooch . . ." *The Letters of Virginia Woolf,* edited by Nigel Nicolson and Joanne Trautmann, vol. 3 (1977), 207.

192   "In the hall I talked to . . ." *Ibid.*

193   "One is in the first chapter . . ." Vera Brittain, *Radclyffe Hall: A Case of Obscenity* (1968), 121–23.

193   "There is no mystery or masquerading . . ." *Ibid.*, 124.

194   "There are plenty of people . . ." *Ibid.*, 125.

194   "The court's view, which is unanimous . . ." *Ibid.*, 125–26.

195   "[T]otal strangers would come up . . ." Richard Ormrod, *Una Troubridge: The Friend of Radclyffe Hall* (1985), 189.

196   "Do you remember the time . . ." Michael Baker, *Our Three Selves: The Life of Radclyffe Hall* (1985), 253.

PAGE

198   "The book here involved . . ." Vera Brittain, *Radclyffe Hall: A Case of Obscenity* (1968), 142.

198   *"Stephen turned to Angela abruptly . . ."* Radclyffe Hall, *The Well of Loneliness.*

199   "The book culminates . . ." Vera Brittain, *Radclyffe Hall: A Case of Obscenity* (1968), 142.

199   "Yet the unnatural and depraved . . ." *Ibid.*

200   "I was so confident of being acquitted . . ." Donald Friede, *The Mechanical Angel* (1948), 141. The American trial of *The Well of Loneliness* is also described by Friede in "Getting Started," *Publishers on Publishing,* edited by Gerald Gross (1961), 326ff.

201   "In Dreiser's case there was . . ." Donald Friede, *The Mechanical Angel* (1948), 138.

202   "Here's to the Saints . . ." Michael Baker, *Our Three Selves: The Life of Radclyffe Hall* (1985), 255.

202   "Or better still a retired ironmonger . . ." *Ibid.,* 253.

203   "And most of us were in it . . ." Donald Friede, *The Mechanical Angel* (1948), 261.

204   "Cape went the color of weak lemonade . . ." Michael Baker, *Our Three Selves: The Life of Radclyffe Hall* (1985), 279.

204   "We stopped for the night as we felt inclined . . ." *Ibid.,* 256.

204   "I am dark red brown all over . . ." *Ibid.*

205   "You may flatter yourself, Lady Troubridge . . ." Richard Ormrod, *Una Troubridge: The Friend of Radclyffe Hall* (1985), 271.

205   "Una met me . . ." *Ibid.,* 270.

205   "At one moment it was my beloved . . ." Michael Baker, *Our Three Selves: The Life of Radclyffe Hall* (1985), 345.

206   Inscription on the brass nameplate, *Ibid.,* 346.

207   "Darling, this isn't just pain . . ." *Ibid.* at 348.

208   "There was nothing to confess." *Ibid.* at 357.

CHAPTER 12: *Like a Phallus Made of Dough*

Frank ("Effendi") Doubleday controlled Doubleday and was chairman of its board until a few months before he died, in 1934, after which his son, Nelson, who was serving as the firm's president, took charge. The next year, according to John Tebbel, Doubleday "acquired as a reader in the editorial department the young man who would one day be perhaps its greatest editor in chief," Ken McCormick; by 1949, McCormick was editor in chief, vice president, and director of Doubleday, now one of the largest book publishers in the world. In 1949 Nelson Doubleday—aptly described by *The New York Herald Tribune* as "one of the world's leading merchants of books"—died of cancer, at the age of fifty-nine. The firm's counsel, Douglas Black, had become president of the company in 1946, the year John Sumner raided the Doubleday chain of bookstores in search of Edmund Wilson's *Hecate County.* Black was one of those responsible for the "Freedom to Read" declaration jointly issued in 1953 by the American Book Publishers Council and the American Library Association. He later became chairman of the ABPC's anti-censorship committee. John Tebbel, *A History of Book Publishing in the United States* 3 (1978), 527–33, and 4 (1981), 105–10.

PAGE

209 "Hecate County might be any community . . ." Edmund Wilson, *Letters on Literature and Politics: 1912–1972* (1977), 433.

210 *"But what struck and astonished me most . . ."* Edmund Wilson, *Memoirs of Hecate County* (1980), 250–51.

210 "Hecate County is my favorite . . ." *Ibid.,* unnumbered front pages. The 1980 edition is a Nonpareil Book, a reprint published by David R. Godine, Publishers, of Boston, of the new edition published by Roger Straus in 1959, under the L. C. Page imprint, as described in the text. For this edition, Wilson said he "made a revised text, which differs in many passages from the version originally published." The sexual passages, however, were unchanged.

211 "Wilson's mother, as far as he could tell . . ." Letter from Mary McCarthy to the author, August 1, 1986.

211 "The book is indecent enough . . ." *Selected Letters of Raymond Chandler,* edited by Frank MacShane (1981), 79, 238.

211 "The descriptions of love are so . . ." Malcolm Cowley, *The New Republic,* March 25, 1946.

211 "For a man who spends so much time . . ." *Harper's* magazine, June 1946.

212 "Our rule of thumb . . ." Author interview with Roger Straus, August 27, 1985.

213 "I liked the work and . . ." S. J. Woolf, "Interview with Our Unofficial Censor," *The New York Times Magazine,* October 20, 1946, 24, 65.

213 "I am not carrying out the ideas . . ." "A Vice Suppressor Looks at Our Morals," *The New York Times,* October 8, 1932.

214 *"I remember one cold winter Sunday . . ."* Edmund Wilson, *Memoirs of Hecate County* (1980).

214 "Mr. Sumner doesn't seem to know . . ." *Publishers Weekly,* July 9, 1946. ACLU-affiliated lawyers such as Whitney North Seymour and Morris Ernst probably had as great an impact on the evolving constitutional law of freedom of expression, including the law of obscenity, through their work as private lawyers as through their work officially on behalf of the ACLU. In obscenity cases these lawyers, and the ACLU as well, long advanced the doctrine that it was unconstitutional to suppress "obscene" publications, or to punish their disseminators, in the absence of proof that the dissemination created a "clear and present danger" of bringing about a substantial evil that the government had a right to prevent. In the *Hecate County* case, both Kenneth Greenawalt (for the ACLU) and Seymour (for Doubleday) presented this argument to the Supreme Court. That four of the eight justices participating in the decision voted to reverse the Doubleday conviction is evidence of the forcefulness of these lawyers' arguments. As described in Chapter 16, the "clear and present danger" doctrine was again advanced on a publisher's behalf in 1957, in the famous case of *Roth* v. *United States.* There the ACLU would again present the "clear and present danger" argument amicus

curiae, whereas the attorney for *Roth* would argue mainly that the Court should invalidate the federal obscenity law because obscenity by its nature was an offense that constitutionally was given to the states, not the national government, to enforce, and also that such laws were unconstitutionally vague. In his opinion for the Court upholding the publisher's conviction, Justice William J. Brennan, Jr., rejected the "clear and present danger" doctrine's applicability to obscenity cases because obscenity was deemed not to be expression of the sort that the constitutional free speech and press guarantees were meant to safeguard, and the other contentions on other grounds. At the same time, Brennan's opinion in *Roth* began the judicial process that ultimately led to the emergence of what in this book is referred to as "the Brennan doctrine," which effectively freed from obscenity-law censorship any sexually oriented expression that was not "utterly without literary, scientific, artistic or other social importance."

215   "Our advisers have read the book . . ." Copy of telegram, undated, to Doubleday, Doran, in author's files.

216   "Freedom of speech covers much more . . ." Zechariah Chafee, *Freedom of Speech* (1920), 545.

217   "Most of us agree that the law . . ." *Ibid.,* 529–30. Elsewhere Chafee said this: "To restate . . . the normal criminal law is interested in preventing crimes and certain non-criminal interferences with governmental functions like refusals to enlist or to subscribe to bonds. It is directed primarily against actual injuries. Such injuries are usually committed by acts, but the law also punishes a few classes of words like obscenity, profanity, and gross libels upon individuals, because the very utterance of such words is considered to inflict a present injury upon listeners, readers, or those defamed, or else to render highly probable an immediate breach of the peace. This is a very different matter from punishing words because they express ideas which are thought to cause a future danger to the State.

"[T]hese verbal peace-time crimes . . . are too well recognized to question their constitutionality, but I believe that if they are properly limited they fall outside the protection of the free speech clauses as I have defined them. My reason is not that they existed at common law before the constitutions, for a similar argument would apply to the crime of sedition, which was abolished by the First Amendment. The existence of a verbal crime at common law shows the presence of a social interest which must be weighed in the balance, but the free speech guaranties, as I have argued at length, enact a countervailing social interest in the attainment and dissemination of truth, which was insufficiently recognized by the common law. Nor do I base my conclusion on the historical fact that the framers of the constitutions wanted to safeguard political discussion, because their own statements of freedom of speech in the address to the people of Quebec, the Virginia Toleration Statute, and the opening clause of the First Amendment itself, prove that they also wanted to safeguard scientific and religious freedom, both of which would be greatly restricted by a sweeping application of the common law of obscenity and blasphemy. The true explanation is that profanity and indecent talk and pictures, which do not form an essential part of any exposition of ideas, have a very slight social value as a step toward truth, which is clearly outweighed by the social interests in order, morality, the training of the young, and the peace of mind of those who hear and see. Words of this type offer little opportunity for the usual process of counter-argument. The harm is done as soon as they are communicated, or is liable to follow almost immediately in the form of retaliatory violence. The only sound explanation of the punishment of obscenity and profanity is that the words are criminal not because of the ideas they communicate, but, like acts, because of their immediate consequences to the five senses" (149–50).

In *Chaplinsky* v. *New Hampshire* (1942), the Supreme Court said this: "Allowing the broadest scope to the language and purpose of the Fourteenth Amendment, it is well understood that the right of free speech is not absolute at all times and under all circumstances. There are certain well-defined and narrowly limited classes of speech, the prevention and punishment of which have never been thought to raise any Constitutional problem. These include the lewd and obscene, the profane, the libelous, and the insulting or "fighting" words—those which by their very utterance inflict injury or tend to incite an immediate breach of the peace. It has been well observed [by Chafee] that such utterances are no essential part of any exposition of ideas, and are of such slight social value as a step to truth that any benefit that may be derived from them is clearly outweighed by the social interest in order and morality. 'Resort to epithets or personal abuse is not in any proper sense communication of information or opinion safeguarded by the Constitution, and its punishment as a criminal act would raise no question under that instrument.' *Cantwell* v. *Connecticut,* 310 U.S. 296, 309, 310."

The reasons for the neglect of Theodore Schroeder's work probably include the facts that Schroeder, unlike Chafee, was not of the academic establishment, and unlike Morris Ernst—perhaps the most popular and influential of legal writers before World War II on the obscenity/free speech problem—was not part of the legal establishment either. Other reasons may have been the radical character of Schroeder's position, which was "absolutist," and the somewhat intemperate, impatient tone of his work. His stated goal was "the judicial annulment of all present State and Federal laws against 'obscene' literature" (*"Obscene" Literature and Constitutional Law,* 1972 edition, 92–93). In an introduction to this edition of Schroeder's *magnum opus,* Professor Jerold S. Auerbach points out that at the core of Schroeder's thesis was the conviction that obscenity laws were void because of vagueness. Terms like "lewd," "indecent," "filthy," and "disgusting" were "outrageously undefinable," and so left the citizen at a loss to know in advance what he could or could not express, judges and juries with no objective criteria to determine guilt, and enforcement officials with enormous discretion: obscenity thereby became a "constructive" offense whose limits were as capacious as Anthony Comstock's imagination (xii). Schroeder's thesis regarding the invalidity of *all* obscenity laws because of the irreducible vagueness of their terms was the thesis ultimately advanced (in 1973) by William

J. Brennan, Jr., for a four-member minority of the Supreme Court, as described in Chapter 26. In my opinion, this will also one day become the Court's majority judgment; the continued upholding of anti-obscenity and anti-pornography laws is today a *political* activity of the Supreme Court's conservative majority inasmuch as it is by now perfectly evident that "obscenity" and "pornography" are concepts whose applications are incompatible with any legal system governed by the rule of law or the principle of legality.

Auerbach's introduction very briefly sketches Schroeder's ideas and career. See also Paul Boyer, *Purity in Print* (1968), 41–43. Boyer credits Schroeder with being "the man who did the most" in the United States to advance the anti-censorship debate during the pre–World War I period.

218   "[I]t had been said of him that he was . . ." Edmund Wilson, *The Thirties* (1980), 309–10.

218   "There is at present a vague border line . . ." " 'I'm No Reformer,' Says Sumner," by Alva Johnson, *The New York Times Book Review and Magazine,* August 20, 1922.

219   "I knew that the profits . . ." Edmund Wilson, *The Cold War and the Income Tax* (1964).

219   "All my books seem to have been examined . . ." *Ibid.*

220   "The case of my book in New York . . ." Edmund Wilson, *Letters on Literature and Politics: 1912–1972* (1977), 439.

221   "The *dénouement* of this plot . . ." *Trial Brief for the People,* 21.

222   "There are 20 separate acts . . ." *Ibid.*

222   "Yet when not detailing bedroom scenes . . ." *Ibid.,* 24–25.

222   "The intense delight . . ." *Ibid.,* 21.

223   "Mr. Wilson's . . . reputation in literary circles . . ." *Record* of the trial on appeal, 40.

223   "[T]he court would not allow . . ." Bennett Cerf, *At Random* (1977), 92–93.

225   "*Hecate County* was convicted in New York . . ." Edmund Wilson, *Letters on Literature and Politics: 1912–1972* (1977), 444.

226   "The decision made thousands of citizens . . ." *Time* magazine, December 9, 1946, 24–25.

226   "Of the three who first heard . . ." Letter dated July 1954 to Roger Straus from Edmund Wilson from Talcottville, R.F.D. Boonville, N.Y. This letter is not included in Wilson's *Letters on Literature and Politics.* I am indebted to Roger Straus for making a copy of the letter available to me.

228   "It is regrettable that because . . ." *Publishers Weekly,* November 6, 1948.

229   "Douglas Black was a strange man . . ." Author interview with Jason Epstein, June 3, 1985.

CHAPTER 13: *She Always Called It "It"*

PAGE

230   "He now said that due . . ." Edmund Wilson, *The Forties,* edited by Leon Edel (1983), 311–12.

PAGE

231   "I reminded him . . ." *Ibid.,* 312.

231   "I've said I was wrong . . ." *Ibid.,* 313.

232   "By today's decision . . ." Edward de Grazia, *Censorship Landmarks* (1969), 136.

233   "We agreed that [Frankfurter] had been much better off . . ." Edmund Wilson, *The Forties* (1983), 313–14.

233   "I said that I had the impression . . ." *Ibid.*

236   "[I]t is my belief that the *Memoirs of Hecate County* . . ." Letter to Mrs. Harriet F. Pilpel from District Attorney Frank Hogan, dated April 27, 1957; copy in author's files. Roger Straus kindly gave me access to his correspondence with Mrs. Pilpel on the subject of *Hecate County.*

237   "For several years, Edmund wanted me . . ." Author interview with Roger Straus, August 27, 1985.

237   "We technically could not achieve . . ." *Ibid.*

237   "So we minimized rubbing the book . . ." *Ibid.*

238   "So we achieved what we wanted . . ." *Ibid.*

238   "Farrar, Straus and Giroux was then . . ." "A Flow of Work," by Roger Straus, *The New York Times,* June 18, 1972.

238   "Years of writing for the periodicals . . ." Edmund Wilson, *The Twenties,* edited by Leon Edel (1975), 245.

239   *"(Anna) She had loved Sam more than me . . ." Ibid.,* 407–8, 410, 413, 445–46.

240   "One reviewer has recently gone so far . . ." Jason Epstein, "Edmund Wilson at Ease," *The New York Review of Books,* October 9, 1986, 7.

240   *"(Margaret) On the dunes: the flies . . ."* Edmund Wilson, *The Thirties* (1980), 252–53.

241   *"(Elena) I loved her body . . ."* Edmund Wilson, *The Forties* (1983), 161–62.

241   "At my age, *sex* becomes less . . ." Edmund Wilson, *The Fifties* (1986), 302–3.

242   "Actually, since I have left the hospital . . ." Unpublished letter dated April 19, 1970, to John Dos Passos from Edmund Wilson, in Wilson collection, Beinecke Rare Book and Manuscript Library, Yale University.

242   "This writing of books is . . ." Edmund Wilson, *Letters on Literature and Politics: 1912–1972* (1977), 740.

CHAPTER 14: *With Your Little Claws, Lolita*

PAGE

243   *"Lolita, light of my life . . ."* Vladimir Nabokov, *Lolita* (1988), 11.

244   "I shall try to explain . . ." Vladimir Nabokov, *Selected Letters,* edited by Dmitri Nabokov and Matthew J. Bruccoli (1989), 142–43.

244   "[We] feel that it is literature . . ." *Ibid.,* 153, note 1.

245   "Dear Laughlin . . ." *Ibid.,* 152–53.

245   "Dear Mr. Straus . . ." *Ibid.,* 152.

PAGE

245   "Nabokov . . . was afraid . . ." Author interview with Roger Straus, August 27, 1985.

245   "At first, on the advice of a wary old friend . . ." Vladimir Nabokov, "On a Book Entitled Lolita," in *Lolita* (1958), 313.

246   "You see, this friend was afraid . . ." Author interview with Dmitri Nabokov, October 26, 1986.

246   "Mystifying, rather, it seemed to me . . ." *The Nabokov-Wilson Letters,* edited by Simon Karlinsky (1979), 288–89.

246   "On the other hand . . ." *Ibid.*

246   "The hero's disgust of grown-up women . . ." *Ibid.,* 289.

247   "I felt there was no way . . ." *The New York Times Book Review,* July 3, 1988.

247   "I know that Roger's *official* position . . ." Letter dated July 22, 1991, from Erica Jong to the author.

247   "Jason fell in love with *Lolita* . . ." Author interview with Barney Rosset, May 21, 1985.

248   "I resigned from Doubleday . . ." Author interview with Jason Epstein, June 3, 1985.

248   "The thing that disturbed Douglas Black . . ." Author interview with Ken McCormick, October 12, 1984.

248   "I would ask Black if he'd read it . . ." Author interview with Jason Epstein, June 3, 1985.

249   "Well, there were several others there . . ." Author interview with Ken McCormick, October 12, 1984.

249   *"Under my glancing finger tips . . ."* Vladimir Nabokov, *Lolita.*

249   "You must remember that Doubleday . . ." Author interview with Jason Epstein, June 3, 1985.

251   "[T]ry to remember the state of . . ." Erica Jong, "Lolita Turns Thirty: A New Introduction," *Lolita* (1988).

252   *"How sweet it was to bring that pot of hot coffee . . ."* Vladimir Nabokov, *Lolita.*

253   "Anyway, after that, it went to . . ." Author interview with Jason Epstein, June 3, 1985.

254   *"Lolita* was finished . . ." Vladimir Nabokov, "Lolita and Mr. Girodias," *Evergreen Review,* February 1967, 38.

254   "One day in the early summer of 1955 . . ." Maurice Girodias, "Lolita, Nabokov and I," *Evergreen Review,* September 1965, 44.

254   "He was recommended to me . . ." Vladimir Nabokov, "Lolita and Mr. Girodias," *Evergreen Review,* February 1967, 38.

254   "[I] quickly succumbed . . ." Maurice Girodias, "Lolita, Nabokov and I," *Evergreen Review,* September 1965, 44.

255   "Dear Mr. Girodias . . ." Vladimir Nabokov, *Selected Letters* (1989), 174–75.

255   "Dear Pat . . ." *Ibid.,* 185.

255   "The truth of the matter . . ." Maurice Girodias, "Lolita, Nabokov and I," *Evergreen Review,* September 1965, 45.

256   "My publishing technique was simple . . ." Introduction, *The Olympia Reader,* edited by Maurice Girodias (1965), 23.

PAGE

256 "The year 1956 . . . found me seated . . ." Marilyn Meeske, "Memoirs of a Female Pornographer," *Esquire,* April 1965, 112–13.

257 "[It] was written in random fashion . . ." *Ibid.,* 114.

257 "During that period . . ." *Ibid.,* 113.

258 "I never met the collector . . ." Anaïs Nin, Preface to *Delta of Venus* (Pocket Books, 1990), ix.

258 " 'Less poetry,' said the voice . . ." *Ibid.*

258 "I would tell him how he almost . . ." *Ibid.,* x.

258 "The homosexuals wrote as if . . ." *Ibid.,* xiii.

259 "On [Graham Greene's] recommendation I bought . . ." *Sunday Express,* January 29, 1956. Greene's recommendation of *Lolita* appeared in *The Sunday Times* for Christmas Day, 1955.

260 "I had not been in Europe since . . ." Vladimir Nabokov, "Lolita and Mr. Girodias," *Evergreen Review,* February 1967, 38.

260 "One day a police inspector . . ." Maurice Girodias, Introduction, *The Olympia Reader,* edited by Maurice Girodias (1965), 27–28.

260 "[T]he twenty-five books the inspector . . ." *Ibid.,* 28.

260 "Dear Mr. Greene . . ." Vladimir Nabokov, *Selected Letters* (1989), 197–98.

261 "Thank you very much . . ." *Ibid.,* 198.

262 "The cover is splendid . . ." Vladimir Nabokov, *Selected Letters* (1989), 217.

262 "When I decided to fight the *Lolita* . . ." Maurice Girodias, "Lolita, Nabokov and I," *Evergreen Review,* September 1965.

262 "My moral defense of the book . . ." Vladimir Nabokov, *Selected Letters* (1989), 210.

263 "He wanted me to defend *Lolita* . . ." Vladimir Nabokov, "Lolita and Mr. Girodias," *Evergreen Review,* February 1967, 40.

263 "Please do keep in touch with me . . ." Vladimir Nabokov, *Selected Letters* (1989), 223.

263 "Alas, those were his last nice words . . ." Maurice Girodias, "Lolita, Nabokov and I," *Evergreen Review,* September 1965, 524.

263 "Had not Graham Greene and John Gordon . . ." Vladimir Nabokov, "Lolita and Mr. Girodias," *Evergreen Review,* February 1967, 40.

264 "In 1957, the *Lolita* affair . . ." *Ibid.*

265 "It would be tedious to continue . . ." *Ibid.,* 40–41.

265 "I took a course in the eighteenth-century novel . . ." Author interview with Walter Minton.

267 "I began to curse my association . . ." Vladimir Nabokov, "Lolita and Mr. Girodias," *Evergreen Review,* February 1967, 38.

267 "Dear Mr. Nabokov . . ." Vladimir Nabokov, *Selected Letters* (1989), 278–79.

269 "The advice one often heard was. . . ." London *Times,* December 17, 1958.

269 "*Bend Sinister* could be sandwiched in between . . ." Vladimir Nabokov, *Selected Letters* (1989), 278–80.

270 "An American writer means . . ." *The New York Times,* July 5, 1977.

270 " 'Sheer laziness' was one of the reasons . . ." *Ibid.*

PAGE
270   "Things went from bad to worse. . . ." Maurice Girodias, "Lolita, Nabokov and I," *Evergreen Review,* September 1965, 29–30.

271   "Such giants as Samuel Beckett . . ." Marilyn Meeske, "Memoirs of a Female Pornographer," *Esquire,* April 1965, 115.

271   "I often wonder what I would have done . . ." Vladimir Nabokov, "Postscript to the Russian Edition of *Lolita,*" in *Nabokov's Fifth Arc,* edited by J. E. Rivers and Charles Nicol (1982), 191.

271   "Then the rigamarole . . ." Maurice Girodias, "Lolita, Nabokov and I," *Evergreen Review,* September 1965, 30–31.

CHAPTER 15: *I'm Just Going to Feed Adolphe*

PAGE
274   "Warren was a terrible prude . . ." Author interview with Justice William J. Brennan, Jr.

275   "[A]dvertisements are made . . ." *American Aphrodite,* vol. 3, no. 12 (1953), 3–4.

280   "I haven't any intention of offering . . ." *Ibid.,* 6.

280   "The score as it stands now . . ." *American Aphrodite,* vol. 4, no. 13 (1954).

281   *"When all was said and done . . ."* "The Story of Venus and Tannhäuser," *American Aphrodite,* vol. 1, no. 3 (1951), 23.

282   "He was supposed, just then, to be dying . . ." Arthur Symons, *Aubrey Beardsley* (1948), 7–9.

282   "We know from his own letters . . ." Introduction to Aubrey Beardsley, *Under the Hill* (New York: Grove Press, 1967).

283   *"Anyhow, Adolphe sniffed as never a man did . . ."* "The Story of Venus and Tannhäuser," *American Aphrodite,* vol. 1, no. 3 (1951), 23–24.

283   "[I]n those brilliant, disconnected . . ." Arthur Symons, *Aubrey Beardsley* (1948), 9.

284   *"The Chevalier was feeling very happy . . ."* "The Story of Venus and Tannhäuser," *American Aphrodite,* vol. 1, no. 3 (1951), 24.

284   "The book [*Venus and Tannhäuser*] is a revelation . . ." Haldane MacFall, *Aubrey Beardsley: The Man and His Work* (1928), 81.

284   "As Beardsley lay a-dying on the 7th . . ." *Ibid.,* 108.

285   "Dear Friend, I implore you to destroy . . ." *Ibid.*

285   "On the sixteenth day of the March . . ." *Ibid.*

285   "It doesn't represent what the whole . . ." *Ibid.*

286   *"And when I stayed at the Harrisons' . . ."* John O'Hara, *Ten North Frederick* (1955), 151.

286   *"They were necking, and I said . . ."* *Ibid.,* 293.

287   "Of course there can be no quibble . . ." Appendix to Appellee's Brief in the U.S. Court of Appeals for the Second Circuit, *United States* v. *Samuel Roth,* 520ff.

287   *"I bent all the way down to her . . ."* Thomas Mann, *The Confessions of Felix Krull* (1955), 173–78.

287   "Yes, that stuff is from Thomas Mann. . . ." Appendix to Appellee's Brief

PAGE

in the U.S. Court of Appeals for the Second Circuit, *United States* v. *Samuel Roth,* 520ff.

288   *"Tentatively, she reached out a hand . . ."* Norman Mailer, *The Deer Park* (1955). The version of this scene quoted by Atlas is from an earlier draft of the novel, not the one ultimately published by Putnam's. Excerpts from this earlier version were subsequently published, several years later, by Mailer in *Advertisements for Myself.*

288   "If Your Honor please, Mr. Atlas, Mr. Foreman . . ." Appendix to Appellee's Brief in the U.S. Court of Appeals for the Second Circuit, *United States* v. *Samuel Roth,* 520ff.

288   "Then we get to this *American Aphrodite . . .*" *Ibid.,* 562–72.

292   "I was Felix Frankfurter's law clerk . . ." Author interview with Paul Bender.

293   "165 years later, President Franklin Roosevelt . . ." *Roth* v. *United States,* reprinted in de Grazia, *Censorship Landmarks* (1969), 274–90.

294   "Some few men stubbornly fight for . . ." *Ibid.*

CHAPTER 16: *Clear and Present Danger of What?*

The depiction of the highlights of the oral argument in Roth's case is based mainly on *Oral Arguments Before the Supreme Court: Obscenity* (1983), edited by Leon Friedman, but I have made use also of *Landmark Briefs and Arguments of the Supreme Court of the United States: Constitutional Law* 53 (1975), edited by Philip Kurland and Gerhard Casper.

PAGE

295   "Mr. Albrecht, you may proceed . . ." *Oral Arguments,* 10.

298   "Does that mean that you . . ." *Ibid.,* 10–11.

300   "Does that include pornography . . ." *Ibid.*

300   "A large part is photographs . . ." *Ibid.,* 19.

301   "All three judges in the Court of Appeals . . ." "Brief of the United States in Opposition," 4, reprinted in *Landmark Briefs and Arguments,* 77.

301   "In attacking the constitutionality . . ." *Ibid.*

302   "Arthur Summerfield . . ." Author interview with Justice William J. Brennan, Jr.

303   "Well, to carve it down to size . . ." *Oral Arguments,* 10.

303   "Yes sir. . . . My contention is that you . . ." *Ibid.,* 11.

303   "One of the books upon which this defendant . . ." *Ibid.,* 14.

304   "Mr. Albrecht, may I suggest . . ." *Landmark Briefs and Arguments,* 488.

304   "Well, Your Honor, in the brief supplied . . ." *Ibid.*

305   "Yes, Your Honor. As I understand it . . ." *Ibid.*

305   "It's customary, isn't it . . ." *Ibid.,* 489.

306   "Now as I see the question . . ." *Ibid.*

306   "Mr. Chief Justice, may it please the . . ." *Ibid.*

307   "Do we have to assume that?" *Oral Arguments,* 16.

PAGE

307   "If it means anything, these advertising . . ." *Landmark Briefs and Arguments*, 490.

309   "Clear and present danger that you be . . ." *Ibid.*, 497.

309   "No, I think that there is an effect . . ." *Ibid.*, 498.

310   "Do you agree that it must . . ." *Ibid.*

310   "One of our key points is that . . ." *Oral Arguments*, 25.

311   "Two other interests. . . . The invasion of . . ." *Landmark Briefs and Arguments*, 499.

311   "It doesn't touch conduct; it . . ." *Ibid.*

311   "You say that Congress can make . . ." *Oral Arguments*, 26.

311   "That some restraint can be imposed on how . . ." *Landmark Briefs and Arguments*, 500.

313   "Mr. Fisher, would you regard . . ." *Ibid.*

313   "It makes all the difference in the . . ." *Oral Arguments*, 17.

314   "The only question, Mr. Justice . . ." *Landmark Briefs and Arguments*, 501.

315   "I don't know what that means!" *Ibid.*, 501–2.

315   "Mr. Chief Justice, may it please the . . ." *Ibid.*, 503–4.

316   "Now, Mr. Justice Frankfurter, I'd like to . . ." *Ibid.*, 504.

316   "Mr. Rogge, since you're quoting . . ." *Ibid.*, 505; *Oral Arguments*, 32.

317   "Well, I assumed that when this Court . . ." *Landmark Briefs and Arguments*, 506.

317   "Do you think that's the same thing . . ." *Ibid.*

317   "Mr. Justice Frankfurter, if this statute . . ." *Ibid.*

317   "I agree with you entirely. But . . ." *Ibid.*

318   "[I]n this connection, I want to draw a . . ." *Ibid.*, 508.

318   "That such action must inevitably . . ." *Commonwealth* v. *Gordon*, reprinted in de Grazia, *Censorship Landmarks* (1969), 165.

319   "[I]t is apparent that the unconditional phrasing . . ." *Roth* v. *United States* (1957), in de Grazia, *Censorship Landmarks* (1969), 290, 292.

322   "The protection given . . ." *Ibid.*

322   "[S]ex and obscenity are . . ." *Ibid.*, 293.

325   "For years, people who believed in more . . ." Author interview with Paul Bender.

CHAPTER 17: *I Was Getting Hard-ons*

This chapter is based mainly on Allen Ginsberg's *Howl: Original Draft Facsimile, Transcript & Variant Versions, Fully Annotated by Author, with Contemporaneous Correspondence, Account of First Public Reading, Legal Skirmishes, Precursor Texts & Bibliography*, edited by Barry Miles (1986); and Barry Miles's *Ginsberg: A Biography* (1989).

The Baraka and Burroughs pieces that attracted the federal police to *Floating Bear* (Number 9) were "From the System of Dante's Hell" and "Routine: Roosevelt After Inauguration." The latter, Burrough's piece, contained this arresting passage: "When the Supreme Court overruled some of the legislations perpetrated by this vile rout, [President Franklin D.] Roosevelt forced that august body, one after the other, on threat of immediate reduction to the rank of Congressional Lavatory Assistants, to submit to intercourse with a purple assed baboon, so that venerable, honored men surrendered themselves to the embraces of a lecherous snarling simian, while Roosevelt and his strumpet wife and the veteran brown nose Harry Hopkins, smoking a communal hookah of hashish, watch the lamentable sight with cackles of obscene laughter. . . . Justice Hockactonsvol had both ears bitten off by the simian, and when Chief Justice Howard P. Herringbone asked to be excused pleading his piles, Roosevelt told him brutally, 'Best thing for piles is a baboon's prick up your ass. Right Harry?' 'Right Chief. I use no other. You heard what the man said. Drop your moth eaten ass over that chair and show the visiting simian some southern hospitality.' He—Roosevelt—then appointed the baboon to replace Justice Blackstrap, 'diseased' . . ." (88–90).

The issue came to the FBI's attention this way, according to Diane di Prima: "There was a person on the *Floating Bear* mailing list, a black poet named Harold Carrington, who was in prison in New Jersey. The censor or somebody read all of his mail, of course, and however it happened issue Number Nine was reported [to the FBI] for obscenity. I think the particular objection was to LeRoi's play *From the System of Dante's Hell,* and to William Burroughs' piece *Routine.* I guess they couldn't stand the idea of FDR and all those baboons. (Harold Carrington, by the way, got out of prison in 1965 at the age of 25, after having been there since he was 18. He went to Atlantic City, spent two weeks there, and O.D.'d. I had a lot of poems and letters from him and they were pretty far out. He'd write, 'I've never seen a play. Is this what plays are like? I've just written one.' Then he would send you a play he had written. It was very strange. Some of them have been printed in England.)"

The arrests took place as follows, according to di Prima: "We were arrested on October 18, 1961, and what went down was more or less like this. I heard a knock on my door early in the morning which I didn't answer because I never open my door early in the morning in New York City. In the morning in New York City is only trouble. It's landlords, it's Con Edison, it's the police, it's your neighbors wanting to know why you made so much noise last night, it's something awful, and before noon I never open my door. The people after being slightly persistent went away, and then I got a phone call which I did answer. It was Hettie, LeRoi's wife, informing me that if anybody came to the house I shouldn't let them in because it would be the postal authorities and the FBI looked to arrest me for *The Floating Bear* and that they had just taken LeRoi away. Hettie had opened the door, still sleepy, and they had marched right into the bedroom which was also the office and gotten LeRoi up. Then they searched it quite thoroughly, taking all kinds of little magazines and manuscripts and even a water pipe that LeRoi had made himself with a cork and some glass tubes. They were looking mainly for the Bear mailing list but I had it, so they took practically everything else in sight, including LeRoi, whom they arrested for sending obscenity through the mails. They asked him where I was, and he said immediately that I had left for California. Half asleep, this was his immediate reply: 'Oh, her, she went away, she's not in New York City.'

"A little before noon they came back a second time and banged on the door again. I had an upstairs neighbor who was a very good friend, Freddie Herko, who had been very close to me for about ten years. We used to always communicate by the fire escape, not the doors that led to the hall. I called Freddie up and said, 'Listen, the FBI's banging on the door. Why don't you come down the fire escape and talk to me.' Freddie and his lover Alan Marlowe, who was later my husband, came down the fire escape to babysit my daughter Jeanne, who was four, and I showered and put on some very expensive clothes, which was how I figured I should go to court. Then I called up Roi's lawyer, Stanley Faulkner, and arranged to meet him at the courthouse to turn myself in so we could get LeRoi out. They wouldn't set bail on him until they had me too, so we went down to the courthouse and did this whole number. Stanley really pulls all kinds of 1930's, sentimental, C.P. tricks. And they work. I had told him we couldn't go to court in June because I was going to have LeRoi's baby then. This was only October, and I didn't even look pregnant yet, but Stanley went rushing around insisting that clerks move out of their offices so I could sit down and rest while the whole thing was going on. He had everybody so frightened that the guy who fingerprinted me kept saying 'Excuse me' every time he took a different finger. He'd say 'Excuse me' and then he would do the next finger, 'Excuse me.'

"Meanwhile LeRoi had been in a very small cell by himself all day and they hadn't allowed him any paper or books. I yelled and screamed and Stanley yelled and screamed, and we finally both got out with no bail. It was the first time for me and probably also for LeRoi of having that unpleasant experience of walking through a place like a courthouse while reporters flash lights at you. (A couple of papers ran stories on the arrest; the *New York Post* was one of them.)

"The case never went to court. LeRoi requested a grand jury hearing on Stanley Faulkner's advice. Only one of us could testify and he did. He spent two days on the stand. The first day he was questioned by the D.A., and the second he brought in a ton of stuff that had one time or another been labeled 'obscene': everything from *Ulysses* to Catullus. He read for hours to the grand jury, and they refused to return an indictment. Of course, we also had letters from people all over the world stating that the work of William Burroughs and LeRoi Jones was 'literature' (whatever that is) and that we should be left alone.

"1962 was a good time for people to be liberal that way with a very nice, literate, still polite, still cool LeRoi. Made them feel good. They had a chance to be really nice, and they haven't had many chances since, with any of us." Diane di Prima, Introduction to *Floating Bear, Nos. 1–37, 1961–1969* (1973), xiii–xv.

PAGE

328   "I was getting hard-ons, rubbing up . . ." Barry Miles, *Ginsberg* (1989), 26.

328   *"A look startled his face . . ." Ibid.,* 96.

328   " 'Frankly I don't trust that kind of . . ." *Ibid.*

328   "Dear Allen, The wire is still on . . ." Allen Ginsberg, *Howl: Original Draft Facsimile* (1986), 156; Barry Miles, *Ginsberg* (1989), 185.

328   "Dear Eugene, . . . God's informers came to . . ." Allen Ginsberg, *Howl, Original Draft Facsimile* (1986), 205.

330   "In the fall of 1955 a group of . . ." *Ibid.,* 165.

330   "I followed the whole gang of howling poets . . ." *Ibid.,* 166.

330   "The Six Gallery was a cooperative . . ." *Ibid.,* 168.

331   "[T]he audience reaction was amazing . . ." *Ibid.,* 167.

331   "The poem was a crucible of cultural change . . ." John Tytell, *Naked Angels* (1976), 104.

331   *"I saw the best minds of my generation . . ."* Allen Ginsberg, *Howl: Original Draft Facsimile* (1986), 3.

PAGE

331	"Dear Allen, I hope this reaches you . . ." *Ibid.*, 156.
332	*"angelheaded hipsters burning for . . ." Ibid.*, 3.
332	"Dear Allen, I am gratified about your new . . ." *Ibid.*, 150.
332	*"Who let themselves be fucked in the ass . . ." Ibid.*, 4.
332	"Dear Allen, I'm afraid I have to tell . . ." *Ibid.*, 156.
333	"The first edition of *Howl* . . ." *Ibid.*, 169.
333	"I had submitted the ms. of *Howl* to . . ." *Ibid.*
333	"Ferlinghetti is the . . ." *Ibid.*, 166.
333	"Then the [San Francisco] police . . ." *Ibid.*, 170.
334	"Imagine being arrested for selling . . ." *Ibid.*
335	"For the trial I wore a cheap, light . . ." *Ibid.*
335	"I presume you understand the whole thing . . ." *Ibid.*, 172.
336	*"who copulated ecstatic and . . ." Ibid.*, 4.
336	"Your Honor, frankly I have only got a . . ." *Ibid.*, 172.
337	"The words he has used are valid . . ." *Ibid.*, 173.
337	"In other words, Your Honor, how far are . . ." *Ibid.*
337	"The first part of *Howl* presents a . . ." *Ibid.*, 174.
338	"The author of *Howl* has used those . . ." *Ibid.*
341	"Obviously a writer can employ . . ." *Grove Press* v. *Christenberry* (1960), reprinted in de Grazia, *Censorship Landmarks* (1969), 339, 341.

On movie censorship: In a case decided in 1954, *Commercial Pictures* v. *Regents,* the Court had struck down a New York law pursuant to which censors had banned as "immoral" and as "tending to corrupt morals" the film *La Ronde;* the Court's decision was a one-line *per curiam* with a citation to the 1952 *Miracle* case (*Burstyn* v. *Wilson*) mentioned earlier, which had struck down a section of New York's movie censorship law authorizing the banning of "sacrilegious" films. The complete texts of both cases are in de Grazia, *Censorship Landmarks* (1969). The New York statute before the Court in the *Kingsley International Pictures* case was a third attempt by New York to fashion a film censorship law that would authorize a state agency that had shown itself to be responsive to the opinions of the Catholic hierarchy in New York (notably Cardinal Spellman) concerning film morality to ban films having "immoral" themes.

In *Kingsley,* a conservative four-justice minority filed separate opinions deploring the liberal majority's action in *striking down* the new New York statute (on its face), arguing that the state had the constitutional power to censor films depicting sexual immorality and that, in this case, the problem was simply that the New York film censors had incorrectly (and unconstitutionally) *applied* the law to a film that was not "sexually immoral"; for that reason they had not dissented from the *result* of the Court's decision, which was to reverse the specific ban on the *Lady Chatterley's Lover* film. It is evident from the opinions (Frankfurter, Harlan, and Clark each wrote a separate concurring opinion) that this bloc was prepared to have the Court sanction governmental censorship of "sexual immorality" just as, in *Roth* (and the companion state case, *Alberts*), the Court held that the free-expression guarantees did not prevent the federal (or state) government from censoring "obscenity."

The constitutional implications of the decisions in *Commercial Pictures* and *Kingsley International Pictures* far exceeded their concrete holdings; it was apparent that a solid Court majority was indisposed to permit the censorship of artistic expression (notably films) on grounds of immorality, sexual or otherwise, and also that the notion of "corruption of morals" that had for so long underlined the enforcement of obscenity law was considered constitutionally untenable. Had the majority invalidated the New York law on vagueness grounds, the implications would have been less promising for freedom of expression and less full of foreboding for moral conservatives, because New York might have returned to the drawing board to design a narrower, more specific, constitutionally acceptable means for suppressing the expression of "immoral" ideas—for example, by enacting a law that specifically prohibited the licensing of films that "advocated," "made alluring," or "incited" "sexually immoral activity." Justice Stewart's opinion for the majority was written in such a way as to be a preemptive strike against the enactment of such a new law.

A few years later, the bloc of anti-censorship justices would be augmented by the retirement of the conservative Frankfurter and his replacement on the bench by the unqualifiedly liberal Arthur Goldberg. Still later, the additions of Abe Fortas and Thurgood Marshall would further strengthen the will and disposition of the Court to disable state and federal systems of censorship over literary and artistic forms of expression.

CHAPTER 18: *El Hombre Invisible*

PAGE

343   "Who are you, living in Tangier . . ." Paul Carroll, "Call It Big Table," *Chicago,* March 1979, 163.

343   "Name Wm Seward Burroughs III . . ." *Ibid.*

344   "For the Chris sake do you actually . . ." Barry Miles, *Ginsberg: A Biography* (1989), 130.

344   "Do you ever wonder what happens . . ." *Chicago Daily News,* October 25, 1958.

344   "I was poetry editor of the *Chicago Review* . . ." Author interview with Paul Carroll.

345   "The 'beat' generation has quite a . . ." *Chicago Daily News,* October 25, 1958.

346   "I had been going around trying to be . . ." Author interview with Allen Ginsberg.

347   "Our house in the Marshan was very fine. . . ." William Burroughs, Jr., "Life With Father," *Esquire,* September 1971.

348   "The rooftops, by custom, are the . . ." William Burroughs, Jr., "Life With Father," *Esquire,* September 1971.

348   "All day I had been finding . . ." William Burroughs, *Letters to Allen Ginsberg 1953–1957* (1982), 17.

348   "He wrote something every day, steadily . . ." Author interview with Allen Ginsberg.

349   "We weren't mounting the barricades to wave . . ." Author interview with Paul Carroll.

350   "It is the fall of 1957 . . ." Paul Carroll, "Call It *Big Table,*" *Chicago,* March 1979, 161.

350   *"The Rube is a social liability . . ."* *Chicago Review* (Autumn 1958), 3ff.

351   "Gregory Corso sent a group of major poems. . . ." Author interview with Allen Ginsberg.

PAGE

351   *"Non-using pushers have a contact habit . . ."* Chicago Review (Autumn 1958), 3ff.

352   *"The Buyer's habit keeps getting heavier . . ."* Chicago Review (Autumn 1958), 3ff.

353   "Dear Irving [Rosenthal], what? Suppression? . . ." *Big Table* 1, no. 1 (Spring 1959), 3.

353   "Larry [Kimpton] called me in . . ." Author interview with Professor Edward Rosenheim.

353   "I wasn't a student at the U. of C. then . . ." Author interview with Paul Carroll.

354   "Hutchins was like an Adonis . . ." Author interview with George Anastaplo.

355   "The most dangerous aspect of public relations . . ." Harry S. Ashmore, *Unseasonable Truths: The Life of Robert Maynard Hutchins* (1989), 310, 300.

355   "The University of Chicago did not exert . . ." *Chicago Maroon,* December 12, 1958.

355   "The Taylor and Stern statements are . . ." *Chicago Maroon,* December 12, 1958.

356   "Sometime during the week of November 3–7 . . ." *Report of the Special Committee of the Student Government in Re: The Chicago Review,* January 28, 1959; copy in author's files.

357   "Since an official publication of the University . . ." *Chicago Maroon,* December 12, 1958 ("Chancellor Tells *Maroon* Views on Review").

357   "Stern took the position that . . ." Author interview with Paul Carroll.

358   " 'Cause it was a big new literature and . . ." Author interview with Allen Ginsberg.

358   "It was with the help of Allen and Gregory . . ." Author interview with Paul Carroll.

358   "The Shaw Society in Chicago proposed . . ." Author interview with Allen Ginsberg.

361   "Jack Olson, who was the Chicago bureau . . ." Author interview with Paul Carroll.

361   "So we got interviewed all over . . ." Author interview with Allen Ginsberg.

362   "Years later, Jim Hoge, who was also . . ." Author interview with Paul Carroll.

362   "The *Chicago Review* is a literary quarterly . . ." *The Saturday Review,* June 27, 1959 ("The Book Burners and Sweet Sixteen").

363   "I don't know . . ." Author interview with Professor Edward Rosenheim.

364   *"Ya damn hogfuckin . . ."* Big Table 1, no. 1 (Spring 1959), 7.

364   *"Clem and Jody, two old time . . ."* Big Table 1, no. 1 (Spring 1959), 79.

CHAPTER 19: *Like a Piece of Lead with Wings on It*

PAGE

366   "At last! . . ." *A Henry Miller Reader,* edited by John Calder (London, 1985), 13.

PAGE

367   "This then? This is not a book." Henry Miller, *Tropic of Cancer* (Grove Press, First Black Cat Edition, 1961), 1–2.

367   "I had imagined on leaving America . . ." Henry Miller, Letter to Stanley Fleishman, December 26, 1962, in Appendix J., *Zeitlin* v. *Arnebergh*, Supreme Court of California, decided July 2, 1963; copy in author's files.

367   "I didn't really know much about Miller . . ." Author interview with Barney Rosset. Gerald Jonas, "The Story of Grove," *The New York Times Magazine*, January 21, 1968.

367n.   The Gotham Book Mart became the seat of the James Joyce Society and a place where the literary avant-garde could congregate, talk, borrow money, and admire one another's works. It also became a bibliophile's dream: here, and seemingly nowhere else, could Gertrude Stein's works, and also *transaction* magazine, be found; Steloff prominently displayed the "little magazines" and stocked the works of young authors, too. In her spacious backyard with outside bookstalls like those by the Seine, parties and authors' readings were given. She even published some books: on Joyce, the Lawrence/Russell letters (edited by Harry T. Moore), and poems by Stein and Wallace Stevens. She had to smuggle in contraband works, like most of Lawrence and Henry Miller, and from time to time she was raided by John Sumner and his smut police. See W. G. Rogers, *Wise Men Fish Here: The Story of Frances Steloff and the Gotham Book Mart* (1965), and the Special Gotham Book Mart Issue of the *Journal of Modern Literature* (April 1975), which contains the memoirs of Frances Steloff and a summary of her bookstore's history. Steloff describes her arrest and quotes from a twenty-minute-long opinion written by New York justice Nathan D. Perlman (the dissenter in the *Hecate County* case), which freed her from the charges that John Sumner brought against her for publishing André Gide's "obscene" novel *If It Die* (768–69). (Perlman's full opinion is reprinted in de Grazia, *Censorship Landmarks*, 103–5.) Bennett Cerf provided her with the services of Random House's lawyer, Horace Manges; she also received the warm support of the editors of *The Saturday Review of Literature, The New Republic,* and *The Nation.* Steloff expressed her free speech philosophy in these words: "No more would I refuse anyone the right to smoke because I am a non-smoker, or to take a drink because I am a teetotaler, or to eat meat because I am a vegetarian, would I condemn a man for reading a book of his own choosing" (771).

     Steloff had a miserable childhood and no formal education beyond the seventh grade. After running away to New York, she landed a job selling corsets in a Brooklyn department store; she fell in love with literature when she was transferred during the Christmas rush to the book department. After that she worked for the next dozen years in a variety of bookstores, where she cultivated her innate taste for the best in modern literature. Although she sold the Gotham in 1967 to "another book lover," Andreas Brown, she continued to live over the store and stayed on as a working consultant until she died, on April 16, 1989, at the age of 101.

368   "By nature, I'm a type of free American . . ." Author interview with Barney Rosset.

PAGE

368   "Barney Rosset had a lot of ideas . . ." Author interview with Eugène Ionesco.

368   "I liked Barney Rosset . . ." *Ibid.*

369   "What was funny was how Barney . . ." Author interview with Alain Robbe-Grillet.

369   "Doubleday contracted to publish *Malcolm X . . .*" Author interview with Barney Rosset.

369   "It was in the summer of '68 that I saw . . ." Author interview with Jean Genet.

369   "Grove's first important censorship battle . . ." Author interview with Barney Rosset.

370   *"I am going to sing for you . . ."* Henry Miller, *Tropic of Cancer* (1961), 2.

370   "Twenty years ago a Swarthmore student . . ." Anthony Lewis, "The Most Recent Troubles of 'Tropic,' " *The New York Times Book Review,* January 21, 1962.

370   *"It is to you Tania . . ."* Henry Miller, *Tropic of Cancer* (1961), 2.

370   "When I found myself a publisher . . ." Author interview with Barney Rosset.

370   *"After me you can take on . . ."* Henry Miller, *Tropic of Cancer* (1961), 5.

370   "One day a *Tropic of Cancer* case . . ." Author interview with Judge Samuel B. Epstein.

371   *"O Tania, where now . . ."* Henry Miller, *Tropic of Cancer* (1961), 5.

371   "Whatever may be said of Daley . . ." Author interview with Judge Samuel B. Epstein.

371   "We published the hardbound edition . . ." Author interview with Barney Rosset.

371   "I did not conduct the trial . . ." Charles Rembar, *The End of Obscenity* (1968), 180.

372   "It is not on sale in Massachusetts . . ." Anthony Lewis, "The Most Recent Troubles of 'Tropic,' " *The New York Times Book Review,* January 21, 1962.

372   "Booksellers were worried because . . ." Author interview with Barney Rosset.

372   "The troubles of *Tropic* had a broader . . ." Anthony Lewis, "The Most Recent Troubles of 'Tropic,' " *The New York Times Book Review,* January 21, 1962.

372   "Of one and a half million . . ." Author interview with Fred Jordan.

373   "That, for me, was the most dramatic trial . . ." Author interview with Barney Rosset.

373   "The owner of the bookstore . . ." Author interview with Judge Samuel B. Epstein.

373   "The Chicago story seems to begin . . ." Hoke Norris, " 'Cancer' in Chicago," *Evergreen Review* no. 25, 4–5.

374   "We stopped at 1 North Main Street . . ." *Ibid.,* 5.

374   *"Llona now, she . . ."* Henry Miller, *Tropic of Cancer* (1961), 6.

374   "I asked Mr. Ullrich . . ." Hoke Norris, " 'Cancer' in Chicago," *Evergreen Review* no. 25, 5.

375   *"I'm dancing with every slut in the place . . ."* Henry Miller, *Tropic of Cancer* (1961).

PAGE

375   "It is very fortunate that we have a judge . . ." Elmer Gertz and Felice F. Lewis, editors, *Henry Miller: Years of Trial and Triumph 1962–1964: The Correspondence of Henry Miller and Elmer Gertz* (1978), 24.

375   "When that book was first called . . ." Author interview with Judge Samuel B. Epstein.

375   "Litigation involving *Tropic of Cancer* was . . ." Elmer Gertz, *A Handful of Clients* (1965), 244.

375   "After considerable thought . . ." Elmer Gertz, *A Handful of Clients* (1965), 262.

375   "The book . . . is definitely a work of . . ." *Ibid.*, 263.

376   *"It is a little after daybreak . . ."* Henry Miller, *Tropic of Cancer* (1961).

376   "Ellmann was an incredible witness . . ." Author interview with Barney Rosset.

376   "Through the device of questioning Dr. Ellmann . . ." and the remarks that follow, Elmer Gertz, *A Handful of Clients* (1965), 264.

376   "Adapting a device suggested by Edward de Grazia . . ." and the remarks that follow, *Ibid.*

376   "We brought out through . . ." and the remarks that follow, *Ibid.*, 265.

377   "We felt we had established . . ." *Ibid.*

377   "I am going to permit questions . . ." and the remarks that follow, *Ibid.*, 266.

377   "Now the cross-examination passed . . ." and the remarks that follow, *Ibid.*, 268.

378   "When Dad said that passage . . ." Author interview with Elliot Epstein.

378   "Yes, Your Honor." Elmer Gertz, *A Handful of Clients* (1965), 268.

378   "After the trial ended somehow I knew . . ." Author interview with Barney Rosset.

378   "I myself didn't know how . . ." Author interview with Judge Samuel B. Epstein.

379   "Dad was not a particularly courageous . . ." Author interview with Elliot Epstein.

379   "In my written opinion, I said: . . ." Author interview with Judge Samuel B. Epstein.

380   "The fact is that Dad was bounced . . ." Author interview with Elliot Epstein.

380   "I received more mail concerning . . ." Author interview with Judge Samuel B. Epstein.

381   "[*Tropic of Cancer*] is nothing more than a compilation . . ." *People* v. *Fritch* (decided July 10, 1963), reprinted in de Grazia, *Censorship Landmarks* (1969), 464.

381   "One day, after two years . . ." Author interview with Judge Samuel B. Epstein.

382   "Milton Perlman of Grove Press . . ." Elmer Gertz, *A Handful of Clients* (1965), 300.

382   "Well, what the Illinois Supreme Court . . ." Author interview with Judge Samuel B. Epstein.

382   "This was . . . a fantastic result . . ." Elmer Gertz, *A Handful of Clients* (1965), 301.

PAGE

382   "And then the Supreme Court of Illinois. . . ." Author interview with Judge Samuel B. Epstein.

382   "When he learned about that . . ." Author interview with Elliot Epstein.

382   "They called in Elmer Gertz . . ." Author interview with Judge Samuel B. Epstein.

382   "On June 18, 1964, this Court . . ." Opinion of the Supreme Court of Illinois, copy in author's file.

383   "Judge Epstein's decision . . ." Elmer Gertz, *A Handful of Clients* (1965), 301.

383   "In Illinois today . . ." Author interview with Elliot Epstein.

CHAPTER 20: *This Was "Star Wars"*

PAGE

384   "So you're Burroughs." Ted Morgan, *Literary Outlaw: The Life and Times of William S. Burroughs* (1988), 335.

384   "So you're Burroughs." *Ibid.*

384   "The only thing he'd said . . ." *Ibid.*

385   "Dear Barney . . ." Letter dated June 15, 1959, from Maurice Girodias to Barney Rosset; copy in author's file.

385   "It *was* a mess until we realized . . ." Author interview with Allen Ginsberg.

386   "So then the problem was . . ." *Ibid.*

387   "When Rosenthal was working on the book . . ." Author interview with Barney Rosset.

387   "So it was a mess and it wasn't a mess . . ." Author interview with Allen Ginsberg.

387   "I remember very well one time . . ." Author interview with Alain Robbe-Grillet.

388   "Maurice was up and down . . ." Author interview with Barney Rosset.

389   "It would be cruel irony indeed . . ." Letter from Maurice Girodias to Barney Rosset; copy in author's file.

389   "The fact is that I had invested . . ." Letter from Barney Rosset to Maurice Girodias; copy in author's file.

390   *"Hassan's Rumpus Room . . ."* William S. Burroughs, *Naked Lunch.*

391   "At the time, '59 or '60, there was a big . . ." Author interview with Barney Rosset.

391   "Dear Maurice, I've tried now for the third . . ." Undated letter from Henry Miller to Maurice Girodias; copy in author's file.

392   "Barney Rosset asked Edward de Grazia . . ." Ted Morgan, *Literary Outlaw: The Life and Times of William S. Burroughs* (1988), 343.

392   "De Grazia was a slim elegant Sicilian . . ." Norman Mailer, *The Armies of the Night* (1968).

393   "Each year in [Calder's] home town . . ." Ted Morgan, *Literary Outlaw: The Life and Times of William S. Burroughs* (1988), 332.

394   "[*Naked Lunch*] is like a neighborhood . . ." Mary McCarthy, "Déjeuner sur l'Herbe," *The New York Review of Books,* February 1963.

PAGE

395   "*Naked Lunch* is one of the most alive . . ." Quoted in letter dated October 30, 1962, from Barney Rosset to booksellers; copy in author's file.

395   "[*Naked Lunch*] is a masterpiece of its own genre . . ." *Ibid*.

395   "This book [is] one of the most impressive . . ." E. S. Seldon, "The Cannibal Feast," *Evergreen Review* 22 (January-February 1962).

395   "[*Naked Lunch*] is a book of great beauty . . ." Quoted in letter dated October 30, 1962, from Barney Rosset to booksellers; copy in author's file.

395   "[*Naked Lunch*] is indeed a masterpiece . . ." *Newsweek*, Nov. 26, 1962.

397   "We decided to go ahead with the case . . ." Author interview with William I. Cowin.

CHAPTER 21: *Who Is His Parish Priest?*

Shortly after Reynolds's attack on Justice Brennan's and Professor Dworkin's jurisprudence, Attorney General Edwin Meese attacked the Warren Court's 1958 landmark decision in *Cooper* v. *Aaron,* and the *per curiam* opinion that the Court announced in that case, believed to have been drafted by Justice Brennan. It was the only opinion in history that was signed by all nine members of the Court, to emphasize their unanimity. In it, the Court said that "the Federal Judiciary is supreme in the exposition of the law of the Constitution," and ruled that its landmark 1954 decision in *Brown* v. *Board of Education* (denouncing racially segregated public schools as unconstitutional) was binding on all state officials as "the supreme law of the land." The *Cooper* case had grown out of an effort by Arkansas governor Orval Faubus to obstruct desegregation of the schools in Little Rock. After Faubus sent the Arkansas National Guard to keep blacks from entering a white school, in disregard of the Supreme Court's ruling in *Brown,* President Eisenhower sent federal troops to Little Rock to enforce a lower court's desegregation order and the Supreme Court's interpretation of the Constitution in *Brown.* Meese's speech assailed the Court's opinion in *Cooper* as involving "a flawed reading of our Constitution" and "an even more faulty syllogism of legal reasoning." "The logic of *Cooper* v. *Aaron,*" Meese charged, "was, and is, at war with the Constitution, at war with the basic principles of democratic government, and at war with the very meaning of the rule of law." Meese implied that Faubus was constitutionally correct in taking the position that inasmuch as he had not been a party to the case, he was not bound by the Supreme Court's declaration in *Brown* that segregated schools violated the Constitution, and that the Supreme Court's rulings were not binding on all persons nor even on state government officials, including judges (speech of October 21, 1986, at Tulane University, New Orleans, La.). See the perspicacious analysis of the Meese speech by Stuart Taylor, Jr., in *The New York Times,* October 27, 1986. A neoconservative academic attack on Brennan's jurisprudence had been made earlier, in the February 1985 issue of *Commentary* magazine, by University of Texas Law School professor Lino A. Graglia ("How the Constitution Disappeared," 19–27). Former judge Robert H. Bork has usually been circumspect in his public criticism of Brennan. See Bork's *The Tempting of America* (1989).

PAGE

402   "My father came from Ireland . . ." Author interview with Justice
        William J. Brennan, Jr.

403   "Much has been written about . . ." Dean Norman Redlich, "William
        J. Brennan, Jr.: New Honor for an Old Friend," *NYU Law School
        Annual Survey of American Law* (1982).

403   "He is not a judge who enjoys . . ." Anthony Lewis, "Robust and
        Uninhibited," *The New York Times,* October 17, 1976.

404   "Lively, even acrimonious, debate . . ." Justice William J. Brennan, Jr.,
        "Abe Fortas," *The Yale Law Journal* 91 (May 1982).

Undiscouraged by the constitutional doctrine "separating" church and state, New York policemen permitted themselves to be used as one of Cardinal Spellman's weapons against literary and artistic sins. The day after Spellman condemned the Broadway theatre piece *Wine, Women and Song* before a gathering at the New York City Police Department's Anchor Club—it was described as "a relatively tame burlesque show featuring a fan dancer and a clown"—the police crashed the gates of the Ambassador Theatre and served summonses on the show's manager and producer. Later, Lenny Bruce, who frequently lampooned the cardinal and other Catholic figures (including the pope), was silenced by the police, reputedly after Spellman complained about him to city officials. See Chapter 24.

Cardinal Spellman, alarmed by what he had heard about *The Miracle*'s plot and theme, and certain things that actors Anna Magnani and Federico Fellini did and said on the screen, rose in St. Patrick's Cathedral to condemn the film and those associated with it. He also saw to it that the movie was condemned by the 400-odd Catholic priests working in his archdiocese. Next, Catholic war veterans and members of the Holy Name Society paraded in front of Manhattan's Paris Theatre, where *The Miracle* was playing, carrying signs that read STAY AWAY FROM THIS THEATRE and INSULT TO EVERY WOMAN NOT TO MENTION CHILDREN and THIS IS THE KIND OF PICTURE THE COMMUNISTS WANT and DON'T BE A COMMUNIST—THE COMMUNISTS ARE INSIDE. It was immaterial to Spellman that the New York film critics had named *The Miracle* the best foreign film of 1950. The censorship and the film are described in de Grazia and Newman, *Banned Films,* 77–83, 231–32.

The New York fire commissioner charged the owner of the Paris Theatre with violations and the city's license commissioner tried to shut the movie house down. Finally, the New York Board of Regents, which had innocently licensed the film's exhibition at the Paris Theatre, summoned Joseph Burstyn, the distributor, to a hearing to show cause why the license should not be revoked because the film was in violation of state law; it was charged with being "sacrilegious." The proceedings that followed resulted in a ban of the film in New York until the Supreme Court reversed the ban in 1952. Spellman had other grievances: "*The Miracle* is a vicious insult to Italian womanhood. It presents the Italian woman as moronic, neurotic and in matters of religion fanatical. Only a perverted mind could so misrepresent so noble a race as women. . . . To those who perpetrate such a crime as *The Miracle* within the law all that we can say is: How long will enemies of decency tear at the heart of America? . . . Divide and conquer is the technique of the greatest enemy of civilization, atheistic communism. God forbid that the producers of racial and religious mockeries should divide and demoralize Americans so that the minions of Moscow might enslave this land of liberty."

Spellman spoke like a Catholic counterpart to secular McCarthyism, but his influence was obviously less. Before the Catholic boycott, *The Miracle* had done poorly at the box office; afterward the lines for each show stretched around the block. Burstyn was one of a small breed of freedom-loving, non-Hollywood-bred independents who, using foreign films, fought against motion picture censorship in the United States. Burstyn fought doggedly for the film's freedom up a hierarchy of New York administrative and judicial bodies to the Supreme Court of the United States, where he was rewarded with a holding that the New York ban violated the constitutional guarantees of freedom of speech and press. Said Justice Tom Clark: "It is not the business of government in our nation to suppress real or imagined attacks upon a particular religious doctrine, whether they appear in publications, speeches, or motion pictures." With this single stroke the Supreme Court abolished the ancient common-law offense of "blasphemous libel." In England, the law of blasphemy has been used: in 1822, to ban Shelley's poem *Queen Mab;* in 1978, to imprison the editor of the newspaper *Gay News* for publishing a poem, "The Love That Dares to Speak Its Name," that depicted the adulatory fellation of Jesus Christ on the cross. The case was *Regina* v. *Lemm,* decided March 17, 1978, in the Court of Appeal (*The Weekly Law Reports,* August 11, 1978, 404). Recently, in England, there was banned the exhibition in movie houses anywhere, or by videotapes at home, of an eighteen-minute film, *Visions of Ecstasy,* which "depicts St. Theresa caressing and kissing Christ and being erotically touched by a female character meant to represent her psyche." See "Ban on Film for Blasphemy Is Upheld in Britain," *The New York Times,* December 16, 1989.

In the States, there were no reported modern cases. However, in striking down New York's ban of *The Miracle,* the Supreme Court had to overturn its own forty-year-old precedent, *Mutual Film Corp.* v. *Ohio,* in which it had held that motion pictures were not a part of the nation's press and so not entitled to constitutional freedom. Still, the Court's action in the *Burstyn* case was not so bold as one might have wished: in closing, Justice Clark made it clear that the Court was not striking down motion picture censorship *in toto.* Wrote Justice Clark: "Since the term 'sacrilegious' is the sole standard under attack here, it is not necessary for us to decide, for example, whether a state may censor motion pictures under a clearly drawn statute designed and applied to prevent the showing of obscene films. That is a very different question from the one before us."

Spellman also used the pulpit to attack "obscene" motion pictures like *Baby Doll,* starring Carroll Baker and directed by Elia Kazan. The film was not officially censored or denied a license, however, but the Catholic boycott Spellman launched was respected by the Catholic movie chain exhibitor Joseph P. Kennedy, JFK's father, and others; this seriously impaired the film's box office returns. See de Grazia and Newman, *Banned Films* (1982), 93–94, 243–44.

The Protestant figure today whose power is most comparable to Spellman's may be the Reverend Donald Wildmon, founder of the American Family Association. Wildmon, too, has learned how to penetrate and enlist governmental bodies— including the U.S. Congress, the Justice Department, and the Federal Communications Commission—in his war on obscenity, blasphemy, secular and religious humanists, and artists.

410   "We're a group of writers who value deeply . . ." Testimony of William Styron in Hearings Before the Committee on the Judiciary, U.S. Senate, 100th Cong., 1st Sess., on the Nomination of Robert H. Bork to be Associate Justice of the Supreme Court of the United States, Part 2, at 1989–91, September 22, 1987.

410   "Constitutional protection should be accorded . . ." *Ibid.,* 1993–94.

410   "As I and my colleagues reread these views . . ." *Ibid.,* 1990–91.

411n.   This "kind of censorship," public school library censorship, presents special problems of First Amendment analysis, somewhat analogous to those presented by the prospect that the National Endowment for the Arts may be instructed by Congress not to fund, or to defund, "obscene," "blasphemous," and otherwise "controversial" art. (See Chapter 30.) The problems were first discussed by the Supreme Court in the 1982 case of *Board of Education* v. *Pico,* which held that the removal by a public school board from the school's library of any book *because of ideas presented in the book* violated the First Amendment. The Court's lead (plurality of four) opinion was written by Justice Brennan, who asserted that the free expression guarantees protected a public school student's "right to receive information and ideas." Chief Justice Burger dissented, claiming that Brennan's opinion "demeans our function of constitutional adjudication." Justice Powell (a former public school board trustee) also dissented, expressing "genuine dismay" at the Court's limiting school board powers in this way, and appended seven pages of excerpts from the nine books that had been removed from the Island Trees school library, namely: *Slaughterhouse-Five,* by Kurt Vonnegut; *The Fixer,* by Bernard Malamud; *The Naked Ape,* by Desmond Morris; *Down These Mean Streets,* by Piri Thomas; *Best Short Stories of Negro Writers,* edited by Langston Hughes; *A Hero Ain't Nothin' But a Sandwich,* by Alice Childress; *Soul on Ice,* by Eldridge Cleaver; *A Reader for Writers,* edited by Jerome Archer; and *Go Ask Alice,* by an anonymous author. A school board press release at the time of removal made plain that the objections were to the books' ideas, for the books were described as "anti-American, anti-Christian, anti-Semitic and just plain filthy"; the board also claimed that it was discharging its duty to protect schoolchildren from "this moral danger." The removal action took place after the board saw the titles listed on a sheet of "objectionable" books circulated by a local moral vigilante group called Parents of New York United. The American Civil Liberties Union praised the Court's ruling as "a major victory that comes against the backdrop of a national epidemic of school book censorship."

     The American Library Association has had an Office for Intellectual Freedom, headed by Judith Krug, since 1967, and a Freedom to Read Foundation, which is the legal defense arm of the ALA's Intellectual Freedom Program. The staffs of the office and the foundation are identical. A newsletter chronicles the struggle of many librarians and the ALA to preserve "the right to receive information and ideas," which Justice Brennan said public school students were entitled to enjoy as a matter of constitutional law. An excellent historical survey of the problem is in

Evelyn Geller's *Forbidden Books in American Public Libraries, 1876–1939* (1984). See also Eric Moon, editor, *Book Selection and Censorship in the Sixties* (1969); and Donna A. Demac, *Liberty Denied* (1988), Chapter 2.

Judith Krug has told me that given the Supreme Court's unwillingness (to date) to abolish obscenity censorship, and given her belief that libraries are the only pure "First Amendment institutions in the country" (which, however, unlike profit-making institutions, have "absolutely no incentive" to promote sexually oriented material, "or, in fact, to go out and defend this material"), she thinks that librarians as a group may soon have to go into court and ask for a First Amendment *exemption* from obscenity laws. Librarians, according to Krug, "have to serve the fringes" because they are "part of our constituency." "And so our collections, if they're really good collections, and if we as professional librarians are really doing our jobs, are really going to have some materials that are totally anathema to a lot of the population, and that's where the problem comes in." (Author interview with Judith Krug.)

413   "Felix was absolutely superb . . ." Jeffrey T. Leeds, "A Life on the Court," *The New York Times Magazine*, October 5, 1986.

413   "I looked to Felix to . . ." *Ibid.*

414   "Everyone thought Felix. . . ." *Ibid.*

CHAPTER 22: *Because We Never Could Agree on a Definition*

The Posner memorandum continued: "New York, as I earlier mentioned, has adopted a test of hard-core pornography, and although I find such a test unsatisfactory, . . . it is plain that the New York courts mean it to free bona fide works of art or information from restrictions under the obscenity laws. Massachusetts' highest court has, as I also mentioned earlier, . . . adopted a similar test, and with similar purposes. Connecticut appears to have followed suit. See *State* v. *Andrews,* 186 A. 2d 546, 551 (Conn. 1962); *State* v. *Su . . .* [not legible], 146 Conn. 78, 147 A. 2d 686 (1958). The currents of liberalism in the interpretation of obscenity laws are running as well in Maryland, *Yudkin* v. *State,* 229 Md. 222, 182 A. 2d 798 (1962), Oregon, *State* v. *Jackson,* 356 P. 2d 495 (Ore. 1960), California, *In re Harris,* 16 Cal. Rep. 889, 366 P. 2d 305 (Sup. Ct. 1961), North Carolina, N.C. Sess. Laws, 1957, c. 1227 (ALI Model Penal Code obscenity provisions adopted), Nebraska, *State* v. *Nelson,* 168 Neb. 394, 95 N. W. 2d 678 (1959), Kansas, Kan. Sess. Laws, 1961, c. 186, § 1(b), and very distinctly, in the federal courts, *Grove Press Inc.* v. *Christenberry,* 276 F. 2d 433 (C. A. 2d Cir. 1960), affirming 175 F. Supp. 488 (S. D. N. Y. 1959); *Zenith Int'l Film Corp.* v. *Chicago,* 291 F. 2d 785 (C. A. 7th Cir. 1961); *Big Table, Inc.* v. *Schroeder,* 186 F. Supp. 254 (N. D. Ill. 1960); *Upham* v. *Dill,* 195 F. Supp. 5 (S. D. N. Y.)."

The *Yudkin* case, mentioned by Posner, involved the reversal on appeal of the obscenity conviction of bookseller Samuel Yudkin for selling *Tropic of Cancer,* a case in which I filed an amicus curiae brief for the American Civil Liberties Union and its Maryland chapter, on Yudkin's side. Sam Yudkin, who lost his bookstore franchise at Washington's National Airport as a result of his prosecution in suburban Maryland, is one of the unsung fallen heroes of the struggle for literary freedom. The *Grove* v. *Christenberry* case involved the freeing of *Lady Chatterley's Lover*. *Big Table* v. *Schroeder* was the case in which the writings of Jack Kerouac and William Burroughs were freed from Post Office restraints, as described in Chapter 18.

PAGE

420   "It remains only to be observed that the law . . ." Copy in author's file.

425   "It has been suggested that . . ." *Jacobellis* v. *Ohio* (1964), reprinted in de Grazia, *Censorship Landmarks* (1969), 423, 425–26.

427   "We are told that the determination . . ." *Ibid.,* 424.

428   "In other areas involving . . ." *Ibid.*

429   "In . . . *Jacobellis* v. *Ohio* . . . Brennan made . . ." Kalven, *A Worthy Tradition* (1987), 38.

429   "The question of the proper standard . . ." de Grazia, *Censorship Landmarks* (1969), 425.

430   "I did not know what it was . . ." Author interview with Justice William J. Brennan, Jr.

A note in *Harvard Law Review* 94 (1981), page 1127, entitled "Plurality Decisions and Judicial Decisionmaking," criticizes the contemporary Supreme Court for the frequency of plurality decisions, which the note's author regards as "pathological decisionmaking." The author is, I believe, misguided, writing no doubt under pressure from the myth mentioned earlier that the law is normally "certain." The law is *ideally* certain but there will always be disagreement among the men and women who interpret and apply it. Expressions of disagreement may be suppressed by agreement, for example, that despite their existence in the minds of the justices, only one opinion will be issued. This gives a *false* impression of certainty, for unless the disagreements themselves are eliminated, they will probably rise again in the next case in which a litigant believes the argument should be made. Doubtless, the suppression of any expression of disagreement existing among the justices will discourage some litigants from raising the suppressed points, and this may slow down the process of change in the law and give an impression of stability. But stability, only one of the law's virtues, can hardly be praised as superior to justice.

The style of law declaration represented by plurality opinions is similar to the *seriatim* style which the Supreme Court used before 1801, and to the traditional *seriatim* practice of the English law lords. From 1801 until 1955, shortly after the beginning of the Warren Court (that is to say, over a period of 154 years), there were only 45 plurality decisions. From 1955 to the end of the Warren Court (say, in 1970) there were 42 plurality decisions. By 1981 the Burger Court alone had issued 88 plurality decisions, more than in the entire previous history of the Court.

In her unpublished monograph "Study of the Records of Supreme Court Justices," Alexandra K. Wigdor says: "Jefferson applauded the system of *seriatim* opinion-giving because it threw greater light on difficult subjects, it was more educative, and it showed whether the judges were unanimous or divided, thus giving more or less weight to the decision as a precedent." Chief Justice Marshall stopped the *seriatim* practice when he took his place on the Court in 1801; at that time the Court was "by far the least prestigious branch of the federal government." The Court was regarded as of so small consequence that it had to meet in a Senate committee room on the main floor of the Capitol—"the architects having forgotten [the Court] entirely when designing the Capitol City." During his tenure, Marshall aimed to increase the Court's prestige, and to establish the supremacy of the national government and the authority of law. He worked at this not only through the famous opinions that he wrote, such as *Marbury* v. *Madison,* which helped establish the bases of our federal constitutional system, but through the practices that he engendered for judicial decision-making immediately upon assuming leadership of the Court. Wigdor: "Marshall convinced his brethren on the bench of the novel proposition that the Court should speak with a single voice, contrary to the traditional practice of delivering opinions *seriatim,* each judge stating in turn the reasons for his judgment. Whatever differences might exist in conference, the Court, he urged, should face the outside world with a united front in the form of a single opinion, preferably written by the Chief Justice." Thus, in the first five years of Marshall's tenure, he personally delivered "the opinion of the Court" in every case, thereby greatly augmenting the secrecy of the Court's processes and effectively monopolizing the process whereby the Court provided definitive principled statements of the law. Although Marshall has been viewed by some scholars as having manipulated his fellow judges "like putty," Wigdor observes that "his seems to have been a pleasant domination, based on camaraderie, force of argument, great energy, and the ability to generate respect in those who worked closely with him." In these respects, of the justices who made up the second most activist bench in the Court's history, the Warren Court, only Justice Brennan will bear comparison with Marshall.

PAGE

432   "[T]he book is now printed in twelve . . ." Elmer Gertz and Felice F. Lewis, editors, *Henry Miller: Years of Trial and Triumph 1962–1964* (1978), 317–18.

432   "British publication [of *Tropic of Cancer*] . . ." *A Henry Miller Reader* (1985), edited by John Calder, Introduction.

432   "When I first became acquainted with Miller . . ." Elmer Gertz and Felice F. Lewis, editors, *Henry Miller* (1978), 331.

433   "Applying steady pressure . . ." Anthony Lewis, "Sex and the Supreme Court," *Esquire,* June 1963.

433   "So, as always, America ends up last!" Elmer Gertz and Felice F. Lewis, editors, *Henry Miller* (1978), 318.

433   "Sure, they made Fortas resign . . ." Author interview with Justice Brennan.

CHAPTER 23: *If All Mankind Minus One*

PAGE

434   "Many Catholics winced . . ." *The Catholic Standard and Times,* July 3, 1964.

PAGE
434   "Mr. Justice Brennan, author of . . ." *Operation Yorkville,* September–
       October 1964.
435   "Religious leaders of all faiths . . ." *The Tablet,* September 3, 1964; *The
       New York Times,* June 23, 1964.
435   "We cannot accept these court . . ." *The Tablet,* August 13, 1964;
       Operation Yorkville, September–October 1964; *The New York Times,*
       August 7, 1964, 31.
436   "[T]hree elements must . . ." de Grazia, *Censorship Landmarks* (1969),
       522.
437   "The terms of this test . . ." Harry Kalven, Jr., *A Worthy Tradition*
       (1987), 38.
437   "I would like to follow . . ." Leon Friedman, ed. *Oral Arguments Before
       the Supreme Court* 2 (1983), 247–48.
438   "Unlike a book such as . . ." *Ibid.*
438   "But the literary value. . . ." *Ibid.,* 249.
439   "Because the Court as a matter of . . ." *Ibid.*
440   "If all mankind minus one . . ." John Stuart Mill, *On Liberty.*
442   "The Supreme Judicial . . ." *"Memoirs"* v. *Attorney General,* reprinted
       in de Grazia, *Censorship Landmarks* (1969), 521, 523.
442   "There is a sense in which . . ." Harry Kalven, Jr., *A Worthy Tradition*
       (1987), 40.
442   "If 'social importance' is to be used . . ." *"Memoirs"* v. *Attorney General,*
       reprinted in de Grazia, *Censorship Landmarks* (1969), 521, 535.
442   "I agree with my brother White that . . ." *Ibid.,* 529.
442   "You have to applaud Brennan for trying . . ." Author interview with
       Paul Bender.
443   "As I look back . . ." John J. Gibbons, "Tribute to Justice Brennan,"
       36 *Rutgers Law Review,* 729.

CHAPTER 24: *The Ideas I Have Are Now Imprisoned Within Me*

Unless otherwise indicated, the quotations of Bruce's "bits" are based on typed transcripts contained in documents that Lenny Bruce gave me in connection with my representation of Bruce for purposes of the filing of the petition for writ of certiorari in the Supreme Court, mentioned in the text.

PAGE
445   "I used a ten-letter word onstage . . ." Lenny Bruce, *How to Talk Dirty
       and Influence People: An Autobiography* (1967), 132–33.
447   "By the winter of 1964 . . ." Albert Goldman (with Lawrence Schiller),
       Ladies and Gentlemen, Lenny Bruce!!! (1974), 520.
448   "Dear Edward, I feel like I have a vise . . ." Letter from Lenny Bruce
       to the author, dated March 16, 1965.
449   "Dear Ephraim, If the court had appointed . . ." Letter from Lenny
       Bruce to Ephraim London, dated September 2, 1964; copy in author's
       file.

PAGE

450   "We sued him for our fees . . ." Author interview with Gary Schwartz, 1990.

451   "I want them to stop prosecuting me . . ." Martin Garbus, *Ready for the Defense* (1971), 141–42.

451   "The judges listened with interest . . ." *Ibid.,* 142.

452   "He concluded with his imitation of the . . ." *Ibid.*

453   "I'm Captain McDermott. I want to tell . . ." Lenny Bruce, *How to Talk Dirty* (1972), 185–86.

454   "What may have been the Cardinal's last . . ." John Cooney, *The American Pope* (1984), 283.

454   "We wanted to believe desperately that . . ." *Ibid.*

454   "Hogan's assistant, Richard Kuh, was a . . ." Martin Garbus, *Ready for the Defense* (1971), 94.

454   "Richard Kuh was a brisk, athletic YMCA . . ." Albert Goldman (with Lawrence Schiller), *Ladies and Gentlemen, Lenny Bruce!!!* (1974), 543.

455   "Hogan was a small graying leprechaun . . ." *Ibid.,* 526.

455   "The third shot, all too . . ." *Time* magazine, December 6, 1963.

456   "Bruce was very funny. I didn't think we . . ." Martin Garbus, *Ready for the Defense* (1971), 95.

457   "Hogan found himself in the unusual . . ." *Ibid.,* 95–96.

457   "Murtagh, the presiding judge, had . . ." *Ibid.,* 98.

457   "Murtagh had the reputation . . ." Author interview with William Hellerstein, 1991.

458   "This once effective panjandrum of social . . ." Richard H. Kuh, *Foolish Figleaves?* (1967), 175–76.

458   "One factor that should discourage . . ." Martin Garbus, *Ready for the Defense* (1971), 96.

458   "Lenny Bruce's principal ploy . . ." Richard H. Kuh, *Foolish Figleaves?* (1967), 177.

459   "Emitting howls of protest, brigades of . . ." *Ibid.*

459   "The men who conceived and executed . . ." Albert Goldman (with Lawrence Schiller), *Ladies and Gentlemen, Lenny Bruce!!!* (1974), 529–30.

460   "The first day of the trial the courtroom . . ." *Ibid.,* 542.

460   "Due to the number of spectators, the case . . ." Martin Garbus, *Ready for the Defense* (1971), 98.

461   "The intellectual journals had also sent . . ." Albert Goldman (with Lawrence Schiller), *Ladies and Gentlemen, Lenny Bruce!!!* (1974), 542.

462   "In [Bruce's] performances, words . . ." *Decision and Opinion* of the Criminal Court of the City of New York, *People* v. *Lenny Bruce.*

463   "2. Jacqueline Kennedy 'hauling ass' . . ." *Ibid.*

464   "4. An accident victim . . ." *Ibid.*

465   "Judge Murtagh's decision was a travesty . . ." Martin Garbus, *Ready for the Defense* (1971), 136.

465   "Ephraim London and I spoke to dozens of . . ." *Ibid.,* 103.

465   "[D]efense witnesses heaped praises upon . . ." Richard H. Kuh, *Foolish Figleaves?* (1967), 201.

465   "Our next witness was one the judges could . . ." Martin Garbus, *Ready for the Defense* (1971), 103. The colloquy among Dorothy Kilgallen, Richard Kuh, Martin Garbus, and Judge Murtagh is based on the ac-

PAGE

counts given by Garbus in *Ready for the Defense* (1971), 103ff., and by Richard H. Kuh, *Foolish Figleaves?* (1967), 202ff.

469 "The entire performance . . ." *People* v. *Lenny Bruce*, 202 N.E.2d 497 (November 24, 1964).

470 "However distasteful it may be . . ." *Decision and Opinion* of the Criminal Court of the City of New York, *People* v. *Lenny Bruce.*

470 "Whether Bruce provided serious social . . ." Richard H. Kuh, *Foolish Figleaves?* (1967), 199–200.

470 "*First,* [the *Jacobellis*] case's language . . ." *Ibid.,* 199.

471 "*Second,* even had a majority of the . . ." *Ibid.*

472 "*Third,* even had much of Bruce's . . ." *Ibid.*

472 "The final irony was the action taken by . . ." Martin Garbus, *Ready for the Defense* (1971), 137.

472 "As I have stated in my complaint, I not . . ." Albert Goldman (with Lawrence Schiller), *Ladies and Gentlemen, Lenny Bruce!!!* (1974), 578.

473 "It is not as if a particular playlet or . . ." *Ibid.,* 579.

473 "His shoulders were hunched, his hands in . . ." Martin Garbus, *Ready for the Defense* (1971), 138.

473 "The ears of his judges were flooded by . . ." Albert Goldman (with Lawrence Schiller), *Ladies and Gentlemen, Lenny Bruce!!!* (1974), 588.

474 "I am a Jew before this court. I would like . . ." *Ibid.,* 589.

474 " 'Spit in my face!' . . ." *Ibid.,* 590–92.

476 "He had not struck his head on the pavement . . ." *Ibid.,* 592.

477 "I feel terrible about Bruce . . ." Martin Garbus, *Ready for the Defense* (1971), 89.

478 "Lenny Bruce will play the Supreme Court . . ." Albert Goldman (with Lawrence Schiller), *Ladies and Gentlemen, Lenny Bruce!!!* (1974), 603.

479 "I've never told anyone but my wife . . ." Author interview with William Hellerstein, July 18, 1990.

There follows the description by Lenny Bruce of his "obscenity" arrests at the Cafe Au Go Go in New York on April 3, 1964 and April 7, 1964. (Spelling and punctuation are reproduced exactly as in document sent by Bruce to the author.)

CHRONOLOGY:

April 3, 1964 plaintiff was arrested, violation of N.Y. penal las 1140A, at the Cafe Au Go Go, 152 Bleeker St., N.Y.C. Plaintiff was appearing in a small variety review, consisting of a folk singer, English comedy team and himself. (see excerpt from people's transcript, reflecting that plaintiff was just part of the show and an actor as was explained by the las. Transcript pages annexed here to.) April 3, before his turn to perform, he was instructed by the owner Howard L. Solomon to go to the back stage of the club, he did so and was promptly arrested by employees of the N.Y.C. Police Dept. Taken to a police station where he was fingerprinted, photographed and put in a jail cell where he was detained. Detained illegally (this conclusion is a result of the plaintiff's interpretation of the las in this area) the cell was 5' by 7' by 7'. In the morning he was taken unbathed and unfed, placed in a police wagon with 15 surly males and was vomited on. Then taken from the police wagon into the building with a long corridor and placed in another cell with some 30 persons, who held contempt for the plaintiff and his odor that the plaintiff's vomit stained clothing did emit.

The owner Howard L. Solomon was arrested for presenting plaintiff, expressed great contempt for the plaintiff and stated that he was "ruined, that he was a stock broker and his reputation was destroyed." He was taken from the cell with several other prisoners and put in an elevator and was called outbye name and brought before a Hon. John J. Murtaugh. A gentleman came to the side of the plaintiff and said I'm representing you, don't worry. Another gentleman announced himself that he was representing the owner, Howard L. Solomon. The bailiff asked the plaintiff if he would waive the reading of the information and the plaintiff respectfully requested that the charges be read to him. For he had been told at the club, by the arresting officer, that he had violated "1040A or 1140A—it's one of those up there." The plaintiff was aware that 1040A was petit treason, murdering one's master or manservant and was fearful that the information might be erroneous, because the arresting officer was not sure of the information. Therefore the request was not a display of legal savvy but a genuine concern for his safety. Judge Murtaugh became annoyed at the request for the reading of the information. It has been the experience of the plaintiff that the prosecution rewrite the law. By altering, deleting or adding thereby changing the legislative intent. Therefore making a defense rather difficult. The man who introduced himself as his representative cautioned him of the mistake of such an affront to Judge Murtaugh and asked the bench if he might have a moment to confer with the plaintiff. Thereupon he explained that this part of the proceeding was of no importance and that I should remain silent and not irk the judge. The plaintiff is a present and always has been, mindful of the necessity of proper behavior in the courts and the only words that he did speak were in response to a question he was asked "do you waive the reading of the information?" The plaintiff explained to the gentleman, that proof of a respect for the bench, is the insistence that one who sits upon it, follows procedure in due process—and his answer was "he was going to run it. "or I was." At that time the judge asked "well have you made up your mind? do you waive the reading?" Again the plaintiff answered no. He would like to hear the charges read to him. The Judge Murtaugh said "very well then, second call." The gentleman explained to the plaintiff that he was to wait until all the other prisoners had been before the bench. Several hours later the plaintiff was recalled to the bench and Judge Murtaugh restated the question and the plaintiff restated his earlier position that he wanted the charges reread to him. The language of law had been changed, the law 1140A rewritten. The owner's attorney immediately made an objection as to the repositioning and deleting of the words in 1140A and he and the D.A. indulged in colloquy and ended by restating the deleted words. The owner was released on his own recognizance and the plaintiff a $1000 bail. The owner instructed the plaintiff to rejoin the show. Several days later on April the 7, 1964, after the plaintiff's appearance in the show two plainclothes police 8 uniformed policemen took the plaintiff from the club without a warrant and informed him that it was a summary arrest. This was the second illegal arrest for a different cause—explained in the memorandum "illegal detention". The owner's wife declared "I am the owner leave my husband alone take me." The woman Ella Solomon, being naive in the construction of our government. And that the police authority have no personal vendetta in any type case that they do not have a system that they pick assignments that meet their fancy. That at all times they were gentle in manner and impersonal. She became petulant and began chanting, and was overheard by several drunken customers who decided to come to her aid. A total of 6 police ca s, tow wagons and three horseback policemen managed to keep the peace as the owner's wife Ella Solomon and the plaintiff were taken to a different jail. Again the plaintiff was fingerprinted and jailed and taken from his friend the Vicar of S^T. Clemens Episcopalian Church, 46th St. New YOrk City, who was in the audience. The plaintiff doesn't bring the priest as a self serving statement but ot demonstrate the mounting of denial of due process in these$_f$ two arrests. For when he came to the police station to see me he was refused admittance. He was to bring me news of counsel and bail money. The denial of a visitor in a misdemeanor on a summary arrest, which is illegal, because of the statutory exemption, provision 4 in 1140A—that was an amendment for the express purpose precluding such summary arrests. And exempted the actor completely. The plaintiff was brought before a Judge Gomez and following that appearance

CHAPTER 25: *Any Writer Who Hasn't Jacked Off*

PAGE

480   "He's the king of the Yads. . . ." *Time* magazine, November 30, 1962.

480   "I had that terrible accident with . . ." William Burroughs, "An Interview," *Paris Review* (Fall 1965), 13, 40.

481   *"Heir's pistol kills his wife . . ."* New York *Daily News,* September 8, 1951.

481   "So Mama was tempestuous . . ." William Burroughs, Jr., "Life With Father," *Esquire,* September 1971.

481   "I was with Joan up to the day before . . ." Author interview with Allen Ginsberg.

482   "He killed his wife. But since his family . . ." Author interview with Jean Genet.

482   "I was aiming for the very tip . . ." Victor Bockris, *With William Burroughs: A Report from the Bunker* (1981), 44–45.

485   *" 'I want!' said the hunchback . . ."* Terry Southern and Mason Hoffenberg, *Candy* (1964).

486   "When Dante dipped the sinners in excrement . . ." Transcript of the trial of *Naked Lunch,* vol. 1, *Massachusetts* v. *Naked Lunch,* Boston, January 11, 1965.

486   "Burroughs has extraordinary style . . ." *Ibid.*

487   "I don't want you to feel hurt . . ." *Ibid.*

487   "What did you say? . . ." *Ibid.*

487   "Do you mean to say, Professor . . ." *Ibid.*

487   *"Naked Lunch* confronts the reader with the . . ." *Ibid.*

488   "But Burroughs's narration is especially . . ." *Ibid.*

488   "Burroughs's use of four-letter words is . . ." *Ibid.*

488   "Would you say then . . ." *Ibid.*

488   "I don't believe so. . . ." *Ibid.*

489   "Any writer who hasn't jacked off . . ." Victor Bockris, *With William Burroughs* (1981), 65.

489   *"On Screen. Red-haired . . ."* William Burroughs, *Naked Lunch* (1966).

PAGE

490   "My name is Gabriele Bernhard Jackson . . ." Transcript of the trial of
      Naked Lunch, vol. 2.

490   *"Mary: 'No, let me.'"* William Burroughs, *Naked Lunch* (1966).

491   "The technique is to find an image . . ." Transcript of the trial of *Naked
      Lunch,* vol. 2.

492   "While we have to take the book as . . ." *Ibid.*

492   "In its day?" *Ibid.*

493   "But what are we headed for?" *Ibid.*

493   "He was a big florid Irishman . . ." Author interview with Norman
      Mailer.

495   "It was fitting that the final battle . . ." Ted Morgan, *Literary Outlaw*
      (1988), 347.

495   "Every gain of freedom carries its price. . . ." Author interview with
      Norman Mailer, January 18, 1988.

In an act of self-censorship, the publisher of *Show Me! A Picture Book of Sex for
Children and Parents* (1975) withdrew the book from sale in the following letter,
dated August 16, 1982, sent by St. Martin's Press to bookdealers across the country
after the Supreme Court upheld the constitutionality of an arguably applicable New
York child pornography law:

> Dear Bookseller,
>
> It is my regretful duty to inform you that the United States Supreme
> Court, in *People v. Ferber,* has reached a decision that forces St. Martin's Press
> to cease publication of *Show Me!* by Dr. Helga Fleischauer-Hardt and Will
> McBride.
>
> The Court ruefully concedes that the decision, aimed at deterring child
> abuse, could have an "overbroad" application to which legitimate works—like
> *National Geographic* or *Show Me!*—might fall prey. But they could not bring
> themselves to find a way around this difficulty.
>
> The result is a vexing erosion of our First Amendment right to read and
> publish, and the loss of a superb and enlightened work of sexual orientation
> for young people. I have no illusions that everyone approves of *Show Me!,*
> but there are many parents, educators, librarians, and psychologists who feel
> as I do that it is the best available book for fostering in young people a healthy
> attitude towards sex.
>
> So I am deeply distressed that such a book must now be suppressed. But
> the Court tells me that it is the law of the land, and I hereby withdraw the
> title from the St. Martin's Press trade list.
>
> Yours,
> Thomas J. McCormack
> President

The book's presence on the shelves of public libraries had previously generated a
score of library censorship incidents.

CHAPTER 26: *Sex Life of a Cop*

PAGE

496   "The sexual content of paperback books . . ." *Report of the Commission on Obscenity and Pornography* (1970).

496   "Those books were meant for the great . . ." Author interview with Stanley Fleishman.

498   "The revolting language . . ." Felice Flannery Lewis, *Literature, Obscenity and Law* (1976), 192–96.

499   "The acts of intercourse . . ." *Ibid.,* 194.

499   "No Government—be it . . ." *Jacobellis* v. *Ohio* (1964), reprinted in de Grazia, *Censorship Landmarks* (1969), 423, 428.

501   "Typical of appellant . . ." *Mishkin* v. *New York* (1966), *Ibid.,* 560, 561.

502   "*Eros* early sought . . ." *Ginzburg* v. *United States* (1966), reprinted in de Grazia, *Censorship Landmarks* (1969), 485, 486.

503   "One can only wonder why the . . ." Harry Kalven, Jr., *A Worthy Tradition* (1987), 43.

504   "We all have a lot to learn in these areas . . ." Author interview with Paul Bender.

505   "I had been told by a former associate . . ." Merle Miller, "Ralph Ginzburg, Middlesex, N.J., and the First Amendment," *The New York Times Magazine,* April 30, 1972.

505   "He was not being the humble defendant . . ." Author interview with Paul Bender.

506   "Much of the contents, by present-day . . ." Merle Miller, "Ralph Ginzburg, Middlesex, N.J., and the First Amendment," *The New York Times Magazine,* April 30, 1972.

507   "[I]t was beautiful; it was a real work of . . ." *Ibid.*

507   "I suppose if you object to a Negro and . . ." Quoted by Justice William O. Douglas, dissenting in *Ginzburg* v. *United States* (1966), reprinted in de Grazia, *Censorship Landmarks* (1969), 566, 567.

507   "I think they are . . ." *Ibid.*

508   "I thought [this was] an extremely . . ." *Ibid.,* 567–68.

508   "Still another article . . ." *Ibid.,* 568.

508   "*Eros* is a carefully contrived . . ." *Ibid.,* 477, 480.

511   "Ginzburg came along with an issue . . ." Victor Navasky, *Kennedy Justice* (1971), 391.

511   "[Bob] was terribly offended . . ." *Ibid.*

511   "Only one stark fact emerges . . ." *Ginzburg* v. *United States* (1966), reprinted in de Grazia, *Censorship Landmarks* (1969), 488.

511   "The Court today appears to . . ." *Ibid.,* 492.

513   "As [Hamling] saw it, the courtroom battle . . ." Gay Talese, *Thy Neighbor's Wife* (1980), 456–57.

515   "Ralph Ginzburg has been sentenced . . ." *Ginzburg* v. *United States,* reprinted in de Grazia, *Censorship Landmarks* (1969), 482–93 (this passage at 492).

516   "Different constitutional questions . . ." *Ibid.*

519   "So I never brought into evidence . . ." Author interview with Stanley Fleishman.

PAGE

520   "In *The Naked and the Dead* I'd chosen . . ." Author interview with Norman Mailer.

521   "Oddly enough, the cancellations we got . . ." Hilary Mills, *Mailer* (1982), 323.

521   "There was a passage in the original . . ." Author interview with Angus Cameron.

521   "This was late fifties, after *Roth*. . . ." Author interview with Stanley Fleishman.

522   "This is an appeal from a . . ." *United States* v. *West Coast News*, 228 F. Supp. 171.

523   "Well, I took it up to the Supreme Court . . ." Author interview with Stanley Fleishman.

CHAPTER 27: *Playing the Role of Revolutionaries*

PAGE

525   "I want to say that I am very happy . . ." Senate Judiciary Committee Hearings, *Nominations of Abe Fortas and Homer Thornberry,* 90th Cong., 2nd sess., 1968.

526   "The idea was Warren was going to retire . . ." Author interview with Paul Bender.

526   "A 'Fortas Court' would . . ." *National Decency Reporter,* July/August 1968.

526   "I think that . . ." Author interview with Abe Krash.

528   "*Playboy* was a little bold at that time . . ." *Ibid.*

529   "One is the extent to which . . ." Bruce Allen Murphy, *Fortas: The Rise and Ruin of a Supreme Court Justice* (1988), 372.

529   "I want that word to ring . . ." Senate Judiciary Committee Hearings, *Nominations of Abe Fortas and Homer Thornberry,* 90th Cong., 2nd sess., 1968.

529   "Senator, because of my respect for . . ." *Ibid.,* Bruce Allen Murphy, *Fortas* (1988), 426–27.

531   "Mr. Chairman, honorable Senators, . . ." Robert Shogan, *A Question of Judgement* (1972), 169.

533   "The film, O-12, was viewed by the court . . ." *Schachtman* v. *Arnebergh,* 258 Fed. Supp. 983 (1966).

534   "I was of the view . . ." Author interview with Arthur Goldberg.

535   "Mr. Clancy, I . . ." Senate Judiciary Committee Hearings, *Nominations of Abe Fortas and Homer Thornberry,* 90th Cong., 2nd sess., 1968.

536   "Could I ask a question?" *Ibid.*

538   "Twenty-one people were huddled . . ." Bruce Allen Murphy, *Fortas* (1988), 441.

539   "I have seen one Fortas . . ." *Ibid.,* 448–49.

539   "[I would] never vote for . . ." *Ibid.,* 449.

539   "From that point on it became obvious . . ." "Fortas Confirmation Defeated," *National Decency Reporter,* September/October 1968.

PAGE

539   "The [Supreme Court] majority's brusque order . . ." James J. Kilpatrick, "Proposal Suggested to Save Time in Fortas Argument," *Washington Star,* August 18, 1968.

541   "The youngster . . ." *Oral Arguments Before the Supreme Court,* edited by Leon Friedman, vol. 2, 278ff.

541   "My Appellant, who received a suspended sentence . . ." *Ibid.*

543   "Do you not agree that it is . . ." Senate Judiciary Committee Hearings, *Nominations of Abe Fortas and Homer Thornberry,* 90th Cong., 2nd sess., 1968.

543   "Mr. Christopher, how much longer . . ." *Ibid.;* Bruce Allen Murphy, *Fortas* (1988), 446.

545   "In the case of Justice Brandeis . . ." Bruce Allen Murphy, *Fortas* (1988), 481.

545   "If President Johnson would take . . ." *Ibid.*

545   "If certain members of the Senate . . ." *The New York Times,* September 14, 1968.

547   "A 16mm movie was prepared by CDL . . ." *National Decency Reporter,* September/October 1968.

549   "It's just as if an automobile hit me . . ." Robert Shogan, *A Question of Judgement* (1972), 261.

549   "Warren, the Chief, was . . ." Bruce Allen Murphy, *Fortas,* 461.

550   "The work, career, and character . . ." Justice William J. Brennan, Jr., "Abe Fortas," *The Yale Law Journal,* vol. 91, no. 6, May 1982.

CHAPTER 28: *A Magna Charta for Pornographers*

PAGE

551   "We are pleased to have with us . . ." *Hearings on "Presidential Commissions" of the Subcommittee on Administrative Practice and Procedure of the Committee on the Judiciary,* Washington, D.C., May 25, 1971, 24.

552   "The recommendation of the commission was . . ." Author interview with Paul Bender.

553   "Bill asked me if I would be general . . ." *Ibid.*

554   "In sum, empirical research designed to . . ." *The Report of the Commission on Obscenity and Pornography* (1970), 32.

554   "Mr. Lockhart, the purpose of this hearing . . ." Statement by Senator Strom Thurmond, inserted into the record of the *Hearings on "Presidential Commissions,"* 96–97.

555   "Statistical studies of the relationship . . ." *The Report of the Commission on Obscenity and Pornography,* 31.

555   "In the [commission's] stampede. . . ." *Ibid.,* 614–16.

556   "Some may wonder how a report . . ." *Hearings on "Presidential Commissions,"* 97.

556   "Lockhart was a natural choice . . ." Author interview with Paul Bender.

556   "Chairman Lockhart and his hand-picked . . ." *Hearings on "Presidential Commissions,"* 97.

PAGE

557   "Dean Lockhart, the position of the . . ." *Hearings on "Presidential Commissions,"* 95.

558   "Bill Lockhart came to see me . . ." Author interview with Paul Bender.

558   "[C]itizen action groups organized . . ." *The Report of the Commission on Obscenity and Pornography,* 37–38.

559   "There were no representatives from . . ." Author interview with Paul Bender.

560   "The Commission's energies were . . ." *Hearings on "Presidential Commissions,"* 86.

560   "And, of course, Nixon's little speech . . ." Author interview with Paul Bender.

560   "The Commission contends that the proliferation . . ." *The New York Times,* October 25, 1970.

560   "American morality is not . . ." *Ibid.*

561   "And that was a big disappointment . . ." Author interview with Paul Bender.

562   "Noticing this volume on a display rack . . ." Introduction to *The Illustrated Report of the Presidential Commission on Obscenity and Pornography.*

562   "Eason didn't have the foggiest . . ." Author interview with Stanley Fleishman.

563   "We can't write a review which simply . . ." Gay Talese, *Thy Neighbor's Wife* (1980), 459.

563   "It would appear that somehow your staff . . ." *Ibid.,* 460–61.

564   "The advertising for the . . ." *Hamling* v. *United States,* 418 U.S. 87 (1974).

565   "I thought we were going to win . . ." Author interview with Stanley Fleishman.

567   "It concerns the tone of society . . ." *Paris Adult Theatre I* v. *Slaton,* reprinted in Stanley Fleishman, editor, *The Supreme Court Obscenity Decisions* (1973), 31.

568   "Such laws are to protect the weak . . ." *Ibid.,* 36–37.

569   "At a minimum, prurient . . ." *Miller* v. *California, Ibid.,* 101.

569   "It is neither realistic nor . . ." *Ibid.*

571   "The First Amendment protects works . . ." *Ibid.,* 110.

572   "Instead of requiring . . . that . . ." *Paris Adult Theatre I* v. *Slaton,* reprinted in Stanley Fleishman, editor, *The Supreme Court Obscenity Decisions,* 72–73.

572   "The most notable change in the test . . ." Harry Kalven, Jr., *A Worthy Tradition* (1987), 50.

573   "We are of the view that . . ." Justice William J. Brennan, Jr., dissenting in *Hamling* v. *United States,* 418 U.S. 87 (1974).

574   "I now agree with the principle . . ." *Ibid.*

575   "This case required the Court . . ." *Ibid.*

575   "Hamling received a long sentence . . ." Author interview with Stanley Fleishman.

576   "This case squarely presents the issue . . ." *Kaplan* v. *United States,* in Stanley Fleishman, editor, *The Supreme Court Obscenity Decisions,* 125, 127.

CHAPTER 29: *Like the Towel-Boy in a Whorehouse*

PAGE

577   "The expression 'going pink' is not mine. . . ." Author interview with Bob Guccione.

577   "I'd been modeling since I was fourteen . . ." Author interview with Dottie Meyer.

578   "*Penthouse* liberated the female pubis. . . ." Author interview with Bob Guccione.

578   "[T]he *Penthouse* centerfold had gone pubic . . ." Russell Miller, *Bunny: The Real Story of Playboy* (1985).

578   "I was very, very unhappy about it . . ." *Ibid.*

578   "Hefner publicly sneered . . ." *Ibid.*

578   "When a guy's peeking at a girl . . ." Author interview with Bob Guccione.

578   "The first pubic Playmate appeared . . ." Russell Miller, *Bunny: The Real Story of Playboy* (1985).

579   "My circulation began to increase . . ." Author interview with Bob Guccione.

579   "You realize, of course . . ." Russell Miller, *Bunny* (1985).

579   "Slowly, the girls in *Playboy* lost their . . ." *Ibid.*

579   "[*Playboy*'s] lowest point was unquestionably . . ." *Ibid.*

579   "There was an uproar after it appeared . . ." *Ibid.*

580   "I had a press conference at which I said . . ." Author interview with Bob Guccione.

581   "I am a citizen of the United States . . ." Proceedings Before the Attorney General's Commission on Pornography.

581   "We did not introduce . . ." Author interview with Bob Guccione.

586   "This father took a *Playboy* magazine . . ." Proceedings Before the Attorney General's Commission on Pornography.

586   "I was sexually abused by my . . ." *Ibid.*

586   "My first association . . ." *Ibid.*

586   "I was extremely suicidal . . ." *Ibid.*

587   "Most [pornographers] are small-time . . ." Andrea Dworkin, "Against the Male Flood: Censorship, Pornography and Equality," *Harvard Women's Law Journal* 8 (Spring 1985).

587   "The first victims of pornography . . ." Catharine A. MacKinnon, "Pornography, Civil Rights, and Speech," *Harvard Civil Rights–Civil Liberties Law Review* 20 (1985), 32.

587   "I was always dubious about the Linda . . ." Author interview with Norman Mailer.

588   "Good morning, Ms. Marciano . . ." Proceedings Before the Attorney General's Commission on Pornography.

589   "*Deep Throat* is available in 8mm and VHS formats . . ." Attorney General's Commission on Pornography, *Final Report* (1986).

591   "It's been said that the . . ." Proceedings Before the Attorney General's Commission on Pornography.

592   "[T]he victims of pornography are . . ." Catharine A. MacKinnon, "Pornography, Civil Rights, and Speech," *Harvard Civil Rights–Civil Liberties Law Review* 20 (1985), 34.

PAGE

593 "Since I had worked with the company . . ." Author interview with Dottie Meyer.

593 "Our next witness is Dottie Meyer . . ." Proceedings Before the Attorney General's Commission on Pornography.

593 "Would you say that the text. . . ." *Ibid.*

594 "Well, is it true that you . . ." *Ibid.*

594 "I don't know. It didn't seem quite fair . . ." Author interview with Dottie Meyer.

595 "We define pornography as . . ." Catharine A. MacKinnon, "Pornography, Civil Rights, and Speech," *Harvard Civil Rights–Civil Liberties Law Review* 20 (1985), 1, 22.

595 "[Pornography] is some creature called . . ." Andrea Dworkin, "Against the Male Flood: Censorship, Pornography and Equality," *Harvard Women's Law Journal* 8 (Spring 1985), 1, 10.

595 *"N is easy to love . . ."* Andrea Dworkin, *Ice and Fire* (1987).

595 "The distinction between what falls . . ." Barbara Ehrenreich, "Pornography as Paradox," *The New York Times Book Review,* September 29, 1985.

596 "The feminists say they are 'anti-porn . . .' " Author interview with Al Goldstein.

596 *"N is slightly more . . ."* Andrea Dworkin, *Ice and Fire* (1987).

596 "It's the repression of sexuality . . ." Author interview with Al Goldstein.

596 *"The beach is a little scummy, empty cans . . ."* Andrea Dworkin, *Ice and Fire* (1987).

597 "Defining pornography as a 'form of . . .' " Barbara Ehrenreich, "Pornography as Paradox," *The New York Times Book Review,* September 29, 1985.

597 "At a bookstore or drugstore a Harlequin . . ." Ann Barr Snitow, "Mass Market Romance," in *Powers of Desire: The Politics of Sexuality,* edited by Ann Snitow (1983), 245, 254.

597 *"She had never felt . . ."* Elizabeth Graham, *Mason's Ridge* (1978).

597 *"The warmth of . . ."* Rebecca Stratton, *The Sign of the Ram* (1977).

598 "The televangelists would yell . . ." Author interview with Bob Guccione.

599 "I don't get the . . ." Proceedings Before the Attorney General's Commission on Pornography.

599 "Dear Authorized Representative . . ." Copy of letter dated February 11, 1986, from Alan E. Sears, in author's files.

600 "Indeed, in the family marketplace 7-Eleven is . . ." "Pornography in the Market Place"; copy in author's files.

601 "The dropping of *Penthouse* from the . . ." Author interview with David Myerson.

602 "Politics may have had . . ." Robert Yoakum, *Columbia Journalism Review,* September/October 1986.

603 "It was the televangelists . . ." Author interview with David Myerson.

603 "The only purpose served by the . . ." *Playboy Enterprises, Inc.,* v. *Meese,* 639 F. Supp. 581 (D.D.C., 1986).

604 "I think there are fairly deep moral . . ." Author interview with Norman Mailer.

PAGE

604   "I don't think you're playing with your . . ." Author interview with
       Marcia Pally.

604   "I had a sugar daddy who was keeping me . . ." "Porn's Busiest Beaver,"
       Hustler, April 1986, quoted in Attorney General's Commission on Por-
       nography, *Final Report* 1 (1986), 859–60.

604   "What was I gonna do when the money . . ." *Exotic X-Film Guide,* May
       1986, quoted *ibid.*

604   "I was making a whopping $76.00 a week . . ." *Adult Video News,* April
       1985, quoted *ibid.*

604   "I directed one film recently where I had . . ." Author interview with
       Norman Mailer.

605   "And there are other knotty issues . . ." Marcia Pally, "Women and
       Porn," *Penthouse,* November 1987.

605   "You can get into very difficult . . ." Author interview with Norman
       Mailer.

605   "Feminism . . . completely misses the blood-lust . . ." Camille Paglia,
       Sexual Personae (1990), 24–25.

608   "The Foreword [of *Tying Up Rebecca*] . . ." Attorney General's Commis-
       sion on Pornography, *Final Report* (1986).

610   "You know, what [the anti-porn feminists] are really opposed to . . ."
       Author interview with Norman Mailer.

610   "I had a show called . . ." Author interview with Holly Hughes.

611   "Sex is that place . . ." Author interview with Norman Mailer.

611   "If we were serious about ensuring . . ." Marcia Pally, "Women and
       Porn," *Penthouse,* November 1987.

The following information concerning the Justice Department unit called the
National Obscenity Enforcement Unit (NOEU) is from a Justice Department
Criminal Division document entitled "Beyond the Pornography Commission: The
Federal Response" (July 1988), published by the U.S. Government Printing Office.

The National Obscenity Enforcement Unit (NOEU) was created by
Attorney General Edwin Meese III, partly in response to recommendations
of the Attorney General's Commission on Pornography. The Unit comprises
the Federal Obscenity Task Force and the Obscenity Law Center. The Task
Force initiates and directs federal investigations and prosecutions of obscenity, racketeering (i.e., R.I.C.O.), child pornography and child sexual exploitation violations. The Task Force is also available to assist state and local
prosecutors and participates in the training of federal, state and local law
enforcement agents and prosecutors.

The Obscenity Law Center serves as a legal resource bank and provides
litigation support to federal, state and local prosecutors. It also provides
information to interested public and private organizations and individuals,
and serves as a clearinghouse for and regularly disseminates accurate information regarding recent developments in obscenity and child pornography case
law and legislation at the state and federal level. . . .

The National Obscenity Enforcement Unit consists of two sections: the
Federal Obscenity Task Force, and the Obscenity Law Center.

The Task Force, working closely with the FBI, IRS, Customs, the Postal Service, and the Organized Crime Strike Forces, is coordinating and spearheading the federal prosecution of obscenity and child pornography violations nationwide. The Task Force is also lending practical assistance to state and local prosecutors in these areas.

The Obscenity Law Center is serving as a vital clearinghouse for legal resources and information on pornography. Furthermore, to date more than 25 states have held or agreed to gather their state and local prosecutors and law enforcement officials for training seminars by the Unit and United States Attorneys on the prosecution of obscenity and child pornography violations. This coordinated national effort will be indispensable to solving the huge obscenity and child pornography problem in America. The Law Center organized these events and prepares specialized training materials. By mid-summer 1988, over 3500 key individuals will have been trained by the Unit in this manner.

In addition to assisting state and local prosecutors across the country, the Unit is utilizing 93 Assistant United States Attorneys trained by the Unit as "Obscenity/Child Exploitation Specialists." Each United States Attorney's office has one such Obscenity/Child Exploitation Specialist to help spearhead and coordinate federal prosecutions of the major distributors and producers of obscenity and child pornography in their respective districts. The Unit is also motivating state and local officials to prosecute similar cases. . . .

One of the first actions taken by the Unit was the drafting of legislation proposed by the Commission on Pornography. On November 10, 1987, President Reagan unveiled the Justice Department's bill—the Child Protection and Obscenity Enforcement Act—in a special White House ceremony. At that time, President Reagan said: "In the last several years, distributors of obscenity and child pornography have expanded into new areas employing new technologies and reaching new audiences. Neither our Constitution, our courts, our people, nor our respect for common decency and human suffering will allow this trafficking in obscene material—which exploits women, children and men alike—to continue. With this Act, and the implementation of the Attorney General's seven-point plan—in which the creation of the National Obscenity Enforcement Unit is the centerpiece—this Administration is putting the purveyors of obscenity and child pornography on notice: your industry's days are numbered."

If passed by Congress this Act (S. 2033, H.R. 3889), presently boasting over 300 Congressional sponsors, will plug existing legal loopholes and allow for more effective prosecution of the producers and distributors of obscenity and child pornography.

The Unit is also involved in a substantial number of major ongoing activities which will be made public at the appropriate time. Significant developments in the child pornography and obscenity enforcement areas will be reported in a bi-monthly newsletter, The "Obscenity Enforcement Reporter," published by the Unit. This newsletter is available free of charge to federal, state and local employees directly involved in these matters. It is also available to the public from: Superintendent of Documents, U.S. Government Printing Office, Washington, DC 20430. Subscription price: $5.00/year (Six issues). Single copy price: $1.00.

The following information regarding the NOEU is from the "Complaint for Declaratory and Injunctive Relief" filed by Washington lawyer Bruce Ennis (Jenner & Block) in *PHE, Inc.* v. *U.S. Department of Justice,* decided in favor of *PHE, Inc.,* on July 23, 1990, by District Court Judge Joyce Hens Green (copy in author's files):

> . . . 55. On February 10, 1987, Attorney General Edwin Meese III created a task force within the Department of Justice, subsequently named the National Obscenity Enforcement Unit (NOEU), 'to coordinate the activities of all Federal enforcement agencies engaged in obscenity investigations and prosecutions,' and appointed H. Robert Showers, who had coordinated defendants' earlier efforts to put plaintiffs out of business, as its first Director and Special Counsel. Under subsequently issued DOJ policies, all U.S. Attorneys are required to consult with the NOEU before instituting obscenity prosecutions, and before instituting a case against large-scale interstate distributors who may be a target of multiple or successive prosecutions. Defendant DOJ and Attorney General Edwin Meese III authorized defendant NOEU to develop and employ prosecutorial methods designed to put distributors of sexually oriented materials out of business.
>
> 56. To aid NOEU in this campaign against nonobscene sexually oriented speech, DOJ has established a training program to instruct United States Attorneys and their assistants on prosecutorial methods designed to put distributors of sexually oriented speech out of business. One of the instructors DOJ appointed for this training program was Alan Sears, the former Executive Director of the Pornography Commission, who was personally involved in the unconstitutional effort to suppress protected speech that was enjoined in *Playboy Enterprises, Inc. v. Meese, supra.* At the time he was an instructor in the NOEU training program, Sears was an officer of Citizens for Decency Through Law (CDL), a private interest group dedicated to the suppression of all sexually oriented speech whether or not obscene under the standards set forth in *Miller v. California.*
>
> 57. Several other instructors in the NOEU training program were also officers or employees of CDL and were equally devoted to the suppression of all sexually oriented speech. One of these CDL officers or employees began training sessions by welcoming the Assistant United States Attorneys as "crusaders for morality." At least one Assistant United States Attorney found this "partisan" practice to be "in very bad taste."
>
> 58. Since its inception, DOJ, NOEU and their cadre of CDL-trained prosecutors have undertaken a number of activities designed to force distributors of nonobscene sexually explicit speech out of business and to otherwise suppress the distribution of constitutionally protected speech. . . .

It is a favorite stratagem of the NOEU to threaten national distributors of constitutionally protected sexually oriented material (now often referred to as "pornography") with two or more criminal trials based on the same material in geographically disparate and politically conservative locales. Defendants readily fold under such pressures and frequently agree to guilty pleas that preempt them from the distribution of "protected" materials, including videocassettes. The emphasis on "local community standards" which the Burger Court laid on the definition of the constitutionally "obscene" facilitates such harassing law enforcement practices.

Paul M. Barrett reported as follows in *The Wall Street Journal* for July 27, 1990:

The effort is being spearheaded by the Justice Department's 10-member obscenity unit, soon to be expanded to 13 members. Former Attorney General Edwin Meese created the unit largely to give speeches and draft state anti-porn laws. His successor, Dick Thornburgh, has turned it into a high-voltage prosecution machine.

Working with postal inspectors and regional U.S. attorneys, the unit last year helped in the indictments of 120 individuals and corporations on obscenity charges, up from only 37 in 1988. Investigations in progress, including one in Southern California, are expected to produce another large batch of indictments in coming months.

By bringing cases that have been ignored by most federal prosecutors for 20 years, Mr. Thornburgh—a former governor of Pennsylvania who is said to harbor higher elective ambitions—has strengthened his ties to the right. His putting more child pornographers behind bars has brought little protest, even from doctrinaire civil libertarians. But the obscenity unit's offensive against adult pornography—especially its efforts against material sent by mail, code-named Project Postporn—has begun to create controversy. . . .

Critics charge that the obscenity unit's hardball tactics breach the First Amendment by bullying defendants into self-censorship. "There can be a chilling effect on all sorts of legitimate artistic expression," says Robert O'Neil, a First Amendment scholar at the University of Virginia. Coming at the same time as local obscenity prosecutions in Fort Lauderdale, Fla., of the rap music group 2 Live Crew and in Cincinnati of a gallery director who displayed Robert Mapplethorpe's homoerotic photographs, Project Postporn raises the danger that "the conscientious artist will restrain expression for fear" of punishment, Mr. O'Neil says. . . .

Justice Department officials say they launched Postporn in response to "hundreds of thousands" of citizen complaints and that cases are brought in areas where large numbers of people object to unsolicited sexually explicit advertisements. But defendants claim that major distributors are being selectively prosecuted and that the government is employing an old legal trick known as "forum shopping." In the obscenity context, that means bringing cases in conservative jurisdictions, where judges and juries are thought to be hostile to pornography.

[The defendant's] legal counterattack asserts that the Justice Department's real goal is to pressure him into self-censorship to avoid multiple prosecutions. Prosecutors deny it. But in a strongly worded opinion released Monday, Washington, D.C., federal Judge Joyce Hens Green said [the defendant] had made credible allegations that prosecutors had violated the First Amendment and acted in "bad faith" by using threats to try to force him to drop distribution of all sexually related material, including Playboy magazine.

Judge Green also preliminarily endorsed [the defendant's] contention that even if he could prevail in different jurisdictions, the burden of fighting multiple prosecutions would violate due process and could destroy his company anyway. [The defendant], the judge wrote, faces "annihilation, by attrition if not conviction."

PAGE

612   "Most pornography may indeed be worthless . . ." Robin West, "The Feminine-Conservative Anti-Pornography Alliance," *American Bar Association Research Journal* 4 (1987), 681.

613   "The idea that pornography should . . ." Author interview with Norman Mailer.

613   "On the evening of July 10 [1984] . . ." Lois P. Sheinfeld, "Banning Porn: The New Censorship," *The Nation,* September 8, 1984.

613   "Perhaps the most bizarre turn . . ." Nat Hentoff, "Is the First Amendment Dangerous to Women?," *Village Voice,* October 16, 1984.

614   "Assisted by MacKinnon, an unlikely . . ." Lois P. Sheinfeld, "Banning Porn: The New Censorship," *The Nation,* September 8, 1984.

614   "Depictions of subordination . . ." Marcia Pally, "Women and Porn," *Penthouse,* November 1987. *American Booksellers* v. *Hudnut,* 771 F. 2d 323 (7th Cir. 1985).

614   "A group of radical feminists . . ." Richard Posner, *Law and Literature: A Misunderstood Relation* (1988), 334–35.

615   "The Indianapolis ordinance does . . ." *American Booksellers* v. *Hudnut,* 771 F. 2d 323 (7th Cir. 1985), affirmed 106 S.Ct. 1172 (1986).

617   "The [Dworkin-MacKinnon] anti-pornography ordinance . . ." Robin West, "The Difference in Women's Hedonic Lives," 3 *Wisconsin Women's Law Journal* (1987), 134–35.

617   "I think there are probably . . ." Ron Bluestein, "Interview with the Pornographer," *Vogue,* April 1986.

617   "Indianapolis justifies the . . ." *Darlene Miller* v. *South Bend,* decided May 24, 1990, 7th Cir. *(en banc).*

618   "Feminism, I think, finally is a right-wing . . ." Author interview with Norman Mailer.

618   "The First Amendment protects . . ." *American Booksellers* v. *Hudnut,* 771 F. 2d 323 (7th Cir. 1985), affirmed 106 S.Ct. 1172 (1986).

619   "The line between the informing and the entertaining . . ." *Burstyn* v. *Wilson* (1952), in de Grazia, *Censorship Landmarks* (1969), 180, 182.

621   "If the only expression that the . . ." *Darlene Miller* v. *South Bend,* decided May 24, 1990, 7th Cir. *(en banc).*

CHAPTER 30: *Just a Pro-Choice Kind of Gal*

PAGE

622   "There's a big difference between . . ." Charles Babington, "Jesse Rides Again," *Museum & Arts: Washington,* November/December 1989.

623   " 'The Perfect Moment' . . . offers a sensible . . ." Ingrid Sischy, "White and Black," *The New Yorker,* November 13, 1989.

623   "Lord have mercy, Jesse, I'm not believing this." *The New York Times,* July 28, 1989.

623   "[My favorite painting] shows an old man . . ." *Ibid.*

624   "Robert Mapplethorpe is perhaps the most . . ." *The New York Times,* July 31, 1988.

624   "Mapplethorpe's flowers can have a . . ." Ingrid Sischy, "White and Black," *The New Yorker,* November 13, 1989.

PAGE

625   "Alice Neel was incredible." Stephen Koch, "Guilt, Grace and Robert Mapplethorpe," *Art in America,* November 1986.

625   "At some point, I picked up a camera . . ." Janet Kardon, interview with Robert Mapplethorpe, in Robert Mapplethorpe, *The Perfect Moment* (1988), 23.

625   "There's irony in Mapplethorpe becoming . . ." Ingrid Sischy, "White and Black," *The New Yorker,* November 13, 1989.

625   "Have you ever seen the X, Y, and Z . . ." Janet Kardon, interview with Robert Mapplethorpe, in Robert Mapplethorpe, *The Perfect Moment* (1988), 28.

626   "Though Mapplethorpe's work in his . . ." *Insight,* July 17, 1989, 9.

626   "There is a long tradition of the erotic . . ." Susan Weiley, "Prince of Darkness, Angel of Light," *ARTnews,* December 1988.

626   "The feeling I got was . . ." *Ibid.*

626   "Mapplethorpe's sexual photographs raise . . ." *Ibid.*

626   "My intent was to open people's eyes . . ." *Ibid.*

626   "The sexual photographs also disturb us . . ." *Ibid.*

627   "If a democratic society cannot . . ." *ARTnews,* October 1989.

627   "The federal government has the power . . ." *Insight,* July 17, 1989, 11.

627   "This matter does not involve . . ." Carole S. Vance, "The War on Culture," *Art in America,* September 1989.

627   "The [eighties] decade has seen . . ." *Ibid.*

627   "As with our rivers and lakes . . ." *Ibid.*

628   "We really felt this exhibit was . . ." *Time,* July 3, 1989.

628   "We've been fighting since April . . ." *The New York Times,* August 31, 1989.

628   "If proceeding with this . . ." *Ibid.*

628   "The Corcoran's savvy board . . ." "Funds for the Enfeebled," *Harper's,* December 1990.

629   "It's pretty bad when a museum is . . ." *Los Angeles Daily News,* July 16, 1989.

629   "The Corcoran's decision [was] also bad . . ." Joshua Smith, "Art Censorship in Washington, D.C.," *New American Writing* No. 5 (Fall 1989), 15ff.

629   "The Corcoran's withdrawal from the . . ." Alan Fern, *Art in America,* November 1986, 145.

629   "How could the Corcoran's director have . . ." Ingrid Sischy, "White and Black," *The New Yorker,* November 13, 1989.

631   "First and foremost ["Piss Christ"] . . ." William H. Honan, "Artist Who Outraged Congress Lives Amid Christian Symbols," *The New York Times,* August 16, 1989.

631   "The Serrano photograph measures . . ." *Ibid.*

631   "If there's been a running theme . . ." *Ibid.*

631   "These are life's bodily fluids . . ." *Ibid.*

631   "One of the few unintended benefits . . ." *Ibid.*

632   "You know, man, I made the picture in my . . ." *Ibid.*

633   "The idea that what the Government does not . . ." Garry Wills, *The New York Times,* July 31, 1989.

PAGE

633   "Mapplethorpe's leitmotif . . ." Andrew Ferguson, *National Review,* August 4, 1989.

633   "I spoke to one of the subjects . . ." Ingrid Sischy, "White and Black," *The New Yorker,* November 13, 1989.

633   "I must have been four or five then . . ." *Ibid.*

635   "I know that we scored . . ." *National Review,* August 4, 1989.

635   "Do we really want it to . . ." *The New York Times,* September 13, 1989.

635   "I suggest you take a look at the . . ." *Ibid.*

636   "Through the 1920s and '30s H. L. Mencken . . ." *The New York Times,* August 10, 1989.

637   "Look at the pictures!" *The Washington Post,* September 29, 1989.

637   "Three times in less than 24 hours . . ." *The Washington Post,* September 30, 1989.

638   "[I]f Senators do not believe me . . ." *Congressional Record—Senate,* October 7, 1989, at S12967ff.

639   "But suppose Mr. Frohnmayer goes . . ." *Ibid.*

639   "I rise in opposition . . ." *Ibid.,* at S12971ff.

640   "I wish the distinguished Senator . . ." *Ibid.,* at S12973.

641   "[G]overnment, through its various . . ." Dean Geoffrey Stone, "Statement Before the Independent Commission on the National Endowment for the Arts," July 31, 1990.

641   "So, Mr. President, a unanimous . . ." *Congressional Record—Senate,* October 7, 1989, at S12973.

641   "There is no doubt that Congress can . . ." Dean Geoffrey Stone, "Statement Before the Independent Commission on the National Endowment for the Arts," July 31, 1990.

642   "The question is . . ." *Congressional Record—Senate,* October 7, 1989, at S12975.

642   "I rise again to . . ." *Ibid.,* at S12976.

642   "Mr. President, I believe that . . ." *Ibid.,* at S12983.

643   "Mr. President, it is all well and good . . ." *Ibid.,* at S12984.

644   "I was concerned that the Endowment not be . . ." *The New York Times,* September 13, 1989.

644   "Political discourse ought to be . . ." *Ibid.*

644   "Instead I went public, hoping to encourage . . ." *The New York Times,* November 19, 1989.

645   "I have great respect for . . ." *The New York Times,* November 10, 1989.

645   "The word 'political,' I'm coming to see . . ." *Ibid.*

645   "I visited Artists Space in New York . . ." *The New York Times,* November 17, 1989.

646   "I do hope that Mr. Frohnmayer is . . ." *Ibid.*

646   "It is a reprieve we are celebrating . . ." *Ibid.*

646   "There may be two . . ." *Ibid.*

647   "Government need not fund any art . . ." Dean Geoffrey Stone, "Statement Before the Independent Commission on the National Endowment for the Arts," July 31, 1990.

648   "I work for the board of trustees . . ." *The Washington Post,* September 22, 1989.

648   "It was the federal funding . . ." *Ibid.*

PAGE

648   "But cancellation did not happen to another . . ." *Ibid.*

648   "I mean, I don't know Washington!" *Ibid.; The New York Times,* September 22, 1989.

649   "We are not talking here about the . . ." *Los Angeles Times,* November 20, 1989.

649   "Look! The unthinkable has occurred!" Author interview with Harry Lunn.

650   "Way back in June [1989], when the Corcoran . . ." *The Washington Post,* March 28, 1990.

650   "We saw the catalogue . . ." *The New York Times,* April 14, 1990.

651   "If Mr. Barrie had exercised better judgment . . ." *Ibid.*

651   "Those photographs are just . . ." *The New York Times,* March 29, 1990.

652   "Police and Sheriff's officers swept into . . ." *The Washington Post,* April 8, 1990.

652   "Absolutely not. It's not even close." *The New York Times,* April 24, 1990.

653   "People don't usually walk into museums to . . ." *Ibid.*

654   "It's a sad commentary . . ." *Ibid.*

654   "The jurors in the . . ." "Justice in Cincinnati," *The New York Times,* October 6, 1990.

654   "The judge hearing . . ." "Rank and File Rebuff to Censorship," *The New York Times,* October 6, 1990.

655   "They did exactly what . . ." *The New York Times,* October 10, 1990.

655   "That's what it boiled down . . ." *Ibid.*

655   "We had to go . . ." *Ibid.*

655   "At one point . . ." *Ibid.*

655   "Unless the political climate . . ." Quoted by David Margolick, *The New York Times,* October 6, 1990.

655   "We have sent a signal . . ." "Cincinnati Museum Quiet After Trial," *The New York Times,* October 7, 1990.

656   *"You can say I'm desperate . . ."* "Me So Horny," from the album *As Nasty As They Wanna Be,* by 2 Live Crew, Skywalker Records, Miami, Florida.

657   "In my time I've had a lot to say . . ." Liz Smith, "2 Live Crew Fuss Not Just a Bad Rap," New York *Daily News,* August 13, 1990.

657   "The issue at the heart . . ." *U.S. News & World Report,* July 2, 1990.

658   "So, is censorship the answer?" Liz Smith, "2 Live Crew Fuss Not Just a Bad Rap," New York *Daily News,* August 13, 1990.

658   "It's nice to see . . ." *New York Post,* August 14, 1990.

658   "They're just giving Luke . . ." Lisa Jones, "The Signifying Monkees," *The Village Voice,* November 6, 1990.

658   "[Their lyrics] do have to do . . ." *Ibid.*

659   "I basically took it as . . ." "2 Live Crew Swiftly Found Not Guilty," *The New York Times,* October 21, 1990.

659   "This was their way . . ." *Ibid.*

659   "There is no cult of . . ." *Ibid.*

659   "The bottom line is . . ." *Ibid.*

661   "To fund or not to fund . . ." *New York Post,* August 14, 1990.

PAGE

661 "Frohnmayer is the Neville Chamberlain of . . ." Author interview with Holly Hughes, August 6, 1990.

662 "I am an advocate for the arts . . ." Christopher Meyers, "Fresh Focus," *University of Chicago Magazine,* April 1991.

662 "Our work *is* controversial . . ." Author interview with Holly Hughes, August 6, 1990.

662 "National Endowment for the Arts Chairman John Frohnmayer, in a secret telephone vote . . ." *The Washington Times,* June 12, 1990.

663 "I feel like the Endowment is . . ." Author interview with Holly Hughes, August 6, 1990.

664 "National Endowment for the Arts Chairman John Frohnmayer has the arts community speculating . . ." *The Washington Times,* July 2, 1990.

664 "Mid-summer [1990] was probably . . ." *University of Chicago Magazine,* April 1991.

665 "Performance art, a form that . . ." *The Washington Post,* July 8, 1990.

665 "Chief Justice Burger devised . . ." Amy M. Adler, "Post-Modern Art and the Death of Obscenity Law," *The Yale Law Journal* 99 (1990), 1359ff.

666 "Karen Finley's subject is . . ." "Karen Finley's Rage, Love, Hate and Hope," *The New York Times,* July 22, 1990.

666 "When I was very young my parents . . ." Author interview with Karen Finley, March 14, 1991.

666 *"It's my body . . ."* "Aunt Mandy," in Karen Finley, *Shock Treatment* (1990).

666 "Finley began performing in . . ." "Unspeakable Practices, Unnatural Acts: The Taboo Art of Karen Finley," *The Village Voice,* June 24, 1986.

667 "People were actually . . ." *Ibid.*

667 "She points to a drawing . . ." *The New York Times,* July 22, 1990.

667 "And the thing that was very strange . . ." *Ibid.*

667 "When she returned to college . . ." *The Village Voice,* June 24, 1986.

667 "When I was very young . . ." author interview with Karen Finley, March 14, 1991.

669 "[Finley and Routh] had installed several . . ." *The Village Voice,* June 24, 1986.

669 "We were drinking beer . . ." Author interview with Karen Finley, March 14, 1991.

669 "Police stopped a couple of her performances . . ." *The Village Voice,* June 24, 1986.

670 "I had this problem . . ." Author interview with Karen Finley, March 14, 1991.

670 *"Even though I'm married . . ."* Karen Finley, *Shock Treatment,* 49–51.

670 "I was to perform . . ." Author interview with Karen Finley, March 14, 1991.

671 "In [Finley] id-speak . . ." *The Village Voice,* June 24, 1986.

671 "I was the first generation of my family . . ." Author interview with Karen Finley, March 14, 1991.

672 "[T]here are actually writers and artists . . ." *The Wall Street Journal,* May 14, 1990.

PAGE

672 "Being awarded an NEA grant . . ." Author interview with Barbara Raskin, May 1991.

672 "[Hughes's] language soars . . ." Laurie Stone, *The Village Voice,* May 19, 1987.

672 *"The woman leans back . . ." Theater Week,* July 16, 1990.

675 "Dear Mr. Gergen, Regarding your article in . . ." Letter dated July 26, 1990, from Cliff Scott to David Gergen; copy in author's file.

676 "Dear Chairman Frohnmayer, In Dave Gergen's . . ." Letter dated August 3, 1990, from Kathryn Bushkin to John Frohnmayer; copy in author's file.

676 "Correction. David Gergen's . . ." Attachment to letter dated August 3, 1990, from Kathryn Bushkin to John Frohnmayer; copy in author's file.

676 "In its laudable desire to maintain . . ." *U.S. News & World Report,* July 30, 1990.

676 "As attacks on the National Endowment . . ." C. Carr, "The Endangered Artists List," *The Village Voice,* August 21, 1990.

677 "So . . . Bill T. Jones . . ." Author interview with Holly Hughes, August 6, 1990.

678 "Discrediting or discarding government . . ." Author interview with Barbara Raskin, May 1991.

679 "[B]ut I would prefer . . ." *The Washington Post,* National Weekly Edition, April 8, 1990.

682 "Mr. Chairman, listen to . . ." *Congressional Record—House,* October 15, 1990, H9681.

683 "The specter of N.E.A. censorship . . ." *The Nation,* April 15, 1991.

685 "Just as the ideas a work represents . . ." *Pope* v. *Illinois,* 481 U.S. 497 (1987).

685 "The proper inquiry is not whether . . ." *Ibid.*

686 "The problem with . . ." *Ibid.*

686 "The problems with . . ." *Ibid.*

687 "This leeway for the jury . . ." Amy M. Adler, "Post-Modern Art and the Death of Obscenity Law," *The Yale Law Journal* 99 (1990), 1359ff.

687 "Since ratiocination has little to do . . ." *Pope* v. *Illinois,* 481 U.S. 497 (1987).

687 "A central purpose of serious art . . ." Dean Geoffrey Stone, "Statement Before the Independent Commission on the National Endowment for the Arts," July 31, 1990.

Select Bibliography

BOOKS

Aldington, Richard. *D. H. Lawrence: Portrait of a Genius But . . .* New York: Collier Books, 1950.

Anastaplo, George. *The Constitutionalist: Notes on the First Amendment.* Dallas: Southern Methodist University Press, 1971.

Anderson, Margaret. *My Thirty Years' War.* London: A. A. Knopf, 1930; New York: Horizon, 1969.

———, ed. *The Little Review Anthology.* New York: Heritage House, 1953.

Ashmore, Harry S. *Unseasonable Truths: The Life of Robert Maynard Hutchins.* Boston: Little, Brown, 1989.

Attorney General's Commission on Pornography. *Final Report.* July 1986.

Baker, Michael. *Our Three Selves: The Life of Radclyffe Hall.* New York: William Morrow, 1985.

Beach, Sylvia. *Shakespeare and Company.* New York: Harcourt Brace, 1959.

Bell, Quentin. *Virginia Woolf: A Biography.* New York: Harcourt Brace Jovanovich, 1972.

Benstock, Shari. *Women of the Left Bank: Paris 1900–1940.* Austin: University of Texas Press, 1986.

Bockris, Victor. *With William Burroughs: A Report from the Bunker.* New York: Seaver Books, 1981.

Bork, Robert H. *The Tempting of America.* New York: Free Press, 1989.

Boyer, Paul S. *Purity in Print.* New York: Scribner, 1968.

Brittain, Vera. *Radclyffe Hall: A Case of Obscenity.* London: Femina Press, 1968.

Broun, Heywood, and Margaret Leech. *Anthony Comstock: Roundsman of the Lord.* New York: A. and C. Boni, 1927.

Bruccoli, Matthew. *The Fortunes of Mitchell Kennerley, Bookman.* San Diego: Harcourt Brace Jovanovich, 1986.

Bruce, Lenny. *How to Talk Dirty and Influence People: An Autobiography.* Chicago: Playboy Pocket Book, 1967.

Burroughs, William S. *Junky.* New York: Penguin, 1977.

———. *Letters to Allen Ginsberg 1953–1957.* Introduction by Allen Ginsberg. New York: Full Court Press, 1982.

———. *Naked Lunch.* New York: Grove Press (Evergreen Black Cat Edition), 1966.

———. *Queer,* New York: Viking Penguin, 1985.

Carter, Angela. *The Sadeian Woman and the Ideology of Pornography.* New York: Pantheon, 1988 (reprint of 1978 edition).

Cerf, Bennett. *At Random.* New York: Random House, 1977.

Chafee, Zechariah, Jr. *Free Speech in the United States.* Cambridge: Harvard University Press, 1941.

———. *Freedom of Speech.* New York: Harcourt Brace and Howe, 1920.

——— *Government and Mass Communication.* Chicago: University of Chicago Press, 1947.

Chandler, Raymond. *Selected Letters of Raymond Chandler.* Edited by Frank Mac-Shane. New York: Columbia University Press, 1981.

Churchill, Allen. *A Literary Decade.* Englewood Cliffs, N.J.: Prentice Hall, 1971.

Cleland, John. *Memoirs of a Woman of Pleasure.* New York: Putnam, 1963.

Cohen, John, ed. *The Essential Lenny Bruce.* New York: Ballantine Books, 1967.

Cooney, John. *The American Pope: The Life and Times of Francis Cardinal Spellman.* New York: Random House, 1984.

Craddock, Ida C. *Advice to a Bridegroom.* Date unknown; a typed remnant is in New York Public Library.

Crompton, Louis. *Byron and Greek Love: Homophobia in Nineteenth-Century England.* Berkeley: University of California Press, 1985.

de Grazia, Edward. *Censorship Landmarks.* New York: Bowker, 1969.

de Grazia, Edward, and Roger K. Newman. *Banned Films: Movies, Censors and the First Amendment.* New York: Bowker, 1982.

Delavenay, Emile. *D. H. Lawrence: The Man and His Work.* Translated by Katharine R. Delavenay. Carbondale: Southern Illinois University Press, 1972.

Dell, Floyd. *Homecoming: An Autobiography.* New York: Farrar and Rinehart, 1933.

Demac, Donna A. *Liberty Denied.* New York: PEN American Center, 1988.

Dickie, George. *Art and the Aesthetic: An Institutional Analysis.* Ithaca: Cornell University Press, 1974.

Doran, George H. *Chronicles of Barabbas.* New York: Harcourt Brace, 1935.

Dreiser, Helen. *My Life with Dreiser.* Cleveland: World Publishing Company, 1951.

Dreiser, Theodore. *An Amateur Laborer.* Edited by Richard W. Dowell, Neda M. Westlake, and James L. West III. Philadelphia: University of Pennsylvania Press, 1984.

———. *The American Diaries: 1902–1926.* Edited by Thomas Riggio, Neda M. Westlake, and James L. West III. Philadelphia: University of Pennsylvania Press, 1983.

———. *An American Tragedy.* New York: Boni and Liveright, 1925.

———. *The Dreiser–Mencken Letters.* Edited by Thomas P. Riggio. 2 vols. Philadelphia: University of Pennsylvania Press, 1986.

———. *The "Genius."* New York: John Lane Company, 1915.

———. *Letters of Theodore Dreiser.* Edited by Robert H. Elias. 3 vols. Philadelphia: University of Pennsylvania Press, 1959.

————. *Sister Carrie.* New York: Doubleday, 1901.

————. *Sister Carrie: The Pennsylvania Edition.* Edited by James L. West III, Alice M. Winters, and Neda M. Westlake. Philadelphia: University of Pennsylvania Press, 1981. With an introduction by Alfred Kazin. New York: Viking Penguin, 1986.

————. *Sister Carrie.* Introduction by E. L. Doctorow. New York: Bantam, 1982.

Dreiser, Vera. *My Uncle Theodore.* With Brett Howard. New York: Nash Publishing Company, 1976.

Dworkin, Andrea. *Ice and Fire.* New York: Grove Weidenfeld, 1987.

Ellmann, Richard. *James Joyce.* New York: Penguin, 1982.

Finley, Karen. *Shock Treatment.* San Francisco: City Lights, 1990.

Fitch, Noel R. *Sylvia Beach and the Lost Generation.* New York: W. W. Norton, 1983.

Fleishman, Stanley, ed. *The Supreme Court Obscenity Decisions.* San Diego: Greenleaf Classic, 1973.

Friede, Donald. *The Mechanical Angel.* New York: A. A. Knopf, 1948.

Friedman, Leon, ed. *Obscenity: The Complete Oral Arguments before the Supreme Court in the Major Obscenity Cases.* 2 vols. New York: Chelsea House, 1983.

Gabler, Neal. *An Empire of Their Own.* New York: Crown, 1988.

Garbus, Martin. *Ready for the Defense.* New York: Farrar, Straus and Giroux, 1971.

Geller, Evelyn. *Forbidden Books in American Public Libraries, 1876–1939.* Des Plaines, Ill.: Greenwood Publishing, 1984.

Gertz, Elmer. *A Handful of Clients.* Chicago: Follett Publishing Company, 1965.

Gertz, Elmer, and Felice F. Lewis, eds. *Henry Miller: Years of Trial and Triumph 1962–1964: The Correspondence of Henry Miller and Elmer Gertz.* Carbondale: Southern Illinois University Press, 1978.

Gilmer, Frank Walker. *Horace Liveright: Publisher of the Twenties.* New York: D. Lewis, 1970.

Ginsberg, Allen. *Howl: Original Draft Facsimile, Transcript & Variant Versions, Fully Annotated by Author, with Contemporaneous Correspondence, Account of First Public Reading, Legal Skirmishes, Precursor Texts & Bibliography.* Edited by Barry Miles. New York: Harper and Row, 1986.

Girodias, Maurice. *The Olympia Reader.* New York: Grove Press, 1965.

Goldman, Albert. *Ladies and Gentlemen, Lenny Bruce!!!* From the journalism of Lawrence Schiller. New York: Random House, 1974.

Graham, Elizabeth. *Mason's Ridge.* New York: Avon, 1978.

Haight, Anne L. *Banned Books: 387 B.C. to 1978 A.D.* Compiled by Chandler B. Grannis and Charles Rembar. New York: Bowker, 1978.

Hall, Radclyffe. *The Well of Loneliness.* With an introduction by Havelock Ellis. London: J. Cape, 1928.

Harris, Frank. *My Life and Loves.* New York: Grove Press, 1963.

Hays, Arthur Garfield. *Let Freedom Ring.* New York: Boni and Liveright, 1928.

Hutchison, Earl R. *Tropic of Cancer on Trial.* New York: Grove Press, 1968.

Journal of the Continental Congress (ed. 1800), vol. 1: *Lettre adressée aux Habitans de la Province de Québec (ci-devant le Canada) de la part du Congrés Général de l'Amérique Septentrionale,* 1774.

Joyce, James. *Letters of James Joyce.* 3 vols. Vol. 1 edited by Stuart Gilbert; vols. 2 and 3 edited by Richard Ellmann. New York: Viking Penguin, 1966.

————. *Selected Letters of James Joyce.* Edited by Richard Ellmann. New York: Penguin, 1975.

————. *Ulysses.* New York: Random House, 1934.

————. *Ulysses: The Corrected Text.* Edited by Hans Walter Gabler. New York: Random House, 1986.

Kalven, Harry, Jr. *A Worthy Tradition: Freedom of Speech in America.* Edited by Jamie Kalven. New York: Harper and Row, 1987.

Kuh, Richard. *Foolish Figleaves?* New York: Macmillan, 1967.

Kurland, Philip, and Gerhard Casper, editors. *Landmark Briefs and Arguments of the Supreme Court of the United States: Constitutional Law.* Vol. 53. Frederick, Maryland: University Publications of America, 1975.

Lawrence, D. H. *The Collected Letters of D. H. Lawrence.* Edited by Harry T. Moore. 2 vols. New York: Viking Penguin, 1962.

————. *D. H. Lawrence: Letters to Thomas and Adele Seltzer.* Edited by Gerald M. Lacy. Santa Rosa, California: Black Sparrow Press, 1976.

————. *Lady Chatterley's Lover.* New York: Grove Press, 1959.

————. *The Letters of D. H. Lawrence.* Edited by Aldous Huxley. London: W. Heinemann, 1932.

————. *The Letters of D. H. Lawrence.* James T. Boulton, general editor. 5 vols. to date. New York: Cambridge University Press, 1979–89.

————. *The Rainbow.* Edited by Mark Kinkead-Weekes. New York: Cambridge University Press, 1989.

————. *Selected Letters.* Edited by Diana Trilling. New York: Farrar, Straus and Cudahy, 1958.

————. *Sex, Literature and Censorship.* Edited by Harry T. Moore. New York: Irvington, 1953.

————. *Women in Love.* Edited by David Farmer, Lindeth Vasey, and John Worthen. New York: Cambridge University Press, 1987.

Lawrence, Frieda. *Not I, But the Wind.* New York: Viking Press, 1934.

————. *The Memoirs and Correspondence.* Edited by E. W. Tedlock. London: Heinemann, 1961.

Lewis, Felice Flannery. *Literature, Obscenity and Law.* Carbondale: Southern Illinois University Press, 1976.

Lingeman, Richard. *Theodore Dreiser.* Vol. 1, *At the Gates of the City 1871–1907.* New York: Putnam, 1986. Vol. 2, *An American Journey.* New York: Putnam, 1990.

MacFall, Haldane. *Aubrey Beardsley: The Man and His Work.* London: John Lane, 1928.

Maddox, Brenda. *Nora: The Real Life of Molly Bloom.* Boston: Houghton Mifflin, 1988.

Mailer, Norman. *Advertisements for Myself.* New York: Putnam, 1959.

————. *The Armies of the Night.* New York: New American Library, 1968.

————. *The Deer Park.* New York: Putnam, 1955.

Mann, Thomas. *The Confessions of Felix Krull, Confidence Man.* New York: Alfred A. Knopf, 1955.

McDonald, Edward D. *A Bibliography of the Writings of D. H. Lawrence.* With a Foreword by D. H. Lawrence. Philadelphia: The Centaur Book Shop, 1925.

Mencken, H. L. *The Diary of H. L. Mencken.* Edited by Charles A. Fecher. New York: Alfred A. Knopf, 1989.

Miles, Barry. *Ginsberg: A Biography.* New York: Simon and Schuster, 1989.

Miller, Henry. *Tropic of Cancer.* New York: Grove Press (Black Cat Edition), 1961.

Miller, Russell. *Bunny: The Real Story of Playboy*. New York: Holt, Rinehart and Winston, 1985.

Mills, Hilary. *Mailer*. New York: Empire Books, 1982.

Moore, George. *Avowals*. New York: Boni and Liveright, 1924.

Moore, Harry T. *The Intelligent Heart: The Story of D. H. Lawrence*. New York: Grove Press, 1962.

———. *The Priest of Love*. New York: Farrar, Straus and Giroux, 1974.

Morgan, Ted. *Literary Outlaw: The Life and Times of William S. Burroughs*. New York: Henry Holt, 1988.

Moscato, Michael, and Leslie LeBlanc, editors. *The United States of America v. One Book Entitled Ulysses by James Joyce*. Introduction by Richard Ellmann. Des Plaines, Illinois: Greenwood Publishing, 1984.

Mumby, Frank Arthur. *Publishing and Bookselling: A History from the Earliest Times to the Present Day*. New York: Bowker, 1931.

Murphy, Bruce Allen. *Fortas: The Rise and Ruin of a Supreme Court Justice*. New York: William Morrow, 1988.

Nabokov, Vladimir. *Lolita*. New York: Putnam, 1958.

———. *Lolita*. Introduction by Erica Jong. New York: Putnam, 1988.

———. *Nabokov's Fifth Arc*. Edited by J. E. Rivers and Charles Nicol. Austin: University of Texas Press, 1982.

———. *The Nabokov–Wilson Letters*. Edited by Simon Karlinsky. New York: Harper and Row, 1979.

———. *Vladimir Nabokov: Selected Letters, 1940–1977*. Edited by Dmitri Nabokov and Matthew J. Bruccoli. San Diego: Harcourt Brace Jovanovich, 1989.

Navasky, Victor. *Kennedy Justice*. New York: Atheneum, 1971.

Nehls, Edward, ed. *D. H. Lawrence: A Composite Biography*. 3 vols. Madison: University of Wisconsin Press, 1957–59.

Nin, Anaïs. *Delta of Venus*. New York: Pocket Books, 1990.

O'Hara, John. *Ten North Frederick*. New York: Random House, 1955.

Ormrod, Richard. *Una Troubridge: The Friend of Radclyffe Hall*. New York: Carroll and Graf, 1985.

Paul, James C. N., and Murray L. Schwartz. *Federal Censorship: Obscenity in the Mail*. New York: Free Press of Glencoe, 1961.

Posner, Richard A. *Law and Literature: A Misunderstood Relation*. Cambridge: Harvard University Press, 1988.

Rembar, Charles. *The End of Obscenity*. New York: Random House, 1968.

The Report of the Commission on Obscenity and Pornography. New York: Bantam Books, 1970.

Robertson, Geoffrey. *Obscenity*. London: Weidenfeld and Nicolson, 1979.

Rolph, C. H., editor. *The Trial of Lady Chatterley*. With a new Foreword by Geoffrey Robertson. New York: Penguin, 1990.

St. John-Stevas, Norman. *Obscenity and the Law*. London: Secker & Warburg, 1956.

Schauer, Frederick. *The Law of Obscenity*. Washington, D.C.: BNA Books, 1976.

Schom, Alan. *Emile Zola: A Biography*. New York: Henry Holt, 1988.

Schwartz, Bernard. *Super Chief: Earl Warren and His Supreme Court*. New York: New York University Press, 1983.

Schwartz, Bernard, with Stephan Lesher. *Inside the Warren Court*. New York: Doubleday, 1983.

Sharaf, Myron. *Fury on Earth: A Biography of Wilhelm Reich*. New York: St. Martin's Press, 1983.

Shnayerson, Robert. *The Illustrated History of the Supreme Court of the United States*. New York: Harry N. Abrams, 1986.

Shogan, Robert. *A Question of Judgement: The Fortas Case and the Struggle for the Supreme Court*. New York: Bobbs-Merrill, 1972.

Southern, Terry, and Mason Hoffenberg. *Candy*. New York: Putnam, 1964.

Stratton, Rebecca. *The Sign of the Ram*. London: Mills and Boon, 1977.

Swanberg, W. A. *Dreiser*. New York: Scribner's, 1965.

Symons, Arthur. *Aubrey Beardsley*. New York: Modern Library, 1925.

Talese, Gay. *Thy Neighbor's Wife*. New York: Dell, 1980.

Tebbel, John. *A History of Book Publishing in the United States*. 4 vols. New York: Bowker, 1972–81.

Thomas, Donald. *A Long Time Burning*. London: Routledge and Kegan Paul, 1969.

Troubridge, Una. *The Life and Death of Radclyffe Hall*. London: Hammond and Hammond, 1961.

Tytell, John. *Naked Angels: The Lives and Literature of the Beat Generation*. New York: McGraw-Hill, 1976.

U.S. Congress. Senate. *Hearings on Presidential Commissions of the Subcommittee on Administrative Practice and Procedure of the Committee on the Judiciary*. Washington, D.C., May 25, 1971.

U.S. Congress. Senate Judiciary Committee. *Hearings on the Nominations of Abe Fortas and Homer Thornberry*. 90th Cong., 2nd sess., 1968.

U.S. Congress. Special Subcommittee of the House Committee on the Judiciary regarding H.R. 920, a resolution impeaching William O. Douglas. *Final Report*. 91st Cong., 2nd sess., September 17, 1970.

Vizetelly, Ernest. *Emile Zola: Novelist and Reformer*. London and New York: John Lane, 1904.

Wilson, Edmund. *The Cold War and the Income Tax*. New York: Farrar, Straus, 1963.

———. *The Fifties*. Edited by Leon Edel. New York: Farrar, Straus and Giroux, 1986.

———. *The Forties*. Edited by Leon Edel. New York: Farrar, Straus and Giroux, 1983.

———. *Letters on Literature and Politics: 1912–1972*. New York: Farrar, Straus and Giroux, 1977.

———. *Memoirs of Hecate County*. New York: L. C. Page, 1959. Boston: David R. Godine, 1980.

———. *The Nabokov–Wilson Letters*. Edited by Simon Karlinsky. New York: Harper and Row, 1979.

———. *The Thirties*. Edited by Leon Edel. New York: Farrar, Straus and Giroux, 1980.

———. *The Twenties*. Edited by Leon Edel. New York: Farrar, Straus and Giroux, 1975.

Woodward, Bob, and Scott Armstrong. *The Brethren: Inside the Supreme Court*. New York: Simon and Schuster, 1979.

Woolf, Virginia. *The Diary of Virginia Woolf*. Edited by Anne O. Bell. 5 vols. New York: Harcourt Brace Jovanovich, 1977–84.

————. *The Letters of Virginia Woolf.* Edited by Nigel Nicolson and Joanne Traut-mann. 5 vols. London: Hogarth Press, 1975–79.

Zola, Emile. *La Terre.* Translated by Ernest Dowson. New York: Boni and Live-right, 1924.

ARTICLES

Adler, Amy M. "Post-Modern Art and the Death of Obscenity Law." *The Yale Law Journal* 99 (1990): 1359ff.

Babington, Charles. "Jesse Rides Again." *Museum & Arts: Washington,* November/December 1989.

Bourjaily, Vance. "Preface." *Discovery No. 4.* New York: Pocket Books, 1954.

Brennan, Justice William J., Jr. "Abe Fortas." *The Yale Law Journal* 91, no. 6 (May 1982).

Burroughs, William S. "An Interview." *Paris Review,* Fall 1965.

Burroughs, William S., Jr. "Life With Father." *Esquire,* September 1971.

Carr, C. "The Endangered Artists List." *The Village Voice,* August 21, 1990.

————. "War on Art." *The Village Voice,* June 5, 1990.

Carroll, Paul. "Call It Big Table." *Chicago,* March 1979.

Cerf, Bennett. "Publishing Ulysses." *Contempo* 3, no. 13 (February 15, 1934): 1–2.

Cohen, Lester. "Theodore Dreiser: A Personal Memoir." *Discovery No. 4.* New York: Pocket Books, 1954.

Corn, David. "Dirty Bookkeeping." *The New Republic,* April 2, 1990.

Crigler, John, and William J. Byrnes. "Decency Redux: The Curious History of the New FCC Broadcast Indecency Policy." *Catholic University Law Review* 38, no. 2 (Winter 1989).

de Grazia, Edward. "Obscenity and the Mail." *Law and Contemporary Problems* 20, no. 4 (1955): 608ff.

Dworkin, Andrea. "Against the Male Flood: Censorship, Pornography and Equal-ity." *Harvard Women's Law Journal* 8 (Spring 1985): 1ff.

Ehrenreich, Barbara. "Pornography as Paradox." *The New York Times Book Review,* September 29, 1985.

Epstein, Jason. "Edmund Wilson at Ease." *The New York Review of Books,* October 9, 1986.

Gibbons, John J. "Tribute to Justice Brennan." *Rutgers Law Review* 36: 729ff.

Girodias, Maurice. "Lolita, Nabokov and I." *Evergreen Review,* September 1965.

Hentoff, Nat. "Is the First Amendment Dangerous to Women?" *The Village Voice,* October 16, 1984.

Jonas, Gerald. "The Story of Grove." *The New York Times Magazine,* January 21, 1968.

Kalven, Harry, Jr. " 'Uninhibited, Robust, and Wide-Open'—A note on Free Speech and the Warren Court." *Michigan Law Review* 67 (1968): 289.

————. "The Metaphysics of Obscenity." *1960 Supreme Court Review* (1960): 1.

————. "The New York Times Case: A Note on 'The Central Meaning of the First Amendment.' " *1964 Supreme Court Review* (1964): 191.

Knopf, Alfred A. "A Balance Sheet—Part II." *The Saturday Review,* November 21, 1964.

Koch, Stephen. "Guilt, Grace and Robert Mapplethorpe." *Art in America,* November 1986.

Leeds, Jeffrey T. "A Life on the Court." *The New York Times Magazine,* October 5, 1986.

Leo, John. "Polluting Our Popular Culture." *U.S. News & World Report,* July 2, 1990.

Lewis, Anthony. "The Most Recent Troubles of 'Tropic.' " *The New York Times Book Review,* January 21, 1962.

———. "Sex and the Supreme Court." *Esquire,* June 1963.

Lockhart, William, and Robert McClure, "Censorship of Obscenity: The Developing Constitutional Standards." *Minnesota Law Review* 45 (1960): 5ff.

———. "Literature, The Law of Obscenity, and the Constitution." *Minnesota Law Review* 38 (1954): 295ff.

MacKinnon, Catharine A. "Pornography, Civil Rights, and Speech." *Harvard Civil Rights–Civil Liberties Law Review* 20 (1985): 1ff.

Marchese, John. "The Bustling Days and Rum-and-Coke Nights of Barney Rosset." *7 Days,* September 6, 1989.

McCarthy, Mary. "Déjeuner sur l'Herbe," *The New York Review of Books* 1, no. 1 (1963): 4–5.

Meeske, Marilyn. "Memoirs of a Female Pornographer." *Esquire,* April 1965.

Miller, Merle. "Ralph Ginzburg, Middlesex, N.J., and the First Amendment." *The New York Times Magazine,* April 30, 1972.

Nabokov, Vladimir. "Lolita and Mr. Girodias." *Evergreen Review,* February 1967.

———. "On a Book Entitled Lolita." *Anchor Review,* no. 2 (1955); and in Nabokov, *Lolita,* New York: Putnam, 1958.

Norris, Hoke. " 'Cancer' in Chicago." *Evergreen Review,* no. 25: 4–5.

Pally, Marcia. "Women and Porn." *Penthouse,* November 1987.

Redlich, Norman. "William J. Brennan, Jr.: New Honor for an Old Friend." *NYU Law School Annual Survey of American Law* (1982).

Redman, Ben Ray. "Obscenity and Censorship." *Scribner's Magazine,* May 1934.

Seldon, E. S. "The Cannibal Feast." *Evergreen Review* 22 (January-February 1962).

Sheinfeld, Lois P. "Banning Porn: The New Censorship." *The Nation,* September 8, 1984.

Simakis, Andrea. "Telephone Love." *The Village Voice,* July 17, 1990.

Sischy, Ingrid. "White and Black." *The New Yorker,* November 13, 1989.

Smith, Joshua. "Art Censorship in Washington, D.C." *New American Writing,* no. 5 (Fall 1989).

Smith, Liz. "2 Live Crew Fuss Not Just a Bad Rap." *New York Daily News,* August 13, 1990.

Snitow, Ann Barr. "Mass Market Romance." In *Powers of Desire: The Politics of Sexuality.* Edited by Ann Snitow, Christine Stangell, and Sharon Thompson. New York: Monthly Review Press, 1983.

Span, Paula, and Carla Hall. "Portraits of the Performers the NEA Refused to Fund." *The Washington Post,* July 8, 1990.

———. "Rejected." *The Washington Post,* July 8, 1990.

Stone, Geoffrey. Statement Before the Independent Commission on the National Endowment for the Arts, July 31, 1990.

Straus, Roger. "A Flow of Work." *The New York Times,* June 18, 1972.

Styron, William. Testimony in Hearings Before the Committee on the Judiciary, U.S. Senate, 100th Cong., 1st sess., on the Nomination of Robert H. Bork to be Associate Justice of the Supreme Court of the United States, September 22, 1987.

Vance, Carole S. "The War on Culture." *Art in America,* September 1989.

Weiley, Susan. "Prince of Darkness, Angel of Light." *ARTnews,* December 1988.

West, Robin. "The Difference in Women's Hedonic Lives: A Phenomenological Critique of Feminist Legal Theory." *Wisconsin Women's Law Journal* 3 (1987): 81ff.

Woolf, S. J. "Interview with Our Unofficial Censor." *The New York Times Magazine,* October 20, 1946.

———. "A Vice Suppressor Looks at Our Morals." *The New York Times,* October 9, 1932.

Index

Abrams, Floyd, 653
Abrams v. United States, 117*n*
Ach, Roger, 650
Acheson, Dean, 413
Acker, Kathy, 667
ACLU, *see* American Civil Liberties Union
Adams, Franklin P., 109
Adams, J. Donald, 253*n*
Adams, John, 617
Adams' Breed (Hall), 165, 170, 171, 174
Adams Theatre Co. v. *Keenan*, 235*n*, 405*n*
Aday, Sanford "Les," 496, 519, 521–24
Adler, Amy M., 665, 686–87
Advice to a Bridegroom (Craddock), 3–4, 5, 570
Aga Khan, 95
Agger, Carolyn, 399*n*, 549*n*
Agnew, Spiro, 552
Alberts, David, 299*n*
Albrecht, David von, 295, 298–300, 303–6
Alcott, Louisa May, 280
Alden, Henry Mills, 99
Aldington, Richard, 56, 62, 87, 90, 94–95, 96, 202, 203, 276
Aldrich, Bailey, 566*n*
Algren, Nelson, 212, 356, 359*n*, 360
Alien and Sedition Acts (1798), 617
Allen, Walter, 268
American Aphrodite, 225, 275–76, 279–84, 288–89, 298, 301, 303*n*, 306, 506
American Arts Alliance, 638
American Book Publishers Council, 308

American Civil Liberties Union (ACLU), 75*n*, 214–15, 308, 354*n*, 358, 363, 380, 446
  Howl defense and, 236–37, 333, 334
  obscenity laws opposed by, 517, 557–58, 559
  on *Tropic of Cancer* cases, 76*n*, 371*n*, 372, 373, 392, 417, 439
American Dream, An (Mailer), 520
American Family Association, 598, 629, 630, 653
American League for National Equity, 133
American Mercury, 134
American Tragedy, An (Dreiser), 30, 132–42, 156, 164
  Boni and Liveright edition of, 128, 132–33, 140, 142, 145*n*
  financial success of, 139–42, 152
  Mencken's critique of, 127*n*, 134–35
  obscenity prosecution for, 75, 91, 98, 123, 131*n*, 135–39, 165, 201, 202
Amyat, Katinka, 168
Anastaplo, George, 354
Anchor Books, 213*n*, 250, 261
Anchor Review, 261–62, 264, 265
Anderson, Margaret, 7–17, 20, 34, 36*n*, 110, 114, 129, 367*n*–68*n*
Anderson, Sherwood, 66, 110, 122, 129, 132*n*, 134, 148, 151, 197, 200, 364
And the Hippos Were Boiled in Their Tanks (Burroughs and Kerouac), 349
Ansen, Alan, 348, 386
Apollinaire, Guillaume, 256, 259*n*

Apuleius, 279
Arabian Nights, The (Burton), 42
Aristophanes, 279, 340, 459
Armey, Richard, 632
Armies of the Night, The (Mailer), 520–21
Armstrong, Scott, 274*n*, 399*n*, 419*n*, 506*n*, 580
Arnold, Fortas and Porter, 527–28, 633, 638
Artists Space, 643–46
Ashmore, Harry S., 218*n*, 354*n*
As Nasty As They Wanna Be, xiii, 455*n*, 656–57, 659
Asquith, Herbert, 44, 59, 62
Asquith, Lady Cynthia, 59, 63*n*, 64
Assommoir, L' (Zola), 48*n*
Atheneum Publishers, 183*n*
Atherton, Gertrude, 76, 129
Atlas, Nicholas, 283, 285, 286–88, 289
At Random (Cerf), 183*n*
Attorney General's Commission on Pornography (Meese commission), 232*n*, 310*n*, 324, 536*n*, 553*n*, 558*n*, 581, 583–86, 588–95, 598–609, 612, 652
Auden, W. H., 386
Augustine, Saint, 487
Austin v. *Kentucky*, 516*n*
Authors' League of America, 78, 121–22, 125

Baby Doll, 510*n*
Bacon, Peggy, 210
Bair, Deirdre, 258*n*–59*n*
Baker, Michael, 168*n*, 186*n*, 189, 192*n*
Baldwin, James, 467
Baldwin v. *New York*, 461*n*
Balzac, Honoré de, 6, 7, 40
Bantam Books, 583
Bantam Books v. *Melko*, 308*n*
Baraka, Amiri (LeRoi Jones), 329, 351*n*, 367*n*
Barker, Colonel (Lillian Smith), 196
Barker, George, 257
Barnes, Djuna, 7*n*
Barnes v. *Glen Theatre*, 235*n*, 621*n*
Barrie, Dennis, xiii, 531*n*, 582*n*, 603*n*, 633, 650–55, 684
Barrymore, John, 144
Baruch, Bernard, 237
Basel, Amos, 71
Bataille, Georges, 256, 259*n*, 335
Batten, Mabel "Ladye," 168, 206
Baudelaire, Charles, 270*n*, 283, 364, 605
Bazelon, David, 527*n*
Beach, Eleanor, 38
Beach, Holly, 39
Beach, Rex, 122
Beach, Sylvia, 15, 21, 38–39, 129, 254
  manuscripts refused by, 54–56, 67*n*, 94, 184

Ulysses published by, 15, 19–21, 23, 25, 27, 38, 54, 144, 174*n*
Beardsley, Aubrey, 66, 281–85, 288–89, 298, 304
Beatles, 361
Beauharnais v. *Illinois*, 275*n*, 312–13, 319*n*, 320
Beck, Julian, 390, 459*n*
Becker, May Lamberton, 175
Beckett, Samuel, 55*n*, 164, 258–59, 271, 368
Bedborough (bookseller), 181
Beerbohm, Max, 66
Bel-Ami (A Ladies' Man) (Maupassant), 48*n*
Bell, Anne Oliver, 178*n*
Bell, Quentin, 178*n*, 180
Bender, Paul, 292, 293*n*, 421*n*, 526
  on Brennan's achievements, 442–43
  on *Ginzburg*, 292, 504–6, 545*n*, 552
  on Lockhart commission, 292, 298*n*, 435*n*, 541*n*, 545*n*, 552, 553, 556, 558–61
  on *Roth* decision, 292, 325–26
Bendich, Albert, 334, 446, 477*n*
Bennett, Arnold, 56*n*, 114, 122, 134, 178, 198, 223
Bennett, Debbie, 658
Benstock, Shari, 7*n*, 10*n*, 19*n*, 21*n*
Bentham, Jeremy, 52–53, 166*n*
Bering-Jensen, Helle, 626
Berkman, Alexander, 101, 111
Berlin, Sir Isaiah, 233*n*, 268
Besig v. *United States*, 76*n*, 400*n*
Bessie, Simon Michael, 183*n*
Bestiary (Olds), 613
Bible, 12, 76, 466, 615
Bickel, Alexander, 422, 567–68
Biddle, Francis, 232, 233
Biedenkapp, F. G., 152
Biggs, John, Jr., 231
Big Table, 237, 307*n*, 312*n*, 354, 362
  debut of, 347, 357–60, 362
  Naked Lunch excerpts in, 237, 338, 341, 357, 360, 363, 364–65, 386, 387, 390, 393
Birkett, Norman, 186–91
Biron, Sir Chartres, 186–89, 190–92, 194, 200
Birrell, Augustine, 62
Bishop, Morris, 245*n*, 263*n*
Black, Douglas, 152, 209, 215, 220, 228–29, 237, 247–48, 250
Black, Hugo, 317, 402, 443, 511, 688
  absolutist free speech approach of, 299, 312*n*, 313*n*, 319*n*, 400–401, 402*n*, 423*n*, 434, 471, 514, 517, 518, 534, 539–40, 542, 575, 686
  Court alliances and, 314*n*, 403, 413–14, 431, 515*n*, 516, 528, 534, 566*n*
  on *Roth*, 295*n*, 318*n*
  on *Tropic of Cancer*, 417, 431, 434, 471

"Black and White in Color," 504, 505, 507, 509
Black Book (Durrell), 385
Black Mountain Review, 351*n*
Blackmun, Harry, 515*n*, 561, 566*n*, 621*n*
Black Spring (Miller), 392
Blake, William, 87
Blanche, Jacques, 282
"Blood Stream" (Serrano), 631
Bloomsday, 38
Blue Hen's Chickens, The (McHugh), 220*n*
Blume, Judy, 596
Boccaccio, Giovanni, 43, 224
Bockris, Victor, 482
Bodenheim, Maxwell, 131
Bodley Head, 114, 261
Body, Ralph C., 505, 508-9
Boissevain, Eugen Jan, 198
Bok, Curtis, 215*n*, 251, 290*n*, 308, 318
Bolsheviki, The (Trotsky), 117, 129
Boni, Albert, 17-18, 72, 124, 127, 143, 184
Boni, Charles, 72, 124, 143, 184
Boni and Liveright, 52*n*, 117
    American Tragedy published by, 128, 132-33, 140, 142, 145*n*
    "Genius" published by, 123, 124, 128, 129
    management of, 72, 80*n*, 129-31, 143, 145-47, 148, 150
    offshoot of, 143, 145, 184, 196
    Ulysses contract sought by, 17-18, 144-45
Bonnemere, Joseph, 40
Bonnierre, Suzanne, 21*n*
Book of Meditations, A (Grigg), 18
Book of Prefaces (Mencken), 125
Bork, Robert H., 216*n*, 293*n*, 399*n*, 401*n*, 405, 409-11, 548, 567, 570, 618*n*
Borzoi imprint, 183*n*-84*n*
Bouguereau, Adolphe-William, 119-20
Bourdet, Edouard, 146*n*
Bourgeois, Louise, 624
Bourget, Paul, 6, 48*n*
Bowers v. *Hardwick*, 166*n*
Bowles, Paul, 256, 347-48, 354, 358
Boyer, Paul, 55*n*, 91*n*, 145*n*, 183
Bradley Reed Smith v. *California*, 372*n*, 418*n*
Brainard, Clinton T., 184, 220
Brand, Dorothea, 73
Brandeis, Louis D., 380, 412, 443, 545
    on clear and present danger, 216, 296*n*, 308, 309, 311, 316
Brandenburg v. *Ohio*, 117*n* 660*n*
Breit, Harvey, 255, 257
Brennan, William J., Jr., 398-416, 434-43
    appointment of, 235, 406, 408-9, 525*n*
    background of, 235, 402, 404-7, 413, 544

Bender praised by, 292
    on child pornography, 582*n*, 609*n*, 610*n*, 652
    Court coalitions built by, 401-3, 412-15, 505-6, 534*n*, 566
    doctrinal leadership of, xiii-xiv, 274-75, 291, 403, 409, 500*n*, 514*n*, 560-62, 573*n*
    on *Fanny Hill*, 422, 436-42, 470*n*, 490, 497-98, 500, 512, 533-34, 517*n*, 571*n*, 574
    on Fortas, 550
    on *Ginsberg*, 540, 541, 542
    on *Ginzburg*, 500, 502-6, 655*n*
    on *Hamling*, 573-75
    Jacobellis/Tropic of Cancer cases and, xii, 274, 275, 302*n*, 306*n*, 321, 324*n*-25*n*, 396, 397, 399-400, 401*n*, 405, 420, 422-31, 434, 436, 442, 470-72, 493, 533-34, 574, 618*n*
    law clerks for, 420-21, 471*n*, 614
    on libelous expression, 113*n*, 275, 313*n*, 325*n*, 411-12, 422
    on limitations of seizures, 212*n*
    on *Miller* v. *California*, 561-62, 565, 572, 574, 646*n*, 684
    obscenity law nationalized by, 33*n*, 201, 234*n*, 274, 275, 425-27, 429
    on obscenity vs. artistic/social value, xii-xiii, 11*n*-12*n*, 31*n*, 113*n*, 195, 365, 409, 420, 423, 493, 497*n*, 535, 574*n*
    opposition to, 401*n*, 404, 433
    on *Osborne*, 537*n*, 609*n*, 610*n*, 618*n*
    on public discussion of sex, 264, 322-23, 429-30, 581
    on redeeming social value, 190*n*, 321, 324, 341-42, 405*n*, 418*n*, 618*n*, 685
    retirement of, 548*n*, 582*n*, 653*n*, 688
    on *Roth* case, 33*n*, 216*n*-17*n*, 263, 264, 266, 273-75, 295*n*, 298*n*, 302-3, 313*n*-16*n*, 319-26, 337, 338, 341, 363*n*, 377*n*, 398, 400, 403*n*, 412*n*, 415, 418*n*, 421, 423, 428-30, 443, 471*n*, 473, 492*n*, 493, 499, 541, 561, 566, 572, 574, 618*n*
    on sex vs. obscenity, 322-23, 429-30
    on vagueness of obscenity law, xii-xiii, 31*n*, 534*n*, 541*n*, 561-62, 573-75, 576, 599, 646, 684
    on Warren's prudishness, 274, 406
Brennan, William J., Sr., 405
Brennan doctrine, xii
    conservative revision of, 218*n*, 234*n*, 324*n*, 440*n*, 501*n*, 565-66, 569-72, 636, 665, 688
    evolution of, 279*n*, 500-501, 512-13, 566
    in *Fanny Hill* case, 436-42, 494, 501, 505, 512, 523*n*, 534, 571*n*

Brennan doctrine (*cont.*)
  liberating effects of, 30*n*, 34*n*, 497–500,
    514
  opposition to, 516–18
  Roth opinion vs., 412*n*, 499
  triple-pronged test described by, 436–37,
    497–98, 514, 533–34, 535
  utterly without social value test in, xii,
    11*n*, 218*n*, 437–42, 469–72, 497,
    516–18, 523*n*, 532*n*, 570, 574*n*,
    655*n*
Brenson, Michael, 631–32
Brentano, Frances, 19
Brethren, The (Woodward and Armstrong),
    399*n*, 419*n*, 506*n*, 580
Brett, Dorothy, 81
Brill, A. A., 164
Brittain, Vera, 176*n*
Broadwater, Bowden, 246
Brockway, Wallace, 243, 247*n*
Brooke, Edward, 396, 397
Brooke, Rupert, 114
Brooks, Latonia, 658
Brooks, Van Wyck, 68
Broun, Heywood, 151, 159
Browder, Earl, 151, 157, 158
Brown, Curtis, 80, 81, 85, 90
Browne, Maurice, 110
Brownell, Herbert, 406, 408
Browning, Elizabeth Barrett, 206
Brown v. *Board of Education*, 298, 402*n*,
    510–11
Bruccoli, Matthew J., 65*n*, 248*n*
Bruce, Honey, 476
Bruce, Lenny, 444–79, 666, 667
  Brennan doctrine and, 469–72
  Chicago case against, 383, 422, 444,
    446–47, 449, 452, 453–54, 469, 470,
    494
  civil suit filed by, 448, 450–52
  counsel for, 233*n*, 334*n*, 446, 447–50
  despair experienced by, 474–77
  manifesto in support of, 122*n*, 458–59
  New York case against, 221*n*, 392*n*,
    431, 436, 447–48, 449, 452–74,
    478–79, 660
  San Francisco case against, 334*n*,
    444–46
  Supreme Court on, 448–49, 450, 452,
    477–78
Bryan, Frederick van Pelt, 340, 341
Bryden, David, 613*n*
Buchanan, Patrick, 627–28
Buckley, John, 635
Buckley, William F., Jr., 585*n*, 627
Budgen, Frank, 23, 36
Bulwark, The (Dreiser), 123, 152, 159,
    160, 162–63
Burger, Warren, 565–72
  appointment of, 415*n*, 424, 515*n*, 528,
    551, 564

Brennan doctrine qualified by, 218*n*,
    234*n*, 324*n*, 405*n*, 426*n*, 431*n*,
    440*n*, 470, 501*n*, 512, 569–72,
    655*n*, 665, 688
  on hard-core pornography, 580, 606
  on *Kaplan* v. *California*, 430*n*, 575–76
  obscenity defined by, xii, xiii, 566–68,
    636, 684, 685
Burger Court, 399*n*, 520*n*, 620*n*
  Court alliances and, 403, 560–62, 565
  on local community standards, 33*n*,
    201, 234*n*, 303*n*, 425, 562*n*, 569,
    652*n*
  pollution metaphor used by, 568–69, 627
  Stanley freedoms limited by, 480*n*,
    516*n*, 537*n*, 566
  Warren Court's progressive law vs.,
    275*n*, 546, 553, 581
  see also specific cases; specific justices
Burress, Phillip, 655–56
Burroughs, Billy, 347, 348, 387*n*, 481
Burroughs, Joan Vollmer, 344*n*, 346,
    387, 480–84
Burroughs, William Seward, III, 259, 328,
    329, 343–55, 359, 369, 384–97
  accidental shooting by, 344, 346, 387,
    391*n*, 480–84
  background of, 343–44
  at Edinburgh Festival, 384, 393–94, 432
  pseudonym used by, 346, 351*n*
  writing process and, 347–49
  see also Naked Lunch
Burstyn, Joseph, 407
Burstyn v. *Wilson*, 233*n*, 293*n*, 312*n*,
    619*n*, 621
Burton, Harold, 295*n*, 307
Burton, Sir Richard, 42
Bush, George, 403*n*, 634, 639*n*, 664,
    666, 676, 678, 679
Bushkin, Kathryn, 675–76
Bushnel, Hyman, 198, 199–200
Butcher, Chester, 158
Butler, Ellis Parker, 122
Butler v. *Michigan*, 74*n*, 252*n*
Byrd, Robert C., 552, 642–43
Byrne, Garrett, 396, 397
Byron, George Gordon, Lord, 52*n*
Byron and Greek Love (Crompton), 52*n*,
    53*n*, 166*n*

CAC, *see* Contemporary Arts Center
Caen, Herb, 362
Calder, John, 384*n*, 393, 432
Caldwell, Erskine, 30, 151, 215*n*, 224,
    251, 278*n*
Cameron, Angus, 19*n*, 520*n*, 521
Campbell, Luther, xiii, 652*n*, 656, 658
Campus Mistress, 498
Canby (Wilson), Margaret, 239, 240–41
Candy (Southern and Hoffenberg), 259*n*,
    265, 288*n*, 484–86

Cape, Jonathan, 172
  New York publishing venture of, 197,
    203–4
  Well of Loneliness published by, 87, 165,
    172–74, 176–97, 207
Cape-Ballou, 204
Captive, The (Bourdet), 146
Carew, Thomas, 33*n*
Carlin, George, 520*n*
Carnal Knowledge, 571
Carpenter, Edward, 166*n*
Carr, C., 633*n*, 663*n*, 666–69, 671,
    676–77
Carroll, Paul, 343, 344–45, 349, 350,
    353–54, 356*n*, 357–58, 360, 361,
    362, 364, 365
Carswell, Catherine, 82, 89
Carter, Jimmy, 682
Carter, John, 57*n*
Caruth, Jane Randolph, 169
Casanova's Homecoming (Schnitzler), 72,
    74, 78, 184
Cashin, John M., 284
Cassell's, 171
Cather, Willa, 122
Catholic Church:
  Bruce prosecution and, 453–54
  judges and, 226–27, 334–35*n*, 406–7,
    408
  Memoirs of Hecate County suppression
    and, 220, 221*n*, 226–27
  NEA grants and, 631, 644
  Tropic of Cancer ruling opposed by,
    434–36
  Ulysses and, 25
CCV, *see* Citizens for Community Values
CDL, *see* National Organization of
    Citizens for Decent Literature
Céline, Louis-Ferdinand, 358, 391, 667
Cenci, The (Shelley), 146
Cerf, Bennett, 17, 151, 183*n*, 220*n*, 285
  background of, 129, 130–31
  on Liveright's style, 141, 143, 144, 148
  Ulysses published by, 22*n*, 27–29, 130,
    197, 223–24, 392*n*
Cézanne, Paul, 85*n*
Chafee, Zechariah, 116*n*, 117*n*, 124*n*,
    216–19, 293*n*, 314, 321*n*, 413
Chains (Dreiser), 145*n*
Chamber Music (Joyce), 37
Chambers, Sir Thomas, 45, 46, 47, 51
Chandler, Raymond, 211
Chant d'Amour, Un, 500*n*–501*n*, 532*n*
Chaplin, Charlie, 163, 248
Chaplinsky v. *New Hampshire,* 219*n*, 291*n*,
    315, 317*n*, 320, 415–16
Chapman, Ed, 586
Chapman, Frederic, 118
Chase, Frank, 135
Chaucer, Geoffrey, 37*n*, 43
Chaucer ABC (Lucia Joyce), 37

Cherkovski, Neeli, 331
Chesterton, G. K., 114
Chicago, University of, 218, 345–46,
    353–57, 362–63
Chicago Review, 344–46, 347, 349–57,
    358, 362–63, 365
Children's Legal Foundation, 585*n*, 650*n*
Christie, Agatha, 114
Christopher, Warren, 543
Churchill, Allen, 175*n*, 183*n*–84*n*
Churchill, Stella, 180
Churchill, Winston, 62, 156
Ciardi, John, 362–63, 365, 376, 395,
    480, 484, 486
Citizens Concerned for Community
    Values, 580, 583*n*–84*n*
Citizens for Community Values (CCV),
    xiii, 650–51
Citizens for Decency Through Law, 585*n*
Citizens for Family First, 656
City Lights Books, 333, 334, 345*n*
Civil Rights Act (1964), 402*n*
Clancy, James J., 232*n*, 531–33, 534,
    535–39, 540, 542, 543, 544, 547
Clark, Charles, 273, 290, 301, 341
Clark, Ramsey, 515*n*, 526, 545
Clark, Sir Kenneth, 85*n*, 660*n*
Clark, Tom, 295, 421*n*, 499, 514, 526,
    566*n*
  on Brennan's revision of *Roth,* 431*n*,
    499
  on information vs. entertainment, 619
  Miracle case and, 235, 414
  obscenity rulings by, 295*n*, 302, 415,
    424, 438, 442, 514, 515, 535, 540
  resignation of, 515*n*, 518, 526*n*, 534
  on social value test, 442, 516–17
Clark, Walter Van Tilburg, 335, 337
Clarke, Arthur C., 359–60
Clarke, Martha, 677
Clarke, Sir Edward, 45, 46, 47, 51
Classics and Commercials (Wilson), 234,
    238
Clean Books League, 74–77, 78, 144, 149
Cleland, John, 193*n*, 251, 436
  see also Memoirs of a Woman of Pleasure
Clements, Marcelle, 666, 667
Cluer, A. R., 45, 49, 50
Cock, Mr., 49–50, 51
Cockburn, Lord, 193, 310*n*
Cohen, Arthur, 656
Cohen, John, 464*n*
Cohen, Lester, 132, 164
Cohen v. *California,* 408*n*, 564*n*
Cole, Marilyn, 579
Colette, 196, 204
Colfax, Schuyler, 4*n*
Colgate, Samuel, 6
Colmer, John, 179*n*
Commonwealth v. *Gordon,* 251, 290*n*,
    308*n*

Communist party, 132*n*, 133, 157–58, 318*n*, 328, 339*n*, 434–35, 509*n*
Comstock, Anthony, 3–7, 31, 65, 69, 70, 91*n*, 102, 113, 309, 588*n*
    successor to, 69, 70, 117, 118, 182, 213
Comstock Act (1873), 296, 297, 301–2, 306, 308, 315, 317, 573, 589
Conboy, Martin, 32, 74
Confessions of Nat Turner, The (Styron), 411
Congress, U.S.:
    on Fortas nomination, 525–48
    on Lockhart commission, 551–58
    on NEA, 293*n*, 340*n*, 627–28, 632–44, 676–84
Connolly, Cyril, 53, 220
Conrad, Joseph, 56*n*, 109
Contempo, 27
Contemporary Arts Center (CAC), xiii, 582*n*, 603*n*, 633, 650–56
Continental Congress, 216–17, 293, 321*n*, 322, 435*n*
Contraception (Stopes), 30*n*
Cooney, John, 406*n*, 408, 454
Corcoran Gallery of Art, 622–23, 628–29, 647–50
Corn, David, 531*n*, 535*n*
Cornell University, 243–46, 255, 262–63, 270
Corso, Gregory, 330, 333, 351, 353, 358–62
Counterattack, 521*n*
Cousins, Norman, 376
Covenant House, 310*n*, 599*n*
Covici, Pascal, 129, 145, 183, 196, 203, 243, 255
Covici-Friede, 27, 145, 184, 196–202, 203
Cowin, William I., 396–97, 438, 484, 488
Cowley, Malcolm, 211, 340
Cox, Archibald, 504–5
Cox, Ray, 601
Craddock, Ida, 3–4, 5–6, 570, 573
Craig, Alec, 189–90
Creel, J. Randall, 461*n*, 462, 469–70, 472, 479
Creeley, Robert, 351, 358
Crompton, Louis, 52–53, 166*n*
Crosby, Caresse, 257
Crothers, Rachel, 122
Cuccia, Vincent, 448, 477
cummings, e. e., 203
Cuomo, Mario, 407*n*

Dahlberg, Edward, 357, 360
Daily Telegraph (London), 60, 176
Daley, Richard J., 370–71, 380
D'Amato, Alphonse, 627, 630, 632, 644
Damiano, Gerard, 590
Dannemeyer, William E., 644, 645
D'Annunzio, Gabriel, 7

Dante Alighieri, 274, 276, 486, 492
Darantière, Maurice, 21, 22, 25
Darlene Miller v. *City of South Bend*, 294*n*, 618–19, 621
Darrow, Clarence, 137, 138
Davidson, Jo, 95
Davis, Murray S., 35*n*
Dawson, Mrs. N. P. 115
Death in the Woods (Anderson), 148
Death of a Hero (Aldington), 202, 203
Decameron (Boccaccio), 76, 224
Deep Throat, 342*n*, 584, 587–92, 596
Deer Park, The (Mailer), 225, 251, 265, 287–88
de Gaulle, Charles, 55*n*, 266
de Grazia, Edward:
    ACLU obscenity position formulated by, 517
    Bruce defense and, 447–49, 450, 452
    I Am Curious—Yellow case and, 229*n*, 335*n*, 422, 497*n*, 517*n*, 548
    on *Lysistrata* case, 279, 340*n*
    Mailer's description of, 392
    Mishkin brief filed by, 620*n*
    Naked Lunch defended by, 139*n*, 167*n*, 392–93, 396, 397, 480, 484–94
    on nonverbal expression, 564*n*, 620*n*
    Oakes brief filed by, 582*n*
    Tropic of Cancer cases and, 76*n*, 122*n*, 229*n*, 312*n*, 372*n*, 375, 376, 382, 392, 397, 417–18, 439, 440–41, 447, 517*n*
DeLacey, James A., 90–91
Delavenay, Emile, 58
Delineator, 111*n*
Dell, Floyd, 109, 110–12, 117, 118, 124, 140, 151, 183
Demac, Donna A., 406*n*
Dennett, Mary, 30*n*, 323*n*
Dennis v. *United States*, 158*n*, 318, 339*n*, 509*n*
de Reszke, Jean, 23
Dershowitz, Alan, 566*n*
Dewar, Helen, 637
Dewey, Thomas E., 221, 237
Diary of Love (Maude Phelps Hutchins), 354*n*
Dickinson, Sir John, 60
Dickson, Lovat, 207
Dietz, Park E., 591–92, 593–94
Dinamov, Sergei, 133, 152
di Prima, Diane, 272*n*, 329–30, 351*n*
Dirksen, Everett McKinley, 546, 547, 548
Divine Comedy (Dante), 486
Dobson, James, 584*n*, 606
Doctorow, E. L., 100
Dodd, Mead, 129, 282
Dodge, William E., Jr., 6
Dollar Library of American Fiction, 104
Donleavy, J. P., 259
Don't Grow Old (Ginsberg), 328

Doran, George H., 68–69, 77, 99, 113, 183n
Doran v. *Salem Inn*, 618n, 621n
Dos Passos, John, 132n, 151, 200, 242, 376
Dostoevsky, Fyodor, 40, 153, 287, 362
Doty, Douglas, 116
Doubleday, Ellen, 249, 250
Doubleday, Frank N. "Effendi," 77, 209
  background of, 98–99, 129, 249–50
  Sister Carrie published by, 98–105, 112, 129, 250
Doubleday, Nelson, 209, 249, 369
Doubleday, Neltje, 99, 100, 104, 209, 249
Doubleday and Company, 151–52, 212n–13n
  Anchor Books, 213n, 250, 261
  books rejected by, 174, 229, 247–50, 253
  Memoirs of Hecate County published by, 75n–76n, 209–12, 214–19, 221–29, 241, 248, 250, 273, 285, 297, 303n, 305
  ownership of, 209, 249–50
Douglas, Alfred, Lord, 66
Douglas, James, 26, 57, 61n, 173–74
Douglas, William O., 299, 313n, 379, 380, 399n, 443, 504n, 688
  absolutist doctrine of free expression advocated by, 317, 400–401, 423n, 434, 471, 514, 517, 518, 539–40, 542, 575
  on Brennan doctrine, 516, 534
  Court alliances and, xii, 314n, 402, 403, 412–13, 414, 417, 431, 528, 565n, 566n, 573
  criticism of, 334n, 433, 546n, 548–49
  Ginzburg dissent written by, 439n, 508
  on *Roth*, 295n, 302, 308, 309, 311–12, 316, 318n, 319n
Downtown Art Company, 663, 674, 675
Dowson, Ernest, 53n, 66, 114
Draper, Albert, 57–58
Dreiser (Swanberg), 109n, 127n
Dreiser, Ed, 107
Dreiser, Emma, 100, 107
Dreiser, Helen Patges Richardson, 132–33n, 134, 151, 153, 154, 156, 158–64
Dreiser, Mame, 105, 107, 132–33
Dreiser, Paul, 161
Dreiser, Sarah Osbourne White "Jug," 100, 102, 105, 106, 109n, 112, 133n, 139, 140
Dreiser, Theodore, 30, 66, 68, 98–142, 150–65, 196, 200
  death of, 151, 152, 162–64
  essays by, 116, 127
  family background of, 101, 107, 128
  finances of, 105, 108, 111n, 114, 124, 139–42, 145n, 150, 157, 164

illnesses of, 105–9, 110, 153–54, 159–62
Mt. Kisco estate of, 139, 151
political beliefs of, 62n, 114, 115–16, 121, 128, 132n, 133, 152–58, 162–63
romantic involvements of, 102, 110–12, 113, 132n–33n, 140, 153, 154, 158–59, 163
  see also American Tragedy, An; Bulwark, The; Financier, The; "Genius," The; Jennie Gerhardt; Sister Carrie; Stoic, The; Titan, The
Dreiser, Vera, 133n
Dreiser Looks at Russia (Dreiser), 145n
Droll Stories (Balzac), 6
Dubliners (Joyce), 20, 24
Dujardin, Edouard, 23
Duke, David, 682
Duncan, Robert, 257, 331, 334, 358
Dunster House Bookshop, 90–91
Dupee, F. W., 252n, 262
Duras, Marguerite, 368
Durham, Monte, 527
Durham v. *United States*, 527n
Durrell, Lawrence, 259n, 376, 385n
Duvall, William A., 363, 365
Dworkin, Andrea, 581, 583, 584, 587, 595, 596–97, 611, 613–15, 616n, 617
Dworkin, Ronald, 401n
Dwyer, James F., 224
Dylan, Bob, 359, 360, 361

Earth, The (Zola), *see Terre, La*
Easterbrook, Frank, 614, 615–16, 617–21
Eastland, James O., 536
Eastland, Terry, 401n
Eastman, Max, 117, 122, 124, 151, 328
Eckerd, Jack, 547
Eckstein, Anthony, 655
Ecstasy, 32
Edel, Leon, 238–39
Edinburgh Arts Festival, 384, 393–94, 432
Edwards, Ruth Dudley, 36n
Egoist, 18
Ehrenreich, Barbara, 595–96, 597
Ehrlich, Jake, 334, 335
Eisenhower, Dwight D., 235n, 291, 302, 406, 408, 525n
Eisenstein, Sergei, 141n
Elder, Paul, 234
Elias, Robert, 162
Eliot, T. S., 22, 277, 376, 386
Ellis, Edith, 180–81
Ellis, Havelock, 52, 166n, 170–71, 174, 176, 180–81, 197, 198, 277
Ellmann, Richard, 22n, 23, 25, 33n, 36, 37n, 84n, 166n
  at *Tropic of Cancer* trial, 373, 375–78
Elvins, Kells, 343–44
Emerson, Ralph Waldo, 332

E. M. Forster (Colmer), 179n
Emile Zola (Vizetelly), 44–45
Emrickson, Clarence, 374
End As a Man (Willingham), 215n, 251
E. P. Dutton, 78, 131
Epstein, Barbara, 213n
Epstein, David, 378
Epstein, Elliot, 378–79, 380, 382, 383
Epstein, Jason, 213n, 228–29, 240, 501n
    Lolita publication and, 213n, 245,
    247–48, 249, 250n, 253, 261, 262,
    264, 265
Epstein, Joseph, 167n, 239n, 663n, 677
Epstein, Richard, 275n
Epstein, Samuel B., 325, 370–71, 373,
    375, 377–80, 381, 382, 383, 574
Ergaz, Doussia, 245n, 254
Ernst, Morris, 28–33, 223, 236, 309n,
    392
    Well of Loneliness case and, 197, 198,
    200–201, 202
Eros, 340n, 436, 502–3, 504, 506–11
Ervin, Sam J., Jr., 530, 552
Erznoznik v. *City of Jackson*, 618n
Evans, Rowland, 662, 674
Everett, Raymond, 521
Evergreen Review, 334, 347, 369, 548
Everyman's Library, 131
Exiles (Joyce), 15
Extraordinary Women (Mackenzie), 172,
    196

Fabri, Ralph, 151
Fadiman, Clifton, 151
Falcon Press, 207
Falwell, Jerry, 583n, 601, 603
Famous Players–Lasky, 140, 141n
Fanfrolico Press, 94, 279n
*Fanny Hill, see Memoirs of a Woman of
    Pleasure*
Fanon, Frantz, 369
Farrar, Straus, and Cudahy, 212
Farrar, Straus & Giroux, 237n, 238
Farrar, Straus, and Young, 234, 245
Farrell, James T., 215n, 278n, 360
Faulkner, William, 130, 215n, 251, 376
Federation of Hungarian Jews in America,
    277
Feiffer, Jules, 454–55, 461, 466n
Fein, Bruce, 652–53
Felix Krull (Mann), 225, 286–87
Ferber, Edna, 200
Ferber v. *New York*, 557n, 582n, 609,
    653n
Ferguson, Andrew, 633
Ferlinghetti, Lawrence, 236, 325, 330,
    332–35, 345n, 349, 350n, 365, 445,
    446
Fields, Suzanne, 661
Financier, The (Dreiser), 109, 110, 114,
    128

Finley, Karen, 620n, 658, 660, 662–65,
    666–72, 673, 674, 677, 681, 684,
    687, 688
Finnegans Wake (Joyce), 38, 144, 364,
    394
First Lady Chatterley, The (Lawrence), 93n,
    224
Fish, Hamilton, 141n
Fisher, Roger, 290–91, 300–301n, 306–7,
    309–15, 317, 321n, 571, 589
Fiss, Owen, 683–84, 688n
Fitch, Noel Riley, 21n
Fitzgerald, F. Scott, 231n
Fitzpatrick, James, 633, 638
Flaming Creatures, 459, 500n–501n,
    532n, 538–39, 545
Flaubert, Gustave, 6, 7, 40, 48n, 224,
    268n, 270n
Fleck, John, 660, 662–65, 673, 674, 684
Fleischer, Max, 76
Fleischhauer-Hardt, Helga, 570
Fleishman, Stanley, 367, 375, 496–97,
    519, 521–24, 535n, 559, 572n
    Hamling represented by, 496, 513,
    562–63, 565, 569, 575
Fles, John, 358n
Fleurs du mal, Les (Baudelaire), 270n
Floating Bear, 329–30
Flower, Newman, 171
Ford, Ford Madox, 56n, 112
Ford, Gerald R., 334n, 546n, 548, 685
Ford, Hugh, 11n
Ford, John, 73–78, 131, 142
Forster, E. M., 52, 167n, 177–78,
    179–80, 185, 187, 189, 277
Fortas, Abe, 399, 404n, 513, 525–50
    as attorney, 309n, 527, 528, 529, 532,
    549–50, 638n
    Chief Justice nomination of, 232n,
    415n, 459, 525–39, 542–48, 551,
    553, 589
    Court alliances and, 403, 470n, 506,
    517, 529
    on criminal rights, 527, 528, 529
    obscenity rulings of, 431n, 500, 501,
    503n–4n, 505n, 514, 517, 528,
    530–45, 559
    resignation of, 298n, 433, 498, 515n,
    527, 549–50, 564, 566, 585n, 688
Fortnightly Review, 48–49
Fortune of the Rougons, The (Zola), 48n
Foster, William Z., 133, 151, 157, 158
Fowlie, Wallace, 376
France, Anatole, 41
Francis, Kay, 144
Frank, Jerome, 201
    on *Roth*, 215n, 217n, 280n, 289–91,
    293, 294, 297, 299, 301, 308, 310,
    316n, 318, 321, 322n, 411
Frank, John P., 295n
Frank, Waldo, 116

Frankfurter, Felix F., 74n, 326, 409, 424, 505, 528, 552, 567
  Butler decision by, 74n, 252n
  on clear and present danger, 308, 310–15
  on community standards, 286n
  Court alliances and, 233, 275, 279n, 291, 314n, 401n, 402, 412–16
  judicial restraint promoted by, 305, 401n, 404, 408n, 409n, 412, 414–15, 440n
  recusal by, 227, 230–31, 232–33, 334n, 549
  on Roth case, 232n, 291–92, 295n, 301n, 304, 305, 307, 309, 310–15, 317, 318, 319–20, 321n, 403n
Frankfurter, Marion, 230
Franklin Furnace Archive, 663–64
Fraser, Donald M., 613
Freedom of Speech (Chafee), 216–17, 218n, 219n, 321n
Freeman, Charles, xiii, 656, 658, 684
Freeman, Louis, 559
Freud, Sigmund, 10, 12n, 31, 34, 72, 129, 279
Freund, Gisele, 38
Freund, Paul, 511n
Frick, Henry Clay, 101
Friede, Donald, 27, 129, 130, 137–38, 142, 143, 144–45, 151, 203
  American Tragedy prosecution and, 123, 135, 136–37, 165, 201, 202
  Well of Loneliness prosecution and, 192–98, 200, 201, 202
  see also Covici-Friede
Friendly, Henry, 450, 473
Frohnmayer, John, 639, 643–46, 648, 650
  grants evaluated by, 611n, 660–64, 674, 675–76, 678, 679, 680, 684
Frost, Robert, 66
Fruitfulness (Zola), 104

Gabler, Hans Walter, 15n
Gallagher, John F., 55n
Gallantz, George G., 224
Gallatin, Francis D., 76
Gallery of Women, A (Dreiser), 145n
Gallimard, 196, 254n, 255, 267
Galsworthy, John, 181
Game of Love, The, 398
Garbus, Martin, 447n, 449, 451, 452, 454, 457, 458, 460–61, 465–69, 472, 473, 477, 606
Garcia, Edward, 599
Garden, Mary, 13
Gates, Henry Louis, Jr., 659
Gautier, Théophile, 193n, 224
Geller, Evelyn, 114n, 332n
General Introduction to Psychoanalysis (Freud), 129

Genet, Jean, 259, 270, 271, 358, 368, 369, 392, 393, 482, 532n, 667
"Genius," The (Dreiser), 62n, 109, 114–27
  Mencken's support for, 121–27, 154
  Sumner's attack on, 66n, 117–24, 128
  unexpurgated edition of, 123, 124, 128, 129
Gent v. Arkansas, 516n
Gergen, David, 674–76
Germinal (Zola), 48n
Gertz, Elmer, 325, 358, 373, 375, 376, 377, 381–82, 383, 423, 432–33
  Tropic of Cancer litigation and, 375–78, 381–82, 383, 432–33
Gibbons, John J., 443
Gide, André, 25, 37–38, 224, 246, 277
Gideon, Clarence Earl, 527
Gilbert, Sandra M., 193n
Gilded Hearse, The (Gorham), 251
Gillers, Stephen, 275n
Gillet, Louis, 37n
Gilman, Richard, 465
Gilmer, Walker, 131n, 142n, 144, 145, 147–48
Ginsberg, Allen, 122n, 327–38, 344, 345, 346–47, 353, 357, 367n, 388, 459, 461
  Big Table debut and, 358–62, 363, 364, 386
  Burroughs and, 328, 344, 346–51, 352n, 363, 385–87, 480–82, 484, 491–92, 493
  family background of, 327–29, 331–32
  see also Howl
Ginsberg, Sam, 540
Ginsberg v. New York, 536, 540–42, 660n
Ginzburg, Ralph, 502–4, 505, 563–64, 575n
Ginzburg v. United States, 274, 436, 500, 502–17, 534, 545, 558, 573
  Eros contents and, 340n, 506–9
  "pandering" doctrine used in, 494n–95n, 503–6, 512, 516, 531, 542, 564, 655n
  political factors in, 509–11
  prosecuting attorney in, 292, 504–6, 545n, 552
  Stewart's dissent in, 511–12, 514, 515–16
  variable obscenity approach and, 423n, 503n, 556n
Girodias, Maurice, 55n, 282n, 366, 484
  Lolita published by, 245n, 254–55, 258–67, 271, 365, 385
  Naked Lunch and, 365, 385, 386, 387–91
  pornography commissioned by, 256–58, 263
  prosecution of, 262, 270–72

Gitlow v. *New York*, 16*n*, 296
Glasco, John, 259*n*, 282–83
God's Little Acre (Caldwell), 30, 215*n*, 224, 251
Gogol, Nikolay, 40, 153
Goldberg, Arthur H., 513
 appointment of, 275, 415, 528
 Court alliances and, 334*n*–35*n*, 403, 415–16, 417, 528
 on *Jacobellis/Tropic of Cancer* cases, 424, 431, 470, 471, 472, 506*n*, 534
 resignation of, 506, 526, 530, 534*n*, 549
Goldin, Nan, 644
Goldman, Albert, 308*n*, 447, 453, 454–55, 459–61, 473–78
Goldman, Emma, 7, 101, 111, 124
Goldstein, Al, 274, 596
Goldstein, Jonah, 72–73
Goldwater, Barry, 445, 467–69, 472, 535*n*
Goncourt, Edmond de, 41
Goodman, Lillian, 161
Goodman, Mark, 161
Goodman, Roy, 682
Gorbachev, Mikhail S., 155, 616*n*
Gordon, John, 259, 260, 263
Gore, Albert, 530*n*
Gorham, Charles O., 251
Gorton, Slade, 632
Gosse, Edmund, 26
Gotham Book Mart, 251*n*, 367, 400*n*
G. P. Putnam's Sons:
 Candy published by, 485
 Fanny Hill published by, 397, 436, 437, 500
 Lolita published by, 237, 265–66, 269–70, 288*n*
 Roth trial and, 285, 287–88
Graham, Elizabeth, 597
Granahan, Kathryn E., 509–10
Grannis, Chandler B., 323*n*
Grapes of Wrath, The (Steinbeck), 203
Greenawalt, Kenneth W., 214*n*
Greene, Graham, 259, 260–61, 263
Gregory, Dick, 445, 467–68
Gregory, Horace, 203, 376
Griffin, Robert, 547
Grigg, E. H., 18
Grigsby, Emily, 113
Grosskurth, Phyllis, 166*n*
Grossman, Albert, 361
Grove Press, 55*n*, 245*n*, 247, 254*n*, 255, 523*n*
 development of, 256, 368–69
 I Am Curious—Yellow and, 335*n*, 548
 Lady Chatterley's Lover published by, 94*n*, 98*n*, 236, 338–41, 363, 369, 375
 Naked Lunch publication and, 385, 387, 388, 389, 395, 397, 480, 486, 491, 492*n*

Tropic of Cancer published by, 358*n*, 367–72, 388–89
Grove Press v. *Gerstein*, 382–83, 400, 417, 429*n*, 499
Grove Weidenfeld, 595*n*
Grundberg, Andy, 624
Gubar, Susan, 193*n*
Guccione, Bob, 577–81, 583, 592, 598
Guesde, Jules, 40
Guest, Morris, 16
Guevara, Che, 334, 369
Guinzburg, Harold K., 129, 151
Gurney, Edward J., 552
Gysin, Brion, 347, 386, 482

Hagar Revelly, 65, 222
Haight, Anne Lyon, 323*n*
Haiman, Franklin, 373
Haley v. *New York Society for the Suppression of Vice*, 74*n*
Hall, Carla, 665
Hall, Marguerite Radclyffe "John," 165–208
 death of, 204, 205–7
 finances of, 182, 184, 186*n*, 195, 202, 207
 lovers of, 168, 170, 196, 198–99, 204–5
 sexuality of, 165, 167–68
 see also Well of Loneliness, The
Hall, Sir Charles, 181
Hamling, William, 274, 495*n*, 496, 513, 527, 528, 530, 532, 559
 "Illustrated Report" issued by, 340*n*, 495*n*, 513*n*, 562–65, 567, 573–75
Hand, Augustus, 14*n*, 31*n*, 33–34, 216, 224
Hand, Learned, 30, 404, 413*n*, 552
 on clear and present danger, 158, 318*n*
 on contemporary community standards, 425*n*
 Hagar Revelly case and, 65, 66, 222
 Masses opinion of, 65, 116–17, 216, 217, 312*n*
 on Supreme Court as arbiter of constitutionality, 290
 Ulysses decisions and, 30, 31*n*, 33, 65
Hand of the Potter, The (Dreiser), 126, 127
Hannegan v. *Esquire*, 239*n*, 316, 619*n*
Hanrahan, William, 333
Harcourt, Alfred, 77
Harcourt, Ellen, 175
Harcourt Brace, 175, 197
Harlan, John Marshall, 399, 408, 564
 Court alliances and, 424, 514, 515, 535, 549
 judicial restraint advocated by, 408*n*, 414, 549
 on obscenity standards, 31*n*, 423*n*, 429*n*, 517, 540, 574*n*
 on *Roth* case, 295*n*, 298–303, 304, 314*n*, 316, 318*n*–19*n*, 574*n*

Harlequin romances, 597
Harper, 99, 109, 112, 114, 184, 220
Harper's, 211, 520–21
Harris, Frank, 49*n*, 54–55, 67, 122, 184, 259*n*, 508
Harris, Jerry, 456–57
Harris, Marguerite, 160
Hartisan, Matthew, 354*n*
Hartman, Geoffrey, 605
Harvey, Alexander, 122, 124
Harvey, George, 129
Hatfield, Mark O., 639*n*
Hauk, A. Andrew, 533–34
Haydn, Hiram, 183*n*
Hays, Arthur Garfield, 136, 137
Hays, Paul, 450, 473, 497*n*
Haywood, W. D. "Big Bill," 124, 154
Head, Sir Henry, 178
Heap, Jane, ix, 7–14, 17, 20, 34, 114
Hearst, William Randolph, 76, 220, 221, 226
Heath, Audrey "Robin," 171, 172, 174, 195, 196, 202, 203, 204
Hecht, Ben, 130, 360
Hefner, Hugh, 527, 528, 563, 578–79, 580, 583, 585–86
Heinemann, William, 65, 90, 104–5, 171–72, 175
Hellerstein, William, 449*n*, 457, 461, 478, 479
Helms, Dorothy, 623, 633
Helms, Jesse, 293, 501*n*–2*n*, 507*n*, 556*n*, 598*n*, 622–25, 629, 630, 645, 646, 662
  Mapplethorpe opposed by, 507*n*, 622, 623, 625, 635, 637, 639
  NEA legislation proposed by, 628, 632, 634–44, 676, 677*n*, 678, 679, 683, 684
Hemingway, Ernest, 25, 130, 142, 153, 164, 172, 200, 203, 277, 278*n*, 346, 376
Henderson, Hubert, 178
Henry, Arthur, 100, 101*n*, 102
Henson, Hensley, 190
Hentoff, Nat, 359, 466*n*, 479*n*, 613
Herlong, Henry, 557–58
Hershey, Judge, 381
Hewes, Laurence I., 448
Heyman, Phil, 504
Hicklin doctrine, *see Regina* v. *Hicklin*
Hill, Clinton S., 456
Hill, Leopold, 177, 180, 190
Hill, Morton, 454*n*, 558, 559
Hirshfeld, Samuel, 160, 161
History of Book Publishing in the United States (Tebbel), 6*n*, 18*n*–19*n*, 213*n*, 220*n*, 237*n*
Hitchcock, Richley, 109*n*
Hitler, Adolf, 617, 668*n*, 669
Hocking, William Ernest, 218*n*
Hofert, Edward, 377

Hoffenberg, Mason, 259*n*, 484–86
Hoffman, Julius J., 338, 341, 365, 386
Hofstadter, Judge, 478*n*
Hogan, Frank, 252
  Bruce prosecuted by, 221*n*, 444, 452–57, 458, 459, 460, 469, 477, 478, 479
  Memoirs of Hecate County case and, 212, 220–22, 224, 226*n*, 227, 234, 236, 238
Hoge, Jim, 362
Hollander, Norman, 487
Hollander, Paul, 487–88
Holmes, John Clellan, 329*n*
Holmes, Oliver Wendell, 117*n*, 404, 412, 436
  on clear and present danger, 31, 116, 158, 216, 296*n*, 308, 309, 311, 316–17, 443
Holroyd-Reece, John, 177, 181–82
Homer, 616
Homo Sapiens (Przbyszewski), 9, 72, 183
Honan, William H., 631
"Honey, 1976" (Mapplethorpe), 633
Hoover, Herbert, 203*n*
Hoover, J. Edgar, 357, 399*n*, 564, 569*n*
Horn, Clayton W., 335, 336, 337–38, 341, 365, 446
Hoskins, Dorothy, 79*n*
Houghton Mifflin, 174, 210
Hour, 18
Housman, A. E., 114
Howells, William Dean, 164
Howl (Ginsberg), 236–37, 330–38, 341, 346, 350*n*, 360, 445, 446*n*
  public readings of, 330–33, 345*n*, 361, 362
  Roth influence and, 252, 312*n*, 325, 337, 338, 365
How to Talk Dirty and Influence People (Bruce), 445
Hudnut, William H., 614
Hudson, Eugene A., 484, 485, 487–89, 491–93
Hudson, Henry E., 310*n*, 585, 588, 593, 607
Huebsch, B. W. "Ben," 66, 78, 129
  Dreiser and, 111, 122, 127, 151, 153
  Lawrence's works published by, 57*n*, 67, 69–71, 79, 80
  Ulysses publication and, 18, 19, 144
Hughes, Charles Evans, 443
Hughes, Holly, 610–11, 620*n*, 660, 661–64, 665, 672–76, 677, 681, 684, 688
Huling, Beth, 210
Hunter, Nan, 611*n*
Hustler, 583, 600*n*
Hutchins, Maude Phelps, 354*n*
Hutchins, Robert Maynard, 218, 354–55, 357, 362
Hutchison, E. R., 371*n*

Huxley, Aldous, 56, 89, 96
Huxley, Julian, 185, 187
Huxley, Maria, 89
Huysmans, Joris-Karl, 41, 184, 605
Hyman, Elaine (Kirah Markham), 110–13, 140, 163

I Am Curious—Yellow, 229*n*, 312*n*, 334*n*, 335*n*, 422, 497*n*, 501*n*, 517, 548–49, 566*n*, 620*n*
Ice and Fire (Dworkin), 595, 596–97, 616*n*
If It Die (Gide), 224
Iliad (Homer), 615, 616
Illustrated Report, 340*n*, 495*n*, 513*n*, 562–65, 567, 573
Industrial Workers of the World (I.W.W.), 124*n*
Inferno (Dante), 486, 492–93
Inge, William, 171
Inskip, Sir Thomas, 193
Institute for Contemporary Art (ICA) (Boston), 656
Institute of Contemporary Art (ICA) (Philadelphia), 624, 629, 634–35, 637
International Labor Defense, 132*n*
International Library Company, 76*n*
International Workers' Aid, 152*n*, 153
"Introduction to These Paintings" (Joyce), 85*n*
Iobst, Anne, 667
Ionesco, Eugene, 368–69
I.W.W. (Industrial Workers of the World), 124*n*

Jackson, Eddie, 601
Jackson, Gabriele Bernhard, 490–91
Jackson, Gardner, 232–33
Jackson, Robert, 305, 427, 616*n*
Jackson case, 317
Jacob, Micki, 205
Jacobellis, Nico, 409, 418
Jacobellis v. *Ohio*, 302*n*, 436, 506*n*, 534, 621
    social value standard in, 401*n*, 405, 418, 422–30, 434, 437, 438, 442*n*, 447, 469, 470–72, 516, 523*n*, 572*n*, 618*n*, 620
Jacobi, Allen, 659
Jacobs v. *New York*, 539*n*
James, Henry, 56*n*
Janet March (Dell), 183
Janeway, Elizabeth, 253*n*
Janson, Horst W., 507
Jeffers, Robinson, 129
Jeffords, James M., 639–40
Jeffrey, Terrence P., 531*n*
Jenkins v. *Georgia*, 571
Jennie Gerhardt (Dreiser), 105, 106, 109, 111, 113, 127

"Jessie McBride" (Mapplethorpe), 633–34
Jewett, Rutger, 105, 106
J. F. Taylor, 105
J. M. Dent, 131
John, Augustus, 87
John Bull, 90
John Lane Company:
    Beardsley published by, 66, 282
    "Genius" published by, 114, 117–18, 121, 123–24, 129
    New York branch of, 66, 114
    Titan published by, 113, 114
Johnson, Carla, 618
Johnson, Forrest, 465, 466*n*
Johnson, Lionel, 66
Johnson, Lyndon B., 293*n*, 434, 445
    justices appointed by, 415*n*, 506*n*, 515*n*, 525–29, 534*n*, 538, 539, 542, 544–45, 549, 566
    Lockhart commission and, 435, 551–52, 556, 585*n*
Jones, Antoinette, 658
Jones, Bill T., 677
Jones, Howard Mumford, 265–66
Jones, J. Jefferson, 66*n*, 114, 117–18, 120, 122, 123, 124, 129
Jones, James, 655
Jones, LeRoi (Amiri Baraka), 329, 351*n*, 367*n*
Jones, Lisa, 658
Jong, Erica, 247, 251
Jordan, Fred, 256, 369, 372–73
Joseph, Stephen C., 644
Journal (Chicago), 112
Journal-American, 220*n*, 221
Joyce, George (Giorgio), 27, 36
Joyce, Helen Kastor, 27, 28
Joyce, James, 7–35
    Beardsley vs., 284
    beat writers influenced by, 358, 364
    death of, 36–37
    Dubliners, 20, 24
    finances of, 29, 35, 36, 38
    Finnegans Wake, 38, 144, 364, 394
    literary stature of, 27, 35, 37–39
    love letters of, 34–35, 239
    poetry by, 84*n*
    Portrait of the Artist, 15, 16, 18
    stylistic influences on, 23
    see also *Ulysses*
Joyce, Lucia, 35–37
Joyce, Nora, 23–24, 34–35, 36, 37–38, 239
Joyce, Stanislaus, 36
Joyce, Stephen, 35*n*
Joynson-Hicks, Sir William "Jix," 85–86, 87, 93, 94, 196
    Well of Loneliness prosecution and, 173–74, 176, 177, 179, 190
Jung, Carl G., 23, 35–36

Junkie (Burroughs), 346, 351*n*
Justice Department, U.S.:
  Meese commission, 232*n*, 310*n*, 324,
    536*n*, 553*n*, 558*n*, 581, 583–86,
    588–95, 598–609, 612, 652
  obscenity enforcement unit of, 582*n*,
    584*n*, 606
Justine (Sade), 52*n*
Juvenal, 193, 459

Kaddish (Ginsberg), 358, 360, 361
Kahane, Eric, 266
Kahane, Jack, 55, 366, 367
Kahn, Otto, 16–17, 144, 147
Kalven, Harry, Jr., 275, 293*n*, 409, 462,
    509*n*, 564*n*
  Bruce defended by, 422, 436*n*, 447,
    449, 469, 477*n*
  on clear and present danger test, 308,
    315, 318*n*
  on *Fanny Hill* ruling, 442
  on free speech protections, 620
  on *Ginzburg* ruling, 503
  on Hugo Black's absolutist views, 312*n*
  on *Jacobellis/Tropic of Cancer,* 431*n*
  Kaplan v. *California,* 430*n*, 575–76
  on political dissent, 116*n*, 117*n*, 158,
    328*n*, 339*n*, 408*n*
  on *Roth* decision, 319*n*, 324–25, 371*n*,
    400, 412*n*, 418–19, 421, 428–29,
    572
  on *Times* v. *Sullivan,* 113*n*, 275*n*
  on triple-pronged test, 437, 572
  on two-level speech classification, 315,
    412*n*, 415, 574*n*
  "worthless" terminology used by, 342*n*,
    371*n*, 422, 423, 438, 440, 441,
    497*n*, 535
Kalven, Jamie, 117*n*, 158*n*
Kardon, Janet, 624
Kasper, Gerhard, 309*n*
Kastor, Robert, 27–28, 29*n*, 37
Katzenbach, Nicholas, 504, 510, 511
Katzenberger, Lehmann Israel, 568*n*
Kauffman, Bill, 672
Kaufman, George S., 142
Kazan, Elia, 510*n*
Kazin, Alfred, 100–101, 340
Kearney, Patrick, 140
Keating, Charles H., Jr., 531, 552, 553*n*,
    555–56, 558, 559, 585*n*, 606, 650*n*,
    651
Kemp, Earl, 562, 563, 564, 565, 573
Kennedy, Anthony, 621*n*
Kennedy, Edward M., 551, 553
Kennedy, Jacqueline, 445, 455–56, 462,
    463
Kennedy, John F., 454, 455–56, 500,
    510–11, 528
Kennedy, Joseph P., 510*n*

Kennedy, Robert F., 504, 509–11
Kennerley, Mitchell, 65–68, 71, 79, 80,
    83, 113, 114, 222
Kennerly, Karen, 410*n*, 646
Kern, Richard, 687
Kerouac, Jack, 346, 350, 360
  beat culture described by, 329*n*, 362*n*
  in literary journals, 338, 341, 351*n*,
    357, 358, 363, 364, 365, 369
  Naked Lunch and, 358*n*, 385, 391*n*
  at poetry readings by, 330, 331, 359
  in Tangier, 334, 347, 349, 385, 386
Kidd, John, 15*n*
Kilgallen, Brian, 377
Kilgallen, Dorothy, 444, 465–69, 472
Kilpatrick, James J., 539, 540
Kimmel, Charles, 499
Kimpton, Lawrence A., 353, 354, 355,
    356–57, 362, 363
Kingsley International Pictures, 139*n*, 250*n*,
    312*n*, 339*n*, 340, 607*n*
Kinkead-Weekes, Mark, 57*n*, 58*n*, 60*n*,
    70*n*
"Kinsey Report," 193*n*
Kipling, Rudyard, 99, 177, 185, 187,
    198
Kipper, Harry, 668–69
Kirk, David, 337
Kirk, Jerry, 584*n*, 606
Kitchen, The, 663
Klaw, Irving, 498–99
Klopfer, Donald, 17*n*, 27, 28, 129,
    130–31, 183*n*
Klubock, Daniel, 484
Knight, Christopher, 649
Knopf, Alfred A., 122, 129, 151, 202,
    213*n*, 225, 521*n*
  censorship battles avoided by, 9, 72,
    182–84
  Dreiser published by, 113, 125
  early career of, 66–67, 71, 80*n*
  as Lawrence's publisher, 81–83, 93, 94,
    369
  physical beauty of books published by,
    183*n*–84*n*
  Roth trial and, 285, 286–87
  Well of Loneliness and, 175–76, 182,
    184, 196, 197
Knopf, Alfred A. "Pat," 183*n*
Knopf, Blanche, 19, 175, 176, 182, 184
Knox, Bernard, 166*n*
Koch, Edward I., 644
Komroff, Manuel, 148
Krash, Abe, 526–27, 528
Kreeger, David Lloyd, 628, 649–50
Kreutzer Sonata, The (Tolstoy), 6, 7
Kristol, Irving, 569
Kronhausen, Eberhard W., 507
Kronhausen, Phyllis C., 507
Krutch, Joseph Wood, 133

796 ❧ Index

Kuh, Richard H., 392, 454–55, 457, 458,
    459, 465, 466, 470–72, 474, 479,
    511n
Kummer, Clare, 161
Kupcinet, Irv, 361
Kurland, Philip B., 309n
Kuspit, Donald, 632
Kyros, Peter, 682

Là-Bas (Huysmans), 184
Lacy, Gerald M., 80n
Ladies' Man, A (Bel-Ami) (Maupassant),
    48n
Lady Chatterley's Lover (Lawrence), 30,
    89–95
    British publication of, 94n, 98n, 190,
        269, 528
    expurgated versions of, 93–94, 224
    movie based on, 139n, 250n, 312n,
        339, 398, 607n
    Penguin edition of, 190, 269
    pirated editions of, 83, 91, 93
    private publication of, 83, 84, 85,
        89–91, 93, 94, 210, 277, 338, 368n
    prosecutions based on, 91, 93n, 94n,
        190, 192n, 252, 339–41, 375, 528
    publishers' rejections of, 55–56, 279n
    seizures of, 55n, 85, 93, 94, 307n
    sexual content of, 91–93
    U.S. publication of, 94n, 98, 236, 251,
        338–41, 363, 369, 375, 528
    writing of, 84, 88–89
Lahr, Charles, 86
Laird and Lee, 53n
Lamantia, Philip, 330n
Lamarr, Hedy, 32
Lane, Allen, 98n
Lane, John, 114
Lane, Robert, 457, 465
Lang, Cosmo, 190
Lanier, Henry W., 102
Lanier, Sidney, 102n
Lapiccirella, Professor, 169
Lasky, Jesse, 140, 141, 144
Lattimore, Owen, 527
Latzko, Andreas, 117, 129
Laughlin, James, 243, 244, 245, 334, 347
Lauriers Sont Coupés, Les (Dujardin), 23
Lausche, Frank, 539
Lawrence, D. H., 55–75, 79–97, 196
    copyright problems of, 56
    death of, 95–97, 98
    finances of, 60n, 67–68, 80–82, 86, 90,
        91, 93
    ill health of, 83–84, 89, 94–97
    pornography condemned by, 298n
    pseudonymous publication of, 64
    Sons and Lovers, 56, 65, 67–69, 104
    in U.S., 63–65, 67, 75, 79, 80–83
    war fever decried by, 62–63
    watercolors painted by, 84, 85, 86–88

    see also Lady Chatterley's Lover; Rainbow,
        The
Lawrence, Frieda von Richthofen, 56, 63,
    65, 67, 68, 94
    Lawrence's death and, 84, 95, 96, 97
    on Lawrence's work, 84, 89, 93n
    publishers and, 79, 81
    at Taos, 75, 79
Lawrence, T. E., 172
Lawson, John Howard, 162
Leach v. Carlile, 316–17
Leaves of Grass (Whitman), 332
Leblanc, Georgette, 7n, 36n
LeBlanc, Leslie, 22n
Leeds, Jeffrey T., 407n, 423n
Legal Realism, 289–90
Lehrman, Nat, 563
Lehrman, Rabbi, 559
Leidholdt, Dorchen, 587–88
Leis, Simon L., Jr., 651
Leisure, George H., 283, 284, 285,
    288–89
Leland, John, 659
Lengel, William, 112, 114
Lenin, V. I., 153, 154
Leo, John, 627n, 657–58
Léon, Paul, 22n, 29n
Lesher, Stephen, 402n
Levi, Edward H., 313n
Levine, Esar, 55n
Levy, David C., 650
Lewis, Anthony, 302, 370, 371, 398–99,
    403, 433, 527n, 635–36
Lewis, Felice Flannery, 89n, 93n, 341,
    383n
Lewis, Jo Ann, 648
Lewis, Sinclair, 122, 144, 151, 172, 197
Lewis, Wyndham, 14n, 216n, 277
Lewisohn, Ludwig, 129, 277
Lezar, Harold "Tex," 585, 599, 652
Liberal Club, 124–25
Lickfold, Mr., 51
Liebman, Ernst, 448
"Life, Art and America" (Dreiser), 116,
    127
Lindsay, Vachel, 66
Lingeman, Richard, 103, 104n, 111n,
    121n
Link, Winfrey C., 558
Lippmann, Walter, 67
Lipschitz, Chaim U., 434n–35n
Little, Brown, 19, 521n
Little Bookshop Around the Corner, 66
Little Leather Library, 130
Little Review, 7–17, 114n, 203, 216n
    management of, 7, 16–17, 36n
    Ulysses episode published in, ix, xi,
        7–17, 20, 22, 215
Little Theatre, 110, 111
Liveright, Horace, 137, 142–49
    authors signed by, 129–32, 142, 145–46

Clean Books League opposed by, 76, 77, 78
Dreiser's relationship with, 127, 129, 140–42, 150
Dreiser's work published by, 123, 124, 126, 129, 132–35, 140, 142, 145n
in Hollywood, 140, 146, 147, 203
parties hosted by, 140, 143–44
publishing firm established by, 72
reversals suffered by, 142–50, 152, 183
theatrical business of, 130, 140–41, 143, 146, 147
Ulysses publication and, 17–18
see also Boni and Liveright
Liveright Publishing Corporation, 148
Liverpool Mercury, 43
Livingston, Edward, 253n
Livingston, Jane, 623, 647
Living Theatre, 459n
Llewellyn, Karl, 477
Lobb, Monty, 651
Locke, William J., 122
Lockhart, William, 560, 561
on ACLU, 557–58
background of, 551n, 553, 556
on Doubleday, 212n
on pornography, 298n, 551
on *Roth* cases, 280n, 302n
on sexual taboos, 497n
variable obscenity doctrine presented by, 423n, 503n, 556n
see also National Commission on Obscenity and Pornography
Logue, Christopher, 259n
Lolita (Nabokov), 243–56, 258–70, 365, 385, 388, 393
British edition of, 261, 266, 267–69, 388
French language edition of, 266–67
French suppression of, 195n, 260, 261, 262–63, 266–67
Olympia Press edition of, 55n, 245n, 254–55, 258–67, 271, 365, 385, 388
publishers approached for, 213n, 229n, 236n, 237, 243–54, 608n
success of, 259, 260, 261, 388, 393
U.S. publication of, 237, 261–64, 265–66, 269–70, 288n, 385n, 388
London, Ephraim, 233n, 400, 407, 418, 422n, 423, 447n
Bruce defended by, 233, 447n, 449–50, 465, 477n
London, Jack, 66
London Evening Standard, 134
London Star, 43, 57
Long, Russell, 532, 539
Longford, Lord, 660n
Lord Campbell's Act (1857), 47, 58–59, 85, 86n, 177, 186
Love Crime, A (Bourget), 48n
Lovelace, Linda, *see* Marciano, Linda

Lovers, The, 33n, 274, 275, 400, 409, 418, 419, 420, 422n, 424–25, 431n, 435, 464, 469, 471n, 478n, 506n, 534, 574, 620
see also Jacobellis v. *Ohio*
Lovett, Robert M., 231
Loving v. *Virginia*, 510n
Lowell, Amy, 67n, 69, 122, 174, 193n
Lowell, Robert, 395
Lubell, Adeline, 520n, 521
Luhan, Mabel Dodge, 68n, 95
Lunn, Harry, 628, 649
Lynd, Robert, 57
Lynn, Amber, 604
Lynn, Barry, 585
Lysistrata (Aristophanes), 278n, 279, 285, 307n, 340n

Mabley, Jack, 344, 345–46, 353, 354, 355
Macaulay, Rose, 129, 185, 187
McBride, Jessie, 633–34
McBride, Will, 570
McCarthy, Desmond, 185, 187, 188, 189
McCarthy, Joseph, 141n, 158, 227, 319n, 378n, 406, 408–9, 445, 586
McCarthy, Mary, 210–11, 242, 246, 365n, 391, 393, 394–95, 432, 439n
McCarthyism, 250–51, 598
McClellan, John L., 532, 545
McClure, Michael, 330–31
McClure, Robert, 212n, 280n, 423n, 497n, 503n, 556n
McClure, S. S., 99
McClure-Phillips, 105
McCormick, Ken, 248, 249, 250
McDermott, Captain, 453
MacDonald, Dwight, 507, 508
MacDonald, James Ramsey, 85
McEntegart, Thomas E., 76
MacFall, Haldane, 284–85
McGrath, C. Peter, 423
McGraw-Hill Book Company, 269
MacGregor, Robert, 244
Machaty, Gustav, 32
McHugh, Vincent, 220n
MacInnis, James Martin, 233–34, 236
McIntosh, Ralph, 335–37
McIntyre, Alfred, 521
McKean, Judge, 6n
McKee, Tom, 103
Mackenzie, Compton, 172, 173, 196, 268
McKinley, William, 296n
MacKinnon, Catharine, 581, 583, 587, 592, 595, 596, 611, 613–15, 617
McLawhorn, Richard, 584n
MacLeish, Archibald, 84n, 277
Macmillan, 184
MacPhee, Chester, 333
McTeague (Norris), 99, 100
Madame Bovary (Flaubert), 48n, 202, 268n, 270n

Maddox, Brenda, 20n–21n, 23n, 24, 29n, 34, 35, 37n, 38n
Madeleine, 184, 220
Mademoiselle de Maupin (Gautier), 30n, 193n, 224
Madison, James, 314, 618
Maeterlinck, Maurice, 66
Mailer, Norman, 251, 278n, 365, 432
 Deer Park, 225, 265, 287–88
 on feminists, 610, 618
 language used by, 467, 520–21
 on *Naked Lunch*, 391, 392, 393, 394, 395, 439n, 480, 484, 486–87, 493, 495
 on pornographic films, 587, 604–5, 611, 613
Maison des Amis des Livres, La, 21, 38
Makers of the New (Symons), 34
Makris, John N., 278, 279–80
Malcolm X, 369
Malina, Judith, 459n
Malle, Louis, 33n, 274, 275, 409, 418, 424, 506n
Mallory v. *United States*, 529
Mandrake Press, 85n
Mann, Heinrich, 63
Mann, Thomas, 225, 286–87
Mannin, Ethel, 169–70, 208
Manning, Estelle, 159, 160, 161, 163
Man Shakespeare, The (Harris), 54, 67
Manton, Martin, 33n
Manual Enterprises v. *Day*, 31n, 415n, 429n, 574n
Mapplethorpe, Robert, 620n
 Cincinnati exhibit of, xiii, 87n, 269, 405n, 441n, 531n, 582n, 603n, 633–34, 650–56, 659
 Helms's criticism of, 507n, 622, 623, 625, 635, 637, 639
 Washington exhibit and, 622–23, 628–29, 630, 633, 634, 647–49
 works of, 623–26, 632, 681, 687
Marbury v. *Madison*, 296
Marciano, Linda ("Lovelace"), 584, 587–88, 589–92, 610
Marcus, Steven, 523n
Marcus v. *Search Warrants*, 415n
Margolick, David, 654
Marker, Lewis Adelbert, 483
Markham, Kirah (Elaine Hyman), 110–12, 140, 163
Marks, Burton, 446
Marlowe, Alan, 329, 351n
Marriage and Morals (Russell), 145–46
Married Love (Stopes), 30n
Marsh, Edward, 63
Marshall, Thurgood, 423n, 513, 573
 appointment of, 515n, 518, 526n, 534
 on Bruce case, 450, 452, 473
 Court coalitions and, xii, 565n, 621n, 652

 on *Stanley* v. *Georgia*, 440, 450n, 516n, 537n, 566, 574
Mashburn, John, 630
Mason's Ridge (Graham), 597
Massachusetts v. *Oakes*, 557n, 582n, 610n
Masses, 65, 116–17, 124, 216, 217, 290n, 312n, 328
Master of the House, The (Hall), 203–4
Masters, Edgar Lee, 110
Masters, Kim, 652
Matarasso, Leo, 266, 271
Matthews, Brander, 122
Maupassant, Guy de, 6, 48n, 506–7
Maure, Dominique, *see* Meyer, Dottie
Mauriac, François, 203, 276
Maurice (Forster), 52, 167n, 179
Mavrikos, Theodore, 395, 396, 397
Meade, Frederick, 87, 88
Mechanical Angel (Friede), 130n
Meese, Edwin, 581
Meese commission, *see* Attorney General's Commission on Pornography
Meeske, Marilyn, 256–58, 271
Meiklejohn, Alexander, 113n, 293n, 409
Mekas, Jonas, 459, 539n
Melody, Jack, 329
Melville, J. B., 193
Memoirs of a Woman of Pleasure (Fanny Hill) (Cleland), 251
 Brennan doctrine on, 436–42, 494, 501, 505, 512, 523n, 534, 571n
 lesbian relations in, 193n,
 Memoirs of Hecate County vs., 210
 Putnam edition of, 288n
 Supreme Court on, 139n, 265–66, 363, 397, 418n, 421n, 422, 430n, 431n, 436–42, 470n, 471n, 478, 490, 494, 497–501, 503, 505n, 511n, 512, 533–34, 542, 571n, 574, 621
Memoirs of Hecate County (Wilson), 30, 209–39, 419n
 British edition of, 219–20, 234
 Doubleday prosecuted for, 75n–76n, 209–12, 214–19, 221–29, 241, 248, 250, 273, 285, 297, 303n, 305
 reissue of, 212, 221, 233–38, 252, 257n
 reviews of, 210–211, 221n, 224
 Supreme Court ruling on, 152n, 212, 214n, 215–16, 218–19, 224–35, 273, 297, 303n, 307, 334n, 427, 549
Memoirs of the Foreign Legion (Lawrence), 81
Mencken, H. L., 66, 197
 books reviewed by, 109, 127n, 134–35
 on cultural intolerance, 635–36
 on Dreiser's career, 150, 163–64
 Dreiser's friendship with, 113–14, 115, 124–27, 135, 151, 159, 162, 163–64
 "Genius" censorship opposed by, 117, 119–20, 121, 122, 123, 124–26, 154
Menken, Helen, 146n

Men in War (Latzko), 117, 129
Merlin, 256
"Metaphysics of the Law of Obscenity,
    The" (Kalven), 342*n*, 421, 572*n*, 620
Metcalf, Herbert, 190
Methodist Times, 43
Methuen, Algernon, 56–58, 61, 71
Methuen and Company, 56–57, 59, 60,
    69, 70
Meyer, Dottie (Dominique Maure),
    577–78, 592–95
Meyers, Jeffrey, 60–61, 82*n*, 84*n*, 85*n*,
    88*n*
Middleton, Henry, 217
Mikva, Abner J., 414
"Mildred Lawson" (Moore), 24
Miles, Barry, 329*n*, 350*n*, 482*n*
Mill, John Stuart, 294, 440
Millay, Edna St. Vincent, 66, 67, 144,
    198
Miller, Clyde C., 580
Miller, Darlene, 294*n*, 618–19, 621
Miller, Eric, 474–76
Miller, Ernest I., 269
Miller, Henry, 393, 595
    Burroughs's meeting with, 384
    career of, 366–67, 432–33
    Olympia Press publication of, 256, 257,
        258, 259*n*
    pulp pornography written by, 257, 258,
        393
    romantic involvements of, 376*n*
    Rossett's college paper on, 251*n*
    on *Tropic of Cancer* litigation, 431–32
    Whitman admired by, 332*n*
    see also Tropic of Cancer
Miller, Jack, 544, 547
Miller, Marvin, 562
Miller, Merle, 505, 506–7, 509
Miller, Mona, 376
Miller, Robert, 625
Miller, Russell, 578–80, 602*n*
Miller, Tim, 660, 664, 665, 674, 684
Miller v. *California*, 405*n*, 470, 560*n*,
    561–62, 564, 574, 575, 620, 652
    Brennan doctrine revised in, 565–72, 636
    obscenity test from, 31*n*, 319*n*,
        566–68, 607*n*, 609, 615, 636, 637,
        640–43, 646*n*, 651*n*, 653*n*, 655,
        660, 665–66, 681, 684–85
    pornography guidelines in, 580, 606
Millin, Sarah, 130
Mills, Hilary, 520*n*
Mills, Wilbur, 535*n*
Minersville School District v. *Gobitis*, 314*n*
Ming, Robert, 447, 449, 477*n*
Minton, Sherman, 235, 406, 408
Minton, Walter, 237, 265–66, 267, 270,
    288*n*, 485, 501*n*
Miracle, The, 233*n*, 234*n*–35*n*, 293*n*,
    407, 414–15, 619*n*

Miranda v. *Arizona*, 527, 529
Mishkin, Edward, 500, 501, 503*n*
Mishkin, Samuel, 436
Mishkin v. *New York*, 499*n*, 501, 503*n*,
    511*n*, 512, 514, 620*n*
Miss Lonelyhearts (West), 148
Mitchell, Joan, 368
Mitchell, John, 546
Modern Library, 130–31, 148*n*, 213*n*
Moeller, Phillip, 10
Monnier, Adrienne, 21, 29*n*, 38, 254*n*
Monroe, Eason, 562–63
Monroe, Harriet, 10*n*, 16*n*–17*n*, 64
Montagu, Ivor, 140*n*, 141*n*, 143*n*
Moods, Cadenced and Declaimed (Dreiser),
    145*n*, 163
Moore, Donald Page, 446
Moore, George, 24, 156
    Henry Vizetelly defended by, 48–49,
        51–52
    library censorship of, 22, 42
    Paris exile of, 52, 64
    publishers for, 40, 41, 42, 66, 104,
        114, 129, 131
    on *Ulysses*, 22–23, 26
Moore, Harry T., 63, 64*n*, 67*n*, 68, 84*n*,
    85, 86, 93*n*
Moore, Henry, 87
Moore, Leonard P., 498–99
Morality in Media, 517–18, 656
Moral Majority, 601, 614
Morgan, J. Pierpont, 6, 114
Morgan, Ted, 343*n*, 346, 352*n*, 355*n*,
    362*n*, 384*n*, 392, 393–94, 482*n*, 495
Morganstern, Bill, 353
Morgenthau, Robert, 479
Morland, Andrew, 96
Morley, Christopher, 99
Morrell, Lady Ottoline, 62*n*–63*n*, 92,
    96*n*, 181
Morrell, Philip, 59, 63*n*, 87
Morris, Robert, 374
Morris, Willie, 520–21
Morrison, Nelly, 89
Morton, W. Scott, 434*n*
Moscato, Michael, 22*n*
Mount-Temple, Lord, 42
Moynihan, Daniel Patrick, 635
Mrs. Warren's Profession (Shaw), 146
Mumby, Frank Arthur, 66*n*
Mundt, Karl E., 535*n*, 559
Murao, Shigeyoshi, 325, 333*n*, 334, 335,
    446*n*
Murphy, Bruce Allen, 503*n*, 504*n*, 538,
    539–40, 544, 546*n*
Murphy, Frank, 219*n*, 227, 314*n*, 317*n*,
    380, 408, 415
Murry, J. Middleton, 25
Murtagh, John M., 457, 459, 461–65,
    466, 467, 469, 470, 472, 474, 478,
    479

Muskett, Herbert G., 60, 87
Mussio, John King, 434n
Mutual Film Corp. v. Ohio, 405n
Myerson, David, 601, 603
My Life (Ellis), 181
My Life and Loves (Harris), 49n, 55, 184, 508
My Life with Dreiser (Helen Dreiser), 163

Nabokov, Dmitri, 245n, 246, 248n, 270
Nabokov, Nicholas, 267
Nabokov, Véra, 243, 244, 254n, 262, 267, 272
Nabokov, Vladimir, 243–72
    as American writer, 270
    at Cornell, 243–46, 255, 262–63, 270
    Edmund Wilson and, 210, 225, 246, 247, 248, 254n, 255, 261
    pseudonym for, 236n, 245–46, 247, 261n
    see also Lolita
Naked and the Dead, The (Mailer), 251, 520, 521
Naked Lunch (Burroughs), 252, 345–65, 384–97
    in Big Table, 237, 338, 341, 357, 360, 363, 364–65, 386, 393
    in Chicago Review, 349–53, 354, 357
    expert witnesses for, 484–92
    prosecutions based on, 139, 167n, 229n, 395–97, 417, 422, 438, 480, 484–95
    Olympia edition of, 55n, 385–91, 393
    Rossett's edition of, 385–94, 439n, 488
    title for, 358n
    writing of, 334–35, 347–50, 385–87, 492n
Nana (Zola), 41, 44, 105, 193n
Nathan, George Jean, 157
Nation, 73, 115–16, 133, 354
National Association of Book Publishers, 77, 78
National Coalition Against Pornography, 584n, 585n, 603, 650n
National Commission on Obscenity and Pornography (Lockhart commission), 497n, 504, 545n, 551–62
    abolition of obscenity laws advocated by, 292, 298n, 435n, 501n, 552–55, 560, 561, 571, 575
    on behavioral effects of pornography, 310, 553–56, 560, 585
    on children's exposure to obscenity, 541n
    establishment of, 435n, 531–32, 551–52, 559, 584
    "Illustrated Report" on, 340n, 495n, 513n, 562–65, 567, 573
    Meese commission vs. 583, 584, 585
    on sex pulp novels, 496

National Decency Reporter, 547
National Endowment for the Arts (NEA), 598n, 622–47, 660–88
    art censored by, 611n, 660–65, 671–76, 684, 687–88
    budget of, 634–35, 637
    grantees of, 610n, 623, 625, 629–30, 632, 634–35, 643–46, 648, 671–72
    legislative control of, 293n, 340n, 556n, 622, 627–28, 632–44, 646–47, 664, 676–84
    oath required by, 647, 650
    religious opposition to, 453n, 643, 678
National Federation for Decency, 598, 601
National Obscenity Enforcement Unit (NOEU), 582n, 584n, 606
National Organization of Citizens for Decent Literature (CDL), 232n, 552, 558, 588n–89n, 650, 651
    Fortas attacked by, 531–47, 559, 585n
National Republican Congressional Committee, 635
National Vigilance Association, xiii, 44
Navarro, Nick, 455n
Navasky, Victor S., 509, 510, 511
NEA, see National Endowment for the Arts
Neel, Alice, 624
Nesbitt, Lowell, 647
Neumann, Julius G., 435n
Neumann, Moshe, 454n
Neusner, Jacob, 663n, 676–77
New Directions, 243, 244, 245, 354n
Newman, Muriel, 359
Newman, Roger, 32n, 312n, 398n, 399, 400, 405n, 415n, 510n, 619n
New Masses, 328
New Republic, 73, 211
New Yorker, 142, 211–12, 242, 244, 255
New York Herald Tribune, 133, 377
New York Public Library, 3
New York Review of Books, 213n
New York Society for the Suppression of Vice:
    Clean Books League bill backed by, 76
    decline of, 237
    establishment of, 4, 6, 61, 91n
    Halsey v., 74n
    Knopf withdrawals and, 175, 176, 182, 183
    Seltzer's publications and, 72, 73, 79
    semigovernmental status accorded, 118n–19n
    see also Sumner, John S.
New York Times, 6, 7, 14, 75, 76, 78, 115, 156, 239, 253n
New York Times v. Sullivan, 113n, 275, 313n, 325, 398n, 401n, 411n–12n, 422, 442–43
New York World, 115
Nexus (Miller), 433

Nichols, Agnes, 167–68
Nichols, Luther, 335, 337
Nicol, Charles, 245*n*
Nicolson, Nigel, 252*n*, 267, 268–69
Niebuhr, Reinhold, 458
Niemoeller, Martin, 677
Nin, Anaïs, 242, 257, 258, 272*n*, 366, 376*n*
Nixon, Richard M., 415*n*, 424, 433*n*, 530, 531*n*, 546*n*, 548, 563, 565, 569, 581
    justices appointed by, 515*n*, 526–27, 544, 554*n*, 561, 564, 685
    Lockhart commission as viewed by, 435*n*, 552, 553*n*, 558, 560, 563, 585
NOEU (National Obscenity Enforcement Unit), 582*n*, 584*n*, 606
No Man's Land (Gilbert and Gubar), 193*n*
Nora (Maddox), 21*n*, 29*n*, 34
Norris, Frank, 99, 100, 101, 102, 104
Norris, Hoke, 365, 373
Novak, Robert, 662, 674
November (Flaubert), 224

Obelisk Press, 55*n*, 257, 366, 367
O'Brien, John Lord, 413
Obscene Publications Act (1959), 190*n*, 266, 267–69, 430*n*
"Obscenity and Censorship" (Redman), 33*n*
O'Connor, John Cardinal, 407*n*, 644, 666
O'Connor, Sandra Day, 419*n*, 420*n*, 621*n*, 653*n*
O'Flaherty, Liam, 130
O'Hara, John, 225, 278*n*, 285, 286
O'Keeffe, Georgia, 240, 624
Okrand, Fred, 419
"Old Angel Midnight" (Kerouac), 363, 364, 365
Olds, Sharon, 613
Olson, Jack, 361
Olympia Press, 55*n*, 256, 272, 282*n*, 484
    Lolita published by, 55*n*, 245*n*, 254–55, 258–67, 271, 385
    Naked Lunch published by, 55*n*, 385–91, 393
    pornography commissioned for, 256–58, 263
O'Meara, Joseph, 404, 436, 544
O'Neal, William, 457
O'Neill, Eugene, 111, 129, 147, 197
O'Neill, Thomas P. "Tip," 535*n*
On Liberty (Mill), 440
On the Road (Kerouac), 360
Operation Yorkville, 434, 454*n*
Orioli, Pino, 56, 84, 85, 89–91, 93, 94, 338
Orlovsky, Peter, 330*n*, 358, 359, 360, 361, 362, 386, 461
Ormrod, Richard, 168*n*

Orr-Cahall, Christina, 622–23, 628–29, 647–49
Orwell, George, 376
Osborne v. *Ohio*, 537*n*, 582*n*, 609*n*, 610*n*, 618*n*, 677*n*
Oscar Wilde (Harris), 67
"O-7," 533–35, 537, 538, 539
Osgood, James, 332*n*
O'Sullivan, Judge, 522–23
Ould, Herman, 181
Our Lady of the Flowers (Genet), 270
Ousler, Fulton, 203
Outlaw, The, 335
Ovid, 193*n*, 279
Owen, Iris, 259*n*
Oxford University Press, 64

Packwood, Bob, 639*n*
Page, L. C., 99, 237, 257*n*
Page, Walter Hines, 99–100, 101, 102, 103
Paget, Mamaine, 219
Paglia, Camille, 605
Pally, Marcia, 167*n*, 595*n*, 604, 605, 611–12
Palmer, Tony, 401*n*
Pansies (Lawrence), 84–85, 86
Parachini, Alan, 638
Paramount Publix Corporation, 141*n*, 147
Paris Adult Theatre v. *Slaton*, 319*n*, 575
Parisi, Peter, 597
Parker, Dorothy, 142
Parker, Helen, 344
Partisan Review, 255, 261
Passaro, Vince, 628
Patchen, Kenneth, 333, 334
Patges, Myrtle, 158
Paul, James, 278*n*, 279*n*
Peattie, Elia W., 114–15, 117
Peck, Harry Thurston, 53*n*
Pegasus Press, 94, 177, 186, 194, 195, 202
Pegler, Westbrook, 521*n*
Pell, Arthur, 143, 145, 147, 148, 150
Pell, Claiborne, 642
PEN, 181, 410–11
Penguin, 94*n*, 98*n*, 190, 269
Penn, John Garrett, 603
Penthouse, 577–81, 583, 585, 586*n*, 592–95, 598
People v. *Berg,* 222
People v. *Brainard,* 74*n*
Perdriat, Hélène, 202
Perkins, Maxwell, 142
Perlman, Milton, 382
Perlman, Nathan D., 225, 226, 419*n*
Pethick-Lawrence, F. W., 85, 86
Petronius, 131
Phipps, Kenneth M., 461*n*, 462, 469, 470, 479
Pilpel, Harriet, 221, 236

Pinker, J. B., 29n, 56, 57, 58, 60n, 64, 69–70, 80n
Piping Hot (Zola), 44
"Piss Christ" (Serrano), 630–32
Playboy, 308, 309n, 310n, 527, 528, 536n, 556, 563, 578–86, 598
Plexus (Miller), 256
Plimpton, George, 256, 259n
Plumed Serpent, The (Lawrence), 84
Pocket Poet Series, 333
Podhoretz, Norman, 362n, 501n
Poe, Edgar Allan, 40, 364
Poetry, 10n, 16n, 64
Points of Rebellion (Douglas), 548
Pomes Penyeach (Joyce), 84n
Pope v. Illinois, 518n, 571n, 685, 686–87
"Pornography and Obscenity" (Lawrence), 84
"Pornography in the Market Place" (Wildmon), 600
Porter, Paul, 543n, 544
Portrait of the Artist as a Young Man, A (Joyce), 15, 16, 18
Posner, Richard A., 294n, 420–21, 422n, 614–15, 619, 621
Potter, Gail, 337
Potter, Ted, 630
Pound, Ezra, 7–8, 10n, 17, 18, 21, 22, 25, 66, 84n, 122, 223, 386
Powell, Lewis F., 515n, 561
Powers, Francis Gary, 456
Powys, John Cowper, 11, 114
Praz, Mario, 209
Prescott, Orville, 253n
Pringle, Henry F., 220n
Prothero, John, 190
Proust, Marcel, 72
Prussian Officer, The (Lawrence), 59
Public Prosecution Act (1879), 44
Public Welfare Pictures v. Brennan, 405n
Published in Paris (Ford), 11n
Publisher Weekly, 66, 67, 71, 77, 82
Purity in Print (Boyer), 91n, 145n, 183
Pursley, Leo A., 434n
Putnam, George Palmer, 77

Quantity of Books v. Kansas, 212n
Queer (Burroughs), 167n, 346
Quinn, John, 8, 10, 12, 13, 16, 20, 65

Rabelais, François, 12, 26, 43
Racht, Leon, 220n
Radclyffe Hall (Brittain), 176n
Rago, Henry, 334
Rahv, Philip, 247, 255, 261n
Rainbow, The (Lawrence), 56–72
  British suppression of, 18, 56–63, 65, 67, 69, 70, 85, 86, 87, 95
  cuts made in, 56–57n, 69–70
  lesbianism in, 193n

sequel to, 72
  U.S. edition of, 57n, 68–71
"Rainbow Prosecution, The" (Carter) 57n
Rainsford, W. S., 6n
Randolph (Caruth), Jane, 169
Randolph, John, 253n
Random House:
  books seized from, 220n
  founding of, 17n, 27
  Knopf merger with, 183n
  Lockhart Report issued by, 583
  Modern Library, 130–31, 148n, 213n
  Roth case and, 225, 285, 286
  Ulysses published by, 22n, 27–32, 33, 35, 130, 197, 223–24, 234, 235, 282, 392n, 493
Raney, Bill, 520
Rankin, J. Lee, 296, 297–98, 302
Rascoe, Burton, 15
Raskin, Barbara, 672, 678
Rathbone, Basil, 146n
Rauschenberg, Robert, 410n
Ray, Nicholas, 359
Read, Herbert, 259n, 268
Ready for the Defense (Garbus), 454n
Reagan, Ronald, 216n, 401n, 419n, 548, 564, 569, 581, 583–85, 599n, 602, 627, 662, 685
Réage, Pauline, 254n, 259n, 523n
Reardon, Judge, 494
Rechy, John, 358, 369, 392
Redfield, Emanuel, 540–41, 542
Redlich, Norman, 403
Redman, Ben Ray, 31–32
Redrup, Robert, 513, 527
Redrupping, 341n, 513, 514, 515
Redrup v. New York, 471n, 505n, 512–18, 523, 532n, 540n, 547n, 573, 621
Reed, John, 66, 122, 124, 129, 154, 328n
Reed, Stanley Forman, 230
Reems, Harry, 590–91, 604
Regan v. Taxation with Representation, 640–41
Regina v. Hicklin, xi, 12, 30, 31, 45, 58, 65, 74n, 137, 187, 192–94, 310n, 325, 576
Rehnquist, William, 201, 403n, 501n, 515n, 564–65
Rehnquist Court, 574n
  Brennan doctrine eroded by, 688
  on child pornography, 537n, 582n
  on Falwell's libel suit, 583n
  on local community standards, 201, 685
  on nude dancing, 235n, 618n, 621n, 688n
  on social value, 518n
  Warren Court's progressive law vs., 275n, 546
Reich, Charles, 528
Reich, Wilhelm, 319, 347, 394

Reinhardt, Max, 261
Reitman, Alan, 557
Reitman, Ben, 111
Rembar, Charles:
  Fanny Hill case and, 418*n*, 422*n*, 430*n*,
    437–39, 440*n*, 441, 497*n*
  on Grove Press *Lady Chatterley's Lover*
    case, 94*n*, 339, 340, 375
  Tropic of Cancer cases and, 139*n*, 371,
    381, 417, 419
Remembrance of Things Past (Proust), 72
Replenishing Jessica (Bodenheim), 131, 149
Resnick, Beverly, 659
Rexroth, Kenneth, 330, 333, 335, 337,
    359
Reynolds, William Bradford, 401*n*
Ribback, Alan, 453
Rice, Anne, 617
Rice, Elmer, 75*n*–76*n*, 214–15
Richards, Grant, 88
Richardson, Helen, *see* Dreiser, Helen
    Patges Richardson
Ridgewell, Rosemary, 265
Riesman, David, 345, 356
Riggio, Thomas P., 111*n*
Rimbaud, Arthur, 358, 364
Rinehart, Ted, 520
Ritter, Bruce, 310*n*, 599
Rivera, Diego, 153
Rivers, J. E., 245*n*
Rivers, Larry, 661
"Road I Came, The" (Dreiser), 163
Robbe-Grillet, Alain, 358, 368, 369,
    387–88
Robbins, Harold, 251, 467
Robert Mapplethorpe Foundation, 646
Roberts, Samuel J., 540*n*
Robertson, Geoffrey, 59, 189, 190*n*,
    194*n*, 269*n*
Robertson, Pat, 632, 643
Robeson, Paul, 144
Robinson, Edwin Arlington, 122
Rogge, O. John, 315–18
Rogow, Bruce, 659
Rogue, 308, 309*n*, 527
Rohrabacher, Dana, 638, 682
Rolland, Romain, 63
Rolph, C. H., 94*n*, 190*n*, 269*n*, 528*n*
Romans, Epistle of Paul to, 193
Roosevelt, Eleanor, 445, 462–63, 465
Roosevelt, Franklin D., 201*n*, 232*n*, 293,
    315*n*, 408, 414
Rosenfeld, Maurice, 447, 449, 477*n*
Rosenheim, Edward, 353, 356, 363
Rosenthal, Irving, 344–45, 347, 350,
    352–57, 362, 363, 365, 386, 387
Rosen v. *United States*, 290*n*
Rosenzweig, Richard, 579
Ross, David, 656
Ross, Mark, 656–57, 659
Rossellini, Roberto, 233*n*, 407

Rosset, Barney, 247, 259, 501*n*
  background of, 251*n*, 367–69
  Ginsberg's work published by, 334, 347
  Grove Press developed by, 256, 368–69
  Lady Chatterley's Lover published by,
    94*n*, 98*n*, 236, 338–41
  Naked Lunch published by, 385, 386,
    387–93, 394, 439*n*, 488
  Tropic of Cancer published by, 367–73,
    376, 378, 385, 391, 417, 432
  see also Grove Press
Roth, Pauline, 273
Roth, Philip, 355–56, 461
Roth, Samuel, 273–94, 506
  background of, 276–78
  criminal convictions of, 215*n*, 273,
    277–78, 289, 318–19, 330, 445,
    474*n*
  numerous imprints used by, 257*n*, 278
  Post Office lectured by, 275–76,
    278–80
  Ulysses excerpts published by, 277, 400
Rothaug, Oswald, 568*n*
Rothko, Mark, 330
Roth v. *Goldman*, 279*n*–80*n*
Roth v. *United States*, 280–326
  Brennan doctrine vs., 412*n*, 499
  briefs amici curiae filed in, 308, 309*n*,
    528
  cases influenced by, 323–26, 337,
    338–42, 363*n*, 365, 377*n*, 398, 399,
    418–19, 423, 428–30, 471*n*, 473,
    575
  at circuit court level, 301, 383–94
  clear and present danger principle in,
    308–15, 541
  Continental Congress letter cited in,
    216*n*–17*n*
  facial unconstitutionality as basis for,
    227*n*, 296–97, 307–8, 573, 576
  Frank's opinion on, 215*n*, 217*n*,
    289–91, 293, 294, 297, 299, 301,
    308, 310, 316*n*, 318, 321, 322*n*, 411
  literary freedom influenced by, 139*n*,
    263–64, 266, 409, 421, 443
  majority opinion written on, 403*n*; *see
    also* Brennan, William J., Jr., on *Roth*
    case
  Memoirs of Hecate County trials vs., 225,
    227*n*, 297, 305
  nude dancing case vs., 294*n*
  pornography discussed in, 297–300,
    316, 412*n*, 571, 589
  social importance test in, 190*n*, 250*n*,
    252, 371*n*, 419, 421–23, 425–26,
    429–30, 435*n*, 445, 457, 472, 492*n*,
    493, 561, 566, 572, 618*n*
  Supreme Court arguments on, 232*n*,
    289, 290–92, 295–326
  two-level approach in, 315, 412*n*,
    415–16, 419, 424, 574

Routh, Brian, 668n, 669
Rubington, Norman, 259n
Rubinstein, Harold, 185
Rubinstein, Nash and Company, 185,
    190n, 192n, 269n
Rudman, Warren, 642
Ruhe, Herbert S., 455, 457, 465
Russell, Bertrand, 142, 145–46
Russell, Vickie, 329
Rutledge, Wiley B., 314n, 317n
Ryan, Michael J., 446, 447
Ryerson, Edward, 353

Sable Communications v. FCC, 683
Sackville-West, Vita, 178, 179, 180, 185,
    193, 394
Sade, Marquis de, 26, 52n, 256, 259n,
    335, 391, 605
Safire, William, 677
St. John-Stevas, Norman, 47n, 97n
St. Martin's Press, 495n
Salome (Wilde), 66
Samson, Maria, 151
Sanctuary (Faulkner), 215n, 251
Sandburg, Carl, 360
Sanger, Margaret, 137–38, 171, 605
Sargent, John Singer, 168
Sartorius, Irving, 27–28
Saturday Review, 134
Satyricon (Petronius), 131
Savoy, 282
Scaife, Roger, 174
Scalia, Antonin, 298n, 569n, 687
SCCA (Southeastern Center for
    Contemporary Art), 629–30, 632,
    634–35
Schachtman v. California, 533, 535, 539,
    540n
Schad v. Mt. Ephraim, 618n, 621n
Schauer, Frederick, 310n, 553n, 585, 606,
    607, 652, 654
Schenck v. United States, 16n, 117n, 436
Schilback, Milton, 223
Schnitzler, Arthur, 72
Schorer, Mark, 335–36
Schroeder, Theodore, 217n
Schuler, J. Carroll, 363
Schuster, M. Lincoln, 150–51
Schuster, Max, 129
Schwartz, Bernard, 274n, 402n
Schwartz, Gary, 450
Schwartz, Louis, 503n
Schwartz, Murray, 278n
Scileppi, John F., 381
Scopes, John, 636
Scott, Barbara, 559
Scott, Cliff, 674–75
Scribner's Magazine, 31–32, 33n
Scribner's Sons, 142, 184, 210
Sears, Alan, 584–85, 599–600, 601, 603
Seaver, Richard, 256, 368, 369, 388

Sebastian, Ellen, 675
Secker, Martin, 61n, 84, 86, 93, 94, 172,
    173
Seiler, Irene, 568n
Selby, Hubert, Jr., 432n
Seldes, Gilbert, 25–26, 73
Seldon, E. S., 395
Seltzer, Adele, 73, 79–80, 81, 82, 83
Seltzer, Thomas, 71, 72–73, 74, 78–84,
    129, 183, 184
Serrano, Andres, 620n, 628–32, 633, 634,
    638, 642, 681
7-Eleven, 600–601, 603
Sex Addicts, The, 499
Sex Life of a Cop, 324, 341, 519, 522–24,
    532
Sex Side of Life, The (Dennett), 323n
Sexton, Lucy, 667
Sexual Inversion (Ellis and Symonds), 52,
    166n, 170–71, 180–81
Sexual Inversion (Westphal), 170
Seymour, Whitney North, 214n, 218,
    224, 227–28, 305n
Shaidell, Donald, 543
Shakespeare, William, 12, 179
Shakespeare and Company, 15n, 20–21,
    25, 27, 35, 38, 54, 144
Shanley, Bernard, 408
Shannon, James, 656
Sharaf, Myron, 347n, 394n
Shaw, George Bernard, 87n, 146n, 177,
    180, 198
Shawn, William, 242
Shay, Felix, 122
Sheen, Bishop Fulton J., 453, 455
Sheinfeld, Lois, 613, 614
Shelley, Percy Bysshe, 146n
Sherman, Stuart Pratt, 115, 133
Shnayerson, Robert, 295n
Shogan, Robert, 525n, 530n
Shorter, Clement, 57, 61n
Shoshana, 507
Show Me! (McBride and
    Fleischhauer-Hardt), 459n, 570
Sign of the Ram, The (Stratton), 597–98
Silone, Mrs. Ignazio, 37
Silvers, Robert, 213n
Simakis, Andrea, 501n
Simon, John F., 402n, 404n, 413n
Simon, Richard, 129
Simon, Sir John, 59, 85, 86
Simon and Schuster, 150–51, 243
Simpson, George, 72–73, 78
Sinclair, Boyd, 232n
Sinclair, Upton, 150, 200
Sirkin, H. Louis, 655
Sischy, Ingrid, 623, 624, 625, 629, 633
Sisco, Elizabeth, 645
Sister Carrie (Dreiser), 98–106, 114
    alterations made in, 100n, 101n, 103,
    104, 109n

Doubleday edition of, 98–105, 112, 129, 250
Jennie Gerhardt vs., 106, 127
later editions of, 100*n*, 101*n*, 104–5, 129
Six Gallery, 330–31
Slaymaker, John Tate, 91
Sloan, John, 661
Smith, Harrison, 197, 203
Smith, Jack, 459
Smith, Joshua, 629
Smith, Lillian (Colonel Barker), 30, 196
Smith, Liz, 657, 658
Smith, Michael, 669
Smith, Samuel, 43–44
Smith, T. R. "Tom," 131, 132, 140, 148, 149
Smith, William French, 583, 585*n*
Smith Act (1940), 158, 318, 509*n*
Smithers, Leonard, 284
Smith v. *California*, 286*n*, 292*n*, 420*n*–21*n*
Snitow, Ann, 597
Snyder, Gary, 330*n*, 349, 350, 387
Society of Authors, 56*n*, 57*n*
Soil, The (Zola), *see Terre, La*
Solomon, Barbara, 358
Solomon, Carl, 346, 350*n*, 352*n*
Solomon, Howard, 444, 447, 449*n*, 457, 458, 478–79
Solomon, Lois, 358
Sons and Lovers (Lawrence), 56, 65, 67–69, 104
Sontag, Susan, 523*n*
Souline, Evgenia, 168, 205, 206
Southeastern Center for Contemporary Art (SCCA), 629–30, 632, 634–35, 637
Southeastern Promotions v. *Conrad*, 621
Southern, Terry, 259, 265, 288*n*, 484–86
Southland Corporation, 600, 601
Span, Paula, 665
Sparkman, John, 535*n*
Spectorsky, A. C., 359
Speiser, Lawrence, 334
Spellman, Francis Cardinal, 226, 227, 235*n*, 406–8, 434, 435, 445, 453, 454, 455, 510*n*, 552
Spelts, Cathryn, 559
Sprayregen, Joel, 237, 363, 365
Sprinkle, Annie, 663, 687
Spritzer, Ralph, 504
Squire, J. C., 63
Stalin, Joseph, 154, 156, 157
Stanley v. *Georgia*, 440, 450*n*, 516*n*, 537*n*, 566, 574, 582*n*
Stein, Gertrude, 25, 193*n*
Steinbeck, John, 203, 278*n*
Steloff, Frances, 251*n*, 367–68, 400*n*
Stephenson, P. R., 85*n*, 86, 87
Stern, Adolph, 73
Stern, Richard, 355, 356, 357, 363

Stevens, John Paul, 621*n*, 652, 685–87
Stevenson, Adlai, 357*n*
Stewart, Ellen, 685*n*
Stewart, Potter:
    as centrist, 540
    Court alliances and, xii, 417, 565*n*, 566*n*
    on *Fanny Hill,* 439
    on *Ginzburg,* 505*n*, 511–12, 515–16
    on *Lady Chatterley* film, 250*n*, 339, 340
    liberal development of, 340*n*, 514–16, 573
    on pornography, 407, 417, 423, 471, 505*n*, 514, 517, 523, 534
    on *Redrup,* 514, 523*n*
    on *Tropic of Cancer* case, 431, 471
Stieglitz, Alfred, 240
Still, Clyfford, 330
Stock, Noel, 8*n*
Stoic, The (Dreiser), 110, 151, 152, 159, 160, 161
Stokes, Rose Pastor, 124
Stone, Geoffrey, 641–42, 647, 653, 687–88
Stone, Harlan, 412
Stone, Laurie, 672
Stopes, Marie C., 30*n*, 171
Story of a Modern Lover, The (Moore), 131
Story of O, The (Réage), 254, 259*n*, 523*n*
Stowe, Harriet Beecher, 40
Strange Fruit (Smith), 30
Stratton, Rebecca, 597–98
Straus, Roger, 212, 221, 226, 233, 234–38, 244–45, 246, 247, 252
Strauss, Peter L., 471*n*
Strunsky, Simeon, 156–57
Studies in the Psychology of Sex (Ellis), 170–71
Studs Lonigan trilogy (Farrell), 215*n*, 251
Sturges, Jock, 606–7, 677
Styron, William, 410–11, 501*n*
Suite 69, 430*n*, 576*n*
Sullivan, Joe, 91
Sullivan, Kathleen, 679
Sullivan, Patrick H., 235
Summerfield, Arthur, 275, 279, 302
Sumner, John S., 135, 147, 218, 231, 588n
    background of, 7, 8–9, 213–14, 237
    Clean Books League backed by, 74, 75, 76, 78
    Comstock succeeded by, 69, 70, 117, 118, 182, 213
    damage suit filed against, 73, 79
    "Genius" censored by, 66*n*, 117–24, 128
    Lady Chatterley's Lover and, 55*n*, 93*n*
    on *Memoirs of Hecate County,* 152*n*, 209, 211, 212, 214–15, 219, 220, 221, 226
    publishers intimidated by, 72, 182–84

Sumner, John S. (*cont.*)
  Ulysses prosecutions and, 7–11, 13, 17*n*
  Well of Loneliness and, 27, 182, 197–98
Sunday Express, 26, 173–74, 175
Sunstein, Cass R., 412*n*, 574*n*, 655
Supreme Court, U.S., 398–416
  alliances among justices of, xii, 31*n*,
    34*n*–35*n*, 233, 274–75, 279*n*, 291,
    314*n*, 401–3, 409, 412–16, 417, 424,
    431, 470*n*, 499, 500–501, 505–6,
    514–17, 528, 529, 534, 535, 549,
    560–62, 565, 566*n*, 573, 621*n*, 652
  Brennan doctrine adopted by, xii,
    11*n*–12*n*, 30*n*
  Catholic judges on, 227, 234, 235*n*
  on child pornography laws, 609*n*–10*n*,
    652
  clear and present danger doctrine of, 31,
    116, 158, 216, 229*n*, 296*n*, 299,
    308–15, 316–17, 318*n*, 443, 541
  confirmation process for, 399*n*, 525*n*,
    530*n*, 547–48
  conservative shift of, 527–28
  constitutional prerogatives of, 290
  courtroom used by, 295*n*
  development of obscenity law by, 139*n*,
    215–16, 266
  on entertainment, 618, 619–21
  on federal postal law, 4–5, 289, 290,
    297–99, 306, 307, 315
  on freedom of artistic expression,
    xii–xiv, 139, 293*n*, 687–88
  homosexual criminalization upheld by,
    166*n*
  institutional restraints on, 547–48
  law clerks for, 399*n*, 419–21
  liberal shift of, 266, 412–15
  on local antipornography statutes, 613,
    614
  McCarthyism and, 158, 227, 406,
    408–9
  obscenity law nationalized by, 33*n*,
    234*n*
  opinion-writing assignments on, 403*n*
  on political speech vs. artistic expression,
    16*n*
  pornography production affected by,
    xii–xiii, 11*n*
  seizures limited by, 87*n*, 212*n*
  state obscenity rulings corrected by, 494
  see also specific cases; specific justices
Suter, Paul, 23
Sutherland, John, 190*n*
Sutro, Gayle, 618
Swaggart, Jimmy, 603
Swanberg, W. A., 101, 102, 106, 109*n*,
  110, 116, 124, 127*n*, 136*n*, 141,
  160*n*, 162–63, 164
Swearingen v. *United States*, 5*n*
Sweeter Than Life (Tryon), 286*n*, 292*n*,
  420*n*

Swift, Jonathan, 12, 395
Swinburne, Algernon Charles, 281
Swope, Herbert Bayard, 144
Symonds, John Addington, 166*n*
Symons, Arthur, 114, 281–82, 283
Symons, Julian, 34

Tablet, 42, 267
Tajiri, Vince, 578
Talese, Gay, 273–74, 513
Tate, Allen, 226*n*, 360
Tatum, Annie, 112–13
Taylor, Joshua, 355, 356
T. B. Peterson and Brothers, 53*n*
Tebbel, John, 6*n*, 18–19*n*, 53*n*, 76*n*,
  148, 102*n*, 103*n*, 213*n*, 220*n*, 237*n*,
  332*n*, 521*n*
Temps, Le, 41
Ten Days That Shook the World (Reed),
  129, 328*n*
Tennery, B. J., 543
Ten North Frederick (O'Hara), 225, 286
Terkel, Studs, 359, 360
Terre, La (The Earth) (Zola), 40–47, 53,
  269, 674
Texas v. *Johnson*, 687*n*
Thayer, Scofield, 11
Theatre of the World Festival, 669–70
"Theodore Dreiser" (Cohen), 132*n*
Thomas, Donald, 52*n*
Thomas, Dylan, 331
Thomas Aquinas, Saint, 391
Thompson, Dorothy, 154
Thompson, Gordon, 565
Thornhill v. *Alabama*, 323
Thornton (Wilson), Elena Mumm, 239,
  241, 242
Three Essays on the Theory of Sexuality
  (Freud), 12*n*
Thurmond, Strom, 411*n*, 459, 548, 552,
  554, 556–57, 589, 627
  Fortas nomination and, 529–30,
    535–37, 538, 539, 540, 542–45, 553,
    589*n*
Thurston, E. Temple, 122
Thurston, Phillip B., 212
Thy Neighbor's Wife (Talese), 273–74
Time, 226
Times (London), 44, 48
Times Film Corp. v. *Chicago*, 414–15
Titan, The (Dreiser), 109, 110, 112–14,
  128
Titus, Edward, 94
Tobey, Esther, 161
Tobriner, Matthew, 419, 422*n*, 429*n*
Tolstoy, Leo, 6, 7, 40, 66, 109
"To the Russian People" (Dreiser), 155
Toynbee, Philip, 268
Trainor, Charles "Chuck," 588, 592
Traveller's Companion Series, 257, 263,
  272

Trefusis, Violet, 180
Tribe, Lawrence, 305n, 613–14n, 646n
Trilling, Diana, 63n
Trilling, Lionel, 22–23, 332, 365
Triumph of Death, The (D'Annunzio), 7
Trocchi, Alex, 256, 259n
Tropic of Cancer (Miller), 366–97, 417–32
  author's work on behalf of, 76n, 122n,
    229n, 312n, 372n, 375, 376, 382,
    392, 397, 417–18, 439, 440–41, 447,
    517n
  Brennan doctrine and, xii, 425–31,
    523n
  California cases on, 122n, 372n, 417,
    418, 419, 519, 572n
  Chicago ban on, 358n, 370–71, 373–80
  Fanny Hill vs., 438
  Florida case on, 372n, 381–83, 396,
    397, 400, 417–18, 424, 426, 431,
    441n, 444, 447, 499n, 532n
  foreign language editions of, 432
  Illinois ruling on, 381–83, 417, 588n
  initial U.S. publication of, 367–72, 385,
    388–89, 391
  Maryland case on, 372n, 392, 417, 439,
    440, 517n
  Massachusetts ruling on, 139, 417,
    418–19
  New York ruling on, 380–81, 417, 423
  Paris edition of, 55n, 366–67
  Supreme Court ruling on, 33n, 122n,
    229n, 234n, 274, 275, 306n, 321,
    324n–25n, 382–83, 396, 397,
    399–400, 405, 407, 420, 422–31,
    434–36, 442, 462, 469, 470–72, 493,
    497–99, 516, 534, 572n, 618n, 620,
    621
Tropic of Capricorn (Miller), 30, 76n, 251,
  392, 410n, 417, 432
Trotsky, Leon, 80n, 117, 129, 153, 154,
  156
Trotter, Philip, 87
Troubridge, Andrea, 174
Troubridge, Una, 167–72, 174, 182,
  192n, 195–96, 198, 202, 204–9
Truman, Harry S, 210, 227, 526n
Tryon, Mark, 292n
Tungelmann, George William de, 63
Twain, Mark, 507
2 Live Crew, xiii, 405n, 441n, 455n,
  620n, 627n, 652n, 656–60, 677, 685
Two Worlds Monthly, 277
Tying Up Rebecca, 607–9
Tytell, John, 331, 334, 391n

Ullrich, Max, 374
Ulysses (Joyce), 7–35
  corrected text of, 15n
  critical reaction to, 25–26, 27, 174n
  Little Review excerpt of, ix, xi, 7–17, 20,
    22, 215

  Martello Tower depicted in, 38–39
  Molly Bloom character in, 23–27
  obscenity test for, xi–xii, 74, 93n, 224n,
    320
  Paris edition of, 15n, 17, 20–21, 25,
    27, 35, 38, 54, 144, 174n
  Samuel Roth's publication of, 277, 400
  seizures of, 28, 32, 54, 174n, 268n,
    367–68n, 406n
  U.S. release of, 17–18, 19, 22n, 27–34,
    35, 65, 130, 144–45, 197, 223–24,
    234, 235, 282, 392n, 493
United States v. *Dennett*, 323n
United States v. *Kennerley*, 425n
Unlit Lamp, The (Hall), 203
Updike, John, 661
Urofsky, Melvin I., 402n
U.S. News and World Report, 674–76

Vance, Carole S., 640n
Vanderbilt, Arthur, 406
Van Doren, Carl, 73
Van Hemert, Susan, 659
van Loon, Hendrick Willem, 129
Van Vechten, Carl, 144
Venus and Tannhäuser (Beardsley), 281–85,
  288, 289n, 298, 304
Victoria, Queen of England, 166
Viking Press, 129, 202, 203, 243
Villiers, 333
Vinson Court, 158n, 233, 248, 318n,
  339n, 509n
Virago, 207n
Visetti, Alberto, 167, 168, 169
Vizetelly, Ernest, 41–42, 44–45, 48,
  49–51
Vizetelly, Henry, xi, 40
  death of, 51n, 52, 71
  imprisonment of, xi, xiii, 47, 51, 52,
    57, 59, 64, 71, 688
  prosecutions of, 44–52, 71
  Zola novels published by, 40–48, 50,
    51, 52
Vizetelly and Company, 40–45, 47–49,
  51, 104
Vollmer (Burroughs), Joan, 344n, 346,
  387, 480–84
Volstead, Andrew, 77n
Volstead Act (1919), 77
von Haselberg, Martin, 668n
von Richtofen, Else, 63
von Richtofen, Friedrich, 63
von Sternberg, Josef, 141n

Wagner, Robert F., 73, 78
Wainhouse, Austyn, 256
Walker, James J. "Jimmy," 75, 77–78, 144
Walker, Samuel, 76n
Walk on the Wild Side (Algren), 212
Wallace, Sir Robert, 193, 194
Wallinger, Aloysius J., 434n

Walpole, Hugh, 122, 185
Wanger, Walter, 140, 141
Warburg, Fredric, 219, 220
Ward v. *Rock Against Racism*, 621
Warhol, Andy, 624, 626
Warren, Dorothy, 87, 88
Warren, Earl:
    appointment of, 235, 408
    Brennan's alliance with, 274–75, 291,
        403, 409, 431*n*, 470*n*, 499,
        500–501, 505–6, 514*n*, 573*n*
    on *Ginzburg*, 500, 502*n*, 503*n*, 505–6,
        512*n*
    popular opposition to, 298, 532*n*
    on profit motive, 572*n*
    puritanical attitudes of, 274, 291, 406,
        409, 412, 499–500, 535
    resignation of, 415*n*, 515*n*, 525–26,
        528, 538, 544, 551, 560*n*, 688
    on review process, 302*n*, 427*n*
    on *Roth* case, 273, 274–75, 295, 305,
        307, 319*n*, 409, 474*n*
    Tropic of Cancer case and, 397, 424
    variable obscenity approach advocated
        by, 423*n*, 556*n*
Warren Court:
    Burger Court's conservativism vs., xii,
        553*n*, 566, 570, 581, 627, 652*n*
    on civil rights cases, 402, 510, 530
    coalitions on, 31*n*, 412–15, 505–6,
        514–17, 566*n*
    on criminal rights cases, 529, 530
    Fortas's admiration for, 459
    on freedom of artistic/sexual expression,
        340, 342, 398–401, 409, 412–15,
        513–19, 539–40, 564*n*, 581, 685
    on freedom of political speech, 117*n*,
        339*n*
    judicial activism of, 296
    Masses doctrine revived by, 117*n*
    obscenity law nationalized by, 201,
        426–29
    pornography permitted by, 298*n*,
        532–43, 554*n*, 582
    progressive decisions of, 30*n*, 236,
        274–75, 450*n*, 513, 546
    public criticism of, 434–36, 439*n*, 511,
        515, 527, 530, 538, 546
    see also specific cases; specific justices
Warren Gallery, 87, 88
Washington Project for the Arts, 633, 648
Washington Times, 598*n*, 662–63, 664,
    674, 675
Waste Land, The (Eliot), 386
Watch and Ward Society, 91, 123, 128,
    135, 174, 183
Watt (Beckett), 55*n*, 258*n*–59*n*
Wayne, Heather, 604
Weaver, Harriet, 18, 145
Wechsler, Herbert, 329, 422
Wedding Night, The (Craddock), 3, 5, 6*n*

Weidenfeld, George, 267–68, 269
Weidenfeld and Nicolson, 266, 267–69
Weiley, Susan, 626–27
Weintraub, Stanley, 283
Weiss, Ted, 682–83
Well of Horniness, The (Hughes), 610–11
Well of Loneliness, The (Hall), 30*n*, 52*n*,
    70, 163–67, 170–82, 184–204
    autobiographical aspect of, 167, 198–99
    Bloomsbury group in support of,
        177–80, 181
    British editions of, 171–74, 176, 207*n*,
        282
    British suppression of, 88, 177–95, 196,
        269
    homosexuality portrayed in, 165–67,
        170–71, 172
    Paris editions of, 176–77, 185, 195,
        196, 202
    success of, 177, 195–96, 202, 207
    U.S. publication of, 27, 145, 174–76,
        182, 184, 196–202, 203
Wells, H. G., 95, 122, 177, 180, 198, 277
Wermiel, Stephen, 677*n*
West, Nathanael, 148
West, Rebecca, 394
West, Robin, 523*n*, 612–13, 617
West, Wilburn C., 434*n*
Western Society for the Suppression of
    Vice, 118
Westphal, Carl, 170
West Virginia Board of Education v.
    Barnette, 308*n*, 314*n*, 616*n*
Whalen, Lawrence, 651
Whalen, Philip, 330*n*, 345, 349
W. H. Allen, 220, 234
White, Byron S.:
    on community values test, 685–86, 687
    Court alliances and, 515, 566*n*, 621*n*
    obscenity rulings by, 424, 431*n*, 534,
        535*n*, 540
    on social importance test, 442, 514,
        516–17
White, G. Edward, 274*n*
White, Katherine A., 244
White, Sarah Osbourne, *see* Dreiser, Sarah
    Osbourne White
Whitehall Review, 42
White Peacock, The (Lawrence), 90
Whitman, Alden, 270
Whitman, Walt, 332
Whittaker, Charles E., 295*n*
Whittenberg, George E., 373–74
Wicke, Lloyd C., 434*n*, 435
Wilde, Oscar, 52, 54, 66, 114, 166, 281
Wilder, George Warren, 111*n*
Wildmon, Allen, 630
Wildmon, Donald, 406*n*–7*n*, 598–99,
    600, 601, 606, 653
    NEA grants and, 629–30, 643, 674*n*,
    678

Wild Palms (Faulkner), 215*n*, 251
Williams, Edward Bennett, 544
Williams, Francis B., 45, 46–47
Williams, Pat, 646, 682
Williams, Tennessee, 467
Williams, William Carlos, 386
Willingham, Calder, 215*n*, 251, 278*n*
Wills, Garry, 633
Wilson, Edmund, 132, 209–42
  career of, 209, 211, 238, 242
  on Chafee's objectivity, 218
  death of, 238, 242
  finances of, 210, 211–12, 219
  journals of, 238–42
  as literary critic, 26, 223, 281, 376
  Nabokov and, 210, 225, 246, 247, 248,
    254*n*, 255, 261
  wives of, 210, 211–12, 219, 239–42
  see also Memoirs of Hecate County
Wilson, Elena Mumm Thornton, 239,
  241, 242
Wilson, John A., 7
Wilson, Margaret Canby, 239, 240–41
Wilson, Robert, 353
Wilson, Woodrow, 116, 124*n*
Wilt, Napier, 355, 356, 357
Winters v. *New York*, 231–32, 310*n*,
  619*n*, 621
Wirin, Al, 419, 422*n*
Wojnarowicz, David, 644
Wolfe, Thomas, 144
Wolfgang, Marvin, 559
Woltman, Frederick, 521
Woman's Life, A (Maupassant), 48*n*
Women Against Pornography, 581, 611
Women in Love (Lawrence), 56, 65, 67
  British publication of, 61*n*, 64
  U.S. publication of, 68, 71, 72–74, 79,
  98
Women of the Left Bank (Benstock), 7*n*,
  10*n*, 19*n*, 21*n*
Wong, Anna May, 144
Wongwon, Chris, 656

Wontner and Sons, 60
Woodruff, Douglas, 267
Woodward, Bob, 274*n*, 399*n*, 419*n*,
  506*n*, 580
Woodward, W. E., 142
Woolf, Leonard, 173, 177, 178, 180, 185,
  187, 189, 192
Woolf, Virginia, 26, 178–80, 181, 185,
  186, 187, 189, 192–93, 277
Woolsey, John M., ix–xii, 29–32, 493
Wooster, Martin Morse, 586*n*
World Publishing Company, 164
Worthy Tradition, A (Kalven), 428–29, 620
Wyatt, Susan, 643–44, 646
Wylie, Andrew, 482
Wylie, Elinor, 144
Wylie, Ida, 173
Wyn, A. A., 346

Yates, Sidney, 634, 636, 637, 638, 641,
  645, 676, 682
Yeats, W. B., 25, 66
Yellow Book, 66, 282
Yerkes, Charles Tyson, 109–10, 113
Yoakum, Robert, 602
Young, Art, 117, 124
Young, Stark, 142
Young Girl's Diary, A, 72, 74, 78, 184
Yudkin, Samuel, 440*n*
Yudkin v. *Maryland*, 440, 517*n*

Zaharias, Mildred "Babe," 464
Zane, Arnie, 677
Zeitlin v. *Arnebergh*, 418, 419, 422*n*,
  429*n*, 497*n*, 572*n*
Zidins, Earle, 446, 477*n*
Zola, Emile, 26, 40–53
  British suppression of, xi, xiii, 6, 47–48,
    50–51, 64, 688
  Dreiser vs., 98, 109, 128
  Nana, 41, 44, 105, 193*n*
  La Terre, 40–47, 53, 269, 674
  U.S. publication of, 99, 100, 104

ABOUT THE AUTHOR

After graduating from the University of Chicago Law School, EDWARD DE GRAZIA practiced communications law and First Amendment law in Washington, D.C. In the course of his career, he has been responsible for freeing from censorship Aristophanes' *Lysistrata,* Henry Miller's *Tropic of Cancer,* William Burroughs's *Naked Lunch,* and the Swedish film *I Am Curious—Yellow.* He has taught at Georgetown University Law School and is a member of the founding faculty of the Benjamin N. Cardozo School of Law (Yeshiva University) in Manhattan. De Grazia is the author of several plays and two previous books, *Censorship Landmarks* and *Banned Films: Movies, Censors and the First Amendment.* A member of PEN American Center's Freedom to Write Committee and a governor of the Law and Humanities Institute, he continues to work for the expansion of literary and artistic freedom. He lives in Greenwich Village.

Windows CE Developer's Handbook

Windows® CE Developer's Handbook™

Terence A. Goggin
with
David L. Heskett and
Jason M. MacLean

SYBEX®

San Francisco • Paris • Düsseldorf • Soest • London

Associate Publisher: Gary Masters
Contracts and Licensing Manager: Kristine O'Callaghan
Acquisitions & Developmental Editor: Brenda Frink
Editor: Sally Engelfried
Project Editor: Bronwyn Shone Erickson
Technical Editor: John Psuik
Book Designer: Kris Warrenburg
Graphic Illustrator: Tony Jonick
Electronic Publishing Specialist: Robin Kibby
Proofreader: Judy Weiss
Project Team Leader: Shannon Murphy
Indexer: Meg Fortune McDonnell
Companion CD: Ginger Warner
Cover Designer: Design Site
Cover Photographer: The Image Bank

Library of Congress Card Number: 99-61299
ISBN: 0-7821-2414-3

Manufactured in the United States of America
10 9 8 7 6 5 4 3 2 1

I dedicate this book to Tim, my brother, my editor, and my best friend. I could not have written this book without you. Your hard work means more to me than I could ever put into words. Thank you.

ACKNOWLEDGMENTS

There are a great many people who made this book possible, and I would like to thank them all.

First, thanks to Ann Goldmann, Brooke Richardson, and Suzanne Lamberton of Waggoner-Eddstrom for helping me on a project that was a little outside of the norm. You really helped me to get started and I want you to know that I appreciate it very much.

To Barry Raymond, Eric Drew, and Norman Hills of Casio's Vertical Markets Division: Thank you for sharing with me some of the unique and exciting projects you've created with Windows CE. Your real-world perspective was extremely helpful and got me started off on the right track.

To Bob Smith, Pat Carrasco, and Cheryl Balbach of Casio New Jersey. It was a pleasure working with you, and I hope you're pleased with the result.

To Scott Crossen, thank you for creating the excellent RAPI source code for Delphi, and thank you for graciously allowing me to reprint it here in this book.

To Helen Chan and Chris Yien of Hewlett-Packard, thank you for your help in completing this book and making sure it contained the very latest information about the newest CE devices.

To everyone at Microsoft who made time to help out: to David Streams, thank you for the initial interview and your insight and advice on what to cover; to Amy Stuhlberg, thank you for stepping in and helping me get in touch with the right people; to Scott Horn and Cyra Richardson, thank you for your advice on what developers want to learn about; to Doug Yip, thank you for putting me in touch with the right people; to Brian Sherrell, thank you for answering all of my questions and helping me sort through the issues; to Scott Henson, thank you for working with me on the promotion of the book before it was even finished; and to Prashant Sridharan, thank you for making sure I had the latest versions of the toolkit. I am indebted to all of you.

To Shirley Macbeth and Liam Cavanagh of Sybase; Neil Shepherd, Jay Botelho, and Etienne Viellard of Oracle; and Larry Lundgren and John Deurbrouck (who wrote the Raima section of Chapter 12) of Raima Corporation, thank you all for providing samples of your products and write-ups of their capabilities.

To Andy Mallinger and Michael Snyders of InstallShield; to Yuko Tanaka, Mike Nydam, Mike Krautkramer, and Dan Spalding of Proxim, Inc.; to Peter Phillips of Socket Communications; and to Tom Carpenter and Mark Gentile of Odyssey Software, thank you for all of your hard work and for making sure that I was able to include your products in the book. I think—and I hope you do, too—that the book is much better for it.

To everyone at Sybex—to Peter Kuhns, who got this whole thing started, thank you for believing in me and in the book. To Brenda Frink and Gary Masters, thank you for taking over and for being so patient. To Bronwyn Erickson, thank you for keeping me organized and focused. Thanks also to Shannon Murphy, Project Team Leader; Robin Kibby, Electronic Publishing Specialist; Kristine O'Callaghan, Contracts and Licensing Manager; and Liz Paulus, Production Technician.

To Sally Engelfried, thank you for doing a great job editing my work. Thank you for being flexible and really working with me on some of the early issues. What more can I say but thank you?

To David Heskett and Jason MacLean, thank you for helping me to complete this book. You guys really pulled through for me, and I appreciate that. You both created some great code, and I hope when it's all done you're as proud of it as I am. But more important than that for me, I wanted to let you know that it was great to work this closely with you both after such a long absence. It's just not the same without you around.

To John Psuik, my technical editor, I've said it before, and I'll say it again: Thank you. Your knowledge, your attention to detail, and your generosity were invaluable. I look forward to working with you on future projects.

Thanks also to Fred Wilf, for your excellent advice.

Last but most, thanks to my dad, who first suggested that I write.

CONTENTS AT A GLANCE

Introduction   *xix*

PART I **Inside the Core Operating System**   **1**

    Chapter 1: What Does CE Do for Me?   3

    Chapter 2: The Three Commandments of Writing for CE   41

    Chapter 3: To C or Not to C?   75

    Chapter 4: CE's Structured Storage   113

PART II **Mastering the Developer's Tools**   **142**

    Chapter 5: CE Toolkit for Visual C++   145

    Chapter 6: Yes, It's Possible—MFC on CE!   173

    Chapter 7: Real MFC Applications Ported to CE   197

    Chapter 8: Visual Basic Toolkit for CE   225

    Chapter 9: A Real VB Application Converted to CE   243

PART III **Advanced Topics**   **278**

    Chapter 10: RAPI: How the Outside World Talks to CE   281

    Chapter 11: How CE Talks to the Outside World   305

    Chapter 12: Third-Party Database Engines   335

    Chapter 13: Windows CE Case Studies and Cost Analysis   361

PART IV   **Finishing Touches**   **373**

Chapter 14: Distributing Your CE Application   375

Chapter 15: Microsoft's Logo Requirements   405

PART V   **Appendices**   **432**

Appendix A: The C Runtime Library Functions of Windows CE   436

Appendix B: The CE 2.0 API   472

Index   *585*

TABLE OF CONTENTS

Introduction		*xix*
PART I	**Inside the Core Operating System**	**1**
1	**What Does CE Do for Me?**	**3**
	What Is CE, Anyway?	4
	Why CE Isn't Windows 98/NT	5
	What Is Unique to CE?	10
	CE Devices	12
	Palm-Size PC Devices	12
	Handheld PC Devices	25
	Handheld PC/Pro Devices	27
	Other Devices	34
	Accessories for CE	36
	Ethernet/Networking Solutions	36
	Bar Code Readers	38
	Summary	38
2	**The Three Commandments of Writing for CE**	**41**
	The First Commandment: Your Application Must Use the Unicode Character Set	42
	Declaring Strings Using Unicode Types Rather Than Char Types	43
	Using Unicode Strings for All Text Literals	46
	Choosing the Correct RTL Functions for Unicode Strings	47
	Equipping Your Program to Handle Two Types of Text Files	48
	The Second Commandment: Your Application Must Be Low-Memory Aware	55
	Keeping the Size and Number of Static Variables to a Minimum	56
	Keeping the EXE File Size Low	56
	Checking the Return Result of Memory Allocation	57
	Mass-Allocating Your Application's Memory	58
	Handling the WM_HIBERNATE Message	60

The Third Commandment: Know Your Form Factor!   61
    The UI of the Application Should Be Tailored to the Device   62
    Maintaining a Single Codebase Is Nearly Impossible   67
    Creating Your Own Conditional Defines   69
    Creating a Runtime Platform Detector   70
Summary   73

3   To C or Not to C?   75

Finding Substitute Functions   77
    calloc()   77
    MoveToEx() / LineTo()   77
    WM_RBUTTONDOWN   78
Changing the Program's Logic: try..catch and Exceptions   79
Writing Your Own Functions   80
    FILE*   81
    fopen()   83
    fclose()   88
    fgetc()   89
    fputc()   90
    fgets()   92
    fputs()   94
    fread()   95
    fwrite()   96
    fprintf()   97
    fscanf()   99
    fseek()   108
Summary   110

4   CE's Structured Storage   113

The Registry   115
    Proper Uses of the CE Registry   116
    Improper Uses of the CE Registry   116
The Windows CE Database Engine   119
    Differences between CE's Database Engine and Familiar
        Database Engines   119
    Similarities between CE's Database Engine and Familiar
        Database Engines   122
The CE Database Engine API   135
Summary   141

PART II   **Mastering the Developer's Tools**   **142**

    5 **CE Toolkit for Visual C++**   **145**

        Using VC++ to Develop for Windows CE   146
            The Windows CE Toolkit for VC++   146
            The Platform SDKs   158
        MFC vs. SDK-Style Coding   160
            Storage Space   161
            Ease of Development   161
        A Sample SDK-Style Application   162
            Displaying a List of Running Tasks   163
            Switching to One of the Tasks   166
            Closing an Application   166
            One Last Snag: Keeping the List of Tasks Current   168
        Summary   170

    6 **Yes, It's Possible—MFC on CE!**   **173**

        New Classes for CE   174
            CCeSocket   175
            CCeDBEnum   176
            CCeDBProp   176
            CCeDBRecord   179
            CCeDBDatabase   179
        Modified Classes   191
            Classes That Lost Functionality   192
            Classes That Gained Functionality   192
        Missing Classes   194
        Summary   194

    7 **Real MFC Applications Ported to CE**   **197**

        The Shopping List Application   198
        Mechanical Issues of Porting   201
            Toolbars and Status Bars   201
            Printing Support   206
            The Grid   207
        Optimizing for CE   217
        One Final Surprise   220
        Summary   222

8   Visual Basic Toolkit for CE   **225**

The Windows CE Toolkit for VB   226
  The Application Templates   226
  The Debugger   228
  The Runtime Files   229
  The Control Manager   230
  The ActiveX Control Pack   231
  The Standard VBCE Controls   235
  The Setup Wizard   236
Changes in the Visual Basic Language   237
A Sample Application   238
Summary   240

9   A Real VB Application Converted to CE   **243**

The Application: International ATM   244
  Porting the ATM Application: Not As Simple As It Looks   246
Mechanical Issues of Porting   249
The Optional Features   262
  Re-Adding the WAV Files   262
  The Country and Flag Bitmaps   266
Optimizing for CE   270
  Eliminating a Form   270
  Eliminating Optional Controls and DLLs   274
  Optimizing the Code Itself   274
Summary   276

PART III   Advanced Topics   **278**

10   RAPI: How the Outside World Talks to CE   **281**

What Is RAPI, Anyway?   282
  General RAPI Management Functions   283
  System Information Functions   285
  Registry Access Functions   287
  File Access Functions   288
  Database Access Functions   292
  Miscellaneous Shell and System Functions   292
A Sample RAPI Application   293
Using Other Languages   298
Summary   302

11 How CE Talks to the Outside World   **305**

What's in the Box?   306
    The Hardware Aspect   306
    The Software Aspect   308
Summary   333

12 Third-Party Database Engines   **335**

Raima's RDM/CE for Data Storage   337
    Network and Relational Data Models   337
    Introducing HpcLadr   338
    Putting RDM to Work   341
Sybase's Adaptive Server Anywhere   341
    Sybase's Adaptive Server Anywhere Sample Application   342
Oracle Lite Introduction   347
    Oracle Lite for Windows CE   348
Comparison of Features   356
Summary   358

13 Windows CE Case Studies and Cost Analysis   **361**

Study 1: Inventory Management System   362
    The Technical Issues   362
    Cost   365
    Conclusion of Study 1   366
Study 2: Insurance Agents in the Field   366
    Solution   367
    The Technical Issues   367
    Cost   368
    Conclusion of Study 2   370
Study 3: Choosing Your Development Machine   370
    Solution   370
    Cost   372
    Conclusion of Study 3   372
Summary   372

PART IV   Finishing Touches   **373**

14 Distributing Your CE Application   **375**

Creating Help for Windows CE   376
    The Two Types of CE Help Files   377

The Single-File Help System   378
The Multiple-File Help System: The HTC File   383
The Multiple-File Help System: The HTP File   386
Getting the Application to the User's Device   389
    The Cab Wizard Option   390
    InstallShield for Windows CE   400
Summary   403

15 Microsoft's Logo Requirements   405

What Is the Logo Program and Why Should You Care?   406
    So What?   407
The Logo Requirements   408
    Installation   409
    UI Requirements   413
    Functionality Requirements   425
    File-Handling Requirements   429
Summary   431

PART V   Appendices   432

A   The C Runtime Library Functions of Windows CE   436

B   The CE 2.0 API   472

Index   *585*

INTRODUCTION

The war on the desktop is over.

Well, okay...maybe it isn't truly *over*, but the focus has definitely shifted a bit.

Suddenly, as if out of nowhere, there appeared a whole new class of Windows-based machines, unlike anything we'd ever seen before. These were the very first Handheld PC (HPC) devices. Soon after, there was a version 2.0 release of Windows CE, and with it, a greater sophistication of devices, as well as a greater variety of form factors and features.

But unlike other flavors of Windows, CE is a brand new Windows operating system, built entirely from scratch. There is no old DOS core—but then again, there's also no backwards compatibility. Instead, CE is a wild mixture of new and old elements. On the one hand, developers can write programs for it using a good portion of the Win32 API. On the other hand, it's amazingly compact and has some very tight memory requirements. Likewise, it's a version of Windows that runs on several different CPUs, yet it has a look and feel that's very close to that of desktop-based Windows.

Developing CE applications is also a strange mix of elements. One moment you're reminded that you're writing applications for a tiny device with a small grayscale screen, and the next moment you think it's just like Windows 98 or NT.

Yes, CE does have some limitations. But in this book, we'll be treating these limitations simply as challenges to be dealt with. Here we'll develop all kinds of applications designed to show off everything that you need to know in order to be a successful CE developer. We'll cover everything from new common controls to memory limitations to dealing with the Unicode character set.

Who Should Read This Book

This book was written with the experienced developer in mind. Perhaps you've been hearing or seeing a lot about Windows CE, and you've decided that you'd like the inside scoop with as little hassle as possible. Or perhaps you've already decided CE is the way to go and you just need a way to dive right in. Or maybe you're interested in CE for some other reason completely.

In any event, this book assumes that you are an experienced Windows developer, with at least the ability to read C/C++, Visual Basic, or Delphi source code. This book assumes that you know the basics of Windows programming tasks such as creating a window, adding items to a list box, etc.

Instead of re-emphasizing the basics, this book concentrates on the differences between Windows 98/NT and Windows CE. It spells out exactly what you need to know to navigate the ins and outs of Windows CE.

What This Book Contains

This book uses numerous examples in C/C++, Visual Basic, and even Delphi to demonstrate Windows CE programming techniques. There is a sample program for each technique discussed in the book, and the source code for each of these programs can be found on the CD.

The book is organized into five major sections:

Part I: Inside the Core Operating System

Part II: Mastering the Developer's Tools

Part III: Getting the Most Out of Windows CE

Part IV: Finishing Touches

Part V: Appendices

Part I: Inside the Core Operating System

The main purpose of this section is to lay out exactly what Windows CE offers developers, both in terms of hardware and software. You'll jump right into code in Chapter 1, learning about the different hardware platforms and how to work with what each one offers. For example, how *do* you use a CE device to output graphics to a VGA monitor?

Chapter 2 details some of the main differences between Windows 98/NT programming and Windows CE programming. Some of the topics covered here include getting your application to look good on all of the CE form factors, working with the Unicode character set, and memory allocation issues.

Chapter 3 highlights some of the functions and features missing from Windows CE and demonstrates solid techniques for replacing or working around the missing functionality. For instance, when you're developing for certain CE platforms, you don't have a `stdio.h` available. Of course, this makes it very difficult to port existing code...unless, of course, you recreate the missing file-access functions of `stdio.h` as we do in this chapter!

In the last chapter of this section, Chapter 4, the book introduces a feature of CE not available on any other operating system: a built-in database engine. Windows CE is one of the few—if not the only—operating systems to offer a database engine as part of the operating system itself, and this chapter shows you how to make the best use of it.

Part II: Mastering the Developer's Tools

In this section, we look at how to best utilize the tools Microsoft makes available for us. Specifically, Chapter 5 discusses the Windows CE toolkit for Visual C++. You'll learn how to deal with common problems encountered with the toolkit. In addition, the chapter analyzes the tradeoffs between SDK-style C programming and MFC programming for CE.

In Chapter 6, we'll look at the differences between MFC on Windows 98/NT and MFC on Windows CE. Specifically, we'll look at some new classes to deal with CE's Database Engine and its communications model. And, as you may have guessed, there are also a few classes that don't exist under CE, and some that have undergone changes.

In Chapter 7, we'll see exactly what it takes to port a real Windows 98/NT MFC application to Windows CE–based MFC. We'll cover issues ranging from the basic port to printing support.

In Chapter 8, we explore the Windows CE toolkit for Visual Basic. There are some areas where the toolkit for Visual Basic can present some real surprises for anyone who's used to working with Visual Basic for Windows 98/NT, and this chapter looks at both the surprises and features.

In Chapter 9, just as we did in Chapter 7, we'll port a real Windows 98/NT Visual Basic application to Windows CE. We'll explore all aspects of what has to happen before we can take a working desktop VB application and produce a solid VB application.

Part III: Getting the Most Out of Windows CE

In this section, we take full advantage of the more advanced features of the CE operating system. Specifically, in Chapter 10, we look at how desktop machines and desktop applications can communicate with Windows CE devices. Using the Remote API (or RAPI), desktop applications can access a surprisingly rich set of features on the CE device. What's more, we'll even see how RAPI programs can be written in any desktop application development language—even a non-Microsoft product like Borland's Delphi can talk to CE devices, thanks to RAPI!

In Chapter 11, we'll explore all forms of Windows CE communications. CE devices have a multitude of possible ways to communicate with the outside world, and this chapter looks at all of them: the serial port, the IR port, modems, PCMCIA devices, and Winsock connections!

In Chapter 12, we look at ways to extend the usefulness of Windows CE devices by examining the features of some third-party CE Database Engines. Oracle, Sybase, and Raima Corporation offer the three leading third-party database engines available for Windows CE. Each of these vendors has created a sample application and a brief article describing the application and/or the features of their engine.

Chapter 13 offers something few programming books do: pseudo case studies. Based on real case studies but modified to be general enough to apply to anyone, these case studies present a view of what it takes to put together a full Windows CE–based solution for your clients, whether you're a consultant or a part of a corporation's IS department.

Part IV: Finishing Touches

In this section, we look at some additional touches you might want to put on your application. In Chapter 14, we look at what it takes to create a help system—whether it's one simple file or multiple files—for your CE application. Also, we'll look at what it takes to create a simple setup program for your application, either by hand or using a third-party tool.

Then, in Chapter 15, we'll explore what the Windows CE Logo Program is all about and how it can help you. We'll see how, in addition to ensuring that your application has a standard consistent look and feel, the Logo Program can help you market your CE application much more effectively.

Part V: Appendices

To round out the book, we've included two of the most useful appendices possible. Appendix A details all of the C runtime library functions guaranteed to be available for *all* CE versions/platforms. Using this appendix as a guide, you can safely pick and choose which runtime functions to use if you're compiling an application for more than one CE version/platform. As an added benefit, the header file and a simple example are provided for each and every function.

Appendix B takes a similar approach to the Windows CE API. In this appendix, we detail every single API call that is unique to Windows CE 2. For every function, we list the header file, a description of the function's purpose, and a sample demonstrating the use of the function.

Perhaps the best feature of this section is that both of these appendices are provided on the CD in PDF form, so that you can easily load each appendix, browse to the function you want, and copy/paste the function's example right into your own code.

About the Examples

The majority of the examples in this book were written in Microsoft Visual C++ 6 with the Windows CE Toolkit for VC++ 6. There are also examples that were created in Visual Basic 5/6, with the appropriate version of the Windows CE toolkit for Visual Basic. Also, in Chapters 10 and 14, there are two samples developed using Borland's Delphi product.

As of this writing, Microsoft has the only C/C++ based compiler that builds applications for the Windows CE operating system. Although there is talk on the newsgroups about a possible GNU compiler port, no such product has yet been released.

PART I

Inside the Core Operating System

■ CHAPTER 1: What Does CE Do for Me?

■ CHAPTER 2: The Three Commandments of Writing for CE

■ CHAPTER 3: To C or Not to C

■ CHAPTER 4: CE's Structured Storage

CHAPTER
ONE

1

What Does CE Do for Me?

■ What is CE, Anyway?

■ Why CE isn't Windows 98/NT

■ Features Unique to CE

■ CE Devices: Shapes, Sizes, and What You Need to Know About Each One

■ CE Accessories

In a promotional video sent out by Microsoft late last year, Harel Kodesh of Microsoft's Consumer Appliances Group was quoted as saying, "CE was built with one thing in mind, and that is powering information appliances." These information appliances give people such a degree of freedom and power in their personal and business lives that they've created an instant market for new software.

A large part of what makes these devices so powerful is that they're not just organizers or wizards. Yes, every CE device comes with pocket versions of Outlook, but you can run real applications on the devices, too.

In many ways, Windows CE puts a virtual desktop computer in the palm of your hand or in your pocket. It's that capability that makes Windows CE a "shrunken head" version of Windows 98/NT, as we'll see in this chapter. We call CE a shrunken head version of Windows because you have to work with far less memory than you are used to, smaller screens, fewer colors, etc.

The questions we'll be answering in this chapter are, "What does CE do for me?" and, "How can I get my programs ported to CE?" To answer them, we'll look at the different types of CE devices and what each one offers in terms of functionality. In many cases, you'll be surprised to find out just how powerful a CE device can be. Despite their small sizes, their CPUs rival those we have in our desktop computers.

We'll also be looking at some of the CE-compatible hardware you can add to your application to make it a more complete CE solution. For instance, what if you need to add some kind of secondary storage to your device because 8MB just isn't enough? That said, let's get right into it with a look at the different device types.

What Is CE, Anyway?

Windows CE is a stripped-down version of Windows 98/NT that's been engineered specifically for small, low-resource, portable devices such as:

- The Palm-size PC
- The Handheld PC
- The Handheld PC/Pro

From an end user's point of view, it is a miniature Windows, complete with a pocket version of Outlook, Start button, and Taskbar. However, there are a few significant differences between CE and 98/NT. After all, if you're going to take the world's most popular desktop operating system and make an embedded, tiny version of it, you end up sacrificing some features.

> **NOTE** According to Microsoft, CE doesn't officially stand for anything at all; however, it's generally assumed that CE means *consumer edition* or *compact edition*.

Why CE Isn't Windows 98/NT

CE and Windows 98 differ in five major ways:

- CE won't run your existing programs
- CE has serious memory constraints
- CE has a reduced runtime library and API
- CE devices usually don't have a mouse
- CE hardware is not very standardized

Of course, there are ways to deal with each of these differences, and we'll be looking at them in more detail in later chapters. For now, here's what all this means.

CE Won't Run Your Existing Programs

Perhaps the biggest difference between the two operating systems is the fact that CE will not run *any* existing Windows applications. This means that all programs must be recompiled especially for the Windows CE operating system. This is a striking departure from the backwards compatibility goals of Windows 98 and NT.

CE Has Serious Memory Constraints

In recent years, the amount of memory in any given PC has gone up astronomically. That's why, under Windows 98, there is usually plenty of memory to go around. Under Windows CE, however, that's not always the case. And, since this is one of the main reasons you can lose your way, we'll pay a lot of attention to it. When it comes to CE's memory constraints, there are three key issues:

- Reduced amounts of physical memory

- User control over memory availability

- Operating system requests to your program

Reduced Amounts of Physical Memory Most CE devices ship with comparatively little physical memory to begin with. The Palm-size PC devices, for example, usually have just 4 or 8MB. For a Windows 98 machine, such a small amount of memory would be ridiculous.

NOTE However, the amount of physical memory in CE devices is set by the manufacturer, and there really isn't a whole lot you, as a developer, can do about it. Most of the makers of Palm-size PC devices seem to feel that 4MB is an adequate amount of RAM for their devices, and, truth be told, they're correct. The operating system and most CE applications will run quite comfortably under these conditions. While it is possible to upgrade the amount of RAM in many of these devices, asking your users to upgrade is not a preferred option. Before doing that, try eliminating some noncritical features to reduce the requirements of your application.

User Control over Memory Availability When Microsoft and the various CE device makers collaborated on the designs and standards for CE devices, they decided that CE devices would not come with hard drives. This was probably so they could hit a lower price point.

To compensate for the lack of true "secondary storage," Microsoft chose to make the physical memory (RAM) serve two purposes: our more traditional understanding of *RAM* (program memory) and a sort of *RAM-disk* (storage memory).

The result of this is that you do not have complete control over how much memory is available for your program. Unfortunately, the user of the device largely controls the allocation of memory into program memory and storage memory. And, although the user can't adjust the settings so that no programs will run, they can adjust it so fewer programs will run. Or, they can adjust it so programs with greater memory needs don't run properly.

With Windows 98, of course, the user has no such control. The amount of physical memory is the amount of RAM, and the size of the disk is the size of the disk.

On the other hand, if enough memory is available on your CE device, your program will continue to steam right along, with the advantage that all the memory it needs is already reserved for its use.

Operating System Requests to Your Program   All CE programs must be able to handle low-memory situations. Specifically, they should try to relinquish some of the memory they're using whenever the operating system requests it. This is a complete departure from what you're used to doing in Windows 98.

For this reason and others, you are going to have to pay infinitely more attention to memory when writing your Windows CE programs. In fact, it may not be going too far to say that memory is, perhaps, the most important CE issue you have to understand before tackling your program. We'll deal with these memory issues in more detail in Chapter 2.

CE Has a Reduced Runtime Library and API

A big difference between Windows CE and the Windows 98/NT platforms is the scaled-down C/C++ runtime library (RTL) and API of Windows CE. Many of the more common ANSI functions have been substituted with Windows API functions or removed entirely. In other words, your existing Windows programs probably won't compile for CE the first time out, and you'll have to make a few modifications. In Chapter 3, we'll look at some of the functions that are missing from the RTL and API, and what we can do to fix this situation.

CE Devices Usually Don't Have a Mouse

Under Windows 98, the mouse is used to control an application and its appearance—that is, select objects, resize windows, drag things around the screen, and navigate menu items. Very few Windows 98 programs can be reasonably operated without a mouse.

However, most Windows CE devices do not have a mouse. Instead, CE devices have a penlike tool called a *stylus*. Unlike a mouse, a stylus has no constant visual representation on the screen. In other words, there's no cursor.

NOTE   There is only one CE device that has a mouse: the Hewlett-Packard Jornada HPC/Pro device, which we'll be looking at later in this chapter.

What You Need to Know about the Stylus Unlike the always-present mouse of Windows 98/NT, CE's stylus only interacts with the operating system and the applications when the user taps (or taps and holds) it to the screen. CE users can still efficiently select objects, navigate menu items, etc. However, there are some areas where the stylus-as-a-mouse substitute just doesn't cut it; for instance, resizing windows and right-clicking. In fact, resizing windows is so difficult with a stylus, Microsoft removed that functionality completely! This means that no CE windows can be resized at all. Under CE, windows are either maximized or fixed at whatever size they're created.

Right-clicking is available, but it can be a chore for a user. When the user wants to right-click on something, they must hold down the Alt key and tap the screen with the stylus at the same time—a very awkward procedure. It's so inconvenient, in fact, that you probably won't want to use pop-up/right-click menus at all.

NOTE If you still want to include right-click functionality in your application, see Chapter 3 for a demonstration of how to trap the Alt-click combination.

The upshot of all this is that it's not a good idea to have your program rely too heavily on right-click operations. Similarly, unless your application is a dialog-based app that doesn't require the full screen, you'll probably want to launch most of your programs in a maximized window, since there's no way for the user to resize the window with the stylus.

WARNING Using the Alt-click combination for right-click functionality only applies to the HPC and HPC/Pro devices—Palm-size PCs don't have any mechanism for right-clicking at all!

CE's Hardware Is Not Very Standardized

With Windows 98, your programs are likely to run on fairly standardized hardware. Everybody's running an Intel (or compatible) chip, some reasonable amount of memory, a 16- or 256-color display, and at least 640 × 480 resolution. With very few limitations, it's expected that everything's going to work the same on any Windows 98 machine.

That's not the case under CE, though. Each manufacturer designs their devices differently, and CE devices don't have a single standard configuration as PCs do. For instance, some CE devices run on a Hitachi microprocessor, while others run on a chip from NEC. Some devices have a color display, while others have only grayscale. And some devices run 640 × 240 display, while others run a 240 × 320 display.

The key differences between manufacturers' CE devices are:

- Chip type
- Display type
- Display size

Chip Type When using Microsoft's CE development tools, you are required to compile your program once for each of the chip types supported by CE. It's then up to you to test your program on each of the chip types, and it's up to your install program to copy the correct executable file when it uploads the file to the user's device. Of course, this also means that unless you want to tie your application to a specific processor or device, you probably want to stay away from any assembler.

Display Type Some of the Handheld PC models have a color display; others have only grayscale. So, unless you are targeting a specific device, model, and manufacturer (e.g., Casio PA-2500), you probably don't want your program to rely too heavily on any color-related operations. Clearly, you wouldn't want your program to tell a user with a grayscale device to "click the red button."

Display Size If you design your application for the Handheld PC devices, they will probably look fine on all of those devices. However, if you merely recompile for the Palm-size PC devices, the application probably won't even be useable. This is because Handheld PCs generally have a display of about 640 × 240, whereas most Palm-size devices have a display of only 240 × 320. This makes it challenging to design one application for multiple devices.

While it might be *possible* to simply recompile an HPC application for the PPC platform, it probably wouldn't be a good idea. If you did, half of your program's main window would likely be outside the visible area of the display! In the next chapter, we will examine how to change a few simple elements of your program in order to make this recompilation possible.

Now that you know how CE isn't Windows 98/NT, let's take a look at some of the features that make CE unique and special.

What Is Unique to CE?

Although there are a lot of things CE doesn't do—from a Windows 98/NT developer's perspective, that is—there are also a lot of things that it does do. And, given the small size of CE, some of these items are quite impressive.

Core OS Features

First, there are the core operating system features. Windows CE is a 32-bit, multitasking, multithreaded operating system. It will address memory using the flat memory model, run multiple programs at once, and support multiple threads in a program. In other words, its architecture is based on 98/NT's architecture.

Networking- /Internet-Related Features

CE supports Winsock 1.1 for writing custom Internet applications and supports portions of the WinInet library so that your CE application can retrieve documents via HTTP operations. CE also supports network shares accessing on Desktop/server-based Windows machines. Later in this chapter, we'll see how it's possible to get your CE device onto your network using some third-party hardware.

Communications

Windows CE devices support communication over a serial port or an Infrared (IR) port. Because the serial port is a standard serial port just like the one(s) on your PC, you can connect standard modems and other serial devices to a CE device's serial port. This can be a big cost saving to your users, who might otherwise believe that only expensive cellular modems will work with CE, when a standard external modem will do the trick.

The IR port is especially efficient if your application needs to transfer data between two CE devices. While it's possible to transfer data between serial ports, the IR port is much faster and much more convenient to the end user. After all, there are no cables to connect—you just point the two devices at each other and click OK.

Databases

When doing database development for Desktop-based Windows platforms, you must select and purchase some kind of third-party database engine, or you must choose a development tool that includes a database engine. One of the qualities that makes CE unique, however, is that the operating system itself has support and functionality for creating and accessing databases from within your programs. CE is the *only* operating system with database functionality built right into the OS itself. Granted, it's not a very sophisticated database engine, but it should meet most simple needs. This will save you the time and money associated with choosing and purchasing a third-party engine.

Just How Powerful Is a CE Device, Anyway?

Most developers are surprised to learn just how powerful a CE device really is. In fact, many of the CE devices sport CPUs that, while impressive by themselves, are even more impressive when compared to a Desktop system's CPU.

For instance, the Casio E-11 features an NEC VR4111, which is a 64-bit chip that runs at 80MHz! The dhrystone rating on this chip is 105. (Dhrystone is a benchmarking test used to rate how fast a chip can do integer-based operations. The score indicates millions of instructions per second, so a higher number is better.)

Similarly, the Hewlett-Packard Jornada HPC/Pro device uses a strongARM processor, which is a 32-bit chip that has a dhrystone rating of 220. Considering that a typical 133MHz Pentium has a dhrystone rating of about 240, these are very impressive numbers!

Here's a practical example, however, that's even more telling than these ratings. When the Palm-size PCs were first released, CE development newsgroups debated whether or not the PPC devices would be powerful enough to play MP3 music files. As you probably know, MP3s are very tightly compressed, very high quality sound recordings. Because they are so tightly compressed, their playback is an incredibly CPU-intensive task—so much so that it's generally assumed that you need a Pentium running at 100MHz just to get decent, uninterrupted listening. Many people argued that the CPUs of the Palm-size devices simply could not process the decompression fast enough to be practical for the playback of MP3s.

After several months, the debate was finally settled when XAudio of Mountain View, California (`http://www.xaudio.com`) released their XAudio MP3 player for Windows CE. Although the product is still in beta form as of this writing, it does, in fact, play MP3 files on any Palm-size PC device. And it does it very well!

If a Palm-size PC can handle the complex operations required to play an MP3 file without skipping and dropping sections of the recording, it ought to be powerful enough to do just about anything (within the limits outlined in this and the next several chapters)!

CE Devices

There are currently four distinct types of CE devices, each with its own purpose:

- Palm-size PC devices
- Handheld PC devices
- Handheld PC/Pro devices
- Devices that don't fall into the above categories

Palm-Size PC Devices

Palm-size PCs (or PPCs) are usually the smallest of the Windows CE devices, with approximately the same dimensions as a package of 3 × 5-inch index cards. They have a long, narrow, portrait-oriented display; no true keyboard; a touch screen; and integrated voice recording features. In addition, all PPC devices have a Compact Flash slot, which can be used to add additional memory or peripheral devices to the PPC.

The shape and portability of PPC devices make them ideal for applications that allow the user instant, "on the road" access to some specific kind of data, with a minimum of data entry. Figure 1.1 shows an example of a Palm-size PC device, the Casio E-11.

There are several features that make PPCs different from other CE devices:

- Display
- Lack of a true keyboard
- The Ink control
- The CapEdit control
- Voice recording and playback services

FIGURE 1.1:

The Casio E-11

Copyright Casio © 1999

Display

The first thing that makes the display on a PPC so unique is that it is portrait-oriented, as illustrated in Figure 1.2. As you probably realize, this is a sharp contrast to the Desktop world, where everything is more landscape-oriented than anything else.

In addition to its unusual orientation, the display on a PPC is very small, typically around 240 × 320 pixels. This, too, contrasts to the Desktop world where we can expect at *least* 640 × 480. Obviously, this means that a lot more thought must go into the design of dialogs and windows to get them to look decent in such a tight space.

The final element of the display that makes it unusual when compared with our Desktop programming is that it is only a four-color grayscale LCD. In the Desktop world, we can count on 16 colors at the bare minimum.

FIGURE 1.2:

Portrait vs. landscape orientation

NOTE As this book was going to press, HP announced a color PPC device.

Together, these elements mean that you're going to have to pay much more attention to your visual design. In many cases, you will end up having to reduce the width of any control on your windows or dialogs simply because you've got to fit everything into such a small space. Figures 1.3 and 1.4 show sample dialogs designed for Windows 98/NT and a Palm-size PC, respectively.

FIGURE 1.3:

A dialog designed for Windows 98/NT

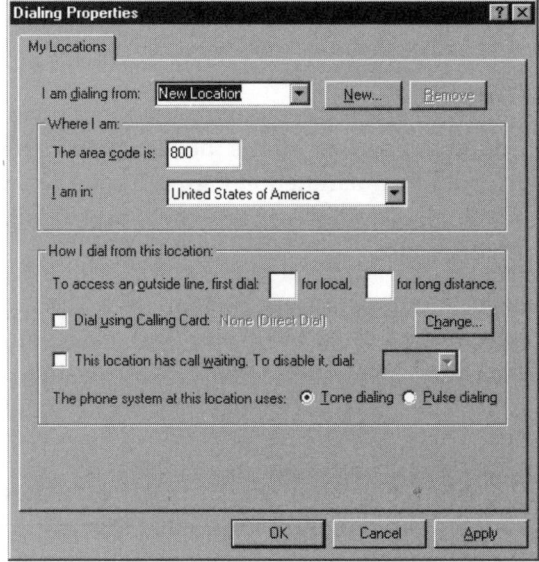

FIGURE 1.4:

A dialog designed for a PPC device

As you can see, making this dialog work on a PPC involved stacking the various controls a little more closely and making each control just a little bit narrower. If we wanted to, we could also have used a tabsheet control to help break up the various controls into two distinct sections.

Lack of a True Keyboard

Palm-size PCs do not have a physical keyboard. Instead, they have a "virtual keyboard," a pop-up panel, called the System Input Panel, that displays letters and numbers in a QWERTY arrangement. The user taps out the keys on this panel with the stylus. The System Input Panel can be raised and lowered as needed, as shown in Figures 1.5 and 1.6, respectively.

As you can imagine, this can create havoc for your program. When the Input Panel is raised, it occupies roughly one-third of the display area. To accommodate it and to give your program some control over how it interacts with the Input Panel, there are two modifications you need to make to any PPC application:

- Programmatically raise and lower the Input Panel
- Detect when the user pops up the Input Panel

FIGURE 1.5:

The Input Panel raised

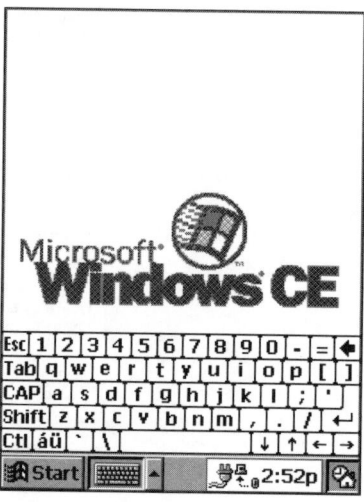

FIGURE 1.6:

The Input Panel lowered

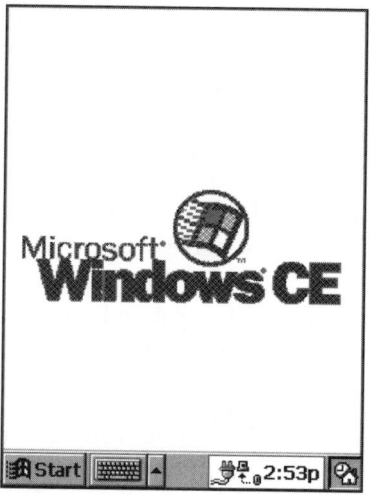

Programmatically Raise and Lower the Input Panel   You need to be able to raise and lower the Input Panel programmatically because not all of your programs will use the Input Panel in the same way, or to the same extent. For example, if you designed a blackjack game for CE, you would probably want to hide the

Input Panel when the game started because the user probably won't need the keyboard in a blackjack game.

Similarly, if you designed some kind of data entry application, it would make your program friendlier if you showed the keyboard when the program started. For these reasons, you need to be able to control the Input Panel's state. In Chapter 15, we'll explore exactly how to do this.

Microsoft already provides code to lower the Input Panel, so you only have to write the code to raise the Input Panel. The original lowering code, as provided by Microsoft, looks like this:

```
BOOL LowerSip( void )
{
    BOOL fRes = FALSE;
    SIPINFO si;
    memset( &si, 0, sizeof( si ) );
    si.cbSize = sizeof( si );
    if( SHSipInfo( SPI_GETSIPINFO, 0, &si, 0 ) )
    {
        si.fdwFlags &= ~SIPF_ON;
        fRes = SHSipInfo( SPI_SETSIPINFO, 0, &si, 0 );
    }
    return fRes;
}
```

What's happening here is that you're first filling a structure (si) of type SIPINFO. For our purposes here, though, you're only interested in one member of the structure, fdwFlags, which you'll use to set the state of the panel. There are three possible values for the fdwFlags member:

- SIPF_ON   The panel is visible.

- SIPF_DOCKED   The panel is attached to the Taskbar.

- SIPF_LOCKE   The panel is locked in place, and its state cannot be changed by the user.

NOTE   These values can then be combined by using the AND (&&) and OR (||) operators. Although the second two fdwFlags values are not of interest to us here, they do have meaning for other programs. For instance, with regard to the second value SIPF_DOCKED, some Input Panels allow themselves to be detached from the toolbar and dragged around the screen much like a dockable toolbar.

To lower the panel, all you have to do is remove the SIPF_ON value from the fdwFlags member. Do this by using AND on the current value of fdwFlags with the logically negated SIPF_ON code. Then, write your si structure back to the Input Panel, and it lowers itself. Return the result of your work, and you're done. The following code is an example of this procedure:

```
si.fdwFlags &= ~SIPF_ON;
```

Then, write your si structure back to the Input Panel, which then lowers itself:

```
fRes = SHSipInfo( SPI_SETSIPINFO, 0, &si, 0 );
```

Return the result of your work, and you're done:

```
return fRes;
```

Using this piece of code as a model, you can see that to get a routine that *raises* the Input Panel, all you need to change is the line that sets the value of fdwFlags. In other words, instead of removing the SIPF_ON flag, use OR on fdwFlags, as in the following:

```
si.fdwFlags |= SIPF_ON;
```

Or, when put into the full routine:

```
BOOL RaiseSip( void )
{
    BOOL fRes = FALSE;
    SIPINFO si;
    memset( &si, 0, sizeof( si ) );
    si.cbSize = sizeof( si );
    if( SHSipInfo( SPI_GETSIPINFO, 0, &si, 0 ) )
    {
        si.fdwFlags |= SIPF_ON;
        fRes = SHSipInfo( SPI_SETSIPINFO, 0, &si, 0 );
    }
    return fRes;
}
```

But raising and lowering the Input Panel is only one of the two requirements you need to take care of to manage the Input Panel's interaction with your programs. The second requirement is much more involved.

Detecting When the User Pops Up the Input Panel You've got to be able to detect when the user pops up the Input Panel because the Input Panel occupies so much of the screen area when it's visible. Your application will be much more user-friendly if it resizes itself and allows the user to scroll the window whenever the Input Panel is shown.

You can observe this behavior in the Owner control panel applet. With the Input Panel lowered, all of the controls are visible and the window does not have a scroll bar, as shown in Figure 1.7. When you show or raise the Input Panel, the Owner window actually resizes itself and adds a scrollbar on its right side, as shown in Figure 1.8. The user can then scroll to that portion of the window that would otherwise be obscured by the Input Panel.

FIGURE 1.7:

The Owner applet with the Input Panel lowered

FIGURE 1.8:

The Owner applet with the Input Panel raised

As you can probably guess, CE provides a way to detect the state change in the Input Panel, and Microsoft even provides a sample of how to do this. However, their sample is incomplete in that it doesn't show how to add the scroll bar to the application based on the state of the Input Panel. To get your application working as smoothly as possible, you'll need to take their sample and make it complete.

This can get a bit confusing, so let's start by looking at some simplistic pseudo-code for the logic at work here:

```
If we're showing our scroll bar
      and If the input panel is not visible
            Then let's hide our scroll bar.
Otherwise (we're not showing our scroll bar)
      and If the input panel is visible
            Then let's show our scroll bar.
```

WARNING This logic assumes that your application doesn't normally need a scroll bar and that it only displays one when the user pops up the Input Panel.

Start by adding a handler for the Windows CE message that tells you one of the system settings has changed. When the Input Panel's state changes, CE will send you a WM_SETTINGCHANGE message with the wParam value set to SPI_SETSIPINFO:

```
case WM_SETTINGCHANGE:
        switch( wParam )
        {
            case SPI_SETSIPINFO:
```

Then, just as you did when you wanted to show or hide the Input Panel, fill your si variable (of type SIPINFO) with information about the Input Panel:

```
memset( &si, 0, sizeof( si ) );
si.cbSize = sizeof( si );
if( SHSipInfo( SPI_GETSIPINFO, 0, &si, 0 ) )
{
```

Your next task is to check whether or not your application already has a scroll bar visible. Do this by retrieving the current window style by calling GetWindowLong()

and passing GWL_STYLE as the second parameter. GetWindowLong() returns a Long integer; store it into a variable called lWndStyle:

```
lWndStyle = GetWindowLong(hWnd, GWL_STYLE);
```

Then check to see if you're already displaying a scroll bar by comparing lWnd-Style against WS_VSCROLL style:

```
if (lWndStyle & WS_VSCROLL)
{
```

If you are already showing a scroll bar, then you've got to decide whether or not to hide it based on whether or not the Input Panel is hidden. You must then check the fdwFlags value of your si (SIPINFO) variable to see if the Input Panel is still visible:

```
if (!(si.fdwFlags & SIPF_ON))
{
```

If the Input Panel is hidden, use AND on lWndStyle and the logical negation of WS_VSCROLL together in order to remove the WS_VSCROLL style and, therefore, the scroll bar itself:

```
lWndStyle &= ~WS_VSCROLL;
```

Finally, make your changes take hold by calling SetWindowLong(), passing in the newly modified style:

```
SetWindowLong(hWnd, GWL_STYLE, lWnd-
Style);
        }
    }
```

If, however, you're not showing your scroll bar and the Input Panel is visible, show your scroll bar by using OR on the WS_VSCROLL style with your lWndStyle:

```
else
{
    if (si.fdwFlags & SIPF_ON)
    {
        lWndStyle |= WS_VSCROLL;
```

Then—just as you did above—make your window take on the new style by calling SetWindowLong(), passing in the new lWndStyle:

```
                              SetWindowLong(hWnd, GWL_STYLE, lWnd-
Style);
                    }
          }
```

Next—and this is the core piece from the Microsoft sample code—resize your window to whatever the visible screen area is. The SIPINFO structure, which has as one of its members a RECT representing the visible desktop area, allows you to do this. In code, the entire operation can be done in one call to MoveWindow():

```
          MoveWindow(
                    hWnd,
                    si.rcVisibleDesktop.left,
                    si.rcVisibleDesktop.top,
                    si.rcVisibleDesktop.right -
si.rcVisibleDesktop.left,
                    si.rcVisibleDesktop.bottom -
                    si.rcVisibleDesktop.top,
                    TRUE );
          }
          break;
```

Finally, to ensure that your application can detect the state of the Input Panel when it starts, you must manually send your program a WM_SETTINGCHANGE message in the WM_CREATE message handler:

```
SendMessage(hWnd, WM_SETTINGCHANGE, SPI_SETSIPINFO, 0);
```

You're finished. Now your applications will behave correctly and interact as efficiently as possible with the Input Panel.

NOTE   You'll also need a message handler for the WM_VSCROLL message to handle any requests that the user might make while the scroll bar is visible. This code is included on the CD in the samples for this chapter.

The Ink Control

Because most of the input to the system is done via a touch screen, it seems only natural that the PPCs have a control that accepts handwriting input. It's called the

Ink control, and it will record any mixture of handwritten and typewritten data. This control is especially useful in applications where a signature is needed.

WARNING   The Ink control does not do any handwriting recognition; any handwritten data that it stores is stored as graphical, rather than textual, data.

Working with the Ink control is a bit trickier than you might imagine. In fact, there are three steps required just to create an individual Ink control within your own application.

1. Initialize the common control library:

    ```
    InitCommonControls();
    ```

2. Specifically initialize the Ink (or InkX as it is alternately called) control:

    ```
    InitInkX();
    ```

3. Call `CreateWindow()`, specifying `WC_INKX` as the window class:

    ```
    hInk = CreateWindow(WC_INKX, TEXT(""),
                        WS_VISIBLE | WS_CHILD | WS_BORDER,
                        5, 90, 200, 160, hWnd,
                        NULL, hInst, NULL);
    ```

WARNING   Note that `WC_INKX` is not an `lpClassName` string, but rather a defined constant to be passed in place of the `lpClassName` string.

The CapEdit Control

To allow for easier data entry, Microsoft added a special kind of edit control called the CapEdit control. The CapEdit control looks and behaves like a standard Edit control, with one exception: the first letter typed in the control is automatically capitalized. This allows users to enter data much faster because they do not have to press the Shift key before entering the first letter.

There are a number of situations where this is important, such as when a user enters an address where, typically, the first letter of every piece of data is capitalized. If the user doesn't have to worry about capitalization, it's easier to enter addresses.

Using the CapEdit control is very easy—all you have to do is call `SHInitExtra-Controls()` to initialize the control, then call `CreateWindow()`, specifying `"CAPEDIT"` instead of `"EDIT"` as the class name, as in this example:

```
#include <aygshell.h> //for SHInitExtraControls

//...

SHInitExtraControls();
hEdit = CreateWindow(TEXT("CAPEDIT"), TEXT(""),
                     WS_VISIBLE | WS_BORDER | WS_CHILD,
                     5, 5, 150, 21, hWnd,
                     NULL, hInst, NULL);
```

Voice Recording and Playback Services

Although all of the CE devices offer some kind of voice recording software, the PPC platform is the only CE platform that exposes this functionality to developers in the form of a control. The "control" in this case is a dialog box that can be launched from within a program. The dialog will then send notification messages to the calling program, indicating the user's actions.

The PPC Taskbar

Although the PPC does follow the Windows 98/NT user interface very closely, there is one subtle difference that can take some getting used to. PPC devices have a Taskbar, but running applications don't show up there as they do under desktop versions of Windows. The reason for this is that the Taskbar is already so narrow because of the form factor of the device itself that there isn't enough room to maintain a button for each application that the user starts.

Instead, it's Microsoft's intent that a PPC program shouldn't really be closed or exited in the normal fashion. As you can see in any of the Microsoft Pocket Outlook applications, it's preferred that a program not have a File ➤ Exit menu, or a system close (X) button.

Instead, as we'll be exploring very shortly, applications are supposed to stay running indefinitely, hidden in the background. It is the responsibility of the developer to ensure that the user cannot start two copies of the same program. When the user tries to start a program, the program should first check if there's already a copy of itself running. If it finds another copy, it should bring that to the front rather than opening a new copy of itself. Likewise, when the system is running low on memory, it will ask the running programs to close down.

Continued on next page

Of course, it's worth pointing out that many developers have ignored the PPC style of program management and have exposed all of the standard means of closing an application. That's probably because they believe that users are more comfortable with a program that can be closed. The examples in this book generally include at least the system close (X) button, as this seems more comfortable to use while debugging and testing.

Handheld PC Devices

Handheld PCs (or HPCs) are usually the midrange models, being moderately larger than the PPCs (about $4 \times 7^1/_2 \times 1$ inches), yet possessing less-than-full-size keyboards. Designing programs for HPCs has a more familiar feel to it since the displays are landscape-oriented and applications are represented on the Taskbar when running. In addition, most HPC devices have both a Compact Flash slot and a PCMCIA (Type II) slot, either of which can be used to add additional memory or peripheral devices to the HPC. However, like the PPCs, HPC devices have a touch screen instead of a mouse.

The shape and portability of HPC devices make them ideal for pocket or mini versions of some Desktop applications, with reduced sets of features and not as much data entry as, say, a Desktop application might require. Figure 1.9 shows an example of a Handheld PC device, the Casio PA-2500.

There are several noteworthy features that make HPCs different from other CE devices:

- Display
- A true keyboard
- The HTML Viewer control

FIGURE 1.9:

The Casio PA-2500

Copyright Casio Business Solutions Group © 1999

Display

The first thing that makes the display on an HPC different from other CE devices is that it is landscape-oriented, just like Desktop machines. In addition, the displays on HPCs typically measure about 640 × 240. That's twice as large as the screens on the PPC devices. Of course, that's still quite small when compared to resolutions available on Desktop machines, but this increase in size does help—especially when you're designing an application that displays lots of information and you really need the extra room.

The final characteristic of HPC displays that makes them unique is that there are *some* color HPCs. However, not all HPCs have color displays, so it's still a good idea to play it safe and not make any assumptions about your user's ability to see colors.

A True Keyboard

Handheld PCs have an actual physical keyboard. From a development standpoint, this means that you can design the HPC version of your program to require some data entry. Of course, because the keyboard is not really a full-size keyboard, you won't want to insist on intensive data entry.

The HTML Viewer Control

Because HPCs have a larger display and are therefore better for viewing data, they have a special control called the HTML Viewer control. As you can guess, it's a control that you can use in your own programs to display HTML pages. The tricky part about this control is that it notifies your application of any HTML-based event. For example, when an HTML page contains a request for an image, the HTML Viewer control notifies your application, passing in the URL of the image, so that you can then download and display the image. Similarly, when a user clicks on a link, the HTML Viewer control notifies your application, passing in the text of the link, so that you can then choose to retrieve and display the requested page.

NOTE The HTML Viewer control does not actually manage the retrieval of documents over the Internet. Rather, it is a means of displaying HTML data. Your application is still responsible for actually fetching the document from a server and then sending it to the HTML control.

WARNING Be aware that if you're developing for both the PPC and the HPC that the HPC does not support the CapEdit control! The Ink control is supported, although it is undocumented as of this writing.

Handheld PC/Pro Devices

Handheld PC/Pro devices (or HPC/Pros) are the top-of-the-line models. They are typically the size of a small laptop, about $10 \times 7 \times 1\frac{1}{2}$ inches. HPC/Pros have a laptop-size keyboard, which is more than adequate for any amount of data entry by the user. Their screen is landscape-oriented and huge compared to the other CE devices, a full 640×480.

Further, at least one HPC/Pro model has a mouse pointer instead of a touch screen. In addition, most HPC/Pro devices have both a Compact Flash slot and a PCMCIA (Type II) slot, either of which can be used to add additional memory or peripheral devices to the HPC/Pro. Of all the CE platforms, the HPC/Pro is the most powerful and the most familiar-looking device. Figure 1.10 shows an example of an HPC/Pro, the Hewlett-Packard Jornada.

FIGURE 1.10:

The Hewlet-Packard
Jornada

Copyright Hewlett-Packard © 1999

The form and design of the HPC/Pro devices make them an ideal platform for doing just about anything short of compiling code. As noted earlier, the keyboard is easy to type with, and the battery on an HPC/Pro device lasts up to 10 hours.

There are several features that make HPC/Pros unique from other CE devices:

- Display
- VGA-out port
- A laptop-size keyboard
- The HTML Viewer control

Display

The displays on HPCs typically measure about 640 × 480. That's twice as large as the screens on the HPC devices, and four times the size of the PPC screens. And it's not too far out of line with the resolutions available on Desktop machines.

The final characteristic of HPC/Pro displays that makes them unique is that all of the HPC/Pros have color displays capable of displaying 256 colors.

VGA-Out Port

Some HPC/Pros, such as the Hewlett-Packard Jornada, offer a VGA-out port, so that your application can send data to a standard VGA monitor in a number of resolutions not supported directly by the CE device's own display. While it does take some additional battery power to drive the VGA-out port, this is still an excellent feature for any application that needs to display presentation-oriented data.

As a demonstration of this feature, let's borrow some simple graphics code that paints simple shapes from one of the MSDN samples and modify it to display its output on the VGA-out port.

In order to activate the VGA-out port, we'll set up a simple window with a large button marked "VGA!!!". When the user clicks the button, we'll change the caption of the button (to "End VGA"), activate the VGA-out port by calling `Cre-ateDC()` with a special parameter, and launch a separate thread (which we'll also write) to do the drawing. When the user clicks the button a second time, we'll change its caption back to the original "VGA!!!", set a flag to stop the drawing, and do any necessary cleanup.

Your first task is to create the handler for the button click event by adding a block of code to your `WM_COMMAND` message handler. First, test to make sure that the `WM_COMMAND` message refers to your button:

```
case WM_COMMAND:
    if ((HWND)lParam == hButton)
    {
```

If it does, next check a Boolean flag, bVGA, to see if you're already displaying something on the VGA-out port:

```
        if (bVGA)
        {
```

If bVGA is set to TRUE, that means you're currently using the VGA-out port. If you arrive at this point, it means that the user would like to end the VGA graphics show. Your first job then is to reset the bVGA flag so that your graphics thread can terminate:

```
bVGA = FALSE;
```

Then delete the special VGA-out HDC you created with a call to CreateDC(), which we'll look at in just a moment. Next, reset the caption of your button so that it now reads "VGA!!!" again:

```
DeleteDC(hVGA);
SetWindowText(hButton, TEXT("VGA!!!"));
```

Then exit the procedure:

```
return TRUE;
}
```

If, however, the bVGA flag was not set, you'll know that you need to initialize the VGA-out port and begin drawing to it. In order to open the VGA-out port, call CreateDC() but pass as the first parameter the name of the DLL that serves as the VGA-out port driver. On the Hewlett-Packard Jornada, there are three such DLLs to choose from, as illustrated in this table:

Driver DLL Name	VGA display resolution
Skvout0.dll	640×480
Skvout1.dll	800×600
Skvout2.dll	1024×768

TIP   This information can be found at runtime by querying the registry under HKEY_CLASSES_ROOT\Drivers\Display\Active\. Any keys under this key represent the different available output devices.

For the purposes of this demonstration, use the 1024×768 driver. Your call to CreateDC() will then look like this:

```
hVGA = CreateDC(TEXT("skvout2.dll"), NULL, NULL, &Init-
Data);
```

Next, test to make sure your call to CreateDC() worked, and, if it didn't, handle the error with a simple message:

```
                if (!hVGA)
                {
                        MessageBox(hWnd, TEXT("Unable to initialize VGA
output device."), TEXT("ERROR:"),MB_OK);
                        return TRUE;
                }
```

If you were successful, set the bVGA flag to true, indicating to other parts of our program both that the VGA-out port is in use and that it's now safe to paint to the hVGA display context.

Set the bVGA flag to true and start your drawing/graphics thread:

```
                bVGA = TRUE;
                StartVal = 0;
                hVGAThread = CreateThread(NULL, 0, &VGAThreadProc,
&StartVal, 0, &dwVGAThreadID);
```

Then, set the button's text to "End VGA" and exit the procedure:

```
                SetWindowText(hButton, TEXT("End VGA"));
                return TRUE;
        }
        break;
```

Now, take a quick look at your drawing/graphics thread. It's fairly standard code, so it will probably look familiar. The first thing to do in this routine after declaring your variables is to initialize a RECT structure to the full dimensions of the VGA resolution you're using:

```
DWORD WINAPI VGAThreadProc(LPVOID lpParameter)
{
    int x1,y1,x2,y2,x3,y3,x4,y4,r,g,b,nObject;
    RECT rect, textrect;
    HBRUSH hBrush;
    LPTSTR DebugMsg;

    rect.top = 0;
    rect.left = 0;
    rect.right = 1024;
    rect.bottom = 768;
```

We'll be using the RECT a little later, but first, paint a black rectangle on the hVGA HDC to clear it out, and start with a clean background:

```
if(hBrush = SelectObject(hVGA,CreateSolidBrush(RGB(0,0,0))))
{
    Rectangle(hVGA, -2, -2, 1026, 770);
    DeleteObject(SelectObject(hVGA,hBrush));
}
```

TIP

Paint the rectangle just a little bit larger than needed to make sure it covers the whole area.

Now, enter a while loop based on the value of bVGA:

```
while (bVGA)
{
```

At this point, begin your drawing code. First, obtain some random color values to draw with by calling the C runtime function, rand(), applying modulus 25 to the result, and then multiplying that value by 10:

```
r = (rand() % 25) * 10;
g = (rand() % 25) * 10;
b = (rand() % 25) *10;
```

Next, create an HBRUSH to paint with and, if that operation is successful, choose some random coordinates at which to do your drawing:

```
if(hBrush = SelectObject(hVGA,CreateSolidBrush(RGB(r,g,b))))
{
    x1 = rand() % rect.right;
    y1 = rand() % rect.bottom;
    x2 = rand() % rect.right;
    y2 = rand() % rect.bottom;
    x3 = rand() % rect.right;
    y3 = rand() % rect.bottom;
    x4 = rand() % rect.right;
    y4 = rand() % rect.bottom;
```

Next, make a random choice as to which of three possible shapes you should draw, and via a `switch..case` block, draw the randomly chosen shape:

```
nObject = rand() % 3;

switch(nObject)
{
    default:
    case OBJ_RECTANGLE:
        Rectangle(hVGA,x1,y1,x2,y2);
        break;

    case OBJ_ELLIPSE:
        Ellipse(hVGA,x1,y1,x2,y2);
        break;

    case OBJ_ROUNDRECT:
        RoundRect(hVGA,x1,y1,x2,y2,x3,y3);
        break;

}
```

Next, clean up by deleting the HBRUSH you created earlier:

```
        DeleteObject(SelectObject(hVGA,hBrush));
    }
```

And, because you don't want this thread to lock the rest of the program, put it to sleep for one second at a time:

```
        Sleep(1000);
    }
```

When your `while` loop exits, it means that the user has clicked on the button a second time, and you've now closed the VGA-out port. Exit the thread and the actual function:

```
    ExitThread(0x0000);
    return TRUE;
}
```

You're done. Although this demonstration only paints ellipses and rectangles, the VGA-out port is a great way to display charts, graphs, or any kind of graphical data. The Jornada even comes with an application that displays the entire CE desktop on the VGA monitor!

A Laptop-Size Keyboard

HPC/Pros' keyboards are very easy to use. This means that you can develop an application for an HPC/Pro device with the expectation that the user can and will be doing a lot of typing. Therefore, it's both possible and reasonable to request some serious data entry from users of an HPC/Pro.

The HTML Viewer Control

Just as HPCs do, the HPC/Pro devices offer the HTML Viewer control. For information on how to use the HTML Viewer control, see the section on HPC devices above.

WARNING   Be aware that if you're developing for both the PPC and the HPC/Pro that the Pro supports the Ink control but not the CapEdit control!

Version Numbering of the CE Operating System

With the release of the HPC/Pro devices, Microsoft announced a new version numbering scheme to help keep track of the different features offered by each version of Windows CE.

The HPC version of CE is known as v2.00 because it was the first second-generation CE operating system. The PPC version of CE is known as v2.01, and the HPC/Pro version is v2.11. It's worth noting that, just as some manufacturers allowed users to upgrade their CE 1.0 devices to CE 2.0 devices, some HPCs can be upgraded to CE v2.11. However, the software upgrade alone does not give them the additional HPC/Pro features, such as longer battery life, etc.

Other Devices

Because Windows CE is also available as an embedded operating system, and because each OEM can customize the operating system, there are any number of devices that offer some unique configuration or sets of features that might be just what you're looking for in your CE-based solution.

Casio's Vertical Markets division puts out one such device, known as the PA-2400. Casio has taken the larger screen of the HPCs and combined it with the software-based keyboards of the PPC devices to create a Handheld PC that doesn't have a keyboard. The result, shown in Figure 1.11, is a tablet-like device, adequate for displaying moderate amounts of data and ideal for bar code/inventory-type applications. From a developer's standpoint, the PA-2400 is just like any other HPC with its 480×240 screen, grayscale, and all of the standard controls available on an HPC.

Of course, the PA-2400 is only one example of the variety of Windows CE devices that exist. By the time you read this, there will also be an Auto-PC device. To accommodate this variety, developers must write code as generically as possible, so that it will run on as many CE platforms as possible with as little modification as possible. Another option is to target a specific device from a specific manufacturer as part of your CE solution.

FIGURE 1.11:

The Casio PA-2400 "tablet" device

Copyright Casio Business Solutions Group © 1999

Accessories for CE

In this section, we'll be looking at Ethernet/networking solutions and a bar code solution, some of the accessories that you can add to a CE device to make your CE solution that much more complete.

Ethernet/Networking Solutions

Adding a network connection to a CE device is one of the most important things you can do to enhance the functionality of a CE solution. Once a CE device is on the network, it can browse files, access data, and (in the case of the HPC/Pro) even print to a network printer.

Furthermore, from a developer's point of view, a network connection can be your best friend thanks to the Ethernet debugging features of VC++. As the name suggests, Ethernet debugging lets you execute and debug your application over a network. Debugging your applications this way is considerably faster and easier than the standard serial connection.

When it comes to networking and CE, there are two solutions to consider:

- A traditional wired connection

- A wireless connection

The tradeoff between a wired connection and a wireless connection can be summarized in one sentence: Can your device be tethered to a network hub, or do you require absolute freedom to go anywhere with your device?

Of course, that question itself is really answered by the application. If you are developing an application that's going to be used, say, all over a warehouse, then you'll definitely need a wireless connection. On the other hand, if your application is more oriented toward a sales rep in the field who only needs to get onto the corporate network once a day, then a wired connection would be the way to go.

Wired Connections

Socket Communications of Newark, California (`http://www.socketcom.com`) is the leader in the field of wired network accessories for CE. They offer two different kinds of Ethernet cards for Windows CE:

- PCMCIA-based "Low Power" Ethernet card
- Compact Flash (CF) Ethernet card

PCMCIA-Based Low-Power Ethernet Card This version of Socket Communications' Ethernet card is ideal for HPCs and HPC/Pros that have a PCMCIA slot available. The biggest feature of this card is that it uses extremely low power, which, of course, is good for the battery life of the user's device. The standard version of the card supports only 10BaseT Ethernet, but the "plus" version supports both 10BaseT and 10Base2 Ethernet.

Compact Flash Ethernet Card The fact that there's a Compact Flash version of this Ethernet card available is no small feat! What this means is that you don't have to use your device's PCMCIA slot to get on your network. Instead, you can get the Compact Flash Ethernet card to use the Compact Flash slot, which you're probably not using anyway! Furthermore, the CF slot is the only way to get a PPC device on the network, as they do not have PCMCIA slots.

A Wireless Connection

With a wireless connection, your CE device can be anywhere—literally—and still have access to every resource on your network. Proxim, Inc. of Mountain View, California (`http://www.proxim.com`) is the leader in the field of wireless Local Area Network solutions for CE. Proxim offers a wireless bridge (a kind of network hub) that has a radius of 500 feet indoors and well over 1000 feet outdoors.

The way the Proxim RangeLAN2 system works is that you have one or more wireless bridges (hubs) which hook up to your existing network. Then, for each CE device that needs to be on the network, you have a PCMCIA-based Ethernet card.

One of the advantages of the Proxim system is that their PCMCIA cards are also designed to use smart power management. For instance, if there is no network traffic after a certain amount of time—and you can set this value yourself—the card will enter a sleep mode, merely signaling the minimum amount to remain connected to the network. This of course, uses less power and improves battery life.

Bar Code Readers

Bar code readers and CE seem to go hand in hand. Many developers are already implementing bar code–based solutions with Windows CE. As far as bar code readers and CE are concerned, Socket Communications is the leader here, too. They have a variety of bar code readers that come in all shapes and sizes, depending on the nature of the application. And, just as with their Ethernet cards, Socket Communications' bar code readers are available in both PCMCIA form as well as CF form.

The great thing about Socket's CE solutions is that when a user scans in a bar code, their drivers make it appear to the application that the user has typed in the information using the keyboard. This means that integrating one of their bar code readers into your CE solution requires no extra coding on your part!

Summary

This chapter gave a general overview of some of the more important CE topics. In the next several chapters and throughout the book, we'll be exploring each of these topics in depth, finding solutions to problems and using whatever new features we find along the way.

CHAPTER

TWO

The Three Commandments of Writing for CE

- ■ The First Commandment: Your Application Must Use the Unicode Character Set

- ■ The Second Commandment: Your Application Must Be Low-Memory Aware

- ■ The Third Commandment: Know Your Form Factor!

The purpose of this chapter is to provide you with a general "heads up" on the unique requirements and considerations you should be aware of when writing for Windows CE. Not all of the items in this chapter will apply specifically to you and your programs, but most of them will. As you already know, writing for CE is definitely not the same as writing for Win32. There are a number of new challenges, and it is those challenges that we'll focus on now.

The Three Commandments that you must follow when programming for CE are as follows:

1. Your application must use the Unicode character set.

2. Your application must be low-memory aware.

3. Know your form factor!

Because these are the three rules that will affect almost every single CE program you will write, we will take a serious, detailed look at each one.

The First Commandment: Your Application Must Use the Unicode Character Set

The First Commandment is that your application must use the Unicode Character Set. Unicode is a worldwide character standard, which theoretically makes it much easier to internationalize your applications.

Windows CE is a Unicode-based operating system. That means that all of the text displayed to the user by the operating system is actually Unicode text. It also means that all of the Edit boxes, List boxes, Combo boxes, etc., display Unicode character string only. From the practical standpoint of working with text strings under Windows CE, however, Unicode is just something that makes your life more difficult.

Unicode will create the following changes in the way your programs work with text:

1. All strings must be declared using Unicode types rather than char types.

2. All text literals in your programs must be Unicode strings.

3. You must choose the correct C runtime library (RTL) functions for Unicode strings.

4. Your program must now handle two types of text files.

Unicode forces you to make these changes because it is a two-byte (16-bit) character set. That means that a single Unicode character is actually two bytes wide—twice as wide as each character in the ANSI character set of Windows 98.

TIP   The Unicode strings are often called *wide* strings, and Unicode characters are *wide* characters. You might see Windows NT source code relying on a variety of functions with the letter *W* prominently in the function names or type declarations. The *W* is what indicates a wide or Unicode string. For example, LPWSTR is a long pointer to a wide string.

Even if you decide that your program(s) will only read and write ANSI-based data files, you'll have to deal with the fact that all of the Windows CE API and standard Windows controls work with only Unicode text. This means that you'll still have to convert that data to Unicode to display it, and then you'll have to convert it from Unicode to read it!

In other words, there's no way to completely avoid Unicode. Your program will be either 100 percent Unicode-based or some mix of Unicode- and ANSI-based.

Let's take a look at each of the five Unicode-related changes and how, exactly, they will affect your code.

Declaring Strings Using Unicode Types Rather Than Char Types

Previously, under Windows 98, you probably declared your strings using char, char *, or LPSTR, as in either of the following examples:

```
char * lpszMessage;
LPSTR lpszMessage;
```

Under CE, however, neither of these string types will display properly, if at all. That's because both char * and LPSTR are ANSI, 8-bit character strings. Therefore, to get your strings to behave correctly under Windows CE, you must declare them using either

- Unicode-specific string types

or

- *Generic* string types

Unicode-Specific String Types

Unicode-specific string types are just that—strings in which each character is explicitly set to be two bytes wide. They are 100 percent compatible with all of the Unicode-based CE API and RTL functions. Table 2.1 shows the Unicode-specific type to ANSI-specific type mappings.

T A B L E 2 . 1 : Unicode-Specific to ANSI-Specific Type Mappings

Type	Description	What It Replaces
WCHAR	2-byte Unicode character	char
WCHAR*	pointer to a string of Unicode characters	char*
LPWSTR	long pointer to a Unicode string	LPSTR
LPCWSTR	long pointer to a Unicode string constant	LPCSTR

NOTE   The code in this book employs both the Unicode-specific string types and the generic string types.

So, when using Unicode-specific strings, your declarations will look like either of the following examples:

```
WCHAR * lpwszMessage;

LPWSTR lpwszMessage;
```

Generic String Types

Generic string types are macros that are mapped at compile time to the correct character set (ANSI or Unicode), depending on the target operating system. In other words, if you are targeting Windows 98—an ANSI-based OS—TCHAR is defined as a 1-byte char. If you are targeting Windows CE, TCHAR is defined as a WCHAR or 2-byte Unicode character. Therefore, if you use generic string types to declare your strings and characters, your program will be Unicode-aware as soon as you compile. Table 2.2 shows the generic string type to ANSI-specific string-type mappings.

TIP Because generic string types change their definitions based on the target platform, you can write string-handling code that will compile for a variety of platforms.

TABLE 2.2: Generic String Type to ANSI-Specific String Type Mappings

Type	Description	What It Replaces
TCHAR	generic character type	char
TCHAR*	pointer to generic character string	char*
LPTSTR	long pointer to generic string	LPSTR
LPCTSTR	long pointer to generic string constant	LPCSTR

If you're using these generic strings type, your declarations will look like either of the following examples:

```
TCHAR * lptszMessage;
```

```
LPTSTR lptszMessage;
```

Of the two methods for declaring strings under CE, the generic method is usually preferred because of the cross-compilation advantage. However, there are times when you may want to use the explicit Unicode types. For instance, you may want to distinguish between functions that require a Unicode string and functions that will require an ANSI string type.

NOTE The Unicode-specific string types are defined in WCHAR.H. The generic string types are defined in TCHAR.H.

Using Unicode Strings for All Text Literals

Text literals are any hard-coded character strings that exist in your program. They can be strings that are explicitly declared, or they can be embedded in some other command and never declared at all, as in the following respective examples:

```
char lpszMessage[] = "Good Morning!";
MessageBox(hwnd, (LPSTR)"Cats and mice do not have fun.", (LPSTR)"Oh
    no!", MB_OK);
```

When you compile the above lines for CE, though, you will get warnings, and your program probably won't run at all.

There's a simple solution to this problem, but it can be time-consuming, especially if you're porting code that contains a fair number of text literals.

To mark your text literals as Unicode, you must enclose them in the TEXT macro, as in the following examples:

```
TCHAR lpszMessage[] = TEXT("Good Morning!");
MessageBox(hwnd, TEXT("Cats and mice do not have fun."), TEXT("Oh
    no!"), MB_OK);
```

The TEXT macro takes care of converting your text literals at compile time—and that's all you need to do to ensure that your text literals will show up properly under CE.

Alternatives to the Text Macro

There are two additional macros that do exactly the same thing as the TEXT macro.

The L macro, which looks like this:

```
TCHAR lpszMessage[] = L"Good Morning!";
```

The only difference between the L macro and the TEXT macro is the lack of parentheses.

The _T macro, which looks like this:

```
TCHAR lpszMessage[] = _T("Good Morning!");
```

The only difference here is that using the _T macro instead of the TEXT macro saves you from typing two characters.

The TEXT, L, and _T macros are all functionally equivalent and choosing between them is strictly a matter of preference. There is no penalty for choosing one over the other.

Choosing the Correct RTL Functions for Unicode Strings

One of the consequences of changing all of your strings over to Unicode-aware string types is that some of the RTL (runtime library) functions are ANSI-based and will not work with Unicode strings. Of course, there is a set of Unicode-based functions that replaces the ANSI-based one, and there are also some generic string-type routines that you can use. The trick is finding and choosing the right ones.

The generic string type routines will work just fine with Unicode-specific strings, and—when you compile for CE, at least—the Unicode-specific functions will work with the generic string types.

As a rule, though, you don't want to mix and match the string types and their related functions. Mixing generic string types with Unicode-specific functions defeats the cross-platform purpose of generic string types and means that your code will be much more difficult to port or reuse later. Furthermore, mixing string types and functions can cause your code to be more difficult to read and debug.

Table 2.3 lists some of the more common ANSI-based RTL functions and their Unicode and generic string equivalents.

TABLE 2.3: ANSI, Unicode, and Generic String Function Equivalents

ANSI Function	Unicode Function	Generic String Function	Description
strlen()	wcslen()	_tcslen()	Returns number of bytes in a string.
atoi()	_wtoi()	_ttoi()	Converts a string to an integer.
strcmp()	_wcscmp()	_tcscmp()	Compares two strings.
atof()	wcstod()	_tcstod()	Converts a string to a floating point value. (There is no direct mapping from atof() to a Unicode or generic string function. Instead, you must use the string to double-precision functions.)

TIP   It's still possible to increment Unicode string pointers as if they were ANSI string pointers, like this: *str++;

Equipping Your Program to Handle Two Types of Text Files

Unicode isn't universal—just because it might be easier for CE programs to store their data using Unicode doesn't mean that other operating systems can read Unicode, nor will they necessarily be providing data in Unicode form. If your program is going to be receiving data in the form of text files, it's a good idea to ensure that you can handle both Unicode data and ANSI data.

The good news is that it's not very difficult to do this. Mostly, you just have to be able to determine whether a given file is Unicode or ANSI. Although ANSI text files do not have any kind of identifying header or signature, Unicode files do. The Unicode signature consists of two bytes (one Unicode character) that appear as the very first data in the file: in hex, FEFF. To determine whether or not a file you're working with is Unicode, simply open it up and read the first two bytes. If those bytes are FEFF, you know the file is a Unicode file. Otherwise, you can safely assume that it's an ANSI file.

WARNING   The FEFF signature is a generally agreed upon standard for working with Unicode files on a PC. It's entirely possible that the data you receive from some other source may completely ignore this standard. Also, the order of the two bytes may depend on the "endian-ness" of the machine producing the file. In other words, in most cases, you can count on the FEFF signature, but it is not always 100 percent guaranteed to be there.

Converting between Unicode and ANSI Character Sets— A Sample Application

One example of an application that would need to properly accommodate files in both ANSI and Unicode formats is a notepadlike application. (After all, NT's notepad handles both Unicode and ANSI files transparently.)

For a demonstration of the techniques and functions required to convert smoothly between one character set and the other, let's build a CE version of the familiar notepad text editor. The finished CE-based notepad is shown in the graphic below.

FIGURE 2.1:

The finished CE notepad application

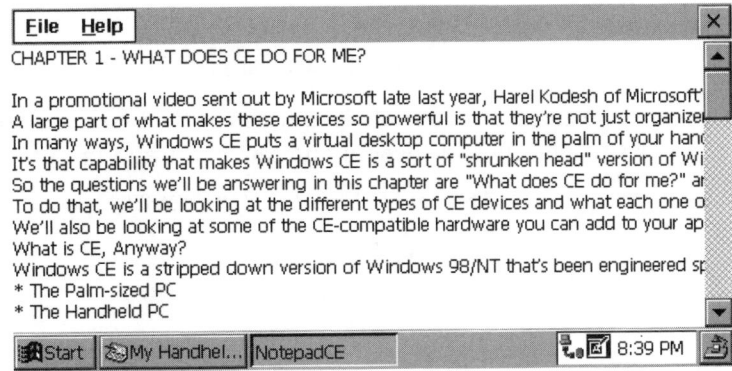

Under Windows 98/NT, creating a notepad application is so simple, it's usually only used as a teaching exercise. However, writing a notepad application for CE requires you to support the two character sets, which makes the project a bit more complicated. There are two tricks that you'll have to employ in order to pull this off:

1. Account for the user opening Unicode- and ANSI-based text files.

2. Save the user's text files in both character sets for maximum compatibility.

Opening Both Unicode- and ANSI-Based Text Files To be able to open both Unicode- and ANSI-based text files, you must be able to auto-detect the character set of the text file you're opening and then read the data correctly. As you know, ANSI text files do not have any kind of header or signature bytes that uniquely identify them as ANSI text files. However, Unicode text files do. The Unicode signature bytes can be defined in C code as

```
#define UNICODE_HEADER  0xFEFF
```

Header bytes enable you to open the file, read the first two bytes, and compare those bytes against the UNICODE_HEADER value.

To check whether a file is Unicode-based, open it and read the first two bytes:

```
if(ReadFile(*fp, buf, 2, &num, NULL))
{
```

Then, so that the calling routine can still treat the file as though it's just been opened, set the file pointer back to the beginning of the file:

```
fseek(fp, 0, SEEK_SET);
```

Next, make the actual comparison of the two bytes you read against the definition of a Unicode header and return the appropriate value:

```
if( (buf[0] == UNICODE_HEADER) )
{
    //it's Unicode!
    return(TRUE);
}
else
{
    // it's ANSI!
    return(FALSE);
}
}
```

Finally, you need to handle the condition of not being able to read from the file in the first place:

```
else
{
    return(-1);  // indicates error
}
```

When your code is assembled into final form, it will look something like the following:

```
int fisunicode(FILE *fp)
{
    unsigned short buf[4];
    DWORD num = 0;

    //initialize buffer
    buf[0] = 0x0000;
    buf[1] = 0x0000;
    buf[2] = 0x0000;

    if(ReadFile(*fp, buf, 2, &num, NULL))
    {
        fseek(fp, 0, SEEK_SET);
        if( (buf[0] == UNICODE_HEADER) )
```

```
          {
              //it's Unicode!
              return(TRUE);
          }
          else
          {
              // it's ANSI!
              return(FALSE);
          }
      }
      else
      {
          return(-1);  // indicates error
      }
}
```

Using this code, your applications can now branch on the file type (Unicode or ANSI) and handle the reading of the file in whatever manner is appropriate. In the case of your notepad application, of course, the appropriate action is to read the text from the file and put it into an edit control.

Saving Unicode- and ANSI-Based Text Files   Merely opening both types of files would be pointless if you couldn't save in both formats, however. In order to account for both text formats, when saving data, you can simply provide an extra Save As menu for the ANSI format, as shown in Figure 2.2.

FIGURE 2.2:

The Save As ANSI menu

Of course, ANSI is an arbitrary choice here, and it could just as easily have been a Save As Unicode menu. However, since it's easier to save a file as a Unicode-based document, it's a good idea to make that the default.

Once you've chosen one character set as the default, implementing the different saving functions becomes quite simple. Before we can take a look at the Unicode-based file-saving code, though, you need a function that can write the Unicode signature bytes out to the file. WriteUnicodeTag() does just that:

```
void WriteUnicodeTag(FILE *fp)
{
    unsigned short buf[4];
    DWORD num = 0;

    buf[0] = UNICODE_HEADER;
    buf[1] = 0x0000;
    buf[2] = 0x0000;

    //now write the bytes to the file
    WriteFile(*fp, buf, 2, &num, NULL);
}
```

> **NOTE**   In these examples, we're using stdio.h file access functions. For more information on using the stdio.h functions on Windows CE, see Chapter 3.

Now you can proceed with the main task of writing the contents of the edit control out to a file. First, open the file for writing and write the Unicode header bytes. The next step is to determine the number of characters you'll be writing to the file, dynamically allocate memory for a string (szChunk), and store the contents of the edit control into that string. Notice that, because GetWindow-TextLength() reports the number of characters and not the number of bytes, you must allocate twice the result of GetWindowText().

```
fp = fopen(ofn.lpstrFile, TEXT("w"));
if (fp != NULL)
{
    WriteUnicodeTag(fp);
```

The next thing you need to do is determine the number of characters you'll be writing to the file, dynamically allocate memory for a string (szChunk), and then store the contents of the edit control into that string. Note that because

GetWindowTextLength() reports the number of characters—not the number of bytes—you have to allocate the result of GetWindowText() twice:

```
filesize = GetWindowTextLength(hEdt) + 1;
szChunk = LocalAlloc(LMEM_ZEROINIT, filesize * sizeof(WCHAR) +
            sizeof(WCHAR));
GetWindowText(hEdt, szChunk, filesize);
```

Next, write that string out to the file, making sure to remove the trailing NULL (which, in the case of Unicode-based strings, is actually two NULL characters):

```
if (fwrite(szChunk, sizeof(byte), filesize * sizeof(WCHAR) -
    sizeof(WCHAR), fp) == 0)
    break; //didn't write anything, so nothing to do
```

Finally, free the memory you allocated and close the file:

```
LocalFree(szChunk);
fclose(fp);
}
```

To save text in ANSI format, you follow roughly the same procedure, with the exception that the text of the edit control—which is in the Unicode character set—must be converted to ANSI before it can be written out to the file. This requires that you create a routine called UnicodetoANSI(), which, as you may have guessed, will take a Unicode-based string and return an ANSI-based string. The work of the conversion itself is done through the API function WideCharToMultiByte(), which takes eight parameters that specify a number of conversion options. For our purposes here, we'll use the simplest settings and specify an ANSI conversion with no options. Your UnicodetoANSI() function, then, looks like this:

```
LPSTR UnicodetoANSI(LPWSTR str)
{
    LPSTR buf;
    int len = 0;
    // return string length - add one for NULL and halve it.
    len = (wstrlen(str) + 1 ) / 2;
    buf = (LPSTR) LocalAlloc(LMEM_ZEROINIT, len);
    // caller's responsibility to free this!
    //CP_ACP == ANSI code page conversion
    WideCharToMultiByte(CP_ACP, 0, str, wcslen(str), buf, len, NULL,
        NULL);
    return (buf);
}
```

Now that we've got that out of the way, let's take a look at how the overall ANSI-based file-saving code works. Just as with the Unicode-based file-saving routine, the first thing to do is open the file for writing:

```
fp = fopen(ofn.lpstrFile,TEXT("w"));
if (fp != NULL)
{
```

Next, as with the Unicode-based file-saving routine, you need to allocate memory for a string (szChunk) and store the edit control's text in that string:

```
filesize = GetWindowTextLength(hEdt) + 1;
szChunk = LocalAlloc(LMEM_ZEROINIT,
                filesize * sizeof(WCHAR) +
                sizeof(WCHAR));
GetWindowText(hEdt, szChunk, filesize);
```

Normally, you'd just save the text to the file at this point, but because you're writing out the ANSI-based version of your text, first call your conversion function, storing the resulting ANSI-based string into a variable (szChunkA), and then write the data to the file:

```
szChunkA = UnicodetoANSI(szChunk);
if (fwrite(szChunkA, sizeof(byte),
    filesize-1, fp) == 0)
        break;
//didn't read anything, so nothing to do
```

Then, as you did before, free the memory you allocated for the strings and close the file:

```
LocalFree(szChunkA);
LocalFree(szChunk);
fclose(fp);
}
```

When assembled, the full routine looks like this:

```
fp = fopen(ofn.lpstrFile,TEXT("w"));
LocalFree(szChunkA);
if (fp != NULL)
{
    filesize = GetWindowTextLength(hEdt) + 1;
    filesize = filesize;
    szChunk = LocalAlloc(LMEM_ZEROINIT,
                filesize);
```

```
GetWindowText(hEdt, szChunk, filesize);
szChunkA = UnicodetoANSI(szChunk);
if (fwrite(szChunkA, sizeof(byte),
        filesize-1, fp) == 0)
    break;
//didn't write anything, so nothing to do
LocalFree(szChunkA);
LocalFree(szChunk);
fclose(fp);
}
```

You have now successfully saved the Unicode data in the ANSI character set. Typically, a few helper functions, such as ffileisunicode(), WriteUnicodeTag(), and UnicodetoANSI() are all that you'll need in order to get your applications to work with both Unicode- and ANSI-based text files.

NOTE   The code for the full CE notepad application can be found on the CD-ROM in the subdirectory for this chapter.

The Second Commandment: Your Application Must Be Low-Memory Aware

As you know, CE devices typically have nowhere near as much memory as a desktop PC. The Second Commandment, therefore, involves tailoring your program for the low-memory environment of a CD device.

In addition to having less memory than a desktop PC, the CE user can adjust both how much of the physical memory is to be used as storage (i.e., simulated hard-disk space) and how much is to be used as program memory (i.e., RAM). As if that isn't enough, the operating system itself can also request that your program free some of its memory whenever the amount of available memory gets below a certain level.

In order to correctly navigate this maze of memory-related requirements, you must make sure your program is doing the following:

1. Keeping the size and number of static variables to a minimum

2. Keeping the EXE file size low

3. Checking the return result of memory allocation

4. Mass-allocating your application's memory

5. Handling the `WM_HIBERNATE` message

Keeping the Size and Number of Static Variables to a Minimum

When you're coding for Windows CE, everything related to memory allocation becomes an issue. Even something like local variables and stack space could be a problem down the road if it's not handled properly from the beginning.

While it's unlikely that you'll actually run out of stack space, it is possible. Windows CE allocates approximately 60K per stack per thread, so you do have quite a bit of room. However, all it takes is some careless static allocation of large strings to quickly push that limit, as in the following code:

```
char LargeString[1024];
```

WARNING   Recursive functions also require special attention, as those that may work fine on a desktop machine might "blow the stack" on a CE device.

Even without the issue of using up the stack space, the general rule is that you don't want to allocate memory you're not using. As Rule 5 in the list above suggests, this could cause trouble for other applications that are running but are not active when your program attempts to grab its memory because, if there's not enough memory for your program, CE will ask the other applications to free up some memory.

Keeping the EXE File Size Low

Keeping the EXE file sizes low is a big issue because programs on CE are executed just as they are in Windows 98/NT; namely, the executable is loaded into RAM and then executed. The very act of launching an executable is, in effect, a memory allocation.

Under Windows 98/NT, you can pretty much use as much disk space as you need, and it's the user's responsibility to ensure that they have enough space to install your application. Under Windows CE, however, there is a fixed amount of memory available. Most users won't be able or willing to upgrade that memory just for one program. And, even if they have the memory to support such a program, they probably won't appreciate the fact that it will keep them from installing other programs down the line. Therefore, you want to ensure that your executable is as small and as tight as it can be.

This involves taking a close look at the resource file that's compiled into your EXE. Have you converted the bitmaps to a lower-quality (i.e., smaller-memory) format? Windows CE supports a number of lower-quality, space-saving bitmap types that can greatly reduce the size of an executable.

If you ported the application from a desktop program, are there resources you're not using in the CE version, such as WAV files or other such resources? Although the WAV file format supported by CE is a low-quality, compressed form, these files can still take up quite a bit of storage space on the device.

TIP   For more information on converting resources, see Chapter 9.

Checking the Return Result of Memory Allocation

This rule is common sense that applies to all types of programming, not just for CE. But because it matters for CE, too, we'll mention it briefly.

As you know, just because you request memory doesn't mean the operating system will be able to allocate it. Here's a simple block of code that demonstrates how easy it is to handle an allocation error:

```
lpStr = LocalAlloc(LMEM_FIXED, 50 * sizeof(TCHAR));
if ( lpStr )
{
    //...
}
else
{
    //handle error here
}
```

Using this simple code can save you a lot of trouble later on.

Mass-Allocating Your Application's Memory

Typically, in a Windows application, memory is allocated as needed. The flow of a program, then, might look something like this:

```
//beginning of program
var1 = LocalAlloc(LMEM_ZEROINIT, 124);
//some additional operations
//...
var2 = LocalAlloc(LMEM_ZEROINIT, 512);
//...
LocalFree(var1);
var3 = LocalAlloc(LMEM_ZEROINIT, sizeof(SOMESTRUCT));
//etc.
//end of program
```

And so on. The problem with this style of program design is that memory is not always going to be available on CE. An application could be in the middle of a complex operation, only to fail at a critical moment because memory could not be allocated. That would mean that all of the work done up to that point would likely be lost, and the user would have to close some additional applications just to retry the operation.

Casio's Vertical Markets division has developed one technique designed to deal with this. This technique is to allocate all (or nearly all) of the memory needed by the application at once. While this might seem a bit unorthodox, it actually solves this problem in a very creative manner. If you were to redesign the above pseudo-code using this technique, it would look something like this:

```
//beginning of program
var1 = LocalAlloc(LMEM_ZEROINIT, 124);
var2 = LocalAlloc(LMEM_ZEROINIT, 512);
var3 = LocalAlloc(LMEM_ZEROINIT, sizeof(SOMESTRUCT));
//now do your work
//...
LocalFree(var1);
//etc.
//end of program
```

Another way to accomplish this is to create a private heap as soon as your application starts, as in the following example:

```
//beginning of program
hHeap = HeapCreate(0, 1024, 1024);
```

```
//...
//anytime later, allocate "off the heap"
var1 = HeapAlloc(hHeap, 0, 124);
var2 = HeapAlloc(hHeap, 0, 512);
var2 = HeapAlloc(hHeap, 0, sizeof(SOMESTRUCT));
//now to your work
//...
HeapFree(hHeap, 0, var1);
//etc.
//...
//just before end of program
HeapDestroy(hHeap);
//end of program
```

The advantage of this kind of coding is twofold:

- If a low-memory condition exists when your program starts up, you'll be able to detect it right away. You can then alert the user as to this condition and take the appropriate action.

- You avoid the possible scenario described above, in that your program will not crash in the middle of an operation due to lack of available memory. This, of course, is the main reason to organize your memory allocation in this manner.

It won't always be possible to organize your memory allocation this way, and there are times when you may find it more efficient to allocate as needed, but whenever possible, this is a technique that's worth using.

Different Types of Memory Allocation

In the examples above, you used two different types of memory allocation.

LocalAlloc() is the default memory allocation function under CE, much as malloc() is in the C runtime library. It gets the memory it allocates from the process heap, which is a general-purpose space for your program's use. The problem with LocalAlloc() is that when you free memory reserved with LocalAlloc() (by calling LocalFree()), the memory is not freed right away. Instead, it is freed after some time, in an almost lazy manner.

Continued on next page

HeapAlloc() works somewhat differently, however. With HeapAlloc(), it is possible to reserve memory from either the process heap or a private heap, that you can create yourself by calling CreateHeap(). The advantage to using the HeapAlloc()-related functions is that HeapFree(), the de-allocation function, frees memory immediately.

VirtualAlloc() is a third type of memory allocation that involves reserving one page (either 1024 or 4096 bytes, as set by the device manufacturer) at a time.

For most uses, LocalAlloc() will do an adequate job. In cases where you're concerned about memory being freed immediately, HeapAlloc() is the way to go. And, if you need to grab really large blocks of memory at once, VirtualAlloc() is something to look into. Whichever function you choose, you'll still want to follow the advice above and allocate as much memory as possible when your program starts up.

Handling the *WM_HIBERNATE* Message

Under Windows NT, when the system is nearing the upper limit of its available memory, a dialog box pops up warning the user that the "system is running low on virtual memory." It's then up to the user to start closing some applications so that memory can be freed and the remaining programs can go about their business.

Similarly, under Windows CE, when memory gets tight, the operating system takes action. Instead of notifying the user right away, however, CE asks inactive programs to release some of the memory they're using. It does this by sending a special message called WM_HIBERNATE to these programs. This message is unique to Windows CE.

The WM_HIBERNATE message is sent to all visible application windows, starting with the window that has been inactive for the longest time. When an application receives the WM_HIBERNATE message, it must free up as much memory as it can and, at the same time, save the state of any unfinished work. Freeing memory might include destroying unused window handles, closing noncritical dialog boxes, and so on. For some applications, merely exiting is appropriate.

When the application is reactivated, it can restore the unfinished work to its previous state, and the user will never know the difference. For example, an application might save the text from any of its edit boxes and then destroy those edit boxes to free some memory. Then, when the application is reactivated, it will re-create the edit boxes and populate them with the saved text.

The most important thing to remember about the WM_HIBERNATE message is that your application *must* respond to it in some way. Even simply closing down and letting the user restart the application later is better than no response at all.

Reactivating Your Application

There is no unique-to-CE message that parallels WM_HIBERNATE to signal your application that it has been reactivated. Instead, CE uses WM_ACTIVATE. The problem with this is that your application will receive WM_ACTIVATE messages in the normal course of business, regardless of whether or not it's currently in a hibernating state. Therefore, you can't expect to restore from hibernation every time you get a WM_ACTIVATE message.

The solution to this is to set a global variable to indicate that the application has gone into hibernation whenever you receive a WM_HIBERNATE message:

```
case WM_HIBERNATE:
    //set hibernation flag
    bHibernating = TRUE;
    //finish with hibernation processing
    //...
case WM_ACTIVATE:
    if (bHibernating)
        //restore from hibernation
    //...
```

This way, you can be assured of proper handling for both the hibernation and the re-awakening actions.

The Third Commandment: Know Your Form Factor!

Form factor is a term used to describe the shape, look, and feel of a given device. The Palm-size PC, for example, is one form factor; the Handheld PC is another form factor.

The tricky part is that each form factor has different design requirements. For instance, the screen of a Palm-size PC is long and narrow, about 240×320. The screen of a Handheld PC, however, is closer to a desktop size, about 640×320. Similarly, programs running on Palm-size devices may want to resize themselves whenever the user pops up the input panel (software-based virtual keyboard).

The difficulty with all of these different form factors and their unique display types is that tailoring your code to each of these machines can create two problems:

1. The UI of the application should be tailored to the device.

2. Maintaining a single codebase is nearly impossible.

Each of these presents a different set of challenges, which we'll now examine.

The UI of the Application Should Be Tailored to the Device

You will probably find that you can compile your applications for both the HPC and PPC platforms without changing a line of code. However, it's not so likely that your application will *look good* on both platforms.

If you design your application first for the HPC, your dialogs will almost certainly be too big for the PPC, assuming they'll even fit into the screen at all. Similarly, if you design your application first for the PPC, the dialogs will look cramped and small on an HPC. Here again, you probably won't even be able to see the bottom one-eighth or so of the dialog, as it will be hidden by the Taskbar. An example of this is shown in Figure 2.3.

FIGURE 2.3:

A PPC application running on an HPC device

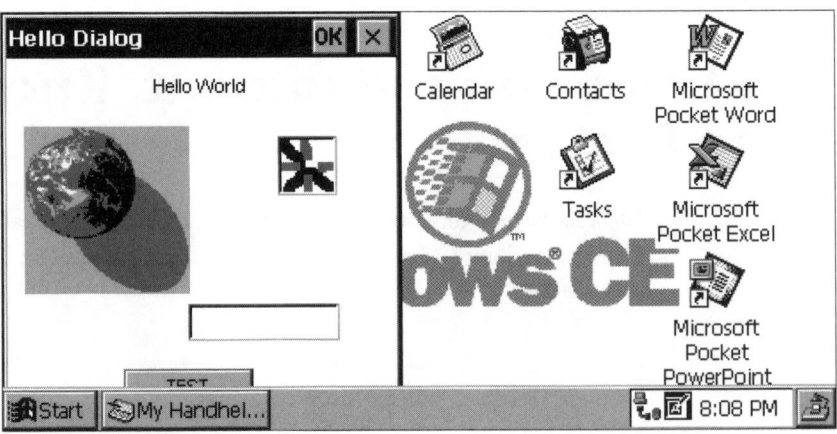

Clearly, even the simplest of programs will require some changes to the UI. The good news is that, in most cases, the changes needed are small and easy to implement.

In the case of the notepad application developed earlier in this chapter, for example, one way you can ensure that the user interface looks good on both device types is to automatically size the window to the screen size. You can do this simply by creating the application's main window with the default size and positioning options set:

```
hwndMain = CreateWindow(szAppName, szTitle,
                              WS_VISIBLE,
                              CW_USEDEFAULT,
                              CW_USEDEFAULT,
                              CW_USEDEFAULT,
                              CW_USEDEFAULT,
                              NULL, NULL, hInstance, NULL );
```

Windows CE sets the default size to be the full screen area. Then, by creating any child window controls—in the case of the notepad application, the edit control—based on the client area of the main window, you can ensure that the notepad application will look good on both the PPC and HPC device types.

Sometimes, however, just ensuring that windows and controls are the right size isn't enough. The DBView sample that Microsoft provides is a perfect example of this. Figures 2.4 and 2.5 show DBView running on an HPC and PPC device, respectively.

FIGURE 2.4:

DBView running on an HPC device

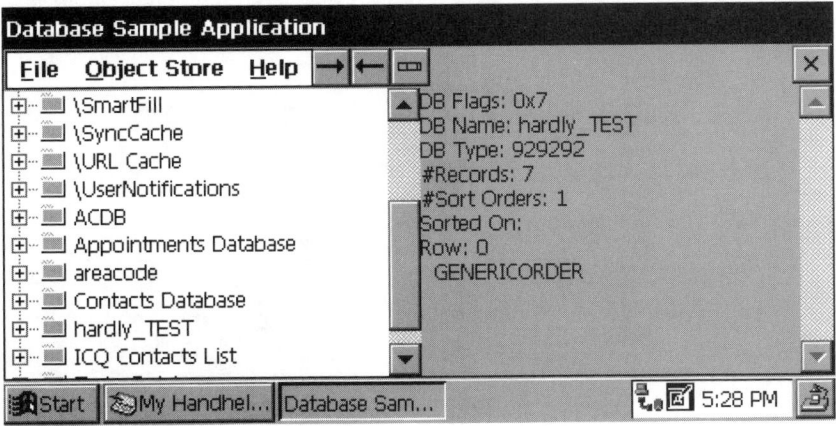

FIGURE 2.5:

DBView running on a PPC
device

As you can see, DBView will compile and run on a PPC or HPC device without
any modifications. However, a TreeView control with a width of about 60 pixels,
as shown in Figure 2.5, is not exactly user-friendly. Most of the items in the Tree-
View cannot be read without using the scrollbar. Modifying the UI would clearly
help. Figure 2.6 shows a possible modification that will definitely make the program easier to use.

FIGURE 2.6:

DBView modified for the
PPC platform

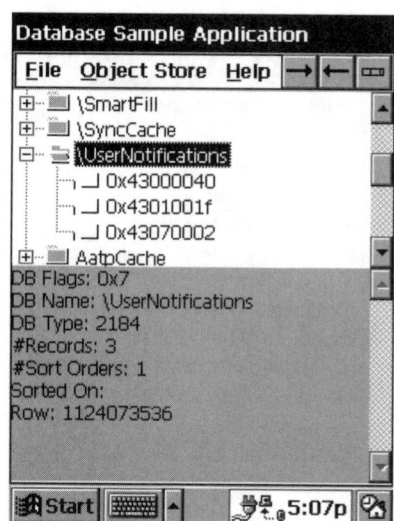

The TreeView and edit controls were originally created so that they'd be alongside each other, as illustrated by this code:

```
GetClientRect(hwnd, &rcClient);
//...
nCommandHeight = CommandBar_Height(hwndCB);
//...
hwndTV = CreateWindowEx(0, WC_TREEVIEW, TEXT("DB View Control"),
            WS_VISIBLE | WS_CHILD | TVS_HASLINES |
            TVS_LINESATROOT | TVS_HASBUTTONS, 0, nCommandHeight,
            rcClient.right/2, rcClient.bottom-nCommandHeight, hwnd,
            (HMENU) IDC_TREEVIEW, g_hInstance, NULL);

hEdit = CreateWindow(TEXT("EDIT"), TEXT("Property Information"),
            WS_VISIBLE | WS_CHILD | ES_MULTILINE |  ES_READONLY |
            WS_VSCROLL,
            rcClient.right/2, nCommandHeight,
            rcClient.right/2, rcClient.bottom-nCommandHeight, hwnd,
            (HMENU) IDC_EDITCONTROL, g_hInstance, NULL);
```

In the modified version, the TreeView control is positioned above the edit control, as shown here:

```
GetClientRect(hwnd, &rcClient);
//...
nCommandHeight = CommandBar_Height(hwndCB);
//...
hwndTV = CreateWindowEx(0, WC_TREEVIEW, TEXT("DB View Control"),
            WS_VISIBLE | WS_CHILD | TVS_HASLINES |
            TVS_LINESATROOT | TVS_HASBUTTONS, 0, nCommandHeight,
            rcClient.right, rcClient.bottom/2-nCommandHeight, hwnd,
            (HMENU) IDC_TREEVIEW, g_hInstance, NULL);

hEdit = CreateWindow(TEXT("EDIT"), TEXT("Property Information"),
            WS_VISIBLE | WS_CHILD | ES_MULTILINE |  ES_READONLY |
            WS_VSCROLL,
            0, rcClient.bottom/2,
            rcClient.right, rcClient.bottom/2, hwnd,
            (HMENU) IDC_EDITCONTROL, g_hInstance, NULL);
```

In many cases, of course, the changes required will be more involved than those required by DBView's main window, and it might be necessary to maintain device- or platform-specific copies of each important dialog used in your application.

For example, if you look again at DBView, you will find that it has a dialog box it uses to allow the user to set which fields in a given table are indexed, and which are not. You'll also find that this dialog box will definitely not work on a PPC device, because it's over 290 pixels wide. Figures 2.7 and 2.8 show the original Modify Indexes dialog box, running on both HPC and PPC devices, respectively.

FIGURE 2.7:

The original Modify Indexes dialog box running on an HPC

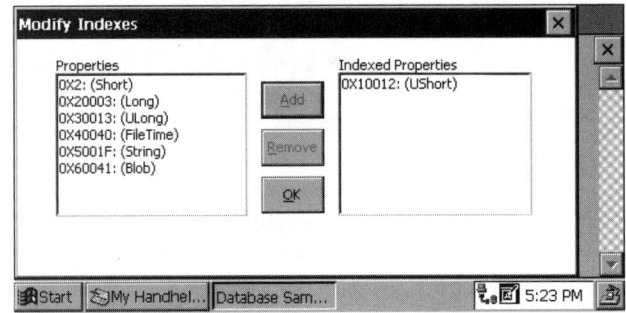

Clearly, the original dialog box is not appropriate for both platforms. This is a perfect example of needing two copies of the same dialog box. Just as you did with the TreeView and edit controls of the main window, you'll need to reorganize the controls on the Modify Indexes dialog box. However, don't actually modify the original dialog. Instead, follow this simple three-step procedure for creating a copy of the original dialog:

1. Create a new dialog and name it something related to the original.

2. Mark and copy all of the controls from the original dialog into the new one. (This ensures that all of the control identifiers will remain the same. You can then essentially swap one dialog for another with a minimum of work.)

3. Resize and rearrange the controls until they're usable on the desired form factor.

When you do this for the Modify Indexes dialog, you end up again rearranging the controls so that they are vertically oriented. The result looks something like Figure 2.9.

The three-step procedure outlined above allows you to make all of your programs useable and give them a professional look, regardless of what device they're running on.

FIGURE 2.8:

The original Modify Indexes dialog box running on a PPC

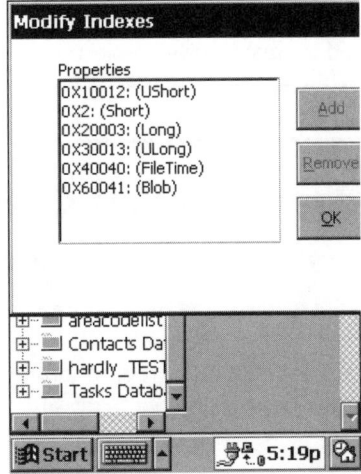

FIGURE 2.9:

The PPC-fixed version of the Modify Indexes dialog box

Maintaining a Single Codebase Is Nearly Impossible

While all of the form factors are running the same operating system, there are subtle differences between each form factor that make it very difficult to maintain a single codebase for your project.

NOTE   The term *codebase* refers to all of the source code, resource files, etc., that are used to create a given project.

Advantages of a Single Codebase

A single codebase can help prevent a situation like this:

You find a bug in, say, the HPC version source code. That same code is also in the PPC version source. Now you've got to make the same fix to both the HPC and the PPC source. When you then run your program on the PPC, you find that the change you've made breaks something else. Naturally, this also affects both versions.

The long and short of it is that you can drive yourself crazy keeping multiple codebases up-to- date and (relatively) bug-free. Therefore, the preferred way is to maintain only one codebase.

Typically, when you want to maintain one codebase that compiles for multiple platforms, you can rely on the availability of compiler defines. *Compiler defines* are global constants available at compile time that exist largely for the purpose of maintaining a single codebase. For example, you might want to perform some operation differently under the Windows CE emulator than you do on the device. For such a situation, you can use the _WIN32_WCE_EMULATION compiler define:

```
#if defined(_WIN32_WCE_EMULATION)
    //Do some emulator-specific code here
    MessageBox(hwnd, TEXT("You are in the emulator"), TEXT("em x86"),
        MB_OK);
  #endif
```

The magic of compiler defines is that they actually control what blocks of code are compiled into the final executable. The above call to MessageBox would not be compiled into an application that was built for any platform other than the x86 emulator.

Visual C++ for Windows CE implements the Windows CE–related compiler defines listed in Table 2.4.

TABLE 2.4: Windows CE-Related Compiler Defines

Compiler Define	Question It Answers
_WIN32_WCE	Are you targeting a CE-based platform?
_WIN32_CE_EMULATION	Are you targeting the x86-based emulator?
MIPS	Are you targeting a MIPS-based device?
_SH3_	Are you targeting an SH3-based device?

You may notice that something important is missing from this list, however; namely, there are no compiler defines that you can use to determine whether your code is targeting an HPC, a PPC, an Auto PC, or some custom device type.

TIP

The AutoPC SDK implements the **#APC** compiler define to help determine whether you're compiling for an AutoPC device.

So, how can you determine what device type you're running on? As far as conditional compilation is concerned, there is no automatic way to do this, but there are two possible solutions to this problem:

1. Create your own conditional defines.

2. Create a runtime platform detector.

Creating Your Own Conditional Defines

The way that Microsoft recommends managing a single codebase is to create your own #define to indicate the platform you're targeting. In other words, if you're building for the Palm-size PC platform, add the following line to the relevant file or files:

```
#define _PPC
```

You then build your project for the Palm-size PC platform, remove or comment out the #define, and build for any other platforms.

TIP   You can also create a `#define` by simply adding it to the "Preprocessor defines" edit control on the C/C++ tab of Visual C++'s Project Settings dialog box.

While this does work, it requires you to remember that you've made this `#define` when you build for other platforms. This can be a bit tricky, so it's best to use this method only when necessary. If you can find a way to implement your platform-specific code without conditional compiles, it will be simpler for you in the long run.

Creating a Runtime Platform Detector

A *runtime platform detector* is a function that attempts to guess the current platform while the program is running. This is useful for all platform operations that don't require major changes to the source code. For instance, in the DBView example above, switching from one version of a dialog box to another is something that can be handled at runtime by a simple platform detector.

Microsoft recommends that you determine the device type by calling `System-ParametersInfo()` and passing `SPI_GETPLATFORMTYPE` as the requested information:

```
SystemParametersInfo(SPI_GETPLATFORMTYPE , 80, (PVOID)plat, 0);
```

The only problem with this is that not all of the OEMs support this item, so you have to use the screen dimensions to guess the platform type. This method is actually fairly reliable, although, eventually, there may be too much variety in the types of devices running CE to depend on it.

The screen-size method works by calling `GetSystemMetrics()` to get the height (pass in the `SM_CYSCREEN` constant) and the width (pass in the `SM_CXSCREEN` constant) of the device's screen:

```
int GuessPlatform()
{
    int iHeight, iWidth;

    iHeight = GetSystemMetrics(SM_CYSCREEN);
    iWidth = GetSystemMetrics(SM_CXSCREEN);
```

Once you have these dimensions, you can make a few simple comparisons to determine the device type. First, check to see if the screen is long and narrow (i.e., is the height greater than the width?). If it is, assume you're running on a Palm-size PC:

```
if (iHeight > iWidth)
{
    return(PLAT_PPC);
}
```

On the other hand, if the device has a screen that's short and wide, you must perform some additional tests to narrow down your choices. First, check if the device has a screen like the HPC Pro devices (assumed to be 640×480).

```
if ((iHeight == HPCPRO_HEIGHT) && (iWidth == HPCPRO_WIDTH))
{
    return(PLAT_HPCPRO);
}
```

Next, check to see if the height of the screen is equal to the height of an Auto PC's screen, assumed to be 16 pixels:

```
else if (rcClient.bottom == APC_HEIGHT)
{
    return(PLAT_APC);
}
```

As the default condition, if the screen size is not that of an HPC Pro and not that of an Auto PC, then assume the device is a standard HPC:

```
else
{
    return(PLAT_HPC);
}
```

Finally, as a catchall condition, if the height and width of the screen are equal, return a value indicating an unknown type:

```
else
{
    return(PLAT_OTHER);
}
```

When it's all put together, the function looks like this:

```
int GuessPlatform()
{
    int iHeight, iWidth;
```

```
iHeight = GetSystemMetrics(SM_CYSCREEN);
iWidth = GetSystemMetrics(SM_CXSCREEN);

if (iHeight > iWidth)
{
    return(PLAT_PPC);
}
else if (iHeight < iWidth)
{
    if ((iHeight == HPCPRO_HEIGHT) && (iWidth == HPCPRO_WIDTH))
    {
        return(PLAT_HPCPRO);
    }
    else if (iHeight == APC_HEIGHT)
    {
        return(PLAT_APC);
    }
    else
    {
        return(PLAT_HPC);
    }
}
else
{
    return(PLAT_OTHER);
}
}
```

Although this runtime platform detector may look easier to implement than the "roll your own" conditional defines, there are some situations that the runtime detector can't handle, and there will be times when you must compile and link different pieces of code into the program depending on the target platform.

In your own applications, you will probably find that you need to employ a combination of the two techniques to successfully deal with any platform-dependant issues that arise.

Summary

In this chapter, you explored some of the issues that you are faced with when programming for Windows CE. Specifically, you learned the ins and outs of the Unicode character set and how it affects CE programming. You also learned how to tailor your code for the low-memory environment of Windows CE. And, finally, you saw how to deal with the different form factors with a minimum of effort.

Although some of these issues might seem difficult to navigate, it only takes a little bit of practice before they become second nature.

CHAPTER
THREE

3

To C or Not to C?

- calloc()

- MoveToEx90/LineTo()

- WM_RBUTTONDOWN

- Recreating the fopen()/FILE*-based functions

This chapter will give the experienced C/C++ programmer a heads up as to what's missing in the C/C++ language for Windows CE. Most importantly, there are a number of programming constructs and functions that have been removed. For instance, there is no `try..catch` construct. Similarly, many standard functions such as `fprintf()` are gone.

The long and short of all this is that whether you're writing a program from scratch or porting an existing application, you'll definitely run into some road-blocks. In this chapter, we'll take a look at what's missing, how to deal with it, and what's still there. The most basic of C library functions do exist for Windows CE, and many API calls also still exist. However, a quick glance at the different include (`.h`) file directories (the standard Visual C++ files and the Windows CE files) reveals just how much of the C/C++ runtime library and Windows API is missing: there are roughly 350 standard include files, but there are less than 120 CE include files. Ouch! Some of the more important functions/constructs that are not available to you when coding for CE are listed below:

- `Calloc()`
- `MoveToEx()/LineTo()`
- `WM_RBUTTONDOWN`
- `try..catch`
- `FILE*`, `fopen()`, `fprintf()`, etc.

When you need to use one of these functions, there are three approaches you can take:

1. Search for a substitute function provided by the CE runtime libraries or perhaps the CE API.

2. Consider changing the logic of your program to work around the missing functionality.

3. Write your own function to perform the same task as the function that's missing.

NOTE CE 2.11 does support the full `stdio.h` library of functions. However, this is of very little practical use to those of us who need to target all of the other devices already on the market.

Let's see how these choices can be applied in a practical way to our list of missing functions.

Finding Substitute Functions

Whenever possible, the best solution to dealing with a missing API function is to find a substitute function that will perform the same operations as the original. In this section, we'll take a look at how this applies to three common operations: `calloc()`, `MoveToEx()` / `LineTo()`, and `WM_RBUTTONDOWN`.

calloc()

As you probably know, `calloc()` is one of the more important functions in the C/C++ language. It is one of the primary ways that you can allocate and initialize a block of memory. Unfortunately, it does not exist in CE's runtime library.

Thankfully, `LocalAlloc()`, another allocation function, *does* exist under CE. The catch is that `calloc()` allocated and initialized the memory, whereas `LocalAlloc()`, requires you to explicitly request that it initialize the memory by specifying the `LMEM_ZEROINIT` flag, like this:

```
ptr = LocalAlloc(LMEM_ZEROINIT, size);
```

MoveToEx() / LineTo()

While perhaps not as important as `calloc()`, `MoveToEx()` and `LineTo()` are important Windows API calls for drawing lines onto an HDC. The two functions are usually used in a pair, as follows:

```
RECT rt;     GetClientRect(hWnd, &rt);
MoveToEx(hdc, 0, 0, NULL);
LineTo(hdc, rt.right, rt.bottom);
```

Unfortunately, they too do not exist under Windows CE.

NOTE   Although MoveToEx()/LineTo() do not exist in the Windows CE API, they do exist in MFC for CE.

A quick search through the API documentation, though, reveals that Poly-Line(), another API function, is the recommended substitute. Using PolyLine(), you can draw exactly the same line that the previous code sample produces, as shown below. (This code can be found on the CD in the directory for this chapter as MoveToEx_LineTo.txt.)

```
POINT Points[2];
RECT rt;
GetClientRect(hWnd, &rt);
Points[0].x = 0;
Points[0].y = 0;
Points[1].x = rt.right;
Points[1].y = rt.bottom;
Polyline(hdc, &Points[0], 2);
```

WM_RBUTTONDOWN

WM_RBUTTONDOWN is the message that Windows sends your program every time the user right-clicks the mouse. Of course, since most CE devices (all of the PPC and HPC class devices, in fact) do not have any mouse at all, there is also no right mouse button, and thus no right-click message. But there are still times when you'd like to be able to offer a pop-up (i.e., right-click) menu. Under Windows CE, a right-click is simulated with a combination of pressing the Alt key and tapping the stylus to the screen, also known as WM_LBUTTONDOWN.

TIP   For a demonstration of the Alt-tap behavior, just try pressing the Alt key while clicking on your HPC device's Desktop.

The way to support pop-up menus and right-click functionality is to handle the stylus tap (which translates to a WM_LBUTTONDOWN message), while checking to see whether the Alt key is depressed. Under Windows 98/NT, you would use code that relies on WM_RBUTTONDOWN:

```
case WM_RBUTTONDOWN:
{
MessageBox(hwnd, TEXT("Show your pop-up menu"), TEXT("wow!"),
MB_OK);
break;        }
```

Under Windows CE, however, your code would instead use WM_LBUTTONDOWN and then test whether the Alt key (VK_MENU virtual key code) was depressed (as shown in the file WM_RBUTTONDOWN.txt).

WM_RBUTTONDOWN.txt

```
case WM_LBUTTONDOWN:
{
      if (GetAsyncKeyState(VK_MENU))
      {
            MessageBox(hwnd, TEXT("Show your popup menu"),
TEXT("wow!"), MB_OK);
      }
      break;
}
```

NOTE   This technique does not apply to Palm-size PCs, since programs running on a PPC device cannot support the Alt-click combination at all. The Input Panel (keyboard) of a PPC device does not have an Alt key.

Changing the Program's Logic: *try..catch* and Exceptions

While some of the missing API functions do have suitable replacements, this isn't always the case. Some constructs have simply been removed entirely, and there are no substitutes available. In those situations, you're forced to alter the actual logic of your programs to work around this fact.

When it comes to having to restructure your program's logic, the worst offender is the try..catch construct. This construct is a wonderfully flexible way for your program to be notified of an error (exception) created in a block of code. Your program can then gracefully handle it in the appropriate manner.

But, as you may have guessed, it does not exist under CE. And, because try..catch is something that the compiler itself, as opposed to a set of functions, must implement, there isn't really a good way to recreate it yourself. Therefore, your only choice is to rework your existing code so that you add enhanced error checking and to make sure that you've thoroughly tested your application before shipping it.

NOTE

This only applies to the C++-based exception-handling methods. All of the Win32 API-based exception handling still exists. However, there are some subtle differences between the two that may make it difficult to port from one to the other.

Writing Your Own Functions

At the beginning of this chapter, we listed five functions that are missing in CE: Calloc(), MoveToEx()/LineTo(), WM_RBUTTONDOWN, try..catch, and FILE* (along with fopen(), fprintf(), etc.). In this list, there is one item that is particularly important, probably because you've come to count on its existence more than on any of the others. Specifically, it's the FILE */fopen()/fprintf() set of functions contained in stdio.h. These are among the most basic file-handling functions of the C language, and almost every C programmer is well versed in their use. However, Microsoft did not implement them on CE. Instead, Microsoft implemented only the following three Win32 API file-access functions:

- CreateFile()
- ReadFile()
- WriteFile()

If you've ever looked at these functions, you know that they don't offer the same functionality of formatted output as, say, fprintf() does. That means those of us who prefer the FILE*-based functions are left with only two choices:

1. Struggle with the CreateFile()family of functions. This means that you have to do extensive work on any FILE*-based code that you want to port to CE. Most people don't like this option for the following reasons:

   - If you were porting legacy code, you'd have to find all of the calls to the FILE*-based functions and convert them over by hand, one at a time.

   - Even if you're not porting legacy code, many longtime C programmers feel more comfortable with the FILE*-based functions and are probably not anxious to learn an entirely new system for file access.

2. Create wrapper functions around the CreateFile()family of functions that will elegantly simulate and recreate the FILE*family of functions in such a way that you can use both sets of functions interchangeably. This also means that you will have a much easier time of porting your existing FILE*-based code to CE.

NOTE

Wrapper functions are functions used to insulate us from or *wrap* functions with complex parameters. For instance, the CreateProcess() function has 10 parameters, but 5 of them are always NULL on Windows CE. Therefore, it might make sense to create a wrapper function for CreateProcess() (say, MyCreateProcess()) that would have 5 parameters. These parameters, in turn, would call CreateProcess(), passing in the 5 values it received, as well as the 5 NULLs.

Naturally, option number two is the one to choose. The up-front investment you must put in to re-create these functions will pale in comparison to the amount of time and energy you would waste trying to port your existing code or learn the API's file-access functions.

FILE*

All of the FILE*-based functions identify an open, active file via a *file pointer*. All of the API's file access functions identify an open, active file via a *file handle*.

The Microsoft Developer Network Glossaries define a file pointer as a pointer to "the next byte to be read or the location to receive the next byte written in a file."

A file handle, in contrast, is "a unique identifier that Windows assigns to a file when the file is opened or created. A file handle is valid until the file is closed."

Your first job then is to try and figure out how to implement the FILE* pointer type, while still remaining compatible with the CreateFile()-based functions of the API. There are two reasons you'd want your file-access routines to remain compatible with the API's routines:

- Even though you're going to be creating some sophisticated file-access functions, you'll still need to be able to use the CreateFile() functions to do the core work.

- By maintaining compatibility between our routines and those of the API, you'll be able to seamlessly mix and match functions from one group with those from another group.

Although there may be other ways to do this, the most elegant way is to first #define the FILE type to be equivalent to, or in this case, another name for, standard Win API HANDLEs:

```
#define FILE HANDLE
```

Then, declare a simulated file pointer just as you would if you were writing a Desktop application:

```
FILE* fp;
```

This means that you've made FILE * equivalent to HANDLE *.

Clearly, though, your new file pointer is not the same file pointer you would have used when writing a Desktop application. However, since you're rewriting those routines from scratch, and since you just want them to *appear* to be the same as the original functions, this substitution is perfectly acceptable.

What that means is that you can design your FILE*-based functions to take this faked file pointer and then simply dereference (i.e., use the contents of the address being pointed to) that file pointer to retrieve the true file handle. Or, using C- pseudocode, we can illustrate it like this:

```
FILE* fp;
//...
fsomefileaccess(fp);
//...
```

Then in the implementation of fsomefileaccess, we would have:

```
//...
```

```
ReadFile(*fp, ...);    //API call : ReadFile
//...
```

Although this doesn't look like much, it meets both of your goals perfectly. You can use your file access functions with your fake file pointer, and you can use all of the API file access functions by dereferencing your file pointer.

Now let's move on to the functions themselves.

NOTE   All of the code for the FILE*-related routines can be found on the CD in the files cestdio.c and cestdio.h.

fopen()

In the standard C runtime library (RTL), fopen() is defined as follows:

```
FILE *fopen( const char *filename, const char *mode );
```

fopen() opens the file specified by filename, and returns either a file pointer or NULL (if the request fails). The mode parameter is a string that specifies the type of file access:

Mode	What It Means
r	For reading
r+	For reading and writing
w	For writing
w+	For reading and writing
a	For appending
a+	For appending and reading

The original runtime library (RTL) fopen() function supports some additional values for the mode parameter, but we've decided not to implement them here since they don't mean anything in Windows CE. For instance, t (for text mode) is a mode value that we do not support because the underlying CE API functions do not support text mode file access. Because the fopen() function takes only character strings as parameters, the first question you must address when creating your own fopen() is whether your fopen() function should require Unicode strings or ANSI strings.

While it is true that the original `fopen()` takes ANSI strings, CE is a Unicode-based operating system, and most, if not all, of the CE API functions that take string parameters require Unicode strings. Therefore, for the sake of consistency with the CE API, use Unicode strings for your `fopen()` function. The CE `fopen()`, then, will be defined as follows:

```
FILE * fopen(LPWSTR filename, LPWSTR mode);
```

As you can see, the `char *` parameters have been replaced with `LPWSTR` parameters. `LPWSTR` stands for "long pointer to wide (Unicode) string."

Next, let's turn our attention to the implementation of our `fopen()` function.

```
LocalAlloc(LMEM_ZEROINIT, LocalFree(
```

The first thing that `fopen()` does is allocate memory for your simulated file pointer, as follows:

```
h = (HANDLE *)LocalAlloc(LMEM_ZEROINIT, 1 * sizeof(HANDLE));
```

This is the magic that makes the entire file-pointer simulation possible, as you'll see when you call the CE API's `CreateFile` function.

Just as your `fopen()` has "flags" that can be set via the `mode` parameter, `CreateFile()` also has a set of flags that must be set to indicate the type of file access desired. The next block of code examines the `mode` string and converts the value(s) passed in that string into the corresponding values for the `CreateFile()` flags.

First, there's a test to determine whether or not a "modifier" (i.e., the "+" character) is specified in the `mode` flags:

```
if(wstrlen(mode) > 1)
{
    modifier = mode[1];
}
```

Then, use a `switch..case` statement to actually set the `CreateFile` flags based on the `mode` string. In the `switch..case` statement, the first character of the `mode` string is examined to see what type of file access is requested:

```
case (TCHAR)'r':
```

NOTE TCHAR is a character type which, in the case of Windows CE and any Unicode-based operating system, equates to a 2-byte or *wide* character. (See Chapter 2 for more information.)

Then, based on this value, the appropriate `CreateFile` flags are set:

```
flag = GENERIC_READ;
opentype = OPEN_EXISTING;
```

This is repeated for each of the possible values and modifiers. The complete `switch..case` statement follows:

```
switch((TCHAR)mode[0])
{
    case (TCHAR)'r':
        flag = GENERIC_READ;
        opentype = OPEN_EXISTING;
        if(modifier == (TCHAR)'+')
        {
            flag = GENERIC_READ | GENERIC_WRITE;
        }
    break;
    case (TCHAR)'w':
        flag = GENERIC_WRITE;
        opentype = CREATE_ALWAYS;
        if(modifier == (TCHAR)'+')
        {
            flag = GENERIC_READ | GENERIC_WRITE;
            opentype = CREATE_ALWAYS;
        }
    break;
    case (TCHAR)'a':
        flag = GENERIC_WRITE;
        opentype = OPEN_ALWAYS;
        if(modifier == (TCHAR)'+')
        {
            flag = GENERIC_READ | GENERIC_WRITE;
            opentype = CREATE_ALWAYS;
        }
    break;
    default:
    break;
}
```

Once you're out of the `switch..case` statement, it's time to call to `Create-File()`, passing in the flags you've just configured:

```
hFiletmp = CreateFile(filename, flag, FILE_SHARE_READ,
NULL, opentype, FILE_ATTRIBUTE_NORMAL, NULL);
```

The first thing you must do now is to test the return value to determine whether or not `CreateFile` was successful. If it was—and this is where the file pointer magic comes in—you then take the file *handle* returned by `CreateFile` and assign that value to the contents of the file *pointer* that will be returned by your `fopen()` function!

```
if(hFiletmp != INVALID_HANDLE_VALUE)
{
    *h = hFiletmp;
}
```

If the call to `CreateFile()` was not successful, however, you must free the memory you allocated for the file pointer and return a NULL to indicate failure:

```
else
{
    LocalFree(h);
    return(NULL);
}
```

Finally, if everything went smoothly, return the file pointer:

```
return(h);
```

That's how to simulate `fopen()`. The complete function is shown below:

```
FILE * fopen(LPWSTR filename, LPWSTR mode)
{
    HANDLE hFiletmp;
    HANDLE *h = NULL;
    DWORD opentype = OPEN_ALWAYS;
    DWORD flag = GENERIC_READ | GENERIC_WRITE;
    TCHAR modifier = (TCHAR)'\0';

    // part of magic to simulate familiar FILE handle
    h = (HANDLE *)LocalAlloc(LMEM_ZEROINIT, 1 * sizeof(HANDLE));

    // use mode flags
```

```
if(wstrlen(mode) > 1)
{
    modifier = mode[1];
}
switch((TCHAR)mode[0])
{
    case (TCHAR)'r':
        flag = GENERIC_READ;
        opentype = OPEN_EXISTING;
        if(modifier == (TCHAR)'+')
        {
            flag = GENERIC_READ | GENERIC_WRITE;
        }
    break;
    case (TCHAR)'w':
        flag = GENERIC_WRITE;
        opentype = CREATE_ALWAYS;
        if(modifier == (TCHAR)'+')
        {
            flag = GENERIC_READ | GENERIC_WRITE;
            opentype = CREATE_ALWAYS;
        }
    break;
    case (TCHAR)'a':
        flag = GENERIC_WRITE;
        opentype = OPEN_ALWAYS;
        if(modifier == (TCHAR)'+')
        {
            flag = GENERIC_READ | GENERIC_WRITE;
            opentype = CREATE_ALWAYS;
        }
    break;
    default:
    break;
}
// actually make the file per params.
hFiletmp = CreateFile(filename, flag, FILE_SHARE_READ,
NULL, opentype, FILE_ATTRIBUTE_NORMAL, NULL);

// if we have a valid handle give it, else we return NULL
if(hFiletmp != INVALID_HANDLE_VALUE)
{
```

```
        *h = hFiletmp;
    }
    else
    {
        LocalFree(h);
        return(NULL);
    }
    return(h);
}
```

Let's now take a look at `fclose()`, which is considerably simpler.

fclose()

The original `fclose()`is defined as follows:

```
int fclose( FILE *stream );
```

As you can see, `fclose()` takes the single FILE* pointer parameter and returns an integer: 0 to indicate success or EOF to indicate an error. Because no strings are involved and because file pointers have been simulated, the CE `fclose()` can follow the existing definition exactly.

The definition done, let's examine the implementation of our `fclose()`. The first step is to attempt to close the file handle you got from your initial call to `CreateFile()` from within `fopen()`. Do this by calling `CloseHandle()`, a fairly generic API function for closing almost any type of open or active handle, whether it's for a file, a process, or other handle type.

Because `CloseHandle()` returns a BOOL, you can easily test the result to determine what type of value you should return from your `fclose()`. So, if `CloseHandle()` fails, free your file pointer—you'd have to do this anyway—and return EOF to indicate an error:

```
if (!CloseHandle(*fp))
{
    LocalFree(fp);
    return(EOF);
}
```

In order to implement `fclose()` properly, you must define the value of EOF because EOF is defined in a header file that does not exist under CE. Furthermore, the `CreateFile()`-based functions do not return such a value themselves, so until now there was no need for EOF to be defined. Therefore, you must define it yourself, as follows:

```
#define EOF        -1
```

It's not terribly complex, but it is important, just the same.

If the call to CloseHandle() was a success, however, free your file pointer—again, something you'd have to do anyway—and return 0 to indicate success:

```
        else
        {
            LocalFree(fp);
            return(0);
        }
```

That's all there is to recreating fclose(). The complete function is shown below:

```
int fclose(FILE * fp)
{
        if (!CloseHandle(*fp))
        {
            LocalFree(fp);
            return(EOF);
        }
        else
        {
            LocalFree(fp);
            return(0);
        }
}
```

Next, let's examine how to re-create some of the simpler FILE*-based functions, and we'll work our way up to the more complex ones.

fgetc()

fgetc() is a function that reads one character from the file and returns that character as an integer value. The original fgetc() is defined as follows:

```
int fgetc( FILE *stream );
```

For our purposes, this definition will work just fine.

However, the original fgetc() returns an integer. You'll be returning a Unicode character, but an integer will work just fine. That's because an integer is 4 bytes long, whereas a Unicode character is only 2 bytes long. Therefore, you can use the existing definition for fgetc() without change.

The heart of this function is the actual call to ReadFile(), which reads a single TCHAR from the file specified by the file handle supplied:

```
ret = ReadFile(*fp, charbuf, sizeof(TCHAR), &num, NULL);
```

Then, as you might expect, a check of the value returned by ReadFile determines what your fgetc() will return. If ReadFile() was not successful, you'll return EOF; otherwise, you'll return the TCHAR read by ReadFile():

```
        if(ret == FALSE)
        {
                return(EOF);
        }
        return(charbuf[0]);

int fgetc( FILE *fp )
{
        BOOL ret = FALSE;
        DWORD num = 0;
        TCHAR charbuf[2];

        ret = ReadFile(*fp, charbuf, sizeof(TCHAR), &num, NULL);
        if(ret == FALSE)
        {
                return(EOF);
        }
        return(charbuf[0]);
}
```

Now that we've looked at reading a single character, let's take a look at writing a single character.

fputc()

fputc() is the other half of fgetc; it writes a single character to the file and returns the character written. The original fputc() is defined as follows:

```
int fputc( int c, FILE *stream );
```

Your `fputc()` will be defined slightly differently in that you'll want to ensure that the first parameter passed—in the case of the original `fputc()`, an integer—is explicitly typed as a TCHAR. This is mostly for consistency's sake. If you feel strongly that you'd like to change it back to an integer, you are welcome to do so. Your definition of `fputc()`, then, looks like this:

```
int fputc(TCHAR value, FILE * fp);
```

To implement it, initialize the data that you'll actually be passing to `WriteFile()`:

```
TCHAR msg[2];
msg[0] = (TCHAR)value;
msg[1] = (TCHAR)'\0';
```

Next, call `WriteFile()` and, as always, check the return value to determine whether to return EOF (failure) or the character written (success):

```
if (!WriteFile(*fp, msg, sizeof(TCHAR), &num, NULL))
{
    return(EOF);
}
else
{
    return(value);
}
```

Again, it's fairly simple logic. The implementation looks like this:

```
int fputc(TCHAR value, FILE * fp)
{
    DWORD num = 0;
    TCHAR msg[2];
    msg[0] = (TCHAR)value;
    msg[1] = (TCHAR)'\0';
    // data
    if (!WriteFile(*fp, msg, sizeof(TCHAR), &num, NULL))
    {
        return(EOF);
    }
    else
    {
        return(value);
    }
}
```

Now, let's move on to writing out full strings, instead of just a single character at a time.

fgets()

fgets() is a function that reads a string from the file specified. It will read up to and including the first newline character or it will read until it has read n characters from the file. fgets() then returns either the string read or EOF to indicate an error. The RTL fgets() is defined as follows:

```
char *fgets( char *string, int n, FILE *stream );
```

As you've probably guessed, your definition will be slightly different, in that you'll need to change all of the char * pointers to Unicode strings (LPWSTR). Your definition of fgets, then, will look like this:

```
LPWSTR fgets(LPWSTR msg, int n, FILE *fp );
```

As you can see, it's very close to the original fgets().

In its implementation, this function basically reads one character at a time, via a do..while loop:

```
do
{
    ret = ReadFile(*fp, charbuf, sizeof(TCHAR), &num, NULL);
```

If ReadFile() fails for any reason, it breaks out of the loop:

```
if(ret == FALSE)
{
    return(EOF);
}
```

The next block is slightly more complex. Here, you read and append every non-NULL character you read to your return value. However, there's an extra if statement embedded in this block of code that will keep you from reading past a newline character:

```
if(charbuf[0] != (TCHAR)'\0')
{
    msg[count] = charbuf[0];
    count++;
    if (charbuf[0] == (TCHAR)'\n')
        break;
}
```

This is consistent with the original `fgets()`, which also would read until a newline character was encountered, or until it had read n characters. This brings you to the end of the `do..while` loop, where it's time to test to ensure that you do not read more than n characters:

```
} while( count <= n );
```

Next, test to make sure that you did, in fact, read something from the file. If you didn't, return EOF to indicate an error:

```
if (count == 0) //no characters read, error
{
    return(EOF);
}
```

If you did manage to read some data from the file, however, return the string that was read:

```
msg[count] = (TCHAR)'\0';
return(msg);
```

You're done! The completed function follows:

```
LPWSTR fgets(LPWSTR msg, int n, FILE *fp )
{
    BOOL ret = FALSE;
    DWORD num = 0;
    TCHAR charbuf[2];
    int count = 0;

    do
    {
        ret = ReadFile(*fp, charbuf, sizeof(TCHAR), &num, NULL);
        if(ret == FALSE)
        {
            return(EOF);
        }
        if(charbuf[0] != (TCHAR)'\0')
        {
            msg[count] = charbuf[0];
            count++;
            if (charbuf[0] == (TCHAR)'\n')
                break;
        }
    } while( count <= n );
```

```
        if (count == 0) //no characters read, error
        {
            return(EOF);
        }
        msg[count] = (TCHAR)'\0';
        return(msg);
    }
```

Now let's take a look at fputs(), the companion function to fgets().

fputs()

fputs() writes a string up to (but not including) its NULL character to the file specified. If successful, it returns a positive number; otherwise, it returns EOF. The original RTL fputs() is defined as follows:

```
int fputs( const char *string, FILE *stream );
```

Your fputs, of course, will change the char * parameter to an LPWSTR, as with the previous functions:

```
int fputs(LPWSTR msg, FILE * fp);
```

The implementation of your fputs() is fairly straightforward. Call Write-File(), and based on the result, return either EOF or the number of bytes written to the file:

```
int fputs(LPWSTR msg, FILE * fp)
{
    DWORD num = 0;

    if (!WriteFile(*fp, msg, wstrlen(msg), &num, NULL))
    {
        return(EOF);
    }
    else
    {
        return(num);
    }
}
```

We'll now look at fread() and fwrite().

wstrlen()—More on Unicode

As you look at the code for the **fputs()** function, you may notice one function that's not defined anywhere in the Microsoft documentation: **wstrlen()**. **wstrlen()** is a function created strictly for the purpose of dealing with Unicode and file access under CE. Simply put, it will return the length, in bytes—not characters—of a Unicode string.

The existing Unicode string length function of CE, **wcslen()**, returns string length in terms of the number of characters in the string. However, **WriteFile()** and other API file-access functions require the number of bytes. You'll recall that Unicode strings are 2 bytes long, hence the difference, making the number of bytes is twice the number of characters. Because of this difference, you need a function that will do the conversion.

```
wstrlen
```

is defined as follows:

```
int wstrlen(LPWSTR wstr)
{
    return(wcslen((LPWSTR)wstr) * sizeof(TCHAR));
}
```

You'll find that **wstrlen()** is used in a number of the functions developed in this chapter.

fread()

The original RTL **fread()** is defined as follows:

```
size_t fread( void *buffer, size_t size, size_t count, FILE *stream );
```

fread() reads **count** items (each one of size **size**) from the file and returns the number of items read or, if there's an error, returns 0 to indicate no items were read. The **size** parameter, then, specifies the number of bytes each item occupies. In other words, to calculate the total number of bytes read, you could multiply **size** by **count**.

Your **fread()** looks and acts exactly the same as the original:

```
int fread(void *buffer, int size, int count, FILE *fp )
{
    BOOL ret = FALSE;
    DWORD num = 0;
```

```
    ret = ReadFile(*fp, buffer, size * count, &num, NULL);
    return(num / size);
}
```

Here, all you have to do is call ReadFile, calculate the total number of bytes to be written (size * count), and return the number of items (num / size) actually written. If there is an error of any kind, num will still be 0, so fread() will correctly return 0 to indicate an error.

Not surprisingly, fwrite() works in much the same manner.

fwrite()

The original RTL fwrite() is defined as follows:

```
size_t fwrite( const void *buffer, size_t size, size_t count, FILE
*stream );
```

fwrite() works exactly like fread(), except that it writes data instead of reading it. fwrite() writes count items (each one of size size) from the file and returns the number of items written. The size parameter, then, specifies the number of bytes each item occupies. In other words, to calculate the total number of bytes to be written, you could multiply size by count. fwrite() returns the number of items written or, if there's an error, returns 0 to indicate no items were written.

Your fwrite() will be defined as follows:

```
int fwrite(const void *buffer, int size, int count, FILE *fp )
{
    DWORD num = 0;
    WriteFile(*fp, buffer, size * count, &num, NULL);
    return(num / size);
}
```

As you can see, fwrite() calls WriteFile(), calculates the total number of bytes (size * count), and returns the number of items read (num / size). Again, just as with fread(), if there is an error of any kind, num will still be 0, so fwrite() will correctly return 0 to indicate an error.

Next, we come to the pair of functions that you will probably use more than any other, fprintf() and fscanf(). These functions are also more complex than those that you've already implemented in this chapter.

But What If I Don't Want to Use Unicode?

On the CD for this book, there are ANSI-based versions of all of the Unicode files implemented here. They are named according to the Win32 API standard for indicating an ANSI-based function; namely, they have a capital letter *A* appended to their name. For instance, the Unicode version of the function `fprintf()` is simply `fprinf()`, while the ANSI-based function is named `fprintfA()`.

These ANSI functions will be of particular interest to anyone who is porting significant volumes of legacy code that explicitly uses `char *` or LPSTR, both of which are ANSI string types.

For more on helping your application to be Unicode-aware, see Chapter 2.

fprintf()

The original RTL `fprintf()` is defined as follows:

```
int fprintf( FILE *stream, const char *format [, argument ]...);
```

According to the Microsoft documentation, `fprintf()` "formats and prints a series of characters and values" to the file specified. "Each function argument (if any) is converted and output according to the corresponding format specification in format." The format string uses the same format-specifiers as `printf()` and `wsprintf()`.

TIP   The three dots in the function definition mean that the function takes a variable and an unknown number of arguments. It is up to the implementers of the function to parse the variable argument list.

The only difference between your `fprintf()` and the original `fprintf()` is that yours will, of course, change the `char *` parameter (the format string) to an LPWSTR Unicode string.

As you can see in the code below, the real trick to implementing `fprintf()` is in the variable argument list:

```
int fprintf(FILE * fp, LPWSTR format, ...)
{
```

```
DWORD num = 0;
TCHAR msg[512];
unsigned short *pmsg = NULL;
int len = 0;
BOOL bResult;

va_list marker;
va_start( marker, format );

pmsg = (TCHAR *)&msg[0];
wvsprintf(pmsg, format, marker);
// get string length for WriteFile call.
len = wstrlen((LPWSTR)pmsg);
bResult = WriteFile(*fp, pmsg, len, &num, NULL);

va_end( marker );
if (bResult)
{
    return(num);
}
else
{
    return(EOF);
}
}
```

Because this function is a bit complex, let's take each part and examine it.

First, you must set up the variable argument list:

```
va_list marker;
va_start( marker, format );
```

Next, declare the argument list with the `va_list` macro. Then, call `va_start()`, passing the variable argument list and the parameter that appears just before the variable argument list in the function declaration.

Next, use the little-known variant of `wsprintf` to help you do your work:

```
pmsg = (TCHAR *)&msg[0];
wvsprintf(pmsg, format, marker);
```

`wvsprintf()` differs from `wsprintf()` in that it takes the entire variable argument list as a single variable (i.e., one declared with the `va_list` macro) instead of the actual arguments themselves. This means that you don't have to do any parsing of the format string and the variable argument list yourself!

Then, call WriteFile(), passing it the string you just got back from wvsprintf():

```
len = wstrlen((LPWSTR)pmsg);
bResult = WriteFile(*fp, pmsg, len, &num, NULL);
```

Now that you're finished with the variable argument list, use the va_end() macro to indicate that:

```
va_end( marker );
```

Finally, check the value you got back from WriteFile() and indicate whether or not your operation has been successful:

```
if (bResult)
{
    return(num);
}
else
{
    return(EOF);
}
```

And you're done. On to fscanf(), the next function on our list.

fscanf()

The Microsoft Developer Network documentation defines fscanf() as:

```
int fscanf( FILE *stream, const char *format [, argument ]... );
```

"The fscanf() function reads data from the current position of stream into the locations given by argument (if any). Each argument must be a pointer to a variable of a type that corresponds to a type specifier in format."

In other words, fscanf() is used to read formatted data from a file. Just as with fprintf(), the format string specifies the data types of the various items being read. And, just as with the other functions you've worked on, the only parameter that needs to change is format, which you can implement as an LPWSTR instead of a char *.

fscanf() is the longest (in terms of lines of code) of our functions, so it's easiest to break it into steps. Begin with the same variable argument handling that you used in fprintf():

```
va_list ap;
va_start(ap, format);
```

Here you declare the argument list "ap" with the va_list macro. Then, call va_start(), passing the variable argument list and the parameter that appears just before the variable argument list in the function declaration.

The next step is to set up a while loop and switch..case statement that will iterate through all of the characters in the format string:

```
while (*format)
{
    count = 0;
    switch(*format++)
    {
```

TIP

The *format++ in the switch statement increments the *format string pointer (**LPWSTR**) so that it automatically points to the next character in the format string.

This is how you know the data type of the items you're reading from the formatted input file. It is also how you know the expected data types of the items in the variable argument list, as you'll see from the case portion of your switch statement. Here's the first condition, which tests for, and then reads, a string from the file:

```
case (TCHAR)'s':          // string
    s = va_arg(ap, TCHAR *);
```

The second line extracts the next variable argument from the list and uses the variable "s" to act as that variable. At the same time, the variable argument list is advanced by the size of a TCHAR pointer.

The next portion of this case is a do..while loop which reads a TCHAR from the file and, if it's not NULL, appends it to the result s:

```
do
{
    ret = ReadFile(*fp, charbuf, sizeof(TCHAR),
&num, NULL);
```

```
                        if(ret == FALSE)
                        {
                            break;
                        }
                        if(charbuf[0] != (TCHAR)'\0')
                        {
                            s[count] = charbuf[0];
                            count++;
                        }
                    } while( (charbuf[0] != (TCHAR)'\n') && (charbuf[0]
    != (TCHAR)'\r')  && (charbuf[0] != (TCHAR)' ') && (charbuf[0] !=
    (TCHAR)'\0'));
                        s[count] = (TCHAR)'\0';
                        break;
```

You'll also notice here that the end of a string is defined by the `while` condition of the `do..while` loop, repeated here for clarity:

```
while( (charbuf[0] != (TCHAR)'\n') && (charbuf[0] != (TCHAR)'\r')  &&
(charbuf[0] != (TCHAR)' ') && (charbuf[0] != (TCHAR)'\0'));
```

What this means is that "whitespace" for our `fscanf()` is defined as any character that is:

- `'\n'` a linefeed

- `'\r'` a carriage return

- `' '` a space

- `'\0'` a NULL

As you can see, all of the conditions in our `switch..case` statement follow the same guidelines for determining whitespace.

The next `case` condition tests for long integers and integers and treats them in the same manner:

```
case (TCHAR)'d':          // int
case (TCHAR)'l':          // int
    d = va_arg(ap, int *);
```

Here again, you are extracting the next item from the list of variable arguments and assigning it to the variable *d*, an integer. The variable argument list is then advanced by the size of an integer pointer. Unlike the string processing code, however, this case condition will first attempt to read any leading blanks from the file before reading the numeric digits:

```
do
    {
        ret = ReadFile(*fp, charbuf, sizeof(TCHAR),
&num, NULL);
        if(ret == FALSE)
        {
            break;
        }
    } while(charbuf[0] == (TCHAR)' ');
```

Then, because you had to read one nonblank character (i.e., a numeric digit) in order to break out of the loop, you must save that extra character:

```
tmp[count] = charbuf[0];
count++;
```

Now that you've stripped out any leading blanks, continue to read digits until you encounter whitespace:

```
do
    {
        ret = ReadFile(*fp, charbuf, sizeof(TCHAR),
&num, NULL);
        if(ret == FALSE)
        {
            break;
        }
        if(charbuf[0] != (TCHAR)'\0')
        {
            tmp[count] = charbuf[0];
            count++;
        }
    } while( (charbuf[0] != (TCHAR)'\n') && (charbuf[0]
!= (TCHAR)'\r')  && (charbuf[0] != (TCHAR)' ') && (charbuf[0] !=
(TCHAR)'\0'));
```

Finally, append a NULL to the end of the string of digits you've collected and convert it to an integer:

```
tmp[count] = (TCHAR)'\0';
*d = _wtoi(tmp);
    break;
```

Floating-point values are handled in much the same way, by grabbing the next argument off the variable argument list and reading the leading blanks:

```
case (TCHAR)'f':              // float
    f = va_arg(ap, float *);
        do
        {
            ret = ReadFile(*fp, charbuf, sizeof(TCHAR),
&num, NULL);

            if(ret == FALSE)
            {
                break;
            }
        } while(charbuf[0] == (TCHAR)' ');
        tmp[count] = charbuf[0];
        count++;
```

Then, read a digit at a time, until you encounter whitespace:

```
        do
        {
            ret = ReadFile(*fp, charbuf, sizeof(TCHAR),
&num, NULL);

            if(ret == FALSE)
            {
                break;
            }
            if(charbuf[0] != (TCHAR)'\0')
            {
                tmp[count] = charbuf[0];
                count++;
            }
        } while( (charbuf[0] != (TCHAR)'\n') && (charbuf[0]
!= (TCHAR)'\r')  && (charbuf[0] != (TCHAR)' ') && (charbuf[0] !=
(TCHAR)'\0'));
```

To finish off, append a NULL to the string of digits you've collected and convert it to a floating-point value using swscanf():

```
        tmp[count] = (TCHAR)'\0';
        swscanf(tmp, TEXT("%f"), f);
        break;
```

NOTE   swscanf() works just like fscanf(), except that it reads and parses formatted data from a string, as opposed to a file.

The last time you will use switch..case is for single characters. Again, start by grabbing the next argument from the variable argument list:

```
case (TCHAR)'c':               // char
    c = va_arg(ap, TCHAR *);
```

Then, because you're only reading a single char, don't scan for whitespace or leading blanks. Instead, just read a single character from the file:

```
    ret = ReadFile(*fp, charbuf, sizeof(TCHAR), &num,
NULL);
```

If the read is not successful for any reason, simply continue to the next iteration of the while loop:

```
    if(ret == FALSE)
    {
        continue;
    }
```

Otherwise, assign the result of our parsing to the appropriate variable:

```
    *c = charbuf[0];
```

Since that's the last of the data types you're checking for, close the switch..case, the while loop, and, finally, the function itself.

Before you're done, however, you must properly reset the variable argument list pointer:

```
    va_end(ap);
```

And that's all there is to re-creating fscanf().

Here is the code in its entirety:

```
int fscanf(FILE * fp, LPWSTR format, ...)
{
    TCHAR *c, *s;
    int *d;
    float *f;
    DWORD num = 0;
    TCHAR charbuf[2];
    TCHAR tmp[80];
```

```
int count = 0;
BOOL ret = FALSE;

va_list ap;
va_start(ap, format);
while (*format)
{
    count = 0;
    switch(*format++)
    {
        case (TCHAR)'s':          // string
            s = va_arg(ap, TCHAR *);
            do
            {
                ret = ReadFile(*fp, charbuf, sizeof(TCHAR),
&num, NULL);

                if(ret == FALSE)
                {
                    break;
                }
                if(charbuf[0] != (TCHAR)'\0')
                {
                    s[count] = charbuf[0];
                    count++;
                }
            } while( (charbuf[0] != (TCHAR)'\n') && (charbuf[0]
!= (TCHAR)'\r')  && (charbuf[0] != (TCHAR)' ') && (charbuf[0] !=
(TCHAR)'\0'));
            s[count] = (TCHAR)'\0';
            break;
        case (TCHAR)'d':          // int
        case (TCHAR)'l':          // int
            d = va_arg(ap, int *);
            do
            {
                ret = ReadFile(*fp, charbuf, sizeof(TCHAR),
&num, NULL);

                if(ret == FALSE)
                {
                    break;
                }
            } while(charbuf[0] == (TCHAR)' ');
            tmp[count] = charbuf[0];
```

```
                    count++;
                    do
                    {
                        ret = ReadFile(*fp, charbuf, sizeof(TCHAR),
&num, NULL);

                        if(ret == FALSE)
                        {
                            break;
                        }
                        if(charbuf[0] != (TCHAR)'\0')
                        {
                            tmp[count] = charbuf[0];
                            count++;
                        }
                    } while( (charbuf[0] != (TCHAR)'\n') && (charbuf[0]
!= (TCHAR)'\r') && (charbuf[0] != (TCHAR)' ') && (charbuf[0] !=
(TCHAR)'\0'));
                    tmp[count] = (TCHAR)'\0';
                    *d = _wtoi(tmp);
                    break;
                case (TCHAR)'f':              // float
                    f = va_arg(ap, float *);
                    do
                    {
                        ret = ReadFile(*fp, charbuf, sizeof(TCHAR),
&num, NULL);

                        if(ret == FALSE)
                        {
                            break;
                        }
                    } while(charbuf[0] == (TCHAR)' ');
                    tmp[count] = charbuf[0];
                    count++;
                    do
                    {
                        ret = ReadFile(*fp, charbuf, sizeof(TCHAR),
&num, NULL);

                        if(ret == FALSE)
                        {
                            break;
                        }
                        if(charbuf[0] != (TCHAR)'\0')
                        {
```

```
                                     tmp[count] = charbuf[0];
                                     count++;
                              }
                        } while( (charbuf[0] != (TCHAR)'\n') && (charbuf[0]
            != (TCHAR)'\r')  && (charbuf[0] != (TCHAR)' ') && (charbuf[0] !=
            (TCHAR)'\0'));
                        tmp[count] = (TCHAR)'\0';
                        swscanf(tmp, TEXT("%f"), f);
                        break;
                  case (TCHAR)'c':              // char
                        c = va_arg(ap, TCHAR *);
                        ret = ReadFile(*fp, charbuf, sizeof(TCHAR), &num,
            NULL);

                        if(ret == FALSE)
                        {
                              continue;
                        }
                        *c = charbuf[0];
                        break;
                  default:
                        break;
            }
      }
      va_end(ap);
      return(1);
}
```

Differences between Our fscanf() and the Original fscanf()

As you may have noticed, this is not a 100 percent perfect recreation of fscanf(). For instance, there are some format specifiers that this fscanf() does not understand:

- "%0x..." hex value specifiers

- "%03d" leading zero specifiers when reading integers into string variables

- Literals embedded in the format string

These limitations aside, however, it is practical for moderate use and can be easily extended or customized to meet specific requirements.

fseek()

The last function in our list of FILE*-based functions to re-create on CE is fseek(). fseek() is used to change the current position of the file. The original RTL fseek() is defined as follows:

```
int fseek( FILE *stream, long offset, int origin );
```

where stream is the file pointer, offset is the number of bytes to move (positive or negative value), and origin specifies the starting point. origin can be one of three values, predefined as constants:

- SEEK_CUR offset is relative to current position in file

- SEEK_END offset is relative to end of file

- SEEK_SET offset is relative to beginning of file

Your fseek() will follow this definition exactly. Here, however, you're really just translating these constants into constants used by the API's SetFilePointer function.

SetFilePointer—a member of the CreateFile-family of functions—does essentially the same thing as fseek() but requires rewriting existing code. fseek(), therefore, is easier to use.

First, map the constants from one function to the constants from another function, using a switch..case statement:

```
switch(origin)
{
    case SEEK_CUR:
    default:
        how = FILE_CURRENT;
        break;
    case SEEK_END:
        how = FILE_END;
        break;
    case SEEK_SET:
        how = FILE_BEGIN;
        break;
}
```

That done, call `SetFilePointer` and then check the result type for an error:

```
ret = SetFilePointer(fp, offset, NULL, how);
if(ret == 0xFFFFFFFF)      // error
     return(1);
return(0);
```

And that's it!

Here is the entire `fseek()` function, as you'll implement it:

```
int fseek( FILE *fp, long offset, int origin )
{
    DWORD how;
    DWORD ret;
    switch(origin)
    {
        case SEEK_CUR:
        default:
            how = FILE_CURRENT;
            break;
        case SEEK_END:
            how = FILE_END;
            break;
        case SEEK_SET:
            how = FILE_BEGIN;
            break;
    }
    ret = SetFilePointer(fp, offset, NULL, how);
    if(ret == 0xFFFFFFFF)      // error
        return(1);
    return(0);
}
```

As you can see, it's fairly simple and straightforward. At this point, with a few functions, some API calls, and a clever `#define`, you have re-created the key `stdio.h` file-access functions.

Summary

In this chapter, we reviewed some of what's missing in the C/C++ language for Windows CE. You learned that, although some favorite constructs and functions are missing from Windows CE, there are ways to work around this. You can find substitute functions, change your program's logic, or re-create the missing functions yourself. In addition to reviewing some of the items that were removed, you also implemented your own FILE*-based functions!

CHAPTER

FOUR

CE's Structured Storage

- The Registry

- The Windows CE Database Engine

- CE's Database Engine vs. Familiar Database Engines

- The CE Database Engine API

Windows CE was designed to power information appliances and, when you think about it, an information appliance without a way to store information is pretty useless. That's why Microsoft provides two kinds of structured storage as part of the CE operating system itself. These two kinds of structured storage are

- The Windows CE registry
- The Windows CE Database Engine

The Windows CE registry is used for the same purpose as the registry in Windows 98/NT: to store user settings and small amounts of user data. As you'll see later in this chapter, there are a few precautions you must take when using the CE registry because, in contrast to the registry of Windows 98/NT, the CE registry has a reduced scope and purpose.

The registry as a form of structured storage has some characteristics in common with a database system, but it really isn't a true database system. Instead, it is a hierarchical data store that allows us to immediately access any specific piece of information. In addition, it provides the functionality for us to search the entire data store for a value. But, as you'll also see, that's about all you can do with the registry.

Windows CE provides an additional, better form of structured storage: it comes with its own database engine. However, the CE Database Engine is significantly different from most of the database engines we're used to. The tables created with the CE Database Engine are closer to text files than to relational structures used by most database systems. Further, the CE Database Engine does not support SQL and does not come with the usual array of database management software. Naturally, these factors will impact your choices when it comes to storing and organizing your data.

Despite its limitations, though, the CE Database Engine does have enough functionality to be very useful for light database work. For instance, just as with the registry, you can search a CE database for a specific value. Likewise, you can immediately access any specific piece of data. Furthermore, the CE Database Engine even allows you to use indexes (called *sort orders*) to order the records of a table. On the whole, the CE databases provide a convenient, no-frills, low-effort, zero-cost way to store and organize your data.

In this chapter, we'll examine the trade-offs of using the registry, when to use it, and when not to use it. In addition, we'll look at when to use the registry vs. when to use the Database Engine. Then we'll examine the trade-offs of using the

Database Engine, when to use it, and when not to use it. We'll finish up with a sample application that shows off the features of the CE Database Engine.

The Registry

In this section, we'll be examining the basics of working with the registry under Windows CE. Data in the registry is organized in a hierarchical fashion, with four major roots, called keys, as outlined in Table 4.1.

TABLE 4.1:   The Roots of the Windows CE Registry Hierarchy

Key Name	Type of Information Stored under Key
HKEY_LOCAL_MACHINE	Hardware information and program settings that apply to the machine as a whole
HKEY_CURRENT_USER	Program settings relating to the preferences of the currently logged-in user
HKEY_USERS	Program settings stored by user name
HKEY_CLASSES_ROOT	ActiveX classes and file types registered with the system

Each of these roots or keys has an unlimited number of branches called subkeys. Each of these subkeys can then have subkeys of their own, and so on, and so on. It is these keys that form the hierarchical structure of the registry.

HKEY_CURRENT_USER and *HKEY_USERS* Under Windows CE

Traditionally, under Windows 98/NT, the HKEY_USERS key retains the settings for all of the users, organized by user name. So, when a user logs into the system, their individual settings are loaded into the HKEY_CURRENT_USER key. Because Windows CE doesn't support multiple users, the HKEY_USERS key exists largely for the purpose of backward compatibility with Desktop Windows applications ported to the CE platform. You can continue to use both the HKEY_USERS and HKEY_CURRENT_USER keys just as you would under 98/NT; however, only HKEY_CURRENT_USER will have any real use under CE.

Proper Uses of the CE Registry

Under Windows CE, there are really only two main uses of the registry:

- Storing system data
- Storing user-specific information

Storing System Data

The operating system itself maintains certain system data in the registry. Typically, this consists of file associations, properties of ActiveX controls, locale settings, owner information, control panel settings, and other information necessary to maintain the state of the system.

Acceptable kinds of information you might write to the registry include your application-specific file associations, persistent state information, and user option settings. Other types of data written to the registry may include COM object registration (i.e., ActiveX controls and input methods) and references to other installed application or data files.

Storing User-Specific Information

The second acceptable use of the registry is to store user-specific information such as color preferences, MRU (most recently used) file lists, default file locations, etc. For example, Microsoft's Pocket Internet Explorer stores its user-specific information under the key HKEY_CLASSES_ROOT\Software\Apps\PocketIE. If you examine the various settings found under this key, you'll find ones like the default search engine, the proxy server address, and even the maximum cache size. The point is that even Microsoft only stores the bare minimum information needed.

Improper Uses of the CE Registry

The basic rule to follow when deciding whether or not to write a specific piece of data out to the CE registry is: "Is this absolutely critical and necessary to the operation of our program?" If you can't answer "yes" to that question, you shouldn't be writing that data to the registry at all. There are two reasons for this:

- Limited storage space
- Decreased system performance

The issue of limited storage space is obvious. CE devices don't have a lot of memory, so you must be conservative in your use of what memory is available. Not quite as obvious is the issue of decreased system performance. This is because every application, including the OS itself, needs to access the registry on an almost constant basis. For example, the simple act of minimizing a window under Windows 98/NT generates *at least six reads* from the registry! The problem here is that if you load the registry down with a lot of unnecessary data, it takes longer to access any specific piece of data. Simply put, if you add lots of data to the registry, its overall size increases. If its overall size increases, it takes longer to either search the registry or to access a specific piece of data. The more bloated the registry becomes, the longer it takes to access the information you're after because the registry-related functions have to wade through data you don't care about.

Unless you feel that there's a compelling reason to do so, there are several types of information that you should avoid writing to the registry:

- Application version information
- BLOB data of any kind
- Redundant information that can be dynamically generated

MFC, Palm-size PCs, and the Registry

One of the problems with MFC on a Palm-size PC is that the usual MFC classes that are used to work with the registry are Active Template Library (ATL) classes. Unfortunately, the ATL is not supported on PPC devices. Therefore, it's probably best to use straight API-based functions for working with the CE registry under MFC. This will ensure that your code will compile for as many platforms as possible. On the CD for this book, there is a sample password application that demonstrates how to use the registry API from within an MFC application. Basically, the application prevents anyone from doing anything on the device until the correct password is entered. The user can also change the password if desired. As you can guess, the application uses the registry to store and retrieve the password.

Application Version Information

Typically, under Windows 98/NT, when an application is installed, it writes some application version information to the registry. For instance, when Windows itself is installed or upgraded, Microsoft writes the version number to the registry under the key HKEY_LOCAL_MACHINE\SOFTWARE\Microsoft\Windows\CurrentVersion\Version. While this is fine to do on a Desktop machine, it would be considered very poor design to write such information to the CE registry because of the limited storage space of a CE device.

Under Windows 98/NT, storage space is theoretically not an issue, so the extra few bytes or so that it takes to write this setting to the registry don't count a great deal. However, under CE if every application vendor wrote such information to the registry, your free space would rapidly disappear. A quick review of the CE registry reveals that almost no vendors at all write this kind of information to the registry. Of course, there are situations in which your application may legitimately need to store this type of data; however, it is best to be as conservative as possible.

BLOB Data of Any Kind

BLOB (Binary Large Object) data is free-form binary data of a certain length that can represent anything from the user's address to a bitmap image. Under CE, just as with Windows 98/NT, it's possible to store BLOB data in the registry. However, it's not necessarily a good idea. The main issue here is, once again, storage space. As a developer, you need to ensure that you do not take up too much storage space, especially in the registry, which is an area that most users do not have the tools or skills to edit directly.

Redundant Information

Information in this category is anything that can be calculated or otherwise retrieved from another source instead of being stored. For instance, you wouldn't want to store the time stamp of a file in the registry because you can always retrieve that information by querying the file itself.

The Registry vs. the Database Engine

When it comes to choosing the registry over the database engine, the main issue is storage space. While it's true that there are some uses for which a database is naturally more suited, there is another issue that makes databases very attractive as a means of structured storage. By default, all databases are compressed. That means that even if you store the same number of characters to the registry and a database, you'll be saving the user some storage space simply by choosing the database method.

The Windows CE Database Engine

In this section, we'll be looking at the CE database engine and what it can and can't do. First, we'll look at the differences and similarities between the CE database engine and other database engines. After that, we'll move on to a sample application.

Differences between CE's Database Engine and Familiar Database Engines

When it comes to CE's database engine, there are a few points you need to know up front. Typically, the most challenging part of getting started with a CE database is getting used to the differences between the CE database engine and other database engines.

These differences come in two forms:

- The engine's organization and naming of data
- Features offered by the engine itself

Organization and Naming of Data

There are three important facts about the organization and naming of data by the CE database engine:

- CE's "databases" are really just tables.

- CE's database engine is not relational.

- Fields are record-specific and not table-specific.

CE's Databases Are Really Just Tables The term *database* is misused under Windows CE. That's because a CE database is what most of us would call a table—an object containing columns and rows of data. Typically, of course, a database is a *collection* of related tables, each table having columns and rows.

CE's Database Engine Is Not Relational The CE Database Engine is not a relational database system. There are no foreign keys or master-detail relationships that the engine will create for us. Instead, it is a system closer in logical appearance to an early version of the DBF file format; that is, a CE database is basically a well-organized text file.

Fields Are Record-Specific and Not Table-Specific The fields of a CE database are record-specific and not table-specific. In other words, it's entirely possible for one record to have three fields and the next record to have five fields. Fields, in fact, are considered to be a record's properties, undefined until the record's contents are actually written out to the database. Consider a standard table of the type you're used to:

ID	NAME	COMPUTER TYPE	DEPARTMENT
34	Jane S.	PII	Engineering
9A	Joe R.	486	Sales
44	Ted W.	586	Sales

A CE Table, on the other hand, might look something like this:

Record 1:

ID	NAME	COMPUTER TYPE	DEPARTMENT
34	Jane S.	PII	Engineering

Record 2:

ID	NAME	COMPUTER TYPE	DEPARTMENT	SALARY	PICTURE
9A	Joe R.	486	Sales	$44,000.00	(BLOB Data)

Record 3:

ID	NAME	COMPUTER TYPE	DEPARTMENT	SALARY
44	Ted W.	586	Sales	$42,500.00

Record 4:

ID	NAME	COMPUTER TYPE	DEPARTMENT
Z7	Betty Y.	K-6	Engineering

Differences in Features Offered by the Engine Itself

The features offered by the CE Database Engine itself make up the additional differences between the CE Database Engine and more traditional database engines. For instance, CE's Database Engine does not support SQL (Structured Query Language) queries. This means that you must use the API and your own code in order to perform searches of a database.

Similarly, the CE Database Engine does not offer the usual package of management tools and utilities that most engines do. Most database engines, for instance, come with some kind of Enterprise Manager application, which provides a graphical way to manage your databases and tables.

Now that you've seen all of the differences between CE's Database Engine and other engines, let's take a look at the similarities.

Similarities between CE's Database Engine and Familiar Database Engines

Despite the differences between CE's Database Engine and other database engines, there are a number of similarities. For instance, CE's Database Engine allows you to do two of the most common database operations:

- Indexing

- Searching

Even when you're performing these more common database operations, there are still some unusual aspects you need to deal with before diving in.

Indexing

Just as most database engines do, CE's Database Engine allows you to create indexes (or "sort orders") for your tables. While these indexes/sort orders allow you to sort the records of a CE database, they do have a few limitations. Before you can understand these limitations and how they'll affect you, however, you need to first understand how databases are created and then opened.

To create a CE database, call `CeCreateDatabase()`. `CeCreateDatabase()` is defined as follows:

```
CEOID CeCreateDatabase(LPWSTR lpszName, DWORD dwDbaseType, WORD wNum-
    SortOrder, SORTORDERSPEC * rgSortSpecs);
```

The first parameter, `lpszName`, is simply the name you're going to assign to the database once it's created.

The second parameter, `dwDbaseType`, is a numeric value that your application uses to uniquely identify one of its databases from another.

The **dwDbaseType** value does not have to be globally unique; only your application uses this value.

The third parameter, **wNumSortOrder**, tells the CE Database Engine how many sort orders you'll be creating.

The fourth parameter, **rgSortSpecs**, is a pointer to an array of SORTORDERSPEC structures, which serve to define the actual sort orders. The SORTORDERSPEC structure has two members:

```
PEGPROPID propid;
DWORD dwFlags;
```

PEGPROPID is a **long** integer, composed of two WORDs. The low-order WORD specifies the field type using one of the eight possible constants defined by Microsoft, as outlined in Table 4.2.

TABLE 4.2:   Field Types of the CE Database Engine

Field Type	Description
CEVT_LPWSTR	The field is a Unicode string, NULL terminated.
CEVT_FILETIME	The field is a FILETIME type.
CEVT_I2	The field is a 16-bit signed int type.
CEVT_I4	The field is a 32-bit signed int type.
CEVT_UI2	The field is a 16-bit unsigned int type.
CEVT_UI4	The field is a 32-bit unsigned int type.
CEVT_R8	The field is a double (floating point) type.
CEVT_BOOL	The field is a Boolean type.
CEVT_BLOB	The field is a BLOB type.

The **CEVT_BLOB** type, which is included here for completeness, cannot be indexed. All other field types can be indexed.

WARNING The CEVT_R8 and CEVT_BOOL types are new to CE 2.11 and are not supported in previous versions. To store a floating point value under CE 2.0x, you must convert the value to a string and store it that way. Similarly, to store a Boolean value under CE 2.0x, you should probably convert it to an integer and store it that way.

The high-order WORD is an application-defined value. It is a numeric value used by the application to uniquely distinguish one field from another. Just as with the dwDbaseType parameter of CeCreateDatabase( ), the high-order WORD here is only intended to be unique within the scope of the application. In other words, it's perfectly acceptable to have one application that used the value *100* for the first field of its database and a second application that also used *100* for the first field of its database.

The second part of the SORTORDERSPEC structure is the dwFlags parameter, which is a bitmask value specifying the way in which the records should be ordered. A complete listing of the possible values and their descriptions is shown in Table 4.3. As indicated in the table, these values can be combined to further customize the sort.

TABLE 4.3: Sort Types Available

Value	Description
CEDB_SORT_GENERICORDER	The default setting, wherein records are sorted in ascending order. (The value *0* will appear before *9*.) You cannot use the OR operator on this value and CEDB_SORT_DESCENDING because they conflict with each other.
CEDB_SORT_DESCENDING	The records are sorted in descending order. (The value *9* will appear before *0*.) You cannot use the OR operator on this value and CEDB_SORT_GENERICORDER because they conflict with each other.
CEDB_SORT_CASEINSENSITIVE	If the field being sorted is a character string, the records are sorted without regard to case. (The value *a* has the same rank as the value *A*.) You can use the OR operator on this value together with any of the other flags.
CEDB_SORT_UNKNOWNFIRST	This flag exists to handle the condition of records that do not contain the field being sorted. As you saw earlier, it's entirely possible for some records to possess a field that is not shared by other records. By default, records that do not possess the field being sorted will be sorted to appear at the end of the database. However, if you use CEDB_SORT_UNKNOWNFIRST, these records will appear at the beginning of the database. You can safely use the OR operator on this value together with any of the other flags.

NOTE The CEOID (CE Object Identifier) return type of CeCreateDatabase() is another globally unique value. CEOIDs are like ID numbers given to all CE system objects, such as files and databases, which CE uses to keep track of them. Even records of a CE database get their own CEOID number.

Now that you know everything that goes into creating a database, let's look at some code that actually does the work of creating a database. This example is from an application we'll be developing throughout the rest of this chapter. Here, we'll create a database to hold a list of area codes and the states they correspond to.

NOTE In the source code for this project, each database-related operation is encapsulated in its own function, named for the operation being performed. For instance, the database creation code you're looking at now is contained in a function called AreaCodeDatabaseCreate().

Your first task when creating a database is to choose the unique value to identify this database type; this will be used for the dwDbaseType parameter of CeCreateDatabase():

```
#define DB_ID        1911
```

You must also define a constant for the name of the database:

```
#define AREACODEDBNAME   TEXT("ACDB")
```

Next, choose values to identify the field types; these values will be used first in your SORTORDERSPEC array:

```
#define PROP_AREACODE    100
#define PROP_STATE    200
```

TIP It's best to define the database type identifier, database name, and field identifiers as constants because you'll be using them throughout your application.

The next step is to create and then fill in the values for your SORTORDERSPEC array. Your array will be two SORTORDERSPECs wide, one sort order for the area code field and one sort order for the state field:

```
SORTORDERSPEC soSortOrders[2];
```

Then fill in the values of the SORTORDERSPEC structures, starting with the SORTORDERSPEC for the area code field, then the state field:

```
soSortOrders[0].propid = MAKELONG(CEVT_LPWSTR,PROP_AREACODE);
soSortOrders[0].dwFlags= CEDB_SORT_GENERICORDER;
soSortOrders[1].propid = MAKELONG(CEVT_LPWSTR,PROP_STATE);
soSortOrders[1].dwFlags= CEDB_SORT_GENERICORDER;
```

Now that you've prepared everything, call CeCreateDatabase(), passing in the database name, the database type ID, the number of sort orders, and a pointer to the sort order array:

```
m_obj = CeCreateDatabase(AREACODEDBNAME, DB_ID, 2, &soSortOrders);
```

You can then test the result and perform some action based on the value of m_obj. In this case, you'll be returning a TRUE or FALSE result from a function:

```
if (!m_obj) //a NULL result from CeCreateDatabase indicates failure
{
    return(FALSE);
}
else
{
    return(TRUE);
}
}
```

When you're all done, your completed AreaCodeDatabaseCreate() function looks like this:

```
BOOL AreaCodeDatabaseCreate()
{
    //fill in the properties of our sort orders before we create the
database
    soSortOrders[0].propid = MAKELONG(CEVT_LPWSTR,PROP_AREACODE);
    soSortOrders[0].dwFlags= CEDB_SORT_GENERICORDER; //Ascending
(default) order
    soSortOrders[1].propid = MAKELONG(CEVT_LPWSTR,PROP_STATE);
    soSortOrders[1].dwFlags= CEDB_SORT_GENERICORDER; //Ascending
(default) order

    m_obj = CeCreateDatabase(AREACODEDBNAME, DB_ID, 2, &soSortOrders);

    if (!m_obj) //a NULL result from CeCreateDatabase indicates failure
    {
```

```
        return(FALSE);
    }
    else
    {
        return(TRUE);
    }
}
```

Let's now proceed to the `AreaCodeDatabaseOpen()` function. To open a database, use the API function `CeOpenDatabase()`, which is defined as follows:

```
HANDLE CeOpenDatabase(PCEOID poid, LPWSTR lpszName, CEPROPID propid,
DWORD dwFlags, HWND hwndNotify);
```

The first parameter, `poid`, is a pointer to a CEOID. Since you probably won't know the CEOID most of the time (you'll probably only know the database name) you can set this value to 0. For example:

```
CEOID oid = 0;
CeOpenDatabase(&oid,...);
```

CE's Database Engine will then write the value of the database's CEOID to the variable passed in as `poid`.

WARNING   Because CE's Database Engine will actually be writing a value to the `poid` parameter, you should never pass 0 as a constant value.

The second parameter, `lpszName`, is the name of the database that you assigned when you created the database. In the case of your area code application, use the same value you used before, AREACODEDBNAME.

The third parameter, `propid`, specifies the sort order you'd like to use. It must be either 0 (for no sort order) or a `long` integer, just like the `propid` value of your SORTORDERSPECS. Therefore, your value for the `propid` parameter will be `MAKELONG(CEVT_LPWSTR, PROP_AREACODE)`.

The fourth parameter, `dwFlags`, specifies what, if anything, will be done to the current record pointer each time you read a record. The choices are

- CEDB_AUTOINCREMENT
- 0 (no operation)

With the CEDB_AUTOINCREMENT value, the CE Database Engine will automatically set the current record pointer to point to the next record in the database each time you read a record. With the value of 0, the CE Database Engine won't do anything to the current record pointer. For your purposes, the auto-increment option will be just fine.

The fifth parameter, hwndNotify, is used if you want to receive notification messages when another program is accessing your database at the same time you are accessing it. You don't need this for your application, so pass in a NULL value.

TIP

The hwndNotify parameter can be used to set up some kind of crude record-locking mechanisms so that the two programs accessing the same data will not overwrite each other's data.

Your actual call to CeOpenDatabase(), then, looks like this:

```
m_Handle = CeOpenDatabase(&oid, AREACODEDBNAME,
MAKELONG(CEVT_LPWSTR,PROP_AREACODE), CEDB_AUTOINCREMENT, NULL);
```

And your entire AreaCodeDatabase() function looks like this:

```
BOOL AreaCodeDatabaseOpen()
{
    CEOID oid       = 0;
    CEPROPID propid  = 0;
    HWND hwndNotify  = NULL;
    m_Handle = CeOpenDatabase(&oid, AREACODEDBNAME, MAKELONG(CEVT_LPW-
STR,PROP_AREACODE), CEDB_AUTOINCREMENT, NULL);
    if(m_Handle == INVALID_HANDLE_VALUE)
    {
        return(FALSE);
    }
    else
    {
        return(TRUE);
    }
}
```

Now that you have a pretty good background on what goes into creating and opening a database and how sort orders are created and used, we can return to our original discussion of database sort orders. As you just learned, these sort orders have a few limitations that may affect how you use them. These limitations are:

- A sort order can only sort records based on one of the database's fields.

- Only one sort order per database can be marked as active.

- A database can have a maximum of four sort orders.

- The sort orders should be created when the table is created.

Let's take a look at these limitations and how to ensure that these sort orders will still work for you.

A Sort Order Can Only Sort Records Based on One of the Database's Fields Typically, with other database engines it would be possible to create an index that ordered records based on multiple fields. However, as you've just seen, you are limited to a *one-field-per-sort-order* rule when you create a sort order.

Only One Sort Order per Database Can Be Marked as Active Unlike ordinary database engines, where an index exists more for the purpose of maintaining a certain relationship between records, CE's sort orders are analogous to a SQL "view" that displays the records of the database in the order specified. Sort orders do not change the physical order of the records in any way. The catch to this is that you can only use one sort order at a time. If you want to change sort orders, you must close the database and then reopen it, specifying a different sort order.

With a CE database, each time you open the database, you have the opportunity to select one of your sort orders (or no sort order at all). One way to think about sort orders is that they are comparable to the columns in a ListView control in the Report View style (pictured in Figure 4.1). By clicking on any of the column headings, you can sort the data according to the values in that column. In much the same way, by selecting one of the sort orders, you will sort the data according to the data in the column that the sort order points to.

FIGURE 4.1:

A ListView control, Report View style

Name	Size	Type	Modified	Attributes
WMIPSDbg		File Folder	1/29/99 6:37 PM	
WMIPSRel		File Folder	2/2/99 12:07 AM	
Acdb.001	21KB	001 File	12/29/98 9:32 PM	A
Acdb.aps	36KB	APS File	2/2/99 12:07 AM	A
ACDB.c	13KB	C File	1/29/99 4:32 AM	A
ACDB.dsp	22KB	DSP File	1/29/99 6:37 PM	A
ACDB.dsw	1KB	DSW File	1/29/99 6:37 PM	A
ACDB.exe	19KB	Application	1/29/99 4:43 AM	A
ACDB.ncb	73KB	NCB File	2/1/99 4:47 PM	A
ACDB.opt	54KB	OPT File	2/2/99 12:07 AM	A
ACDB.plg	2KB	PLG File	2/2/99 12:07 AM	A
ACDB.rc	4KB	RC File	2/2/99 12:07 AM	A
areacodes.txt	6KB	Text Docu...	1/23/99 3:37 PM	A
db.c	16KB	C File	1/29/99 4:38 AM	A
db.h	3KB	H File	1/29/99 3:43 AM	A
icon1.ico	1KB	Icon	12/1/98 5:54 PM	A
resource.h	2KB	H File	1/29/99 3:27 AM	A

TIP

If you don't select a sort order, the records will appear in the order in which they were entered into the database.

A Database Can Have a Maximum of Four Sort Orders An additional limitation of sort orders is that you can only create a maximum of four indexes per table. This probably won't affect most of your applications, but it's worth knowing about before you get too far into your application.

The Sort Orders Should Be Created When the Table Is Created The final limitation of the CE sort orders is that it is best to create them when the table is created. This is because the CE Database Engine operates more efficiently when building the indexes as the records are entered, as opposed to creating an index after the database has been populated with records.

In version 2.11 of Windows CE, however, Microsoft did add a feature that makes it possible to add and delete indexes after you've created and populated the table. As is usually the case, there are trade-offs to this option. First, there is the fact that it only works on CE version 2.11, which limits your code to HPC/Pro devices (or upgraded HPCs). The second trade-off is that building new sort orders is a very resource-intensive task that can take several minutes to complete. Therefore, it's always best to create the sort orders at the same time you create the table.

Searching

Despite its lack of support for SQL, CE's database engine does allow you to search the databases. The catch here is that the engine does not allow wildcard matching as SQL does. Instead, the CE Database Engine provides one function, CeSeekDatabase(), which serves as a way to both search the database and manipulate the current record pointer. CeSeekDatabase() is defined as follows:

```
CEOID CeSeekDatabase(HANDLE hDatabase, DWORD dwSeekType, DWORD dwValue,
LPDWORD lpdwIndex);
```

The first parameter, hDatabase, is a handle to an open database.

TIP
The second parameter, dwSeekType, specifies the type of seek or search operation you want to perform. In this way, you tell the CE Database Engine whether you're searching for a value or merely moving the current record pointer. When you do a search, a sort order must be active. That's because CE's database engine only searches on the sort order field. For the purpose of this discussion, *searching* means that you are attempting to find a value in the database matching the one supplied; *seeking* means simply moving the current record pointer to some relative or absolute position in the database.

The third parameter, dwValue, specifies the value you're searching for or is a numeric value specifying how the current record pointer should be moved.

The fourth parameter, lpdwIndex, is a pointer to a WORD that the CE Database Engine will fill in with the number of records from the start of the database to the record that was found.

There are eight different types of search or seek operations you can perform. When searching, you can look for a record that has a

- Certain CEOID
- Value smaller than the value you're searching for
- Value greater than the value you're searching for
- Value equal to the value you're searching for

When seeking, you can move the current record pointer to the record that is

- The next record having a value equal to the value you just searched for (used with the last search operation above)

- A given number of records from the first record in the database

- A given number of records from the last record in the database

- A given number of records from the current record

A Record That Has a Certain *CEOID*   This is a search operation that attempts to find a record that has a CEOID matching the one you specify in the dwValue parameter. To perform this type of search, pass in the value CEDB_SEEK_CEOID to CeSeekDatabase():

```
CeSeekDatabase(m_Handle, CEDB_SEEK_CEOID, oidValue, &dwIndex);
```

While this search is very efficient, it's unlikely that you'll know the CEOID for your records. Therefore, you probably won't be performing this type of search very often.

A Record That Has Smaller Value than the Value You're Searching For
This is a search operation that finds the largest value that is smaller than the search value. So, if you had a database with the following records:

ID
42
43
47
56

and you were searching for the value 44 and specifying the CEDB_SEEK_VALUE-SMALLER flag, the result of your search would point to the record with the ID value of 43. The code to perform this search looks like this:

```
CeSeekDatabase(m_Handle, CEDB_SEEK_VALUESMALLER, 44, &dwIndex);
```

A Record That Has a Value Greater than the Value You're Searching

For This is a search operation that finds the smallest value that is greater than the search value. So, if you had a database with these records:

ID
42
43
47
56

and you were searching for the value 44 and specifying the CEDB_SEEK_ VALUEGREATER flag, the result of your search would point to the record with the ID value of 47. The code to perform this search looks like this:

```
CeSeekDatabase(m_Handle, CEDB_SEEK_VALUEGREATER, 43, &dwIndex);
```

A Record That Has a Value Equal to the Value You're Searching For

This is a search operation that finds the first value that's equal to the search value. So, if you had a database with these records:

ID
42
43
47
56

and you were searching for the value 43 and specifying the CEDB_SEEK_VALUE- FIRSTEQUAL flag, the result of your search would point to the record with the ID value of 43. Similarly, if you were searching for the value 44 or some other value that doesn't exist in the table, the result of your search would point to the end of the table. The code to perform this kind of search looks like this:

```
CeSeekDatabase(m_Handle, CEDB_SEEK_VALUEFIRSTEQUAL, 43, &dwIndex);
```

The Record That Is the Next Record Equal to the Search Criteria This is a seek operation that is used in conjunction with the search operation you just looked at. Simply put, if you have a database with these records:

ID
42
43
43
57

and if you just searched for the value 43 specifying the CEDB_SEEK_VALUEFIRST-EQUAL flag, the result of your search would point to the first record with the ID value of 43. If you then called CeSeekDatabase(), specifying the CEDB_SEEK_VALUENEXTEQUAL flag, your database cursor would be positioned at the second record with the ID value of 43. The code to perform this type of operation looks like this:

```
CeSeekDatabase(m_Handle, CEDB_SEEK_VALUENEXTEQUAL, 43, &dwIndex);
```

The Record That Is a Given Number of Records from the Beginning of the Database This seek operation positions the current record pointer to a record that is dwValue records from the first record in the database. One use of this function is to position the cursor to the beginning of the database by specifying 0 as the dwValue parameter. The code to perform this type of operation looks like this:

```
CeSeekDatabase(m_Handle, CEDB_SEEK_BEGINNING, 0, &dwIndex);
```

The Record That Is a Given Number of Records from the End of the Database This seek operation positions the current record pointer to a record that is dwValue records from the last record in the database. One use of this function is to position the cursor at the last record of the database by specifying 0 as the dwValue parameter. The code to perform this type of operation looks like this:

```
CeSeekDatabase(m_Handle, CEDB_SEEK_END, 0, &dwIndex);
```

The Record That Is a Given Number of Records from the Current Record This seek operation positions the current record pointer to a record that is dwValue records from the current record in the database. For example, the code to advance the cursor by one record looks something like this:

```
CeSeekDatabase(m_Handle, CEDB_SEEK_CURRENT, 1, &dwIndex);
```

The CE Database Engine API

Although we've previewed it a little bit, let's now concentrate on creating a database application that will show off some of the lessons you've just learned. The application you'll create will be an area code lookup utility, which will enable the user to either:

- Find an area code if they know the state *or*

- Find a state if they know the area code

For the sake of simplicity, we'll make it a dialog-based application. The final dialog will look something like Figure 4.2.

FIGURE 4.3:

The Edit/Add Record dialog

The idea here is that the large list box will display the area codes and states. The user will have the option via two radio buttons to sort the list by area code or by state. They'll also be able to add or delete records using the buttons along the bottom of the form. When the user chooses to add a record, a separate dialog, shown in Figure 4.3, will appear, prompting them for an area code and a state.

FIGURE 4.3:

The Edit/Add Record dialog

Your first task will be to create a library of database-related functions, as you'll be performing many of these operations several times throughout the running of the program. You'll create a wrapper function for each one of the database operations your application will perform.

NOTE   We'll examine only the highlights of the application's code here. The full code is provided on the CD-ROM, of course.

At this point, the only routines you still need to develop are

- `AreaCodeDatabaseRead()` for reading records from the database
- `AreaCodeDatabaseInsert()` for adding records to the database
- `AreaCodeDatabaseDeleteRecord()` for deleting records from the database
- `AreaCodeDatabaseFinish()` for performing any cleanup operations

AreaCodeDatabaseRead()

Reading a record from a CE database is accomplished via `CeReadRecordProps()`, which is defined as follows:

```
CEOID CeReadRecordProps(HANDLE hDbase, DWORD dwFlags, LPWORD lpcPropID,
CEPROPID * rgPropID, LPBYTE * lplpBuffer, LPDWORD lpcbBuffer);
```

The first parameter, hDbase, is a handle to an open database.

The second parameter, dwFlags, tells the CE Database Engine whether or not it can reallocate memory if the memory pointed to by the fifth parameter is too small. To allow the database engine to reallocate the memory, pass in CEDB_ALLOWREALLOC; to insist that it *not* reallocate the memory, pass in 0.

WARNING   Although it's possible to pass in 0 for this parameter, you'll almost always want to let the system reallocate memory as needed. Otherwise, your function call could fail, and you'll have to reallocate the buffer yourself.

The third parameter, lpcPropID, is a pointer to a long integer specifying the number of properties to be read. If you set this value to NULL, the variable you pass as lpcPropID will receive an integer value specifying the number of properties read. Recall that database fields are referred to as *properties* of a record.

The fourth parameter, rgPropID, is a pointer to an array of CEPROPID structures specifying which properties are to be read. If you set this parameter to NULL, all properties will be read.

NOTE   This is the same type of structure used to specify the active sort order when calling CeOpenDatabase().

The fifth parameter, lplpBuffer, is a pointer to a pointer to an array of CEPROPVAL structures. This is where the properties you requested will actually be returned. CEPROPVAL is a somewhat complicated structure that has four members:

- CEPROPID propid
- WORD wLenData
- WORD wFlags
- CEVALUNION val

The propid member is just like all the other CEPROPIDs you've seen in this chapter: a long integer comprised of two WORDs that tell you about the field you're looking at. wLenData is officially unused, and wFlags will only be one of two values:

- CEDB_PROPNOTFOUND if you're reading a record and the requested property doesn't exist

- CEDB_PROPDELETE if you're removing a property from a record

That leaves just one member of the CEPROPVAL structure: val, a CEVALUNION, which is a union type that changes its contents based on the type of the field itself. This is a bit confusing at first, but it will become clear as soon as you begin to look at the code.

The final parameter of CeReadRecordProps() is lpcbBuffer, which is a pointer to an integer that will receive the size of the buffer that is the fourth parameter.

To look at AreaCodeDatabaseRead() from a coding perspective, what you have is a WORD used to store the number of properties read, a CEPROPVAL pointer (your buffer), and the number of bytes in the reallocated buffer:

```
BOOL AreaCodeDatabaseRead()
{
    WORD cProps;

    CEPROPVAL * pBuf;

    DWORD cbBuf;
```

Then, you call CeReadRecordProps():

```
    if (!CeReadRecordProps(m_Handle,    // handle to the database
                    CEDB_ALLOWREALLOC,  // allow pBuf allocation
                    &cProps,  // return count of properties
                    NULL,   // retrieve all properties
                    (LPBYTE *)&pBuf,    // buffer to return prop data
                    &cbBuf))  // count of bytes in pBuf
```

Then, you return a BOOL value based on the result of the call:

```
    {
        return FALSE;
    }
```

```
        else
        {
            return TRUE;
        }
    }
```

NOTE You may not have encountered an error, even if `CeReadRecordProps()` returns a 0. It's up to the calling procedure to check `GetLastError()` to determine whether an error occurred or whether you merely reached the end of the database.

AreaCodeDatabaseInsert()

Your next task is inserting or adding records to your database. The function that does this is called `CeWriteRecordProps()` and is defined as follows:

```
CEOID CeWriteRecordProps(HANDLE hDbase, CEOID oidRecord, WORD cPropID,
CEPROPVAL * rgPropVal);
```

The first parameter, `hDbase`, is a handle to an open database. The second parameter, `oidRecord`, is the CEOID of an existing record. If this parameter contains a value, the record being written will actually overwrite the existing record. If this parameter is 0, the record being written will be added as a new record. The third parameter, `cPropID`, is the number of properties you're writing. Finally, the `rgPropVal` parameter is a pointer to an array of CEPROPVAL structures, just as you saw above with `CeReadRecordProps()`.

In order to write a new record to your database, then, you need a function like this:

```
BOOL AreaCodeDatabaseInsert(LPTSTR szCode, LPTSTR szState)
{
    CEPROPVAL pvPropVals[2];
```

In this case, you are receiving the values for the area code property and the state property. You use these values passed in to your function as the values of the properties you'll write to the database:

```
pvPropVals[0].propid = MAKELONG(CEVT_LPWSTR, PROP_AREACODE);
pvPropVals[0].wFlags = 0;
pvPropVals[0].val.lpwstr = szCode;
pvPropVals[1].propid = MAKELONG(CEVT_LPWSTR, PROP_STATE);
pvPropVals[1].wFlags = 0;
pvPropVals[1].val.lpwstr = szState;
```

Once you've initialized your CEPROPVAL array, you can then call CeWriteRecordProps():

```
if (!CeWriteRecordProps(m_Handle, 0, 2, &pvPropVals))
```

You then return a value based on the result of CeWriteRecordProps():

```
        return(FALSE);
    else
        return(TRUE);
}
```

AreaCodeDatabaseDelete()

To delete a record, you use a function called CeDeleteRecord(). So, in the context of this application, to delete a record from your database, you would have a function like the following, where you pass in a string containing the CEOID of the record to be deleted:

```
BOOL AreaCodeDatabaseDeleteRecord(LPWSTR data)
{
```

The next step is to convert the string to a numeric value:

```
CEOID oidRecord;
oidRecord = (CEOID)_wol(data);
```

Once that's done, all you have to do is call CeDeleteRecord():

```
ret = CeDeleteRecord(m_Handle, oidRecord);
return(ret);
}
```

And that's all there is to deleting records from a database.

AreaCodeDatabaseFinish()

The only action you really have to take here is to remember to close the database and free any memory still in use. To close a database, call CloseHandle() and pass in the handle to the open database:

```
void AreaCodeDatabaseFinish()
{
    CloseHandle(m_Handle);
}
```

Summary

In this chapter, we looked at the basics of CE's structured storage types. There's a lot of information to master here, and it can be quite dizzying at first. With a little bit of practicing on the examples provided here, however, you're sure to have it down in no time.

In Chapter 12, we'll look at some alternatives to API-based database access. Specifically, we'll be looking at MFC's approach to databases, as well as some database engines provided by third-party vendors.

PART II

Mastering the Developer's Tools

- CHAPTER 5: CE Toolkit for Visual C++

- CHAPTER 6: Yes, It's Possible—MFC on CE

- CHAPTER 7: Real MFC Applications Ported to CE

- CHAPTER 8: Visual Basic Toolkit for CE

- CHAPTER 9: A Real VB Application Converted to CE

CHAPTER
FIVE

CE Toolkit for Visual C++

- Using VC++ to Develop for Windows CE

- The Windows CE Toolkit for VC++

- The Platform SDKs

- MFC versus SDK-Style Coding

The purpose of this chapter is to show off the Windows CE Toolkit for Visual C++ (VC++). After reading this chapter, you will have a thorough understanding of the most important features of the toolkit and will know how to integrate the toolkit into VC++ as smoothly as possible. You'll also have a sense of what sort of common problems crop up from time to time when using the toolkit. (There are a few, but not too many.)

Along the way, you'll develop a Wizard for VC++ to help you prototype CE applications with a minimum of code and effort by creating small, dialog-based applications! Next, we'll examine the tradeoffs of coding in Microsoft Foundation Classes (MFC) vs. SDK-style coding. Of course, we'll be picking up MFC again in a later chapter. Finally, we'll present a simple SDK-style application, written specifically for the PPC devices, which will illustrate the differences—if any—between "regular" (i.e., desktop) applications and CE applications.

Using VC++ to Develop for Windows CE

When we use Visual C++ to build programs for Windows CE, we're really using two products at once.

The first product is the Microsoft Windows CE Toolkit for Visual C++. The toolkit consists of the core files needed to build and debug executables for the various Windows CE platforms.

The second product is the Software Development Kit (SDK) for the platform we're targeting. The SDK consists of additional tools to help prototype and debug our applications, such as the Windows CE emulators.

In this section, we'll look at the components that make up both the toolkit and the emulator and show you what you really need to know about each.

The Windows CE Toolkit for VC++

As noted, the toolkit is the core that makes it possible for Visual C++ to build executables for the Windows CE operating system, including such tools as

- The compilers
- The Platform Manager
- The Project Wizards

The Compilers

Because CE is an operating system that runs on a variety of chip types, several compilers are included in the toolkit, one for each chip. While the fact that you have more than one compiler might seem unusual to many Windows developers, the compilers are generally fairly transparent. However, there are times when it can be useful to know a bit about them.

The major issue that you'll experience from time to time is that of the compilers not being able to find the correct path or location of certain .h or .lib files that it needs in order to build and link your project successfully. This issue may appear trivial, but it's not! In fact, questions relating to directories and linking are among the most commonly asked by those new to CE programming.

If you're using the toolkit for VC++ 5, the paths are

BIN

%WCESDK%\wce\emul\hpc\windows

%WCETOOLKIT%\Bin

%WCESDK%\wce\bin

INCLUDE

%WCETOOLKIT%\Include\WCE200

%WCETOOLKIT%\MFC\Include\WCE200

%WCETOOLKIT%\ATL\Include

LIB

%WCETOOLKIT%\LIB\wce200\%CHIPTYPE%

%WCETOOLKIT%\MFC\LIB\wce200\%CHIPTYPE%

For VC++ 6, the paths are

BIN

%WCETOOLS%\Bin

INCLUDE

%WCETOOLS%\WCE200\%PLATFORM%\Include

%WCETOOLS%\MFC\ WCE200\%PLATFORM%\Include

%WCETOOLS%\WCE200\ATL\%PLATFORM%\Include

INCLUDE

%WCETOOLS%\WCE200\%PLATFORM%\Lib\%CHIPTYPE%

%WCETOOLS%\MFC\ WCE200\%PLATFORM%\ Lib\%CHIPTYPE%

%WCETOOLS%\WCE200\ATL\%PLATFORM%\ Lib\%CHIPTYPE%

NOTE   There are special assemblers for each of the chips.

The Platform Manager

The Platform Manager is a new tool provided in the toolkit for VC++ 6 that makes it much easier to specify the target device and the preferred connection method for EXE file uploading and debugging purposes. As shown in Figure 5.1, the Platform Manager can maintain a listing of all your CE devices, organized by platform type.

By right-clicking on one of the platform types (e.g., Palm-size PC 2.01) and selecting the Property menu, you can view information about the platform type, including which version of CE is supported and which chip types and architectures are supported. The Platform Property dialog is shown in Figure 5.2.

FIGURE 5.1:

The main view of Platform
Manager

FIGURE 5.2:

The Platform Property
dialog

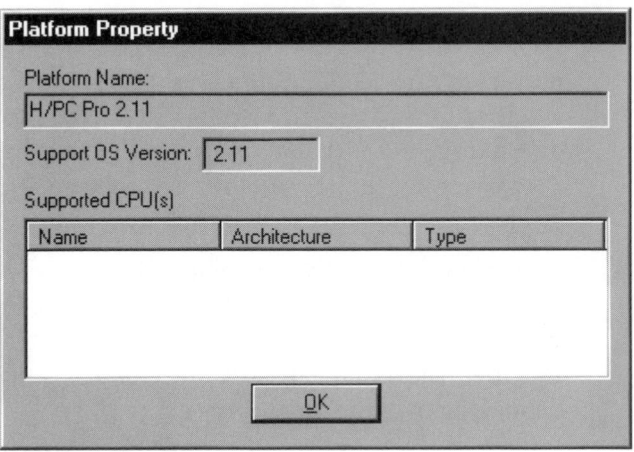

Additionally, Platform Manager allows you to set the properties for each device registered with the system. By right-clicking on a device and selecting Property, you can tell Platform Manager how you would like the CE development tools to connect to your CE devices. There are three possible ways to connect to a CE device, as shown in Figure 5.3: PPP Transport for Windows CE, TCP/IP Transport for Windows CE, or Windows CE Services.

FIGURE 5.3:

The Device Property dialog

Of the three, Windows CE Services is probably the most common means of connecting to a device. CE Services is the standard, serial-line connection that is usually used for Active Syncing devices with the Desktop. The drawback to debugging over a serial line is that it's very slow. In fact, you'll find that it takes so long to execute a single line of source code while debugging over the serial port that you can actually count the seconds. Obviously, this can be very frustrating.

That's why the debugging method that most developers will probably want to use is the TCP/IP Transport for Windows CE. Basically, this allows you to set up your CE devices and all of the CE-related tools so that they use debugging over Ethernet. The immediate advantage of this is that it is many times faster than debugging over the serial connection.

Ethernet Debugging

When it comes to debugging your applications, the Ethernet TCP/IP Transport is about as fast as it gets. It's so useful and such a time saver, in fact, that it's really worth the investment to get your CE device connected to your LAN.

As mentioned in Chapter 1, there are two options available to get your CE device on your LAN. The first is a wireless LAN solution from Proxim, Inc. of Mountain View, California (http://www.proxim.com). Proxim offers a product called the RangeLan2 Bridge, which serves as a kind of wireless hub or access point to the network. The other part of this solution is a PC Card (PCMCIA Card) that you use with the CE Device itself.

Your second option for Ethernet debugging is a solution provided by Socket Communications of Newark, California (http://www.socketcom.com). Socket Communications offers a PC Card (PCMCIA Card) or Compact Flash Card that provides an instant (wired) connection to the network. Both the PC Card and the Compact Flash solution are easy to configure. However, the Compact Flash version has the added benefit of taking advantage of a slot you're probably not using, and it will run on Palm-size PC devices, too.

The Project Wizards

The Project Wizards are the add-ins to VC++ that appear whenever you choose File ➤ New and highlight the Projects tab, as shown in Figure 5.4. Although there are over 20 Wizards in all, there are 7 Wizards that help to speed up Windows CE development. They are

- WCE Application
- WCE ATL COM AppWizard
- WCE Dynamic-Link Library
- WCE MFC ActiveX Control
- WCE MFC AppWizard (DLL)
- WCE MFC AppWizard (EXE)
- WCE Static Library

However, of these seven Wizards, you'll probably only use two of them on a regular basis, the WCE Application Wizard and EXE version of the WCE MFC AppWizard.

WCE Application Wizard Using the WCE Application Wizard is the simplest way to create a full-fledged SDK-style Windows CE application. In less than three steps, the WCE Application Wizard will create

- An empty project, with no source files whatsoever

- A Simple Windows CE Application, which merely has an empty `WinMain()`

- A "Hello World"–style application, complete with a simple window, `Wnd-Proc()` function, and an icon, as shown in Figure 5.5

WCE MFC AppWizard The WCE MFC AppWizard is the one you'll use for every CE-based MFC Application you create. It's very similar to the standard MFC AppWizard that you've probably used to create Desktop-based MFC applications. However, there are a few noticeable differences between the CE version and the Desktop version.

The biggest potential problem to watch out for relates to choosing the correct implementation of CommandBars for your application. On the second page of the Wizard (shown in Figure 5.6), you are asked to choose the type of Command-Bar you'd like for your application.

FIGURE 3.5:

The "Hello World" application

FIGURE 5.6:

The WCE MFC AppWizard

The Wizard presents you with four options:

- Basic CommandBar
- CommandBar with toolbar buttons
- Internet Explorer ReBars
- MFC 2.0–compatible CommandBar

The problem is that unless you explicitly choose the fourth option, you will only be able to compile for CE 2.01 or CE 2.11, which are the versions of CE that PPC and HPC/Pro devices are running; all of the HPC devices are running CE 2! And, while it's true that some OEMs will be offering customers the ability to upgrade to CE 2.11, not all of them will. This means that if you don't choose the MFC 2–compatible CommandBar, you will be ignoring a potentially huge market for your software.

Of course, everything has its tradeoffs. When you do choose the 2.0–compatible CommandBar, you lose the option of having a status bar and support for printing, both of which are only available for CE 2.01 and 2.11. The end result of this is that you either have to explicitly target only PPC and HPC/Pro devices, or you have to write your own printing and status bar code.

As of this writing, there are no commercially available HPC devices running CE 2.11; only the HPC/Pro devices run CE 2.11. The Palm-size PCs run CE 2.01. However, as mentioned in Chapter 1, some HPC manufacturers do offer a software or ROM upgrade from CE 2 to CE 2.11.

Creating A Wizard for Dialog-Based Applications—A Sample Application In previous versions of the toolkit, the array of Wizards was not nearly so complete. In fact, there was no way to quickly prototype an application at all. Even with the current toolkit's extensive list of Wizards, there may be a variety of custom applications or frameworks that you'd also like to be able to use for quick development.

For instance, there's no way to quickly and easily create a dialog-based application. In many situations, dialog-based applications represent a very handy tool in prototyping or rapidly developing an application that would take much longer to create if you used any other method.

To remedy this situation, let's create our own Wizard for VC++ in 10 easy steps, first creating a simple, dialog-based application and the Wizard based on the application.

1. To create the dialog-based application, create a new WCE Application with the Simple Windows CE Application option specified.

2. After VC++ creates the source files and places you in the project, create a simple, generic dialog, as shown in Figure 5.7.

FIGURE 5.7:

The generic dialog

3. Your next task is to create a simple `DialogProc()`. So that your project is generic enough to be useful for a variety of applications, make it handle two messages:

    ```
    WM_INITDIALOG
    WM_COMMAND
    ```

    (You may also want to handle `WM_CTLCOLORDLG` if you find that your dialog paints strangely on some devices.)

    When you're finished, you have a fairly basic-looking `DialogProc()`:

    ```
    BOOL CALLBACK DlgProc (HWND hwnd, UINT uMsg, WPARAM wParam,
    LPARAM lParam)
    {
        switch (uMsg)
        {
            case WM_INITDIALOG:
            {
                    return TRUE;
            }
    ```

```
            case WM_CTLCOLORDLG:
            {
                    SetBkColor((HDC)wParam, LTGRAY_BRUSH);
                    return FALSE; //for occasional strange painting
            }
            case WM_COMMAND:
            {
                    switch(LOWORD(wParam))
                    {
                        case IDCANCEL:
                        case IDOK:
                        {
                                EndDialog(hwnd, 0);
                                return TRUE;
                        }
                    }
            }
            default:
                    return FALSE;
    }
```

4. The only thing left to do is to edit your `WinMain()` function to launch the dialog:

    ```
    DialogBox ((HANDLE) hInstance, MAKEINTRESOURCE(IDD_DIALOG1), NULL,
    (DLGPROC)DlgProc);
    return 0 ;
    ```

    You are now done creating your template application.

5. Now to create the Wizard. Choose File➤New in VC++. Then choose the Projects tab, and select CustomAppWizard from the list. Enter a name for your new Wizard such as **WCE Dialog–based Application**. Click Next.

6. When you've done this, you'll be presented with a list of options, as shown in Figure 5. 8.

7. Choose An Existing Project as the starting point for your Wizard, and click the Next button.

8. In the dialog that appears, enter the name of the application you created in steps 1–4. Click Next. You'll then be asked to confirm your options; click Done to finish.

FIGURE 5.8:

The Custom App
Wizard dialog

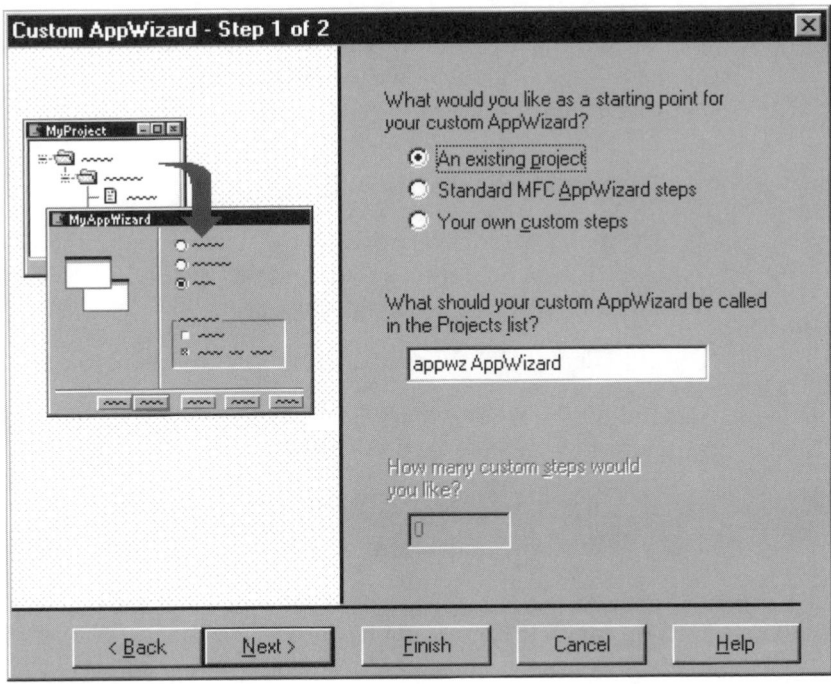

9.   When VC++ places you into the project, NEWPROJ.INF should read some-
     thing like the following:

```
=:ICON1.ICO    icon1.ico
RESOURCE.H     resource.h
=SIMPLE.C      simple.c
ROOT.RC        $$root$$.rc
```

Change this so that the line referencing simple.c—or the name of your
application's main C/C++ file—now reads

```
=SIMPLE.C      $$root$$.c
```

This ensures that your main C/C++ file will be renamed to reflect whatever
project name is entered into your Wizard when someone creates a new project.

10. Next, compile your Wizard—and it's ready to use!

The Platform SDKs

The platform SDKs can be regarded as two separate packages: First, there are the generic tools that will work for any CE platform. Second, there are the platform-specific tools, such as the emulators.

The Generic Tools

The major part of every SDK is the supplementary tools and utilities designed to make it easier to target and debug the Windows CE platforms. Some of the tools currently shipping with the SDKs are

- Remote File Viewer, a Desktop-based Explorer for CE Devices

- Remote Heap Viewer, which allows you to view information about Heap allocation on your device

- Remote Process Viewer, a kind of Desktop-based task manager for CE

- Remote Registry Editor, which allows you to edit the registry of your CE device

- Remote Spy++, which allows you to view class information and messages for the various windows, both hidden and active, on your CE device

- Remote Zoomin, a tool for taking screenshots of programs running on your device

These tools are included in all of the SDKs and should work with any CE devices, regardless of form factor. However, in each toolkit there is a unique tool that can help you develop for a CE-based form factor, even if you do not own a device.

TIP

All SDK tools are simple RAPI applications, which means that you can easily create your own CE tools for debugging! For more on RAPI and creating RAPI applications, see Chapter 10.

The Emulators

Each of the SDKs comes with a Desktop-based emulator for the platform the SDK is targeting. For example, the AutoPC SDK comes with an emulator for the AutoPC.

The emulators can be a wonderful tool for prototyping and debugging your application before you begin testing it on a device.

There are, however a few drawbacks to using the emulators. The first disadvantage is that they're not true emulators. You must compile a special version of your program just for the emulator.

Second, the emulators only run on Windows NT; they will not run under Windows 98. This is because the emulators, like Windows CE itself, are Unicode-based, while Windows 98 is ANSI-based. It is true that 98 does have stub code for some Unicode operations, but it is not enough to support the CE emulators.

WARNING   Because the emulators and many of the SDK tools do not run under Windows 95/98, it is recommended that you use Windows NT as your development platform. Although the emulators do not work under 95/98, two of the SDK tools will run just fine: Remote Zoomin and Heap Viewer.

The typical CE application development cycle, then, is to first compile for the emulator of your choice (yes, you must actually do a special compilation just for the emulator). Next, test and debug your application in the emulator as thoroughly as possible. Finally, when you believe that your application is ready, upload it to the CE device and repeat the process. Of course, since testing and debugging on a CE device may be quite time-consuming, being able to debug on the Desktop is a serious advantage.

The third real disadvantage of using the emulators is that they tend to be more forgiving of bad code than the devices are. What that means is that even though your code works in the emulator, you may still have some work to do before it will work on the device. Simply put, the emulators are not a 100 percent–reliable measure of how your code will work on a device. For instance, in the HPC emulator, the following code either crashes or runs and displays the desired result:

```
case WM_INITDIALOG:
{
        LPSYSTEMTIME lpSystemTime; //system time struct
        TCHAR chTime[254]; //string to display system time
        GetSystemTime(SystemTime);
        wsprintf((LPTSTR)chTime, TEXT("Today's date: %d/%d/%d"),
lpSystemTime->wMonth, lpSystemTime->wDay, lpSystemTime->wYear);
        SetWindowText(hwnd, TEXT("Hello WinCE!"));
```

```
              SendDlgItemMessage(hwnd, IDC_DATETEXT, WM_SETTEXT, 0,
(LPARAM) (LPTSTR)chTime);
              return TRUE;
      }
```

At first glance, it seems like acceptable code, but look closely. The lpSystem-Time structure is never initialized to point to a valid memory location before it is passed to GetSystemTime(). When this same code is executed on an HPC device, the program runs and behaves relatively normally, with the exception that there is an area of the dialog box that, instead of showing the date, shows the word *Static*.

The corrected code looks like this:

```
      case WM_INITDIALOG:
      {
              SYSTEMTIME SystemTime; //system time struct
              TCHAR chTime[254]; //string to display system time
              GetSystemTime(&SystemTime);
              wsprintf((LPTSTR)chTime, TEXT("Today's date: %d/%d/%d"),
SystemTime.wMonth, SystemTime.wDay, SystemTime.wYear);
              SetWindowText(hwnd, TEXT("Hello WinCE!"));
              SendDlgItemMessage(hwnd, IDC_DATETEXT, WM_SETTEXT, 0,
(LPARAM) (LPTSTR)chTime);
              return TRUE;
      }
```

Here, the *address* of a SYSTEMTIME variable (not just an LPSYSTEMTIME variable, as before) is passed to GetSystemTime(), which will return the correct values on a device or in the emulator.

MFC vs. SDK-Style Coding

There's ongoing debate about using MFC or SDK-style code. And, in the case of Windows CE, both SDK-style programmers and MFC programmers have had to give up a little. As demonstrated in Chapters 3 and 6, many API calls are missing from the CE API and some MFC classes have been modified or dropped completely on CE. In the end, however, it comes down to two simple issues: storage space and ease of development.

Storage Space

If you create the simplest possible SDK-style application and the simplest possible MFC application, you'll get the following results:

MFC or SDK	EXE Size	Additional DLLs	Total Storage Space
SDK	8.5K	(none)	8.5K
MFC	10K	356K	366K

When developers first started writing for CE, this 350K difference was a big reason that so much SDK-style development was done. However, CE devices and their uses are changing in a couple of ways that make MFC more attractive.

First, many applications are being developed as vertical market applications, which means that the device will likely be running just that one application. In that case, it obviously doesn't matter how much storage space your program occupies, because you have the entire device to yourself.

The second changing aspect of CE devices is that OEMs are now starting to include the MFC runtimes in the ROM of the devices themselves. This means that it will no longer be necessary for you to ship a 350K DLL with your applications.

Of course, not all devices have the DLL in ROM, so this is still an issue for the time being. And, SDK-style programmers will correctly point out that they can still write tighter, more compact code than that which MFC can produce.

Ease of Development

Ease of development is more of an individual decision. If you happen to have an existing program that you're looking to port to Windows CE, you're almost certainly going to choose whichever style of coding the existing program was originally written in.

Only a few MFC classes have not been implemented on CE, so it is typically easier to port existing MFC code than it is to port existing SDK-style code. This is especially true as large numbers of the API and C-runtime library functions have not been implemented for CE. However, just as with the issue of storage space, some of these objections are also fading away. For instance, with the release of

CE 2.11, Microsoft significantly enhanced the available C-runtime libraries, making it easier to port existing code and to write new code.

The end result of this is that the line dividing MFC and SDK-style CE developers is becoming almost invisible. With the release of CE 2.11 and future releases, you'll likely see both styles of coding become equally popular, with no clear benefit to either one. In the next chapters, we'll examine MFC and SDK-style programming in more detail. We'll look at the benefits of each and tell you how to work around what's missing from each when it comes to Windows CE.

A Sample SDK-Style Application

At this point, let's take a look at a sample SDK-style application for CE and examine how it differs from a standard Win32 application. For this demonstration, let's make a simple Task Manager–style application for the Palm-size PC. Currently, the only way to see all of the programs running on your PPC device and close a program that's running requires you to go to Start ➤ Settings ➤ System, then click the Task Manager tab, as shown in Figure 5.9. In our sample application, we will change this so that our Task Manager will allow the user to close any application with one click.

FIGURE 5.9:

The PPC device
Task Manager

Using the Dialog-based App Wizard that you just created, you will now create a simple, dialog-based application from which you'll begin your Task Manager. Your Task Manager will have three purposes:

- To display a list of running tasks

- To allow the user to switch to any of the tasks

- To allow the user to close any of the tasks

We will cover each of these purposes separately in the following sections.

Displaying a List of Running Tasks

The first step in this process is to add a list box to your dialog box that will show the list of running tasks once they've been retrieved from the system. Using the dialog editor of VC++, go ahead and add a list box by selecting the ListBox icon from the toolbar and dragging in onto your form. Then, right-click the list box, select Properties, and rename its identifier to IDC_LISTTASKS. Since you'll also need an End Task and a Switch To button, go ahead and add them to the form now. Give the End Task button an identifier of IDC_ENDTASK and the Switch To button an identifier of IDC_SWITCHTO.

Now, on to the list of tasks. Filling the list box with the list of windows on the system is quite easy. First, make sure to clear out any existing contents of the list box:

```
SendMessage(hwndCtrl, LB_RESETCONTENT, 0, 0);
```

Then, begin looping through all of the windows on the system with successive calls to GetWindow():

```
hWndAWindow = GetWindow(hwnd, GW_HWNDFIRST);
while (hWndAWindow != 0)
{
```

Be careful to filter out your own application, any hidden windows, any child windows, and, of course, the Desktop itself:

```
if ((hWndAWindow != hwnd) &&
        IsWindowVisible(hWndAWindow) &&
        (GetWindow(hWndAWindow, GW_OWNER) == 0) &&
        (GetWindowText(hWndAWindow, szBuff, MAX_PATH) != 0)
&&
        (lstrcmpi (szBuff, TEXT("Desktop")) != 0))
```

If the window you find passes these tests, simply add its caption to your list box and retrieve the next window handle:

```
                        SendMessage(hwndCtrl, LB_ADDSTRING, 0, (LPARAM)
(LPCTSTR) szBuff);
                hWndAWindow = GetWindow(hWndAWindow, GW_HWNDNEXT);
        }
```

When it's all put together, it looks like this:

```
        SendMessage(hwndCtrl, LB_RESETCONTENT, 0, 0);
        hWndAWindow = GetWindow(hwnd, GW_HWNDFIRST);
        while (hWndAWindow != 0)
        {
                if ((hWndAWindow != hwnd) && IsWindowVisible(hWndAWin-
dow) &&
                        (GetWindow(hWndAWindow, GW_OWNER) == 0) &&
                        (GetWindowText(hWndAWindow, szBuff, MAX_PATH) != 0)
&&
                        (lstrcmpi (szBuff, TEXT("Desktop")) != 0))
                                SendMessage(hwndCtrl, LB_ADDSTRING, 0, (LPARAM)
(LPCTSTR) szBuff);
                        hWndAWindow = GetWindow(hWndAWindow, GW_HWNDNEXT);
        }
```

A Missing API Call and Some Recycled Code

With a few changes, the above code can double as a replacement for GetDesktop Window(), one of the API calls that's missing from the CE API. GetDesktopWindow() is used to get the window handle of the desktop. This has many uses, including retrieving the device context (DC) of the desktop so that you can paint directly on it. However, although it is used quite commonly in desktop PC programming, GetDesktopWindow() is not supported under Windows CE.

If you look at the code we just wrote, though, you'll note that we're making sure not to add the Desktop window to our task list. Therefore, it stands to reason that there is a window calling itself the Desktop. If you know this, you can get its handle. For instance, if you modified your existing block of code from the example above so that you are explicitly looking for that Desktop window, you can simulate GetDesktopWindow().

Continued on next page

The modified code for a `GetDesktopWindow()`-style routine has the same `GetWindow()` loop as the above example:

```
hWndAWindow = GetWindow(hwnd, GW_HWNDFIRST);
while (hWndAWindow != 0)
{
```

Again, it retrieves the caption of each window:

```
GetWindowText(hWndAWindow, szBuff, MAX_PATH);
```

This time, however, it only quits if it finds one whose caption matches the word *Desktop:*

```
if (lstrcmpi (szBuff, TEXT("Desktop")) == 0)
{
            break;
}
```

Otherwise, it continues to retrieve the next window:

```
hWndAWindow = GetWindow(hWndAWindow, GW_HWND-
NEXT);
}
```

When assembled, the entire block of code looks like this:

```
hWndAWindow = GetWindow(hwnd, GW_HWNDFIRST);
while (hWndAWindow != 0)
{
    GetWindowText(hWndAWindow, szBuff, MAX_PATH);
    if (lstrcmpi (szBuff, TEXT("Desktop")) == 0)
    {

        break;
    }
    hWndAWindow = GetWindow(hWndAWindow, GW_HWND-
NEXT);
}
```

With just a few lines of mostly recycled and borrowed code, you've just managed to simulate one of the missing API calls. Of course, you might not be so lucky all the time—for more on working around missing API calls, see Chapter 3.

Switching to One of the Tasks

Switching to one of the tasks in the task window is extremely simple. All you have to do is to add a handler for the WM_COMMAND message, since the user will be clicking a button in order to make this work. First, make sure that the user actually did select an item from the list:

```
                   cbCnt = (int)SendMessage(GetDlgItem(hwnd,
    IDC_LISTTASKS), LB_GETCURSEL, 0, OL);
                   if ((cbCnt < 0))
                   {
                           MessageBox(hwnd, TEXT("You must first
    select a task."), TEXT("Error: No task"), MB_OK | MB_ICONSTOP);
                           return TRUE;
                   }
```

If they did select an item, retrieve the text of the currently selected item:

```
                   SendMessage(GetDlgItem(hwnd, IDC_LISTTASKS),
                   LB_GETTEXT,
                   (WPARAM)SendMessage(GetDlgItem(hwnd,
    IDC_LISTTASKS), LB_GETCURSEL, 0, OL),
                   (LPARAM)(LPSTR)szBuff);
```

Then, make sure the window still exists by calling FindWindow():

```
                   if (FindWindow(NULL, szBuff) != NULL)
                   {
```

If it does, call SetForegroudWindow():

```
                   hWndAWindow = FindWindow(NULL, szBuff);
                   SetForegroundWindow(hWndAWindow);
```

This done, the only job remaining is to add the logic for closing a running application.

Closing an Application

You may have noticed that in the last code example, which switches to an application, the if (FindWindow(NULL, szBuff) != NULL) block was never actually finished. This is because with just another few lines of code, you can make the same routine serve to close an application as well. All you have to add to the above code is:

```
                   if (LOWORD(wParam) == IDC_ENDTASK)
                   {
```

```
                                          SendMessage(hWndAWindow, WM_CLOSE, 0,
0);
                                    }
```

Then, add one additional line to close the Task Manager:

```
                              SendMessage(hwnd, WM_CLOSE, 0, 0);
```

NOTE

Close the Task Manager after the user has switched to another program or closed a program to be consistent with the behavior of the Windows 98 Task Manager, which does the same thing.

At first, this handling of two button events with the same WM_COMMAND message handler might seem a bit confusing, so let's take a look at the entire message handler block of code:

```
          case WM_COMMAND:
          {
                  switch(LOWORD(wParam))
                  {
                        case IDCANCEL:
                        case IDOK:
                        {
                            EndDialog(hwnd, 0);
                            return TRUE;
                        }
                        case IDC_ENDTASK:
                        case IDC_SWITCHTO:
                        {
                            int     cbCnt;
                            TCHAR   szBuff[MAX_PATH];
                            HWND    hWndAWindow;
                            cbCnt = (int)SendMessage(GetDlgItem(hwnd,
IDC_LISTTASKS), LB_GETCURSEL, 0, 0L);
                            if ((cbCnt < 0))
                            {
                                  MessageBox(hwnd, TEXT("You must first
select a task."), TEXT("Error: No task"), MB_OK | MB_ICONSTOP);
                                  return TRUE;
                            }
                            SendMessage(GetDlgItem(hwnd, IDC_LISTTASKS),
                                  LB_GETTEXT,
```

```
                                (WPARAM)SendMessage(GetDlgItem(hwnd,
IDC_LISTTASKS), LB_GETCURSEL, 0, 0L),
                                (LPARAM)(LPSTR)szBuff);
                        if (FindWindow(NULL, szBuff) != NULL) //the
window still exists!
                        {
                                hWndAWindow = FindWindow(NULL, szBuff);
                                SetForegroundWindow(hWndAWindow);
                                if (LOWORD(wParam) == IDC_ENDTASK)
                                {
                                        SendMessage(hWndAWindow, WM_CLOSE, 0,
0);
                                }
                                SendMessage(hwnd, WM_CLOSE, 0, 0);
                                return TRUE;
                        }
                        else //if you didn't find the app, it's time to
refresh the list of tasks
                                SendMessage(hwnd, WM_USER + 200, 0, 0);
                        break ;
                }
        }
```

As you can see, it makes sense to handle both the IDC_ENDTASK and the IDC_SWITCHTO button clicks in the same handler because, with the exception of the very last if statement, they need to do exactly the same thing. Both of them need to make sure the user selected an item from the list, and both of them need to make sure that if they did select an item, that item is still a valid window. By combining the two button handlers into one, you can make the application much more efficient.

One Last Snag: Keeping the List of Tasks Current

If you look closely at the entire WM_COMMAND message handler, you'll notice that there's one extra line of code at the end that we haven't yet discussed. It reads

```
SendMessage(hwnd, WM_USER + 200, 0, 0);
```

This simple line of code exists to solve a common Task Manager problem: it ensures that the list of tasks in the list box is current. In other words, you don't want the application to display a task that's no longer running. Normally, you might handle something like this by setting up a timer, but here that's not necessarily the most efficient way to accomplish this.

Instead, take the code that fills up your list box and move it to a custom message (say, WM_USER+200) handler, like this:

```
case WM_USER + 200:
{
    //fill list box code get moved here...
}
```

Then, ensure that the Task Manager application sends itself this WM_USER + 200 message on any one of the following three occasions:

- When the program starts up

- When the program receives a WM_CTLCOLORDLG message (the closest thing to WM_PAINT when working with dialogs)

- Whenever the user selects a task from the list that no longer exists

The first case can be handled by amending the WM_INITDIALOG handler to read

```
case WM_INITDIALOG:
{
    SendMessage(hwnd, WM_USER + 200, 0, 0);
    return TRUE;
}
```

The second case can be implemented similarly with regard to the WM_CTLCOL-ORDIALOG message:

```
case WM_CTLCOLORDLG:
{
    SendMessage(hwnd, WM_USER + 200, 0, 0);
    return TRUE;
}
```

The third item, as you saw already, is implemented in the WM_COMMAND handler by trapping the condition of the selected item not being a valid window handle. This is shown in the last line of this block of code:

```
            if (FindWindow(NULL, szBuff) != NULL) //the
window still exists!
            {
                hWndAWindow = FindWindow(NULL, szBuff);
                SetForegroundWindow(hWndAWindow);
                if (LOWORD(wParam) == IDC_ENDTASK)
                {
```

```
                                      SendMessage(hWndAWindow, WM_CLOSE, 0,
0);
                             }
                             SendMessage(hwnd, WM_CLOSE, 0, 0);
                             return TRUE;
                    }
                    else //if you didn't find the app, it's time to
refresh the list of tasks
                             SendMessage(hwnd, WM_USER + 200, 0, 0);
```

When you're finished, you'll have a professional-looking application that will make the Palm-size PC devices much easier to use.

TIP   There's absolutely no reason you can't run your Task Manager on an HPC device, too.

As you can see, SDK-style coding for CE doesn't look all that different from SDK-style coding for desktop PCs. The main difference between SDK-style coding and any Win32 code you may have written is the use of the TEXT macro to account for Unicode strings. Of course, you can and *should* use this macro when coding for 98 or NT, but most programmers still regard it as optional.

Summary

In this chapter, we learned the basics of using Visual C++ to build applications for Windows CE. We also examined some of the advantages of both MFC and SDK-style coding. Finally, we made a simple Task Manager application to make our Palm-size PCs more user-friendly.w

In the next chapters, we'll be exploring more MFC on CE as well as Visual Basic on CE. MFC has several "new" classes that exist only on the CE platform, and we'll be looking at each of them and how to use them. Similarly, Visual Basic on CE has a number of unique tools and features that we'll learn to master.

CHAPTER
SIX

Yes, It's Possible—MFC on CE!

- New Classes for CE

- Modified Classes

- Classes That Lost Functionality

- Classes That Gained Functionality

- Missing Classes

In chapter 5, we looked at some of the differences between coding in an SDK-style versus using MFC. In this chapter, we'll explore the differences between MFC on the Desktop and MFC on a CE device. While most of MFC remains unchanged, there are a few changes we need to know about. Generally, these changes fall into three categories:

- New classes and how to use them

- Modified classes and how to deal with them

- Deleted classes and how to live without them

We'll be taking a look at each of these areas and how they'll affect our applications.

New Classes for CE

Because some of the functionality offered by the Windows CE API was so different from anything in the desktop world, Microsoft found it necessary to add five new classes to the MFC class library. They are:

- CCeSocket

- CCeDBEnum

- CCeDBDatabase

- CCeDBProp

- CCeDBRecord

The first of these classes, CCeSocket, handles the limited Winsock operations supported by Windows CE. The remaining four classes allow MFC programs to use the Windows CE database engine.

CCeSocket

The CCeSocket is a very unusual class. Mostly, that's because all of its documentation advises us that CAsyncSocket is not supported under Windows CE and that we should use CCeSocket instead. However, this is only partially true.

In fact, we should use CCeSocket for all Winsock-based communication under Windows CE. That's because CE doesn't support true asynchronous communication. Instead, CCeSocket simulates asynchronous events by creating two threads that watch for socket-related operations and events. When an event occurs, the threads pass the notification to the correct message handler. That's the part of the statement about CAsyncSocket and CCeSocket that's true.

The part that isn't true is that there is, in fact, a CAsyncSocket on Windows CE. It's just that it's buried about three levels deep and exists only as a base class upon which the other two socket classes of Windows CE (CSocket and CCeSocket) are built.

Under Windows 98/NT, the object hierarchy for socket classes looks something like the diagram in Figure 6.1.

FIGURE 6.1:

Socket classes object hierarchy under Windows 98/NT

Under Windows CE, there is one extra class, as shown in Figure 6.2.

FIGURE 6.2:

Socket classes object hierarchy under Windows CE

TIP
For more on communication with Windows CE, see Chapter 11.

TIP
MFC for CE also defines a custom Windows message, WM_SOCKET_NOTIFY, for use with the **CCeSocket** class. However, since this message appears to be used only internally, it should not affect our development at all.

The remaining four classes in our list are CE database classes and exist strictly for the purpose of encapsulating the Windows CE Database Engine. In this section, we'll take a look at each class and how to use it.

CCeDBEnum

CCeDBEnum is a class that wraps the CeFindFirstDatabase()/CeFindNextDatabase() functions. When you create a CCeDBEnum object—just as with the CeFindFirstDatabase() function—you can pass in a database-type identifier to look for a specific type of database, or you can pass in 0 to tell the object to enumerate all databases. You can then retrieve the CEOID of each database matching your criteria by calling the class's Next() method.

In code, retrieving a listing of all databases might look something like this:

```
CCeDBEnum DBEnum;
DBEnum = new CCeDBEnum(0);
while (idCEOID = DBEnum.Next())
{
   //...do some processing here
}
//...
```

CCeDBProp

The CCeDBProp class encapsulates the CEPROPVAL structure used to set and retrieve values for properties (fields) of a database record. Table 6.1 shows the methods of CCeDBProp and the members of the CEPROPVAL structure to which they correspond.

TABLE 6.1: CCeDBProp Methods and Corresponding CEPROPVAL Members

Method	CEPROPVAL members	Description
GetBlob()	myCEPROPVAL.val.blob	Retrieves the CEBLOB value of the property
GetFiletime()	myCEPROPVAL.val.filetime	Retrieves the FILETIME value of the property
GetIdent()	HIWORD(myCEPROPVAL.propid)	Retrieves the identifier of the property
GetLong()	myCEPROPVAL.val.lVal	Retrieves the long int value of the property
GetShort()	myCEPROPVAL.val.iVal	Retrieves the int value of the property
GetSortFlags()	myCEPROPVAL.wFlags	Retrieves the flags specifying how the property is sorted
GetString()	myCEPROPVAL.val.lpwstr	Retrieves the wide string value of the property
GetType()	LOWORD(myCEPROPVAL.propid)	Retrieves the type of the property
GetULong()	myCEPROPVAL.val.ulVal	Retrieves the unsigned long int value of the property
GetUShort()	myCEPROPVAL.val.uVal	Retrieves the unsigned int value of the property
SetBlob()	myCEPROPVAL.val.blob	Retrieves the CEBLOB value of the property
SetFiletime()	myCEPROPVAL.val.filetime	Sets the FILETIME value of the property
SetIdent()	HIWORD(myCEPROPVAL.propid)	Sets the identifier of the property
SetLong()	myCEPROPVAL.val.lVal	Sets the long int value of the property
SetShort()	myCEPROPVAL.val.uVal	Sets the unsigned int value of the property
SetSortFlags()	myCEPROPVAL.wFlags	Sets the flags specifying how the property is sorted
SetString()	myCEPROPVAL.val.lpwstr	Sets the wide string value of the property
SetType()	LOWORD(myCEPROPVAL.propid)	Sets the type of the property
SetULong()	myCEPROPVAL.val.ulVal	Sets the unsigned long int value of the property
SetUShort()	myCEPROPVAL.val.uVal	Sets the unsigned int value of the property

The one point you must be aware of here is that these methods to set and retrieve a value of a certain type do not perform any conversions. If you attempt to read a numeric value from a property that contains a string, you will likely get invalid data and cause an error. In other words, you must always check the type of the property before reading its data.

Although there are lots of ways to accomplish this, the most generic—and, it would seem, most popular—is through the use of a switch..case block based on the value returned by the GetType() method:

```
switch(MyCeDBProp.GetType())
{
  case CEVT_I2:
    wsprintf(szBuf, TEXT("%d"), MyCeDBProp.GetShort());
    break;
  case CEVT_UI2:
    wsprintf(szBuf, TEXT("%d"), MyCeDBProp.GetUShort());
    break;
  case CEVT_I4:
    wsprintf(szBuf, TEXT("%d"), MyCeDBProp.GetLong());
    break;
  case CEVT_UI4:
    wsprintf(szBuf, TEXT("%d"), MyCeDBProp.GetULong());
    break;
  case CEVT_FILETIME:
    wsprintf(szBuf, TEXT("FILETIME DATA"));
    break;
  case CEVT_LPWSTR:
    wsprintf(szBuf, MyCeDBProp.GetString());
    break;
  case CEVT_BLOB:
    wsprintf(szBuf, TEXT("BLOB_DATA"));
    break;
}
```

This switch..case block is very similar to the one we'll create later in Chapter 10. One of the reasons for this is that although the MFC classes for accessing data do provide some abstraction from the API, they do not provide the same level of abstraction as, say, CString provides.

CCeDBRecord

The CCeDBRecord class serves mostly as a way to group a set of CCeDBProp objects together so that they may be treated as a record. In reality, this class is little more than a wrapper for a CObArray object. This means that the methods of CCeDBRecord do not have any API equivalents, and they have absolutely no effect on the underlying data. They exist only to provide a friendly, logical way to associate CCeDBProp objects. Table 6.2 lists the CCeDBRecord methods and reveals what each method actually does.

TABLE 6.2: CCeDBRecord Methods and What They Do

Method	Description
AddProp()	Calls the CObArray.Add() method
AddProps()	Calls the CObArray.Add() method for each property passed in
DeleteAllProps()	Removes all elements from the CObArray and frees all used memory
DeleteProp()	Removes specified property from CObArray
GetNumProps()	Returns number of elements in CObArray
GetPropFromIdent()	Finds specified property and returns CCeDBProp object
GetPropFromIndex()	Returns nth CCeDBProp from CObArray

CCeDBDatabase

The CCeDBDatabase class encapsulates all of the API calls dealing with database creation and seeking and accessing records. In short, CCeDBDatabase makes it possible for us to treat a CE database as an object. Table 6.3 lists the methods of the CCeDBDatabase class and shows the API function that each method corresponds to.

NOTE   In Table 6.3, only the key values have been filled in for each API function.

TABLE 6.3: CCeDBDatabase Methods and Corresponding API Functions

CCeDBDatabase Method	API function	Description
AddRecord()	CeWriteRecordProps(... ,0,...,...)	Writes the specified **CCeDBRecord** to the database. Used for appending a new record to the database.
Close()	CloseHandle()	Closes the database.
Delete()	CeDeleteDatabase(idCEOID)	Deletes the database.
DeleteCurrRecord()	CeDeleteRecord(hDatabase, idCEOID)	Deletes the record with the specified CEOID from the database.
DeleteCurrRecordProps()	cepvPropVal.wFlags = CEDB_PROPDELETE	Equivalent to setting the **wFlags** of a **CEPROPVAL** to **CEDB_PROPDELTE**. Deletes the specified property or properties from the current record.
Exists()	CeOpenDatabase()	Attempts to open specified database; if not found, function returns **FALSE**.
GetCurrIndex()	CeSeekDatabase(...,CED B_SEEK_CURRENT,...,&dw Index)	Calls **CeSeekDatabase()** to retrieve the index value returned in the fourth parameter.
GetCurrRecord()	CeSeekDatabase(...,CED B_SEEK_CURRENT,...,...)	Retrieves the current record.
GetIdent()	CeOidGetInfo(idCEOID,...)	Calls **CeOidGetInfo()** to retrieve the database type identifier.
GetLastModified()	CeOidGetInfo(idCEOID,...)	Calls **CeOidGetInfo()** to retrieve the date that the database was last modified.
GetName()	CeOidGetInfo(idCEOID,...)	Calls **CeOidGetInfo()** to retrieve the database name.
GetNumRecords()	CeOidGetInfo(idCEOID,...)	Calls **CeOidGetInfo()** to retrieve the number of records in the database.
GetSize()	CeOidGetInfo(idCEOID,...)	Calls **CeOidGetInfo()** to retrieve the database size.
GetSortProps()	CeOidGetInfo(idCEOID,...)	Calls **CeOidGetInfo()** to retrieve the database's **SORTORDERSPEC** array.

TABLE 6.3 CONTINUED: CCeDBDatabase Methods and Corresponding API Functions

CCeDBDatabase Method	API function	Description
Open()	CeOpenDatabase()	Calls CeOpenDatabase() to open the database.
ReadCurrRecord()	CeReadRecordProps()	Calls CeReadRecordProps() to read in the current record.
SeekFirst()	CeSeekDatabase(...,CEDB_SEEK_BEGINNING,0,...)	Calls CeSeekDatabase() and passes in CEDB_SEEK_BEGINNING.
SeekFirstEqual()	CeSeekDatabase(...,CEDB_SEEK_VALUEFIRSTEQUAL,cepvPropToMatch,...)	Calls CeSeekDatabase() and tells it to try to match a specific value/property.
SeekLast()	CeSeekDatabase(...,CEDB_SEEK_END,0,...)	Calls CeSeekDatabase() and passes in CEDB_SEEK_END.
SeekNext()	CeSeekDatabase(...,CEDB_SEEK_CURRENT,1,...)	Calls CeSeekDatabase() and tells it to advance the record pointer by one record.
SeekNextEqual()	CeSeekDatabase(...,CEDB_SEEK_NEXTEQUAL,...,...)	Calls CeSeekDatabase() and passes in CEDB_SEEK_NEXTEQUAL.
SeekPrev()	CeSeekDatabase(...,CEDB_SEEK_CURRENT,-1,0)	Calls CeSeekDatabase() and tells it to move the record pointer back by one record.
SeekToIndex()	CeSeekDatabase(...,CEDB_SEEK_END,-lval,...) or CeSeekDatabase(...,CEDB_SEEK_BEGINNING,lval,...)	Calls CeSeekDatabase() and tells it to seek from the beginning or end of the database if the number of records to seek is positive or negative, respectively.
SeekToRecord()	CeSeekDatabase(...,CEDB_SEEK_CEOID,idCEOID,...)	Calls CeSeekDatabase() and tells it to find the record with a matching CEOID.
SeekValueGreater()	CeSeekDatabase(...,CEDB_SEEK_VALUEGREATER,cepvPropToMatch,...)	Calls CeSeekDatabase() and tells it to find the first value/property greater than that specified.
SeekValueSmaller()	CeSeekDatabase(...,CEDB_SEEK_VALUESMALLER,cepvPropToMatch,...)	Calls CeSeekDatabase() and tells it to find the first value/property smaller than that specified.

TABLE 6.3 CONTINUED: CCeDBDatabase Methods and Corresponding API Functions

CCeDBDatabase Method	API function	Description
SetIdent()	CeSetDatabaseInfo (idCEOID,...)	Calls CeSetDatabaseInfo () to set the database type identifier.
SetLastModified()	CeSetDatabaseInfo (idCEOID,...)	Calls CeSetDatabaseInfo () to set the last modified date.
SetName()	CeSetDatabaseInfo (idCEOID,...)	Calls CeSetDatabaseInfo () to set the database name.
SetSortProps()	CeSetDatabaseInfo (idCEOID,...)	Calls CeSetDatabaseInfo () to set the database's SORTORDERSPEC array.
WriteCurrRecord()	CeWriteRecordProps(...,idCEOID,...,...)	Calls CeWriteRecordProps() to save changes to current record. Used for editing an existing record.

Using the *CCeDB* Classes: Database as Document

In this section, we'll look at how to integrate the CCeDB classes into an MFC application. Specifically, we'll take an existing Windows CE MFC application and convert it so that it stores data in a database instead of in a file.

> **TIP**
>
> Although the techniques outlined here apply to any file-based MFC application, the project we're using is the one we'll be working with in the next chapter.

The first thing you need to know about using the CCeDB classes is that in the MFC Document/View architecture, the database itself becomes the Document. In order to make this happen, you need to add one member data element to the public section of our CShoppingListDoc class. This will be a CCeDBDatabase object called m_Mydb. Or, in code:

```
// Attributes
public:
    CCeDBDatabase m_Mydb;
```

Previously, in the file-based version of this application, the CShoppingListDoc class had only public member data and no methods. The example here assumes that you have already deleted the existing member data elements.

In addition to that data element, you'll also add four methods to our CShoppingListDoc class:

- CreateDB()
- OpenDB()
- CloseDB()
- AddRecord()

Before you implement these methods, though, you need to define some global constants. The first of these is the database type identifier, DB_IDENT:

```
const DWORD DB_IDENT    = 13245;
```

Next, define a constant to hold the name of the database:

```
const WCHAR DB_NAME[] = _T("ShoppingCEDatabase");
```

Finally, declare the property type identifiers, one for each of the record properties:

```
const WORD  PROP_DESCRIPTION = 101,
    PROP_QTY = 102,
    PROP_STORE1 = 103,
    PROP_STORE2 = 104,
    PROP_STORE3 = 105,
    PROP_STORE4 = 106;
```

CreateDB() The CreateDB() will be responsible for creating the actual database that your application will use to store the user's shopping list data. First, declare a variable of type CEOID that you'll use in just a moment when you create the database:

```
BOOL CShoppingListDoc::CreateDB()
{
    CEOID poid;
```

Next, set up the sort order for your database. To do this, create a one-cell array of type CCeDBProp. The property for which you're creating the sort order is a string property, identified by the value PROP_DESCRIPTION. The sort order will be ascending, case insensitive:

```
CCeDBProp SortProps[1] =
{
    CCeDBProp(CCeDBProp::Type_String, PROP_DESCRIPTION,
        CCeDBProp::Sort_Ascending | CCeDBProp::Sort_CaseInsensi-
tive)
};
```

Next, it's time to attempt to create the database. At the same time you do that, store the result (a CEOID) as well and verify that the creation was successful:

```
if (!(poid = m_Mydb.Create(DB_NAME,DB_IDENT,1,SortProps)))
    return FALSE;
```

Next, call CShoppingListDoc::OpenDB()

```
return ::OpenDB();
}
```

OpenDB() The next method you'll implement is your OpenDB() function. This function tests whether or not the database has already been created by calling the Exists() method of the CCeDBDatabase class:

```
BOOL CShoppingListDoc::OpenDB()
{
    if (!CCeDBDatabase::Exists(DB_NAME))
    {
```

NOTE   Exists() is a static method of the **CCeDBDatabase** class, which means you should not call it as a member function of a specific object; instead, you should call it as you would any other globally available function.

If the database does not exist, you must attempt to create it. This accounts for first-time uses of the program where the database isn't necessarily created ahead of time:

```
if (!CreateDB())
    return FALSE;
}
```

Otherwise, if the database does exist, simply open it, calling the Open() method of your CCeDBDatabase object, m_Mydb:

```
    else
    {
        m_Mydb.Open(DB_NAME);
    }
    return TRUE;
}
```

CloseDB() The CloseDB() method is the simplest of the ones you're creating here. All it does is call the Close() method of our CCeDBDatabase object, m_Mydb:

```
BOOL CShoppingListDoc::CloseDB()
{
    m_Mydb.Close();
    return TRUE;
}
```

AddRecord() The next method you'll create is the AddRecord() method. This is the function that will receive the data from the Add Item dialog and write it to the database. Your first job is to convert the float values representing the stores' prices into strings, because the CE database engine does not support floating point values. The quickest and easiest way to perform this conversion is via swprintf(), as shown below:

```
BOOL CShoppingListDoc::AddRecord(CString sDescription, int nQTY, float
fStore1, float fStore2, float fStore3, float fStore4)
{
    WCHAR wcDescription[255], wcStore1[10], wcStore2[10], wcStore3[10],
wcStore4[10];

    swprintf(wcDescription,_T("%s"),sDescription);
    swprintf(wcStore1,_T("%.2f"),fStore1);
    swprintf(wcStore2,_T("%.2f"),fStore2);
    swprintf(wcStore3,_T("%.2f"),fStore3);
    swprintf(wcStore4,_T("%.2f"),fStore4);
```

NOTE   CE 2.11 has added support for floats as a standard datatype but, as of this writing, that support has not been added to MFC.

Next, declare an object of type CCeDBRecord:

```
CCeDBRecord rec;
```

And declare a six-cell array of type CCeDBProp, which will hold all of the information about our record's properties:

```
CCeDBProp props[6];
```

Then, create and initialize all of the CCeDBProp objects in that array:

```
props[0] = CCeDBProp(wcDescription,PROP_DESCRIPTION);
props[1] = CCeDBProp((USHORT)nQTY,   PROP_QTY);
props[2] = CCeDBProp(wcStore1, PROP_STORE1);
props[3] = CCeDBProp(wcStore2,PROP_STORE2);
props[4] = CCeDBProp(wcStore3,PROP_STORE3);
props[5] = CCeDBProp(wcStore4,PROP_STORE4);
```

You then add these properties to your CCeDBRecord object, rec:

```
rec.AddProps(props,6);
```

Now, write the record out to the database:

```
if (!m_Mydb.AddRecord(&rec))
    return FALSE;
```

Finally, clean up your used memory by calling the DeleteAllProps() method of rec:

```
rec.DeleteAllProps();
return TRUE;
}
```

Now that you've managed to implement the Document part of your database work, let's take a look at the second half of the equation and see what it takes to get the database to integrate into the View portion of your application.

Using the *CCeDB* Classes: Database as View

Of course, just making the database your document isn't quite enough. You also have to integrate this new type of document into your application from the View side of the application. This means writing new code to populate the ListView control and handle deletion of records. It also means writing a slightly different handler for the user inserting a new record. Those three methods of your `CShoppingListView` class are

- `UpdateListBox()`
- `OnDelete()`
- `OnInsert()`

Let's take a look at each of these methods now and see exactly how the database Document interacts with your View.

UpdateListBox()   In the file-based version of the Shopping List application, `UpdateListBox()` was the function responsible for reading the data out of the file and then populating the ListView. In the database-aware version, however, `UpdateListBox()` will be reading data in from the database object and populating the ListView with the records.

The first thing you need to do here is clear out the ListView so that you can start fresh:

```
void CShoppingListView::UpdateListBox()
{
    m_ListBox.DeleteAllItems();
```

Next, declare some local variables to be used as temporary placeholders for the data as you read it from the database and store it momentarily before putting into the ListView control:

```
CString    sProductName, sTemp;
int        nQty;
CString    sStore1Price;
CString    sStore2Price;
CString    sStore3Price;
CString    sStore4Price;
```

Then declare a `CCeDBRecord`, which you'll be using to access the data:

```
CCeDBRecord rec;
```

Next, declare pointers to `CCeDBProp` objects, so that you have a means of accessing the individual properties once they're read into your `CCeDBRecord` object, which you just declared above:

```
CCeDBProp *pPropDescription,
          *pPropQty,
```

```
*pPropStore1,
*pPropStore2,
*pPropStore3,
*pPropStore4;
```

The first action is to close and then reopen the database using the `CloseDB()` and `OpenDB()` methods of our Document:

```
GetDocument()->CloseDB();
GetDocument()->OpenDB();
```

Next, seek to the first record, using the `SeekFirst()` method of your Document's m_Mydb member object:

```
GetDocument()->m_Mydb.SeekFirst();
```

Next, set the m_bAutoSeekNext flag of m_Mydb to indicate that you want the record pointer to be automatically advanced to the next record each time you read a record:

```
GetDocument()->m_Mydb.m_bAutoSeekNext = TRUE;
```

Now, retrieve the number of records in the database by calling the `GetNumRecords()` method of m_Mydb:

```
int nNumOfRecs = 0;
nNumOfRecs = (int)GetDocument()->m_Mydb.GetNumRecords();
```

Then reserve that number of rows in your ListView control:

```
for (int t = 0; t <= nNumOfRecs; t++)
{
    m_ListBox.InsertItem(t, NULL);
}
```

Now you can begin to populate the ListView with the data in the database. Do this via a `for` loop based on the record count we retrieved earlier:

```
for (int i = 0; i < nNumOfRecs; i++)
{
```

The first thing to do is to read the current record from the database:

```
GetDocument()->m_Mydb.ReadCurrRecord(&rec);
```

TIP	This is where the **m_bAutoSeekNext** flag comes in: each time you call ReadCurr-Record(), the record pointer is automatically positioned on the next record. You don't have to worry about it at all.

Now, extract **CCeDBProp** objects from the **CCeDBRec** object (rec) using the constants you declared at the beginning of the program:

```
pPropDescription = rec.GetPropFromIdent(PROP_DESCRIPTION);
        pPropQty          = rec.GetPropFromIdent(PROP_QTY);
        pPropStore1       = rec.GetPropFromIdent(PROP_STORE1);
        pPropStore2       = rec.GetPropFromIdent(PROP_STORE2);
        pPropStore3          = rec.GetPropFromIdent(PROP_STORE3);
        pPropStore4          = rec.GetPropFromIdent(PROP_STORE4);
```

Then extract the actual property values into your local variables, which you declared earlier in this function:

```
sProductName = pPropDescription->GetString();
nQty         = pPropQty->GetUShort();
sStore1Price = pPropStore1->GetString();
sStore2Price = pPropStore2->GetString();
sStore3Price = pPropStore3->GetString();
sStore4Price = pPropStore4->GetString();
```

Next, add the items to the list box, one column at a time:

```
m_ListBox.SetItemText(i, 0, sProductName);
sTemp.Format(_T("%i"),nQty);
m_ListBox.SetItemText(i, 1, sTemp);
m_ListBox.SetItemText(i, 2, sStore1Price);
m_ListBox.SetItemText(i, 3, sStore2Price);
m_ListBox.SetItemText(i, 4, sStore3Price);
m_ListBox.SetItemText(i, 5, sStore4Price);
}
```

Finally, just as you did with the file-based version, create a row indicating the total cost for each store:

```
CreateTotals();
}
```

OnDelete()   The CShoppingListView's OnDelete() method has changed considerably from that of the file-based version of your application. Now, rather than just removing the item from an array, you're going to immediately delete it from the database.

The first thing to do is to ensure that the currently selected item in the ListView represents a valid record. You can do this by testing that the index of that item—the number of records between the selected record and the first item in the ListView—is less than the number of records in the database and greater than or equal to 0:

```
void CShoppingListView::OnDelete()
{
    if (m_nListBoxIndex <= GetDocument()->m_Mydb.GetNumRecords()  &&
m_nListBoxIndex >= 0)
    {
```

If it is, tell your Document's m_Mydb to seek to that record in the database:

```
        CCeDBRecord rec;
        GetDocument()->m_Mydb.SeekToIndex(m_nListBoxIndex);
```

Then ask the user to confirm that they want to delete the record:

```
        if (AfxMessageBox(_T("Are you sure you want to delete "
            + m_ListBox.GetItemText(m_nListBoxIndex, 0) + "
?"),MB_OKCANCEL) == IDOK)
            {
```

If they do, go ahead and delete the record from the database by calling the DeleteCurrentRecord() method of your Document's m_Mydb:

```
GetDocument()->m_Mydb.DeleteCurrRecord();
            UpdateListBox();
            }
        }
    }
}
```

OnInsert() The database-aware OnInsert() has changed very little from the file-based version of the function. You still use it to launch the Add Item dialog:

```
void CShoppingListView::OnInsert()
{
    CInsertDlg dlg;
    if (dlg.DoModal() == IDOK)
        {
```

You also still retrieve the values from the dialog and store them into local variables:

```
int      nQty = dlg.m_nQty;
CString  sProductName = dlg.m_sPdtName;
float fStore1Price = dlg.m_fStore1;
float fStore2Price = dlg.m_fStore2;
float fStore3Price = dlg.m_fStore3;
float fStore4Price = dlg.m_fStore4;
```

But instead of adding these values to a set of arrays, you then call the AddRecord() method of your Document class, passing in the local variables we just created:

```
    GetDocument()->AddRecord(sProductName, nQty, fStore1Price,
fStore2Price, fStore3Price, fStore4Price);
    }
    UpdateListBox();
}
```

And that's how to integrate databases into the View side of the Document/View architecture. Of course, the various pieces of making the database work within the Document/View architecture will vary with each application's needs, but this does provide you with a good model to follow.

Now that you know all about the new classes of MFC for CE, let's move on to the classes that have been altered in some way to conform to the CE operating system.

Modified Classes

It would seem that all of MFC's classes, including CString, have been modified some way when they were ported to the CE operating system. Thankfully, most of these changes are minor and should not affect us. Although space does not permit a full listing of each of the changed classes and their changed elements, we will review some of the more common classes and how their changes might affect us.

The modified classes fall into two categories:

1. Classes that lost some functionality

2. Classes that gained some functionality

Classes That Lost Functionality

Most of the modified classes lost some degree of functionality. After all, CE as an operating system doesn't have as much functionality as Windows 98/NT, so it only makes sense that some classes would lose a feature or two. The more important classes that have lost some functionality are

- CFrameWnd
- CWnd
- CDC

CFrameWnd

Most of the functionality that CFrameWnd has lost relates to the fact that CE itself does not offer support for dockable toolbars. For instance, of the 13 methods no longer supported by CFrameWnd, 7 are directly related to the lack of dockable toolbars. The remaining unsupported methods can also be traced directly to some feature of Windows 98/NT that is not supported by CE.

CWnd

Similarly, the methods that are not supported by CWnd are also closely tied into missing features of the CE operating system. There are 97 missing functions in all! While that seems daunting at first, many of these functions probably won't affect you directly. In fact, 20 of these missing functions are directly related to the fact that most CE devices don't have a mouse.

CDC

Almost as bad as CWnd is CDC, which has lost 86 of its functions. Here again, most of these functions do not work under CE simply because the operating system does not offer them.

Classes That Gained Functionality

While many classes lost some features, a few classes actually gained functionality. It seems strange, but there are actually some features offered by CE that

Windows 98/NT doesn't offer. The more important classes that have gained functionality are

- CFrameWnd
- CWnd

CFrameWnd

CFrameWnd actually gained functions for the same reason it lost them! Although CE doesn't offer dockable toolbars, it does offer CommandBars. So, CFrameWnd picked up all of the functions for dealing with CommandBars:

- AddAdornments()
- AddBitmap()
- AddComboBoxString()
- GetComboCount()
- GetComboCurSel()
- InsertButtons()
- InsertComboBox()
- InsertMenu()
- SetComboCurSel()

TIP   For more information on how to use these new functions, see Chapter 7.

CWnd

As a class, CWnd didn't pick up any new members. But it did get something very important under Windows CE: the ability to process the WM_HIBERNATE message. As we saw in Chapter 2, the WM_HIBERNATE message is sent by the operating system under low-memory conditions as a way to request that running applications free some memory. Of course, this new feature is relatively transparent to you, except for the fact that you can now create your own handler for WM_HIBERNATE within the context of a CWnd object.

Missing Classes

Some classes are gone completely. In most of these cases, the class is unsupported because the underlying control does not exist in Windows CE. For instance, there is no Font Selection Dialog, so `CFontDialog` is not supported. Likewise, there is no Printer Setup Dialog in Windows CE, so `CPrintSetupDialog` is not supported. And, of course, all of the Windows 98/NT–specific common controls that don't exist under CE (`AnimateCtrl`, `CheckListBox`, etc.) are also not supported by MFC.

NOTE   `CPrintDialog` is still supported by MFC 2.10; it's only `CPrintSetupDialog` that doesn't exist under Windows CE.

Summary

In this chapter, we learned about the new classes that MFC offers for CE. Specifically, we saw that `CCeSocket` is almost exactly the same as `CAsyncSocket`. In addition, we learned how to work with databases and the Windows CE database engine. Then we took a brief look at some of the classes that have changed a bit from their Desktop-based counterparts. Finally, we learned what to expect in the way of classes that aren't supported at all under CE.

CHAPTER
SEVEN

7

Real MFC Applications Ported to CE

- The Shopping List Application

- Mechanical Issues of Porting

- Toolbars and Status Bars

- Printing Support

- Optimizing for CE

In the last chapter, you examined what sort of things were and were not supported by MFC for CE. In this chapter, you'll be converting a real MFC application to Windows CE. When you're done, you'll have an understanding of what's involved in converting even the simplest of MFC Desktop applications to the CE platform.

First you'll take a look at the project as it exists now. Then, starting with the simpler tasks, you'll work your way through the conversion to CE to get a no-frills version of the application running on a CE device. Next, you'll look at porting some of the optional features and at optimizing the user interface and the code for the Windows CE platform. Finally, you'll see how to optimize your program for the CE platform and why it may be necessary to drop or add certain features.

The Shopping List Application

The Shopping List application that you'll be porting is a program designed to help you keep track of your purchases so you can determine which store, if any, really has better prices on the items you want to buy. The program itself is designed primarily for supermarkets, where a user might have time to collect prices from various stores by shopping at each of them a few times. They can then enter prices of various items at a variety of stores and sit back and let the program show them how much they actually spent. The main window of this application is shown in Figure 7.1.

FIGURE 7.1:

The Desktop version of the Shopping List application

	Qty	Product Name	Got	Lucky	Vons	Ralphs
1	1	Soda	☑	1.99	2.15	2.35
2	1	Cereal	☑	1.35	2.00	1.15
3	5	Bottled Water	☐	0.59	0.62	0.68
4			☐			
5			☐			
6			☐			
7			☐			
8			☐			
9			☐			
10			☐			

You'll note that most of the user interface of this program is taken up with a large grid. The user can navigate the grid with the keyboard or the mouse, entering quantity, item description, and the prices at each of the stores. This data can then be serialized out to a text file whenever the user clicks the Save button. The user also has the option of changing the names of the supermarkets/stores at which they're doing their price comparisons.

NOTE   The grid you see in Figure 7.1 is not part of MFC itself; it is a third-party MFC library. This grid handles its own serialization and contains built-in functionality for simple operations such as summing a column.

At first glance, the application looks pretty much like it could run on a CE device without any modifications at all. However, there are a number of changes you'll have to make to this application just to get a minimal version working on CE. The areas of this application that you'll have to either eliminate or alter to get your application running on a CE device are

- Toolbars and status bars
- Printing support
- The grid

When you first look at this list, you might think that you'd need to change everything that makes this application what it is. After all, the items on this list basically represent the entire graphical portion application, and, especially without a gridlike control to display the pricing information to the user, the Shopping List application seems at a definite disadvantage.

But it's not as bad as it first appears. Some of these items are easy to fix and involve nothing more than choosing a different option in the WCE MFC App-Wizard. Now that you have an idea of what portions of your Shopping List application might need some reworking, let's take each item and begin to port the application, performing the tasks in order of complexity.

How, Exactly, Do You Get a Desktop MFC Application to Compile for CE?

In Toolkit for VC++ 5, it was very easy to compile an existing Desktop application for Windows CE. All you had to do was choose Build➤Configurations from the menu, click the Add button on the dialog shown below, and add a CE-based configuration. Assuming your code was written in such a way that all of your classes were available under CE, a port was merely one build away.

Even if major pieces of code had to change, this was still the simplest way to start a port of a desktop program to CE. (Although if you knew you were going to be changing major pieces of code, it was probably advisable to make a copy of your project and then begin the work of porting it.)

If you were going to do a full port, you'd simply add all of the CE configurations that you needed and then remove the Desktop configurations. That's all it took to get a 100 percent CE-based project from your existing Desktop project.

As you may know, however, VC++ 6 does not allow projects to contain both Desktop and CE configurations. The unfortunate truth is that, unless Microsoft announces some kind of patch or special tool to make this possible, you'll have to re-create your application from scratch, cutting and pasting code and files as appropriate.

For this reason, it may actually be advisable to keep a copy of VC++ 5 and the earlier toolkit on one of your machines. There is simply no other way to create an application that will build for both Desktop and CE platforms. Further, there is no easier way to get started with a port of an existing program to CE.

In the case of the application in this chapter, you will employ the cut-and-paste method of porting so that some of the changes are more manageable. This will apply to many applications that require major changes; the cut-and-paste method will probably be easier in the long run, as opposed to attempting to compile your project for both Desktop- and CE-based platforms at once.

Mechanical Issues of Porting

Some of the items that won't port are easier to fix than others. We'll work from the easiest to fix to the most difficult.

Toolbars and Status Bars

The easiest items to fix, at least in terms of actual coding required, are the status bar and the toolbar. In fact, fixing these items requires that you do nothing more than correctly check off some of the options on the WCE MFC AppWizard. However, deciding *which* options to check off is sometimes not that simple. As you learned in Chapter 5, there are a number of subtle differences between MFC for CE version 2.0 and MFC for CE version 2.1.

Probably, the most notable of these differences is the multiple types of command bars. You'll recall that of the four possible command-bar types offered by the WCE MFC AppWizard, only one of them (the fourth) can compile and run on both the PPC, HPC, and HPC/Pro devices. The first three will only run on PPC and HPC/Pro devices. In the current context of having to port a status bar and a toolbar, this 2.0/2.1 version difference affects us in several ways.

First and foremost, you must choose which devices you really want to target with your application. If you'd like to run it on all of the three major CE platforms, then you must choose the fourth type of command bar. However, by doing this, you are explicitly setting your application to be 100 percent compatible with MFC 2.0 and thus eliminating the option of having a status bar for your application, since status bars are only supported in MFC 2.1. How frustrating! This means that some elements of the design and visual appearance of your program may be limited simply because you want to reach the widest possible market for your program.

MFC 2.0 vs. MFC 2.1

So, why are there different versions of MFC on an operating system and platform that are basically brand new?

With the release of CE 2.0—the version that's running on all of the Handheld and Palm-size PCs currently on the market—there was also a 2.0 release of MFC. Officially, the 2.0 version of MFC would work only on the Handheld devices, not the Palm-size.

Of course, that didn't stop a large number of developers from copying the MFC DLLs to their PPCs and trying to run their applications anyway. What they found was that although their MFC programs could and did run, they were rather slow at times.

When Microsoft released Windows CE version 2.11—that's the version that runs on HPC/Pro devices, such as the HP Jornada—they also released a new version of MFC, dubbed 2.1.

One of the major advantages of this new MFC is that you can now officially use it to build programs for Palm-size devices. In addition, MFC 2.1 added features such as new command bar styles, status bars, and printing support. The following table summarizes the features in each version.

MFC Version	Devices supported		Toolbars		Status Bar	Printing
2	HPC	1	style		No	No
2.1	PPC, HPC/Pro	4	styles		Yes	Yes

As you can see, the configuration that gives you the most flexibility in terms of devices to target also takes away your ability to print and/or provide a status bar. Which configuration you decide to use comes down to whether support for printing is more important than being able to sell your product to owners of a standard HPC device.

In the case of the project that we're porting now, let's opt to support the PPC, HPC, and HPC/Pro devices, even though this means that you'll lose your status bar. To support all three devices, make sure that you select the fourth command bar type when you're going through the WCE MFC AppWizard.

As it turns out, the status bar isn't a great loss. You weren't really using it for much, so letting it go does not really affect your application. In practical terms, all it means is that you must remove the following lines of code from your CMain-Frame's `OnCreate()` event:

```
if (!m_wndStatusBar.Create(this) ||
    !m_wndStatusBar.SetIndicators(indicators,
      sizeof(indicators)/sizeof(UINT)))
{
    TRACE0("Failed to create status bar\n");
    return -1;      // fail to create
}
```

It's worth noting that, with one simple choice in a wizard, we've managed to deal with two of the items on the list of possible problem areas that appeared earlier in the chapter. As far as the command bar is concerned, the original code to create the toolbar in the Desktop application is called from within the CMain-Frame's `OnCreate()` event handler. There, you create the toolbar object and populate it with the buttons contained in the IDR_MAINFRAME resource, as follows:

```
if (!m_wndToolBar.Create(this) ||
    !m_wndToolBar.LoadToolBar(IDR_MAINFRAME))
{
    TRACE0("Failed to create toolbar\n");
    return -1;      // fail to create
}
```

Then, set the style of the toolbar, so that it will give the ToolTip hints and be resizable:

```
m_wndToolBar.SetBarStyle(m_wndToolBar.GetBarStyle() |
    CBRS_TOOLTIPS | CBRS_FLYBY | CBRS_SIZE_DYNAMIC);
```

Finally, make it possible for the user to dock and undock the toolbar:

```
m_wndToolBar.EnableDocking(CBRS_ALIGN_ANY);
EnableDocking(CBRS_ALIGN_ANY);
DockControlBar(&m_wndToolBar);
```

In the Windows CE version of your `CMainFrame::OnCreate()`, the code to create the Command Bar looks somewhat different. All you have to do here is call the `CFrameWnd::InsertButtons()` member function, as follows:

```
if (!InsertButtons( g_tbSTDButton,
    sizeof(g_tbSTDButton)/sizeof(TBBUTTON),
    IDR_MAINFRAME,
    6 ))
```

```
        {
            TRACE0("Failed to add command bar buttons\n");
            return -1;
        }
```

In the above code, `g_tbSTDButton` is an array of properties that describe how the buttons are to be displayed and `IDR_MAINFRAME` is the resource ID for the Command Bar images.

WARNING   The `InsertButtons()` call can be the cause of some very odd behavior if it's not called with the correct number of buttons specified as the final parameter. If the value is less than the number of actual buttons, the *X* (or Close) button of the application will have the same image as the last button on the toolbar. If the value is greater than the number of actual buttons, the *X* button will have absolutely no image at all!

More on *CMainFrame: InsertButtons()*

`InsertButtons()` takes an array of type TBBUTTON. TBBUTTON is a structure that defines properties for each of the buttons to be displayed and is defined as follows:

```
typedef struct _TBBUTTON {

int iBitmap;

int idCommand;

BYTE fsState;

BYTE fsStyle;

DWORD dwData;

int iString;

} TBBUTTON, NEAR* PTBBUTTON, FAR* LPTBBUTTON;

typedef const TBBUTTON FAR* LPCTBBUTTON;
```

Of the items in the structure, the most important ones to you will be

- `iBitmap`, which specifies the order of the button/image in the Command Bar

Continued on next page

- **idCommand**, which makes your Command Bar button act like a true button in that the value specified in **idCommand** will be passed to the application's WM_COMMAND handler when the button is clicked

- **fsState**, which specifies that the state (hidden, enabled, etc.) will typically be **0** (disabled), **TBSTATE_ENABLED**, or **TBSTATE_HIDDEN**

- **fsStyle**, which specifies whether you're creating a checkbox, a button, or a separator

The rest of the values in the structure are simply set to –1 or 0, as shown below. A standard **TBBUTTON** array would look something like this:

```
static TBBUTTON g_tbSTDButton[] = {
    {0, 0, TBSTATE_ENABLED, TBSTYLE_SEP, 0, 0, 0, 0},
    {0, ID_FILE_NEW, TBSTATE_ENABLED, TBSTYLE_BUTTON, 0, 0, 0, -1},
    {1, ID_FILE_OPEN, TBSTATE_ENABLED, TBSTYLE_BUTTON, 0, 0, 0, -1},
    {2, ID_FILE_SAVE, TBSTATE_ENABLED, TBSTYLE_BUTTON, 0, 0, 0, -1},
    {0, 0, TBSTATE_ENABLED, TBSTYLE_SEP, 0, 0, 0, -1},
    {3, ID_EDIT_CUT, TBSTATE_ENABLED, TBSTYLE_BUTTON, 0, 0, 0, -1},
    {4, ID_EDIT_COPY, TBSTATE_ENABLED, TBSTYLE_BUTTON, 0, 0, 0, -1},
    {5, ID_EDIT_PASTE, TBSTATE_ENABLED, TBSTYLE_BUTTON, 0, 0, 0, -1},
    {0, 0, TBSTATE_ENABLED, TBSTYLE_SEP, 0, 0, 0, -1},
    { 0, 0, TBSTATE_ENABLED, TBSTYLE_SEP, 0, 0, 0, 0}
};
```

If you had custom buttons to add, you'd simply draw them in the Resource Editor, as shown below, and then add their properties to this array.

Continued on next page

The modified TBBUTTON array, then, would look like this:

```
static TBBUTTON g_tbSTDButton[] = {
    {0, 0, TBSTATE_ENABLED, TBSTYLE_SEP,    0, 0, 0,  0},
    {0, ID_FILE_NEW, TBSTATE_ENABLED, TBSTYLE_BUTTON, 0, 0, 0, -1},
    {1, ID_FILE_OPEN, TBSTATE_ENABLED, TBSTYLE_BUTTON, 0, 0, 0, -1},
    {2, ID_FILE_SAVE, TBSTATE_ENABLED, TBSTYLE_BUTTON, 0, 0, 0, -1},
    {0, 0, TBSTATE_ENABLED, TBSTYLE_SEP,    0, 0, 0, -1},
    {3, ID_EDIT_CUT, 0, TBSTYLE_BUTTON, 0, 0, 0, -1},
    {4, ID_EDIT_COPY, TBSTATE_ENABLED, TBSTYLE_BUTTON, 0, 0, 0, -1},
    {5, ID_EDIT_PASTE, TBSTATE_ENABLED, TBSTYLE_BUTTON, 0, 0, 0, -1},
    {0, 0, TBSTATE_ENABLED, TBSTYLE_SEP,    0, 0, 0, -1},
    {0, 0, TBSTATE_ENABLED, TBSTYLE_SEP,    0, 0, 0,  0},
    //A new button!
    {6, ID_NEWBUTTON, TBSTATE_ENABLED, TBSTYLE_BUTTON, 0, 0, 0, -1},
};
```

Then, you'd simply update the value you passed to InsertButtons() to reflect the new button count:

```
InsertButtons( g_tbSTDButton,
        sizeof(g_tbSTDButton)/sizeof(TBBUTTON),
        IDR_MAINFRAME,
        7 );    //now there are 7 buttons.
```

This simple change is, in fact, one you'll be making a little later in the process of porting your Shopping List application.

Although you did have to drop a status bar, the port here was relatively simple. However, you'll see that, as you progress into the application, your next porting issues may not be so easy.

Printing Support

The second major consequence of choosing to target all three of the major CE platforms is that we've now lost the ability to offer printing support in your application. This is yet another of the subtle differences between MFC 2.0 and 2.1. If you want to support all three CE-based device types, you won't be able to use MFC's printing support.

However, there are a few possible solutions to this dilemma. The first is that you could drop printing support altogether. After all, the majority of CE devices do not have access to a printer, and there is only one printer that's even specifically targeted to the CE market.

TIP   The printer specifically targeted to the CE market is the PocketJet II from Pentax Technologies. For more information, visit `http://www.pentaxtech.com`.

The second option is for you to create your own printing object that would encapsulate all of the API's own printing routines. The problem with this, of course, is that it can be quite time-consuming, and requires you to learn more about the API's methods of printing than you probably want to know.

These two options might seem a little bleak, but there is a third that is ideal for certain types of applications. If the application in question is already being tailored to a wireless environment, the solution to consider is one provided by Odyssey Software (`http://www.odysseysoftware.com`). As part of an extensive package called CEFusion that exposes many of the NT/BackOffice products to CE developers, Odyssey offers a CE-based client product that makes it possible for developers to write code to print to any Windows NT-based network printer. The kind of printing that CEFusion allows you to do is fairly basic, but if the application really needs to be able to print and you're already considering a wireless environment, this could be the ideal solution.

The Grid

The most complex change you'll probably have to make is to the grid that now occupies most of the main form of your application. Because you're using a third-party MFC class that hasn't yet been ported to CE, you're in a tight spot with this issue.

Of course, if the third-party grid existed on CE, you'd be all set, and the porting process would pretty much be done by now. Instead, what you'll have to do is to select a replacement grid or control that you can use in the same way. As far as selecting a new grid control is concerned, you have two options:

- The Microsoft ActiveX Grid Control
- A replacement control

Unfortunately, there's no ideal solution here. Whatever you choose will likely require serious reworking of your code. While that's never really a pleasant task, it may still be the best—if not the only—way to successfully port your application.

Microsoft's ActiveX Grid Control

Microsoft provides a simple, no-frills grid control in the form of an ActiveX control. This control is available either from the ActiveX control pack, which is freely downloadable from the Microsoft Web site, or from the Windows CE toolkit for Visual Basic 6. As grid controls go, the ActiveX grid control is more than adequate for your needs. There are, however, a few disadvantages to using it.

The first disadvantage is that it's really designed for Visual Basic. That's not to say that you couldn't use it, but VC++ doesn't come with the Control Manager tool for registering ActiveX controls on the device or in the emulator. That means that you have to manage the registration of this component yourself instead of having VB take care of it for you. Plus, assuming that you don't have the latest toolkit for Visual Basic, you'd have to use the version of the control that comes with the ActiveX control pack. Because the ActiveX control pack was created before the development of CE 2.11, the ARM and SH4 processors aren't supported, which means that you would not be able target some of the HPC/Pro devices.

NOTE
The Control Manager tool from the Visual Basic toolkit is covered in more detail in Chapter 8.

The other problem with using the Microsoft Grid ActiveX control, or any ActiveX control, for that matter, is the additional disk space it requires. The Grid control itself is about 100K in size, and on devices with limited resources, 100K can represent a good deal of space. Instead of using the ActiveX grid, then, let's look at a solution that works well with VC++ and doesn't use too much additional space.

A Replacement Control

When it comes to finding a replacement for your grid that won't occupy any additional space and will still allow you the same or similar functionality, one control stands out: the CListView control. ListView controls can perform almost all of the functions that a grid can perform, and using a ListView doesn't add 100K to the size of the files you'll have to distribute.

However, ListView controls will require you to write code to handle the editing and display of the user's data. Previously, of course, the grid handled all of this work itself. The basic tasks that you've got to handle on your own are

- Managing the user's data while the program is running

- Displaying the user's data

- Allowing the user to enter and delete data

Let's take a look at how you can implement each one and finish getting your application ported to CE.

Managing the User's Data While the Program Is Running The task at hand is to store all of the user's data as they enter it, so that you can display it to the CListView control, serialize it out to a file, etc. To accomplish this, you'll need to add several arrays to the CDocument class. In all, there will be seven arrays:

- An array to maintain the names of the stores on your shopping list:
  ```
  CStringArray        m_sStoreNames;
  ```

- An array to store the quantities of the items you'll be price comparing:
  ```
  CArray<int,int>     m_Qty;
  ```

- An array to store the names of the actual products you'll be price comparing:
  ```
  CStringArray        m_sProductName;
  ```

- Four arrays to store the prices for each item at each of the four stores on your shopping list:
  ```
  CArray<float,float> m_fStore1Price;
  CArray<float,float> m_fStore2Price;
  CArray<float,float> m_fStore3Price;
  CArray<float,float> m_fStore4Price;
  ```

With these arrays, you can store all of the user's data while the program is running. Now, you must handle the task of displaying this data to the user.

Displaying the User's Data Given your list of arrays, your first task whenever the user requests a new document is to set up default values for the store names and clear out the other arrays. In the CShoppingListDoc::OnNewDocument() event, first clear out the m_sStoreNames array:

```
m_sStoreNames.RemoveAll();
```

Then, initialize the array with default values:

```
m_sStoreNames.Add(_T("Store 1"));
m_sStoreNames.Add(_T("Store 2"));
m_sStoreNames.Add(_T("Store 3"));
m_sStoreNames.Add(_T("Store 4"));
```

Next, clear out the other arrays, so that everything is reset for the next shopping list:

```
m_fStore1Price.RemoveAll();
m_fStore2Price.RemoveAll();
m_fStore3Price.RemoveAll();
m_fStore4Price.RemoveAll();
m_Qty.RemoveAll();
m_sProductName.RemoveAll();
```

The next step is to set up the column headers on the CListView control, so that the data has some meaning to the user and they know what it is they're looking at. Do this in the CShoppingListView::CreateListBoxHeader() method. First, retrieve the store names from the m_sStoreNames CStringArray and store those names in local variables:

```
CString sStore1Name = GetDocument()->m_sStoreNames[0];
CString sStore2Name = GetDocument()->m_sStoreNames[1];
CString sStore3Name = GetDocument()->m_sStoreNames[2];
CString sStore4Name = GetDocument()->m_sStoreNames[3];
```

Then, delete and then re-create each column as you change its heading:

```
m_ListBox.DeleteColumn(0);
m_ListBox.InsertColumn( 0, _T("Product Name") , LVCFMT_LEFT, 175 );
m_ListBox.DeleteColumn(1);
m_ListBox.InsertColumn( 1, _T("Qty")          , LVCFMT_LEFT, 50 );
m_ListBox.DeleteColumn(2);
m_ListBox.InsertColumn( 2, sStore1Name , LVCFMT_RIGHT, 95 );
m_ListBox.DeleteColumn(3);
m_ListBox.InsertColumn( 3, sStore2Name , LVCFMT_RIGHT, 95 );
```

```
m_ListBox.DeleteColumn(4);
m_ListBox.InsertColumn( 4, sStore3Name , LVCFMT_RIGHT, 95 );
m_ListBox.DeleteColumn(5);
m_ListBox.InsertColumn( 5, sStore4Name , LVCFMT_RIGHT, 95 );
```

You do this to ensure that the heading text is properly refreshed each time.

NOTE   This is also where you could change the width of a column if you wanted to; just change the value of the fourth parameter in the calls to `InsertColumn()`.

The next step is to add code to get the data from these arrays that you created into your CListView control. This is done in the CShoppingListView::UpdateListBox() method. First, clear out the CListView:

```
m_ListBox.DeleteAllItems();
```

Next, pre-reserve all of the rows you'll need in the CListView:

```
//how many product names do we have?
int nIndex = GetDocument()->m_sProductName.GetSize();
for (int t = 0; t <= nIndex; t++){
    m_ListBox.InsertItem(t, NULL);
}
```

Then loop through the arrays, adding their information to your replacement grid, CListView:

```
for (int i = 0; i < nIndex; i++)
{
```

Here, you retrieve the array values and store them in local variables temporarily:

```
nQty        = GetDocument()->m_Qty[i];
fStore1Price = GetDocument()->m_fStore1Price[i];
fStore2Price = GetDocument()->m_fStore2Price[i];
fStore3Price = GetDocument()->m_fStore3Price[i];
fStore4Price = GetDocument()->m_fStore4Price[i];
sProductName = GetDocument()->m_sProductName[i];
```

Then, add the product name to the 0th column:

```
m_ListBox.SetItemText(i, 0, sProductName);
```

Now, add the quantity to the first column:

```
sTemp.Format(_T("%i"),nQty);
m_ListBox.SetItemText(i, 1, sTemp);
```

Add the first store's price to the second column:

```
sTemp.Format(_T("%.2f"),fStore1Price);
m_ListBox.SetItemText(i, 2, sTemp);
```

You repeat this process for each of the remaining pieces of data:

```
sTemp.Format(_T("%.2f"),fStore2Price);
m_ListBox.SetItemText(i, 3, sTemp);

sTemp.Format(_T("%.2f"),fStore3Price);
m_ListBox.SetItemText(i, 4, sTemp);

sTemp.Format(_T("%.2f"),fStore4Price);
m_ListBox.SetItemText(i, 5, sTemp);

}
```

So far, so good! Now let's move on to allowing the user to enter and delete data.

Allowing the User to Enter and Delete Data   Your first task is to allow the user to enter data into the CListView control. However, instead of letting them simply click on the CListView and add whatever they'd like, add a button to the toolbar that, when clicked, will pop up a dialog box. This dialog will ask the user to enter information about the product that they're adding to their shopping list. This dialog-based approach allows for greater validation on your part because it's easier to limit the number of ways that data can be entered into the system. The first step is to go to the Resource Editor and create a new button that will be for adding records. For the sake of simplicity, just type a large letter *A* on the button face, as shown in Figure 7.2.

FIGURE 7.2 :

The Add button

The next step to getting your new button loaded onto the Command Bar is to add it to the TBBUTTON array discussed earlier. So, add an entry to that array as follows:

```
{6, ID_INSERT, TBSTATE_ENABLED, TBSTYLE_BUTTON, 0, 0, 0, -1}
```

Then you've got to change one value in your call to CMainFrame::InsertButtons(). Previously, you had:

```
if (!InsertButtons( g_tbSTDButton,
    sizeof(g_tbSTDButton)/sizeof(TBBUTTON),
    IDR_MAINFRAME,
    6 ))
//...
```

Now, because you've added an additional button, you must increase the number of buttons (six, in the above code) to seven. Therefore, your call to Insert-Buttons() should now read:

```
if (!InsertButtons( g_tbSTDButton,
    sizeof(g_tbSTDButton)/sizeof(TBBUTTON),
    IDR_MAINFRAME,
    7 ))
//...
```

Now that you've added an Add button onto the Command Bar, you must create the Add dialog. To do this, use the Resource Editor to insert a new dialog. You can now add controls to the dialog according to the data you'll need to get from the user. In this case, the dialog should have six edit boxes:

- One edit box to record the quantity of the item being added

- One edit box to record the name of the product

- Four edit boxes to record the price of the item at each store

Figure 7.3 shows a possible design for this dialog.

FIGURE 7.3:

The Add/Insert dialog

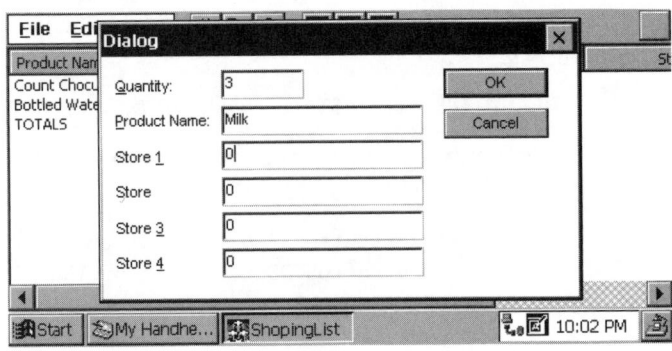

Now create a class to act as a wrapper for the dialog. Simply double-clicking anywhere on the dialog while in the Resource Editor will do the trick. Call your class CInsertDialog. Then, using the Class Wizard, create member variables for CInsertDialog to store the data entered by the user and add code to launch the dialog in the CShoppingListView::OnInsert() event:

```
CInsertDlg dlg;
if (dlg.DoModal() == IDOK)
    {
```

If the user clicked the OK button, go ahead and get the values that they entered and store them into local variables:

```
int      nQty = dlg.m_nQty;
CString  sProductName = dlg.m_sPdtName;
float fStore1Price = dlg.m_fStore1;
float fStore2Price = dlg.m_fStore2;
float fStore3Price = dlg.m_fStore3;
float fStore4Price = dlg.m_fStore4;
```

Then add the values you just retrieved from the dialog into your arrays:

```
GetDocument()->m_Qty.Add(nQty);
    GetDocument()->m_sProductName.Add(sProductName);
    GetDocument()->m_fStore1Price.Add(fStore1Price);
    GetDocument()->m_fStore2Price.Add(fStore2Price);
    GetDocument()->m_fStore3Price.Add(fStore3Price);
    GetDocument()->m_fStore4Price.Add(fStore4Price);
    }
```

Finally, make sure that you indicate that the data has changed, and update the CListView control:

```
GetDocument()->SetModifiedFlag(TRUE);
UpdateListBox();
```

The next step in allowing the user to enter and delete data is to allow them to change the names of the four supermarkets/stores at which you're performing your price comparisons. Just as you did with the Add dialog, start by creating a button (using, let's say, a capital *S* for stores) and add it to the TBBUTTON array:

```
{7, ID_STORE_NAMES, TBSTATE_ENABLED, TBSTYLE_BUTTON, 0, 0, 0, -1},
```

Again, change the call to CMainFrame::InsertButtons() to reflect the additional button:

```
if (!InsertButtons( g_tbSTDButton,
    sizeof(g_tbSTDButton)/sizeof(TBBUTTON),
    IDR_MAINFRAME,
    8 ))    //changed to '8' from '7'
```

To launch the dialog, create an OnStoreNames() event in your CShoppingListView class. However, unlike in the Add dialog, put some initial values into the dialog box:

```
CChgStrNameDlg dlg;
dlg.m_sStore1Name = GetDocument()->m_sStoreNames[0];
dlg.m_sStore2Name = GetDocument()->m_sStoreNames[1];
dlg.m_sStore3Name = GetDocument()->m_sStoreNames[2];
dlg.m_sStore4Name = GetDocument()->m_sStoreNames[3];
```

Then, if the user clicks the OK button, retrieve their values and store them in the m_sStoreNames array:

```
if (dlg.DoModal() == IDOK)
{
    GetDocument()->m_sStoreNames[0] = dlg.m_sStore1Name;
    GetDocument()->m_sStoreNames[1] = dlg.m_sStore2Name;
    GetDocument()->m_sStoreNames[2] = dlg.m_sStore3Name;
    GetDocument()->m_sStoreNames[3] = dlg.m_sStore4Name;
}
```

When you're all done, refresh the column headings:

```
CreateListBoxHeader();
```

At this point the only thing left to do is to add functionality to allow the user to delete items from their Shopping List. Here again, start by creating a button (with a capital *D* for delete) and adding it to the TBBUTTON array:

```
{8, ID_DELETE,      TBSTATE_ENABLED, TBSTYLE_BUTTON, 0, 0, 0, -1},
```

Again, change the call to CMainFrame::InsertButtons() to reflect the additional button:

```
if (!InsertButtons( g_tbSTDButton,
    sizeof(g_tbSTDButton)/sizeof(TBBUTTON),
    IDR_MAINFRAME,
    9 ))    //changed to '9' from '8'
```

To actually delete the selected record, you'll need to create a CShoppingListView::OnDelete() method which will do the actual work of deleting the item out of the array.

First, make sure that the index of the selected item is valid by ensuring that it's less than the number of items available and greater than 0:

```
if (nListBoxIndex <= GetDocument()->m_sProductName.GetSize() &&
nListBoxIndex >= 0)
    {
```

Next, confirm with the user that they do want to delete the record in question:

```
if (AfxMessageBox(_T("Are you sure you want to delete "
    + GetDocument()->m_sProductName[nListBoxIndex] +
"?"),MB_OKCANCEL) == IDOK)
        {
```

If they do want to delete the item, give them the various arrays to delete the values at the appropriate index:

```
GetDocument()->m_Qty.RemoveAt(nListBoxIndex,1);
GetDocument()->m_sProductName.RemoveAt(nListBoxIndex,1);
GetDocument()->m_fStore1Price.RemoveAt(nListBoxIndex,1);
GetDocument()->m_fStore2Price.RemoveAt(nListBoxIndex,1);
GetDocument()->m_fStore3Price.RemoveAt(nListBoxIndex,1);
GetDocument()->m_fStore4Price.RemoveAt(nListBoxIndex,1);
```

Finally, set the modified flag, and update the contents of the CListView:

```
GetDocument()->SetModifiedFlag(TRUE);
UpdateListBox();
        }
    }
```

When you're all done, you should have an application that looks something like the one shown in Figure 7.4.

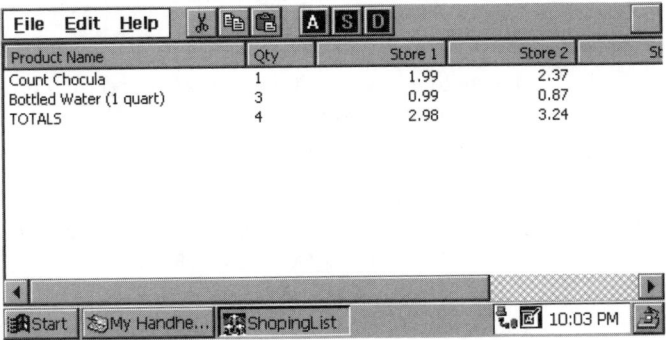

Although it looks very different from the application you started with, you can see that the two applications are functionally very similar. Of course, this is merely a rough port. There's a lot you can do to enhance and optimize this application to be more in tune with the features and limitations of a CE device.

Optimizing for CE

You now have a port of your application to CE, and, technically, you're finished. However, there are a few steps you can take to make your application run just a little bit more smoothly on a CE device. The first one, which takes almost no effort on your part, is to limit the application to only opening one true Shopping List file. Currently, the user can create any number of shopping list files. However, given the limited storage space of a CE device and the fact that you don't really want the user to litter their CE device with dozens of shopping list files, it would be much better to simply enforce a single-file policy. Fortunately, it only takes one line of code in order to ensure that ShoppingList.dat is always the file opened by the application:

```
OpenDocumentFile(_T("ShoppingList.dat"));
```

You'll also want to fix the Command Bar so that it does not have any buttons relating to New and Open. To do that, first edit the resource containing the toolbar buttons, so that the first three buttons are deleted, then edit the TBBUTTON array so that it now reflects the true number of button images available.

TIP

To delete a button, either click on it and then press the delete key, or click and drag it off the screen with your mouse.

```
static TBBUTTON g_tbSTDButton[] = {
    {0, 0, TBSTATE_ENABLED, TBSTYLE_SEP, 0, 0, 0, 0},
    {0, 0, TBSTATE_ENABLED, TBSTYLE_SEP, 0, 0, 0, -1},
    {0, ID_EDIT_CUT, TBSTATE_ENABLED, TBSTYLE_BUTTON, 0, 0, 0, -1},
    {1, ID_EDIT_COPY, TBSTATE_ENABLED, TBSTYLE_BUTTON, 0, 0, 0, -1},
    {2, ID_EDIT_PASTE, TBSTATE_ENABLED, TBSTYLE_BUTTON, 0, 0, 0, -1},
    {0, 0, TBSTATE_ENABLED, TBSTYLE_SEP, 0, 0, 0, -1},
    {0, 0, TBSTATE_ENABLED, TBSTYLE_SEP, 0, 0, 0,  0},
    {3, ID_INSERT, TBSTATE_ENABLED, TBSTYLE_BUTTON, 0, 0, 0, -1},
    {4, ID_STORE_NAMES, TBSTATE_ENABLED, TBSTYLE_BUTTON, 0, 0, 0, -1},
    {5, ID_DELETE, TBSTATE_ENABLED, TBSTYLE_BUTTON, 0, 0, 0, -1},
    {0, 0, TBSTATE_ENABLED, TBSTYLE_SEP, 0, 0, 0,  0}
};
```

You'll notice that the first three buttons have now been removed, and the index values for the remaining buttons have all been appropriately adjusted.

Naturally, you must also alter your call to `CMainFrame::InsertButtons()`:

```
if (!InsertButtons( g_tbSTDButton,
    sizeof(g_tbSTDButton)/sizeof(TBBUTTON),
    IDR_MAINFRAME,
    6 ))    //reflects loss of 3 buttons
```

This modification helps to cut down on possible excessive storage space use and does so with only a minimal loss in functionality.

There's one additional optimization that you can make here that would improve the efficiency and memory usage of your application. When you originally performed the port on this application, there were a number of occasions where, for debugging and illustration purposes, you stored values from an array into a local variable and then displayed them to the user. The step of storing the values into local variables can be entirely eliminated. In fact, to be truly low-memory aware, you should eliminate as many nonessential variables as possible, as they are essentially memory allocations. Let's take a look at how one of these blocks of code might change.

You'll recall that in the CShoppingListView::CreateListBoxHeader() method you retrieve the store names from the m_sStoreNames CStringArray and put the values into local variables:

```
CString sStore1Name = GetDocument()->m_sStoreNames[0];
CString sStore2Name = GetDocument()->m_sStoreNames[1];
CString sStore3Name = GetDocument()->m_sStoreNames[2];
CString sStore4Name = GetDocument()->m_sStoreNames[3];
```

Then, you refresh the actual heading text, passing the local variables to the InsertColumn() method, where appropriate:

```
m_ListBox.DeleteColumn(0);
m_ListBox.InsertColumn( 0, _T("Product Name"), LVCFMT_LEFT, 175 );
m_ListBox.DeleteColumn(1);
m_ListBox.InsertColumn( 1, _T("Qty"), LVCFMT_LEFT, 50 );
m_ListBox.DeleteColumn(2);
m_ListBox.InsertColumn( 2, sStore1Name, LVCFMT_RIGHT, 95 );
m_ListBox.DeleteColumn(3);
m_ListBox.InsertColumn( 3, sStore2Name, LVCFMT_RIGHT, 95 );
m_ListBox.DeleteColumn(4);
m_ListBox.InsertColumn( 4, sStore3Name, LVCFMT_RIGHT, 95 );
m_ListBox.DeleteColumn(5);
m_ListBox.InsertColumn( 5, sStore4Name, LVCFMT_RIGHT, 95 );
```

Although this does make it easier to debug this procedure, there's no reason at all to leave the code organized in this way for the final shipping product. Instead, you'd do much better to pass the array values directly to the InsertColumn() method, thus eliminating the need for local variables entirely:

```
m_ListBox.DeleteColumn(0);
m_ListBox.InsertColumn( 0, _T("Product Name"), LVCFMT_LEFT, 175 );
m_ListBox.DeleteColumn(1);
m_ListBox.InsertColumn( 1, _T("Qty"), LVCFMT_LEFT, 50 );
m_ListBox.DeleteColumn(2);
m_ListBox.InsertColumn( 2, GetDocument()->m_sStoreNames[0],
LVCFMT_RIGHT, 95 );
m_ListBox.DeleteColumn(3);
m_ListBox.InsertColumn( 3, GetDocument()->m_sStoreNames[1],
LVCFMT_RIGHT, 95 );
m_ListBox.DeleteColumn(4);
```

```
    m_ListBox.InsertColumn( 4, GetDocument()->m_sStoreNames[2],
LVCFMT_RIGHT, 95 );
    m_ListBox.DeleteColumn(5);
    m_ListBox.InsertColumn( 5, GetDocument()->m_sStoreNames[3],
LVCFMT_RIGHT, 95 );
```

If you make this simple change everywhere else it's needed in the source, you will have saved quite a bit of needless memory allocation.

One Final Surprise

Although it wasn't demonstrated in the porting of the Shopping List application, there is one additional surprise that you need to know about when you're porting to CE.

Under Windows 98 or NT, there are a number of cases where you rely on another program to do a task for you, rather than attempting to duplicate that functionality on your own. For instance, many programs that don't require a full-fledged reporting engine of their own may opt to use Microsoft Word as a reporting engine. Typically, the developer will create template documents for Word. Then, via a service known as OLE Automation, it's possible to launch Word in a hidden state, pass it values to insert into the template document, and even ask it to print the document for you. All this is done without the user's knowledge that Word has been invoked at all. For instance, in your `CWinApp`'s `InitInstance()` method, you might actually launch a hidden copy of Excel with code that looks something like this:

```
m_pExcelWS = new IWorksheetFunction;
ASSERT (m_pExcelWS!= NULL);
if (!m_pExcelWS->CreateDispatch("Excel.Application"))
    return AfxMessageBox("Failed to Connect, Please make sure you have
    Excel 97 Installed");
```

The problem is that under CE, the programs that are most commonly used as OLE Automation servers—namely, the Microsoft Office Suite of applications—do not offer any OLE Automation features. So, if you had an application like the one pictured in Figure 7.5, which uses Excel as an OLE Automation server to perform an interest calculation, you would be facing an additional porting task.

FIGURE 7.5:

The Desktop version
of CarCalc

This application imports all of the functions Excel makes available. Then, using a pointer to the Excel object, it lets Excel perform the calculation:

```
m_nMonthlyPayment = pApp->m_pExcelWS->Pmt(dInt, m_nNumOfMonths,
m_nAmountBorrowed, d, e);
```

In this way, you have a fully functional application without having to do any of the interest payment algorithms yourself. However, when you port this CarCalc application to CE, you soon find that you're not so lucky because, in order to get this application to run on a CE device, you have to do all of the math yourself. What was previously one simple line of code is now an entire algorithm for calculating monthly payments:

```
if (m_nNumOfMonths > 0)
{

    double pow = 1;
    double value;
    double dTempAPR = m_nAPR / 12;

    for (int i = 0; i < m_nNumOfMonths; i++){
        pow = pow * (1 + dTempAPR);
        value = (m_nAmountBorrowed * pow * dTempAPR) / (pow - 1);
    }

    m_nMonthlyPayment = value;
```

```
sTemp.Format(_T("%.2f"),m_nMonthlyPayment);
m_nMonthlyPayment = (double)wcstod(sTemp,'\0');
}
```

All of your code that relies on OLE Automation will almost certainly have to change in a similar fashion.

Summary

In this chapter, you examined the porting of a Desktop-based MFC application to a CE-based MFC application. You learned what sort of perils can arise and looked at some common solutions for these problems. In addition, you took a look at some of the services provided by a third-party application (Office) and what you could do to compensate for the fact that the Pocket versions of those applications did not provide the same features.

In the coming chapters, you'll be looking at the Visual Basic side of programming for CE. You'll then explore some features that are unique to the Windows CE operating system.

CHAPTER
EIGHT

Visual Basic Toolkit for CE

■ The Application Templates

■ The Debugger

■ The Runtime Files

■ The Control Manager

■ The ActiveX Control Pack

■ The Standard VBCE Controls

■ The Setup Wizard

The purpose of this chapter is to show off the Windows CE toolkit for Visual Basic. We'll take a look at some of the things you can do with VBCE and what exactly the toolkit offers. We'll also take a look at the special debugger for CE-based applications. In addition, we'll pay special attention to VBCE's own Application Setup Wizard, a special tool available only for Visual Basic. Then we'll move on to changes in the actual Visual Basic language for CE. Finally, we'll present a sample Visual Basic application.

The Windows CE Toolkit for VB

When you use the Windows CE toolkit for Visual Basic to build programs, you're really using a collection of tools and products all at once. Unlike VC++, where the various SDKs and toolkit features seem to be one product, VB's toolkit is distinct and different from any tools provided with the SDK. The toolkit for VB consists of the following core components:

- The application templates
- The debugger
- The runtime files
- The Control Manager
- The ActiveX Control Pack
- The Standard VBCE controls
- The Setup Wizard

The Application Templates

The application templates, as shown in Figure 8.1, are the three types of Windows CE applications that you can create with VBCE. They are

- Windows CE HPC Project
- Windows CE HPC/Pro Project
- Windows CE Formless Project

FIGURE 8.1:

FIGURE 8.1:

The Application Templates

The first of these templates has existed since the toolkit for VB 5 and is the standard project that you can create for any HPC device. The other two templates are new to the VB 6 toolkit. As you might guess, the HPC/Pro template allows you to create applications for HPC/Pro devices, such as the HP Jornada.

TIP   An HPC/Pro VBCE application will also run on HPCs that have been upgraded to Windows CE version 2.11.

The last of these templates, the Formless Project, may not make sense at first. Starting with the toolkit for VB 6, we can now use Visual Basic to create applications that are formless. The main purpose of such an application would be to develop applications to run on embedded versions of Windows CE.

Embedded Applications with VB

As you may know, Microsoft offers a version of Windows CE for developers of embedded systems. The way it works is that a developer who wants to use CE for an embedded device must purchase the Embedded Toolkit for VC++. The developer then builds a special, completely customized version of Windows CE, according to the specific needs of their application or device.

Continued on next page

However, when they're finished building their custom version of CE, they don't get the attractive Windows 98–like shell. Instead, their version of CE has either a minimal shell or is a text-mode operating system. This lack of a standard shell is the reason for the formless VB application type.

With the advent of the formless VB application, you can build your custom version of CE itself using the Embedded Toolkit and VC++, then code all of your embedded applications using Visual Basic.

The Debugger

Unlike the standard Visual Basic debugger, the debugger for CE-based applications is actually a completely separate program from the IDE. This makes it a little more difficult to use in a number of ways.

1. *Setting breakpoints in your code becomes a challenge in itself.* The problem is that, because the debugger is a separate executable, you can't set breakpoints from within the VB IDE itself. Instead, you must manually set your breakpoints while your application is running in the debugger. When your program is passed to the debugger, there are three distinct events that take place:

   a. First, if appropriate, the debugger launches the Desktop emulator.

   b. Next, the debugger launches your program.

   c. Finally, your program, as shown in Figure 8.2, is displayed in the debugger.

What this means to you is that it's extremely difficult to set any breakpoints on anything that executes as part of the initialization code for your project's startup object. You literally have to race to get to the code in time to put a breakpoint on any of it.

NOTE   In the newest version of the toolkit (for VB 6) there is a Step Into option in the IDE that goes a long way toward fixing the problem. However, it's still not very efficient if your application does a lot of processing at startup and you only want to break toward the end of the operation.

FIGURE 8.2:

An application as viewed in the debugger

```
Windows CE Toolkit for Visual Basic Debugger - [TimerDemo:Form1]
Debug  View  Window  Help

Option Explicit
Dim i
Private Sub cmdStart_Click()
  i = 0
  Timer1.Enabled = True
  txtStart.Text = Time
End Sub
Private Sub cmdStop_Click()
  Timer1.Enabled = False
  txtEnd.Text = Time
  txtDifference.Text = i & " seconds elapsed"
End Sub
Private Sub Timer1_Timer()
    i = i + 1
End Sub
```

2. *Your breakpoints are only temporary.* As soon as you exit the debugger, they're lost. So, if you want to debug the same code more than once, you must set all the breakpoints each time.

3. *When your program is finished running, the debugger asks you if you want to close the debugger as well.* This can be quite annoying.

NOTE

It is expected that the debugger will no longer ask you if you want to close the debugger in the final release version of the toolkit; however, as of this writing, only the beta version of the toolkit was available.

In conclusion, the VBCE debugger still needs some work before it will be as user-friendly or as easy to use as VB's standard debugger.

The Runtime Files

VBCE's runtime files are not the same as the VBRUNx00.dll files that exist in the Desktop VB world. Instead, the VBCE runtime engine is a CE port of Microsoft's

Visual Basic Script engine! This means that when you're writing a VBCE program, you're really working with an enhanced version of the VBScript language.

Although the toolkit for VB 5 only supported two processors, VBCE 6 supports nine different processors and devices. They are

- Strong ARM
- Intel 486
- MIPS 39xx
- MIPS 41xx
- MIPS 43xx
- Power PC 821
- SA 1100
- SH3
- SH4

The actual runtime files, should you ever need to manually copy them, are

- pvbload.exe
- pvbform2.dll
- pvbhost2.dll
- vbscript.dll
- vbsen.dll

The Control Manager

The Control Manager is an application designed to help developers know which ActiveX controls are registered on which devices. When it starts, Control Manager queries the Desktop operating system for a list of all registered Windows CE controls. It then queries the Emulator and the currently connected Windows CE device (if any) for the same information.

When finished, Control Manager displays the list of all the CE ActiveX controls available and whether or not they exist on the device and the Emulator. You can then register (or delete) controls as needed. Of course, when you distribute your application it will be the responsibility of your setup program to register controls on the user's device. That's why Control Manager is so useful: it saves you from having to create that setup program every time you add or remove a control from your project.

The ActiveX Control Pack

The original version of the toolkit didn't come with anywhere near the variety of ActiveX controls that VB developers have come to expect. To remedy this situation, Microsoft released the ActiveX Control Pack, which contains six additional ActiveX controls for Windows CE. Although these controls are now shipped as part of the toolkit, they're worth mentioning separately in the event that you're using the VBCE toolkit for VB 5.

The ActiveX Control Pack includes the following controls:

- Grid
- TabStrip
- TreeView
- ListView
- ImageList
- Common Dialog

Grid

The Grid control of the ActiveX Control Pack is a simple, low-powered version of the MSFlexGrid control that comes with VB 6. While the grid is fine for displaying and organizing small amounts of data, it is read-only and doesn't support features such as FixedRows. For most applications, you're probably better off purchasing a third-party grid or modifying your project to use a ListView control. Figure 8.3 shows the Grid control at runtime.

FIGURE 8.3:

The Grid control at runtime

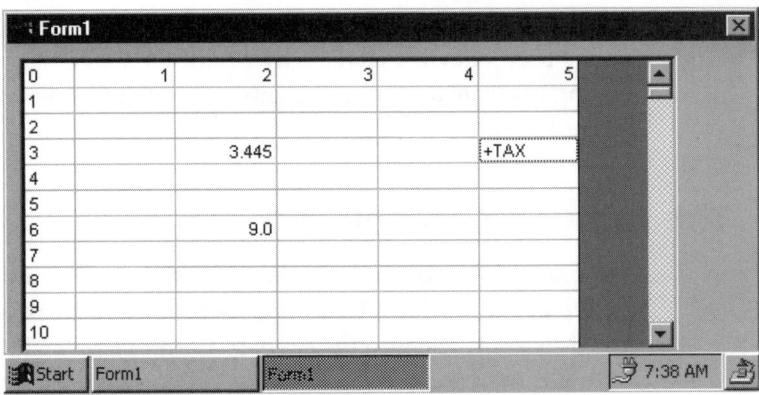

Solving the Read-Only Problem

For many of us, a read-only grid is not worth very much at all. Typically, users like to be able to edit the data they see in a grid, and CE users are certainly no exception. Unfortunately, the standard Grid control of the ActiveX Control Pack is read-only, just like its Desktop cousin, the MSFlexGrid.

If you've worked with the MSFlexGrid control for any length of time, you've probably seen the MSDN sample code that demonstrates how to simulate in-place editing with the MSFlexGrid. However, the problem with that code is that it doesn't work on CE without some modification. Although there are lots of issues related to porting Desktop VB code to VBCE that we'll deal with in the next chapter, this MSDN code fails for one simple reason: CE-based controls do not respect the Z-order set at design time. (As you probably know, Z-order refers to the order in which controls sit "on top of" one another—the BringToFront and SendToBack menu options available at design time.)

The problem comes from the fact that the Grid control always seems to place itself at the top of the Z-order, obscuring all the controls previously above it. The solution to this problem is to hide the Grid control, then reshow it *after* you show the Edit control.

The original MSDN code to position and show the Edit control looked like this:

```
Edt.Move MSHFlexGrid.Left + MSHFlexGrid.CellLeft, _
    MSHFlexGrid.Top + MSHFlexGrid.CellTop, _
    MSHFlexGrid.CellWidth - 8, _
    MSHFlexGrid.CellHeight - 8
Edt.Visible = True
Edt.SetFocus
```

Continued on next page

To make the Grid control effective, that code must now be changed to hide and then show the Grid control:

```
Edt.Move MSHFlexGrid.Left + MSHFlexGrid.CellLeft, _
    MSHFlexGrid.Top + MSHFlexGrid.CellTop, MSHFlexGrid.CellWidth -
8, _
    MSHFlexGrid.CellHeight - 8
MSHFlexGrid.Visible = False   'Hide the Grid
Edt.Visible = True            'Show the Edit control
MSHFlexGrid.Visible = True    'Show the Grid again
Edt.SetFocus
```

This fix correctly causes the Grid control to be shown "under" the Edit control, completing the illusion of in-place editing.

TabStrip

The TabStrip control is another rather simplistic control, but it's one that can be quite useful when you have too many controls for one form. Using the TabStrip control, you can logically group related UI elements so that when the user clicks on a tab, a different set of controls is shown. (This behavior can also be seen on any Windows 98/NT property sheet dialog.) Figure 8.4 shows the TabStrip control at runtime.

FIGURE 8.4:

The TabStrip control at runtime

WARNING The TabStrip control does not actually manage the showing and hiding of related controls. You must write the code to do this yourself.

TreeView

The TreeView control is simply an implementation of the standard Windows CE TreeView control.

ListView

Similarly, the ListView control is an implementation of the standard Windows CE ListView control. It supports the four standard views of data supported by the Desktop ListView control: Large Icon, Small Icon, List, and Report.

ImageList

The ImageList control is an implementation of the standard Windows CE ImageList control. As you probably know, the ImageList control is used to manage bitmaps that are then accessed by other controls, such as TreeViews and ListViews.

Common Dialog

The Common Dialog control is a control that serves as a wrapper for the four common dialogs:

- File Open
- File SaveAs
- Color Selection
- Font Selection

In addition, the Common Dialog control can also be used to display a help file using the CE Help system. The methods of the Common Dialog control are outlined in Table 8.1.

TABLE 8.1: Methods of the Common Dialog Control

Method	What It Does
ShowOpen	Launches the FileOpen dialog. The selected FileName is returned in the FileName property.
ShowSave	Launches the FileSaveAs dialog. The FileName is returned in the FileName property.
ShowColor	Launches the Color Selection dialog. The value of the selected color is returned in the Color property.
ShowFont	Launches the Font Selection dialog. The selected FontName, FontSize, and other attributes are returned in the similarly named properties of the control.
ShowHelp	Launches `PegHelp.exe`, the Windows CE Help Viewer. Invokes the Windows Help Engine. The HelpFile property specifies the complete path of the application's help file.

The Standard VBCE Controls

Of course, the ActiveX Control Pack is only intended to supplement the core controls offered by VBCE. Some of these controls are implemented as ActiveX controls, while others are included as part of the VBCE language itself. Wherever possible, you'll want to stick to the native VBCE controls instead of the ActiveX controls. That's because each ActiveX control you use adds to the total storage space requirement of your program, and, on a CE device, storage space is always at a premium.

Table 8.2 below lists the controls available to VBCE programmers and describes what type of control each is as well as the purpose of each control.

TABLE 8.2: The Standard VBCE Controls

Control	Implemented As	Purpose
CheckBox	Native VBCE control	Standard CheckBox control
ComboBox	Native VBCE control	Standard ComboBox control
Comm	ActiveX control	Similar to Desktop Comm control; provides access to serial communications

TABLE 8.2 CONTINUED: The Standard VBCE Controls

Control	Implemented As	Purpose
CommandBar	ActiveX control	Windows CE CommandBar; helps to improve CE-like appearance of VBCE applications
File	ActiveX control	Provides read-and-write access functions for working with files
FileSystem	ActiveX control	Exposes file-system functions such as FileCopy
Finance	ActiveX control	Provides financial functions such as PMT
Frame	Native VBCE control	Standard Frame control
Image	ActiveX control	Similar to Desktop Image control; used for displaying bitmaps, but does not support any drawing operations
Label	Native VBCE control	Standard Label control
Line	Native VBCE control	Standard Line control
ListBox	Native VBCE control	Standard ListBox control
Menu	Native VBCE control	Standard Menu control
OptionButton	Native VBCE control	Standard OptionButton control
PictureBox	ActiveX control	Similar to Desktop PictureBox control; used for displaying bitmaps; offers several drawing functions
Scrollbar	Native VBCE control	Standard Scrollbar control
Shape	Native VBCE control	Standard Shape control
TextBox	Native VBCE control	Standard TextBox control
Timer	Native VBCE control	Standard Timer control
Winsock	ActiveX control	Provides Winsock functions for communication over the IR port of the CE device

The Setup Wizard

One of the most useful tools provided with VBCE is the Setup Wizard. As you'll see in Chapter 14, creating a correct, working Windows CE setup application is a task no one welcomes. That's where the Setup Wizard comes in.

The Setup Wizard is a tool that takes your application, any related files, and the VBCE runtime engine, and creates a setup program for you. All you have to do in order to create this setup program is to give the wizard the following information:

1. Which VB (application) file you want to install

2. Where you want your files to end up when copied to the device

3. Which ActiveX controls or additional files you want installed

4. Whether or not to copy the VBCE runtime files

That's all there is to creating a setup. As you'll see in Chapter 14, creating setup programs for Windows CE is usually considerably more complex unless you opt for a third-party tool like InstallShield for Windows CE. However, with VBCE's Setup Wizard, it's a breeze.

Changes in the Visual Basic Language

As you probably know, VBCE is really a souped-up version of the VBScript language. VBScript is a language that was designed to compete with JavaScript; in other words, it's a simple language for scripting Web pages. However, VBScript is loosely based on Visual Basic, and these languages really aren't that diffeent from one another.

But not all features of the Visual Basic language exist on CE and, as you'd expect, the features that do exist are not the same in the version 5 toolkit as they are in the version 6 toolkit.

The version 5 toolkit is fairly restrictive in what it offers in terms of the Visual Basic language. As a general rule, it seems to be much closer to VBScript than to Visual Basic. For instance, the `Dim variable As Type` syntax is not supported. You can still declare your variables using `Dim`, but you cannot specify an explicit type. That's because VBScript is basically a typeless language; every variable is a variant.

The toolkit for Visual Basic version 6 is, as the Microsoft documentation says, "essentially identical to the earlier version." However, there are a number of familiar statements and other language features that have been added. Table 8.3 shows some of the more common Visual Basic for CE Language features and which versions of the toolkit, if either, offer those features.

TABLE 8.3: Visual Basic for CE Language Features

Language Feature	Supported by Version 5 of Toolkit?	Supported by Version 6 of Toolkit?
#If...#Else	No	No
DoEvents	No	No
GoTo	No	No
With...End With	No	No
End	No	No
Debug.Print	No	No
Declare	No	Yes
Dim Variable As Type	No	Yes
LoadResString	No	Yes

In addition to the above list, all file access and financial functions are now encapsulated in ActiveX controls. However, the following standard Visual Basic controls are unsupported:

- Directory List Box
- Drive List Box
- File List Box
- Data
- OLE

A Sample Application

In order to get familiar with the Visual Basic for CE environment and language, let's create a sample application based on one of the old tutorial examples from early versions of VB. Specifically, you'll make a simple stopwatch-like application. It will record the starting and ending times, as well as the number of seconds elapsed.

Start by creating a new HPC or HPC/Pro Project by choosing File ➤ New Project off of the main menu. The Application Properties window will appear. When you finish filling out the Properties window, you'll be presented with a standard-looking blank form.

Let's begin the visual design of the application by adding three edit controls to the form. Stack them so they appear one on top of the other. Name these edit controls `txtStart`, `txtEnd`, and `txtDifference`. When you're done with that, add three label controls to identify the edit controls' purposes as Starting Time, Ending Time, and Difference.

Now, add two buttons to the form. Name the first button `cmdStart` and change its caption to Start. Name the second button `cmdStop` and change its caption to Stop.

Finally, add a timer control to your form. The default name of `Timer1` will be fine, but change the interval to 1000. This will cause the `Timer()` event to be triggered every 1000 milliseconds, or once a second. When you're all finished, you should have a form that looks something like that shown in Figure 8.5.

FIGURE 8.5:

The Stopwatch form at design time

Now you'll add some code to the form to make it actually do something! Start by declaring the variable `i`. Do this just under the `Option Explicit` line at the top of your code. When you're done, the first two lines of your code should read

```
Option Explicit
Dim i As Integer
```

Next, add some code for the cmdStart button's Click() event. Specifically, you'll be initializing i, starting the timer control, and recording the starting time in the txtStart edit control:

```
Private Sub cmdStart_Click()
  i = 0                    'initialize i
  Timer1.Enabled = True    'start the timer
  txtStart.Text = Time     'record starting time
End Sub
```

Then, add some code for the timer control's Timer() event. Specifically, increment i by 1 whenever the Timer() event is triggered:

```
Private Sub Timer1_Timer()
    i = i + 1
End Sub
```

Finally, add some code to the cmdStop button's Click() event. Here, you'll stop the timer, record the ending time in the txtEnd edit box, and display the number of seconds elapsed by writing the value of i to the txtDifference edit box:

```
Private Sub cmdStop_Click()
  Timer1.Enabled = False     'stop the timer
  txtEnd.Text = Time         'record the ending time
  txtDifference.Text = i & " seconds elapsed"  'display elapsed time
End Sub
```

You're done! You now have a CE stopwatch application, created in only a few minutes, with a minimum of coding and controls.

Summary

In this chapter, you examined Visual Basic for Windows CE. First, you saw what the toolkit had to offer. You looked at some of the special tools and utilities we'll need to build and distribute VBCE applications. You also examined some of the language differences between the VB you're used to and VBCE. Finally, to familiarize yourself with VBCE, you created a simple application.

In the next chapter, you'll look at what it takes to get a Desktop Visual Basic application ported to Windows CE and how to make that process go as smoothly as possible.

CHAPTER
NINE

A Real VB Application
Converted to CE

- A Sample Application: International ATM

- Mechanical Issues of Porting

- Optional Features

- Optimizing for CE

In this chapter, we'll be converting a real Visual Basic application to Windows CE. When we're done, you'll have an understanding of what's involved in converting even the simplest of Visual Basic desktop applications to the CE platform. In addition, you'll see why you have to drop certain features and that you may be inspired to add new ones.

At this point, you already have an understanding of which Visual Basic features are and are not supported under Windows CE. It probably comes as no surprise that Microsoft's recommendation for porting existing Visual Basic applications to CE is: *don't!* Microsoft believes that you're better off starting from scratch. However, that's simply not realistic, since many of you already have significant investments in your existing Visual Basic code, and you're probably not willing to rewrite everything. The steps to porting a VB application to CE are covered in the following order:

1. We'll take a look at the project as it exists now.

2. We'll work our way through the conversion, starting with the simpler tasks. The goal is to get a no-frills version of the application running on a CE device.

3. During the conversion, we'll consider porting some optional features.

4. We'll look at optimizing the user interface and the code for the Windows CE platform.

The Application: International ATM

The application we'll be porting is one you're probably already familiar with—it's the ATM sample that ships with VB5. In case you've never run into it before, though, let's take a quick look at it.

NOTE   This chapter uses the ATM sample application that comes with Visual Basic 5. You can find this application in the `VB\Samples\Pguide\ATM` directory on the VB 5 CD-ROM.

The ATM program is a simple demonstration of a multilingual cash machine. When you first start it, the application presents the flags of five countries with a button next to each one, as shown in Figure 9.1.

FIGURE 9.1:

The opening form of the ATM application

As you move your mouse over each of the buttons, your cursor changes to indicate that you can click on the buttons. Clicking on one of the buttons selects your preferred language for the rest of your transaction. Upon selecting your preferred language, you are presented with another form, asking for two pieces of information (see Figure 9.2):

- Your PIN number

- The amount you want to withdraw in U.S. dollars

FIGURE 9.2:

The controls on the form display text in whatever language the user chose.

Another form then pops up and asks you to confirm the amount of your withdrawal in U.S. dollars, as shown in Figure 9.3. (Naturally, the program performs the currency conversion for you.)

FIGURE 9.3:

The ATM application performs the currency conversion.

Finally, once the transaction is finished, the program plays a "thank you" message as a WAV file in your chosen language.

Porting the ATM Application: Not As Simple As It Looks

At first glance, it doesn't look like there's anything here that would be difficult to port. After all, there are only about 8 buttons, 4 edit boxes, and just over 150 lines of code in the whole project—it really looks like this is going to be a piece of cake.

As soon as you look a little more closely, however, you can see that there are quite a few things in the ATM program that absolutely will not port to CE under any circumstances. For instance, the "thank you" WAV file in the example requires the following Declare statement to play:

```
Declare Function sndPlaySound Lib "WINMM.DLL" Alias "sndPlaySoundA"
(ByVal lpszSoundName As Any, ByVal uFlags As Long)
```

VBCE, however, has no Declare statement and no support for calling external DLLs, so the code for the existing WAV files simply will not port to CE. If you still want to play WAV files, you must find another way.

NOTE

This has been remedied with the VB 6 Toolkit for Windows CE, in which the core VBCE language was modified to include the Declare statement. At the time of this writing, both the version 5 and 6 toolkits are still in popular use. Therefore, in the porting process of this chapter, we have followed the more restrictive standards of the VB 5 toolkit for illustration purposes. Additionally, the majority of the issues discussed here are still relevant to the VB 6 Toolkit for Windows CE.

How, Exactly, Do You Port from VB (Desktop) to VBCE?

There are two ways to get the forms from one project to the other when porting from an existing VB (desktop) application to a VBCE application:

- Start a new CE project, and then attempt to add the existing desktop forms to the new CE project (Project ➤ Add Form on the main menu).

- Start two copies of Visual Basic, open the existing project in one copy of VB, and open the new project in the other copy of VB. Then create a form in the new project. Go back to the old project and proceed to cut and paste controls (one at a time or all at once) and code from one to the other until you are finished.

Officially, Microsoft does not recommend the first method. However, both options produce essentially the same result: as you add the existing form to the new project, or as you paste one or more controls, VB will notify you about each control that is not supported under CE and will then remove it from the form. The only distinct advantage of the second method is that your forms will be automatically sized to the HPC screens by default. With the first method, you have to make sure your forms fit the smaller screens. Aside from this difference, however, both methods appear to work equally well, and which one you choose is a question of personal preference.

Planning the Porting Process

Before you start to dissect the application for porting, perhaps the best thing to do is to make a list of everything that will not port to CE without modifications of some kind. This way, you can get a sense of the work involved and can begin researching some clever workarounds or fixes.

When you take a look at everything that needs to be fixed or changed for the ATM project to compile and run under CE, the list looks like this:

- Several Global Const declarations. Although it doesn't appear to be documented anywhere, VBCE does not support Global declarations.

- All the project's variable declarations that specify a data type must be changed. For example:

  ```
  Dim ConversionValue As Currency
  ```

  must be changed to

  ```
  Dim ConversionValue
  ```

- An array of currency values initialized with the following line of code:

  ```
  ConversionTable = Array(1@, 4.8635@, 1.3978@, 1614@, 119.07@,
  89.075@)
  ```

  This will not compile under CE because it uses explicit typing; specifically, the values in the array are being cast to the currency type by the @ sign placed at the end of each value. Other explicit casting operations used in the ATM project also will not port, such as Val() or CCur().

- The Flag pictures on frmOpen must be changed from standard Image Controls to controls supported under CE, such as the CE Image Control. (The same change must be made to the two other forms in the application, as they also use an Image Control.)

- The WAV-playing functions, as mentioned previously, will not port to CE.

- The changing of the cursor as you pass over the buttons on frmOpen will not port to CE, as CE has no mouse cursors.

- The manner in which the secondary forms (i.e., not the main form) are shown modally will not port to CE, as VBCE does not support modal forms.

NOTE A modal form is one that locks out other parts of the program until the user dismisses or closes it, typically by clicking an OK or Cancel button.

- The very core of the ATM application itself, namely, the ability to load language-specific strings and images from a resource file, will not port to Windows CE because VBCE doesn't support the necessary `LoadResString` and `LoadResPicture` functions.

When you look at this list, porting the ATM application to VBCE can appear to be somewhat daunting. Yes, there are some items that are rather easy to fix and may involve nothing more than a bit of editing and a few REM statements. On the other hand, the ATM application relies upon being able to show a form modally and being able to load strings from a resource file. If it can't change the language of the buttons and labels dynamically, it doesn't have a purpose anymore.

Now that we have a better sense of parts of the ATM project that won't immediately port, let's come up with an action plan so that we can manage and rank the tasks in order of importance and complexity.

Mechanical Issues of Porting

When you look at the list of things that won't port, it's clear that some of them will be easier to fix than others. Let's start with the easier parts first.

Change `Global` to `Public`   Probably the easiest change to make is that of replacing the word `Global` with the word `Public`. This can be done with a simple Find..Replace operation that searches all files in the current project. This takes very little effort and fixes the problem completely. After all, the word `Global` only appears about three or four times in the entire ATM application!

Explicit type declarations   The next easiest changes to make are the Explicit Type declarations. To fix these, search for `As` on all files in the project. Each time you find an occurrence, stop and edit the code to remove the `As` and the type name after the `As`. Again, there are only a few such occurrences in the ATM project, so fixing them is pretty simple.

Explicit Types   While you're working on data-type-specific issues, you should also fix the currency conversion array. This occurs on line 26 of the modATM.bas module. Before the fix, it reads:

```
ConversionTable = Array(1@, 4.8635@, 1.3978@, 1614@, 119.07@,
89.075@)
```

To fix it, change it to read:

```
ConversionTable = Array(1, 4.8635, 1.3978, 1614, 119.07, 89.075)
```

Typecasts   Let's move on to removing the Val() and CCur() typecasts that are used on lines 20 and 21 of the code for frmAmountWithdrawn. They now read:

```
txtUSDollarsAmt = Val(frmInput.txtUSDollarsAmt.Text)
txtConvertedAmt = ConversionValue * CCur(txtUSDollarsAmt.Text)
```

To fix it, change it to read:

```
txtUSDollarsAmt = frmInput.txtUSDollarsAmt.Text
txtConvertedAmt = ConversionValue * txtUSDollarsAmt.Text
```

Bitmaps, icons, and the Image Control   Then there's the question of the Image Controls and the little flag pictures. As we discovered earlier, the standard Image Control doesn't exist on CE. While it's true that there is a substitute CE Image Control that you can use for this purpose, that may not be the best action to take, as we'll examine shortly. For the time being, simply leave the flags off the form.

Now that we've finished the simpler tasks, let's move on to some of the more complex conversions and fixes.

Converting WAV Files

First, let's deal with the WAV-playing functionality. Because VBCE offers no way to call an external DLL, and since it does not provide any multimedia functions of its own, you will have to Rem out and/or delete most of the WAV-related code for the time being. You should delete:

- The Declare statement(s)

- The actual DLL calls

- Any constants associated with the sound functions

Then, stub the existing Sub procedures, so as not to break any other code that may be calling those procedures. *Stubbing* is the process of removing the code from a procedure while keeping the Sub and End Sub blocks. Stubbing these procedures reduces the chance that something dependent on these routines will break when the routine is no longer there; it also ensures that other parts of the program still have a subroutine—even an empty one—that they can reference or call without breaking.

Currently, toward the top of your modATM.bas file, you should have some code that looks like this:

```
' ...
' High level sound support API
#If Win32 Then
Declare Function sndPlaySound Lib "WINMM.DLL" Alias
    "sndPlaySoundA" _ (ByVal lpszSoundName As Any, ByVal
    uFlags As Long)As Long
#Else
    Declare Function sndPlaySound Lib "MMSYSTEM.DLL" _
        (ByVal lpszSoundName As Any, ByVal wFlags As Integer) As
    Integer
#End If
Public Const SND_ASYNC = &H1       ' Play asynchronously
Public Const SND_NODEFAULT = &H2 ' Don't use default sound
Public Const SND_MEMORY = &H4      ' lpszSoundName points to mem

Public SoundBuffer
' ...
```

Mark and delete all of the code. When you're finished with the conversion, no portion of it should remain.

TIP   Even if VBCE did have a Declare statement, you'd still have to do some work on the section of code that references the WAV-playing functions. That's because VBCE doesn't support the conditional compile directives (#If..#Else..#End If) that are used heavily in this block of code.

A little further down in that same module, some additional code must be modified.

```
Sub BeginPlaySound(ByVal ResourceId As Integer)
    Dim Ret As Variant
    #If Win32 Then
  SoundBuffer = StrConv(LoadResData(ResourceId,
      "ATM_SOUND"), vbUnicode)
    #Else
        SoundBuffer = LoadResData(ResourceId, "ATM_SOUND")
    #End If
    Ret = sndPlaySound(SoundBuffer, SND_ASYNC Or SND_NODEFAULT
            Or SND_MEMORY)
    ' Important: This function is neccessary for playing sound
        ' asynchronously
    DoEvents
End Sub

Sub EndPlaySound()
    Dim Ret As Variant
    Ret = sndPlaySound(0&, 0&)
End Sub
```

To convert it, change the block of code to now read:

```
Sub BeginPlaySound(ByVal ResourceId As Integer)
End Sub

Sub EndPlaySound()
End Sub
```

What you did here was remove all of the code from the body of the BeginPlaySound and EndPlaySound procedures. Here again, by stubbing these routines, you ensure that any procedures attempting to call the BeginPlaySound or EndPlaySound procedures will be able to proceed as if the sound was still started or stopped.

Modifying Mouse/Cursor Code for CE

As we've covered in previous chapters, most CE devices do not have a mouse. And, clearly, if there's no mouse, there's also no mouse cursor. Therefore, to ensure that the ATM application will be compatible with as many CE devices as possible, all of the cursor-related code will have to go. But, as before, let's stub the procedures related to the cursor operations—just in case. For example, the following block of code is from modATM.bas:

```
Sub Cursor_Initialize()
    Set curSelect = LoadResPicture(1, vbResCursor)
End Sub

Sub SetCursor(Button As CommandButton)
    Button.MousePointer = 99
    Button.MouseIcon = curSelect
End Sub
```

To stub the cursor operator procedures, modify this segment of code to read:

```
Sub Cursor_Initialize()
    'CE: no cursors
End Sub

Sub SetCursor(Button)
    'CE: no cursors
End Sub
```

Again, you're completely gutting these procedures by deleting all of the code between the Sub and End Sub lines. The reason to leave the functions here, although they're empty, is to accommodate other parts of the program that may still contain a call to one of these procedures. Of course, you should still go back and try to remove all references to the empty procedures, but you might not catch all of them.

Converting Modal Forms

Now that you've finished the smaller stuff, you come to one of the bigger difficulties of porting the ATM application to CE—the fact that VBCE doesn't support modal forms. It's simple to compile the application:

1. Use a Find operation for the string Show 1. Every time you find a match, delete the 1.

2. Make sure there are no Unload Me commands below a Show 1 command. In the ATM project, an example of this can be found in the Sub cmdOK_click() event of frmInput. Before conversion, the code reads:

    ```
    frmAmountWithdrawn.Show 1
    Unload Me
    ```

Unload Me lines should be remmed out or deleted because Step 1 (changing the Show 1 command to read Show) will cause an error when frmInput attempts to unload itself while its child form, frmAmountWithdrawn, is still visible. Removing the Unload Me command suppresses this error.

Snag! It Works, but the Forms Aren't Modal Anymore! Once you've made these changes, you're on your way...or, are you? As you may have realized, this fix leaves the ATM application with a serious problem. Specifically, none of the forms wait for the active (formerly modal) form to be properly dismissed! This is a disaster for any program that depends on modal forms—not just the ATM application. Although there are several popular workarounds, none truly simulate a modal form perfectly. However, we have an application to port, so let's apply some workarounds and see if we like the final result once it's all done.

The most popular workaround for this problem seems to be to show the fake modal form and then immediately hide the parent form. Then, when the fake modal form is dismissed (as a true modal form would be), it will be up to the fake modal form to show the parent form again. For example, in the parent form, you might have code that looks like this:

```
frmFakeModal.Show        ' first show the fake modal form
Hide                     ' then hide the parent form...
```

Then, in the frmFakeModal.Unload event, you might have code that looks like this:

```
frmParent.Show           ' show the parent form again
```

For our purposes, this is a fairly good workaround for the lack of true modal forms. However, for larger projects, involving a greater number of forms, this could get a bit complicated.

To fix this problem with this project, you've got to find every place that a form was previously shown or unloaded and replace that code with your workaround code. In the case of the ATM project, you must add code similar to the code listed above wherever there is a Command Button click event on each form.

As an example, let's take a look at frmOpen and one of the language selection Command Buttons. The code for the Click event of the button marked Español (Command5) currently looks like this:

```
Sub Command5_Click()
    i = 144                ' User chose Spanish.
    frmInput.Show
End Sub
```

To add the modal form workaround, modify this code to read:

```
Sub Command5_Click()
    i = 144                 ' User chose Spanish.
    frmInput.Show
    Hide
End Sub
```

The next step is to repeat this operation for the remaining five buttons on frmInput. Once you've done that, you'll need to add this code to the Unload event of frmInput, as follows:

```
    frmOpen.Show
```

You're not finished yet! You still must add the same logic to the Command Buttons of frmInput and frmAmountWithdrawn. For frmInput, the cmdOK Click event should be modified to look something like this:

```
Sub cmdOK_click()
    'MsgBox (LoadResString(7 + i))   ' Remmed for the moment
    Hide     ' Hide yourself before showing the next form...
    frmAmountWithdrawn.Show
End Sub
```

For frmAmountWithdrawn, add the following two lines of code to the end of the cmdOKEnd Click event:

```
frmOpen.Show
Hide
```

That will solve the modal form problem!

To recap, here's what we just did:

- Added the workaround code to the Command Buttons of frmOpen

- Modified the Unload event of frmInput

- Modified the cmdOK Click event (on frmInput)

- Modified the cmdOKEnd Click event (on frmAmountWithdrawn)

Modifying Resource Loads

Now, we move to the last—and perhaps most important—porting issue of the ATM application: specifically, the lack of support for loading resources from a resource file. The main feature of the ATM application is that it can dynamically change its language. It does this by loading all of its string resources (not to mention, flag pictures) from a resource file. In some sense, then, if we cannot port this feature or find a workaround that allows the ATM application to dynamically change its captions and other text, the entire application will be worthless.

At this point, you have a couple of options:

- You can scrap the idea of dynamically changing the language of the program and instead create six separate executables, one for each language.

- You can store the string resources in some kind of separate file to be distributed along with the executable.

- You can use some cleverly designed arrays to store the string resources.

Of these ideas, the last one is probably the most elegant and appropriate solution, because the final CE version of the ATM application will be very similar to the original one. There won't be, as in the case of the second choice, any additional files to distribute along with the executable, not to mention the task of writing the appropriate file reading code. Also, the third option doesn't waste disk space, while the first option clearly does. For these reasons, we'll try to implement the third option.

TIP   There are cases when having the different language strings in a separate file is beneficial. For instance, it's easier to change the text of a particular message, as you wouldn't have to recompile the application.

When you examine the actual resource file (using Developer Studio (see Figure 9.4) or your favorite resource editor), you find that for each language, there are actually only 11 messages.

Currently, the ATM project already has one array that it uses to perform the math for the currency conversion figures displayed by frmAmountWithdrawn. That array contains one value (representing how many units of the chosen currency it takes to equal one U.S. dollar) for each language, or six entries in all.

FIGURE 9.4:

The resource file as viewed in Developer Studio

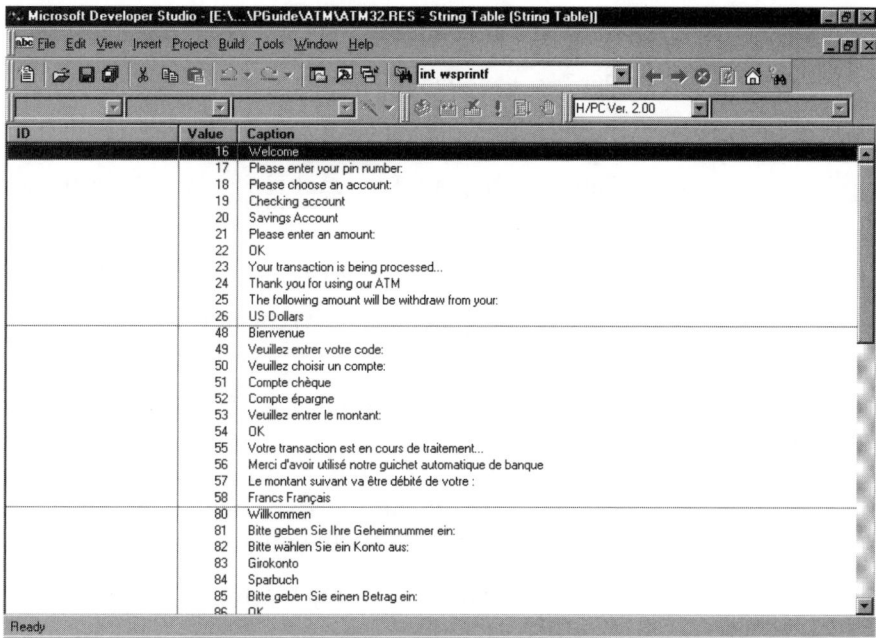

Using this existing concept, we're going to make 11 additional arrays (one for each of the messages) Each array will have six entries (one for each of the languages).

1. Your first step is to declare an array for each of the 11 messages. Each of these arrays will then contain a single phrase in each of the six languages. Declare these arrays in the modATM.bas module because all forms of the project will use them. This table shows the declarations for the arrays, as well as the English translation of the message each one will store.

Array Declaration	Messages
Public LanguageWelcome	"Welcome"
Public LanguagePinNumber	"Please enter your PIN number:"
Public LanguageChooseAccount	"Please choose an account:"
Public LanguageChecking	"Checking account"

Array Declaration	**Messages**
`Public LanguageSavings`	"Savings account"
`Public LanguageEnterAmount`	"Please enter an amount:"
`Public LanguageOK`	"OK"
`Public LanguageTransaction`	"Your transaction is being processed..."
`Public LanguageThankYou`	"Thank you for using our ATM."
`Public LanguageAmountWithdrawn`	"The following amount will be withdrawn from your:"
`Public LanguageCurrency`	"U.S. Dollars"

2. Now that you've declared the arrays, write the code to initialize and populate them with the translated messages. Put this code in the Load event of frmOpen, as that's where the original ATM project did its initialization.

Your code to initialize the array for the Welcome messages will look like this:

```
LanguageWelcome = Array("Welcome", "Bienvenue", "Willkommen", "Ben-
venuti", "Bienvenido", "TRANSLATE: Welcome")
```

NOTE Microsoft did not provide translations for the Japanese messages in the original ATM program, so they are not translated here.

Then add the array containing the different "Insert Pin Number" prompts, as follows:

```
LanguagePinNumber = Array("Please enter your pin number:", "Veuillez
entrer votre code:", "Bitte geben Sie Ihre Geheimnummer ein:",
"Digitare il proprio codice segreto:", "Por favor, ingrese su número de
identificación secreto:", "TRANSLATE: Please enter your pin number:")
```

Next, the array containing the different "choose an account" prompts looks like this:

```
LanguageChooseAccount = Array("Please choose an account:", "Veuillez
choisir un compte:", "Bitte wählen Sie ein Konto aus:", "Scegliere il
tipo di conto:", "Por favor, elija una cuenta:", "TRANSLATE: Please
choose an account")
```

The array containing the different checking account labels follows:

```
LanguageChecking = Array("Checking account", "Compte chèque",
"Girokonto", "Conto corrente", "Conto corrente", "TRANSLATE: Checking
account")
```

Then add the array containing the different savings account labels:

```
LanguageSavings = Array("Savings Account", "Compte épargne", "Spar-
buch", "Libretto di risparmio", "Cuenta de ahorros", "TRANSLATE: Sav-
ings Account")
```

Then add the array containing the different "enter an account" prompts:

```
LanguageEnterAmount = Array("Please enter an amount:", "Veuillez
entrer le montant:", "Bitte geben Sie einen Betrag ein:", "Digitare la
cifra richiesta:", "Por favor, ingrese un importe:", "TRANSLATE: Please
enter an amount:")
```

Next add the array containing the translations of "OK":

```
LanguageOK = Array("OK", "OK", "OK", "Attendere", "Aceptar",
"TRANSLATE: OK")
```

Then add the array containing the "transaction is being processed" status messages:

```
LanguageTransaction = Array("Your transaction is being processed...",
"Votre transaction est en cours de traitement...", "Ihr Auftrag wird
bearbeitet...", "La vostra operazione è in corso di esecuzione...", "Su
transacción se está procesando...", "TRANSLATE: Your transaction is
being processed...")
```

Next, add the array containing the different "thank you" messages:

```
LanguageThankYou = Array("Thank you for using our ATM", "Merci
d'avoir utilisé notre guichet automatique de banque", "Vielen Dank daß
Sie unseren Geldautomaten verwendet haben.", "Grazie e arrivederci",
"Le agradecemos que haya usado nuestro cajero automático", "TRANSLATE:
Thank you for using our ATM")
```

Next, add the array with the different "amount withdrawn" messages:

```
LanguageAmountWithdrawn = Array("The following amount will be withdrawn
from your:", "Le montant suivant va être débité de votre :", "Die fol-
gende Summe wird abgebucht von Ihrem:", "La seguente cifra verrà prele-
vata dal vostro:", "La siguiente cantidad será retirada de su:",
"TRANSLATE: The following amount will be withdraw from your :")
```

Then add the array holding the different currency names:

```
LanguageCurrency = Array("US Dollars", "Francs Français", "DM", "Lire
Italiane", "Pesetas", "TRANSLATE: US Dollars")
```

With your arrays prepared in this manner, you will be able to minimize the number of changes you must make to the code. All you need to do is steal the code that currently does the lookup into the currency conversion array and modify it to work with your new string arrays. The code that performs the conversion lookup is as follows:

```
Dim ConversionValue
ConversionValue = ConversionTable((i - 16) \ 32)
```

Based on that, you would change a line of code that looked like this:

```
MsgBox LoadResString(8 + i)
```

This references the new Language Arrays as follows:

```
MsgBox LanguageThankYou((i - 16) \ 32)
```

3. Your next task is to go through the source, looking for calls to LoadResString. (As with the changes you made earlier, this can probably be accomplished most efficiently by doing a Find operation on all files in the project for the text LoadResString.)

When you find a call to LoadResString, you must determine which message the ATM program is really looking for. This can usually be determined from the context of the surrounding code, or from the object being referenced. (However, if you get stuck, you can always run the original desktop ATM application.)

WARNING   After you've made all of your conversions from LoadResString to the Language Arrays, you may notice that the controls on the secondary forms (frmInput and frmAmountWithdrawn) do not change their text once they've been loaded for the first time. This is one of the consequences of the lack of true modal forms and using the workaround we were forced to use. What's happening is that those forms' Load events are only being called once—when the form is first shown. The way to get around this problem is to move all of the code that loads the language-specific text into the Form_Activate event instead.

Preparing the ATM's frmAmountWithdrawn Form

Once you've finished replacing all the LoadResString code, you should have a functional version of the ATM application. Upon running it, however, you may notice some errors coming from the Load event of frmAmountWithdrawn. To get the ATM program to work correctly, you'll have to make a few more changes to the code in that event.

1. The first surprise is related to the If statement, which, if you've finished your language conversion code, should look like this:

```
lblAmountWith = LanguageAmountWithdrawn((i - 16) \ 32) & " " & _
IIf(frmInput.optChecking, LanguageChecking((i - 16) \ 32),
LanguageSavings((i - 16) \ 32))
```

For reasons that are not clear, VBCE did not care for this statement. Instead, it works well to convert the IIf statement to an If..Else..End If block, like this:

```
If frmInput.optChecking.Value Then
   lblAmountWith = LanguageAmountWithdrawn((i - 16) \ 32) & " " &
      LanguageChecking((i - 16) \ 32)
Else
   lblAmountWith = LanguageAmountWithdrawn((i - 16) \ 32) & " " &
      LanguageSavings((i - 16) \ 32)
End If
```

2. In that same procedure, the following line may also create errors under certain conditions:

```
txtUSDollarsAmt = frmInput.txtUSDollarsAmt.Text
```

The error occurs when the user has not typed a value in the frmInput .txtUSDollarsAmt text box. VBCE is unable to convert the empty string value to a numeric value, and the operation fails. To fix this, insert this block of code just before the above line of code:

```
If frmInput.txtUSDollarsAmt.Text = "" Then
   frmInput.txtUSDollarsAmt.Text = "0"
End If
```

That will prevent that situation from causing an error.

As it now stands, you have an application that will run on CE and perform all of the basic tasks that the desktop version of the same application performed.

The Optional Features

In case you were wondering, yes, we do have an application that is a CE-based port of an existing desktop application. And, for all practical purposes, it works.

But, it still doesn't play any sounds. It also doesn't show any flag pictures. The ATM application does not depend on these features to run properly, so they are an optional part of the porting process. In fact, when we get into optimizing the application for CE, we'll probably decide not to include them in the final product.

Now, however, let's take a look at each of these features and determine:

- If it's possible to port them

and

- Whether or not they should be ported

Re-Adding the WAV Files

First, there's the issue of the WAV files that the original ATM application played at the end of the transaction. These WAV files are recordings of someone saying something to the effect of "thank you for using the ATM" in the chosen language. As we've already learned, VBCE has no way to call the WAV-playing functions of Windows CE directly. In addition, VBCE does not have any kind of CE Multimedia control. That leaves only one option: to look for a third-party control that will play WAV files.

Fortunately, just such a control exists. And, as if this isn't enough, it's also free and can be downloaded from the CD included with this book or from the Internet by visiting http://www.vbce.com. The name of the control is VBCE Miscellaneous Utility Control and, as the name implies, it's a collection of miscellaneous routines and functions that weren't included in VBCE itself.

One of the procedures this control offers is PlayWaveFile, which, naturally, plays a WAV file.

1. The first step is to extract the WAV files from the resource file. This is simple and can be easily done with Visual Studio (or any other resource editor). You must perform the extraction for two reasons:

   - VBCE doesn't support loading anything from resource data.

   - The VBCE Miscellaneous Utility Control requires the actual name of a physical WAV file rather than a resource stored in the executable.

To extract the WAV files from the resource file using Visual Studio:

    a. Open ATM32.res in Visual Studio.

    b. Find the ATM_SOUND resource type, and expand it. It will reveal six WAV files.

    c. To extract them to individual files, right-click on each one, and choose Export.

    d. When prompted with a Save File As... dialog box, change the file extension to .wav, but do not change the file name. For example, the first WAV file in the resource file is named 112. When you've extracted it, you should have a file called 112.wav.

2. Once you've extracted the WAV files, copy them to the emulator and the device in a directory of your choice. (The examples on the CD-ROM use the \Windows directory.) Then, go back to Visual Basic and find the line of code that previously played the WAV file in the Click event for cmdOKEnd handler. The line of code in question previously read:

```
BeginPlaySound i
```

3. If you haven't already commented that line out, do that now.

4. Next, if you haven't already installed the VBCE Miscellaneous Utility Control and added it to your toolbox, do that now. (Right-click on the toolbox and select Components.)

   Once you've done that, add a VBCE Miscellaneous Utility Control to frmAmountInput.

5. Next, head back to the code for the cmdOKEnd Click event and add the following line where the previous WAV-playing code was located:

```
VBCEUtil1.PlayWaveFile ("\windows\" & i & ".wav")
```

Snag! WAV Files, but Still No Sound! And that's all there is to it.... Or is it? You may notice one rather interesting problem when you go to test this program. It still doesn't play the sounds! Not on the emulator, nor on the device! Yet, both the emulator and the device *can* play WAV files, so what's the difference?

A comparison of the properties of WAV files that do play on the device (i.e., Alarm1.wav) with those that don't play reveals that the WAV files we're working with are in a different WAV file format.

There are two WAV file formats involved here:

1. PCM, 11.025kHz, 8-bit, Mono, which plays on the CE device

2. Microsoft ADPCM, 8.000kHz, 4-bit, Mono, which came with the ATM project but does not play on the CE device

NOTE   It's puzzling that CE will play the higher quality 8-bit format, but not the 4-bit format. However, CE insists on the PCM,11.025kHz, 8-bit, Mono format and will not play anything but that.

So, our next task is to convert the WAV files to the correct format, which we can do with a tool as simple as the standard Windows Sound Recorder.

To convert the WAV files to the correct format:

1. Open them one at a time in Sound Recorder. Choose File ➤ Properties from the main menu. You will see a Properties dialog like that pictured in Figure 9.5.

FIGURE 9.5:

The WAV file properties dialog of Sound Recorder

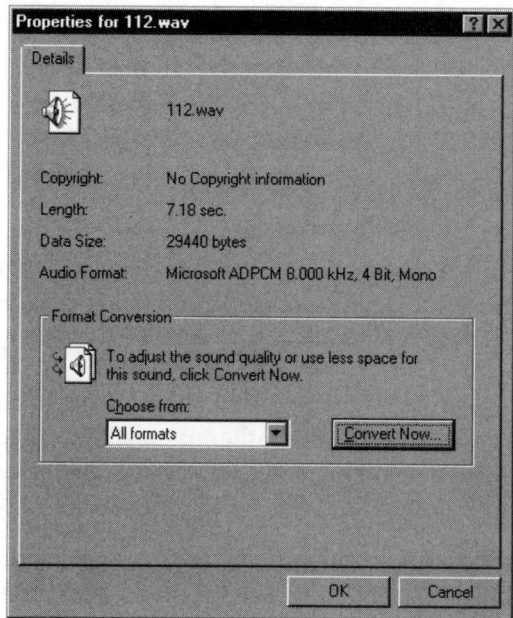

2. Click the Convert Now button, and you will see the Sound Selection dialog box, which allows you to choose a new format for the WAV file. This is shown in Figure 9.6.

FIGURE 9.6:

The Sound Selection
dialog box

3. Choose PCM, 11.025 kHz, 8 Bit, Mono from the Attributes list box and click the OK button. Then close the Properties dialog.

4. From the Sound Recorder's main menu, select File ➤ Save. Now, simply recopy the WAV files to the device, and they should play just fine.

NOTE   The WAV files do not play in the emulator, regardless of the file format. This may be an issue related to the emulator or the VBCE Miscellaneous Utility Control. (They do, however, play correctly on the device after conversion to the correct file format.)

Size Matters   One issue that almost evaded us while we were converting WAV files to the correct format is the need to monitor the size of the WAV files. Because the original format of the WAV files was a lesser quality format, the files were smaller than after the conversion.

In fact, their size after the conversion is now more than double what it was before. The total size of all the WAV files before the conversion was 157K; after the conversion their total size was 404K!

This difference cannot be ignored on a platform where space is at such a premium. So, although it's possible to port the WAV file functionality, you may want to think twice about doing it because of the resources required. You might be better off just playing Alarm1.wav instead of the other WAV files.

TIP   The VBCE Miscellaneous Utility Control will not cause an error if the WAV file does not exist. This is very helpful because you can add the code to play the WAV files and, if you decide later that you'd rather not distribute them, you won't have to rebuild your program.

The Country and Flag Bitmaps

Now we come to the issue of the images of the different countries' flags and geographical shapes and whether they should be included in the final application. In the original ATM application, the flag images were icons displayed by an Image Control, and the country images were loaded from resources just like the WAV files. As we've already discovered, resources and the resource-related functions are not supported under CE. However, all is not lost.

Although it's true that the standard Image Control does not support resources, it will load a bitmap directly from a file. Therefore, it will probably still suit our purposes.

1. First, let's extract the country bitmaps from the resource file of the original ATM project, following the same procedures we did when extracting the WAV files earlier.

    Extract the country bitmaps following the same steps as before:

    a. Open ATM32.res in Visual Studio.

    b. Find the bitmap resource type, and expand it to reveal six items. These are the individual bitmaps.

    c. Right-click on each one and choose Export.

    d. When prompted with the Save File As... dialog, accept the default file name, which should be the same as the resource ID. For example, the first bitmap file in the resource file is marked as 112. When you've extracted it, you should have a file called 112.bmp.

    When you're finished with the extracting process, you should have a 112.bmp, a 144.bmp, etc.

2. Copy these files to the emulator and the device in a directory of your choice. (As with the WAV files, the examples on the CD-ROM use the \Windows directory.)

    If you haven't already added the CE Image Control to your toolbox, do that now.

3. Right-click on the toolbox and select Components. Add a CE Image Control to *both* frmInput and frmAmountWithdrawn, in about the same place they were in the original ATM project (Left: 120, Top: 120). For the sake of consistency with the original ATM project, name both of these CE Image Controls imgFlag.

4. In the Form_Activate procedure for both of the forms, add the following line of code:

    ```
    ImgFlag.Picture = "\windows\" & i & ".bmp"
    ```

Both forms are restored to the way they looked in the original ATM application, but frmOpen still does not have the flag icons next to each button. Of course, the icons themselves are readily available—they don't even have to be exported from a resource file, as they're just some of the standard icons that come with Visual Basic (they're located in the \Graphics\Icons\Flags directory). The problem occurring this time is that neither of the image-handling controls of VBCE support icons!

So, if you want to put these flags back on the main form, you'll have to convert them to bitmaps first.

1. You can use a variety of graphics packages or utilities to do this. In Corel Photo-Paint, for example, after opening the icon, select Image ➢ Convert To ➢ Paletted (8-bit). Then, choose the Optimized palette, and select 16 colors. (The images on the CD-ROM were also cropped to 16 × 16 instead of 32 × 32.)

NOTE   Just as with WAV files, Windows CE is limited to the types of bitmap formats it recognizes. Although the documentation claims that CE will recognize bitmaps that use up to 32 bits per pixel, 8 bits per pixel seems to be preferred.

For these conversions, follow your existing naming convention of using the numeric identifier (established in the original ATM project) for each language. This time, though, since you already have a 112.bmp, 144.bmp and so on, name this new batch of flag bitmaps with a prefix of flg so that you can distinguish them from the country bitmaps. The list of file conversions looks something like this:

Original File Name	Becomes...
FlgUSA02.ico	Flg16.bmp
FlgFran.ico	Flg48.bmp
FlgGerm.ico	Flg80.bmp
FlgItaly.ico	Flg112.bmp
FlgSpain.ico	Flg144.bmp
FlgJapan.ico	Flg176.bmp

TIP

The converted resources (WAV and bitmap files) are located in the directory for this chapter on the CD.

2. When you finish converting the icons to bitmaps, copy the bitmaps to the emulator or the device. (Again, the examples on the CD-ROM use the \Windows directory.)

3. When you're ready, go back to Visual Basic and complete the operation by adding six CE Image Controls to frmOpen. As in the original ATM project, add one CE Image Control next to each button.

NOTE

In the original ATM project, the Image Controls were defined as one control array. However, there doesn't seem to be any particular reason for this, so it's up to you whether you'd like to make the CE Image Controls one array, or six individual controls.

4. Set each CE Image Control's Picture property to reflect the path of the correct flag bitmap. The first CE Image Control's Picture property should be set to \windows\Flg16.bmp, the second control's Picture property should be set to \windows\Flg48.bmp, and so on. (This can be done via the Property Inspector.)

When you've completed these steps, the project should be ready to run.

WARNING   The CE Image Controls do not appear to honor their Visible property if the Visible property is set to False. In other words, they will not hide themselves. In the context of this project, that's only a problem with the Japanese flag. In the original ATM project, the Japanese flag and button are simply hidden to prevent their being shown on a non-Kanji system. However, since the CE Image Control doesn't hide itself, the Japanese flag is always visible—even though the button is not. To resolve this, you may find it easier to simply remove the CE Image Control for the Japanese flag entirely, or show the Japanese button regardless of whether the system supports Kanji.

At this point, we come to the question of whether the bitmaps are a worthwhile feature to port to CE. The WAV files, you'll recall, took up quite a bit of space—nearly half a megabyte! The bitmaps, on the other hand, take up almost no space at all—about 7K. Even on a platform like CE, where all the resources are precious, the bitmaps are not a big concern.

However, as a file, the CE Image Control itself does occupy about 67K, so you should be concerned about it if you start adding lots of other controls or large files to the project.

NOTE   If you haven't already done so, you can freely remove the `ATM32.res` file from the ATM project. Simply find it in the VB Project window (under Related Documents), right-click it and select Remove.

The only other noticeable disadvantage to using the CE Image Controls is that `frmOpen` takes longer to load. You will have to decide for yourself whether the delay in loading is justified by the enhanced user interface. If you don't mind the delay, the bitmaps offer an enhancement with a minimum of cost.

At this point, you've successfully ported the ATM application to Windows CE. Everything that the original application did, the CE application does. Congratulations!

Optimizing for CE

We now come to the third and final issue of the design side of porting a desktop application to CE: optimizing and polishing the application for the constraints of a CE device.

We've already ensured that all the features are included; now we must determine which ones to eliminate to make the ATM project a better CE application.

Even though the program does work in its current state, it could use some optimization and cleaning for the low-resource environment of a CE device.

Here are some issues that need to be considered:

- Reducing the number of forms used in the application from three to two

- Eliminating any noncritical controls and DLLs

- Optimizing the code to improve overall performance

Eliminating a Form

First, there is the question of whether we can reduce the number of forms used in the application. As a general rule, reducing the number of forms or dialogs in any application will help improve the application in a number of ways:

- The file size of the executable will be reduced, because less data is compiled into the program.

- The speed of the application will be improved—if there's one less form to display and manage, there's that much more time for other operations in the program.

When you take a close look at the ATM project, you realize that frmOpen serves no real purpose—at least not so important a purpose that it requires a separate form. In fact, if we can reduce the language selection process to a single combo box, we can eliminate frmOpen from the project.

1. Start by adding a ComboBox to frmInput and calling it CboLanguages.

2. Populate its List property with the names of the various languages offered by the ATM project. When you're finished, frmInput should look something like the one pictured in Figure 9.7.

FIGURE 9.7:

frmInput with the Languages ComboBox added

3. That done, populate the ItemData property of CboLanguages with the existing language identifiers (i.e., 16= English, 48= French, etc.) so that the language names in the List property correspond to the language identifiers in the ItemData property.

4. Set the language ID variable (i) with this line of code, to be placed in the Click event of CboLanguages.

```
i = CboLanguages.ItemData(CboLanguages.ListIndex)
```

5. Then take all of the code that's in the frmInput Activate event handler, and move it to just below that line of code in the CboLanguage Click event handler.

TIP

With just a single line of code, we've theoretically already eliminated six event handlers—one for each of the language-selection buttons located on frmOpen.

This way, all of the controls that change their `Caption` or `Text` properties will refresh themselves every time the user chooses a different language.

To facilitate `frmInput` being our start-up form, we'll remove all of the initialization code from the `frmOpen` Load event, and paste it into the `frmInput` Load event.

1. In Visual Basic, find the Load event of `frmOpen`. It should currently look something like this:

```
Private Sub Form_Load()
    ' Initialize the currency conversion table.
    ConversionTable_Initialize
    LanguageWelcome = Array("Welcome", "Bienvenue", "Willkommen",
"Benvenuti", "Bienvenido", "TRANSLATE: Welcome")
    LanguagePinNumber = Array("Please enter your pin number:",
"Veuillez entrer votre code:", "Bitte geben Sie Ihre Geheimnummer
ein:", "Digitare il proprio codice segreto:", "Por favor, ingrese
su número de identificacier of ways:
no space at all—about 7Ker your pin number:")
    LanguageChooseAccount = Array("Please choose an account:",
"Veuillez choisir un compte:", "Bitte wählen Sie ein Konto aus:",
"Scegliere il tipo di conto:", "Por favor, elija una cuenta:",
"TRANSLATE: Please choose an account")
    LanguageChecking = Array("Checking account", "Compte chèque",
"Girokonto", "Conto corrente", "Conto corrente", "TRANSLATE:
Checking account")
    LanguageSavings = Array("Savings Account", "Compte épargne",
"Sparbuch", "Libretto di risparmio", "Cuenta de ahorros", "TRANS-
LATE: Savings Account")
    LanguageEnterAmount = Array("Please enter an amount:",
"Veuillez entrer le montant:", "Bitte geben Sie einen Betrag
ein:", "Digitare la cifra richiesta:", "Por favor, ingrese un
importe:", "TRANSLATE: Please enter an amount:")
    LanguageOK = Array("OK", "OK", "OK", "Attendere", "Aceptar",
"TRANSLATE: OK")
    LanguageTransaction = Array("Your transaction is being
processed...", "Votre transaction est en cours de traitement...",
"Ihr Auftrag wird bearbeitet...", "La vostra operazione è in corso
di esecuzione...", "Su transacción se está procesando...", "TRANS-
LATE: Your transaction is being processed...")
    LanguageThankYou = Array("Thank you for using our ATM", "Merci
d'avoir utilisé notre guichet automatique de banque", "Vielen Dank
```

```
daß Sie unseren Geldautomaten verwendet haben.", "Grazie e
arrivederci", "Le agradecemos que haya usado nuestro cajero
automático", "TRANSLATE: Thank you for using our ATM")
    LanguageAmountWithdrawn = Array("The following amount will be
withdrawn from your:", "Le montant suivant va être débité de votre
:", "Die folgende Summe wird abgebucht von Ihrem:", "La seguente
cifra verrà prelevata dal vostro:", "La siguiente cantidad será
retirada de su:", "TRANSLATE: The following amount will be with-
draw from your :")
    LanguageCurrency = Array("US Dollars", "Francs Français",
"DM", "Lire Italiane", "Pesetas", "TRANSLATE: US Dollars")
End Sub
```

2. Mark and cut the entire body of the Load event handler.

3. Find the Load event of `frmInput`. (If it does not already exist, you can create it by going to the code view window of Visual Basic, selecting `frmInput` in the Object ComboBox, and Load in the Procedure ComboBox.)

4. Paste the code into this event.

    Now you must remove all references to `frmOpen` from the other forms. Fortunately, there are only two such references, and they're both the exact the same line of code:

    ```
    frmOpen.Show
    ```

    The first of these references to `frmOpen` occurs in the Unload event of `frmInput`, and we can simply comment it out, as it no longer applies. The next reference to `frmOpen` occurs in the `cmdOKEnd` Click() event of `frm-AmountWithdrawn`. To reflect the fact that `frmInput` is now our main form, this reference must be changed to:

    ```
    frmInput.Show
    ```

5. Remove `frmOpen` from the project by right-clicking on it in the Project window (under Forms), and selecting the Remove option.

6. To complete the removal of `frmOpen` from the ATM project, you need to set `frmInput` as the start-up form.

    To do that, select Project ➤ Properties from the main menu. Then, find the ComboBox marked Startup Object and select `frmInput`.

You have now successfully removed frmOpen from the project, and the project has only two forms. This means there is one less form to manage, and, because the new start-up form does not have the images to paint (as did frmOpen), the entire program loads considerably faster.

Eliminating Optional Controls and DLLs

Continuing our exercise in optimization, let's also remove the remaining CE Image Controls from frmInput and frmAmountWithdrawn. In addition, let's also remove the VBCE Miscellaneous Utility Control. This will let us see how far we can compress the resources required by the application. After all, if we don't use these two controls, there are two fewer DLLs we'll have to copy onto the user's device.

Eliminating these controls from the project saves us 140K of space on the device. Further, because we've eliminated these controls, we no longer have to worry about the 400K of WAV files that we'd have to distribute with the application. Now, let's move one step further, to optimizing the actual code of the ATM project.

Optimizing the Code Itself

As you may have already realized, every time a language-specific string is loaded from an array, a separate calculation is done:

```
(i - 16) \ 32
```

When we started out, we retained the original language identifiers (i.e., 16= English, 48= French, etc.) because it seemed easier to port that way, as so much of the code was related to the resource file and the various bitmaps and WAV files. However, since you've eliminated all ties to the resource file, there's really no need to stick with the default language IDs. Further, by changing these language IDs to something simpler, you can eliminate the need to do 12 or 13 calculations whenever the user selects a different language.

Therefore, one of the simplest and easiest optimizations we can perform is to re-do all of the language identifiers so that they make more sense. And, since you're already using the ItemData property of CboLanguages to load the correct language-specific strings, all you have to do is edit the values of ItemData as follows:

Language	Old ItemData Value	New Value
English	16	0
French	48	1
German	80	2
Italian	112	3
Spanish	144	4
Japanese	176	5

Clearly, if you can load the language-specific strings based on a constant value rather than an equation, it will be faster and use less processor time. For example, code that previously read:

```
Caption = LanguageWelcome((i - 16) \ 32)
```

should now read:

```
Caption = LanguageWelcome(i)
```

This will execute faster on any platform—not just CE!

Once you've edited the ItemData values, there is only one step that remains. Perform a Find…Replace command on all files in the project, searching for (i-16) \ 32 and replacing it with i. It's that easy!

On the surface, it may appear that for all of your optimizations, you haven't really saved or optimized all that much. The size of the PVB file (VBCE executable) only shrunk from 24K to 17K, not a terrific savings. However, our program is now much faster. In fact, if you run the project now, you'll find that the main form loads faster and, every time you change the language, the various controls update themselves faster, as well.

More importantly, by eliminating the pictures, WAV files, and the controls associated with them, *you've reduced the amount of space the ATM application requires by well over 500K!*

Summary

In this chapter, you converted a desktop Visual Basic application to Windows CE. In fact, you now have a full-featured port (as well as an optimized, stripped-down version) of the application we started with.

FIGURE 9.8:

The final, optimized ATM application

You found that, although it did take some work at times, you were able to complete the porting process and then go back through your code and optimize it for the limited resources of a CE device.

Interestingly enough, with the exception of the custom cursors that the original ATM application had, *we could port every feature to the CE platform*! Considering that Microsoft doesn't recommend the porting approach, that's quite an accomplishment.

Of course, not every application will port as well as this one did, but all of them will likely present similar issues and problems along the way.

PART III

Advanced Topics

- CHAPTER 10: RAPI: How the Outside World Talks to CE
- CHAPTER 11: How CE Talks to the Outside World
- CHAPTER 12: Third-Party Database Engines
- CHAPTER 13: Windows CE Case Studies and Cost Analysis

CHAPTER
TEN

RAPI: How the Outside World Talks to CE

- What Is RAPI, Anyway?

- General RAPI Management Functions

- A Sample RAPI Application

- Using Other Languages

Okay, so you've just written a killer Windows CE application that collects data, stores it into a CE database, lets the user query the data, runs reports, and maybe even has the ability to share data with other CE devices.

Now comes the tough part: You need a way to get that data into the desktop version of your software so that it can be stored in your database server along with the rest of the company's corporate data.

How do you do that?

Well, if your data is contact information, appointments or tasks, it will be automatically synched up with Outlook. But your data doesn't fall into any of those categories, and you're not using Outlook. That means there's only one way to export that data from your CE device and import it to your desktop software: RAPI.

RAPI, or Remote API, is a special set of functions that allows developers in situations like yours to access any files, databases, or system information on a CE device, regardless of what type of chip it's running or what version of CE it has. You don't even have to worry about any of the mechanics of making the connection to the device or anything like that. All you have to do is ask RAPI to make sure a device is connected, and then you're set to go.

One of the best things about RAPI is that, because it's a standard Win32 API and the code runs only on Desktop Windows, you can use any development tool that will produce Win32 executables. This is the one area of CE where you don't have to be concerned about chip types or cross-compilers!

In this chapter, we'll be looking at some of the features of RAPI and what it can do for us. We'll start with a general overview of the more important areas of RAPI, then move on to some sample applications, including one that will help solve the problem described above. Finally, we'll demonstrate that we can use any development tool to write RAPI applications by creating a sample program using Borland's Delphi tool.

What Is RAPI, Anyway?

The thing to remember about the majority of the RAPI functions is that if you know how to write CE code, you also know how to write RAPI code. All but one or two of the RAPI functions have a CE-based counterpart that behaves in exactly the same manner, takes the same parameter types, etc.

RAPI is actually just one DLL called—not surprisingly—Rapi.dll. In all, there are some 80 functions to RAPI, which can be broken down into the following four basic categories:

- General RAPI management functions
- System information functions
- Registry access functions
- File access functions
- Database access functions
- Miscellaneous Shell and System functions

General RAPI Management Functions

The general RAPI management functions are those functions used to load and unload the RAPI DLL and establish a connection to the currently connected device. The two functions in this group that you'll use most often are

- CeRapiInit()
- CeRapiUninit()

You must call the CeRapiInit() function before you do anything else. CeRapi-Init() attempts to connect you with a CE device. In order to test whether or not you are able to connect to an actual device, use the Win32 API's FAILED() macro, which should look something like this:

```
//...
HRESULT hRapiResult;
hRapiResult = CeRapiInit();
if (FAILED(hRapiResult))
{
    MessageBox(hwnd, TEXT("Unable to connect to CE Device and RAPI
services"), TEXT("Error:"), MB_OK);
    SendMessage(hwnd, WM_DESTROY, 0, 0);
    return TRUE;
}
//...
```

As the code demonstrates, CeRapiInit() returns an HRESULT value that we can then use to see if there is a device for our application to talk to.

The next function that you'll be using a lot is CeRapiUninit(). It must be called to properly disconnect your application when you're all done working with the CE device:

```
//...
CeRapiUninit();
```

With these two management functions, your application can use any other RAPI functions.

It's worth noting that just because you use some of the RAPI functions in your application, the CE device does not have to be connected to the Desktop machine the entire time your program is running—only while you're actually using the RAPI library. It's quite possible to have your application connect to the device through RAPI, perform some action, and then immediately disconnect from the RAPI services. For instance, if you wanted to know what version of the CE operating system was running on the device, you might do something like this:

```
//...
hRapiResult = CeRapiInit();
if (FAILED(hRapiResult))
{
    MessageBox(hwnd, TEXT("Unable to connect to CE Device and RAPI
services"), TEXT("Error:"), MB_OK);
    SendMessage(hwnd, WM_DESTROY, 0, 0);
    return TRUE;
}
OsInfo.wOSVersionInfoSize = sizeof(OSInfo);
CeGetVersionEx(&OSInfo);
wsprintf(szBuf, TEXT("You are running CE Version %d.%d"),
OSInfo.dwMajorVersion, OsInfo.DwMinorVersion);
MessageBox(hwnd, szBuf, TEXT("About your device."), MB_OK);
CeRapiUninit();
//...
```

This way, the application would only be connected to RAPI and the CE device for as long or as short a time as it needs. Remember that, unless your application is going to be constantly interacting with the device, there's no need to stay connected to RAPI for any length of time.

System Information Functions

The next group of RAPI functions is the group of system information functions. These functions provide basic information about the device's hardware. The most common ones in this group are

- CeGetSystemInfo()

- CeGetVersionInfo()

- CeGlobalMemoryStatus()

- CeGetDesktopDeviceCaps()

- CeOIDGetEx()

- CeGetSystemPowerStatusEx()

Of these functions, the most useful is probably CeGetSystemInfo(). It does everything that the Windows 98/NT version of that function (called GetSystem-Info()) does. CeGetSystemInfo() can be used to determine the device's CPU, platform type, and OS version. To call it, just pass the address of a SYSTEM_INFO structure. The SYSTEM_INFO structure is defined as follows:

```
typedef struct _SYSTEM_INFO {
DWORD dwOemId;
DWORD dwPageSize;
LPVOID lpMinimumApplicationAddress;
LPVOID lpMaximumApplicationAddress;
DWORD dwActiveProcessorMask;
DWORD dwNumberOfProcessors;
DWORD dwProcessorType;
DWORD dwAllocationGranularity;
DWORD dwReserved;
} SYSTEM_INFO;
```

Likewise, CeGetVersionEx() tells us what version of Windows CE is running on the device. To call it, pass in the address of an OSVERSIONINFO structure. The OSVERSIONINFO structure is defined as follows:

```
typedef struct _OSVERSIONINFO{
DWORD dwOSVersionInfoSize;
DWORD dwMajorVersion;
DWORD dwMinorVersion;
```

```
DWORD dwBuildNumber;
DWORD dwPlatformId;
TCHAR szCSDVersion[128];
} OSVERSIONINFO;
```

CeGlobalMemoryStatus() tells you everything you need to know about the available memory on the device. When you call CeGlobalMemoryStatus(), you pass in a pointer to a MEMORYSTATUS structure, which is defined as follows:

```
typedef struct _MEMORYSTATUS {
    DWORD dwLength;        // sizeof(MEMORYSTATUS)
    DWORD dwMemoryLoad;    // percent of memory in use
    DWORD dwTotalPhys;     // bytes of physical memory
    DWORD dwAvailPhys;     // free physical memory bytes
    DWORD dwTotalPageFile; // bytes of paging file
    DWORD dwAvailPageFile; // free bytes of paging file
    DWORD dwTotalVirtual;  // user bytes of address space
    DWORD dwAvailVirtual;  // free user bytes }
MEMORYSTATUS;
```

You can then use the information in this MEMORYSTATUS structure in any way you like.

CeGetDesktopDeviceCaps() retrieves the value of certain system variables. To use it, pass in an identifier indicating the system variable you'd like, and the function will return the requested value. For most purposes, the values you'll be requesting are shown in Table 10.1.

TABLE 10.1: Common CeGetDesktopDeviceCaps() Identifiers

Parameter	What the device returns
HORZSIZE	Physical screen width (millimeters)
VERTSIZE	Physical screen height (millimeters)
HORZRES	Screen width (pixels)
VERTRES	Screen height (raster lines)

Registry Access Functions

The registry access functions make it possible for our Desktop applications to access the system registry of the device as if it were the registry on the Desktop machine. The functions involved here are

- CeRegOpenKeyEx()

- CeRegEnumKeyEx()

- CeRegCreateKeyEx()

- CeRegCloseKey()

- CeRegDeleteKey()

- CeRegEnumValue()

- CeRegDeleteValue()

- CeRegQueryInfoKey()

- CeRegQueryValueEx()

- CeRegSetValueEx()

One of the great things about these functions is that they operate just like the Desktop registry functions of the same name. For instance, to open a key in a Desktop program, you might have code that looks like this:

```
retCode = RegOpenKeyEx (*hKeyRoot,
                        RegPath,
                        0,
                        KEY_ENUMERATE_SUB_KEYS |
                        KEY_EXECUTE |
                        KEY_QUERY_VALUE,
                        &hKey);

if (retCode != ERROR_SUCCESS)
{
  if (retCode == ERROR_ACCESS_DENIED)
     wsprintf (Buf, TEXT("Error: unable to open key.  Probably due
to security reasons."));
     else
        wsprintf (Buf, TEXT("Error: Unable to open key, RegOpenKey =
%d, Line = %d"), retCode, __LINE__);
```

```
MessageBox (hDlg, Buf, TEXT(""), MB_OK);
PostMessage (hDlg, WM_COMMAND, IDB_BACK, 0);
return;
}
```

If you were writing for RAPI, the only difference between the above code and the RAPI-based code would be the addition of the "Ce-" prefix to RegOpenKeyEx():

```
retCode = CeRegOpenKeyEx (*hKeyRoot,
                          RegPath,
                          0,
                          KEY_ENUMERATE_SUB_KEYS |
                          KEY_EXECUTE |
                          KEY_QUERY_VALUE,
                          &hKey);

    if (retCode != ERROR_SUCCESS)
    {
      if (retCode == ERROR_ACCESS_DENIED)
         wsprintf (Buf, TEXT("Error: unable to open key.  Probably due
to security reasons."));
      else
         wsprintf (Buf, TEXT("Error: Unable to open key, RegOpenKey =
%d, Line = %d"),
                  retCode, __LINE__);

    MessageBox (hDlg, Buf, TEXT(""), MB_OK);
    PostMessage (hDlg, WM_COMMAND, IDB_BACK, 0);
    return;
    }
```

File Access Functions

The file access functions are those functions that allow you to create directories, read and write files, and find files matching a certain criteria. In this category, these are the most important functions:

- CeFindFirstFile()

- CeFindNextFile()

- CeFindClose()

- CeCreateFile()

- CeReadFile()

- CeWriteFile()

- CeCloseHandle()

- CeGetSpecialFolderPath()

- CeGetTempPath()

The first three functions—CeFindFirstFile(), CeFindNextFile(), CeFind-Close()—all work together to perform file searches, much in the way that the similarly named functions work together on the Desktop. For example, if you want to find all files in the \Windows directory called "win*.*", simply call CeFindFirstFile(), passing in your file mask and an empty CE_FIND_DATA structure:

```
hFind = CeFindFirstFile( TEXT("\\windows\\win*.*"), &wfd);
```

NOTE   The CE_FIND_DATA parallels the FIND_DATA structure of the Win32 (Desktop-based) API.

WARNING   Keep in mind that all of the RAPI functions are Unicode-based, just like the Windows CE API. That means that you must convert from Unicode to ANSI when writing a RAPI program for Windows 98. Because Windows NT is already Unicode-based, no conversion is necessary.

After checking the return result of that function call, enter a do..while loop based on the result of CeFindNextFile(). Continue to loop until there are no more matching files:

```
if (INVALID_HANDLE_VALUE == hFind)
{
    CeRapiUninit();
    return 1;
}
do
{
    _tprintf(TEXT("%s\n"), wfd.cFileName);

}while(CeFindNextFile(hFind, &wfd));
```

When you've found all the matching files, free the memory allocated by the functions by calling CeFindClose():

```
CeFindClose( hFind);
```

Working with the CeCreateFile() set of functions is also just like working with the similarly named Desktop-based functions. For instance, to open a file in a Desktop program, you might have code that looked something like this:

```
hSrc = CreateFile(
            wszSrcFile,
            GENERIC_READ,
            FILE_SHARE_READ,
            NULL,
            OPEN_EXISTING,
            FILE_ATTRIBUTE_NORMAL,
            NULL);
if (INVALID_HANDLE_VALUE == hSrc)
{
    MessageBox(hWnd, TEXT("Error opening file."), TEXT("ERROR"),
MB_OK);
}
```

This is fairly standard code for opening the file for reading. If you perform the same operation under CE, your code will look like this:

```
hSrc = CeCreateFile(
            wszSrcFile,
            GENERIC_READ,
            FILE_SHARE_READ,
            NULL,
            OPEN_EXISTING,
            FILE_ATTRIBUTE_NORMAL,
            NULL);
if (INVALID_HANDLE_VALUE == hSrc)
{
    MessageBox(hWnd, TEXT("Error opening file."), TEXT("ERROR"),
MB_OK);
}
```

As you can see, the CE code is virtually indistinguishable from standard, Desktop-specific file access code.

CeGetSpecialFolderPath()

CeGetSpecialFolderPath() is an often-overlooked function that can be very useful at times. It can retrieve the true path of certain system-defined directories, such as the location of the recycle bin, the Desktop directory, etc.

CeGetSpecialFolderPath() is defined as follows:

```
DWORD CeGetSpecialFolderPath( int nFolder, DWORD nBufferLength,
LPWSTR lpBuffer);
```

The first parameter, nFolder, specifies an identifier for the folder we're interested in. It should be one of the following values:

CSIDL_BITBUCKET   The Recycle Bin

CSIDL_COMMON_PROGRAMS   The Start ➢ Programs menu folder

CSIDL_CONTROLS   The Control Panel folder

CSIDL_DESKTOP   The root directory

CSIDL_DESKTOPDIRECTORY   The Desktop folder

CSIDL_FONTS   The Fonts directory

CSIDL_PERSONAL   The My Documents folder

CSIDL_PROGRAMS   Location of the user's program groups

CSIDL_RECENT   The Start ➢ Documents folder

CSIDL_STARTMENU   The Start menu folder

CSIDL_STARTUP   The StartUp folder

CSIDL_TEMPLATES   The Templates directory

The second parameter, nBufferLength, specifies the length of the buffer you've allocated to hold the actual path. The third parameter, lpBuffer, specifies the actual buffer to hold the path.

Database Access Functions

The database access functions expose all of the functionality of the CE database engine to your Desktop-based RAPI program. Using these functions, you can view and edit databases stored on the CE device. These functions include

- CeCreateDatabase()
- CeDeleteDatabase()
- CeDeleteRecord()
- CeFindFirstDatabase()
- CeFindNextDatabase()
- CeOpenDatabase()
- CeReadRecordProps()
- CeSeekDatabase()
- CeSetDatabaseInfo()
- CeWriteRecordProps()

When it comes to database access, these functions work exactly like the CE-based versions—the only difference is the "Ce-" prefix on the function names. For a complete CE database reference, see Chapter 4.

Miscellaneous Shell and System Functions

The last and final category of RAPI functions is a set of miscellaneous shell and system functions that allow you to retrieve information about the various applications running on the CE device, work with CE shortcuts, and start CE applications remotely. These include

- CeCreateProcess()
- CeSHCreateShortcut()
- CeSHGetShortcutTarget()
- CeGetWindow()
- CeGetWindowLong()
- CeGetWindowText()

- CeGetClassName()

Here again, you have a set of functions that work exactly like their Desktop-based counterparts, with the exception being that they have the "Ce-" prefix. For example, if you call GetWindowLong() from a Desktop program, your code will look something like this:

```
lWndStyle = GetWindowLong(hWnd, GWL_STYLE);
```

Similarly, if you call the RAPI version of GetWindowLong(), CeGetWindowLong(), your code will look like this:

```
lWndStyle = CeGetWindowLong(hWnd, GWL_STYLE);
```

A Sample RAPI Application

Now that you have some idea of what RAPI is all about, let's see what it can do for you. Let's fulfill the purpose outlined at the beginning of this chapter and create an application that will export all of the records from a CE database into a comma-delimited text file. Of course, you could integrate this application with your existing applications and transfer the data directly into your Desktop application's database, but this way you can use the data with any program that can read delimited text files. You can also use your CE data with any other applications. The final application will look something like the one pictured in Figure 10.1.

NOTE   Of course, before you do anything else, you must call CeRapiInit().

Your first job will be to enumerate all of the databases on the CE device, adding them to a list box as you find them. To do this, first call CeFindFirstDatabase(), passing in 0 as the parameter.

```
if( (hEnumObject = CeFindFirstDatabase(0)) != INVALID_HANDLE_VALUE)
{
```

The 0 value tells CeFindFirstDatabase() that you're going to be retrieving a list of all of the databases, so it will return a handle to the first database on the device.

FIGURE 10.1:

The final RapiDBSave application

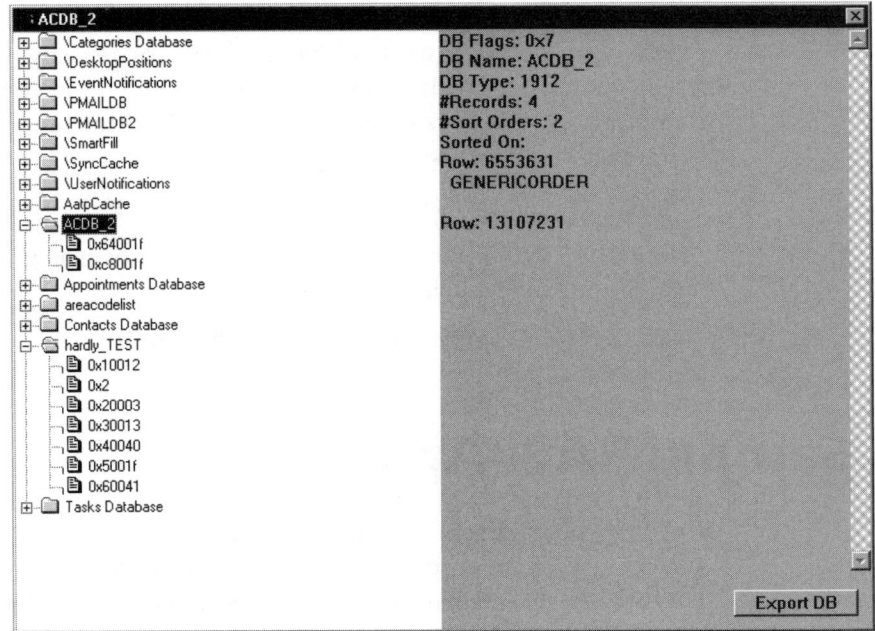

Next, begin to iterate through the databases by calling `CeFindNextDatabase()`, this time passing in the handle of the previous database:

```
while( (ObjectID = CeFindNextDatabase(hEnumObject)) != 0)
    {
```

Then, retrieve the database's name and test whether or not you were successful in this effort:

```
if ( !CeOidGetInfo(ObjectID, &CeObject) )
    {
        wsprintf(szBuf, TEXT("CeOidGetInfo failed with
error (%ld)"), CeGetLastError());
        MessageBox(NULL, szBuf, TEXT("Error"), MB_OK);
        break;
    }
```

If you were successful, add the database's name to your list box:

```
else
    {
```

```
                     // add database name to treeview
if (!SendMessage(hwndLB, LB_ADDITEM, CeObject.infDatabase.szDbaseName,
0, 0))

                    }

          }
```

Finally, if you've exited your `while` loop, check to make sure that you did not encounter any errors along the way:

```
    if ( (rc=CeGetLastError()) != ERROR_NO_MORE_ITEMS )
    {
        wsprintf(szBuf, TEXT("CeFindFirstDatabase failed with error
(%ld)"), rc);
        MessageBox(NULL, szBuf, TEXT("Error"), MB_OK);
    }
```

Your next task is to handle the saving of the database to a text file. To do this, you need to provide a button control on the main form of the application. When the user clicks the button, you'll get the name of the currently selected database in the list box and then export the data. The first step is to make sure that a database name is highlighted in your `WM_COMMAND` message handler:

```
    if (hwndCtl == hButton) //the export button was clicked!
    {
        if (!szCurrentDBName)
            return 0L;
```

If the user did select a database from the list, create a text file (called dbdump.txt) to hold the exported records:

```
        hFile = CreateFile(
                    TEXT(".\\dbdump.txt"),
                    GENERIC_WRITE,
                    FILE_SHARE_READ,
                    NULL,
                    CREATE_ALWAYS,
                    FILE_ATTRIBUTE_NORMAL,
                    NULL);

        if (INVALID_HANDLE_VALUE == hFile)
        {
            MessageBox(hwnd, TEXT("Unable to open file for export."),
TEXT("Error:"), MB_OK);
            return 1;
        }
```

If you were able to successfully create the text file, begin to export the database's records by first ensuring that you can open the database:

```
hOpenDB = CeOpenDatabase(&CeOID, szCurrentDBName, 0,
CEDB_AUTOINCREMENT, NULL);
        if (hOpenDB == INVALID_HANDLE_VALUE)
            MessageBox(NULL, TEXT("CeOpenDatabase failed after creating
DB"), TEXT("Error"), MB_OK);
```

NOTE

> Note the use of the **CEDB_AUTOINCREMENT** flag so that as you read each record in the database, the record pointer will automatically move to the next record in the database. For more information, see Chapter 4.

Then, if you were able to open the database, read in all of the properties or fields of the database:

```
        else
        {
            while ( (CeRecObj = CeReadRecordProps(hOpenDB,
CEDB_ALLOWREALLOC,
                    &wNumRecProps, NULL, &lpRecProps, &cbRecProps)) )
            {
                if ( lpRecProps )
                {
                    if ( wNumRecProps )
                    {
                        pCePropVal = (PCEPROPVAL)lpRecProps;
```

NOTE

> Again, we don't go into the purpose of the database-related functions here because they are explained in detail in Chapter 4.

Next, take each field and stream it out to your text file, based on the field's data type:

```
                for ( i= 0 ; i < wNumRecProps; i++)
                {

                        switch(
TypeFromPropID(pCePropVal[i].propid) )
                        {
```

If it's one of the four numeric types, convert it to a string:

```
                            case CEVT_I2:
                            case CEVT_UI2:
                            case CEVT_I4:
                            case CEVT_UI4:
                                    wsprintf(szBuf, TEXT("%d"), pCe-
PropVal[i].val.ulVal);

                                    break;
```

If it's a date/time value, convert the FILETIME value to a SYSTEMTIME value, and then copy the portions of the date that you want into a string:

```
                            case CEVT_FILETIME:
FileTimeToSystemTime(pCePropVal[i].val.filetime, &stSystemTime);
                                    wsprintf(szBuf, TEXT("%d/%d/%d"),
stSystemTime.wDay, stSystemTime.wMonth, stSystemTime.wYear);
                                    break;
```

If it's a string, just copy it into a string, and you're done:

```
                            case CEVT_LPWSTR:  //and this one
                                    wsprintf(szBuf,
pCePropVal[i].val.lpwstr);

                                    break;
                            default:
                                    break;


                            }
```

NOTE

The strings here are wide or Unicode-based strings. In this example, you're writing them to the text file as Unicode strings. Just as with all of the RAPI functions, you'd have to convert these strings to ANSI string if you were targeting Windows 98.

WARNING

In this example, we're not accounting for the **CEVT_BLOB** type. That's because BLOBs (Binary Large Objects) can contain any type of data of any length. Further, the data in a BLOB field is very application-specific and likely requires special processing depending on the nature of the data. This, of course, makes it difficult to handle BLOBs in any kind of generic manner.

Then, simply write the string containing the contents of the field out to the file, with the appropriate error checking:

```
        if (!WriteFile(hFile, szBuf, _tcslen(szBuf)
* sizeof(TCHAR), &dwNumWritten, NULL))
        {
                MessageBox(hwnd,TEXT("Unable to write
record props to text file."), TEXT("Error"), MB_OK);
                break;
        }
```

Now, it's time to write the field separator out to the file. As with all standard comma-delimited text files, only write the comma if you're not at the end of a line. The way to do that here is to make sure you're not writing out the last field or property of the current record:

```
        if (i != wNumRecProps-1)
                WriteFile(hFile, TEXT(","),
_tcslen(TEXT(",")) * sizeof(TCHAR), &dwNumWritten, NULL);
                }
            }
        }
```

Then, when you're finished writing the entire record, tack on a carriage return and linefeed:

```
        WriteFile(hFile, TEXT("\r\n"), _tcslen(TEXT("\r\n")) *
sizeof(TCHAR), &dwNumWritten, NULL);

        }
    }
```

Finally, close the handle to the database, free the record buffer, and close the text file:

```
    CeCloseHandle(hOpenDB);
    LocalFree(lpRecProps);
    CloseHandle(hFile);
    return 0L;
}
```

Using Other Languages

As you learned at the beginning of this chapter, one of the great things about RAPI is that you can use any development tool to create RAPI applications. At the time of this writing, there is already one RAPI ActiveX control for Visual Basic, and there's also some free RAPI source code for Delphi. In this section, we'll build a simple database properties viewer in Delphi using the RAPI source code unit. The final Delphi application is shown in Figure 10.2.

FIGURE 10.2:

The final Delphi application

Static vs. Dynamic Linking

Static linking is when you let the compiler hard code the addresses of the functions you'll be calling. Dynamic linking is when you load the DLL(s) at runtime and then attempt to resolve the addresses of the functions you're looking for. Static linking is faster, but it requires that the DLL you call be present on the user's machine when your application starts. If the DLL isn't there, you'll get an error message, the program will likely shut down, and you'll have no control at all.

You have more control with dynamic linking because you can attempt to load the DLL you're after and, if you can't find it, you can handle the situation in any way you like.

The Pascal unit you'll use to create our Delphi RAPI application is a freeware unit, generously provided by Scott Crossen. Crossen created a Pascal-/Delphi-based import of all of the functions, types, and constants listed in Rapi.h. This in itself is no small feat—many of the structures in Rapi.h are quite complex and were probably very difficult to port. But the best thing about the Rapi.pas unit that Crossen created is that all of the functions are loaded dynamically.

In C/C++, when you use the default Rapi.h, the compiler statically links Rapi.lib into your program. When the program starts on the user's machine and they're not running CE Services, it will crash before it even gets off the ground.

What Crossen did differently was to attempt to find and load Rapi.dll at run-time. If you can't find Rapi.dll, you exit gracefully and return an error code. In contrast to linking in rapi.lib, Crossen's implementation first checks to see if RAPI is available. If RAPI isn't available on the user's machine, the program won't crash; it can still perform every non-RAPI feature just fine.

If you look at the code to do this, you'll see it starts with a call to LoadLibrary(), passing in 'RAPI.DLL' as the library to load:

```
RapiModule := LoadLibrary('RAPI.DLL');
```

Check to make sure that the library was successfully loaded:

```
if RapiModule > HINSTANCE_ERROR then
begin
  Result := True;
```

Next, proceed to retrieve the addresses of all of the RAPI functions, one at a time:

```
@mCeRapiInit := GetProcAddress(RapiModule, 'CeRapiInit');
//...and repeat for each RAPI function
@mCeGetSystemPowerStatusEx:= GetProcAddress(RapiModule, 'CeGet-
SystemPowerStatusEx');

end
else
  Result := False;
end;
```

You've managed to successfully dynamically load all of the RAPI functions at once. The amazing thing about the "any Desktop development tool" aspect of

RAPI is that the code to retrieve all of the databases looks virtually the same in Pascal as it does in C/C++.

For instance, when you retrieve the list of databases in your Delphi application, the code is virtually identical to that of the C/C++ version:

```
hEnumContext := CeFindFirstDatabase(DBType);
if hEnumContext = INVALID_HANDLE_VALUE then
begin
  ShowMessage('Error retrieving DB Info');
  Exit;
end;
for i := 1 to TVCEDB.Items.Count-1 do
  if Assigned(TVCEDB.Items[i].Data) then
    Dispose(TVCEDB.Items[i].Data);
TVCEDB.Items.Clear;
Node := TVCEDB.Items.Add(nil, 'Device Databases');
Node.ImageIndex := 0;
Node.SelectedIndex := 0;
ObjID := CeFindNextDatabase(hEnumContext);
while ((ObjID <> 0) and (ObjID <> ERROR_NO_MORE_ITEMS) and (ObjID <>
ERROR_INVALID_PARAMETER)) do
  begin
    CeOidGetInfo(ObjID, CeOIDInfo);
    if CeOIDInfo.wObjType <> OBJTYPE_DATABASE then
    begin
      ObjID := CeFindNextDatabase(hEnumContext);
      Continue;
    end;
    Application.ProcessMessages;
```

The only difference comes when you actually add the items to your TreeView, in that you're adding some data along with the actual text:

```
with Node, CeOIDInfo.infDatabase do
begin
  Node := TVCEDB.Items.AddChild(TVCEDB.Items[0], String(szDbase-
Name));
    Data := new(PCeOIContainerStruct);
    TCeOIContainerStruct(Data^).OID := ObjID;
    TCeOIContainerStruct(Data^).OIDInfo := CeOIDInfo;
    ImageIndex := 1;
    SelectedIndex := 3;
```

```
      end;
      ObjID := CeFindNextDatabase(hEnumContext);
   end;
   if ObjID = ERROR_INVALID_PARAMETER then
      ShowMessage('An Error occured while retrieving information from the
CE device.');
   TVCEDB.Items[0].Expand(True);
```

With that one simple exception, the two sets of source code are virtually the same.

By using some free source code, you can give your Delphi applications access to the entire RAPI library. And, since Inprise (formerly Borland) does not appear to have plans for a Delphi that compiles a true CE-based executable, this is definitely the next best thing.

Summary

RAPI helps extend the CE application into the Desktop by giving the other machines in your system access to the data and files on the CE device. This is especially important given that the data on these devices wouldn't be worth very much if you couldn't get that data circulated to other machines and other pieces of software. In this chapter, you saw how you could get a Desktop program to perform the very same types of data access possible on the CE devices themselves. In addition, you saw how it was possible to extend even non-Microsoft development products so that they, too, could access and talk to a CE device.

CHAPTER

ELEVEN

How CE Talks to the Outside World

- Serial Communications Issues

- Modem-Based Communications Issues

- PC Card/PCMCIA Communications Issues

- Winsock Commmunications Issues

In the last chapter, you saw how Desktop programs can talk to a CE device. In this chapter, we'll be looking at how to get your CE device talking to the outside world, including all of your other devices, Desktop machines, or any other piece of equipment you might have in mind. We'll explore all areas of CE-based communication from serial I/O to CE's Winsock support, starting with a brief overview of your options when it comes to CE communications. Then we'll look at each of the options in detail.

What's in the Box?

There are two aspects to Windows CE-based communication:

- The hardware aspect
- The software aspect

Although this may seem like an obvious distinction, it's not. That's because under Windows 98/NT, an application could open a serial port or begin a Winsock operation without paying much attention to the underlying hardware. Windows CE is closer to the hardware level, however, so you generally have no such luxury. And, as you've seen in previous chapters, each manufacturer may expose different features.

The Hardware Aspect

When it comes to hardware, there are only two ports you can count on:

- A serial port
- An Infrared (IR) port

In addition to these ports, there is an entire set of uncertain hardware, including:

- Modems
- PCMCIA cards

The Serial Port

The default serial port is usually the same one used to connect to the Desktop computer, and it is usually COM1. For the most part, it behaves like a serial port on a Desktop machine. Just as in Windows 98/NT, you can open the port in CE with a call to `CreateFile()`, read from it with `ReadFile()`, and so on. Most of your existing Windows-based serial communications code should port to CE rather easily.

The IR Port

The IR port is more of a gray area, however. Although all commercial CE devices offer an IR port, the port number (i.e., COM1, COM2, etc.) changes from one device to the next.

Also, some manufacturers configure their devices so that both the serial port and the IR port appear as COM1. In this case, the only way to specify which one you want is to open the port and then try to set it into IR mode.

And, as if it isn't confusing enough already, some devices allow you to open a serial port *and* an IR port at the same time. This goes against everything we've ever been told about CE allowing only one serial connection at a time.

Modems and PCMCIA Cards

As for devices that may or may not be available to you, some devices, such as the HP Jornada, have a built-in modem; other devices offer it as an upgrade; and some don't offer a modem at all. Similarly, the PCCard (PCMCIA) slot opens the device up to such hardware as networking cards, cell phone modems, additional serial ports, or higher-speed modems.

TIP   If your application calls for additional serial ports, your best bet is either the serial I/O card or the dual serial I/O card offered by Socket Communications of Newark, California (`http://www.socketcom.com`). Both are PCMCIA cards that instantly add one or two RS-232 ports to your CE device.

All of this hardware variety only makes it more of a challenge to design reliable communications-related software.

The Software Aspect

Obviously, with so much possible hardware available on a CE device, there's some complexity to the software as well. When it comes to communications, Windows CE supports a mix of everything from Win32 serial communications functions to Winsock to special blends of Winsock and IR.

Serial Communications

Serial communications haven't changed very much from Windows 98/NT to Windows CE. CE supports 16 of the 23 communications-related API calls, and the ones that aren't there probably won't affect your applications much, if at all. The seven unsupported functions are

- `BuildCommDCB()`
- `BuildCommDCBAndTimeouts()`
- `CommConfigDialog()`
- `GetCommConfig()`
- `GetDefaultCommConfig()`
- `SetCommConfig()`
- `SetDefaultCommConfig()`

It is possible to do almost everything these functions do with the functions that are supported by Windows CE. For instance, most of the functionality of `GetCommConfig()` can easily be replaced with the function `GetCommState()`, which is supported by CE.

The following is a list of the 16 functions that are supported under Windows CE:

- `ClearCommBreak()`
- `ClearCommError()`
- `EscapeCommFunction()`
- `GetCommMask()`
- `GetCommModemStatus()`
- `GetCommProperties()`

- GetCommState()

- GetCommTimeouts()

- PurgeComm()

- SetCommBreak()

- SetCommMask()

- SetCommState()

- SetCommTimeouts()

- SetupComm()

- TransmitCommChar()

- WaitCommEvent()

With this many supported functions, it's clear that the few functions that are missing shouldn't affect you too much.

NOTE   For more information on some of the missing API functions, see Chapter 3.

IR Communications

IR communications on a CE device are available in three classes:

- Raw IR

- IrCOMM

- Infrared Sockets (IrSock)

Raw IR *Raw IR* means that you'll be using the IR port as though it was any other serial port. There is no special handshaking and no error handling.

The most difficult part about using the IR port as a raw serial port comes from the fact that, as noted above, every manufacturer seems to assign a different port number to the IR port. With some of the earlier CE devices, it was possible to query a certain key in the registry to determine the IR port number, but it seems that all manufacturers do not store that information in the same place.

The only truly reliable way to determine the logical designation of the IR port is to loop through all of the ports and ask each one if it's the IR port.

The way to ask a port whether it is an IR port or a standard serial port is to call EscapeCommFunction() and pass in the handle to the open port and a flag (SETIR) indicating that you want to put the port into IR mode:

```
EscapeCommFunction(hPort, SETIR);
```

Since this function only returns TRUE if the port is an IR port, it's safe to assume that if the call fails, the port is not an IR port, and you need to keep looking. The most efficient and effective way to use this trick is probably to create a routine to detect the presence of the IR port. To do this, first initialize the result of the function to 0 to indicate that an IR port could not be found and then allocate memory to store the "name" (COM1, COM2, etc.) of the comm port:

```
result = 0; //zero indicates error, could not find port
szPort = (TCHAR *)LocalAlloc(LMEM_ZEROINIT, MAX_PATH);
```

Then, loop from 1—the lowest comm port number—to MAX_PORTS, a predefined constant indicating the highest port number to test:

```
for (i=1; i <= MAX_PORTS; i++)
{
```

WARNING   The MAX_PORTS value differs greatly from one device to another. On some devices, such as the Casio E-10, the highest comm port number is COM3; on the Casio 2400, the highest comm port number is COM4; and on the HP Jornada, the highest comm port number is COM6!

Next, construct the name of the comm port using the value of i as the number of the comm port:

```
_tcscpy(szPort, TEXT("COM"));
_itow(i, szNum, 10); //convert i to string
_tcscat(szPort, szNum);
_tcscat(szPort, TEXT(":"));
```

NOTE   In the above code, there is a call to the RTL function _itow(), which only works with Unicode-based strings. Ideally, the function to use is _itot(), which works with the generic-string types. However, _itot() is not supported on all of the CE platforms. See Appendix A for more information.

WARNING   You'll notice that the last step in the above code is to append a colon to the port name. Although Windows 98 and Windows NT do not require that the port name be followed with a colon, Windows CE does.

The next step is to open the port whose name you've just created. Just as you would on Windows 98/NT, do this using the `CreateFile()` function:

```
hPort = CreateFile(szPort, GENERIC_READ | GENERIC_WRITE,
  0, NULL, OPEN_EXISTING, FILE_ATTRIBUTE_NORMAL, NULL);
if (hPort != INVALID_HANDLE_VALUE)
{
```

Now, if you've been able to successfully open the port, you can apply the trick of attempting to set the port to IR mode. If it returns TRUE, that means you found the IR port:

```
if (EscapeCommFunction(hPort, SETIR))
{
  //Ir Port Found!!!
  result = i;
  CloseHandle(hPort);
  break;
}
}
```

The rest of the function is just clean up and remembering to return the numeric value representing the IR comm port:

```
CloseHandle(hPort);
}
LocalFree(szPort);
return result;
}
```

When fully assembled (and with some function calls to display the status of your search in a list box), the full function looks like this:

```
int DetectIRPort(void)
{
  int i, result;
  TCHAR * szPort;
  TCHAR szNum[4];
  HANDLE hPort;
```

```
result = 0; //zero indicates error, could not find port
szPort = (TCHAR *)LocalAlloc(LMEM_ZEROINIT, MAX_PATH);
for (i=1; i <= MAX_PORTS; i++)
{
  _tcscpy(szPort, TEXT("COM"));
  _itow(i, szNum, 10); //convert i to string
  _tcscat(szPort, szNum);
  _tcscat(szPort, TEXT(":"));
  SendMessage(hListBox, LB_ADDSTRING, 0, (LPARAM)TEXT("Now testing
    port:"));
  SendMessage(hListBox, LB_ADDSTRING, 0, (LPARAM)szPort);
  SendMessage(hListBox, LB_ADDSTRING, 0, (LPARAM)TEXT("..."));
  hPort = CreateFile(szPort, GENERIC_READ | GENERIC_WRITE,
    0, NULL, OPEN_EXISTING, FILE_ATTRIBUTE_NORMAL, NULL);
  if (hPort != INVALID_HANDLE_VALUE)
  {
    if (EscapeCommFunction(hPort, SETIR))
    {
      SendMessage(hListBox, LB_ADDSTRING, 0, (LPARAM)TEXT("IR Port
        Found!!!!!!!!!!!!!!!!!!!!!"));
      SendMessage(hListBox, LB_ADDSTRING, 0, (LPARAM)szPort);
      result = i;
      CloseHandle(hPort);
      break;
    }
  }
  CloseHandle(hPort);
  }
  LocalFree(szPort);
  return result;
}
```

When integrated into a sample test application, the result looks like the application shown in Figure 11.1.

IrCOMM In addition to the raw IR, which we've just examined, there is another kind of IR communication available under Windows CE, IrCOMM. This is a more reliable form of IR serial communication that provides handshaking, error handling, and many other features that make it an attractive alternative to raw IR.

FIGURE 11.1:

The IrDetect application

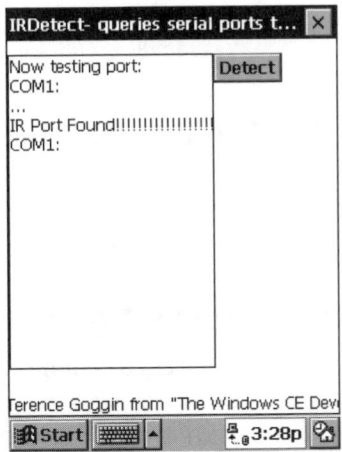

The best part about all of these additional features is that they're completely transparent—as far as your code is concerned, the IrCOMM port is just like any other serial port. In other words, the IrCOMM port can be used as though it were a standard serial port. That means you can call CreateFile(), ReadFile(), etc., while still enjoying the benefits of a more reliable connection.

In fact, the only difference between raw IR and IrCOMM that you'll actually notice is that the IrCOMM port is on a different logical comm port number than the raw IR port! To ensure that you open the correct IrCOMM port, you'll need to consult the registry. The key containing the information about the IrCOMM port is HKEY_ LOCAL_MACHINE\Drivers\BuiltIn\IrCOMM. The actual port number is contained in the value Index under this key. Or, as it would appear in code:

```
HKEY hKeyIR;
if (ERROR_SUCCESS == RegOpenKeyEx (HKEY_LOCAL_MACHINE,
TEXT("Drivers\\BuiltIn\\IrCOMM"), 0, KEY_READ, &hKeyIR))
{
    DWORD dwIRport;
    DWORD dwSizeData = sizeof (DWORD);
    if (ERROR_SUCCESS == RegQueryValueEx (hKeyIR, TEXT("Index"),
       NULL, NULL, (LPBYTE)&dwIRport, &dwSizeData))
    {
        WCHAR wszMsg[64];
```

```
wsprintf (wszMsg, TEXT"IrCOMM port number is: %u"),
  dwIRport);
MessageBox (NULL, wszMsg, TEXT("IR Port Info"), MB_OK);
}
```

Infrared Sockets (IrSock) Infrared Sockets is a Winsock-like wrapper for communicating over the Infrared port. Refer to the "Winsock-Based Communications" section later in this chapter to see what it takes to convert a simple Winsock-based application to an Infrared Sockets application.

Modem-Based Communications

There are really three classes of modems when it comes to CE:

- Standard external modems connected via the serial port

- Built-in modems

- PC Card/PCMCIA modems

Standard External Modems Standard external modems are just that: standard. There is nothing special about opening a serial port and dialing a modem connected to that serial port when working with Windows 98/NT, and that's true under Windows CE as well.

Built-in Modems It's tempting to conclude that built-in modems work just like external modems—and they do. The trick, however, is finding the internal modem, or more correctly, finding the comm port of the internal modem. The way to do this is to iterate through the HKEY_LOCAL_MACHINE\ExtModems key of the registry. Under this key, there will be a key for each of the modems the device knows about. For example, all CE devices have a default Hayes Compatible modem setting that refers to any external modem on COM1. Therefore, under the HKEY_LOCAL_MACHINE\ExtModems key, there is a Hayes Compatible key. To get the actual comm port name, which you can then use to open the port, simply retrieve the string stored in the Port value of the Hayes Compatible key. Or, in code, open the ExtModems key under HKEY_LOCAL_MACHINE as the first step:

```
RegOpenKeyEx (HKEY_LOCAL_MACHINE, TEXT("ExtModems"), 0, KEY_READ,
  &hKey);
if (hKey)
{
```

Next, create a `while` loop that retrieves the names of the subkeys under the `ExtModems` key (i.e., the subkeys for each of the different modems).

```
retCode = ERROR_SUCCESS;
i = 0;
while (retCode == ERROR_SUCCESS)
{
  cbName = MAX_PATH;
  memset(szSubKeyName, 0, MAX_PATH);
  retCode = RegEnumKeyEx(hKey, i, szKeyName,&cbName, NULL, NULL,
NULL, NULL);
  i++;
```

If you are able to successfully enumerate the key, then try to open the key so you can retrieve the values you're after:

```
if (retCode == (DWORD)ERROR_SUCCESS)
{
  memset(szModemInfo, 0, MAX_PATH);
  memset(szPortInfo, 0, MAX_PATH);
  memset(szDevName, 0, MAX_PATH);
RegOpenKeyEx (hKey, szKeyName, 0, KEY_READ, &hSubKey);
```

If you are able to open the key, you can retrieve the `Port` value and the `FriendlyName` of the modem:

```
if (hSubKey)
{
  dwBytes = MAX_PATH;
  RegQueryValueEx (hSubKey, TEXT("Port"), NULL, &dwType,
    (LPBYTE)szPortInfo, &dwBytes);
  dwBytes = MAX_PATH;
  RegQueryValueExW(hSubKey, TEXT("FriendlyName"), NULL, &dwType,
    (LPBYTE)szDevName, &dwBytes);
```

Optionally, you could then format the two strings retrieved and add the formatted string to a ComboBox:

```
wsprintf (szModemInfo, TEXT("%s %s"), szPortInfo, szDevName);
SendDlgItemMessage(hwnd, IDC_CBOMODEMS, CB_ADDSTRING, 0,
  (LPARAM)szModemInfo);
```

Finally, clear out your strings for the run through the next subkey:

```
memset(szModemInfo, 0, MAX_PATH);
memset(szPortInfo, 0, MAX_PATH);
```

```
        memset(szDevName, 0, MAX_PATH);
        RegCloseKey(hSubKey);
      }
     }
    }
  }
```

If you then create a simple dialog with a ComboBox and put this code into, say, a WM_INITDIALOG message handler, the final assembled message handler looks like this:

```
case WM_INITDIALOG:
{
    HKEY   hKey, hSubKey;
    DWORD dwDisposition;
    DWORD dwType;
    DWORD dwBytes = 0;
    TCHAR *szSubKeyName;
    TCHAR *szKeyName;
    TCHAR ClassName[MAX_PATH] = TEXT(""); // Buffer for class name.
    DWORD cbName;
    TCHAR *szPortInfo;
    TCHAR *szDevName;
    TCHAR *szModemInfo;
    DWORD retCode;
    int i;

    szSubKeyName = (TCHAR *)LocalAlloc(LMEM_ZEROINIT, MAX_PATH);
    szKeyName   = (TCHAR *)LocalAlloc(LMEM_ZEROINIT, MAX_PATH);
    szPortInfo  = (TCHAR *)LocalAlloc(LMEM_ZEROINIT, MAX_PATH);
    szDevName   = (TCHAR *)LocalAlloc(LMEM_ZEROINIT, MAX_PATH);
    szModemInfo = (TCHAR *)LocalAlloc(LMEM_ZEROINIT, MAX_PATH);

    RegOpenKeyEx (HKEY_LOCAL_MACHINE, TEXT("ExtModems"), 0, KEY_READ,
      &hKey);
    if (hKey)
    {
      retCode = ERROR_SUCCESS;
      i = 0;
      while (retCode == ERROR_SUCCESS)
      {
        cbName = MAX_PATH;
        memset(szSubKeyName, 0, MAX_PATH);
```

```
        retCode = RegEnumKeyEx(hKey, i, szKeyName,&cbName, NULL,
         NULL, NULL, NULL);

        i++;
        if (retCode == (DWORD)ERROR_SUCCESS)
        {
          memset(szModemInfo, 0, MAX_PATH);
          memset(szPortInfo, 0, MAX_PATH);
          memset(szDevName, 0, MAX_PATH);
          RegOpenKeyEx (hKey, szKeyName, 0, KEY_READ, &hSubKey);
          if (hSubKey)
          {
            dwBytes = MAX_PATH;
            RegQueryValueEx (hSubKey, TEXT("Port"), NULL, &dwType,
              (LPBYTE)szPortInfo, &dwBytes);
            dwBytes = MAX_PATH;
            RegQueryValueExW(hSubKey, TEXT("FriendlyName"), NULL,
              &dwType, (LPBYTE)szDevName, &dwBytes);
            wsprintf (szModemInfo, TEXT("%s %s"), szPortInfo,
              szDevName);
            SendDlgItemMessage(hwnd, IDC_CBOMODEMS, CB_ADDSTRING, 0,
              (LPARAM)szModemInfo);
            memset(szModemInfo, 0, MAX_PATH);
            memset(szPortInfo, 0, MAX_PATH);
            memset(szDevName, 0, MAX_PATH);
            RegCloseKey(hSubKey);
          }
        }
      }
    }
    LocalFree(szSubKeyName);
    LocalFree(szKeyName);
    LocalFree(szPortInfo);
    LocalFree(szDevName);
    LocalFree(szModemInfo);
    return TRUE;
}
```

The resulting Modem Selector dialog looks something like the one pictured in Figure 11.2.

PC Cards/PCMCIA Modems PCMCIA modems are really just another kind of PCMCIA device. In the next section, we'll be looking at all PCMCIA devices as a group, regardless of whether the actual card is a modem, a serial I/O card, or a network interface card.

PC Cards/PCMCIA Cards and Communications

PC cards/PCMCIA cards are fairly transparent when it comes to communications. Your application could open a comm port and never really know that the port it just opened was really, say, a PCMCIA modem.

However, there *are* two occasions when your application will care about the PCMCIA slot:

- When the application starts and needs to find out if the desired card/port is inserted into the slot and available for use

- When the application is running and the card in the slot changes (i.e., a card is added or removed)

When the Application Starts Officially, the Microsoft documentation says that when your application starts, you can use a function called EnumPnpIds() to retrieve a double-NULL terminated list of strings representing the device(s) currently inserted in the PCMCIA slot(s). However, there is one problem with this function: it doesn't exist in any of the .h files for any versions of Windows CE!

TIP The Pnp in EnumPnpIds() stands for *Plug and Play*.

This doesn't mean you can't get a list of available PCMCIA cards when your program starts, however; you just can't get that list using the EnumPnpIds()

function. Instead, you can create a function that does the exact same thing by querying the registry.

In this case, the key you're interested in is HKEY_LOCAL_MACHINE\Drivers\ Active. In this key you will find a set of double-digit subkeys numbered 00 to nn, where nn is a double-digit integer.

NOTE   Each of these double-digit subkeys specifies a different driver or hardware component that is currently being used by the device. The values of **nn** are assigned
somewhat sequentially, with the OEM system components taking the lower numbers first. For instance, on many systems, the **00** entry contains information about
the sound component, WAV1:. The value of **nn** assigned to a PCMCIA card
depends on the number of times any cards have been inserted since the device
was last reset. If the OEM has used, say **00** through **09** for system devices, the first
PCMCIA card inserted will get an **nn** value of **10**, the second card a value of **11**,
and so on. Also, if a card is inserted, removed, and then inserted at a later time
(but before a reset) that card may or may not be assigned a different value than
the one it had the last time it was used.

The way this set of double-digit subkeys helps make it possible to get information about the PCMCIA cards currently available on the device is that all PCMCIA-
related subkeys will have a value called PnpId. If an entry has this value and a
Name value containing the string COM, then it is a serial communications card of
some kind.

NOTE   Note that this method also detects compact flash cards, so if your application
expects a comm port in the form of a compact flash card, this technique will work
to detect its presence as well.

Using the same logic employed above in the modem detection routine, you can
start by opening the HKEY_LOCAL_MACHINE\Drivers\Active key:

```
RegOpenKeyEx (HKEY_LOCAL_MACHINE, TEXT("Drivers\\Active"), 0, KEY_READ,
&hKey);
```

NOTE   We present only a portion of the full code here so as to avoid duplicating the
modem detection code above. The full code for the **PnpId** enumeration is on the
CD for this book, in the directory for this chapter.

Just as before, you can enumerate the nn subkeys:

```
RegEnumKeyEx(hKey, i, szKeyName,&cbName, NULL, NULL, NULL, NULL);
```

And for each subkey enumerated, you can attempt to retrieve the PnpId and the device name (i.e., COM1, COM2, etc.):

```
//...
RegQueryValueEx (hSubKey, TEXT("PnpId"), NULL, &dwType,
  (LPBYTE)szPnpId, &dwBytes);
//...
RegQueryValueExW(hSubKey, TEXT("Name"), NULL, &dwType,
  (LPBYTE)szDevName, &dwBytes);
```

If the string retrieved from the PnpId value is non-NULL, add this item to your list box of PCMCIA devices:

```
if (_tcscmp(szPnpId, TEXT("")) != 0) //there was a PnpId
{
    wsprintf (szDevName, TEXT("%s %s"), szDevName, szPnpId);
    SendDlgItemMessage(hwnd, IDC_LSTPNPIDS, LB_ADDSTRING, 0,
      (LPARAM)szDevName);
}
```

When this code is hooked up to a dialog box with a ListBox on it, the result is something like Figure 11.3.

FIGURE 11.3:

PCMCIA-PnpIds application

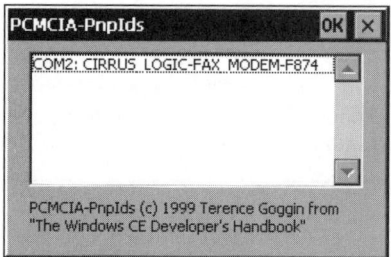

It turns out that the **EnumPnpIds()** actually does exist, it's just completely undocumented. John Psuik, technical editor of this book, has included a sample on the CD documenting how to call this function, if you prefer to go the undocumented route.

When the Card in the Slot Changes   If you are doing serial communications in your application, you're going to have to know when the card in the PCMCIA slot changes.

Why? Well, first you have the issue of error prevention or detection. If your application is in the middle of a file transfer over a PCMCIA-based serial port, and the user pulls the card out, your application will immediately know an error has occurred. However, your application will be much more robust if it is able to determine that the source of the error was the user removing the card and not, say, a problem with the other computer.

Second, even if your application is not actually using a comm port at the moment a card is removed or added, you'll probably want to update the comm port options that you offer the user. If the user inserted a modem or a serial I/O card, it's a safe guess they want to use that port with your program, and they don't want to have to restart your application in order to refresh the list of available comm ports.

Now that we know the advantages of monitoring changes in the PCMCIA slot, let's investigate how to do it. Like the techniques outlined in the section above, detecting a change in the current PCMCIA card requires some undocumented—or at least under-documented—CE tricks. Here again, the documentation says that an application need only respond to the WM_DEVICECHANGE message in order to be notified when a PCMCIA card is inserted or removed. However, there appears to be a small problem with this in that other portions of the documentation indicate that WM_DEVICECHANGE doesn't even exist on CE!

So what's the truth?

The WM_DEVICECHANGE message *does* exist, but it's not defined in the winuser.h header file where all of the other WM_ messages are defined. Instead, the WM_DEVICECHANGE message and a number of related constants and structures are all defined in a separate header file called dbt.h.

The first step, then, in handling the WM_DEVICECHANGE message is including this header file.

The second step is correctly interpreting the wParam value that the WM_DEVICECHANGE message passes to your application. From testing, it appears that there are only two values that matter under Windows CE:

- DBT_DEVICEARRIVAL   A card has just been inserted into the slot.

- DBT_DEVICEREMOVECOMPLETE   A card has just been removed from the slot.

Code to handle the wParam of the message, then, might look like this:

```
switch(wParam)
{
case DBT_DEVICEARRIVAL:
  //Card was inserted
  break;
case DBT_DEVICEREMOVECOMPLETE:
  //Card was removed
  break;
}
```

The lParam of WM_DEVICECHANGE is a pointer to a structure that should tell you a little bit of information about the device. The trick to using the lParam is that it points to one of several possible structures, depending on what type of card has been inserted. In order to determine what type of card and, therefore, which structure lParam is pointing to, you must first cast the lParam to a generic structure and read one of that structure's members.

The generic structure is called DEV_BROADCAST_HEADER and is defined as follows:

```
struct _DEV_BROADCAST_HEADER
{
  DWORD    dbcd_size;
  DWORD    dbcd_devicetype;
  DWORD    dbcd_reserved;
};
```

In order to determine the type of card that was just inserted or removed, you must examine the value of the structure's dbcd_devicetype member. The possible values for dbcd_devicetype are

- DBT_DEVTYP_OEM   Unspecified OEM type card

- DBT_DEVTYP_PORT   Serial or parallel port

- DBT_DEVTYP_NET   Network resource

NOTE   There are other possible values for the **dbcd_devicetype** member, but they do not appear to have meaning under Windows CE.

Once you've tested the dbcd_devicetype value, you can cast the lParam to a more detailed structure specific to the card's type. For some reason, however, it appears that CE reports all PCMCIA cards as being DBT_DEVTYP_PORT cards—in other words, it considers all cards to be serial- or parallel-port cards.

The positive side of this is that you only have to worry about casting the lParam to one type of structure; the negative side is that you'll have to work even harder to differentiate the comm port cards from the other types of cards.

The comm port–specific structure is called DEV_BROADCAST_PORT and is defined as follows:

```
typedef struct _DEV_BROADCAST_PORT_W
{
  DWORD    dbcp_size;
  DWORD    dbcp_devicetype;
  DWORD    dbcp_reserved;
  wchar_t  dbcp_name[1];
};
```

As you may have guessed, the member of this structure that actually makes it possible to determine whether or not the card in question is a comm port is dbcp_name[1]. If the card is a comm port, the name will contain the text "COM" followed by a number and a colon. The good news about this is that the name is all you need in order to call CreateFile()and open that port.

If you now put everything that you know about PCMCIA cards into a simple testing utility, you'll wind up with something like the application pictured in Figure 11.4.

FIGURE 11.4:

The PCMCIA Detect application

PCMCIA-detect - detects when a PCCard/PCMCIA card is inserted into... ☒

WM_DEVICECHANGE:
Card was inserted.
wParam: 8000
Device is a serial/parallel port.
COM2:
lParam: 18040004

WM_DEVICECHANGE:
Card was removed.
wParam: 8004
Device is a serial/parallel port.

PCMCIA-detect (c) 1999 Terence Goggin from "The Windows CE Developers' Handbook

Start | My Handhel... | PCMCIA-detect ... | 3:24 PM

Of course, the WM_DEVICECHANGE message handler does the real work of this application:

```
case WM_DEVICECHANGE:
TCHAR * szParam;
TCHAR szNum[MAX_PATH];
PDEV_BROADCAST_HDR pdbhDeviceHeader; //the generic card structure
```

First, add a status message to a list box to let the user know that notification was received:

```
SendMessage(hListBox, LB_ADDSTRING, 0,
  (LPARAM)TEXT("WM_DEVICECHANGE:"));
```

Next, based on the value of wParam, alert the user as to whether the card is being inserted or removed:

```
switch(wParam)
{
case DBT_DEVICEARRIVAL:
  SendMessage(hListBox, LB_ADDSTRING, 0, (LPARAM)TEXT("Card was
    inserted."));
  break;
case DBT_DEVICEREMOVECOMPLETE:
  SendMessage(hListBox, LB_ADDSTRING, 0, (LPARAM)TEXT("Card was
    removed."));
  break;
}
```

Next, you can convert wParam and lParam to strings and display their actual values:

```
szParam = (TCHAR *)LocalAlloc(LMEM_ZEROINIT, MAX_PATH);
_tcscpy(szParam, TEXT("wParam: "));
_ltow(wParam, szNum, 16); //convert i to hex string
_tcscat(szParam, szNum);
SendMessage(hListBox, LB_ADDSTRING, 0, (LPARAM)szParam);
memset(szParam, 0, MAX_PATH);
_tcscpy(szParam, TEXT("lParam: "));
_ltow(lParam, szNum, 16); //convert i to hex string
_tcscat(szParam, szNum);
```

Now, treat the lParam as the generic device information structure:

```
pdbhDeviceHeader = (PDEV_BROADCAST_HDR)lParam;
```

Then, attempt to determine the type of card:

```
switch(pdbhDeviceHeader->dbch_devicetype)
{
```

If it's a serial or parallel port, go ahead and treat the lParam as a specific DEV_BROADCAST_PORT structure:

```
case DBT_DEVTYP_PORT:
  PDEV_BROADCAST_PORT pdbpPortDeviceHeader;
  pdbpPortDeviceHeader = (PDEV_BROADCAST_PORT)lParam;
```

You can also let the user know the type of card, and, from the DEV_BROADCAST _PORT structure, the name of the port, as well:

```
SendMessage(hListBox, LB_ADDSTRING, 0, (LPARAM)TEXT("Device is a
  serial/parallel port."));
SendMessage(hListBox, LB_ADDSTRING, 0, (LPARAM)pdbpPortDevice
  Header->dbcp_name);
break;
```

As noted before, all PCMCIA cards appear to be recognized by CE as serial or parallel ports. Therefore, the default clause here is mostly for the sake of good coding:

```
default:
  SendMessage(hListBox, LB_ADDSTRING, 0, (LPARAM)TEXT("Device is of
    an unknown type."));
}
```

When fully assembled, the entire message handler looks like this:

```
case WM_DEVICECHANGE:
  TCHAR * szParam;
  TCHAR szNum[MAX_PATH];
  PDEV_BROADCAST_HDR pdbhDeviceHeader;
  SendMessage(hListBox, LB_ADDSTRING, 0,
    (LPARAM)TEXT("WM_DEVICECHANGE:"));
  switch(wParam)
  {
  case DBT_DEVICEARRIVAL:
    SendMessage(hListBox, LB_ADDSTRING, 0, (LPARAM)TEXT("Card was
      inserted."));
    break;
  case DBT_DEVICEREMOVECOMPLETE:
```

```
  SendMessage(hListBox, LB_ADDSTRING, 0, (LPARAM)TEXT("Card was
    removed."));
  break;
}
szParam = (TCHAR *)LocalAlloc(LMEM_ZEROINIT, MAX_PATH);
_tcscpy(szParam, TEXT("wParam: "));
_ltow(wParam, szNum, 16); //convert i to hex string
_tcscat(szParam, szNum);
SendMessage(hListBox, LB_ADDSTRING, 0, (LPARAM)szParam);
memset(szParam, 0, MAX_PATH);
_tcscpy(szParam, TEXT("lParam: "));
_ltow(lParam, szNum, 16); //convert i to hex string
_tcscat(szParam, szNum);
pdbhDeviceHeader = (PDEV_BROADCAST_HDR)lParam;
switch(pdbhDeviceHeader->dbch_devicetype)
{
case DBT_DEVTYP_PORT:
  PDEV_BROADCAST_PORT pdbpPortDeviceHeader;
  pdbpPortDeviceHeader = (PDEV_BROADCAST_PORT)lParam;
  SendMessage(hListBox, LB_ADDSTRING, 0, (LPARAM)TEXT("Device is a
    serial/parallel port."));
  SendMessage(hListBox, LB_ADDSTRING, 0, (LPARAM)pdbpPortDevice
    Header->dbcp_name);
  break;
case DBT_DEVTYP_NET:
  SendMessage(hListBox, LB_ADDSTRING, 0, (LPARAM)TEXT("Device is a
    network interface card."));
  break;
default:
  SendMessage(hListBox, LB_ADDSTRING, 0, (LPARAM)TEXT("Device is of
    an unknown type."));
}
SendMessage(hListBox, LB_ADDSTRING, 0, (LPARAM)szParam);
LocalFree(szParam);
SendMessage(hListBox, LB_ADDSTRING, 0, (LPARAM)TEXT(""));
break;
```

You now have a complete set of PCMCIA detection routines.

TIP   This **WM_DEVICECHANGE** code should also work quite nicely under Windows 98/NT!

Winsock-Based Communications

Windows CE supports a subset of the Winsock 1.1 specifications. What this means on a practical level, though, is that most of your Windows 98/NT Winsock-based code will not port to Windows CE. If, however, you have some Windows 3.*x* code that you want to port, that process will probably go very smoothly.

Of course, there's still a lot you can do with Winsock 1.1. In fact, you can really do just about everything you can do with Winsock 2, but your code will look very different. For instance, under Winsock 1.1, there is no WSAAsyncSelect() function to help you process socket-related events. In fact, there are only five WSA functions supported under Windows CE:

- WSACleanup()
- WSAGetLastError()
- WSAIocl()
- WSASetLastError()
- WSAStartup()

All of the WSA–related functionality is only accessible through Berkeley Sockets–style functions, such as accept(), bind(), and receive().

Winsock 1.1 To learn how to make the Winsock 1.1 functions actually do something, let's create a simple *whois* client. As you know, *whois* is a very simple protocol used to retrieve registration information about domain names. All the client does is connect to the server, send the request in the form whois somedomain.com, and wait for the result. The server will return some text containing the desired information or a message indicating that the domain is available.

First, create a simple dialog, with an Edit control, a multiline Edit control, and a button, so that when you're done, you have a dialog looking something like the one in Figure 11.5.

The user will be able to enter a domain name to look up in the single-line Edit control and view the results in the multiline Edit control. The actual look-up code will be triggered whenever the user clicks the button.

FIGURE 11.5:

The whois program

The first step to take in the WM_COMMAND event handler for the button when coding your whois client is to initialize Winsock with the WSAStartup() function, just as you would under Winsock 2:

```
if (WSAStartup(wVersionRequested, &wsaData))
{
    WSACleanup();
    return TRUE;
}
```

Next, create the client socket with a call to the socket() function:

```
sockWhois = socket(AF_INET, SOCK_STREAM, IPPROTO_TCP);
if (sockWhois == INVALID_SOCKET)
{
    WSACleanup();
}
```

Then, populate a SOCKADDR_IN structure with information about the whois server's address and port number to connect on:

```
saddrInternic.sin_family = AF_INET;
//198.41.0.6 - whois.internic.net *the* whois server
saddrInternic.sin_addr.S_un.S_un_b.s_b1 = 198;
saddrInternic.sin_addr.S_un.S_un_b.s_b2 = 41;
saddrInternic.sin_addr.S_un.S_un_b.s_b3 = 0;
saddrInternic.sin_addr.S_un.S_un_b.s_b4 = 6;
saddrInternic.sin_port = htons(43); //whois port number
```

Now, attempt to connect to the server:

```
if (connect(sockWhois, (LPSOCKADDR)&saddrInternic,
    sizeof(SOCKADDR_IN)) == SOCKET_ERROR)
{
    closesocket(sockWhois);
    WSACleanup();
}
```

Next, construct the string that will be your request to the server by concatenating "whois " with the domain name the user entered into the edit box:

```
strcpy(szWhois, "whois ");
GetDlgItemText(hwnd, IDC_DOMAIN, szUnicodeDomain, MAX_PATH);
WideCharToMultiByte(CP_ACP, 0, szUnicodeDomain, wcslen(szUnicode-
    Domain) * sizeof(TCHAR), szTemp, MAX_PATH, NULL, NULL);
strcat(szWhois, szTemp);
```

WARNING Note the use of the `WideCharToMultiByte()` function above. Although CE is Unicode-based, all of the Internet protocols still use ANSI text strings. Therefore, you must convert the Unicode-string of the edit box to an ANSI string. For more information on working with Unicode, see Chapter 2.

You can now send this request string to the whois server:

```
if (send(sockWhois, szWhois, strlen(szWhois), 0) == SOCKET_ERROR)
{
    closesocket(sockWhois);
    WSACleanup();
}
```

Loop until you receive the full text of the reply from the server, calling the `recv()` function to get a small portion of the text each time through the loop:

```
do
{
    iResult = recv(sockWhois, szTemp, sizeof(szTemp), 0);
    if (iResult == SOCKET_ERROR)
        break;
    strcat(szWhois, szTemp);
    memset(szTemp, 0, MAX_PATH);
}while (iResult != 0);
```

Now you can close the socket and clean up:

```
closesocket(sockWhois);
WSACleanup();
```

When some code to display the errors to the user is added and the entire routine is assembled, it looks like this:

```
case IDC_BTNLOOKUP:
  {
    WORD wVersionRequested = MAKEWORD(1,1);
    WSADATA wsaData;
    SOCKET    sockWhois;
    int iResult;
    SOCKADDR_IN saddrInternic;
    char *szWhois;
    char *szTemp;
    TCHAR *szUnicodeDomain;
    DWORD dwNumWritten;
    SendMessage(hEdtInfo, WM_SETTEXT, 0, (LPARAM)TEXT("Initializing
      Winsock."));
    if (WSAStartup(wVersionRequested, &wsaData))
    {
        SendMessage(hEdtInfo, WM_SETTEXT, 0, (LPARAM)TEXT("ERR: Unable
          to initialize Winsock."));
        WSACleanup();
        return TRUE;
    }
    sockWhois = socket(AF_INET, SOCK_STREAM, IPPROTO_TCP);
    if (sockWhois == INVALID_SOCKET)
    {
        SendMessage(hEdtInfo, WM_SETTEXT, 0, (LPARAM)TEXT("ERR: Unable
          to create client socket."));
        WSACleanup();
        return TRUE;
    }
    SendMessage(hEdtInfo, WM_SETTEXT, 0, (LPARAM)TEXT("Socket
      created."));
    saddrInternic.sin_port = htons(43); //whois port
    saddrInternic.sin_family = AF_INET;
    //198.41.0.6 - whois.internic.net *the* whois server
    saddrInternic.sin_addr.S_un.S_un_b.s_b1 = 198;
    saddrInternic.sin_addr.S_un.S_un_b.s_b2 = 41;
```

```
saddrInternic.sin_addr.S_un.S_un_b.s_b3 = 0;
saddrInternic.sin_addr.S_un.S_un_b.s_b4 = 6;
if (connect(sockWhois, (LPSOCKADDR)&saddrInternic, sizeof(SOCKADDR
  _IN)) == SOCKET_ERROR)
{
    SendMessage(hEdtInfo, WM_SETTEXT, 0, (LPARAM)TEXT("ERR: Unable
      to connect to server."));
    closesocket(sockWhois);
    WSACleanup();
    return TRUE;
}
SendMessage(hEdtInfo, WM_SETTEXT, 0, (LPARAM)TEXT("Connected to
  server."));
szWhois = (char *)LocalAlloc(LMEM_ZEROINIT, MAX_PATH * 2);
szUnicodeDomain = (TCHAR *)LocalAlloc(LMEM_ZEROINIT, MAX_PATH * 2 *
  sizeof(TCHAR));
szTemp = (char *)LocalAlloc(LMEM_ZEROINIT, MAX_PATH);
strcpy(szWhois, "whois ");
GetDlgItemText(hwnd, IDC_DOMAIN, szUnicodeDomain, MAX_PATH);
WideCharToMultiByte(CP_ACP, 0, szUnicodeDomain, wcslen(szUnicodeDo-
  main) * sizeof(TCHAR), szTemp, MAX_PATH, NULL, NULL);
strcat(szWhois, szTemp);
SendMessage(hEdtInfo, WM_SETTEXT, 0, (LPARAM)TEXT("Sending
  request."));
if (send(sockWhois, szWhois, strlen(szWhois), 0) == SOCKET_ERROR)
{
    SendMessage(hEdtInfo, WM_SETTEXT, 0, (LPARAM)TEXT("ERR: Unable
      to send request to server."));
    closesocket(sockWhois);
    WSACleanup();
    return TRUE;
}
memset(szWhois, 0, MAX_PATH * 2);
strcpy(szWhois, " ");
memset(szTemp, 0, MAX_PATH);
SendMessage(hEdtInfo, WM_SETTEXT, 0, (LPARAM)TEXT("Receiving
  reply."));
do
{
    iResult = recv(sockWhois, szTemp, sizeof(szTemp), 0);
    if (iResult == SOCKET_ERROR)
        break;
```

```
        strcat(szWhois, szTemp);
        memset(szTemp, 0, MAX_PATH);
    }while (iResult != 0);
    closesocket(sockWhois);
    WSACleanup();
    MultiByteToWideChar(CP_ACP, 0, szWhois, strlen(szWhois), szUnicode-
        Domain, MAX_PATH * 2 * sizeof(TCHAR));
    SendMessage(hEdtInfo, WM_SETTEXT, 0, (LPARAM)szUnicodeDomain);
    WriteFile(hFile, szUnicodeDomain, _tcslen(szUnicodeDomain) *
        sizeof(TCHAR), &dwNumWritten, NULL);
    LocalFree(szWhois);
    LocalFree(szUnicodeDomain);
    LocalFree(szTemp);
}
```

When you actually look at this code, you can see that Winsock 1.1, while crude compared to Winsock 2, is not too difficult to use and should be adequate for most of your communications needs.

Infrared Sockets (IrSock) Infrared Sockets is version of Winsock 1.1 that uses the IR port as a transport medium. There really isn't a whole lot of difference between IrSock and Winsock—in fact, just make sure you take these precautions when converting your Winsock code to IrSock code:

- Always include the af_irda.h header file.

- Use AF_IRDA instead of AF_INET when creating a socket.

- Use the SOCKADDR_IRDA structure instead of the SOCKADDR_IN structure.

With these three exceptions, *everything* else is exactly the same as standard Winsock operations.

TIP MFC's CCeSocket does provide some rudimentary support for asynchronous notification; you may want to consider using MFC if code that you are porting depends heavily on asynchronous notification.

Summary

In this chapter, you've explored CE's communications hardware and software sides, and you saw how to smoothly integrate the two in order to make our applications as robust and as flexible as possible. You started with simple serial communications and moved up to Infrared ports. You learned how to detect internal modems on a CE device and you even delved into a bit of undocumented Windows CE in order to detect changes in the PCMCIA hardware. Finally, you took a look at Winsock 1.1 and IrSock technologies.

CHAPTER

TWELVE

Third-Party Database Engines

- Raima's RDM/CE

- Sybase's Adaptive Server Anywhere

- Oracle Lite

- Comparison of Features

In Part I of this book, you learned about the database engine that Windows CE provides as part of the API. As you saw, CE's database engine has some quirks and limitations that may affect its usefulness, depending on your purpose. To summarize, the real strengths of the CE database engine are:

- Zero cost: it's part of the CE operating system/API.

- Automatic Data Compression: all CE databases are compressed by default.

- Simple searches: simple searches of the indexed field can be performed.

- Simple sorts: simple sorts through sort orders can be performed.

However, the CE database engine falls a little short in these areas:

- Unusual table structures/organization

- Complex API calls

- No data relationships

- No support for SQL

NOTE In addition to the above list, there are a number of reports on the CE newsgroups and mailing lists that bog down the CE database engine since it's dealing with such large amounts of data.

In this chapter, we'll address the issue of what to do when the CE database engine doesn't meet your needs. Specifically, we'll be looking at some of the third-party database engines that are available for Windows CE.

When it comes to data access on CE, there are three leading third-party vendors:

- Raima offers Raima Data Manager for CE

- Sybase offers Adaptive Server Anywhere for CE

- Oracle offers Oracle Lite for CE

A little experimentation is necessary to ensure that you choose the best database engine for your needs. Therefore, each of these three vendors has prepared a sample application as well as some introductory text about their database engine.

These three sections will comprise the bulk of this chapter. After that, we'll do a feature-by-feature comparison of the engines so that you can pick the one that best meets your development needs.

Raima's RDM/CE for Data Storage

When you need to store more data access it in ways that are difficult using CE's native facilities, it's time to look at a more robust data manager. You can write your own, or use a third-party product. In this section, we examine one of those third-party products, Raima Data Manager for Windows CE (RDM/CE).

RDM/CE is a network model database with extensive indexing and navigation capabilities. Its data files are binary compatible with RDM for Win32, Win16, and even DOS, so you can prepare data on whichever platform is most convenient to you.

Network and Relational Data Models

While Windows CE offers incredible computing speed for the price, current platforms are limited in the amount of data they can store. On some platforms, main memory is shared with mass storage and can be as small as 2MB. If your application requires a lot of data storage, finding the most compact data format can make your application a real winner. As with any tool for CE development, you'll want to consider the files size of the DLL involved. More important in database management, though, is the size of the data files themselves as you add your data.

The most commonly used data storage format in business computing is the relational model. Relational technology uses common fields and indexes to allow navigation from one record to another. For example, consider an invoicing system in which you have CUSTOMER, INVOICE and INVOICE_ITEM tables. Each CUSTOMER will have a unique CUST_ID, and the CUST_ID will likely be indexed. Each INVOICE will have its INV_ID, which will also be indexed, along with the INV_CUST_ID stored in the INVOICE table. Similarly, each INVOICE_ITEM record will contain an indexed field, the II_INV_ID.

Navigating from a specific customer record involves first retrieving the CUSTOMER record. This gives you the CUST_ID. You then must look in the INV_CUST_ID index for the INVOICE table, retrieving each INVOICE record in turn, as you find it in the index. Retrieving all the INVOICE_ITEM records involves the II_INV_ID index, since the INV_ID is the key to retrieving the data.

This technology is easy to understand, practical, and flexible. But in a constrained environment like Windows CE, how can you cut some corners, save some space, and still get the data retrieval you need? The network model can offer a real advantage.

Rather than relying on a common field and performing index lookups to do a JOIN, the network model offers direct record-to-record navigation, either manually or using what RDM calls *sets*. In an RDM set, one record is designated an owner, and one or more record types serve as members.

In the example above, the CUSTOMER record would be the owner of the INVOICE record, and the INVOICE record would in turn be the owner of the INV_ITEM record. Embedded in each CUSTOMER record are the physical addresses of the first and last INVOICE records. Each INVOICE record contains the physical address of the related CUSTOMER record and the physical addresses of the next and previous INVOICE records for the same customer.

Navigating the data is more direct, since reading the CUSTOMER record immediately yields the physical address of the first INVOICE record. Reading the INVOICE record instantly yields the address of the first INV_ITEM record.

In RDM, this physical address is called the database address, or DB_ADDR. Sets can be managed using a number of set functions, or DB_ADDR fields can be stored in your own programs during processing. They can even be added to the other fields in your database definition.

This direct record-to-record navigation, with its advantage of speed and optional elimination of indexes, makes network databases like RDM an excellent match for Windows CE.

Introducing HpcLadr

A ladder puzzle is an old word game. An example of a ladder puzzle is, given a start word of CAP and a destination word of PIN, you can transform one letter at a time thus: CAP, CAN, PAN, PIN. HpcLadr is a Windows CE application that makes it possible to create these puzzles yourself; it also allows you to solve the puzzles it creates. Figure 12.1 shows the completed HpcLadr running on a CE device.

FIGURE 12.1:

HpcLadr running on a
CE device

The first item you need so you can write a program like HpcLadr is a database of words. You can prepare this database with an application running on Windows NT, using RDM for Windows NT. This program, called LadrPrep, is also in the \LADDER directory. When you run it, you will find it has only two actions it can perform:

- Import words

- Export words

HpcLadr comes complete with a set of data and index files; you will only need to use LadrPrep if you wish to change the words in the HpcLadr database.

The database that LadrPrep creates is structurally simple. Each word is entered into a table of similarly sized words. The database is searched for other words that could be adjacent in a ladder puzzle, and mutual DB_ADDR pointers are added. For example, CAP points to CAN, and CAN points to CAP.

In designing the database, you must take into account how you intend to use it. In this case, you know that your only use for the database is to find a specific word and from it find all ladder-adjacent words. Therefore, instead of using RDM's full set capabilities, it makes sense to use a very simple database entry for each word, such as this record definition for three-letter words:

```
record word3 { char w3[3]; DB_ADDR adjacent; }
```

In the adjacent field, store the physical address of the first related word you find. The size of the entire record is only 7 bytes. However, rather than pointing to the actual word, the DB_ADDR points to a junction record (only 8 bytes and no index necessary):

```
record junction { DB_ADDR target_word; DB_ADDR next_adjacent; }
```

The logic of adding the word CAP to a database already containing CAN could be represented with pseudocode that looks something like this:

```
Add new word to database; its DB_ADDR is db_new
Search database for adjacent words
For each adjacent word db_adj
     Create two new junction records, j1 and j2
     Set j1's next_adjacent to db_adj's adjacent
     Set j1's target_word to db_adj
     Set db_adj's adjacent to j1
     Set j2's next_adjacent to db_new's adjacent
     Set j2's target_word to db_new
     Set db_new's adjacent to j2
End for
```

The ability to directly store physical database addresses here gives you both speed and compactness of data representation. Using relational technology, the junction set has to contain not two 32-bit quantities, but one column for the target word and one column for the adjacent word. Even if you limit yourself to seven-letter words, a 14-byte record is required instead of an 8-byte record. In addition, for practical use the junction table must be indexed, adding overhead of at least 11 bytes per record, for a total of 25 bytes instead of RDM's 8 bytes.

This may seem like a contrived example, but think about the data in your own application: how much data access travels along predictable paths, parent record to child record? Could you speed up your application *and* reduce storage requirements by trying network technology?

Adding a list of words to LadrPrep creates a database in which every word is directly linked to all words that differ by only one letter. It will also contain a number of words, like xylophone, which aren't linked to any others, because no other word differs from them by only one letter. Therefore, the LadrPrep function's Export Word List only exports words that have links.

If you decide to create your own database for HpcLadr using LadrPrep, you will get the smallest database by performing the following steps:

1. Import the word list.

2. Export the word list.

3. Import the word list once more.

This will ensure that the database is as compact as possible.

Once the database is prepared, writing HpcLadr is pretty easy. In its Make a Ladder mode, HpcLadr simply displays a list from which you may choose words. Once you choose a step in your ladder, HpcLadr shows all the adjacent words, eliminating any that are closer to the beginning of the ladder than the current step. This way, you are guaranteed that any puzzle you construct using HpcLadr will use the shortest possible route between your chosen words, given the vocabulary used by the program.

In its Solve a Ladder mode, HpcLadr shows the starting word, the ending word, and a varying number of hint words. You fill in the ladder by typing in the adjacent words or by clicking on the words in the hint list.

Implementing both modes is quite easy using RDM and the database you designed. Given a specific word, retrieve its record and read the junction record's DB_ADDR. Each junction record contains a DB_ADDR `target_word`. Retrieve that and add a word to the list of words displayed as adjacent to your original word. Navigate to the junction record's `next_adjacent`, and you're at a new junction record. Simple, direct, fast, and there's no need for indexes.

Putting RDM to Work

You can find the file `RaimaDM.zip` in the `\Raima` directory on this book's companion CD. It contains two files: `README.txt` and `RDMCE.zip`. Please read the license agreement in `README.txt`; if you agree with the terms, you are welcome to try the full RDM/CE product, encrypted with a key disclosed in the license agreement. More information is available direct from Raima at `http://www.raima.com`.

Sybase's Adaptive Server Anywhere

As part of their SQL Anywhere Studio, Sybase offers Adaptive Server Anywhere (ASA) for Windows CE. ASA builds on Sybase's technology to deliver a small-footprint, self-tuning, fully functional RDBMS engine for applications operating in remote or mobile computing environments.

In the next section, we'll be looking at a sample application provided by Sybase for the purpose of demonstrating some of the features and benefits of ASA for Windows CE.

Sybase's Adaptive Server Anywhere Sample Application

This sample application demonstrates database access, multi-user features/user rights, and report generation using SQL stored procedures. The application allows a user to log in to the database. Based on their user rights, they will be able to choose a report to view. The reports are stored in the database as stored procedures. When the user selects a report to view, the ASA database engine will execute a stored procedure. The application will then display the results of this procedure.

TIP   Stored procedures are complex SQL statements, stored and managed by the database engine, which can then be executed and referenced like other SQL functions.

A major advantage of storing the reports as stored procedures is that very little SQL code needs to be hard-coded into the application. For example, if a new report needs to be created, it can simply be added to the database without having to recompile and test the application. Similarly, through the replication and synching features of ASA, these new reports can be added to a central database and then populated to all of the CE devices that connect to that central database. Database replication can also be very useful in cases where the data is changing on a consistent basis.

NOTE   This sample application does not include database synching functionality, but it is a very simple task to include it.

The Database Schema

The application uses two types of tables:

- Fake sales data
- Report data

For our purposes, the table that's of interest is the Report table. The Report table is organized as follows:

report_id   A unique integer column used as the table's primary key.

report_name   The "friendly" name of the report. The application uses this column to display the list of available reports.

proc_name   The name of the SQL stored procedure that generates the report.

security_level   A numeric value used to determine the user's rights.

Administering and Managing ASA for CE Databases

Due to the limited resources of Windows CE, Sybase does not provide database administration tools that run on CE devices. Therefore, you have two options for administering these databases:

- Active Sync
- File copy

Administering the database with Active Sync might be easy for users who are familiar with the Active Sync process. However, as you know, transferring data over the serial port is incredibly slow. Therefore, this option can be fairly time consuming, especially if there are a large number of records that need to be synched.

The second alternative is to copy the database (.db) and transaction log (.log) from the CE device to your desktop. This, of course, can be done with an Ethernet connection or any other way you prefer to get your CE device connected to your desktop. This method is almost always quicker than synching over a serial connection.

TIP   Since the databases are completely binary compatible, you can start this database on your desktop and administer it directly from Sybase Central. Once the changes are complete, you can recopy it down to your CE device.

Configuring the Application

To set up the demo, follow these steps:

1. Install ASA for CE on the device.

2. Once the setup has been completed, copy both the application and the database files to the root directory of the CE device.

3. Start up the database server by running the following command:

   ```
   "\program files\asa\dbsrv6" -x "TCPIP" -z -n demo asademo.db
   ```

After the database has started, you are ready to start the application.

ASA for CE Command Line Options

In this example, you're starting the ASA server with several command line options that allow you to tweak the server's operation for your individual needs. For instance, the -x "TCPIP" option assumes that the device is connected to the network and that you'll be connecting to it via TCP/IP. If you're not connected to the desktop, simply use -x " " instead.

Similarly, the -z option gives you debugging information and is not required. The -n option assigns the name **demo** to the current session of the server. The **asademo.db** tells the server to start the **asademo.db** database.

Incidentally, Sybase recommends creating a shortcut specifying your most common configuration to avoid typing the full command line each time.

NOTE The default database administrator userid is **dba** and the password is **sql**.

The Demo

In the previous section, you started the database server. Now you'll start the application by launching **asademo.exe**. Figure 12.2 shows the login window. When prompted, you'll enter a userid of **clark** and a password of **sales**.

FIGURE 12.2:

The Login dialog

When you click OK, the application executes the Logon method of the CDemoDB class:

```
result = m_db.Logon(m_user, m_password);
```

Next, the application will attempt to log in to the database. If unsuccessful, it will return an error message. If successful, the application will display the Report dialog, as shown in Figure 12.3.

FIGURE 12.3:

The Report dialog

The server returns the employee ID in the bottom right corner of the page, as well as the user rights assigned to this user in the bottom left corner. Based on these user rights, the application displays all of the reports that this user can access. If you click on Customer List in the CListBox labeled Reports List, the application calls the appropriate stored procedure, which is executed by the ASA Server. The application then displays the results of the stored procedure in the CListView control. This is shown in Figure 12.4.

FIGURE 12.4:

Results of running the Customer List report

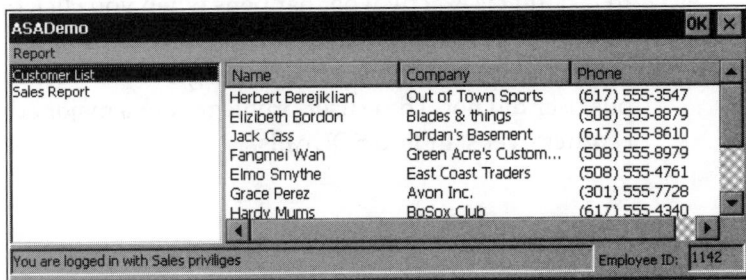

The code performing this operation first retrieves the name of the report from the CListBox control (called m_reports):

```
TCHAR Buffer[60];
m_reports.GetText( m_reports.GetCurSel(), Buffer );
```

Next, translate the friendly name of the selected report into the name of the stored procedure, again using your CDemoDB class:

```
m_db.GetReportProcedure(Buffer, m_empid);   //m_db is of class
CDemoDB
```

Then, after setting up the CListView control, add one record at a time to the CListView, looping until there are no more records to display:

```
for (;;)
{
    if (m_db.GetNextReportRow() == false)
        break;
    FillListCtrl(m_db.m_result1,m_db.m_result2,m_db.m_result3);
}
```

If you now click on Sales Report, the Server will run the Sales Report stored procedure. Once again, the appropriate stored procedure is called, which brings back all of the sales this person has made. As before, the resulting set of data is displayed in the ListView control.

If you then close the application and start it again, this time logging in as a different user, you will see the user rights features at work. This time, log in with a user ID of kelly and a password of manager.

Once you're logged in, you'll see the same dialog as before. However, this time the employee ID in the bottom right corner is different, and the privileges assigned to this user are different than those of the previous user. For instance, this user has rights to view three reports, as opposed to the previous user who could only view two reports. It stands to reason that the results of their reports will also differ.

In fact, that is exactly what happens when you click on Customer List. This time, the stored procedure returns a list of all the customers. The reason the full list is displayed is that this user has privileges to view all customers, whereas the previous user did not. These user privileges are a major advantage of using stored procedures over standard SQL calls.

In conclusion, ASA for CE offers all of the same functionality you've come to expect from a high-performance database engine with all the compactness of a CE application. Keep in mind that the above application shows off only a small portion of the features and benefits offered by Adaptive Server Anywhere for CE.

Oracle Lite Introduction

Oracle Lite is a powerful object-relational client database for mobile enterprise applications. Its built-in replication engine enables data to be synchronized with Oracle 7.3 (or higher) data servers. Its small footprint allows it to run on laptops and PDAs, including Windows CE devices.

Oracle Lite is an enabling technology that allows large-scale deployment of Windows CE devices for enterprise applications such as sales force automation, maintenance crew support, outpatient care support, etc.

Although widely used for personal information management, PDAs have not become mainstream business tools yet for two main reasons:

- The cost of accessing corporate data from mobile devices is prohibitive.
- PDAs could not previously do complex data management and processing.

Prohibitive Cost

Traditionally, the only available technology for accessing corporate data from PDAs has been wireless distant database querying and file exchanges. Wireless communication has two obvious handicaps, however: high cost and slow communication. These handicaps normally make permanent wireless connection of large fleets of PDAs with corporate databases and file systems too expensive.

Lack of Processing Power

Until now, there was no true object-relational database on the Windows CE platform that seriously impaired any development of data-intensive enterprise applications. Oracle Lite changes this.

Oracle Lite solves these two problems and enables large-scale deployment of Windows CE devices for business applications by doing the following:

- It allows fast and inexpensive access to corporate data on mobile devices.

- It enables data-intensive applications on PDAs.

Fast and Inexpensive Access to Corporate Data on Mobile Devices

Thanks to replication technology, a subset of the larger corporate database populates the local database. After the local database is populated, the mobile application accesses and modifies this local subset of data. This allows much faster transactions than wireless database queries. At regular intervals, the local database is synchronized with the master database. During synchronization, only the changes, not the entire subsets, are transferred between the central database and the local databases; the process is very bandwidth-efficient. Overall bandwidth cost is a fraction of that of wireless distant queries, with the same end user benefits.

Data-Intensive Applications on PDAs

Oracle Lite is a true object-relational database on the Windows CE platform and may be accessed through standard methods, such as ODBC. Because Oracle Lite is ODBC compliant, programming is truly easy and uses standard SQL statements. Oracle Lite is the database of choice for building any mobile enterprise application on the Windows CE platform and enables a wide range of mobile applications to be developed. These applications reduce the cost of tasks performed by mobile workers.

For further information regarding Oracle Lite solutions in your industry, visit the Oracle Lite Industry Solutions Guide at www.oracle.com/mobile/olite/. To download the Oracle Lite database engine, visit www.oracle.com/mobile/.

Oracle Lite for Windows CE

The Oracle Lite database engine is available on all Windows CE Handheld PC (HPC) and tablet devices running Windows CE 2 (and higher). With Oracle Lite, enterprise applications using standard SQL can run on Windows CE and have their data automatically synchronized with enterprise servers. Like Oracle Lite on the desktop or laptop, Oracle Lite on Windows CE offers a standard ODBC interface and takes full advantage of Oracle Advanced Replication.

Key Features

The key features of Oracle Lite are:

- Fully object-relational Oracle database for Windows CE

- Small footprint: 350KB core engine, 750KB with ODBC support

- Built-in bidirectional replication to Oracle data servers over multiple protocols

- Built-in subsetting and conflict resolution to support multiple unique clients

- Support for wireless client applications

ODBC Support

With the Oracle Lite ODBC driver for Windows CE, porting an existing SQL-based application can be as simple as recompiling it for the target Handheld PC using a tool such as Visual C++. Alternatively, an application can be developed from the ground up that supports complex SQL queries to be executed on the Handheld device. Oracle Lite for Windows CE leverages your investment in the tools and applications you already have by providing open data access. In addition, tools such as Oracle Navigator and SQL*Plus can be used from the desktop to access the Oracle Lite database on Windows CE through the Remote ODBC feature. Using this feature with Oracle Navigator, you can even drag and drop a table from a mainframe to Windows CE or from an Oracle server to Oracle Lite.

Application Development Support

Applications for the Handheld PC are most often developed and tested first on the desktop, after which they are then downloaded to the actual Handheld device. Oracle Lite for Windows CE provides support for this kind of cross-development environment, and developers have three different models to choose from:

- Applications can be developed using Oracle Lite for 95/98/NT first. Once perfected, the applications can then be recompiled for the target CE device.

- Developers can use the CE emulation mode support on an NT workstation. This allows rapid development and testing cycles without having to download to the CE device after every recompilation.

- Applications can be tested directly on the CE device to ensure proper functionality on the target platform.

In addition, Oracle Lite for Windows CE comes with a download utility to simplify application deployment to the CE device.

TIP

Currently, Oracle Lite on Windows CE only works with Visual C++ for CE. Other development tools will be supported as they become available for Windows CE.

Sample Application

The following code samples illustrate how the Oracle Lite database can be accessed on the CE device. The first segment defines an Execute primitive that allows a SQL statement to be passed and a result set to be returned.

```
// Execute a Statement and Return a Result Set
//
CSQLResult* COLiteDB :: Execute (LPCTSTR pszSQL)
{
  SWORD    len;
  SWORD    nCol;
  HSTMT    stmt;
  CWaitCursor wait;

  if (::SQLAllocStmt (m_dbc, &stmt) == SQL_SUCCESS)
  {
    if (::SQLExecDirect (stmt, (BYTE*)::MakeChar (pszSQL), SQL_NTS)
  == SQL_SUCCESS)
    {
      g_szBuff[0] = 0;
      if (::SQLNumResultCols (stmt, &nCol) == SQL_SUCCESS && nCol > 0)
      {
        CSQLResult* result = new CSQLResult (stmt, TRUE); //N Columns

        for (int i = 1; i <= nCol; i++)
        {
```

```
            if (::SQLDescribeCol (stmt, i, (BYTE*)g_szBuff,
sizeof(g_szBuff),
                &len, NULL, NULL, NULL, NULL) == SQL_SUCCESS)
                  result->AddColumn ((const char*)g_szBuff);
          }
          return result;
        }
        ::SQLFreeStmt (stmt, SQL_CLOSE);
        ::SQLExecDirect (stmt, g_pszCommit, SQL_NTS);
      }
      else
      {
        UCHAR state[32];
        SDWORD err;
        UCHAR msg[1024];
        SWORD len;

        ::SQLError (m_env, m_dbc, stmt, state, &err, msg, 1024, &len);
        state[6] = 0;
        wsprintf (g_szBuff, TEXT ("SQLExecDirect: Native=%d
message=%s"), err, MakeWideChar ((char*)state));
        ::SQLFreeStmt (stmt, SQL_CLOSE);
      }
      ::SQLFreeStmt (stmt, SQL_DROP);
    }
    return NULL;
  }
```

The code segment below shows how the Execute primitive can be called to create a table and insert rows.

```
///////////////////////////////////////////////////////////////////
//////
// CSampleApp initialization

BOOL CSampleApp::InitInstance()
{
  COLiteDB db;
  if (db.Connect())
  {
    db.Execute (_T ("CREATE TABLE TT (COL1 VARCHAR2(40), COL2
    VARCHAR2 (50))"));
    if (*db.GetError())
```

```
        AfxMessageBox (db.GetError());

    db.Execute (_T ("INSERT INTO TT VALUES ('TEST1', 'TEST2')"));
    if (*db.GetError())
      AfxMessageBox (db.GetError());

    db.Execute (_T ("UPDATE TT SET COL2 = 'TESTING ORACLE LITE'
WHERE COL1='TEST1'"));

    if (*db.GetError())
      AfxMessageBox (db.GetError());

    CSQLResult* pres = db.Execute (_T ("SELECT * FROM TT"));
    if (pres != NULL)
    {
      const CRowObj* pobj = pres->Fetch();
      while (pobj)
      {
        CString str = (LPCTSTR)pobj->GetAt (0);
        str += TEXT ("  ");
        str += (LPCTSTR)pobj->GetAt (1);
        AfxMessageBox (str);

        pobj = pres->Fetch();
      }
      delete pres;
    }
  }
  // Since the dialog has been closed, return FALSE so that we
  exit the
  // application, rather than start the application's message
  pump.return FALSE;
}
```

The full code sample can be found on the Oracle Lite 3.5 CD.

Oracle Lite Replication

Oracle Lite enables subquery subsetting for mobile users. Subquery subsetting is a technique that allows the server to identify the exact, unique subset of information that each user needs to see or is authorized to see. For instance, each sales representative gets only the information relating to his or her accounts. This subsetting capability extends to any tables in one-to-one, many-to-one, many-to-many, or one-to-many relationships between relevant tables. Not only do sales reps receive only the customer records unique to them, that uniqueness extends to any dependent or associated records in other tables such as order numbers, addresses, or other related information.

Subquery subsetting works hand in hand with Oracle Lite's extensive, powerful replication capabilities. Users receive only the records of interest to them; in addition, users can update only the records that are their responsiblity. Oracle Lite's replication functionality allows you to automatically copy information between Oracle Lite and Oracle servers. More than just a copy mechanism, replication takes two tables with the same structure and automatically merges them together at two or more locations, giving distributed users data synchronization with a centralized Oracle7 or Oracle8 server running anywhere in your enterprise.

Oracle Lite for CE offers three replication options:

- Wireless replication using Oracle Mobile Agents
- Internet replication
- File-based replication and disk file replication

Wireless Replication Using Oracle Mobile Agents   Oracle Lite allows users to do wireless replication using a store-and-forward method. This replication strategy uses Oracle Mobile Agents to pass changes to a replication agent on the server side and receive updated information from the server. The agent then handles all communication with the master site, applying and receiving changes on behalf of the snapshot site. Changes are then batched and returned to the snapshot site.

Oracle Mobile Agents is described more thoroughly in the "Oracle Mobile Agents" section later in this chapter.

Internet Replication   With a connection to the Internet, users can invoke replication and send the changes from the snapshot site to a Web application server through HTTP or MIME protocols. The Web application server then communicates with the master site (behind a firewall) to apply changes, receive changes intended for the snapshot site, and send those changes back over the Internet to the snapshot site. Changes can be sent almost any way the Internet allows, even via e-mail.

Internet replication allows any user who has an Internet connection to perform replication with the master site. It also minimizes the number of connections users have to make. For example, if they connect to the Internet to check mail or to browse, they can also send and receive database changes.

File-Based Replication and Disk File Replication With file-based replication mechanisms, Oracle Lite exposes its replication capabilities so that a developer can execute replication and post the snapshot changes to a file. The developer can then choose to move this file to the master site in whatever manner desired including MAPI, FTP, sneaker net, or flash memory cards. The master site will then apply the changes to the master table and place its changes in a file that the developer can move back to the snapshot site so as to apply the snapshot.

File-based replication gives developers control over how replication changes are moved to the master site. It also provides flexibility in how replication is performed during other types of connections (i.e., mail transfers).

Security

Oracle Lite can be made secure either for local data protection purposes or for transmission purposes. Users or user applications can encrypt an Oracle Lite database with a key as a password, send the database to a master site, and then connect to the encrypted database using the same key.

Oracle Mobile Agents

As an integral part of Oracle's mobile computing strategy, Oracle Mobile Agents provides the connectivity required for mobile computing. This flexible, standards-based solution provides the connectivity for all mobile users, whether LAN based, dial-up, or wireless, on a wide variety of platforms.

Anytime, Anywhere Oracle Mobile Agents is a mobile middleware product, that is, an asynchronous, secure, store-and-forward messaging system that provides the foundation on which to quickly build and deploy mobile applications. Oracle Mobile Agents supports a variety of wireless networks, including packet data networks and dial-up and LAN connections. Its scaleable architecture can add mobility to and enhance the productivity of any application in the enterprise.

Optimized for the Mobile Environment The client/agent/server architecture used by Oracle Mobile Agents minimizes traffic over the wireless link, which is often slower and less reliable than a LAN; this is a key feature for any mobile application. It minimizes traffic by using a software agent to work on behalf of the mobile client. While traditional client/server operations require the client to remain connected for the duration of a transaction, Oracle Mobile Agents requires the client to remain connected only long enough to submit a request to an agent. With combined data compression and carefully optimized message size, expensive connect time can be kept to a minimum. From a user perspective, application performance over wireless links becomes comparable to a LAN connection.

Wireless Replication with Oracle Lite   Oracle Lite exploits the features of Oracle Mobile Agents to provide wireless replication. Replication is the synchronization of data between databases, in this case an Oracle Lite database on a client and a server side Oracle7 or Oracle8 database. Wireless replication provides flexibility to a mobile user to replicate data at any time—for example, right after a large order has been entered into the client database—to ensure that the order-processing commences immediately. Using Oracle Mobile Agents for wireless replication requires no additional programming.

Developing Applications and Agents   The Oracle Mobile Agents architecture requires that a client application be modified (or written from scratch) to communicate with the flexible Oracle Mobile Agents' API. Client applications can access Oracle Mobile Agents via OLE v2, or Windows' DLLs, or by using the ActiveX interface. For new applications, all of the typical development packages can be used.

An agent must also be written that will act on behalf of the application at the server, and this agent will also communicate with the Oracle Mobile Agents infrastructure via the same API. The role of the agent is to keep all of the highly interactive network traffic within the corporate network, thus minimizing network round trips over the mobile link. Additionally, the agent allows work to be performed for the client even when the client is not active or connected to the system. Agents are a combination of code you write and a code library, called the Agent Event Manager, supplied as part of Oracle Mobile Agents.

Secure and Reliable   The public nature of most wireless services raises valid security concerns. Oracle Mobile Agents addresses these concerns by providing configurable authentication, encryption, and tamper proofing, all of which are implemented using industry standard algorithms. Further, Oracle Mobile Agents' store-and-forward architecture guarantees message delivery. If a mobile worker is unavailable or suddenly loses coverage, messages are queued rather than discarded. Together, these services allow the mobile worker to work when and where they want, without worrying about network availability and knowing that corporate information is safe.

Samples

The sample program in the Odbc directory creates the table tt (in the database \oracle\polite.odb) and inserts one new row into the table tt containing the data:

```
'Test1'|'Testing Oracle Lite'
```

TIP   The statements used to create the table and insert data into the table may be seen in the file SAMPLE.CPP located in the Odbc directory.

The program then prints out the contents of all rows in tt in separate dialog boxes on the Windows CE device.

The REPSVR sample under the replication subdirectory demonstrates bi-directional replication between the Windows CE device and an Oracle Web Server.

When compiling REPSVR.exe, the application is copied to the Windows CE device. The first logon screen requires the server user name, password, connect string, the <Server URL>\repcartx, and the Communication Type (HTTP or OMA). A sample URL is: HTTP://testserver.us.oracle.com/repcartx. The second logon screen requires the local user name, password, and ODBC DSN (such as POLITE).

The main screen gives you the option to create a snapshot, add a snapshot to the snapshot group, drop a snapshot, or replicate.

Comparison of Features

Because the different vendors' sample applications only show off a small portion of each product's full potential, in this section we'll look at some comparison tables that show what each one offers. This way, you can pick the one that best suits your needs. In addition, for the purposes of having a full and complete picture, we'll also include the CE database engine in the tables.

The features we'll be examining are:

- Is the data automatically compressed?

- How does the data get copied to/synched with desktop data?

- How much storage space does the engine require?
- Does it support SQL?
- Does it support stored procedures?
- Does it support user privileges?

Is the Data Automatically Compressed?

CE	Raima	Sybase	Oracle
Yes	No	No	No

CE's own native engine is the only one that automatically compresses data, unless you explicitly tell it not to.

How Does the Data Get Copied To/Synched with Desktop Data?

CE	Raima	Sybase	Oracle
Custom Coding (some automatic functionality)	Custom Coding	Automated for us	Automated for us

How Much Storage Space Does the Engine Require?

CE	Raima	Sybase	Oracle
None (part of the OS)	500K	1MB	1MB

Does the Engine Support SQL?

CE	Raima	Sybase	Oracle
No	Subset	Yes	Yes

Does the Engine Support Stored Procedures?

CE	Raima	Sybase	Oracle
No	No	Yes	Yes

Does the Engine Support User Privileges?

CE	Raima	Sybase	Oracle
No	No	Yes	Yes

Summary

In this chapter, we looked at some of the features offered by third-party databases for Windows CE. We also compared the CE database engine to those of Raima, Sybase, and Oracle, with the following results:

- CE's database engine is towards the low end, but it is still very attractive due to its compression and its zero footprint.

- Raima's RDM/CE is somewhere towards the high-middle range, with a number of professional features, such as true indexing and very small footprint.

- Oracle and Sybase are very high end, with features that we've come to expect from these two database engine leaders.

Just as with any technical implementation issue, there are always tradeoffs. Choosing the database engine that's right for you is no different. For many applications, the CE database engine will be adequate, if not overkill. For others, stored procedures will be a must.

CHAPTER

THIRTEEN

Windows CE Case Studies and Cost Analysis

- Study 1: Inventory Management System

- Study 2: Insurance Agents in the Field

- Study 3: Choosing Your Development Machine

In this chapter, we'll look at several example case studies that are based on real case studies and stories about how CE devices are being used in the real world. The purpose of this chapter is to provide some sample ideas on how CE is being used or could be used and the costs of implementing CE-based solutions.

Study 1: Inventory Management System

An inventory management system is perhaps the most frequently cited ideal Windows CE solution. The vision of CE devices as an inventory management tool often goes something like this:

"The user performing the actual inventorying would walk through the warehouse with either a Palm-size PC or Handheld PC and a bar-code scanner attached to this device. They would travel the warehouse and scan in the bar-codes on the boxes as they went. The information could be automatically recorded in a database and then synchronized with the main database when the device is attached to a Desktop computer sometime later."

But is the technical implementation of this process correct? Is it cost-effective for the company? Is this really the best use of some CE devices? In short, does it make sense for the company to do this?

Of course, some of these questions are really a matter of opinion (and some might even cause fierce debate), but others can be answered with a careful analysis of the plan.

The Technical Issues

First, let's examine the technical details. When it comes to the technical details, there are really only three major questions:

- Is the bar-code scanner attachment the most efficient way to implement this solution?

- Is it best to synchronize the data afterward or is there a better alternative?

- Which form factors can be used?

The Bar-Code Scanner

It seems that a bar-code scanner is, in fact, the best way to implement this solution, for a number of reasons. First, bar codes are extremely efficient. In fact, it's safe to say that almost every large inventory management system uses bar codes in some way.

Second, as you saw in Chapter 1, the leading bar-code devices for Windows CE scan the bar code and enter the input into the keyboard buffer as though the numeric values of the bar code were typed in by the user. The advantage of such a system is that you don't have to write any special code to support a bar-code scanner. Simply write your application to accept keyboard input, then hook up the bar-code scanner. This means that you can deliver a fully functional solution, even if the customer/user decides not to include the bar-code scanner in the final package. Further, since these readers are available in either PCMCIA or CF (compact flash) implementations, you still have maximum flexibility in terms of any unused port(s) on the CE device.

NOTE   As mentioned in Chapter 1, the maker of these CE barcode readers is Socket Communications (`http://www.socketcom.com`).

Synchronization vs. a Wireless Connection

The next issue to look at is whether the data should be synchronized after it's been collected or whether you should use a wireless connection to ensure that the data is always accurate up to the minute.

The main benefit of synchronization is its low cost of implementation. CE devices are automatically configured to hook up to a Desktop machine and transfer data over a serial cable. The downside to a synchronization-based solution is that your main databases will never be 100 percent accurate and will always lag behind the real count of items in your warehouse by at least eight hours.

A wireless LAN solution, however, ensures that the data in your main databases is at most a few seconds old. But there is also a higher cost associated with this way of updating your main database.

Also, the size of the warehouse becomes an issue here because a wireless LAN hub has a range of approximately 500 square feet. This means that it might well require more than one or two wireless LAN hubs to cover the entire warehouse. While this might appear to be expensive, it may be that the benefit of having all of the inventory data updated as the information is being scanned in far outweighs the cost of the wireless LAN hubs.

The main difference between this issue and the bar-code issue is that this one must be decided before any application development is begun. If you're going to connect to a database server, you'll need to build the application with support for some kind of wireless client libraries. As you can imagine, this is a much more complicated task once the application's already been written.

Form Factor Choices

As with any part of this system, there are trade-offs when it comes to choosing the right form factor. For inventory management, though, there are really only two practical form factors available:

- Palm-size PC
- Handheld PC

Palm-Size PC The advantages of the Palm-size PC for this application are somewhat obvious: their small size means that the user is free to move about and can access harder-to-reach areas more easily. The disadvantage of a Palm-size PC for this solution is that PPCs only have a single CF (compact flash) slot. This means that there is no way to connect them to a wireless LAN, as the wireless LAN cards are PCMCIA based. And, even if there were wireless LAN cards that worked off of the CF slot, there wouldn't be any place for the bar-code scanner to attach to the device if the CF slot were used for the LAN connection. Clearly, then, the PPC devices are only a good solution in cases where the data does not need to be updated live but can be synched later.

Handheld PC The Handheld PC devices have that extra slot that makes them a more powerful solution to this problem. HPCs have a place for a bar-code scanner (the CF slot) and a place for a wireless LAN connector (the PCMCIA slot). However, the HPC devices are almost always more expensive and somewhat larger in bulk. Low cost is still one advantage possessed by the PPCs.

Cost

Let's now take a look at the costs of implementing such a solution to this inventory management problem. Depending on the system purchased, traditional, non-CE–based inventory management devices can cost upward of $2000 per unit; let's see how that compares to the possible Windows CE–based solutions.

WARNING   Please note that all prices should be considered approximate guides only. Prices may—and probably will—change by the time you read this.

Palm-Size PC–Based Solution Cost Analysis

Table 13.1 shows the Palm-size PC–related form factor expenses.

TABLE 13.1:   Palm-Size PC–Related Expenses

Item	Maker	Model	Cost
Palm-size PC	Casio	E-11	$299
Bar-code Scanner CF card	Socket Communications	N/A	$180 (est.)
Total Cost			**$479**

Handheld PC–Based Solution Cost Analysis

Table 13.2 shows the Handheld PC–related form factor expenses. The main difference here is that you must figure in the additional costs for the wireless LAN hardware.

TABLE 13.2:   Handheld PC–Related Expenses

Item	Maker	Model	Cost
Handheld PC	Casio	PA-2400	$499 (est.)
Bar-code Scanner CF card	Socket Communications	N/A	$180 (est.)
RangeLAN2 PCMCIA card	Proxim	N/A	$595
Total Cost			**$1274**

In addition to these expenses, which are per-device costs, there is the cost of one or more wireless hubs (about one hub per 500–1000 square feet). This cost is displayed in Table 13.3.

TABLE 13.3: Wireless LAN Hub Cost

Item	Maker	Model	Cost
RangeLAN2 Ethernet Access Point	Proxim	N/A	$1895

NOTE   As mentioned in Chapter 1, you should be using Proxim's (`http://www.proxim.com`) RangeLAN2 family of products for your wireless LAN calculations.

Although the HPC solution costs more, it also offers much more in the way of network connectivity and, more specifically, data access.

Conclusion of Study 1

This example is a very popular real world use of CE devices. It turns out that in many cases, the benefits of either solution—whether you choose the PPC or the HPC—far outweigh the cost. As mentioned above, most bar-code-based inventory systems cost more than $2000 per unit. At a cost of approximately $500, the PPC-based solution is not only very high-tech, it's also very, very cheap!

Study 2: Insurance Agents in the Field

One issue that seems to have a lot of consumers' attention is the benefits of an HPC/Pro device, such as the Hewlett-Packard Jornada, over a standard Windows 98/NT laptop. One of the advantages that's often cited is the 10-hour (or greater) battery life of an HPC/Pro device as compared with the one-and-a-half to two-hour battery life of a laptop.

Here's a practical example that shows just how much of a difference an HPC/Pro device can make.

Consider insurance agents working on claims in the field. They need to take pictures of property damage and then file those pictures, along with their reports, once they return to the office. Currently, however, they have no really good way to preview their pictures and make sure that the pictures did the job.

Solution

If these agents could use digital cameras that store images on compact flash memory cards, they could transfer the pictures over to the handheld device using the CF slot. Their HPC/Pro devices, using Sierra Imaging's Image Expert for CE, would allow them to preview and, if necessary, retake any pictures that didn't turn out as they expected.

Here again, you are faced with a similar set of questions: Is this the best use of the insurance agency's money? What are they really getting for their money?

Let's examine how well this solution meets the agents' needs.

The Technical Issues

There are really two technical issues that need to be addressed here:

- Is a digital camera the right tool for the job?
- Is a CE-based HPC/Pro the right tool for the job?

Digital Camera

First, let's examine the question of whether or not a digital camera is the right tool for the job.

Many people who rely on some kind of photography in their professions have probably already begun to switch to digital cameras. There are many advantages to digital cameras, such as more pictures, not having to get your pictures developed, being able to preview your pictures, etc.

So a digital camera is probably the right tool for this job on its technical merit alone. As you'll see in the cost analysis section, there's another very compelling reason to go to a digital camera.

HPC/Pro

The HPC/Pro is an obvious choice here simply based on the battery life. If the agents were to use a laptop instead, they would only be able to work with it on battery power for a maximum of 2 hours. The HPC/Pro class devices all run for 10 or more hours on a fully charged battery.

The extra eight hours of battery life means that the agents could easily spend a full eight-hour day in the field without worrying about their computer going down.

Further, there's already very inexpensive image editing/viewing software available for CE devices, so there's no real difference between the CE-based solution and the laptop-based solution in terms of the functionality needed for this purpose.

Cost

Now, let's take a look at cost and see if our technical conclusions are justified. First, you've got to select your hardware.

For the camera, let's use the Canon PowerShot A5, which seems to be a fairly popular model of digital camera. It uses compact flash memory and costs about $699.

And, since we'll be doing a pricing comparison here, let's choose a laptop. Most reviews seem to like comparing the HPC/Pro devices to the Sony Vaio ultrathin laptop, which costs about $1999.

Now let's see how this stacks up against the Windows CE–based solution.

WARNING Again, please note that all prices should be considered approximate guides only. Prices may—and probably will—change by the time you read this.

Laptop-Based Solution Cost Analysis

Table 13.4 shows the laptop-related expenses, if you decide to choose that type of hardware.

TABLE 13.4: Laptop-Related Expenses

Item	Maker	Model	Cost
Laptop	Sony	Vaio	$1999 (est.)
Digital Camera	Canon	PowerShot A5	$699 (est.)
Total Cost			**$2698**

HPC/Pro-Based Solution Cost Analysis

Now let's look at the HPC/Pro-based solution. Table 13.5 shows the Handheld PC–related expenses, if you decide to choose that form factor. The main difference here is that you must figure in the additional costs for the wireless LAN hardware.

TABLE 13.5: HPC/Pro-Related Expenses

Item	Maker	Model	Cost
HPC/Pro	Hewlett-Packard	Jornada	$899 (est.)
Digital Camera	Canon	PowerShot A5	$699 (est.)
Graphics S/W	Sierra Imaging	Image Expert	$50
Total Cost			**$1648**

NOTE   Sierra Imaging's (`http://www.sierraimaging.com`) Image Expert for CE is the leading graphics software for Windows CE.

In addition to being the right choice based strictly on technical merit, the Windows CE–based solution is also significantly cheaper—by $1050, to be exact.

Conclusion of Study 2

An HPC/Pro device proved to clearly be the winner on technical merits, as well as the winner on price. This is a perfect example of putting CE to work.

Study 3: Choosing Your Development Machine

One type of study that will probably be of the most interest to you as a developer is how to choose your first CE device for development purposes.

Unless you're committing to CE full time, chances are you'll want to test the waters, so to speak, by purchasing one device and working with it as your development machine until you have had a chance to fully evaluate Windows CE. Yes, you can theoretically develop an entire application in the emulator, but it's not generally recommended practice. At some point, you'll need or want to test your application on a real, honest-to-goodness device, just to make sure that the emulator didn't give you a false impression of how your program was running.

Solution

In this case, there really is no clear-cut solution. But let's take a look at the pros and cons of each device type and from that, perhaps, you'll be able to find the one that's right for you.

PPC Devices

Palm-size PCs are great for applications where

- Minimal data entry is required
- Heavy reading isn't required
- The lack of a PCMCIA slot is acceptable
- The information displayed can be made to fit in the 320×240 display area

If your future application is likely to be OK with those constraints, by all means, consider a PPC device. Their main advantage from the prospective CE developer's point of view, as we'll see in a moment, is their cost. As a development tool, the PPC devices are more demanding than an HPC/Pro because getting an application to look good on a PPC device requires more work than on either of the other platforms.

HPC Devices

HPCs offer a midrange option for applications where

- A keyboard is required
- A PCMCIA slot is required
- A larger screen is required

If that sounds like your future application, then an HPC is the way to go. One additional advantage of an HPC is that most HPCs are still running CE 2. If your program runs on an HPC running CE 2, it should run on all of the CE platforms.

HPC/Pro Devices

HPC/Pros occupy a unique niche in the array of portable devices available. They are near-laptops with just about everything a laptop offers. They're perfect for applications where

- A keyboard is required
- A PCMCIA slot is required
- A much larger screen is required

If your future application fits the bill, then you'll want to consider an HPC/Pro device. And if you don't already own a laptop, you'll want to *seriously* consider the HPC/Pro devices. As a laptop substitute, the HPC/Pro devices will likely prove very adequate for most uses. One thing to watch out for, though, is that HPC/Pros run CE 2.11, which offers a number of features not available on other versions of CE. In other words, if you want your application to compile for all of the 2.*x* versions of CE, you will have to be extra cautious when coding to make sure that you use only those functions available on all CE devices.

Cost

Table 13.6 shows the different approximate costs of each of the form factors.

TABLE 13.6: CE Form Factors and Their Approximate Costs

Form Factor	Cost
PPC	$200–$299
HPC	$400–$499
HPC/Pro	$899

As of this writing, most PPC devices are priced right around $300, but some have been priced as low as $200. This means that for a relatively small investment (the cost of a new hard drive, perhaps), you can have an actual CE device to test and develop with.

HPC devices are getting cheaper all the time, with the price hovering around the $400–$499 range, while HPC/Pros are still the most expensive of the lot, priced at around $899.

Conclusion of Study 3

The conclusion you make really depends on your own personal CE needs and plans. If you're just experimenting, the PPC devices are probably the best low-risk, low-investment strategy. If cost is not an issue, however, either the HPC or the HPC/Pro devices will serve you quite nicely.

Summary

In this chapter, you saw at two examples of how CE devices can be used. In addition, you examined the pros and cons of each CE device so that you can pick the most appropriate CE device for your development purposes.

In the next chapter, you'll see how to put the finishing touches on a Windows CE application.

PART IV

Finishing Touches

■ Chapter 14: Distributing Your CE Application

■ Chapter 15: Microsoft's Logo Requirements

Distributing Your CE Application

- Creating Help for Windows CE

- The Two Types of CE Help Files

- Installing Your Software

In this chapter, we'll explore what it takes to put the finishing touches on your CE applications. Specifically, you'll learn how to create help files for Windows CE, what the different types of help files are, and what the advantages and disadvantages of each one are. Then, to round out the chapter, we'll look at the available options as far as setup or install programs are concerned.

Creating Help for Windows CE

If you've ever written help files for Windows 3.*x*, 98, or NT, you know what a pain they can be… Some of their more notable problems are that

- The text portion of the help files has to be written in an arcane set of formatting commands known as RTF

- The pictures and text all have to be compiled into an HLP file

- If any portion of the help file is incorrect, the whole thing has to be recompiled from scratch

The whole process was much more complex and time-consuming than it needed to be. Thankfully, though, Windows CE has done away with the Windows 98/NT help-file system completely!

Instead, the CE help system uses a unique subset of HTML—the same set of universally supported formatting commands used to create Web pages.

TIP

One of the nice things about an HTML-based help system is that testing and debugging your help is a much quicker process. That's because you can actually edit the help files *on the device* if you find a small mistake and want to correct it immediately. This means you can test your fix right away, without having the delay of copying the help file from the Desktop to the device.

The Two Types of CE Help Files

Just like the Windows 98/NT help system, which has the .cnt, or Contents, file and the .hlp file formats, Windows CE also has two help file-types:

1. .htc, or Help Contents file (comparable to the .cnt file of 98/NT)

2. .htp, or Help Topic file (comparable to the .hlp file of 98/NT)

NOTE A file extension of .html will also work for help files; in fact, this is the required file extension for PPC help files.

The HTC/Contents format is used, as you've probably guessed, to store a table of contents, almost like a home page that contains links to one or more Help Topics. Each of these Help Topics is then contained in a separate HTP/Topic file.

The HTC/Contents file has only one purpose, but the HTP/Topic files have two possible purposes:

- Use as a file containing one or more single topics (subpages of an HTC file)

- Use as a standalone, self-contained help file, with a reduced table of contents and multiple smaller topics.

One way to organize your program's help system is to use one HTC/Contents file and multiple HTP/Topic files. This is the way you'd probably organize your help system if you had, say, a complex program with multiple features in which the user might need additional instruction. The tradeoffs of this multiple-file help system can best be viewed in this way:

Multiple-File Help System	(HTC File Paired with One or More HTP Files)
Advantages	With minor tweaking, can be created with an off-the-shelf HTML editor.
	Topic files may be stored anywhere on device.
Disadvantage	More difficult to maintain and test.
	All files must be located in the \Windows directory.

The other way to organize your program's help system is to put everything (including a brief contents page) into one single HTP/Topic file. This is almost certainly the way you'd organize your help if you were writing an application on the scale of complexity close to a notepad-like application. The trade-offs of the single-file system can best be viewed in this way:

Single-File Help System	(Stand-Alone HTP File)
Advantage	Easier to maintain and test a single help file.
Disadvantages	Can't be easily created with an off-the-shelf HTML editor. See the "FrontPage and HTP Files" sidebar below for more information.
	Help files can be anywhere on the device, but links must then contain full paths, even if the link points to the same file in which it appears.
	The only exceptions to this is when the file is in the \Windows directory, in which case your internal links do not have to include the full path.

NOTE   Most of the applications that are already on your CE device, including those written by Microsoft, use the single-file help system.

Let's examine each help system in detail, dissecting a sample system in each style.

The Single-File Help System

First, let's take a look at the simpler single-file help system, where all of the help topics and the contents are placed in a single HTP file.

At first glance, the source for one such HTP file might look a little like a Web site desperately in need of content. Figure 14.1 shows a simple HTP file, which has one Contents entry and one topic.

FIGURE 14.1:

A simple HTP help file, as it would be viewed on a CE device

This is the source of that same HTP file:

```
<HTML>
<HEAD>
<META HTTP-EQUIV="Content-Type" Content="template.htp#contents">
<title>Template Single-File Help System</title>
</HEAD>
<BODY BGCOLOR=#FFFFFF TEXT=#000000>
<!-- PegHelp -->
<p>
<a name="contents"></a><b>The Contents</b>
</p>
<p>
<a href="template.htp#topic_1">Topic #1</a>
</p>
<!--now include a link (image) to next topic-->
<div align=right>
<a href="template.htp#topic_1">
<img src="arrowr.2bp" border=0></a>
</div>
<!-- PegHelp -->
<a name="topic_1"></a>
<b>Topic #1</b>
<!--now include a link (image) to the "main" page or topic-->
<div align=right>
<a href="template.htp#contents">
<img src="arrowl.2bp" border=0>
</a>
```

```
<!-- PegHelp -->
</BODY>
</HTML>
```

As you can see, it's not very complex. However, as with most CE development tasks, everything has to be done just right. So, in order to get a better understanding of the various parts of this help file, let's take it one step at a time.

The Header

Let's take a look at a typical CE help-file header, which looks very similar to the header of a standard HTML document:

```
<!DOCTYPE HTML PUBLIC "-//W3C//DTD HTML 3.2 Final//EN">
<HTML>
<HEAD>
<META HTTP-EQUIV="Content-Type" Content="template.htp#contents">
<title>Template Single-File Help System</title>
</HEAD>
<BODY BGCOLOR=#FFFFFF TEXT=#000000>
```

The main difference between an HTML document and an HTP document is that the HTP single-file help system requires that the META HTTP-EQUIV "Content-Type" tag contain the name of the help file (template.htp), followed by the pound sign (#), followed by the name or anchor of the first Contents entry. Hence the line:

```
<META HTTP-EQUIV="Content-Type" Content="template.htp#contents">
```

FrontPage and HTP Files

Incidentally, it is this customization of the "Content-Type" entry that makes it difficult to create single-file HTP help systems with off-the-shelf HTML editors such as Microsoft FrontPage 98. Although FrontPage will allow you to add, modify, and delete most other HTTP-EQUIV tags, it does not allow you to change the "Content-Type" entry. Like most documents, help files often require multiple revisions. The consequence of this is that each time you save your help file for testing, you must manually edit this line. As you can imagine, this can be quite annoying. That's why it's easier to simply use Notepad to create and edit the single-file system HTP help files.

The *<!--PegHelp-->* Comment

The next thing you'll probably notice about the HTP source is the line that reads:

```
<!-- PegHelp -->
```

Yes, this is just a fairly standard-looking comment tag, but the PegHelp text means that it serves a special purpose for the CE help viewer. The `<!-- PegHelp -->` comment is used as a separator between sections. It must also appear before the contents and after the final topic.

The next chunk of the HTP file is the only entry on the Contents page:

```
<p>
<a name="contents"></a><b>The Contents</b>
```

Here's where you could list the entire contents of your help file, along with some introductory text, perhaps:

```
</p>
<p>
<a href="template.htp#topic_1">Topic #1</a>
</p>
```

For the most part, this is fairly standard HTML. The href tag is what's of real interest here. It looks and works just like a standard href tag, and in the case of single-file HTP files, it's how you provide a link to a topic—subtopic_1 in this case.

Next, you have a link to subtopic_1, this time via an image.

```
<!--now include a link (image) to next topic-->
<div align=right>
<a href="template.htp#topic_1">
<img src="arrowr.2bp" border=0></a>
</div>
```

Here again, this is fairly standard HTML, and all that's really worth noting is that the image is a 2-bit-per-pixel bitmap file, instead of a more traditional GIF or JPEG file format.

WARNING The Windows CE Help Viewer does not support GIF and JPEG images; only Windows CE bitmap types can be displayed in help files. Be especially careful of this if you're porting some existing HTML-based help documents to CE.

The Rest of the HTP file

The next section of the HTP file is the first actual topic of the help file, again, beginning with the `<!-- PegHelp -->` comment:

```
<!-- PegHelp -->
<a name="topic_1"></a>
<b>Topic #1</b>
```

Here's where you could provide some information about topic #1 to the user. For instance, maybe they need advice about how to use the help system.

Next, just as with the end of the Contents entry, you have a link (again via an image), this time taking the user back to the previous topic:

```
<!--now include a link (image) to the "main" page or topic-->
<div align=right>
<a href="template.htp#contents">
<img src="arrow1.2bp" border=0>
</a>
```

Finally, you have a closing `<!-- PegHelp -->` comment, followed by the standard HTML closing tags.

```
<!-- PegHelp -->
</BODY>
</HTML>
```

Additional HTP File Tricks!

There's one additional trick that you can make your HTP files do, and that is to display some static text (or links) at the beginning of every topic in the help file.

Simply by inserting any valid HTP/HTML tag after the `<BODY BGCOLOR=#FFFFFF TEXT=#000000>` tag and before the first `<!-- PegHelp -->` comment, you can cause that text to appear as the first thing on every page in the help file.

You might want to exploit this trick to let the user know that they can always find the latest information on your Web site, as in this example:

```
<!-- ... -->
<BODY BGCOLOR=#FFFFFF TEXT=#000000>
<i>Please visit http://www.ce-faq.com</i><hr>
<!-- PegHelp -->
<!-- ... -->
```

Continued on next page

When viewed on a CE device, the HTP file looks like this:

Don't forget: The single-file help system requires you to either use full paths in your links or that you put all of your HTP files in the \Windows\ directory!

The Multiple-File Help System: The HTC File

The layout of the multiple-file help system is even closer to standard HTML than the HTP file you just examined. And, the best part about the multiple-file help system is that the files are so close to standard HTML that you can create and edit them using an off-the-shelf HTML editor such as FrontPage 98.

To develop a multiple-file help system, you must first create an HTC/Contents file. Figure 14.2 shows what a fairly standard HTC file might look like when viewed on a CE device.

Here's what the source code for that HTC file looks like:

```
<html>
<head>
<title>This is the Main Topic</title>
<meta http-equiv=refer content="">
</head>
<body>
<h3>This is the Table of Contents for our help file!</h3>
```

```
<p><a href="file://this_is_topic1.htp">this way to topic #1</a></p>
<p><a href="file://this_is_topic2.htp">or topic #2, if you
prefer</a></p>
</body>
</html>
```

FIGURE 14.2:

A standard HTC as viewed on a CE device

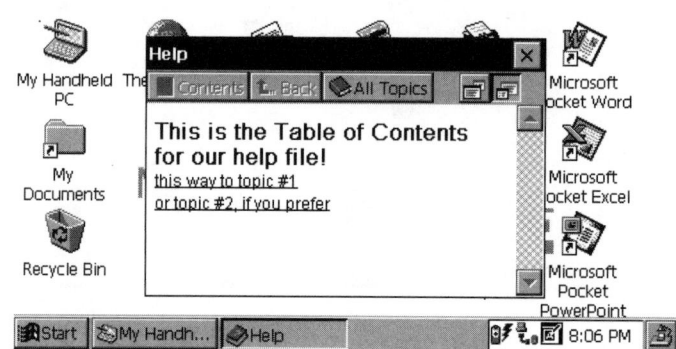

Probably the first thing you noticed about this HTC file is that it's even simpler than the HTP file you just examined. But just to be sure that you understand everything in it, let's once again take it apart, one section at a time.

The Header

First, let's take a look at a standard HTC file header:

```
<html>
<head>
<title>This is the Main Topic</title>
<meta http-equiv=refer content="">
</head>
```

The only point of real interest in this header is the fact that it's truly a standard HTML header. Unlike the HTP file you just looked at, this one has nothing unique or custom about it, and that's one of the main reasons it's possible to create these files with a standard HTML editor.

The Table of Contents

Now you come to the Table of Contents section for your HTC file. This is literally the body of your document:

```
<body>
<h3>This is the Table of Contents for your help file!</h3>

<p><a href="file://this_is_topic1.htp">this way to topic #1</a></p>
<p><a href="file://this_is_topic2.htp">or topic #2, if you
prefer</a></p>
</body>
</html>
```

In this example, the Table of Contents consists of a line announcing the table of contents:

```
<h3>This is the Table of Contents for your help file!</h3>
```

This is then followed by links to the two topics in our minimal help system:

```
<p><a href="file://this_is_topic1.htp">this way to topic #1</a></p>
<p><a href="file://this_is_topic2.htp">or topic #2, if you prefer</a></p>
```

The important point about these links is that they're just standard HTML code. This is just another reason why the multiple-file help systems are much easier to create.

Also, note that because there really aren't any topics, there aren't any of the `<!-- PegHelp -->` tags which pepper the single-file help system's HTP files.

TIP   Although Microsoft's sample help files show tags such as `<a href="file:/ /this_is_topic1.htp">` omitting the double slashes after "`file:`", this does not appear to matter.

Table of Contents Entry Tags

In this sample HTC file, the Table of Contents entries are listed as individual paragraphs, as demonstrated by the use of the `<p>` and `</p>` tags. However, which tags you use is largely a matter of personal preference, and you can use any number of tags to list the entries in your Table of Contents.

Continued on next page

Officially, Microsoft's documentation recommends the use of the <menu> tag, which can be used to list any number of items so that they are indented and appear as one block of text. The following illustration shows what your simple HTC file would look like if you had used the **menu** tag instead of individual paragraphs.

It's also worth noting that Microsoft and many others do not use the <menu> tag at all but instead choose *list tags*, such as <UL> and <LI>.

Now that we've seen how simple an HTC file can be, let's see how simple a multiple-file help system's HTP files can be.

The Multiple-File Help System: The HTP File

When creating a multiple-file help system, you can use HTP files to contain

- multiple topics per file, *or*

- one topic per file.

If you choose the first option, the document source of your HTP file will end up looking exactly like a single-file help system's HTP file—in fact, it will look exactly like the one featured in the second section of this chapter. This, of course, means that you're back to HTP files that can't easily be created with off-the-shelf HTML editors. In other words, you could end up losing all of the advantages of the multiple-file help system.

However, if you choose the second option, the document source of your HTP file will look very different from the single-file help system's doocument source. Figure 14.3 shows one such HTP file as it looks in the CE Help Viewer.

FIGURE 14.3:

Multiple-file help
system HTP file

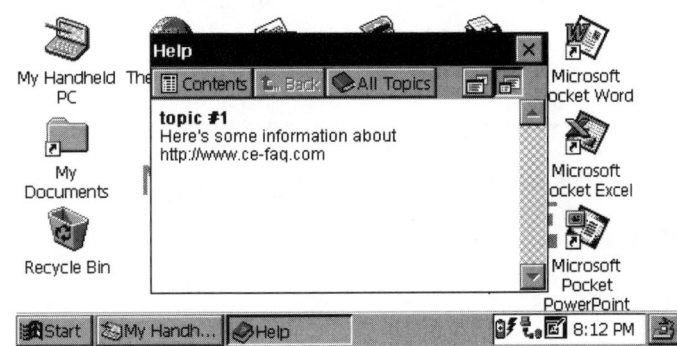

The source for this document is amazingly simple:

```
<html>
<head>
<meta http-equiv="refer" content="file://the_contents.htc">
<title>some stuff</title>
</head>
<body>

<b>topic #1</b><br>

<p>Here's some information about
http://www.ce-faq.com</p>
</body>
</html>
```

The first point you'll notice about this HTP file is that it is almost entirely standard HTML formatting commands. In fact, there's only one line in the entire file that's CE-specific: an entry in the `<meta>` tag section of the header.

The Custom *<Meta>* Tag

The FrontPage 98 help defines `<meta>` tag as, "An HTML tag that must appear in the `<head>` portion of the page. `<Meta>` tags supply information about a page but do not affect its appearance."

The <meta> tag in your HTP file looks like this:

```
<meta http-equiv="refer" content="file://the_contents.htc">
```

In this case, your <meta> tag is used to tell the CE Help Viewer that your HTP file refers to a certain HTC file; specifically, the_contents.htc. Aside from that, everything else in the HTP file is standard HTML and can easily be generated with FrontPage 98 or any other HTML editor.

Creating the Custom <*Meta*> Tag / *HTTP_EQUIV* Values within FrontPage 98

1. Open an existing HTP document, or create a new document.

2. Right-click on the document and select Page Properties from the pop-up menu.

3. Click the Custom tab, as shown below.

4. Click the Add button. The System Meta Value dialog box appears.

5. In the box marked Name, type **refer**.

6. In the box marked Value, type **file://**, followed by the CE path and file name of your contents file.

7. Click OK. That's it!

Now you know everything there is to know about CE help systems and how to create them. The next issue to tackle is the setup program—in short, how do you get your applications onto the end user's device?

Launching CE's Help Viewer from Your Application

Under Windows 98/NT, the help-viewer application is called `winhlp32.exe`; under Windows CE, the help-viewer application is called `peghelp.exe`. To launch the help viewer and cause it to bring up a specific help file, use code that looks something like this:

```
case WM_HELP: //handling a WM_HELP message
     PROCESS_INFORMATION pi;
     TCHAR szAppName[MAX_PATH] = TEXT("peghelp.exe");
     TCHAR szCmdLine[MAX_PATH] = TEXT("\\My App\\MyHelp.HTP");
     dwCreate = 0;
     CreateProcess(szAppName, szCmdLine, NULL, NULL, FALSE,
dwCreate, NULL, NULL, NULL, &pi);
```

Getting the Application to the User's Device

When it comes to installing your program on a user's CE device, you have two options.

The first option is to create a set of arcane, confusing, and generally difficult-to-use files and tools. If you decide to do this, you will need to create a setup program of your own design. This type of installation doesn't have to be fancy, though—it just needs to be able to copy files and launch another program. The advantage to this method is that it is free. The tools that you'll use, while difficult to master, are usually included with the CE toolkits or should be available from the Microsoft Web site. Let's call this option the Cab Wizard option, named for the tool you'll be using to create your installations, `cabwiz.exe`.

The second option is to use a graphical, familiar tool that allows you to create the setup in a few simple steps. You won't have to create your own setup program, and you'll have a complete, customized installation quickly and easily. This is the InstallShield for CE option.

In the following sections, we'll create a setup program for the TaskCE application developed in Chapter 5. First, we'll create a Cab file–based setup, and then we'll create an InstallShield-based setup.

The Cab Wizard Option

When it comes to the Cab Wizard option, there are three steps you need to complete in order to install your application on a user's CE device:

1. Create the Cab, or archive, files, one for each device or platform you've got an EXE for.

2. Next, create an INI file that contains some user-friendly information about your application, such as the application name, author, and so on.

3. Finally, create a Desktop PC-based setup program of your own.

Creating the Cab File

Cab files are a special kind of compressed archive file that Microsoft designed specifically for installations. To make Cab files for Windows CE installations, you'll have to use a program called Cab Wizard.

The creation of a Cab file can be broken down into two distinct steps:

- Creating an INF file to tell Cab Wizard which files to use

- Running Cab Wizard to create the Cab archive

Creating an INF File   Cab Wizard is not your typical interactive wizard program; instead, it's a command-line utility that gets all of the information it needs from a complicated text file. It's this text file, known as the INF file, which you must create before you do anything else. The INF file is a basic settings file; a common INF file for creating CE applications has about a dozen sections, each one identified with a unique name enclosed in brackets, with several settings per section.

Before you start, note that this is the most complicated and confusing part of creating a Windows CE installation. While it's true that the INF file is basically an INI file, and therefore nothing you haven't seen before, it's also a good deal more complex than a standard INI file. For instance, there are several places in the INF file where settings in one section refer to settings in another section, which then refer to something else entirely. However, it should also be noted that CE developers create INF files regularly, so it isn't an impossible task.

The first section to be found in any INF file is the [Version] section, which usually looks like this:

```
[Version]
Signature = "$Windows NT$"
Provider = "doctorce.com"
CESignature = "$Windows CE$"
```

The Signature specifies the development machine; it is usually set to either "$Windows NT$" or "$Windows 95$". The Provider is the company or individual who wrote the software. Finally, the CESignature tells CabWizard that it must build CE-specific Cab files. This value is always set to "$Windows CE$".

The next section in an INF file is the [CEStrings] section. This is where to set up any paths or strings that you'll be using throughout the INF file. For example, your [CEStrings] section will look like this:

```
[CEStrings]
AppName = taskCE
InstallDir = %CE1%
```

TIP   The reference to **%CE1%** is explained in detail in the "Predefined Destination Directories" sidebar below.

AppName and InstallDir are now available to be used throughout the INF file. This means that you can later specify the following elsewhere in the INF file:

```
SomeSetting=%InstallDir%\thefile.txt
```

AppName, of course, is the name of the application, and InstallDir is the destination directory on the device.

The Predefined Destination Directories

When you specified your InstallDir above, you used an identifier enclosed in percent symbols:

```
InstallDir = %CE1%
```

The **%CE1%** is part of a list of 17 predefined destination directories that you can use when creating your INF file. They can be used as the full path, as shown above, or they can be combined with string literals to specify a customized destination:

```
InstallDir = %CE1%\doctorce.com\TaskCE
```

Continued on next page

Obviously, the reason they're provided is to save you from retyping the more common paths and to prevent simple errors. These 17 predefined paths are listed in the following table:

Macro String	HPC Devices' Directory	Palm PC Devices' Directory
%CE1%	\Program Files	\Program Files
%CE2%	\Windows	\Windows
%CE3%	\Windows\Desktop	
%CE4%	\Windows\StartUp	\Windows\StartUp
%CE5%	\My Documents	\My Documents
%CE6%	\Program Files\Accessories	\Program Files\Accessories
%CE7%	\Program Files\Communication	\Program Files\Communication
%CE8%	\Program Files\Games	\Program Files\Games
%CE9%	\Program Files\Pocket Outlook	
%CE10%	\Program Files\Office	
%CE11%	\Windows\Programs	\Windows\Start Menu\Programs
%CE12%	\Windows\Programs\Accessories	\Windows\StartMenu\Programs\Accessories
%CE13%	\Windows\Programs\Communications	\Windows\StartMenu\Programs\Communications
%CE14%	\Windows\Programs\Games	\Windows\StartMenu\Programs\Games
%CE15%	\Windows\Fonts\Windows\Fonts	
%CE16%	\Windows\Recent	
%CE17%	\Windows\Favorites	\Windows\Start Menu

The next sections to create are the [CEDevice.ChipType] sections. These sections specify the chips you're targeting, so you need to create one [CEDevice.ChipType] section for each chip. In addition, in each section you'll need to indicate the processor type(s) you're supporting:

```
[CEDevice.SH3]
ProcessorType = 10003
[CEDevice.MIPS]
ProcessorType = 4000
```

The next section we'll deal with is the [DefaultInstall] section. This is where to tell Cab Wizard which additional sections of the INF file are to be processed, regardless of what type of device the user has. Options that might appear here include registry settings, readme files, help files, and so on. Your [DefaultInstall] section for TaskCE merely contains a reference to a section that will contain information about a shortcut that you might like to create a little later on:

```
[DefaultInstall]
CEShortcuts = Shortcuts.All
```

It might also contain registry settings for both MIPS and SH3 installations.

The next sections you'll need to create are the [DefaultInstall.ChipType] sections. Just as you did with the generic [DefaultInstall] section, in the [DefaultInstall.ChipType] sections, you'll need to refer to later sections that contain settings for chip-specific files:

```
[DefaultInstall.SH3]
CopyFiles = Files.Common, Files.SH3

[DefaultInstall.MIPS]
CopyFiles = Files.Common, Files.MIPS
```

So, in the above example, Files.Common, Files.SH3, and Files.MIPS are all sections that appear later in the INF file.

Next, create a set of [SourceDiskNames] sections in which each source directory is identified with a unique number.

```
[SourceDisksNames]
1 = ,"Common Files",,"h:\"

[SourceDisksNames.SH3]
2 = ,"SH3 Files",,"h:\sh3"

[SourceDisksNames.MIPS]
2 = ,"MIPS Files",,"h:\mips"
```

Now that you've identified each source directory, you can tell Cab Wizard which files to add to the archive and where to find each file. You do this in three [SourceDiskFiles] sections:

```
[SourceDisksFiles]
 readme.txt = 1

[SourceDisksFiles.SH3]
 taskCE.exe = 2

[SourceDisksFiles.MIPS]
 taskCE.exe = 2
```

From the settings in these sections, Cab Wizard knows to look for the common file readme.txt in the directory marked 1 under the [SourceDiskNames] section above.

Next, tell Cab Wizard where you want all of these files to end up once they're on the CE device. This section, [DestinationDirs], is fairly self-explanatory. Each previously outlined section is assigned a destination directory where all of the files will eventually be copied:

WARNING   The %InstallDir% path is subject to change; the only thing it really specifies is the default installation path, which the user may change when installing the software via App Manager.

```
[DestinationDirs]
Shortcuts.All = 0,%CE3%
Files.Common = 0,%InstallDir%
Files.SH3 = 0,%InstallDir%
Files.MIPS = 0,%InstallDir%
DefaultDestDir = 0,%InstallDir%
```

The Shortcuts.All entry specifies the destination for all shortcuts, the Files.Common specifies the destination for all common files, and so on.

NOTE   The 0 that precedes each directory is a feature normally found in Desktop PC INF files, but Windows CE does not support this feature.

Next, you get to specify options for each of the files we're copying. In the [Files.Common] section, tell Cab Wizard to rename readme.txt to readthis.txt. The executables (in [Files.SH3] and [Files.MIPS]), however, will remain unchanged:

```
[Files.Common]
readme.txt,readthis.txt,,0

[Files.SH3]
taskCE.exe,,,0

[Files.MIPS]
taskCE.exe,,,0
```

Finally, tell Cab Wizard that you'll want a shortcut for your TaskCE application to be placed on the Desktop:

```
[Shortcuts.All]
taskCE,0,taskCE.exe
```

The entry under [Shortcuts.All] can be broken down in this way: the first item is the name of the shortcut, the 0 indicates that this is a shortcut to a file, and the last value specifies the name of the executable the shortcut is pointing to.

You can also specify a shortcut to a folder by changing the 0 to any other number. Similarly, you can specify that a shortcut be created in a directory other than that specified in [DestinationDirs] by simply appending your desired directory to the existing entry. So, in the above example, if you wanted that shortcut to appear in \Windows\Program Files\Accessories instead of the default directory, you would set it up as

```
[Shortcuts.All]
taskCE,0,taskCE.exe,%CE6%
```

That's the full picture on INF files. As you've probably realized, they're not very easy to create or friendly to use. It's generally regarded that once you create one that does what you need, you ought to simply use it as a template for all future installations. Naturally, the INF file we've created here is provided on the CD for this book so that you can use it as a template for your installations.

Running Cab Wizard to Create the Cab Archive Now that you've finished with your INF file, the next step is to run the Cab Wizard against your INF file so that it can create the Cab archives for you. Of the two steps, this is definitely the simpler one.

All you have to do to create your Cab files is open a command prompt window, go to the directory where `CabWiz.exe` is located and type:

```
CabWiz.exe "C:\TaskCE\TaskCE.INF" /err errors.txt /cpu mips sh3
```

The Cab files will be created for you and placed in the same directory as `Cab-Wiz.exe`. In the case of your TaskCE project, the resulting Cab files will be named `TaskCE.SH3.cab` and `TaskCE.MIPS.cab`—one Cab file for each chip type specified after the `/cpu` command line option. If Cab Wizard cannot create the Cab files for any reason, the errors will appear in the `errors.txt` file you specified with the `/err` option.

Now that your Cab file creation is completed, it's time to create an INI file.

Creating an INI File

The INI file you're going to create now is the INI file that will be used by your setup program to register your application with the CE Application Manager, shown in Figure 14.4.

FIGURE 14.4:

The CE Application Manager

This INI file has only two sections and can be created very quickly.

The first section, [CEAppManager], specifies two values:

- The version of CE App Manager, which should always be 1.0

- The name of the next section in the INI file

Or, as it appears in the actual INI file:

```
[CEAppManager]
Version=1.0
Component=TaskCE
```

The second section, named for the Component setting of the first section (in your case [TaskCE]), specifies several additional values used by the CE Application Manager:

```
[TaskCE]
Description=TaskCE
CabFiles=taskce.sh3.CAB,taskce.mips.CAB
```

The Description setting specifies the text that CE Application Manager will display when the user highlights your application in the list of available programs. The CabFiles option tells CE Application Manager the names of your Cab files. The most important point to know about the CabFiles setting is that there should not be any spaces following the equal sign or the comma(s); a space on this line can actually cause your installation to fail!

As you can see, the INI file is very simple. Here again, it's a good idea to create one that works, and then use it as a template for future installations.

Creating Your Own Setup Program

The next step in the Cab file method of installing your software is to create your own setup program. The only real task that the setup program must perform is to copy the Cab files and the INI files to a subdirectory under the directory in which the CE Application Manager is located. We'll design your setup program to be as generic as possible so that when it's done, all you have to do is include it in the same directory as your INI and Cab files, and it will do the rest!

Although you can create your setup program using just about any tool, including batch files, let's use Delphi as a quick-and-dirty solution. We'll create a blank project without any forms so that what you're left with will be a single DPR file with a minimal Uses clause.

TIP Removing the forms and reducing the **Uses** clause keeps your EXE file size low.

The first thing your setup must do is locate your INI file, which should exist in the same directory as the setup program itself. Use the FindFirst function to search for the first INI file in your directory:

```
AppExePath := ExtractFilePath(ParamStr(0));
if (FindFirst(AppExePath + '*.ini', faAnyFile, SearchRec) <> 0) then
begin
```

If no INI file is found, report the error and quit:

```
  MessageBox(NULL, PChar('No Ini file found. Aborting.'),
PChar('Error'),MB_OK);
    Exit;
  end
```

If the INI file was found, however, the next step is to locate the CE Application Manager. The way to do this is by querying the registry. When CE Services are installed on the user's machine, a set of values are added to the registry under HKEY_LOCAL_MACHINE \SOFTWARE\Microsoft\Windows CE Services\. One of these values in particular, InstalledDir, tells you where the CE Services files, including the CE Application Manager, are installed. Your next step, then, is to retrieve that value using Delphi's TRegistry object:

```
  else
  begin
    RegIni := TRegistry.Create;
    RegIni.CloseKey;
    RegIni.RootKey := HKEY_LOCAL_MACHINE;
    RegIni.OpenKey('\SOFTWARE\Microsoft\Windows CE Services\', False);
    //CEAppMgrPath := RegIni.ReadString('', '', '') + '\ceappmgr.exe';
    CEAppMgrPath := RegIni.ReadString('InstalledDir');
    RegIni.Free;
  end;
```

The next step is to open the INI file you located earlier and retrieve the Component value from the [CEAppManager] section:

```
  AppIni := TIniFile.Create(AppExePath + IniFileName);
  DestinationDir := AppIni.ReadString('CEAppManager', 'Component', '');
  AppIni.Free;
```

You'll use this value as the name of the subdirectory where you'll copy the INI and Cab files. If this value is empty or does not exist, report the error to the user and quit:

```
if DestinationDir = '' then
begin
   MessageBox(NULL, PChar('Error in INI file. Aborting.'),
PChar('Error'),MB_OK);
   Exit;
end;
```

Next, create the destination subdirectory (under the path of the CE Application Manager):

```
CreateDirectory(PChar(CEAppMgrPath + '\' + DestinationDir), nil);
```

Then loop through all of the files in the same directory as the setup program, copying them into the destination directory and making sure not to copy the setup program itself:

```
iResult := FindFirst(AppExePath + '*.*', faAnyFile, SearchRec);
while (iResult <> 0) do
begin
   if (SearchRec.Name <> ExtractFileName(ParamStr(0))) then
      CopyFile(PChar(AppExePath + SearchRec.Name),
        PChar(CEAppMgrPath + '\' + DestinationDir + '\' +
SearchRec.Name), TRUE);
   iResult := FindNext(SearchRec);
end;
FindClose(SearchRec);
```

Finally, launch the CE Application Manager, specifying the INI file you just copied as the command line parameter:

```
WinExec(PChar(CEAppMgrPath + '\ceappmgr.exe "' + CEAppMgrPath + '\' +
DestinationDir + '\' + IniFileName + '"'), SW_NORMAL);
```

TIP   If the CE Application Manager ever gives you an error message, you can turn on its debugging feature by adding the /**report** option to the command line just before the name of the INI file.

NOTE   It is also possible for a user to download a CAB file directly onto their CE device and install the software by double-tapping the actual CAB file. For more information, see Chapter 15.

And that's how to create a complete Cab file–based setup. While there are quite a few steps to manage and some of them are a bit confusing, many CE applications are installed in just this way without any additional tools.

However, if you prefer an easier route, there is a third-party tool that can be a big help.

InstallShield for Windows CE

Install Shield for Windows CE is a tool that can help you to quickly and easily create installation files for Windows CE–based applications. InstallShield for Windows CE automatically knows about the different devices and chip types and makes it possible to target multiple platforms with ease.

When you start InstallShield and create a new project, you are first asked to enter some basic information about the application.

Next, the wizard asks you to specify the default destination folder of the application on the CE device. By default, InstallShield selects the `\Program Files\ <Company Name>\<Application Name>` folder. You may specify another destination folder by selecting the desired destination in the TreeView, as shown in Figure 14.5.

FIGURE 14.5:

Specifying the default destination folder

Next, you're asked to specify all of the files you'll be installing to the user's device. The Files dialog, as shown in Figure 14.6, displays the name, destination folder, source folder, device type, supported processor type(s), and the size of each file you specify to include with your application. The Add File button allows you to add any files needed to run your application on the device.

FIGURE 14.6:

The Files dialog displays all of the files you'll be installing.

For your TaskCE application, browse to the location of the TaskCE files, select both the MIPS and SH3 files, and click Open. You can then add any additional files, such as the `readme.txt` file, in the same way.

In the next step, you can specify unique properties in the File Properties dialog for all of the files you've added using the Add File button. As shown in Figure 14.7, you can specify:

- Different destination folders

- Special copying options (i.e., Always update older file on target)

- Target chip type of file

In the next step, you can specify any shortcuts that you'll need. So, for your TaskCE project, you'll need to create a shortcut on the Desktop. Identify the shortcut target, the destination for the shortcut, and a name. You can rename shortcuts or change the destination folder of the shortcut by selecting the desired shortcut from the list in the Shortcuts dialog and clicking the Properties button. The Shortcut Properties dialog is shown in Figure 14.8.

FIGURE 14.7:

The File Properties dialog

FIGURE 14.8:

The Shortcut Properties dialog

In the next few steps, InstallShield allows you to specify additional options for your application, such as file associations and registry keys. While TaskCE does not have any file associations or registry keys associated with it, it's worth noting how easily these items can be configured with InstallShield.

Finally, when you're all finished setting up the application and any additional options, InstallShield displays a confirmation/summary of the options you've specified, as shown in Figure 14.9.

FIGURE 14.9:

The Summary or Confirmation dialog

Confirm the options you've set, and InstallShield will create the INI, INF, and Cab files for you. You then have one set of distributable files that you can use for all of the chip types you're targeting.

Clearly, when it comes to CE installs, there's an easy way and a hard way to do it. You may prefer to create your own INF files so that you have more control over the install process, but the ease of using InstallShield for CE is a definite timesaver.

Summary

In this chapter, you learned how to put the finishing touches on a CE application. The help files are relatively easy to create, and there are a number of options that you can choose from to get the job done. CE installs, on the other hand, can be a bit time-consuming unless you use a third-party tool to help you.

CHAPTER
FIFTEEN

Microsoft's Logo Requirements

- ■ Installation Requirements

- ■ UI Requirements

- ■ Functionality Requirements

- ■ File-Handling Requirements

In this chapter, we'll be exploring the Logo process and what it takes to get your applications approved for the "Powered By Windows CE" Logo. The Logo program is often touted as a way for users to judge the quality of an application. In some sense, it may help to give the potential customer a sense that Microsoft or the powers that be have approved your application.

What Is the Logo Program and Why Should You Care?

The Logo program is not a computer program; rather, it is a type of program that developers can participate in. If your application conforms to these standards and rules, you can pay to have it certified by Microsoft's approved testing labs, Veritest. If your application passes the tests and is certified as conforming to the standards outlined by Microsoft, you earn the right to put the "Powered By Windows CE" logo on your application's box, advertisements, and so on.

TIP   As of this writing, the cost to have an application tested by Veritest is $300 per application.

The general idea is that a potential customer for your software sees this Logo and concludes that your software has been tested and certified to be OK. As you'll see, the Logo is not a mark of quality or reliability of the software, but rather a certification that the program looks and feels a certain way.

NOTE   *Logo'd* is the official Microsoft term for a product that has been verified as conforming to the Logo requirements.

Most of the freeware or shareware Windows CE programs do not conform to the Logo requirements. In fact, some of the Logo requirements may actually be in direct opposition to the wants of your users. For instance, it is required that certain Palm-size PC applications not show the file system or directory hierarchy in any way. For experienced users, not including an explorer or file manager-type application because of this requirement is extremely frustrating. To remedy this,

Casio provides a Find File utility, which can also be used to browse directories and files. Of course, this application would never be approved for a Logo, but it is extremely useful and probably quite popular.

Many other programs are already in compliance with the majority of the Logo requirements, and adding or modifying a few features here and there probably wouldn't be a major effort.

So What?

The real question is what benefit do you get from having your application Logo'd? It's certainly true that many potential customers may never notice the Logo on your program's box. Some may not care even if they do notice it. So why go to all of this trouble?

Well, of course, there is the argument that some potential customers do care. They want to know that launching your PPC application when there's already a copy running won't start two instances of it, but will instead bring the existing one to the foreground. They care that your HPC application supports mouse cursors, and that it will resize itself to account for the user's taskbar preferences.

However, the real benefits of the Logo program are in the perks that Microsoft provides to you. If you had your application certified for that reason alone, it would be worth the time and expense. Some of the more important benefits Microsoft provides for Logo'd applications include:

- Listing of your company and product on the Third-Party Showcase on the Microsoft Web site. This showcase is only for third parties that have qualified for the Logo.

- Microsoft quote provided if you are announcing in a press release that your company recently received the Logo.

- Discounts and special premium invitations to participate in the Windows CE-based Application CD samplers that are distributed to qualified Microsoft customers and at various trade shows.

- Invitation to participate in co-op advertising campaigns focused around Microsoft product launches.

- Invitation to participate in direct mail campaigns, joint seminars, and training events focused around Microsoft product launches.

- Opportunity to participate in Microsoft Partner Pavilions at trade shows, such as Windows World and COMDEX.

- Inclusion of your company and Logo'd product in the Windows CE-based Product Spotlight.

- Opportunity to participate in magazine advertisement discount offers of 10 percent (for new ad contracts only). To receive this discount, your product must be Logo'd and the Powered by Windows CE Logo must appear in the advertisement.

Clearly, there's a real, tangible benefit here that goes beyond just putting some additional art on a product's box. Assuming you've decided the Logo program is something you want to participate in, you then need to know what sort of modifications you'll have to make in order to get your programs to conform to the standards and rules.

In most cases, you won't have to do much of anything at all. If you've followed the UI guidelines and the model provided by the Microsoft applications, you'll probably be just fine. To see how the Logo rules will likely affect you, let's take a look at the most important ones for each platform, starting with the Palm-sized PC and then the Handheld PC (which includes HPC/Pro).

The Logo Requirements

For the rest of this chapter, we'll examine the four major areas in which the Logo requirements are likely to affect your application. They are:

- Installation
- UI Design
- Functionality
- File Handling

Although there are other sections to the Logo specifications, these are the items that are likely to affect you more than the others.

Installation

When it comes to installing your software on the user's device, there are a number of rules you need to follow to ensure that you get Logo'd. Most of them make good sense anyway, and the others are relatively minor.

1. Your application must install using CAB files and/or the CE Application Manager.

HPC	PPC
Required	Required

Simply put, Microsoft wants you to use their system of CAB files and the CE Application Manager to install applications to the CE Device.

NOTE When the user downloads a CAB file from the Internet directly to their device, the installation is performed by a CE-based utility called WCELoad.

---

2. Your application must register the CAB files for all processors with CE AppManager when installed from the desktop.

HPC	PPC
Required	Required

Along with Installation Rule #7, this rule's purpose is to make sure that CE AppManager knows about the CAB files for processors other than the one used in the device hooked up at the time of install.

3. All nonshared program files must be installed to your application's directory.

HPC	PPC
Required	Required

All EXE and DLL files must be installed to the application directory, as long as these files will be used by your program and your program alone.

4. All shared program files must be installed to the Windows directory.

HPC   **PPC**

Required   Required

All EXE and DLL files which might be used by more than one application should be installed to the \Windows directory.

NOTE   In the official documents from Microsoft, Installation Rules #3 and #4 are combined into one rule for the PPC platform.

---

5. When your application is uninstalled, you must remove the user settings from the Windows CE registry

HPC   **PPC**

Required   Required

When your application is uninstalled, you must remove all traces of it from the registry.

6. When installing from the desktop to the device, you should first copy all of the files to a subdirectory of the CE AppManager Path.

HPC   **PPC**

Recommended   Recommended

This technique is demonstrated by the sample setup described in the previous chapter.

7. CAB files for all processors should be copied to the desktop when the user is installing from the desktop to the device.

HPC   **PPC**

Recommended   Recommended

The idea here is that even if the end user only has a MIPS device, you must copy the CAB files for the other processors to their desktop machine. Although users typically only have one CE device, they could very easily upgrade or purchase a new device that uses a different chipset. Therefore, it's best to provide a way for them to install your software to their new device, if needed.

TIP   MIPS R3910 binaries will run on all of the MIPS chips.

---

8. When allowing the user to install from the Internet to a device, you should instruct them on choosing the correct CAB file for their device.

HPC	PPC
Recommended	N/A

This rule applies only to HPC devices, as PPC devices are not configured to allow a direct Internet-to-device installation.

Determining the User's CPU Type over the Internet

Microsoft recommends that you set up your Web site to automatically choose the correct CAB file for the user. This is possible because Pocket IE sends a special HTTP variable indicating the CPU type of the device. To determine the User Agent CPU, you can reference the environment variable HTTP_UA_CPU.

For example, here is a simple Perl script that tells the user what type of browser and CPU their device is running:

```perl
#!/usr/local/bin/perl
print "Content-type: text/plain \n\n";
print "Your browser type is: ";
print $ENV{'HTTP_USER_AGENT'};
print "\n\nYour CPU type is: ";
print $ENV{'HTTP_UA_CPU'};
exit;
```

You could then easily use this HTTP_UA_CPU variable to direct the user's browser to the specific CAB file that's right for their device.

9. When your application is uninstalled, you must either remove the data files or alert the user to the fact that you did not remove these files.

HPC   **PPC**

Recommended   Recommended

If you choose not to delete these files, Microsoft recommends that you advise the user to move the data files to the desktop, then recopy them to the device as needed.

10. If you do remove user data files, you must alert the users and give them the option of saving these files.

HPC   **PPC**

Recommended   Recommended

As a corollary to Installation Rule #10, if you are going to delete the user's data files, you must give the users the option of copying these files to the desktop first.

11. You must use meaningful, unique names for program files.

HPC   **PPC**

Recommended   Recommended

The idea here is that you would like to avoid installing a shared DLL from your application to the Windows directory when a similarly named file from another vendor may already exist. So, naming your DLL "OurCompany_OurApplication_Our-DLL.DLL" would be unique and, therefore, unlikely to conflict with any other vendor's DLLs.

12. You must support installation to a compact flash card.

HPC   **PPC**

N/A   Required

When your application is installed, the user will have the option (via CE App-Manager) of installing to a compact flash card. If the user chooses this option, you must copy as many files as possible to the compact flash card.

13. You must create a shortcut on the Start menu for your application.

HPC	PPC
Recommended	Required

When installing your application to a *PPC* device, you need to create a shortcut to your application under the \Windows\Start Menu\Programs\ directory on the device. While it is a good idea to do this on both platforms, it is especially important on the PPC device, as there is no Explorer-type application by which the user could otherwise find and run your application once it is installed.

When installing to an *HPC* device, Microsoft recommends that you create shortcuts to your application in the \Program Files\ directory instead of the desktop.

UI Requirements

In this section, we'll look at all of the UI and shell-related requirements. The rules in this section are designed to ensure that all Windows CE programs present a consistent look and feel.

1. The command bar and rebars must appear at the top of the screen.

HPC	PPC
Required	Required

Although Microsoft allows you to offer the option of hiding the command bar, they do require you to, by default, show the command bar and to place it at the top of your application's main window.

NOTE   Games and other applications that wouldn't ordinarily have menus or toolbars may not be required to follow this rule.

---

2. Menus must appear in the left-hand portion of the command bar, while buttons must use the right-hand portion.

HPC	PPC
Required	Required

This organization can be seen on just about any of the Microsoft applications that ship with a CE device.

3. Your Help "?" button must be placed to the right of the screen, just to the left of the Close "X" button.

HPC	PPC
Required	N/A

This UI-related rule, as well as the next one, does not apply to PPC devices, as the help system on PPC devices works slightly different than on HPC devices. For the PPC version, see UI Rule #5.

4. Your application must allow the user to press Alt+H to bring up Help.

HPC	PPC
Required	N/A

This rule is intended to ensure that users will be able to click or tap the "?" button and receive help. If for some reason you do not want to offer this functionality, Microsoft gives you the option of adding a Help menu to your command bar, which could then be accessed via the Alt+H key combination.

Here again, this rule does not apply to PPC devices; for PPC devices, see UI Rule #5.

5. Your applications must not show a "?" Help button on the command bar.

HPC	PPC
N/A	Required

As you saw in the previous chapter, PPC users access the help system off of the Start menu. In order to be consistent, your applications should not offer any different means of accessing help. This, of course, is also why UI Rules #4 and #5 do not apply to applications running on PPC devices.

6. Standard menu items must appear in a set order.

HPC	PPC
Required	Required

UI Rules #6, #7, and #8 all go together. They are concerned with making sure that your applications present the same look and feel as other applications, at least as far as the command bar is concerned. This rule, for instance, says that if your application includes the standard File, Edit, etc. menus, you must arrange them in the usual set order, from left to right, of:

```
File, Edit, View, Insert, Format, Tools, Window
```

7. Standard buttons must appear in a set order.

HPC	PPC
Required	Required

This rule parallels UI Rule #6 and says that if your application includes the standard New, Open, etc. buttons, you must arrange them in the usual set order, from left to right, of:

```
New, Open, Save, Print
```

8. Standard functions must appear in a set order.

HPC	PPC
Required	Required

This rule also parallels UI Rule #6 and says that if your application includes the standard text-formatting functionality, the buttons or drop-down combos that provide that functionality must appear in the following order, from left to right:

```
Style, Font, Font Size, Bold, Italic, Underline
```

9. Users can not close the application themselves.

HPC	PPC
N/A	Required

This rule requires that your PPC applications not have a Close "X" button or a File ➢ Exit menu. The reason for this is that Microsoft does not want the user to have to worry about managing memory; instead, the operating system itself closes the applications as memory is needed.

TIP

Because the Close "X" button is probably more comfortable to you as a developer, you may want to include the Close button until you're all finished testing the application, then remove it before shipping.

Finding the Previous Instance

One of the consequences of UI Rule #9 is that every time the user starts an instance of your application, you must make sure you check to see that no other instance is already running. To do this, you can use `FindWindow()` from within your `WinMain()` function. For example:

```
int WINAPI WinMain(HINSTANCE hInstance,
                   HINSTANCE hPrevInstance,
                   LPTSTR    lpCmdLine,
                   int       nCmdShow)
{
    HWND hWnd;
```

Assuming that **szAppName** is your application's window class name, and **szTitle** is the caption of your application's main window, call `FindWindow()`:

```
    hWnd = FindWindow(szAppName, szTitle);
```

If `FindWindow()` finds a window matching your criteria, it will return a handle to that window. So, if **hWnd** contains a valid window handle:

```
    if IsWindow(hWnd)
    {
```

set the focus to that window, bringing it to the front, and then exit from the second instance:

```
        SetForegroundWindow(hWnd);
        return 0;
    }
```

10. Command bar buttons must offer tool tips.

HPC	PPC
Required	Required

All of the buttons—if there are any—on your command bar must offer tool tip hints so that the user can hold their stylus over the button for a few seconds and receive a "yellow balloon hint" as to that button's purpose. Further, while both the PPC and HPC platforms require these tool tips, Microsoft has rules on how the hints are to be worded for each platform.

10a. Hints for HPC Applications must give the button's function and its keyboard shortcut. In other words, a hint for a button on an HPC application that printed the application's data might read "`Print (Ctrl+P)`."

10b. Hints for PPC Applications must give the button's function *but not its keyboard shortcut*. In other words, a hint for a button on a PPC application that printed the application's data might read "`Print`" (notice the omission of "`Ctrl+P`").

11. Applications must provide small (16 x 16) and large (32 x 32) icons for the main executable and all registered file types.

HPC	PPC
Required	Required

This is a common sense rule that's something you'd want to do with any Windows application.

12. Your applications must not duplicate the functionality of the Address Book API.

HPC	PPC
Required	Required

This rule, which affects mostly PIM (Personal Information Manager) applications, is designed to conserve storage space on the CE Device. Simply put, Microsoft does not want each PIM application to create its own database in addition to the Contacts application database that's already on the system. If all PIM applications use the same database, there will theoretically be less wasted storage space. Therefore, if your application performs any kind of contacts-related operations, you must use the existing Contacts database and the Contacts database functions.

13. Your applications must not duplicate the functionality of the msgstore API.

HPC	PPC
Required	Required

Just as UI Rule #12 requires you to use the Contacts database and related functions, this rule deals with messages and message-related applications. If you have an application that stores messages similar to e-mail messages, you must use the msgstore database and the related msgstore functions.

14. If your applications use the IR port, you must adhere to the IrDA standards.

HPC	PPC
Required	Required

The purpose of this rule is merely to ensure that all CE-based applications use the IrDA standards.

15. Your applications must use the hourglass or wait cursor whenever necessary.

HPC	PPC
Required	Required

Although the HP Jornada is the only CE device with a mouse, all CE devices support an hourglass or wait cursor, although it looks slightly different from a regular Windows 98/NT wait cursor. The CE wait cursor appears as a small window, about 32 × 32, which displays an animation of a wait cursor.

16. Your applications must resize themselves depending on the taskbar settings.

HPC	PPC
Required	Required

Because the user can always choose to auto-hide the taskbar, your application must be able to accommodate the taskbar settings and use the full screen area.

Working with the Taskbar

There are really only two things you must do to work with the taskbar and use the full screen area for our main window.

1. The first time you need to be concerned about the taskbar is when you create our main window.

2. The second time you need to be concerned about the taskbar is if the user changes their taskbar preferences while your application is running.

1. Creating the Main Window

When you create your application's main window, you should specify its dimensions as 0, 0, CW_DEFAULT, CW_DEFAULT. Your call to CreateWindow(), then, might look like this:

```
hWnd = CreateWindow(szWindowClass, szTitle, WS_VISIBLE | WS_SYS-
MENU | WS_CAPTION, 0, 0, CW_USEDEFAULT, CW_USEDEFAULT, NULL, NULL,
hInstance, NULL);
```

The CW_DEFAULT value on Windows CE ensures that your application will occupy the full screen area, taking into account the taskbar settings.

2. Watching for Taskbar Changes While Your Application Is Running

Since the user can also change their taskbar settings while your application is running, you need to be able to resize your window at runtime. The way to accomplish this is to handle the WM_SETTINGCHANGE message. When you receive this message, you can call System-ParametersInfo() and request the dimensions of the working area (i.e., the screen size

Continued on next page

minus the taskbar size). You can then call MoveWindow() to resize your window accordingly. Or, in code:

```
case WM_SETTINGCHANGE:
    RECT rcWorkArea;
    //Get the working area
    SystemParametersInfo(SPI_GETWORKAREA, 0, &rcWorkArea, 0);
    //resize the window
    return MoveWindow(hWnd, rcWorkArea.top, rcWorkArea.left,
rcWorkArea.right, rcWorkArea.bottom, TRUE);
    break;
```

With these two changes in place, your application will be able to perfectly adapt to the user's taskbar preferences, making your application that much closer to being Logo'd.

17. Your applications must support Alt+tap for pop-up menus and Alt+Enter for property sheets.

HPC	PPC
Required	N/A

While pop-up menus and property sheets are by no means required components of a Logo'd application, if the application does offer those items, Microsoft requires that the user be able to access them in a certain way.

NOTE This rule does not apply to PPC devices, as the default Input Panel keyboard has no Alt key.

TIP Chapter 3 has a demonstration of handing an Alt+tap event.

18. Your applications must support mouse cursors.

HPC	PPC
Required	N/A

On CE devices that have a mouse, your applications must accommodate the mouse, especially in regard to selection operations and right-clicking.

WM_RBUTTONUP and Pop-up Menus

As you saw in Chapter 3, the WM_RBUTTONUP message was removed from the CE API, simply because CE devices didn't have a mouse. However, with the advent of CE devices such as the HP Jornada, which does offer a mouse, the WM_RBUTTONUP message has been added back into the CE API. So, in order to get an application to compile for (and behave correctly on) multiple CE platforms with regards to right-click handling, you must put an #ifdef around your WM_RBUTTONUP message handler:

```
#ifdef WM_RBUTTONUP
    //if there's true mouse support...
    case WM_RBUTTONUP:
        PopupMenuHandler();
    break;
#endif
```

---

19. Your applications should use the default system font (9-point Tahoma) whenever possible.

HPC	PPC
Required	N/A

This is the simplest of the UI Rules, requiring you to do absolutely nothing when it comes to fonts. Tahoma (9-point) is the default system font, so as long as you don't specify any font settings, you'll be in compliance with this rule automatically.

20. Your dialogs should be centered on the screen.

HPC	PPC
Recommended	N/A

Microsoft recommends centering dialogs in the nontaskbar area of the screen to improve the overall look and feel of your applications.

21. Your dialogs shouldn't be any larger than 466 x 198.

HPC	PPC
Recommended	N/A

Since the smallest HPC resolution is 480×240, you can safely design your dialogs to be 466×198 and be assured that they'll look good on any of the HPC devices.

22. Your buttons should use a bold font style to improve readability.

HPC	PPC
Recommended	N/A

Microsoft recommends using a bold font on command buttons to improve readability and to be consistent with other HPC applications.

23. Your applications must deal with the showing/hiding of the Input Panel.

HPC	PPC
N/A	Required

Specifically, your windows and dialogs must be arranged so that an Input Panel does not hide any edit boxes. (Input Panels are assumed to be 80 pixels high for the purpose of this rule). It's worth noting that it is apparently OK to have an edit box that's hidden by an Input Panel, as long as the window has a scroll bar available so the user can scroll the edit box into view. This, in fact, is the way many Microsoft PPC applications work.

NOTE   Chapter 1 demonstrates how to add and remove a scroll bar whenever the Input Panel's state changes.

---

24. If you choose not to provide a tray icon or Start menu shortcut to your applications, you must ensure that the applications use the desktop as their parent window.

HPC	PPC
N/A	Required

This rule seems to be somewhat pointless, considering that any application not providing a Start menu shortcut would be in direct conflict with Installation Rule #13.

25. Your applications should not display underlined accelerators (Alt+letter) or shortcut keys (Ctrl+letter) in menus or dialogs.

HPC	PPC
N/A	Recommended

It is perfectly acceptable to use underlined accelerators in HPC applications; this rule applies only to PPC applications where there is no Alt key on the standard Input Panel keyboard.

Similarly, although PPC keyboards do have the Ctrl key, it is usually a more complex process for the user to tap out Ctrl+X than it would be for them to go directly to that menu item. Therefore, it's recommended that you not display the shortcut keys in our menu items' text.

26. Toolbar buttons should have keyboard equivalents.

HPC	PPC
Recommended	Recommended

Despite UI Rule #10b, which says that you must not show keyboard shortcuts in your tool tips, Microsoft recommends that you provide keyboard equivalents just the same.

27. Your buttons should support pop-up help.

HPC	PPC
N/A	Recommended

Many of the PPC applications support pop-up help, so Microsoft recommends that, for consistency's sake, your applications should offer it, too.

28. Your applications' windows should not be overlapping or resizable.

HPC	PPC
Recommended	Recommended

Microsoft strongly recommends that applications take advantage of the full screen area to the maximum amount possible. Further, CE devices do not allow the user to resize windows. Therefore, it is recommended that none of your applications' windows overlap any existing windows.

29. Your applications should use HTML-based help.

HPC	PPC
Recommended	Recommended

As the Windows CE help viewer uses HTML-based help files, it's strongly recommended that your applications use HTML-based help, as opposed to using some other help system.

30. Your applications' windows should not display a title bar.

HPC	PPC
Recommended	Recommended

As screen real estate on CE devices is already somewhat limited, you should do everything you can to maximize the space you do have available. One of the modifications you can make is to eliminate title bars from your applications and simply avoid putting the name of the applications anywhere on the top of the main window.

31. Your applications' closing and launching should execute as quickly as possible.

HPC	PPC
Recommended	Recommended

The idea behind this rule is that your applications should mimic as closely as possible the "instant on" feature of a CE device. The user will come to expect everything on a CE device to be instantaneous and, to maintain this appearance, your applications should start and close immediately.

32. Your applications' ListView controls should allow for drag multi-select.

HPC	PPC
N/A	Recommended

Because it's somewhat difficult to press the Ctrl or Shift keys on a PPC device while selecting items in a ListView, Microsoft recommends that you allow the user to simply mark the items they want by pressing and dragging the stylus around the items they want to select.

NOTE   This is the default behavior for a ListView control and will require no extra work on your part.

Functionality Requirements

Although the Powered by Windows CE Logo is not intended to be an indication that the application behaves as advertised, there are some functionality-related rules that an application must follow in order to be approved.

1. Your applications must run on all of the CE-supported CPUs.

HPC	PPC
Required	Required

Unless you've included some kind of chip-specific assembly language in your application, you should have no trouble at all meeting this requirement.

TIP   The exception to this rule is that if there is no commercially available device that uses a certain CPU, then your application will not be tested and is not required to be compatible with that CPU.

---

2. Your applications must be fully functional when submitted for testing.

HPC	PPC
Required	Required

Microsoft requires that all of the parts of your application are working and functional at the time you submit the application for testing. This rule simply exists so that your application can be fully tested for compatibility with the rules.

3. Your applications' windows and graphical components must resize themselves based on resolution and screen size.

HPC	PPC
Required	N/A

For the most part, this rule is covered if you simply create your window using the default values for width and height, as illustrated in UI Rule #16. However, it may be necessary to incorporate, say, a scroll bar on the left of your applications' main forms, so that it will still be possible for the user to access all of the controls on a smaller screen.

TIP   The reason this doesn't apply to PPC devices is that all of the PPC devices available have the same display size.

---

4. Your help files must be working when you submit our applications for testing.

HPC	PPC
Required	Required

Although it's not required that your help files actually be fully written, they must at least display the correct topic when the user asks for help.

5. Your applications must use RAPI where applicable.

HPC   **PPC**

Required   Required

Simply put, Logo'd applications may not use any custom means of communicating with desktop or companion applications.

6. Your applications must use Winsock where applicable.

HPC   **PPC**

Required   Required

Here again, where possible and applicable, your applications should use Winsock to communicate with desktop or companion applications.

7. Your application must respond to WM_HIBERNATE messages by reducing the amount of memory used.

HPC   **PPC**

Required   Required

The only element not specified by this rule is the *amount* by which your application should reduce its memory usage. However, Microsoft does recommend a 25 percent reduction.

8. Your applications must exit without user intervention.

HPC   **PPC**

N/A   Required

This special PPC-specific rule is related to UI Rule #9, regarding the fact that users should not be able to close the applications themselves. Because the PPC OS closes applications as memory is needed, it's important that your applications don't require any user intervention to be closed. In this way, the automatic closing of applications is seamless, and the user never knows what's going on behind the scenes.

9. Our applications must store and load their state.

HPC	PPC
N/A	Required

This rule is also related to the way in which the PPC OS closes applications automatically. Part of the way the automatic closing process is supposed to work is that when the user starts up your applications for the second time, everything must appear exactly as they left it—again, this is so that they don't know what's going on behind the scenes. It's up to you to ensure that your applications save and restore their state to carry off the illusion of everything appearing as they left it.

10. Your applications' dialogs must not obscure the Input Panel.

HPC	PPC
N/A	Required

This applies only to dialogs that are not full-screen dialogs. If the dialog is long enough that it will obscure some portion of the Input Panel regardless, it must be positioned so that it is flush with the top of the display area.

11. Your applications should capitalize the first letter of any text in an edit box.

HPC	PPC
N/A	Recommended

This rule is designed to make it easier for PPC users to enter data with the Input Panel, especially contact-type data, where the first character of the text is capitalized anyway.

12. Your applications should support color.

HPC	PPC
Recommended	Recommended

There is a wide variety of devices available today, and your applications should look good on all of them.

13. Your applications must support long file names in all file-related operations.

HPC	PPC
Required	Required

Where appropriate, your applications must support and use long file names for saving/opening files, displaying file names, and so on. Further, it is recommended that your applications hide the three-digit file extension.

Here are the tests that Microsoft recommends in order to verify that your applications properly handle LFNs. If your applications follow the rules of this table, then you're handling LFNs just fine.

What the user enters	What the result should be
Test	Test.ext
Test test test test	test test test test.ext
Test 1234567890[...to 250 chars]	Test 1234567890[...].ext
test (3 blank spaces @ beginning of file name)	test.ext (no blanks)
test (3 blank spaces @ end of file name)	test.ext (no blanks)
test ; + , = [ ]	test ; + , = [ ].ext

In addition, files with invalid names (i.e., those containing characters such as question marks) should not save.

File-Handling Requirements

This set of rules relates to applications that mainly open, create, and edit documents.

1. Your applications must use common dialog boxes whenever appropriate.

HPC	PPC
Required	Required

This is another common-sense rule that applies across all Windows platforms.

2. Your applications should display the name of the open document on their taskbar buttons.

HPC	PPC
Required	N/A

For an example of this, look at Pocket Word.

> This rule does not apply to PPC devices, as PPC applications do not have buttons in the taskbar.

3. Your applications should not be multi-instance.

HPC	PPC
N/A	Required

Again, in relation to UI Rule #9, your PPC-based applications must only allow a single instance of themselves to be running at once.

4. Your applications must not show the file system in any way.

HPC	PPC
N/A	Required

Perhaps in order to make PPC devices more accessible to some users, Microsoft is attempting to insulate them from having to know the file system of their device. At any rate, if you stick to the common dialogs for file access, you should be just fine with this rule.

5. Your applications should create a shortcut to a recently used document in the Start Menu ➤ Documents menu.

HPC	PPC
Recommended	N/A

Microsoft recommends that you create a shortcut for a recently used document under the \Windows\Recent directory so that it will appear on the Start Menu ➤ Documents menu.

6. Your applications should have their own MRU lists.

HPC	PPC
Recommended	N/A

In addition to adding recently opened files to the system's Documents menu, your application should also maintain its own MRU list.

7. Your applications should support IR transfer of files, if appropriate.

HPC	PPC
N/A	Recommended

As there is no Explorer-type application on PPC devices that offers this functionality at a system level, it's recommended that you provide this feature from within your applications.

8. Your applications should offer the ability to e-mail files.

HPC	PPC
N/A	Recommended

Again, since this functionality is not offered in any other way on the PPC devices, it's up to you to provide it as a feature of your applications.

Summary

In this chapter, we've seen some of the more important Logo requirements and how they may or may not affect your applications. And, while there are other requirements, such as those for companion desktop applications, they generally won't affect the majority of the CE applications you create. Joining the Logo program is one of the best things you can do for your application, and, in most cases, shouldn't require more than $300 and some minor cosmetic changes.

PART V

Appendices

■ Appendix A: The C Runtime Library Functions of Windows CE

■ Appendix B: The CE 2.0 API

APPENDIX

A

The C Runtime Library Functions of Windows CE

This appendix contains all of the C runtime library functions that are supported on all versions of Windows CE. In other words, you can safely use any of the functions listed here on any 2.*x* version of Windows CE. Although CE 2.11 supports many additional functions, they are of very little benefit to anyone who needs to target a wide range of CE devices. The format that we will use to describe these functions is as follows:

Function name

```
#include <Header file to be included>
```

Brief description

Example (if appropriate)

TIP

There are several places where Microsoft's online help contains an excellent example of some of these functions. In those cases, we have opted not to include an example, as it would only duplicate the help files. Instead, we refer you to the online help in a boxed tip like this one.

_cabs()

```
#include <math.h>
```

Returns a `double` containing the absolute value of a complex number.

Example:

```
struct _complex number = { 3.0, 4.0 };
double d;
d = _cabs( number );
printf( "The absolute value of %f + %fi is %f\n",
        number.x, number.y, d );
```

_chgsign()

```
#include <float.h>
```

Changes the sign of a `double` from positive to negative and vice versa.

Example:

```
_chgsign(-3.90923);  //returns 3.90923
```

_clearfp()

```
#include <float.h>
```

Clears the floating-point status WORD.

Example:

```
_clearfp();
```

_controlfp()

```
#include <float.h>
```

Sets the value of the floating-point status WORD.

Example:

```
_control87( _PC_64, MCW_PC ); //sets precision to 64 bit
```

_copysign ()

```
#include <float.h>
```

Returns the first value with the sign of the second.

Example:

```
_copysign(9.54, -8.6);  //returns -9.54
```

_ecvt()

```
#include <stdlib.h>
```

Converts a double numeric value to an ANSI string.

Example:

```
int dec, sign;
char *szNum;
szNum = _ecvt(3.7834, 4, &dec, &sign );  //szNum = "3.7834"
```

_fcvt()

```
#include <stdlib.h>
```

Converts a floating-point number to a string.

Example:

```
int dec, sign;
char *szNum;
szNum = _fcvt(3.7834, 4, &dec, &sign );  //szNum = "3.7834"
```

_finite()

```
#include <float.h>
```

Determines whether given double value is finite.

Example:

```
if (_finite(99.74))
{
    //...do something
}
else
{
    //...this code will never be reached
}
```

_fpclass()

```
#include <float.h>
```

Returns status word containing information on floating-point class.

Example:

```
double dVal;
// some code
int icls = _fpclass (dVal);
if (_FPCLASS_SNAN == icls || _FPCLASS_QNAN == icls)
{
    // show error, dVal is a Non-number
}
```

fpieee_flt()

Invokes user-defined trap handler for IEEE floating-point exceptions.

TIP   The online help contains an excellent example of this function.

_fpreset()

Resets the floating-point package.

TIP   The online help contains an excellent example of this function.

_gcvt()

```
#include <stdlib.h>
```

Given a floating-point value and the precision, converts the value to a string.

Example:

```
_gcvt(9.00213, 6, szDest);
```

_hypot()

```
#include <math.h>
```

Given floating-point lengths of two sides of a triangle, returns the hypotenuse.

Example:

```
fLengthC = _hypot(fLengthA, fLengthB );
```

_isnan()

```
#include <float.h>
```

Checks given double-precision floating-point value for not a number (NaN).

Example:

```
if (_isnan (fValue))
    {
        // handle non-number value, show error, etc..
    }
```

_itoa()

```
#include <stdlib.h>
```

Given an integer and the base (radix), converts the integer to an ANSI string.

Example:

```
_itoa(iNum, szBuff, 16);
```

_itow()

```
#include <stdlib.h>
```

Given an integer and the base (radix), converts the integer to a Unicode string.

Example:

```
_itow(iNum, szBuff, 16);
```

_j0()

```
#include <math.h>
```

Computes the Bessel function.

Example:

```
_j0(3.987);
```

_j1()

```
#include <math.h>
```

Computes the Bessel function.

Example:

```
_j1(3.987);
```

_jn()

```
#include <math.h>
```

Given the order of the function to compute, computes the Bessel function.

Example:

```
_jn(iOrder, 3.987);
```

_logb()

```
#include <float.h>
```

Extracts exponential value of **double** argument.

Example:

```
double dExp = _logb (7.775);
```

_lrotl()

```
#include <stdlib.h>
```

Left rotates a Long integer value by *n* bits.

Example:

```
_lrotl(0x759fe, nBitsToRotate);
```

_lrotr()

#include <stdlib.h>

Right rotates a Long integer value by *n* bits.

Example:

```
_lrotl(0x759fe, nBitsToRotate);
```

_ltoa()

#include <stdlib.h>

Given a Long integer and the base (radix), converts the integer to an ANSI string.

Example:

```
_ltoa(lVal, szNum, 16);
```

_ltow()

#include <stdlib.h>

Given a Long integer and the base (radix), converts the integer to a Unicode string.

Example:

```
_ltow(lVal, szNum, 16);
```

_matherr()

#include <math.h>

Handles math errors.

TIP   The online help contains an excellent example of this function.

_memccpy()

`#include <memory.h>`

(or `string.h`)

Copies characters from a buffer until iNumToCopy characters have been copied, or until the cToStopAt character is found in the source.

Example:

```
char szWalrus[13] = "IAmTheWalrus\0";
char szCopy[13];
int iNumToCopy = 13;
char cToStopAt = "\0";
_memccpy(szCopy, szWalrus, cToStopAt, iNumToCopy
```

_memicmp()

`#include <memory.h>`

(or `string.h`)

Performs a case-insensitive comparison on iNum characters in two strings.

Example:

```
char szComp1[] = "Red house over";
char szComp2[] = "RED HOUSE OVER yonder";
int iNum = 14;
_memicmp(szComp1, szComp2, iNum);
```

_msize()

`#include <malloc.h>`

Returns size in bytes of a memory block allocated with malloc().

Example:

```
iSize = _msize(pMemLocation);
```

_nextafter()

`#include <float.h>`

Returns next representable neighbor of x in the direction of y.

Example:

```
double x, y, result;
    x = 200.39434399999;
    y = 1000.99999;
    result = _nextafter(x, y);
```

WARNING This function seems to consistently return the value passed in as *x*. For instance, in this example, you would expect the function to return 200.394344; however, it seems to consistently return 200.39434399999.

_rotl()

```
#include <stdlib.h>
```

Left rotates an integer value by *n* bits.

Example:

```
    _rotl (0x759fe, nBitsToRotate);
```

_rotr()

```
#include <stdlib.h>
```

Right rotates an integer value by *n* bits.

Example:

```
    _rotr(0x759fe, nBitsToRotate);
```

_scalb()

```
#include <float.h>
```

Calculates the value of $x * 2^y$.

Example:

```
    _scalb(x, y);
```

_statusfp()

```
#include <float.h>
```

Gets the floating-point status word.

TIP The online help contains an excellent example of this function.

_swab()

`#include <stdlib.h>`

Swaps *n* bytes from one byte or char array to another.

Example:

```
_swab(szSource, szDest, nBytesToCopy);
```

_ultoa()

`#include <stdlib.h>`

Given an unsigned Long integer and the base (radix), converts the integer to an ANSI string.

Example:

```
_ultoa(lVal, szNum, 16);
```

_ultow()

`#include <stdlib.h>`

Given a Long integer and the base (radix), converts the integer to a Unicode string.

Example:

```
_ultow(lVal, szNum, 16);
```

_wcsdup()

`#include <string.h>`

(or `wchar.h`)

Allocates a Unicode string buffer and then copies the contents of `szSource` into the new string. The new string will be created with `malloc()`, and it is the responsibility of the calling program to `free()` the string at some point.

Example:

```
szNewString = _wcsdup(szSource);
```

_wcsicmp()

#include <string.h>

(or wchar.h)

Compares lower-cased versions of two Unicode strings.

Example:

```
WCHAR szFirst[] = TEXT("Windows CE is great!");
WCHAR szSecond[] = TEXT("WINDOWS CE IS GREAT!");
iResult = _wcsicmp(szFirst, szSecond); //these strings will be
equal.
```

_wcslwr()

#include <string.h>

(or wchar.h)

Lowercases a Unicode string.

Example:

```
WCHAR szUpper[] = TEXT("WINDOWS CE IS GREAT!");
_wcslwr(szUpper);
```

_wcsnicmp()

#include <string.h>

(or wchar.h)

Performs a case-insensitive comparison on iNum characters in two strings.

Example:

```
WCHAR szComp1[] = "Red house over";
WCHAR szComp2[] = "RED HOUSE OVER yonder";
int iNum = 14;
_wcsicmp(szComp1, szComp2, iNum);
```

_wcsnset()

#include <string.h>

(or wchar.h)

Replaces iNum characters of a Unicode string with the character specified; see also memset().

Example:

```
WCHAR szString[] = TEXT("Red house over");
_wcsnset(szString, TEXT('@'), 10);
```

_wcsrev()

```
#include <string.h>
```

(or wchar.h)

Reverses characters in a Unicode string.

Example:

```
WCHAR szString[] = "Red house over";
_wcsrev(szString);
```

_wcsset()

```
#include <string.h>
```

(or wchar.h)

Replaces all characters of a Unicode string with the specified character.

Example:

```
WCHAR szString[] = "Red house over";
_wcsset(szString, TEXT('@'));
```

_wcsupr()

```
#include <string.h>
```

(or wchar.h)

Uppercases a Unicode string.

Example:

```
WCHAR szUpper[] = TEXT("windows ce is great!");
_wcslwr(szUpper);
```

_wtoi()

```
#include <stdlib.h>
```

(or wchar.h)

Converts a Unicode string to an integer.

Example:

```
WCHAR szNum [] = TEXT("12345");
iNum = _wtoi(szNum);
```

_wtol()

```
#include <stdlib.h>
```

(or wchar.h)

Converts a Unicode string to a Long integer.

Example:

```
WCHAR szNum [] = TEXT("12345");
iNum = _wtol(szNum);
```

_y0()

```
#include <math.h>
```

Computes the Bessel function.

Example:

```
_y0(3.987);
```

_y1()

```
#include <math.h>
```

Computes the Bessel function.

Example:

```
_y1(3.987);
```

_yn()

```
#include <math.h>
```

Computes the Bessel function of order *x*.

Example:

```
_y0(x, 3.987);
```

abs()

```
#include <stdlib.h>
```

(or math.h)

Calculates the absolute value of an integer.

Example:

```
iAbsoluteVal = abs(-8000);
```

acos()

```
#include <math.h>
```

Calculates the arccosine of an angle of *x* radians.

Example:

```
fArcCos = acos(x);
```

asin()

```
#include <math.h>
```

Calculates the arcsine of *x* radians.

Example:

```
fArcSin = asin(x);
```

atan()

```
#include <math.h>
```

Calculates the arctangent of *x* radians.

Example:

```
fArcTan = atan(x);
```

atan2()

```
#include <math.h>
```

Calculates the arctangent of *x*/*y* radians.

Example:

```
fArcSin = atan2(y/x);
```

atoi()

```
#include <stdlib.h>
```

Converts an ANSI string to an integer.

Example:

```
char szNum [] = "12345";
iNum = atoi(szNum);
```

atol()

```
#include <stdlib.h>
```

Converts an ANSI string to a Long integer.

Example:

```
char szNum [] = "12345";
iNum = atol(szNum);
```

ceil()

```
#include <math.h>
```

Calculates the ceiling of a floating-point value.

Example:

```
fCeiling = ceil(x);
```

cos()

```
#include <math.h>
```

Calculates the cosine of *x* radians.

Example:

```
fCosine = cos(x);
```

cosh()

```
#include <math.h>
```

Calculates the hyperbolic cosine of *x* radians.

Example:

```
fHypCosine = cosh(x);
```

difftime()

```
#include <time.h>
```

Returns the difference between two time_t times.

Example:

```
time_t starting, ending, difference;
time(&starting);
//...do something time consuming
time(&ending);
difference = difftime(starting, ending);
```

div()

```
#include <stdlib.h>
```

Given numerator and denominator, calculates quotient and remainder, returning result in div_t structure.

Example:

```
div_t result;
result = div(3, 5); //3 divided by 5
```

exp()

```
#include <math.h>
```

Given a floating-point value, calculates the exponential.

```
y = exp(9.012847);
```

fabs()

#include <math.h>

Calculates the absolute value of an integer.

Example:

```
fAbsoluteVal = fabs(-4.36742);
```

floor()

#include <math.h>

Calculates the floor of a floating-point value.

Example:

```
fFloor = floor(x);
```

fmod()

#include <math.h>

Returns the modulus of a floating-point division.

Example:

```
fModulus = fmod(3.00, 5.00); //3.00 divided by 5.00
```

free()

#include <stdlib.h>

(or malloc.h)

Deallocates or releases memory allocated with malloc().

Example:

```
free(szDynamicString);
```

frexp()

#include <math.h>

Returns the mantissa and the exponent for a given floating-point value; performs the reverse operation of ldexp().

Example:

```
fMantissa = frexp(fFloatVal, &iExponent);
```

iswalnum()

```
#include <ctype.h>
```

(or wchar.h)

Returns true if the Unicode character falls in one of these ranges: A–Z, a–z, or 0–9.

Example:

```
bResult = iswalnum(TEXT('s'));
```

iswalpha()

```
#include <ctype.h>
```

(or wchar.h)

Returns true if the Unicode character falls in either of these ranges: A–Z or a–z.

Example:

```
bResult = iswalpha(TEXT('s'));
```

iswascii()

```
#include <ctype.h>
```

(or wchar.h)

Returns true if the Unicode character is an ASCII character.

Example:

```
bResult = iswascii('s');
```

iswcntrl()

```
#include <ctype.h>
```

(or wchar.h)

Returns true if the Unicode character is a control character.

Example:

```
bResult = iswcntrl(TEXT('\t'));
```

iswctype()

```
#include <ctype.h>
```

Tests the character c for the specified property.

Example:

```
int i = iswctype('D', _ALPHA|_UPPER);
```

iswgraph()

```
#include <ctype.h>
```

(or wchar.h)

Returns true if the Unicode character is a printable character and not a space.

Example:

```
bResult = iswgraph(TEXT('~'));
```

iswlower()

```
#include <ctype.h>
```

(or wchar.h)

Returns true if the Unicode character is a lowercase character.

Example:

```
bResult = iswalnum(TEXT('t'));
```

iswprint()

```
#include <ctype.h>
```

(or wchar.h)

Returns true if the Unicode character is a printable character.

Example:

```
bResult = iswprint(TEXT('*'));
```

iswpunct()

```
#include <ctype.h>
```

(or wchar.h)

Returns true if the Unicode character is a punctuation mark.

Example:

```
bResult = iswpunct(TEXT('!'));
```

iswspace()

```
#include <ctype.h>
```

(or wchar.h)

Returns true if the Unicode character is a space.

Example:

```
bResult = iswpunct(TEXT(' '));
```

iswupper()

```
#include <ctype.h>
```

(or wchar.h)

Returns true if the Unicode character is an uppercase character.

Example:

```
bResult = iswupper(TEXT('E'));
```

iswxdigit()

```
#include <ctype.h>
```

(or wchar.h)

Returns true if the Unicode character is a hexadecimal digit; that is, a character that falls in one of these ranges: 0–9, A–F, or a–f.

Example:

```
bResult = iswxdigit(TEXT('d'));
```

labs()

#include <stdlib.h>

(or math.h)

Calculates the absolute value of a Long integer.

Example:

```
lAbsoluteVal = abs(-4,568,992);
```

ldexp()

#include <math.h>

Given the mantissa and the exponent, calculates a floating-point value; performs the reverse operation of frexp().

Example:

```
fFloatVal = frexp(fMantissa, &iExponent);
```

ldiv()

#include <stdlib.h>

Given numerator and denominator, calculates quotient and remainder, returning result in ldiv_t structure; Long integer version of div().

Example:

```
ldiv_t result;
result = div(39873, 574359); //39873 divided by 574359
```

log()

#include <math.h>

Calculates the logarithm of a given floating-point value.

Example:

```
y = log(x);
```

log10()

```
#include <math.h>
```

Calculates the natural (or base 10) logarithm of a given floating-point value.

Example:

```
y = log(x);
```

longjmp()

```
#include <setjmp.h>
```

Restores stack environment and execution locale.

TIP   The online help contains an excellent example of this function.

---

malloc()

```
#include <stdlib.h>
```

(or malloc.h)

Allocates or reserves memory blocks.

Example:

```
szString = (TCHAR *) malloc(100 * sizeof(TCHAR));
```

mbstowcs()

```
#include <stdlib.h>
```

Converts a sequence of multibyte or ANSI characters to a corresponding sequence of wide or Unicode characters.

Example:

```
mbstowcs(szWideString, szANSIString, strlen(szANSIString));
```

memchr()

#include <memory.h>

(or string.h)

Searches iCount characters of the szString buffer for the character cChar; returns a pointer to the first occurrence of the cChar.

Example:

```
szMatch = memchr(szString, cChar, iCount);
```

memcmp()

#include <memory.h>

(or string.h)

Compares iCount characters of two buffers.

Example:

```
iResult = memcmp(szStr1, szStr2, iCount);
```

memcpy()

#include <memory.h>

(or string.h)

Copies iCount characters from szSource to szDest buffers.

Example:

```
memcpy(szDest, szSource, iCount);
```

memmove()

#include <string.h>

(or memory.h)

Copies iCount characters from szSource to szDest buffers.

Example:

```
memmove(szDest, szSource, iCount);
```

memset()

#include <string.h>

(or memory.h)

Replaces iNum characters of an ANSI string or char buffer with the character specified; see also _wcsnset().

Example:

```
char szString[] = "Red house over";
memset(szString, '@', 10);
```

modf()

#include <math.h>

Extracts the integer portion and decimal portion of a floating-point number.

Example:

```
fDecimalPortion = modf(fFloatVal, &iIntPortion);
```

pow()

#include <math.h>

Returns x to the y power.

Example:

```
pow(x, y);
```

qsort()

#include <stdlib.h>

Performs a quick sort.

Example:

```
qsort (infoarray, numelements, sizeof(DWORD), fnCompare);
```

rand()

#include <stdlib.h>

Returns a pseudorandom number.

Example:

```
iWinningLottoNum = rand();
```

realloc()

```
#include <stdlib.h>
```

(or `malloc.h`)

Reallocates memory blocks originally allocated with `malloc()`.

Example:

```
realloc(szBuffer, iNewSize);
```

sin()

```
#include <math.h>
```

Calculates the sine of *x*.

Example:

```
sin(x);
```

sinh()

```
#include <math.h>
```

Calculates the hyperbolic sine of *x*.

Example:

```
sinh(x);
```

sqrt()

```
#include <math.h>
```

Calculates the square root of a given floating-point value.

Example:

```
sqrt(4.00);
```

srand()

```
#include <stdlib.h>
```

Seeds the random number generation function, rand(), with a starting value.

Example:

```
srand(8945373);
```

strcat()

```
#include <string.h>
```

Concatenates or adds the contents szString2 to the end of szString1, where szString1 and szString2 are both ANSI strings.

Example:

```
strcat(szString1, szString2);
```

strchr()

```
#include <string.h>
```

Finds an ANSI character in an ANSI string and returns a pointer to the first occurrence of that character in the string.

Example:

```
strchr(szString, 'c');
```

strcmp()

```
#include <string.h>
```

Compares contents of two NULL-terminated ANSI strings; performs a case-sensitive comparison.

Example:

```
iResult = strcmp(szStr1, szStr2);
```

strcpy()

```
#include <string.h>
```

Copies the contents of one ANSI string to another.

Example:

```
strcpy(szDest, szSource);
```

strcspn()

```
#include <string.h>
```

Searches an ANSI string szToSearch for an ANSI substring szSub; returns an integer specifying the number of characters in szToSearch before one of the characters in szSub occurs.

Example:

```
char szToSearch[] = "789areyou?";
char szSub[] = "eyou?";
strcspn(szToSearch, szSub); //result will be 5
```

strlen()

```
#include <string.h>
```

Returns the length in bytes of an ANSI string.

Example:

```
strlen("Hello, World!"); //result will be 13
```

strncat()

```
#include <string.h>
```

Appends at most iCount characters from ANSI string szSource to ANSI string szDest.

Example:

```
strncat(szDest, szSource, iCount);
```

strncmp()

```
#include <string.h>
```

Compares iCount characters of two ANSI strings.

Example:

```
iResult = strncmp(szStr1, szStr2, iCount); //compare the first
 iCount characters
```

strncpy()

```
#include <string.h>
```

Copies iCount characters from ANSI string szSource to ANSI string szDest.

Example:

```
strncpy(szDest+5, szSource, iCount); //copy first iCount characters
of szSource to szDest, starting at szDest's 5th character
```

strstr()

```
#include <string.h>
```

Finds an ANSI substring szSub in an ANSI string szString; returns a pointer to the first occurrence of szSub in szString.

Example:

```
szFirstOccurrence = strstr(szString, szSub);
```

strtok()

```
#include <string.h>
```

Parses an ANSI string by searching for single ANSI character delimiters in the string; returns a pointer to the next token.

Example:

```
char szStrToParse[] = "Windows CE version 2.11";
char* szToken = strtok(szStrToParse, " "); //szToken will point to
"Windows"
szToken = strtok(NULL, " "); //szToken will point to "CE"
//...etc.
```

swprintf()

```
#include <stdio.h>
```

(or wchar.h)

A printf()-like function that "prints" the data elements to a Unicode string instead of a console.

Example:

```
swprintf(szMsg, TEXT("%d:%d -%s"), 5024, 898, szTemp);
```

swscanf()

`#include <stdio.h>`

(or `wchar.h`)

Reads data elements from a formatted Unicode string; essentially performs the reverse function of `swprintf()`.

Example:

```
    swscanf("3 9 4 yes!", "%d %d %d %s", iInt1, iInt2, iInt3,
szString); //iInt1, etc. will all be filled with correct values from
the string
```

tan()

`#include <math.h>`

Calculates the tangent of x.

Example:

```
    fTangent = tan(x);
```

tanh()

`#include <math.h>`

Calculates the hyperbolic tangent of x.

Example:

```
    fHypTangent = tanh(x);
```

towlower()

`#include <ctype.h>`

(or `wchar.h`)

Converts a Unicode character to lowercase; characters already lowercased are ignored.

Example:

```
    towlower('P');
```

towupper()

```
#include <ctype.h>
```

(or wchar.h)

Converts a Unicode character to uppercase; characters already uppercased are ignored.

Example:

```
towupper('P');
```

vswprintf()

```
#include <stdlib.h>
```

Writes formatted output using a pointer to a list of arguments.

Example:

```
WCHAR wszBufferX[100];
mywsprintf (wszBufferX, TEXT("Number: %u, Text: %s"), 1234, 31415,
TEXT("Hello"));

//wraps a wsprintf function
void mywsprintf (LPWSTR pszTarget, LPWSTR pszFormat, int iCustom-
Value, ...)
{
    va_list varlist;
    va_start (varlist, iCustomValue);
    vswprintf (pszTarget, pszFormat, varlist);
}
```

wcscat()

```
#include <string.h>
```

(or wchar.h)

Concatenates or adds the contents szString2 to the end of szString1, where szString1 and szString2 are both Unicode strings.

Example:

```
wstrcat(szString1, szString2);
```

wcschr()

#include <string.h>

(or wchar.h)

Finds a Unicode character in a Unicode string and returns a pointer to the first occurrence of that character in the string.

Example:

```
wcschr(szString, TEXT("c"));
```

wcscmp()

#include <string.h>

(or wchar.h)

Compares contents of two Unicode strings; performs a case-sensitive comparison.

Example:

```
iResult = wcscmp(szStr1, szStr2);
```

wcscpy()

#include <string.h>

(or wchar.h)

Copies the contents of one Unicode string to another.

Example:

```
wcscpy(szDest, szSource);
```

wcscspn()

#include <string.h>

(or wchar.h)

Searches a Unicode string szToSearch for a Unicode substring szSub; returns an integer specifying the number of characters in szToSearch before one of the characters in szSub occurs.

Example:

```
WCHAR szToSearch[] = TEXT("789areyou?");
WCHAR szSub[] = TEXT("eyou?");
wcscspn(szToSearch, szSub); //result will be 5
```

wcslen()

`#include <string.h>`

(or `wchar.h`)

Returns the length in characters of a Unicode string.

WARNING   You'll recall that Unicode characters are actually two bytes wide, which means that you must multiply the return value of `wsclen()` by 2 if you want to determine the number of bytes the Unicode string occupies.

Example:

```
wcslen(TEXT("Hello, World!")); //result will be 13
```

wcsncat()

`#include <string.h>`

Appends at most `iCount` characters from Unicode string `szSource` to Unicode string `szDest`.

Example:

```
wcsncat(szDest, szSource, iCount);
```

wcsncmp()

`#include <string.h>`

(or `wchar.h`)

Compares `iCount` characters of two Unicode strings.

Example:

```
iResult = wcsncmp(szStr1, szStr2, 7); //compare the first 7 charac-
ters
```

wcsncpy()

`#include <string.h>`

(or `wchar.h`)

Copies iCount characters from Unicode string szSource to Unicode string szDest.

Example:

```
wcsncpy(szDest+5, szSource, 6); //copy first 6 characters of
szSource to szDest, starting at szDest's 5th character
```

wcspbrk()

```
#include <string.h>
```

Scans strings for characters in specified character sets.

Example:

```
LPWSTR wszStr = TEXT("Test+String");
LPWSTR wszSearchChars = TEXT("+");

//locate the first occurence of any character in the wszSearchChars
list
LPWSTR pszFound = wcspbrk(wszStr, wszSearchChars);    //pszFound
should point to "+String"
```

wcsrchr()

```
#include <string.h>
```

(or wchar.h)

Finds a Unicode character in a Unicode string and returns a pointer to the first occurrence of that character in the string.

Example:

```
wcsrchr(szString, 'c');
```

wcsspn()

```
#include <string.h>
```

(or wchar.h)

Searches a Unicode string szToSearch for a Unicode substring szSub; returns an integer specifying the number of characters in szToSearch before one of the characters in szSub occurs.

Example:

```
WCHAR szToSearch[] = TEXT("789areyou?");
WCHAR szSub[] = TEXT("eyou?");
wcsspn (szToSearch, szSub); //result will be 5
```

wcsstr()

```
#include <string.h>
```

(or wchar.h)

Finds a Unicode substring szSub in a Unicode string szString; returns a pointer to the first occurrence of szSub in szString.

Example:

```
szFirstOccurrence = wcsstr(szString, szSub);
```

wcstod()

```
#include <string.h>
```

(or wchar.h)

Converts a string szNum to a (double) floating-point value; stops scanning at first non-numeric character and returns a pointer to this first non-numeric character as szStopAt.

Example:

```
fFloatVal = wcstod(szNum, &szStopAt);
```

wcstok()

```
#include <string.h>
```

(or wchar.h)

Parses a Unicode string by searching for single Unicode character delimiters in the string; returns a pointer to the next token.

Example:

```
WCHAR szStrToParse[] = TEXT("Windows CE version 2.11");
WCHAR* szToken = wcstok(szStrToParse, TEXT(" ")); //szToken will
point to "Windows"
szToken = wcstok(NULL, TEXT(" ")); //szToken will point to "CE"
//...etc.
```

wcstol()

#include <string.h>

(or wchar.h)

Converts a string szNum to a Long integer value; stops scanning at first non-numeric character and returns a pointer to this first non-numeric character as szStopAt.

Example:

```
fLongIntVal = wcstol(szNum, &szStopAt);
```

wcstombs()

#include <string.h>

(or wchar.h)

Converts a sequence of Unicode characters to a corresponding sequence of multibyte or ANSI characters.

Example:

```
wcstombs(szANSIString, szWideString, wcslen(szWideString) *
sizeof(WCHAR));
```

wcstoul()

#include <string.h>

(or wchar.h)

Converts a string szNum to a Long unsigned integer value; stops scanning at first non-numeric character and returns a pointer to this first non-numeric character as szStopAt.

Example:

```
fUIntVal = wcstoul(szNum, &szStopAt);
```

wsprintf()

#include <winbase.h>

A printf()-like function that "prints" the result to a string instead of a console.

Example:

```
wsprintf(szMsg, TEXT("%d:%d -%s"), 5024, 898, szTemp);
```

APPENDIX

B

The CE 2.0 API

This appendix contains a list of those API functions specific to Windows CE 2.0. The format that we will use to describe these functions is as follows:

Function Name

```
#include <Header file to be included>
```

Brief description

Example

Explanation of example

Unless otherwise explicitly stated, all strings are assumed to be Unicode-based or wide strings. If a function has a RAPI version that is named the same as the CE-based version, the CE-based header file will be given first, with `rapi.h` following on the next line to indicate that a RAPI version of that function (with that name) also exists.

AddAddressCard()

```
#include <addrstor.h>
```

One of the Contacts database functions; adds a new entry to the Contacts database.

Example:

```
AddAddressCard(&ac, &oidCard, &index);
```

Where:

- `ac` is an AddressCard holding the information to be added to the database.

- `oidCard` is a CEOID; the function will return the CEOID of the record after it has been added.

- `index` is an integer; the function will return the index of the record after it has been added.

The AddressCard structure is defined as follows:

```
typedef struct _AddressCard {
SYSTEMTIME stBirthday;
SYSTEMTIME stAnniversary;
TCHAR *pszBusinessFax;
TCHAR *pszCompany;
```

```
TCHAR *pszDepartment;
TCHAR *pszEmail;
TCHAR *pszMobilePhone;
TCHAR *pszOfficeLocation;
TCHAR *pszPager;
TCHAR *pszWorkPhone;
TCHAR *pszTitle;
TCHAR *pszHomePhone;
TCHAR *pszEmail2;
TCHAR *pszSpouse;
TCHAR *pszNotes;
TCHAR *pszEmail3;
TCHAR *pszHomePhone2;
TCHAR *pszHomeFax;
TCHAR *pszCarPhone;
TCHAR *pszAssistant;
TCHAR *pszAssistantPhone;
TCHAR *pszChildren;
TCHAR *pszCategory;
TCHAR *pszWebPage;
TCHAR *pszWorkPhone2;
TCHAR *pszNamePrefix;
TCHAR *pszGivenName;
TCHAR *pszMiddleName;
TCHAR *pszSurname;
TCHAR *pszGeneration;
TCHAR *pszHomeAddrStreet;
TCHAR *pszHomeAddrCity;
TCHAR *pszHomeAddrState;
TCHAR *pszHomeAddrPostalCode;
TCHAR *pszHomeAddrCountry;
TCHAR *pszOtherAddrStreet;
TCHAR *pszOtherAddrCity;
TCHAR *pszOtherAddrState;
TCHAR *pszOtherAddrPostalCode;
TCHAR *pszOtherAddrCountry;
TCHAR *pszOfficeAddrStreet;
TCHAR *pszOfficeAddrCity;
TCHAR *pszOfficeAddrState;
TCHAR *pszOfficeAddrPostalCode;
TCHAR *pszOfficeAddrCountry;
BYTE *rgbReserved[84]
} AddressCard;
```

BatteryNotifyOfTimeChange()

```
#include <winbase.h>
```

Notifies battery of system time change. Used by OS to recalculate battery elapsed time when user or an application changes system time.

Example:

```
SYSTEMTIME st;
FILETIME ft;
BOOL bAhead;
GetSystemTime(&st);
bAhead = TRUE;
st.wHour = st.wHour + 1; //daylight savings? spring ahead
SetSystemTime(&st);
memset(&st, "/0", sizeof(st));
st.wHour = 1;
SystemTimeToFileTime(&st, &ft)
BatteryNotifyOfTimeChange(bAhead, &ft);
```

Where:

- bAhead is a BOOL indicating whether the time is being set ahead (TRUE) or backward (FALSE).

- ft is a FILETIME 64-bit time structure.

TIP

It is almost always easier to use the SYSTEMTIME structure and then convert to a FILETIME, as opposed to attempting to directly manipulate the FILETIME structure. This is shown in the above example.

CeCheckPassword()

```
#include <winbase.h>
```

(or rapi.h)

Checks supplied password against system password.

Example:

```
TCHAR szPwd[MAX_PATH] = TEXT("IamTheWalrus");
CeCheckPassword(szPwd);
```

Where:

- szPwd is a string specifying the password to be checked.

CeClearUserNotification()

`#include <notify.h>`

Removes or clears a User Notification created with a prior call to CeSetUser-Notification().

Example:

```
CeClearNotification(hNotification);
```

Where:

- hNotification is a handle to an existing notification.

CeCloseHandle()

`#include <rapi.h>`

RAPI version of the CloseHandle() function; closes an active handle to an object.

Example:

```
CeCloseHandle(hCeObject);
```

Where:

- hCeObject is an active handle to a CE system object such as a file.

TIP   Although CeFindClose() is used to close a CeFindFirstFile() search, CeCloseHandle() should be used to close a CeFindFirstDatabase() search.

CeCopyFile()

`#include <rapi.h>`

RAPI version of the CopyFile() function; copies an existing file on the CE device to a new path/file on the CE device.

Example:

```
TCHAR szSource[MAX_PATH] = TEXT("\\source.txt");
TCHAR szDest[MAX_PATH] = TEXT("\\dest.txt");
bFailOnExist = FALSE;
CeCopyFile(szSource, szDest, bFailOnExist);
```

Where:

- szSource is the source file.

- szDest is the destination file.

- bFailOnExist is a BOOL indicating whether the function should fail if the destination file already exists.

CeCreateDatabase()

#include <winbase.h>

(or rapi.h)

Part of the CE database engine; creates a database.

Example:

```
TCHAR szName[MAX_PATH] = TEXT("MasterDB"); //set name of database
//set up sort orders
soSortOrders[SORT_ORDER_CODE].propid =
MAKELONG(CEVT_LPWSTR,PROP_CODE);
    soSortOrders[SORT_ORDER_CODE].dwFlags= CEDB_SORT_GENERICORDER;
//Ascending (default) order
    soSortOrders[SORT_ORDER_STATE].propid =
MAKELONG(CEVT_LPWSTR,PROP_STATE);
    soSortOrders[SORT_ORDER_CODE].dwFlags= CEDB_SORT_GENERICORDER;
//Ascending (default) order
    wCount = 2;   //two sort orders
    oidObjId = CeCreateDatabase(szName, DB_ID, wCount, soSortOrders);
```

Where:

- szName is a string containing the name of the database.

- DB_ID is an integer identifying the database. The database ID is intended to be used as a unique ID by which applications may reference a database instead of using the database's name, usually a #define constant.

- wCount is a WORD specifying the number of sort orders (maximum is 4).

- soSortOrders is an array of SORTORDERSPEC structures used to specify the sort orders of the database.

- oidObjId is a CEOID. The function will return the CEOID of the database created.

The SORTORDERSPEC structure is defined as follows:

```
typedef struct _SORTORDERSPEC {
PEGPROPID propid;
DWORD dwFlags;
} SORTORDERSPEC;
```

CeCreateDirectory()

```
#include <rapi.h>
```

RAPI version of CreateDirectory() function; creates a directory on the CE device.

Example:

```
TCHAR szPath[MAX_PATH] = TEXT("\\My Documents\\My App");
CeCreateDirectory(szPath, NULL);
```

Where:

- szPath is a string specifying the directory to be created.

TIP The second parameter is always NULL on CE; on 98/NT it would specify the security attributes of the directory.

CeCreateFile()

```
#include <rapi.h>
```

RAPI version of CreateFile() function; creates a file for reading or writing and returns an active handle to that file.

Example:

```
TCHAR szFileName[MAX_PATH] = TEXT("\\data.txt");
wAccess = GENERIC_WRITE;
wShare = 0;
```

```
dwCreate = CREATE_ALWAYS;
dwFlags = FILE_ATTRIBUTE_NORMAL;
hSrc = CeCreateFile(
szFileName,
wAccess,
wShare,
NULL,
dwCreate,
dwFlags,
NULL);
```

Where:

- szFileName is a string specifying the name of the file to open.

- wAccess is a WORD specifying the type of access (GENERIC_READ and/or GENERIC_WRITE).

- wShare is a WORD specifying under what conditions another application may open or modify the file while you are using it (0 for no access, FILE_SHARE_READ to permit read access, and FILE_SHARE_WRITE to permit write access).

- dwCreate is a DWORD specifying whether you are attempting to open an existing file or create a file (CREATE_ALWAYS always creates the file, OPEN_EXISTING attempts to open an existing file, etc.).

- dwFlags is a DWORD specifying additional file attributes, such as the archive, hidden, or read-only flags.

TIP   The fourth parameter specifies security attributes and the seventh specifies a template file. Both are always NULL on CE.

CeCreateProcess()

```
#include <rapi.h>
```

RAPI version of CreateProcess() function; launches a program on the CE device.

Example:

```
//launches Pocket Word
TCHAR szAppName[MAX_PATH] = TEXT("\\windows\\pword.exe");
TCHAR szCmdLine[MAX_PATH] = TEXT("\\My Documents\\AWordFile.doc");
dwCreate = 0;
CeCreateProcess(szAppName, szCmdLine, NULL, NULL, FALSE, dwCreate,
NULL, NULL, NULL, &pi);
```

Where:

- szAppName is the path and file name of the application to be started on the CE device.

- szCmdLine is a string specifying the command line to be passed to the application being started; can be NULL.

- dwCreate is a DWORD specifying creation options, such as whether the process is to be created suspended, and so on. In this example, we set dwCreate to 0 so that the process will be launched immediately.

- pi is a structure of type PROCESS_INFORMATION; used to return information about the started process to the calling application.

The PROCESS_INFORMATION structure is defined as follows:

```
typedef struct _PROCESS_INFORMATION {
HANDLE hProcess;
HANDLE hThread;
DWORD dwProcessId;
DWORD dwThreadId;
} PROCESS_INFORMATION;
```

CeDeleteDatabase()

```
#include <winbase.h>
```

(or rapi.h)

Deletes a database from the CE device.

Example:

```
CeDeleteDatabase(CeOid);
```

Where:

- CeOid is a CEOID of a valid, existing database.

WARNING Although `CeDeleteDatabase()` is sensitive to sharing violations (i.e., it will not delete the database if it is being actively used by another process), it does not check to ensure that the database is empty before deleting it. In other words, it is entirely possible to delete a database with perfectly good data in it.

CeDeleteFile()

```
#include <rapi.h>
```

RAPI version of `DeleteFile()` function; deletes a file from the CE device.

Example:

```
TCHAR szFileName[MAX_PATH] = TEXT("\\deleteme.txt");
CeDeleteFile(szFileName);
```

Where:

- `szFileName` is the name of the file to be deleted.

CeDeleteRecord()

```
#include <winbase.h>
```

(or `rapi.h`)

Deletes the specified record from the specified database.

Example:

```
CeDeleteRecord( hDatabase, oid );
```

Where:

- `hDatabase` is a valid handle to a database.
- `oid` is the `CEOID` of the record to be deleted.

CeFindAllDatabases()

```
#include <rapi.h>
```

RAPI function that returns a list of all databases of a certain type on the CE device.

Example:

```
dwType = 0;
LPCEDB_FIND_DATA pFindData;
wFlags = FAD_OID | FAD_FLAGS | FAD_NAME | FAD_TYPE FAD_NUM_RECORDS
| FAD_NUM_SORT_ORDER | FAD_SORT_SPECS;
    CeFindAllDatabases( DbType, 0xFF, &cFound, &pFindData);
```

Where:

- dwType is a DWORD specifying the database type ID to search for; 0 retrieves all databases.

- wFlags is a WORD specifying what pieces of information the function should retrieve. (In the example above, all possible flags are retrieved; the same effect could be achieved by setting this parameter to 0xFF.)

- cFound is an integer used by the function to indicate the number of matching databases found.

- pFindData is a pointer to an array of cFindData elements, where each element is a CEDB_FIND_DATA structure.

The CEDB_FIND_DATA structure is defined as follows:

```
struct CEDB_FIND_DATA {
CEOID OidDb;
CEDBASEINFO DbInfo;
};
```

The CEDBASEINFO, which you'll notice is a member of the CEDB_FIND_DATA structure, is defined as follows:

```
typedef struct _CEDBASEINFO {
DWORD dwFlags;
WCHAR szDbaseName[CEDB_MAXDBASENAMELEN];
DWORD dwDbaseType;
WORD wNumRecords;
WORD wNumSortOrder;
DWORD dwSize;
FILETIME ftLastModified;
SORTORDERSPEC rgSortSpecs[CEDB_MAXSORTORDER];
} CEDBASEINFO;
```

CeFindAllFiles()

```
#include <rapi.h>
```

RAPI function that returns a list of all files on the CE device matching the specified criteria.

Example:

```
TCHAR szSearchPath[MAX_PATH] = TEXT("\\*.txt");
dwAttributes = FAF_ATTRIBUTES | FAF_NAME;
CeFindAllFiles(szSearchPath, dwAttributes, &cFound, &pFindData);
```

Where:

- szSearchPath is a string specifying the path and/or filename to search for; can contain wildcards.

- dwAttributes is a DWORD used to set searching options; can be used to filter certain file types and tell the function which pieces of information you want it to return to your program.

- cFound is an integer used by the function to return the number of matching files found.

- pFindData is a pointer to an array of cFound elements where each element is a CE_FIND_DATA structure.

The CE_FIND_DATA structure is defined as follows:

```
typedef struct _CE_FIND_DATA {
DWORD dwFileAttributes;
FILETIME ftCreationTime;
FILETIME ftLastAccessTime;
FILETIME ftLastWriteTime;
DWORD nFileSizeHigh;
DWORD nFileSizeLow;
DWORD dwOID;
WCHAR cFileName[MAX_PATH];
} CE_FIND_DATA;
```

CeFindClose()

```
#include <rapi.h>
```

RAPI version of FindClose() function; closes a search handle and frees memory associated with Find operation.

Example:

```
hFind = CeFindFirstFile( TEXT("\\*.exe"), &wfd);
do
{
    //do something with found files
}while(CeFindNextFile(hFind, &wfd));
CeFindClose(hFind);
```

Where:

- hFind is a handle to the search operation.

CeFindFirstDatabase()

`#include <winbase.h>`

(or rapi.h)

Finds the first database matching the criteria.

Example:

```
dwDatabaseType = 0;
hFind = CeFindFirstDatabase(dwDatabaseType);
do
{
    //...
} while (oid = CeFindNextDatabase( hFind ));
CloseHandle( hFind );
```

Where:

- dwDatabaseType is a DWORD specifying either the database type ID to search for, or 0 to retrieve all databases.

CeFindFirstFile()

`#include <rapi.h>`

RAPI version of FindFirstFile() function; finds first file matching specified criteria.

Example:

```
TCHAR szFileSpec[MAX_PATH] = TEXT("\\*.exe");
hFind = CeFindFirstFile(szFileSpec, &wfd);
```

```
do
{
    //do something with found files
}while(CeFindNextFile(hFind, &wfd));
CeFindClose(hFind);
```

Where:

- szFileSpec is a string specifying the filename to match; can contain wild-cards.

CeFindNextDatabase()

```
#include <winbase.h>
```

(or rapi.h)

Finds the next database matching the criteria; used in conjunction with
CeFindFirstDatabase().

Example:

```
dwDatabaseType = 0;
hFind = CeFindFirstDatabase(dwDatabaseType);
do
{
    //...
} while (oid = CeFindNextDatabase( hFind ));
CloseHandle( hFind );
```

Where:

- hFind is a valid handle returned by CeFindFirstDatabase().

CeFindNextFile()

```
#include <rapi.h>
```

RAPI version of FindNextFile() function; finds next file matching specified
criteria.

Example:

```
TCHAR szFileSpec[MAX_PATH] = TEXT("\\*.exe");
hFind = CeFindFirstFile(szFileSpec, &wfd);
do
{
```

```
    //do something with found files
  }while(CeFindNextFile(hFind, &wfd));
  CeFindClose(hFind);
```

Where:

- szFileSpec is a string specifying the filename to match; can contain wild-cards.

CeGetClassName()

```
#include <rapi.h>
```

Retrieves the class name of a given window handle.

Example:

```
GetClassName(hWnd, szClass, iLength);
```

Where:

- hWnd is the handle of the window whose class name is being requested.

- szClass is a string the function will use to store the class name of the window.

- iLength is the maximum length, in number of characters, of szClass.

CeGetDesktopDeviceCaps()

```
#include <rapi.h>
```

RAPI version of GetDeviceCaps() function; retrieves one of several possible pieces of information about the CE device.

Example:

```
iParamToRetrieve = HORZSIZE;
iWidth = CeGetDesktopDeviceCaps(iParamToRetrieve);
```

Where:

- iParamToRetrieve is an integer specifying one of several possible flags that tell the function which piece of information to retrieve. The value returned will be an integer containing the value requested. Some common flags specified are

    HORZSIZE   Function retrieves the horizontal dimensions of the device's screen.

VERTSIZE Function retrieves the vertical dimensions of the device's screen.

HORZRES Function retrieves the horizontal resolution of the device's screen.

VERTRES Function retrieves the vertical resolution of the device's screen.

CeGetDeviceId()

```
#include <ceutil.h>
```

Retrieves the ID of the currently selected device. Although the CE devices registered with the system appear as "friendly names" in the Mobile Devices window, they are actually identified in the Desktop machine's registry via a unique ID assigned to each device when it first connects to the system. This function, then, is useful in enabling you to work with the registry to retrieve various settings and properties of the connected device.

Example:

```
iCurrentDeviceId = CeGetDeviceId();
```

Where:

- `iCurrentDeviceId` is an integer that will store the ID of the currently connected device.

TIP

The device ID is a subkey of the `HKEY_CURRENT_USER\Software\Microsoft\Windows CE Services\Partners` key.

NOTE

This is a Desktop-based function designed for working with registry entries related to CE Services. Unlike RAPI functions, you do *not* need to have a CE device connected in order to use the **ceutil** functions.

CeGetFileAttributes()

```
#include <rapi.h>
```

RAPI version of `GetFileAttributes()` function; retrieves attributes for a file, given the file name.

Example:

```
TCHAR szFile[MAX_PATH] = TEXT("\\windows\\pword.exe");
dwAttribs = CeGetFileAttributes(szFile);
```

Where:

- `szFile` is a string containing the name of the file whose attributes the function should retrieve.

- `dwAttribs` is a `DWORD` into which the function will return the file's attributes. In addition to the usual archive, read-only, etc. flags, Windows CE introduces two new file attributes:

    FILE_ATTRIBUTE_INROM   A nonexecutable ROM file. Can be opened for read-only access.

    FILE_ATTRIBUTE_ROMMODULE   An executable ROM file. Cannot be opened as a file, but must instead be executed (if an executable) or loaded (if a DLL).

CeGetFileSize()

```
#include <rapi.h>
```

RAPI version of `GetFileSize()` function; retrieves size of a file.

Example:

```
DWORD dwHigh;
dwSize = GetFileSize (hFile, &dwHigh);
```

Where:

- `hFile` is a handle to an open file.

- `dwSize` will receive the low 32 bits of the file's size.

- `dwHigh` will receive the high 32 bits of the file's size; may be NULL if files are known to have a size of 4GB or less.

CeGetFileTime()

`#include <rapi.h>`

RAPI version of `GetFileTime()` function; retrieves the created, last accessed, and last modified date-time stamps for a file.

Example:

```
CeGetFileTime(hFile, &ftCreate, &ftAccess, &ftModified);
```

Where:

- `hFile` is a handle to an open file.

- `ftCreate` is a FILETIME structure the function will use to return the created date-time.

- `ftAccess` is a FILETIME structure the function will use to return the created date-time.

- `ftModified` is a FILETIME structure the function will use to return the created date-time.

TIP   See `BatteryNotifyOfTimeChange()` for more information about the `FILETIME` structure and how to best use it.

WARNING   Only files stored on a Compact Flash card will report the same values for `ftModified` and `ftCreate`. Files stored in main storage (not a Compact Flash card) will always report all three `FILETIME` values as being the same as the last modified date `ftModified`.

CeGetLastError()

`#include <rapi.h>`

RAPI version of `GetLastError()` function; returns numeric value of last error generated due to error on the CE device itself.

Example:

```
hErrorCode = CeGetLastError();
```

Where:

- hErrorCode is an HRESULT value.

CeGetSelectedDeviceId()

```
#include <ceutil.h>
```

Related to CeGetDeviceId(); part of the RAPI-like ceutil.h functions.

Example:

```
dwDeviceId = CeGetSelectedDeviceId();
```

Where:

- dwDeviceID is a DWORD that will store the device ID returned by the function.

CeGetSpecialFolderPath()

```
#include <rapi.h>
```

RAPI version of the GetSpecialFolderPath() function; retrieves the true path of a system "special folder."

Example:

```
CeGetSpecialFolderPath(CSIDL_BITBUCKET, MAX_PATH, szPath);
```

Where:

- The first parameter specifies which path (i.e., special folder) to retrieve; in this case, the recycle bin.
- The second parameter specifies the length of szPath.
- szPath is a string that will hold the actual path of the special folder.

NOTE For more information on this function and its parameters, see Chapter 10.

CeGetStoreInformation()

```
#include <rapi.h>
```

RAPI version of GetStoreInformation() function; retrieves information about the CE object store (i.e., that part of RAM used as storage space).

Example:

```
CeGetStoreInformation(&siStoreInfo);
```

Where:

- siStoreInfo is a STORE_INFORMATION structure.

The STORE_INFORMATION structure is defined as follows:

```
typedef struct STORE_INFORMATION {
DWORD dwStoreSize;
DWORD dwFreeSize;
} STORE_INFORMATION;
```

CeGetSystemInfo()

```
#include <rapi.h>
```

RAPI version of GetSystemInfo(); retrieves generic operating system information about the CE device.

Example:

```
CeGetSystemInfo(&siSystemInfo);
```

Where:

- siSystemInfo is a SYSTEM_INFO structure.

The SYSTEM_INFO structure is defined as follows:

```
typedef struct _SYSTEM_INFO {
DWORD dwOemId;
DWORD dwPageSize;
LPVOID lpMinimumApplicationAddress;
LPVOID lpMaximumApplicationAddress;
DWORD dwActiveProcessorMask;
DWORD dwNumberOfProcessors;
DWORD dwProcessorType;
DWORD dwAllocationGranularity;
DWORD dwReserved;
} SYSTEM_INFO;
```

CeGetSystemMetrics()

```
#include <rapi.h>
```

RAPI version of `GetSystemMetrics()` function; retrieves sizes (in pixels) of certain graphical elements.

Example:

```
    iWidth = CeGetSystemMetrics(SM_CXSCREEN); //retrieves width of
screen
```

Where:

- `iWidth` is an integer that will store the value returned by the function. Common values for this parameter are

  SM_CXSCREEN   Retrieves the width of the screen.

  SM_CYSCREEN   Retrieves the height of the screen.

CeGetSystemPowerStatusEx()

```
#include <rapi.h>
```

RAPI version of `GetSystemPowerStatusEx()` function; retrieves information about the CE device's power source.

Example:

```
    bMostCurrentInfo = FALSE;
    CeGetSystemPowerStatusEx(&psPowerStatus, bMostCurrentInfo);
```

Where:

- `psPowerStatus` is a SYSTEM_POWER_STATUS_EX structure.

- `bMostCurrentInfo` is a BOOL value indicating whether the function should query the device driver directly for the most up-to-date information or whether it should use cached information that may be several seconds old.

The SYSTEM_POWER_STATUS_EX structure is defined as follows:

```
typedef struct _SYSTEM_POWER_STATUS_EX {
BYTE ACLineStatus;
BYTE BatteryFlag;
BYTE BatteryLifePercent;
BYTE Reserved1;
```

```
DWORD BatteryLifeTime;
DWORD BatteryFullLifeTime;
BYTE Reserved2;
BYTE BackupBatteryFlag;
BYTE BackupBatteryLifePercent;
BYTE Reserved3;
DWORD BackupBatteryLifeTime;
DWORD BackupBatteryFullLifeTime;
} SYSTEM_POWER_STATUS_EX;
```

CeGetTempPath()

```
#include <rapi.h>
```

Retrieves the CE device's TEMP path.

Example:

```
CeGetTempPath(dwStrLen, szPath);
```

Where:

- dwStrLen is a DWORD specifying the length of szPath.

- szPath is a string the function will use to return the TEMP path.

CeGetUserNotificationPreferences()

```
#include <notify.h>
```

Launches the Notification Options dialog with the options you set. The dialog allows the user to set options about how they'd like a notification to appear. The user's changes to the notification options are then returned via the structure passed as the second parameter.

Example:

```
unNotify.ActionFlags =  PUN_LED | PUN_DIALOG;
unNotify.pwszDialogTitle = TEXT("Notification!");
unNotify.pwszDialogText = TEXT("Your notification.");
CeGetUserNotificationPreferences(hWnd, &unNotify);
```

Where:

- hWnd is the handle of the calling application.

- unNotify is a CE_USER_NOTIFICATION structure. (PUN_LED specifies that the LED on the device should be blinked; PUN_DIALOG specifies that the user should be notified via a dialog box.)

The CE_USER_NOTIFICATION structure is defined as follows:

```
typedef struct UserNotificationType {
DWORD ActionFlags;
TCHAR *pwszDialogTitle;
TCHAR *pwszDialogText;
TCHAR *pwszSound;
DWORD nMaxSound;
DWORD dwReserved;
} CE_USER_NOTIFICATION
```

WARNING   Calling the CeGetUserNotificationPreferences() function and displaying the Options dialog does not actually create or set the actual notification. The application must still call CeSetUserNotification() itself.

NOTE   Giving the user the option to alter the notification settings is purely optional; it's possible to create a notification using any combination of preferences and settings without ever consulting the user.

CeGetVersionEx()

```
#include <rapi.h>
```

RAPI version of GetVersionEx() function; returns version information.

Example:

```
CeGetVersionEx(&viOSVerInfo);
```

Where:

- viOSVerInfo is an OSVERSIONINFO structure.

The OSVERSIONINFO structure is defined as follows:

```
typedef struct _OSVERSIONINFO{
DWORD dwOSVersionInfoSize;
DWORD dwMajorVersion;
```

```
DWORD dwMinorVersion;
DWORD dwBuildNumber;
DWORD dwPlatformId;
TCHAR szCSDVersion[128];
} OSVERSIONINFO;
```

CeGetWindow()

```
#include <rapi.h>
```

RAPI version of GetWindow() function; returns the handle of a window matching the criteria specified.

Example:

```
uWndType = GW_HWNDFIRST;
hMatchingWnd = CeGetWindow(hWnd, uWndType);
```

Where:

- hWnd is the handle to a window, usually that of the calling application.

- uWndType is a UINT specifying the criteria of the window to search for, in this case, the window at the top of the Z-order.

- hMatchingWnd is a handle to the window matching the criteria, or NULL if no window matches.

CeGetWindowLong()

```
#include <rapi.h>
```

RAPI version of GetWindowLong() function; retrieves extended information about the window specified.

Example:

```
iVal = GWL_WNDPROC;
DefEditProc = GetWindowLong(hWnd, iVal);
```

Where:

- hWnd is the handle to the window whose information the function should retrieve.

- iVal is an integer specifying the piece of information the function should retrieve, in this case, the address of the hWnd's WndProc() function.

CeGetWindowText()

```
#include <rapi.h>
```

RAPI version of GetWindowText() function; retrieves the caption or text displayed by the window specified.

Example:

```
GetWindowText(hWnd, szText, iSize);
```

Where:

- hWnd is a handle to a window.

- szText is a string that will receive the window's text.

- iSize is the size or maximum length of szText.

CeGlobalMemoryStatus()

```
#include <rapi.h>
```

RAPI version of GlobalMemoryStatus() function; retrieves information about memory of the CE device.

Example:

```
CeGlobalMemoryStatus(&msMemStatus);
```

Where:

- msMemStatus is a MEMORYSTATUS structure.

The MEMORYSTATUS structure is defined as follows:

```
typedef struct _MEMORYSTATUS {
DWORD dwLength;
DWORD dwMemoryLoad;
DWORD dwTotalPhys;
DWORD dwAvailPhys;
DWORD dwTotalPageFile;
DWORD dwAvailPageFile;
DWORD dwTotalVirtual;
DWORD dwAvailVirtual;
} MEMORYSTATUS
```

CeHandleAppNotifications()

```
#include <notify.h>
```

Marks all "triggered" notifications created by the calling application as handled.

Example:

```
CeHandleAppNotifications(szAppName);
```

Where:

- szAppName is a string containing the name of the application, as it was specified in calls to CeSetUserNotification().

CeMoveFile()

```
#include <rapi.h>
```

RAPI version of MoveFile() function; moves (i.e., renames) a file or directory on the CE device.

Example:

```
CeMoveFile(szOldName, szNewName);
```

Where:

- szOldName is a string specifying the current name of the file or directory.

- szNewName is a string specifying the new name of the file or directory.

CeOidGetInfo()

```
#include <winbase.h>
```

(or rapi.h)

Retrieves information about a CEOID; can be used to identify the type of object specified, etc.

Example:

```
CeOidGetInfo(oid, &oiOidInfo) ;
```

Where:

- oid is a CEOID whose properties the function is to retrieve.

- oiOidInfo is a CEOIDINFO structure.

The CEOIDINFO structure is defined as follows:

```
typedef struct _CEOIDINFO {
WORD wObjType;
DWORD dwSize;
WORD wPad;
union {
CEFILEINFO infFile;
CEDIRINFO infDirectory;
CEDBASEINFO infDatabase;
CERECORDINFO infRecord;
};
} CEOIDINFO;
```

CeOpenDatabase()

```
#include <winbase.h>
```

(or rapi.h)

Part of the CE database engine; opens a CE database.

Example:

```
oid = 0;
TCHAR szDBName[MAX_PATH] = TEXT("My DB");
m_Handle = CeOpenDatabase(&oid, szDBName, 0, 0, NULL);
```

Where:

- oid is a CEOID (can be 0, if the CEOID of the database is unknown, but the szDBName is supplied. In that case, the CEOID of the database will be written back to oid).

- szDBName is a string containing the name of the database to be opened.

TIP

The remaining parameters are explored in greater detail in Chapter 4.

CeRapiFreeBuffer()

#include <rapi.h>

Frees memory allocated by calls to RAPI functions such as CeFindAllDatabases(), CeFindAllFiles(), or CeReadRecordProps().

Example:

```
CeFindAllDatabases(DbType, 0xFF, &cFound, &pFindData);
//do something with info...then, when done...
CeRapiFreeBuffer(pFindData);
```

Where:

• pFindData is a pointer to an array created by a call to CeFindDatabases().

CeRapiGetError()

#include <rapi.h>

Returns an error value if a call to a RAPI function failed due to a RAPI-related problem (e.g., the device was suddenly disconnected) as opposed to a CE-related problem (e.g., one of the parameters contained an illegal value).

Example:

```
if (CeRapiGetError() != NO_ERROR)
{
    //Function failed due to RAPI-related problem
}
```

NOTE This function takes no parameters and returns either NO_ERROR or an error-specific code.

CeRapiInit()

#include <rapi.h>

Ensures a device is connected and initializes RAPI library.

Example:

```
if ( CeRapiInit() != E_FAIL )
{
    //Connected to device successfully!
}
```

| **NOTE** | This function takes no parameters and returns E_FAIL if unsuccessful. |

CeRapiInitEx()

```
#include <rapi.h>
```

"Connects" to device, initializes RAPI library, and returns an event handle.

Example:

```
riRapiInit.cbSize = sizeof(RAPIINIT);
CeRapiInitEx(&riRapiInit);
```

Where:

* riRapiInit is a RAPIINIT structure, which the function uses to return the event handle.

The RAPIINIT structure is defined as follows:

```
typedef struct _RAPIINIT {
DWORD cbSize;
HANDLE heRapiInit;
HANDLE hrRapiInit;
} RAPIINIT;
```

CeRapiInvoke()

```
#include <rapi.h>
```

Executes a function in a DLL located on the CE device.

Example:

```
WCHAR szDllName[MAX_PATH] = TEXT("\\Windows\\mydll.dll");
WCHAR szTmp[MAX_PATH];
WCHAR szFxn[MAX_PATH];
WCHAR szInput[MAX_PATH];
LPTSTR szOut = NULL;
BOOL fStream = FALSE;
IRAPIStream *pStream = NULL;
DWORD dwInput = 0;
DWORD dwOut = MAX_PATH;
TCHAR sz[MAX_PATH];
```

```
//...
CeRapiInit();
//...
HRESULT  hr = CeRapiInvoke(szDllName, szFxn, dwInput, (BYTE *)
szInput, &dwOut, (BYTE **)&szOut, fStream ? &pStream : NULL, NULL);
```

Where:

- szDllName is a string specifying the name of the DLL.

- szFxn is a string specifying the name of the function.

- dwInput is a DWORD specifying the length in bytes of szInput.

- szInput is a string specifying the input to the function.

- dwOut is a DWORD that will receive the length in bytes of szOut.

- szOut is an ANSI string that will receive the output data.

- pStream is an IRAPIStream interface.

NOTE   The last parameter of this function is always NULL.

CeRapiUninit()

```
#include <rapi.h>
```

"Disconnects" from device and uninitializes RAPI library.

Example:

```
CeRapiUninit();
```

NOTE   This function takes no parameters and returns E_FAIL only if the RAPI libraries were not initialized to begin with.

CeReadFile()

```
#include <rapi.h>
```

RAPI version of ReadFile() function; reads data from a file opened with CreateFile().

Example:

```
CeReadFile(hFile, &szData, dwBytesToRead, &dwBytesRead, NULL);
```

Where:

- hFile is a handle to a file.

- szData is a string or buffer to hold the data being read.

- dwBytesToRead is a DWORD specifying number of bytes to read.

- dwBytesRead is a DWORD used by the function to indicate number of bytes actually read.

TIP   The last parameter of CeReadFile() is always NULL.

CeReadRecordProps()

```
#include <winbase.h>
```

(or rapi.h)

Reads the properties (fields) of a record in a CE database.

Example:

```
objId = CeReadRecordProps(hDB,CEDB_ALLOWREALLOC,
&cProps,  NULL, (LPBYTE *)&pBuf, &cbBuf);
```

Where:

- hDB is a handle to an open database.

- CEDB_ALLOWREALLOC is a flag that tells the function it can reallocate the buffer passed as the fifth parameter if necessary; can be 0 for no reallocation.

- cProps is an integer used by the function to return the number of properties read.

- NULL specifies that you want the function to read all of the record's properties.

- pBuf is a pointer to an array of CEPROPVAL structures.

- cbBuf is a DWORD specifying the size of pBuf in bytes; useful mostly if CEDB_ALLOWREALLOC is not specified.

The CEPROPVAL structure is defined as follows:

```
typedef struct _CEPROPVAL {
CEPROPID propid;
WORD wLenData;
WORD wFlags;
CEVALUNION val;
} CEPROPVAL;
```

CeRegCloseKey()

```
#include <rapi.h>
```

RAPI version of RegCloseKey() function; closes handle to a specified registry key on the CE device.

Example:

```
CeRegCloseKey (hKey);
```

Where:

• hKey is a handle to a registry key.

CeRegCreateKeyEx()

```
#include <rapi.h>
```

RAPI version of RegCreateKeyEx() function; creates a registry key on the CE device.

Example:

```
HKEY  hKeyResult;
DWORD dwCreateStatus;
DWORD dwType;
DWORD dwBytes = 0;
TCHAR szKeyName[MAX_PATH] = TEXT("Preferences");
CeRegCreateKeyEx(hKey, szKeyName, 0, NULL, 0, 0 NULL, &hKeyResult,
&dwCreateStatus);
```

Where:

- hKey is a handle to the key under which the new key will be created. This parameter can be a handle to a key or any of the following predefined constants:

  - HKEY_CLASSES_ROOT

  - HKEY_CURRENT_USER

  - HKEY_LOCAL_MACHINE

  - HKEY_USERS

- szKeyName is the name of the new key.

- hKeyResult is a handle to receive the handle of the newly created key.

- dwCreateStatus is a DWORD used by the function to indicate whether the key was created (REG_CREATED_NEW_KEY) or whether it already existed (REG_OPENED_EXISTING_KEY).

CeRegDeleteKey()

```
#include <rapi.h>
```

RAPI version of RegDeleteKey(); deletes the specified key and any subkeys from the registry.

Example:

```
TCHAR szKeyName[MAX_PATH] = TEXT("Preferences");
//delete key created in example for CeRegCreateKeyEx() above
CeRegDeleteKey(HKEY_CURRENT_USER, szKeyName);
```

Where:

- HKEY_CURRENT_USER is a predefined constant value. This parameter can be a handle to a key or any of the following predefined constants:

  - HKEY_CLASSES_ROOT

  - HKEY_CURRENT_USER

  - HKEY_LOCAL_MACHINE

  - HKEY_USERS

- szKeyName is a string specifying the name of the key to be deleted.

CeRegDeleteValue()

```
#include <rapi.h>
```

RAPI version of RegDeleteValue() function; deletes the specified value from the registry of the CE device.

Example:

```
TCHAR szValName[MAX_PATH] = TEXT("value2");
LONG CeRegDeleteValue(hKey, szValName);
```

Where:

- hKey is a handle to a registry key. This parameter can be a handle to a key or any of the following predefined constants:

  - HKEY_CLASSES_ROOT

  - HKEY_CURRENT_USER

  - HKEY_LOCAL_MACHINE

  - HKEY_USERS

- szValName is a string specifying the value to be deleted.

CeRegEnumKeyEx()

```
#include <rapi.h>
```

RAPI version of RegEnumKeyEx() function; lists subkeys of the specified registry key on the CE device.

Example:

```
    while (ERROR_NO_MORE_ITEMS != CeRegEnumKeyEx(hKey, iIndex,
szKeyName, &cbKeyName, NULL, szClassName, &cbClassName, NULL )
    {
        //do something...
        iIndex++; //always increment index value
        cbClassName = 0; //these values must be reset each time
        cbKeyName = 0;
    }
```

Where:

- hKey is a handle to a registry key. This parameter can be a handle to a key or any of the following predefined constants:

  - HKEY_CLASSES_ROOT

  - HKEY_CURRENT_USER

  - HKEY_LOCAL_MACHINE

  - HKEY_USERS

- iIndex is an integer specifying the index of the subkey to be enumerated.

- szKeyName is a string to receive the name of the subkey.

- cbKeyName is an integer specifying the maximum length of szKeyName in bytes.

- szClassName is a string to receive the class name of the subkey.

- cbClassName is an integer specifying the maximum length of szClassName in bytes.

TIP The fifth and eighth parameters of this function are always NULL.

CeRegEnumValue()

```
#include <rapi.h>
```

RAPI version of RegEnumValue(); lists values belonging to the specified key.

Example:

```
    retValue = CeRegEnumValue (hKey, dwIndex, szValName, &dwValLen,
NULL, &dwValType, (LPBYTE)szData, &dwDataLen);
```

Where:

- hKey is a handle to a key. This parameter can be a handle to a key or any of the following predefined constants:

  - HKEY_CLASSES_ROOT

  - HKEY_CURRENT_USER

  - HKEY_LOCAL_MACHINE

  - HKEY_USERS

- dwIndex is a DWORD specifying the index of the value to retrieve; this value should be 0 on the first call to the function and incremented before each additional call.

- szValName is a string used by the function to return the name of the value.

- dwValLen is a DWORD specifying the size of the szValName buffer.

- dwValType is a DWORD used by the function to return the type of the value. The most common values returned to this parameter are

    REG_BINARY   Binary data

    REG_DWORD   A DWORD

    REG_SZ   A string

- szData is a string or byte array used to hold the data being returned.

- dwDataLen specifies the length of the szData buffer in bytes.

NOTE   The fifth parameter of this function is always NULL.

CeRegOpenKeyEx()

```
#include <rapi.h>
```

RAPI version of RegOpenKeyEx(); opens the specified registry key.

Example:

```
CeRegOpenKeyEx (hKey, szKeyName, 0, KEY_READ, &hSubKey);
```

Where:

- hKey is a handle to a key. This parameter can be a handle to a key or any of the following predefined constants:

    - HKEY_CLASSES_ROOT

    - HKEY_CURRENT_USER

    - HKEY_LOCAL_MACHINE

    - HKEY_USERS

- szKeyName specifies the name of the key to be opened. This key must be a subkey of the key specified by hKey.

- KEY_READ specifies the type of access/operation we'll be performing. Some common values are

  - KEY_READ

  - KEY_WRITE

  - KEY_ALL_ACCESS

- hSubKey is a handle to the key specified by szKeyName, if the function was successful.

CeRegQueryInfoKey()

RAPI version of RegQueryInfoKey(); retrieves information about the specified registry key.

Example:

```
CeRegQueryInfoKey(hKey, szClassName, &dwClassLen, NULL,
&dwSubKeyCount, &dwMaxSubKeyLen, &dwMaxClassLen, &dwValueCount,
&dwMaxValueName, NULL, NULL, NULL);
```

Where:

- hKey is a handle to a key. This parameter can be a handle to a key or any of the following predefined constants:

  - HKEY_CLASSES_ROOT

  - HKEY_CURRENT_USER

  - HKEY_LOCAL_MACHINE

  - HKEY_USERS

- szClassName is a string the function uses to return the class name of the key.

- dwClassLen is the size of the szClassName buffer.

- dwSubKeys is a DWORD the function uses to return the number of subkeys.

- dwMaxSubKeyLen is a DWORD the function uses to return the length of the longest subkey.

- dwMaxClassLen is a DWORD the function uses to return the length of the longest class name of a subkey.

- dwValueCount is a DWORD the function uses to return the number of values belonging to the key.

- dwMaxValueLen is a DWORD the function uses to return the length of the longest value name.

NOTE The fourth, tenth, eleventh, and twelfth parameters of this function are always NULL.

CeRegQueryValueEx()

`#include <rapi.h>`

RAPI version of RegQueryValueEx(); retrieves data and information about a specified value.

Example:

```
RegQueryValueEx (hKey, szValName, NULL, &dwValType, (LPBYTE)szData,
&dwDataLen);
```

Where:

- hKey is a handle to a key. This parameter can be a handle to a key or any of the following predefined constants:

  - HKEY_CLASSES_ROOT

  - HKEY_CURRENT_USER

  - HKEY_LOCAL_MACHINE

  - HKEY_USERS

- szValName is a string specifying the name of the value to retrieve.

- dwValType is a DWORD used by the function to return the type of the value. The most common values returned to this parameter are

    REG_BINARY   Binary data

    REG_DWORD   A DWORD

    REG_SZ   A string

- szData is a string or byte array used to hold the data being returned.

- dwDataLen specifies the length of the szData buffer in bytes.

NOTE   The third parameter of this function is always NULL.

CeRegSetValueEx()

```
#include <rapi.h>
```

RAPI version of RegSetValueEx(); writes data to the specified registry value.

Example:

```
CeRegSetValueEx(hKey, szValName, NULL, dwValType, (LPBYTE)szData,
dwDataLen);
```

Where:

- hKey is a handle to a key. This parameter can be a handle to a key or any of the following predefined constants:

  - HKEY_CLASSES_ROOT

  - HKEY_CURRENT_USER

  - HKEY_LOCAL_MACHINE

  - HKEY_USERS

- szValName is a string specifying the name of the value to retrieve.

- dwValType is a DWORD used by the function to return the type of the value. The most common values returned to this parameter are

  REG_BINARY   Binary data

  REG_DWORD   A DWORD

  REG_SZ   A string

- szData is a string or byte array used to hold the data being returned.

- dwDataLen specifies the length of the szData buffer in bytes.

NOTE

The third parameter of this function is always NULL.

CeRemoveDirectory()

`#include <rapi.h>`

RAPI version of `RemoveDirectory()`; deletes a directory. The directory must be empty before it can be removed.

Example:

```
TCHAR szDir[MAX_PATH] = TEXT("\\AppTempDir");
CeRemoveDirectory(szDir);
```

Where:

- `szDir` is the name of the directory to remove.

CeRunAppAtEvent()

`#include <notify.h>`

Runs the specified application when the specified system-level event occurs; similar to `CeRunAppAtTime()`.

Example:

```
TCHAR szAppName[MAX_PATH] = TEXT("\\windows\\pword.exe");
CeRunAppAtEvent(szAppName, NOTIFICATION_EVENT_TIME_CHANGE);
```

Where:

- `szAppName` is a string specifying the application to run.

- `NOTIFICATION_EVENT_TIME_CHANGE` is a predefined constant. Possible values for this second parameter are

    NOTIFICATION_EVENT_SYNC_END   When the device is finished syncing with the Desktop.

    NOTIFICATION_EVENT_DEVICE_CHANGE   When a PCMCIA card is removed or inserted.

    NOTIFICATION_EVENT_RS232_DETECTED   When a serial port connection is made.

NOTIFICATION_EVENT_TIME_CHANGE   When the system time has been changed.

NOTIFICATION_EVENT_RESTORE_END   When a device data restore operation is completed.

To remove a previously set notification, the value to pass for the second parameter is

NOTIFICATION_EVENT_NONE   Removes run-at settings for the specified application.

CeRunAppAtTime()

```
#include <notify.h>
```

Runs the specified application at the specified time; similar to CeRunAppAt-Event().

Example:

```
TCHAR szAppName[MAX_PATH] = TEXT("\\windows\\pword.exe");
CeRunAppAtTime(szAppName, &stSystemTime);
```

Where:

- szAppName is a string specifying the application to run.

- stSystemTime is either a pointer to a SYSTEMTIME structure or NULL. If NULL, any previously set run-at-time events for the specified application will be cleared.

TIP

For more information on working with the SYSTEMTIME structure, see Bat-teryNotifyOfTimeChange() earlier in this appendix.

CeSeekDatabase()

```
#include <winbase.h>
```

(or rapi.h)

Part of the CE database engine; serves as a way to both search the database and manipulate the current record pointer (seek).

Example:

```
CeSeekDatabase(hDb, dwSeekType, dwValue, &dwIndex);
```

Where:

- hDb is a handle to an open database.

- dwSeekType specifies the type of search/seek to perform.

- dwValue is the value you're searching for or is a numeric value specifying how the current record pointer should be moved.

- dwIndex is a DWORD that the CE Database Engine uses to return the number of records from the start of the database to the record that was found.

NOTE   This function, and the dwSeekType parameter in particular, is fully documented in Chapter 4.

CeSetDatabaseInfo()

```
#include <winbase.h>
```

(or rapi.h)

Part of the CE Database Engine; sets various properties of the database.

Example:

```
CeSetDatabaseInfo(oid, &dbiDatabaseInfo);
```

Where:

- oid is the CEOID of the database whose properties are to be changed.

- dbiDatabaseInfo is a CEDBASEINFO structure.

The CEDBASEINFO is defined as

```
typedef struct _CEDBASEINFO {
DWORD dwFlags;
WCHAR szDbaseName[CEDB_MAXDBASENAMELEN];
DWORD dwDbaseType;
WORD wNumRecords;
WORD wNumSortOrder;
DWORD dwSize;
```

```
FILETIME ftLastModified;
SORTORDERSPEC rgSortSpecs[CEDB_MAXSORTORDER];
} CEDBASEINFO;
```

CeSetEndOfFile()

```
#include <rapi.h>
```

RAPI version of `SetEndOfFile()`; marks current position as the end of the file.

Example:

```
CeSetEndOfFile(hFile);
```

Where:

- `hFile` is a handle to an open file on the CE device; you must have write access to the file in order to successfully set the EOF of that file.

CeSetFileAttributes()

```
#include <rapi.h>
```

RAPI version of `SetFileAttributes()`; sets attributes of a file on the CE device.

Example:

```
TCHAR szFileName[MAX_PATH] = TEXT("\\myappdata.txt");
dwFileAttributes = FILE_ATTRIBUTE_NORMAL;
CeSetFileAttributes(szFileName, dwFileAttributes);
```

Where:

- `szFileName` is the name of the file whose attributes you want to change.

- `dwFileAttributes` is a DWORD specifying the attributes to set. It can be any combination of the following values:

    FILE_ATTRIBUTE_ARCHIVE   Sets the archive flag.

    FILE_ATTRIBUTE_HIDDEN   Sets the hidden flag.

    FILE_ATTRIBUTE_NORMAL   Clears all other attributes; cannot be combined with other attributes.

    FILE_ATTRIBUTE_OFFLINE   File has been moved to offline storage.

    FILE_ATTRIBUTE_READONLY   Sets the read-only flag.

FILE_ATTRIBUTE_SYSTEM   Sets the system flag.

FILE_ATTRIBUTE_TEMPORARY   Marks the file as being for temporary use only, which can improve access time. It is still the responsibility of the application to remove the temporary file when finished with it.

CeSetFilePointer()

```
#include <rapi.h>
```

RAPI version of `SetFilePointer()`; advances or reverses the file pointer of an open file.

Example:

```
CeSetFilePointer(hFile, 3000, NULL, FILE_BEGIN);
```

Where:

- `hFile` is a handle to an open file.

- 3000 is the number of bytes to move.

- `FILE_BEGIN` is the point that the file pointer will move relative to. In other words, in the above example, the file pointer will be positioned 3000 bytes from the beginning of the file. Other possible values for this parameter are

  FILE_CURRENT   Distance to move is relative to the current position of the file pointer.

  FILE_END   Distance to move is relative to the EOF.

NOTE   The third parameter can either be NULL, as in the example here, or it can serve as the high-order `DWORD` if the distance to move is a 64-bit value. In that case, the second parameter would be the low-order `DWORD`.

CeSetFileTime()

```
#include <rapi.h>
```

RAPI version of `SetFileTime()`; sets the creation, last accessed, and/or last modified date-time stamps of the specified file.

Example:

```
SYSTEMTIME st;
FILETIME ftCreate, ftAccess, ftModify;
BOOL bAhead;
GetSystemTime(&st);
//set all three dates equal to current date-time stamp
SystemTimeToFileTime(&st, &ftCreate);
SystemTimeToFileTime(&st, &ftAccess);
SystemTimeToFileTime(&st, &ftModify);
CeSetFileTime(hFile, &ftCreate, &ftAccess, &ftModify);
```

Where:

- hFile is a handle to an open file.

- ftCreate is a FILETIME structure specifying the new creation date-time stamp of the file.

- ftAccess is a FILETIME structure specifying the new last accessed date-time stamp of the file.

- ftModify is a FILETIME structure specifying the new last modified date-time stamp of the file.

CeSetUserNotification()

```
#include <notify.h>
```

Creates or updates a user notification.

Example:

```
BOOL ret;
SYSTEMTIME stTime, stFuture;
CE_USER_NOTIFICATION unNotify;
HANDLE hNotification;
TCHAR szAppFullPath[MAX_PATH] = TEXT("\\Windows\\Start Menu\\
helloworld.exe");
GetLocalTime(&stTime);
stFuture = stTime;
stFuture.wMinute = stFuture.wMinute + 1;
unNotify.ActionFlags =  PUN_LED | PUN_DIALOG;
unNotify.pwszDialogTitle = TEXT("Notification!");
unNotify.pwszDialogText = TEXT("Your notification is here!");
```

```
 hNotification = NULL;
 hNotification = CeSetUserNotification(hNotification, szAppFullPath,
&stFuture, &unNotify);
```

Where:

- hNotification is NULL to create a notification (as in this example) or the handle to an existing notification.

- szAppFullPath is a string specifying the full path to the executable creating the notification. This is the application whose icon will appear in the notification dialog box and the application that will be executed if the user clicks the Open button on the notification dialog.

- stFuture is a SYSTEMTIME structure specifying the date-time stamp at which the notification is to occur.

- unNotify is a CE_USER_NOTIFICATION structure, specifying various notification options.

The CE_USER_NOTIFICATION structure is defined as follows:

```
typedef struct UserNotificationType {
DWORD ActionFlags;
TCHAR *pwszDialogTitle;
TCHAR *pwszDialogText;
TCHAR *pwszSound;
DWORD nMaxSound;
DWORD dwReserved;
} CE_USER_NOTIFICATION
```

CeSHCreateShortcut()

```
#include <rapi.h>
```

RAPI version of SHCreateShortcut(); creates a shortcut.

Example:

```
TCHAR szShortcutFile[MAX_PATH];
TCHAR szActualExe[MAX_PATH];
szShortcutFile = TEXT("\\MyApp.lnk");
szActualExe = TEXT("\\Windows\\MyApp.exe");
CeSHCreateShortcut(szShortcutFile, szActualExe);
```

Where:

- szShortcutFile is a string specifying the full path of the shortcut file.

- szActualExe is a string specifying the full path to the actual executable file.

CeSHGetShortcutTarget()

RAPI version of SHGetShortcutTarget(); retrieves the path to the target executable of the specified shortcut.

Example:

```
TCHAR szShortcutFile[MAX_PATH];
TCHAR szActualExe[MAX_PATH];
int iActualExeLen = MAX_PATH;
szShortcutFile = TEXT("\\MyApp.lnk");
CeSHGetShortcutTarget(szShortcutFile, szActualExe, iActualExeLen);
```

Where:

- szShortcutFile is a string specifying the full path of the shortcut file.

- szActualExe is a string the function uses to return the full path to the actual executable file.

- iActualExeLen is an integer specifying the maximum possible length of szActualExe.

CeWriteFile()

```
#include <rapi.h>
```

RAPI version of WriteFile(); writes data to an open file.

Example:

```
CeWriteFile(hFile, szBuf, dwBufSize, &dwNumWritten, NULL));
```

Where:

- hFile is a handle to an open file.

- szBuf is a buffer of some kind.

- dwBufSize is a DWORD specifying the size of szBuf in bytes.

- dwNumWritten is a DWORD the function uses to return the number of bytes written to the file.

| WARNING | When using `CeWriteFile()` to write Unicode data to the file, remember that `dwBufSize` is the number of bytes—not characters—in the buffer. When writing Unicode text, you must remember to double the number of characters to get the number of bytes. |

CeWriteRecordProps()

```
#include <winbase.h>
```

(or `rapi.h`)

Part of the CE Database Engine; creates or modifies a record in a database.

Example:

```
CEOID oidRecord;
WORD wPropCount;
CEPROPVAL pvPropVals[2];
pvPropVals[0].propid = MAKELONG(CEVT_LPWSTR, PROP_CODE);
pvPropVals[0].wFlags = 0;
pvPropVals[0].val.lpwstr = szCode;
pvPropVals[1].propid = MAKELONG(CEVT_LPWSTR, PROP_STATE);
pvPropVals[1].wFlags = 0;
pvPropVals[1].val.lpwstr = szState;
wPropCount = 2;
//...
//get a value for the record's oid & store in oidRecord
//...
CeWriteRecordProps(hDb, oidRecord, wPropCount, pvPropVals);
```

Where:

- hDb is a handle to an open database.

- oidRecord is the CEOID of the record being modified; if adding a new record, this value should be set to 0.

- wPropCount is a WORD indicating the number of properties being written to.

- pvPropVals is an array of CEPROPVAL structures.

The CEPROPVAL structure is defined as follows:

```
typedef struct _CEPROPVAL {
CEPROPID propid;
WORD wLenData;
WORD wFlags;
CEVALUNION val;
} CEPROPVAL;
typedef CEPROPVAL;
```

CloseAddressBook()

```
#include <addrstor.h>
```

Closes the Contacts database; part of the AddressBook family of functions.

Example:

```
CloseAddressBook();
```

NOTE   This function takes no parameters and does not return a value.

CommandBands_AddAdornments()

```
#include <commctrl.h>
```

Adds the Close (X) button to the CommandBands control. Can also add Help (?) and/or OK buttons. These buttons are considered separate *adornments bands*.

Example:

```
DWORD dwFlags = CMDBAR_HELP | CMDBAR_OK;
REBARBANDINFO rbiInfo;
rbiInfo.cbSize = sizeof (REBARBANDINFO);
rbiInfo.fMask = RBBIM_ID;
rbiInfo.wID = 300;
CommandBands_AddAdornments(hBands, hInstance, dwFlags, &rbiInfo);
```

Where:

- hBands is a handle to the window's CommandBands control.

- hInstance is a handle to the instance of the application.

- dwFlags is a DWORD specifying one or more of the following values:

  CMDBAR_HELP Add the Help (?) button.

  CMDBAR_OK Add the OK button.

- rbiInfo is optionally NULL or a REBARBANDINFO structure, which can be used to override the default ID for the adornments band. Usually, the ID of the adornments band is set to 0xFFFFFFFF; the example above sets it to 300.

The REBARBANDINFO structure is defined as follows:

```
typedef struct tagREBARBANDINFO{
UINT cbSize;
UINT fMask;
UINT fStyle;
COLORREF clrFore;
COLORREF clrBack;
LPTSTR lpText;
UINT cch;
int iImage;
HWND hwndChild;
UINT cxMinChild;
UINT cyMinChild;
UINT cx;
HBITMAP hbmBack;
UINT wID;
UINT cyChild;
UINT cyMaxChild;
UINT cyIntegral;
UINT cxIdeal;
LPARAM lParam;
} REBARBANDINFO;
```

CommandBands_AddBands()

```
#include <commctrl.h>
```

Adds bands to the CommandBands control.

Example:

```
REBARBANDINFO rbiInfo[2];
UINT iBandCount = 2; //add 2 bands
rbiInfo[0].cbSize = sizeof (REBARBANDINFO);
rbiInfo[0].fMask = RBBIM_ID | RBBIM_STYLE;
```

```
rbiInfo[0].fStyle = RBBS_GRIPPERALWAYS | RBBS_FIXEDSIZE;
rbiInfo[0].wID = 0;
rbiInfo[0].iImage = 0;
rbiInfo[1].cbSize = sizeof (REBARBANDINFO);
rbiInfo[1].fMask = RBBIM_ID | RBBIM_STYLE;
rbiInfo[1].fStyle = RBBS_GRIPPERALWAYS | RBBS_FIXEDSIZE;
rbiInfo[1].wID = 1;
rbiInfo[1].iImage = 1;
CommandBands_AddBands(hBands, hInstance, iBandCount, &rbiInfo);
```

Where:

- hBands is a handle to the CommandBands control.

- hInstance is a handle to the application instance.

- iBandCount is an integer specifying the number of bands to add.

- rbiInfo is an array containing iBandCount REBARBANDINFO structures.

CommandBands_Create()

```
#include <commctrl.h>
```

Creates a new CommandBands control.

Example:

```
DWORD dwStyles = CCS_VERT | RBS_VERTICALGRIPPER; //create a
vertical band with the proper vertical gripper
WORD wID = ID_CMDBAND;
hBands = CommandBands_Create (hInstance, hWnd, wID, dwStyles,
hImgList);
```

Where:

- hBands is the handle of the newly created CommandBands control if the function is successful.

- hWnd is the handle to the window that will own the CommandBands control.

- hInstance is a handle to the application instance.

- wID is a WORD specifying the numeric ID of the CommandBands control to be used in notification messages for that CommandBands control.

- dwStyles is a DWORD specifying how the CommandBands control is to appear. This value a combination of the following constants:

  CCS_VERT CommandBands control should appear vertically.

  RBS_AUTOSIZE CommandBands control's size will change automatically as needed.

  RBS_BANDBORDERS CommandBands control will be drawn with borders.

  RBS_FIXEDORDER The order of the CommandBands control's individual bands cannot be changed.

  RBS_SMARTLABELS CommandBands control's bands will only show their icon when minimized.

  RBS_VARHEIGHT CommandBands control will occupy the minimum possible vertical space.

  RBS_VERTICALGRIPPER CommandBands control will have a vertical gripper; for vertical CommandBands only.

- hImgList is a handle to an Image List.

CommandBands_GetCommandBar()

```
#include <commctrl.h>
```

Retrieves the handle to a CommandBar child control in a band of the CommandBands control.

Example:

```
HWND CommandBands_GetCommandBar( HWND hwndCmdBands, UINT uBand);
```

Where:

- hwndCmdBands is the handle to a CommandBand.

- uBand is a UINT zero-based index specifying which CommandBar within the CommandBand you want to retrieve the handle of.

WARNING The uBand index value applies to the currently displayed order of the CommandBars and may be altered by user repositioning.

CommandBands_GetRestoreInformation()

`#include <commctrl.h>`

Retrieves information to restore a band's current state.

Example:

```
CommandBands_GetRestoreInformation(hBands, uBand, &cbrRestoreInfo);
```

Where:

- hBands is a handle to the CommandBands' control window.

- uBands is the index of the CommandBands control whose restore info the function should retrieve.

- cbrRestoreInfo is a COMMANDBANDSRESTOREINFO structure that the function will use to return the information.

The LPCOMMANDBANDSRESTOREINFO is defined as follows:

```
typedef struct tagCOMMANDBANDSRESTOREINFO {
UINT cbSize;
UINT wID;
UINT fStyle;
UINT cxRestored;
BOOL fMaximized;
} COMMANDBANDSRESTOREINFO;
```

CommandBands_Height()

`#include <commctrl.h>`

Returns the height (in pixels) of a CommandBands control.

Example:

```
CommandBands_Height(hBands);
```

Where:

- hBands is a handle to the CommandBands control you want to get the height of.

CommandBands_IsVisible()

```
#include <commctrl.h>
```

Determines whether or not the CommandBands control is visible.

Example:

```
BOOL CommandBands_IsVisible (hBands);
```

Where:

- hBands is a handle to the CommandBands control.

CommandBands_Show()

```
#include <commctrl.h>
```

Shows or hides the CommandBands control.

Example:

```
bShow = TRUE;
CommandBands_Show(hBands, bShow);
```

Where:

- hBands is a handle to the CommandBands control.

- bShow is a BOOL value indicating whether the function should show (TRUE) or hide (FALSE) the CommandBands control.

CommandBar_AddAdornments()

```
#include <commctrl.h>
```

Adds the Close button (X) to the CommandBar. You can also use it to add the Help button (?) and the OK button.

Example:

```
DWORD dwFlags = CMDBAR_HELP | CMDBAR_OK;
CommandBar_AddAdornments(hCB, dwFlags, 0);
```

Where:

- hCB is the handle to the CommandBar.

- dwFlags is a DWORD specifying one or more of the following values:

    CMDBAR_HELP   Add the Help (?) button.

    CMDBAR_OK   Add the OK button.

NOTE   The last parameter of this function is reserved and should always be 0.

CommandBar_AddBitmap()

```
#include <commctrl.h>
```

Adds a bitmap containing button images to the available CommandBar button images.

Example:

```
hCB = CommandBar_Create(hInstance, hwnd, 1);
iBmpID = IDB_BUTTONS;
iNumImages = 3;
CommandBar_AddBitmap(hCB, hInstance, iBmpID, iNumImages, 0, 0);
```

Where:

- hCB is a handle to the CommandBar.
- hInstance is an instance handle to the module containing the bitmap.
- iBmpID is the identifier of the bitmap resource.
- iNumImages is the number of 16×16 images contained in the bitmap.

NOTE   The last two parameters of this function are reserved; it appears that it is safe to pass any integer values.

CommandBar_AddButtons()

```
#include <commctrl.h>
```

Adds buttons to an existing CommandBar.

Example:

```
CommandBar_AddButtons(hCB, iNumButtons, tbButtons);
```

Where:

- hCB is a handle to the CommandBar.

- iNumButtons is the number of buttons to be added.

- tbButtons is an array of TBBUTTON structures.

The TBBUTTON structure is defined as follows:

```
typedef struct _TBBUTTON {
int iBitmap;
int idCommand;
BYTE fsState;
BYTE fsStyle;
DWORD dwData;
int iString;
} TBBUTTON;
```

CommandBar_AddToolTips()

```
#include <commctrl.h>
```

Adds ToolTips hints to the buttons of a CommandBar.

Example:

```
CommandBar_AddToolTips(hCB, uNumTips, lpszTips);
```

Where:

- hCB is a handle to the CommandBar.

- uNumTips is the number of ToolTip strings to add.

- lpszTips is an array containing uNumTips strings containing the tips.

CommandBar_Create()

```
#include <commctrl.h>
```

Creates a CommandBar control.

Example:

```
iCmdID = 1;
hCB = CommandBar_Create(hInstance, hWnd, iCmdID);
```

Where:

- hInstance is the instance handle of the application.

- hWnd is the handle of the parent window of the CommandBar to be created.

- iCmdID is an integer used to identify this CommandBar from other CommandBars used in the application.

CommandBar_DrawMenuBar()

```
#include <commctrl.h>
```

Redraws the CommandBar after one of its menus has been modified.

Example:

```
CommandBar_DrawMenuBar(hCB, iMenuBar);
```

Where:

- hCB is a handle to a CommandBar.

- iMenuBar is the index of the menu within the CommandBar that you wish to redraw.

CommandBar_GetMenu()

```
#include <commctrl.h>
```

Retrieves the handle to a menu of the CommandBar.

Example:

```
hCmdBarMenu = CommandBar_GetMenu(hCB,  iButton);
```

Where:

- hCB is a handle to a CommandBar.

- iButton is the index of the CommandBar separator button holding the menu; in most cases, this will be 0.

CommandBar_Height()

```
#include <commctrl.h>
```

Returns the height of the CommandBar in pixels.

Example:

```
CommandBar_Height(hCB);
```

Where:

• hCB is a handle to the CommandBar whose height you want to know.

CommandBar_InsertButton()

```
#include <commctrl.h>
```

Inserts a button into the CommandBar.

Example:

```
CommandBar_InsertButton(hCB, iButton, &tbButton);
```

Where:

• hCB is a handle to a CommandBar.

• iButton is the index of the button that this new button will be placed to the left of.

• tbButton is a TBBUTTON structure.

CommandBar_InsertComboBox()

```
#include <commctrl.h>
```

Inserts a combo box control into the CommandBar.

Example:

```
    iComboID = 300;
    iButton = 4;
    hCombo = CommandBar_InsertComboBox(hCB, hInstance, 120,
CBS_DROPDOWNLIST, ID_CMDCOMBO, iButton);
```

Where:

• hCombo is the handle to the newly created combo box if the function is successful.

• hCB is a handle to a CommandBar.

• hInstance is the instance handle of the application.

- CBS_DROPDOWNLIST is a constant specifying the style of combo box to be created. Any valid "Window Style" constants can be combined for this parameter.

- iComboID is an integer used to identify this combo box from other combo boxes used in the application.

- iButton is the index of the button that the combo box will be placed to the left of.

CommandBar_InsertMenubar()

```
#include <commctrl.h>
```

Inserts a MenuBar into the CommandBar.

Example:

```
CommandBar_InsertMenubar(hCB,  hInstance, idMenu, iButton);
```

Where:

- hCB is a handle to a CommandBar.

- hInstance is the instance handle of the application.

- idMenu is an integer used to identify this combo box from other combo boxes used in the application.

- iButton is the index of the button that the combo box will be placed to the left of.

CommandBar_InsertMenubarEx()

```
#include <commctrl.h>
```

Inserts a menu into a CommandBar.

Example:

```
CommandBar_InsertMenubarEx(hCB, hInstance, lpszMenuName, iButton);
```

Where:

- hCB is the handle to the CommandBar.

- hInstance is the instance handle of the application.

- lpszMenuName is the name of the menu resource.

- iButton is the index of the button that the combo box will be placed to the left of.

TIP   The main difference between CommandBar_InsertMenubar() and Command-Bar_InsertMenubarEx() is that with the "-Ex()" version, the menu to be inserted can be identified by a resource name or by its handle if it has already been created.

CommandBar_IsVisible()

#include <commctrl.h>

Determines whether or not the CommandBar is visible.

Example:

```
CommandBar_IsVisible(hCB);
```

Where:

- hCB is the handle to the CommandBar.

CommandBar_Show()

#include <commctrl.h>

Shows or hides the CommandBar.

Example:

```
bShow = TRUE;
BOOL CommandBar_Show(hCB, bShow);
```

Where:

- hCB is a handle to the CommandBar control.

- bShow is a BOOL value indicating whether the function should show (TRUE) or hide (FALSE) the CommandBar control.

CreateAddressBook()

```
#include <addrstor.h>
```

Creates the Contacts database if it doesn't exist.

Example:

```
    int iSortOrderCount = 4;
    HHPRTAG hPrTagList[4] = {HHPR_COMPANY_NAME, HHPR_FILEAS,
HHPR_GIVEN_NAME, HHPR_TITLE};
    CreateAddressBook (hPrTagList, iSortOrderCount);
```

Where:

- hPrTagList is an array of HHPRTAG constants specifying the possible sort orders for the Contacts database. It may contain up to four HHPRTAGs.

- iSortOrderCount is an integer specifying the number of HHPRTAGs in the hPrTagList array.

CreateFileForMapping()

```
#include <winbase.h>
```

Creates a memory-mapped file.

Example:

```
    TCHAR szFileName[MAX_PATH] = TEXT("\\data.txt");
    wAccess = GENERIC_WRITE;
    wShare = 0;
    dwCreate = CREATE_ALWAYS;
    dwFlags = FILE_ATTRIBUTE_NORMAL;
    hSrc = CreateFileForMapping(
    szFileName,
    wAccess,
    wShare,
    NULL,
    dwCreate,
    dwFlags,
    NULL);
```

Where:

- szFileName is a string specifying the name of the file to open.

- wAccess is a WORD specifying the type of access (GENERIC_READ and/or GENERIC_WRITE).

- wShare is a WORD specifying under what conditions another application may open or modify the file while you are using it (0 for no access, FILE_SHARE_READ to permit read access, and FILE_SHARE_WRITE to permit write access).

- dwCreate is a DWORD specifying whether you are attempting to open an existing file or create a file (CREATE_ALWAYS always creates the file, OPEN_EXISTING attempts to open an existing file, etc.).

- dwFlags is a DWORD specifying additional file attributes, such as the archive, hidden, or read-only flags.

TIP

The fourth parameter specifies security attributes and the seventh specifies a template file. Both are always NULL on CE.

DeleteAddressCard()

```
#include <addrstor.h>
```

Deletes the specified entry from the Contacts database.

Example:

```
DeleteAddressCard(oidToDelete);
```

Where:

- oidToDelete is a CEOID specifying the entry (record) to delete.

DeleteAndRenameFile()

```
#include <winbase.h>
```

Copies source file to destination file, then deletes source file.

Example:

```
TCHAR szSource[MAX_PATH] = TEXT("\\MyData.txt");
TCHAR szDest[MAX_PATH] = TEXT("\\Archived\\MyData.txt");
DeleteAndRenameFile(szDest, szSource);
```

Where:

- szDest is a string specifying the name of the destination file.

- szSource is a string specifying the name of the source file.

DeregisterDevice()

```
#include <winbase.h>
```

Deregisters a device previously registered with a call to RegisterDevice().

Example:

```
DeregisterDevice(hDev);
```

Where:

- hDev is a handle to a device.

EnableEUDC()

```
#include <wingdi.h>
```

Enables or disables end user–defined characters (EUDCs). Applies to Asian-language versions of Windows CE.

Example:

```
BOOL bEnable;
if (IDYES == MessageBox(hWnd, TEXT("Do you want enable EUDCs?"),
TEXT("Question"), MB_YESNO))
{
    bEnable = TRUE;
}
else
{
    bEnable = FALSE;
}
EnableEUDC(bEnable);
```

Where:

- bEnable is a BOOL specifying whether EUDCs are to be enabled (TRUE) or disabled (FALSE).

EnableHardwareKeyboard()

```
#include <winuser.h>
```

If the device has a hardware keyboard, this function can be used to turn it on or off.

Example:

```
BOOL bEnable;
if (IDYES == MessageBox(hWnd, TEXT("Do you want to turn on the
keyboard again?"), TEXT("Question"), MB_YESNO))
{
    bEnable = TRUE;
}
else
{
    bEnable = FALSE;
}
EnableHardwareKeyboard(bEnable);
```

Where:

- bEnable is a BOOL specifying whether EUDCs are to be enabled (TRUE) or disabled (FALSE).

TIP   This function might be useful in situations where the user is concerned about accidentally striking keys (for example, when they are entering data with the stylus for an extended period of time).

FindFirstEntry()

```
#include <addrstor.h>
```

Searches the object store for the first item that *follows* the specified value; returns the oid of the matching item.

Example:

```
if (OpenAddressBook (NULL, HHPR_FILEAS))
{
    TCHAR szToMatch[MAX_PATH] = TEXT("J"); //find first *following*
value
    dwFlags = 0;
    oid = FindFirstEntry(szToMatch, HHPR_FILEAS, &iIndex, dwFlags);
```

Where:

- oid is the CEOID of the first item following the searched-for value.

- szToMatch is a string specifying a value to search for.

- HHPR_COMPANY_NAME is an HHPRTAG, one of numerous possible constants specifying the property (field) to search on. Other possible values include

  - HHPR_ANNIVERSARY

  - HHPR_ASSISTANT_NAME

  - HHPR_ASSISTANT_TELEPHONE_NUMBER

  - HHPR_BIRTHDAY

  - HHPR_BUSINESS_FAX_NUMBER

  - HHPR_CAR_TELEPHONE_NUMBER

  - HHPR_CATEGORY

  - HHPR_CHILDREN_NAME

  - HHPR_COMPANY_NAME

  - HHPR_CUSTOM_DISPLAY_FIELDS

  - HHPR_DEPARTMENT_NAME

  - HHPR_EMAIL1_EMAIL_ADDRESS

  - HHPR_EMAIL2_EMAIL_ADDRESS

  - HHPR_EMAIL3_EMAIL_ADDRESS

  - HHPR_GENERATION

  - HHPR_GIVEN_NAME

  - HHPR_HOME2_TELEPHONE_NUMBER

- HHPR_HOME_ADDRESS_CITY
- HHPR_HOME_ADDRESS_COUNTRY
- HHPR_HOME_ADDRESS_POSTAL_CODE
- HHPR_HOME_ADDRESS_STATE
- HHPR_HOME_ADDRESS_STREET
- HHPR_HOME_FAX_NUMBER
- HHPR_HOME_TELEPHONE_NUMBER
- HHPR_MIDDLE_NAME
- HHPR_MOBILE_TELEPHONE_NUMBER
- HHPR_NAME_PREFIX
- HHPR_NOTES
- HHPR_OFFICE_ADDRESS_CITY
- HHPR_OFFICE_ADDRESS_COUNTRY
- HHPR_OFFICE_ADDRESS_POSTAL_CODE
- HHPR_OFFICE_ADDRESS_STATE
- HHPR_OFFICE_ADDRESS_STREET
- HHPR_OFFICE_LOCATION
- HHPR_OFFICE_TELEPHONE_NUMBER
- HHPR_OFFICE2_TELEPHONE_NUMBER
- HHPR_OTHER_ADDRESS_CITY
- HHPR_OTHER_ADDRESS_COUNTRY
- HHPR_OTHER_ADDRESS_POSTAL_CODE
- HHPR_OTHER_ADDRESS_STATE
- HHPR_OTHER_ADDRESS_STREET
- HHPR_PAGER_NUMBER
- HHPR_SPOUSE_NAME

- HHPR_SURNAME

- HHPR_TITLE

- HHPR_WEB_PAGE

- HHPR_YOMI_NAME   //Japanese CE only

- HHPR_YOMI_COMPANY   //Japanese CE only

- iIndex is an integer used by the function to return the index of the matching item.

- dwFlags is either 0 or FFE_CONTAINS. Specifying FFE_CONTAINS searches for the first value following and containing szToMatch.

FreeAddressCard()

```
#include <addrstor.h>
```

Frees memory allocated by calls to OpenAddressCard() or GetAddressCardProperties().

Example:

```
AddressCard ac;
GetAddressCardProperties(oidCard, &ac, 8, rghhProp);
//...do something...
FreeAddressCard(&ac);
```

Where:

- ac is an AddressCard structure.

The AddressCard structure is defined as follows:

```
typedef struct _AddressCard {
SYSTEMTIME stBirthday;
SYSTEMTIME stAnniversary;
TCHAR *pszBusinessFax;
TCHAR *pszCompany;
TCHAR *pszDepartment;
TCHAR *pszEmail;
TCHAR *pszMobilePhone;
TCHAR *pszOfficeLocation;
TCHAR *pszPager;
TCHAR *pszWorkPhone;
```

```
TCHAR *pszTitle;
TCHAR *pszHomePhone;
TCHAR *pszEmail2;
TCHAR *pszSpouse;
TCHAR *pszNotes;
TCHAR *pszEmail3;
TCHAR *pszHomePhone2;
TCHAR *pszHomeFax;
TCHAR *pszCarPhone;
TCHAR *pszAssistant;
TCHAR *pszAssistantPhone;
TCHAR *pszChildren;
TCHAR *pszCategory;
TCHAR *pszWebPage;
TCHAR *pszWorkPhone2;
TCHAR *pszNamePrefix;
TCHAR *pszGivenName;
TCHAR *pszMiddleName;
TCHAR *pszSurname;
TCHAR *pszGeneration;
TCHAR *pszHomeAddrStreet;
TCHAR *pszHomeAddrCity;
TCHAR *pszHomeAddrState;
TCHAR *pszHomeAddrPostalCode;
TCHAR *pszHomeAddrCountry;
TCHAR *pszOtherAddrStreet;
TCHAR *pszOtherAddrCity;
TCHAR *pszOtherAddrState;
TCHAR *pszOtherAddrPostalCode;
TCHAR *pszOtherAddrCountry;
TCHAR *pszOfficeAddrStreet;
TCHAR *pszOfficeAddrCity;
TCHAR *pszOfficeAddrState;
TCHAR *pszOfficeAddrPostalCode;
TCHAR *pszOfficeAddrCountry;
BYTE *rgbReserved[84]
} AddressCard;
```

FtpCommand()

```
#include <wininet.h>
```

Sends the specified command to an FTP server.

Example:

```
BOOL bResponse = TRUE;
char szCmd[MAX_PATH] = "HELP\r\n";
DWORD dwFlags = FTP_TRANSFER_TYPE_ASCII;
DWORD dwContext = 100;
WINAPI FtpCommand(hFtpSession, bResponse, dwFlags, szCmd,
dwContext);
```

Where:

- hFtpSession is a handle to an open FTP session.

- bResponse is a BOOL indicating whether the command being sent will generate a response; in this example, it will generate a response.

- dwFlag is a DWORD specifying the type of data being sent. Can be one (but not both) of the following:

    FTP_TRANSFER_TYPE_ASCII   ASCII data transfer

    FTP_TRANSFER_TYPE_BINARY   Binary data transfer

- szCmd is a string containing the command to send to the server.

- dwContext is a DWORD used to uniquely identify this command for use with the status callback functions.

GetAddressCardIndex()

```
#include <addrstor.h>
```

Retrieves index of an address card in the contacts database, given its CEOID.

Example:

```
iIndex = GetAddressCardIndex(oidAC);
```

Where:

- iIndex is an integer that will receive the index of the address card or a value indicating an error. This zero-based index is based on the current sort order of the Address Book.

- oidAC is the CEOID of the address card whose index the function will retrieve.

GetAddressCardOid()

#include <addrstor.h>

Retrieves the CEOID of an address card given its index.

Example:

```
oidAC = GetAddressCardOid(iIndex);
```

Where:

- oidAC is the CEOID of the address card whose index is being passed to the function.

- iIndex is an integer specifying the index of the address card.

GetAddressCardProperties()

#include <addrstor.h>

Opens an address card and returns its properties.

Example:

```
AddressCard ac;
int iPropCount = 7; //retrieve 7 properties
HHPRTAG ptProps[7] = {HHPR_SURNAME, HHPR_GIVEN_NAME, HHPR_TITLE,
HHPR_OFFICE_LOCATION, HHPR_OFFICE_TELEPHONE_NUMBER,
HHPR_BUSINESS_FAX_NUMBER, HHPR_ANNIVERSARY};
    GetAddressCardProperties(oidCard,&ac,iPropCount, ptProps);
```

Where:

- oidCard is the CEOID of the card whose properties the function will retrieve.

- ac is an AddressCard structure. The members of the AddressCard structure that correspond to the properties requested will contain the values of those properties when the function returns.

- iPropCount is an integer specifying the number of properties requested.

- ptProps is an array containing iPropCount HHPRTAG values. See Find-FirstEntry() for a list of possible values for this parameter.

GetClipboardDataAlloc()

```
#include <winuser.h>
```

Allocates memory for and returns a handle to the data in the clipboard. This handle to memory must be freed later by the application via a call to `Local-Free()`.

Example:

```
UINT uTypeOfData = CF_TEXT;
TCHAR *szClipData;
szClipData = (TCHAR *) GetClipboardDataAlloc(uTypeOfData);
```

Where:

- `szClipData` is a buffer (in this case, a TCHAR buffer) that will point to the data in the clipboard when the function returns.

- `uTypeOfData` is UINT specifying the format of the clipboard data. Common values include

  CF_UNICODETEXT   The clipboard contains (Unicode) text data.

  CF_BITMAP   The clipboard contains bitmap data.

GetColumnProperties()

```
#include <addrstor.h>
```

Retrieves an array of properties representing the properties on which the Contacts database can be sorted.

Example:

```
    int iColCount = 4; //maximum # of properties the function can
return.
    HHPRTAG ptProps[4]; //reserve enough space for maximum # of
properties
    GetColumnProperties(&ptProps[0], &iColCount);
```

Where:

- `ptProps` is an array of HHPRTAG property specifiers. See `GetAddressCard-Properties()` for a list of possible HHPRTAG values. The function returns a maximum of four HHPRTAG values in the array.

- `iColCount` is an integer specifying the number of HHPRTAG props actually returned by the function.

GetMatchingEntry()

```
#include <addrstor.h>
```

Searches specified text-based property of the Contacts database for a matching value.

Example:

```
    CEOID oidMatch;
    HHPRTAG ptProp;
    TCHAR szToMatch[MAX_PATH] = TEXT("billg@microsoft.com"); //find
matching value
    iToMatchLen = _tcslen(szToMatch);
    TCHAR szPropToSearch[MAX_PATH] = TEXT("Internet");
    if (OpenAddressBook (NULL,NULL))
    {
        GetMatchingEntry(szToMatch, iToMatchLen, szPropToSearch,
&oidMatch, &ptProp);
        //...
```

Where:

- szToMatch is a string specifying a value to search for.

- iToMatchLen is an integer specifying the length of szToMatch.

- szPropToSearch is the name of the Contacts database property (field) to search.

- oidMatch is a CEOID the function uses to return the CEOID of the matching record.

- ptProp is an HHPRTAG value the function uses to return the HHPRTAG of the matching record. See GetAddressCardProperties() for a list of possible HHPRTAG values.

GetMessageSource()

```
#include <winuser.h>
```

Used to determine the origin of a keyboard-related message.

Example:

```
    UINT iMsgSource;
    iMessageSource = GetMessageSource();
```

Where:

- iMessageSource is a UINT value, which when the function returns will contain one of the following values:

  MSGSRC_SOFTWARE_POST   Another application generated the sent or posted the keyboard message to our application.

  MSGSRC_HARDWARE_KEYBOARD   The user actually struck a key on the keyboard to generate this message.

  MSGSRC_UNKNOWN   Source of the keyboard message is unknown.

GetMouseMovePoints()

```
#include <winuser.h>
```

Retrieves an array of POINTs indicating all of the points the mouse or stylus has been at for the current mouse-/stylus-related message. The advantage of this is that typically these points are recorded at too high a rate for an application to properly handle them. This function, then, allows for higher-resolution tracking of the stylus or mouse.

Example:

```
POINT ptPointArray[10]; //reserve room for up to 10 POINT
structures
UINT uPointCount = 10; //# of elements in array
UINT uPointsRetrieved;
GetMouseMovePoints(&ptPointArray, uPointCount, &uPointsRetreived);
```

Where:

- ptPointArray is an array of POINT structures.

- uPointsCount is a UINT specifying the number of POINT structures in ptPointArray.

- uPointsRetrieved is a UINT the function will use to indicate how many points it actually wrote to ptPointArray.

WARNING   This function does not exist under the CE emulators!

GetNumberOfAddressCards()

```
#include <addrstor.h>
```

Retrieves the number of address cards (records) in the Contacts database.

Example:

```
int iAddressCardCount;
iAddressCardCount = GetNumberOfAddressCards();
```

Where:

- iAddressCardCount is an integer that will receive the return value indicating the number of address cards.

GetPropertyDataStruct()

```
#include <addrstor.h>
```

Retrieves information about a property in the Contacts database.

Example:

```
int fFlag = GPDS_PROPERTY;
ULONG uPropID = HHPR_COMPANY_NAME;
PropertyDataStruct pds;
GetPropertyDataStruct(fFlag, uPropID, &pds);
```

Where:

- fFlag is an integer specifying how the function should search for the property. Possible values are

  GPDS_INDEX Treat the function's second parameter as the index of the property to search for.

  GPDS_NAME Treat the function's second parameter as a string specifying the name of the function.

  GPDS_PROPERTY Treat the function's second parameter as an HHPROPTAG value, as in the example above.

- uPropID is a ULONG value. Its purpose depends on the value of the first parameter.

- pds is a PropertyDataStruct structure the function will use to return information about the specified property.

GetSortOrder()

#include <addrstor.h>

Retrieves the property on which the Contacts database is currently sorted. Returns the property tag of this property.

Example:

```
BOOL bTrueSort = TRUE;
HHPRTAG hptPropSortOrder;
hptPropSortOrder = GetSortOrder(bTrueSort);
```

Where:

- hptPropSortOrder is an HHPRTAG value that is being used to store the return value of the function, identifying the property on which the Contacts database is currently sorted.

- bTrueSort is a BOOL specifying whether the function should return the property tag of the property the database is actually sorted on (TRUE), or the property tag of the property the user *thinks* the database is sorted on (FALSE). For example, although the database might be sorted on the HHPR_GIVEN_NAME, it would appear to the user to be sorted on the HHPR_FIRST_LAST_NAME property.

GetStoreInformation()

#include <winbase.h>

Returns information about free space of the CE device's object store.

Example:

```
STORE_INFORMATION siInfo;
CeGetStoreInformation(&siInfo);
```

Where:

- siInfo is a STORE_INFORMATION structure to be filled with the information about the object store.

The STORE_INFORMATION structure is defined as follows:

```
typedef struct STORE_INFORMATION {
DWORD dwStoreSize;
DWORD dwFreeSize;
} STORE_INFORMATION
```

GetSystemPowerStatusEx()

```
#include <winbase.h>
```

Retrieves information about the CE device's power source.

Example:

```
bMostCurrentInfo = FALSE;
CeGetSystemPowerStatusEx(&psPowerStatus, bMostCurrentInfo);
```

Where:

- psPowerStatus is a SYSTEM_POWER_STATUS_EX structure.

- bMostCurrentInfo is a BOOL value indicating whether the function should query the device driver directly for the most up-to-date information, or whether it should use cached information that may be several seconds old.

The SYSTEM_POWER_STATUS_EX structure is defined as follows:

```
typedef struct _SYSTEM_POWER_STATUS_EX {
BYTE ACLineStatus;
BYTE BatteryFlag;
BYTE BatteryLifePercent;
BYTE Reserved1;
DWORD BatteryLifeTime;
DWORD BatteryFullLifeTime;
BYTE Reserved2;
BYTE BackupBatteryFlag;
BYTE BackupBatteryLifePercent;
BYTE Reserved3;
DWORD BackupBatteryLifeTime;
DWORD BackupBatteryFullLifeTime;
} SYSTEM_POWER_STATUS_EX;
```

ImageList_Duplicate()

```
#include <commctrl.h>
```

Creates a duplicate or copy of an existing image list.

Example:

```
HIMAGELIST hImgListNew;
hImgListNew = ImageList_Duplicate(hImgListOld);
```

Where:

- hImgListNew is a handle to an image list. If the function is successful, hImgListNew will be a handle to a new image list containing the same images as hImgListOld.

- hImgListOld is a handle to the image list to be copied.

InitCommonControlsEx()

```
#include <commctrl.h>
```

Initializes the commctrl.dll library and makes the requested controls available to the calling application.

Example:

```
INITCOMMONCONTROLSEX icInitCommCtrl;
icInitCommCtrl.dwSize = sizeof(INITCOMMONCONTROLSEX);
icInitCommCtrl.dwICC = ICC_TREEVIEW_CLASSES;
InitCommonControlsEx(&icInitCommCtrl);
```

Where:

- icInitCommCtrl is an INITCOMMONCONTROLSEX structure. The dwICC member of this structure specifies which controls are being requested from the commctrl.dll. The dwICC member can be any combination of the following values:

    ICC_BAR_CLASSES   "Bar" controls: toolbar, status bar, trackbar, and CommandBar

    ICC_COOL_CLASSES   Rebar control

    ICC_DATE_CLASSES   Date and date-time picker controls

    ICC_LISTVIEW_CLASSES   Listview and header controls

    ICC_PROGRESS_CLASS   ProgressBar control.

    ICC_TAB_CLASSES   Tab controls

    ICC_TREEVIEW_CLASSES   Treeview control

    ICC_UPDOWN_CLASS   Up-down control

The INITCOMMONCONTROLSEX structure is defined as follows:

```
typedef struct tagINITCOMMONCONTROLSEX {
DWORD dwSize;
DWORD dwICC;
 } INITCOMMONCONTROLSEX;
```

InitInkX()

```
#include <richink.h>
```

Initializes the Ink control libraries; must be called before attempting to use the Ink control.

Example:

```
InitInkX();
```

NOTE   This function takes no parameters and does not return a value.

WARNING   You must always call `InitCommonControls()` before calling `InitInkX()`.

InitHTMLControl()

```
#include <htmlctrl.h>
```

Initializes the HTML control.

Example:

```
InitHTMLControl(hInstance);
```

Where:

• hInstance is a handle to the application's instance.

TIP   Although the documentation says, "An application must load the HTML control library `Htmlview.dll`" before calling `InitHTMLControl()`, this is not necessary. Simply calling `InitHTMLControl()` is enough.

InterlockedTestExchange()

`#include <winbase.h>`

Conditionally sets the value of a LONG variable, guaranteeing that the values will be successfully exchanged via synchronization in the case of multiple threads accessing the variables.

Example:

```
LONG lTarget = 444;
LONG lOldVal = 444;
LONG lNewVal = 42;
InterlockedTestExchange(lTarget, lOldVal, lNewVal);
```

Where:

- lTarget is a LONG variable whose value the function will conditionally replace.

- lOldVal is a LONG value the function uses to determine whether or not it should replace the value of lTarget. If lTarget and lOldVal are equal, then the function will replace the value of lTarget.

- lNewVal is a LONG value the function will assign to lTarget providing that lTarget is equal to lOldVal.

MailClose()

`#include <msgstore.h>`

Closes an open message store handle.

Example:

```
MailClose(hMsgStore);
```

Where:

- hMsgStore is an open handle to the message store.

MailDelete()

`#include <msgstore.h>`

Deletes a mail message from the message store.

Example:

```
MailDelete(hMsgStore, &mmMsg);
```

Where:

- hMsgStore is an open handle to the message store.

- mmMsg is a MailMsg structure specifying the message to be deleted.

The MailMsg structure is defined as follows:

```
typedef struct MailMsg {
DWORD dwMsgId;
DWORD dwFlags;
DWORD dwMsgLen;
WORD wBodyLen;
FILETIME ftDate;
LPWSTR szSvcId;
LPWSTR szSvcNam;
WCHAR *pwcHeaders;
LPWSTR szBody;
CEOID oid;
HANDLE hHeap
} MailMsg;
```

MailDeleteAttachment()

```
#include <msgstore.h>
```

Deletes a mail message's attachment.

Example:

```
BOOL bDeleteEntire = TRUE;
MailDeleteAttachment (hMsgStore, &mmMsg, maAttach, bDeleteEntire);
```

Where:

- hMsgStore is an open handle to the message store.

- mmMsg is a MailMsg structure specifying the mail message to which the attachment belongs.

- maAttach is a MailAtt structure specifying the attachment to be deleted.

- bDeleteEntire specifies whether the entire attachment is to be deleted (TRUE) or whether the header of the attachment should be retained (FALSE).

The `MailAtt` structure is defined as follows:

```
typedef struct MailAtt_s {
UINT uiAttachmentNumber;
DWORD dwFlags;
ULONG ulCharacterPosition;
ULONG ulSize;
LPWSTR szOriginalName;
LPWSTR szLocalName;
} MailAtt;
```

MailError()

```
#include <msgstore.h>
```

Comparable to `GetLastError()`; returns a numeric code for the last error that was caused by a Message Store function.

Example:

```
int iError;
iError = MailError(hMsgStore);
```

Where:

- `iError` is an integer used to store the result of the function.

- `hMsgStore` is an open handle to the message store.

MailErrorMsg()

```
#include <msgstore.h>
```

Comparable to `FormatMessage()`; formats a string error message based on the last error that was caused by a Message Store function. Also provides the numeric identifier of the last error as its return value.

Example:

```
int iError;
int iLineNo;
TCHAR szError[MAX_PATH];
iError = MailError(hMsgStore, szError, MAX_PATH, &iLineNo);
```

Where:

- `iError` is an integer used to store the result of the function.

- `hMsgStore` is an open handle to the message store.

- szError is a string that, if the function is sucessful, will contain a text message indicating the error that occurred.

- MAX_PATH specifies the length, in bytes, of szError.

- iLineNo is an integer the function uses to return the line number on which the error occurred.

WARNING   This function is provided as an alternative to MailError().

MailFirst()

```
#include <msgstore.h>
```

Retrieves the first message matching the specified criteria.

Example:

```
if (MailOpen(&hMsgStore, FALSE))
{
    mmMsg.dwFlags = MAIL_FOLDER_INBOX | MAIL_FULL;
    MailFirst(hMsgStore, &mmMsg);
    //...
}
MailClose(hMsgStore);
```

Where:

- hMsgStore is an open handle to the message store.

- mmMsg is a MailMsg structure specifying the mail message to retrieve.

The MailMsg structure is defined as follows:

```
typedef struct MailMsg {
DWORD dwMsgId;
DWORD dwFlags;
DWORD dwMsgLen;
WORD wBodyLen;
FILETIME ftDate;
LPWSTR szSvcId;
LPWSTR szSvcNam;
WCHAR *pwcHeaders;
LPWSTR szBody;
```

```
CEOID oid;
HANDLE hHeap
} MailMsg;
```

MailFree()

```
#include <msgstore.h>
```

Frees memory allocated by calls to MailFirst(), MailGet(), or MailNext().

Example:

```
if (MailOpen(&hMsgStore, FALSE))
{
    mmMsg.dwFlags = MAIL_FOLDER_INBOX | MAIL_FULL;
    MailFirst(hMsgStore, &mmMsg);
    //...
    //...done w/ message, so free memory
    MailFree(&mmMsg);
}
MailClose(hMsgStore);
```

Where:

- hMsgStore is an open handle to the message store.

- mmMsg is a MailMsg structure specifying the mail message to retrieve.

MailGet()

```
#include <msgstore.h>
```

Retrieves specified mail entry from the message store.

Example:

```
if (MailOpen(&hMsgStore, FALSE))
{
    memset(&mmMsg, 0, sizeof(MailMsg));
    mmMsg.dwFlags = MAIL_FOLDER_INBOX | MAIL_FULL;
    MailGet(hMsgStore, &mmMsg);
    //...
    //...done w/ message, so free memory
    MailFree(&mmMsg);
}
MailClose(hMsgStore);
```

Where:

- hMsgStore is an open handle to the message store.

- mmMsg is a MailMsg structure specifying the mail message to retrieve.

MailGetAttachment()

```
#include <msgstore.h>
```

Retrieves an attachment to a mail message.

Example:

```
MailAtt maAtt;
    MailMsg mmMsg;
    if (MailFirst(hMsgStore, &mmMsg))
    {
        // see if any attachments in this message
        if (mmMsg.dwFlags & MAIL_STATUS_ATTACHMENTS)
        {
            MailGetAttachment (hMsgStore, &mmMsg, &maAtt);
        }
    }
```

Where:

- hMsgStore is an open handle to the message store.

- mmMsg is a MailMsg structure specifying the mail message whose attachment you want to retrieve.

- maAttachment is a MailAtt structure the function will use to return the attachment.

The MailAtt structure is defined as follows:

```
typedef struct MailAtt_s {
UINT uiAttachmentNumber;
DWORD dwFlags;
ULONG ulCharacterPosition;
ULONG ulSize;
LPWSTR szOriginalName;
LPWSTR szLocalName;
} MailAtt;
```

MailGetField()

```
#include <msgstore.h>
```

Retrieves a specified header field from the mail message.

Example:

```
LPWSTR szFieldName = TEXT("Subject");
bGetName = FALSE;
MailGetField(&mmMsg, szFieldName, bGetName);
```

Where:

- mmMsg is a MailMessage previously retrieved with a call to MailFirst(), MailGet(), etc.

- szFieldName is the name of the mail message field to retrieve. Possible values include

    "Subject"   Retrieves the subject field of the message.

    "To"   Retrieves the recipient field of the message.

    "From"   Retrieves the sender field of the message.

    "CC"   Retrieves the carbon-copy-recipient field.

- bGetName is a BOOL indicating whether the function should retrieve the name of the field (e.g., "Subject") or the actual contents of the field. A TRUE value retrieves the field name; a FALSE value retrieves the contents.

MailGetFolderId()

```
#include <msgstore.h>
```

Retrieves the ID number of a mail folder from the message store.

Example:

```
BYTE iFolderID; //will receive ID of folder if successful.
LPWSTR szFolderName = TEXT("Inbox");
MailGetFolderId(hMsgStore, &iFolderID, szFolderName);
```

Where:

- hMsgStore is an open handle to the message store.

- iFolderID is an integer the function will use to return the ID number of the folder specified.

- szFolderName is a string specifying the name of the folder whose ID you want to retrieve.

MailGetFolderName()

```
#include <msgstore.h>
```

Retrieves the name of a mail folder from the message store.

Example:

```
WCHAR szFolderName[MAX_PATH];
    int iLen = MAX_PATH;
    int iFolderID = MAIL_FOLDER_OUTBOX;
    MailGetFolderName(hMsgStore, &iFolderID, &iLen, szFolderName);
```

Where:

- hMsgStore is an open handle to the message store.

- iFolderID is an integer the function will use to return the ID number of the folder specified. Predefined system folder IDs include

    MAIL_FOLDER_INBOX   Inbox Folder

    MAIL_FOLDER_OUTBOX   Outbox Folder

    MAIL_FOLDER_SENT   Sent Folder

- iLen is the maximum length of szFolderName.

- szFolderName is a string specifying the name of the folder whose ID you want to retrieve.

MailGetSort()

```
#include <msgstore.h>
```

Retrieves the information about the current sort order of the open message store.

Example:

```
MAILSORTINFO msiSortInfo;
if (MailGetSort (hMsgStore, &msiSortInfo))
{
    if (msiSortInfo == MAIL_SORT_FROM)
    {
        //do something...
    }
}
```

Where:

- hMsgStore is an open handle to the message store.

- msiSortInfo is a MAILSORTINFO structure.

The MAILSORTINFO structure is defined as follows:

```
typedef struct _MAILSORTINFO {
MAILSORTFIELD iSort;
BOOL fAscending;
int cMsgs;
} MAILSORTINFO;
```

MailGetSvcId()

```
#include <msgstore.h>
```

Retrieves the CEOID (object identifier) of a mail message from the message store based on the value of the szSvcId and szSvcNam (service identifier) fields of the MailMsg structure.

Example:

```
MailGetSvcId(hMsgStore, &mmMsg);
```

Where:

- hMsgStore is an open handle to the message store.

- mmMsg is a MailMessage structure that contains values for the szSvcId and szSvcNam fields.

TIP   The "service identifier" is a string that uniquely identifies a mail message.

MailHeaderLen()

`#include <msgstore.h>`

Returns the size, in characters, of a mail message's header.

Example:

```
DWORD dwHeaderLen;
dwHeaderLen = MailHeaderLen(&mmMailMsg);
```

Where:

- dwHeaderLen is a DWORD used to store the return value of the function.

- mmMailMsg is a MailMsg structure.

MailLocalAttachmentLen()

`#include <msgstore.h>`

Returns the total size of a mail message's attachments.

Example:

```
DWORD dwTotalAttSize;
MailLocalAttachmentLen(hMsgStore, &mmMsg);
```

Where:

- dwTotalAttSize is a DWORD used to store the return value of the function.

- mmMailMsg is a MailMsg structure.

MailNext()

`#include <msgstore.h>`

Used in conjunction with MailFirst(); retrieves the next mail message matching the criteria specified in MailFirst().

Example:

```
MailNext(hMsgStore, &mmMailMsg);
```

Where:

- hMsgStore is an open handle to the message store.

- mmMsg is a MailMessage structure that the function will use to return the next matching message.

MailOpen()

```
#include <msgstore.h>
```

Opens the message store and obtains a handle to the mail context.

Example:

```
HANDLE hMsgStore;
BOOL bAllowCreate = TRUE;
MailOpen(&hMsgStore, bAllowCreate);
```

Where:

- hMsgStore is a handle; if the function is successful, it will be a handle to the message store.

- bAllowCreate is a BOOL specifying whether you'd like the message store to be created if it does not exist.

MailOpenNotify()

```
#include <msgstore.h>
```

Opens the message store, obtains a handle to the mail context, and specifies that the calling application should receive notification if the message store is modified while the application is accessing it.

Example:

```
HANDLE hMsgStore;
BOOL bAllowCreate = TRUE;
MailOpenNotify(&hMsgStore, bAllowCreate, hWnd);
```

Where:

- hMsgStore is a handle; if the function is successful, it will be a handle to the message store.

- bAllowCreate is a BOOL specifying whether you'd like the message store to be created if it does not exist.

- hWnd is the handle to the window that should receive the notification messages.

MailPut()

```
#include <msgstore.h>
```

Retrieves specified mail entry from the message store.

Example:

```
if (MailOpen(&hMsgStore, FALSE))
{
    //...
    //fill in mmMsg structure here
    //...
    MailPut(hMsgStore, &mmMsg);
    //...
}
MailClose(hMsgStore);
```

Where:

- hMsgStore is an open handle to the message store.

- mmMsg is a MailMsg structure specifying the mail message to retrieve.

MailPutAttachment()

```
#include <msgstore.h>
```

Appends or modifies an attachment to a mail message.

Example:

```
MailAtt maAtt;
MailMsg mmMsg;
if (MailFirst(hMsgStore, &mmMsg))
{
    //...
    //make any modifications to maAtt here
    //
    MailPutAttachment (hMsgStore, &mmMsg, &maAtt);
}
```

Where:

- hMsgStore is an open handle to the message store.

- mmMsg is a MailMsg structure specifying the mail message whose attachment you want to retrieve.

- maAttachment is a MailAtt structure the function will use to return the attachment

---

NOTE   To append the attachment to the mail message, set uiAttachmentNumber member of the MailAtt structure to be one higher than the uiAttachmentNumber of the last attachment of the message; to update an existing attachment, set uiAttachmentNumber to the uiAttachmentNumber value of the existing attachment.

MailPutFolder()

```
#include <msgstore.h>
```

Creates, deletes, or renames mail folders.

Example:

```
//create a folder
LPWSTR szFolderName = TEXT("Spam Mail");
BYTE iFolderID = 224;
MailPutFolder(hMsgStore, &iFolderID, szFolderName);
```

Where:

- hMsgStore is an open handle to the message store.

- iFolderID is an integer used to uniquely identify the folder; must be between 0 and 255.

- szFolderName is a string specifying the name of the folder to create or rename. To delete a folder, set this value to NULL.

MailRequestAttachment()

```
#include <msgstore.h>
```

Requests and/or downloads an attachment to a mail message that has not yet been saved to the local machine.

Example:

```
MailAtt maAtt;
MailMsg mmMsg;
BOOL bDownload = TRUE;
if (MailFirst(hMsgStore, &mmMsg))
{
    // see if there are un-retrieved attachments
    if (mmMsg.dwFlags & MAIL_STATUS_ATT_REQ)
    {
        MailRequestAttachment(hMsgStore, &mmMsg, &maAtt,
bDownload);
    }
}
```

Where:

- hMsgStore is an open handle to the message store.

- mmMsg is a MailMsg structure specifying the mail message whose attachment you want to download.

- maAttachment is a MailAtt structure the function will use to return the attachment.

- bDownload is a BOOL value specifying whether to download the attachment (TRUE) or cancel a previous request (FALSE) to download the attachment.

MailSetField()

```
#include <msgstore.h>
```

Sets a specified header field from the mail message.

Example:

```
LPWSTR szFieldName = TEXT("Subject");
LPWSTR szVal = TEXT("A New Subject!");
MailSetField(&mmMsg, szFieldName, szVal);
```

Where:

- mmMsg is a MailMessage previously retrieved with a call to MailFirst(), MailGet(), etc.

- `szFieldName` is the name of the mail message field to retrieve. Possible values include

    "Subject"   Retrieves the subject field of the message.

    "To"   Retrieves the recipient field of the message.

    "From"   Retrieves the sender field of the message.

    "CC"   Retrieves the carbon-copy-recipient field…or any custom header you'd like to add to the message.

- `szVal` is a string specifying a value for the header field. If this parameter is NULL, the header field will be deleted.

MailSetSort()

```
#include <msgstore.h>
```

Sets the sort order for the messages of an open message store handle.

Example:

```
MAILSORTFIELD msfSort = MAIL_SORT_DATE;
MailSetSort(hMsgStore, &msfSort)
```

Where:

- `hMsgStore` is an open handle to the message store.

- `msfSort` is a `MAILSORTFIELD` value specifying how the messages are to be sorted.

The `MAILSORTFIELD` is an enumeration defined as follows:

```
typedef enum {
MAIL_SORT_FROM,
MAIL_SORT_SUBJ,
MAIL_SORT_DATE,
MAIL_SORT_SIZE
} MAILSORTFIELD;
```

MailUpdate()

```
#include <msgstore.h>
```

Updates an existing mail message entry in the message store.

Example:

```
BOOL bUpdateAllFields = TRUE;
MailUpdate(hMsgStore, &mmMsg, bUpdateAllFields);
```

Where:

- hMsgStore is an open handle to the message store.

- mmMsg is a MailMessage structure that contains the updated information.

- bUpdateAllFields is a BOOL specifying whether all of the existing message's fields should be overwritten (TRUE) or just those specified in the dwFlags member of mmMsg.

ModifyAddressCard()

```
#include <addrstor.h>
```

Saves changes to an address card back to the Contacts database.

Example:

```
AddressCard ac;
CEOID oid;
int iIndex;
//...
//obtain oid of card to modify...then
//populate AddressCard ac
//...
ModifyAddressCard(&ac, oid,  &iIndex);
```

Where:

- ac is an AddressCard structure containing the values to be written back to the Contacts database.

- oid is the CEOID of the card (record) to modify.

- iIndex is an integer the function will use to return the index of the modified record.

The AddressCard structure is defined as follows:

```
typedef struct _AddressCard {
SYSTEMTIME stBirthday;
SYSTEMTIME stAnniversary;
TCHAR *pszBusinessFax;
TCHAR *pszCompany;
TCHAR *pszDepartment;
TCHAR *pszEmail;
TCHAR *pszMobilePhone;
TCHAR *pszOfficeLocation;
TCHAR *pszPager;
TCHAR *pszWorkPhone;
TCHAR *pszTitle;
TCHAR *pszHomePhone;
TCHAR *pszEmail2;
TCHAR *pszSpouse;
TCHAR *pszNotes;
TCHAR *pszEmail3;
TCHAR *pszHomePhone2;
TCHAR *pszHomeFax;
TCHAR *pszCarPhone;
TCHAR *pszAssistant;
TCHAR *pszAssistantPhone;
TCHAR *pszChildren;
TCHAR *pszCategory;
TCHAR *pszWebPage;
TCHAR *pszWorkPhone2;
TCHAR *pszNamePrefix;
TCHAR *pszGivenName;
TCHAR *pszMiddleName;
TCHAR *pszSurname;
TCHAR *pszGeneration;
TCHAR *pszHomeAddrStreet;
TCHAR *pszHomeAddrCity;
TCHAR *pszHomeAddrState;
TCHAR *pszHomeAddrPostalCode;
TCHAR *pszHomeAddrCountry;
TCHAR *pszOtherAddrStreet;
TCHAR *pszOtherAddrCity;
TCHAR *pszOtherAddrState;
TCHAR *pszOtherAddrPostalCode;
```

```
TCHAR *pszOtherAddrCountry;
TCHAR *pszOfficeAddrStreet;
TCHAR *pszOfficeAddrCity;
TCHAR *pszOfficeAddrState;
TCHAR *pszOfficeAddrPostalCode;
TCHAR *pszOfficeAddrCountry;
BYTE *rgbReserved[84]
} AddressCard;
```

OpenAddressBook()

```
#include <addrstor.h>
```

Opens the Address Book; returns a nonzero value if successful.

Example:

```
HANDLE hWnd = NULL;
HHPRTAG hptProp = HHPR_FILEAS;
OpenAddressBook(hWnd, hptProp);
```

Where:

- hWnd is a handle to a window or NULL. Uses a window handle to receive notification if the Contacts database is modified while your application is accessing it.

- hptProp is an HHPRTAG value specifying the sort order to apply to the Contacts database while in use by your application.

OpenAddressCard()

```
#include <addrstor.h>
```

Retrieves all properties of an address card, given the card's CEOID.

Example:

```
ULONG uFlag = OAC_ALLOCATE;
OpenAddressCard (oidContact, &ac, uFlag);
```

Where:

- oidContact is the CEOID of the address card whose properties the function is to retrieve. The CEOID of the card must be known ahead of time; you can get the CEOID of a card by calling functions like FindFirstEntry() and GetMatchingEntry().

- ac is an AddressCard structure that the function uses to return the address card's properties.

- uFlag is a ULONG value that can be one of the following values:

    OAC_ALLOCATE   Specifies that the function should allocate additional memory to accommodate any possible modifications to string properties.

    0   Specifies that the function should not allocate the additional memory and essentially makes the card read-only.

Random()

```
#include <winbase.h>
```

Returns a DWORD random number.

Example:

```
DWORD dwRandom;
dwRandom = Random();
```

Where:

- dwRandom is a DWORD used to store the return value of the function.

NOTE   This function takes no parameters.

RapiFreeBuffer()

```
#include <rapi.h>
```

Frees memory allocated by the RAPI functions CeFindAllDatabases(), CeFindAllFiles(), and CeReadRecordProps().

Example:

```
dwType = 0;
LPCEDB_FIND_DATA pFindData;
wFlags = FAD_OID | FAD_FLAGS | FAD_NAME | FAD_TYPE FAD_NUM_RECORDS
| FAD_NUM_SORT_ORDER | FAD_SORT_SPECS;
CeFindAllDatabases( DbType, 0xFF, &cFound, &pFindData);
//...
```

```
//do something with found databases...
//then, when finished....
RapiFreeBuffer(pFindData);
```

Where:

- pFindData is a buffer allocated by one of the RAPI functions listed above; in this case, CeFindAllDatabases().

RasGetEntryDevConfig()

Although still provided for backward compatibility, this function has been replaced by RasGetEntryProperties(), which is supported on all versions of Windows, including 98 and NT.

RasSetEntryDevConfig()

Although still provided for backward compatibility, this function has been replaced by RasSetEntryProperties(), which is supported on all versions of Windows, including 98 and NT.

RecountCards()

```
#include <addrstor.h>
```

Causes the system to recount the number of cards in the Contacts database. Useful if your application is set up to receive notification when the Contacts database is modified while your application is using it.

Example:

```
RecountCards();
```

NOTE   This function has no parameters and does not return a value.

RegisterDevice()

```
#include <winbase.h>
```

Registers a hardware device.

Example:

```
HANDLE hDev;
DWORD dwIndex;
DWORD dwInstanceInfo; //depends on device being registered
TCHAR szDevType[MAX_PATH] = TEXT("WAV");
TCHAR szDriverName[MAX_PATH] = TEXT("snd.dll");
dwIndex = 2;
hDev = RegisterDevice(szDevType, dwIndex, szDriverName,
dwInstanceInfo);
```

Where:

- hDev is a handle to the device if the function is successful.

- szDevType is a string identifying the type of device.

- dwIndex is a DWORD specifying the index of the device.

- szDriverName is a string containing the name of the driver for the device being registered.

- dwInstanceInfo is a DWORD specifying the instance information of the device. For example, this might be a hexidecimal memory address.

SetColumnProperties()

```
#include <addrstor.h>
```

Sets the available sort orders for the Contacts database.

Example:

```
HHPRTAG hptProps[4]; //max. 4 properties to sort on
hptProps[0] = HHPR_SURNAME;
int iColumnCount = 1;
SetColumnProperties(&hptProps, iColumnCount);
```

Where:

- hptProps is an array of HHPRTAG values, specifying the properties on which the Contacts database is to be sorted.

- iColumnCount specifies the number of positions in the array containing valid HHPRTAG values. The maximum value for this parameter is 4.

SetDaylightTime()

```
#include <winbase.h>
```

Specifies to the CE operating system whether or not daylight saving time is in effect.

Example:

```
DWORD dwDaylight = 1;
SetDaylightTime(dwDaylight);
```

Where:

- dwDaylight is a DWORD value specifying:

    - **1** daylight saving time is currently in effect.

    - **0** daylight saving time is not currently in effect.

SetMask()

```
#include <addrstor.h>
```

Indicates which of the properties in an AddressCard structure are being used by the application.

Example:

```
AddressCard ac;
HHPRTAG hptTag;
memset (&ac, 0, sizeof (AddressCard));
ac.pszGivenName = TEXT("Karen");
ac.pszSurname = TEXT("Johnson");
ac.pszCompany = TEXT("Widget Co.");
ac.pszEmail = TEXT("Karen@widgetco.com");
// tell system which properties we are setting.
hptTag = HHPR_GIVEN_NAME;
SetMask (&ac, hptTag);
hptTag = HHPR_SURNAME;
SetMask (&ac, hptTag);
hptTag = HHPR_COMPANY_NAME;
SetMask (&ac, hptTag);
hptTag = HHPR_EMAIL1_EMAIL_ADDRESS
SetMask (&ac, hptTag);
```

Where:

- ac is an AddressCard structure.

- hptTag is an HHPRTAG value specifying which members of the AddressCard structure you're using.

SetSortOrder()

```
#include <addrstor.h>
```

Selects one of the available sort orders and marks it as active. The sort order selected must be one of the sort orders specified with a call to OpenAddress-Book() or SetColumnProperties().

Example:

```
HHPRTAG hptProps[4]; //max. 4 properties to sort on
HHPRTAG hptProp;
hptProps[0] = HHPR_SURNAME;
int iColumnCount = 1;
SetColumnProperties(&hptProps, iColumnCount);
hptProp = HHPR_SURNAME;
SetSortOrder(hptProp);
```

Where:

- hptProp is an HHPRTAG value specifying the sort order to use.

SHCreateShortcut()

```
#include <shellapi.h>
```

Creates a shortcut.

Example:

```
TCHAR szShortcutFile[MAX_PATH];
TCHAR szActualExe[MAX_PATH];
szShortcutFile = TEXT("\\MyApp.lnk");
szActualExe = TEXT("\\Windows\\MyApp.exe");
SHCreateShortcut(szShortcutFile, szActualExe);
```

Where:

- szShortcutFile is a string specifying the full path of the shortcut file.

- szActualExe is a string specifying the full path to the actual executable file.

SHGetShortcutTarget()

```
#include <shellapi.h>
```

Retrieves the path to the target executable of the specified shortcut.

Example:

```
TCHAR szShortcutFile[MAX_PATH];
TCHAR szActualExe[MAX_PATH];
int iActualExeLen = MAX_PATH;
szShortcutFile = TEXT("\\MyApp.lnk");
SHGetShortcutTarget(szShortcutFile, szActualExe, iActualExeLen);
```

Where:

- szShortcutFile is a string specifying the full path of the shortcut file.

- szActualExe is a string the function uses to return the full path to the actual executable file.

- iActualExeLen is an integer specifying the maximum possible length of szActualExe.

SHLoadDIBitmap()

```
#include <shellapi.h>
```

Loads a bitmap from a file and returns a handle to that bitmap if successful.

Example:

```
HBITMAP hBmp;
TCHAR szBmpName[MAX_PATH] = TEXT("\\MyApp\\resources\\logo.bmp");
hBmp = SHLoadDIBitmap(szBmpName);
```

Where:

- hBmp is the handle of the bitmap returned by the function if the call is successful.

- szBmpName is a string specifying the name of the bitmap file.

SHShowOutOfMemory()

```
#include <shellapi.h>
```

Shows the Out of Memory message.

Example:

```
SHShowOutOfMemory(hWnd, 0);
```

Where:

- hWnd is the handle of the window that will own the dialog.

NOTE   The second parameter of this function is always 0.

TIP   It is recommended that you use this function if your application runs low on memory. This function will work under low-memory conditions, whereas creating your own new dialog box may fail under low-memory conditions.

TransparentImage()

```
#include <wingdi.h>
```

Copies the contents of one HDC to another, with the ability to specify that one of the colors in the source HDC is to be considered a transparent color.

Example:

```
HDC hdcDest, hdcSource;
COLORREF clrTrans;
LONG DstX, DstY, DstCx, DstCy;
LONG SrcX, SrcY, SrcCx, SrcCy;
//...
//set up hdcDest and hdcSource...
//...
DstX = 0;
DstY = 0;
DstCx = 16;
DstCy = 16;
SrcX = 0;
SrcY = 0;
```

```
    SrcCx = 16;
    SrcCy = 16;
    clrTrans = 0x00FFFFFF; //white is the transparent color
    TransparentImage(hdcDest,DstX, DstY, DstCx, DstCy, hdcSource, SrcX,
SrcY, SrcCx, SrcCy, clrTrans);
```

Where:

- hdcDest is the destination HDC.

- DstX is a LONG integer specifying the destination *x* coordinate.

- DstY is a LONG integer specifying the destination *x* coordinate.

- DstCx is a LONG integer specifying the destination *x* coordinate.

- DstCy is a LONG integer specifying the destination *x* coordinate.

- hdcSource is the source HDC.

- SrcX is a LONG integer specifying the destination *x* coordinate.

- SrcY is a LONG integer specifying the destination *x* coordinate.

- SrcCx is a LONG integer specifying the destination *x* coordinate.

- SrcCy is a LONG integer specifying the destination *x* coordinate.

- clrTrans is a COLORREF value specifying the transparent color. A COLORREF is a 32-bit value specifying the RGB value for a color. COLORREFs have the form 0x00rrggbb, where rr is the red component, gg is the green component, and bb is the blue component.

TIP   Essentially, TransparentImage() is a BitBlt() that supports transparency.

---

*Var*YYYY*From*ZZZZ*()* Family of Functions

```
#include <oleauto.h>
```

All of the functions having the form Var*YYYY*From*XXXX*() are part of the OLE automation of Windows CE. Instead of listing each individual function here (there are approximately 170 different functions), we will provide a description of the general form and detail the different data types involved.

Each of these Var*YYYY*From*XXXX*() functions converts from a variant type to a nonvariant type. Table B.1 shows the abbreviations for each of these data types and their meanings.

TABLE B.1: Variant Data Types

Abbreviation	Data Type
Bool	Boolean
Bstr	BSTR
Cy	currency
Date	date
Dec	decimal
Disp	IDispatch
R4	float
R8	double
I1	char
I2	short
I4	long
I8	double
Str	char*
UI1	byte
UI2	unsigned short
UI4	unsigned long

A full listing of all of the conversion functions follows:

- VarBoolFromCy()
- VarBoolFromDate()
- VarBoolFromDec()

- VarBoolFromDisp()
- VarBoolFromI1()
- VarBoolFromI2()
- VarBoolFromI4()
- VarBoolFromR4()
- VarBoolFromR8()
- VarBoolFromStr()
- VarBoolFromUI1()
- VarBoolFromUI2()
- VarBoolFromUI4()
- VarBstrFromBool()
- VarBstrFromCy()
- VarBstrFromDate()
- VarBstrFromDec()
- VarBstrFromDisp()
- VarBstrFromI1()
- VarBstrFromI2()
- VarBstrFromI4()
- VarBstrFromR4()
- VarBstrFromR8()
- VarBstrFromUI1()
- VarBstrFromUI2()
- VarBstrFromUI4()
- VarCyFromBool()
- VarCyFromDate()
- VarCyFromDec()

- VarCyFromDisp()
- VarCyFromI1()
- VarCyFromI2()
- VarCyFromI4()
- VarCyFromR4()
- VarCyFromR8()
- VarCyFromStr()
- VarCyFromUI1()
- VarCyFromUI2()
- VarCyFromUI4()
- VarDateFromBool()
- VarDateFromCy()
- VarDateFromDec()
- VarDateFromDisp()
- VarDateFromI1()
- VarDateFromI2()
- VarDateFromI4()
- VarDateFromR4()
- VarDateFromR8()
- VarDateFromStr()
- VarDateFromUdate()
- VarDateFromUI1()
- VarDateFromUI2()
- VarDateFromUI4()
- VarDecFromBool()
- VarDecFromCy()

- VarDecFromDate()
- VarDecFromDisp()
- VarDecFromI1()
- VarDecFromI2()
- VarDecFromI4()
- VarDecFromR4()
- VarDecFromR8()
- VarDecFromStr()
- VarDecFromUI1()
- VarDecFromUI2()
- VarDecFromUI4()
- VarI1FromBool()
- VarI1FromCy()
- VarI1FromDate()
- VarI1FromDec()
- VarI1FromDisp()
- VarI1FromI2()
- VarI1FromI4()
- VarI1FromR4()
- VarI1FromR8()
- VarI1FromStr()
- VarI1FromUI1()
- VarI1FromUI2()
- VarI1FromUI4()
- VarI2FromBool()
- VarI2FromCy()

- `VarI2FromDate()`
- `VarI2FromDec()`
- `VarI2FromDisp()`
- `VarI2FromI1()`
- `VarI2FromI4()`
- `VarI2FromR4()`
- `VarI2FromR8()`
- `VarI2FromStr()`
- `VarI2FromUI1()`
- `VarI2FromUI2()`
- `VarI2FromUI4()`
- `VarI4FromBool()`
- `VarI4FromCy()`
- `VarI4FromDate()`
- `VarI4FromDec()`
- `VarI4FromDisp()`
- `VarI4FromI1()`
- `VarI4FromI2()`
- `VarI4FromR4()`
- `VarI4FromR8()`
- `VarI4FromStr()`
- `VarI4FromUI1()`
- `VarI4FromUI2()`
- `VarI4FromUI4()`
- `VarR4FromBool()`
- `VarR4FromCy()`

- VarR4FromDate()
- VarR4FromDec()
- VarR4FromDisp()
- VarR4FromI1()
- VarR4FromI2()
- VarR4FromI4()
- VarR4FromR8()
- VarR4FromStr()
- VarR4FromUI1()
- VarR4FromUI2()
- VarR4FromUI4()
- VarR8FromBool()
- VarR8FromCy()
- VarR8FromDate()
- VarR8FromDec()
- VarR8FromDisp()
- VarR8FromI1()
- VarR8FromI2()
- VarR8FromI4()
- VarR8FromR4()
- VarR8FromStr()
- VarR8FromUI1()
- VarR8FromUI2()
- VarR8FromUI4()
- VarUI1FromBool()
- VarUI1FromCy()

- `VarUI1FromDate()`
- `VarUI1FromDec()`
- `VarUI1FromDisp()`
- `VarUI1FromI1()`
- `VarUI1FromI2()`
- `VarUI1FromI4()`
- `VarUI1FromR4()`
- `VarUI1FromR8()`
- `VarUI1FromStr()`
- `VarUI1FromUI2()`
- `VarUI1FromUI4()`
- `VarUI2FromBool()`
- `VarUI2FromCy()`
- `VarUI2FromDate()`
- `VarUI2FromDec()`
- `VarUI2FromDisp()`
- `VarUI2FromI1()`
- `VarUI2FromI2()`
- `VarUI2FromI4()`
- `VarUI2FromR4()`
- `VarUI2FromR8()`
- `VarUI2FromStr()`
- `VarUI2FromUI1()`
- `VarUI2FromUI4()`
- `VarUI4FromBool()`
- `VarUI4FromCy()`

- VarUI4FromDate()
- VarUI4FromDec()
- VarUI4FromDisp()
- VarUI4FromI1()
- VarUI4FromI2()
- VarUI4FromI4()
- VarUI4FromR4()
- VarUI4FromR8()
- VarUI4FromStr()
- VarUI4FromUI1()
- VarUI4FromUI2()

INDEX

Note to the Reader: Throughout this index **boldfaced** page numbers indicate primary discussions of a topic. *Italicized* page numbers indicate illustrations.

A

abs(), **450**
accelerators, **425**
accessories, **36–38**
acos(), **450**
Active Sync, **343**
ActiveX Control Pack
    Common Dialog, **234–235**, *235*
    grid, **231–232**, *232*
    ImageList, **234**
    ListView, **234**
    overview, **231**
    solving read-only problem, **232–233**
    tab strip, **233–234**, *234*
    TreeView, **234**
adding
    Add button, **212–213**, *212*
    Add/Insert dialog, **214**, *214*
    AddAddressCard(), **474–475**
    AddRecord(), **180**, **185–186**
    EditAdd Record, **135–136**, *135*, *136*
Address Book API, **419–420**
allocating memory
    AreaCodeDatabaseRead(), **137**
    calloc(), **77**
    checking return results of, **57**
    EXE file size, **56–57**
    LMEM_ZEROINIT, **77**
    LocalAlloc(), **58–60**, **77**, **84**
    mass, **58–59**
    overview, **56**
    types of, **59–60**
Alt+Enter for property sheets, **422**
Alt+letter for underlined accelerators, **425**
Alt+tap for pop-up menus, **422**
Alt-click combination for right-click functionality, **8**
Alt-tap behavior, **78**
ANSI
    ANSI-based RTL functions, **47**, *47*

ANSI-specific string type mappings, **44**, *44*
    converting between Unicode- and ANSI-based
        text files, **49–51**, *49*, *51*
    vs. Unicode files, **97**
API
    Address Book, **419–420**
    vs. CCeDBDatabase methods, **180–182**
    functions for Windows CE 2.0. *See* API functions
        for Windows CE 2.0
    msgstore, **420**
    Polyline(), **78**
    reduction of, **7**
    Remote API. *See* RAPI (Remote API)
    replacing GetDesktopWindow(), **164–165**
    SetFilePointer, **108–109**
    structured storage
        AreaCodeDatabaseDelete(), **140**
        AreaCodeDatabaseFinish(), **140**
        AreaCodeDatabaseInsert(), **139–140**
        AreaCodeDatabaseRead(), **136–139**
    substituting for missing functions
        calloc(), **77**
        MoveToEx()/Line To(), **77–78**
        WM_RBUTTONDOWN, **78–79**
    Unicode text and, **43**
API functions for Windows CE 2.0
    AddAddressCard(), **474–475**
    BatteryNotifyOfTimeChange(), **476**
    CeCheckPassword(), **476–477**
    CeClearUserNotification(), **477**
    CeCloseHandle(), **289**, **477**
    CeCopyFile(), **477–478**
    CeCreateDatabase, **122**, **292**, **478–479**
    CeCreateDirectory(), **479**
    CeCreateFile(), **289**, **479–480**
    CeCreateProcess(), **292**, **480–481**
    CeDeleteDatabase(), **180**, **292**, **481–482**
    CeDeleteFile(), **289**, **482**
    CeDeleteRecord(), **140**, **292**, **482**
    CeFindAllDatabases(), **482–483**

CeFindAllFiles(), **484**

CeFindClose(), 288, **484–485**

CeFindNextDatabase(), 176, 292, **486**

CeFindNextFile(), 288, **486–487**

CeGetClassName(), 293, **487**

CeGetDesktopDeviceCaps(), 285, 286, *286*, **487–488**

CeGetDeviceId(), **488**

CeGetFileAttributes(), **489**

CeGetFileSize(), **489**

CeGetFileTime(), **490**

CeGetLastError(), **490–491**

CeGetSelectedDeviceId(), **491**

CeGetSpecialFolderPath(), 289, 291, **491**

CeGetStoreInformation(), **492**

CeGetSystemInfo(), 285, **492**

CeGetSystemMetrics(), **493**

CeGetSystemPowerStatusEx(), 285, **493–494**

CeGetTempPath(), 289, **494**

CeGetUserNotificationPreferences(), **494–495**

CeGetVersionEx(), 285, **495–496**

CeGetVersionInfo(), **285**

CeGetWindow(), 292, **496**

CeGetWindowText(), 292, **497**

CeGlobalMemoryStatus(), 285, 286, **497**

CeHandleAppNotifications(), **498**

CeMoveFile(), **498, 498**

CeOIDGetEx(), 285

CeOidGetInfo(), 180, **498–499**

CeOpenDatabase(), 128, 137, 180, 181, 292, **499**

CeRapiFreeBuffer(), **500**

CeRapiGetError(), **500**

CeRapiInit(), 283–284, 293, **500–501**

CeRapiInitEx(), **501**

CeRapiInvoke(), **501–502**

CeRapiUninit(), 283–284, **502**

CeReadFile(), 289, **502–503**

CeReadRecordProps(), 136, 138, 292, **503–504**

CeRegCloseKey(), 287, **504**

CeRegCreateKeyEx(), 287, **504–505**

CeRegDeleteKey(), 287, **505**

CeRegDeleteValue(), 287, **506**

CeRegEnumKeyEx(), 287, **506–507**

CeRegEnumValue(), 287, **507–508**

CeRegOpenKeyEx(), 287, **508–509**

CeRegQueryInfoKey(), 287, **509–510**

CeRegQueryValueEx(), 287, **510–511**

CeRegSetValueEx(), 287, **511–512**

CeRemoveDirectory(), **512**

CeRunAppAtEvent(), **512–513**

CeRunAppAtTime(), **513**

CeSeekDatabase(), 131, 132, 133, 134, 135, 180, 181, 292, **513–514**

CeSetDatabaseInfo(), 182, 292, **514–515**

CeSetEndOfFile(), **515**

CeSetFileAttributes(), **515–516**

CeSetFilePointer(), **516**

CeSetFileTime(), **516–517**

CeSetUserNotification(), **517–518**

CeSHCreateShortcut(), 292, **518–519**

CeSHGetShortcutTarget(), 292, **519**

CeWriteFile(), 289, **519–520**

CeWriteRecordProps(), 139–140, 292, **520–521**

CloseAddressBook(), **521**

CommandBands_AddAdornments(), **521–522**

CommandBands_AddBands(), **522–523**

CommandBands_Create(), **523–524**

CommandBands_GetCommandBar(), **524**

CommandBands_GetRestoreInformation(), **525**

CommandBands_Height(), **525**

CommandBands_IsInvisible(), **526**

CommandBands_Show(), **526**

CommandBar_AddAdornments(), **526–527**

CommandBar_AddButtons(), 527–528

CommandBar_AddToolTips(), **528**

CommandBar_Create(), **528–529**

CommandBar_DrawMenuBar(), **529**

CommandBar_GetMenu(), **529**

CommandBar_Height(), **529–530**

CommandBar_InsertButton(), **530**

CommandBar_InsertComboBox(), **530–531**

CommandBar_InsertMenubar(), **531**

CommandBar_InsertMenubarEx(), **531–532**

CommandBar_IsVisible(), **532**

CommandBar_Show(), **532**

CreateAddressBook(), **533**

CreateFileForMapping(), **533–534**

DeleteAddressCard(), **534**

DeleteAndRenameFile(), **534–535**

DeregisterDevice(), **535**

EnableEUDC(), **535–536**

EnableHardwareKeyboard(), **536**

FindFirstEntry(), **536–539**

FreeAddressCard(), **539–540**

FtpCommand(), 540–541
GetAddressCardIndex(), 541
GetAddressCardOid(), 542
GetAddressCardProperties(), 542
GetClipboardDataAlloc(), 543
GetColumnProperties(), 543
GetMatchingEntry(), 544
GetMessageSource(), 544–545
GetMouseMovePoints(), 545
GetNumberOfAddressCards(), 546
GetPropertyDataStruct(), 546
GetSortOrder(), 547
GetStoreInformation(), 547
GetSystemPowerStatusEx(), 548
ImageList_Duplicate(), 548–549
InitCommonControlsEx(), 549–550
InitHTMLControl(), 550
InitInkX(), 550
InterlockedTestExchange(), 551
MailClose(), 551
MailDelete, 551–552
MailDeleteAttachment(), 552–553
MailErrorMsg(), 553–554
MailFirst(), 554–555
MailFree(), 555
MailGet(), 555–556
MailGetAttachment(), 556
MailGetField(), 557
MailGetFolderId(), 557–558
MailGetFolderName(), 558
MailGetSort(), 558–559
MailGetSvcId(), 559
MailHeaderLen(), 560
MailLocalAttachmentLen(), 560
MailNext(), 560
MailOpen(), 561
MailOpenNotify(), 561
MailPut(), 562
MailPutAttachment(), 562–563
MailPutFolder(), 563
MailRequestAttachment(), 563–564
MailSetField(), 564–565
MailSetSort(), 565
MailUpdate(), 566
ModifyAddressCard(), 566–568
OpenAddressBook(), 568
OpenAddressCard(), 568–569

Random(), 569
RapiFreeBuffer(), 569–570
RasGetEntryDevConfig(), 570
RasSetEntryDevConfig(), 570
RecountCards(), 570
RegisterDevice(), 570–571
SetColumnProperties(), 571
SetDaylightTime(), 572
SetMask(), 572–573
SetSortOrder(), 573
SHCreateShortcut(), 573–574
SHGetShortcutTarget(), 574
SHLoadDIBitmap(), 574
SHShowOutOfMemory(), 575
TransparentImage(), 575–576
VarYYYYFromZZZZ() functions, 576–584
Application Manager
    creating INI files, 398–399, *398*
    creating setup programs, 399–402
    Logo program installation, **411**, *412*
application templates, **226–227**, *227*
area code lookup utility
    AreaCodeDataBaseCreate(), **125–126**
    AreaCodeDatabaseDelete(), **140**
    AreaCodeDatabaseFinish(), **140**
    AreaCodeDatabaseInsert(), **139–140**
    AreaCodeDatabaseRead(), **136–139**
    Edit/Add Record dialog, **135–135**, *135, 136*
    overview, **135–135**, *135, 136*
array declarations, **256–260**, *257*
ASA (Adaptive Server Anywhere)
    administration and management, **343**
    command line options, **344**
    comparison of features, **356–358**
    configuring application, **344**
    copying data to desktop, **357**
    Customer List report, **345–346**, *345*
    data compression, **357**
    database schema, **342–343**
    demo, **344–347**, *345*
    Login dialog, **344–345**, *345*
    overview, **341**
    proc_name, **343**
    Report dialog, **345**, *345*
    report_id, **343**
    report_name, **343**
    Sales Report, **346**

sample application, **342–347**, *345*
security_level, **343**
SQL support, **357**
storage requirements, **357**
stored procedures, **357**
synching data with desktop, **357**
user privileges, **358**
asademo.db, **344**
atan(), **450**
atan2(), **451**
ATM conversion,
  array declarations, **256–260**, *257*
  Bitmaps, **250**
  change Global to Public, **249**
  country and bit maps, **266–269**
  Declare statements, **246–247**
  eliminating code, **274–275**
  eliminating forms, **270–274**, *271*
  eliminating optional controls and DLLs, **274**
  Explicit Type declarations, **249**
  Explicit Types, **249**
  icons, **250**
  Image Control, **250**
  mechanical issues, **249–261**, *257*
  modal forms, 248, **253–255**
  modifying resource loads, **255–260**, *257*
  mouse/cursor code, **252–253**
  optimizing, **270–275**
  optional features, **262–269**, *264, 265*
  overview, **244–249**, *245, 246, 276, 276*
  planning porting process, **247–249**
  porting from VB to VBCE, **247**
  preparing frmAmountWithdrawn Form, **261**
  sound, **263–265**, *264, 265*
  Typecasts, **250**
  using Developer Studio, **256–257**, *257*
  WAV files, **250–253**, *262–266, 264, 265*
atoi(), **451**
atol(), **451**
AutoPC SDK, **69**

B

bar code scanners, 38, **363**, *365*
BatteryNotifyOfTimeChange(), **476**
Bin paths, **147–148**

bitmaps, 250, **266–269**
BLOB (Binary Large Object) data, **118**, 297
buttons
  Add button, **212–213**, *212*
  Close "X" button, 25, 204, **418**
  displaying open documents, **432**
  Help "?" button, **416**
  HPC applications, **419**
  InsertButtons(), **204–206**
  Logo program
    taskbar buttons, **432**
    UI requirements, **416**, 417, 419, 424, 425
  WM_BUTTONDOWN, **78–79**
  WM_BUTTONUP, **423**

C

C runtime library functions
  abs(), **450**
  acos(), **450**
  asin(), **450**
  atan(), **450**
  atan2(), **451**
  atoi(), **451**
  atol(), **451**
  _cabs(), **438**
  _chsign(), **438**
  _clearfp(), **439**
  _controlfp(), **439**
  _copysign(), **439**
  cos(), **451**
  cosh(), **452**
  difftime(), **452**
  div(), **452**
  _evct(), **439**
  exp(), **452**
  fabs(), **453**
  _fcvt(), **439**
  _finite(), **440**
  floor(), **453**
  fmod(), **453**
  _fpclass(), **440**
  fpieee_flt(), **440**
  _fpreset(), **440**
  free(), **453**
  frexp(), **453**

_gcvt(), **441**

_hypot(), **441**

_isnan(), **441**

iswalnum(), **454**

iswalpha(), **454**

iswascii(), **454**

iswcntrl(), **454**

iswctype(), **455**

iswgraph(), **455**

iswlower(), **455**

iswprint(), **455**

iswpunct(), **456**

iswspace(), **456**

iswupper(), **456**

iswxdigit(), **456**

_itoa(), **441**

_itow(), **441**

_j0(), **442**

_j1(), **442**

_jn(), **442**

labs(), **457**

ldexp(), **457**

ldiv(), **457**

log(), **457**

log10(), **458**

_logb(), **442**

longjmp(), **458**

_lrotl(), **442**

_lrotr(), **443**

_ltoa(), **443**

_ltow(), **443**

malloc(), **458**

_matherr(), **443**

mbstowcs(), **458**

_memccpy(), **444**

memchr(), **459**

memcmp(), **459**

memcpy(), **459**

_memicmp(), **444**

memmove(), **459**

memset(), **460**

modf(), **460**

_msize(), **444**

_nextafter(), **444–445**

pow(), **460**

qsort(), **460**

rand(), **460–461**

realloc(), **461**

_rotl(), **445**

_rotr(), **445**

_scalb(), **445**

sin(), **461**

sinh(), **461**

sqrt(), **461**

srand(), **462**

_statusfp(), **445**

strcat(), **462**

strchr(), **462**

strcmp(), **462**

strcpy(), **462**

strcspn(), **463**

strlen(), **463**

strncat(), **463**

strncmp(), **463**

strncpy, **463–464**

strstr(), **464**

strtok(), **464**

_swab(), **446**

swprintf(), **464**

swscan(), **465**

tan(), **465**

tanh(), **465**

towlower(), **465**

towupper(), **466**

_ultoa(), **446**

_ultow(), **446**

vswprintf(), **466**

wcscat(), **466**

wcschr(), **467**

wcscmp(), **467**

wcscpy(), **467**

wcscspn(), **467**

_wcsdup(), **446**

_wcsicmp(), **447**

wcslen(), **468**

_wcslwr(), **447**

wcsncat(), **468**

wcsncmp(), **468**

wcsncpy(), **468–469**

_wcsnicmp(), **447**

_wcsnset(), **447–448**

wcspbrk(), **469**

wcsrchr(), **469**

_wcsrev(), **448**

_wcsset(), **448**
wcsspn(), **469–470**
wcsstr(), **470**
wcstod(), **470**
wcstok(), **470**
wcstol(), **471**
wcstombs(), **471**
wcstoul(), **471**
_wcsupr(), **448**
wsprintf(), **471**
_wtoi(), **449**
_wtol(), **449**
_y0(), **449**
_y1(), **449**
_yn(), **450**
CAB files Logo program installation, **411**, 412, 413
Cab Wizard
    creating Cab files
        Cab archive, **397–398**
        INF files, **392–397**
        INI files, **398–399**, *398*
    creating setup programs, **399–402**
    overview, **391–392**
    predefined destination directories, **393–394**
_cabs(), **438**
Canon PowerShot A5, 368
CapEdit control
    Handheld PC/Pro devices (HPC/Pros), **34**
    Handheld PCs (HPCs), **27**
    Palm-size PCs (PPCs), **23–24**
Carcalc, **221–222**, *221*
case studies
    choosing development machine
        conclusion, **372**
        cost analysis, **372**
        HPC devices, **371**
        HPC/Pro devices, **371**
        overview, **370**
        PPC devices, **370–371**
        solution, **370**
    insurance field agents
        conclusion, **370**
        cost analysis, **368–369**, *369*
        digital cameras, **367**
        HPC/Pro, **368**
        HPC/Pro-based cost analysis, **369**, *369*
        lap-top based cost analysis, **368–369**, *369*

        overview, **366–367**
        solution, **367**
        technical issues, **367–368**
    Inventory Management System
        conclusion, **366**
        cost, **365–366**
        overview, **362**
        technical issues, **362–364**
Casio
    PA-2400 "tablet" device, **35**, *35*
    PA-2500 Handheld PC (HPC), **25**, *26*
    Vertical Markets division, **58**
C/C++ language for CE
    calloc(), **77**
    changing program logic, **79–80**
    CreateFile(), **80–81**
    CreateProcess(), **81**
    exception handling methods, **79–80**
    fclose(), **88–89**
    fgetc(), **89–90**
    fgets(), **92–94**
    FILE*, **81–83**
    fopen(), **83–88**
    fprint(), **97–99**
    fputc(), **90–91**
    fputs(), **94–95**
    fread(), **95–96**
    fscanf(), **99–107**
    fseek(), **108–109**
    fwrite(), **96–97**
    MoveToEx()/Line To(), **77–78**
    overview, **76–77**
    Readfile(), **80**
    swscanf(), **99–107**
    try..catch, **79–80**
    Unicode and file access, 95
    Win32 API file-access functions, **80–81**
    WM_RBUTTONDOWN, **78–79**
    wrapper functions, **81**
    Writefile(), **80**
    wstrlen(), **95**
CCeDBDatabase, 174, **179–182**, *180–182*
CCeDBEnum, 174, **176**
CCeDBProp, 174, **176–178**, *177*, 186
CCeDBRecord, 174, **179**, *179*
CCeSocket, 174, **175–176**, *175*
CDC, **192**

CE communications
    hardware aspects
        IR ports, **307**
        modems, **307**
        overview, **306**
        PCMICIA cards, **307**
        serial ports, **307**
    overview, **306**
    PC cards/PCMCIA cards
        application start, **318–320**, *320*
        card changes, **321–326**, *323*
        overview, **318**
    PC cards/PCMCIA modems, **318**
    software aspects
        built-in modems, **314–317**, *318*
        Infrared Sockets (IrSock), **314**, 332
        IR communications, **308–314**, *313*
        IrCOMM, **312–314**, *313*
        modem-based communications, **314–318**, *318*
        overview, **308**
        Raw IR, **309–312**
        serial communications, **308–309**
        standard external modems, **314**
    Winsock-based
        Infrared Sockets (IrSock), 314, **332**
        overview, **327**
        Winsock 1.1, **327–332**, *328*
CE devices. *See also* Windows CE
    accessories, **36-38**
    bar code readers, **38**
    Handheld PCs (HPCs). *See* Handheld PCs
        (HPCs)
    other, **34–35**, *35*
    overview of types, **12**
    Palm-size PCs (PPCs). *See* Palm-size PCs (PPCs)
    tablet devices, **35**, *35*
CeCheckPassword(), **476–477**
CeClearUserNotification(), **477**
CeCloseHandle(), 289, **477**
CeCopyFile(), **477–478**
CeCreateDatabase(), 122, 292, **478–479**
CeCreateDirectory(), **479**
CeCreateFile(), 289, **479–480**
CeCreateProcess(), 292, **480–481**
CEDB_AUTOINCREMENT flag, **296**
CEDB_sort types, **124**
CeDeleteDatabase(), 180, 292, **481–482**

CeDeleteFile(), **482**
CeDeleteRecord(), 140, 292, **482**
CeFindAllDatabases(), **482–483**
CeFindAllFiles(), **484**
CeFindClose(), 288, **484–485**
CE_FIND_DATA, **289**
CeFindFirstDatabase(), **292**, 293
CeFindFirstFile(), **288**
CeFindNextDatabase(), 176, 292, **486**
CeFindNextFile(), 288, **486–487**
CeGetClassName(), 293, **487**
CeGetDesktopDeviceCaps(), 285, 286, *286*, **487–488**
CeGetDeviceId(), **488**
CeGetFileAttributes(), **489**
CeGetFileSize(), **489**
CeGetFileTime(), **490**
CeGetLastError(), **490–491**
CeGetSelectedDeviceId(), **491**
CeGetSpecialFolderPath(), 289, 291, **491**
CeGetStoreInformation(), **492**
CeGetSystemInfo(), 285, **492**
CeGetSystemMetrics(), **493**
CeGetSystemPowerStatusEx(), 285, **493–494**
CeGetTempPath(), 289, **494**
CeGetUserNotificationPreferences(), **494–495**
CeGetVersionEx(), 288, **495–496**
CeGetVersionInfo(), **285**
CeGetWindow(), 292, **496**
CeGetWindowText(), 292, **497**
CeGlobalMemoryStatus(), 285, 286, **497**
CeHandleAppNotifications(), **498**
CeMoveFile(), **498**
CEOID (Ce Object Identifier), **125**, 127, 132
CeOIDGetEx(), **285**
CeOidGetInfo(), 180, **498–499**
CeOpenDatabase(), 128, 137, 180, 181, 292, **499**
CEPROVAL structures, **137–139**, 176–177
CeRapiFreeBuffer(), **500**
CeRapiGetError(), **500**
CeRapiInit(), 283–284, 293, **500–501**
CeRapiInitEx(), **501**
CeRapiInvoke(), **501–502**
CeRapiUninit(), **283–284**, 502
CeReadFile(), 289, **502–503**
CeReadRecordProps(), 136, 138, 292, **503–504**
CeRegCloseKey(), 287, **504**
CeRegCreateKeyEx(), 287, **504–505**

CeRegDeleteKey(), 287, **505**
CeRegDeleteValue(), 287, **506**
CeRegEnumKeyEx(), 287, **506–507**
CeRegEnumValue(), 287, **507–508**
CeRegOpenKeyEx(), 287, **508–509**
CeRegQueryInfoKey(), 287, **509–510**
CeRegQueryValueEx(), 287, **510–511**
CeRegSetValueEx(), 287, **511–512**
CeRemoveDirectory(), **512**
CeRunAppAtEvent(), **512–513**
CeRunAppAtTime(), **513**
CeSeekDatabase(), 131, 132, 133, 134, 135, 180, 181, 292, **513–514**
CeSetDatabaseInfo(), 182, 292, **514–515**
CeSetEndOfFile(), **515**
CeSetFileAttributes(), **515–516**
CeSetFilePointer(), **516**
CeSetFileTime(), **516–517**
CeSetUserNotification(), **517–518**
CeSHCreateShortcut(), 292, **518–519**
CeSHGetShortcutTarget(), 292, **519**
CEVT_BLOB type, **297**
CEVT_field types, **123–124**
CeWriteFile(), 289, **519–520**
CeWriteRecordProps(), 139–140, 292, **520–521**
CFrameWnd, **192**, **193**
char types, **43–46**
checking return result of memory allocation, **57**
chips
    CE device type, **9**
    compilers and, **147–148**
_chsign(), **438**
_clearfp(), **439**
CListView control. *See* ListView controls
closing
    applications, **166–168**
    AreaCodeDatabaseFinish(), **140**
    close (X) button, 25, 204, **418**
    CloseAddressBook(), **521**
    CloseDB(), **185**
    CloseHandle, **88–89**
    debuggers, **229**
    fclose(), **88–89**
    Logo program applications, **418**
    Task Manager, **167**
CMainFrame
    InsertButtons(), **204–206**
    OnCreate() event, **203**

CObArray, **179**
codebase defined, **68**
color
    Handheld PC/Pro devices (HPC/Pros), **29**
    Handheld PCs (HPCs), **26**
    support for, **430**
    Task Manager, **169**
ComboBox, **270–271**, *271*
command bars, **415**, 416, 419
command line options, **344**
CommandBands_AddAdornments(), **521–522**
CommandBands_AddBands(), **522–523**
CommandBands_Create(), **523–524**
CommandBands_GetCommandBar(), **524**
CommandBands_GetRestoreInformation(), **525**
CommandBands_Height(), **525**
CommandBands_IsInvisible(), **526**
CommandBands_Show(), **526**
CommandBar_AddAdornments(), **526–527**
CommandBar_AddButtons(), 527–528
CommandBar_AddToolTips(), **528**
CommandBar_Create, **528–529**
CommandBar_DrawMenuBar(), **529**
CommandBar_GetMenu(), **529**
CommandBar_Height(), **529–530**
CommandBar_InsertButton(), **530**
CommandBar_InsertComboBox(), **530–531**
CommandBar_InsertMenuBar(), **531**
CommandBar_InsertMenubarEx(), **531–532**
CommandBar_IsVisible(), **532**
CommandBar_Show(), **532**
commandments for writing for Windows CE. *See* writing for Windows CE
Common Dialog, **234–235**, *235*
communications from CE to outside world. *See* CE communications
Compact Flash (CF) cards
    detecting, **319**
    Ethernet, **37**
    supporting installation to, **414–415**
compiling
    chips, **147–148**
    compiler defines, **68–69**, *69*
    conditional defines, **69–70**
    generic string types, **44–45**
    MFC applications for Windows CE, **200**
    runtime platform detectors, 69, **70–72**
    text literals, **46**
    toolkit for VC++, **146–147**

compressing data, **357**
conditional defines, **69–70**
configuring applications, **344**
connecting to CE devices, **150**
controls
    ActiveX Control Pack, **231–235**, *232*, *235*
    Control Manager
        grid control, **208**
        VBCE, **230–231**
    _controlfp(), **439**
    Image Controls, **250**, 268–269
    standard VBCE controls, **235**, *235–236*
    unsupported standard VB controls, **238**
converting
    MFC applications to CE
        Carcalc, **221–222**, *221*
        mechanical issues. *See* MFC applications
            ported to CE
    VB applications to CE
        array declarations, **256–260**, *257*
        ATM conversion overview, **244–249**, *245*, *246*,
            276, *276*
        Bitmaps, **250**
        change Global to Public, **249**
        country and bit maps, **266–269**
        Declare statements, **246–247**
        eliminating code, **274–275**
        eliminating forms, **270–274**, *271*
        eliminating optional controls and DLLs, **274**
        Explicit Type declarations, **249**
        Explicit Types, **249**
        icons, **250**
        Image Control, **250**
        mechanical issues, **249–261**, *257*
        modal forms, 248, **253–255**
        modifying resource loads, **255–260**, *257*
        mouse/cursor code, **252–253**
        optimizing, **270–275**
        optional features, **262–269**, *264*, *265*
        planning porting process, **247–249**
        porting from VB to VBCE, **247**
        preparing frmAmountWithdrawn Form, **261**
        sound, **263–265**, *264*, *265*
        Typecasts, **250**
        using Developer Studio, **256–257**, *257*
        WAV files, **250–253**, 262–266, *264*, *265*
    Unicode- to ANSI-based text files, **49–51**, *49*, *51*

copying
    comparison between third-party database
        engines, **357**
    _copysign(), **439**
    file copy in database administration, **343**
cos(), **451**
cosh(), **452**
cost analysis
    application testing, **408**
    development machine choices, **372**
    HPC/Pros, 369, *369*, 372
    HPCs, 365, 372
    laptops, **368**, *369*
    mobile devices, **348**
    Oracle Lite, **347**
    PPCs, 364, 365, 372
country bitmaps, **266–269**
CPrintDialog, **194**
CPUs
    determining type over Internet, **413**
    Logo program requirements, **427**
creating
    Cab archive, **397–398**
    Cab Wizard setup programs, **399–402**
    CE database, **122–127**
    conditional defines, **69–70**
    CreateAddressBook(), **533**
    CreateDB(), **183–184**
    CreateDC(), **30–31**
    CreateFile(), **80–81**
    CreateFileForMapping(), **533–534**
    CreateHeap(), **60**
    CreateProcess(), **81**
    custom<Meta>Tag, **390**
    INF files, **392–397**
    INI files, **398–399**, *398*
    multiple-file help system files, **385–391**, *389*
    Project Wizards for dialog-based applications,
        154–157, *155*, *157*
    runtime platform detectors, **70–72**
    setup programs, **399–402**
    single-file help system files, **380–385**
CShoppingListDoc, **182–183**
CShoppingListView
    methods of, **187**
    OnDelete(), **189–190**
    UpdateListBox(), **187–189**

Ctrl+letter, **425**
currency conversions, **246**
cursors, 420, 422–423
custom <meta> tags, **389–391**
Custom App Wizard dialog, *157*
Customer List report, **345–346**, *345*
Cwnd, **192**, **193**

D

databases
  access functions, **292**
  engines. *See* Windows CE Database Engine
  schema, **342–343**
dbcd_devicetype, **322–323**
DBView, **63–66**, *63, 64, 66, 67*
debugging
  closing debugger, **229**
  Ethernet, 36, **151**
  generic SDK tools, **158**
  HTML-based help, **378**
  TCP/IP Transport, **150–151**
  VB IDE, **228**
  VBCE, **228–229**, *229*
  Windows CE services, **150**
declaring
  Unicode strings, **43–45**, *44, 45*
  VB alternatives to, **246–247**, *251*
defaults
  database administrator userid, **344**
  drag multi-select, **427**
  ListView controls, **427**
  specifying default destination folders, **402**, *402*
  system fonts, **423**
#define, **69–70**
deleting
  AreaCodeDatabaseDelete(), **125–126**, 140
  CCeDBDatabase methods for, **180**
  CeDeleteDatabase(), 180, **481–482**
  CeDeleteFile(), **482**
  CeDeleteRecord(), 140, **482**
  data in ListView control, **212–217**, *214, 217*
  DDLS, **274**
  DeleteAddressCard(), **534**
  DeleteAndRenameFile(), **534–535**
  forms from VB applications converting to CE,
    270–274, *271*

indexes, **130**
OnDelete(), **189–190**
optional controls, **274**
using EditAdd Record, **136**, *136*
Delphi
  Cab Wizard setup programs, **399–402**
  properties viewer, **299–302**, *299*
demo, **344–347**, *345*
DeregisterDevice(), **535**
Developer Studio, *257*
development machine choices
  conclusion, **372**
  cost analysis, **372**
  HPC devices, **371**
  HPC/Pro devices, **371**
  overview, **370**
  PPC devices, **370–371**
Device Property dialog, **150**
dhrystone ratings, **10–11**
dialog-based applications, **154–157**, *155, 157*
difftime(), **452**
digital cameras, **367**, *369*
disk file replication, **354**
displays
  display size CE devices, **9**
  display type CE devices, **9**
  Handheld PC/Pro devices (HCP/Pros), **29**
  Handheld PCs (HPCs), **26**
  Palm-size PCs (PPCs), **12–15**, *14, 15*
  user data in ListView control, **210–212**
distributing CE applications
  help files
    creating, **378**
    multiple-file system, **388–391**
    single-file system, **380–385**, *381*
    types of, **379–380**
  installing programs on user's CE device
    Cab Wizard option, **392–402**, *398*
    InstallShield, **402–405**, *402, 403, 404, 405*
    overview, **391–392**
  overview, **378**
div(), **452**
DLLs
  converting WAV files, **250**
  deleting, **274**
  driver names, **30**
  RAPI as, **283**
  storage space, **161**
  VGA-out port, **29–30**

dwSeekType, **131**
dynamic vs. static linking, **299**

E

editing
    capitalization in edit boxes, **430**
    Edit/Add Record dialog, **135–135**, *135*, *136*
    grid data, **232–233**
embedded applications with VB, **227–228**
emulation
    emulators for platform SDKs, **158–160**
    WAV files, **265**
    _WIN32_WCE_EMULATION, **68–69**
EnableEUDC(), **535–536**
EnableHardwareKeyboard(), **536**
Enterprise Manager applications, **122**
entry tags, **387–388**
EnumPnpIds(), **318**
Ethernet
    debugging, 36, **151**
    networking solutions
        Compact Flash (CF) Ethernet cards, **37**
        overview, **36**
        PCMCIA-based "Low Power" Ethernet
            cards, **37**
        Proxim Range LAN2, **37**, 151, 366
        Socket Communications, **37**
        wired connections, **37**
_evct(), **439**
exception handling methods, **79–80**
EXE file size, **56–57**, 161
Exists(), **184**
Exiting
    Logo program requirements, **429**
    Palm-size PCs (PPCs), **24–25**
exp(), **452**
Explicit Type declarations change, **249**
Explicit Types change, **250**

F

fabs(), **453**
fclose(), **88–89**
_fcvt(), **439**

FEFF signature, **48**
fgetc(), **89–90**
fgets(), **92–94**
fields
    not table-specific, **120–121**
    sorting based on one, **129**
files
    FILE*-based functions, **81–83**
    file access functions, **288–290**
    file handles defined, **81–82**
    file pointers defined, **81**
    file-based replication, Oracle Lite for CE, **354**
    Files dialog, **403–404**, *403*, *404*
    Logo program file-handling requirements,
        431–433
    RAPI file access functions, **288–290**
finding
    FindFirstEntry(), **536–539**
    previous instance, **418**
    substitute functions using C/C++ language,
        77–79
_finite(), **440**
flag bitmaps, **266–269**
floats, **185**
floor(), **453**
fmod(), **453**
form factors
    compiler defines, **68–69**, *69*
    creating conditional defines, **69–70**
    creating runtime platform detectors, **70–72**
    DBView, **63–66**, *63*, *64*, *66*, *67*
    overview, **61–62**
    single codebases, **67–69**
    tailoring application UI to device, **62–67**, *63*, *64*,
        66, *67*
format string pointer, **100**. *See also* LPWSTR
_fpclass(), **440**
fpieee_flt(), **440**
_fpreset(), **440**
fprint(), **97–99**
fputc(), **90–91**
fputs(), **94–95**
free(), **453**
FreeAddressCard(), **539–540**
frmAmountWithdrawn, **261**
frmInput, **270–273**
frmOpen, **270–274**

fscanf(), **99–107**
fseek(), **108–109**
FtpCommand(), **540–541**
fwrite(), **96–97**

G

_gcvt(), **441**
generic
    dialog base for Project Wizard, **154–157**, *155*, *157*
    platform SDKs, **158**
    string types, **44–45**, *45*
GetAddressCardIndex(), **541**
GetAddressCardOid(), **542**
GetAddressCardProperties(), **542**
GetClipboardDataAlloc(), **543**
GetColumnProperties(), **543**
GetDesktopWindow(), **164–165**
GetMatchingEntry, **544**
GetMessageSource(), **544–545**
GetMouseMovePoints(), **545**
GetNumberOfAddressCards(), **546**
GetPropertyDataStruct(), **546**
GetSortOrder(), **547**
GetStoreInformation(), **547**
GetSystemMetrics, **70**, 72
GetSystemPowerStatusEx(), **548**
GetSystemTime(), **159–160**
GetType(), **178**
GetWindowText(), **53**
Global to Public change, **249**
Grids
    MFC applications ported to CE, **207–217**, *214*, *217*
    runtime and, *232*
    solving read-only problem, **232–233**
    third-party MFC library, **199**
    VCBE, **231–233**, *232*

H

Handheld PC/Pro devices (HPC/Pros). *See also*
    Hewlett-Packard Jornada HPC/Pro
    devices
    application templates, **226–227**

CapEdit control, **34**
choosing development machine, **371**
choosing machine for development, **371**
cost analysis, 369, *369*, 372
displays, **29**
HTML Viewer controls, **34**
Ink control, **34**
insurance field agents case study, **368**, 369, *369*
Handheld PCs (HPCs)
    Alt-tap behavior, **78**
    application templates, **226–227**
    CapEdit control, **27**
    choosing machine for development, **371**
    cost analysis, **365**, *365*, 372
    DBView, **63–67**, *63*, *64*
    displays, **26**, 29
    form factor choices, **364**
    Handheld PC/Pro devices (HPC/Pros)
        overview, **27–28**, *28*
        version numbering of operating system, **34**
        VGA-out ports, **29–33**
    HTML Viewer control, 25, **27**
    Ink control, **27**
    Internet document retrieval, **27**
    keyboards, **26**
    Logo program
        functionality requirements, **427–431**
        installation requirements, **411–415**
        UI requirements, **415–427**
    overview, 25, *26*
    predefined destination directories, **394**
    tailoring application UI to, **62–67**, *62*, *63*, *66*
    version numbering of operating system, **34**
HANDLE, **82**, 84, 86
handwritten data, **23**
hardware aspects of CE communications
    IR ports, **307**
    modems, **307**
    overview, **306**
    PCMICIA cards, **307**
    serial ports, **307**
HBRUSH, **31–33**
headers, **386**
HeapAlloc(), **59–60**
"Hello World" application, *153*
Help "?" button, **416**
help files

creating, **378–379**
help viewer, **391**
HTML-based, 378, **426**
Logo program testing, **428**
multiple-file system
   FrontPage, **390**
   header, **386**
   launching help viewer, **391**
   overview, **385–386**, *386*
   table of contents, **387–388**
pop-up, **425–426**
single-file system
   <!—PegHelp—> comment, **383**
   additional HTP file tricks, **384–385**
   FrontPage, **382**
   headers, **382**
   HTP files, **382**
   overview, **380–382**, *381*
Hewlett-Packard Jornada HPC/Pro devices
   Alt-click combination, **8**
   application templates, **227**
   mouse, **7**
   overview, **27–28**, *28*
hierarchy in registry, **115**, *115*
HKEY_CLASSES_ROOT, **115**
HKEY_CURRENT_USER, **115**
HKEY_LOCAL_MACHINE, **115**, 118, 314, 319
HKEY_USER, **115**
hourglass or wait cursor, **420**
HPC/Pros. See Handheld PC/Pro devices
    (HPC/Pros)
HpcLadr, **338–341**, *339*
HPCs. *See* Handheld PCs (HPCs)
HTC files
   header, **386**
   overview, **385–386**, *386*
   table of contents, **387**
   table of contents entry tags, **387–388**
HTML
   help, **426**
   InitHTMLControl(), **550**
   Viewer controls
      Handheld PC/Pro devices (HPC/Pros), **34**
      Handheld PCs (HPCs), 25, **27**
HTP files
   <—PegHelp—> comment, **383**
   additional tricks, **384–385**

custom<Meta>Tag, **390**
in multiple-file help system, **388–389**, *389*
overview, **380–382**, *381*
_hypot(), **441**

I

icons, **250**, 425
IDC_LISTTASKS, **163–168**
Image Controls, **250**, 268–269
ImageList
   ImageList_Duplicate(), **548–549**
   VBCE, **234**
improper uses of Windows CE registry, **116–119**
Include paths, **147–148**
indexing
   creating sort order at table creation, **130**
   deleting indexes, **130**
   four sort order maximum, **129–130**, *130*
   Modify Indexes dialog box, **66**, *66*, *67*
   only one active sort order per database, **129–130**
   overview, 114, **122–129**
   sorting based on one field, **129**
INF files, **392–397**
Infrared Sockets (IrSock), **314**, 332
INI files, **398–399**, *398*
InitCommonControlsEx(), **549–550**
InitHTMLControl(), **550**
InitInkX(), **550**
Ink control
   Handheld PC/Pro devices (HPC/Pros), **34**
   Handheld PCs (HPCs), **27**
   Palm-size PCs (PPCs), **18–22**, *19*
Input Panels
   Logo program requirements, 424, 430
   Owner applet, **19–22**, *19*
   Palm-size PCs (PPCs), 15, 16–18, **18–22**, *19*,
      20–22, 79
   raising and lowering, **16–18**, *16*
   scroll bars, 20–22
inserting
   AreaCodeDatabaseInsert(), **139–140**
   InsertButtons(), **204–206**
   mechanical issues porting MFC applications to
      CE, **204–206**

installing
    InstallDir, **393**, 396
    Logo program requirements, **411–415**
    programs to user's CE device
        Cab Wizard, **392–402**, *398*
        InstallShield, **402–405**, *402, 403, 404, 405*
insurance field agents case study
    conclusion, **370**
    cost analysis, **368–369**, *369*
    overview, **366–367**
    technical issues
        digital cameras, **367**
        HPC/Pro, **368**
        overview, **367**
InterlockedTestExchange(), **551**
Internet
    determining user's CPU type over, **413**
    document retrieval, **27**
    Logo program installation, 411, **413**
    Oracle Lite for CE, **353–354**
    replication, **353–354**
Inventory Management System
    case study
        bar code scanner, **363**
        conclusion, **366**
        cost analysis, **365–366**, *365, 366*
        form factor choices, **364**
        Handheld PC (HPC), **364**
        Palm-size PC (PPC), **364**
        synchronization vs. wireless connection,
            363–364
        technical issues, **362–364**
    overview, **362**
invoicing systems, **337–338**
IR communications
    Infrared Sockets (IrSock), **314**, 332
    IR ports, **307**, 420
    IR transfer of files, **433**
    IrCOMM, **312–314**, *313*
    IrDA standards, **420**
    IrDetect application, *313*
    overview, **309**
    Raw IR, **309–312**
IrDetect application, *313*
_isnan(), **441**
iswalnum(), **454**
iswalpha(), **454**

iswascii(), **454**
iswcntrl(), **454**
iswctype(), **455**
iswgraph(), **455**
iswlower(), **455**
iswprint(), **455**
iswpunct(), **456**
iswspace(), **456**
iswupper(), **456**
iswxdigit(), **456**
_itoa(), **441**
_itot(), **310**
_itow(), 310, **441**

J

_j0(), **442**
_j1(), **442**
_jn(), **442**

K

keyboards
    EnableHardwareKeyboard(), **536**
    Handheld PCs (HPCs), **26**
    hints for HPC applications, **419**
    Palm-size PCs (PPCs) lacking, **15**
    toolbar button equivalents, **425**
keys defined, **115**

L

labs(), **457**
ladder puzzles, **338**
language selection, **245**, 274–275
laptops
    case study of use of, **368–369**, *369*
    vs. HPC/Pros devices, **366**
    HPC/Pros keyboard size comparison, **34**
    Sony Vaio, 368
ldexp(), **457**
ldiv(), **457**
LIB paths, **147**
license agreement, **341**

linking, **299**
ListView controls
    database administration, **346**
    deleting data, **212–217**, *214*, *217*
    displaying user data, **210–212**
    drag multi-select, **427**
    grid replacements, **208–209**
    managing user data while program runs, **209**
    as replacement control, **208–209**
    Report View style, **129**, *130*
    user entry, **212–217**, *214*, *217*
    VBCE, **234**
LMEM_ZEROINIT, **77**
LoadResString, **260**
LocalAlloc(), **58–60**, *77*, *84*
log(), **457**
log10(), **458**
_logb(), **442**
Login dialog, **344–345**, *345*
Logo program
    file handling requirements
        common dialog boxes, **431**
        e-mailing files, **433**
        file system display, **432**
        IR file transfers, **433**
        MRU lists, **433**
        multi-instance applications, **432**
        open document name display, **432**
        shortcut to recently used documents,
            432–433
        taskbar buttons, **432**
    functionality requirements
        applications storing and loading their state,
            430
        capitalization in edit boxes, **430**
        CE-supported CPUS, **427**
        color support, **430**
        dialogs and Input Panel, **430**
        exiting without user intervention, **429**
        graphical components, **428**
        help files, **428**
        long names in file-related operations, **431**
        RAPI, **429**
        testing, **428**
        windows, **428**
        Winsock, **429**
        WM_HIBERNATE messages, **429**

installation requirements
    Application Manager, **411**
    Cab files, **411**, *412*
    compact flash cards, **414–415**
    copying files to subdirectory of CEAppMan-
        ager Path, **412**
    installing from desktop to device, **412**
    installing from Internet to device, **413**
    naming program files, **414**
    nonshared files, **411**
    removing user settings from CE registry, **412**
    shared program files, **412**
    shortcut on Start menus, **415**
    uninstalling, **412**, *414*
overview, **408–410**
UI requirements
    Address Book API, **419–420**
    Alt+Enter, **422**
    Alt+H for Help, **416**
    Alt+letter, **425**
    Alt+tap, **422**
    buttons, **416**, *417*, *419*, *424*, *425*
    centering dialogs, **423**
    closing, **418**, *426–427*
    command bars, **415**, *416*, *419*
    Ctrl+letter, **425**
    default system font, **423**
    desktop as parent window, **425**
    drag multi-select, **427**
    finding previous instance, **418**
    games, **415**
    Help "?" buttons, **416**
    hints for HPC Applications, **419**
    hints for PPC Applications, **419**
    hourglass or wait cursor, **420**
    HTML-based help, **426**
    icons for files types, **419**
    IR port, **420**
    IrDA standards, **420**
    keyboard equivalents for toolbar buttons,
        425
    keyboard shortcuts, **419**
    launching, **426–427**
    ListView controls, **427**
    menus, **416**, *417*, *422*, *423*
    mouse cursors, **422–423**
    msgstore API, **420**

order of standard functions, **417**
pop-up help, **425**
pop-up menus, **422**, 423
property sheets, **422**
rebars, **415**
resizing, **421–422**
shortcut keys, **425**
showing/hiding Input Panel, **424**
size of dialogs, **424**
Start menu shortcuts, **425**
taskbar settings, **421–422**
title bar, **426**
tool tips, **419**
tray icons, **425**
underlined accelerators, **425**
windows, **426**
WM_RBUTTONUP, **423**
longjmp(), **458**
lowering
  System Input Panels
    codes provided for, **16–18**, *16*
    Owner applet, **19**, *19*
low-memory environment
  checking return result of memory allocation, **56–57**
  different types of memory allocation, **59–60**
  EXE file size, **56–57**
  handling WM_HIBERNATE message, **60–61**
  mass-allocating application memory, **58–60**
  minimizing static variables, **56**
  overview, **55–56**
  reactivating application, **61**
LPCTSTR, **45**
LPTSTR, **45**
LPWSTR, **44**, 84, 92–93, 94, 97
_lrotl(), **442**
_lrotr(), **443**
_ltoa(), **443**
_ltow(), **443**

M

macros
  generic string types, **44–45**, *45*
  macro strings, **394**
  TEXT, **46**

MailClose(), **551**
MailDelete(), **551–552**
MailDeleteAttachment(), **552–553**
MailErrorMsg(), **553–554**
MailFirst(), **554–555**
MailFree(), **555**
MailGet(), **555–556**
MailGetAttachment(), **556**
MailGetField(), **557**
MailGetFolderId(), **557–558**
MailGetFolderName(), **558**
MailGetSort(), **558–559**
MailGetSvcId(), **559**
MailHeaderLen(), **560**
MailLocalAttachmentLen(), **560**
MailNext(), **560**
MailOpen(), **561**
MailOpenNotify(), **561**
MailPut(), **562**
MailPutAttachment(), **562–563**
MailPutFolder(), **563**
MailRequestAttachment(), **563–564**
MailSetField(), **564–565**
MailSetSort(), **565**
MailUpdate(), **566**
malloc(), **458**
mass-allocating application memory, **58–60**
_matherr(), **443**
MAX_PORTS, **310**
mbstowcs(), **458**
_memccpy(), **444**
memchr(), **459**
memcmp(), **459**
memcpy(), **459**
_memicmp(), **444**
memmove(), **459**
memory
  allocating. *See* allocating memory
  constraints in Windows CE, **5–7**
  low-memory environment. *See* low-memory environment
  WM_HIBERNATE messages, **429**
memset(), **460**
menus
  Logo program UI requirements, **416**, 417, 422, 423
  pop-up, **422**, 423

Save As ANSI menu, **51**, *51*
Start menu shortcuts, **425**
MFC applications
  missing classes, **194**
  modified classes, **191–193**
  modified classes that gained functionality
    CFrameWnd, **193**
    CWnd, **193**
    overview, **192–193**
  modified classes that lost functionality
    CDC, **192**
    CFrameWnd, **192**
    CWnd, **192**
    overview, **192**
  MoveToEx()/LineTo(), **78**
  new classes for CE
    CCeDBDatabase, 174, **179–182**, *180–182*
    CCeDBEnum, 174, **176**
    CCeDBProp, 174, **176–178**, *177*
    CCeDBRecord, 174, **179**, *179*
    CCeSocket, 174, **175–176**, *175*
    overview, **174**
  Palm-size PCs (PPCs), **117**
  porting to CE. *See* MFC applications ported to
    CE
  vs. SDK-style coding, **160–162**
  using CCeDB classes
    AddRecord(), **185–186**
    CloseDB(), **185**
    CreateDB(), **183–184**
    database as document, **182–186**
    database as View, **186–191**
    OnDelete(), **189–190**
    OnInsert(), **190–191**
    OpenDB(), **184–185**
    UpdateListbox(), **187–189**
MFC applications ported to CE
  Carcalc, **221–222**, *221*
  mechanical issues
    ActiveX Grid control, **208**
    grid control, **207–217**, *214, 217*
    InsertButtons(), **204–206**
    ListView control, **208–217**
    MFC 2.0 vs. MFC 2.1, **202**
    printing support, **206–207**
    status bars, **201–206**
    toolbars, **201–206**

OLE Automation, **220–222**, *221*
optimizing for CE, **217–220**
overview, **198**
Shopping List application, **198–200**, *198*
minimizing, **56–57**
mobile devices, **348**. *See also* Oracle Mobile Agents
modal forms, 248, **253–255**
modems
  built-in, **314–318**, *318*
  classes of, **314**
  hardware aspects, **307**
  Modem Selector dialog, **318**
  PCMCIA, **318**
  standard external, **314**
modf(), **460**
Modify Indexes dialog box, **66**, *66, 67*
ModifyAddressCard(), **566–568**
mouse
  converting VB codes for, **252–253**
  Hewlett-Packard Jornada HPC/Pro device, **7**
  Logo program support for mouse cursors,
    422–423
MoveToEx()/Line To(), **77–78**
MRU lists, **433**
msgstore, API, **420**
_msize(), **444**
multi-instance applications, **432**
multiple-file help system
  header, **386**
  HTP files in
    custom <meta> tags, **389–391**
    overview, **388–389**, *389*
  launching help viewer, **391**
  overview, **385–386**, *386*
  table of contents, **387–388**

N

networking solutions. *See* Ethernet
_nextafter(), **444–445**
nonshared program files, **411**
notepad, **48–55**, *49, 51*

O

ODBC support, **349**
Odyssey Software, **207**
OLE Automation, **220–222**, *221*
OnDelete(), **189–190**
opening
    CE database, **127–128**
    fopen(), **83–88**
    OpenAddressBook(), **568**
    OpenAddressCard(), **568–569**
    OpenDB(), **184–185**
    Unicode- and ANSI-based text files, **49–51**
optimizing
    MFC applications ported to CE, **217–220**
    VB code for CE, **274–275**
Oracle Lite for CE
    application development support, **349–350**
    copying data to desktop, **357**
    data compression, **357**
    disk file replication, **354**
    file-based replication, **254**
    Internet replication, **353–354**
    key features, **349**
    ODBC support, **349**
    overview, **347–349**
    replication, **352–354**
    sample applications, **350–352, 356**
    security, **254**
    SQL support, **357**
    storage requirements, **357**
    stored procedures, **357**
    synching data with desktop, **357**
    user privileges, **358**
    wireless replication, **353**, *355*
Oracle Mobile Agents
    anytime, anywhere, **354**
    developing applications and agents, **355**
    optimized for mobile environment, **354–355**
    overview, **354**
    reliability, **355**
    security, **355**
    wireless replication, **355**
Owner applet, **19–22**, *19*

P

Palm-size PCs (PPCs)
    CapEdit control, **23–24**
    choosing machine for development, **370–371**
    cost analysis, **364–365**, *365*, 372
    display, **12–15**, *14*, *15*
    exiting, **24–25**
    form factor choices, **364**
    Ink control, **22–23**
    keyboard vs. Input Panel, 15, 16–17, **18–22**, *19*,
        20–22, 79
    Logo program
        file-handling requirements, **431–433**
        functionality requirements, **427–431**
        installation requirements, **411–415**
        UI requirements, **415–427**
    MFC applications, **117**
    overview, **12**, *13*
    physical memory, **6**
    predefined destination directories, **394**
    right-clicking, **8**
    System Input Panels
        detecting when user pops up, **18–22**, *19*
        no Alt key, **79**
        overview, **15**
        raising and lowering, **16–18**, *16*
        scroll bars, **20–22**
    tailoring application UI to, **62–67**, *62*, *64*, *67*
    Task Manager, **162–163**, *162*
    Taskbar, **24–25**
    version numbering of operating system, **34**
    voice recording and playback, **24–25**
    WM_RBUTTONDOWN message, **79**
passwords, 117, 344
PC/PCMCIA cards
    hardware aspects, **307**
    "Low Power" Ethernet cards, **37**
    software aspects
        PCMCIA slot overview, **318**
        when application starts, **318–320**, *320*
        when card changes, **321–326**, *323*
PDAs, **347–348**
Pentax Technologies, **207**
PIM (Personal Information Manager) applications,
    419–420
Platform Manager, **148–150**, *149*, *150*

platform SDKs
    emulators, **158–160**
    generic, **158**
    overview, **158**
plug and play, **318**
PnpIds, **318–320**, *320*
PocketJet II printer, **207**
poid parameters, **127**
Poly-Line(), **78**
porting. *See* converting
pow(), **460**
predefined destination directories, **393–394**
Preprocessor defines, **70**
printing
    CPrintDialog, **194**
    MFC applications ported to CE, **206–207**
    PocketJet II, **207**
proc_name, **343**
Project Wizards
    for dialog-based applications, **154–157**, *155, 157*
    overview, **151–152**, *152*
    WCE Application Wizard, **157**
    WCE MFC AppWizard, **152–154**, *153*
proper uses of Windows CE registry, **116**
properties defined, **137**
property sheets, **422**
Proxim Range LAN2, **37**, 151, 366

Q

qsort(), **460**

R

raising
    System Input Panels
        Owner applet, **19**, *19*
        writing codes for, **16–18**, *16*
rand(), **460–461**
Random(), **569**
RangeLAN2, **37**, 151, 365–366
RAPI (Remote API)
    CeGetSpecialFolderPath(), **291**
    database access functions, **292**
    file access functions, **288–290**

general management functions, **283–284**
Logo program requirements, **429**
miscellaneous shell and system functions,
    292–293
overview, **282–283**
registry access functions, **287–288**
sample application, **293–298**, *294*
SDK tools and, **158**
system information functions, **285–286**, *286*
Unicode-based, **289**
using Delphi, **299–302**, *299*
RapiDBSave application, **293–294**, *294*
RapiFreeBuffer(), **569–570**
RasGetEntryDevConfig(), **570**
RasSetEntryDevConfig(), **570**
Raw IR, **309–312**
RDM/CE (Raima Data Manager for CE)
    copying data to desktop, **357**
    data compression, **357**
    HpcLadr, **338–341**, *339*
    license agreement, **341**
    network models, **337–338**
    relational data models, **337–338**
    SQL support, **357**
    storage requirements, **357**
    stored procedures, **357**
    synching data with desktop, **357**
    user privileges, **358**
reactivating application, **61**
reading
    AreaCodeDatabaseRead(), **136–139**
    ReadFile, **80–81**, 90
    read-only Grid control problem, **232–233**
realloc(), **461**
rebars, **415**
RecountCards(), **570**
recursive functions, **56**
RegisterDevice(), **570–571**
registry
    access functions, **287–288**
    application vs. information, **118**
    BLOB (Binary Large Object) data, **118**
    vs. database engine, **119**
    hierarchy, **115**, *115*
    improper uses of, **116–119**
    MFC applications and Palm-size PCs (PPCs),
        117

proper uses of, **116**
redundant information, **118**
removing user settings from, **412**
storing system data, **116**
storing user-specific information, **116**
relational database systems, **120**, 337–338
remote functions
    Remote File Viewer, **158**
    Remote Heap Viewer, **158**, 159
    Remote Process Viewer, **158**
    Remote Registry Editor, **158**
    Remote Spy++, **158**
    Remote Zoomin, **158**, 159
replacement controls, **208–209**
replication
    bi-directional, **356**
    disk file, **354**
    file-based, **354**
    Internet, 353–354
    Oracle Lite for CE, **352–354**
    Oracle Mobile Agents, **355**
    wireless, **355**
reports
    Report dialog, **345**, *345*
    report_id, **343**
    report_name, ASA (Adaptive Server Any-
        where), **343**
REPSVR, **356**
resource loads, **255–260**, *257*
return result of memory allocation, **57**
_rotl(), **445**
_rotr(), **445**
RTL (runtime library) functions
    choosing for Unicode strings, **47**, *47*
    fgets(), **92**
    fopen(), **83**
    fprintf(), **97**
    fputs(), **94**
    fread(), **95**
    fseek(), **108**
    fwrite(), **96**
    in Windows CE, **7**
runtime
    grid control, *232*
    library functions. *See* RTL (runtime library)
        functions
    platform detectors, 69, **70–72**

TabStrip control, **233–234**, *233*
VBCE files, **229–230**

S

Sales Report, **346**
sample application
    area code lookup utility, **135–140**
    ASA (Sample Application Anywhere), **342–347**,
        345
    ATM conversion, **244–276**, *245*, *246*, *276*
    converting between Unicode and ANSI Charac-
        ter Sets, **48–55**, *49*, *51*
    Oracle Lite for CE, **350–352**, 356
    RAPI (Remote API), **293–298**, *294*
    sample program in Odbc directory, **356**
    Shopping List application, **198–200**, *198*
    Stopwatch-like, **238–240**, *239*
    Task Manager, **162–163**, *162*
    Wizard for dialog-based applications, **154–157**,
        157
saving Unicode- and ANSI-based text files, **51–55**,
    51
_scalb(), **445**
scroll bars, **20–22**
SDK (Software Development Kit)
    AutoPC SDK, **69**
    platform, **158–160**
    sample application
        closing application, **166–168**
        displaying task lists, **163–164**
        keeping task list current, **168–170**
        overview, **162–163**, *162*
        replacing GetDesktopWindow(), **164–165**
        switching to one task, **166**
    using VC++, 146
searching
    CCeDBDatabase seek methods, **181**
    CeSeekDatabase(), 131, 132, 133, 134, 135, 180,
        181, **513–514**
    dwSeekType, **131**
    given number of records, **134–135**
    matching CEOID records, **132**
    next record equal to search criteria, **134**
    overview, **131–132**
    records with equal value, **133**

records with greater values, **133**
records with smaller values, **132**
vs. seeking, **131**
using API for, **121**
security
    ASA security_level, **343**
    Oracle Lite for CE, **354**
    Oracle Mobile Agents, **355**
serial communications, **308–309**
serial ports, **307**
SetColumnProperties(), **571**
SetDaylightTime(), **572**
SetFilePointer, **108–109**
SetMask(), **572–573**
SetSortOrder(), **573**
Setup programs, **399–402**
Setup Wizards
    Cab Wizard, **399–402**
    for VBCE, **236–237**
shared program files, **412**
SHCreateShortcut(), **573–574**
shell and system functions, **292–293**
SHGetShortcutTarget(), **574**
SHLoadDIBitmap(), **574**
Shopping List application, **198–200**, *198*
shortcuts
    destination directories, **397**
    displaying keys for, **425**
    hints for HPC applications, **419**
    Shortcut Properties dialog, **403**, *404*
    Start menu, 425, 432
showing
    Common Dialog control, **235**
    SHShowOutOfMemory(), **575**
Sierra Imaging, **369**
sin(), **461**
single codebase, **67–69**
sinh(), **461**
size
    dialogs, **424**
    EXE files, **56–57**, 161
    Handheld PC/Pro devices (HPC/Pros), **27**
    Handheld PCs (HPCs), **25**, 62
    Palm-size PCs (PPCs), 62
    resizing based on taskbar settings, **421–422**
    screen, 62, 70–72
    string, **56**

of WAV files, **265–266**
windows resizing based on screen size, **428**
Socket Communications
    bar code readers, **38**, 363
    cost analysis, *365*
    Ethernet debugging, **151**
    serial I/O cards, **307**
    wired network accessories, **37**
software aspects of CE communications
    built-in modems, **314–317**, *318*
    Infrared Sockets (IrSock), **314**, 332
    IR communications, **308–314**, *313*
    IrCOMM, **312–314**, *313*
    modem-based communications, **314–318**, *318*
    overview, **308**
    Raw IR, **309–312**
    serial communications, **308–309**
    standard external modems, **314**
Sony Vaio, 368
sort orders. *See* indexing
SORTORDERSPEC, **123–127**
sound, 250–253, **262–266**, *264*, *265*
SQL (Structured Query Language)
    alternate program's support for, **357**
    CE database engine support for, **121**, 357
    stored procedures, **342**
sqrt(), **461**
srand(), **462**
static variables, **56**
static vs. dynamic linking, **299**
status bars, **201–206**
_statusfp(), **445**
stdio.h file access functions, 52, 77
Stopwatch-like sample application, **238–240**, *239*
storage
    misuse of CE registry, **116–117**
    registry vs. database engines, **119**
    structured. *See* structured storage
    of system data, **116**
    third-party database engines requirements, **357**
    of user-specific information, **116**
    VC++ (Visual C++), **161**
stored procedures, **342**, 357
strcat(), **462**
strchr(), **462**
strcmp(), **462**
strcpy(), **462**

strcspn(), **463**

strings

allocating memory for (szChunk), **52–55**

ANSI-based RTL functions, **47**, *47*

ANSI-specific string type mappings

generic to, **44–45**, *45*

Unicode-specific to, **44**, *44*

choosing RTL (runtime library) functions for

Unicode, **47**, *47*

declaring, **43–45**, *44*, *45*

generic types, **44–45**, *45*

macro, **394**

size limits, **56**

Unicode-specific types, **44**, *44*

using Unicode strings for all text literals, **46**

using Unicode types vs. char types, overview,

42–44

wide, **43**, 297

strlen(), **463**

strncat(), **463**

strncmp(), **463**

strncpy, **463–464**

strstr(), **464**

strtok(), **464**

structured storage

CE Database Engine API

AreaCodeDatabaseDelete(), **140**

AreaCodeDatabaseFinish(), **140**

AreaCodeDatabaseInsert(), **139–140**

AreaCodeDatabaseRead(), **136–139**

overview, **135–136**, *135*, *136*

indexing

creating sort order at table creation, **130**

four sort order maximum, **129–130**, *130*

only one active sort order per database,

129–130

overview, **122–129**

sorting based on one field, **129**

overview, **114–115**

registry

application vs. information, **118**

BLOB (Binary Large Object) data, **118**

hierarchy, **115**, *115*

improper uses of, **116–119**

MFC applications and Palm-size PCs (PPCs),

117

proper uses of, **116**

storing system data, **116**

storing user-specific information, **116**

searching

given number of records from beginning of

database, **134**

given number of records from current

record, **135**

given number of records from end of data-

base, **134**

matching CEOID records, **132**

next record equal to search criteria, **134**

overview, **131–132**

records with equal value, **133**

records with greater values, **133**

records with smaller values, **132**

Windows CE database engine, vs. the registry,

118

stubbing, **251–253**

stylus vs. mouse, **7–8**

substitute functions, **77–79**

Summary/confirmation dialog, **405**, *405*

_swab(), **446**

switch..case blocks, **178**

switch statements, **100**

swprintf(), **464**

swscan(), 104, **465**

swscanf(), **104**

Sybase's ASA (Adaptive Server Anywhere). *See*

ASA (Adaptive Server Anywhere)

synching data

Active Sync, **343**

comparison between third-party database

engines, **357**

stored procedures, **342**

vs. wireless connection, **363–364**

system information functions, **285–286**, *286*

System Input Panels

detecting when user pops up, **18–22**, *19*

lowering, **16–18**, *16*

Owner applet, **19–22**, *19*

raising, **16–18**, *16*

scroll bars, **20–22**

SystemParametersInfo(), **70**

szChunk, **52–55**

T

table of contents, **387–388**
tables, **120–121**
tablet devices, **35**, *35*
TabStrip control, **233–234**, *233*
Tahoma (9-point), **423**
tan(), **465**
tanh(), **465**
task lists, displaying, **163–164**, 168–170
Task Manager, **162–163**, *162*, 167
Taskbars
    changes while application running, **421–422**
    creating main window, **421**
    displaying open documents, **432**
    Logo program, **421–422**
    Palm-size PCs (PPCs), **24–25**
TCHAR, 45, 46, 57, **84**, 85–88, 90, 91, 94, 98,
    100–107, 346
text literals, **46**
TEXT macros, **46**
Third-party database engines
    ASA (Adaptive Server Anywhere)
        administration and management, **343**
        command line options, **344**
        configuring application, **344**
        copying data to desktop, **357**
        Customer List report, **345–346**, *345*
        data compression, **357**
        database schema, **342–343**
        demo, **344–347**, *345*
        Login dialog, **344–345**, *345*
        overview, **341**
        proc_name, **343**
        Report dialog, **345**, *345*
        report_id, **343**
        report_name, **343**
        Sales Report, **346**
        sample application, **342–347**, *345*
        security_level, **343**
        SQL support, **357**
        storage space requirements, **357**
        stored procedures, **357**
        synching data with desktop, **357**
        user privileges, **358**
    comparison of features, **356–358**

Oracle Lite
    access to corporate data on mobile devices,
        348
    copying data to desktop, **357**
    costs, **347**
    data compression, **357**
    data-intensive applications on PDAs, **348**
    overview, **347**
    processing power deficiency, **347–348**
    SQL support, **357**
    storage requirements, **357**
    stored procedures, **357**
    synching data with desktop, **357**
    user privileges, **358**
Oracle Lite for CE
    application development support, **349–350**
    disk file replication, **354**
    file-based replication, **254**
    Internet replication, **353–354**
    key features, **349**
    ODBC support, **349**
    overview, **348–349**
    replication, **352–354**
    sample application, **350–352**, 356
    security, **254**
    wireless replication, **353**
Oracle Mobile Agents
    anytime, anywhere, **354**
    developing applications and agents, **355**
    optimized for mobile environment, **354–355**
    overview, **354**
    reliability, **355**
    security, **255**
    wireless replication, **355**
overview, **336–337**
RDM/CE (Raima Data Manager for CE)
    copying data to desktop, **357**
    data compression, **357**
    HpcLadr, **338–341**, *339*
    license agreement, **341**
    network models, **337**
    overview, **337**
    SQL support, **357**
    storage requirements, **357**
    stored procedures, **357**
    synching data with desktop, **357**
    user privileges, **358**

title bars, **426**
tool tips, **419**
toolbars, **201–206**, 425
toolkits
    for VB (Visual Basic language). *See* VB (Visual
        Basic language)
    for VC++. *See* Windows CE toolkit for VC++
towlower(), **465**
towupper(), **466**
TransparentImage(), **575–576**
tray icons, **425**
TreeView
    vs. DBView, **65**
    VBCE, **234**
try..catch, **79–80**
Typecasts change, **250**

U

UI
    Logo program requirements, **415–427**
    tailoring to device, **62–67**, *62, 63, 64, 66, 67*
_ultoa(), **446**
_ultow(), **446**
underlined accelerators, **425**
Unicode Character Set
    vs. ANSI-based functions, **97**
    applications must use, **42–43**
    converting between Unicode and ANSI
        opening text files, **49–51**
        overview, **48–49**, *49*
        saving text files, **51–55**, *51*
    declaring strings using Unicode vs. char types
        generic string types, **44–45**, *45*
        overview, **43–44**
        Unicode-specific string types, **44**, *44*
    FEFF signature, **48**
    file access, **95**
    fopen(), **84**
    RTL functions for Unicode strings, **47**, *47*
    string function equivalents, **47**, *47*
    using with other text files, **48**
    using Unicode strings for all text literals, **46**
    wstrlen(), **95**
UpdateListBox(), **187–189**
user privileges, **358**

V

variable argument lists, **97–107**
VarYYYYFromZZZZ() functions, **576–584**
VB (Visual Basic language)
    changes in, **237–238**, *238*
    converting real VB application to CE
        array declarations, **256–260**, *257*
        ATM conversion overview, **244–249**, *245, 246,*
            276, 276
        Bitmaps, **250**
        change Global to Public, **249**
        country and bit maps, **266–269**
        Declare statements, **246–247**
        eliminating code, **274–275**
        eliminating forms, **270–274**, *271*
        eliminating optional controls and DLLs, **274**
        Explicit Type declarations, **249**
        Explicit Types, **249**
        icons, **250**
        Image Control, **250**
        mechanical issues, **249–261**, *257*
        modal forms, **248**, **253–255**
        modifying resource loads, **255–260**, *257*
        mouse/cursor code, **252–253**
        optimizing, **270–275**
        optional features, **262–269**, *264, 265*
        planning porting process, **247–249**
        porting from VB to VBCE, **247**
        preparing frmAmountWithdrawn Form, **261**
        sound, **263–265**, *264, 265*
        Typecasts, **250**
        using Developer Studio, **256–257**, *257*
        WAV files, **250–253**, **262–266**, *264, 265*
    standard controls, **235**, *235–236*
    Stopwatch-like application, **238–240**, *239*
    toolkit for CE
        ActiveX Control Pack, **231–235**, *235*
        application templates, **226–227**, *227*
        control manager, **230–231**
        debugger, **228–229**, *229*
        embedded applications, **227–228**
        overview, **226**
        runtime files, **229–230**
        Setup Wizard, **236–237**
        standard VBCE controls, **235**, *235–236*
        versions 5 and, 6, **238**

VBCE Miscellaneous Utility Control, **266**
VBScript, **237**
VC++ (Visual C++)
    using to develop for Windows CE, **146**
    Windows CE toolkit for
        compilers, **146–147**
        debugging, **150–151**
        Embedded Toolkit, **227–228**
        MFC vs. SDK-style coding, **160–162**
        overview, **146**
        Platform Manager, **148–150**, *149*, *150*
        platform SDKs, **158–160**
        Project Wizards, **151–157**, *152*, *153*, *155*, *157*
Veritest, **408**
version numbering of CE operating systems, **34**
VGA-out ports, Handheld PC/Pro devices
        (HPC/Pros), **29–33**
VirtualAlloc(), **60**
vswprintf(), **466**

W

WAV files, 250–253, **262–266**, *264*, *265*
WCE Application Wizard, **157**
WCE MFC AppWizard, **152–154**, *153*
WCHAR, **44**, 45
wcscat(), **466**
wcschr(), **467**
wcscmp(), **467**
wcscpy(), **467**
wcscspn(), **467**
_wcsdup(), **446**
_wcsicmp(), **447**
wcslen(), **468**
_wcslwr(), **447**
wcsncat(), **468**
wcsncmp(), **468**
wcsncpy(), **468–469**
_wcsnicmp(), **447**
_wcsnset(), **447–448**
wcspbrk(), **469**
wcsrchr(), **469**
_wcsrev(), **448**
_wcsset(), **448**
wcsspn(), **469–470**
wcsstr(), **470**

wcstod(), **470**
wcstok(), **470**
wcstol(), **471**
wcstombs(), **471**
wcstoul(), **471**
_wcsupr(), **448**
whitespace, **101**, 102, 103
whois program, **327–332**, *328*
wide strings, **43**, 297
Windows CE
    database engine. *See* Windows CE Database
        Engine
    overview of. *See* Windows CE overview
    registry hierarchy. *See* registry
    toolkit for VC++. *See* Windows CE toolkit for
        VC++
    vs. Windows 98/NT, **5–9**
    writing for. *See* writing for Windows CE
Windows CE Database Engine
    API
        AreaCodeDatabaseDelete(), **140**
        AreaCodeDatabaseFinish(), **140**
        AreaCodeDatabaseInsert(), **139–140**
        AreaCodeDatabaseRead(), **136–139**
        overview, **135–136**, *135*, *136*
    vs. other familiar database engines
        databases as tables, **120**
        Enterprise Manager applications, **122**
        indexing, **122–130**
        management tools and utilities, **121–122**
        not relational, **120**
        organization and naming of data, **120**
        overview, **119**
        record-specific vs. table-specific fields,
            120–121
        searching, **131–135**
        similarities, **122–135**
        SQL (Structured Query Language) queries,
            121
    vs. the registry, **119**
Windows CE overview
    CE defined, **4–5**
    communications, **10**
    core OS features, **10**
    databases, **10–11**
    dhrystone ratings, **10–11**
    display size and type, **9**

hardware standardization, **8–9**
Internet features, **10**
low-memory situations, **6–7**
memory constraints, **5–7**
networking features, **10**
operating system requests, **6–7**
physical memory, **6**
power of, **11**
reduced API, **7**
reduced runtime library (RLT), **7**
resizing windows, **8**
right-clicking, **8**
running existing programs, **5**
stylus vs. mouse, **7–8**
unique features, **10–11**
user control over memory availability, **6–7**
vs. Windows 98/NT, **5–9**
Winsock 1.1, **10**
vs. x86 Intel platform, **9**
Windows CE toolkit for VC++
   compilers, **146**
   debugging, **150–151**
   #define, **70**
   GetDesktopWindow(), **164–165**
   MFC vs. SDK-style coding
      ease of development, **161–162**
      overview, **160**
      storage space, **161**
   overview, **146**
   Platform Manager, **148–150**, *149, 150*
   platform SDKs
      emulators, **158–160**
      generic tools, **158**
      overview, **158**
   Preprocessors defines, **70**
   Project Wizards
      for dialog-based applications, **154–157**, *155, 157*
      overview, **151–152**, *152*
      WCE Application Wizard, **157**
      WCE MFC AppWizard, **152–154**, *153*
   sample SDK-style application
      closing application, **166–168**
      displaying tasks, **163–164**
      keeping task lists current, **168–170**
      overview, **162–163**, *162*
      switching to one task, **166**

Windows NT, 159, 175, 192, 289, 326
Winsock 1.1
   in CE communications, **327–332**
   Infrared Sockets (IrSock), **314**, 332
   Logo program requirements, **429**
   overview, **10**
Wired network accessories for CE devices, **36–37**
wireless connections
   accessories for CE devices, **36–37**
   LAN Hub cost analysis, **366**
   Oracle Mobile Agents, **355**
   replication, **353**, 355
   synching vs., **363–364**
Wizards
   Cab Wizard, **392–402**, *398*
   Project Wizards, 151–152, *152*, **154–157**, *155, 157*
   Setup Wizard for VBCE, **236–237**
   WCE Application Wizard, **157**
   WCE MFC AppWizard, **152–154**, *153*
WM_ACTIVATE, **61**
WM_COMMAND, **29**, 166, 167, 168
WM_DEVICECHANGE, **321–322**, 324, 326
WM_HIBERNATE, **60–61**, 193, 429
WM_INITDIALOG, **159–160**, 316
WM_RBUTTONDOWN, **78–79**
WM_RBUTTONUP, **423**
WM_SOCKET_NOTIFY, **176**
wrapper functions, **81**
WriteFile, **80–81**, 91
writing for Windows CE
   first commandment of, **42–55**
   form factors
      compiler defines, **68–69**, *69*
      creating conditional defines, **69–70**
      creating runtime platform detectors, **70–72**
      DBView, **63–66**, *63, 64, 66, 67*
      overview, **61–62**
      single codebases, **67–69**
      tailoring application UI to device, **62–67**, *63, 64, 66, 67*
   low-memory environment
      checking return results of memory allocation, **57**
      different types of memory allocation, **59–60**
      EXE file size, **56–57**
      handling WM_HIBERATE message, **60–61**
      mass-allocating application memory, **58–60**

minimizing static variables, **56**
overview, **55–56**
reactivating application, **61**
overview, **42**
second commandment of, **55–61**
third commandment of, **61–72**
using Unicode Character set
declaring strings using Unicode types vs.
char types, **43–46**, *44, 45*
generic string types, **44–45**, *45*
overview, **42–43**
RTL (runtime library) functions, **47**, *47*
text literals, **46**
Unicode-specific string types, **44**, *44*
using with ANSI-based text files, **48–55**, *49,
51*
wide strings, **43**
writing your own functions
fclose(), **88–89**
fgetc(), **89–90**
fgets(), **92–94**
FILE*-based functions, **81–83**
fopen(), **83–88**
fprintf(), **97–99**
fputs(), **94**
fputz(), **90–92**
fread(), **95–96**
fscanf(), **99–107**
fseek(), **108–109**
fwrite(), **96**
overview, **80–81**
wstrlen(), **95**
WSA-related functions, **327**
wsprintf(), **471**
wstrlen(), 84, **95**
_wtoi(), **449**
_wtol(), **449**

X

x86 Intel platform, **9**

Y

_y0(), **449**
_y1(), **449**
_yn(), **450**

GET MCSD CERTIFIED WITH SYBEX

THE CERTIFICATION EXPERTS

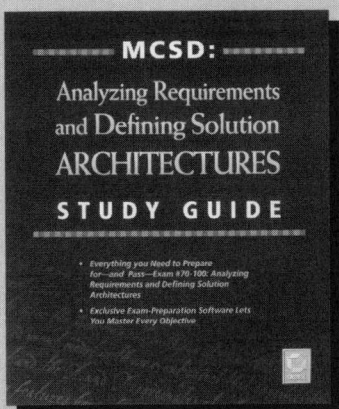

Ben Ezzell
ISBN 0-7821-2431-3

- Complete coverage of every Microsoft objective

- Hundreds of challenging review questions, in the book and on the CD

- Hands-on exercises that let you apply the concepts you've learned

- Page count: 592-752; Hardcover; Trim: 7½" x 9"; Price: $44.99; CD included

Other MCSD Study Guides Available from Sybex:

*MCSD: Visual Basic® 6 Desktop Applications
Study Guide*
Michael McKelvy
ISBN 0-7821-2438-0

*MCSD: Visual Basic® 6 Distributed
Applications Study Guide*
Michael Lee with Clark Christensen
ISBN 0-7821-2433-X

MCSD: Access® 95 Study Guide
Peter Vogel & Helen Feddema
ISBN 0-7821-2282-5

MCSD: Windows® Architecture I Study Guide
Ben Ezzell
ISBN 0-7821-2271-X

MCSD: Windows® Architecture II Study Guide
Michael Lee & Kevin Wolford
ISBN 0-7821-2274-4

*MCSD: SQL Server® 6.5 Database Design
Study Guide*
Kevin Hough
ISBN 0-7821-2269-8

MCSD: Visual Basic® 5 Study Guide
Mike McKelvy
ISBN 0-7821-2228-0

Available Summer '99:
*MCSD: Visual C++® 6 Desktop and
Distributed Applications Study Guide*
Peter Thorsteinson
ISBN 0-7821-2570-0; $49.99

Available Summer '99:
*MCSE/MCSD: SQL Server® 7 Database
Design Study Guide*
Kevin Hough & Ed Larkin
ISBN 0-7821-2586-7

Available Summer '99:
*MCSD Visual Basic® 6
Core Requirements Box*
Michael McKelvy,
Michael Lee with
Clark Christensen &
Ben Ezzell
ISBN 0-7821-2582-4
$109.97
Contains:
*MCSD: Analyzing Requirements and
Defining Solution Architectures Study Guide*
*MCSD: Visual Basic® 6 Desktop
Applications Study Guide*
*MCSD: Visual Basic® 6 Distributed
Applications Study Guide*

A savings of $25!

SYBEX®

www.sybex.com